THE AMERICANA ANNUAL

2000

AN ENCYCLOPEDIA
OF THE EVENTS OF 1999

YEARBOOK OF THE
ENCYCLOPEDIA AMERICANA

GROLIER

This annual has been prepared as a yearbook for general encyclopedias.
It is also published as *Encyclopedia Year Book.*

Library of Congress Catalog Card Number: 23-10041
ISBN: 0-7172-0324-7
ISSN: 0196-0180

Printed and manufactured in the United States of America

EDITORIAL

Publisher	Philip Friedman
Executive Editor	James E. Churchill, Jr.
Art Director	Claudia Durrell
Editors	Meghan O'Reilly Fiero Susan H. McClung
Director, Annuals	Doris E. Lechner
Managing Editor	Kenneth W. Leish
Director, Art and Design	Nancy A. Hamlen
Contributing Editors	William E. Shapiro Jim Anderson Kristi Vaughan
Assistant Editor	Jone E. Baltzell
Editorial Assistant	Gayle M. Wanag
Chief Indexer	Pauline M. Sholtys
Indexer	Linda King
Production Editor	Jeanne A. Schipper
Director, Photo Research	Cindy Joyce
Photo Researcher	June Lundborg Whitworth
Manager, Picture Library	Jane H. Carruth
Financial Manager	Joseph Cantone
Editorial Librarian	Charles Chang
Assistant Vice-President, Network Services/Publishing Technology	Adrianne Beauchamp
Project Leader	Gail G. Dell
Publishing Systems Manager	Linda Dillon
Senior Publishing Systems Analyst	Emilia Urra Smith
Compositor	Karen Calise
Staff Assistants	Amy N. Deacon Louise D. Wyman

MANUFACTURING

Vice-President, Manufacturing	Joseph J. Corlett
Director, Reference Publications	Christine L. Matta
Production Manager	Barbara L. Persan
Production Assistant	Andrea L. Lauri

CONTENTS

20TH CENTURY—A REMEMBRANCE

International Affairs • 8
U.S. Affairs • 18
Arts and Entertainment • 26
Business and Industry • 36
Medicine and Health • 44
Science and Technology • 50
Sports • 60

A Review of the Year 1999 • 66
Chronology • 68

SPECIAL FEATURES

The Kosovo Crisis • 78

Dr. Janusz Bugajski, director of East European Studies at the Center for Strategic and International Studies in Washington, DC, analyzes the 1999 crisis involving Yugoslavia and ethnic Albanians over the issue of independence for Kosovo—the background, the diplomacy, the fighting, and the aftermath. Separate sidebars discuss the role of the North Atlantic Treaty Organization in the dispute—including its bombing campaign—and the sudden and huge exodus of refugees.

Sleep and Its Disorders • 91

With the study of sleep becoming one of the fastest-growing and most exciting areas of medicine, Dr. Clete A. Kushida, director of the Stanford Center for Human Sleep Research in Stanford, CA, describes the sleep process and reports on the most common sleep disorders prevalent today.

Pop Music's New Diversity: Latin, Jazz, Swing ... • 97

Pop-music writer and critic John Milward explains that the adults of today, who grew up listening to rock 'n' roll, have become more diversified in terms of their music. The Latin beat—with such performers as Ricky Martin, Jennifer Lopez, and Marc Anthony—has become the "in" style; the renown of trumpeter Wynton Marsalis testifies to the renewed interest in jazz; and swing—so popular more than a half century earlier—has enjoyed a definite revival.

***Breitling Orbiter 3*—A Dream Is Realized • 104**

For some 200 years, man had dreamed of traveling around the Earth in a balloon propelled solely by wind. In 1999 the Breitling Orbiter 3, *with Dr. Bertrand Piccard and Brian Jones aboard, accomplished that goal. Balloon enthusiast Malcolm W. Browne of* The New York Times *comments on the 19-day flight and on other historic moments in the sport.*

See page 594 for illustration credits for page 4.

THE ALPHABETICAL SECTION

Entries on the continents and major nations of the world will be found under their own alphabetical headings.

Economics and Industry

Government, Human Welfare, Law, and Politics

Humanities, Arts, and Hobbies

Science and Technology

Miscellaneous

Special Reports and Sidebars

20TH CENTURY A REMEMBRANCE

Historians well may judge the 20th century as an exciting and adventurous 100 years. The airplane was invented and became a common means of travel; television became a household fixture; discoveries such as the wonder drugs advanced the world of medicine; the space and nuclear ages were born; and the computer altered almost everything. India's Mother Teresa devoted her life to the poor; Elvis Presley popularized rock 'n' roll; Babe Ruth and Michael Jordan were among the heroes of sports. African-Americans sought and gained new rights. Yet the period was not without tragedy—two world wars, senseless regional conflicts, and horrible natural disasters. Mohandas Gandhi, John F. Kennedy, and Martin Luther King, Jr., were among those whose lives were cut short by assassins' bullets.

In addressing the United Nations General Assembly on Sept. 21, 1999, U.S. President Bill Clinton noted that the 20th century "taught us much of what we need to know

about the promise of tomorrow. We have learned a great deal over the last 100 years: how to produce enough food for a growing world population; how human activity affects the environment; the mysteries of the human gene; an information revolution that now holds the promise of universal access to knowledge."

Although a century is a relatively short, artificial period in the annals of time, it offers one a chance to look back, recall the past, and assess the pluses and minuses of 100 years. It is with this in mind that this annual opens with the following chronology of 20th-century highlights. The list is divided into world affairs, U.S. affairs, arts and entertainment, business and industry, medicine and health, science and technology, and sports.

See page 594 for illustration credits for pages 6–7.

NASA

The planet Earth is photographed during the "Apollo 17" space mission, December 1972.

1900

Aug. 14. The antiforeign Boxer uprising by Chinese nationalists is ended when an eight-nation military force lifts the siege of Beijing (Peking).

1901

Jan. 1. The Commonwealth of Australia is founded.

Jan. 22. After a reign of nearly 64 years, Queen Victoria of England, *photo below*, dies and is succeeded by her son, who will reign as Edward VII.

© Brown Brothers

1902

May 20. Cuba gains its independence from Spain.

May 31. The Boer War between Britain and the Dutch in South Africa comes to an end.

1905

Jan. 9. Civil disturbances known as the Revolution of 1905 begin in Russia, forcing Czar Nicholas II to grant some civil rights.

Sept. 5. The Treaty of Portsmouth ends the Russo-Japanese War.

Oct. 26. Norway gains independence from Sweden.

1910

May 31. The Union of South Africa is established.

Aug. 22. Japan formally annexes Korea.

1911

Sept. 9. Italy declares war on the Ottoman Turks and annexes Libya, Tripolitania, and Cyrenaica in North Africa.

1912

Feb. 12. China's boy emperor Hsüan T'ung announces his abdication, ending the Manchu Ch'ing dynasty. The Republic of China is established subsequently.

1914

June 28. Archduke Franz Ferdinand, heir to the Austro-Hungarian throne, is assassinated in Sarajevo, Bosnia, precipitating World War I.

July 28. World War I starts when Austria-Hungary declares war on Serbia.

Aug. 1–4. Germany declares war on Russia and France, and invades Belgium; Britain declares war on Germany.

Aug. 10. Austria-Hungary invades Russia.

Aug. 15. The Panama Canal, across the isthmus of Panama, is opened.

Sept. 12. The Allies halt the German offensive in France.

Oct. 31. The Ottoman Empire (Turkey) joins the Central Powers (Germany, Austria-Hungary, and Bulgaria), declaring war on the Allies.

"All the News That's Fit to Print." **The New York Times.** EXTRA

LUSITANIA SUNK BY A SUBMARINE, PROBABLY 1,260 DEAD; TWICE TORPEDOED OFF IRISH COAST; SINKS IN 15 MINUTES; CAPT. TURNER SAVED, FROHMAN AND VANDERBILT MISSING; WASHINGTON BELIEVES THAT A GRAVE CRISIS IS AT HAND

NOTICE!

IMPERIAL GERMAN EMBASSY

© Corbis-Bettmann

1915

April 22. At the Second Battle of Ypres, Germany is the first nation to use poison gas.

May 7. A German submarine sinks the British passenger ship *Lusitania*, killing 1,198 passengers, *photo of "New York Times" headlines above.*

May 23. Italy joins the Allies, declaring war on Austria-Hungary.

1916

Dec. 18. The ten-month-long Battle of Verdun ends.

1917

March 15. Czar Nicholas II of Russia abdicates.

April 6. The United States declares war on Germany.

July 7. Aleksandr Kerensky forms a provisional government in Russia.

Nov. 2. The British Balfour Declaration endorses "the establishment in Palestine of a national home for the Jewish people."

Nov. 7. The Bolsheviks (Communists) under V.I. Lenin seize power in Russia.

1918

June–July. Civil war breaks out in Russia between Communists and anti-Communists.

July 16. Russian Communists execute Czar Nicholas II and his family.

Nov. 11. Germany and the Allies sign an armistice, ending World War I.

1919

June 28. Following negotiations among the Allies in Paris, *photo below*, the Treaty of Versailles ends World War I.

Sept. 10. The Treaty of St.-Germain-en-Laye ends the state of war between Austria and the Allies; Austria recognizes the independence of Czechoslovakia, Poland, Hungary, and Yugoslavia.

1920

November. The Communists defeat the anti-Communists, ending Russia's civil war.

Nov. 15. The League of Nations meets for the first time in Geneva, Switzerland.

1921

Dec. 6. The Catholic Irish Free State becomes a self-governing dominion of Britain.

© Granger Collection

1922

March 15. After Egypt gains nominal independence from Britain, Fuad I assumes the title of king.

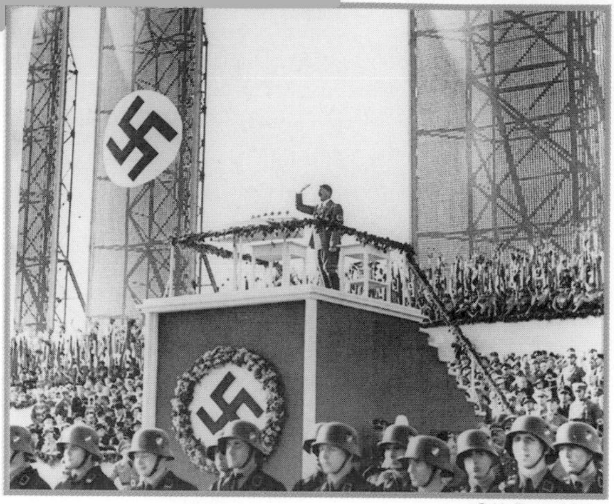

© H. Roger Viollet

Oct. 31. Fascist Benito Mussolini becomes prime minister of Italy.

1923

July 6. The Union of Soviet Socialist Republics (USSR) is established.

Oct. 29. Turkey becomes a republic following the dissolution of the Ottoman Empire.

1924

Jan. 21. Lenin dies, and Joseph Stalin fights his rivals for leadership of the Soviet Union.

1925

Dec. 1. The Locarno Pact finalizes the treaties between the World War I protagonists.

1926

Dec. 25. Japan's Taisho emperor dies; his son will reign as Emperor Hirohito.

1928

Oct. 6. War-torn China is reunited under Nationalist leader Chiang Kai-shek.

1929

June 7. The Lateran Treaty reestablishes the independence of Vatican City.

Oct. 29. The Wall Street stock market crashes, precipitating the Great Depression.

1930

Nov. 2. Haile Selassie I is crowned emperor of Ethiopia.

1931

April 14. King Alfonso XIII leaves Spain after a 45-year reign; Spain becomes a republic.

Sept. 21. Japanese forces begin to occupy Manchuria, China's northeast territory.

1932

March 9. Eamon de Valera is elected president of Ireland.

1933

Jan. 30. Adolf Hitler, *photo above*, becomes chancellor of Germany.

Nov. 16. The United States and the Soviet Union establish diplomatic relations.

1935

Sept. 15. Germany's Nuremberg Laws deprive Jews of their citizenship.

Oct. 3. Italian forces invade Abyssinia (now Ethiopia).

1936

March 7. German forces reoccupy the Rhineland in violation of the Versailles Treaty.

July 18. The Spanish Civil War begins.

Dec. 10. King Edward VIII (the duke of Windsor), *photo right*, abdicates the British throne to marry American divorcée Wallis Warfield Simpson; he is succeeded by George VI.

© Hulton Getty/Liaison Agency

1937

July 7. Japanese troops invade China.

1938

March 14. Adolf Hitler proclaims a union (Anschluss) of Germany and Austria.

Sept. 30. British and French appeasement of Hitler at the Munich Conference, *photo left*, leads to German occupation

© AP/Wide World Photos

of the Sudetenland region of western Czechoslovakia.

© Archive Photos

1939

March 15. German forces occupy the rest of Czechoslovakia.

March 28. The Spanish Civil War ends.

Aug. 23. The Soviet Union and Germany sign a nonaggression pact.

Sept. 1. World War II begins as Germany invades Poland.

Sept. 3. France and Britain declare war on Germany.

Sept. 17. Soviet forces invade Poland; the Soviet Union and Germany partition Poland.

1940

March 12. The Russo-Finnish War ends with Finland's surrender.

April 9. Germany invades Denmark and Norway.

May 7. Winston Churchill becomes British prime minister.

May 10. Germany invades Belgium, France, the Netherlands, and Luxembourg.

June 10. Italy declares war on France and Britain.

July 21. Lithuania, Estonia, and Latvia are annexed by the Soviet Union.

Oct. 31. The British air victory in the Battle of Britain prevents the German invasion of Britain.

1941

June 22. Germany invades the Soviet Union.

July. German "killing squads" begin to kill Soviet Jews—a significant development in the Holocaust, the murder of 6 million European Jews.

Dec. 7. Japanese planes bomb U.S. military bases at Pearl Harbor, Hawaii.

Dec. 8. Great Britain, Canada, and the United States declare war on Japan.

Dec. 11. Germany and Italy declare war on the United States.

1942

May 6. The Japanese seize control of the Philippines.

June 4–6. Japanese expansion in the Pacific is ended at the Battle of Midway.

1943

Feb. 2. The German siege of Stalingrad, *photo above*, ends.

May 12. Allied forces defeat the Axis powers in North Africa.

Sept. 3. Allied forces invade southern Italy after capturing Sicily.

Oct. 13. Italy signs an armistice with the Allies and declares war on Germany.

1944

June 6. On D-Day, Allied invasion forces land at Normandy in northern France.

Aug. 25. Allied forces liberate Paris.

Oct. 20. Allied forces invade the Philippines.

1945

Feb. 11. U.S. President Franklin Roosevelt confers with British Prime Minister Churchill and Soviet Premier Joseph Stalin at Yalta. The three leaders had conferred at the Tehran Conference, *photo right*, in late 1943.

March 22. The Arab League is founded.

April 30. Hitler commits suicide.

May 7. Germany surrenders to the Allies.

Aug. 14. Japan surrenders, ending World War II, days after the United States drops atomic bombs on the cities of Hiroshima and Nagasaki.

Photo Courtesy, Franklin D. Roosevelt Library

© George Holton/Photo Researchers, Inc.

Oct. 24. The United Nations (UN) comes into being. UN headquarters, *photo left*, are completed in New York City in 1952.

1946

April 14. The civil war between Communists and Nationalists resumes in China.

May 25. Transjordan becomes a sovereign state.

July 4. The Philippines gains its independence from the United States.

Oct. 1. The Nuremberg Tribunal sentences 12 Nazis to death.

Dec. 20. Full-scale guerrilla warfare between Vietminh partisans and French troops begins in Indochina (Vietnam).

1947

May 31. Communists seize control of Hungary.

Aug. 15. India gains independence from Great Britain and is divided into the nations of India and Pakistan.

Nov. 29. The UN General Assembly votes to partition Palestine into Arab and Jewish states.

1948

Jan. 30. Indian leader Mohandas Gandhi is assassinated.

Feb. 25. Communists take over Czechoslovakia.

April 30. The Organization of American States (OAS) is founded.

May 14. Palestinian Jews establish the state of Israel, *photo directly below*.

May 15. Arab armies invade Israel.

July 24. Soviet forces in Germany blockade West Berlin; a U.S.-British airlift begins the following day.

Aug. 15. The Republic of Korea (South Korea) is established.

Sept. 9. The People's Republic of Korea (North Korea) is established.

© UPI/Corbis-Bettmann

1949

Feb. 24. Israel and Egypt sign an armistice, which leads to an end to the Arab-Israeli war.

April 4. The North Atlantic Treaty Organization (NATO) is formed.

April 18. The Republic of Ireland is established formally.

May 12. The Soviet Union lifts the Berlin blockade.

May 23. The Republic of Germany (West Germany) is established.

Oct. 1. Communist forces defeat the Nationalists and establish the People's Republic of China; the Nationalists flee to the island of Taiwan.

Oct. 7. The German Democratic Republic (East Germany) is established.

Dec. 27. Indonesia gains its independence from the Netherlands.

1950

June 25. North Korea invades South Korea, beginning the Korean War, *photo right*.

Nov. 26. Chinese forces enter the Korean War.

© Archive Photos

1951

May 3. The Japanese Peace Treaty is signed; Allied military rule of Japan ends; and Japan regains its sovereignty.

1953

March 5. Soviet dictator Joseph Stalin dies.

June 2. The coronation of Queen Elizabeth II occurs at London's Westminster Abbey, *photo right.* She had become the British monarch after the death of her father, George VI, on Feb. 6, 1952.

July 27. The Korean War ends.

© European/FPG International

1954

April 18. Col. Gamal Abdel Nasser becomes premier of Egypt.

July 21. Vietnam is partitioned into North Vietnam and South Vietnam.

1955

May 5. The Federal Republic of Germany (West Germany) attains sovereignty.

May 14. The Warsaw Pact, the Eastern European Communist bloc's mutual-defense treaty, comes into being.

Sept. 19. Argentine President Juan Perón is ousted by a military coup.

1956

March. Morocco and Tunisia gain their independence from France.

April 19. Monaco's Prince Rainier III and U.S. actress Grace Kelly are married in religious ceremonies in Monte Carlo. Civil ceremonies were held on April 18.

Nov. 14. Soviet troops and tanks crush an antigovernment uprising in Hungary.

Dec. 22. A crisis over Egypt's nationalization of the Suez Canal ends, as invading British and French forces evacuate Egypt; the Israelis will withdraw later.

1957

March 6. Ghana is the first sub-Saharan African state to gain its independence from a European colonial power.

1958

Jan. 1. The European Economic Community (EEC) is established.

May 31. Charles de Gaulle becomes premier of France.

1959

Feb. 16. Fidel Castro, *photo below*, seizes power in Cuba.

March 31. The Dalai Lama flees to India, after China crushes an uprising in Tibet.

1960

June 30. Following the independence of the Congo, Katanga province secedes.

1961

Jan. 3. The United States severs relations with Communist Cuba.

Aug. 17. Communist East Germany completes the construction of the Berlin Wall.

Sept. 18. UN Secretary-General Dag Hammarskjöld is killed in a plane crash in Northern Rhodesia.

1962

July 3. Algeria gains its independence from France.

Nov. 20. The monthlong Cuban missile crisis ends; the Soviet Union withdraws its missiles and bombers from Cuba, and the United States ends its blockade of the island.

© Archive Photos

1963

May 25. The Organization of African Unity (OAU) is established.

Oct. 10. The United States, the USSR, and Great Britain conclude a partial nuclear-test-ban treaty.

Dec. 4. The Ecumenical Council Vatican II concludes.

Dec. 12. Kenya becomes independent of Britain.

1964

Aug. 5. U.S. planes bomb North Vietnam after it attacks U.S. ships in the Gulf of Tonkin; U.S. involvement in Vietnam escalates.

Oct. 15. Nikita Khrushchev is ousted as leader of the Soviet Union.

Oct. 16. Communist China explodes an atomic bomb.

© Gilles Caron/Liaison Agency

1965

Nov. 11. Rhodesia unilaterally declares its independence from Britain.

1967

May 30. Civil war erupts in Nigeria when the state of Biafra secedes, *photo right*.

June 5. The Six-Day War between Israel and its Arab neighbors begins; a victorious Israel will seize Arab Jerusalem, the West Bank, and the Golan Heights.

1968

Aug. 20. Warsaw Pact troops invade Czechoslovakia to end liberalization.

1970

Jan. 12. Nigeria's civil war ends.

Jan. 16. Col. Muammar el-Qaddafi becomes premier of Libya.

Oct. 14. Anwar el-Sadat becomes president of Egypt following the death of Nasser.

Nov. 19. Hafiz al-Assad seizes power in Syria.

1971

Feb. 13. South Vietnamese troops, backed by U.S. air and artillery support, invade Laos.

March 26. East Pakistan (Bangladesh) declares its independence from Pakistan.

April 21. Haitian dictator François Duvalier dies and is succeeded by his son, Jean-Claude.

June 10. The United States ends its 21-year trade embargo of China.

Oct. 23. The UN General Assembly votes to expel Taiwan and seat Communist China.

1972

Feb. 20. President Nixon meets with Chinese leader Mao Zedong in Beijing, *photo below*.

April 1. North Vietnamese and Vietcong troops renew their offensive in South Vietnam.

Sept. 5. Arab terrorists kill 11 Israeli athletes at the Munich Olympics.

1973

Jan. 1. Britain, Ireland, Denmark, and Norway join the EEC.

Sept. 11. A coup in Chile overthrows President Salvador Allende's Marxist government.

Sept. 23. Juan Perón returns to power as president of Argentina.

Oct. 24. The two-and-one-half-week Yom Kippur War ends with Israel's defeat of Egypt and Syria.

© Liaison Agency

1974

April 25. A military coup in Portugal leads to democratic reforms.

July 20. Turkey invades Cyprus; the nation later will be partitioned into Greek and Turkish zones.

Sept. 12. Emperor Haile Selassie of Ethiopia is ousted in a military coup.

1975

April 5. Nationalist Chinese leader Chiang Kai-shek dies.

April 16. The Khmer Rouge rebels win control of Cambodia and begin a reign of terror that will kill millions of people.

April 30. Saigon, capital of South Vietnam, surrenders to North Vietnamese forces.

Nov. 11. Angola gains its independence from Portugal, and civil war breaks out.

Nov. 22. Juan Carlos I, *photo right*, becomes king of Spain following the death of Gen. Francisco Franco on November 20.

Also in 1975. Civil war between Muslims and Christians erupts in Lebanon.

© UPI/Corbis-Bettmann

1976

July 2. North and South Vietnam are reunited officially.

Sept. 9. Chinese leader Mao Zedong dies.

1977

Sept. 7. Panama and the United States sign two treaties that will transfer the Panama Canal to Panama in 2000.

1978

April 27. Pro-Soviet Marxists seize control of Afghanistan.

Oct. 16. Cardinal Karol Wojtyla of Poland is the first non-Italian in nearly 500 years to be elected pope. He becomes Pope John Paul II.

1979

March 26. Israel and Egypt sign a treaty ending the 31-year state of war between them.

April 1. Ayatollah Ruhollah Khomeini proclaims Iran an Islamic republic.

May 4. Conservative Party leader Margaret Thatcher, *with her husband in photo right*, becomes Britain's first woman prime minister.

July 16. Gen. Saddam Hussein becomes president of Iraq.

Dec. 24. Soviet troops occupy Afghanistan in support of the country's Marxist government, precipitating a guerrilla war by Islamic *mujahidin*.

© Hulton Getty/Liaison Agency

1980

April 17–18. Rhodesia becomes the independent nation of Zimbabwe.

Sept. 1. Poland's Solidarity, led by Lech Walesa, becomes the first independent union in a Communist country.

Sept. 22. A border dispute leads to open warfare between Iran and Iraq.

1981

Jan. 20. Iran releases the U.S. hostages it has held since late 1979.

May 13. Pope John Paul II is shot and wounded by a Turkish gunman.

Oct. 6. Egyptian President Anwar el-Sadat is assassinated; Hosni Mubarak becomes president.

1982

April 2. Argentina invades the British-held Falkland Islands.

June 14. British troops recapture the Falkland Islands from Argentina.

1983

Sept. 1. A Soviet jet fighter shoots down a Korean Air Lines plane, killing 269 people.

1984

Oct. 31. Prime Minister Indira Gandhi of India is assassinated.

Dec. 3. More than 2,000 people die from a toxic-gas leak at a pesticide plant in Bhopal, India.

© Sovfoto/Eastfoto

1985

March 11. Mikhail Gorbachev, *photo left*, is named chairman of the Soviet Communist Party.

Oct. 7. Palestinian terrorists hijack the Italian cruise ship *Achille Lauro.*

1986

Feb. 26. Corazon Aquino becomes president of the Philippines, as Ferdinand Marcos goes into exile.

Feb. 28. Swedish Prime Minister Olof Palme is assassinated.

1987

Nov. 7. Tunisian President Habib Bourguiba is overthrown.

Dec. 8. U.S. President Ronald Reagan and Soviet leader Gorbachev sign a treaty on the elimination of intermediate-range nuclear forces.

Dec. 9. West Bank Palestinians launch an uprising against Israeli occupation.

1988

March 11. A cease-fire is declared in the war between Iran and Iraq.

Oct. 1. Gorbachev assumes the Soviet presidency.

Dec. 21. A terrorist bomb blows up a Pan Am Boeing 747 over the Scottish village of Lockerbie.

1989

Jan. 7. Crown Prince Akihito becomes emperor of Japan following the death of his father, Emperor Hirohito.

February. Soviet troops withdraw from Afghanistan, but the civil war continues.

June 4. Chinese troops kill hundreds of pro-democracy demonstrators in Beijing's Tiananmen Square, *photo right.*

Aug. 18. Communist rule ends in Poland. The Communists also will lose power in Hungary and Romania, and demonstrations in East Germany will lead to the demolition of the Berlin Wall.

© Jacques Langevin/Corbis-Sygma

1990

March 21. Namibia, Africa's last territory, becomes an independent nation.

April 25. Marxist Sandinista rule ends in Nicaragua.

Aug. 2. Iraq invades Kuwait.

Oct. 3. East and West Germany are reunited.

Dec. 9. Lech Walesa, leader of the Solidarity movement, wins the first direct presidential elections in Poland's history.

Dec. 16. Jean-Bertrand Aristide is elected president in Haiti's first free elections.

1991

Jan. 16–March 3. A U.S.-led international force defeats Iraq and liberates Kuwait in the Persian Gulf war.

June 25. Slovenia and Croatia declare their independence of Yugoslavia; Macedonia also will declare its independence.

July 31. U.S. President George Bush and Soviet President Gorbachev sign the Strategic Arms Reduction Treaty.

Sept. 6. The USSR recognizes the independence of Latvia, Lithuania, and Estonia.

Dec. 8. The Commonwealth of Independent States is established to replace the USSR.
Dec. 25. The Soviet Union itself collapses.

© Peter Turnley/Black Star

1992
Jan. 16. El Salvador's 12-year-old civil war ends.
March 1. Voters in Bosnia and Herzegovina vote to become independent of Yugoslavia.
Sept. 22. Yugoslavia is expelled from the UN because of its role in the war in Bosnia.
Oct. 4. A 16-year-long civil war in Mozambique ends.

1993
Jan. 1. Czechoslovakia splits into two countries, the Czech Republic and Slovakia.
Jan. 3. U.S. President George Bush and Russian President Boris Yeltsin sign the second Strategic Arms Reduction Treaty.
May 24. The Ethiopian province of Eritrea declares itself an independent nation.
Sept. 13. Israeli and Palestinian leaders sign an agreement that will lead to Palestinian self-rule in the Gaza Strip and some parts of the West Bank.

1994
May 2. Nelson Mandela, *photo above*, is elected president of South Africa after winning that nation's first all-race elections.
July 8. North Korean President Kim Il Sung dies; his son Kim Jong Il assumes power.
July 25. Israel and Jordan formally end their 46-year-long state of war.

1995
Nov. 4. Israeli Prime Minister Yitzhak Rabin is assassinated by a Jewish extremist opposed to Rabin's plans to make peace with the Palestinians.

1996
Jan. 20. Palestinians choose a new self-rule Palestinian Authority government; Yasir Arafat of the Palestine Liberation Organization (PLO) is elected as its president.

1997
July 1. China resumes sovereignty over Hong Kong, ending 165 years of British rule, *photo below.*
Aug. 31. Diana, princess of Wales, dies following a car crash in Paris, France.

1998
April 10. In Northern Ireland, leaders of Great Britain and Ireland, and Protestant and Catholic groups, reach an agreement designed to bring peace to the region.
May. India and Pakistan each conduct a series of underground nuclear tests.

William E. Shapiro

© Peter Turnley/Black Star

The United States celebrates its bicentennial, July 4, 1976.

1900

Nov. 6. Republican William McKinley, the 25th president, is reelected.

1901

Sept. 14. Following the assassination of President McKinley, Vice-President Theodore Roosevelt is sworn in as the 26th president.

1903

Nov. 18. Through a treaty with Panama, the United States acquires the rights to the Panama Canal Zone.

1904

Nov. 8. Theodore Roosevelt is elected to a full presidential term.

1906

April 18–19. Most of San Francisco, CA, is destroyed by an earthquake, *photo below.*
June 30. The Pure Food and Drug Act is passed by Congress.

1907

March 21. U.S. Marines are sent to Honduras to put down a revolution.
Nov. 16. Oklahoma becomes the 46th state.

1908

Nov. 3. Republican William Howard Taft is elected the 27th president.

1909

Feb. 12. The National Association for the Advancement of Colored People (NAACP) is founded.

1912

Jan. 6. New Mexico becomes the 47th state.

Feb. 14. Arizona becomes the 48th state.

Nov. 5. Democrat Woodrow Wilson, *photo below*, is elected the 28th president.

© Culver Pictures, Inc.

IN SAFE WATERS AT LAST

1913

May 31. The 17th Amendment to the Constitution, establishing direct election of senators, is ratified. The 16th Amendment, calling for a graduated income tax, was approved on Feb. 25, 1913, *cartoon right.*

Dec. 23. The Federal Reserve Bill, a basic reform of the U.S. banking system, is signed into law by President Wilson.

1914

Aug. 18. President Wilson proclaims U.S. neutrality in World War I.

1915

July 28. U.S. Marines land in Haiti, beginning a 20-year period of military occupation.

1916

March 15. Gen. John J. Pershing leads U.S. troops into Mexico to punish revolutionary Pancho Villa, who had raided New Mexico a week earlier. The forces will withdraw on Feb. 5, 1917.

May 15. U.S. Marines land in the Dominican Republic to restore order and will occupy the country until 1924.

Nov. 7. President Wilson is reelected.

1917

March 2. The Jones Act is enacted, making Puerto Rico a U.S. territory and Puerto Ricans U.S. citizens.

March 31. The Virgin Islands, purchased from Denmark, become a U.S. territory.

April 6. The United States declares war on Germany, entering World War I.

© Brown Brothers

1918

Jan. 8. President Wilson announces his Fourteen Points as the basis for peace following World War I.

Nov. 11. World War I ends.

1919

Jan. 16. The 18th Amendment to the U.S. Constitution, which prohibits the transportation and sale of alcoholic beverages, is ratified; Prohibition will go into effect on Jan. 16, 1920.

1920

Nov. 2. Republican Warren G. Harding is elected the 29th president.

1922

Feb. 27. The U.S. Supreme Court declares the 19th Amendment to the Constitution, which gives women the right to vote, to be constitutional; it was ratified in 1920.

1923

Aug. 3. Vice-President Calvin Coolidge is inaugurated as the 30th U.S. president, after the death of President Harding the previous day.

1924

May 10. J. Edgar Hoover is named director of the Federal Bureau of Investigation (FBI).

June 15. Congress approves a law making all American Indians born in the United States citizens.

Nov. 4. President Coolidge is elected to a full term as president.

1925

July 21. John T. Scopes is tried and found guilty of teaching the theory of evolution in a Dayton, TN, high school.

1926

May 2. U.S. Marines land in Nicaragua to put down a revolt and protect U.S. interests. They will depart in 1933.

© Granger Collection

1928

Nov. 6. Republican Herbert Hoover is elected the 31st president.

1929

Oct. 29. The Wall Street stock market crashes, precipitating a worldwide economic depression, *photo right.*

1930

July 3. The Veterans Administration is established.

1932

March 1. The infant son of aviation hero Charles A. Lindbergh is kidnapped; he will be found dead on May 12.

Nov. 8. Democrat Franklin D. Roosevelt is elected the 32d president.

1933

March 4. Frances Perkins becomes the first woman cabinet member in U.S. history when President Roosevelt appoints her secretary of labor.

March 9. Congress passes the first of Roosevelt's New Deal programs, which are designed to counter the effects of the depression.

Dec. 5. The 21st Amendment to the U.S. Constitution, ending Prohibition, is ratified.

1935

Aug. 14. President Roosevelt signs legislation establishing the Social Security System, *photo below.*

Sept. 8. Huey P. Long, Louisiana senator and former governor, is assassinated.

1936

Nov. 3. Roosevelt is reelected president.

© AP/Wide World Photos

1938

May 26. The House of Representatives sets up the Dies Committee to investigate un-American groups, including Nazis and Communists.

1939

Sept. 5. Four days after the outbreak of World War II in Europe, the United States declares its neutrality.

1940

Sept. 16. The first U.S. peacetime draft is enacted by Congress.

Nov. 5. President Roosevelt is reelected to a third term.

1941

March 11. President Roosevelt signs the Lend-Lease Bill, allowing the transfer of U.S. war materiel to those nations whose defense the president considers vital.

Dec. 7. The Japanese bomb U.S. military bases at Pearl Harbor, Hawaii.
Dec. 8. The United States declares war on Japan.
Dec. 11. The United States declares war on Germany and Italy.

© AP/Wide World Photos

1942
Feb. 19. The U.S. government orders the internment of 110,000 West Coast Japanese-Americans.
June 4–6. A U.S. fleet defeats a Japanese fleet at the Battle of Midway, ending Japanese expansion in the Pacific.

1944
June 6. On D-Day, American and other Allied forces land at Normandy, France.
Nov. 7. Roosevelt is reelected for an unprecedented fourth term; Harry S. Truman is chosen vice-president.

1945
February. The U.S. flag is raised on Mount Suribachi, Iwo Jima, following severe fighting, *photo above*.
April 12. President Roosevelt dies; Vice-President Truman is inaugurated as the 33d president.
May 7. Germany surrenders to the United States and the Allies.
Aug. 14. Japan surrenders to the United States and the Allies, days after the United States drops atomic bombs on the Japanese cities of Hiroshima and Nagasaki.

1946
July 4. The United States grants independence to the Philippines.

1947
March 12. President Truman outlines the Truman Doctrine, a plan to help Greece and Turkey resist Communist aggression.
June 5. The U.S. Marshall Plan for the postwar economic recovery of Europe is proposed.
June 23. The Taft-Hartley labor bill becomes law.

© Byron Rollins/AP/Wide World Photos

1948
Nov. 2. Surprising many polls and newspapers, *photo left*, Truman defeats Republican Thomas E. Dewey and is elected to a full term as president.

1950
June 27. Two days after North Korea invades South Korea, the United States, with a mandate from the UN, orders American forces to the area to assist South Korea.

1951
Feb. 26. The 22d Amendment to the U.S. Constitution, restricting American presidents to two terms, goes into effect.
April 11. President Truman dismisses Gen. Douglas MacArthur from all of his posts, including that of supreme commander in Korea.

© Granger Collection

1952
July 25. The U.S. Commonwealth of Puerto Rico is established.
Nov. 1. The United States tests the first hydrogen bomb.
Nov. 4. With "I like Ike" as a campaign slogan, *photo right*, Dwight D. Eisenhower is elected the 34th president; Sen. Richard M. Nixon is his running mate.

1953
June 19. Julius and Ethel Rosenberg are executed for atomic espionage.
July 27. The Korean war ends.

© UPI/Corbis-Bettmann

1954

May 17. Racial segregation in public schools is declared unconstitutional by the U.S. Supreme Court.

Dec. 2. Sen. Joseph R. McCarthy (R-WI) is condemned by the Senate for his abuse of the Senate.

1955

Nov. 25. The Interstate Commerce Commission bans racial segregation on interstate trains and buses.

Dec. 1. Rosa Parks, a 42-year-old African-American seamstress, refuses to give up her seat on a Montgomery, AL, bus to a white man, *photo left*. The incident inaugurates the civil-rights movement.

1956

Nov. 6. The Eisenhower-Nixon ticket is reelected.

1957

Sept. 24. President Eisenhower sends federal troops to Little Rock, AR, to enforce school integration.

1958

July 15. U.S. Marines land in Beirut, Lebanon, to protect the nation's pro-Western government; they will withdraw by October 25.

July 29. The National Aeronautics and Space Administration (NASA) is established.

1959

Jan. 3. Alaska becomes the 49th state.

Aug. 21. Hawaii becomes the 50th state.

1960

May 1. An American U-2 spy plane is shot down over the Soviet Union.

Nov. 8. Democratic Sen. John F. Kennedy defeats Vice-President Nixon to win the U.S. presidential election. Kennedy and his running mate, Lyndon B. Johnson, take office on Jan. 20, 1961, *photo right*.

© UPI/Corbis-Bettmann

1961

March 1. President Kennedy establishes the Peace Corps.

April 17. Cuban exiles, backed by the U.S. Central Intelligence Agency, attempt the unsuccessful Bay of Pigs invasion.

1962

Nov. 20. The Cuban missile crisis ends, as Soviet missiles and bombers are withdrawn from Cuba, and the United States ends its blockade of Cuba.

1963

Aug. 28. More than 200,000 people attend the March on Washington for civil rights in Washington, DC, and hear Martin Luther King, Jr., declare, "I have a dream."

Nov. 22. President Kennedy is assassinated in Dallas, TX; Vice-President Johnson is inaugurated as the 36th president, *photo right*.

© Cecil Stoughton/LBJ Library Collection

1964

Feb. 23. The 24th Amendment to the U.S. Constitution, prohibiting poll taxes in federal elections, is ratified.

July 2. The Civil Rights Act of 1964 becomes law.
Oct. 14. Civil-rights leader Martin Luther King, Jr., is named the winner of the Nobel Peace Prize.
Nov. 3. President Johnson is elected to a full term.

© Fabian Bachrach

1965

Feb. 21. Black Muslim leader Malcolm X is shot fatally in New York City.
March 9. The first U.S. combat troops arrive in South Vietnam.
Aug. 11–16. Race riots in the Watts section of Los Angeles leave 35 dead.

1966

As U.S. involvement in Vietnam increases, antiwar demonstrations are held in various American cities.

1967

Feb. 10. The 25th Amendment to the U.S. Constitution, requiring the appointment of a vice-president when that office becomes vacant and instituting new measures in the event of presidential disability, is ratified.
Oct. 2. Thurgood Marshall, *photo above*, becomes the first African-American member of the U.S. Supreme Court.

1968

April 4. Civil-rights leader Martin Luther King, Jr., is assassinated.
June 6. Sen. Robert F. Kennedy dies after being shot while campaigning for the Democratic presidential nomination.
July 1. The United States—along with the Soviet Union, Britain, and 58 other countries—signs the nuclear nonproliferation treaty.
Nov. 5. Former Vice-President Nixon is elected the 37th president.

1969

June 8. President Nixon announces the start of U.S. troop withdrawals from Vietnam.
June 23. Warren E. Burger succeeds Earl Warren as chief justice of the U.S. Supreme Court.

1970

May 4. Ohio National Guardsmen kill four Kent State University students during an anti–Vietnam war protest, *photo right*.

© John Paul Filo

1971

June 30. The 26th Amendment to the U.S. Constitution, lowering the voting age to 18, is ratified.
Sept. 13. Forty-three people, including 11 prison guards and 32 prisoners, are killed in a four-day revolt at Attica state prison in New York.

1972

Feb. 20. President Nixon begins a historic trip to Beijing, China.
May 15. Alabama Gov. George C. Wallace is shot and paralyzed while campaigning for the presidency.
June 17. The Watergate affair begins with the arrest of five burglars, all working for the reelection of President Nixon, at Democratic Party headquarters in the Watergate complex in Washington, DC.
Nov. 7. Nixon is reelected president.

1973

March 29. The last U.S. troops leave South Vietnam.
Oct. 10. Charged with income-tax evasion, Vice-President Spiro Agnew resigns.

© Dirck Halstead/Liaison Agency

Dec. 6. Gerald R. Ford, Republican House of Representatives leader, becomes vice-president.

1974

Aug. 9. Facing three articles of impeachment, President Nixon resigns, *photo left*; Vice-President Ford takes the oath as the 38th president.

1975

Nov. 12. William O. Douglas announces his resignation from the Supreme Court after 36 years on the bench.

1976

July 4. The United States celebrates its bicentennial.

Nov. 2. Democrat James Earl ("Jimmy") Carter is elected the 39th president.

1977

Sept. 7. The United States and Panama sign two treaties that will transfer the Panama Canal to Panama in the year 2000.

1978

Sept. 6–17. President Carter oversees the Camp David peace accords between Egyptian President Anwar Sadat and Israeli Prime Minister Menahem Begin, *photo right.*

Nov. 18. More than 900 members of a religious cult led by Jim Jones, most of them Americans, commit suicide at Jonestown, Guyana.

Courtesy, Jimmy Carter Library

1979

Jan. 1. The United States establishes diplomatic relations with Communist China.

Nov. 4. The U.S. embassy in Tehran, Iran, is taken over by revolutionaries; various people are taken hostage.

1980

April 7. The United States breaks diplomatic relations with Iran.

Nov. 4. Republican Ronald Reagan is elected the 40th president.

1981

Jan. 20. The U.S. hostages in Iran are released.

Sept. 25. Sandra Day O'Connor is sworn in as the first woman member of the Supreme Court.

1983

Oct. 23. Terrorists blow up the U.S. Marine Corps headquarters in Beirut, Lebanon, killing 241 servicemen.

Oct. 25. U.S. forces invade the Caribbean island of Grenada to oust a pro-Cuban regime.

1984

Nov. 6. President Reagan is reelected.

1985

Nov. 19–21. President Reagan and Soviet leader Mikhail Gorbachev hold a summit meeting in Geneva, Switzerland, *photo left.*

© Terry Arthur/The White House

© Renato Rotolo/Liaison Agency

1986

Sept. 26. Following the retirement of Warren Burger, William H. Rehnquist becomes chief justice of the Supreme Court.

Nov. 3. The Northern Mariana Islands become a self-governing commonwealth of the United States.

1988

Nov. 8. Republican Vice-President George Bush is elected the 41st president.

1989

Dec. 20. U.S. forces invade Panama and depose Gen. Manuel Antonio Noriega as Panama's strongman.

1991

Jan. 16–March 3. A U.S.-led international force liberates Kuwait and defeats Iraq in the Persian Gulf war.

1992

May 3. Five days of rioting and looting end in Los Angeles, following the acquittal of four white police officers in the beating of an African-American Los Angeles motorist; 53 people were killed in the disturbance.

May 7. The 27th Amendment to the U.S. Constitution, barring Congress from enacting midterm pay increases, is approved.

Nov. 3. Democrat Bill Clinton is elected the 42d president.

Dec. 17. The United States, Canada, and Mexico sign the North American Free Trade Agreement.

1993

Feb. 26. Six persons are killed when terrorists explode a bomb at New York City's World Trade Center, *photo above.*

April 19. More than 80 members of the Branch Davidian cult die, as the FBI mounts an attack and their Waco, TX, compound burns down.

1994

Oct 1. Palau, a U.S. trust territory in the Pacific Ocean, becomes independent.

1995

April 19. A car bomb explodes outside a federal office building in Oklahoma City, OK, killing 168 people.

Oct. 3. Former football star O.J. Simpson is found not guilty of first-degree murder in the deaths of his former wife Nicole Brown Simpson and her friend Ronald L. Goldman.

1996

Nov. 5. Bill Clinton is reelected president.

1997

April 24. The U.S. Senate ratifies the Chemical Weapons Convention, a global treaty that bans the development, production, storage, and use of chemical weapons.

1998

Aug. 7. Two bombs explode outside the U.S. embassies in Nairobi, Kenya, and Dar es Salaam, Tanzania, killing more than 200 people. Osama bin Laden, a Saudi-born millionaire believed to be living in Afghanistan, later is indicted by a U.S. federal grand jury in connection with the attacks.

Dec. 19. The U.S. House of Representatives votes to impeach President Clinton for lying under oath and for obstructing justice.

1999

Feb. 12. The U.S. Senate acquits President Clinton of impeachment charges, *photo right.*

William E. Shapiro

© CBS Photo-Warnecke & Lautenberger

The Beatles launch their first U.S. tour by appearing on television's "Ed Sullivan Show," February 1964.

1901

Ethel Barrymore is hailed by critics as America's most outstanding younger actress for her starring role in Broadway's *Captain Jinks of the Horse Marines*.

1902

The 18-year career of Enrico Caruso, *photo below*, as a recording star begins....Arthur Conan Doyle writes the Sherlock Holmes adventure *The Hound of the Baskervilles*.

1903

Film audiences begin enjoying the Western *The Great Train Robbery*.

© "Opera News"

1904

Feb. 17. Giacomo Puccini's *Madama Butterfly* is performed for the first time at La Scala in Milan.

1905

J.M. Barrie's musical *Peter Pan* opens in New York, starring actress Maud Adams.

1906

Dec. 24. Reginald Fessenden makes the first radio broadcast.

Also in 1906. William Sidney Porter (O. Henry) publishes his first collection of short stories....Upton Sinclair publishes *The Jungle*, leading to the passage of U.S. federal food and drug laws....Norwegian playwright Henrik Ibsen, known for such works as *A Doll's House* and *Ghosts* and regarded by later writers as the father of modern theater, dies at age 78.

© Culver Pictures, Inc.

1909

May. The first performance of the Ballets Russes de Sergei Diaghilev occurs in Paris.

Also in 1909. U.S. architect Frank Lloyd Wright constructs the Frederick G. Robie House in Chicago.

1911

Nestor Film Company of Bayonne, NJ, establishes the first motion-picture studio in Hollywood....Irving Berlin's hit "Alexander's Ragtime Band" popularizes ragtime music.

1912

Leopold Stokowski takes over as conductor of the Philadelphia Orchestra—a post he will hold until 1936.

1913

Feb. 17. The Armory Show—a full-scale exhibition of contemporary painting, organized by the Association of Painters and Sculptors—opens at the 69th Regiment Armory in New York City.

May 29. Igor Stravinsky's composition *The Rite of Spring* premieres in Paris.

1914

George Bernard Shaw's play *Pygmalion* makes its London debut.

1915

D.W. Griffith directs the three-hour-long Civil War motion picture *The Birth of a Nation*....Ruth St. Denis and Ted Shawn organize the Denishawn dance company....Somerset Maugham publishes *Of Human Bondage*.

1916

Poet Carl Sandburg publishes his first book, *Chicago Poems*.

1917

The Original Dixieland Jazz Band makes the first-ever jazz recording, "The Darktown Strutters' Ball."

1919

Walter Gropius establishes the Bauhaus school of design in Germany.

1920

Sinclair Lewis publishes *Main Street*.

1922

Robert Flaherty's documentary *Nanook of the North* is presented....*Reader's Digest* is founded....Irish novelist James Joyce publishes *Ulysses*....T.S. Eliot's poem "The Waste Land" is published....John Barrymore's turn in the title role of Shakespeare's *Hamlet*, *photo above*, brings a modernist, Freudian slant to the play and receives critical acclaim.

1923

The iconoscope, the first television transmission tube, is patented by Vladimir Zworykin....*Time* magazine is founded.

1924

Austrian-born composer Arnold Schoenberg uses his new 12-tone system for the first time in his composition *Quintet for Winds*.

1925

Soviet director Sergei Eisenstein demonstrates the art of film editing in *Battleship Potemkin*....Charlie Chaplin opens in the film *Gold Rush*....Jazz trumpeter Louis Armstrong revolutionizes jazz as he begins leading his own bands, the Hot Five and Hot Seven....F. Scott Fitzgerald, *photo right*, publishes *The Great Gatsby*.

© Corbis-Bettmann

1926

Greta Garbo appears in *The Torrent*, her first film for MGM, and becomes an overnight success....English author A.A. Milne publishes the children's book *Winnie-the-Pooh*.

1927

July. In Paris, Isadora Duncan, a pioneer of modern dance, gives her final performance.

Dec. 27. Jerome Kern and Oscar Hammerstein's production of *Show Boat* premieres on Broadway, ushering in a new era of realism and topicalism in musicals.

Also in 1927. Al Jolson stars in the first "talkie," *The Jazz Singer*....Electronic television is demonstrated for the first time, by Philo Taylor Farnsworth, in San Francisco.

1928

Aug. 31. *The Threepenny Opera* by Bertolt Brecht and Kurt Weill is received well in Germany.

Also in 1928. Walt Disney presents *Steamboat Willie*, introducing Mickey Mouse to film audiences....Spanish classical guitarist Andrés Segovia stages a 40-city tour—his first performances in the United States....General Electric presents the first dramatic television production: *The Queen's Messenger*....*Amos 'n' Andy* is introduced to radio audiences.

1929

The Academy Awards are presented for the first time. *Wings, poster left*, is judged the year's best film....New York City's Museum of Modern Art (MoMA) is founded....Erich Maria Remarque publishes *All Quiet on the Western Front*....*A Farewell to Arms*, by Ernest Hemingway, is published.

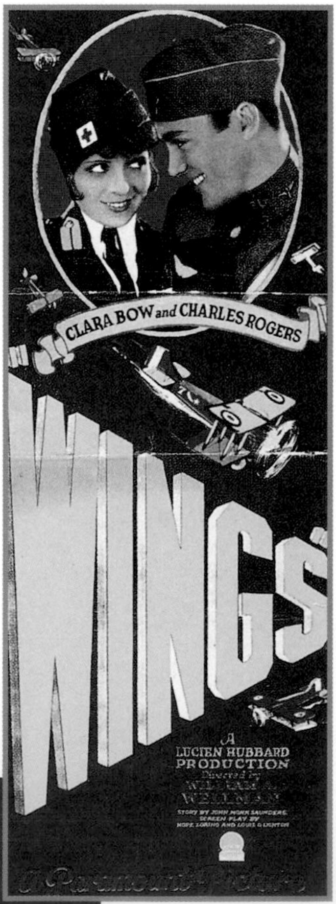

© Archive Photos

1931

Jan. 23. Renowned Russian ballerina Anna Pavlova dies in The Hague, the Netherlands.

May 1. The 102-story Empire State Building opens in New York City.

Also in 1931. Boris Karloff is featured in the film *Frankenstein*....The form of jazz music is expanded with Duke Ellington's composition *Creole Rhapsody*....Pearl Buck publishes *The Good Earth*.

1932

The Royal Shakespeare Theatre opens at Stratford-upon-Avon, England....Radio City Music Hall opens in Rockefeller Center in New York City.

1933

The film *King Kong* is released.

1934

Claudette Colbert and Clark Gable star in the film comedy *It Happened One Night*....Lincoln Kirstein and choreographer George Balanchine establish the School of American Ballet.

1935

Oct. 10. George and Ira Gershwin's *Porgy and Bess* begins a 16-week run in New York City.

Also in 1935. Jazz music enters the swing era, with big bands gaining in popularity.

1936

Life magazine, which will elevate the photo essay to an art form, is introduced....*Gone With the Wind*, by Margaret Mitchell, is published.

Institut Amatller d'Art Hispànic

1937

Walt Disney's *Snow White and the Seven Dwarfs* is the first full-length animated musical motion picture....Pablo Picasso paints "Guernica," *right*, depicting the bombing of that Basque town during the Spanish Civil War....The British Broadcasting Corporation (BBC) begins regular television service.

1938

Oct. 30. Orson Welles' Mercury Theater of the Air production of *War of the Worlds* is so realistic that many radio listeners believe that Martians actually have landed on Earth.

1939

November. *Life with Father*, a play by Howard Lindsay and Russel Crouse, begins a record Broadway run of 3,224 performances.

Also in 1939. The films *Gone With the Wind*, *photo left*, and the *Wizard of Oz* open. They come to rank among the most popular motion pictures of all time....The first public demonstration of television in the United States takes place at the New York World's Fair....John Steinbeck publishes *The Grapes of Wrath*.

© The Kobal Collection, Ltd.

1941

Orson Welles directs and stars in *Citizen Kane*.

1942

Casablanca, starring Humphrey Bogart and Ingrid Bergman, is released....Edward Hopper depicts city loneliness in his painting "Nighthawks."...Singer Bing Crosby records "White Christmas"...Singer Frank Sinatra's solo appearance at New York City's Paramount Theater vaults him to stardom....French author Albert Camus publishes *L'étranger*.

1943

Nov. 14. Leonard Bernstein has his debut with the New York Philharmonic.

Also in 1943. French writer Jean-Paul Sartre publishes the existentialist work *Being and Nothingness*....The Richard Rodgers and Oscar Hammerstein musical *Oklahoma!*, *photo below*, opens on Broadway.

1944

Martha Graham dances in *Appalachian Spring*, which features music by Aaron Copland....Leonard Bernstein's musical *On the Town* premieres on Broadway.

1945

Bebop, a new jazz style, emerges with the first collaborative recordings by Dizzy Gillespie and Charlie "Yardbird" Parker, marking a breaking off of jazz from mainstream pop music of the day.

© Photofest

1946

It's a Wonderful Life, photo right, opens in movie houses.

© Movie Still Archives

1947

Full-scale commercial TV broadcasting begins in the United States....*Kraft Television Theatre* begins televising original television dramas. Together with such later dramatic anthology series as *Studio One* and *Playhouse 90*, the shows will represent television's "Golden Age."...Among important new theatrical dramas is *A Streetcar Named Desire*, by Tennessee Williams; the play makes actor Marlon Brando a star.

1948

June. *The Texaco Star Theater* (later *The Milton Berle Show*) makes its debut. The program features television's first superstar, "Mr. Television"—Milton Berle....*Toast of the Town* (later *The Ed Sullivan Show*), a Sunday-night variety show, begins a 23-year run.

Also in 1948. The New York City Ballet, organized from the American Ballet by George Balanchine, gives its first performance....American painter Andrew Wyeth completes his "Christina's World," which becomes a very popular painting.

1949

George Orwell, a British author, publishes *1984*....Arthur Miller's *Death of a Salesman* challenges the "American dream" of material wealth.

1950

Recent paintings by Jackson Pollock and Willem de Kooning illustrate a new movement—abstract expressionism.

© CBS Photo Archive

1951

Dec. 24. Television viewers watch Gian Carlo Menotti's *Amahl and the Night Visitors*, the first opera written expressly for television.

Also in 1951. *I Love Lucy, photo left,* makes its debut....J.D. Salinger publishes *The Catcher in the Rye*.

1952

November. Agatha Christie's *The Mousetrap* opens in London. It will become the world's longest-running play.

Also in 1952. The "adult" Western *High Noon* enjoys tremendous popularity....Gene Kelly delights filmgoers in the musical *Singin' in the Rain*.

1953

African-American writer James Baldwin publishes his first novel, *Go Tell It on the Mountain*....The play *Waiting for Godot* by Samuel Beckett is popular.

1954

April 4. Arturo Toscanini retires as conductor of the NBC Symphony Orchestra.

Nov. 3. French painter Henri Matisse dies in Nice.

1955

Jan. 7. Contralto Marian Anderson, *photo right,* is the first African-American to sing at New York's Metropolitan Opera.

Also in 1955. One of the first rock 'n' roll hits, "Maybellene" by Chuck Berry, goes to Number 1 on the rhythm-and-blues chart....*The Honeymooners* premieres.

© FPG International

1956

Oct. 29. Maria Callas makes her Metropolitan Opera debut in *Norma*.

Also in 1956. Singer Elvis Presley has his first hit, "Heartbreak Hotel"; it is followed by several more before year's end....With the release of such song hits as "Jamaica Farewell" and "The Banana Boat Song," Harry Belafonte introduces calypso music to the mainstream....*My Fair Lady*, by Alan Jay Lerner and Frederick Loewe, based on Shaw's *Pygmalion*, is a hit on Broadway.

1957

Jack Kerouac's *On the Road*, as well as Allen Ginsberg's 1956 *Howl*, typify the writings and concerns of the "beat" generation....Jerome Robbins' musical *West Side Story* opens on Broadway....Eugene O'Neill's *Long Day's Journey into Night* receives a Pulitzer Prize.

1958

March 30. The Alvin Ailey American Dance Theater gives its initial performance.

April 14. Harry L. (Van) Cliburn wins the International Tchaikovsky piano competition.

Also in 1958. New York City's Seagram Building, designed by Mies van der Rohe, is completed....Revelations occur regarding the rigging of popular quiz shows such as *Twenty-One*....Russian writer Boris Pasternak declines the Nobel Prize for literature, a year after *Doctor Zhivago* is published.

© Rafael Macia/Photo Researchers, Inc.

1959

Frank Lloyd Wright's Guggenheim Museum, *photo left*, opens in New York City.

1960

A debate between presidential contenders is televised for the first time and is watched by some 75 million viewers—the largest television audience ever, up to that time....Alfred Hitchcock's *Psycho* begins to terrorize filmgoers.... The film epic *Ben Hur* wins the Oscar for best film....The Dave Brubeck Quartet, a jazz band, has a crossover hit with "Take Five," which hits the top 25 on the pop chart....John Updike's second novel, *Rabbit, Run*, marks his ascendance in popularity and spawns three eventual sequels.

1961

Joseph Heller's satiric *Catch-22* is published.

1962

February. Rudolf Nureyev, formerly of the Kirov Ballet, who defected to the West in June 1961, dances with Margot Fonteyn in the Royal Ballet's production of *Giselle*.

Also in 1962. Peter O'Toole stars in the film *Lawrence of Arabia*....The British pop group The Beatles makes its first recordings....*Who's Afraid of Virginia Woolf?* brings Edward Albee popular acclaim and wins both a Tony and a New York Drama Critics Circle Award.

1964

Pop art—featuring the works of Roy Lichtenstein, Claes Oldenburg, Andy Warhol, and others—enjoys popularity....The musical *Fiddler on the Roof*, directed and choreographed by Jerome Robbins, opens on Broadway.

1965

Aug. 27. French architect, city planner, printer, and author Le Corbusier (Charles Édouard Jeanneret) dies while swimming off Cap-Martin, France.

Also in 1965. The Rolling Stones, *photo right*, a blues-tinged British rock band, become international stars with their hit song "(I Can't Get No) Satisfaction," which

© Baron Wolman/The Image Works

sells more than 1 million copies in the United States and reaches Number 1 on the U.S. charts....All television programs begin to be broadcast in color....*I Spy*, the first weekly TV drama to feature an African-American in a starring role (Bill Cosby) debuts on NBC.

1966

Sept. 16. The new Metropolitan Opera House at New York City's Lincoln Center opens with a performance of Samuel Barber's *Antony and Cleopatra*.

1967

Katharine Hepburn and Spencer Tracy star in their last film together, *Guess Who's Coming to Dinner?*....The U.S. Congress creates television's Public Broadcasting System (PBS), a nonprofit corporation....*One Hundred Years of Solitude*, by Colombian author Gabriel García Márquez, brings to the world's attention the Latin American literary form of "magic realism" and helps pave the way for international recognition for other Latin American authors....The rock musical *Hair* is a hit with its celebrations of the lifestyle of "hippies."

1969

A music festival held near Woodstock, NY, *photo above*, in August attracts a crowd of some 400,000....The British rock group The Who creates *Tommy*, the first "rock opera"; it is the first rock-music work ever to be staged at New York's Metropolitan Opera House....On PBS, the children's educational program *Sesame Street*, *photo right*, debuts.

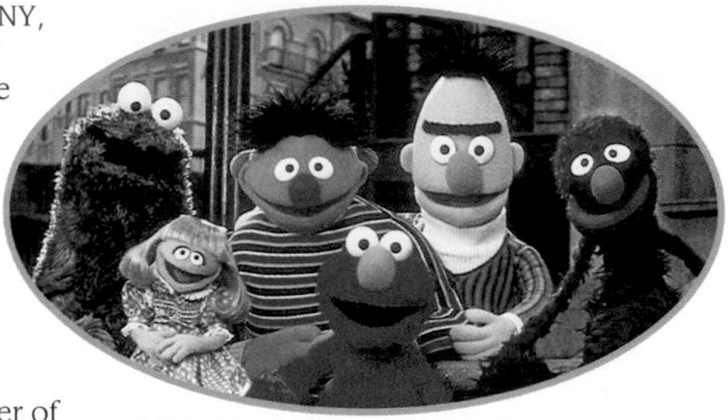

© Richard Termine/Children's Television Workshop

1970

Jan. 16. Buckminster Fuller, the designer of the geodesic dome, is awarded the Gold Medal of the American Institute of Architects.

Also in 1970. The deaths of two of rock music's major stars, Jimi Hendrix and Janis Joplin, herald the beginning of hard times for the counterculture.

1971

Sept. 8. The John F. Kennedy Center for the Performing Arts in Washington, DC, is inaugurated with the premiere of Leonard Bernstein's *Mass*.

Oct. 24. Spanish-born cellist Pablo Casals conducts the premiere of his *Hymn to the United Nations*, with text by W.H. Auden, at UN Day in New York.

Also in 1971. The British band Led Zeppelin, one of the most popular rock groups in history, releases its soon-to-be-classic song "Stairway to Heaven."...*All in the Family*, *photo left*, premieres on CBS....Chile's Pablo Neruda wins the Nobel Prize for literature for his internationally popular poetry....Andrew Lloyd Webber becomes one of theater's dominant figures with the hit musical *Jesus Christ Superstar*.

© Globe Photos

1972

Francis Ford Coppola directs Marlon Brando in *The Godfather*....Sir Rudolf Bing's 22-year reign as general manager of the Metropolitan Opera ends...."Glitter rock" attains popularity as British musician David Bowie launches an international tour to promote his album *The Rise and Fall of Ziggy Stardust and the Spiders from Mars*....The comedy series *M*A*S*H* makes its debut.

1973

March 25. American photographer Edward Steichen, who helped turn photography into a fine art, dies in West Redding, CT. He had served as director of photography at the Museum of Modern Art (1947–62).

Also in 1973. The album *Dark Side of the Moon*, by the British band Pink Floyd, is released; it will have the longest top-200 run ever, spending 741 weeks on the U.S. charts....Thomas Pynchon's *Gravity's Rainbow* is published; some critics find it unbearably complicated, while others hail it as a successor to Joyce's *Ulysses*....The Broadway musical *A Little Night Music* marks Stephen Sondheim's ascendance in the theater world.

© Everett Collection, Inc.

1974

The International Center of Photography opens in New York City....A new comedy series on ABC, *Happy Days*, debuts; set in the 1950s, it becomes a hit when the character "Fonzie," played by Henry Winkler, becomes a national star.

1975

April 7. Beverly Sills, longtime coloratura with New York City Opera, makes her debut at the Metropolitan Opera in Gioacchino Rossini's *Siege of Corinth*.

July 25. *A Chorus Line* debuts on Broadway, where it remains for a record 6,137 performances until closing in 1990. The musical earns nine Tony Awards and a Pulitzer Prize.

Oct. 11. The late-night comedy show *Saturday Night Live* premieres, becoming a major hit and the source of some of television and film's major comedy stars of the 1980s and beyond.

Also in 1975. Singer-guitarist Bruce Springsteen releases a hit album, *Born to Run*, to much acclaim; he is hailed as a major star and appears on the covers of *Time* and *Newsweek*....Home Box Office (HBO), a New York–based pay cable channel, goes national through the use of satellites and helps revolutionize the cable and television industries.

1976

British guitarist and teen idol Peter Frampton's *Frampton Comes Alive* becomes the biggest-selling live pop album ever.

1977

Aug. 16. The death of Elvis Presley elevates him to the status of a cult figure, and his home in Memphis, "Graceland," becomes a shrine for fans.

Also in 1977. George Lucas' film *Star Wars, photo above,* is released and becomes a big success....The Spoleto Festival USA holds its inaugural season in Charleston, SC....The landmark TV miniseries *Roots*—following the fictionalized family history of African-American journalist Alex Haley—is broadcast in January, garnering an audience of some 130 million and winning six Emmy Awards.

1978

Feb. 26. Russian-born pianist Vladimir Horowitz marks the 50th anniversary of his U.S. debut with a performance at the White House.

Also in 1978. The December 1977 release of the hit film *Saturday Night Fever*, with a soundtrack by the BeeGees, turns the dance music known as disco into a worldwide craze....Yiddish-language writer Isaac Bashevis Singer wins the Nobel Prize for literature.

1979

"Moonrise, Hernandez," a landscape photograph taken by Ansel Adams in 1941, sells at auction for $15,000, a record amount at the time.

1980

Country-music star Loretta Lynn, the first woman in that genre to earn $1 million, is named performer of the decade by the Academy of Country Music....Entrepreneur Ted Turner

establishes the satellite-broadcast Cable News Network (CNN), the first TV network devoted entirely to news. The reports of corrrespondent Peter Arnett, *photo at bottom of page 33*, from world trouble spots become a CNN fixture.

1981

The first 24-hour music channel, Music Television or MTV, is introduced by Warner Amex Satellite Entertainment Company.

© Tom Gates/Pictorial Parade/ Archive Photos

1982

The release of the album *Thriller* turns Michael Jackson, *photo right*, into an international superstar. The album produces seven top-ten singles and becomes the best-selling record of all time....The sitcom *Cheers* premieres on NBC.

1983

David Mamet's Pulitzer Prize–winning drama *Glengarry Glen Ross* premieres in London; it opens in New York the following year.

1984

Run-D.M.C.'s self-titled album becomes the first rap album ever to sell 500,000 copies and to have a video appear on MTV....Music videos are pervasive and hold an increasingly important place in pop-music culture; the trend is reflected in the creation of the annual MTV Video Music Awards.

1985

The Boston Pops Orchestra celebrates its 100th anniversary.

1986

September. Oprah Winfrey's talk show, based in Chicago, goes into national syndication; soon Winfrey is one of the most-recognized figures in the United States.

Also in 1986. Nigeria's Wole Soyinka becomes the first black author to win the Nobel Prize for literature.

1988

Oct. 18. Adding sarcasm and realism to the world of sitcoms, *Roseanne* debuts on ABC.

Also in 1988. Two years after its London premiere, the Andrew Lloyd Webber musical *Phantom of the Opera* opens on Broadway and becomes a long-running fixture.

1990

February. "Monet in the '90s," the most comprehensive exhibit ever of the series paintings of Claude Monet, opens at Boston's Museum of Fine Arts.

July. With Zubin Mehta conducting, Plácido Domingo, José Carreras, and Luciano Pavarotti give the first of what will develop into a series of "Three Tenors" concerts at Rome's Baths of Caracalla. The concert becomes a best-selling recording.

Also in 1990. A ensemble comedy "about nothing," *Seinfeld*—starring stand-up comedian Jerry Seinfeld—debuts on NBC; it becomes one of history's most popular sitcoms and influences comedy shows for years to come.

© NBC/Globe Photos

1991

May 5. New York City's Carnegie Hall marks its 100th anniversary.

1992

May 22. Johnny Carson, *photo left*, host of NBC's *The Tonight Show* for 20 years, retires and is replaced by frequent guest host Jay Leno.

1993

April 3. The new Norman Rockwell Museum opens in Stockbridge, MA.

May 2. An exhibit of 80 paintings from the collection of Dr. Albert C. Barnes opens at Washington's National Gallery of Art.

© Timothy Greenfield-Sanders/Courtesy, Knopf

Also in 1993. Italian mezzo-soprano Cecilia Bartoli makes her U.S. debut in the Houston Grand Opera production of *The Barber of Seville*....Author Toni Morrison, *photo left*, wins the Nobel Prize for literature, becoming the first black woman to win a Nobel; among her novels are *The Bluest Eye* and *Beloved*....Tony Kushner's two-part drama *Angels in America* opens on Broadway. Part I, *Millennium Approaches*, wins the Pulitzer Prize for drama.

1994

April. Kurt Cobain, leader of the band Nirvana—one of the leaders of Seattle-based "grunge" music—commits suicide.

Also in 1994. Steven Spielberg's "Schindler's List" wins Oscars for best film and best director.

1995

September. The $92 million Rock and Roll Hall of Fame, designed by architect I.M. Pei, opens in Cleveland, OH, marking the final "legitimization" of rock music.

1996

June 15. Jazz great Ella Fitzgerald, known as "the first lady of song," dies at age 79.

1997

April 30. The ABC comedy series *Ellen* makes television history when its lead character "comes out" as a lesbian, as does its star, Ellen DeGeneres.

July. A museum devoted to the works of American artist Georgia O'Keeffe opens in Santa Fe, NM.

Also in 1997. The J. Paul Getty Center, which includes a major museum and allied facilities, opens in Los Angeles....*Cats*, a Broadway musical that opened on Oct. 7, 1982, becomes the longest-running show in Broadway history.

1998

May 14. Singer and actor Frank Sinatra, *photo right*, one of the century's best-known public figures, dies at age 82.

© Santi Visalli Inc./Archive Photos

Also in 1998. *Titanic*, *photo below*, becomes the biggest financial success in motion-picture history....The exhibit "Van Gogh's Van Goghs: Masterpieces from the Van Gogh Museum in Amsterdam" opens at Washington's National Gallery of Art....*60 Minutes*, television's first newsmagazine show, marks its 30th anniversary.

The Editors

© AP/Wide World Photos

© Jeff Christensen/Liaison Agency

The New York Stock Exchange experiences a volatile day in 1998.

1900

Feb. 1. Eastman Kodak Co. introduces the $1 Brownie box camera.

Aug. 3. Firestone Tire & Rubber Co. is founded.

1901

March 11. U.S. Steel, the world's first billion-dollar corporation, is formed, as industrialists led by J.P. Morgan buy Carnegie Steel Corp., making Andrew Carnegie the world's richest man.

Items introduced: electric typewriters, safety razors, instant coffee.

1902

The Pepsi-Cola Co. is founded.

Items introduced: Crayola crayons, Teddy bears, Barnum's Animal Crackers.

1903

June 16. Ford Motor Co. is founded with ten employees and begins producing its first car—the Model A.

Dec. 17. The Wright brothers take flight in Kitty Hawk, NC, *photo below*, launching the aviation industry.

1904

A.P. Giannini, a retired produce merchant, establishes the Bank of Italy in San Francisco, which evolves into Bank of America.

Items introduced: Campbell's Pork and Beans, tea bags.

© National Advisory Committee for Aeronautics

1906

June 30. The U.S. Congress passes the Meat Inspection Act and the Pure Food and Drug Act to protect consumers.

Items introduced: the Victrola, electric washing machines, Mack trucks, Fuller Brush Co.

1907

Oct. 22. The Panic of 1907 begins as depositors, fearing the collapse of the banking system, begin withdrawing money from many New York banks. The government is unable to help, but J.P. Morgan and other financiers bail out the ailing banks to stave off a depression.

1908

Sept. 16. William C. Durant founds General Motors Co. by merging the Buick and Olds car companies.

Oct. 1. Ford Motor Co. assembles the first Model T, which at a purchase price of $850 revolutionizes the market for affordable cars.

1909

Items introduced: Kewpie dolls, electric toasters.

1910

Items introduced: food mixers, trench coats, Hallmark cards.

1911

May 15. The U.S. Supreme Court orders the breakup of John D. Rockefeller's Standard Oil Company.

June 15. Computing-Tabulating-Recording Co., later renamed International Business Machines (IBM) Corp., is incorporated in the state of New York.

1913

Dec. 1. Ford's new movable assembly line ushers in the era of mass production, *photo above.*

Dec. 13. The Federal Reserve System is established as the first U.S. central bank.

1914

Sept. 26. The U.S. Federal Trade Commission is established as the government's corporate watchdog.

1915

Jan. 25. Alexander Graham Bell places the first transcontinental phone call, from New York to San Francisco.

Items introduced: Pyrex, aspirin tablets.

1916

July 15. Pacific Aero Products Co., later renamed Boeing Co., is incorporated.

Also in 1916. The eight-hour workday begins to become the industrial standard.

1917

Ford rolls out the first commercially successful tractor.

1918

Items introduced: pop-up toasters, Raggedy Ann dolls (*photo right*), airmail postage, rental cars.

1920

Nov. 2. The country's first commercial radio station, Westinghouse's KDKA in Pittsburgh, makes its first broadcast—the Warren Harding–James Cox presidential-election results.

1921

Items introduced: Chanel No. 5 perfume, Wise potato chips, Band-Aids.

1923

March 3. The first issue of *Time* magazine, *photo right*, is published.

© Time Inc.

1924

July 3. Clarence Birdseye founds the General Seafood Corp., starting the frozen-foods industry, *photo below*.

Items introduced: Wheaties, Kleenex, Metro-Goldywn-Mayer (MGM).

1925

June 6. The Maxwell Motor Co. transfers all rights and obligations to the newly formed Chrysler Corp.

Oct. 2. Scottish inventor John Logie Baird completes the first transmission of moving images, the forebear of television.

Also in 1925. The first motor hotel (motel) in the United States opens in San Luis Obispo, CA.

© Corbis-Bettmann

1926

Nov. 15. The National Broadcasting Co. (NBC) makes its first network radio broadcast with a four-hour "spectacular."

1927

Jan. 27. United Independent Broadcasters Inc. starts a radio network of 16 stations and later becomes the Columbia Broadcasting System (CBS).

Items introduced: Gerber baby food, Hostess cakes.

1929

Oct. 23–29. The Dow Jones Industrial Average, the symbol of Wall Street, plunges, starting the stock-market crash that begins the Great Depression.

1930

Worldwide unemployment reaches 21 million, and more than 1,300 U.S. banks close....Western Air Express merges with Transcontinental Air Transport to become Transcontinental and Western Air (later Trans World Airlines). Other airline companies, including American Airlines and United Airlines, also are developing at this time.

1931

Items introduced: electric razors, Bisquick, Alka-Seltzer (*shown at right in a 1950s advertisement*).

© Bayer Corporation

1932

March 23. The Norris-LaGuardia Act establishes workers' right to strike.

1933

Franklin D. Roosevelt's first "100 Days" as president produce a wealth of economic and social reforms aimed at lifting the country from the Great Depression. The president declares a "bank holiday," and the Banking Act of 1933 establishes the Federal Deposit Insurance Corporation....Inventor Edwin Armstrong receives patents for FM radio-broadcasting technology.

1934

April 18. The world's first Laundromat opens in Fort Worth, TX.

Also in 1934. Such U.S. government agencies as the Securities and Exchange Commission and the Federal Communications Commission are born.

1935

The initial Howard Johnson franchise restaurant opens.

1937

August. Toyota Motor Co. is established.
Item introduced: Spam.

1939

Jan. 1. The Hewlett-Packard partnership is formed.
June 28. Pan American Airways begins the first transatlantic passenger service.
Items introduced: automatic dishwashers, pressure cookers.

1940

Item introduced: Jeeps.

1941

April 10. Ford becomes the last major automaker to recognize the United Auto Workers as the representative for its workers.
Items introduced: Cheerios, aerosol bug sprays, M&M's candies.

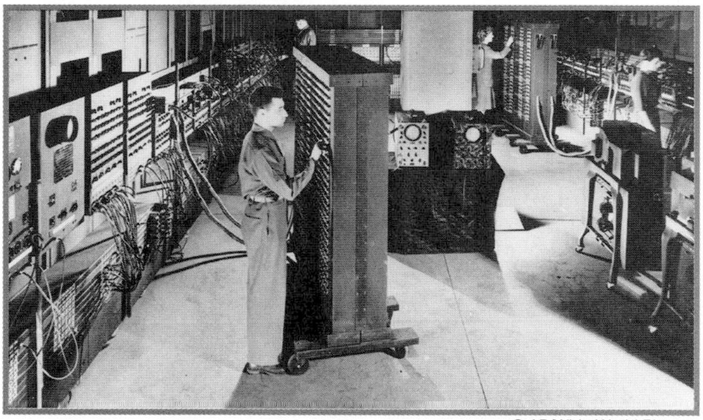

© AP/Wide World Photos

1943

July 1. The U.S. government begins automatically withholding federal income tax from paychecks.
Also in 1943. RCA sells NBC Blue, one of its two NBC radio networks, to Lifesavers candy inventor Edward Noble. It is renamed the American Broadcasting Co. (ABC).

1945

Items introduced: frozen orange juice, zoom lens, Tupperware, *Ebony* magazine.

1946

Feb. 14. The world's first general-purpose electronic computer, the ENIAC (Electronic Numerical Integrator and Computer), built at the University of Pennsylvania, is unveiled, *photo above*.
May 7. Tokyo Telecommunications Engineering Corp., later called Sony, is born.
Items introduced: bikinis, the Slinky, Timex watches.

1947

Feb. 21. Inventor Edwin H. Land unveils instant photography, leading to sales of Polaroid Land Cameras the following year.
October. Construction of Cape Cod and ranch-style houses begins on a former potato field on Long Island, *photo below*; the development will become Levittown, NY.
Dec. 23. Bell Labs invents the transistor, launching an electronics revolution.

1948

Items introduced: Porsche cars, long-playing vinyl records (LPs), Velcro.

1949

Items introduced: the game Scrabble, Silly Putty, Legos.

1950

Items introduced: Minute Rice, Diners Club credit cards.

Joe Scherschel/"Life" Magazine/© Time Inc.

© Steve Winter/Black Star

1952

The first Kentucky Fried Chicken franchise opens.

Item introduced: transistor radios.

1954

France introduces the first value-added tax—a fee imposed during the manufacture of a product.

Items introduced: TV dinners, *Sports Illustrated* magazine.

1955

April. Ray Kroc's first McDonald's franchise opens in Des Plaines, IL, jump-starting the fast-food industry, *photo above.*

July 17. Disneyland Park opens in Anaheim, CA.

Dec. 5. The American Federation of Labor (AFL) and the Congress of Industrial Organizations (CIO) merge. George Meany, *photo below*, is elected president of the new AFL-CIO.

Also in 1955. H&R Block, a company that specializes in the preparation of tax returns, is established.

1957

March. Representatives of Belgium, France, West Germany, Italy, Luxembourg, and the Netherlands sign the Treaty of Rome, establishing the European Economic Community—the EEC (later the European Union—the EU).

Item introduced: Frisbees.

© "Daily Mirror"/Corbis-Bettmann

1958

Oct. 4. British Overseas Airways Corp. offers the first transatlantic passenger jet service.

Items introduced: Hula-Hoops, Sweet 'N' Low, American Express cards.

1959

Jan. 12. Berry Gordy, a former boxer, borrows $800 to found his Motown record empire.

Items introduced: Barbie dolls, panty hose.

1960

Sept. 14. The Organization of Petroleum Exporting Countries is formed by Iran, Iraq, Kuwait, Saudi Arabia, and Venezuela.

Also in 1960. The Interpublic Group of Companies, the first holding company for advertising agencies, is formed.

1962

April 13. Major U.S. steel companies rescind announced price increases in the wake of pressure against the hikes by the John F. Kennedy administration.

Also in 1962. The first Wal-Mart (Rogers, AR) and Kmart (Garden City, MI) stores open.

1963

Betty Friedan's book *The Feminine Mystique* calls for equal rights for women and helps to launch the women's-liberation movement. More and more women will join the workforce as a result of the movement.

1964

Item introduced: Ford Mustangs, *photo right*.

Courtesy, Ford Motor Co.

1965

July 27. The Federal Cigarette Labeling and Advertising Act, requiring health warnings on all cigarette packages, is signed into law.

Also in 1965. Ralph Nader's book *Unsafe at Any Speed* details the safety hazards of U.S. automobiles. The book is a best-seller, and Nader becomes the leader of a growing consumerism movement.

© Richard Lord/The Image Works

1966

Items introduced: MasterCharge (later MasterCard), fiber-optic telephone cable.

1968

Item introduced: the cruise ship *Queen Elizabeth II*.

1969

Feb. 9. The first Boeing 747 jumbo jet takes flight.

Also in 1969. Various U.S. government agencies begin investigations of the conglomerate phenomenon—corporations taking over completely unrelated companies....The Defense Department sets up a computer network that will evolve into the Internet.

Item introduced: automatic teller machines, *photo right*.

1970

April 1. The Public Health Cigarette Smoking Act, banning cigarette advertising on radio and television after Jan. 1, 1971, is signed.

November. Lee Iacocca is installed as head of the Chrysler Corp. four months after being dismissed as president of Ford Motors.

Also in 1970. Billboard operator Ted Turner buys an Atlanta UHF TV station in the first step toward building a cable-television empire.

1971

Feb. 8. The Nasdaq stock-market index is born.

May 1. The National Railroad Passenger Corp. (Amtrak), established by the U.S. Congress to run the nation's intercity railroads, begins operation.

November. Intel Corp. debuts the microprocessor, which first is used in calculators but becomes the foundation for the personal-computer revolution.

Items introduced: floppy discs; Walt Disney World in Orlando, FL; Starbucks Coffee Company.

1972

Nov. 14. The Dow closes above 1,000 for the first time....Blue Ribbon Sports becomes Nike.

Also in 1972. Time Incorporated's popular magazine *Life* ceases publication with its year-end issue. The final issue of *The Saturday Evening Post*, a Curtis publication that began in 1821, had been published early in 1969.

1973

April. Federal Express, *photo right*, begins operation.

© Reuters/Ken Dedeno/Archive Photos

1975

Jan. 1. *Popular Electronics* magazine heralds the invention of a personal computer, the Altair, developed by a company called MITS using an Intel microprocessor. The PC era begins.

Nov. 29. Bill Gates coins the name Microsoft for the company he and friend Paul Allen form to write the BASIC computer language for the Altair.

1976

April 1. Apple Computer is born, selling its first computer, the Apple I, in July for $666.66.

1979

Jan. 1. The United States and Communist China establish diplomatic relations, leading to increased trade and financial agreements between the two countries.

July 1. Sony introduces the Walkman.

Wendy's

Also in 1979. The price of gasoline in the United States exceeds $1 per gallon.

1980

Jan. 7. President Jimmy Carter signs legislation authorizing loans of $1.5 billion to bail out the Chrysler Corp., as Japanese competition, among other factors, hammers the U.S. auto industry.

1981

Aug. 12. IBM unveils its first PC.

Items introduced: Pac-Man, *Jane Fonda's Workout Book.*

1982

More U.S. companies go bankrupt in 1982 than in any year since the Great Depression.

Item introduced: *USA Today.*

1983

Items introduced: compact discs, Cabbage Patch dolls.

1984

Jan. 1. The government-ordered breakup of AT&T takes effect, creating new regional "Baby Bell" phone companies.

Jan. 22. Apple introduces the Macintosh, the first computer to use point-and-click technology.

Item introduced: Wendy's "Where's the beef?" advertisement, *photo above.*

1985

Feb. 20. The American Agriculture Movement and other farm groups stage a major march on Washington, as declining farm income and a tightening of farm credit lead to an unusual number of farm foreclosures in the United States.

April 23. Coca-Cola unveils "New Coke," a $35 million failure.

Also in 1985. Montgomery Ward closes its century-old catalog business.

Item introduced: Nintendo home video games.

1987

April 12. Texaco, the country's third-largest oil company, files for bankruptcy protection after failing to settle a legal dispute with the Pennzoil Co.

Oct. 19. "Black Monday" sweeps Wall Street, as the Dow plunges nearly 23%, or 508 points—the worst sell-off ever in percentage terms.

1989

Feb. 9. Kohlberg Kravis Roberts and Co. completes the $25 billion purchase of RJR Nabisco Inc., then the richest takeover ever.

1990

Jan. 10. Time Inc. and Warner Communications Inc. complete a $14 billion merger to create the world's biggest entertainment company, Time Warner.

April 24. Drexel Burnham Lambert's 1980s junk-bond king Michael Milken pleads guilty to six felonies and agrees to a $600 million penalty; he later is sentenced to ten years in prison.

1991

July 5. International regulators shut down the Pakistani-managed, Abu Dhabi–owned Bank of Credit and Commerce International (BCCI) as a result of management fraud.

Also in 1991. Pan-American World Airways, Eastern Airlines, and Midway Airlines go out of business.

1992

Aug. 11. The nation's largest mall, the Mall of America, opens in Bloomington, MN, *photo at top of page 43.*

1993

July 8. Lincoln Savings chief Charles Keating is sentenced to 12 years and seven months in prison for his role in defrauding investors in the now-defunct Lincoln Savings & Loan Association. Keating, currently serving a ten-year jail sentence for violating California's securities laws and other related fraud charges, was found guilty in January by a federal jury on 73 counts of fraud and racketeering.

July 27. IBM's new chairman, Louis V. Gerstner, Jr., announces an $8.9 billion program to cut the company's costs.

© Carolyn Schaefer/Liaison Agency

1994

Jan. 1. The North American Free Trade Agreement—a regional trading group that includes the United States, Canada, and Mexico—takes effect.

April 15. The World Trade Organization is established, succeeding the General Agreement on Tariffs and Trade that was negotiated in 1947.

1995

July 2. *Forbes* magazine reports Microsoft's 39-year-old chairman, Bill Gates, is now the world's richest man, worth $12.9 billion—a figure that will climb to approximately $77 billion by 1999.

July 17. The Nasdaq composite stock index rises above 1,000 for the first time.

July 31. The Walt Disney Co. announces the $19 billion acquisition of Capital Cities/ABC, the richest media merger of all time.

Aug. 1. Westinghouse announces the $5.4 billion takeover of CBS.

Sept. 20. AT&T unveils a plan to break into three companies—telecom services, communications-equipment making, and computer making.

Nov. 21. The Dow closes above 5,000 for the first time, at 5,023.55.

© Bebeto Matthews/AP/ Wide World Photos

1996

Nov. 15. Texaco agrees to pay $176 million to settle a race-discrimination lawsuit.

Item introduced: Tickle Me Elmo doll, *photo right.*

1997

Oct. 28. The Dow gains a record 337.17 points, or 5%, in a quick rebound after plunging a record 554.26 points, or 7%, to 7,161.15, on October 27.

Also in 1997. ITT, MCI, and McDonnell Douglas are among companies swallowed in the late-1990s merger wave....F.W. Woolworth, a U.S. discount variety store that was founded in 1879, announces that it is closing its 400 remaining U.S. stores.

1998

May 18. The federal government and 20 states file an antitrust lawsuit against Microsoft.

Nov. 12. Germany's Daimler-Benz completes a merger with Chrysler, forming Daimler-Chrysler AG.

Nov. 20. Forty-six states agree to a $206 billion settlement of health claims against the tobacco industry, which also agrees to give up billboard advertising of cigarettes.

Dec. 1. Exxon announces the $74 billion takeover of Mobil, in the biggest merger ever.

Also in 1998. Shopping sales on the Internet exceed an estimated $6 billion for the year.

1999

March 29. The Dow closes above 10,000 for the first time, at 10,006.78.

Eric Quiñones

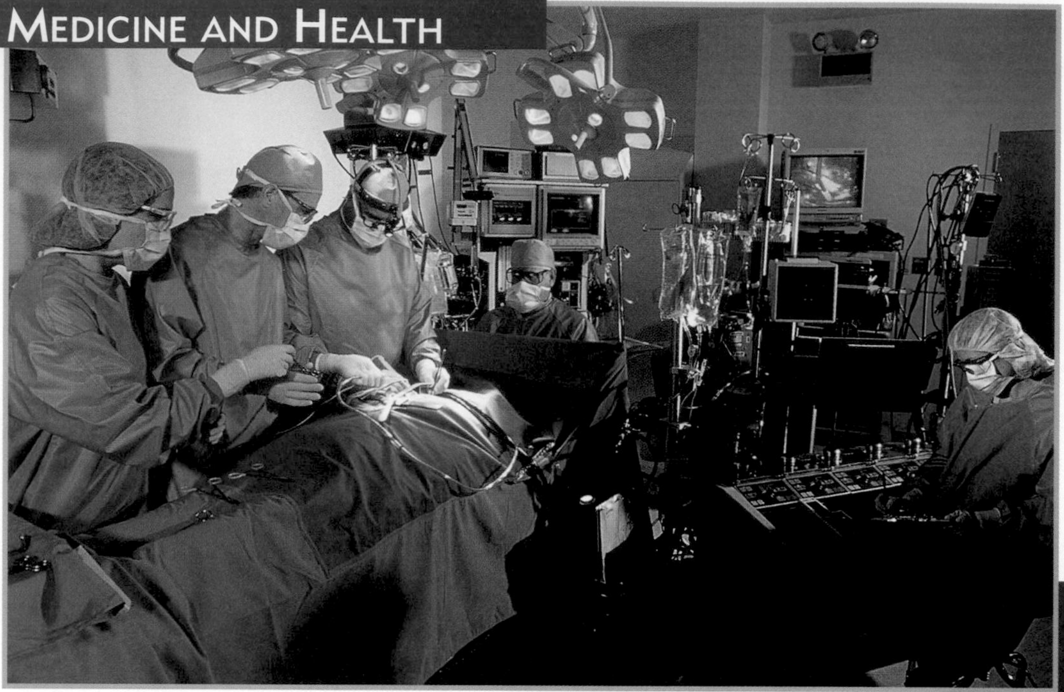

© Pete Saloutos/The Stock Market

The technological advances of the 20th century make surgery safer and more effective.

1900

Austrian psychoanalyst Sigmund Freud, *photo below,* publishes *The Interpretation of Dreams*....Austrian doctor Karl Landsteiner discovers the blood groups A, B, and O....Walter Reed proves that mosquitoes transmit yellow fever.

1901

Austrian psychoanalyst Sigmund Freud introduces the concept of the "Freudian slip."...German chemist Adolf Windaus shows that ergosterol can be activated by ultraviolet light into vitamin D....Eugene Opie discovers that destruction of the islets of Langerhans in the pancreas causes diabetes mellitus.

1902

Austrian doctor Karl Landsteiner discovers the fourth blood group, AB.

1903

Dutch physiologist Willem Einthoven invents the string galvanometer, forerunner of the electrocardiograph....German surgeon Georg Perthes discovers that X rays inhibit the growth of tumors.

© UPI/Corbis-Bettmann

1905

Albert Einhorn synthesizes procaine (Novocaine), which becomes the most widely used dental anesthetic....In France the first version of the Binet-Simon intelligence test is issued....In Germany, Fritz Schaudinn and Erich Hoffmann discover the bacterium that causes syphilis.

1906

German bacteriologist Albert von Wassermann develops a test for syphilis....In England, Frederick G. Hopkins asserts that certain "accessory food factors"—later called vitamins—are essential to life.

1909

French physician Charles-Jules-Henri Nicolle reports that typhus is transmitted by body lice.

1910

Salvarsan, discovered by German bacteriologist Paul Ehrlich, is used successfully to treat syphilis, marking the beginning of modern chemotherapy.

1911

The gastroscope, an instrument for viewing the inside of a patient's stomach, is developed by London doctor William Hill.

1912

Swiss psychiatrist Carl Jung publishes *The Psychology of the Unconscious*....Austrian psychiatrist Alfred Adler publishes *The Neurotic Constitution*.

1913

In Vienna, Béla Schick develops a test for determining susceptibility to diphtheria....William D. Coolidge invents an X-ray tube that enables medicine to make practical use of X rays.

1916

The first birth-control clinic is opened by Margaret Sanger in Brooklyn, NY.

1918

An influenza pandemic that will kill more than 21 million people begins to sweep through Europe, Asia, and the Americas....The use of stored blood for transfusions is begun, by Oswald H. Robertson....Francis Benedict creates the basal metabolism test for measuring the rate of body metabolism.

© Brown Brothers

1921

July 27. Canadian biochemist Frederick Banting and associates announce the discovery of the hormone insulin.

Also in 1921. British bacteriologist Alexander Fleming, *photo right*, discovers an antibacterial agent, lysozyme, in saliva, mucus, and tears....Swiss psychiatrist Hermann Rorschach devises the inkblot test for use in personality studies....French bacteriologists Albert Calmette and Camille Guérin develop the tuberculosis vaccine BCG.

1925

Joseph Goldberger announces that the disease pellagra is caused by a niacin deficiency.

1926

Canadian biochemist James B. Collip extracts and purifies the hormone parathormone from the parathyroid gland.

1928

Sept. 15. British bacteriologist Alexander Fleming discovers the antibiotic penicillin in the mold *Penicillium notatum*.

Also in 1928. George Papanicolaou develops the Pap test for detecting cancer of the cervix and uterus.

1929

Germany's Hans Berger develops the electroencephalogram (EEG)....German doctor Werner Forssmann performs the first cardiac catheterization—on his own heart!

1936

Portuguese neurologist António Moniz first uses prefrontal lobotomy as a treatment for mental illness....At the Pasteur Institute in Paris, Daniel Bovet discovers sulfanilamide, the first sulfa drug.

1937

At the Pasteur Institute in Paris, Daniel Bovet develops the first antihistamine....South African Max Theiler develops a vaccine against yellow fever....The first modern blood bank is established, at the Cook County Hospital in Chicago.

1938

March 28. In Italy psychiatrists demonstrate the use of electric-shock therapy for treating certain mental illnesses.

Also in 1938. England's Philip Wiles develops the first total artificial hip replacement.

1939

René Dubos isolates tyrothricin, the first antibiotic commercially produced and used.

1940

In England, Howard Florey and Ernst Chain extract and purify penicillin, and the compound later becomes available as a clinical drug....In New York, Karl Landsteiner reports the discovery of the Rhesus (Rh) blood factor, an inherited characteristic of red blood cells.

1943

Dutch doctor Wilhelm Kolff designs the first kidney dialysis machine.

1944

Selman Waksman and his assistants announce the discovery of the antibiotic streptomycin....Alfred Blalock and Helen Taussig perform the first operation to correct the congenital heart defect in "blue babies."

1945

April 12. Organization of the first eye bank, Eye Bank for Sight Restoration, is announced in New York.

© Hella Hammid/Rapho/Photo Researchers, Inc.

1946

Dr. Benjamin Spock, *photo right*, publishes *The Common Sense Book of Baby and Child Care*.

1947

In the first use of a broad-spectrum antibiotic, Eugene Payne uses chloromycetin to treat typhus patients.

1948

April 7. The United Nations' World Health Organization begins operation.

Also in 1948. Corneal contact lenses are introduced by optician Kevin Tuohy.

1949

April 13. Philip S. Hench and associates announce that cortisone, a steroid hormone, is an effective treatment for rheumatoid arthritis.

Aug. 29. A nuclear device is used for the first time to treat cancer patients, at the University of Illinois.

1951

John Gibbon invents the heart-lung machine.

1952

Dec. 1. It is announced that the first successful sex-change operation has been performed, in Denmark on American George Jorgensen, who assumes the name Christine.

Also in 1952. In Great Britain, Douglas Bevis describes the use of amniocentesis to test for abnormalities in the human fetus.

1953

Sept. 24. The discovery of a new antibiotic, tetracycline, is reported.

Also in 1953. John Gibbon uses his heart-lung machine as he performs the first successful open-heart operation.

1954

Feb. 23. Inoculations of children using a polio vaccine developed by Jonas Salk begin, *photo at top of page 47*.

March 4. Peter Bent Brigham Hospital in Boston reports the first successful kidney transplant.

June 21. The American Cancer Society reports significantly higher death rates among cigarette smokers than among nonsmokers.

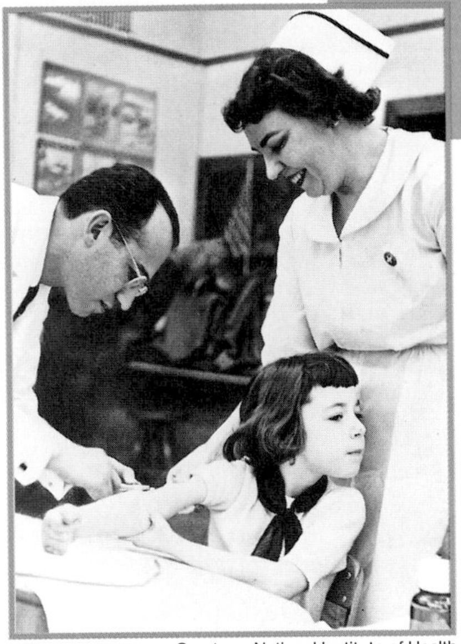

Courtesy, National Institute of Health

1956

Hemodialysis—cleansing blood in an artificial kidney machine—is begun by U.S. doctors.

1957

Scientists working in Great Britain discover interferons, proteins produced by the body that fight viruses....Albert Sabin develops a polio vaccine—based upon live, weakened viruses—that can be given orally.

1958

The first implantable pacemaker is implanted by Swedish surgeon Ake Senning....Scotland's Ian Donald pioneers the use of ultrasound to examine the human fetus.

1959

The first bone-marrow bank is opened by the Vienna (Austria) Cancer Institute.

1960

May 9. For the first time, the U.S. Food and Drug Administration (FDA) approves for sale an oral birth-control pill.

1961

The drug thalidomide is found to cause malformations in newborn babies.

1962

IDU—the first drug to cure a virus-caused disease in humans—is discovered.

1963

An effective vaccine for measles, developed by John F. Enders, is approved....Thomas E. Starzl performs the first human liver-transplant operation....The first successful transplantation of nerves is achieved at Los Angeles Medical School.

1964

The first lung transplant is performed by James D. Hardy at the University of Mississippi....Michael DeBakey and associates perform the first coronary-artery bypass, using part of a vein from the patient's leg....Taxol is identified in the bark of Pacific yew trees and becomes a promising drug for fighting certain cancers....The *U.S. Surgeon-General's Report on Smoking and Health* reports that cigarette smoking is a health hazard.

1965

July 30. President Lyndon Johnson signs into law amendments to the Social Security Act of 1935 that establish Medicare and Medicaid.

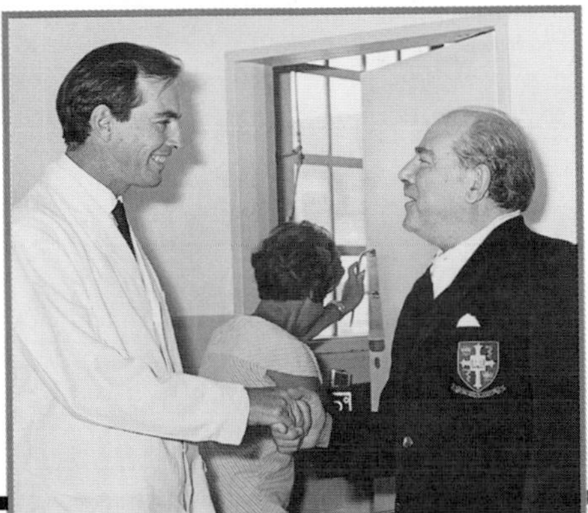

© Pictorial Parade/Archive Photos

1966

Aug. 8. Michael DeBakey is the first surgeon to install an artificial heart pump in a patient.

Also in 1966. Paul Parkman and Harry Meyer develop a vaccine for rubella (German measles)....Insulin is synthesized independently by scientists in the United States and China; it is the first hormone to be synthesized.

1967

Dec. 3. In South Africa, Christiaan Barnard, *at left in photo left*, performs the first successful human heart transplant.

1969

April 4. Surgeons led by Denton A. Cooley replace the diseased heart of a patient with an artificial heart.

Also in 1969. The viral infection that comes to be called Lassa fever is isolated; it is named after the Nigerian village in which it first was found.

1970

Following demonstrations by researchers of the effectiveness of L-dopa therapy in treating patients with Parkinson's disease, the drug is approved by the FDA.

1972

Aug. 25. Computerized axial tomography (CAT scan) is introduced in Great Britain.

Also in 1972. Swiss biochemist Jean Borel discovers cyclosporine, which will revolutionize drug therapy for organ transplants.

1973

April 24. Albert Sabin reports that herpesviruses are factors in nine kinds of cancer.

Also in 1973. The nuclear magnetic resonator (NMR), later called the magnetic resonance imager (MRI), is introduced in Great Britain.

1975

Lyme disease first is identified, in Lyme, CT. It is caused by the spirochete *Borrelia burgdorferi, photo right*, a type of bacteria that lives in the midgut of the black-legged deer tick.

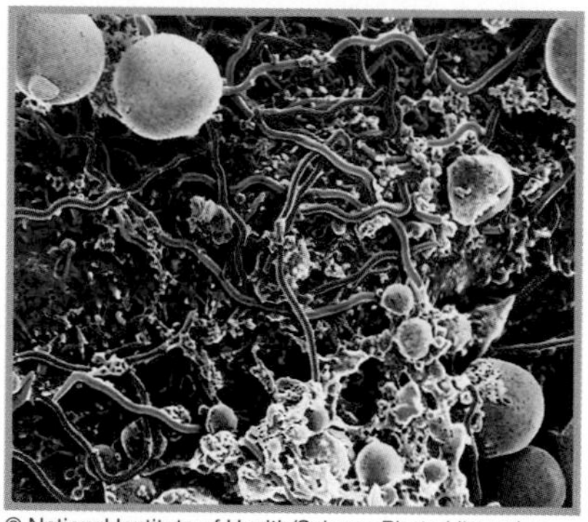

© National Institute of Health/Science Photo Library/ Photo Researchers, Inc.

1976

The first outbreak of Legionnaires' disease occurs in Philadelphia, PA....The first recognized outbreak of Ebola kills more than 400 people in Zaire and Sudan.

1977

Andreas R. Gruentzig invents balloon angioplasty, a method for opening diseased coronary arteries.

1978

July 25. Louise Brown, the first "test-tube baby," is born in England.

Also in 1978. The U.S. Congress establishes the President's Commission for the Study of Ethical Problems in Medicine and Biomedical and Behavioral Research, as continuing medical breakthroughs pose new and troubling ethical questions.

1979

The World Health Organization declares that smallpox has been eradicated totally.

1980

In Germany, Dornier Medical Systems develops the lithotripter, a device that uses sound waves to break up kidney stones.

1981

Nov. 16. A vaccine for hepatitis B developed at Merck Institute for Therapeutic Research is approved.

Also in 1981. Scientists identify a previously unknown disease, acquired immune deficiency syndrome (AIDS)....Surgeons at the University of California at San Francisco perform the first successful operation on a fetus.

1982

Dec. 2. A team led by William DeVries performs the first successful transplant of an artificial heart.

Also in 1982. The FDA approves the first commercial product of genetic engineering, human insulin made by bacteria....Researchers at Stanford University report the first successful use of monoclonal antibodies to treat cancer.

1983

Feb. 14. A 6-year-old boy becomes the first person to receive heart and liver transplants in the same operation.

Also in 1983. Genetic markers are found for Duchenne muscular dystrophy and Huntington's disease....In California, John Buster and Maria Bustillo perform the first successful human embryo transfer.

1984

April 21. Luc Montagnier of France reports isolating the virus believed to cause AIDS.

Also in 1984. The first baby produced from a frozen embryo is born in Australia.

1985

The FDA approves the defibrillator, a device implanted in patients to control abnormally rapid or irregular heartbeat....Human growth hormone made by bacteria—a product of genetic engineering—is approved by the FDA....Tumor angiogenesis factor, which simulates growth of new blood vessels, is found....Genetic markers are found for cystic fibrosis and polycystic kidney disease....Lasers are used for the first time to clean out clogged arteries.

© Camille Tokerud/Liaison Agency

1986

July 23. The FDA approves the first genetically altered vaccine for humans, designed to protect against hepatitis B.

1987

Eli Lilly & Co. introduces Prozac, which becomes the world's best-selling antidepressant....Scientists announce the discovery of the calcium release channel, which regulates passage of calcium into and out of muscle cells.

1990

Sept. 4. A 4-year-old girl becomes the first person to receive gene therapy.

1992

Health organizations recommend that infants sleep on their backs or sides, *as in the photo above*, to reduce the risk of sudden-infant-death syndrome (SIDS).

1993

Oct. 27. Amid skyrocketing health-care costs and an increase in the number of Americans lacking health-care coverage, President Bill Clinton and First Lady Hillary Rodham Clinton present to Congress a plan for comprehensive health-care reform—the Health Security Act. The plan is defeated in 1994.

Also in 1993. The U.S. Environmental Protection Agency (EPA) designates environmental tobacco smoke ("secondhand smoke") as a human carcinogen. "No smoking" signs and symbols, *such as the one by the Action on Smoking and Health group at left,* become more common.

1995

The FDA approves the first U.S. vaccine for chicken pox.

1996

In Great Britain scientists announce the possibility that the agent that causes bovine spongiform encephalopathy ("mad cow disease") can spread to humans via infected beef, causing Creutzfeld-Jakob disease.

1998

March 27. Viagra, the first pill for male impotence, is approved.

July 17. Biologists report that they have deciphered the genome (genetic map) of the syphilis bacterium.

Sept. 23. A successful transplant of a cadaver hand and forearm occurs in France.

Dec. 21. The first vaccine for Lyme disease is approved.

Jenny Tesar

SCIENCE AND TECHNOLOGY

NASA

U.S. astronaut Mark Lee floats freely in space, Sept. 16, 1994.

1900

Three Europeans independently rediscover Gregor Mendel's laws of genetics....England's Frederick G. Hopkins and Sydney William Cole discover the first essential amino acid, tryptophan....Max Planck of Germany, *photo right*, formulates the quantum theory....Paul Villard of France is the first to observe gamma rays....British archaeologist Arthur Evans discovers the Palace of Minos on Crete.

© Hulton-Getty/ Liaison Agency

1901

Dec. 12. The first radio message is sent across the Atlantic, from England to Newfoundland.

Also in 1901. Japanese chemist Jokichi Takamine isolates adrenaline, the first hormone to be isolated....Russian physiologist Ivan Pavlov demonstrates the phenomenon he terms a "conditioned reflex."

1902

French excavators at Susa, the ancient capital of Elam, now in Iran, discover the Code of Hammurabi....Willis H. Carrier designs the first air conditioner.

1903

Dec. 17. At Kitty Hawk, NC, Orville and Wilbur Wright make the first successful flight in a gasoline-powered airplane.

1904

England's Frederick S. Kipping discovers silicones....England's John Fleming patents the first vacuum tube, a diode....England's Arthur Harden discovers the existence of coenzymes (compounds that activate enzymes).

© AP/Wide World Photos

1905

In Germany, Albert Einstein, *photo left*, proposes his special theory of relativity and the law $E=mc^2$....Italy's Enrico Forlanini builds the first successful hydrofoil boat.

1906

Dec. 24. Using a transmitter at Brant Rock, MA, Reginald A. Fessenden makes the world's first radio broadcast.

Also in 1906. Physicist Heike Kamerlingh Onnes of the Netherlands liquefies hydrogen (and helium in 1908)....Great Britain launches the HMS *Dreadnought*, the first modern battleship.

1907

Bertram B. Boltwood demonstrates that the decay of uranium to lead can be used to determine the age of rocks....Lee De Forest patents the Audion vacuum tube, a triode for amplifying radio signals, revolutionizing communications.

1908

In Germany, Fritz Haber develops an inexpensive process for making ammonia....In England, Hans Geiger and Ernest Rutherford develop an instrument for detecting the presence of radiation, which comes to be called the Geiger counter....Swiss chemist Jacques Brandenberger develops cellophane.

1909

Croatian geophysicist Andrija Mohorovicic discovers the boundary between Earth's crust and mantle, now known as the Mohorovicic discontinuity....Leo Baekeland patents the plastic Bakelite, one of the first artificial substitutes for a natural product.

1910

French engineer Georges Claude invents the neon light.

1911

Jan. 26. The first successful seaplane is flown by its inventor, Glenn H. Curtiss.

Also in 1911. In England, Ernest Rutherford formulates his theory that an atom has a positively charged nucleus surrounded by negative electrons....Dutch physicist Heike Kamerlingh Onnes discovers the superconductivity of metals at very low temperatures....In Austria physicist Victor F. Hess discovers cosmic radiation.

1912

German geophysicist Alfred Wegener proposes his theory of continental drift....German physicist Max von Laue develops his theories on the diffraction of X rays by crystals, opening the way to X-ray spectroscopy

1913

English physicist Joseph J. Thomson provides the first confirmation that isotopes of an element are possible....The ozone layer in the upper atmosphere is discovered by French physicist Charles Fabry....In Russia, Igor Sikorsky builds and flies the first multiengine airplane....Swedish engineer Gideon Sundback perfects the zipper when he develops the first practical slide fastener.

1914

Aug. 15. The Panama Canal, *photo right*, opens to commercial vehicles.

Also in 1914. Edward C. Kendall crystallizes and identifies the thyroid hormone thyroxine.

© Hulton-Getty/Liaison Agency

1915

Jan. 25. The first official transcontinental telephone call takes place, between Alexander Graham Bell in New York and Thomas A. Watson in San Francisco.

Also in 1915. In England, Frederick W. Twort discovers bacteriophages (viruses that prey on bacteria)....Albert Einstein announces a new theory of gravitation—general relativity—that identifies gravity with the curvature of space-time.

1918

Harlow Shapley discovers the dimensions of the Milky Way.

1919

England's Sir Frank W. Dyson announces that photographs of a solar eclipse confirm Einstein's theory of gravitation....English physicist Francis W. Aston develops the mass spectrograph and uses it to discover many isotopes.

1920

German chemist Hermann Staudinger shows that polymers are giant molecules consisting of smaller, linked molecules.

1922

Nov. 26. English archaeologist Howard Carter opens the virtually intact tomb of ancient Egypt's King Tutankhamen.

Also in 1922. The first fossilized dinosaur eggs are discovered in Mongolia.

1924

The first fossil of an australopithecine, a relative of early humans, is discovered at Taung, South Africa....French physicist Louis Victor de Broglie proposes that particles have a wave-like nature....Austrian physicist Wolfgang Pauli, *photo below right*, argues that a fourth quantum number is needed to represent the "spin" of an electron.

© Corbis-Bettmann

1925

Edwin Hubble composes a classification scheme for galaxies....Austrian physicist Wolfgang Pauli proposes the exclusion principle, which states that no two electrons in an atom can share the same quantum numbers.

1926

March 16. Robert Goddard launches the first liquid-fuel rocket.

Also in 1926. James B. Sumner isolates crystals of urease and shows that enzymes are proteins.

1927

Excavations near Beijing (Peking) unearth the first fossil remains of "Peking man," a race of *Homo erectus*....The first version of the Big Bang theory of the origin of the universe is advanced by Belgium's Georges F. Lemaître....German physicist Werner K. Heisenberg states his uncertainty principle: that the position and momentum of a subatomic particle cannot be precisely determined at the same time....Transatlantic radiotelephone service is established between the United States and Great Britain.

1928

Margaret Mead's *Coming of Age in Samoa* is published....English physicist Paul Dirac formulates a mathematical description of elementary particles.

1929

Edwin Hubble discovers a relationship between the distance to a remote galaxy and its redshift (Hubble's law), providing evidence that the universe is expanding....Vladimir Zworykin introduces the iconoscope, the first television camera tube.

© Hulton-Getty/Liaison Agency

1930

Feb. 18. The planet Pluto is discovered by Clyde Tombaugh as a result of photographs he took in January 1930.

Also in 1930. Vannevar Bush builds the Differential Analyzer, the first reliable analog computer....Philo T. Farnsworth develops an electronic scanning system that makes TV pictures suitable for the home....British engineer Frank Whittle patents a gas turbine engine for jet aircraft.

1932

In Germany, Hans A. Krebs discovers the urea cycle, the first metabolic cycle to be described....The first particle accelerator is built at the Cavendish Laboratory in England....English physicist James Chadwick confirms the existence of the neutron....Wallace H. Carothers invents nylon, which becomes the first successful synthetic fiber and leads to the development of nylon stockings, *photo at bottom of page 52.*

1933
Karl G. Jansky reports his discovery of radio waves of interstellar origin....Ernst A.F. Ruska of Germany produces the first practical electron microscope.

1934
French physicists Frédéric and Irène Joliot-Curie achieve the first artificial production of a radioisotope.

1935
Nov. 6. Edwin H. Armstrong announces his development of FM broadcasting.

Also in 1935. Charles F. Richter devises a scale for comparing the power of earthquakes....Scottish physicist Robert A. Watson-Watt patents a radiolocator that forms the basis of British wartime radar.

1936
Boulder Dam (later renamed Hoover Dam) begins operation.

1937
May 6. The German airship *Hindenburg* explodes at Lakehurst, NJ.

Also in 1937. In England, Hans A. Krebs discovers the citric acid (Krebs) cycle in respiration....The muon (mu meson) is discovered by Carl D. Anderson....In Italy physicists Emilio Segrè and Carlo Perrier synthesize technetium, the first artificial element....Chester F. Carlson invents xerography, the first photocopying process.

1938
April 1. The first commercially successful fluorescent lamps are introduced.

Also in 1938. In Germany, Otto Hahn and Fritz Strassmann split the uranium atom....In Germany, Konrad Zuse builds the first computing machine to use the binary system.

1939
Aug. 28. The first successful flight of a jet-propelled airplane, a German Heinkel He 178, takes place.

Sept. 14. America's first successful helicopter, developed by Igor Sikorsky, makes its maiden flight.

Also in 1939. Swiss chemist Paul Müller discovers the great insect-killing properties of DDT....French physicists Frédéric and Irène Joliot-Curie demonstrate the possibility of nuclear chain reactions and thus of the atomic nucleus as an energy source....DuMont Laboratories makes the first television sets for the public.

© Corbis-Bettmann

1940
Sept. 12. Prehistoric cave paintings are discovered at Lascaux in France.

Also in 1940. England's John Rex Whinfield produces the synthetic fiber Terylene, later marketed as Dacron.

1942
Dec. 2. A team led by Enrico Fermi, *photo right,* achieves the first controlled nuclear chain reaction.

1943
Howard Aiken completes construction of the Mark 1, a programmable computer....In France, Jacques-Yves Cousteau and Émile Gagnan develop the Aqua-Lung.

1944
Canadian researchers led by Oswald Avery prove that DNA is the hereditary material of the cell....British chemists Archer J.P. Martin and Richard L.M. Synge develop paper chromatography.

Courtesy, Polaroid Corporate Archives

1945

July 16. The first atomic bomb is detonated near Alamogordo, NM.

1946

Joshua Lederberg and Edward Tatum announce their discovery of genetic recombination....J. Presper Eckert, Jr., and John W. Mauchly complete ENIAC, the first general-purpose electronic digital computer....John von Neumann describes the concept of stored computer programs.

1947

Feb. 21. Polaroid Corp.'s Edwin Land, *photo left*, demonstrates a new camera that delivers a print in about a minute.

Oct. 14. Chuck Yeager breaks the sound barrier, flying in the Bell X-1 test plane.

Also in 1947. The Dead Sea Scrolls, a collection of ancient Hebrew documents, are discovered near Khirbet Qumran....Fritz A. Lipmann discovers coenzyme A, an important compound in sugar metabolism....English physicist Cecil Frank Powell and associates discover the pion, the first known meson, in cosmic rays....Willard F. Libby reasons that radiocarbon dating can be used to determine the age of previously living materials....British scientist Dennis Gabor invents holography, a method of photography that generates a three-dimensional image....The transistor is invented at Bell Laboratories.

1948

The first stored program is run on the Manchester Mark 1 computer in England....Eckert and Mauchly's EDVAC is the first computer to use magnetic disks for storing data.

1949

The first jet-propelled passenger airplane, the British de Haviland Comet, is test-flown.

1950

The field of artificial intelligence begins with the publication of British logician Alan M. Turing's *Computing Machinery and Intelligence*.

1951

June 14. UNIVAC, the first computer designed for commercial purposes and the first to use magnetic tape for input, goes into operation.

June 25. CBS airs the first commercial television broadcast in color.

Also in 1951. Grace M. Hopper devises the first compiler to convert a computer programmer's instructions into machine (binary) language....The MASER (Microwaves Amplified by the Stimulated Emission of Radiation) concept is proposed by Charles H. Townes....Electricity is generated from a nuclear plant in Idaho.

1952

Nov. 1. The United States detonates the first hydrogen bomb, on Eniwetok Atoll.

Also in 1952. Donald A. Glaser invents the bubble chamber.

1953

Nov. 21. British Natural History Museum authorities say "Piltdown Man," fragments of which first were discovered in 1911, is a hoax.

Also in 1953. James D. Watson and Britain's Francis Crick—*left and right, respectively, in photo at right*—propose the double-helix structure of DNA...Murray Gell-Mann

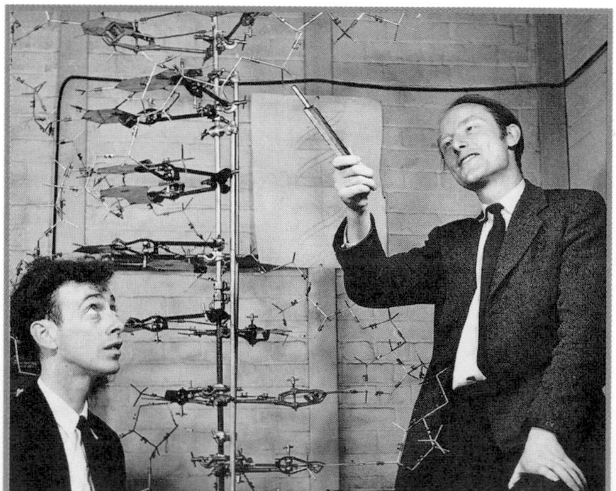
© A. Barrington Brown/Science Source/Photo Researchers, Inc.

proposes the strangeness property of some subatomic particles....IBM introduces its first electronic computer, the 701.

© Hulton-Getty/Liaison Agency

1954

Jan. 21. The USS *Nautilus* (*photo right*), the first nuclear submarine, is launched.

Also in 1954. Researchers at Bell Laboratories develop the photovoltaic cell, which converts solar radiation into electricity.

1955

Owen Chamberlain and others prove the existence of antiprotons (particles of the same mass and spin as protons but having an opposite electric charge)....The first artificial diamonds for industrial use are created.

1956

Sept. 25. The first transatlantic telephone-cable system, between Newfoundland and Scotland, begins operation.

Also in 1956. The neutrino, a subatomic particle whose existence was predicted in 1931, is detected.

1957

Oct. 4. The Soviet Union launches Sputnik 1, the first artificial Earth satellite.

1958

May 1. James Van Allen reports that two radiation belts encircle Earth.

Also in 1958. At Texas Instruments, Jack St. Clair Kilby creates the first integrated circuit....Kitts Peak National Observatory opens near Tucson, AZ.

1959

April 25. The St. Lawrence Seaway, connecting the Great Lakes and the Atlantic Ocean, is opened to traffic.

Sept. 12. The Soviet Union launches Luna 2, the first space probe to reach the Moon, impacting on Sept. 13.

Also in 1959. Grace M. Hopper and others develop COBOL, which becomes the common language for business data processing.

1960

Jan. 23. The U.S. Navy bathyscaphe *Trieste*, with two men aboard, descends to a record 35,800 ft (10 920 m) in the Marianas Trench off Guam.

April 1. The United States launches the first weather satellite, Tiros 1.

Aug. 12. The United States launches the first communications satellite, a large plastic balloon named Echo 1.

Also in 1960. Theodore H. Maiman uses a ruby crystal to obtain the first pulsed laser action....Digital Equipment Corp. begins deliveries of the PDP-1, the first commercial computer to use a keyboard and monitor instead of punched cards.

© UPI/Corbis-Bettmann

1961

April 12. Yuri Gagarin of the USSR, *photo above right*, becomes the first human to orbit Earth.

May 5. Alan B. Shepard, Jr., *photo right*, makes the first U.S. suborbital spaceflight.

Also in 1961. Marshall W. Nirenberg begins to decipher the sequences of nucleotides that make up the genetic

NASA

code....Murray Gell-Mann develops a scheme for classifying subatomic particles, based on the "eightfold way."...The first continuously operating laser is announced by scientists at Bell Laboratories....The first commercial industrial robots are marketed by Unimation Inc.

© AP/Wide World Photos

1962

Feb. 20. John Glenn becomes the first American to orbit Earth.

Aug. 27. The United States launches Mariner 2, which becomes the first space probe to reach the vicinity of another planet, Venus.

Also in 1962. England's John Gurdon creates the first successful clones of an amphibian....Rachel Carson, *photo right*, publishes *Silent Spring*, which warns of the dangers of the indiscriminate use of pesticides.

1963

June 16. Valentina Tereshkova, *photo below right*, becomes the first woman in space, aboard the USSR's *Vostok 6*.

Nov. 1. The USSR launches Polyot 1, the first satellite capable of maneuvering in all directions and able to change its orbit.

Nov. 5. Archaeologists find the remains of a Viking settlement at L'Anse aux Meadows, Newfoundland.

Also in 1963. Maarten Schmidt determines that certain starlike objects called quasars lie far outside our galaxy.

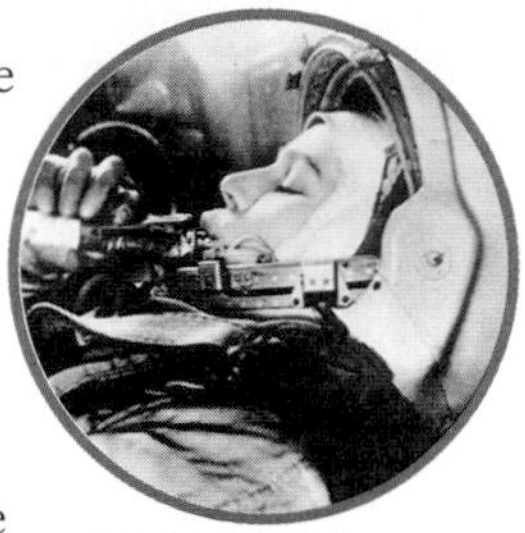

© UPI/Corbis-Bettmann

1964

Arno A. Penzias and Robert W. Wilson discover the existence of cosmic background radiation....Murray Gell-Mann, *photo left*, proposes the quark theory....John G. Kemeny and Thomas E. Kurtz demonstrate BASIC, the first general-purpose computer-programming language.

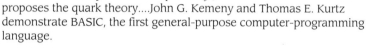

California Institute of Technology

1965

June 7. The U.S. *Gemini 4* completes a mission that features the first space walk by an American.

June 28. The first commercial satellite, Early Bird (Intelsat II), begins communications service.

July 14. The U.S. Mariner 4 becomes the first spacecraft to visit Mars.

Dec. 16. The first rendezvous in space occurs between the U.S. spacecraft *Gemini 6* and *Gemini 7*.

Also in 1965. Cosmic microwave radiation is detected by Arno Penzias and Robert Wilson, providing evidence of the Big Bang....The first chemical laser is made by scientists at the University of California by reacting hydrogen and chlorine.

1966

March 1. The Soviet Union's Venera 3 crashes on Venus, becoming the first space probe to impact another planet.

March 31. The Soviet Union launches Luna 10, which becomes the first spacecraft to enter a lunar orbit.

Also in 1966. The British Hawker Harrier, the first V/STOL (vertical or short takeoff and landing) aircraft, becomes operational.

1967

At Cambridge University, Jocelyn Bell discovers the first pulsar, or "pulsating radio star."

1968

Sept. 21. The USSR probe Zond 5 returns to Earth, completing the first unmanned round-trip flight to the Moon.

1969

March 2. The Anglo-French supersonic transport Concorde, *photo right*, makes its first test flight at Toulouse, France.

July 20. Neil Armstrong and Edwin ("Buzz") Aldrin become the first people to walk on the Moon.

Also in 1969. Arpanet, which eventually grows into the Internet, connects computers at four research institutions.

Air et Cosmos

1970

June 3. Har Gobind Khorana and colleagues announce the first synthesis of a gene from chemical components.

Nov. 17. The USSR probe Luna 17 lands on the Moon and releases Lunokhod 1, the first automated Moon-roving vehicle.

Dec. 15. A capsule released by the USSR probe Venera 7 transmits the first data received on Earth from the surface of another planet, Venus.

Also in 1970. Howard M. Temin and David Baltimore discover the enzyme reverse transcriptase, which becomes important in DNA research....The floppy disk is introduced, greatly speeding access to computer data....Egypt's Aswan High Dam is completed.

1971

April 19. The USSR's *Salyut 1*, the first space station, is launched into orbit around Earth.

Nov. 13. The U.S. spacecraft Mariner 9 becomes the first spacecraft to orbit another planet, Mars.

Also in 1971. Intel Corp. introduces the first microprocessor, developed by Marcian E. Hoff.

1972

July 23. The United States launches Landsat 1 (ERTS-1), the first Earth-resources satellite.

Also in 1972. The pesticide DDT is banned in the United States....Scientists at Bell Laboratories patent an experimental computer that transforms printed text into synthetic speech.

1973

May 14. *Skylab* (*photo below*), the first U.S. space station, is launched and placed into Earth orbit.

Dec. 3. The U.S. Pioneer 10 becomes the first space probe to study Jupiter.

Also in 1973. American biochemists fuse a gene for antibiotic resistance into a bacterium's genetic material, the first demonstration of genetic engineering.

1974

"Lucy," a nearly complete female skeleton of the early hominid species *Australopithecus afarensis*, is uncovered in Ethiopia....An army of life-size pottery figures is discovered in a Ch'in dynasty tomb in China....The U.S. Mariner 10 visits Venus and Mercury....The first tunable, continuously operating, color-center laser is developed at Bell Laboratories.

NASA

1975

MITS introduces the Altair 8800, the first personal computer.

1976

July 20. The U.S. Viking I lands on Mars and sends back the first photographs from the planet's surface.

1977

June 20. The Trans-Alaska Pipeline begins operation.

1978

June 22. James W. Christy and Robert S. Harrington discover the only known moon of Pluto, which is named Charon.

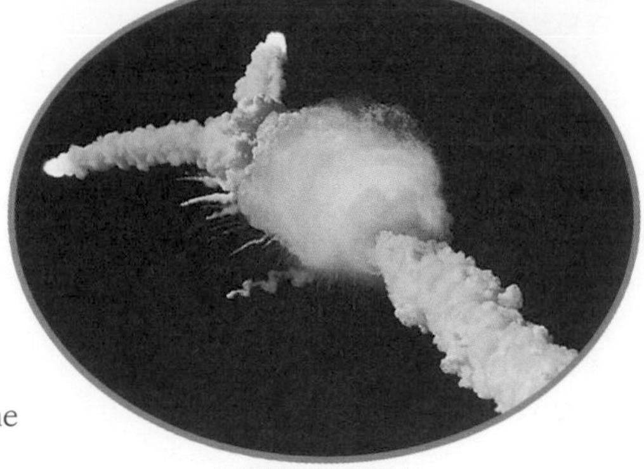

© AP/Wide World Photos

1979

March 28. A nuclear-power reactor at Three Mile Island in Middletown, PA, overheats and suffers a partial meltdown.

Sept. 1. The U.S. Pioneer 11 becomes the first spacecraft to visit Saturn.

Also in 1979. In Japan, Sony introduces the Walkman.

1980

Love Canal, NY, is declared a disaster area because of chemical contamination.

1981

April 14. *Columbia*, the first U.S. space shuttle, completes a three-day test flight.

Also in 1981. IBM introduces its first PC, the IBM PC, using an operating system (PC-DOS) designed by Microsoft.

1983

June 13. Pioneer 10, launched by the United States on March 3, 1972, becomes the first man-made object to escape the solar system.

1984

Dec. 3. A toxic-gas leak at a pesticide plant in Bhopal, India, kills some 2,000 people.

Also in 1984. Denmark's Steen Willadsen produces the first successful mammal clone, a sheep, using embryonic cells.

1985

The first in-flight rotation of space crews occurs as the USSR *Soyuz T-14* docks with the *Salyut 7* space station....Fullerenes—cagelike molecules of carbon atoms—are discovered.

1986

Jan. 24. The U.S. Voyager 2 becomes the first spacecraft to visit Uranus.

Jan. 28. The U.S. space shuttle *Challenger* explodes after launch, *photo above*, killing a crew of seven.

Feb. 19. The Soviet Union launches the space station *Mir*.

April 26. A fire in the Chernobyl nuclear-power plant in the Soviet Ukraine results in the release of substantial radioactivity.

Also in 1986. European physicists Karl Alexander Müller and Johannes Bednorz discover the first high-temperature superconducting compound....Scientists report the formation of a "hole" in the ozone layer over Antarctica.

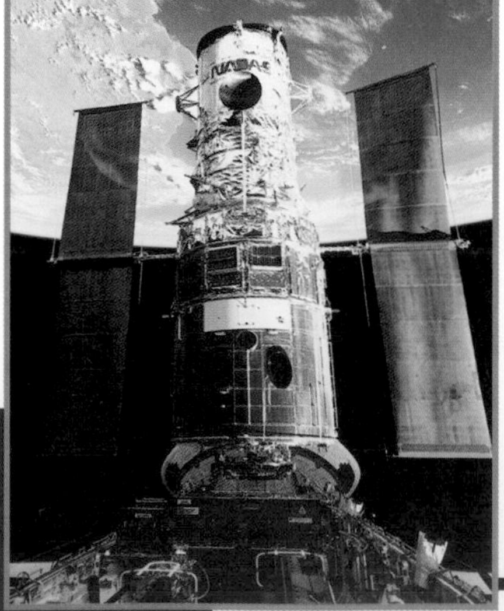

NASA

1987

Feb. 24. An exploding supernova is discovered in the Large Magellanic Cloud galaxy, the nearest visible from Earth since 1604.

April 19. The last California condor known to be in the wild is captured and placed in a breeding program at the San Diego Wild Animal Park.

April 24. Strawberry plants are sprayed with genetically engineered bacteria to protect them from frost formation—the first planned release of genetically engineered microorganisms into the environment.

1988

Dec. 14. The first transatlantic underwater fiber-optic cable goes into service.

1989

Feb. 14. The first satellite of the Global Positioning System is placed in orbit.

March 24. The supertanker *Exxon Valdez* runs aground in Alaska's Prince William Sound, causing a massive oil spill.

July 1. The Montreal Protocol, an international treaty limiting the production of ozone-destroying chemicals, takes effect.

© Yves Forestier/Corbis-Sygma

1990

April 25. The U.S. Hubble Space Telescope, *photo at bottom of page 58*, is placed into orbit.

Also in 1990. At CERN, the European Organization for Nuclear Research in Geneva, Tim Berners-Lee conceives the World Wide Web.

1991

Oct. 29. The U.S. Galileo spacecraft becomes the first to visit an asteroid, Gaspra.

1992

Sept. 14. Astronomers announce the first evidence of the existence of a reservoir of comets (the Kuiper belt) beyond the planet Pluto.

Also in 1992. Astronomers announce the discovery of planets circling a star other than the Sun....Persuasive confirmation of the Big Bang theory is provided by the U.S. Cosmic Background Explorer (COBE) satellite.

1993

Dec. 13. The U.S. space shuttle *Endeavour* completes a successful mission to repair the Hubble Space Telescope.

Also in 1993. Ice cores drilled in the Greenland Ice Sheet Project provide a 250,000-year snowfall record....The U.S. Congress cancels funding for the Superconducting Super Collider (SSC), which was to be built in Waxahatchie, TX.

1994

May 6. The Chunnel (*photo above*), a tunnel under the English Channel that links England and France, is opened officially.

Also in 1994. Astronomers report evidence for the existence of a powerful black hole at the core of the galaxy M87.

1995

Physicists at the Fermi National Accelerator Laboratory in Batavia, IL, announce the discovery of the subatomic particle known as the top quark....Swiss astronomers announce the detection of the first planet known to orbit a star that resembles the Sun.

© Murdo Macleod/FSP/Liaison Agency

1997

July 4. The U.S. spacecraft Mars Pathfinder touches down on Mars and deploys a rover named Sojourner to gather data about the surface.

Also in 1997. In Scotland, Ian Wilmut introduces a sheep named Dolly (*photo left*), the first genetic clone of an adult mammal.

1998

Nov. 1. Iridium inaugurates the first handheld, global satellite phone and paging system.

Also in 1998. Extremely dense stars known as magnetars, whose existence had been proposed in 1992, are discovered....Fossils of two species of dinosaurs showing clear evidence of feathers are uncovered in northeastern China.

Jenny Tesar

© V.J. Lovero/"Sports Illustrated"

Mark McGwire of the St. Louis Cardinals hits his historic 70th home run, Sept. 28, 1998.

1900

Jan. 29. Baseball's American League is formed, based on the merger of the Western League with independent eastern teams.

Aug. 8–10. In tennis' first Davis Cup series, held in Boston, the U.S. team defeats Great Britain, three matches to zero.

Also in 1900. The concept of "par" is introduced in the sport of golf.

1901

Connie Mack takes over as manager of the Philadelphia Athletics. He will remain in the post until 1950, becoming a legend.

1902

Jan. 1. College football's first Tournament of Roses game (later the Rose Bowl) is held; Michigan defeats Stanford, 49–0.

1903

Oct. 13. In baseball's first World Series, the American League's Boston Pilgrims (later the Red Sox) defeat the National League's Pittsburgh Pirates, five games to three.

1904

May 5. Baseball's first perfect game under modern rules is pitched by Cy Young of Boston; he beats the Philadelphia Athletics, 3–0.

1906

March 31. Because of the high number of injuries and deaths in amateur sports, the Intercollegiate Athletic Association of the United States is founded to set rules. The organization becomes the National Collegiate Athletic Association in 1910.

1907

Hawaiian-born George Freeth introduces surfing to the mainland United States at Redondo Beach, CA.

1910

July 4. African-American Jack Johnson defends his heavyweight title in a 15-round knockout of former champion and "great white hope" James J. Jeffries.

1911

May 30. Ray Harroun wins the first Indianapolis Sweepstakes (later the Indianapolis 500) auto race, averaging a speed of 74.59 mph (120.03 km/hr).

September. Baseball pitcher Cy Young retires after a 22-year career, having set records for most complete games (750) and most wins (511).

Nov. 11. In one of the great college-football upsets, Jim Thorpe scores a touchdown and kicks four field goals as little-known Carlisle (PA) Indian School beats Harvard.

1912

May 5–July 22. At the Summer Olympics in Stockholm, Jim Thorpe, *photo left*, wins gold in both the decathlon and the pentathlon.

1913

Nov. 1. In the first use of the forward pass as a main offensive weapon in football, Notre Dame defeats Army, 35–13; Notre Dame quarterback Gus Dorais completes 13 of 17 passes.

1915

Baseball's Ty Cobb of the Detroit Tigers steals a record 96 bases in one season.

1919

Oct. 1–9. Eight players on the Chicago White Sox conspire to lose the World Series to the underdog Cincinnati Reds.

Also in 1919. The first Triple Crown in horse racing is won by Sir Barton, ridden by jockey Johnny Loftus.

1920

Jan. 5. In professional baseball, the New York Yankees purchase Babe Ruth from the Boston Red Sox for a record $125,000; Ruth responds by hitting a record 54 home runs during the season.

Sept. 17. Representatives of ten football teams meet in Canton, OH, to form a professional league, the American Professional Football Association. The league is renamed the National Football League (NFL) in 1922.

1924

Jan. 25–Feb. 4. The first Olympic Winter Games are held in Chamonix, France.

Oct. 18. In the greatest one-man performance in college football, Red Grange of Illinois, *photo below*, scores four touchdowns in the first 12 minutes of a game against Michigan; in the second half, Grange scores a fifth touchdown, intercepts a pass, and throws a touchdown pass.

1926

Aug. 6. Gertrude Ederle of the United States is the first woman to swim the English Channel.

1927

June 4. In the first Ryder Cup international golf competition, the United States defeats Britain, $9^1/_2$ to $2^1/_2$.

Sept. 30. Babe Ruth breaks his own record by hitting his 60th home run.

1930

July 30. Uruguay wins soccer's first World Cup, beating Argentina, 4–2.

Also in 1930. Amateur Bobby Jones becomes the only golfer to win the early form of the Grand Slam, as he takes the British Amateur championship, the British Open, the U.S. Open, and the U.S. Amateur.

© AP/Wide World Photos

1932

July 30–Aug. 14. Mildred "Babe" Didrikson, *photo left*, wins Olympic gold medals in the javelin throw and the 80-m hurdles; she wins a third gold in the high jump but is disqualified because of her then-unorthodox style.

1933

Dec. 17. The Chicago Bears defeat the New York Giants, 23–21, in the National Football League's first interdivisional championship game.

1935

May 25. Ohio State's Jesse Owens breaks three world track records and ties a fourth, all in 45 minutes.

1938

June 22. Avenging an earlier defeat, heavyweight-boxing champion Joe Louis demolishes Max Schmeling in 124 seconds.

1939

May 2. After playing in 2,130 consecutive baseball games, beginning on June 1, 1925, an ailing Lou Gehrig of the New York Yankees benches himself.

1941

May 15–July 17. Yankees star Joe DiMaggio hits safely in 56 consecutive games.

Sept. 28. Ted Williams of the Boston Red Sox becomes the last major-league baseball player of the century to bat more than .400 for a season.

© Archive Photos

1947

April 10. Jackie Robinson, *photo right*, joins the Brooklyn Dodgers as major-league baseball's first African-American player of the modern era. He subsequently is named rookie of the year.

1950

Feb. 8. The Associated Press names Jim Thorpe and Babe Didrikson Zaharias the greatest male and female athletes of the first half of the 20th century.

April 23. The Minneapolis Lakers win the first National Basketball Association (NBA) championship by beating the Syracuse Nationals, four games to two.

1951

Oct. 3. In a dramatic ending to baseball's regular season, Bobby Thompson hits a bottom-of-the-ninth home run in the third game of a best-of-three play-off series to beat the Brooklyn Dodgers and win the pennant for the New York Giants.

1952

Feb. 14–25. At the VI Winter Games in Oslo, Norway, Andrea Mead Lawrence is the first American to win two gold medals in Olympic skiing.

© UPI/Corbis-Bettmann

1953

Ben Hogan becomes the first golfer to win three of the four major championships in one year—the Masters, the U.S. Open, and the British Open.

1954

May 6. At a minor track meet in England, British medical student Roger Bannister becomes the first to run a mile in less than four minutes.

July 4. In a thrilling soccer World Cup final, a well-organized West German team defeats the seemingly unbeatable Hungarian squad, 3–2.

1956

Oct. 8. The Yankees' Don Larsen, *photo left*, pitches the only perfect game in World Series history.

1957

April 13. The Boston Celtics win their first NBA championship, defeating the St. Louis Hawks, 125–123, in Game 7 of the play-offs.

1958

March 25. Boxer Sugar Ray Robinson regains the middleweight title for the fifth time, defeating Carmen Basilio in a 15-round decision.

June 29. With 17-year-old future soccer great Pelé scoring a goal, Brazil defeats Sweden, 5–2, to capture the World Cup.

Dec. 28. The Baltimore Colts win the NFL championship in a thrilling overtime game, beating the New York Giants, 23–17.

1960

May. In a mesmerizing display of soccer skill and power, Real Madrid scores 31 goals in seven games to win the European Cup for a fifth straight time.

Oct. 13. Bill Mazeroski's home run in the bottom of the ninth inning wins the World Series for the Pittsburgh Pirates over the New York Yankees.

1961

Oct. 1. In the last game of the regular season, Roger Maris of the New York Yankees hits his 61st home run, breaking Babe Ruth's record.

1962

March 2. Basketball's Wilt Chamberlain of the Philadelphia Warriors scores an NBA-game-record 100 points against the New York Knicks; the contest's final score is 169–147.

1964

Feb. 25. Boxer Cassius Clay (later Muhammad Ali), *photo right*, becomes heavyweight-boxing champ in an upset victory over Sonny Liston.

Nov. 1. Running back Jim Brown of the Cleveland Browns becomes the first football player to exceed 10,000 yards rushing.

Courtesy, "The Ring" Magazine

1965

Sept. 25. At age 59, Satchel Paige pitches three shutout innings for the Kansas City Athletics against the Boston Red Sox.

1967

Jan. 15. The Green Bay Packers defeat the Kansas City Chiefs, 35–10, in pro football's first Super Bowl.

Dec. 31. In the first "Ice Bowl"—which many call the greatest football game ever played—the Green Bay Packers beat the Dallas Cowboys, 21–17, as game-time temperatures register –13°F (–33°C).

1968

Oct. 18. At the Summer Olympics in Mexico City, Bob Beamon of the United States sets a record of 29′2½″ (8.90 m) in the long jump. The mark remains unbroken until Aug. 30, 1991, when Mike Powell of the United States jumps 29′4½″ (8.95 m).

1969

Jan. 12. With Joe Namath as quarterback, the underdog New York Jets beat the Baltimore Colts, 16–7, to win Super Bowl III, *photo right.*

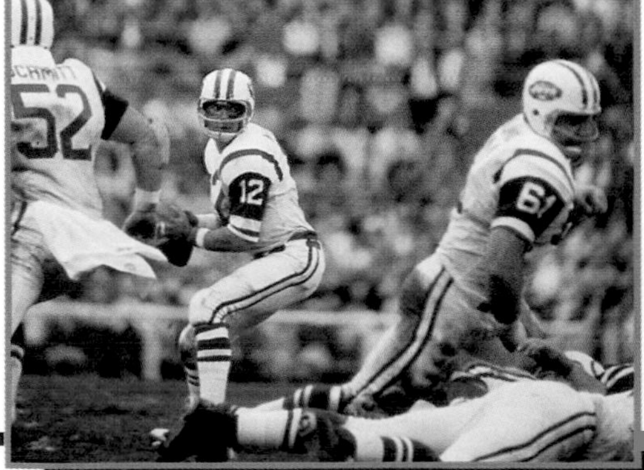

1970

April 6. Bobby Orr of the Boston Bruins changes the way pro hockey is played by becoming the first defenseman to win the National Hockey League's (NHL's) scoring title.

Also in 1970. The merger of the American Football League, which was formed in 1959, and the NFL is completed.

© Allsport

1971

March 8. Joe Frazier defends his heavyweight-boxing championship, winning a 15-round unanimous decision over Muhammad Ali.

Also in 1971. Tennis star Billie Jean King—*photographed at left with 1975 Wimbledon trophy*—becomes the first woman athlete to win $100,000 in one year.

1972

Sept. 4. U.S. swimmer Mark Spitz, *photo below*, wins a record seventh gold medal in the Olympic Games. World records are set in his seven events.

1973

Sept. 20. In an exhibition tennis match that will become a milestone in women's sports, Billie Jean King beats Bobby Riggs in three straight sets.

Dec. 16. O.J. Simpson of the Buffalo Bills runs for 200 yards against the New York Jets to become the first pro-football player to rush for more than 2,000 yards in one season.

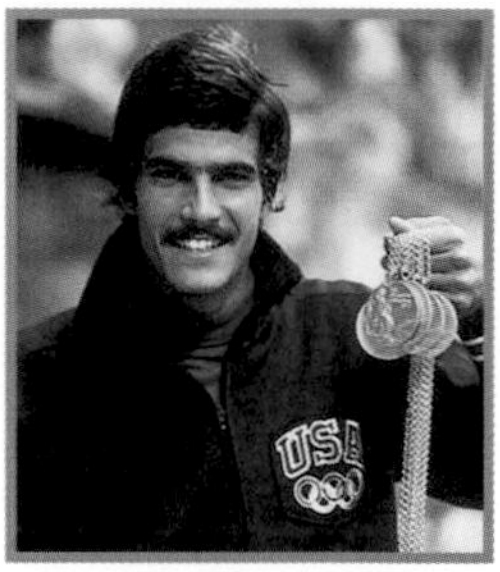

© UPI/Corbis-Bettmann

1974

April 8. Hank Aaron of the Atlanta Braves hits his 715th career home run, breaking Babe Ruth's record as the sport's leading home-run hitter.

Oct. 30. Muhammad Ali regains his heavyweight-boxing title by knocking out heavily favored George Foreman in the eighth round in a bout in Kinshasa, Zaire.

1975

July 5. In a rare display of tennis finesse over power, Arthur Ashe becomes the first African-American to win the Wimbledon men's singles championship, besting a heavily favored Jimmy Connors in four sets.

1976

June 4. The Boston Celtics win what may be basketball's greatest game, a triple-overtime endurance contest against Phoenix in Game 5 of the NBA finals. Boston goes on to take the series on June 6.

1977

Seattle Slew becomes the first undefeated horse to win the Triple Crown. Seventeen-year-old jockey Steve Cauthen captures 487 races.

1980

Feb. 24. In a memorable upset at the XIII Winter Olympics, the U.S. hockey team takes the gold medal. The United States had defeated the favored Russians, 4–3, in a dramatic semifinal game.

1982

Rickey Henderson of baseball's Oakland Athletics establishes a season record of 130 stolen bases.

1983

Sept. 26. For the first time in 132 years, a U.S. yacht loses the America's Cup, as *Australia II* bests *Liberty*, four races to three.

1984

Nov. 23. In a thrilling college-football game, Boston College defeats Miami, 47–45, on quarterback Doug Flutie's last-second 64-yard pass.

1986

July 27. Greg LeMond of the United States is the first non-European to capture the Tour de France cycling race.

1989

Kareem Abdul-Jabbar (*photo right*), the NBA's all-time highest scorer (38,387 points), retires as a player after 20 seasons with the Milwaukee Bucks and the Los Angeles Lakers.

© Joe Kennedy/Los Angeles Times Syndicate

1990

July 7. Tennis star Martina Navratilova wins a record ninth Wimbledon women's singles title.

1991

March 15. Sergei Bubka of the Soviet Union becomes the first pole vaulter to clear 20′ (6.1 m).

Nov. 30. In the first Women's World Cup in soccer, the U.S. team defeats Norway, 2–1, in the finals.

1992

Aug. 8. The U.S. basketball "Dream Team," made up of NBA stars, easily wins the gold medal at the Barcelona Olympics by defeating Croatia, 117–85, in the finals. On August 2, Jackie Joyner-Kersee, *photo below right*, took the gold medal in the heptathlon for a second consecutive time.

1993

June 9. The Montreal Canadiens win their 24th Stanley Cup, underlining their status as hockey's greatest dynasty.

© Tony Duffy/Allsport

1994

Feb. 12–27. The XVII Olympic Winter Games are held in Lillehammer, Norway, as the timing of the Olympic Games is changed. The Winter Games still will be staged every four years but will be two years apart from the Summer Games. The next Summer Games will be held in Atlanta, GA, in 1996.

July 17. Brazil wins a record fourth World Cup in soccer, defeating Italy, 3–2, on penalty kicks.

Aug. 12. A players' strike ends the Major League Baseball season after 117 games, causing the first cancellation of the World Series since 1904.

1995

Jan. 29. San Francisco quarterback Steve Young throws a record six touchdown passes as the 49ers win Super Bowl XXIX over the San Diego Chargers, 49–26; the 49ers become the first team to win five Super Bowls.

1997

April 13. Eldrick "Tiger" Woods, *photo below*, becomes the first African-American and the youngest golfer to win the Masters, with a tournament-record score of 270.

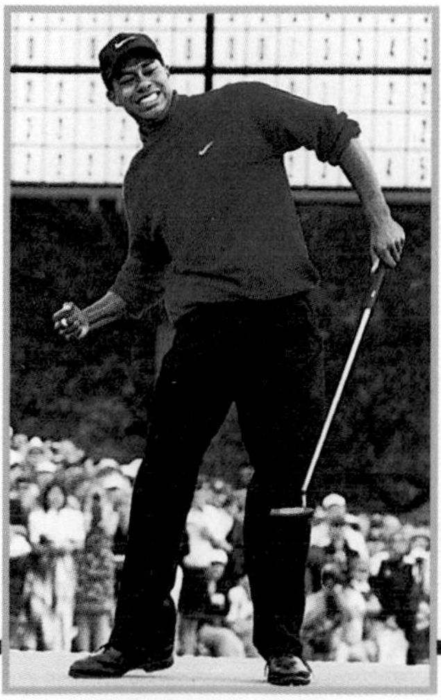

© Steve Munday/Allsport

1998

Sept. 20. Cal Ripken, Jr., of the Baltimore Orioles, after playing in every game since May 30, 1982, ends his record streak at 2,632.

Sept. 27. Mark McGwire of the St. Louis Cardinals hits two home runs to bring his season total to 70, exceeding Roger Maris' record of 61; Sammy Sosa of the Chicago Cubs ends the season with 66.

1999

Such sports luminaries as basketball's Michael Jordan, hockey's Wayne Gretzky, football's John Elway, and tennis' Steffi Graf of Germany announce the ends of their respective playing careers.

Jim Anderson

A Review of the Year 1999

© Ron Sachs/Corbis-Sygma

© Ilkka Uimonen/Corbis-Sygma

With an exciting 100-year period coming to an end, 1999 obviously was a time to reflect, recollect, and reminisce. Numerous books were written about the milestones of the 1900s; special features and news segments on the century dominated television; and all kinds of lists of the "best"—the most influential personalities, the leading fiction, the outstanding athletes—were prepared and analyzed. Thus it is no wonder that when New Year's Eve 1999 finally came, elaborate celebrations were held worldwide—from the islands of the Pacific to the pyramids of Egypt, to the capitals of Europe, to Washington, DC, *photo, top,* and, of course, to New York City's Times Square, *photo, right.*

Despite the fact that looking back was so prevalent in 1999, the year, in a real sense, was one of looking forward, of trying to glance into the future, of anticipating. Computer experts, government officials, and the general public wondered throughout 1999 if the world's computers, so vital a part of today's society, could cope with the arrival of the year 2000. Billions of dollars were spent to avert "Y2K bug" problems; fortunately, no serious ones occurred. As the North Atlantic Treaty Organization (NATO) launched a major bombing campaign to halt Yugoslavia's continued crackdown against the Albanian majority in the Serbian province of Kosovo in the spring, many wondered not only about the future of Kosovo and the numerous refugees resulting from the crisis, but about what effect NATO's actions would have on the organization as well as on world diplomacy and military affairs. As new leaders took over in Israel, Jordan, and Morocco, and as Syria and Israel reopened the door of negotiation, permanent peace in the Middle East remained a future dream. As China marked its 50th anniversary under communism in October, sinologists stopped to consider what the next 50 years would bring for the world's most populated country. As the United Nations (UN) sought to reassert itself as a major force, diplomats contemplated how successful the world body would be as a peacekeeper in the 21st century—not only in Kosovo, but also in East Timor, which underwent a violent struggle for independence from Indonesia in 1999, and in the nations of Africa where civil wars continued to rage. As Boris Yeltsin suddenly resigned the presidency of Russia and designated Vladimir Putin (*l-r, photo, right*) as acting president at year's end, there was anxiety about the future of democracy in that world power. As India continued its missile-development program, and the elected government in Pakistan was removed in a coup, escalating hostilities between the two neighbors caused concern. As the Panama Canal was transferred from U.S. to Panamanian control in December, questions arose about what effect the change would have on this major waterway. As the euro became a common currency in 11 nations of the European Union (EU), the next steps in the continent's unity process were being considered.

© Itar-Tass/Reuters/Archive Photos

On the U.S. scene, the year opened with Bill Clinton being acquitted in the second presidential-impeachment trial in the nation's history. Presidential scholars debated the effect of the episode on the presidency. Meanwhile, parents were soul-searching to discover what was leading children to go on shooting sprees in their schools. Although the next presidential election was months away, candidates in both parties were on the campaign trail, engaging in televised debates, and awaiting the primaries, nominating conventions, and election day 2000. As the Dow Jones industrial average exceeded 10,000 and then 11,000 for the first times, Americans looked for the economic expansion to continue.

Space experts, meanwhile, had to decide the next steps in the Mars program following two setbacks in 1999, and an outbreak of West Nile fever in New York challenged the medical community. Broadway theatergoers awaited the November opening of the first revival of Cole Porter's *Kiss Me Kate*; music lovers tried to imagine *The Great Gatsby* as an opera; and television viewers were glad to learn that the new quiz show, *Who Wants to Be a Millionaire?*, would be back in January 2000. For sports fans, the questions were: What will pro basketball be without Michael Jordan?; Will ice hockey ever have another Wayne Gretzky?; and Will the New York Yankees win a third consecutive world championship in 2000? In turn, the typical American was forced to think of life without Charlie Brown and his "Peanuts" friends; cartoonist Charles Schulz announced his retirement in December.

THE EDITORS ■

JANUARY

1 The euro, the new common currency of the European Union (EU), comes into existence, with 11 EU members participating.

6 The first session of the 106th U.S. Congress convenes. Rep. Dennis Hastert (R-IL) is elected speaker of the House.

7 The impeachment trial of President Bill Clinton formally opens in the U.S. Senate. The House of Representatives had impeached President Clinton in December 1998 for lying under oath and for obstructing justice in an effort to hide a sexual relationship he had had with Monica Lewinsky, a White House intern.

8 British Prime Minister Tony Blair concludes a three-day visit to South Africa.

13 Michael Jordan announces his retirement as a professional-basketball player. The announcement comes one week after the National Basketball Association (NBA) and its players agreed to a tentative labor agreement to end a six-month lockout.

17 A new minority government, headed by Bulent Ecevit of the Grand National Assembly, is formed in Turkey.

19 In the annual State of the Union address, President Bill Clinton outlines his program to save Social Security.

27 Pope John Paul II concludes a six-day visit to Mexico and St. Louis, MO.

28 The Ford Motor Company announces plans to purchase Volvo Cars.

31 The Denver Broncos defeat the Atlanta Falcons, 34–19, to win pro football's Super Bowl XXXIII.

FEBRUARY

1 President Clinton presents to Congress a $1.77 trillion budget proposal for fiscal year 2000.

2 Hugo Chávez Frías, who was elected president of Venezuela in December 1998, takes office.

6 Heavy fighting resumes along the common border between Ethiopia and Eritrea.

7 King Hussein of Jordan dies of cancer at the age of 63; his eldest son, Abdullah, succeeds him.

12 The U.S. Senate acquits President Clinton of both articles of impeachment that were approved by the House of Representatives in December 1998. From the White House Rose Garden, the president then asks for "a time of reconciliation and renewal for America," *photo below*.

15 President Clinton and Mexico's President Ernesto Zedillo Ponce de León conclude a two-day meeting in the Mexican state of Yucatán.

21 India's Prime Minister Atal Bihari Vajpayee concludes two days of meetings with Pakistan's Prime Minister Mohammad Nawaz Sharif.

25 China's Prime Minister Zhu Rongji and Russia's President Boris Yeltsin discuss trade and other issues in Moscow.

27 Nigeria returns to civilian rule as Gen. Olusegun Obasanjo, a former military ruler, becomes the nation's first elected president since August 1983.

MARCH

7 In El Salvador, Francisco Flores Pérez of the ruling Nationalist Republican Alliance (Arena) is elected president.

11 President Clinton completes a four-day, four-nation visit to Central America.

12 The Czech Republic, Hungary, and Poland become members of the North Atlantic Treaty Organization (NATO). The foreign ministers of the three nations join U.S. Secretary of State Madeleine Albright at the expansion-agreement ceremony, *photo below*.

© Jeff Taylor/Reuters/Archive Photos

15 Eleven passengers are killed and more than 100 are injured as an Amtrak passenger train crashes into a semitrailer truck at a railroad crossing in Bourbonnais, IL.

16 The 20 members of the European Union's European Commission announce their resignations amid allegations of corruption and financial mismanagement.

21 Dr. Bertrand Piccard, a Swiss psychiatrist, and Britain's Brian Jones complete a 19-day, around-the-world trip in the balloon *Breitling Orbiter 3*. They are the first balloonists to circle the world nonstop.

24 NATO begins a sustained campaign of air strikes against Yugoslavia (Serbia, Montenegro, and the former autonomous regions of Kosovo and Vojvodina). The bombings are in response to Serbia's refusal to sign a peace treaty with ethnic Albanians who are seeking independence for the province of Kosovo.

26 A Michigan jury convicts Dr. Jack Kevorkian, a proponent of assisted suicide, of second-degree murder for the killing of a terminally ill man by lethal injection.

28 Paraguay's President Raúl Cubas Grau resigns after protests inspired by the assassination of Vice-President Luis María Argaña on March 23 led to several deaths. The nation's Congress had blamed Cubas and his political associate, Gen. Lino César Oviedo, for Cubas' murder. Senate President Luis González Macchi takes office as Paraguay's new chief executive.

29 On the New York Stock Exchange, the Dow Jones industrial average of 30 industrial stocks closes above the 10,000 mark for the first time in history.

APRIL

1 The new Canadian territory of Nunavut, carved from the eastern part of the Northwest Territories and covering some 772,000 sq mi (nearly 2 million km^2), comes into existence.

5 Two Libyans charged in the United States and Great Britain with the bombing of Pan Am Flight 103 over Scotland in 1988 arrive in the Netherlands to stand trial. Libya long had been unwilling to release the suspects, and its doing so results in the suspension of UN sanctions against Libya.

9 In Djibouti, Ismail Omar Guelleh of the ruling Popular Rally for Progress and the Front for the Restoration of Unity and Democracy is elected president.

11 Daouda Malam Wanke is designated president of Niger following the assassination of President Ibrahim Baré Maïnassara on April 9.

Spain's José María Olazábal wins the 63d Masters golf tournament at Augusta, GA.

12 A federal jury in Little Rock, AR, acquits Susan McDougal of obstruction of justice for refusing to testify against President Clinton and First Lady Hillary Rodham Clinton in the Whitewater land-development case and other business arrangements.

14 Chinese Premier Zhu Rongji concludes a nine-day visit to the United States without reaching an anticipated comprehensive trade agreement with President Clinton.

15 In Algeria former Foreign Minister Abdelaziz Bouteflika is elected president. All opposition candidates had claimed that the vote was fraudulent and had withdrawn from the election.

A panel of two Lahore High Court judges in Rawalpindi, Pakistan, convicts former Prime Minister Benazir Bhutto and her husband, Asif Ali Zardari, of corruption.

© Michael S. Green/AP/Wide World Photos

Following inconclusive elections on March 21 in Finland, a new five-party coalition government, headed by Paavo Lipponen as premier, takes office.

17 In India the government of Prime Minister Atal Bihari Vajpayee collapses after losing a vote of confidence.

18 In parliamentary elections in Turkey, the Democratic Left Party of Premier Bulent Ecevit wins a plurality of the votes cast.

20 In a Littleton, CO, high school, two students kill 12 other students, a teacher, and themselves in a shooting rampage. The incident causes grief, *photo above*, and soul-searching regarding the causes for such violence nationwide.

23 The heads of state and government of the 19 member nations of NATO gather in Washington to mark the organization's 50th anniversary.

May

1 On Nepal's Mount Everest, a group of U.S. mountain climbers discovers the body of a man identified as George Mallory, who had died in June 1924 while attempting to be the first person to reach the summit of Everest. It was not known immediately whether or not Mallory had reached the mountain's peak.

2 In Panama, Mireya Moscoso de Grubar of the opposition Arnulfista Party is elected president.

3 Some 49 people are killed as a series of tornadoes strikes Oklahoma, Kansas, Nebraska, Texas, and South Dakota.

Meeting in Washington, Japan's Prime Minister Keizo Obuchi and President Clinton announce a series of measures intended to deregulate Japan's economy.

6 Britain's Labour Party wins the largest number of seats in the first elections for Scotland's new Parliament and Wales' new Assembly.

7 Three Chinese citizens are killed, and an additional 20 are wounded, as a NATO plane mistakenly drops bombs on the Chinese embassy in Belgrade, Yugoslavia.

In Guinea-Bissau the government of President João Bernardo Vieira is ousted in a military coup.

12 Robert E. Rubin announces his resignation as secretary of the treasury. President Clinton designates Lawrence H. Summers as Rubin's successor and Stuart E. Eizenstat to succeed Summers as deputy secretary of the treasury.

Russia's President Boris Yeltsin dismisses Prime Minister Yevgeny Primakov and names Interior Minister Sergei Stepashin as his successor.

15 Efforts in the lower house of the Russian parliament, the State Duma, to impeach President Boris Yeltsin fail.

17 Israel selects a new parliament and elects Ehud Barak (*photographed voting with his wife at right*) as prime minister. The Labor Party leader captures some 56% of the vote, against 44% for Benjamin Netanyahu of the Likud Party, in the race for prime minister.

20 At Heritage High School in Conyers, GA, a 15-year-old student with two guns shoots and injures six fellow students. He then surrenders to an assistant principal at the school.

25 A report by the U.S. House of Representatives Select Committee on U.S. National Security and Military/Commercial Concerns with the People's Republic of China concludes that China "has stolen design information on the U.S. most-advanced thermonuclear weapons." The select committee also judges that China's next generation of thermonuclear weapons "will exploit elements of stolen U.S. design information," and that China's penetration of U.S. weapons laboratories "spans at least the past several decades and almost certainly continues today."

27 The International Criminal Tribunal for the Former Yugoslavia issues an indictment against Yugoslav President Slobodan Milosevic and four other Serbian officials for crimes against humanity in Kosovo.

© Chip Hires/Liaison Agency

JUNE

2 In elections for Parliament and nine provincial administrations in South Africa, the African National Congress (ANC) wins a major victory. ANC leader Thabo Mbeki is to succeed Nelson Mandela as the nation's president.

3 President Clinton informs Congress that he intends to renew "normal trade relations" (formerly known as "most-favored-nation" status) with China for another year.

7 Voters go to the polls in Indonesia.

9 Yugoslavia signs a peace agreement with NATO pledging to withdraw all of its forces from Kosovo. The agreement paves the way for a halting of NATO's bombing of Yugoslavia.

12 NATO peacekeeping forces enter the province of Kosovo in Yugoslavia.

15 South Korean naval forces sink a North Korean torpedo boat during an exchange in the disputed Yellow Sea.

16 U.S. Vice-President Al Gore formally announces his candidacy for the Democratic presidential nomination in 2000.

20 The Dallas Stars defeat the Buffalo Sabres, four games to two, to take the National Hockey League's Stanley Cup.

22 The U.S. Supreme Court rules that persons with remediable handicaps cannot claim discrimination in employment under the Americans with Disabilities Act.

25 Israel and the Shiite Muslim group Hezbollah exchange air attacks along the Israeli-Lebanon border.

The San Antonio Spurs defeat the New York Knickerbockers, four games to one, to capture the National Basketball Association championship.

JULY

1 The U.S. Justice Department releases new regulations granting the attorney general sole power to appoint and oversee special counsels. The new rules follow the expiration of the 1978 independent-counsel statute on June 30.

7 In Sierra Leone, President Ahmad Tejan Kabbah and rebel leader Foday Sankoh sign a pact to end the nation's civil war.

8 Iranian students, protesting restrictions against the press imposed by the Islamic establishment, begin to clash with police.

10 The heads of six African nations with troops in the Democratic Republic of the Congo sign a cease-fire agreement to end the civil war in that nation.

The U.S. women's soccer team defeats China to capture the 1999 World Cup tournament.

12 In Belgium, King Albert II administers the oath of office to a new government headed by Guy Verhofstadt of the Liberal Party, which is based in the Flemish-speaking region. The two Christian Democratic parties and the two Socialist parties in the former government had suffered electoral setbacks in June.

16 John F. Kennedy, Jr., the son of the late U.S. president; his wife, Carolyn Bessette Kennedy; and his sister-in-law, Lauren Bessette, are killed in the crash of a single-engine plane into the Atlantic Ocean near Martha's Vineyard.

23 Morocco's King Hassan II, 70, dies of a heart attack in Rabat, the nation's capital. He is succeeded by his eldest son, Sidi Mohammed, who becomes King Mohammed VI.

27 The U.S. space shuttle *Columbia* completes a five-day mission. It was the first shuttle mission to be commanded by a woman, Air Force Col. Eileen Collins.

29 In Atlanta, GA, Mark Barton, a 44-year-old securities day trader, kills nine office workers during a shooting rampage and then commits suicide. He earlier had killed his wife and two children and had been a suspect in the 1993 deaths of his first wife and her mother.

U.S. Federal Judge Susan Webber Wright orders President Clinton to pay about $89,000 in legal expenses that resulted from his "intentionally false" testimony regarding his relationship with Monica Lewinsky.

August

2 In eastern India two passenger trains collide, killing nearly 300 persons and injuring some 500.

5 The U.S. Senate confirms the nomination of Richard Holbrooke as U.S. ambassador to the United Nations. Investigations into ethic allegations against Holbrooke had delayed the confirmation vote.

10 In an India-Pakistan border area, an Indian fighter jet shoots down a Pakistani naval aircraft. Sixteen persons aboard the Pakistani craft are killed.

11 Buford Furrow, Jr., a member of white supremacist groups in the U.S. Pacific Northwest, surrenders to the Federal Bureau of Investigation (FBI) in Las Vegas, NV, admitting that he was the gunman who wounded three children and two staff members at a Jewish community center in Los Angeles on August 10. According to authorities, the gunman also killed a postal worker while fleeing from the shooting spree.

In Guyana, Finance Minister Bharrat Jagdeo is sworn in as president, succeeding Janet Jagan, who had resigned for reasons of health.

16 In Russia the lower house of parliament confirms Vladimir V. Putin as prime minister. On August 9, President Yeltsin had dismissed Sergei V. Stepashin as prime minister and nominated the 46-year-old former security-services official to the post. The change marked the fourth Russian government shake-up in 17 months.

17 A powerful earthquake strikes northwestern Turkey, *photo right*, killing some 15,600 persons and devastating several major cities.

19 Thousands of Serbs attend a rally in Belgrade to demand the resignation of Yugoslavia's President Slobodan Milosevic.

27 The final crew of the Russian space station *Mir* departs the station and begins the return to Earth. Financial considerations forced Russia to abandon *Mir*.

September

4 The United Nations announces that residents of East Timor overwhelmingly voted for independence from Indonesia in a referendum held on August 30. Pro-Indonesian militias go on a rampage in Dili, East Timor's capital, attacking independence supporters, burning buildings, blowing up bridges, and destroying telecommunication facilities.

5 Israel's Prime Minister Ehud Barak and Palestinian leader Yasir Arafat sign an accord reviving the stalled Middle East peace process.

7 The White House announces that 12 jailed members of the Armed Forces of National Liberation, a Puerto Rican independence group, have accepted a clemency offer proposed by the president.

Viacom Inc., the media conglomerate, announces that it plans to buy CBS Corp.

8 U.S. Attorney General Janet Reno names former U.S. Sen. John Danforth (R-MO) to head an independent investigation into the 1993 assault by federal agents on the Branch Davidian compound near Waco, TX.

Former U.S. Sen. Bill Bradley of New Jersey announces that he is a candidate for the Democratic presidential nomination in 2000.

11 While in New Zealand for the annual meeting of the Asia-Pacific Economic Cooperation (APEC) forum, President Clinton meets with China's President Jiang Zemin for the first time since June 1998.

12 Andre Agassi wins the men's singles titles at the U.S. Open tennis tournament. Serena Williams had taken the women's crown on September 11.

15 The United Nations approves the deployment of a multinational peacekeeping force in East Timor.

16 In another in a series of bomb blasts in Russia, an apartment in Volgodonsk is destroyed, and at least 17 people are killed. The attacks are attributed to Chechen militants seeking independence from Russia.

17 North Carolina is hit particularly hard by Hurricane Floyd; rivers and creeks in the state overflow, causing heavy damage.

21 A major earthquake strikes Taiwan, killing 2,100 people and injuring 8,000.

30 Radiation escapes a Japanese nuclear facility in Tokaimura, after workers accidentally set off an uncontrolled nuclear chain reaction.

October

1 The 50th anniversary of the founding of the People's Republic of China is marked in Beijing.

5 MCI WorldCom Inc. and Sprint Corp. announce plans to merge.

10 Portugal's Socialist Party is reelected in parliamentary elections.

12 In Pakistan the democratically elected government of Prime Minister Nawaz Sharif is toppled in a bloodless coup d'état.

13 The U.S. Senate rejects ratification of the Comprehensive Test Ban Treaty (CTBT).

In India, Atal Bihari Vajpayee is sworn in for another term as prime minister. Vajpayee heads a newly formed coalition of more than 20 parties, led by his Bharatiya Janata Party, which won 182 seats in the 545-seat lower house of Parliament, the Lok Sabha, in monthlong elections that ended on October 5.

15 The Norwegian Nobel Committee names Doctors Without Borders, a group of medical personnel that provides medical relief in some 80 countries, the winner of the 1999 Nobel Peace Prize.

18 Kenneth Starr resigns as U.S. independent counsel. Robert Ray, a former federal prosecutor, is sworn in as his successor to complete the final stages of Starr's investigations of President Clinton.

21 In Indonesia the People's Consultative Assembly elects Megawati Sukarnoputri as the nation's vice-president, one day after selecting Abdurrahman Wahid as president in a surprise vote. General elections had been held in June, with Megawati's Democratic Party of Struggle winning a parliamentary plurality.

22 The UN Security Council votes to send 6,000 peacekeepers to Sierra Leone to oversee a peace plan signed in July.

24 Buenos Aires Mayor Fernando de la Rúa of the center-left Alianza coalition is elected president of Argentina.

27 Armenia's Prime Minister Vazgen Sarkisian and seven other government officials are killed during a parliamentary session. The gunmen reportedly were staging a coup.

In Major League Baseball, the New York Yankees defeat the Atlanta Braves, four games to none, to win their second consecutive World Series.

29 A powerful cyclone devastates the Indian state of Orissa.

31 EgyptAir Flight 990, a Boeing 767 jetliner bound for Cairo, Egypt, from New York's John F. Kennedy International Airport, crashes into the Atlantic Ocean south of Nantucket Island, MA, killing all 217 people on board.

Leaders from the Roman Catholic Church and the Lutheran Church sign the Joint Declaration on the Doctrine of Justification, ending a centuries-old doctrinal dispute over the nature of faith and salvation.

November

2 Israeli Prime Minister Ehud Barak, Palestinian leader Yasir Arafat, and President Clinton meet in Oslo, Norway, *photo below*.

Off-year elections are held in the United States.

5 In a 207-page "finding of facts," U.S. Judge Thomas Penfield Jackson finds that the computer-software maker Microsoft Corp. enjoys "monopoly power."

A 12-day conference on global warming, attended by delegates from 170 nations, concludes in Bonn, Germany.

6 In a national referendum in Australia, voters retain the British monarchy as the nation's head of state.

Tajikistan's President Imomali Rahmonov is reelected to a second term.

12 President Clinton signs into law the Financial Services Management Act, overhauling the regulatory framework of the financial-services industry.

14 The UN imposes economic sanctions against the Taliban militia that controls much of Afghanistan. The sanctions follow Taliban's refusal to release to the United States Osama bin Laden, who has been charged with masterminding the 1998 bombings of the U.S. embassies in Kenya and Tanzania. The United States had imposed similar sanctions in July.

© Corbis-Sygma

Ukraine's President Leonid Kuchma is reelected to a second term in a runoff election.

15 Representatives of China and the United States sign a major trade agreement involving China's membership in the World Trade Organization (WTO).

19 Concluding a two-day summit in Istanbul, Turkey, the Organization for Security and Cooperation in Europe (OSCE) adopts a new arms accord. During the conference, Russia was the target of international criticism for its military campaign against Chechnya's separatist movement.

Anti-U.S. protests occur in Athens, as President Clinton, who had attended the OSCE summit, begins a brief visit to Greece.

21 China announces that it has test-launched an unmanned space capsule that is designed for manned spaceflight.

27 New Zealand's Labour Party leader, Helen Clark, is elected prime minister.

28 In a runoff election in Uruguay, Sen. Jorge Batlle of the ruling Colorado Party is elected president.

29 President Clinton signs a $390 billion omnibus spending bill.

In Malaysia the ruling coalition of Mahathir bin Mohamad is victorious in parliamentary elections.

DECEMBER

2 The British government transfers political power over the province of Northern Ireland to a new provincial government; the Northern Ireland Executive, a new provincial cabinet, is installed. On November 27 the Ulster Unionist Party, Northern Ireland's largest Protestant party, had voted to allow Sinn Fein, the political wing of the Catholic Provisional Irish Republican Army (IRA), to join the cabinet.

3 The World Trade Organization (WTO) concludes a four-day meeting in Seattle, WA, without setting an agenda for a new round of trade talks. Fierce protests against unrestricted trade and the WTO generally by various groups had occurred during the conference.

The National Aeronautics and Space Administration (NASA) loses radio contact with the Mars Polar Lander, an unmanned spacecraft, as it enters Mars' atmosphere.

7 A U.S. federal grand jury in Texas indicts a former convict in the 1995 disappearance of atheist leader Madalyn Murray O'Hair.

8 Russia and Belarus agree in principle to form an economic and political confederation.

10 Croatia's President Franjo Tudjman dies at the age of 77.

12 Chile's presidential election ends in a deadlock; a runoff election is scheduled for January 2000.

14 In a public ceremony at the Panama Canal, Panama's President Mireya Moscoso de Grubar and former President Jimmy Carter, representing the United States, exchange documents transferring control of the canal from the United States to the Republic of Panama.

15 For the first time since 1996, Israel and Syria engage in peace talks, as Israel's Prime Minister Barak and Syria's Foreign Minister Farouk al-Sharaa meet in Washington, DC.

19 Parliamentary elections are held in Russia. Although the Communist Party wins the most party-list votes, moderates and pro-government blocs score major gains.

Floods and mud slides continue to ravage Venezuela, taking thousands of lives, *photo, below*.

20 Sovereignty over the colony of Macao is transferred from Portugal to China.

24 Ivory Coast's President Henri Konan Bédié is overthrown in a coup.

26 In a runoff election in Guatemala, Alfonso Portillo of the opposition Republican Front is chosen president.

31 Boris Yeltsin resigns as president of Russia. Prime Minister Vladimir Putin is designated acting president.

In Afghanistan more than 150 hostages on an Indian Airlines plane are freed after the Indian government frees three Kashmir militants from prison. The plane had been seized on December 24 during a flight from Katmandu, Nepal, to New Delhi, and eventually was flown to Afghanistan.

Observances begin worldwide to mark the end of the 1900s and the beginning of the year 2000.

Special Features

© Stephen Simpson/FPG International

During the early months of 1999, the eyes of the world were on the Federal Republic of Yugoslavia (Serbia, Montenegro, and the former autonomous republics of Kosovo and Vojvodina). For some time, ethnic Albanians had desired independence for the province of Kosovo, leading to an escalating conflict in 1998. After Serbia refused to sign a peace treaty with Kosovo in February–March 1999, the North Atlantic Treaty Organization (NATO) began sustained air strikes against Serbia and Serbian forces on March 24. The air strikes, which focused attention on NATO as it was marking its 50th anniversary, lasted until June. Meanwhile, hundreds of thousands of ethnic Albanians had been driven from their homes during the hostilities. In light of these developments, the feature section opens with a detailed report on the Kosovo crisis. Subarticles discuss NATO's new role and the refugee crisis (*photos at top of page 77*).

Also in 1999, Bertrand Piccard and Brian Jones (*left and right, respectively, photo at bottom of page 77*) were awarded a trophy and a $1 million prize after becoming the first hot-air balloonists to circle the globe nonstop; the medical community was giving greater emphasis to the study of sleep

© Doug Martin/Photo Researchers, Inc.

© Sharon Abbady/Black Star

(*photo at bottom of page 76*); and in pop-music circles, jazz and swing (*photo at top of page 76*) were enjoying renewed popularity as Latin music was creating a major stir. Accordingly, sleep and its disorders, popular music's new diversity, and the historic flight of the *Breitling Orbiter 3* were chosen as topics for Special Feature coverage. ■

© Noel Quidu/Liaison Agency

© Khue Bui/AP/Wide World Photos

© Yannis Behrakis/Reuters/Archive Photos

The Kosovo Crisis

By Janusz Bugajski

As Yugoslav President Slobodan Milosevic continued his violent crackdown against the Albanian majority in the Serbian province of Kosovo, a Kosovar woman, above, *led a group of refugees in pleading their cause to the Macedonian police. During the crisis, Macedonia became a temporary home for numerous refugees from Kosovo.*

Late in 1998, the regime of Yugoslav President Slobodan Milosevic launched a violent crackdown against the Albanian majority in the Serbian province of Kosovo. Belgrade's objective was to expel most of the roughly 2 million Albanians living in the province and eliminate any resistance to Serbian rule. In response to Milosevic's policies, the North Atlantic Treaty Organization (NATO) engaged in its first major international military offensive since the end of the Cold War, successfully expelling Yugoslav military and Serb paramilitary formations from Kosovo.

After the war ended, NATO dispatched about 50,000 troops to the province under a United Nations (UN) mandate and effectively terminated Belgrade's military and political control. However, the future status of the territory remained undetermined, which contributed to rising fears among the Kosovar Albanians that they again would be subjected to Belgrade's control once the Western alliance vacated the territory.

Restlessness and Repression. A decade of passive resistance by the Albanian population of Kosovo had failed to restore political autonomy to this restless province of Serbia. Albanians constituted more than 90% of Kosovo's population, and their leaders demanded independence from Serbia. However, the majority were denied even the most basic political, civic, and human rights. Fearing the Albanians' determination to gain statehood for Kosovo, Belgrade maintained a virtual police state in the province.

In early 1999, Belgrade stepped up its campaign of repression and attacked a number of Albanian villages believed to be strongholds of the Kosovo Liberation Army (KLA), a guerrilla force fighting for Kosovo's independence. As a result of Serbian attacks, by February more than 210,000 Albanians in Kosovo reportedly were displaced from their homes, and more than 60,000 refugees had found shelter in neighboring states.

In January, Belgrade expelled William Walker, head of the Kosovo Verification Mission, which had been established in fall 1998 by the Organization for Security and Cooperation in Europe (OSCE). Walker was accused of meddling in Serbian politics. In February the mission withdrew its monitors from Kosovo, citing a lack of security and cooperation from Serbian authorities. OSCE Chairman Knut Vollebaek asserted that the Serbian government failed to provide OSCE staff with information, support, or access to suspected mass-murder sites in the province.

The eight-nation Contact Group (including the United States and Russia) set up negotiations between the Serbian authorities and the Kosovar Albanian leadership, which took place in Rambouillet, France. After several weeks of discussion and pressure from Western leaders, the Albanian representatives signed an agreement in mid-March. The accords postponed the question of Kosovo's independence for a transitional period of three years and focused on restoring autonomy and multiethnic institutions in the province. Rambouillet also dictated the presence of a NATO force in Kosovo to help monitor the agreement.

© Jacques Langevin/Corbis-Sygma

In February 1999 the foreign ministers of Great Britain, France, the United States, and Italy—(l-r) *Robin Cook, Hubert Védrine, Madeleine Albright, and Lamberto Dini—attended a conference in Rambouillet, France, that sought an accord on Kosovo's autonomy. After the Serbian delegation rejected an agreement on the issue, the North Atlantic Treaty Organization (NATO) launched air strikes against Yugoslavia.*

The Albanian delegation to the peace talks formed a provisional government headed by the political commander of the KLA, Hashim Thaci. This government, including representatives of several smaller Kosovo parties, was established in direct opposition to the already existing Kosovar government headed by Ibrahim Rugova, the leader of the Democratic League of Kosovo (DLK).

Belgrade refused to sign the Rambouillet accords, arguing that the agreement favored the Albanians. It strongly opposed the prospect of a NATO presence in Kosovo, on the grounds that it would violate Yugoslav sovereignty. Kosovar

Albanian leaders maintained that, without a sizable NATO deployment, Milosevic could not be trusted to implement the autonomy agreement. The Contact Group threatened military action if either side rejected the Rambouillet agreement, a move that was endorsed fully by NATO's leaders. The Serbs continued their opposition, and the peace talks were suspended on March 19.

Serbia's War with NATO. In February and March the Serbian government launched a major military campaign against the Albanian population of Kosovo on the pretext of eradicating the KLA "terrorists." Dozens of villages were bombed by Yugoslav troops, and tens of thousands of Albanians were forced to flee their homes. Several hundred Kosovars reportedly were killed by Yugoslav soldiers and Serb paramilitary detachments. German Foreign Minister Joschka Fischer claimed that this offensive, dubbed "Operation Horseshoe," was masterminded by Milosevic in order to expel or eradicate the Albanian population from Kosovo and to alter the ethnic balance in favor of Serbs.

After Belgrade persistently ignored all ultimatums to halt its offensive in Kosovo, NATO began an aerial bombing campaign against Yugoslav and Serb forces on March 25. The operation, code-named "Joint Guardian," was intended to dislodge Yugoslav and Serb forces from Kosovo and to provide protection for the besieged Albanian population. In retaliation for the bombing, Milosevic intensified his systematic "ethnic cleansing" campaign, with the intention of driving the bulk of the Kosovar Albanian majority out of the province. At least 11,000 Albanians were believed murdered by Serbian paramilitaries, and approximately 1.5 million people were expelled from or fled their homes.

NATO announced that the bombing would continue until Belgrade met five key demands: an end to the killing and expulsion of civilians, the withdrawal of armed forces from Kosovo, the acceptance of international peacekeepers in the province, the return of expelled refugees, and the official acceptance of the Rambouillet accords. Belgrade refused to comply, calculating that as the war continued, NATO's cohesion would unravel, and Serbia could gain more-favorable conditions from the international community.

During the war, disputes within NATO became evident between proponents of more-widespread and -intensive military strikes and voices calling for moderation and compromise. The question of whether the alliance should prepare for a ground invasion also created rifts. Above all, some military leaders—including the American NATO commander, Gen. Wesley Clark—complained that interference by civilian Western leaders was hindering the military operation.

The NATO campaign initially consisted of air strikes against Yugoslav and Serbian military targets. When Belgrade refused to capitulate, the bombing was intensified and expanded to include various governmental, infrastructural, and transportation targets throughout Yugoslavia. Dozens of Serb cities were shelled, and several hundred soldiers and

About the Author. Janusz Bugajski is director of the Eastern Europe Project at the Center for Strategic and International Studies in Washington, DC. Formerly a senior research analyst for Radio Free Europe in Munich, he has worked as a consultant on East European affairs for several organizations, including the U.S. Agency for International Development, the U.S. Department of Defense, and the British Broadcasting Corporation (BBC). Dr. Bugajski has written several books, including *Ethnic Politics in Eastern Europe: A Guide to Nationality, Policies, Organizations, and Parties* and *Nations in Turmoil: Conflict and Cooperation in Eastern Europe*, as well as numerous journal and newspaper articles on Eastern Europe.

© AP/Wide World Photos

The NATO air campaign, below, left and top, *began on March 24 and lasted for 78 days. A Belgrade residence of Yugoslav President Milosevic,* left, *was among the many buildings damaged during the attacks. Three U.S. servicemen,* below, middle, *were captured by Serbs near the Serbia-Macedonia border on March 31 and held for a month. U.S. Army Gen. Wesley Clark and George Robertson* (bottom, l-r) *were supreme commander of NATO and Great Britain's defense secretary, respectively, throughout the hostilities. In August, Robertson was appointed secretary-general of NATO.*

© Brennan Linsley/AP/Wide World Photos

© Stan Parker/U.S. Air Force/Liaison Agency

© Corbis-Sygma

© Corbis-Sygma

civilians reportedly perished in the NATO bombing. Belgrade used the pretext of Serbia's war footing to stifle further any domestic opposition to Milosevic's repressive rule.

As a result of Milosevic's offensive in Kosovo, hundreds of thousands of Albanians fled into neighboring Albania, Macedonia, and Montenegro (*see* SIDEBAR, page 82). Of these, more than 650,000 found refuge in Albania. The refugees provided gruesome accounts of atrocities and executions by

(Continued on page 84.)

The Spotlight Turns to the Refugees

© Antonello Nusca/Liaison Agency

At the height of the Kosovo crisis in April, Albanians who had fled to a refugee camp in Macedonia scrambled for food donated by humanitarian agencies. The massive number of refugees taxed the capabilities of such organizations.

The most dramatic and heartrending aspect of the Kosovo crisis was the sudden and huge exodus of desperate refugees to neighboring Albania, Macedonia, and Montenegro. The outflow of people was staggering. They did not simply flee; they were expelled forcibly from their homes in a brutal ethnic cleansing. The arrival of so many refugees in neighboring countries created serious protection and logistics problems for the international humanitarian agencies. The return home of refugees, when it occurred just three months after the outflow started, was an even faster exodus in reverse. As the Albanian Kosovars streamed home, Serbs and gypsies fled Kosovo, generating yet another refugee crisis.

Origins of the Crisis. The seeds of the refugee crisis in Kosovo can be traced back many decades, even centuries. By the late 1980s, in an estimated population of 2 million, ethnic Albanians—most of whom follow Islam—outnumbered Serbs by a ratio of around nine to one. When Serbian leader Slobodan Milosevic inflamed Serbian nationalistic passions by revoking Kosovo's autonomous status in 1989, he set the stage for a showdown between the two groups. Between 1989 and 1998, as Serbian repression of Albanians escalated, some 350,000 Albanian Kosovars sought refuge in Europe. Widespread fighting between Serbs and Albanians in Kosovo erupted in March 1998. Within months, another 350,000 civilians were displaced inside the province or fled abroad.

When political negotiations failed to resolve the crisis, NATO launched an air war over Yugoslavia and Kosovo on March 24, 1999. Almost immediately, Milosevic unleashed the Serb army, police, and paramilitary forces on Kosovo's largely defenseless ethnic Albanians, turning hundreds of thousands of them into refugees within days. Serbian militias moved from village to village and from house to house, searching for members of the Kosovo Liberation Army (KLA). Draft-age men were separated from women, children, and the elderly and were detained or were taken away at gunpoint to be executed. Masses of civilians were forced onto roads leading out of the country to Albania, while tens of thousands of others were packed onto trains by Serbian authorities for the journey to Macedonia. Houses were turned into piles of rubble after being torched deliberately and then bulldozed. In the Serbian rampage across Kosovo, more than one quarter of all buildings were destroyed or badly damaged.

Over the 11-week bombing campaign, a total of 848,100 Albanians fled or were expelled, including 444,600 to Albania, 242,300 to Macedonia, and 69,700 to Montenegro. Another 600,000 people were displaced within the province, hiding in the mountains or trekking from village to village, sheltering for weeks in basements and barns.

Instability in Host Countries and the Region. The regional repercussions of the conflict and the ensuing refugee crisis were immense. Serbia itself was crippled by the effects of the bombing campaign and became a virtual international outcast. Bosnia hosted more than 21,700 Kosovars, and its own internal problems remained sensitive to regional developments. But the greatest effects were felt in the major host countries. Within three days of the beginning of NATO bombing, ethnic Albanians began to arrive in the neighboring states of Albania, Macedonia, and Montenegro, causing serious security problems in all three regions. Albania, the poorest country in Europe, hosted the majority of refugees. Kukes, a border town of just 28,000 people, handled a sudden influx of destitute and terrified refugees—about 16 times its own population. Most refugees eventually moved away from the sensitive border zone to places further inside Albania, and a large number of Kosovars were taken in by local families. Despite Albania's generosity, the massive influx of refugees seriously destabilized the country. The KLA actively recruited among the refugees, and the Albanian border was shelled constantly by Serbian forces.

The political situations in Macedonia and Montenegro were particularly fragile. The Macedonian government, fearful that a massive influx of ethnic Albanians could destabilize its own finely tuned ethnic balance of Macedonian Slavs and Albanians, kept tens of thousands of new arrivals stranded in an open field on the Kosovo-Macedonia border. These refugees had virtually no medical assistance, little food, and limited access to humanitarian-aid agencies. At one point, the Macedonian authorities suddenly and forcibly cleared the field of refugees, bundled people on flights to Turkey, and shipped others to Albania and to hastily constructed camps nearby. After the Skopje government made it clear that it could not absorb any more people, nearly 92,000 refugees were airlifted outside the region for temporary safety.

While the numbers of refugees crossing into the Yugoslav republic of Montenegro were small compared to those in Albania and Macedonia, the Kosovars represented more than 10% of the tiny republic's population, and there was widespread concern that their presence would create ethnic instability and worsen the economic crisis brought on by the war. Of special concern to Montenegro's leadership was their fear that Belgrade would use these events as an excuse to unseat the local government.

An International Emergency. The Kosovo emergency was as difficult and complex as any that the international community had faced in recent years. Despite several early warnings that conflict was inevitable, no one had anticipated a deliberate, well-planned policy to cleanse the entire province of Albanian Kosovars. Until the last minute, it had been hoped that peace talks in Rambouillet, France, would piece together a compromise political solution. International-aid agencies were criticized for not being able to deliver emergency supplies once the influx began or to build camps quickly enough. The agencies, for their part, were almost entirely dependent on government financial support to carry out operations, and the governments did not provide them with resources early enough to do the job.

The Refugees Return. In early June a cease-fire accord was signed, ending the fighting in Kosovo. Within three weeks, despite warnings to stay where they were until Kosovo could be made safe and habitable again, the bulk of the refugees returned home in one of the swiftest and largest repatriations in modern history. The return of the Albanians led to the flight of most of Kosovo's 200,000 Serbs and gypsies, who feared violent retribution as revenge killings and other atrocities swept through the province. The widespread destruction of houses, schools, and health centers, as well as the limited availability of food because of the halt in agricultural production during the war, made the international reconstruction and rehabilitation effort extremely difficult.

Delays by governments in committing funds and other bureaucratic and logistical hurdles prevented a rapid start-up of the reconstruction effort. In November, European Union (EU) officials reported that about 300,000 Kosovars lacked adequate shelter because so many homes had been destroyed by the Serbs. The advent of winter added a further dimension to the NATO and UN effort, as aid agencies raced against time to help the returning refugees survive the onset of subfreezing temperatures and snowstorms.

GIL LOESCHER, *University of Notre Dame*

(Continued from page 81.)

Serb forces. At the end of May, Louise Arbour, the chief prosecutor at the Hague-based war-crimes tribunal, announced that under mounting evidence, the court was indicting Slobodan Milosevic on three counts of crimes against humanity in Kosovo. The court also indicted Serbian President Milan Milutinovic, Yugoslav Deputy Prime Minister Nikola Sainovic, Gen. Dragoljub Ojdanic (the chief of staff of the Yugoslav army), and Serbian Interior Minister Vlajko Stojilkovic for their role in deporting, murdering, and persecuting the Kosovars.

Several other measures were undertaken by the Western countries against the Milosevic government. They included a travel ban imposed against top government officials, a ban on shipments of oil and oil products to Serbia, a ban on export credits guaranteed by private banks, a tightening of restrictions on investments, and the prevention of companies from providing technical assistance to targets destroyed by NATO. All commercial air links with Belgrade also were suspended by the NATO countries.

Serbia's Surrender. In early June the Serbian authorities capitulated after NATO intensified its bombing against the country's military establishment and its economic infrastructure. Belgrade accepted a peace plan of the Group of 8 (G-8) major industrial democracies that was brought to Belgrade by Finnish President Martti Ahtisaari, the special envoy of the European Union (EU), and Russian envoy Viktor Chernomyrdin. The plan called for the withdrawal of all Serb forces, the return of refugees, and the installment of troops under a UN flag, many of which would be under NATO's command. The G-8 plan received a UN mandate.

War damage to the Serbian economy was estimated at several billion dollars. Most of the bridges along the Danube were destroyed by NATO planes. Factories, power stations,

Viktor Chernomyrdin (center), Russia's envoy to Kosovo, met various times with Yugoslav President Slobodan Milosevic (right). On June 2, Chernomyrdin presented Milosevic with the principles of a peace accord drawn up by the Group of 8 (G-8) major industrial democracies. The plan was accepted by the Serbian parliament the following day.

Leaders of Western nations assembled in Sarajevo, the capital of Bosnia and Herzegovina, in late July to endorse the Stability Pact, which was launched to bring peace, democracy, market economics, and regional cooperation to the war-torn region of the Balkans. Yugoslavia (Serbia) was omitted from the pact. U.S. President Bill Clinton noted that the Western nations "certainly want to make clear to the Serbian people that we want Serbia to be part of the regional negotiation process, but that is not possible as long as [Slobodan] Milosevic is in power."

electricity grids, and oil-storage facilities were also among the targets whose annihilation began to cripple the economy. The republic of Montenegro was spared from most of the attacks, as NATO calculated that dropping bombs there would alienate the pro-Western government of President Milo Djukanovic and strengthen Milosevic's influence in Montenegro.

Throughout the war, NATO had built up its ground forces in neighboring Macedonia and Albania in preparation for a possible land invasion into Serbia. Although NATO leaders denied that such an incursion was being planned, Serbian leaders calculated that that scenario could materialize by the end of the summer and could result in the destruction of the Yugoslav armed forces. They therefore presented the evacuation of their military and paramilitary units from Kosovo as a tactical withdrawal in the face of overwhelming odds.

Under a UN Security Council mandate, NATO's entry into Kosovo on June 14 was placed under the authority of the United Nations Mission in Kosovo (UNMIK). For the next several years, NATO was given the task of ensuring security; the UN was responsible for establishing a political authority and providing humanitarian assistance; the OSCE was charged with developing public institutions (including local police forces), monitoring human rights, and organizing general elections; and the EU was empowered to coordinate economic reconstruction.

(Continued on page 88.)

NATO at 50

© Brad Markel/Liaison Agency

Founded in April 1949 as a mutual-defense pact of the United States, Canada, and ten West European countries, the North Atlantic Treaty Organization (NATO) had concentrated exclusively on preparations to repel an armed attack on one of its members, until the breakup of the Soviet bloc in 1989–90 brought into question its continuing need to exist. Rather than disband, however, NATO undertook ambitious new tasks.

First, it extended its membership to former members of the Warsaw Pact in Eastern Europe—beginning with the Czech Republic, Hungary, and Poland in March 1999—and opened negotiations with other East European countries on their eventual admittance. Secondly, it sought to institutionalize military cooperation with Russia and 26 other former Soviet states and neutral countries by forming Partnerships for Peace for joint military planning and exercises, and by establishing with Russia a NATO Russia Permanent Joint Council. Third, it broadened the geographical area of its military responsibilities from the North Atlantic area alone to include the safeguarding of newly democratic regimes, prevention of international terrorism or crimes against humanity, and peacekeeping operations. The vicious civil and ethnic war in Bosnia, following the breakup of Yugoslavia in 1991–92, forced NATO to engage for the first time in a ground-force operation outside the North Atlantic area.

Initial Responsibilities in the Balkans. Although the United Nations (UN) took primary responsibility for ending the conflict among Muslims, Croats, and Serbs in Bosnia in 1992–95, NATO decided in 1992 to support the UN actions, by sending naval forces to the Adriatic to enforce a UN embargo on sending weapons to the belligerents and by flying assault missions to enforce the UN-declared no-fly zone over Bosnia and to break the Serb siege of Sarajevo. On Feb. 28, 1994, NATO planes shot down four Bosnian Serb planes in the no-fly zone, in the first military combat ever undertaken by NATO. Bombing strikes also were carried out near Sarajevo and other Bosnian towns. When a peace plan was agreed upon in Dayton, OH, in November 1995, NATO forces replaced those of the UN in Bosnia, working as an Implementation Force (IFOR) to end hostilities, rebuild the infrastructure, and attempt to restore a unified government. In December 1996, IFOR was reduced in size by half and became a Stabilization Force (SFOR), keeping the peace while civilian government was reorganized. In 1998 its mission was extended indefinitely.

With its Balkan responsibilities seemingly reduced, NATO began reconsideration of its future role, preparing a new statement of strategic principles that was to be approved at the 50th-anniversary summit in Washington in April 1999. Debate centered on which countries to admit next; the geographical area and objectives of future NATO activity; the role of the European Union (EU) in European defense; and the need for European powers to invest more in advanced military technology. But the crisis in Kosovo made practical decisions imperative.

Kosovo Crisis. As conflict escalated in Kosovo in 1998 between ethnic Albanians and Serb security forces, and large-scale expulsion of civilians from their homes began, NATO threatened air strikes and forced the Serb government to agree to accept the presence in Kosovo of 2,000 unarmed observers and to begin withdrawing its forces. NATO troops were sent to Macedonia to extricate the observers if necessary. After the failure of the Rambouillet conference of February–March 1999, with 250,000 ethnic Albanians already driven from their homes, NATO ordered massive air strikes to begin on March 24 against Serbia itself and against Serbian forces in Kosovo. The decision was controversial, because it had not been authorized by the United Nations; it was intervention in what, under international law, was a civil war within a sovereign state; and it was outside the area NATO was supposed to defend under the North Atlantic Pact. Greece and Italy, within the pact, and Russia, outside, expressed strong misgivings over the action. The military tactics also came under attack, because it was at once clear that NATO—and especially the United States—believed that a war with a medium-sized European power could be won by air strikes alone, through the use of smart bombs, with minimum casualties to NATO and even to civilians in the areas attacked, and without the use of ground troops. Worse, when the air attacks were followed by greater Serb attacks on ethnic Albanians, up to 90% of whom were expelled from their homes and thousands of whom were murdered, critics of NATO charged that the alliance was partly responsible for the atrocities.

50th-Anniversary Summit. NATO held its 50th-anniversary summit on April 23–24, *photo, page 86,* with the participation of the 19 NATO members and all its new Partners for Peace except Russia and Belarus. The latter two nations boycotted the meeting in protest against the bombing of Serbia. NATO reaffirmed its intention of continuing the bombing of Yugoslavia until it received compliance with its demands, but it did not authorize a ground invasion. The summit's final declaration emphasized a willingness to admit new, prepared members from Eastern Europe; to strengthen ties with Russia and other Partners for Peace; to prevent proliferation of weapons of mass destruction; and to support autonomous European military preparations through the EU. The new Strategic Concept permitted NATO intervention beyond the territory of its members but within the Euro-Atlantic area, as in Kosovo, to end conflicts threatening the area's stability through "crisis management, including crisis response operations."

© Karim Daher/Liaison Agency

Acceptance in June by Yugoslavia of NATO's peace terms forestalled a debate that threatened to split NATO over the effectiveness of waging war by "smart," largely American weapons and planes rather than with simultaneous use of largely European ground forces. It also confirmed the need for NATO to act in certain restricted areas, such as southeastern Europe, where inhuman crimes were being committed and where regional conflicts would threaten its own security. Creation of the largely NATO Kosovo Force (KFOR), *photo above,* for the interim administration of Kosovo, combined with the renewal of the mandate of NATO forces in Bosnia, were regarded as proof of NATO's commitment to its expanded role as the alliance entered its second half century.

F. Roy Willis
University of California, Davis

(Continued from page 85.)

The Russian government was opposed adamantly to the NATO bombing campaign, and it suspended various contacts with the NATO states during the war. Moscow's warnings to NATO may have been interpreted by Serbia as evidence that Russia was planning to send military assistance to Serb forces—an incorrect assumption that may have stiffened Belgrade's resolve even more. During the introduction of peacekeepers into Kosovo, a Russian contingent from Bosnia, with Serb cooperation, rushed to take the airport in Pristina, the Kosovar capital, in a show of defiance against NATO. However, despite Moscow's demands, Russian forces were not allocated a separate sector within Kosovo, as Western leaders feared that such an action would lead to the partition of the territory.

Postwar Operations. The bulk of Albanian refugees, numbering more than 1 million, returned to the province shortly after the successful NATO operation. Under the UN mandate, NATO established a Kosovo Force (KFOR) in the territory, consisting of approximately 50,000 troops that included 7,000 Americans, 7,000 French, 13,000 Britons, 5,000 Italians, and 10,000 Russians. Kosovo was divided into five military operational sectors, controlled by the United States, Britain, France, Germany, and Italy.

While all Serbian forces, both regular and irregular, left Kosovo ahead of the NATO intervention, much of the Serbian minority also fled, fearing revenge attacks by returning Albanians. An OSCE report published in late 1999 described the province as completely polarized ethnically, with both Serbs and Albanians subjected to violence by gunmen and vigilantes. Attacks on Serb civilians were particularly worrisome. At least 200 reportedly were murdered in revenge killings in the first three months of the UN administration. In addition, Serb properties were burned or confiscated, and harassment of civilians was widespread. Of a prewar Serbian population of some 200,000, only 70,000 were believed to be remaining in Kosovo by the fall.

Although Serb leaders accused NATO of turning a blind eye to the abuses, military commanders responded that they simply did not possess the manpower to patrol every neighborhood in Kosovo. Meanwhile, there were persistent delays in the training and deployment of an indigenous police force and the establishment of a credible and professional judiciary system that could have promoted law and order in the territory.

In a careful investigation of Serbian atrocities during the war, international war-crimes experts estimated that mass graves in Kosovo contained the bodies of approximately 11,000 Albanians. The exact figure was unknown, because Serb forces reportedly burned thousands of bodies and carefully disguised the evidence of mass murder. In addition, more than 2,000 Albanians were taken hostage by retreating Serb units and were incarcerated in various Serbian prisons. Some were believed to have been tortured and killed.

© Tomislav Peternek/Corbis-Sygma

In accordance with the June peace agreement, ethnic Albanian refugees, right, *returned to their Kosovo villages, and Serbian troops,* above, *withdrew from the province.*

© Santiago Lyon/AP/Wide World Photos

Despite substantial resistance, the KLA was disbanded officially in September. A section of the KLA was transformed into a Kosovo Protection Corps (KPC) that was to contain 3,000 full-time members and 2,000 reservists, and would be empowered to respond to civilian emergencies throughout the territory. Several Serbian members of the UN-sponsored Kosovo Transitional Council resigned to protest the creation of the KPC. They argued that the largely Albanian force could be employed against Serb civilians and would promote Kosovo's ultimate separation from Serbia.

Disputes between the major Albanian factions continued to hinder the establishment of a single indigenous authority in Kosovo. The DLK leadership refused to recognize the legitimacy of the KLA commanders and the provisional government established by KLA leader Thaci. Conversely, KLA commanders dismissed the DLK and President Rugova as an anachronism in the postwar setting.

Attempts by the international community to bring the two sides together failed persistently. Moreover, observers feared that criminal organizations had become active in the province and undermined the emergence of a democratic, law-abiding society. Some of the gangs were operating from Albania and engaged in various forms of smuggling, intimidation, and even assassinations.

Kosovo's Uncertain Status. The OSCE originally had planned to hold local elections in Kosovo in the spring of 2000 and to make preparations for general elections to a central authority later in the year. But there was a lack of clarity as to how much power the proposed central government in Pristina should have, as well as to the government's relationship with the UN authorities and the Serbian and Yugoslav governments in Belgrade. One suggestion being considered was to create a consultative body with limited powers for the time being rather than a full parliament. As of December, local elections were planned for no earlier than summer 2000.

While the overwhelming majority of Albanians continued to demand Kosovo's independence, some Serbian leaders pushed for the province's cantonization. They wanted Serb-majority districts in parts of northern Kosovo to gain their own local administration and to retain special ties with Serbia. This proposal was rejected by UN Special Representative Bernard Kouchner, on the grounds that it would herald a formal partition of Kosovo along ethnic lines. Albanian leaders adamantly opposed such a solution and demanded full territorial integrity under a single government.

Various measures were taken by the international community to create a workable administration and a functioning economy in Kosovo. For example, the German mark was made the legal currency in the province (over Serbia's angry objections), new license plates were introduced, and various public institutions were established outside Belgrade's supervision. In mid-December, Kouchner and Albanian leaders signed an agreement to create a new interim administration to run the province that would absorb both Rugova's and Thaci's governments. The plan also called for representation from the Serb minority in the new administration, but the Serbs refused to participate. In effect, by the end of 1999 the Serbian regime gradually was losing political, economic, and legal control over the province, although the international community still had not decided Kosovo's final status.

Western leaders believed that postponing the decision on Kosovo's status would allow for democratic changes to take place inside Serbia (possibly including Milosevic's ouster) and enable a new relationship to emerge between Serbia and Kosovo. However, critics charged that NATO would be faced with escalating anger in the Albanian community if the UN insisted on preserving Kosovo within Serbia, regardless of any leadership changes in Belgrade. Meanwhile, for the foreseeable future, Kosovo looked set to remain both a UN and a NATO protectorate.

© Index Stock Imagery

SLEEP and Its DISORDERS

© Al Cook/Stock, Boston

Adults typically require about eight hours of sleep nightly. The inability to fall asleep or remain asleep is a major problem and annoyance. In a 1999 poll, 56% of the sampled adults had symptoms of insomnia.

By Clete A. Kushida

Although sleep occupies one third of people's lives, little was known about it and its disorders until the last 50 years. However, since the mid-20th century, the study of sleep has become one of the newest, fastest-growing, and most-exciting areas of medicine.

Sleep and Its Organization. Sleep occurs in all mammals and birds studied to date; however, there is controversy over whether other species sleep. Sleep is divided into NREM (nonrapid eye movement) and REM (rapid eye movement) sleep. NREM sleep, in turn, is divided into four stages, 1–4, which are identified through recordings of the electrical activity of the brain, eyes, and muscle. NREM stages 3 and 4 sleep also are called deep or slow-wave sleep; of the NREM stages, stage 1 is the lightest and stage 4 is the deepest sleep. During REM sleep, rapid eye movements and the majority of dreams occur; brain-wave activity resembles that of waking; voluntary muscle activity is inhibited; and an irregular heart rate and breathing are present.

REM sleep alternates with NREM sleep at intervals of approximately 90 minutes in adults and 60 minutes in infants. It is not unusual for newborn babies to sleep 17–18 hours daily, with REM sleep comprising 50% of their sleep. Adults typically sleep eight hours nightly, with REM sleep comprising approximately 20% of their sleep. The elderly typically sleep six and one half hours daily, with minimal amounts of slow-wave or REM sleep. There is also a circadian-rhythm component—a regular and persistent alteration in sleep—in which the sleep of adolescents is phase-delayed naturally. Thus, adolescents desire late bedtimes and late-morning awakenings. Most elderly are phase-advanced and therefore desire early bedtimes and early-morning awakenings. Although the exact mechanisms and structures responsible for sleep are unknown, the pons in the brainstem is necessary and sufficient for REM-sleep generation, and acetylcholine, a neurotransmitter, is involved in REM sleep.

Is sleep important? Following a poor night's sleep, humans typically suffer from microsleeps, decreased concentration and short-term memory, irritability, and lapses of attention. Such conditions put people at risk for work-related and motor-vehicle-related accidents. In addition, a series of experiments conducted by Dr. Allan Rechtschaffen and his colleagues at the University of Chicago demonstrated that rats deprived of either total sleep, REM sleep, or slow-wave sleep became debilitated and died after a few weeks. Although long-term sleep-deprivation experiments in humans have not revealed serious physical debilitation, studies have supported the theory that the immune system may be compromised with sleep loss.

Widespread Problems. A 1999 U.S. poll conducted by the National Sleep Foundation revealed a high prevalence of daytime sleepiness in today's population, as well as the fact that sleep problems are underrecognized and undertreated. Fifty-eight percent of the sampled adults reported that daytime sleepiness interfered with their daily activities, and 65% of the surveyed adults obtained less than eight hours of sleep daily during the workweek. Sixty-two percent of the sampled adults reported driving while drowsy in the previous year, and 27% had dozed off behind the wheel. Fifteen percent of children fell asleep in school. Although 56% of the sampled adults had symptoms of insomnia, just 6% of the cases were diagnosed, and only 3% were treated.

Sleep Disorders. Sleep disorders are highly prevalent, yet largely are unrecognized, misdiagnosed, and untreated. The International Classification of Sleep Disorders by the American Academy of Sleep Medicine recognizes 88 distinct sleep disorders; the most common are:

Insomnia. Patients with insomnia have difficulty initiating and maintaining sleep. They typically suffer from chronic fatigue and tiredness, irritability, and concentration and memory impairment. In diagnosing and treating insomnia, there must be a thorough evaluation of poor sleep habits, coexisting circadian-rhythm disorders, depression or anxiety disorders, hypnotic or stimulant abuse, and significant medical and neurological problems (e.g., asthma and degenerative arthritis), since such conditions adversely affect sleep. The mainstay of insomnia treatment is the implementation of behavioral techniques. These include: (1) the adoption of a regular sleep-wake schedule, without naps; (2) the avoidance of remaining in bed for extended periods while awake, to prevent being conditioned for wakefulness in the bedroom environment; (3) the decreased use of caffeine, nicotine, and alcohol, and limits on heavy exercise, meals, and fluid intake near bedtime; and (4) the avoidance of reading and watching television in bed

About the Author. Dr. Clete A. Kushida is director of the Stanford Center for Human Sleep Research in Stanford, CA, and serves as a staff physician and clinical instructor at the Stanford Sleep Disorders Clinic. Dr. Kushida has studied the sleep process and its disorders for more than 20 years. He has written numerous articles and papers on the topic.

(unless these activities result in drowsiness). Stimulus-control therapy (reassociating the bedroom environment with rapid sleep onset), sleep restriction (programmed reduction in the duration of time spent in bed), and relaxation therapy (meditation, self-hypnosis, progressive muscle relaxation, and electromyographic biofeedback) also may be beneficial in improving insomnia. Lastly, mild hypnotic medications (e.g., zolpidem) may be used as a supplement to behavioral therapy in intractable cases of insomnia.

Obstructive Sleep Apnea Syndrome. Obstructive sleep apnea (OSA) refers to breathing pauses during sleep. Daytime sleepiness, combined with sleep-related breathing pauses, characterize the obstructive sleep apnea syndrome. Based on studies by Dr. Terry Young and her colleagues at the University of Wisconsin in Madison in 1993, it is estimated that up to one quarter of men and one tenth of women between the ages of 30 and 60 years show evidence of this condition. Besides placing the patient at greater risk for motor-vehicle and work-related accidents, this disorder is associated with cardiovascular conditions such as hypertension, stroke, myocardial infarction, dysrhythmias, and cardiac failure, as well as with neurocognitive problems such as decreased short-term memory.

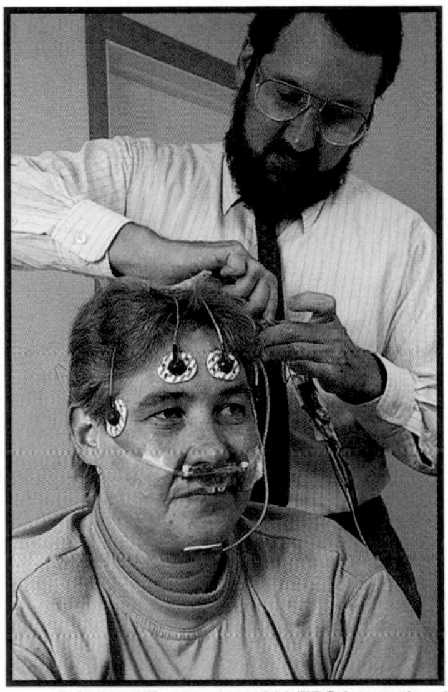

Suctions and tubes are attached to a patient to monitor sleep apnea—breathing pauses during sleep. Some 25% of men and 10% of women between the ages of 30 and 60 show evidence of obstructive sleep apnea (OSA).

The diagnosis of the obstructive sleep apnea syndrome is confirmed by a sleep study, which reveals the repetitive abnormal breathing events characteristic of this disorder. Although obesity is a risk factor, craniofacial abnormalities (a narrow, posteriorly displaced mandible and an elongated, high, arched soft palate), hypertrophied adenotonsillar tissue (particularly in children), redundant peritonsillar tissue, and an enlarged uvula and tongue typically are found in patients who snore or who have the obstructive sleep apnea syndrome or the upper airway resistance syndrome (a milder sleep-related breathing disorder). Nasal obstruction may predispose the patient to develop sleep-disordered breathing or may worsen an existing case. Treatment consists of weight loss; cervical-positioning devices; oral appliances (devices that move the tongue or mandible forward); nasal CPAP (continuous positive airway pressure), which provides a pressure splint to the upper airway; or upper-airway surgery.

Narcolepsy. The disorder known as narcolepsy is characterized by sudden and uncontrollable periods of sleep. It is estimated to affect approximately 200,000 Americans, and there appears to be a genetic predisposition for its development. Narcolepsy most commonly occurs in the second decade of life (teen years) and affects men and women equally. It is indicated by the following symptoms: (1) attacks of sudden daytime sleepiness; (2) cataplexy, or the sudden loss of postural muscle tone, typically precipitated by strong emotion; (3) hypnagogic (sleep-onset) hallucinations, which may be fleeting sounds (e.g., voices), visions, or full-blown auditory, visual, tactile, or kinetic hallucinations; and (4) sleep paralysis, typically at the transition from sleep to wake-

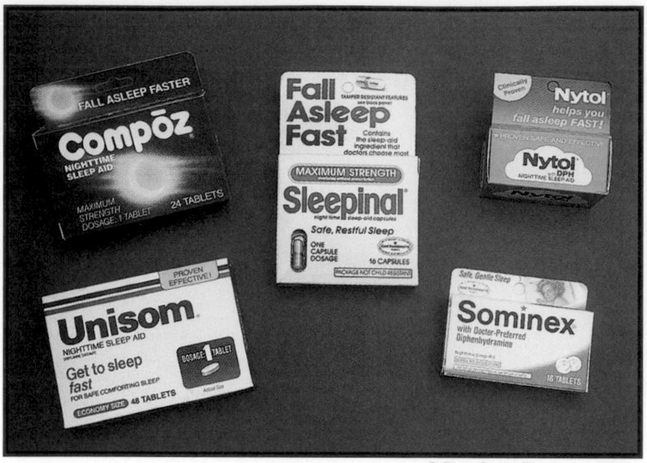

© Dion Ogust/The Image Works

A wide variety of over-the-counter medicines and supplements for occasional sleeplessness now are available. Safer and more effective prescription sleeping pills also have been developed.

fulness. The diagnosis of narcolepsy is established by the presence of symptoms and is confirmed by the multiple sleep latency test (MSLT), in which a subject's tendency to fall asleep is assessed during five daytime naps. This disorder typically is treated with scheduled naps and stimulants to ward off the daytime sleepiness, and with anticataplectic medications (typically, tricyclic antidepressants).

Restless Legs Syndrome and Periodic Limb Movement Disorder. The restless legs syndrome is characterized by unpleasant sensations ("creeping," "crawling," "itching," or pain) in the limbs that result in an irresistible urge to move the limbs. Although these symptoms can occur anytime throughout the day, they may worsen at night, ultimately resulting in insomnia or daytime sleepiness. The syndrome commonly occurs in middle age and equally affects both men and women. Pregnant women and individuals with uremia or rheumatoid arthritis appear susceptible to this disorder. The diagnosis typically is made by the patient's history. First-line treatment consists of dopaminergic agents (e.g., carbidopa/levodopa). Benzodiazepines (e.g., clonazepam), opiates, and anticonvulsants (e.g., gabapentin) have variable effectiveness in treating this disorder.

Periodic limb movement disorder is characterized by daytime sleepiness resulting from repetitive limb movements during sleep. Although the peak onset of this disorder is in middle age, its incidence increases with age. Patients suspected of having this disorder are evaluated by polysomnography—the use of electrodes to measure the activity of the brain, muscles, eyes, heart, and lungs—and treatment consists of the same medications used to treat restless legs syndrome.

Circadian Rhythm Disorders. Circadian rhythm disorders should be considered in patients who have an unusual sleep-wake pattern, accompanied by either insomnia or excessive daytime sleepiness. Time-zone-change (jet-lag) syndrome and shift-work sleep disorder are characterized by the effects of external factors on the patient's sleep. Delayed or advanced sleep-phase syndrome correspond to a chronic delay or advance, respectively, of the timing of the natural sleep period with respect to the desired bedtime or awakening time. These disorders frequently are recognized by the patient's history; sleep logs and actigraphy (the use of a wristwatch-like device to measure activity) may be useful in establishing the diagnosis. The treatment used to help insomnia patients frequently is beneficial in helping patients with circadian-rhythm disorders. Treatment also consists of behavioral-conditioning techniques, such as stimulus-control therapy and relaxation therapy. A mild hypnotic medication may be necessary to initiate sleep at the desired time.

Sleep Terrors, Sleepwalking, and REM Sleep-Behavior Disorder. Sleep terrors and sleepwalking (somnambulism) occur during slow-wave sleep and are characterized by screaming and ambulating, respectively. In addition, victims do not recall the episodes. Typically, between 1% and 15% of the general population experience these familial disorders. It is estimated that between 15% and 30% of healthy children have walked in their sleep at least once.

The diagnosis is established by clinical history. For sleepwalking, polysomnography is important to exclude nocturnal seizures; also, certain polysomnographic features often are found in sleepwalkers. Nighttime safety precautions must be taken in the homes of sleepwalkers. For example, dangerous objects must be removed from the paths of those who sleepwalk, and houseguests should be informed of the condition. Medications (benzodiazepines and tricyclic antidepressants), and occasionally hypnosis and psychotherapy, may control the conditions.

REM sleep-behavior disorder may mimic sleepwalking. However, individuals with this disorder are typically men over the age of 60 years; they frequently "act out" their dreams during REM sleep (as opposed to sleepwalking, which occurs during slow-wave sleep, typically without dream recall). The treatment is identical to that for sleepwalking.

Sleep talking, sleep starts (sudden contractions of the body at sleep onset), nocturnal leg cramps, nightmares, bruxism (teeth grinding), enuresis (bedwetting), and primary snoring are typically more nuisances than clinically significant problems. Such conditions become problems when the episodes are frequent, severe, and/or disruptive to the patient or his or her bed partner.

Diagnostic Tests. Polysomnography is used to confirm the presence and to assess the severity of a sleep disorder, such as the obstructive sleep apnea syndrome, sleep terrors or

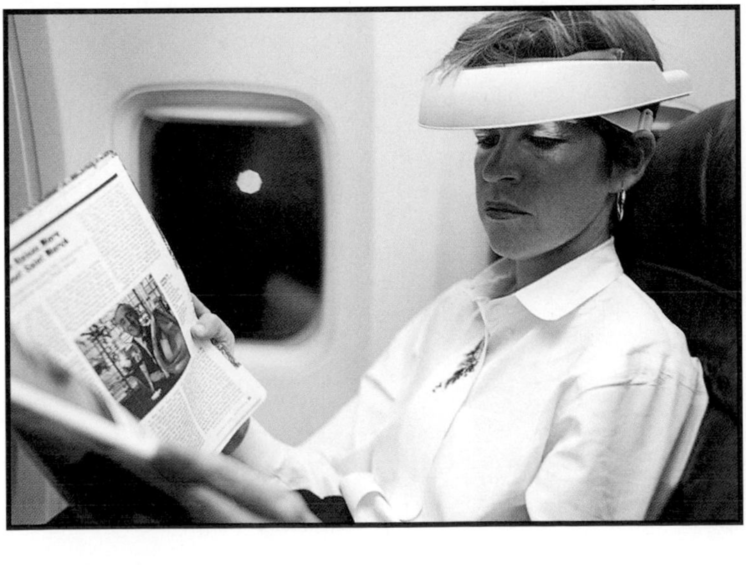

An airline traveler reads a magazine while wearing a bright-light visor designed to combat jet lag. Long airline flights through several time zones tend to disrupt sleep patterns and cause fatigue and irritability.

sleepwalking, nocturnal epilepsy, or periodic limb movement disorder. The subject is connected to electrodes that measure the activity of the brain, eyes, heart, and chin and leg muscles. The electrodes also measure snoring intensity, oronasal airflow, chest and abdominal movement, and oxygen saturation throughout the night. Esophageal-pressure monitoring is useful in the diagnosis of mild sleep-related breathing conditions. Assessment of daytime sleepiness can be measured objectively by the multiple sleep latency test (MSLT). This test also can be used to confirm a diagnosis of narcolepsy, in which the mean sleep latency (average of the time from lights out to sleep onset for five naps) is in the pathologic range of sleepiness (less than five minutes), and REM sleep is present in two or more of the naps.

A maintenance-of-wakefulness test (MWT) uses the same equipment and schedule as the MSLT, with the exception that the subject is sitting and is instructed to resist sleep. Tests such as the psychomotor-vigilance task help to assess vigilance. Other tests—including pulmonary- and thyroid-function tests for patients with sleep-disordered breathing and renal-function tests and the measurement of ferritin levels to identify causes of restless legs syndrome—may be helpful. Genetic tests (e.g., HLA typing) may be useful in diagnosing narcolepsy. Actigraphy—the detection of activity, typically by a wristwatch-like device—may help in the evaluation of insomnia or circadian rhythm disorders. Video monitoring and sleep-deprived electroencephalography aid in the diagnosis of nocturnal seizures.

Unanswered Questions. Despite the growth in knowledge regarding sleep and its disorders, many questions remain unanswered. For example, what is the function of sleep? In addition, the causes of many sleep disorders are not known. Experts hope that breakthroughs in sleep research will continue and eventually will provide relief to the millions who suffer from debilitating sleep disorders.

© LeDuc/Monkmeyer

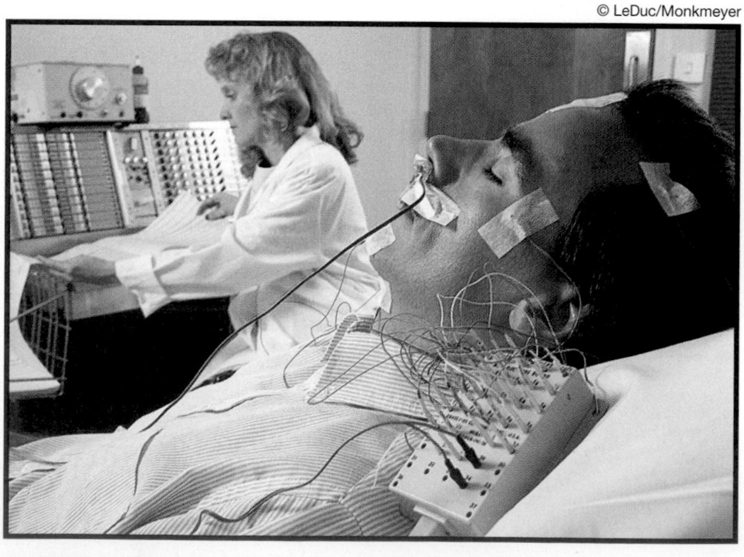

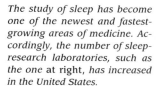

The study of sleep has become one of the newest and fastest-growing areas of medicine. Accordingly, the number of sleep-research laboratories, such as the one at right, has increased in the United States.

Pop Music's New Diversity

LATIN, JAZZ, SWING...

© Mark Richards/PhotoEdit

As swing music enjoys renewed popularity, music fans young and old have found that an evening out at a nightclub's "swing night"—during which dance lessons often are offered—is an enjoyable way to spend time.

By John Milward

As the century turns, a big story in popular music is the growing influence of Latin music, but while the world was tapping its collective foot to Ricky Martin's huge hit "La Vida Loca," a very different Latin recording also was speaking to the diversity of the contemporary music market. *The Buena Vista Social Club* (1997) is a largely acoustic, Spanish-language recording featuring Cuban songs and styles that preceded the 1959 revolution in that country. Guitarist Ry Cooder, who himself is steeped in a wide variety of folk styles, coproduced the album and helped to search out players like singer Ibrahim Ferrer and pianist Rubén Gonzáles, two stars of the record who had not played professionally for years. The record became a hit among adults more likely to listen to National Public Radio than to watch MTV.

Latin music has caused a stir with pop singers like Ricky Martin, Jennifer Lopez, and Marc Anthony reaching the top of the charts, but that is just the tip of the international ice-

Young pop stars such as Jennifer Lopez, above left, *and Ricky Martin,* above right, *have brought a new trendiness to Latin music. Meanwhile, more-established Spanish-language musicians also have benefited from Latin music's increasing popularity; the Argentinian group the Fabulosos Cadillacs,* right, *in 1998 won the first Grammy Award for best Latin rock/alternative performance, for "Fabulosos Calavera."*

Photo credits: top left, © Mitch Gerber/Corbis; top right, © Dalle Luche/Sestini/Grazia Neri/Corbis-Sygma; above, © Reuters/Jeff Christensen/Archive Photos

berg. Brazilian artists such as Gilberto Gil and Caetano Veloso are known around the world; Cesaria Evora of Cape Verde is one of the latest international musical treasures to please Western ears. Cross-cultural collaborations have become increasingly common, such as 1999's *Kulanjan*, in which the African-American blues artist Taj Mahal finds common ground with musicians from Mali, including Toumani Diabate, a master of the kora, a kind of African harp-lute. Such internationally inclined recordings might not be big sellers, but increasingly, they can circulate throughout the world and influence both popular tastes and the imaginations of local musicians.

One reason for this new diversity is that adults have become an increasingly large segment of the music-buying public. The Recording Industry Association of America (RIAA), a music-business trade group, conducted a consumer profile in 1998 that reported a drop in purchases among consumers aged 15 to 29 (to 28% of the market) and a growth in sales to those 35 and older (to 39% of the mar-

About the Author. John Milward is a freelance writer and critic. His work appears regularly in a variety of publications, including *The New York Times* and *The Los Angeles Times*.

ket). The report also found that women were buying a little more music than men.

While kids propelled the day's hot rapper (DMX), rock band (Limp Bizkit), or teen group (Backstreet Boys) to the top of the charts, their parents were buying an album by Shania Twain, the sound track to *Titanic*, or maybe that recording by those old Cuban musicians they read about in the paper. In 1999, a year after *The Buena Vista Social Club* won a Grammy, a similarly titled documentary film about the musicians, directed by Wim Wenders, continued to stoke interest in a disc that was expected to sell a million copies in the United States, a staggering amount for a recording that typically would be filed under "world music."

The RIAA survey explains more about the diversity of today's music market. Among musical genres, rock accounts for about 26% of the recordings sold, with country the second-most-popular style at about 14%. Comparatively esoteric styles of music showed great percentage jumps between 1997 and 1998—including gospel, which surged from 4.5% to 6.3% due to the increased popularity of artists who perform contemporary pop songs with overtly Christian lyrics. Classical music saw a slighter increase, accounting for 3.3% of the market.

None of this has prevented such teen-oriented acts as 'N Sync and Britney Spears from selling millions of records, nor has it put a dent in the chart-topping success of rap and hip-hop performers like Jay-Z and the Wu-Tang Clan. But the survey demonstrates that, although earlier generations tended to buy less music as they reached middle age, the children of rock 'n' roll have not all stopped buying new music—and they are open to diverse styles, including Latin, jazz, and even 1940s "swing," as well as innovative combinations of differing genres.

New swing bands such as Big Bad Voodoo Daddy, below, *have helped revive many of the fashions of the big-band era as well as its music.*

© Karen Mason Blair/Corbis

© Scott Harrison/Archive Photos

The 17-piece Brian Setzer Orchestra, led by Brian Setzer, above, *helped publicize big-band music—and triggered a swell of interest in swing-dance lessons—with an appearance in a commercial for Gap clothing.*

The increased fragmentation of the music market also is encouraged by the strict formats of radio stations, which tailor their programming to attract a very specific demographic group. In addition, the burgeoning sales of recordings through Internet outlets has made an extraordinary amount of music available to consumers with the click of a mouse. Internet stores give rural music fans access to the kind of variety that was once the exclusive province of big-city superstores. Commercial sites typically recommend recordings not just in genres like rock and hip-hop, but also in such specialized fields as "new age," "bluegrass," and "techno." The sites also are designed to encourage the shopper to discover new music through the use of audio clips, record reviews, and other supplementary material.

Musical Fusions. Sales are only part of the story of musical diversity. Adventuresome musicians always have tested the boundaries between genres, with classical composers quick to borrow from folk themes, and contemporary musicians creating such hybrid styles as country-rock or jazz-rock fusion. A major recent trend in rock has found bands like Korn and Limp Bizkit cultivating a style that combines elements of rap and heavy metal. At the same time, rap performers like Puff Daddy and Lauryn Hill have enjoyed hits that have incorporated live instruments and samples that are just as apt to draw from rock or funk as pop or country. Shania Twain has become a huge star by turbocharging her nominally country tunes with elements of pop and rock. Tricky's latest album, *Play*, finds the dance-music deejay and musician weaving samples of obscure country blues and early-20th-century field recordings into his modern dance music.

Musical styles do not disappear as much as recombine or return in the form of revivals. The recent resurgence in swing music is an example of such a phenomenon, with Squirrel Nut Zippers evoking the sound of early big-band swing with their 1997 hit single "Hell." Part of the song's success was due to sheer novelty; it also did not hurt that the fashions and dance styles that accompanied the swing revival made for popular music videos. Brian Setzer, who found success in the 1980s reviving rockabilly with the Stray Cats, came back in the late 1990s playing jump blues and swing with a 17-piece big band. It was totally in keeping with today's media-saturated environment that Setzer's music was promoted not just with music videos, but by his band's appearance in a commercial for the Gap. This television exposure brought on an upsurge in the popularity of swing-dancing classes throughout the United States.

Ska, a rhythmic precursor to Jamaican reggae that was in vogue during the late 1970s, also has enjoyed a recent revival in the hands of bands like No Doubt and Sublime. Ska and swing are intermingled in the repertoire of Cherry Poppin' Daddies, and the blend is reflective of the sampling techniques used in hip-hop recordings. Other acts that mix and match in search of hits include the Mighty Mighty Bosstones, Royal Crown Revue, and Sugar Ray.

© Tim Mosenfelder/Corbis

The Squirrel Nut Zippers, above, *helped set off the swing-music explosion with their 1998 hit "Hell." The group's innovative music fuses the 1940s-style big-band sound with bluegrass, country, jazz, and even calypso.*

Jazz is a musical form that thrives on diversity; indeed, whereas Latin influences just now are becoming prominent in pop music, they have been a part of the jazz palette for more than 50 years. Trumpeter Wynton Marsalis has been the best-known musician in jazz for more than a decade and won the first Pulitzer Prize awarded to a jazz composition for 1997's *Blood on the Fields*. He forged an important link between jazz and the cultural mainstream by acting as the musical director of the Lincoln Center Jazz Orchestra. Marsalis is significant both as a musician and as an educator, effectively using his celebrity to hasten the acceptance of jazz as one of the preeminent forms of American art. Marsalis has drawn scorn from some jazz critics for his conservative tastes—he is dismissive of jazz-rock fusion and much of the avant-garde—but nobody denies his superior musicianship. As a player who writes music in a variety of forms, including dance scores for the Alvin Ailey Dance Troupe, Marsalis is himself an example of musical diversity.

Jazz lives through its individual voices, and among the significant players who have emerged in the last few years are pianist Brad Mehldau, whose playing incorporates classical influences into jazzy improvisations, and Diana Krall, a pianist and singer whose snappy recordings of the past few years never have been far from the top of the jazz charts. Adventurous musicians also have found both musical and spiritual sustenance in klezmer music, the traditional instrumental music of East European Jews that was all but forgotten until it was rediscovered and revived by jazz and folk musicians.

Violinist Nigel Kennedy's untraditional appearance and recordings of rock anthems as well as classical pieces help him appeal to younger, pop-oriented fans as well as to classical-music lovers.

© NTB/Corbis

© Gregory Pace/Corbis-Sygma

Thirty-four-year-old Canadian jazz musician Diana Krall's sultry voice and talent at the piano bring a fresh new twist to jazz standards. Krall's sold-out tours and top-selling albums are evidence of her appeal, and of music fans' renewed interest in jazz.

Recording artists of all kinds have learned lessons from the book of pop-music careers. An obvious example are the successful tours and albums by the Three Tenors, an operatic supergroup consisting of Luciano Pavarotti, Plácido Domingo, and José Carreras. Younger classical artists naturally are drawn to the sizzle of pop. Celebrated violinist Nigel Kennedy, for example, has recorded songs by Jimi Hendrix alongside the classical repertoire. He lately has started to bill himself as "Kennedy," a clear allusion to such one-named pop stars as Cher and Madonna. Andrea Bocelli is an Italian opera singer who became a romantic recording star without even toiling in the world's opera halls. His 1997 album *Romanze* has sold more than 10 million copies.

The Technological Revolution. Computer technology and the Internet also are having a huge impact on musicians and the music business. Digital recording equipment has slashed the price of building a home studio, offering musicians the luxury of time and economy. In recent years, it has become an increasingly common career path for young musicians to develop a grassroots following through live shows and self-produced compact discs and tapes. The homegrown act has more leverage if and when it pursues a contract with a major record label. Where debut acts typically sign deals offering low royalty rates, a band with a proven sales record is likely to obtain far more desirable terms.

Besides the establishment of on-line music stores, many major labels have dabbled in selling recordings directly to the consumer via Web sites. But a more significant development has been the move toward delivering digital music directly into the consumer's home computer. The recording industry was shaken by the introduction and relatively rapid proliferation of MP3, a computer-based technology that allows the efficient downloading of compressed digital music,

The tremendous popularity attained by the group of legendary Cuban musicians assembled by guitarist Ry Cooder and known as the Buena Vista Social Club, below, *demonstrates the diversity of today's contemporary music. The group's Grammy-winning 1997 album was a celebration of Cuban musical styles dating from before the 1959 revolution.*

© G. Lewis/Corbis-Sygma

© Isaac Diggs/Jazz at Lincoln Center

© Culver Pictures, Inc.

Wynton Marsalis, artistic director of jazz at Lincoln Center, led a 1999 celebration of the 100th birthday of late jazz great Duke Ellington, left. *As part of the festivities, the Lincoln Center Jazz Orchestra—with musicians from the Metropolitan Transportation Authority Arts for Transit's Music under New York—paraded up New York City's Broadway,* above, *in April.*

leaving recording-industry executives fearful of how to keep this digital genie in the bottle until it can figure out how to protect copyrighted materials. Technologies like MP3 make it possible for the music of just about anybody to be made available to a potentially huge audience without the participation of a record label. That does not mean the music will be worth hearing, but its very existence will denote both diversity and creativity.

Global Music. A common cliché is that "music is the international language," and that statement is certainly true at the dawn of the 21st century. The amount of music available to consumers is extraordinary. In 1960 blues fans would search attics and flea markets for 78-rpm recordings by all-but-forgotten artists like Mississippi John Hurt and Robert Johnson. Now, virtually every significant recording of any genre is available on compact disc. As communication makes the world seem smaller, so does the ability of music to cross borders. The success of Ricky Martin shows how people of many cultures now can dance to the same music. And at the same time, the proudly traditional music of the Buena Vista Social Club confirms how music need go no further than the heart to strike a universal chord.

© AP/Wide World Photos

Breitling Orbiter 3
A Dream Is Realized

By Malcolm W. Browne

After taking off from Chateau d'Oex, Switzerland, on March 1, 1999, the "Breitling Orbiter 3" flew over the Swiss Alps, above. *Nineteen days later, it became the first balloon to complete a transglobal flight.*

Ever since Nov. 21, 1783, when Jean Pilâtre de Rozier and the Marquis d'Arlandes became the first human beings to rise untethered into the sky, aeronauts had dreamed of a day when a balloon propelled solely by the wind might carry a pilot all the way around the Earth. That dream finally was realized on March 20, 1999, when a Swiss psychiatrist and his English copilot crossed the transglobal finish line.

After speeding past Mauritania and the longitude from which they began their voyage, Dr. Bertrand Piccard and Brian Jones continued on to Egypt, remaining aloft for a record 19 days, 21 hours, and 55 minutes aboard their *Breitling Orbiter 3*. In the course of an exhausting and sometimes hair-raising trip, they had floated over 26 countries and covered 29,055 mi (46 758 km) without landing or refueling.

Despite previous attempts by dozens of balloonists to circle the Earth nonstop, none ever had come close to that mark. The crew gondola of the *Breitling Orbiter 3* was to go on permanent exhibition at the National Air and Space Museum in Washington, DC, joining the Wright brothers' plane and the *Voyager*, which Dick Rutan and Jeana Yeager flew around the world nonstop in 1986.

Besides capturing a permanent perch in the record books, Piccard and Jones were awarded a prize of $1 million from the Anheuser-Busch brewing company. The planning that led to their feat was comparable to that of a military campaign.

The Technology and Expertise. Many would-be balloonists during the last two centuries have patched together rigs that more or less could fly. One of the riskiest in modern times was a lawn chair supported by 45 weather balloons, which in 1982 carried Larry Walters, a Los Angeles truck driver, on a 20-mi (32-km) flight that reached an altitude of 16,000 ft (4 877 m). But long-distance ballooning generally has been the domain of well-heeled experts.

For a balloon to stand a chance at breaking records, it must be enormous—typically the height of a 15-story building—and it must incorporate all kinds of cutting-edge technology. Such a balloon typically costs millions of dollars.

A balloon crew must have the courage and stamina to withstand bitter cold, cramped discomfort, exposure to oxygen starvation, and many other stresses. Each member must be skilled not only in balloon piloting—which involves some of the principles used in maneuvering submarines—but in navigation and survival skills. The team must be backed by an experienced staff of meteorologists, a large mission-control headquarters, a search-and-rescue network, and a gift for diplomacy in dealing with xenophobic governments.

Failure to mend diplomatic fences can have tragic consequences. On Sept. 12, 1995, two Americans, Alan Fraenckel and John Stuart-Jervis, were competing in Europe in the annual Gordon Bennett Balloon Race when their hydrogen-filled balloon drifted eastward from Poland over Belarus, a nation created by the breakup of the Soviet Union. Charging violation of Belarusian airspace, the Minsk authorities sent up a military helicopter that shot down the balloon in flames, killing both pilots. The tacit threat of similar incidents continues in many regions of the world. China and Russia, among other countries, persistently have denied overflight permission to balloonists—an obstacle that enormously complicated the routing of transglobal balloon attempts, including the *Breitling Orbiter 3*.

About the Author. Malcolm W. Browne is a prizewinning science writer for *The New York Times*. As a foreign correspondent earlier in his career, he covered Southeast Asia, Latin America, and East Europe, and was awarded a Pulitzer Prize, an Overseas Press Club Award, and a George Polk Award.

With ballooning as a hobby, Mr. Browne has served as the "unofficial" ballooning correspondent for the *Times* for the past two decades. He has been aloft in hot-air balloons in various major competitions.

Brian Jones was born in Bristol, England, on March 27, 1947. After learning to fly at age 16, he dropped out of school the following year and spent 13 years in the Royal Air Force. He then joined a catering business and began to take up ballooning professionally in the mid-1980s. In 1989, Jones became a ballooning instructor and was certified as an examiner for balloon flight licenses. His wife, Joanna, also is a balloonist. He is the father of two children and has three grandchildren.

Bertrand Piccard, who was born in 1958, is descended from a famous family of Swiss adventurers, inventors, and scientists. His grandfather, Dr. Auguste Piccard, who like Bertrand was a medical doctor, invented the pressurized balloon-crew gondola and in 1931 became the first man to ascend into the stratosphere. He also invented the bathyscaphe—a deep-diving submersible. Auguste's son Jacques, Bertrand's father, was the first to pilot a submersible to the deepest ocean depth in the world—the Marianas Trench—which is some 35,800 ft (10 920 m) deep. Bertrand Piccard became a hang-gliding enthusiast at the age of 16 and made his first hot-air-balloon flight in 1979. A medical doctor who specializes in psychiatry, he is adept at hypnotizing both himself and his balloon crewmates to enable them to sleep during flights. Dr. Piccard is married and the father of three daughters.

Photo Credits: © Alain Morvan/Liaison Agency, top; © Piccard/Jones/Liaison Agency

The Balloons. Balloons are at the mercy of winds and cannot steer themselves. But winds at different altitudes blow at different speeds and in varying directions, and meteorologists tracking weather patterns from minute to minute can advise a flight crew to rise or descend into a current that will take them in the right direction. A well-guided balloon thereby can avoid dead air, storms, hostile airspace, and other hazards. Frequent changes of altitude, however, tend to use up the gas or hot-air burner fuel on which a balloon depends for lift, and thereby limit its endurance. A balloon team must maintain a fine balance between the demands of navigation and the need to conserve fuel.

The design of balloons has evolved over the centuries, but surprisingly, recent champions have flown balloon systems that originated in the 18th century. Nearly all the top contenders for the round-the-world goal during the 1990s flew in rozier balloons. Most of them were built by Britain's Cameron Balloons, Ltd.

The rozier is named for Pilâtre de Rozier, one of the world's first two balloonists. Abandoning the Montgolfier hot-air balloons in which he made his first ascents, Rozier conceived a hybrid design inflated partly with hydrogen lifting gas. Because gas is lost when a balloon climbs above a certain height, and lift is lost when the remaining gas cools at night, Rozier built a second compartment into his balloon, to which he could add hot air from a crude burner, thereby making up for lost hydrogen lift. Unfortunately, while Rozier was making a flight in 1785 with his hybrid balloon, the hot-air burner ignited the balloon's hydrogen, setting the craft on fire and killing its pilot. Rozier thus became history's first air fatality.

Ballooning with hot air—usually heated by propane burners today—always has been cheaper and more accessible than ballooning with gas—either hydrogen or nonflammable helium. But while hot air is the lifting medium preferred by most sport balloonists, long-duration flights are limited by the weight of the steel propane tanks such balloons must carry. Gas balloons, which require no propane tanks, therefore are used in most long-distance flights.

In January 1991, Richard Branson (below left), *chairman of the Virgin Group of companies, and balloon builder Per Lindstrand became the first to cross the Pacific Ocean in a hot-air balloon.*

© Eriko Sugita/Reuters/Corbis-Bettmann

Other Major Flights. In 1978 champion U.S. balloonists Ben Abruzzo, Maxie Anderson, and Larry Newman used only helium to lift their *Double Eagle II* for the first completed crossing of the Atlantic Ocean by balloon. In 1981, Abruzzo, Newman, and two other crew members—Rocky Aoki and Ron Clark—became the first balloonists to cross the Pacific, flying the *Double Eagle V*, which, like the *Double Eagle II*, was lifted by helium.

Meanwhile, however, the technology of hot-air balloons was advancing rapidly, and several propane-fired hot-air balloons made spectacularly long flights. In 1987 the British billionaire Richard Branson, chairman of the Virgin Group of companies, and balloon builder Per Lindstrand set a new endurance record for a hot-air balloon, flying 2,900 mi (4 665 km) in 33 hours in an attempt that fell just short of crossing the Atlantic. In 1991 the same two pilots became the first to cross the Pacific in a hot-air balloon, a 46-hour flight from Japan to Canada.

New polymer films and fabrics for gas-tight balloons, improved burners, pressurized crew gondolas, special insulation to reduce the expansion of gas by solar heating and reduce nighttime cooling, and other innovations convinced both Lindstrand, chairman of Lindstrand Balloons, Ltd., and his main competitor, Don Cameron, chairman of Cameron Balloons, that the time had come to experiment with the old rozier system, adapted to the technologies of the 1990s.

Very similar roziers were purchased by all of the leading round-the-world contenders of the 1990s, but their captains adopted contrasting styles of airmanship. Branson directed a vigorous publicity campaign on behalf of his *Virgin Global Challenger* balloon, which was built by Lindstrand's company and had a pressurized cabin, a three-man crew, and many physical comforts. The opposite approach was taken by Steve Fossett, a Colorado commodities broker, in the Spartan design of his Cameron-built *Solo Spirit*. Fossett's craft was unpressurized; his equipment was limited to the bare essentials; and he flew alone. For several weeks prior to each of his flights, he slept each night in a low-pressure chamber simulating the thin air of high altitudes to condition his body.

In August 1998, Fossett nearly was killed during a round-the-world attempt in the Southern Hemisphere that began in Argentina and ended 14,244 mi (22 923 km) later with a violent storm and a crash in the Coral Sea, several hundred miles east of Australia. A few months later, Fossett—a yacht racer, mountain climber, Iditarod-sled-dog racer, and swimmer—decided to accept an invitation to join Branson's balloon crew. The hopes of this "dream team," as Branson called it, were to be dashed. Their new balloon, the *ICO Global Challenge*, ran into adverse weather conditions in the Pacific after traveling nearly halfway around the world, and Branson, Lindstrand, and Fossett ditched in the ocean near Hawaii on Christmas Day, 1998.

Intermediate in style between Branson and Fossett was Piccard, who made two unsuccessful round-the-world attempts with three-man crews before picking Jones as his sole copilot for his historic flight. At the close of the millennium, long-duration balloonists were discussing the possibility of holding a round-the-world race. But there never will be another first global circumnavigation. The 1999 achievement of Piccard and Jones will stand forever.

In August 1978 the "Double Eagle II" (above) *with three businessmen from Albuquerque, NM—Ben Abruzzo, Maxie Anderson, and Larry Newman—aboard was the first balloon to cross the Atlantic Ocean.*

THE ALPHABETICAL SECTION

© Reuters/Natalie Behring/Archive Photos

The 50th anniversary of the founding of Communist China was marked in 1999. Accordingly, an elaborate parade, featuring the nation's latest military hardware as well as floats celebrating the achievements of China under communism, was held in Beijing's Tiananmen Square on October 1. Sun Yat-sen *(portrait above)*, considered the father of modern China, was remembered throughout the festivities. Meanwhile a Chinese treasure, the giant panda, one of the world's rarest animals, was much in the news. Yang Yang, a 2-year-old male, and Lun Lun, a 2-year-old female, *photo, top, page 109,* took up residence at Zoo Atlanta in November, as the U.S. capital mourned the death of Hsing-Hsing, a giant panda given to the United States in honor of President Richard Nixon's 1972 trip to China, at the National Zoo.

The computer became even more of a part of everyday life in 1999, and Microsoft's Bill Gates, *photo, center right, page 109,* responded after a U.S. District Court judge in Washington, DC, issued preliminary findings that the software company enjoyed "monopoly power." Thousands of demonstrators, *photo, bottom left, page 109,* representing a variety of groups, protested against free trade and the power of the World Trade Organization (WTO), as trade ministers from some 135 nations assembled in Seattle, WA, in late November for a major conference. The meeting ended without accomplishing a major objective—setting an agenda for a new round of trade talks.

The works of Norman Rockwell, including his 1955 painting "Art Critic," *photo, bottom right, page 109,* long have been popular with the public but looked down upon by the art world. Therefore, the retrospective "Norman Rockwell: Pictures for the American People," which opened at Atlanta's High Museum of Art and was to travel to six other locales, offered everyone a chance to reevaluate Rockwell's view of the American scene. ■

© Ric Feld/AP/Wide World Photos

Microsoft

© Laura Rauch/AP/Wide World Photos

FREE
to exploit
people & nature

© Stephane/Liaison Agency

Printed by permission of the Norman Rockwell Family Trust; © 1955, the Norman Rockwell Family Trust

Accidents and Disasters

AVIATION

Jan. 21—A Nicaraguan military plane crashes while en route from Managua to Bluefields; all 28 persons aboard are killed.
Feb. 24—A Chinese passenger jet explodes and crashes in Ruian, China, as it prepares to land in nearby Wenzhou, killing all 61 aboard.
June 1—Eleven persons are killed and 80 injured when a passenger jet speeds off the runway and crashes after landing at Little Rock, AR.
Aug. 31—A passenger jet crashes shortly after takeoff from Buenos Aires, Argentina, killing at least 64 persons aboard the plane and some ten on the ground.
Oct. 31—Two hundred seventeen persons are killed when an EgyptAir passenger plane en route from New York to Egypt crashes near the island of Nantucket, MA.
Nov. 9—A passenger jet flying from Uruapan to Mexico City, Mexico, crashes shortly after takeoff, killing 18 persons.
Nov. 12—A plane chartered by the United Nations World Food Program crashes into a mountain in Kosovo, Yugoslavia; all 24 aboard are killed.

FIRES AND EXPLOSIONS

March 24—Some 42 persons are killed in a fire that erupts inside the Mont Blanc tunnel through the Alps, which connects France and Italy.
May 29—At least 12 are killed when a traffic accident triggers a series of explosions and a fire in the Tauern tunnel through the Alps, connecting Germany and northern Austria with Italy and the Balkans.
June 30—Twenty-three children are killed when fire breaks out in the dormitory of a nursery school in Seoul, South Korea, where more than 500 children are sleeping.
Sept. 19—At least 23 persons are killed when two explosions destroy a factory near Chiang Mai, Thailand.
Sept. 26—An explosion triggered by fireworks sets off a fire and further explosions in Celaya, Mexico; at least 56 persons are killed.
Oct. 30—At least 54 persons are killed in a fire that breaks out in a shopping complex in Inchon, South Korea.

LAND AND SEA TRANSPORTATION

Jan. 25—Some 22 persons are killed when a passenger bus plunges from an overpass in Cairo, Egypt, and lands in a busy city square.
Feb. 6—A cargo ship sinks in rough seas between the Indonesian islands of Borneo and Sumatra; some 300 persons are left dead.
March 15—A passenger train collides with a truck at a railway crossing in Bourbonnais, IL; 11 passengers are killed, and more than 100 are injured.
March 24—Thirty-two persons are killed when a passenger train en route from Nairobi to Mombasa, Kenya, derails inside Tsavo East National Park.
April 27—A crowded passenger bus crashes into a speeding train in Jhukia, India, leaving at least 45 persons dead.
May 1—Thirteen persons drown when an amphibious craft carrying tourists on Lake Hamilton, AR, sinks suddenly, shortly after leaving shore.
May 9—Twenty-two persons are left dead when a chartered bus crosses several lanes of highway traffic and goes over an embankment in New Orleans, LA.
June 7—An overcrowded bus plunges into a lake in Davanagere, India, killing at least 94 passengers.
July 1—A cable car taking passengers to the top of a mountain in the French Alps falls 260 ft (80 m) to the ground, killing all 20 aboard.
Aug. 2—At least 282 persons are left dead when two passenger trains collide at a railroad station in Gaisan, India.
Sept. 27—A bus carrying British tourists loses its brakes on a steep hill near Lydenburg, South Africa, and crashes, killing 26 persons.
Oct. 5—At least 30 are killed when two commuter trains collide during rush hour near Paddington Station, London, England, triggering a fire.
Oct. 18—Hundreds of persons are feared dead after a ship sinks in a remote location off the coast of western New Guinea, an Indonesian island.
Nov. 24—Some 280 persons are killed when a passenger ferry burns and breaks apart in stormy waters off the coast of Yantai, China.

STORMS, FLOODS, AND EARTHQUAKES

Jan. 25—At least 1,185 persons are killed when a strong earthquake shakes western Colombia.
Feb. 11—Some 70 persons are killed when an earthquake shakes Afghanistan.
Feb. 23–24—Two huge avalanches strike the resort villages of Galtür and Valzur in the Austrian Alps, leaving 38 dead.
March 29—At least 100 persons are killed when an earthquake hits India's lower Himalaya region.
April 2—Dozens of illegal immigrants are trapped in a spring snowstorm while crossing mountainous terrain east of San Diego, CA; at least 12 are left dead.
April 15—More than 40 persons are killed as two mud slides triggered by weeks of rain hit Argelia, Colombia.
May 3—Forty-nine persons are killed when severe tornadoes rip through Oklahoma and Kansas, destroying entire neighborhoods.
July 27—A flash flood kills 21 people who are engaged in the sport of "canyoning" in Saxeten Brook, near Interlaken, Switzerland.
Aug. 4—More than 100 are feared dead after several days of rain, flooding, and landslides in North and South Korea.
Aug. 7—Some 725 persons have been killed since June, due to flooding in China's Yangtze River Valley.
Aug. 11—Nearly two weeks of heavy rains in the Philippines cause floods and landslides that kill at least 160 persons.
Aug. 17—Western Turkey is struck by a devastating earthquake centered near the city of Izmit; more than 15,600 persons are killed.
Sept. 7—The strongest earthquake to hit Athens, Greece, in almost a century leaves at least 143 persons dead in that city.
Sept. 20—A powerful earthquake centered about 90 mi (150 km) southwest of Taipei, Taiwan, leaves more than 2,000 persons dead.
Sept. 23—At least 51 persons have been killed in North Carolina by severe flooding caused by Hurricanes Dennis and Floyd.
Sept. 30—Thirty-three persons are killed by an earthquake centered in Oaxaca state, Mexico.
Oct. 6—Nigerian officials open the floodgates of two dams on the Niger River when rising water threatens to cause Shiriro Lake to overflow; 400 villages are submerged, and some 500 persons are left dead.
Oct. 8—At least 400 persons are left dead in central and southern Mexico after a week of heavy rains causes extensive flooding and mud slides.
Oct. 29—At least 9,400 are feared dead in the wake of a huge cyclone that rips through eastern India, causing severe flooding.
Nov. 12—A second major earthquake strikes northwestern Turkey, killing several hundred persons.
Dec. 6—At least 105 persons are left dead due to severe flooding in the central coastal region of Vietnam; a month earlier, some 590 persons were killed by even more massive flooding in the same area.
Dec. 20—At least 20,000 persons—and possibly as many as 30,000—are left dead after severe flooding leads to mud slides in Vargas state, on the Caribbean coast of Venezuela. It is the nation's worst natural disaster in 100 years.
Dec. 29—Dangerous storms strike much of Europe, leaving some 116 dead across the continent.

MISCELLANEOUS

Jan. 14—A 60-ft (20-m) hillock in Pamba, India, partially collapses under the weight of Hindu pilgrims gathered there to watch a ritual; 51 persons are left dead.
May 30—Fifty-two persons are trampled to death when teenagers at an outdoor concert in Minsk, Belarus, stampede while trying to escape a sudden storm.
Nov. 11—At least 52 are left dead when an apartment building collapses in Foggia, Italy.
Nov. 18—Twelve persons are killed when a tower of logs being built for a traditional football bonfire collapses at Texas A&M University.
Dec. 8—Some 47 persons die in the collapse of a poorly constructed five-story apartment building in Fez, Morocco.

Advertising

The U.S. advertising industry got "wired" in 1999, as the boom in Internet companies flooded the marketplace with new accounts. In an ironic twist, "new media" Internet companies turned to "old media"—traditional advertising in print and broadcast outlets—to attract attention to their services. Meanwhile, a still-booming U.S. economy led to record profits for many media outlets, while mergers and acquisitions continued to rock ad agencies.

Ad Spending. Advertising expenditures continued to prosper in 1999, outpacing the overall economy. Ad agency McCann-Erickson projected that advertising spending would reach $213.9 billion in 1999, a gain of more than 6% over $201.6 billion in 1998. The agency predicted that spending in 2000 would be just as strong or even stronger, possibly increasing as much as 7.5% to $230 billion. Factors that could contribute to increased spending included the fact that 2000 is both an election year and an Olympic year, when ad spending traditionally is healthier than usual, as well as events surrounding the new millennium.

Agencies. It was a prosperous year for leading U.S. advertising agencies. From January through June, the top seven U.S. agency-holding companies reported average revenue gains of $7.8 billion, a 13% increase over 1998. Pretax profits rose almost 15%, from $805 million in 1998 to $924 million in 1999. Acquisitions drove those figures in many cases, but the investment community also believed that these companies were serving their stockholders well.

The continuing consolidation of agencies was being driven by the need of agencies to expand in order to satisfy their clients' growing demand for a full range of marketing and communications services. Significant mergers and acquisitions in late 1998 and 1999 included the acquisition of the MacManus Group by Leo Group, which combined several major agencies under a single holding company dubbed BDM. The agencies included MacManus' D'Arcy Masius Benton & Bowles and Leo Group's Leo Burnett Co. The Interpublic Group of Cos. merged two of its agency units, Ammirati Puis Lintas and Lowe & Partners Worldwide, into a single agency. Other top deals included the purchase of Mullen Advertising by Lowe & Partners; and Euro RSCG's purchases of Jordan McGrath Case & Partners and Citron Haligman Bedecarre.

The Internet. While advertising *on* Internet sites stayed relatively static, advertising *about* Internet sites and capabilities showed tremendous gains in 1999. Remaining skeptical of the Internet as an advertising medium, major advertisers spent slightly more in 1999 than the $2.1 billion spent the previous year, but their outlay still represented only about 1% of their advertising budgets. In an August report, Internet research firm Jupiter Communications said that the on-line audience in the United States was expected to increase from the current 38 million households to 64 million by 2003, and that advertising spending should rise to $11.5 billion by that time.

The proliferation of "dot.com" companies vying for consumer attention in 1999 led to scores of new accounts for advertising agencies. *Adweek* magazine reported that almost 100 dot.com advertising accounts were awarded between August 1998 and August 1999, and predicted that these companies would spend about $2 billion on traditional media advertising in 1999. Investment-oriented Web sites, which offered users the capability to make stock trades and purchases over the Internet for discounted fees, led much of this activity.

Creative. One of the most talked-about television ad campaigns of 1999 was unusual in many ways, but perhaps the most remarkable thing about it was that it was not created by a traditional advertising agency. The campaign, developed for The Gap clothing stores by an in-house creative department, featured fresh-faced, khaki-clad young people jitterbugging to 1940s bandleader Louis Prima's song "Jump, Jive, and Wail." The ad's popularity was credited with sparking a revival of swing music in the United States, and its success led to several follow-ups featuring other kinds of music and dancing. Meanwhile, the top awards for print and television advertising at the 46th International Advertising Festival in Cannes, France, went to two London-based agencies. Lowe Howard-Spink won the Grand Prix Award in the television-commercial category for "Litany," a black-and-white spot for *The Independent*, a British newspaper, which featured a more serious tone than that of recent winners. In the print category, the top award went to TBWA Simons Palmer GGT for an ad for Sony Playstation that depicted children with the product protruding from their chests.

JOHN WOLFE
American Association of Advertising Agencies

Afghanistan

In 1999, it was clear that Taliban rule over most of Afghanistan had succeeded only in impoverishing and debasing the country, and in isolating it from the outside world.

Civil War. The mainly Pashtun Taliban army, though aided by some 8,000 Pakistani and Arab volunteers, failed to score a decisive victory during its regular summer offensive. Its Northern Alliance opponents—made up of Tajiks, Uzbeks, and Hazaras—kept control of about 15% of the country. A September counteroffensive under the command of Ahmad Shah Massoud advanced toward Kabul but was thrown back as Taliban rallied.

Both sides were guilty of atrocities against civilians on the battlefield. As winter approached, exposure and starvation faced some 130,000 refugees made homeless by the war.

Economy. The Afghan currency, the afghani, continued its free fall. In November the average government salary was $7.00 a month, yet the price of 1 kg (2.2 lb) of flour during that month rose from $1.50 to $3.50. Most Afghans had not tasted meat in the past year. At least 70% of Kabul remained in ruins; in 1999 only six of the country's 220 factories in operation in 1979 still were running.

By the end of 1999, Afghan production of opium (4,600 metric tons) was by far the greatest in the world, and 96% of it was grown on land that was under Taliban control. Despite giving lip service to the idea of trying to halt opium cultivation, Taliban organized agricultural schools for opium growers. Drug dealers ran the country's only banking system, giving farmers advances on their next year's crop. Taliban financed its military operations mostly via a 20% tax on the opium trade and a similar tax on the smuggling of some $5 billion worth of duty-free contraband into Pakistan.

AFGHANISTAN • Information Highlights

Official Name: Islamic State of Afghanistan.
Location: Central Asia.
Area: 250,000 sq mi (647 500 km²).
Population (July 1999 est.): 25,824,882.
Chief Cities (1988 est.): Kabul, the capital, 1,424,400; Kandahar, 225,500; Herat, 177,300.
Government: Declared an "Islamic state" by the Taliban militia group in 1996. De facto government is under Taliban, administered by an interim Council of Ministers.
Monetary Unit: Afghani (4,714.4351 afghanis equal U.S.$1, official rate, Dec. 1, 1999).
Gross Domestic Product (1998 est. U.S.$): $20,000,000,000 (purchasing power parity).

Society. Taliban's rigid view of Islam—enforced by its Department for the Promotion of Virtue and Prevention of Vice—continued to restrict Afghan freedoms, especially for women, who were not allowed on the street except when accompanied by a male relative. They also were denied jobs and education beyond the eighth grade and were required to wear the *burqa*, a dress hiding even their faces. Some 45,000 war widows and their children in Kabul were reduced to begging for survival. About 12,500 displaced Tajik dependents, including 8,000 children, were crowded into the former Soviet-embassy compound.

Men were required to wear beards, and regular attendance at a mosque was mandatory. Both men and women were beaten publicly for violations of Taliban rules. Public amputations for thieves were staged in Kabul's stadium, and those books not burned as heretical had all photos blacked out with marking pens. There were no movies, no television, no public music, and few permitted amusements of any kind.

Foreign Affairs. Pakistan, the United Arab Emirates, and Saudi Arabia remained the only countries to recognize Taliban rule, and even the Saudis suspended diplomatic relations. As Taliban gained financial independence via drug and smuggling operations, the influence wielded by its former foreign supporters weakened.

Russia, Tajikistan, Uzbekistan, Kyrgyzstan, and Iran supported the Northern Alliance. Taliban provided military-training facilities for exiled dissidents from these neighbors and from China, posing long-term threats to regional stability.

On November 14 the United Nations (UN) imposed sanctions on Afghanistan for its refusal to hand over Osama bin Laden for trial abroad. Bin Laden, a Saudi millionaire renegade, was implicated in the 1998 bombings of U.S. embassies in Kenya and Tanzania. The UN action grounded the Afghan airline, Ariana; shut down international postal service to the country; and resulted in mob demonstrations against UN offices in five Afghan cities.

UN humanitarian aid, however, continued, including a massive immunization program for 3.6 million Afghan children against poliomyelitis and other diseases, and a $52 million relief operation for civil-war refugees. These operations slowed as winter snows blocked the high passes.

ANTHONY ARNOLD
Freelance Writer on Afghanistan

Africa

In 1999, Africa continued to plod its way toward democracy and the free market. The continent saw several Western countries, including the United States, pass trade and investment measures intended to promote Africa's deepening involvement in world markets. Also, various African debt-relief schemes were unveiled.

New rounds of democratic elections were completed in Malawi, the Central African Republic, Namibia, Nigeria, Mozambique, and South Africa. Meanwhile, military coups occurred in such places as Niger, Guinea-Bissau, and the Ivory Coast. But the coup leaders in both Niger and Guinea-Bissau promised a speedy return to civilian rule and democracy—and kept their word. The continent faced several transnational threats, including wars and other physical violence, crime, diseases such as tuberculosis and AIDS, and environmental degradation.

Several high-level U.S. government officials went to Africa in 1999 in a continuing attempt to emphasize the continent as a high priority on the U.S. foreign-policy agenda. The visiting dignitaries included Secretary of State Madeleine Albright; Richard Holbrooke, the U.S. ambassador to the United Nations (UN); Secretary of Transportation Rodney Slater; and Secretary of Commerce William Daley. In October, Albright traveled to Guinea, Sierra Leone, Mali, Nigeria, Kenya, and Tanzania in her third visit to Africa since becoming secretary of state and her seventh since she joined President Bill Clinton's administration. The purpose of her trip was to highlight the partnership that the United States has built with Africa during the Clinton administration and to advance key U.S. policy goals, such as encouraging the continent's steady and rapid integration into the global economy through expanded trade opportunities, continued development assistance, and foreign private investment. Directly related to this was the need to work with African partners to resolve conflicts and promote democracy and human rights in the region.

The United States continued to work with those forces on the continent seeking to end the most-serious threats to the continent's stability, including the conflicts in the Sudan, the Democratic Republic of the Congo, Rwanda, Burundi, Sierra Leone, and Angola. It had provided material and diplomatic support, for example, to the Economic Community of West African States Monitoring Group (ECOMOG) as it tried to bring peace to Sierra Leone, and to the Inter-Governmental Authority on Development (IGAD), which was attempting to broker peace in Sudan and in Somalia. In March, Washington hosted the first U.S.-Africa ministerial meeting, which was attended by representatives from 46 African countries. The topics discussed included conflict resolution, good governance and the global economy, the environment, human rights, and telecommunications and information technology. In addition, the U.S. Congress, at the Clinton

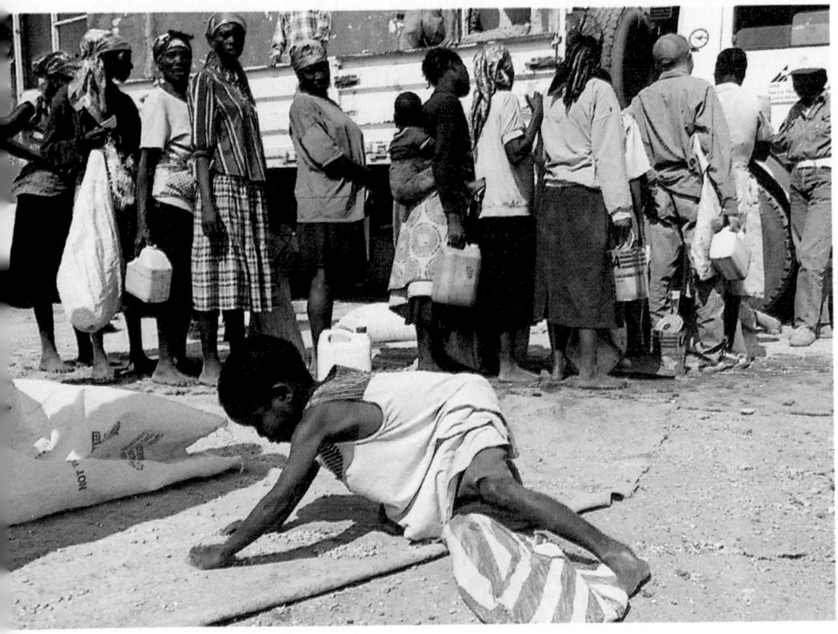

Angola's 25-year-old civil war, which resumed in late 1998 after a brief pause, continued to rage on throughout 1999, with no sign of resolution. The fighting displaced thousands of Angolans, including women and children, left, *exacerbating the already-serious poverty and hunger problems in the country.*

administration's urging, approved debt relief for several African countries.

Despite its efforts, the United States was castigated by some critics for making empty promises or for not being committed to financing some of the grand initiatives it purported to support. The Clinton administration countered that it was better to keep Africa on the public agenda and set lofty goals, even if they could not be achieved at the present time.

The year also witnessed new initiatives by African leaders to find African solutions to African problems. For example, Libya and the Organization of African Unity (OAU) negotiated a peace between various Somali factions and Ethiopia, which reduced tensions along the Ethiopian-Somali border. Until his death in October, former Tanzanian President Julius Nyerere worked to diffuse tensions in Burundi. South Africa's former president, Nelson Mandela, took over that role from Nyerere.

Perhaps one of the most interesting developments relating to intra-Africa cooperation occurred in early September, when 44 African leaders met in Libya and adopted a resolution calling for an African union similar to the European Union (EU). The concept, which dated back to the period immediately following World War II, was to create a United States of Africa, with a central bank, supreme court, monetary fund, and investment bank. The idea was spearheaded by Libyan leader Muammar el-Qaddafi, who saw it as the best way for the continent to face the challenges of globalization in the new millennium.

Sierra Leone. In early January combatants in the Armed Forces Revolutionary Council (AFRC) and the Revolutionary United Front (RUF), which at the time controlled more than 60% of Sierra Leone, attacked the capital city of Freetown. They held large parts of the city for four days before being driven back by ECOMOG. The siege resulted in 3,000 to 5,000 deaths and the severe mutilation of scores of civilians. Up to 150,000 people were displaced in and around the city, and large numbers of public buildings and homes were destroyed. This was a humiliating event for the Nigerian army, which provided the core leadership and largest number of units in ECOMOG. The humiliation was exacerbated by the fact that the Nigerian troops assigned to ECOMOG had gone several months without pay.

The first half of 1999 was spent pursuing both military and political solutions to the conflict. Pressure was brought to bear on Ahmad Tejan Kabbah, Sierra Leone's president, to negotiate seriously with the opposition to bring about a political settlement. In a signal that he was prepared to do so, Kabbah visited several key countries in West Africa—including the Ivory Coast, Ghana, Nigeria, and Togo—in March to discuss possible options. In April he released RUF leader Foday Sankoh from prison so that he could travel to Togo to meet with his commanders. Sankoh was successful in getting them to agree to join peace talks.

A new cease-fire came into effect in late May, and talks commenced shortly afterward in Lomé, Togo, hosted and mediated by Gnassingbé Eyadéma, Togo's president and the current chairman of the Economic Community of West African States (ECOWAS). A facilitation committee consisting of the UN, the OAU, ECOWAS, the Commonwealth of Nations, and Francis Okelo, the UN special representative to Sierra Leone, supported the meetings.

On July 7 the Lomé Peace Agreement was signed by the warring parties; President Eyadéma; the presidents of Burkina Faso, Nigeria, and Liberia; and high-level representatives from Ghana, the Ivory Coast, ECOWAS, OAU, the Commonwealth, and the UN. The pact called for a permanent end to hostilities, the transformation of the RUF into a political party with access to public office, the creation of a coalition government that included RUF members, and the appointment of Sankoh to head a commission on minerals and national reconstruction—a position with a status equivalent to the vice-presidency. One of the more controversial aspects of the agreement was the provision that Sankoh and his fighters be given complete amnesty for any crimes they committed during the civil war. The public in Sierra Leone objected strongly to this, because the rebels allegedly were responsible for the killing and mutilation of thousands of civilians. Okelo signed the agreement with a notation warning that the UN would not recognize the amnesty "as applying to gross violations of human rights."

The UN committed 6,000 troops to monitor the cease-fire and disarm rebel fighters. It was expected that ECOMOG would remain in charge of security, but the organization felt uncomfortable not having the peacekeeping function under one command, and Nigeria indicated in December that it would be withdrawing its forces from Sierra Leone. Ghana and Guinea also indicated

© Corbis

A breakaway military faction led by Brig. Gen. Ansumane Mane overthrew the government of Guinea-Bissau in May 1999, looting and burning the presidential palace, left. *President João Bernardo Vieira, who took refuge in the Portuguese embassy after the siege, later was exiled to Portugal.*

that they were planning to withdraw their troops. To make up for the departure of ECOMOG troops, UN Secretary-General Kofi Annan recommended that the UN force be increased by about 4,000 soldiers and that its mandate be broadened to include the security functions ECOMOG had been performing. By the end of the year, the UN Security Council had not acted on Annan's request.

After the cease-fire went into force, Sierra Leone began rebuilding its police force and army. Efforts also were under way to locate the families of thousands of missing children and to demobilize and rehabilitate thousands of child soldiers from both sides. Humanitarian activities in general were increased greatly as well, but observers predicted it would be years before the country returned to normal.

Guinea-Bissau. In late January a cease-fire that had been implemented in November 1998 broke down. Fighting between Senegalese troops supporting President João Bernardo Vieira and a breakaway army faction headed by Brig. Gen. Ansumane Mane continued for four days, with more than 100 fatalities, before Togolese mediators secured a truce. By late February, 600 ECOMOG peacekeepers arrived, adding to the 1,000 Senegalese troops already in the country.

In June, Vieira was exiled following a military coup, and an interim government was installed while the country prepared for democratic elections. On November 28 presidential and parliamentary elections were held. Kumba Yala of the opposition Party for Social Renewal (PSR) secured 39% of the vote, while acting President Malam Bacai Sanha of the African Independence Party of Guinea and Cape Verde (PAIGC) finished second with 23%. Since no candidate received a majority of the vote, a runoff between Yala and Sanha was scheduled for January 16. Yala indicated that if he were to win the second round, he would form a government of national unity. In the parliamentary elections, the PSR won 38 of the 102 seats, followed by the Resistance of Guinea-Bissau-Bafata Movement with 28 and PAIGC with 24. Five parties shared the remaining 12 seats.

Burundi. Armed clashes between government forces in Burundi and Hutu rebel groups operating out of the Democratic Republic of the Congo continued throughout the year, but intensified during the summer. In July, Pierre Buyoya's presidential palace was attacked, and instability in and around the capital city of Bujumbura increased dramatically. One major attack took place on August 28, resulting in 58 deaths.

The fourth round of mediation talks aimed at ending Burundi's six-year civil war began in January. The talks lasted for two weeks but made little progress. The main sticking points were power sharing, the ethnic composition of the army, and which rebel groups would be represented at the negotiations. In particular, mediator Julius Nyerere had refused to allow the Forces for the Defense of Democracy (FDD), a hard-line

Hutu faction, to participate in peace negotiations. The FDD leaders regularly indicated that since they were not invited to the peace talks, they were forced to assert their importance through military means. Nyerere's successor as mediator, Nelson Mandela, said that he would allow all parties to the conflict to take part in the next round of talks, scheduled for January.

Meanwhile, leaders of eastern and central African countries decided in January to suspend sanctions against Burundi that had been in place for almost three years, in the hope that this act of goodwill would persuade the Buyoya government to show more flexibility in the negotiations.

Near the end of 1999, rumors abounded that a military overthrow of Buyoya's government was a distinct possibility. Between September and December, the government set up makeshift camps on hills surrounding Bujumbura and herded an estimated 350,000 people, mostly poor farm families, into them. Some critics suggested that this was clear evidence that the government could not guarantee their security.

Angola. After resuming late in 1998, Angola's long civil war plodded along during 1999. The government, led by President José Eduardo dos Santos, succeeded in making some advances in areas controlled by the União Nacional para a Independencia Total de Angola (UNITA), but not enough to change the situation very much. As the year ended, the Forcas Armadas Angolanas (FAA), the Angolan national army, launched a major offensive, advancing on UNITA headquarters in the central highlands on four fronts.

Despite international sanctions against UNITA, its leader, Jonas Savimbi, financed his fighters by using his control of Angola's vast diamond mines to produce gems that were sold to private traders and governments. In an attempt to close this loophole, the UN and the Angolan government agreed in 1999 to take a more systematic approach to imposing the UNITA sanctions. In addition, the United States pressured the International Monetary Fund (IMF) to approve loans to Angola to encourage the government to negotiate with UNITA, but not with Savimbi. At the end of the year, Savimbi was calling upon the UN to broker a cease-fire; release UNITA assets that it had frozen because of the sanctions; and begin the process of reopening peace talks between the Angolan government and UNITA.

In Washington, DC, in February, Ghanaian President Jerry Rawlings, above, *advocated forging stronger ties between the United States and African countries.*

Niger. In April, Niger's President Ibrahim Bare Mainassara was assassinated by his own presidential guard. Mainassara had seized power from a democratically elected government in January 1996. During his rule, Mainassara had attempted to clothe himself as a democrat, but few believed him. Daouda Malam Wanke succeeded him. A 14-member National Reconciliation Commission was set up to govern the country while a new constitution was drawn up and preparations were made for parliamentary elections. The new constitution, ratified in July, called for a system in which executive power was to be shared by a president, elected by popular vote, and a prime minister, chosen by a unicameral parliament.

The first round of presidential elections took place on October 18. Mamadou Tandja of the Mouvement National de la Société de Développement (MNSD) finished first, followed by Mahamadou Issoufou of Parti Nigérien pour la Démocratie et le Socialisme. Tandja was the winner of the runoff held on November 24. In parliamentary elections, also held on November 24, the MNSD won 38 of the 83 seats and the Convention Démocratique et Sociale (CDS) won 17. The new prime minister was Hama Amadou, the general secretary of the MNSD, and the new speaker of the Assembly was former President Mahamane Ousmane of the CDS.

See INDEX for African nations on which there are separate articles.

EDMOND J. KELLER
University of California, Los Angeles

Agriculture

Global food supplies tightened slightly in 1999, due to adverse weather that reduced crops in parts of Africa and the southern and eastern United States. Adverse weather and inadequate financing to purchase production inputs in Russia, Ukraine, and other former Soviet republics led to sharply below normal crops in these areas as well, for the second consecutive year. While food supplies and costs for most of the world's consumers were not affected noticeably, the United States, the European Union (EU), and Canada provided substantial food aid to Russia and other nations with limited purchasing power. A severely depressed Russian ruble prevented Russian farmers from purchasing needed fertilizer, seed, and other essential inputs that must be imported.

International Food Aid. In the most aggressive food-aid program in years, the United States donated wheat, feed grain, oilseeds, and meat to 31 nations where food supplies and/or purchasing power were limited. Recipients included 11 countries in Africa; five former Soviet republics; seven nations in Latin America; one country in Eastern Europe; and seven Asian nations, including China and North Korea. Low Russian production of food and feed crops in 1999, on the heels of the short 1998 crops, set the stage for continued food assistance to Russia late in 1999 and in early 2000.

U.S. Weather Problems. In the United States severe drought struck important crop-producing areas from Indiana eastward to New Jersey and southward to parts of Florida, as well as some mid-South areas. After the drought, heavy rains drenched the East Coast, causing devastation to unharvested crops over a wide area. In North Carolina extreme rains also caused severe damage to livestock and poultry farms, drowning an estimated 28,000 head of hogs, more than 2.8 million head of poultry, and nearly 1,200 head of cattle. While impacts on local farmers were extremely severe, national impacts were offset by better weather, large livestock production, and good to excellent crop yields in the west north-central region, which is a major producer of grain, oilseeds, milk, poultry, and other livestock products.

U.S. production of citrus fruit declined by 23% from the record crop of the previous year because of frost and drought damage. In California's Central Valley, production dropped by 45%. Higher prices about offset the lower production, leaving the value of the crop nearly the same as in 1998. Tart-cherry production was 23% below that of a year earlier, due to similar weather problems in several major producing states. Apple production declined 7%, while peach and grape production increased. Potato production was up substantially, along with nearly a one-fifth increase in U.S. cotton production.

Low Prices. Despite a 0.5% decline from the previous year in global grain production and almost no change in global utilization, farm prices for livestock and major field crops remained extremely depressed in the United States and other nations. Prices for soybeans, the second-most-important crop in the United States, fell to the lowest level (without adjusting for inflation) since late 1972. Costs of crop production had gone up several fold since that time. U.S. hog prices fell early in the year to levels not seen since the Great Depression of the 1930s. With severely depressed farm prices, many farm families in the United States and Canada found themselves in a moderately to severely weak financial condition.

An Iowa State University study showed that more than one third of Iowa farmers would be in weak to severely depressed financial condition by mid-2000, unless further assistance from the government was provided. A weak financial status was defined as the need to sell significant farm assets and/or take on as much new debt as possible, and in some cases to cease producing livestock. Farm families with severely depressed financial conditions faced the need to sell their farms.

Farmers from Indiana and Ohio eastward and southward faced even more severe financial pressures because of drought and low crop yields. Low farm incomes had negative effects on main-street businesses of predominantly rural communities in the western north-central and Great Plains regions. The U.S. Congress in late 1999 passed an $8.7 billion farm-assistance bill to help farmers through difficult financial times and to provide government assistance for farmers who purchase higher levels of coverage on commercial crop insurance. New types of U.S. crop insurance guaranteed a minimum level of income per acre for farmers, in contrast to older types that insured only the physical units of crop production. The minimum insured level of income was based on historical production and prices offered by the commodity-futures markets.

Further innovations in farm-income insurance—including a possible livestock-

Low milk prices, land consolidation, and pressures on land prices are among the reasons for a decline in the number of dairy farms operating in the United States during the 1990s.

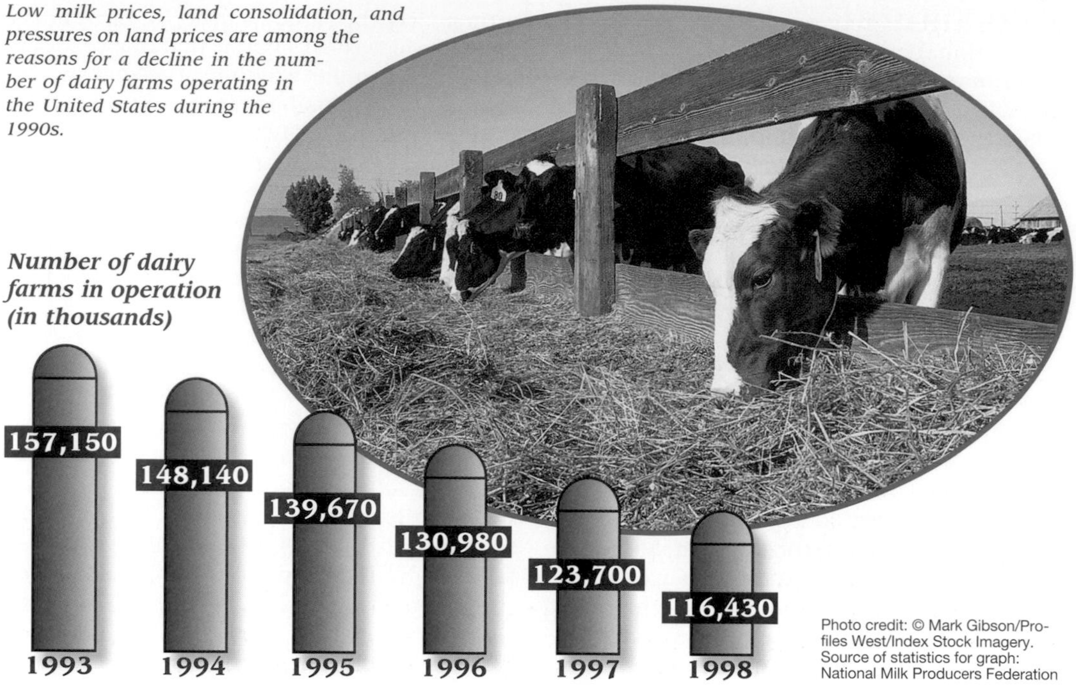

Photo credit: © Mark Gibson/Profiles West/Index Stock Imagery. Source of statistics for graph: National Milk Producers Federation

revenue insurance, patterned after the crop-revenue insurances—were considered. Also actively considered were environmentally friendly crop insurances that would allow farmers to forgo application of certain insecticides on corn. If insect damage beyond a predetermined threshold occurred, the farmer then would receive an indemnity payment. A similar type of insurance was considered for delaying the application of nitrogen fertilizer on corn until the risk of groundwater contamination was at a seasonal low level. If the delay and adverse weather later on prevented the farmer from applying needed nitrogen fertilizer, the insurance would provide partially offsetting benefits.

Agribusiness. The severely depressed prices for major grains, oilseeds, and livestock took a significant toll on manufacturers of farm machinery and fertilizer. The impact occurred as net farm incomes fell to low levels, and a carryover of unpaid loans from the previous year caused many grain and livestock farmers to look for all possible ways to curtail investments and costs. U.S. machinery manufacturers laid off workers, severely curtailing production of tractors, harvesting equipment, and other farm machinery because of depressed sales stemming from low farm incomes. Fertilizer manufacturers closed some plants in response to decreased fertilizer sales. In parts of the Midwest, farmers could reduce certain types of fertilizer use for one year without severe impacts on crop yields. However, several years of failing to replace lost soil fertility would decrease yields. Areas of agribusiness less severely affected included grain-, livestock-, and milk-processing plants.

Computer Use. A U.S. Department of Agriculture survey revealed that U.S. farmers were moving rapidly to incorporate computers in their farming operations. Forty-seven percent of U.S. farmers reported owning or having access to computers in 1999, up from 38% two years earlier. Twenty-nine percent had access to the Internet. Several farm-supply firms made plans to serve larger farm customers through Internet sales of major agricultural inputs. Use of precision farming technology that allows farmers to adjust application rates of key inputs, such as fertilizer and chemicals for varying soil conditions in individual fields, also increased. This technology utilizes signals from satellites and computers to identify the exact location of equipment within a field. It then uses additional information such as a computer file of a soil-type map or crop-yield map for input data. Harvesting equipment produces yield maps for individual fields, showing geographic yield variations.

Agricultural Industries. Major consolidation and increased concentration occurred in the farm-supply and marketing sectors of agriculture, as well as in the hog (or swine) and pork-production sector. Cargill Inc., the world's largest grain/oilseed exporter and a major global merchandiser and processor of grain, purchased the grain business of its largest competitor, Continental Grain Co. U.S. antitrust authorities required Cargill to sell some of Continental's facilities at strategic locations where competition might be affected adversely. Large regional cooperatives Farmland and Harvest States took steps to combine some of their grain operations. New Holland, a German-owned manufacturer of farm machinery, took steps to acquire a major U.S. farm-machinery manufacturer, Case-IH. The latter had been the second-largest manufacturer of agricultural machinery in the United States.

Smithfield Foods Inc., a major integrated producer of swine and pork, purchased its largest competitor, Murphy Family Farms. Smithfield also bought the swine operations of Tyson Foods Inc., Carroll's Foods Inc., and two other sizable swine-producing firms. Together, these acquisitions give Smithfield about 12.5% of the nation's hog-producing capacity. Smithfield also owns pork-processing facilities and sells branded products to retail stores. The acquisitions were subject to approval by antitrust authorities. Major chemical companies acquired some field-crop-seed-producing firms, as they positioned themselves to compete in a biotechnology world where genetically modified crops may eliminate the need for traditional insecticides and may reduce the need for herbicides. A small number of these firms control key patents on newly designed biotech crops.

New Crop Technology and Markets. U.S. farmers as well as those in Argentina rapidly adopted genetically modified corn and soybeans. These types of crops were produced from seed that received genes transplanted from unrelated plants. The main type of genetically modified (GM) corn is Bt corn, with internal resistance to the insect pest the European corn borer. Corn borers attack the corn stalk, reducing yield potential and increasing the risk that stalks will break off before harvest, making the crop difficult or impossible to harvest. Official estimates indicate that 38% of the U.S. corn area was planted to Bt corn. Fifty-seven percent of the nation's soybean crop was estimated to have been planted to varieties that are resistant to the herbicide Round-Up. Round-Up is a broad-spectrum weed killer that controls a wide range of weeds, reducing the need for successive applications of different herbicides. It works well with the recent trend toward little or no tillage and solid seeding of soybeans.

In contrast to U.S. and Argentine farmers, consumers and food retailers in Europe and Japan showed reluctance to embrace genetically engineered foods. The EU adopted food labeling requiring identification of ingredients by genetic origin. Japan's food-labeling program, to be implemented in April 2001, was being developed. Many EU food establishments—including restaurants, institutional food services, school-lunch programs, and supermarket chains—indicated they would sell non-GM foods. In Japan several food processors and brewers also indicated they intended to shift to non-GM food ingredients. Australia, New Zealand, the Philippines, and South Korea also considered implementing food labels that identify type of genetic origin, and a Mexican corn processor shifted its purchases to non-GM corn. Some U.S. processors and exporters requested that farmers and grain elevators segregate corn and soybean supplies by genetic origin. Consumer concerns about genetically modified food centered on safety and environmental impacts. Brazil's government delayed approval for planting of GM soybeans for another two years, while it monitors international demand. The U.S. wheat crop remained genetically unmodified.

Areas being researched for potential genetic improvements in crop production included drought resistance, built-in nitrogen fertilizer generation for corn and other grain crops, and additional insect resistance. Crops with improved nutritional characteristics, and for possible industrial and pharmaceutical use, also were being researched. A new type of biodegradable plastic from soybeans was developed at Iowa State University. Lower-income nations worried that a "terminator gene," making seeds from the current year's harvest unusable for seed the next year, would create serious economic hardships for their farmers.

Work by researchers at Texas A&M University indicated that a proposed U.S. ban on two important groups of agricultural insecticides—the organophosphates and carbamates—would result in more U.S. food imports from farm nations and higher food prices. Impacts on farmers would include lower crop yields and increased crop-production costs.

See also FOOD.

ROBERT N. WISNER
Iowa State University

Albania

After eight years of intensive domestic turmoil, Albania remained a weak state that had veered from hard-line communism toward political fragility and ungovernability. During 1999 the country's economic development was undermined by a number of negative factors, including political polarization, the spread of organized crime and corruption, and the impact of the war in neighboring Kosovo (*see* THE KOSOVO CRISIS, page 78).

Political Polarization and Paralysis. Albania remained dangerously polarized between the governing Socialist Party and the opposition Democratic Party, with no real middle ground of dialogue and compromise. Most of the smaller parties—including Republicans, Monarchists, and Social Democrats—were tied in with one of the major parties. Cronyism and nepotism were rampant in an unstable economic climate. After a prolonged boycott, the return to parliament of the Democratic Party, led by former President Sali Berisha, proved insufficient to engender political stability and institutional reform. The differences between Socialists and Democrats had little to do with ideology or policy and more to do with access to power and resources. Both government and parliament remained largely paralyzed amid bitter power battles and personality struggles.

In September, Berisha was reelected head of the Democratic Party. In October his arch rival, Fatos Nano, was elected chairman of the Socialist Party, defeating Prime Minister Pandeli Majko for the post. In October, Majko resigned from the premiership because of falling confidence in his leadership and was replaced by his deputy, 30-year-old Ilir Meta. Nano's selection by the Socialists as their new head further sharpened conflicts with the Democrats.

The political standstill was likely to endure, unless some cross-party government of national reconstruction was formed. The Democrats called for early general elections, before the scheduled 2001 date, in order to provide renewed legitimacy to Tiranë in the aftermath of the Kosovo conflict and on the eve of international plans for Balkan reconstruction. The Socialists were opposed to an early ballot. The public exhibited little trust either in the government or in the opposition. No credible centrist party had emerged, and young people invariably shunned politics altogether.

Economic Standstill. The Albanian economy continued to flounder in 1999. The gross domestic product (GDP) was projected to fall by almost 7%, after some growth was registered the previous year. Meanwhile, unemployment stood at about 30% of the working population. Economic problems were compounded by rampant fiscal evasion in paying taxes and customs duties, widespread corruption and criminality, and the impact of the refugee crisis from neighboring Kosovo. During the spring, more than 500,000 Kosovar refugees poured into Albania and overburdened the country's fragile economy. The overwhelming majority of refugees returned to Kosovo after the North Atlantic Treaty Organization's (NATO's) successful military campaign against Serbia.

Many young professionals continued to leave Albania because of limited opportunities and general disillusionment. There were also fears that financial remittances from thousands of Albanians working abroad would decrease, depriving the country of tens of millions of dollars in essential revenues.

Politics and Crime. Albania remained a weak state where the central and local governments simply did not control much of the countryside. The government basically had failed in restoring public order. Even more worrisome was the evident symbiosis between politics and crime, in which politicians and policemen were believed to be corrupt, mafia gangs controlled substantial sectors of the economy, and law and order remained at the mercy of mobsters and their political protectors.

Albania increasingly became a transit point for cross-Balkan smuggling, money-laundering, and trafficking routes. It also developed a vibrant home industry of crime,

ALBANIA • Information Highlights

Official Name: Republic of Albania.
Location: Southern Europe, Balkan peninsula.
Area: 11,100 sq mi (28 750 km²).
Population (July 1999 est.): 3,364,571.
Chief City (1990 est.): Tiranë, the capital, 244,200.
Government: *Head of state,* Rexhep Mejdani, president (took office July 1997). *Head of government,* Ilir Meta, prime minister (appointed October 1999). *Legislature* (unicameral)—People's Assembly.
Monetary Unit: Lek (134.300 leks equal U.S.$1, Nov. 16, 1999).
Gross Domestic Product (1998 est. U.S.$): $5,000,-000,000 (purchasing power parity).
Economic Index (1998, 1992 = 100): *Consumer Prices,* all items, 442.6; food, 433.2.
Foreign Trade (1998 est. U.S.$): *Imports,* $788,000,000; *exports,* $205,000,000.

including prostitution, cigarette smuggling, refugee smuggling, drug and arms trafficking, and sanctions busting vis-à-vis Yugoslavia. The state lost enormous amounts of money on customs and tax evasion, while members of the administration as well as local police chiefs were believed widely to be profiting from corruption and criminal involvement. Under international pressure, the government launched a campaign against the country's most notorious criminal gangs. Several gang leaders were arrested. However, the new minister responsible for public order acknowledged in October that some politicians were putting pressure on police and justice officials to have a number of gang leaders released.

The Kosovo Factor. Albania clearly passed some major tests during the two-month war between NATO and Serbia. Regarding NATO, Tiranë opened up the country to the allies with no hesitation and assisted the alliance in its mission against the Slobodan Milosevic regime in Serbia. Regarding regional stability, the Albanian people spontaneously opened up their homes to Kosovar refugees. They also significantly helped to ease a potentially heavy burden on the European Union (EU) and the United Nations.

But the bigger test for Albania began at the close of the year. Both the major Albanian parties had established connections with the nascent Kosovar parties. The influence of the Albanian parties will prove negative if they primarily replicate the cleavages evident in Tiranë. Close and exclusive links between Socialists and the Kosovo Liberation Army (KLA), and between Democrats and the more moderate Democratic League of Kosovo (DLK), will promote polarization and paralysis that could stifle any attempts to forge a broad-based reformist agenda in Kosovo. There were also indications during 1999 that criminal elements were moving into Kosovo from Albania to replace the Serbian mobsters who had ruled the territory for the past decade.

Both Albania and Kosovo remained highly dependent on the international community. But long-term external dependence also could breed economic and political stagnation. Because of political paralysis and rampant criminality, most foreign investors have shied away from Albania. The international community maintained a sizeable presence there. NATO troops were stationed in the country to provide logistical support to the large allied presence in neighboring Kosovo after Serbian forces fled the province in early June. Albania also obtained a commitment from NATO to a longer-term troop presence in the country as part of the effort to stabilize Kosovo and surrounding states. Tiranë continued to participate in NATO's Partnership for Peace (PfP) program.

In July, Albania was included in the South East European Stability Pact sponsored by the EU. The purpose of this initiative was to marshal resources for the political development and economic reconstruction of the whole Balkan region. Tiranë continued to develop good relations with several of its Balkan neighbors, including Greece, Macedonia, and Bulgaria.

JANUSZ BUGAJSKI
Center for Strategic and International Studies

Algeria

Abdelaziz Bouteflika was elected president of Algeria on April 15, 1999. Despite doubts about the legitimacy of his mandate, the new president threw himself into the task of addressing the more-than-seven-year civil war.

The Election. Bouteflika, who served as foreign minister of Algeria from 1963 to 1979, left the country after the 1978 death of his political patron, Houari Boumedienne, the military strongman who ruled from 1965 to 1978. He returned in the 1990s to a deeply divided country and announced his intention to run for president in December 1998, a few months after the surprise announcement of Liamine Zeroual that he would end his term early. Several other candidates—including former reformist Prime Minister Mouloud Hamrouche, former Foreign Minister Ahmed Taleb Ibrahimi, and the long-standing Kabyle opposition leader Hocine Ait Ahmed—followed Bouteflika into the presidential race.

Most of the candidates, including Bouteflika, ran officially as independents, but he was the clear front-runner in the seven-man race, with endorsements from the National Liberation Front (FLN), the National Democratic Rally (RDN, the "presidential party" created by Zeroual for the 1997 parliamentary elections), and En Nahda, a minor Islamic party. Only Ait Ahmed ran as the recognized leader of a political party, the Socialist Forces Front. The three minor candidates were Mokhdad Sifi, once prime minister under Zeroual; Youcef El-Khatib, a na-

ALGERIA • Information Highlights

Official Name: Democratic and Popular Republic of Algeria.
Location: North Africa.
Area: 919,591 sq mi (2 381 740 km²).
Population (July 1999 est.): 31,133,486.
Chief Cities (1987 census): Algiers, the capital, 1,507,241; Oran, 628,558; Constantine, 440,842.
Government: *Head of state,* Abdelaziz Bouteflika, president (elected April 15, 1999). *Head of government,* Ahmed Benbitour, prime minister (named December 1999). *Legislature*—Parliament: National People's Assembly and Council of Nations.
Monetary Unit: Dinar (67.730 dinars equal U.S.$1, Nov. 16, 1999).
Gross Domestic Product (1998 est. U.S.$): $140,200,000,000 (purchasing power parity).
Economic Indexes: *Consumer Prices* (Algiers, 1998; 1990 = 100): all items, 440.7; food, 465.0. *Industrial Production* (1998, 1990 = 100): 82.2.
Foreign Trade (1997 est. U.S.$): *Imports,* $8,500,000,000; *exports,* $14,000,000,000.

tionalist war hero; and Abdellah Djaballah, the former head of En Nahda, who refused to accept his party's endorsement of Bouteflika. The banned Islamic Salvation Front (FIS) issued instructions to its supporters to vote for Taleb Ibrahimi, the son of a revered Muslim leader of the nationalist period.

Zeroual assured the public that the election would be "healthy and democratic, free, transparent, and credible." He criticized several members of the government and an influential retired general who had endorsed Bouteflika. The army stated in its official monthly organ, *El Djeich*, that it was neutral, ostensibly breaking with its practice as kingmaker. The candidates held rallies in what seemed to be an open competitive process.

On the eve of the election, however, the six "opposition" candidates claimed that the itinerant voting booths that had opened early in the Sahara and the special polls that customarily have been organized in the barracks so that soldiers and policemen could vote early (and then provide security on election day) were being stuffed to assure Bouteflika's victory. On April 14 the six announced that they were withdrawing. Zeroual refused to hear their plea for a postponement of the election; suddenly Bouteflika was the single candidate. Objective observers reported that the turnout on April 15 appeared to be very low. The ministry of the interior nonetheless announced that 60% of the electorate had voted, and that 74% had cast votes for Bouteflika. Leaks from the ministry, however, suggested that both official figures were inflated greatly.

The New President. President Bouteflika immediately tackled the security issue. By 1999 the military largely had reclaimed control of the security situation in the country. The brutal massacres of civilian populations in villages that had marked 1997 and 1998 were much less frequent. The army even carried out some operations with the support of the forces of Madani Mezrag, commander of the Islamic Salvation Army (AIS, the armed wing of the FIS), against the remnants of the terrorist Armed Islamic Group (GIA).

Bouteflika emphasized a policy of clemency for participants in the armed rebellion who were ready to reintegrate society peacefully. In June, Mezrag announced "the definitive halt of the armed struggle" in return for a broad amnesty. Abassi Madani, the best-known politician of the FIS, who was under house arrest, supported Mezrag's initiative on June 11, calling for all combatants to respect the halt in hostilities. Later, Bouteflika would acknowledge that the war had taken some 100,000 lives, a figure much higher than previously acknowledged by the government. The president instructed the government to prepare an amnesty law and announced that he would submit it to a nationwide referendum. The electorate massively approved the referendum on September 16.

On December 27, Bouteflika named Finance Minister Ahmed Benbitour as premier. Benbitour succeeded Smail Hamdani, who had been appointed in December 1998 by Zeroual to serve during the transition to a new president.

President Bouteflika hosted the July summit of the Organization of African Unity and the first high-level meeting in years of the Arab Maghreb Union, and met with French Premier Lionel Jospin at the United Nations. He represented Algeria at the funeral of King Hassan of Morocco, but relations with that state remained tense over an Islamist raid on a border village in which Algerian authorities implicated Morocco.

Economic Affairs. Fluctuating oil prices hurt the economy over the first half of the year, with energy revenues down 6.5% for that period. Industrial growth, however, was up by 3.2% for the first quarter, primarily attributable to repairs at the El-Hadjar steel foundry. Privatization of the economy continued, with the first private airlines and several private Internet suppliers.

The national trade-union federation warned of economic crisis, reporting some 400,000 jobs lost, causing a 30% unemployment rate. The International Monetary Fund issued a harsh report on business conditions and development prospects in January but later gave a $300 million loan.

ROBERT MORTIMER, *Haverford College*

Anthropology

The conclusion of researchers who discovered the 24,500-year-old skeleton of a child added a controversial new chapter to the scientific debate over the nature of modern human origins.

Hybrid Child. Researchers who discovered and examined the 24,500-year-old skeleton of a child in Portugal said that it possessed a mix of anatomical traits that could have resulted only from extensive interbreeding between modern *Homo sapiens* and Neanderthals. The roughly 4-year-old fossil child lay in a shallow grave resembling previously unearthed Stone Age human burials in Europe. Much of its skull was crushed, but the rest of the skeleton remained largely intact. Modern human features of the skeleton include a distinct chin and fairly small lower arms, according to Erik Trinkaus of Washington University in St. Louis, who examined the find. A huge jaw, large front teeth, and short legs are among the signs of a Neanderthal heritage, Trinkaus says. Neanderthals and modern humans interbred for at least several thousand years in southwestern Europe as members of the same species, in his view.

Scientists who argue that modern humans evolved at about the same time in two or more parts of the world during the past 1 million years welcomed Trinkaus' report. Those who support more-recent human origins in Africa—with minimal or no Neanderthal influence on human origins—said that the fossil child simply may have been a stocky modern human.

Chimp Cultures. Groups of wild chimpanzees develop unique cultural traditions, just as people do, reported a group of scientists who synthesized decades of field observations. Other than humans, only chimps have demonstrated a tendency to pass on styles of tool use, grooming, and other behaviors through teaching and imitation, the researchers said. Cultural customs vary from one chimp community to another. Chimp culture falls well short of the complexity found in human culture.

The researchers examined evidence from seven chimp populations in Africa that were studied for periods ranging from eight to 38 years. They identified 39 cultural acts, which were defined as behaviors found consistently in only one or a few groups. These included cracking nuts using pieces of wood as hammer and anvil, sucking ants off sticks, and slapping tree branches to get attention.

Fossil Ancestor. A site in East Africa yielded 2.5-million-year-old fossils assigned to a new species in the human evolutionary family. The species, *Australopithecus garhi*, may have been an ancestor of the *Homo* lineage, to which modern humans belong.

Few fossils have been found for human ancestors that lived between 3 million and 2 million years ago. The new discoveries come from an area of Ethiopia where three desert valleys intersect. Beginning in 1996, investigators found limb and skull fossils on the banks of what once was an ancient lake.

An unusual combination of anatomical traits led the researchers to dub the species *A. garhi*. The word *garhi* means "surprise" in the language of the Afar people who live near the fossil site. The new species has much larger teeth than *Australopithecus afarensis*, which lived in East Africa from 4 million to 3 million years ago and is best known for the specimen called Lucy. Much like Lucy's kind, *A. garhi*'s face projected forward from a small braincase with a bony crest. It had a long, apelike forearm and a relatively long upper leg like those of later human ancestors.

Ancient Ape. A partial skeleton of a 15-million-year-old African ape represents a previously unknown line of creatures in the primate family, its discoverers asserted. Ancient apes branched out in more evolutionary directions than has been assumed, they said. The find, which comes from a site in Kenya, was assigned to a new genus dubbed *Equatorius*. One of two *Kenyapithecus* species—African fossil apes dating to between 15 million and 14 million years ago—actually belong to *Equatorius*, the researchers concluded. *Equatorius* may have existed at or near the evolutionary root of modern apes and humans, they suggested. The partial skeleton, from an adult male, includes a lower jaw with most of its teeth, two teeth from the upper jaw, and bones from the spine, chest, shoulders, arms, wrists, and fingers. *Equatorius* appears to have moved frequently about on the ground, much like fossil apes that emerged later.

BRUCE BOWER, *"Science News"*

Archaeology

A stone-tool site in Kenya, an Egyptian mayoral mansion in a 3,700-year-old town, Chinese flutes, and a prehistoric circle cut into limestone bedrock in Miami, FL, were headline items in archaeology in 1999.

Eastern Hemisphere

Stone Tools. A stone-tool site in Kenya dating to 2.3 million years ago yielded evidence of surprisingly complex production skills. The finds are at least 700,000 years older than previously unearthed stone tools of comparable complexity. Toolmakers at the Kenya location either may have belonged to the evolutionary group *Homo*, which includes modern humans, or to a smaller, more apelike group of creatures.

Investigators pieced together many of the more than 2,000 stone flakes that they found, reconstructing about 60 of the larger stones from which they had been struck, each of which was about the size of a loaf of bread. Ancient toolmakers carefully had chipped off as many as 30 sharp flakes from a single rock. The removal of each flake left a new surface suitable for striking, an indication of careful planning.

In a related discovery, researchers who unearthed the 2.5-million-year-old bones of a previously unknown species in the human evolutionary family said that the specimen had been found among animal bones bearing incisions of stone tools.

Egyptian Mummies. Investigators announced the discovery of a large 2,000-year-old cemetery at an oasis 230 mi (370 km) southwest of Cairo. Tombs there contain an unprecedented number of mummies. The mummies, fitted with elaborate masks and gold-covered waistcoats, come from an affluent population that apparently concentrated on making wine from dates and grapes in Roman times. Four tombs explored by late 1999 housed 105 mummies of men, women, and children. Families appear to have been buried together in preparation for the afterlife. Many more tombs at the site, now known as the Valley of the Golden Mummies, extend over more than 2 sq mi (5.2 km^2).

Neanderthal Hunter. Excavations on the slope of a desert plateau in Syria uncovered the remains of a stone spear point that probably was used by a Neanderthal hunter more than 50,000 years ago. The point, which once had been attached to a shaft or a handle, was found embedded in a neck bone of a wild ass, an extinct ancestor of donkeys. As a Neanderthal thrust the spear into the prehistoric animal's neck, both the point's tip and its base broke off, leaving an inch-long piece of a triangular, sharpened stone point. This discovery provided clear evidence that Neanderthals procured meat by hunting with spears rather than solely by scavenging carcasses abandoned by predators, as some researchers have theorized.

Mayoral Mansion. Government bureaucrats attained considerable power alongside Egypt's pharaohs, according to investigators of a mayoral mansion at a 3,700-year-old Egyptian town. The large structure includes a generous living area, a grain-storage facility, and extensive working areas. The ancient town was occupied from about 1850 B.C. to 1700 B.C. It was organized around a mortuary temple for King Senwosret III, who died in 1841 B.C. Seal impressions on clay fragments found in and around the mansion name at least four mayors who held office there. Household artifacts, such as jewelry and cosmetics, indicate that the mayors were wealthy. The mansion's granary may have allowed the mayor to control a vital food source for the town of about 1,000 people.

A separate investigation at this site produced the oldest known examples of writing in Egypt, dating to between 3400 B.C. and 3200 B.C. The writing—consisting of simple pictures that represented a specific place, object, or quantity—appeared on bone and ivory tags attached to containers for fabric and other trade goods.

Russian Tomb. A grave dating to the early third century B.C. was found in southern Russia and may help to clarify that region's cultural history. The burial occurred at a time when the Scythian culture of the southern Russian steppes was giving way to the Sarmatian culture, although it is not clear whether the Sarmatians borrowed heavily from Scythian traditions or largely replaced them with their own customs. A woman's skeleton lay in the ancient grave, accompanied by gold jewelry, a dagger in a gold-covered scabbard, pottery, and other offerings. Some features of the artifacts exhibit a typically Scythian style. Other artifacts bear Sarmatian influences.

Chinese Flutes. A prehistoric Chinese village yielded a set of six complete bone flutes that date to nearly 9,000 years ago. A musician was able to play one of the flutes, which allowed researchers to analyze the pattern of sounds that it makes. Preliminary work showed that a tiny opening drilled next to one of the seven holes on the playable flute corrected a slightly off-pitch tone. Construction of replicas of each bone flute will allow for a comparison of their musical scales to two current Chinese musical scales. The usable flute is the earliest known complete, playable musical instrument, according to its discoverers.

© Johan Reinhard/National Geographic Image Collection

The mummified remains of three children sacrificed some 500 years ago as part of an Inca ritual were discovered by an American-Argentine-Peruvian archaeological team in the spring of 1999 atop Argentina's Mount Llullaillaco. Johan Reinhard of the Mountain Institute in Franklin, WV, left, *was coleader of the expedition.*

Western Hemisphere

Inca Mummies. Investigations at a South American volcano yielded the mummified remains of three children sacrificed around 500 years ago as part of an Inca ritual. The bodies lay under 5 ft (1.5 m) of rock and earth, at the top of Argentina's Mount Llullaillaco. The two girls and a boy were buried along with offerings to Inca gods, including statuettes, pottery, and bundles of woven material. Extremely cold, arid weather at the volcano's 22,000-ft (6 706-m)-high summit freeze-dried the children's bodies. Initial scientific analyses of the mummies revealed intact internal organs and some blood still left in the heart and lungs. The cause of the youngsters' deaths remained unknown.

Mysterious Circle. Archaeologists discovered a huge, prehistoric circle cut into limestone bedrock in downtown Miami. The circle, which measures 38 ft (11.6 m) in diameter, was discovered after bulldozers demolished a three-story apartment building in preparation for building a new luxury tower. Excavators found at least 20 manmade holes, ranging in size from 1 to 3 ft (.3 to .9 m) across, that formed a circle. Postholes and a rock carving similar to an eye appear on the western and eastern sides of the circle. Several offerings, including two stone axes and the skeletal remains of a 5-ft (1.5-m)-long shark deliberately buried in the circle, also turned up. The circle's function is unknown. It may have been the foundation for a chief's house among the Tequesta Indians, who once inhabited the region. Pottery styles found at the circle suggest it may date to between A.D. 1200 and A.D. 1500.

Maya Finds. Ongoing work at the ancient Maya city of Palenque, located in a jungle in Chiapas, Mexico, yielded a tomb decorated with painted murals, a 12-ft (3.6-m)-tall sculptured support pier with portraits of a ruler and his subjects, and a limestone bench or throne inscribed with more than 200 glyphs. Palenque was inhabited from around A.D. 379 to A.D. 799, near the end of the Classic period of Maya civilization. All of the new discoveries lie at one end of a central plaza in Palenque. Murals in the tomb include an image of God K, the celestial lightning god. Writing on the limestone bench surrounds 12 carved figures, including the ruler of Palenque from A.D. 721 to A.D. 764. The inscriptions describe the mythological history of the site's three patron gods and the king's relationship to them.

Pyramid Finds. An ongoing excavation beneath the Pyramid of the Moon at Teotihuacán has uncovered a tomb, dating to between A.D. 100 and A.D. 200, that apparently served to dedicate the fifth phase of the pyramid's construction. The burial contains four human skeletons, animal bones, large conch shells, jewelry, obsidian blades, and many other offerings. Archaeologists working at the site identified some six construction stages for the Pyramid of the Moon, with inhabitants of Teotihuacán building successively larger pyramids on top of previous monuments. The fifth stage involved a significant expansion and redesign of the pyramid to align it with the precise grid structure now seen in the city's 8 sq mi (20.7 km^2) of ruins. Little is known about Teotihuacán's civilization.

BRUCE BOWER, *"Science News"*

Architecture

Renewed environmental concerns, plus an interest in the psychological impact of buildings on users, were among the issues that dominated architecture in 1999.

Impact on Human Behavior. In 1999 the world's top award in architecture, the Pritzker Prize, went to English architect Sir Norman Foster. He was cited for his pioneering technology and environmental interests, such as the quality of users' surroundings. Many of his buildings—including the Hong Kong and Shanghai Bank in Hong Kong and the Commerzbank in Frankfurt—and his proposal for the city of London's assembly building took on forcefully futuristic appearances based on introducing outside light and unique air-handling systems.

Foster's concerns were mirrored in the United States by the findings of research into architecture's influence on inhabitants' behavior. Among those findings were negative human reactions to deprivation from sunlight, privacy, and control over immediate surroundings. Popular design theory had advocated open-plan offices and classrooms in economic large floor areas, requiring mechanical ventilation and more electric lighting. Windowless schools were meant to eliminate distracting outside views. Theory, contended author Winifred Gallagher, produced results contrary to claimed benefits. For example, open offices decreased the sociability and productivity of occupants by increasing confusing noises, irritations, and personality clashes.

Architects asked why more natural light and ventilation, even for tall buildings, could not be introduced in the United States. In Europe occupant-controlled natural-ventilation systems had been normal for almost a decade. The construction industry's response was that costs would be higher, but concerns with users' surroundings pointed to increasing use in the 21st century.

The Environment. Hand in hand with architectural journals' interest in interior environments came new interest in preserving open land and natural resources used in construction. Writing in *Preservation*, the magazine of the National Trust for Historic Preservation, Edward Hoagland stated: "Having presumed that God gave us the Earth to spend, we've positively splurged, and are already groping in some emptied

Photo by Andrew Ward/Courtesy, Foster and Partners

Photo by Ian Lambot/Courtesy, Foster and Partners

British architect Sir Norman Foster, above, *was awarded the 1999 Pritzker Prize, which he considered "a recognition of the importance of architecture itself." Foster's works include the headquarters of Commerzbank in Frankfurt, Germany,* right, *which rotates thin office floors around glazed light courts that spiral up the building's exterior.*

pockets." In the same issue, author Anne Matthews predicted that, if the past 50 years had been any indication, 80% of people in the world soon would be living in cities, because there would be no alternative.

There were 200 state and local referendums on restricting new construction and preserving open land during 1999, and most were passed. As a result, governments set aside major funding to preserve large tracts. The movement was active abroad as well.

To encourage more-livable cities, the 1999 American Institute of Architects (AIA) Honor Awards recognized five urban-design projects, ranging from Robert A.M. Stern Associates' plans for the revival of 42d Street in New York City to Daniel Williams Architect and town planner Erick Valle's South Dade Watershed project in South Dade county, FL. The latter would set aside many acres south of Miami, FL, for water conservation and management.

Preservation. Projects completed in 1999 included the $300 million preservation of San Francisco's City Hall by the city's Bureau of Architecture and Heller Manus Architects with Komorous-Towey and Finger & Moy. The 1912 Beaux Arts landmark required seismic-foundation rebuilding, designed by engineers Forrel and Elsassor, as well as interior and exterior restorations. A renewed New York Life Building in Kansas City, MO, opened to reveal work by Gastinger Walker Harden Architects.

Preservation projects, including Norman Foster's redesign of the Reichstag in Berlin, went much further than simple restorations and renovations. The Reichstag's interiors were sleekly modernist, while the exterior largely was restored with the exception of the dominant dome above the main chamber. The dome received a new profile and glass walls containing a suspended inverted-cone-shaped natural exhaust stack covered with mirrors and surrounded by a spiraling ramp used by visitors to view the city.

Of the nine preservation projects receiving AIA awards, only two—the Thomas Jefferson Building of the Library of Congress in Washington, DC, by Arthur Cotton Moore/Associates, and the Old State Capitol in Baton Rouge, LA, by E. Eean McNaughton Architects—could be classified as restoration. Most other projects transformed the buildings with very modern redesigns. For example, a glass-and-steel superstructure by Bohlin Cywinski Jackson atop a historic structure at Carnegie Mellon University in Pittsburgh, PA, gave the original building a very different roofline and proportions. Renovation by Gabellini Associates of offices inside a landmark mid-19th-century villa in Hamburg, Germany, preserved much of the grander neoclassic moldings and spaces, but introduced flat surfaces and steel-pipe railings elsewhere.

A growing source of work for architects was the renovation of mid-20th-century office buildings, which contained outmoded wiring and plumbing and failing structures. In addition, many of the exterior curtain walls were threatening to collapse. Yet the costs of demolition and new construction outweighed repairing and replacing existing systems. While few of these buildings were distinguished, renovation gave architects and engineers a chance to introduce new efficiencies in mechanical systems and floor layouts. Better-looking exteriors that were more functional also could be introduced.

Modernism. Both the AIA and the professional press veered away from promoting a wide range of styles, including classicism, toward praise of familiar boxy glass modernism or buildings designed by a few much-published architects. The latter included Frank Gehry, who received the 1999 AIA Gold Medal for such buildings as his sinuous titanium-covered Guggenheim Museum in Bilbao, Spain. Such awards countered popular taste that called for styles based on historic precedent.

Of the 29 buildings and interiors receiving AIA honor awards in 1999, all but the two restorations and a rustic park rest area in Brooks county, TX, by Richter Architects, were exclusively modernist. Award winners included the Nomentana House in Stoneham, ME, by Scogin Elam & Bray Architects; the Kiasma Museum of Contemporary Art in Helsinki, Finland, by Steven Holl Architects; Inventure Place in Akron, OH, by the Polshek Partnership; the first building for the new Olympic College in Shelton, WA, by the Miller/Hull Partnership; the McNitt Building, for a concrete-panel manufacturer in Oklahoma City, OK, by Elliot + Associates Architects; Minneapolis Pathways, a health-crisis center, by Anmahian Winton Architects; the World Bank in Washington, DC, a sleek glass building that combined two 1960s structures to speed the project to completion ten years ahead of schedule, by Kohn Pedersen Fox Associates; and the Gagosian Gallery in Beverly Hills, CA, by Richard Meier & Partners.

CHARLES K. HOYT
Fellow, American Institute of Architects

Argentina

The Peronist regime in Argentina was replaced in 1999 national elections, but its economic policies were to be continued by the incoming parties. The country was mired in yet another recession. Relations with Great Britain improved, in contrast to those with Brazil and Paraguay.

Politics and Government. Fernando de la Rúa, mayor of Buenos Aires, led his opposition Alliance coalition to a landslide victory in the three-way presidential contest on October 24, winning 49% of the votes. Thus ended a decade-long domination of the executive branch by the Peronist (PJ) Party, whose populist candidate was Eduardo Duhalde, governor of Buenos Aires province. Domingo Cavallo, a former member of the current government of President Carlos Menem, was an also-ran. The Alliance was composed of the century-old Radical Civic Union and the new center-left Front for the Country in Solidarity (Frepaso), a splinter from the Peronists.

The Alliance's presidential triumph was more a consequence of the voters' widespread desire to rid themselves of the Menem government's pervasive corruption than of an attractive alternative to the official candidate. Alliance forces failed to win control either of the National Congress or of a majority of the provincial governments. Cavallo's pro-market Action for the Republic party picked up nine to ten congressional seats. However, the PJ remained in control of the Senate, at least until 2001, and dominated the judiciary. In other contests, the Peronists retained the governorship of Buenos Aires province.

Although de la Rúa revealed few of his plans during the presidential campaign, after the election he quickly gave the public glimpses of what to expect. As the economic situation was more bleak than he had supposed, there would be sharp cuts in public spending. Troops serving as peacekeepers would be brought home. Foreign policy would be more isolationist, moving away from the United States. De la Rúa visited Brazil on November 4, to express the incoming government's interest in strengthening bilateral relations and regional integration. After attending an international socialist gathering in Paris, he was hospitalized for lung surgery. He recovered in time for his December 10 inaugural, however.

Economy. As the country continued its slide into recession, tax and customs collections fell. The gross domestic product (GDP) for 1999 was projected to fall by 3%. Industrial output in the first seven months of the year was off by 12.5% compared with 1998, although it improved somewhat thereafter. Agricultural production fell by nearly 16%. The shortfall forced the administration to borrow heavily to cover its deficit. The outgoing regime admitted to a possible deficit of $5.8 billion, but outside sources feared an imbalance of up to $12 billion.

An effort to curb expenditure through cuts in school funding brought student strikes and, in May, the protest resignation of Minister of Education Susana Decibe. At midyear, Congress approved a fiscal-convertibility law that had been called for by the International Monetary Fund (IMF), setting a ceiling on public expenditure. In December, Congress approved a $1.4 billion spending cut and a $2 billion tax increase to counteract an expected deficit of $4.5 billion in 2000. Unemployment by July had risen to 14.5%, or 2.2% above the rate of a year earlier. Distribution of wealth was worsening, with 13.4 million inhabitants living below the poverty level and the middle class losing its relative share.

Fearing a flood of cheaper Brazilian imports after that nation's currency devaluation in January, Argentina adopted protectionist measures on shoes, textiles, and bed linens. Trade in these products approached $300 million. By September, Brazil had imposed restrictions on 90% of Argentine imports and referred the textile quotas to the World Trade Organization (WTO). Although negotiations remained stalled, agreements were reached in September temporarily limiting exports on some items.

The trade feud hampered progress toward forging a united position against

ARGENTINA • Information Highlights

Official Name: Argentine Republic.
Location: Southern South America.
Area: 1,068,297 sq mi (2 766 890 km²).
Population (July 1999 est.): 36,737,664.
Chief Cities (1991 census): Buenos Aires, the capital, 2,960,976; Cordoba, 1,148,305; San Justo, 1,111,811; Rosario, 894,645.
Government: *Head of state and government,* Fernando de la Rúa, president (inaugurated Dec. 10, 1999). *Legislature*—National Congress: Senate and Chamber of Deputies.
Monetary Unit: Peso (1.000 peso equals U.S.$1, Jan. 3, 2000).
Gross Domestic Product (1998 est. U.S.$): $374,000,000,000 (purchasing power parity).
Economic Index (Buenos Aires, 1997; 1988 = 100): *Consumer Prices,* all items, 323,667.6; food, 274,621.4.
Foreign Trade (1998 U.S.$): *Imports,* $31,402,000,000; *exports,* $25,227,000,000.

farm subsidies in international forums. A summit on trade between Mercosur (the South American Common Market) and the European Union (EU) was held in Rio de Janeiro, June 28–29. President Menem and Brazil's President Fernando Henrique Cardoso indicated that the summit would produce positive results only if the EU agreed to eliminate its obstacles to trade in farm products. Some 40% of Mercosur's exports to the EU were agricultural. However, the ongoing opposition of France to free farm trade blocked establishment of a timetable for reaching a free-trade pact between the trading blocs.

President Menem had advocated a single currency for Mercosur since 1998. Early in 1999, with the chaos accompanying Brazil's deep devaluation, Menem began to push for acceptance of the U.S. dollar as the regional currency and as a guard against future devaluations. Neither the United States nor Brazil encouraged him in this effort, although Cavallo did endorse the concept of a common currency for the region.

With a $13.4 billion stock purchase in June, Repsol, Spain's biggest oil company, gained almost complete control of YPF, the largest oil company in Argentina. Repsol planned to sell other holdings in Argentina in an effort to avoid violating antitrust laws.

Foreign Affairs. Relations with Brazil deteriorated rapidly throughout the year, threatening the existence of Mercosur. Argentina's attempt to gain membership in the North Atlantic Treaty Organization (NATO) and its rumored offer to participate in a U.S. effort to assist Colombia combat its prolonged guerrilla insurgency upset Brazil. Argentina was affected deeply by the devaluation of the Brazilian currency in January and the resultant trade war. Equally upsetting was Brazil's unilateral launching of talks with the Andean trade pact.

Relations with Paraguay were strained when Lino Oviedo, a fugitive Paraguayan former general, was given refuge in Argentina after the assassination on March 23 of the Paraguayan vice-president, Luis María Argaña. Already implicated in the assassination, Oviedo continued actions from exile that were considered harmful to the government of Paraguay, which requested his extradition. Argentina refused, but it did banish him to distant Patagonia.

On Dec. 17, 1998, Britain had eased its embargo on arms sales to Argentina, imposed in 1982 during the Falklands/Malvinas conflict. Henceforth, such materials could be sold to Argentina, but must not be used to threaten the security of the Falklands or other British territories in the South Atlantic. The policy change was attributed to Menem's pledge during a state visit to Lon-

© Corbis

DE LA RÚA, FERNANDO

Fernando de la Rúa, 62, was elected president of Argentina on Oct. 24, 1999, with about 49% of the popular vote, beating Eduardo Duhalde of the ruling Peronist (PJ) Party. To be successful at the national level, de la Rúa had had to expand the electoral base of his centrist Radical Civic Union (UCR), which was accomplished in 1997 by forming an Alliance with the leftist Front for a Country of Solidarity (Frepaso).

De la Rúa was seen as a middle-class and dour man, not given to kissing strangers or exchanging small talk. A reserved and somber consensus builder, he was viewed as the opposite of the flamboyant incumbent, Carlos Menem.

Fernando de la Rúa was born on Sept. 15, 1937, in Córdoba, a city in northern Argentina. At age 18, he joined the UCR. He earned a law degree from the National University of Córdoba at age 21. At the age of 26, he joined the interior ministry of the UCR government under Arturo Illia. Illia was forced out of office by a military coup in 1966. When Argentina returned to democracy in 1973, de la Rúa was elected to the Senate, representing Buenos Aires. After another military coup shut down the government in 1976, he went into exile, lecturing at universities in the United States, Mexico, and Venezuela. He returned to his Senate seat after the military government was ousted in 1983. In 1996 he left the Senate to become the first elected mayor of the newly created capital district of Buenos Aires.

De la Rúa has written five books on legal procedures. After graduating from law school, he married and had three sons. He enjoys soccer, chess, and golf.

LARRY PIPPIN

don that force never again would be used in pursuit of Argentine claims to sovereignty over the disputed islands. The political decision against the use of force to regain sovereignty over the Malvinas was incorporated into a White Paper on defense, which was prepared in the first weeks of 1999.

With the ratification in early June of an Ice Fields Treaty by the legislatures of both Argentina and Chile, demarcation of their common border was completed. The disputed area was a glaciated zone along the western border of Patagonia.

LARRY L. PIPPIN, *University of the Pacific*

Armenia

Armenian leaders, including President Robert Kocharian, were hoping that 1999 would be an improvement over 1998, which was characterized by the forced (and, some said, unconstitutional) resignation of President Levon Ter-Petrosian, flawed elections, violence, and economic decline. But Kocharian's administration made little progress in keeping its promises to reform the constitution, improve the economy, and end corruption. Questionable democratic practices, human-rights abuses, political murders, and economic and social crises continued to characterize Armenian politics.

Domestic Affairs. The first five months of 1999 were dominated by campaigns for the parliamentary elections. A new law introduced a mixed system of proportional representation and individual candidacies for parliament seats. In elections held in May, Miasnutyun (Unity Bloc), a new alliance led by Karen Demirchian of the People's Party of Armenia and the Republican Party's powerful Defense Minister Vazgen Sarkisian, gained 57 of the 131 seats in parliament, becoming the dominant political force. Sarkisian became prime minister and Demirchian parliamentary speaker.

Despite Miasnutyun's populist platform, Sarkisian's cabinet continued the former government's policies of economic reform and privatization. It had to deal with a 31-billion-dram ($58 million) budget deficit; a serious downturn in trade with Russia, its main trading partner; a $315.7 million trade deficit; and $800 million in foreign debt. Under pressure from the International Monetary Fund (IMF), the new government introduced austerity measures that included increased taxes and cuts in "nonessential" expenditures in the social, education, and health sectors. The economy did show some signs of improvement during the year, however. Inflation remained in single digits; industrial growth began to recover; and the delayed tranches of aid from the IMF and World Bank were granted in the fall.

In the summer, a power rivalry among the leadership of Nagorno-Karabakh, the disputed territory between Armenia and Azerbaijan, led to the dismissal of its entire cabinet. Threatened with a dangerous split in Nagorno-Karabakh's military, Kocharian quickly intervened. This crisis was followed by a shocking event on October 27, as five gunmen entered a parliament session and killed Sarkisian, Demirchian, and six other members. Kocharian formed a new cabinet with the goal of retaining the balance of power between Armenia's political parties. He appointed Aram Sarkisian, Sarkisian's brother, as prime minister.

Foreign Affairs. Kocharian met with Azerbaijani President Heydar Aliyev for four rounds of direct talks over the summer, creating speculation that they would sign a formal framework agreement for resolving the Nagorno-Karabakh dispute at the November conference of the Organization for Security and Cooperation in Europe (OSCE) in Istanbul. But Kocharian was not strong enough politically to push the necessary compromises through parliament.

Armenia's foreign policy continued to be pro-Russian in 1999, though greater emphasis was placed on agreements and alliances with the West. In July, Foreign Minister Vartan Oskanian said Armenia's ultimate goal was to join the European Union (EU). Armenia also established agreements in 1999 with Kazakhstan and Bulgaria that could help it link up with European plans to develop a Caucasian trade corridor—a move essential for the Armenian economy.

STEPHEN F. JONES, *Mount Holyoke College*

ARMENIA • Information Highlights

Official Name: Republic of Armenia.
Location: Southwest Asia.
Area: 11,506 sq mi (29 800 km²).
Population (July 1999 est.): 3,409,234.
Chief Cities (July 1990 est.): Yerevan, the capital, 1,254,400; Gyumri, 206,600; Vanadzor, 170,200.
Government: *Head of state,* Robert Kocharian, president (sworn in April 9, 1998). *Head of government,* Aram Sarkisian, prime minister (appointed November 1999). *Legislature* (unicameral)—National Assembly.
Monetary Unit: Dram (518.935 dram equal U.S.$1, Jan. 3, 2000).
Gross Domestic Product (1998 est. U.S.$): $9,200,000,000 (purchasing power parity).
Foreign Trade (1998 est.U.S.$): *Imports,* $896,000,000; *exports,* $223,000,000.

Art

Controversies over art exhibitions and ownership continued during 1999. Museums across the United States reported record-breaking attendance figures for 1998 and mounted exhibitions of national and international significance. Leonardo da Vinci's "Last Supper" mural was unveiled after decades of restoration, and Leo Castelli, an entrepreneurial gallery director who helped to transform New York's Soho neighborhood into the heart of the contemporary art scene in the 1970s, died at the age of 91. Castelli had used his gallery to showcase the first one-man shows of important artists such as Jasper Johns and Robert Rauschenberg.

Controversies. "Sensation: Young British Artists from the Saatchi Collection" at the Brooklyn Museum of Art created a stir in fall 1999. New York City Mayor Rudolph Giuliani objected to the controversial topics and style of many of the exhibit's works, from the collection of British advertising mogul Charles Saatchi. Giuliani particularly criticized a painting by Chris Ofili called "The Holy Virgin Mary" (1996), which portrayed a cartoonish female figure hovering in a field of gold paint, surrounded by cutouts from pornographic magazines and decorated (or, the mayor claimed, desecrated) with elephant dung. Clearly designed to raise some hackles, the work also raises questions about the fusion of different cultural traditions, including Ofili's own Catholicism and his African heritage, in which dung often is used artistically. The furor increased when the mayor threatened to freeze city funds to the museum (which accounted for about one third of its budget) if it went ahead with the exhibit. When the show opened on October 2, the city withheld its monthly check of $497,554 and then threatened to evict the museum from its building. The museum responded by suing the city on 1st Amendment grounds, and in November a federal judge ordered the city to restore the museum's funding. Meanwhile, the Seattle Art Museum canceled a show featuring contemporary artist Mike Kelley and scheduled for the summer of 2000 because of an uproar surrounding Kelley's 1988 work "Pay for Your Pleasure," which included works by convicted killers.

The reparation of stolen artworks continued to be an issue. When "Dead City" (1911) and "Portrait of Wally" (1912), two paintings by Austrian expressionist Egon Schiele, arrived for an exhibition at New York's Museum of Modern Art in 1997, descendants of Austrian Jews claimed that the Nazis had looted the paintings from their family, and in spring 1998, Manhattan District Attorney Robert Morgenthau blocked the return of the artworks to Austria until the matter was resolved. In September 1999 the New York Court of Appeals invalidated Morgenthau's action, clearing the way for the paintings' return; but only days later, the U.S. Customs Department seized "Portrait of Wally" on the grounds that it was stolen property, and left open the possibility of confiscating "Dead City" at a later date.

© Seattle Art Museum/AP/Wide World Photos

The Seattle Art Museum returned Matisse's "Odalisque," above, *to the heirs of Jewish collector Paul Rosenberg, from whom it was confiscated by the Nazis in 1941.*

Earlier in the year, Austria returned some 250 objects that had been in its state museums to the Rothschild banking family, but it refused to cede possession of five paintings by Gustav Klimt, which were claimed by the heirs of Adele and Ferdinand Bloch-Bauer. The Seattle Art Museum voted in June to return Henri Matisse's 1928 painting "Odalisque" to the heirs of Jewish collector Paul Rosenberg.

The Pew Charitable Trust, a $4.7 billion foundation, announced in August that over the next five years it would commit $50 million to study the potential for the United States to establish a cultural policy to address conflicts over art content and ownership, as well as questions of intellectual property rights, historic district zoning, and school arts curricula.

"The Last Supper." Leonardo da Vinci's 1498 "Last Supper" mural in the refectory of Santa Maria delle Grazie monastery in

Milan, Italy, which had been under scaffolding for two decades while undergoing restoration, was revealed in May 1999. Previously invisible flowers, bread, knives, and plates could be seen on the table, and the apostle Matthew's hair was no longer brown, but blond. Some experts reacted unfavorably, however, charging that the restoration disfigured the work's original appearance and intention.

Exhibitions. Art museums continued to outdraw sports teams across the United States. The most-attended single exhibition of 1998 was "Monet in the 20th Century" at the Museum of Fine Arts, Boston, which attracted 528,267 visitors.

The Venice Biennale, a contemporary-art extravaganza staged every other summer in Venice, Italy, was held again in 1999. The show, with pavilions of current art from dozens of countries, was more global than ever before, and it also integrated more of Venice's unique urban spaces into its displays. Italy's pavilion, which won the Golden Lion for best national entry, featured the work of five young women: Monica Bonvicini, Bruna Esposito, Luisa Lambri, Paola Pivi, and Grazia Toderi.

In the United States the third Site Santa Fe biennial took place during the summer. "Looking for a Place" was described by curator Rosa Martínez as "an invitation to journey—physically and intellectually." Among the participants were Bonvicini, American sculptor and performance artist Janine Antoni, American sculptor Louise Bourgeois, Chinese sculptor and painter Cai Guo-qiang, and 1999 MacArthur Foundation "genius" grant recipients Elizabeth Diller and Ricardo Scofidio.

Several exhibitions of the works of late-19th-century American painter John Singer Sargent opened in summer 1999, including major retrospectives at the National Gallery of Art in Washington, DC, and at Boston's Museum of Fine Arts. Exhibitions of Sargent's drawings were presented at the Fogg Art Museum at Harvard University in Cambridge, MA, and at New York University's Grey Art Gallery. Landscape paintings were on view at the Isabella Stewart Gardner Museum in Boston, and the Jewish Museum in New York dedicated a show to the society painter's "Portraits of the Wertheimer Family." The achievement of 20th-century U.S. illustrator Norman Rockwell, hugely popular with the public but long-shunned by the art world, was recognized in a retrospective that opened in November at the High Museum of Art in Atlanta, GA; it was to travel to a number of U.S. venues, ending at the Guggenheim Museum in New York in November 2001.

The Whitney Museum of American Art in New York ended the millennium with a two-part exhibition, "The American Century: Art & Culture 1900–2000." The museum described the show, which featured more than 1,200 works, as "the largest and most ambitious exhibition ever presented of American art and culture of the 20th century." Marking its 25th anniversary in 1999, the Hirshhorn Museum in Washington, DC, mounted a show called "Regarding Beauty." Artists included such contemporary figures as Janine Antoni and Matthew Barney, as well as many of their precursors, such as Picasso. In another celebration of beauty, an exhibit of 50 gorgeous paintings by often-neglected Italian Renaissance painter Dosso Dossi (whose real name was Giovanni Francesco di Luteri) was shown at the Metropolitan Museum and the J. Paul Getty Museum in Los Angeles. "Goya: Another Look," an exhibit that opened at the Musée des Beaux Arts in Lille, France, in December 1998 and moved to the Philadelphia Museum of Art the following April, displayed

Photo by Graydon Wood, Philadelphia Museum of Art: Given by Anna Warren Ingersoll

"The Seesaw" was part of the "Goya: Another Look" exhibit, which traveled to the Philadelphia Museum of Art in April 1999 after opening in Lille, France, in December 1998.

© Nicholas Whitman, Courtesy, MASS MoCA

A former factory complex in North Adams, MA, was converted into the Massachusetts Museum of Contemporary Art (MASS MoCA), the largest museum of contemporary fine and performing arts in the United States.

35 important paintings and numerous works on paper by the Spanish master of the darker side of human nature.

Permanence as well as beauty were much in evidence in "Egyptian Art in the Age of the Pyramids," an exhibit of art from Egypt's Old Kingdom era (2650–2150 B.C.), displayed at the Grand Palais in Paris and then traveling to the Metropolitan Museum and the Royal Art Museum in Toronto, Ontario. Works from the Amarna Age, when Pharaoh Akhenaten and Queen Nefertiti discarded the traditional pantheon of Egyptian gods and made art more expressive and naturalistic, were seen in "Pharaohs of the Sun: Akenaten, Nefertiti, and Tutankhamen," organized by the Museum of Fine Arts, Boston, and traveling to Los Angeles, Chicago, and the Netherlands.

"Masks: Faces of Culture," organized by the St. Louis (MO) Art Museum, presented more than 150 works ranging from prehistoric times to *Star Wars*. From St. Louis, the collection of masks and costumes traveled to the Field Museum in Chicago and the Museum of Fine Arts in Houston, TX.

Transitions and Renovations. Graham W.J. Beal resigned as the director of the Los Angeles County Museum to take the same position at the Detroit Institute of Arts; he was replaced by the museum's president and CEO, Andrea L. Rich. Jeremy Strick succeeded Richard Koshalek as the director of the Museum of Contemporary Art in Los Angeles. Other new directors in 1999 included John R. (Jack) Lane at the Dallas (TX) Museum of Art; Brent Benjamin at the St. Louis Art Museum; Susan Lubowsky Talbott at the Des Moines (IA) Art Center; and Sharon Patton at the Allen Memorial Art Museum at Oberlin College, Oberlin, OH.

In late 1999 the Museum of Fine Arts in Houston was finishing its 15-year, $115 million expansion, which will double its exhibition space to 85,400 sq ft (7 942 m^2) and make it the sixth-largest art museum in the United States. Designed by Spanish architect Rafael Moneo, the Audrey Jones Beck Building was scheduled to open in March 2000. The Heard Museum in Phoenix, AZ, completed an $18.1 million expansion that increased its space by 50,000 sq ft (4 645 m^2).

The long-awaited Massachusetts Museum of Contemporary Art (MASS MoCA) opened in a 13-acre (5.26-ha) former factory complex in North Adams. The $26 million renovation connected 27 different structures into the largest museum of contemporary fine and performing arts in the United States. The Dia Center for the Arts in New York City acquired a factory building in Beacon, NY, to display some of its huge works, such as Richard Serra's massive Minimalist sculptures, "Torqued Ellipses." The new building was due to open in 2001.

The Jack S. Blanton Museum of Art at the University of Texas in Austin chose the Swiss architectural team of Herzog and de Meuron to design its new 100,000-sq-ft (9 290-m^2) structure, due for completion in 2002. The Museum of Fine Arts, Boston, chose English architect Norman Foster, winner of the 1999 Pritzker Prize, to design its expansion and renovation.

PETER CHAMETZKY
Southern Illinois University, Carbondale

Art Market

The roof came off the art market in 1999. Prices climbed—and at times soared—in all fields. And the high-tech world of the Internet worked to find a way into the elitist world of art and antiques. First, Internet auction company eBay bought Butterfield & Butterfield, the California auction house, for $260 million. Then on-line retailer Amazon.com agreed to buy a $45.4 million stake in Sotheby's to help it set up a joint venture—sothebys.amazon.com; the authenticity of items sold on the Web site would be guaranteed by the auction house.

In the old-fashioned auction world, Impressionist and Modern paintings continued to fetch the highest prices. Paul Cézanne's stately "Still Life with Curtain, Pitcher, and Bowl of Fruit" fetched $60.5 million, and Georges Seurat's "Landscape, Island of the Grande Jatte" brought $35.2 million. The Seurat sold to Mirage Resorts chief Steve Wynn, who in the past three years had spent more than $300 million to fit out the company's Bellagio Gallery of Fine Art. Edgar Degas' pastel drawing of an exhausted dancer, "Dancer at Rest," brought $27.9 million. Claude Monet's 1906 "Nymphéas" sold for $22.5 million.

Pablo Picasso's portrait of his young, blonde mistress, "Nude on a Black Armchair," fetched $45.1 million, while his more angular and jazzy portrait of his brooding mistress Dora Maar, "Woman Sitting in a Garden," sold for $49.5 million. Post–World War II contemporary artist Mark Rothko's "No. 15" fetched $11 million, while Jasper Johns' "Two Flags" brought $7.15 million, and Lucian Freud's "The Painter's Mother" went for $3.3 million.

The most startling price of the season was reached by George Bellows' large and colorful "Polo Crowd." Bellows is respected in the art world, but his works are considered more decorative than innovative. Even so, the painting fetched a whopping $27.7 million, becoming the most expensive American painting ever sold at auction.

While prices in the field of Old Masters (pre-1840) continued to lag well behind those of later works, one piece in particular did quite well. A painting of Saint Rufina dating from the 1630s, long considered to be by Bartolomé Esteban Murillo, had been shown by recent X rays and other scientific techniques to be a work of the more artistically important Diego de Silva y Velazquez; it sold for $8.9 million.

The sale of the year was of art and antiques once owned by Barons Nathaniel and Albert von Rothschild. The paintings, commodes, and other works of art fetched $89.98 million. The property had been owned by the Austrian branch of the Rothschild family until 1938, when the family fled Austria after the Nazi takeover. From 1945 to 1999, the Austrian government had claimed the property as its own, but a new stance of making amends to Holocaust victims led Austria to return the artworks.

ANDREW DECKER, *Freelance Art Journalist*

© Robin Nowacki/AP/Wide World Photos

Art and antiques from the collection of Barons Nathaniel and Albert von Rothschild, including a painting of Dutch merchant Tieleman Roosterman by Frans Hal (right) *and a 16th-century missal (being held by Christie's Elizabeth Lane), were auctioned for $89.98 million in July 1999. The Rothschilds had owned the property until 1938, when the family fled Austria to escape the Nazis. The Austrian government had returned the artworks to the family earlier in 1999.*

Asia

The year 1999 witnessed an economic rebound from the two preceding years of crisis in East Asia, though financial and structural problems persisted. Meanwhile, regional organizations were attempting to cope with serious Asian security issues.

Economic Recovery. After almost two years of economic stagnation, the Asian Development Bank declared in mid-1999 that currency volatility had calmed, regional stock markets had rebounded, and economic activity had revived throughout most of East Asia. The economies of South Korea, Thailand, and Malaysia showed the greatest growth, while Indonesia, with its attendant political turmoil, lagged. Whether the International Monetary Fund's (IMF's) bitter medicine for South Korea and Thailand—in the form of fiscal and monetary austerity, combined with open financial markets—was a better solution than Malaysia's imposition of capital controls remained an open question.

By the end of the year, South Korea was anticipating 9% growth, while Malaysia, Taiwan, and Singapore were expecting to achieve 5%. Thailand's growth rate could reach 3%; and even Indonesia seemed to have bottomed out. It must be remembered, however, that Asia's economies were coming out of deep recessions; thus, growth was bound to be exaggerated in the early stages. Nevertheless, confidence in the region was bolstered.

Asia was not yet out of the woods, however. Slowing growth in China and massive budget deficits in Japan were worrisome, since both nations are normally major importers from the rest of the region. Moreover, at midyear, 64% of Indonesian companies still were not earning enough cash to cover their interest obligations to banks and bondholders. Some 27% of Korean companies, 26% of Malaysian companies, and 28% of Thai companies were in the same condition. Nor had corporate reform proceeded. The World Bank estimated that in Thailand, the Philippines, and Indonesia, more than 50% of corporate ownership still remained in the hands of 15 powerful families. In Taiwan, Malaysia, Singapore, Hong Kong, and South Korea, the top 15 families controlled from 20% to 38% of big business.

The region's banking systems still were a mess. The absence of bankruptcy laws, as well as a lack of transparency and due diligence, left the playing field disturbingly uneven for investors who did not have the

In Auckland, New Zealand, in September 1999, representatives of the 21 member nations of the Asia-Pacific Economic Cooperation (APEC) forum, below, *called on the World Trade Organization (WTO) to end agricultural export subsidies.*

needed business and political connections. Many of the old corporate names and their friends in government—who led the region into the crisis—still were running the show.

Nevertheless, the record was not relentlessly bleak. Malaysia had made progress in getting bad debt off its banks' books and encouraging consolidation in the financial sector. Thailand and South Korea had sold troubled local banks to foreign partners. Only Indonesia had made scant progress. Banks had been so discredited that businesses were scrambling to find a safe haven for the funds offshore. Debt write-offs in Indonesia could approach $70 billion.

Despite the acknowledged need among Asian nations for a simultaneous regional recovery, the fact that exports were the primary method of that recovery would lead to increased competition. As the nations pushed to increase exports, they could undercut each other in an attempt to gain market share and foreign currency.

ASEAN Affairs. ASEAN's annual July foreign ministers' meeting—held in Singapore in 1999—started to explore some contentious issues, including a proposed draft code of conduct for claimants to the South China Sea Spratly Islands, nuclear disarmament, civil societies, and—behind closed doors—the nettlesome issue of human rights. The sixth annual ASEAN Regional Forum (ARF) followed the ASEAN foreign ministers' meeting. In addition to addressing the South China Sea dispute, the ARF expressed concern over North Korean missile developments that could have "serious consequences" for the region.

Recurring violence in the South China Sea led several countries at the ARF meeting, including the United States, to urge a relaxation of military tensions and a more diligent search for a diplomatic settlement. The Philippines offered to draft a code of conduct for claimants' consideration, though China insisted that the Spratlys be treated only bilaterally. At the informal November ASEAN summit in Manila, the Philippines presented its draft on the South China Sea, calling for a "halt to any new occupation of reefs, shoals, and islets in the disputed area." While China rejected the Philippine proposal, Beijing subsequently stated that it would agree to joint development of the islands.

In other business at the Manila meeting, ASEAN accelerated its move toward free trade among its founding members, shifting the deadline forward from 2015 to 2010. The four newest members—Vietnam, Laos, Cambodia, and Myanmar—would drive their own deadlines forward by three years, to 2015. As for Indonesia's political future, the ASEAN leaders took the unprecedented step of issuing a statement expressing "full respect for the sovereignty and territorial integrity of the Republic of Indonesia."

ASEAN members' reaction to Indonesia's political turmoil over East Timor (*see* INDONESIA—*East Timor*) reflected the region's consternation at the potential political breakup of its linchpin state. The military-induced chaos in East Timor that followed its vote for independence perplexed ASEAN. On the one hand, ASEAN members wanted to participate in any peacekeeping force in East Timor, to demonstrate that regional crises could be handled by members of the region. On the other hand, their armed forces were not prepared to manage this kind of intervention; and the prospect of ASEAN troops confronting Indonesian forces was unthinkable. So, although Australia led the military expedition into East Timor, smaller contingents from Malaysia, Singapore, Brunei, Thailand, the Philippines, and South Korea also participated; 4,303 out of the 5,651 troops were Australian, however. The next phase of peacekeeping, scheduled for January 2000, would see Asian states play the dominant role.

Northeast Asia. In Northeast Asia, meanwhile, the United States, Japan, and South Korea moved toward formalizing their relationship in dealing with North Korea. Based on the proposal of former U.S. Defense Secretary William Perry, the three countries established the Trilateral Coordination and Oversight Group (TCOG). In a sense, TCOG was a follow-on to the Korean Peninsula Energy Development Organization (KEDO), created in 1994 to provide North Korea with new light-water nuclear reactors that would not produce weapons-grade plutonium as a by-product. (Japan, South Korea, and the United States also were the key members of KEDO.) By coordinating threats and promises to North Korea, the TCOG was able to convince the North not to test a new missile with intercontinental capabilities. In turn, the United States eased some of its long-standing economic sanctions and opened new talks with the North in Berlin, Germany. It was hoped that these talks would convince Pyongyang to cancel its missile development, in exchange for the restoration of U.S. diplomatic relations and economic aid.

SHELDON W. SIMON, *Arizona State University*

Astronomy

Images of Saturn's moon Titan, evidence of the first multiple planetary system beyond the solar system, new evidence regarding the age of the universe, and the dedication of the first Gemini telescopes near Hawaii's Mauna Kea were among 1999 highlights in astronomy.

Our Planetary System. In mid-November 1998 astronomers at the McDonald Observatory in Texas found a tail of sodium gas stretching at least 500,000 mi (800 000 km) out from the Moon and changing its appearance over three consecutive nights.

Analysis of data from the National Aeronautics and Space Administration's (NASA's) Lunar Prospector spacecraft confirmed that the Moon has a small core, supporting the theory that the bulk of the Moon was ripped away from the early Earth when an object the size of Mars collided with the Earth. When scientists crashed the robotic Lunar Prospector into a lunar crater near the Moon's south pole on July 31, 1999, they used terrestrial and space-based telescopes to look for signs of water vapor being ejected by the blast. They found none.

Scientists have discovered the source of fountains of electrified gas that flow from the Sun like water gushing through cracks in a dam. Called the "high-speed solar wind," this gas rushes out into space at 2 million mph (3.2 million km/hr) from the edges of honeycomb-shaped patterns of magnetic fields on the Sun.

Violent winds—known as "auroral electrojets"—have been found to race around the poles of Jupiter at thousands of miles an hour like cars around a racetrack. Scientists feel this may help explain why temperatures at the top of the Jovian atmosphere are much higher than one would expect for a planet 500 million mi (800 million km) from the Sun.

A dramatic time-lapse movie, assembled from Hubble Space Telescope images, shows for the first time dynamic seasonal changes on Uranus, and the planet's fragile ring system that seems to wobble like an unbalanced wagon wheel.

The best images ever taken of Saturn's mysterious moon Titan—shot with the Keck Telescope on Hawaii's Mauna Kea—reveal a complex surface that may be home to ice and rock continents or highlands, and frigid seas of liquid hydrocarbons.

In the Milky Way. After 11 years of gathering data, astronomers from four research institutions found evidence of the first multiple planetary system to be discovered beyond our own solar system. Three planets are known to orbit the nearby star Upsilon Andromedae.

At 4:47 A.M. EST on Jan. 23, 1999, astronomers using the Earth-orbiting Compton Gamma Ray Observatory with ground-based telescopes witnessed, for the first time, the visible light emitted at the same time as a powerful and mysterious gamma-ray burst. The burst had the power of nearly 10 million billion Suns, and its light became so brilliant that it could have been seen by anyone aiming binoculars in its direction.

© Zia Mazhar/AP/Wide World Photos

Solar Eclipse

At 9:31 A.M. Greenwich Mean Time on Aug. 11, 1999, a dark shadow appeared in the sky over the coast of Nova Scotia, Canada. From there, it raced across the Atlantic, passing over Europe, Turkey, Iraq, Iran, Pakistan, and India before finally disappearing over the Bay of Bengal. This shadow, known as an umbra, was caused by the Moon passing briefly between the Earth and the Sun, temporarily blotting out the sunlight—a solar eclipse.

Total solar eclipses always have held great fascination for humans, and this one was no exception. Not only was it the last eclipse of the millennium, but its path crossed a good deal of densely populated terrain, making it easy for a large number of people to view it. And view it they did: Thousands of skygazers, both professional and amateur, flocked to vantage points throughout Europe and Asia. Millions more watched the event on television. The classic view of the corona peeking around the edges of the Moon was seen most clearly in Eastern Europe and Turkey, but the experience of watching the Sun disappear was memorable even in areas where the sky was cloudy. Many observers—awed by the wondrous sight of an eerie, gray dawn rising in the west instead of the usual east—immediately made plans to catch the next eclipse, scheduled to appear over Angola in 2001.

A 60-story-high NASA balloon sent to the highest regions of Earth's atmosphere collected particles of some of the rarest material in the universe: antimatter. This finding suggests that structures as large as antimatter galaxies may exist.

Using the advanced imaging system attached to the Keck I Telescope on Hawaii's Mauna Kea, astronomers from the University of California at Berkeley discovered a star with a dramatic spiral dust tail. They believe that the tail around Wolf-Rayet 104 is produced by two separate hot stars orbiting one another, generating cool dust and spraying it out in a spiral, much as a lawn sprinkler spews water droplets.

In November 1998 astronomers from England, Australia, Italy, and the United States announced that they had found the 1,000th pulsar in our galaxy. A new class of "middleweight" black holes has been found—weighing only as much as 100 to 10,000 Suns. In addition, Australian astronomers announced their finding that some black holes are not black at all, but bright pink. The "pink holes" were discovered with telescopes at Parkes and Coonabarabran on the western plains of New South Wales between 1994 and 1998.

The Universe Beyond. Astronomers obtained the clearest view yet of the center of the Andromeda galaxy. They learned that the apparent "double nucleus" of this galaxy may be caused by stars orbiting the galaxy's black hole in a lopsided path and piling up in the region of their orbits farthest from the galaxy's central black hole.

In January 1999 an international team of astronomers using NASA's Hubble Space Telescope announced the discovery of a system of star clusters that seems to have been created, or perhaps orphaned, during the destruction of a galaxy by the galaxy NGC 1316.

In May, after an eight-year study of galactic distances with the Hubble Space Telescope, a team of scientists concluded that the universe is about 12 billion years old, with a maximum possible age, depending on a number of variables, of 15 billion years. Previous estimates of the universe's age had ranged between 10 billion and 20 billion years. The team also decided that the value of the Hubble constant—the rate of the universe's expansion—was approximately 70, meaning a galaxy would appear to be receding at the rate of about 44 mi (70 km) per second for every megaparsec (3.26 million light-years) of distance from Earth.

Though only in its beginning stages, the multinational Sloan Digital Sky Survey—using the 100-inch (2.5-m)-diameter telescope at Apache Point, NM—discovered three of the four farthest known quasars. By 2004 the project will produce a 10-terabyte "digital encyclopedia" of the sky that reaches some 50 times farther into space than the famed Palomar Observatory Sky Survey.

Astro-Technology. During 1999 the second 325-inch (8.2-m)-diameter Very Large Telescope (VLT) of the European Southern Observatory (ESO) in Paranal, Chile, saw its "first light." In January astronomers from the National Astronomical Observatory of Japan presented the first astronomical images from the latest telescope atop Hawaii's Mauna Kea—the 329-inch (8.3-m)-diameter Subaru Telescope. The images included Jupiter, Saturn, the Orion Nebula, a galaxy cluster, and a distant quasar.

A survey of 2,500 images and 17 hours of video from the February 1987 Hubble Space Telescope servicing mission revealed 788 potential debris impacts on the orbiting observatory. Beginning on May 17, 500,000 people from 96 countries began helping in the search for extraterrestrial intelligence by using their desktop computers to examine data gathered by some of the world's largest radio telescopes. Within a month the number of volunteers had jumped to 600,000 from 205 countries.

Also in May, the Hobby-Eberly Telescope Consortium announced the first light of the Marcario Low-Resolution Spectrograph (LRS) attached to the Hobby-Eberly Telescope (HET)—the third-largest telescope in the world. Built for a fraction of the cost of a conventional telescope of its size, the HET has a primary mirror 436 inches (11 m) across consisting of 91 mirror segments. On June 25 the first of the twin 317-inch (8.1-m) Gemini telescopes, equipped with adaptive optics from the University of Hawaii, was dedicated near the summit of Hawaii's Mauna Kea. The Gemini Observatory Project is a multinational effort to build two nearly identical 317-inch (8.1-m) telescopes that together can explore the entire sky in both optical and infrared light. In November the Hubble Space Telescope ceased its operations because of a faulty gyroscope. A service mission to fix the problem was completed successfully in late December.

DENNIS MAMMANA
Reuben H. Fleet Space Theater and Science Center

Australia

Australians were in a restless and reflective mood in 1999. The nation undertook increased regional commitments and enjoyed strong economic growth but faced a continuing gulf between affluent city dwellers and poorer rural residents. The government passed major tax reforms. Sydney continued to prepare to host the Summer Olympics in 2000. Meanwhile, voters rejected a proposal to replace the constitutional monarchy with a republic.

Politics. The merits of seeking a new national identity through constitutional change were debated widely, with the media and the Australian Labor Party (ALP) taking a pro-republic stand. The most prominent supporters of a republic were leading lawyers and Labor politicians (and former prime ministers), two former governors-general, and some Liberal members of the cabinet. Opponents included Liberal Prime Minister John Howard (a firm supporter of the constitutional monarchy), former Governor-General Bill Hayden, and the National Party.

Preliminary polls revealed a clear preference for a popularly elected president to replace the governor-general. But the actual referendum, which proposed that the president be elected by the Federal Parliament, caused dissension among the pro-republic forces. The Australian Republican Movement supported the referendum, but other republicans said the president should be chosen directly by the people. On November 6 the question was defeated by a margin of 55% to 45%, and all six states also voted it down. The rejection was seen as reflecting general dissatisfaction with "the elites, perceived, real, or otherwise," and widespread disappointment arising from unfulfilled expectations and, more particularly, from the hardships resulting from globalization and adverse costs that destroyed the viability of traditional rural and manufacturing industries. Immediately after the vote, opposition leader Kim Beazley promised that the ALP would make support for a republic a major electoral issue; however, caucus members, concerned by the referendum's rejection, retreated from that position.

With employment trends continuing to reduce union strength, the ALP faced funding pressures, with reports indicating that "the party's trade union base [was now] weaker than at any time in the 20th century." Coupled with declines in union membership was a weakening of stable employment—another element in the challenge facing Labor in defining its future policy course. In November, ALP National Secretary Gary Grey announced his resignation, effective in March 2000.

In a Nov. 6, 1999, referendum, 45% of Australia's electorate voted "yes" in favor of changing Australia into a republic with a parliamentarily-elected president; 55% voted "no," retaining the British monarch as the nation's head of state.

AUSTRALIA • Information Highlights

Official Name: Commonwealth of Australia.
Location: Southwestern Pacific Ocean.
Area: 2,967,896 sq mi (7 686 850 km^2).
Population (July 1999 est.): 18,783,551.
Chief Cities (mid-1993 est., metro. areas): Canberra, the capital, 325,400; Sydney, 3,719,000; Melbourne, 3,187,500; Brisbane, 1,421,700.
Government: *Head of state,* Elizabeth II, queen; represented by Sir William Deane, governor-general (took office February 1996). *Head of government,* John Howard, prime minister (took office March 1996). *Legislature*—Federal Parliament: Senate and House of Representatives.
Monetary Unit: Australian dollar (0.6460 A$ equals U.S.$1, Dec. 28, 1999).
Gross Domestic Product (1998 est. U.S.$): $393,900,-000,000 (purchasing power parity).
Economic Indexes (1998, 1990 = 100): *Consumer Prices,* all items, 117.3; food, 122.3. *Industrial Production,* 118.0.
Foreign Trade (1998 U.S.$): *Imports,* $64,668,000,000; *exports,* $55,895,000,000.

Other political events during 1999 showed that the electorate no longer favored big-picture politics and political brashness. A return to more-traditional values was evident in September in the surprise defeat, after seven years in office, of Victoria's Liberal Premier Jeff Kennett by the Labor Party's Steve Bracks. Kennett, the nation's highest-profile premier, had projected arrogance, calling the race an "unloseable election." In the poll, the divide between inner-city "elites" and outer-suburban and rural residents was translated into an uprising in popular sentiment. By contrast, Howard's continued good showing in opinion polls owed much to his attention to "the concerns of ordinary people."

In June the High Court invalidated the October 1998 election of Heather Hill, One Nation's only member of the federal legislature. The court said that Hill was ineligible to take her Senate seat, because she had not renounced her British citizenship at the time of the election. The seat was awarded to another One Nation candidate.

In November, Prime Minister Howard initiated a government-funded $70 million program to restore basic transactions services, including banking, to struggling rural towns. At the same time, a new philanthropic foundation, Australian Rural Partnership, was launched to encourage business, communities, and government to take innovative steps to develop the economy and create jobs in rural communities. The federal government contributed $11 million as a start-up for a $100 million fund aimed at generating support for corporate giving and investment to improve the social, cultural, environmental, and economic well-being of rural Australia.

Foreign Policy and Defense. A major reorientation in foreign policy led to an enlarged regional role for Australia during 1999. Australian leaders participated prominently in discussions leading to a referendum on the future status of the Indonesian province of East Timor. The country led a multinational military force to stop the violence that erupted in East Timor after its residents voted overwhelmingly on August 30 to break away from Indonesia. Earlier, the Australia-Indonesia Security Agreement, which had been signed with President Suharto in December 1995, was suspended. These moves indicated Australia's new willingness to accept a regional leadership role. Heavier defense outlays were foreshadowed and significant funds committed to help launch East Timor as a new nation.

Jiang Zemin's visit to Australia in September was the first by a Chinese president. It resulted in closer ties between Canberra and Beijing—a development unaffected by Australia's trade relationship with Taiwan.

Economy. Federal surpluses continued to reflect the nation's economic growth. The 1999–2000 budget presented in May by Treasurer Peter Costello anticipated a $5.4 billion surplus after the continuing reduction in federal debt made possible by a selldown to 51% in the government's share of telecommunications leader Telstra. Costello forecast a 3% growth in gross domestic product (GDP), which subsequently was revised to 4%, as well as unemployment under 7% and 2% inflation for the year ending June 2000. New funding of $800 million was provided for the biotechnology industry, cited as a generator of income growth.

Legislation to implement a 10% goods and services tax (GST) from July 1, 2000, was approved by the Senate after concessions to the Australian Democrats; passage by the House of Representatives was a formality. The GST was a key element of a comprehensive tax-reform program to enable cuts in personal income taxes (with major benefits going to those earning less than $55,000 a year) and corporate taxes.

To add to pledged commercial funding, the federal government and the governments of South Australia and the Northern Territory each provided $165 million toward a $1.23 billion project to construct a south-north Alice Springs–Darwin rail link. In addition, $250 million was allocated to improving the nation's rail infrastructure.

R. M. YOUNGER
Author, "Australia and the Australians"

Austria

The strong performance of outsider Jorg Haider, head of the right-wing Freedom Party (FPÖ), in parliamentary elections in October 1999 threw Austria's coalition government into turmoil.

Domestic Affairs. In the months prior to the elections, tensions increased within the ruling coalition of the Social Democratic Party of Austria (SPÖ), led by Federal Chancellor Viktor Klima, and the Christian Democratic Austrian People's Party (ÖVP), headed by Vice-Chancellor and Foreign Minister Wolfgang Schüssel. The coalition wrangled over such issues as the status of Austria's neutrality, the country's relationship with the North Atlantic Treaty Organization (NATO), and reforms related to taxation, social welfare, and retirement.

The FPÖ's growing popularity also put considerable pressure on the SPÖ and ÖVP. The party campaigned not only by criticizing the heritage of the SPÖ (the longest-ruling social democratic government in Europe since 1970) and the coalition, but also by appealing to "protest voters" wanting to express dissatisfaction with the government's practices of political privilege and patronage. Haider, a right-wing populist, touched a chord of anti–European Union (EU) and xenophobic sentiment in his supporters. Many observers both in and out of the country found the party's success disturbing, and Haider himself was accused by some foreign media of being a "neo-Nazi."

Before the October elections, the SPÖ stated that it would not consider forming a coalition government with the FPÖ, and the ÖVP promised to go into opposition should it finish lower than second place. On election day the FPÖ made a substantial gain at the polls, picking up 11 parliamentary seats. While the SPÖ finished first with 33.1% of the vote and 65 seats, this represented a loss of 4.9% and six seats compared with 1995 results. Meanwhile, the ÖVP and FPÖ won the same percentage of the vote (26.9%) and earned the same number of seats in parliament (52 each); however, the final count showed that the FPÖ had beaten the ÖVP by the slimmest of margins—a mere 415 votes. The Liberal Forum received only 3.65% of the vote and fell below the threshold necessary to be represented in parliament.

After the elections, the ÖVP said it would honor its promise to go into opposition, which ruled out the possibility of keeping the old coalition in power. However, in mid-December it stated its preparedness to enter a coalition government and began negotiations with the SPÖ. At the end of 1999, Austria remained in a parliamentary deadlock, and the previous government continued to serve in a transitional capacity.

The Austrian economy experienced a modest growth rate of 2% in 1999. Inflation reached a 40-year low at 0.5%, and unemployment shrank to 4.2%, the third-lowest rate in the EU and considerably lower than the EU average of 9.2%.

European Union. Austria, which completed its six-month term in the presidency of the EU at the end of 1998, was among the 11 EU member states to participate in the introduction of the euro on Jan. 1, 1999. The country needed to maintain a restrictive budget policy because of the so-called convergence criteria of the Maastricht Treaty, which established benchmarks for government spending and deficits for EU members.

Austria's elections for the European Parliament, held on June 13, were notable for the low voter turnout (49%). The SPÖ received 31.7% of the vote and held seven seats, picking up one; the ÖVP won 30.7% and maintained its seven seats; the FPÖ took 23.5%, losing one seat to hold five; and the Greens earned 9.3%, adding one seat for a total of four.

Avalanche. On February 23 and 24, massive snowslides hit the small ski towns of Galtür and Valzur, located in a region of Austria that had not seen a major avalanche since at least the 17th century. A total of 38 persons were killed, and about 10,000 stranded tourists needed to be flown out of the area by helicopter.

LONNIE JOHNSON, *Author*
"Central Europe: Enemies, Neighbors, Friends"

AUSTRIA • Information Highlights

Official Name: Republic of Austria.
Location: Central Europe.
Area: 32,378 sq mi (83 858 km^2).
Population (July 1999 est.): 8,139,299.
Chief Cities (Dec. 31, 1997 est.): Vienna, the capital, 1,609,600; Graz, 239,990; Linz, 190,136; Salzburg, 144,692; Innsbruck, 110,454.
Government: *Head of state,* Thomas Klestil, president (took office July 8, 1992). *Head of government,* Viktor Klima, chancellor (took office January 1997). *Legislature*—Federal Assembly: Federal Council and National Council.
Monetary Unit: Schilling (13.6803 schillings equal U.S. $1, Dec. 14, 1999).
Gross Domestic Product (1998 est. U.S.$): $184,500,-000,000 (purchasing power parity).
Economic Indexes (1998, 1990 = 100): *Consumer Prices,* all items, 122.0; food, 117.7. *Industrial Production,* 132.3.
Foreign Trade (1998 U.S.$): *Imports,* $68,194,000,000; *exports,* $62,740,000,000.

Automobiles

Reorganized top managements at each of the Big Three automakers—General Motors (GM), Ford, and the merged DaimlerChrysler (DC)—helped by a buoyant U.S. economy, drove U.S. new-car and truck sales to an all-time record in 1999. Analysts forecast that 1999 sales comfortably would eclipse the previous record of 16,026,426 retail deliveries, set in 1986.

For the first eight months of 1999 alone, sales by dealers ran nearly 1 million vehicles ahead of the comparable 1986 pace. A continuing surge in demand for light trucks, including minivans and sports-utility vehicles (SUVs), more than made up for a decline from 1986 of about 1.5 million units in sales of new passenger cars. In the January–August period, the light-truck category accounted for 5,507,804 retail sales, up nearly 2.5 million from the same level in the previous record year. New-car sales, meanwhile, tumbled to 6,009,157 in the first eight months of 1999, and analysts predicted that the gap between cars and trucks would narrow even more in the year 2000.

As the 2000-model year began, optimism continued for extension of the brisk automotive sales pace, based on seven consecutive years of sales exceeding 15 million in the United States. Low interest rates, growth in short-term leasing, and increases in two- and three-vehicle families helped to keep consumer demand high.

In the past, the bullish atmosphere would have served to retain the status quo in management teams of the new-car manufacturers. But that was not the case in 1999. As top executives savored record profits and compensation packages, GM, Ford, and the merged and reorganized DaimlerChrysler (DC) dramatically revamped their administrative structures. Complacency was the enemy, and global vision into the new millennium was the overarching theme.

DaimlerChrysler introduced the newly designed PT Cruiser, resembling a cross between a London taxi and a 1937 Plymouth. It was set to go on sale in May 2000.

Courtesy, DaimlerChrysler

Courtesy, Honda

In 1999, Honda presented the S2000 convertible, a brand-new, two-seater roadster with a 240-horsepower engine. It features an electronic start button.

General Motors. With GM's market share fallen to the 29% level in the United States, GM's chairman and chief executive officer (CEO), John F. (Jack) Smith, Jr., 62, in late 1998 had appointed two younger executives to orchestrate a turnaround for the Number 1 automaker. Named president and chief operating officer was G. Richard Wagoner, Jr., 46. To succeed Wagoner as president of North American operations, Smith assigned a relative newcomer to GM, marketing expert Ronald L. Zarrella, 50.

As advocates of "brand management" throughout GM's sales and marketing systems, Wagoner and Zarrella directed a revamping in 1999. General managers were replaced by "brand managers" at Buick, Chevrolet, Oldsmobile, and Pontiac-GMC. Only Cadillac and Saturn retained a general-manager style of management.

Ford. At Ford a dynamic acquisition and management-reshuffling program was put into place in January upon the installation of Jacques A. Nasser, 52, as president and CEO, and of William Clay Ford, Jr., 42, as nonexecutive chairman. After Ford purchased Sweden's Volvo Car Corporation early in the year for about $6.5 billion, the Australian-raised Nasser set the tone by creating an international five-brand luxury-car group, led by the former Number 2 executive at Germany's BMW automaker, Wolfgang Reitzle, 51.

Along with Reitzle, Nasser brought in 15 senior executives from other automakers or manufacturers to streamline Ford's operations. The influx prompted an outgo of seven entrenched senior executives, the foremost being the chief financial officer, John M. Devine, 55.

In a company-wide commitment long pursued by the new chairman, William Ford—the first member of the founding Ford family to occupy the chairmanship since his uncle, Henry Ford II, retired in 1980—the company served notice it would seek to replace GM and become the top-producing automaker in the world by 2005. At the same time, Ford would address global environmental issues for all of its products.

DaimlerChrysler (DC). Globalization also became an overriding organizational force, as the youngest member of the "Big Three"—Chrysler Corporation—linked up with Germany's Daimler-Benz in 1998. The chairmen and CEOs of Daimler-Benz and Chrysler—Jürgen Schrempp, 55, and Robert J. Eaton, 60, respectively—sought to depict the newly formed DaimlerChrysler as a "merger" rather than an acquisition, even though Daimler-Benz purchased the majority of Chrysler's common stock. Schrempp and Eaton cast themselves as chairmen and co-CEOs of DC, with "coexisting" headquarters in Stuttgart, Germany, and Auburn Hills, MI.

But by October 1999, it was obvious that the 75-year-old Chrysler Corporation had given up its independent status, and the controlling power had moved to Stuttgart. A gradual departure of senior executives that had begun early in 1999 wound up in September with a reorganization in which DC President Thomas T. Stallkamp, 53, agreed to retire as of Dec. 31, 1999. Sharp differences of opinion between Stallkamp, who had led the integration of the U.S. company's operations with those of Daimler-Benz, and Schrempp led to the American's downfall.

Stallkamp's replacement as president of the DC sales division was the company's former chief of U.S. sales and marketing, James P. Holden, 48. Further disruptions in the Chrysler part of the DC lineup were expected. Eaton himself reportedly was preparing to bow out as co-CEO well before his contractual retirement date of Dec. 31, 2001.

In the midst of the furor preceding the realignment in the executive suite, DC and the UAW agreed to one of the most generous contracts in auto-industry history. The first four-year contract in the industry, later adopted in principle by GM and Ford, gave the 400,000 UAW autoworkers in the United States a 3% annual raise, plus cost-of-living increases; a $1,350 signing bonus; "lifetime" employment for those with ten years' seniority; increased pensions; continued profit-sharing plans; and an unprecedented promise not to close or sell any UAW-represented plant. UAW President Stephen Yokich, who at 63 was serving his last term, called the contract "among the best" in the union's 63-year history. The record-breaking sales year and its positive impact on profits also helped melt employer resistance to the UAW's demands. Net income at GM rose from $2 billion in the first half of 1998 to $3.9 billion in the same period of 1999; Ford's net income increased from $3.9 billion to $4.3 billion; and DC saw its net income jump from $2.9 billion to $3.2 billion.

Global Trends. Toyota became the first foreign-headquartered automaker to introduce a full-size truck in the United States. Called the Tundra and equipped with a V-8 engine, it was built in a new plant in Princeton, IN. Honda announced plans to build a new plant for a minivan in Lincoln, AL. Production would start in 2002. France's Renault made a controlling investment in Japan's embattled Nissan Motor. Renault senior executive Carlos Ghosn took charge of Nissan operations. Japan's Mazda Motor was being operated similarly by its U.S. "parent," Ford.

The Plymouth and Mercury brand names were phased out of the Canadian market, and DC advised dealers it was planning to drop the 71-year-old Plymouth nameplate in the United States by 2002.

A manufacturing manager, Cynthia Trudell, was named president and CEO of GM's Saturn car division, becoming the first woman to head a U.S. automaking operation. Saturn, after ten years of building only subcompact cars, added a midsize LS series in Wilmington, DE.

South Korea's Daewoo entered the U.S. market with three car models—the midsize Leganza, the compact Nubira, and the subcompact Lanos. Korean car sales, also including Hyundai and its new subsidiary, Kia,

Saturn's new series of sedans (LS) and station wagons (LW) are assembled in Wilmington, DE. The LW2 wagon, below, offers a four-speed automatic transmission.

Courtesy, Saturn

Courtesy, Toyota

The Echo, Toyota's new subcompact for 2000, has a suggested retail price of $9,995. It is roomier than the Tercel it replaces and features interior storage bins.

jumped in 1999 to 2.5% of the U.S. market, with about 300,000 sales.

The 2000/2001 Models. With better-built new vehicles helping U.S. producers catch up with their foreign-based competitors in quality and durability, styling departments figured more prominently in the battles for volume and market share. "Styling sells" was a focus heard in every executive suite.

Swooping hood and fender lines, enlarged and curvaceous taillight pods, and even reconfigured door handles stamped new cars and trucks in all price segments. Among styling pacesetters for 2000 and 2001 were DC's Chrysler PT Cruiser and Dodge Dakota pickup club cab, Ford's Focus compact and Lincoln LS sedans, GM's Chevrolet Impala and Saturn LS sedans, and Nissan's Frontier four-door pickup and Maxima sedan. A long-lagging two-seater segment was revitalized by Honda's new S2000 roadster and the restyled Mitsubishi Eclipse and Porsche Boxster coupes.

At the extremes of the market, Toyota made news when its new Echo subcompact went on sale for suggested retail prices starting at $9,995, while Ford introduced the largest SUV of all—the Excursion—in the $35,000–$40,000 range.

All-electric-powered cars, hurt by limited driving ranges between time-consuming battery recharges, suffered a severe sales snag. Honda dropped its battery-powered EV Plus but quickly replaced it with the Insight hybrid sedan, which offered both a small gasoline engine for city driving and battery power for rural trips. Toyota's Prius hybrid sedan was due to join the Insight on the U.S. market in the fall of 2000.

A retro look set apart both the 2001 Chrysler PT Cruiser, with a vertical double grille recalling British cabs of the 1930s, and Volkswagen's 2000 New Beetle, built in Mexico as an update of the classic rear-engine "Bug." SUVs drew increased design attention as their sales numbers expanded along with those of four-door and two-door pickup trucks and minivans, but an effort to tighten federal fuel-economy standards on trucks to match those on passenger cars was defeated in the U.S. Congress. Automakers and the UAW lobbied against the proposal.

Motoring Briefs. Two of Oldsmobile's oldest nameplates, Cutlass and 88, were discontinued. Republic Industries, after purchasing 270 dealerships in three years to become the largest U.S. network in retail auto sales, changed its name to AutoNation, Inc., and estimated that its annual sales would approach $20 billion. In step with DaimlerChrysler, Ford/Jaguar/Mazda/Volvo, GM/Saab/Isuzu, and Renault/Nissan, six major independents—BMW, Fiat, Mitsubishi, Daewoo, Subaru, and Peugeot-Citroen—were in play as prospective global partners. The American Automobile Manufacturers Association, left with only two U.S.-based members after the marriage of Daimler-Benz and Chrysler, ceased operations.

MAYNARD M. GORDON, *Senior Editor "Ward's Dealer Business Magazine"*

WORLD MOTOR VEHICLE PRODUCTION, 1998

Country	Passenger Car Production	Light Truck Production	% Change from 1997—Cars, Trucks, and Buses
Argentina	353,068	81,929	3%
Australia	350,000	30,000	10%
Austria	91,264	268	–4%
Belgium	318,528	84,647	–6%
Brazil	1,244,463	243,908	–24%
Canada	1,122,287	1,001,638	–4%
China	507,103	1,079,872	3%
Czech Republic	368,328	35,218	12%
France	2,603,021	301,544	15%
Germany	5,348,115	224,769	14%
Hungary	89,738	0	16%
India	384,139	57,331	–14%
Italy	1,402,382	251,514	–7%
Japan	8,055,763	1,147,671	–8%
Malaysia	126,410	7,339	–50%
Mexico	952,909	464,911	7%
The Netherlands	242,989	0	24%
Poland	380,000	30,000	29%
Portugal	138,890	16,540	7%
Romania	92,163	21,388	–10%
Russia	903,355	144,193	–13%
Serbia	12,908	1,911	19%
Slovenia	103,212	14,825	23%
South Korea	1,625,125	284,369	–31%
Spain	2,216,571	588,031	10%
Sweden	368,305	0	1%
Taiwan	293,009	106,194	6%
Ukraine*	11,316	7	—
United Kingdom	1,748,277	210,443	2%
United States	5,554,390	6,109,264	–1%
Uzbekistan	65,000	0	8%
Total**	37,236,644	12,599,442	–2%

Source: "Ward's Automotive Reports"

*First year of production.

**Production figures exclude 1,632,406 vehicles from "Assembly" plants, including 659,583 from Belgium; 286,367 from South Africa; 158,130 from Thailand; 125,145 from Slovak Republic; and 111,920 from Portugal.

Azerbaijan

In 1999, Heydar Aliyev celebrated 30 years in power in Azerbaijan, first as party boss under communism, and since 1993 as president. However, the country's uncertain future became evident in April, when the 75-year-old Aliyev underwent coronary bypass surgery in the United States. Few decisions could be made during his six-week absence—an indication of the political vacuum that is likely to occur in Azerbaijan when the president is no longer in office.

AZERBAIJAN • Information Highlights

Official Name: Azerbaijani Republic.
Location: Southwest Asia.
Area: 33,436 sq mi (86 600 km²).
Population (July 1999 est.): 7,908,224.
Chief Cities (January 1990 est.): Baku, the capital, 1,149,000; Gyanja, 281,000; Sumgait, 235,000.
Government: *Head of state,* Heydar Aliyev, president (took office June 1993). *Head of government,* Artur Rasizade, prime minister (took office November 1996). *Legislature* (unicameral)—National Assembly.
Monetary Unit: Manat (4,373.0 manats equal U.S.$1, Jan. 3, 2000).
Gross Domestic Product (1998 est. U.S.$): $12,900,-000,000 (purchasing power parity).
Economic Index (1998, 1993 = 100): *Consumer Prices,* all items, 11,131.0; food, 10,816.9.
Foreign Trade (1997 U.S.$): *Imports,* $794,000,000; *exports,* $781,000,000.

Domestic Affairs. Despite Aliyev's suggestion that he might consider running for president a third time in 2003, his son Ilkham was being promoted as a likely successor. At the December congress of the ruling Yeni Azerbaijan (New Azerbaijan) party, President Aliyev was elected chairman and his son deputy chairman.

Although the opposition continued to be beset by rivalries, it organized significant resistance to the regime in 1999. The slander trial of former President Abulfaz Elchibey, chairman of the opposition Azerbaijan Popular Front, began in January, but it was dropped shortly afterward—a small victory for the government's opponents. The following month, several Yeni Azerbaijan members of parliament defected to the opposition, saying that the party leadership was undemocratic. The opposition in parliament created a group called the Democratic Bloc, which then joined with the 23-party Movement for Democracy to campaign against a new draft law on local elections, a bill that could be used to impose more restrictions on the media, and government policy in the dispute with Armenia over the Nagorno-Karabakh territory. The election law was amended somewhat, but the opposition still found itself with few opportunities for control and supervision of elections to prevent fraud.

Nevertheless, the opposition, which boycotted the October 1998 presidential elections, participated in the local elections, held on December 12. But the results, which overwhelmingly favored Yeni Azerbaijan, immediately came under fire not only by the opposition, but also by Council of Europe observers, who claimed to have seen ballot stuffing and other illegalities. Although there was government harassment, the opposition formed a body to collect evidence of electoral misconduct during the vote.

Despite the beginning of oil exports to Georgia in March, the discovery of new gas fields, increased oil prices, low inflation, and up to 10% growth in Azerbaijan's gross domestic product (GDP), the economic situation remained largely grim. To deal with Azerbaijan's poverty and high unemployment, President Aliyev announced in December the formation of a new "state oil fund" designed to use profits from oil sales to finance investments in infrastructure and social programs.

Foreign Affairs. The issue of Nagorno-Karabakh continued to dominate foreign policy. Direct talks between President Aliyev and Armenian President Robert Kocharian in the summer, sharply criticized by the opposition, went nowhere. The resignation in the fall of three top government officials—Aliyev's foreign-policy adviser Vafa Guluzade, Foreign Minister Tofik Zulfugarov, and Eldar Namazov, head of the presidential administrative secretariat—reinforced speculation that the Nagorno-Karabakh issue was dividing the leadership. Meanwhile, Azerbaijan continued to have tense relations with Russia and Iran. In January, Guluzade asked for a North Atlantic Treaty Organization (NATO) base to be established in Azerbaijan, but was refused. Nevertheless, the request reflected the country's increasing ties with the West. Azerbaijan's closest allies in the Caucasus in 1999 were Georgia and Turkey, with which Azerbaijan signed an agreement on the construction of a Baku-Ceyhan oil pipeline.

STEPHEN F. JONES, *Mount Holyoke College*

Baltic Republics

The Russian economic crisis of late 1998, as well as the indigenous politics of language and citizenship in the Baltic region, significantly affected politics and economic policy in Estonia, Latvia, and Lithuania during 1999. Estonia elected a new parliament, and Latvia a new president, while policy differences with the president of Lithuania led to turnover in the office of prime minister. Foreign relations in the three countries continued along a Westward path, while the Baltics recognized the necessity of coexisting with their powerful neighbor, Russia.

Politics. The paramount event in Estonia was the election of a new Riigikogu (parliament) in March. A late-1998 law banning electoral alliances had the desired effect of reducing the number of parties in the new parliament from 12 to seven. The left populist Centre Party won the most seats, 28 of 101, but was excluded from the center-right coalition that formed the new government with a bare majority of 53 votes. Mart Laar, a 39-year-old historian and former prime minister (1992–94), headed the government, which offered a strong pro-Western and free-market economic program.

In June the Latvian Saeima (parliament) elected a new president, Vaira Vike-Freiberga. She became the first democratically elected woman to serve as head of state in a former communist country, and the second North American émigré to assume that office in the Baltic region. A Latvian by birth, Vike-Freiberga spent her adult life in Canada as a professor of psychology at the University of Montreal.

In Latvia in June 1999, Vaira Vike-Freiberga, above, *became the first democratically elected female head of state in the formerly communist countries of Europe.*

While no elections occurred in Lithuania in 1999, three different prime ministers held office during the year. The conflict was driven as much by personality and cultural differences as by policy disputes. As a former U.S. public official, President Valdas Adamkus brought with him a sense of the presidency as a bully pulpit. During the spring, he crossed swords with Prime Minister Gediminas Vagnorius, declaring on national television that he had no confidence in his leadership. Parliament rebuked Adamkus by voting its confidence in Vagnorius, but to no avail. The president, with an approval rating of 88%, prevailed, and the prime minister resigned.

He was succeeded by Rolandas Paksas, the 42-year-old mayor of Vilnius, the capital. Prime Minister Paksas agreed to abide by a pending international deal to privatize the Lithuanian oil complex. However, in the fall, when the time came to conclude the sale to a U.S. firm, Williams International Company, Paksas balked. He insisted that the financial terms were unfavorable to Lithuania. The cabinet rebelled, voting to close the deal, and the prime minister resigned in protest. President Adamkus then asked Andrius Kubilius, the 42-year-old deputy speaker of parliament, to form a new government. The sale was completed, but Lithuanian public opinion opposed the privatization, and in

BALTIC REPUBLICS • Information Highlights

Nation	Population (in millions)	Area (sq mi)	Area (km^2)	Capital	Head of State and Government
Estonia	1.4	17,462	45 226	Tallinn	Lennart Meri, president Mart Laar, prime minister
Latvia	2.4	24,938	64 589	Riga	Vaira Vike-Freiberga, president Andris Skele, prime minister
Lithuania	3.6	25,174	65 200	Vilnius	Valdas Adamkus, president Andrius Kubilius, prime minister

less than a month the president's approval rating plummeted to 47% from 82%.

Politics were less volatile in the other Baltic states. In late 1998 both Latvia and Estonia had liberalized parts of their citizenship law under pressure from the European Union (EU) as well as Russia. In effect, both states allowed ethnic Russian children who were born to stateless parents in the 1990s and who were under certain ages to become citizens. However, during 1999 both countries were putting in place language laws unfavorable to their Russian minorities and considered restrictive by European standards. In Latvia, President Vike-Freiberga was only partially successful in persuading parliament to soften the law, which received final approval in December.

Economy. Because of its foreign trade with Russia, the Baltic region was hit hard by the Russian economic crisis of August 1998. Estonia, which had succeeded in reorienting more of its foreign trade Westward, was affected the least, while Lithuania suffered the greatest impact. In Estonia, Russia's problems caused a sharp economic decline. Bankruptcies occurred, unemployment increased, and the gross domestic product (GDP) fell, leading to a budget crisis, since the government had anticipated higher tax revenue and increased domestic spending. The impact was greatest in the predominantly ethnic-Russian northeast, where unemployment soared from the nationwide average of 5.3% to 9.5%. Estonian trade with Russia as a percentage of its total trade declined from double digits to 8.7% by January 1999. By April the government was cutting the budget and lowering its growth estimates for the year. First-quarter GDP dropped by 5.6%, but in the second quarter it fell only 2.4%, leading the Central Bank to conclude that the economy was rebounding and would end with zero growth. A bright spot was that Moody's gave Estonia an A1 rating for domestic-currency obligations, reflecting the country's small domestic-currency debt.

Latvia, for which Russia was the second-largest market, felt the crisis in three waves. Initially, it hit the companies selling directly to Russia; next, the companies supplying the exporters; and, finally, all firms selling to consumers, since rising unemployment reduced domestic demand. By May 1999 unemployment reached 10.2%, with the unofficial rate estimated at 16%–17%. During the first quarter, GDP fell by 2.3%, but it was down only 1.8% in the second quarter, suggesting a leveling off and a better second half. Still, by September the budget had to be cut due to a shortfall in revenue, as many of the hardest-hit export firms had to request tax-payment extensions. Nevertheless, Standard and Poor's gave Latvia a vote of confidence by reaffirming its credit rating of BBB, indicating a favorable environment for foreign investment.

The effect of the Russian crisis on Lithuania was the worst and lasted the longest. Russia was Lithuania's biggest trade partner, at nearly a quarter of all exports and imports. Industries reliant on this trade equaled 30% of GDP, which fell by 4.8% in the first quarter, precipitating a budget crisis. By fall 1999 salaries were delayed for all but the most important government employees in order to avoid defaulting on international obligations. Compounding Lithuania's economic problems, a Russian oil company, trying to block the sale of the oil complex to the Williams Company, cut off the supply of crude oil to the refinery.

Foreign Relations. There were signs that post-Soviet unity among the Baltic states on their common foreign-policy goals was more expedient than durable. Estonia's foreign minister observed that the concept of "the Baltic states" was a Western construct, and that in fact they were on divergent paths. Viewing itself as a Nordic country, Estonia was moving toward Finland and Sweden. Lithuania, with its Central European identity, gravitated toward Poland. Nonetheless, the three countries continued to work together toward gaining admission to the North Atlantic Treaty Organization (NATO). In this connection, several common steps were taken in 1999, including domestic commitments to raise defense spending to 2% of GDP—the NATO benchmark—over the next several years; to open a Baltic defense college in Estonia to train officers to meet NATO standards; and to support the NATO air strikes in the campaign over Kosovo.

Lithuania's parliament ratified a border treaty with Russia, as well as a bilateral agreement on economic exploitation of the continental shelf for fishing and future oil drilling. Latvia gained admission to the World Trade Organization (WTO) in February and "graduated" from the U.S. foreign-aid program at midyear. Finally, in March, Estonia initialed a border treaty with Russia after seven years of negotiations, and joined the WTO in November.

ROBERT SHARLET, *Union College*

Bangladesh

During 1999, Bangladesh continued to struggle with many problems, including internal political strife, an increase in terrorism and other violence, and an economic slowdown.

Politics. Throughout the year, the Bangladesh Nationalist Party (BNP) led numerous demonstrations and *hartals* (strikes) to protest police actions against opposition activists, price hikes, the deterioration of law and order, and other issues. The opposition also demanded early general elections and the immediate resignation of Prime Minister Sheikh Hasina Wajed's Awami League (AL) government. The government reacted to the *hartals* by confronting participants on the streets, increasing the tension. Meanwhile, public sentiment against *hartals* grew.

In February the government held elections in 30 *pourasavas* (municipalities) across the country. They were boycotted by the opposition, which demanded the removal of the chief election commissioner and called a 66-hour countrywide *hartal* to counter the elections. In late 1999 the government was preparing to hold *upazila* (subdistrict) elections, and again the opposition threatened not to participate unless the elections were held under a caretaker administration.

In April the Jatiya Party (JP) of former president Gen. Hussain Mohammad Ershad split into two groups. Ershad's deputy, Mizanur Rahman Chowdhury, formed a separate executive committee with himself as chairman, criticizing Ershad for shifting his support from the AL government to the BNP. Nearly half of the JP members of parliament, including a government minister, joined the new faction.

BANGLADESH • Information Highlights

Official Name: People's Republic of Bangladesh.
Location: South Asia.
Area: 55,598 sq mi (144 000 km^2).
Population (July 1999 est.): 127,117,967.
Chief Cities (1991 census): Dhaka, the capital, 3,637,892; Chittagong, 1,566,070; Khulna, 601,051.
Government: *Head of state,* Shahabuddin Ahmed, president (took office October 1996). *Head of government,* Sheikh Hasina Wajed, prime minister (sworn in June 1996). *Legislature*—unicameral National Parliament.
Monetary Unit: Taka (49.50 takas equal U.S.$1, Nov. 2, 1999).
Gross Domestic Product (1998 est. U.S.$): $175,500,-000,000 (purchasing power parity).
Economic Indexes: *Consumer Prices* (1997, 1990 = 100): all items, 132.9; food, 134.0. *Industrial Production* (1998, 1990 = 100): 179.7.
Foreign Trade (1998 U.S.$): *Imports,* $7,146,000,000; *exports,* $3,831,000,000.

Economy. The Bangladeshi economy not only suffered from the frequent *hartals* and increasing political polarization in the country, but also from the slow pace of institutional reforms and the lack of good governance. The political instability disrupted the flow of exports, discouraged foreign and domestic capital investment, and prevented many Bangladeshis from making a living. Although the recent discovery of substantial natural-gas reserves was a positive sign, initial exploration contracts became mired in political controversy and bureaucratic red tape. Although the devastating flood of 1998 diminished growth prospects, the level of food production in 1999 set an all-time high. Despite accusations of corruption and inefficiency from opposition parties, government emergency assistance reached the needy in time to avert widespread famine.

Social Issues. Crime—particularly the smuggling of foreign goods, drugs, alcohol, and guns into Bangladesh and a rise in murder, terrorism, rape, and other violence—caused major problems. In an attempt to address the issue, the prime minister replaced Home Affairs Minister Rafiqul Islam with Mohammad Nasim in March. The new home minister promptly identified Dhaka's slums as a major source of crime and ordered the eviction of slum dwellers, a move criticized by donor agencies, human-rights groups, and nongovernment organizations (NGOs). In the subsequent months, however, many criminals were arrested, and the law-and-order situation improved slightly.

In June a health survey reported that arsenic was prevalent in underground drinking-water supplies in 42 of the country's 64 districts, and that nearly two thirds of the population was at risk. The government responded by launching the Arsenic Mitigation Water Supply Project, a $44.4 million project cofunded by the World Bank, in July.

Foreign Relations. Bangladesh and India made several attempts to improve relations, including an agreement by the AL government to allow the transshipment of Indian goods through Bangladesh and the establishment in June of a bus line between Dhaka and Calcutta. But India's continued deportation of people it claimed were illegal Bangladeshi aliens sparked several border clashes. Bangladesh's purchase of eight MiG-29 jets from Russia in July was criticized both by opposition parties within the country and by foreign countries, including the United States.

BIMAL KANTI PAUL, *Kansas State University*

Banking and Finance

In late 1999 the U.S. Congress finally passed financial-modernization legislation that repealed the Glass-Steagall Act of 1933 and allowed banks, securities firms, and insurance companies to affiliate. It was also a year in which the largest bank mergers took place outside the United States, surcharges at automatic teller machines (ATMs) continued to be controversial and debated, and the profitability of the banking industry remained high.

Legislation. The Financial Services Modernization Act of 1999 (also called the Gramm-Leach-Bliley Financial Modernization Act) was signed into law by President Bill Clinton on November 12. While Congress had been considering legislation to enhance competition in the financial-services sector for more than 20 years, the banking, securities, and insurance industries had become more entwined through regulatory changes, court cases, and acquisitions. The Financial Services Modernization Act effectively repealed the Glass-Steagall Act of 1933, which required the separation of commercial and investment banking. The new law allowed for the creation of financial holding companies that engage in banking and insurance and securities underwriting, merchant banking, and real-estate development. These companies would be overseen by the Federal Reserve Board and other regulators. Unitary-thrift holding companies (in which a savings institution is owned by any kind of commercial business, e.g., Ford Motor Company) no longer would be permitted to obtain a charter from the Office of Thrift Supervision, and existing unitary thrifts could be sold only to financial companies. In addition, under the new legislation, access to the Federal Home Loan Bank System will be decentralized and its membership expanded.

Several sections of the new law dealt directly with consumer issues such as privacy, the Community Reinvestment Act (CRA) of 1977, and ATMs. Banks were required to disclose clearly their privacy policies covering the sharing of customer information with affiliates and third parties. Bank customers would be given the opportunity to "opt out" of allowing this information to be shared with third parties. Credit-card and account-number information would not be given to third-party marketers. The CRA, which encouraged banks to lend to minorities and make investments in their communities, would not be repealed in any way, and bank holding companies would not be allowed to merge with insurance or securities firms or to expand into new businesses if any member bank had an unsatisfactory CRA rating. Banks must make full disclosure of any agreement they reach with community groups regarding CRA issues, and those groups must report on how the money involved was spent. Finally, banks were required to disclose any surcharge for the use of an ATM and to allow customers to cancel transactions before any fee was imposed.

On the issue of bankruptcy reform, Congress adjourned before a vote was taken in the Senate on pending legislation. While the

© Jim Bourg/Liaison Agency

In March 1999, Fleet Financial Group announced plans to acquire the BankBoston Corporation. The new corporation would be known as the FleetBoston Corporation and would be the largest bank in New England. Although the bank-merger trend continued in the United States in 1999, most large bank mergers occurred abroad.

House of Representatives passed a bill in May, the legislation stalled in the Senate when controversial amendments were introduced. Meanwhile, the trend of increasing personal-bankruptcy filings seemed to have ended. The forecast for 1999 was for 1.3 million new bankruptcies—100,000 less than in 1998.

Regulatory Agencies. John D. Hawke, Jr., who had been named comptroller of the currency in December 1998 by President Clinton in a recess appointment, was confirmed for a full five-year term by the Senate in October. Roger W. Ferguson, Jr., was nominated in August to succeed Alice M. Rivlin as vice-chairman of the Federal Reserve Board. He became the first African-American to hold that post. Carol J. Parry, head of the community-development group at Chase Manhattan, also was named to the board. Senate action on confirmation of Parry's nomination awaited the new year, however.

The Federal Reserve's Open Market Committee raised the federal funds rate (the rate commercial banks charge each other for overnight loans) three times in 1999. The June increase was to 5%, with another 25 basis points being added in August and again in November, to make the rate 5.5% at the end of 1999. The Federal Reserve's discount rate (the rate it charges banks for loans) was raised to 4.75% in August and to 5% in November.

Mergers. While U.S. banks continued to announce mergers in 1999, none of the largest banks combined as they had in previous years. Perhaps following the U.S. trend, the largest bank mergers took place overseas instead. In Japan there was increased merger activity caused by the recent banking crisis. Dai-Ichi Kangyo Bank, Industrial Bank of Japan, and Fuji Bank agreed in August to merge to form the world's largest bank, with $1.26 trillion in assets. In October, Sumitomo Bank and Sakura Bank announced a merger that would create the world's second-largest bank.

Meanwhile, a number of hostile takeover bids were announced among the largest banks in Europe. In France, Banque Nationale de Paris failed in its attempt to acquire both Société Générale and Paribas, which would have created Europe's largest bank. Instead, it settled for acquiring Paribas alone. In Great Britain the Bank of Scotland and the Royal Bank of Scotland made separate hostile offers to take over National Westminster PLC. NatWest was determined to fight off any acquisition.

Bank and Thrift Profitability. The commercial banking industry's earnings totaled $34.9 billion for the first six months of 1999—9.1% higher than the same time period in 1998. Deposits rose 5% and assets increased 5.5% since June 1998, while equity capital decreased for the first time since 1989. The number of banks continued to decline, with a total of 8,675 in June. There were 217 banks absorbed by mergers, seven bank failures, and 117 new banks chartered in the first six months. The thrift industry had one of its best quarters ever, earning $2.9 billion in the second quarter. Profitability among thrifts was variable, however, with the smaller institutions trailing the rest of the industry.

One of the largest bank failures in two decades took place on September 1, when the Federal Deposit Insurance Corporation (FDIC) closed the First National Bank of Keystone, WV. This bank, with about $1.1 billion in assets, had listed $515 million in loans as assets when they actually had been sold. Fraud was suspected; two bank executives were arrested; and the Federal Bureau of Investigation (FBI) was looking into the case in late 1999. In another instance of possible fraud, three Russian immigrants, one of whom was an employee of the Bank of New York, were indicted in October for illegally transferring almost $7 billion over a period of three and a half years. The FBI suspected this was a case of Russian funds being laundered through a U.S. bank and continued to conduct its investigation.

Consumer Issues. The number of ATMs in the United States passed the 200,000 mark for the first time in 1999. While the availability of ATMs had increased greatly in the past few years, surcharges (fees for the use of ATMs) continued to be controversial. An increasing number of banks charged noncustomers a fee to withdraw money from an ATM, and those people also would pay a fee to their own bank for the same withdrawal. Many consumer advocates criticized this practice as charging twice for a single transaction. Banks, on the other hand, maintained that they had the right to charge for a service and to cover the cost of offering such convenience to consumers.

In November, San Francisco voters passed a measure that banned banks from charging fees to noncustomers at their ATMs. The Santa Monica city council approved a similar law at about the same time. The California Bankers Association, Bank of America, and Wells Fargo filed suit against San Francisco and Santa Monica, alleging that cities did not have the authority to regulate bank fees. Bank of America and Wells Fargo also stopped allowing noncustomers in Santa Monica to withdraw money from their ATMs. A federal judge imposed a preliminary injunction on the new ordinances until a trial could be held on their constitutionality.

ANN KESSLER
American Bankers Association

Belarus

BELARUS • Information Highlights

Official Name: Republic of Belarus.
Location: Eastern Europe.
Area: 80,155 sq mi (207 600 km²).
Population (July 1999 est.): 10,401,784.
Chief Cities (January 1998 est.): Minsk, the capital, 1,712,900; Gomel, 501,900; Mogilev, 368,900.
Government: *Head of state,* Aleksandr Lukashenko, president (took office July 1994). *Head of government,* Sergey Ling, prime minister (took office November 1996). *Legislature*—Parliament: Council of the Republic and Chamber of Representatives.
Monetary Unit: Belarusian ruble (318,000 rubles equal U.S.$1, Dec. 17, 1999).
Gross Domestic Product (1998 est. U.S.$): $53,700,-000,000.
Economic Index (1998, 1992 = 100): *Consumer Prices,* all items, 1,049,047.0; food, 1,275,657.0.
Foreign Trade (1998 est. U.S.$): *Imports,* $8,549,000,000; *exports,* $7,070,000,000.

In 1999, Belarus continued its erratic course toward political authoritarianism, an administered economy, and estrangement from the West. The only bright spot was the signing and ratification of a unification treaty with Russia in December.

Domestic Affairs. Despite his dictatorial tendencies, the nation's president, Aleksandr Lukashenko, continued to enjoy public popularity in 1999. A survey taken in the spring showed strong public approval for his government's timely payment of wages and pensions, its maintenance of an adequate food supply, and its support for public education. Much lower marks, however, were recorded for combating crime and corruption, controlling inflation, and protecting civil rights. The latter lapses continued to give Lukashenko a negative image abroad. During 1999 leading opposition politicians, human-rights activists, and independent journalists were harassed, arrested, and even, in several prominent cases, caused to "disappear" without public knowledge of their whereabouts. The regime hounded the country's critical press in various ways—via defamation lawsuits, tax fines and penalties, and suspension or revocation of publishing licenses on flimsy pretexts.

In October a major public demonstration of 15,000 to 20,000 people in Minsk, the capital, was met with force by the police and was followed by criminal proceedings against the organizers. The marchers, carrying the banned Belarusian national flag, protested the unification process with Russia and called for free parliamentary and presidential elections, in view of the fact that Lukashenko (whose term was supposed to end in July) had extended his presidency unlawfully and had organized a handpicked Parliament.

Foreign Affairs. Political repression in Belarus was condemned throughout 1999 by the United States, the Council of Europe, and the Organization for Security and Cooperation in Europe (OSCE), to little avail. The year's only positive step in relations with the West was the return of the U.S. and European ambassadors to Minsk, after President Lukashenko made amends for evicting them from the diplomatic complex in 1998.

In December, Lukashenko achieved a major foreign-policy objective with the formal signing, with President Boris Yeltsin of Russia, of a framework treaty for unifying the two countries. The parliaments of both countries overwhelmingly ratified the agreement, although the implementation of the treaty was deferred to the future by Russia.

Economy. By late summer, the Belarusian economy still was experiencing the adverse effects of Russia's financial crisis of August 1998. The high economic growth of the preceding two years had slowed to 2%; internal capital investment had decreased; and foreign trade was down sharply, particularly with Russia, Belarus' largest export market. Inflation rose from 67% in 1998 to 358% in 1999, in spite of Soviet-style price controls on many consumer goods. The Belarusian ruble remained weak, with its official exchange rate still hovering around 300,000 to $1 at the end of the year. The government reported that 17.5% of all enterprises were producing losses and that more than half of the industrial enterprises either were without working capital or were operating with insufficient capital. Because of a poor harvest, Minsk asked private entrepreneurs to donate money for grain imports. Lukashenko criticized his ministers, but no easy economic solutions were in sight as the year came to an end.

ROBERT SHARLET, *Union College*

Belgium

Food-contamination scares and electoral change dominated the 1999 Belgian scene.

Political Disaffection. For some time, the Belgian public had been disturbed by apparent bureaucratic callousness, complacency, inefficiency, and cronyism in governmental agencies. The bumbling by police and judicial magistrates in prosecuting alleged pedophile serial killer Marc Dutroux brought demonstrations and sharp criticism by parliamentary committees. In April accusations of a government cover-up in the pedophile case were revived by the chief magistrate's insistence on further medical examination of the dead children. Suspicion of corruption also had been confirmed at the close of 1998. Three former ministers—including Willy Claes, former economics minister and secretary-general of the North Atlantic Treaty Organization (NATO)—were found guilty of accepting bribes from French and Italian firms for military contracts.

Suddenly, on May 28, Health Minister Marcel Colla banned the sale of chickens and eggs, because they might carry cancer-causing dioxin. On June 2 the European Union (EU) banned export of Belgian chickens and eggs and products containing Belgian chicken and eggs, and soon the ban included beef and pork. The problem was caused by tainted livestock feed made from fats contaminated with dioxin. Though Prime Minister Jean-Luc Dehaene claimed 95% of Belgian produce was safe to eat, the EU demanded proof.

The anger of Belgians and the EU toward the government was augmented when it was learned that the government had known of the problem since March. Colla and Minister for Agriculture Karel Pinxten resigned promptly. The ban on the export and sale of Belgian foods visited financial disaster on Belgian farmers. An estimated $1.5 billion was lost in production costs and exports. The EU took legal action against Belgium on June 21, the same day that thousands of farmers demonstrated in Brussels against the EU ban and against government mishandling of the affair.

Elections. By that time, Belgium was operating under a caretaker government, as Dehaene's coalition had suffered defeat in June 13 elections. His Flemish Christian People's Party received 14% of the vote, compared with 17% garnered in 1995. Together with the Walloon Christian Social Party, the two groups controlled only 32 seats in the 150-seat chamber, a decrease of nine. The Walloon and Flemish Socialist Parties, also members of the governing coalition, won 33 seats, a loss of eight. The free-market Liberal parties gained slightly, winning the plurality of the vote and 41 seats. The two Green parties increased their number of seats to 20 from 11. The right-wing, separatist, anti-immigrant Flemish nationalist Vlaams Blok also made gains, receiving 10% of the vote and 15 seats.

King Albert II turned to Guy Verhofstadt, leader of the Liberals, to form a cabinet. Verhofstadt joined with the Socialists and Greens on July 4, becoming the first Liberal premier in more than 100 years. His cabinet was the first one in 41 years that did not include a representative from one of the Christian Democratic parties. Two Greens were the first members of their parties to serve in a Belgian government.

In elections for the European Parliament, the Belgian Liberals held their six seats. The Socialists lost one seat, and the Christian Democrats were down two, each being left with five. The Greens picked up all three.

Coca-Cola. On June 14 the resigning government banned the sale of all bottled and canned beverages produced by Coca-Cola. Headaches and diarrhea experienced by children in Bornem, Kortrijk, and Lochristi were blamed on the drink. The company soon traced the cause to poor-quality carbon dioxide used at a plant in Antwerp and to transportation pallets treated with antifungal preservative at a plant in Dunkirk, France. Although the government lifted the ban within ten days after a massive recall, it remained critical of the company's explanations.

JONATHAN E. HELMREICH, *Allegheny College*

BELGIUM • Information Highlights

Official Name: Kingdom of Belgium.
Location: Northwestern Europe.
Area: 11,780 sq mi (30 510 km²).
Population (July 1999 est.): 10,182,034.
Chief Cities (Dec. 31, 1997): Brussels, the capital (incl. suburbs), 953,175; Antwerp (including suburbs), 449,745; Ghent, 224,545; Charleroi, 203,853; Liège, 188,568; Bruges, 115,573.
Government: *Head of state,* Albert II, king (acceded Aug. 9, 1993). *Head of government,* Guy Verhofstadt, prime minister (took office July 1999). *Legislature*—Parliament: Senate and Chamber of Deputies.
Monetary Unit: Franc (39.2469 francs equal U.S.$1, Nov. 19, 1999).
Gross Domestic Product (1998 est. U.S.$): $236,000,000,000 (purchasing power parity).
Economic Indexes (1998, 1990 = 100): *Consumer Prices,* all items, 118.2; food, 109.1. *Industrial Production,* 109.6.
Foreign Trade (1998 with Luxembourg, U.S.$): *Imports,* $162,209,000,000; *exports,* $177,662,000,000.

Biochemistry

Cancer research remained a dominant activity of biochemists in 1998–99.

Mitochondria and Apoptosis. Researchers had known that in the presence of a proper signal, cells activate an intracellular death program and kill themselves in a controlled manner—a process known as apoptosis. Apoptotic cells round up and shrink, and then are engulfed by neighboring cells. The death signal can be delivered by killer lymphocytes that produce a protein—called the fas ligand—that binds to the fas receptor protein located on the surface of affected cells, causing the fas receptors to aggregate. The aggregation causes proteins—called procaspases—to be activated to caspases inside the target cell. The activated caspases act as executioners that degrade key cellular proteins and cause fragmentation of the cell's DNA. The stressed or damaged cells can activate their own suicide machinery without an external signal. One of the earliest changes in apoptosis is the movement of a negatively charged molecule—called phosphatidylserine—from the inner to the outer surface of the cell's membrane, where it helps to mark the cell's surface so that the cell destined to die is recognized quickly.

In early 1999 biochemists led by Santos Susin discovered that several of the key molecules involved in apoptosis normally reside in the space between the inner and outer membranes of the mitochondria. Apparently, when a cell receives a death signal, the outer mitochondrial membrane becomes leaky, and the molecules that amplify the death response are released. Two such death-inducing molecules were identified—apoptosis-inducing factor (AIF) and cytochrome c. The latter is normally an obligatory component of the respiratory chain in mitochondria that generates most of the cell's ATP, the main energy carrier in cells. Once released from the mitochondria, however, cytochrome c triggers DNA fragmentation. Similarly, AIF, once released from the mitochondria, travels to the nucleus, where it also degrades DNA, and the cell dies. This research led to the view that the mitochondria are both essential for a cell's life and the reservoir for key components in its death.

Not only do the caspases help damaged cells commit suicide, but they also appear to play a critical role in the death of brain cells observed in Huntington's disease. Junying Yuan and her colleagues at Harvard Medical School reported that certain features of the mutant protein made in Huntington's disease—called polyglutamine repeats—help activate one of the caspases found in mammalian cells. Rat-brain cells that contain a protein with such repeats ultimately commit suicide. A caspase inhibitor added to such cells prevents them from dying.

Scientists headed by Laurie Owen-Schaub at the University of Texas found that the skin cells genetically damaged by the Sun's ultraviolet light make the fas protein that induces the cells to die, eliminating mutated cells that might lead to cancer. In some cancers, however, the tumor cells outwit the killer lymphocytes by acquiring the ability to synthesize a phony, ineffective fas receptor. Avi Ashkenazi of Genentech discovered that many lung- and colon-cancer cells possessed large quantities of a decoy fas receptor that hooked up with the killer lymphocytes' fas ligand. This prevented the real fas receptors in the cancer cells from receiving the death signal.

Heparanase. Biochemists succeeded in cloning a gene that helps cancer cells spread to other parts of the body, a process called metastasis. However, in order to metastasize, the cancer cells must penetrate through the barriers that hold the tissue cells together and the dense extracellular matrix (ECM), consisting of proteins and a complex carbohydrate called heparan sulfate. Biochemists had identified several protease enzymes that chew through the ECM proteins, but efforts to find heparanase—the enzyme that degrades heparan sulfate—had been unsuccessful.

Australian and Israeli teams of biochemists, working independently, succeeded in cloning the gene that encodes heparanase. The Australian team also reported that a highly metastatic line of cancer cells possessed much higher levels of heparanase than did tumor cells that normally do not metastasize. The Israeli team found direct evidence for the importance of heparanase in metastasis. It reported that when the purified heparanase gene was added to cancer cells that rarely metastasize and was injected into mice, the engineered—not the original—cells spread rapidly to various organs and quickly killed the animals. Indeed, the Australian team found that blocking the heparanase enzyme with an inhibitor called PI-88 strongly inhibited the formation of lung tumors formed by breast-cancer cells injected into rats.

PREM P. BATRA, *Wright State University*

Biography

A selection of profiles of 1999 newsmakers appears on pages 154–64. The affiliation of each contributor is listed on pages 591–94 or on page 3. Included are profiles of:

Staff-prepared sketches of the U.S. presidential candidates also are included in this section, pages 160–61.

ABDULLAH II

Crown Prince Abdullah became the king of Jordan on Feb. 7, 1999, after the death of his father, King Hussein, who had reigned for nearly 46 years. He was precipitated into the kingship as the result of a surprise decision by the dying Hussein at the end of January.

For decades the designated heir had been Hussein's younger brother, Hassan, who as crown prince of Jordan since 1965 had served his brother faithfully, representing him at many conferences and on other international occasions. Abdullah had been crown prince from 1962—the year of his birth—until 1965. This was normal, as he was King Hussein's eldest son. His mother was Antoinette Gardiner, an Englishwoman whom the king divorced in 1972. Abdullah's replacement as crown prince by Hassan, however, was understandable in the circumstances of the mid-1960s. Hussein had seen his grandfather assassinated in 1951, and there had been attempts on his own life, as well as continuing threats. It was risking the very existence of the kingdom and the dynasty to leave open the possibility of King Hussein's being succeeded by an infant. There was the further, slightly awkward fact that his mother was a Christian.

Over the next three decades, much changed in Jordan. Abdullah's mother was no longer queen, and Hussein's children all had grown up. Some of them, like the 37-year-old Abdullah, were not particularly young. Thus there was considerable speculation—stimulated by the king's repeated ill health in the 1990s and by rumors of dissensions and jealousies within the royal family—about the possibility of Hussein's again changing his successor. The king always had quashed this speculation firmly, up until the moment that he confirmed it. Such guesswork, however, had not focused on Abdullah. The prevailing theory was that one of his half brothers would be chosen to succeed the king. Until his designation as crown prince, Abdullah remained virtually unknown to most Jordanians, at least until seen on television in May 1998 leading a spectacular roundup of an armed gang that had murdered an Iraqi diplomat and 11 other people.

Jordan's King Abdullah II

© Corbis

Upon his accession, King Abdullah II emphatically underlined his intention to continue the foreign and domestic policies of his late father. He has the solid support of the armed forces, with whom he is very popular. Although Abdullah was still largely an unknown quantity, in his first year as king he displayed the self-confidence and drive of a senior military man given a responsible new posting. His deft immediate appointment of his 18-year-old half brother, Prince Hamzeh bin al-Hussein, son of Queen Noor, as crown prince was hailed as likely to create good family relations. In August he began an emphatic crackdown on the Palestinian group Hamas (which was illegal in Jordan, but previously had been tolerated), suggesting that his policies might show less of the graceful ambiguity that was typical of his father.

Background. Very much in the family tradition, Abdullah bin al-Hussein was Western-educated. Born on Jan. 30, 1962, he attended Deerfield Academy in Massachusetts, and later the Royal Military Academy at Sandhurst (as had his father). He studied international relations at both Oxford and Georgetown, and he also returned twice for short courses in Britain, at the Infantry School and at the Command and Staff College at Camberley.

In Jordan he made the military his career, climbing to the rank of major general on the basis of ability rather than influence. He became the Jordanian army's chief of security and its expert on counterterrorism. He has been quoted as saying, "I have a lot of good friends in the Pentagon."

Something of a playboy and risk-taker earlier in his life, he settled down notably after his marriage in 1993 to Rania al-Yasinne, a Palestinian whose family came from Tulkarm in the West Bank. Abdullah and his wife have a son, Hussein, and a daughter, Iman. The new king is a qualified frogman, pilot, and parachutist. Car racing and water sports are among his interests.

Arthur Campbell Turner

AGASSI, Andre

Over the past few years, Andre Agassi's tennis career has been as erratic as a kite in a windstorm. In 1999, however, the 29-year-old Agassi won two major tournaments and reached the finals of a third. By September he was ranked Number 1 in the world. It was a notable comeback for a player who had showed great promise early in his career, but had gone into a long slump.

Agassi entered the French Open in May 1999 as something of an underdog. Less than two years earlier, he had been ranked a lowly 141st, and many players and fans thought his best days were behind him. Over the winter and spring, however, Agassi had undertaken a ferocious training program, and he came to the tournament in excellent physical and mental shape. Reaching the finals against Andrei Medvedev, Agassi badly lost the first two sets, then rallied to win the match. His world ranking jumped from 14 to 4.

After losing to Pete Sampras at Wimbledon, Agassi came back strongly at the U.S. Open in September, winning most of his matches in straight sets on the way to the final against Todd Martin. In a 3-hour, 23-minute contest, Agassi narrowly lost the second and third sets, then overwhelmed Martin in the fourth and fifth. By winning the Open, Agassi had solidified his comeback and propelled himself to the Number 1 ranking.

Background. Andre Agassi was born in Las Vegas, NV, on April 29, 1970. His father, a former Olympic boxer for Iran who emigrated to the United States, was fascinated by the game of tennis and determined to teach it to his children. In Andre's case, the lessons began while he was still a baby—his father tied a tennis ball over his crib to help develop his eye coordination.

While still in grade school, Agassi was good enough to practice with such stars as Jimmy Connors and Bjorn Borg at exhibition matches. By age 13, he was studying with professional coach Nick Bollettieri. At 16 he turned pro and immediately was rewarded with a lucrative endorsement contract from Nike.

Agassi played very well and was ranked Number 3 in the world when he was 18—the youngest player ever to hold that position. With his ready smile and long, sun-bleached hair, he became as popular as a rock star; as in the case of a rock star, his flamboyant attitude charmed some and angered others.

In time, Agassi's game became wildly uneven. He won Wimbledon at age 22, then went into a two-year slump before recovering to capture the U.S. Open in 1994 and the Australian Open the following year. After marrying actress/model Brooke Shields in 1997 (they divorced two years later), he played so poorly his ranking dropped to 141. Overweight and depressed, Agassi turned to trainer Gil Reyes, who put him on a punishing five-hour-a-day fitness routine that restored his vigor and desire to win, just in time for the French Open and yet another masterful comeback. With his victory in France, he became only the fifth male player to win all four of the major championships in tennis.

JIM ANDERSON

© Michael Baz/Liaison Agency

Andre Agassi

ARMSTRONG, C(harles) Michael

Just two years into his brief but turbulent tenure as chief executive of AT&T, C. Michael Armstrong began to transform the nation's biggest long-distance telephone company into the country's largest cable company as well. Armstrong's bold moves and eye-popping spending habits transformed AT&T from its traditional "Ma Bell" image—the safe, steady phone company with the most widely held stock in the United States—into a vibrant, risk-taking enterprise pinning its future on an unproven, faster path of communication.

In May 1999, AT&T surprised Wall Street by bidding $62 billion to acquire MediaOne, the nation's fourth-largest cable company, months after completing its $53.5 billion takeover of the second-largest cable company, Tele-Communications Inc. Suddenly, AT&T had committed more than $115 billion to cable, even as phone rivals MCI Worldcom and Sprint continued to erode AT&T's share of its traditional business—long distance. With his huge bets on cable, however, Armstrong envisions creating an even greater communications company, supplying millions of homes with television programming, local and long-distance phone calls, and the Internet, all through one cable wire.

After leaving Hughes Electronics to take over AT&T in November 1997, the self-assured, motorcycle-riding Armstrong was greeted with open arms by shareholders and analysts. But his drastic makeover of a U.S. business icon began to show some signs of stress. Several high-ranking executives departed AT&T following Armstrong's arrival, and the company's stock price in 1999 began to suffer from worries that the chairman's spending would hamper AT&T's profitability. Upgrading the cable links to millions of homes would be a long and expensive process, and there were lingering doubts about the viability of cable lines as a conduit for phone and Internet traffic. In addition, MCI Worldcom in October announced a $129 billion takeover of Sprint—the largest merger in history—to create an even more potent threat to AT&T's struggling long-distance business.

Background. Charles Michael Armstrong was born on Oct. 18, 1938, in Detroit, MI. He met his future wife, Anne, at age 14; she lived 16 houses down the street. Armstrong earned a football scholarship to Miami University in Oxford, OH, from which he was graduated with a business degree in 1961. He married shortly afterward.

After college, Armstrong went to work at IBM as a systems engineer and remained for 31 years, holding various executive positions, including running the personal-computer division. Realizing he was not in line for IBM's chief executive officer (CEO) post, he left in 1993 to run Hughes Electronics. During his tenure at Hughes, he phased the company out of the struggling defense business and made it a power in satellite television by launching the DirecTV home satellite system. Armstrong interviewed for AT&T's presidency in 1996 but reportedly turned the job down because CEO Robert Allen would not step down immediately. When John Walter, who had been hired to succeed the retiring Allen, was fired by AT&T in 1997, Armstrong was courted again and this time took the job.

Armstrong and his wife live in suburban New Jersey, near AT&T's headquarters. They have three daughters and seven grandchildren.

ERIC QUIÑONES

C. Michael Armstrong

© Porter Gifford/Liaison Agency

ARMSTRONG, Lance

Nobody expected Lance Armstrong to win the 1999 Tour de France. Less than three years earlier, Armstrong had lain on an operating table, a hole cut in his skull, as doctors cleared two cancerous lesions from his brain. For weeks afterward he received powerful and debilitating chemotherapy for up to four hours a day. It was simply impossible for a world-class athlete, no matter how well-trained and dedicated, to come back so quickly from such a devastating illness.

But Armstrong and his team—the United States Postal Service—had a plan for 1999's most prestigious cycling race: Do well in the early, flat stages; build up a lead; then try with all your heart to defend it when the course goes into the mountains, and everything favors the climbing specialists. Armstrong, 27, had ridden in four previous Tours; he never had been a climbing specialist.

By stage 8 of the 1999 race, Armstrong had taken the leader's yellow jersey. The Alps began the next day—six climbs, including two listed as category one (the most difficult rating) and another so hard it was rated "above category." If the mountains were going to break Armstrong, this was where it would happen. Armstrong planned to ride this stage strategically, racing not for one day's win but to keep the overall lead while conserving energy. Then something happened on the final climb. Although he still was ahead overall and did not need the day's victory, Armstrong attacked. In a cold afternoon rain, he surged past the astonished leaders to win stage 9 by 31 seconds. After that, the question for the racers became, simply, who would finish second?

Armstrong crossed the finish line in Paris on July 25. He had ridden the fastest Tour ever, averaging almost 25 mph (40.2 km/hr) for 2,288 mi (3 682 km) over 22 days. As he stood at the finish line in Paris, Lance Armstrong reflected: "I never expected to be here. I hope it sends out a fantastic message of hope to all cancer patients and all cancer survivors around the world."

Background. Lance Armstrong was born on Sept. 18, 1971, in Plano, a small Texas town. A natural athlete with a fierce competitive streak, he won the Iron Kids triathlon at 13 and was a professional triathlete by 16. Triathlons involve running, swimming, and bicycle riding, and by the time he was graduated from high school in 1988, Armstrong had decided he was "born to race bikes." In 1991 he was the U.S. National Amateur Champion; in 1992 (and again in 1996) he was in the Olympics. By 1996 he was ranked the Number 1 cyclist in the world. Then, one day, excruciating pain forced him off his bike.

Tests in October showed that a lethal form of testicular cancer had spread to his brain, lungs, and abdomen. Three operations and 12 weeks of cutting-edge platinum chemotherapy followed. Between bouts of chemo, even as he was losing muscle mass, Armstrong continued to exercise. By February 1997, X rays and blood work showed no traces of cancer in his body. In May 1998 he marked his return to cycling by winning the Sprint 56K—one part of the IKON's Ride for the Roses—in Austin, TX.

On May 8, 1998, he married Kristin Richard; the couple had a son, Luke David Armstrong, in October 1999. Meanwhile, Armstrong had founded the Lance Armstrong Foundation to help people survive cancer. Various endorsement contracts would follow his Tour de France win. His autobiography was scheduled for publication in May 2000.

JIM ANDERSON

© Laurent Rebours/AP/Wide World Photos

Lance Armstrong

BARAK, Ehud

Ehud Barak, the tenth person to serve as Israel's prime minister, was elected in May 1999. When he assumed office in early July, the new prime minister presented an ambitious program topped by a pledge to end the conflict with the Arabs in a year and a half. He promised to remove Israeli forces from Lebanon by July 2000, to sign a final peace agreement with the Palestinians in 18 months, and to renew and conclude an agreement with Syria that had been broken off in 1997. Although Barak scored the largest electoral victory in Israel's history, his One Israel Party, a union of Labor and several other factions, received so few votes in the election that he had to form a government coalition of eight parties representing a diverse range of political, economic, and social perspectives: secular and orthodox Jews, doves and hawks, and market-oriented planners and socialists.

Until entering politics in 1995, Barak spent his career in the military, where he was acclaimed as Israel's most highly decorated soldier. Among his exploits as a commando officer was a daring mission in which he disguised himself as an Arab woman to infiltrate the headquarters of the Palestine Liberation Organization (PLO) in Beirut and assassinate Palestinian commandos.

Background. The third Israeli prime minister to be a sabra (native), Barak was born on Feb. 12, 1942, on Kibbutz Mishmar Hasharon, a communal farm in the Heffer valley, near the Lebanese border. He joined the Israel Defense Forces (IDF) at the age of 17, rising through the ranks to become a lieutenant general and then, in 1991, chief of staff. In the IDF, Barak commanded elite units, including a tank brigade, an armored division, and intelligence and planning branches; he also served as the deputy commander of IDF forces in Lebanon and as the head of Israeli forces in Gaza and Jericho. He played a role in Israel's peace negotiations with Jordan, and he met with Syrian Chief of Staff Hikmat Shehabi.

While he served in the army, Barak received a bachelor of science degree in physics and math from the Hebrew University in 1976, and a master's in science in economic engineering systems at Stanford University in 1978. He was a protégé of Prime Minister Yitzhak Rabin, joining the cabinet upon retiring from the army in 1995. After Rabin's assassination, Barak became foreign minister in the government of the new prime minister, Shimon Peres. In 1996 he was elected chairman of the Labor Party over three other candidates by a 50.33% majority.

To strengthen Labor's position in the 1999 Knesset election, Barak renamed his electoral list One Israel and included the Gesher and Meimad factions as partners. Barak has a reputation as a cautious but skillful planner and a firm commander reluctant to delegate significant tasks to others. After becoming prime minister, Barak also took over the defense ministry. Some of his appointments to the cabinet and top government positions surprised many observers and caused disquiet among other Labor Party leaders. Although Barak originally refused to vote for the Oslo agreement and expressed reservations about the Wye River Plantation accords signed in 1998, he and PLO leader Yasir Arafat reached an agreement in September to move forward on their implementation, which had been frozen since January. The prime minister insisted on slowing down the transfer of land to the

Palestinians, however, as well as soliciting more assurances from the PLO about where the peace process was headed. In November, Barak and Arafat began talks to work out the final phase of the peace process.

Barak and his wife, Nawa, have been married for 30 years and have three children.

DON PERETZ

COLLINS, Eileen Marie

© NASA/Liaison Agency

Eileen Collins

Thirty years after a man made aeronautical history by setting foot on the Moon, Eileen Collins made history by becoming the first woman to command a space shuttle. From July 22, 1999, to July 27, 1999, she was in command of the space shuttle *Columbia* when it delivered the Chandra X-ray Observatory to its position in space. The X-ray telescope will allow astronomers to see further into the universe than previously was possible.

Becoming a space-shuttle commander was a dream come true for Collins, who was inspired in her teens by the biographies of famous women pilots, including Amelia Earhart and the Women Airforce Service Pilots (WASPs). She saved her money and got her pilot's license while in college.

Being first was nothing new to Collins. She was one of the first women to go straight from college into U.S. Air Force pilot training, and, as a result, was among the first group of women to fly for the U.S. Air Force—in which she holds the rank of colonel. She also was the first woman pilot of a NASA space shuttle.

Background. Born in Elmira, NY, on Nov. 19, 1956, Eileen Marie Collins is the daughter of James and Rose Marie Collins. She has two brothers and one sister. She was graduated from Elmira Free Academy in 1974 and received an associate's degree in mathematics/science from Corning Community College in 1976 and a bachelor's degree in mathematics and economics from Syracuse University in 1978. After graduation, she enrolled in the air force, graduating from Air Force Undergraduate Pilot Training at Vance Air Force Base (AFB) in Oklahoma in 1979. She was at Vance AFB until 1982 and at Travis AFB in California until 1985, when she enrolled at the Air Force Institute of Technology.

Collins received a master of science degree in operations research from Stanford University in 1986 and a master of arts degree in space-systems management from Webster University in 1989. From 1986 until 1989, she was an assistant professor in mathematics and a T-41 instructor pilot at the Air Force Academy in Colorado. In 1990 she attended the Air Force Test Pilot School at Edwards AFB. That same year, Collins was selected for the astronaut program.

Prior to the 1999 mission, Collins had logged more than 5,000 hours in different types of aircraft and more than 537 hours in space. She first went into space in 1995 as the pilot of the space shuttle *Discovery* when it rendezvoused with the Russian space station *Mir*. Her second mission was in May 1997, when she traveled 3.8 million mi (6.1 million km) in 145 orbits of the Earth over a nine-day period.

Collins is married to Pat Youngs, a Delta Airlines pilot, whom she met while they both were flying C-141s. Their daughter, Bridget, was born in 1996.

KRISTI VAUGHAN

DENCH, Judi

Judi Dench

© Brendan Beirne/Corbis-Sygma

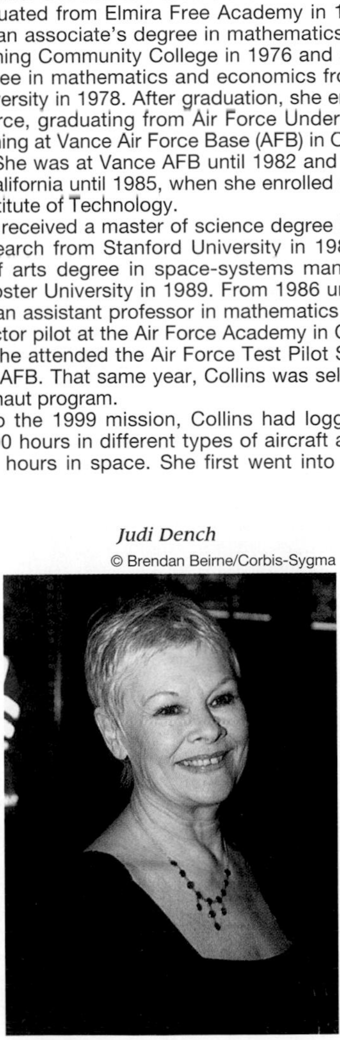

The British have admired Judi Dench's acting for nearly four decades, but it has only been in recent years—as she was nominated in 1998 for an Oscar and then, a year later, won both an Oscar and a Tony Award—that Dench has drawn the attention of U.S. audiences.

Dench was nominated for the best-actress Oscar for her performance as Queen Victoria in *Mrs. Brown* (1997) and received the best-supporting-actress award for playing another queen, Elizabeth I, in *Shakespeare in Love* (1998). She won the Tony for her role as aging actress Esme Allen in *Amy's View*.

In 1999, Dench could be seen in Franco Zeffirelli's film *Tea with Mussolini* and the newest James Bond film, *The World Is Not Enough*. She left *Amy's View* in June, when she learned that Michael Williams, her husband of 28 years, had cancer.

Better known in her native England for her work on stage and television, the 5′ 1″ (1.5-m) Dench is a versatile and humble actress who says she is most at ease on the stage. It is there, she says, that she can refine her art on a daily basis and, if need be, respond to the unique qualities of each specific audience.

Background. Judi Dench was born on Dec. 9, 1934, in York, England. She began acting at the encouragement of her brother, Jeffrey, enrolling at the Central School of Speech and Drama in London. Her first important role, Ophelia in Shakespeare's *Hamlet*, came in 1957. Over the next ten years she made her mark on the stage, winning numerous awards. In 1961 she joined the Royal Shakespeare Company (RSC) and played a wide variety of parts, including Isabella in *Measure for Measure* and Titania in *A Midsummer Night's Dream*.

After a successful nine-month run as Sally Bowles in the musical *Cabaret*, Dench returned to the RSC, touring Africa, Japan, and Australia. In the early 1980s she also worked in television and film, including taking on the role of a very suburban Englishwoman on the British television series *A Fine Romance*, in which she costarred with her husband. For this role, she won the British Association of Film and Television Arts (BAFTA) Award for best actress in a comedy series. In the 1990s she also starred in another television comedy series, *As Time Goes By*, which has been shown on Public Broadcasting Service (PBS) stations in the United States. In 1988, Dench was given the title of Dame of the British Empire.

During the 1980s and 1990s, Dench appeared in several films, but always in supporting parts. In the United States she was probably best known for her work in two

© Ron Edmonds/AP/Wide World Photos

J. Dennis Hastert

James Bond movies, *Goldeneye* (1995) and *Tomorrow Never Dies* (1997), playing M, Agent 007's superior. It was not until *Mrs. Brown* that she received a leading movie role.

Over the years, Dench has earned many awards for her craft. She won two Oliviers (the British equivalent of the Tony) in 1995 for her performances in *Absolute Hell* and *A Little Night Music*. She received BAFTA awards for best supporting actress in a motion picture for *A Room with a View* (1986) and *A Handful of Dust* (1988), as well as for best actress for *Mrs. Brown*. She also won a Golden Globe and a Golden Satellite Award for her work in *Mrs. Brown*, and, in addition to her Oscar nomination, she was nominated for a Screen Actors Guild Award for her role in that film.

Dench and Williams have one daughter, Tara—an actress who is better known in the theater world as Finty—and one grandchild.

KRISTI VAUGHAN

HASTERT, J. Dennis

When Republicans chose J. Dennis Hastert as speaker of the U.S. House of Representatives in January 1999, the main question was whether the low-keyed conciliatory style of the 57-year-old, seven-term representative from Illinois would be the solution to the problems of the fractious and narrow GOP majority in the chamber. The answer after Hastert's first months on the job was yes and no.

On the positive side, Hastert lived up to hopes of many of his supporters by not behaving like his controversial predecessor, Newt Gingrich, whose abrasive manner irritated Republicans as well as Democrats among his peers, and whose outspoken conservatism made him a symbol to the public of GOP extremism. "There is zero meanness in his spirit," said Rep. James A. Leach, an Iowa Republican widely respected in both parties.

But while everyone acknowledged Hastert's geniality, critics complained that he needed to exhibit more decisiveness to be a genuine leader. The most notorious case in point was the House's failure in the spring to adopt a resolution supporting the use of air strikes against Yugoslavia during the undeclared war over Kosovo. Hastert supported the measure but declined to lobby for it, while House Republican whip Tom DeLay of Texas vigorously rallied votes in opposition. That result, along with Hastert's temporizing on other issues such as gun control and taxes, bolstered the impression that DeLay, whom Hastert once served as deputy, was the man really in charge of House Republicans.

In the speaker's defense, his friends pointed to the GOP's small majority—ten seats, with one Independent, by late 1999—as a daunting obstacle to effective leadership by Hastert or anyone else. In the face of this handicap, Hastert demonstrated the determination to put his acknowledged skills as a negotiator to constructive use. With Republican conservatives and moderates sharply divided over a proposed tax cut, the centerpiece of the GOP legislative agenda, Hastert wooed moderates by pledging not to enlarge the national debt and persuaded conservatives to accept an alternative to their demands for increased tax relief for married couples. The result was a midsummer compromise victory that saved face for the new speaker and his party.

Background. Born Jan. 2, 1942, and raised in Illinois farm country, about 50 mi (80 km) from Chicago, J. Dennis Hastert earned a bachelor's degree at Wheaton College, an evangelical Christian school, and then a master's degree from Northern Illinois University. Starting his working life as a high-school government and history teacher and wrestling coach, Hastert entered politics as a state legislator and served in Springfield for six years, beginning in January 1981, before winning election to the House from Illinois' 14th District in November 1986.

On Capitol Hill he made his mark early on in health reform, helping to write the 1996 health-care-reform act. In 1998, Hastert headed a panel of GOP lawmakers that drafted the legislation offered by Republicans as an alternative to Democratic proposals to regulate HMOs. The path to the speakership opened for him suddenly in December 1998, when Rep. Robert Livingston of Louisiana—the GOP's first choice to fill the vacancy created by Gingrich's post-midterm-election resignation—withdrew in the midst of impeachment proceedings against President Bill Clinton, after it was disclosed that Livingston had carried on an extramarital affair.

Hastert is married to the former Jean Kahl, whom he met when she was a high-school physical-education teacher. The couple have two children.

ROBERT SHOGAN

HILL, Lauryn

Lauryn Hill, one of the most significant pop performers to emerge in the 1990s, brings a unique lyrical vision to her music, which smoothly blends rap, soul, and reggae. Many hip-hop artists succeed with songs and videos that trade on violent imagery and sexist attitudes. But the 24-year-old Hill has succeeded by following a more refined artistic muse, both as a member of the hip-hop group the Fugees and on her own wildly successful solo album, *The Miseducation of Lauryn Hill*.

Background. Born in 1975 in South Orange, NJ, Lauryn Hill is the daughter of an English-teacher mother and a computer-consultant father; she has one older brother. Her home was filled with the kind of soulful music that came to influence her own work, including records by Stevie Wonder, Marvin Gaye, Carlos Santana, and Bob Marley and the Wailers. At the age of 13, she sang Smokey Robinson's "Who's Loving You?" during an amateur night at New York's Apollo Theater. While in high school, she not only found time to play an abused teenager in the soap opera *As the World Turns* and a high-school diva in the Whoopi Goldberg film *Sister Act 2*, but formed the Fugees with childhood friends Wyclef Jean and Prakazrel Michel.

The Fugees (the name is short for "refugees") produced its debut album, *Blunted on Reality*, while Hill was a freshman at Columbia University. The album bombed, but a live tour by the group created a buzz of interest, and a far more mature album, 1996's *The Score*, became a mainstream success that drew new listeners to hip-hop and achieved worldwide sales of more than 17 million copies. Much of this interest was generated by Hill's soulful singing, especially on the hit-single cover of Roberta Flack's "Killing Me Softly."

If doubts persisted that Hill might be better at reviving old hits than creating new ones, they were dispelled instantly with the release of *The Miseducation of Lauryn Hill*, a consensus choice among critics as one of the finest albums of 1998, and a winner of five 1999 Grammy Awards, including those for best new artist and album of the year. *Miseducation* impressed with its organic mix of musical styles and its savvy blend of live instruments, recorded samples, singing, and rapping. Hill's lyrics were equally striking, fusing the personal and the political into a vision that was as smart as it was unique.

Like Jamaican reggae, Hill's music draws much of its power from its easy mix of music and politics. It seems oddly appropriate, then, that she has two children with partner Rohan Marley, the son of reggae legend Bob Marley. Hill's own activism is reflected by the Refugee Project, a program she founded in 1996 to send underprivileged children to camp.

JOHN MILWARD

KELLEY, David E.

© Frank Trapper/Corbis-Sygma

David E. Kelley

In 1999 television writer and producer David E. Kelley did what no one else had done before—he won Emmys for two outstanding series (a comedy and a drama) in the same year. His accomplishment came as he had three shows running on prime-time television (on three different networks) and two more premiering in the fall.

Just as remarkable was that Kelley not only created the shows, produced them, and hired the directors, crews, and actors, but in the 1998–99 season he was writing virtually all the scripts for the winning comedy, *Ally McBeal*, and the winning drama, *The Practice*, while creating a detective show, *Snoops*, for the fall 1999 season. Also for fall 1999, he launched *Ally*, a half-hour repackaging of existing hour-long *Ally McBeal* episodes.

And as Hollywood has learned, first with the early 1990s series *Picket Fences* and in fall 1999 with *Chicago Hope*, the Kelley touch can be critical. In the case of both shows, Kelley had turned the writing over to others but was called back to revive them after they slipped in popularity. He was unable to save *Picket Fences*.

Background. A Maine native, David E. Kelley was born around 1956. His father was a hockey coach. He was graduated from Princeton University in 1979 and received a law degree from Boston University Law School in 1983. For several years he worked in the litigation department of Fine & Ambrogne, a Boston firm. While there, he got an idea for a movie about an ambitious lawyer with questionable ethics. That script, which ultimately was produced as the movie *From the Hip*, proved to be his entrance to television writing. His agent sent a copy to producer Steve Bochco, who was looking for writers with a legal background to work on his new series, *L.A. Law*. Kelley was hired as the show's story editor, but he hedged his bets, only asking for a leave of absence from his job rather than quitting outright. A year later he gave up his position with the law firm.

Kelley's talents were recognized quickly. By the show's second season, 1987–88, he had been named executive story editor. In rapid succession, he then became coproducer, supervising producer, co-executive producer, and—when Bochco left at the end of the third season—executive producer. At the time, *L.A. Law* was television's leading show.

Kelley stayed with *L.A. Law* until the end of the 1991–92 season. In those years the show won three Emmys for outstanding drama series, and Kelley won two for outstanding writing in a drama series. In 1994 the show was canceled, following what critics said was a noticeable decline in the quality of its writing. Kelley's success continued, however, as he had launched a new television series, *Picket Fences*, in 1992. The show won three Emmys in 1993—for best drama, best actress, and best actor—but it never achieved ratings success. In 1996, one year after Kelley relinquished creative control of the show, it was canceled. He, meanwhile, had created *Chicago Hope*, which debuted in 1994.

He also had met and, in 1993, married actress Michelle Pfeiffer, for whom he wrote the screenplay for *To Gillian on Her 37th Birthday*. The film received mixed reviews, and Kelley returned to television in the 1997–98 season with *McBeal* and *The Practice*.

Kelley and Pfeiffer have a son and a daughter.

KRISTI VAUGHAN

Lauryn Hill

© Reed Saxon/AP/Wide World Photos

MARTIN, Ricky

Ricky Martin burst onto the U.S. pop-music scene with his hip-shaking appearance on the 1999 Grammy Awards, singing "La Copa de la Vida" ("The Cup of Life"), the official song of the 1998 World Cup, which already had been a Number 1 single in more than 30 countries. It was not the first time television had helped to ignite a pop career—Elvis Presley, the Beatles, and Michael Jackson all exploded out of the tube. But the subsequent success of Martin's English-language-debut album, *Ricky Martin*—powered by "Livin' La Vida Loca," the best-selling single in the history of Columbia Records—was hardly the stuff of an overnight success. Martin had been rehearsing for this moment for most of his young life.

Background. Enrique Martin IV was born in San Juan, Puerto Rico, on Dec. 24, 1971. He was acting in television commercials at the age of 6. (Today he can be seen in ads promoting Puerto Rican tourism.) He auditioned for Menudo, a popular Puerto Rican teenage singing group, three times before he was accepted at the age of 12. Martin made his Menudo debut at Radio City Music Hall in New York City. For the next five years, he recorded and toured with the group, which was known to dismiss members of a certain age. At 17, Martin was an unemployed show-biz veteran, unsure of his next step.

(Continues on page 162.)

Election 2000—The Candidates

As 1999 ended, the campaign for the White House in November 2000 was in full swing. Two Democrats—Bill Bradley and Al Gore—were seeking the Democratic presidential nomination. Six Republicans—Gary L. Bauer, George W. Bush, Malcolm S. Forbes, Jr., Orrin G. Hatch, Alan L. Keyes, and John S. McCain III—remained in the race for the GOP's nod after several well-known Republicans had dropped out. Meanwhile, former Republican Patrick J. Buchanan was seeking the Reform Party's presidential nomination, and real-estate magnate Donald Trump was considering challenging Buchanan for that party's endorsement. The Reform Party had been founded by businessman Ross Perot in 1992. Biographical sketches of the ten candidates follow:

The Democratic Party

William W. (Bill) Bradley

A former three-term U.S. senator from New Jersey, Bill Bradley declared that health care for all, the fight against racial strife, and campaign-finance reform would be focal points in his campaign for the presidency. Since leaving the Senate, Bradley has been a teacher, lecturer, and author. Born in Crystal City, MO, on July 28, 1943, Bradley was graduated from Princeton University and was a Rhodes scholar at Oxford University. An outstanding college basketball player, he played professionally for the New York Knicks (1967–77) and was elected to the Basketball Hall of Fame. He is married and the father of one daughter.

Albert Gore, Jr.

Albert Gore, Jr., has served as vice-president under Bill Clinton since 1993. Previously he was a U.S. senator from Tennessee (1985–93) and U.S. congressman (1977–85). Born in Washington, DC, on March 31, 1948, he grew up in Washington. His father was a U.S. senator. A graduate of Harvard University and Vanderbilt University School of Law, Gore is married and the father of four children. Gore promised to bring "moral leadership" to the presidency, "to fight for America's family," and to maintain the nation's economic prosperity. This is Gore's second try for the Democratic presidential nomination; he previously ran in 1988.

The Republican Party

Gary L. Bauer

Gary L. Bauer, who was on leave as president of the socially conservative Family Research Council and as chairman of the Campaign for Working Families in 1999, pledged an "unapologetic pro-family, pro-life, and pro-growth" presidential campaign. Bauer never has held elected office but served in the White House Office for Policy Development during the Ronald Reagan administration and in the Department of Education (1982–87). Born in Covington, KY, on May 4, 1946, he was graduated from Georgetown (KY) College and Georgetown University Law School. He is married and the father of three children.

George W. Bush

© Mary Ann Chastain/AP/Wide World Photos

George W. Bush

George W. Bush was born on July 6, 1946, in New Haven, CT, the son of future President George Bush. George W., as the presidential candidate is known, was graduated from Yale University and received a master's degree from Harvard Business School. He was a general partner of the Texas Rangers Major League Baseball team before being elected to the first of two terms as governor of Texas in 1994. The governor declared "compassionate conservatism" as the theme of his presidential campaign. He is married and the father of twin daughters. Not only is his father a former president, but his brother Jeb is governor of Florida.

© Jim Cole/AP/Wide World Photos

(l-r): *Orrin G. Hatch, John S. McCain III, Alan L. Keyes, Gary L. Bauer, Malcolm S. Forbes, Jr.*

Malcolm S. Forbes, Jr.

Steve Forbes formally announced his presidential candidacy on the Internet. "You and I are entering the information age, and the Washington politicians are stuck in the Stone Age," he declared. A leading proponent of the flat tax, Forbes took tax reform as his campaign focus. The son of the late publisher Malcolm Forbes, he has held various editorial, advertising, and administrative positions with Forbes Inc., including editor in chief and chief executive, since 1970. An unsuccessful candidate for the Republican presidential nomination in 1996, he never has held elected office. The candidate was born in Morristown, NJ, on July 18, 1947, and received his degree from Princeton University. He is married and the father of five children.

Bill Bradley *Al Gore, Jr.*

© John Mottern/AP/Wide World Photos

Orrin G. Hatch

A member of the U.S. Senate since 1977, Orrin G. Hatch of Utah was chairman of the Senate Judiciary Committee in 1999. A conservative Republican, Hatch has a reputation of being able to work with Democrats, sponsoring major legislation with Sen. Edward Kennedy (D-MA). He said that he was running for the presidency because he was tired of "divisiveness" and wanted to strengthen the military. Prior to his political career, the senator practiced law in both Pennsylvania and Utah. Born on March 22, 1934, in Pittsburgh, PA, Hatch was awarded a bachelor's degree by Brigham Young University and a law degree by the University of Pittsburgh. He is married and the father of six children. Hatch has produced several albums of patriotic and religious music.

Alan L. Keyes

Television and radio host and commentator Alan L. Keyes was seeking the presidency as an outspoken religious conservative. His strong antiabortion stance had excited pro-lifers during his first campaign for the GOP nomination in 1996. Keyes served in the Reagan administration as U.S. ambassador to the UN Economic and Social Council (1983–85) and as assistant secretary of state for international organizations (1985–87). He unsuccessfully sought a U.S. Senate seat from Maryland in 1988 and 1992. Born in New York City on Aug. 7, 1950, Keyes was educated at Harvard University, being awarded a bachelor's degree in 1972 and a doctorate in 1979. He is married and the father of three children.

John S. McCain III

John S. McCain III of Arizona was elected to the U.S. Senate in 1986 and reelected in 1992 and 1998. He was a member of the U.S. House of Representatives (1983–87). A navy aviator during the Vietnam war, McCain spent five and one-half years as a prisoner of war during that conflict. The son and grandson of U.S. Navy admirals, McCain was born on Aug. 29, 1936, in the Panama Canal Zone. He is a 1958 graduate of the U.S. Naval Academy and was a U.S. Navy officer (1958–81). He is the father of four children from his present marriage and three from a previous one. In announcing his presidential candidacy, McCain urged Americans to join him in the fight "to take our government back from power brokers and special interests and return it to the people."

The Reform Party

Patrick J. Buchanan

Patrick J. Buchanan, an unsuccessful candidate for the Republican presidential nomination in 1992 and 1996, announced on Oct. 25, 1999, that he was bolting the GOP to seek the presidential nomination of the Reform Party. As a Reform Party candidate, he vowed to rescue the nation from the "cultural and moral pit" into which it had fallen. Buchanan was born in Washington, DC, on Nov. 2, 1938, was graduated from Georgetown University, and was the recipient of a master's degree from Columbia School of Journalism. A speechwriter and adviser to President Richard Nixon and director of communications for the Reagan White House (1985–87), he has been a syndicated newspaper columnist and cohost of CNN's *Firing Line*. He is married and does not have children.

Donald J. Trump

Real-estate developer and hotel and casino owner Donald Trump also announced in October 1999 that he was switching his political affiliation from the Republican Party to the Reform Party. Although not officially a declared candidate for the party's presidential nomination, he filed the paperwork establishing an authorized presidential exploratory committee. Trump has outlined his position on issues in his book *The America We Deserve,* which was published late in 1999. An opponent of the North American Free Trade Agreement (NAFTA), he pledged to stop "the rip-off of the United States" by its trading partners. Trump was born in New York City on June 14, 1946, and was graduated from the Wharton School of Business. Twice divorced, he is the father of four children.

Patrick J. Buchanan

© John Gaps III/AP/Wide World Photos

Donald J. Trump

© Peter Morgan/Reuters/Archive Photos

(Continued from page 159.)

After relocating to Mexico City, he worked as a stage actor and became a cast member of a television soap opera. The exposure gave him the clout to resume his musical career. By 1994 he had moved to Los Angeles, where he quickly won a role on the soap opera *General Hospital*, playing a bartender and part-time nightclub singer. His third album, 1995's *A Medio Vivir*, found Martin reuniting with a Menudo colleague, Robi Rosa, who helped him zero in on his breakthrough style, a savvy combination of Latin music, contemporary dance music, and rock 'n' roll. Martin also spent a year portraying Marius in the Broadway production of *Les Misérables*.

The release of 1998's *Vuelve*, which won Martin a Grammy for best Latin pop album, made him an international star, and the recording of an English-language record became all but inevitable. Produced over the course of two years, the album was built for success, employing such established industry heavyweights as songwriter Diane Warren, songwriter-producer Desmond Child, and producer Emilio Estefan. The icing on the commercial cake came when, after his breakthrough Grammy performance, Madonna eagerly recorded a last-minute duet with the Latin heartthrob.

In the blink of an eye, "Livin' La Vida Loca" was on its way to becoming the summer single of 1999, and Ricky Martin was the subject of cover stories in magazines from *Time* to *Rolling Stone*. Martin's success is part of a larger trend in which Latin music and culture is exerting an increasing influence on mainstream popular culture (*see* FEATURE ARTICLE, page 97).

JOHN MILWARD

MARTINEZ, Pedro

© Jim Rogash/AP/Wide World Photos

Pedro Martinez

Pedro Martinez was only 27 years old in 1999, when he had one of the most dominating seasons of any pitcher in baseball history. Playing for the Boston Red Sox, the right-hander won the American League's triple crown of pitching, topping the league in wins (23), earned-run average (ERA) (2.07), and strikeouts (313). For this effort, Martinez became only the fourth unanimous winner of the American League's Cy Young Award and finished a close second in the voting as the league's most valuable player. He joined Gaylord Perry and Randy Johnson as the only pitchers to win the Cy Young in both leagues.

Since the Red Sox went 26–5 in his 31 appearances, Martinez was a major factor in Boston's ability to claim the American League's wild-card play-off berth for the second straight season. It was the first time since 1915–16 that the Bosox reached postseason play in consecutive years. The first player voted pitcher of the month four times in one season, Martinez also became the first to strike out the first four hitters he faced in an All-Star game. Pitching in front of his home crowd at Boston's Fenway Park on July 13, 1999, he fanned five in his two-inning stint, was the game's winning pitcher, and was named most valuable player (MVP) of the game. Three months later, his six innings of no-hit relief enabled the Red Sox to win the decisive Game 5 of the American League (AL) Division Series, and his seven shutout innings in AL Championship Series Game 3 enabled Boston to pin the Yankees with a 13–1 defeat—New York's only loss in 12 postseason games.

At 5′11″ and 170 lb (1.8 m and 77 kg), the right-hander is much smaller than his older brother, Ramon, who also pitched for the 1999 Red Sox, but has more power. En route to a Boston club record for strikeouts, Martinez fanned at least 15 men in a game six times.

Background. Pedro Jaime Martinez was born in Manoguayabo, the Dominican Republic, on Oct. 25, 1971. He and brother Ramon had four other siblings plus a father, Paulino, who played amateur ball. Though Pedro never saw his father pitch, he remembers how hard his father threw in backyard games of catch. He also remembers his father, who worked as a supervisor of school employees, telling him always to keep his poise and avoid getting upset. He tries to follow that advice.

On June 18, 1988, Martinez signed with the Los Angeles Dodgers as an undrafted free agent. He reached Los Angeles in 1992, spent all of 1993 in the Dodger bullpen, then became a starter for Montreal in 1994, after he was traded to the Expos. Although he won the National League's (NL's) Cy Young Award after a 17–8 season and 1.90 ERA in 1997, the budget-conscious Expos swapped him to Boston for Carl Pavano and Tony Armas, Jr., on Nov. 18, 1997. He later signed a six-year, $75 million contract with the Red Sox that runs through the 2003 season, with a club option for 2004.

The four-time All-Star has been a double-digit winner in all but one of his eight big-league seasons. He throws strikes and has pinpoint control. Red Sox pitching coach Joe Kerrigan says he is different than other pitchers, because he can win with finesse as well as power.

Martinez enjoys a low-key lifestyle. He likes dancing, driving his sports-utility vehicle cross-country, and a wide variety of music. The pitcher reads the Bible daily. Martinez learned English by listening to music, watching TV, and pretending to broadcast spring-training games.

DAN SCHLOSSBERG

MBEKI, Thabo

South Africa's second president in the post-apartheid era is Thabo Mbeki, who was elected in June 1999 to succeed Nelson Mandela. By the time of the election, many people thought Mbeki had been, in effect, running the country for the latter years of Mandela's term.

Background. Thabo Mvuyelwa Mbeki was born on June 18, 1942, in Idutywa, in the Transkei. Both his parents worked as teachers and were active in nationalist politics. He himself became politically active at a young age and has remarked that he "was born into the struggle." His father, Govan Mbeki, was a leader of the African National Congress (ANC) and was sentenced to life imprisonment with Nelson Mandela in 1964.

His parents ensured that the young Thabo would have a solid education, including attending Lovedale Institution, a Presbyterian secondary school that educated many of South Africa's black elite. He joined the ANC Youth League at the age of 14, and in his senior year he participated in a student strike that temporarily closed Lovedale and resulted in his expulsion. He had to finish his high-school education by studying at home, taking the matriculation examination at St. John's High School in Umtata, in the Transkei, in 1959.

After the ANC was banned in 1960, Mbeki left South Africa in 1962 to attend Sussex University in England, where he continued his political activities. In 1966 he earned his master's degree in economics, after which he served in a variety of posts with the ANC in exile. He quickly moved up the ANC hierarchy; an assistant secretary to the Revolutionary Council in 1971, he became the youngest member of the National Executive in 1975 and took the position of political secretary to ANC President Oliver Tambo in 1978. In the 1980s he accompanied Tambo on numerous diplomatic trips. He also participated in early discussions with leading white South Africans in Lusaka, Zambia, in 1985 and in Dakar, Senegal, in 1988—talks that eventually led to negotiations between the South African government and the ANC in 1990 over the country's future. During this period, Mbeki also made the distressing discovery that both his younger brother and his son, a child he had fathered out of wedlock when he was 16, had been detained and presumably killed by South African security forces in 1975.

Mbeki returned to South Africa after the ANC was unbanned in 1990, ending 28 years in exile. As the country moved toward a negotiated settlement and a new interim constitution, he was involved in many of the key discussions with the government. Initially it appeared that Cyril Ramaphosa, a union leader who also played a key role in negotiating the constitution, was being groomed as Mandela's successor. In 1993, however, Mbeki succeeded Tambo as chairman of the ANC, and when Mandela was elected president in 1994, he appointed Mbeki deputy president of the new South African government.

President Mbeki lacks the charisma of his predecessor and likely will place less emphasis on reconciliation and more on delivering real change for the majority of South Africans than Mandela did.

Mbeki is married to Zanele Dlamini, a social worker who now heads a bank for rural women.

PATRICK O'MEARA and N. BRIAN WINCHESTER

MUNDELL, Robert A.

Supply-side economists cheered when Robert A. Mundell, a professor at Columbia University in New York City, was awarded the 1999 Nobel Memorial Prize in Economic Sciences. "It's gratifying to see the Royal Swedish Academy of Sciences recognize his eminence," proclaimed *The Wall Street Journal*, a fan of cuts in marginal tax rates and other supply-side ideas.

The Canadian economist was not recognized for his influence on what was eventually dubbed "Reaganomics," but for his contributions to international economics. The academy praised him for his "almost prophetic" accuracy in predicting, in the 1960s, future developments in international monetary arrangements and capital markets. "His work on monetary dynamics and optimum currency areas has inspired generations of researchers," the academy noted.

Robert A. Mundell

© Phil Long/AP/Wide World Photos

Professor Mundell theorized that when money moves freely across borders, governments must choose between exchange-rate stability and an independent monetary policy, with its options for interest-rate changes. Mundell's conclusion, according to the Stockholm citation, was that "under a floating exchange rate, monetary policy becomes powerful and fiscal policy powerless, whereas the opposite is true under a fixed exchange rate." That view is commonplace now. In the 1960s, however, most nations controlled movements of capital across their borders. Although the United States supposedly offered free capital movement, it attempted to discourage dollar outflows through a special equalization tax on interest on international loans when its balance-of-payments deficits piled up. Mundell's theory helped him foresee the breakdown of the postwar system of fixed exchange rates in 1971 and the subsequent devaluation of the dollar.

In 1961 he also addressed the question of when it would make economic sense for nations to give up an independent monetary policy in favor of a common currency. Thus he laid the intellectual foundation for the euro, a common currency adopted by 11 of the 15 members of the European Union (EU) at the start of 1999.

Mundell himself traces the supply-side movement to a 1971 meeting of prominent economists, including Paul Volcker, who later became chairman of the Federal Reserve, and Paul Samuelson, a professor at the Massachusetts Institute of Technology (MIT) in Cambridge, MA, who also won the Nobel Prize. At that time, economists were puzzling over how to break out of stagflation—a combination of inflation, a troubled dollar, and persistent unemployment. Mundell urged an unorthodox idea: Cut taxes to boost the economy, and raise interest rates to protect the dollar. The concept was ignored then, but it was picked up during the first term of President Ronald Reagan in the 1980s. Taxes were cut, but that action, combined with a recession, produced a huge budget deficit.

Background. Born in Canada in 1932 and still a Canadian citizen, Robert A. Mundell studied at the University of British Columbia in Vancouver and did postgraduate work at the University of Washington in Seattle and at MIT, where he earned his doctorate. By the age of 29, the talented young man was the chief international economist at the International Monetary Fund (IMF) in Washington, DC. He taught at several universities before joining the faculty of Columbia in 1974. Two years earlier, he had divorced his first wife, Barbara, with whom he had three children. His second wife, Valerie, gave birth to their first son, Nicholas, in December 1997.

The white-haired economist indicated that he planned to use some of his $975,000 prize to further fix up a crumbling, 16th-century Italian castle that he had bought as a hedge against inflation in 1969 for the equivalent of $10,000—a structure that he estimated in 1999 was worth 100 times that amount.

DAVID FRANCIS

ROBERTS, Julia

Famous for an effervescent personality and sparkling smile, actress Julia Roberts was particularly in the spotlight in 1999 with her roles in the hit romantic comedies *Notting Hill* and *Runaway Bride*. The dark-haired young actress first had won her way into filmgoers' hearts in 1988's *Mystic Pizza*. Throughout the next decade, she appeared in a series of hit films and became a major star.

Regarded by critics as moderately talented and very professional, with an unusual measure of charisma and star power, the 32-year-old Roberts is Hollywood's most highly paid actress. In 1999 she reached a new threshold, joining only a few male actors who are able to ask $20 million a picture.

© Victor Malafronte/Archive Photos

Julia Roberts

Background. Julia Roberts was born Oct. 28, 1967, in Smyrna, GA, the youngest of Walter and Betty Roberts' three children. Her parents operated a playwrights' workshop in Atlanta during the 1960s, and both her older siblings, Lisa and Eric, early on decided they would become actors. Roberts' parents divorced in 1971, and her father died a few years later.

Despite an early ambition to become a veterinarian, Roberts joined her older sister in New York City after graduating from Campbell High School, with hopes of becoming an actress. She modeled briefly; then her brother, Eric, got her her first film role, in 1986's low-budget *Blood Red*. She appeared in three 1988 films, one of which was the coming-of-age movie *Mystic Pizza*, in which she had her first substantial part. The film received mixed reviews, but most critics were taken with Roberts, sensing a powerful "star quality" in her.

On the strength of *Mystic Pizza*, Roberts won an important role in *Steel Magnolias* (1989), whose cast included Shirley MacLaine, Sally Field, Olympia Dukakis, Daryl Hannah, and Dolly Parton. As the doomed young heroine of the film, Roberts secured an Oscar nomination for best supporting actress. She broke through to true stardom in her next film, 1990's *Pretty Woman*, with her turn as a charming call girl who wins the heart of a corporate raider, played by Richard Gere. She again was nominated for an Oscar, this time for best actress, for her *Pretty Woman* role.

Two more hits followed—*Flatliners* (1990) and *Sleeping with the Enemy* (1991)—but then things began to go downhill. First, 1991's *Dying Young* was a box-office failure, and rumors began to circulate that Roberts was difficult to work with. In addition, her much-publicized wedding to actor Kiefer Sutherland was called off only a few days in advance, and Roberts fled to Ireland with another actor, Jason Patric.

For a time, Roberts kept a low profile, appearing in only one film in 1992, *The Player*. Upon reemerging in the 1993 hit *The Pelican Brief*, Roberts showed a new maturity, and surprised the press by marrying singer-songwriter Lyle Lovett. (The couple divorced less than two years later.) Despite following *Pelican Brief* with several less-successful movies, she nonetheless garnered some favorable critical reviews and remained a top box-office draw. With 1997's romantic-comedy hit *My Best Friend's Wedding*, Roberts was back as Hollywood's most visible—and one of its most popular—young actresses.

MEGHAN O'REILLY FIERO

SUMMERS, Lawrence H.

Barely days after being sworn in as the 71st U.S. secretary of the treasury on July 2, 1999, Lawrence H. Summers saw the U.S. dollar begin to slide against the Japanese yen and other major currencies on the foreign-exchange markets. Summers stuck to the line employed successfully by his predecessor, Robert Rubin: "A strong dollar is in the national interest of the United States, because of its implications for inflation, capital costs, and the purchasing power of American workers." But by late September the yen was up more than 15% against the dollar.

The fall of the dollar, of course, was not Summers' fault. It reflected record U.S. trade deficits and a pickup in growth in both Japan and Europe. But it was one indication that Summers faced a tough assignment in succeeding Rubin. After all, Rubin had presided at Treasury during most of a record-breaking, low-inflation economic recovery, an astounding bull stock market, and the switch of the federal budget from massive deficits to healthy surpluses. He had helped guide the U.S. economy relatively unscathed through financial crises in Mexico, Asia, and Russia. As a result, Rubin was seen by some in the financial community as a legend—one whose shoes would be hard, if not impossible, to fill.

Background. Intellectually, Summers was considered more than prepared for the task. Born on Nov. 30, 1954, in New Haven, CT, Lawrence H. Summers earned his bachelor's degree at the Massachusetts Institute of Technology in 1975 and was an economics professor there from 1979 to 1982. He was awarded a Ph.D. from Harvard University in 1982, and then was a staff economist at the Council of Economic Advisers for two years under President Ronald Reagan. He became the youngest professor ever to be tenured at Harvard, where he was on staff from 1983 to 1993. He was awarded the John Bates Clark Medal in 1993, given every two years to the outstanding U.S. economist under the age of 40. Beginning in 1991, he served a two-year stint as chief economist at the World Bank before moving to the Treasury as undersecretary for international affairs in 1993 and becoming Rubin's deputy in 1995.

By most accounts, he served his Treasury apprenticeship well. At first, however, the Washington establishment was offended by what they saw as Summers' arrogance. Members of Congress complained of being treated as errant students when he appeared at hearings. A quick learner, Summers developed a certain deference to his political superiors, sometimes seeking their advice. In addition, his prominent role in several financial crises in the world brought some fire from critics of the International Monetary Fund's (IMF's) bailouts and of the United States' heavy involvement. Some politicians in financially besieged nations did not like his backing of the IMF's tough prescriptions for reforms. And Japanese officials got tired of his forceful pleas to stimulate their stagnant economy.

But Summers' early tenure as Treasury secretary did not prompt great criticism at home. He apparently took seriously Rubin's advice to be "cautious" and Federal Reserve Chairman Alan Greenspan's suggestion to be "opaque."

Summers and his wife, Victoria, a tax lawyer, have three children. Two of his uncles, Paul Samuelson and Kenneth Arrow, won the Nobel Prize in economics.

DAVID R. FRANCIS

Lawrence H. Summers

© Corbis

Biotechnology

The year 1999 brought investigations on enhancement of the nutritional content of rice, the use of pig organs in humans, the ecological effects of using genetically modified corn plants, and the use of insect saliva as a vaccine.

Nutritional Enhancement of Rice. Most attempts to improve the world's food supply have involved increasing world food production. This is especially true for rice, a staple food in the world's developing countries. Rice, unfortunately, contains no beta-carotene, which the human body converts to vitamin A, and is poor in iron. Vitamin A deficiency affects some 400 million people worldwide, leaving them vulnerable to infections and blindness. Iron deficiency also affects millions of individuals worldwide, leading to anemia.

In August 1999, I. Potrykus at the Swiss Federal Institute of Technology, Zurich, Switzerland, reported on the transfer to rice plants of four genes that together provide the biochemical pathway for making beta-carotene. The genes were obtained from daffodil plants, which have the ability to produce beta-carotene. In order to increase the iron level of rice grains, a gene that provides for the formation of the iron storage protein ferritin was transferred from French-bean plants. It is hoped that bioengineered rice will be available in the developing countries within three to five years.

Pig-to-Human Transplants. For those people requiring a transplant, pig organs may offer a solution to the shortage of human organs. However, there is concern about the cross-species transmission of pig viruses, with feared disastrous effects. Many of these viruses can be eliminated from the strains of pigs to be used for transplants by pathogen-free closed breeding of the animals. However, the porcine endogenous retrovirus (PERV) cannot be eliminated, because it is integrated permanently in the pig genome.

K. Paradis at Novartis, a biotechnology company in England, and other investigators reported on 160 patients who had been treated with living pig tissues. These included individuals who were treated with fetal pig nerve cells for Parkinson's and Huntington's diseases, those who were treated with pig pancreatic islet cells for diabetes, and those in need of renal dialysis treatment whose blood was perfused through pig kidneys. No patient was found to be infected with PERV. This report will encourage pig-organ transplantations when human organs are not available.

Genetically Modified Corn. In 1999 more than 40% of the corn planted in the United States was sowed with plants whose cells contained a gene that produced an insecticidal protein. The gene had its origin in the bacterial species *Bacillus thuringiensis*. Use of the genetically modified corn, known as Bt corn, for human consumption was approved by the U.S. Food and Drug Administration in 1993.

Results of a laboratory study on the effects of consumption of Bt corn pollen by larvae of a non-corn-eating insect—namely, the monarch butterfly—was reported by J. Losey and his colleagues at Cornell University. The butterfly lays its eggs on the leaves of milkweed plants, which the emerging caterpillars eat as their sole source of food. The investigators dusted the leaves of milkweed plants with Bt corn pollen, regular corn pollen, or no pollen. Half of the larvae that ingested the Bt corn pollen died, whereas the others survived. Whether the laboratory findings reflect what is happening in nature now is being investigated through studies of the monarch-butterfly populations in areas where Bt corn is grown.

Insect Saliva as Vaccine. Leishmaniasis, an infectious protozoan disease afflicting millions of people in tropical and subtropical areas, is transmitted by blood-feeding sand flies. In addition to causing severe skin infections, leishmania microbes can invade internal organs and cause death. When piercing the skin of a person, the sand fly deposits some of its saliva into the wound. The saliva prevents blood clotting at the wound and also promotes the transfer of the protozoans.

D. Sacks and his research team at the National Institute of Allergy and Infectious Diseases in Bethesda, MD, exposed a group of mice, for a short period of time, to sand flies that were free of leishmania. After a one-month interval, the mice were exposed to microbe-containing sand flies, as was a group of mice that never had been exposed to the insects. Only those mice that had been bitten previously by microbe-free sand flies were resistant to leishmania infection.

This finding opens the possibility of using sand-fly saliva as an anti-leishmania vaccine and might help in the development of vaccines against other insect-transmitted infectious diseases.

LOUIS LEVINE, *City College of New York*

Bolivia

The government of President Hugo Banzer entered its third year in Bolivia in August 1999. Although it was hampered by charges of widespread administrative corruption and weakened by an economic downturn, it was buoyed to an extent by encouraging developments in the natural-gas sector.

Corruption. During the year, accusations of high-level skulduggery proliferated. In late April, Labor Minister Leopoldo López was dismissed from his post for allegedly covering up a smuggling ring. Health Minister Tonchi Marinkovic was sacked at about the same time, in connection with overpayments made on shipments of vaccine. On June 1, German Monroy Chazarreta, the mayor of La Paz, the capital, was forced to resign in the face of charges of personal corruption. And in mid-August, Gaby Candia, a former mayor of La Paz, was ordered arrested and held on similar accusations.

Economy. The textile and garment industries of both Bolivia and Peru were hit hard by economic downturn, especially the crisis in Brazil. Traditionally the outlet for 35% of Bolivian production, Brazil cut its textile imports from Bolivia to almost nothing early in the year. Three textile mills in La Paz laid off some 200 workers, following Brazil's devaluation of its currency in January.

The agricultural sector registered a mixed performance. Overall, agricultural output was up slightly (1.1%) during the 1998–99 crop year. However, a combination of drought and flooding caused by El Niño seriously affected the soybean industry in the Santa Cruz region, destroying nearly 193,000 acres (78 000 ha) in plantings.

BOLIVIA • Information Highlights

Official Name: Republic of Bolivia.
Location: West-central South America.
Area: 424,162 sq mi (1 098 580 km^2).
Population (July 1999 est.): 7,982,850.
Chief Cities: Sucre, the legal capital (1993 est.), 144,994; La Paz, the administrative capital (1998 est.), 894,000; Santa Cruz de la Sierra (1998 est.), 953,000; Cochabamba (1993 est.), 448,756.
Government: *Head of state and government,* Hugo Banzer Suarez, president (took office August 1997). *Legislature*—National Congress: Chamber of Senators and Chamber of Deputies.
Monetary Unit: Boliviano (5.940 bolivianos equal U.S.$1, Nov. 23, 1999).
Gross Domestic Product (1998 est. U.S.$): $23,400,-000,000 (purchasing power parity).
Economic Indexes (1998): *Consumer Prices* (1991 = 100): all items, 184.9; food, 185.7. *Industrial Production* (1990 = 100): 137.3.
Foreign Trade (1998 U.S.$): *Imports,* $1,983,000,000; *exports,* $1,103,000,000.

Mining and Hydrocarbons. Mining, still a formidable part of Bolivia's economic spectrum, accounts for 35% of the country's total exports, with a 1998 value of $320 million. Nonetheless, investment in the mining sector has declined steadily in recent years. From a 1995 level of $115 million, investment in mining projects fell to $48 million in 1998. Of 40 foreign-owned mining companies active in Bolivia during 1996, only eight remained active in 1999. Due to the world economic downturn—especially the 1997–98 Asian crisis—Bolivia's overall mining output dropped by 2.8% in 1998.

A Canadian-owned firm, the Vista Gold Co., closed its mines at Potosí in early August, citing the low international price for gold. Some 400 miners were laid off. Earlier in the year, Comibol, the state mining company, had proposed reform of Bolivia's taxation regime to halt the slide in mining investment and to promote new input into mining ventures.

A somewhat brighter economic picture was painted by the performance of the natural-gas industry. In July natural-gas sales to Brazil were inaugurated through the new Santa Cruz–to–São Paulo pipeline at the rate of up to 1.06 billion cu ft (30 million m^3) per day. Plans were being developed for another pipeline—from Yacuiba in southeast Bolivia to Porto Alegre, Brazil, via Asunción, Paraguay.

Bolivia has estimated natural-gas reserves of 8.5 trillion cu ft (240 billion m^3), which could rise to 20 trillion cu ft (566 billion m^3) in the future. In 1999 it signed a memo of understanding with Peru for the construction of a 260-mi (420-km), 8-inch (20-cm) gas pipeline between La Paz and the Peruvian port of Ilo, at a cost of approximately $175 million. A 310-mi (500-km) all-weather road between La Paz and Ilo was scheduled for completion by the end of the year. Bolivia, a landlocked country, ships the bulk of its exports and imports through Peru and Chile.

Drugs. The UN Food and Agricultural Organization and the UN Drug Control Program signed an agreement with Bolivia on May 10 to continue, for three years, support for the alternative-development project in the coca-growing areas of the Chaparé Valley. The project, begun in 1996, involves developing fruit growing and forestry to supplant coca growing by campesinos. About 10,000 families were expected to participate in the project.

RICHARD SCHROEDER, *Freelance Writer*

Bosnia and Herzegovina

The process of reconstructing Bosnia and Herzegovina as a single sovereign state continued throughout 1999, but the international community faced serious difficulties in promoting a central political authority and in stimulating long-term economic recovery. Nationalist politicians continued to block the process of Bosnian integration.

Political Standstill. The country remained polarized along ethnic lines as nationalist parties continued to control decision-making in Bosnia's two entities, the Muslim-Croat Bosnian Federation and the Serb Republic. With municipal elections scheduled for April 2000, the Organization for Cooperation and Security in Europe (OSCE) drafted a Permanent Election Law in July that was supposed to promote multiethnic politics. However, the draft came under severe criticism from various observers because it failed to go far enough in promoting voting along nonnationalist and cross-ethnic lines.

Human-rights violations against rival ethnic groups continued in the country. This included discrimination in obtaining housing, education, pensions, and employment, as well as sporadic acts of violence against returning refugees. Serbian leaders in particular continued to block the return of Muslim residents expelled from their homes during the 1992–95 war.

In August, Muslim deputies threatened to withdraw their support for the government of moderate Serb leader Milorad Dodik unless it actively facilitated the return of Muslim and Croat refugees to the Serb entity. Reportedly, only 10,500 non-Serb refugees had been allowed to return to their homes in the Serb Republic since 1995, while 840,000 Bosnian citizens remained displaced within the country, and a further 350,000 remained as refugees abroad.

Organized criminality remained a serious problem. In March a bomb explosion in Sarajevo led to the death of Jozo Leutar, a Croat and deputy interior minister of the Bosnian Federation. Leutar was known as a determined enemy of organized crime, although some commentators suspected that the attack was politically motivated.

International Involvement. The international community continued to press for the marginalization of nationalist hard-liners among all three ethnic groups. International High Representative Carlos Westendorp dismissed the president of the Serb Republic, Nikola Poplasen, for interfering in the country's democratic process and for favoring partition. This led to protests from Bosnian Serb leaders and to their temporary boycott of Bosnia's central political institutions.

Serbian nationalists suffered a further setback in March, when the strategically positioned town of Brcko in northern Bosnia was removed from unilateral Serb control and placed under a joint multiethnic mandate with continuing international supervision. Serb leaders protested that this decision effectively split the Serb Republic into two parts and rewarded the Muslim side.

In August, Westendorp was succeeded by Austrian diplomat Wolfgang Petrisch, the former European Union (EU) representative for Kosovo. Meanwhile, U.S. envoy Jacques Klein replaced Elisabeth Rehn as

Jozo Leutar, a Croat and deputy interior minister of the Bosnian Federation, died as a result of injuries sustained in a car-bomb explosion in the Bosnian capital of Sarajevo in mid-March 1999.

BOSNIA AND HERZEGOVINA
Information Highlights

Official Name: Bosnia and Herzegovina.
Location: Southeastern Europe.
Area: 19,781 sq mi (51 233 km²).
Population (July 1999 est.): 3,482,495.
Chief Cities (1991 census): Sarajevo, the capital, 415,631; Banja Luka, 142,644.
Government: *Head of state,* Alija Izetbegovic (Muslim), Zivko Radisic (Serb), Ante Jelavic (Croat), presidents. *Head of government,* Haris Silajdzic, Svetozar Mihajlovic, co-prime ministers. *Legislature*—Parliamentary Assembly: National House of Representatives and House of Peoples.
Gross Domestic Product (1998 est. U.S.$): $5,800,000,000 (purchasing power parity).

the United Nations (UN) representative to Bosnia and Herzegovina. Petrisch and Klein began to concentrate their efforts on reforming Bosnia's corrupt judicial system, buttressing its precarious independent mass media, and improving its educational system. Klein also attacked the activities of the Croatian Herzegovinian "mafia," which thwarted the development of a functioning democracy and prevented the emergence of a competitive market economy. He criticized the government in Croatia for supporting illicit structures inside Bosnia and for harboring designs on Bosnian territory.

Yugoslav President Slobodan Milosevic and Croatian President Franjo Tudjman continued to meddle in Bosnian politics. In September, Milosevic hosted the ousted Bosnian Serb president Poplasen and the former Serb member of Bosnia's joint presidency, Momcilo Krajisnik. The move was condemned by the international community for fanning opposition to the moderate Dodik government.

Meanwhile, some members of President Tudjman's ruling party in Croatia called for the creation of separate Croatian and Muslim entities in Bosnia to replace the current Bosnian Federation. Muslim leaders considered this a move toward Croatian separatism, and Bosnia's Deputy Prime Minister Haris Silajdzic declared that Tudjman should be sent to The Hague tribunal for his role in war crimes committed during the 1993–94 Muslim-Croat war. By contrast, Croatia's democratic opposition called for the decentralization of political power rather than the creation of three entities. They believed that Bosnia's cantons (or districts) should become the main centers of political authority, in which the three ethnic groups could gain greater representation.

International organizations continued to be criticized for failing to arrest the two most-senior indicted war criminals—former Serbian leaders Radovan Karadzic and Gen. Ratko Mladic. The French, in particular, were accused of dragging their heels in apprehending them, as both men were believed to operate in the French sector of the S-FOR (Stabilization Force) operation of the North Atlantic Treaty Organization (NATO). In July and August two senior Serb leaders—former Deputy Prime Minister Radoslav Brdjanin and army chief of staff Gen. Momir Talic—were arrested for war crimes. Talic became the highest-ranking Serbian war criminal to be brought to the international war-crimes tribunal in The Hague.

In the light of the new operation in Kosovo, NATO planned to scale down its military mission in Bosnia during 2000. The force of some 31,000 was to be cut to about 16,500 troops, with the U.S. share of the deployment dropping from 6,200 to 4,000.

Economic Drift. Real growth in the Bosnian economy slowed down during 1999 as a consequence of numerous factors, including widespread corruption and mismanagement, overdependence on international agencies, limited economic development, and the crisis in nearby Kosovo. The gross domestic product (GDP) was projected to grow at less than 5% for the year, despite initial forecasts of a double-digit increase. This marked a significant decline from the 18% growth registered in 1998.

Bosnia continued to benefit from substantial foreign economic aid, particularly from the World Bank and the International Monetary Fund (IMF). About $165 million worth of new projects was approved for the country between July 1998 and June 1999. The Bosnian currency remained fairly stable as it was pegged to the German mark, and inflation was held steady during the year. However, unemployment remained high, at some 35% of the economically active population.

In August there were reports that Serbian, Croatian, and Muslim leaders had stolen up to $1 billion from public funds or from international-aid projects since the Dayton peace agreement was signed in November 1995. The embezzled funds were believed to amount to about 20% of all state money in the country. The allegations were denied vehemently by nationalist leaders in both entities, but they soured the climate for foreign assistance and investment.

JANUSZ BUGAJSKI
Center for Strategic and International Studies

Brazil

After a sharp currency devaluation in January 1999, President Fernando Henrique Cardoso persuaded the International Monetary Fund (IMF) to renegotiate a bailout of the nation's troubled economy, provided the government implemented tough economic policies. Retrenchment sparked anti-IMF protests from bureaucrats, teachers, peasants, and other groups demanding more, not less, expenditures on social programs. This prompted Cardoso to announce a major increase in government spending.

Politics. Even though Brazilians would not elect their next chief executive for three years, politicians began maneuvering to succeed Cardoso, who cannot run for a third term. Some potential candidates, including several within Cardoso's own Brazilian Social Democratic Party (PSDB), began slamming the government's neoliberal strategy in order to capitalize on widespread discontent over Cardoso's free-market policies and garner national attention. At a late-summer PSDB forum, for example, Development Minister Clóvis Carvalho—with Finance Minister Pedro Malan seated alongside him—blasted the regime's economic approach. Cardoso demanded Carvalho's resignation, but the cabinet member refused to tender it, forcing the president to fire him.

On the heels of this action, Cardoso unveiled a four-year, $580 billion spending plan in hopes of boosting employment and his low public-approval rating. According to the budget ministry, these outlays would come from all levels of government, state companies, and private firms.

In December the Senate took advantage of Cardoso's anemic public-approval rating to approve a constitutional limitation on the chief executive's ability to implement so-called "provisional measures" without waiting for the legislature to vote on them. The lower house was expected to endorse the initiative early in 2000.

Economics. The year started badly for Cardoso. On January 15 the central bank announced that it would allow Brazil's currency, the real, to float. Within a week, the currency had fallen 42% against the dollar, prompting massive capital flight. To defend the currency, authorities raised interest rates, which peaked at 45% in early March.

In late 1998 the Brazilians had signed a three-year, $41.5 billion accord with the IMF to stabilize their economy. Although Cardoso failed to notify the IMF in advance of the currency devaluation, the Fund agreed to renegotiate the understanding in return for Brazil's tightening its belt, raising taxes, and accelerating the privatization of state-owned industries. Meanwhile, the International Finance Corporation, an arm of the World Bank, created a $4 billion fund to assist Brazilian corporations facing heavy foreign-debt repayments.

© Paulo Fridman/Corbis-Sygma

A January 1999 financial crisis that led to the floating of Brazil's currency, the real, caused nervous moments and anxiety in the financial markets of São Paulo, above.

The shock of devaluation and its attendant austerity measures gave rise to public outcries. In July thousands of truck drivers blockaded the nation's major cities to protest high tolls on privatized highways and the rising cost of diesel fuel.

In response to international pressures and the prospect of hyperinflation, Cardoso persuaded Congress to pass long-stalled reforms of the retirement system. The lawmakers reluctantly agreed to raise pension-fund payments by current state workers and to require more than 400,000 retired public employees to pay 11% of their benefits in contributions. The levies, which took effect on May 1 and would have generated $1.6 billion, were designed to turn the projected budget deficit of 13% of gross domestic product (GDP) into a 3.1% surplus—with a 3.25% target for 2000. Although the amount of anticipated revenues constituted only one tenth of the social-security shortfall for the year, the government viewed the legislation as a vital first step in revamping one of the world's most expensive retirement schemes.

Brazil's 918,000 retired civil servants receive substantially larger payments than do their private-sector counterparts. Worse still from the perspective of finance officials, the country lacks a retirement age. Thus, so-called "precocious pensioners"—individuals like the 33-year-old farmhand who convinced auditors that he had been working since age 3—can draw benefits when they are young and continue to collect annuity checks even if they take another job and retire again.

The president claimed that his changes and his bold new spending program would expand GDP, which declined by 0.5% in 1999, to 4% annually. He also vowed that prices would rise by only 6% in 2000, down from a 10% increase, while real public-debt payments would plummet from 7.5% to 2.4% of GDP.

Such rosy predictions occurred before the Supreme Court declared unconstitutional the two congressionally approved changes in the pension law. To recoup the lost monies, Finance Minister Malan stated that the government would slash spending by $620 million in 2000 and would raise additional funds by changing the rules governing payment of the corporate social-security tax. Moreover, Malan pledged to submit to Congress legislation increasing taxes on interest-rate remittances sent abroad. The government also lowered restrictions on short-term capital inflows in an effort to lure foreign investors back to the country and halt the continued devaluation of the real. Still, economists feared that the weakness of the currency would reignite inflationary pressures and curb economic growth.

Malan's announcements further angered some 6,000 teachers, parents, students, and other demonstrators, who marched through the capital demanding that the government earmark 10% of GDP for education. All told, they wanted a threefold increase in educational funding over the next decade and a $460 monthly minimum wage for teachers. Other protesters arrived from Rio de Janeiro to lambaste the government's austerity policies, the IMF, and "the paralysis of agrarian reform."

In mid-October mass demonstrations called the "Latin American Cry of the Excluded" took place in 13 regions to excoriate the impact of IMF and U.S. policies on Latin America. "People are really indigent now," said the leader of the People Without Land Movement. "If we are already talking about a new president three years before the elections, it shows the seriousness of the economic crisis." Cardoso responded to such rhetoric by defending his record on social issues and insisting that interest rates were falling, growth was resuming, and the jobless rate soon would decline. The president complemented his rejoinder by convening a meeting of the 27 governors in late October. A majority of the state chiefs agreed to back a constitutional amendment reversing the Supreme Court's decision on social-security withholding. As expected, leaders of the three impoverished states run by the leftist Workers' Party—Rio Grande do Sul, Mato Grasso do Sul, and Acre—turned thumbs down on Cardoso's request.

Foreign Policy. Soon after winning the Argentine presidency in October, Fernando de la Rúa sought to diminish the Argentine-Brazilian frictions that had arisen over the mounting protectionism that accompanied Brazil's economic woes. Nonetheless, Cardoso showed little enthusiasm for de la Rúa's proposal to create permanent arbitration panels within the Mercosur free-trade area to resolve commercial disputes among private sectors in member states.

In early September, Gen. Charles Wilhelm, chief of the U.S. Southern Command, flew to Brasília to drum up support for the fight against Colombian guerrillas, who are linked closely to narcotraffickers. At first, the Brazilians downplayed the threat that the Colombia crisis posed to the hemisphere and adamantly rejected initiatives that might constitute interference in the affairs of another nation. Brazilian officials showed greater concern about terrorists when 2,500 representatives of Latin American rebel organizations met in Belém, in northern Brazil, in early December.

George W. Grayson
College of William & Mary

BRAZIL • Information Highlights

Official Name: Federative Republic of Brazil.
Location: Eastern South America.
Area: 3,286,473 sq mi (8 511 965 km²).
Population (July 1999 est.): 171,853,126.
Chief Cities (Aug. 1, 1996): Brasília, the capital, 1,821,946; São Paulo, 9,839,436; Rio de Janeiro, 5,551,538; Salvador, 2,211,539; Belo Horizonte, 2,091,448.
Government: *Head of state and government,* Fernando Henrique Cardoso, president (sworn in Jan. 1, 1995). *Legislature*—National Congress: Federal Senate and Chamber of Deputies.
Monetary Unit: Real (1.8550 reales equal U.S.$1, Dec. 13, 1999).
Gross Domestic Product (1998 est. U.S.$): $1,035,200,-000,000 (purchasing power parity).
Economic Indexes: *Consumer Prices* (1998, 1992 = 100): all items, 93,533.3; food, 84,787.4. *Industrial Production* (1998, 1990 = 100): 114.2.
Foreign Trade (1998 U.S.$): *Imports,* $57,550,000,000; *exports,* $51,120,000,000.

Bulgaria

During 1999, Bulgaria continued to stabilize its economy, improved its bilateral ties with several Balkan neighbors, supported the military operation by the North Atlantic Treaty Organization (NATO) against Serbia, and advanced toward membership in the European Union (EU).

Politics and the Economy. The parliamentary majority held by the Union of Democratic Forces (UDF) ensured that Bulgaria's reform program was not challenged seriously by the Socialist opposition. President Petar Stoyanov retained his high popularity despite the government's painful austerity program. The UDF faced unexpected difficulty in October's local elections, however; although it defeated the Socialists in most municipalities—including Sofia and Plovdiv—the margin of victory was narrow in many cases. Growing public frustration with layoffs and state spending cuts was evident in the low voter turnout of about 50%.

Bulgaria's major domestic priority was completing structural market reforms, particularly privatizing the major state-owned enterprises. By mid-1999, more than one third of state assets were privatized, as was 90% of agricultural land. The country's gross domestic product (GDP) was projected to grow for the second consecutive year at a rate of about 2%, while inflation was nearly 0%. But Bulgaria lost trade commerce as a result of the Serbian conflict, primarily through the blockage of traffic on the Danube River inside Serbia; some experts said the GDP could have grown by another 2% or more if not for the war. Despite Bulgaria's economic recovery, the International Monetary Fund (IMF) stressed the importance of speeding up privatization to avoid delays in foreign investment.

To show confidence in the nation's financial system, the lev was redenominated, making its face value equal to that of the German mark. Both old and new currency would be valid until year's end.

Regional Relations. Bulgaria made substantial progress in developing its relations with its Balkan neighbors as well with NATO. The most significant development was a breakthrough with Macedonia, symbolized by a declaration the two countries signed in February stating that Bulgaria recognized Macedonian as a separate language and that Bulgaria and Macedonia harbored no territorial claims against each other. Other deals, including investment pacts, were signed. The planned creation of a free-trade area in January 2000 was negotiated.

BULGARIA • Information Highlights

Official Name: Republic of Bulgaria.
Location: Southeastern Europe.
Area: 42,823 sq mi (110 910 km²).
Population (July 1999 est.): 8,194,772.
Chief Cities (Dec. 31, 1994 est.): Sofia, the capital, 1,116,454; Plovdiv, 346,330; Varna, 304,499.
Government: *Head of state,* Petar Stoyanov, president (elected November 1996). *Head of government,* Ivan Kostov, prime minister (elected April 1997). *Legislature* (unicameral)—National Assembly.
Monetary Unit: Lev (1.8549 leva equal U.S.$1, Nov. 3, 1999).
Gross Domestic Product (1998 est. U.S.$): $33,600,-000,000 (purchasing power parity).
Economic Index (1998, 1990 = 100): *Consumer Prices,* all items, 148,529.5; food, 170,085.2.
Foreign Trade (1998 U.S.$): *Imports,* $4,976,000,000; *exports,* $4,292,000,000.

Sofia's support of NATO during the Kosovo conflict, as well as its open criticism of Serbian leader Slobodan Milosevic for causing Balkan instability, further soured relations with Serbia. However, Bulgaria continued to develop good relations with both Greece and Turkey. It signed four bilateral agreements with Turkey concerning tourism, environmental protection, prevention of nuclear accidents, and the establishment of new borders. Sofia also signed a protocol with Ankara under which Turkish companies will build highways and dams in Bulgaria in exchange for electricity. Meanwhile, Greece promised to press for Bulgaria's removal from the EU's visa blacklist, and the two countries agreed that joint projects would be implemented under the EU-sponsored South-East European Stability Pact. In October finance ministers from Bulgaria, Macedonia, and Albania negotiated a common approach to infrastructural projects in southeastern Europe.

Foreign Affairs. In October the European Commission recommended that accession negotiations to the EU should be extended to five East European states, including Bulgaria. But to qualify for EU membership, the government must maintain its economic progress, close its nuclear reactor in Kozloduy, intensify its anticorruption campaign, and adopt a body of EU-related legislation.

In November, Bill Clinton became the first U.S. president to visit Bulgaria. He urged Bulgaria to "stay the course" in building democracy and to avoid ethnic conflicts.

JANUSZ BUGAJSKI
Center for Strategic and International Studies

Burma. *See* MYANMAR.

Business and Corporate Affairs

It was a year in which the Internet emerged as the fulcrum of economic change, enabling upstarts to seize market share and compelling older companies to adapt or lose customers. In 1999 the Internet's signature was written onto every aspect of corporate life—profits, huge mergers, marketing skills, inventories, personnel, product design, advertising, workdays, education, and, perhaps most importantly, raised productivity.

While still accounting for only a small but growing percentage of retail sales, the Internet offered almost everything—for example, houses, cars, travel, and stocks. Business communications, including contracts, were as likely to be routed in an instant via E-mail or facsimile as sent by overnight carriers.

The Internet was but one of the major changes that kept executives on their toes in 1999. While new companies emerged in the public marketplace at a previously unmatched rate, older and larger companies sought global power and competitive strength in consolidations. Reminded constantly by U.S. Federal Reserve Chairman Alan Greenspan, businesses large and small were forced to consider the possibility that inflation might emerge. Many businesses—particularly in tobacco, utilities, vitamins, and guns—remained in costly litigation, and lawyers expanded their interests to include health care and other insurers. Throughout the year, Microsoft, with the greatest market valuation of any company, fought a long Justice Department antitrust suit that culminated in a federal judge's ruling that the company frustrated competition and denied choice to computer users. European sales of Coca-Cola, another symbol of American marketing power, were pummeled by accusations of product contamination. Whatever the cause, corporate chiefs had to deal with more than the usual pressures, and some failed to do so.

High-Tech Companies. The year's most spectacular continuing news was the soaring sales and stock prices of high-tech and Internet stocks. With employee 401 (k) and corporate pension plans providing a steady stream of funds, popular averages reached record highs. Benefiting from the almost manic desire for new technology shares were companies such as Cisco, Sun Microsystems, Oracle, America Online, and Qualcomm. On the basis of wireless-technology patents, Qualcomm profits quadrupled, and its shares rose by as much as 15-fold in a year, sometimes by as much as 30 points a day, leading to a planned 4-for-1 stock split in December.

Such examples of high-tech fever were not isolated. By offering their shares to the public, innovative private companies quickly acquired market valuations close to $1 billion, and the paper assets of their founders suddenly placed them among the nation's wealthiest individuals. Akamai, with sales of just $1.3 million and losses of $28.3 million in the first nine months of the year, raised $234 million on an offering of 9 million shares in late October. The share price vaulted in one day from an initial offering price of $26 to more than $145, giving the company—which provides speedier downloading of image-intensive sections of Web pages—a total market value of $13 billion. And yet, its 458% one-day surge made it only the fourth-hottest initial offering ever, behind theglobe.com, which rose 606% on opening day, and the respective first-day gains of 525% and 474% by Foundry Networks and Marketwatch.com. Many hot new issues cooled within months, but great fortunes were made by founders of relatively new public companies. *Fortune* magazine's list of "America's Forty Richest under Forty" was led by the founder of Dell Computer, Michael Dell, 34, whose assets totaled $21.49 billion. The list included ten billionaires, and its smallest fortune was $243 million. Indicative of such newer fortunes was a $150 million gift to Stanford University by James H. Clark, a former faculty member and more recently a founder of Silicon Graphics and cofounder of Netscape Communications.

While the new economy provided opportunities, it also imposed demands, especially on companies and institutions attuned to the old. Xerox, once considered a leader in advanced technology, saw profits fall as computers and E-mail cut into copier sales. In the spirit of the global economy and changing marketplace, the New York Stock Exchange voted to extend its trading hours and to eradicate the last vestiges of its centuries-old private-club image. Emulating the companies whose shares it listed, it laid plans to become a publicly traded corporation. Acknowledging the vast mutations in U.S. industry, Dow Jones changed the component companies of its venerable industrial average. Dropped from the 30-company list were Sears Roebuck, Goodyear, Chevron, and Union Carbide. Added were Intel, Microsoft, Home Depot, and SBC Communications. Symbolic of marketplace changes,

International Business Machines (IBM), increasingly involved in selling its know-how and services rather than computer hardware, announced it would cease selling desktop computers through traditional retail outlets, and would sell them only via the Internet. And after decades of effort, the White House and Congress agreed to revise the Depression-era Glass-Steagall financial-services law. Signing of the provision effectively ended limitations on banking, insurance, and securities firms entering each other's fields. (*See also* BANKING AND FINANCE.)

Mergers. Mergers were frequent, massive, and otherwise of unusual significance, and maneuvering by corporate boards and executives added to the intensity of transactions. The brokerage firm Donaldson, Lufkin & Jenrette estimated that global mergers would far exceed 1998's $2.4 trillion valuation, and said that "consolidation had become the most consistently recurring investment theme of significance across most of the world's industries." The motivation might have been the quest for economies of scale, but the result, it said, was increasingly oligopolistic markets.

Much of the merger activity was among companies involved in electronics and communications. In the largest merger ever, MCI-Worldcom, the second-largest U.S. telephone company, offered $108 billion for third-largest Sprint Corp. The boards of both companies approved the merger, despite indications that BellSouth Corp. would raise its original bid of $100 billion. The move quickened the pace of consolidation in the industry, in which companies strived to offer local, long-distance, wireless, and data services to businesses and consumers. Much smaller in size but of equal and maybe greater significance, Sumner Redstone's Viacom acquired CBS in a deal valued at $37.3 billion. The merger created a company with $18.9 billion in annual revenue, making it the third-largest media concern behind Time Warner and Walt Disney. However, what disturbed critics more than the new company's mammoth size was the thrust it gave to concentration in the ways people received information and entertainment. The new Viacom included Paramount (movies), MTV and Nickelodeon (cable-television programmers), Simon and Schuster (book publishing), copyrights to more than 100,000 songs, the CBS (broadcasting) network, and five amusement parks.

Consolidation was a major theme in pharmaceuticals, too, where patent ownership of the latest in health-care drugs could mean billions of dollars in sales and enhanced research facilities. Shortly after American Home Products and Warner-Lambert announced they were merging in a $72 billion deal, Pfizer Inc. made an $82.4 billion "hostile" offer for Warner-Lambert. No matter which company won, the deal, when completed, would produce the world's largest prescription drug maker. Another major deal was announced in December, when Monsanto and Pharmacia & Upjohn agreed to merge to create one of the world's largest pharmaceutical and biotechnology companies, worth an estimated $52 billion.

Global markets were creating bigness throughout industry. Size, always important

© Jonathan Elderfield/Liaison Agency

Sumner Redstone, chief executive officer of Viacom, and Mel Karmazin (right), *president of CBS, announced the merger of the two companies in September 1999. The merged company would become the third-largest media corporation behind Time Warner and Disney.*

in oil, was becoming more so. The European Union (EU) approved Exxon's $81 billion purchase of Mobil Oil. However, the deal bogged down in negotiations with the U.S. Federal Trade Commission (FTC) until November 30, when federal officials announced their approval after ordering the companies to sell off more than $2 billion worth of gas stations, pipelines, and other assets. The merger reunited two parts of the Rockefeller oil empire broken up by the U.S. government in 1911.

Troubles for Microsoft and the Tobacco Industry. No company had more headline-making troubles—offset to some extent by great and continued successes—than Bill Gates' Microsoft Corp., which now had a market value of more than $400 billion. In a finding of facts preceding an actual court judgment, federal district-court judge Thomas Penfield Jackson found the company to be a predatory monopolist. In his report on November 5, Jackson said the company employed a "business strategy of directing its monopoly power toward inducing other companies to abandon projects that threaten Microsoft and toward punishing those companies that resist." Among companies affected by such actions, he said, were Netscape, Intel, Apple, and Real Networks. IBM—itself the target years earlier of government monopoly charges that eventually were dropped—also was named. While not ruling out a peaceful settlement rather than going to trial, Gates indicated he felt duty bound to defend what he described as the company's right to innovate. Federal Judge Richard Posner, chief judge of the U.S. Court of Appeals in Chicago, was named to mediate talks toward a resolution.

Meanwhile, the serial problems of the tobacco industry added new episodes, and its affairs seemed to grow even more complex. It remained under a decades-old siege from individuals (the first liability suit was filed in 1954) and institutions. Relief came only briefly, when the federal government decided to close a five-year criminal probe. But civil suits, which on paper already had cost the industry hundreds of billions of dollars, continued. The Justice Department added another in September, when it sued to recover what it said were additional billions of dollars spent on smoking-related health care. It accused cigarette makers of a "coordinated campaign of fraud and deceit." Shortly afterward and to public amazement, Philip Morris Cos., parent of the largest tobacco company, conceded that tobacco was unsafe. In a new Web site, part of a $100 million advertising campaign to improve its image, the company blandly announced, "There is overwhelming medical and scientific consensus that cigarette smoking causes lung cancer, heart disease, emphysema, and other serious diseases in smokers."

A Volatile Executive Suite. The intense competition and changing marketplace created volatility in the executive suite. AT&T's top cable and Internet officer, Leo Hindery, quit suddenly and without explanation. This raised more questions about AT&T's ability to spread its cable range from television to local phone service and Internet access. Amid shareholder insistence that the Dun & Bradstreet's shares lagged the market, Volney Taylor, 59, resigned as chairman, chief executive, and director of the old-line information and credit-rating company, whose massive data files had seemed ready-made for the Internet age. Marc Andreesen, cofounder of Netscape, resigned as America Online's chief technology officer to become founding chairman of Loudcloud Inc., a start-up aimed at helping companies adjust to the Internet. Directors of Rite-Aid, the third-largest drugstore chain, removed chief executive officer (CEO) Marvin L. Grass after a series of management missteps that collapsed the company's profits and share price.

And in a development that stunned the international business world, Coca-Cola announced in December the resignation of M. Douglas Ivester, 52, after only two years as chairman and CEO. The resignation, scheduled for April 2000, followed a rocky tenure that included a decline in the price of the company's shares, a suit by a group of current and former African-American employees over alleged discrimination, and accusations of product contamination that damaged European sales.

In appointments significant for their racial connotations, Franklin Raines became chairman of Fannie Mae, the nation's largest mortgage company, and Barry Rand, former Xerox executive vice-president, assumed the chairmanship of Avis. They were the first African-Americans to head Fortune 1000 companies. Perhaps equally significant, Carleton Fiorina was named to head Hewlett-Packard, an electronics firm, and Andrea Jung was named chief at Avon Products, joining Jill Bard of Mattel toys and Marion Sandler of Golden West Financial as female chief executives on *Fortune*'s list of the 500 largest companies. Catalyst, a research orga-

© Ben Margot/AP/Wide World Photos

CARLETON S. FIORINA

Described by *Fortune* magazine as the most powerful woman in American business, Carleton (Carly) S. Fiorina, 44, was named president and chief executive officer of Hewlett-Packard, the second-largest U.S. computer company, in July 1999. Previously she had been employed by AT&T and Lucent Technologies for nearly 20 years. For the last two years she had been president of Lucent Technologies' Global Service Provider Business—a division that enjoyed dramatic growth during that period.

A graduate of Stanford University, Fiorina earned a master's degree in business administration from the University of Maryland and a master's in science from MIT's Sloan School.

nization, said women held 11.9% of 11,681 high executive jobs in 1999 at America's 500 largest companies, up from 11.2% in 1998 and 8.7% in 1994. If such appointments were indicative of a new era, the announcement of the retirement of General Electric chairman John F. Welch, Jr., was seen as another. Welch, who in two decades as CEO grew the company to annual sales of more than $100 billion while diversifying into services and pioneering management concepts, said he would retire in April 2001.

Negative Items. Less pleasant matters also intruded on what was, in all, a prosperous and, in most aspects, highly successful year for business. About $7 billion of what appeared to be "laundered" money flowed through the Bank of New York from Russia, leading to suspicions of high-level government corruption within Russia and raising U.S.-Russian tensions. Good times breed rascals, too, and 1999 had more than its share. Martin Frankel fled from his mansion in Greenwich, CT, and was arrested in Germany after allegedly bilking insurance companies of at least $200 million. Within days, Martin Armstrong, an investment guru, also was arrested and accused of swindling investors out of millions of dollars. And in San Antonio, a group called InverWorld was accused by the U.S. Securities and Exchange Commission (SEC) of defrauding Mexican investors to the tune of nearly $500 million. Senior-level executives Terry Church and Michael Graham were indicated on charges they interfered with regulators examining records of the First National Bank of Keystone. The bank was closed after the regulators found $515 million in loans missing. Giancarlo Parretti, a former Hollywood financier who had masterminded a $1.3 billion takeover of Metro-Goldwyn-Mayer almost a decade earlier—and then had fled after bringing the company to near financial ruin—was arrested near Rome on perjury and other fraud warrants.

Optimism. Such negative items, however, were buried under an avalanche of optimism that continued throughout the year. The strength of corporate profits surprised many economists, especially those who viewed the long expansion—due to reach a record 107th month in February 2000—as being prone to the ravages of old age. That view had been expressed by U.S. Federal Reserve officials, especially chairman Greenspan, and it led the Fed to raise interest rates one quarter of a point three times during the year. But Greenspan also conceded that technology-driven increases in productivity had made the scenario different in 1999 than it had been a decade earlier. He indicated that those increases, which meant products and services were being delivered at lowered costs, had defused a great deal of the inflation argument. Defined as the amount of output for each hour worked, the increases amounted to 2.9% through September but shot up as the year ended. At the same time, unit labor costs rose more slowly.

As the figures came in, corporate fears of a downturn seemed to lessen even more, and businesses continued to pour funds into computers and other technology. A U.S. trade agreement with China in November was welcomed enthusiastically by computer hardware and software makers. Business also spent heavily on preparing for the transition to a new millennium. As the new year approached, the Commerce Department fixed the Y2K bill for government and industry at about $100 billion.

JOHN CUNNIFF, *The Associated Press*

Cambodia

CAMBODIA • Information Highlights
Official Name: Kingdom of Cambodia.
Location: Southeast Asia.
Area: 69,900 sq mi (181 040 km²).
Population (July 1999 est.): 11,626,520.
Chief City (1991 est.): Phnom Penh, the capital, 900,000.
Government: *Head of state,* Norodom Sihanouk, king (acceded Sept. 24, 1993). *Head of government,* Hun Sen, prime minister (named Sept. 24, 1993). *Legislature*—National Assembly and Senate.
Monetary Unit: Riel (3,820.0 riels equal U.S.$1, official rate, July 1999).
Gross Domestic Product (1998 est. U.S.$): $7,800,000,000 (purchasing power parity).
Foreign Trade (1997 est. U.S.$): *Imports,* $1,100,000,000; *exports,* $736,000,000.

Political stability returned to Cambodia in 1999, as Prime Minister Hun Sen and former First Prime Minister Prince Norodom Ranariddh maintained a new government coalition and established a bicameral parliament. For the first time in decades, the regime did not face a significant armed threat, and former Khmer Rouge (KR) guerrillas were integrated back into society. Cambodia's stability and renewed commitment to economic reform attracted foreign financial aid.

Politics. During the year, Hun Sen clearly established himself as the dominant political figure, while Ranariddh pursued his new duties as National Assembly president. Both men seemingly put aside their strong differences when they cooperated in March to create a new 61-seat Senate, headed by former National Assembly President Chea Sim. Opposition leader Sam Rainsy organized several demonstrations on issues such as illegal land seizures and claimed the government illegally ignored 30 opposition questions posed to the National Assembly. The venerable King Norodom Sihanouk was called on less to play his traditional mediator role. He spent two months in China for medical checkups.

While some KR guerrillas who "defected" received government and military positions, others living in western Cambodia closely monitored negotiations between Hun Sen and the international community on creating a court to try former KR members for genocide. Only two KR leaders—former military commander Ta Mok and a former prison warden known as Duch—had been captured by late 1999. The prime minister argued that an international tribunal could disrupt the fragile peace and spark renewed fighting. In October he agreed to a U.S. proposal of a court composed of three Cambodian and two foreign judges.

Economy. After two years of economic malaise following a 1997 coup and the regional economic crisis, the Consultative Group of foreign donors—which funds about 40% of the government's budget—was encouraged by the truce between Hun Sen and Ranariddh. In February the group pledged $470 million in aid to Cambodia. In October the International Monetary Fund (IMF) approved a fresh loan of $81.6 million to be distributed in seven installments. Cambodian leaders promised to institute reforms that included cutting the size of the military and administration. Phnom Penh predicted that the economy would grow between 4% and 5% in 1999, and that inflation would remain under 10%.

The government's ability to raise sufficient revenue to reduce its dependence on foreign aid, however, was challenged by serious crime and corruption problems, inadequate tax collection, and high spending on the military. While international loans helped renew road-building and other improvement projects, most Cambodians still dealt with little or no electricity, a poor water supply, and disease problems.

Foreign Affairs. Cambodia became the tenth member of the Association of Southeast Asian Nations (ASEAN) in April, marking its acceptance as a regional player. New Cambodian embassies in Brunei, Myanmar, the Philippines, and Singapore—as well as Hun Sen's official visits to six Asian nations—demonstrated his commitment to regional interconnectivity. Both Cambodia and Thailand agreed to clear more mines along their common border.

Beyond Southeast Asia, Hun Sen and an Assembly delegation led by Ranariddh visited Beijing, and Phnom Penh and China signed several agreements that increased their political and economic ties. King Sihanouk in August reiterated Phnom Penh's steadfast commitment to the "one-China" policy. Relations with Taiwan were tense, and the number of Taiwanese foreign investors declined sharply. In June, Hun Sen requested that Kuwait give Cambodia technical assistance in oil exploration. But relations with the United States were strained by the refusal of the U.S. Congress to provide direct aid to Cambodia, as well as by the conflicts over trying KR guerrillas and regarding Hun Sen's alleged involvement in a 1997 attack on an opposition rally.

CHRISTINE VAN ZANDT
U.S. Government Analyst on East Asian Affairs

Canada

Canadians will remember 1999 for extreme weather, provincial elections, debates on how to spend government surpluses, the creation in April of a new northern territory called Nunavut (*see* SPECIAL REPORT), Canada's participation in military action in Kosovo and East Timor, and the appointment of a onetime Chinese refugee as governor-general.

Politics. Liberals fared poorly in 1999 provincial elections. In June, Ontario voters reelected their Progressive Conservative (PC) government, and the PCs also upset the Liberals in New Brunswick in June and took Nova Scotia in July. In Saskatchewan the right-wing Saskatchewan Party finished first in the popular vote, but it failed to win a majority, allowing the second-place New Democratic Party (NDP) to retain its hold on government for a third term by forming a coalition with the Liberals. A week later, Manitobans replaced a three-term PC government with the NDP.

Reform leader Preston Manning campaigned to combine his party with the PCs into a "United Alternative" (UA). At a national Reform meeting in February, approximately 55% of those who voted approved the UA (about 300 of the 1,500 attendees abstained); however, the PCs flatly rejected it in October.

Critics complained of Prime Minister Jean Chrétien's inertia, patronage appointments, and personal vengefulness. Still, opinion polls showed the prime minister far ahead of his prospective opponents. After an August 4 cabinet shuffle, Chrétien, 65, pledged to lead the Liberal government into the next election. In October the prime minister prorogued the old parliamentary session and opened a new one, promising a "family agenda" aimed at lowering taxes on families and helping a parent stay home to raise children.

After years of fighting deficits, Ottawa boasted a budget surplus, and politicians debated whether to spend it on tax cuts, debt reduction, or restoring earlier cuts to Canada's health-care system. Most Canadians favored reinvestment, but the Business Council on National Issues insisted that only drastic tax cuts would attract foreign investors to Canada and keep the country's most talented people from emigrating. Finance Minister Paul Martin delivered his budget on February 16. Out of a projected C$7 billion ($4.7 billion) surplus, Martin allocated significant funds for health care and research and promised middle-class tax relief for the year 2000. Meanwhile, governments at all levels worried that Medicare might become an onerous burden on their budgets in spite of the surpluses.

Canada's 26th governor-general, Adrienne Clarkson, was installed on October 4. She became the first immigrant to hold the country's top ceremonial post. Born Adrienne Poy in Hong Kong in 1939, she and her family fled to Ottawa in 1942 to escape the Japanese invasion. A brilliant student, she

Adrienne Clarkson and her husband, John Ralston Saul, were escorted in a landau to greet the crowd after she was invested as the 26th governor-general of Canada on Oct. 4, 1999.

On Feb. 4, 1999, Canada's Prime Minister Jean Chrétien (center) *and the leaders of nine of the ten provinces and two territories signed the "Framework to Improve the Social Union for Canadians," a partnership between the federal and provincial governments to implement social programs. Quebec's Premier Lucien Bouchard refused to sign the agreement, because a province could not withdraw from it.*

© Jim Young/Reuters/Archive Photos

married political scientist Stephen Clarkson in 1963, divorced him in the mid-1970s, and married her companion, philosopher-author John Ralston Saul, shortly before her appointment. Most Canadians knew her as a popular, impeccably dressed television personality. Beyond barbed comments on the gossip circuit and complaints that the post should be elective, the appointment was well received.

The issue of people-smuggling—a profitable arm of organized crime—came to the fore with the interception of three boatloads of illegal Chinese immigrants off the coast of British Columbia during the summer. The incident strained the traditional sympathy for newcomers among Liberals.

Justice. A British Columbia appeals court ruled in January that a new child-pornography law threatened free speech. In May the Supreme Court redefined the meaning of "spouse" under the Family Law Act to give same-sex couples in Ontario the same rights as partners in a failed marriage. These and other controversial decisions led to a spate of marked criticism directed at judges. In July, Chief Justice Antonio Lamer made a rare public response, accusing critics of "judge bashing" and arguing that the courts were listening to the will of the people. A month later he announced he would retire in January 2000. Appeals-court judge and United Nations (UN) war-crimes prosecutor Louise Arbour was appointed in September to fill an Ontario vacancy on the nine-member Supreme Court.

The crime rate in 1998 fell to only 8,102 incidents per 100,000 people, its lowest level in 20 years, and the homicide rate dropped to 1.8 per 100,000, the lowest level since 1968. Some experts attributed the reduction to the aging of Canada's population. At the same time, some polls showed that Canadians felt less safe, in spite of the rosy statistics.

Foreign Affairs and Defense. In 1999 the World Trade Organization (WTO) opened Canada's markets to U.S. magazines, knocked the base from the 1965 Canada-U.S. Auto Trade Pact, and threatened Canada's farmer-controlled marketing boards. In a surprising move, Canada replaced its WTO representative, John Weekes, with former trade minister Sergio Marchi.

A seven-year dispute between Canada and the United States over salmon fishing along the Pacific coast was settled by two state governors, 28 U.S. native groups, and Canadian Fisheries Minister David Anderson. The United States got a bigger share of Fraser River salmon, but both countries agreed to adjust quotas to salmon stocks.

Like its allies in the North Atlantic Treaty Organization (NATO), Ottawa accused the Serbs of committing atrocities in the province of Kosovo. Most Canadians eventually favored the NATO bombing campaign against Serbia, as well as Ottawa's

CANADA • Information Highlights

Official Name: Canada.
Location: Northern North America.
Area: 3,851,792 sq mi (9 976 140 km²).
Population (July 1999 est.): 31,006,347.
Chief Cities (May 1996 census [metro. areas]): Ottawa, the capital (incl. Hull),1,010,498; Toronto, 4,263,757; Montreal, 3,326,510; Vancouver, 1,831,665.
Government: *Head of state,* Elizabeth II, queen; represented by Adrienne Clarkson, governor-general (took office Oct. 4, 1999). *Head of government,* Jean Chrétien, prime minister (took office Nov. 4, 1993). *Legislature*—Parliament: Senate and House of Commons.
Monetary Unit: Canadian dollar (1.4782 dollars equal U.S.$1, Dec. 8, 1999).
Gross Domestic Product (1998 est. U.S.$): $688,300,000,000 (purchasing power parity).
Economic Indexes (1998, 1990 = 100): *Consumer Prices,* all items, 116.4; food, 114.1. *Industrial Production,* 123.6.
Foreign Trade (1998 U.S.$): *Imports,* $201,060,000,000; *exports,* $214,335,000,000.

decision to contribute 800 troops to NATO's occupation force after the conflict was resolved. In September, Canada sent air transport and a company of infantry as part of the Australian-led UN security force in the Indonesian province of East Timor, which was wracked by violence after the province voted for independence.

These new commitments put additional strain on Canada's already-taxed armed forces. Reports that some soldiers had to deliver pizza and visit food banks to support their families prodded the government to approve salary raises, but defense officials warned that further cuts to personnel, aircraft, and other expenses might be needed to pay for them.

Economics, Business, and Labor. Most sectors and regions of Canada enjoyed increased prosperity during 1999. Inflation, at only 1.8%, remained within Bank of Canada targets, but prices rose for petroleum products, vehicles, and food. In June unemployment fell to 7.6%, a nine-year low. British Columbia, still feeling the effects of the Asian financial crisis, was an exception to the general improvement trend. The lowest grain prices in 50 years bankrupted prairie farmers, while disaster-assistance payments proved inadequate.

Some familiar business names vanished or changed owners in 1999; the best known of these was T. Eaton Company, the family-owned nationwide department-store chain. In late August, Eaton declared bankruptcy, although Sears bought some of its downtown stores and promised to keep the name. Mutual Life was renamed Clarica Ltd. after subscribers agreed to demutualization; and Gerry Schwartz's Onex Corporation, backed by American Airlines, promised to buy and merge Canada's two airlines, Air Canada and Canadian. Air Canada, backed by Star Alliance partners Lufthansa and United Airlines, fought the Onex bid. A Quebec court quashed the deal in November, ruling that it violated a Canadian law limiting Air Canada shareholders to a maximum holding of 10%.

Both the Bank of Montreal and the Canadian Imperial Bank of Commerce, which were denied permission to merge by the finance minister in December 1998, changed presidents and fired some staff members. In other developments, British-American Tobacco bought IMASCO, and the Canada Trust became part of the Toronto-Dominion Bank. Québécor spent $2.7 billion to acquire World Color Press, becoming the world's largest printing company.

When the Canadian Labour Congress (CLC) met in May, statisticians reported union membership was down from 37.1% in 1978 to 34.1% in 1997. Retiring CLC president Bob White was replaced by British Columbia Federation of Labour leader Ken Georgetti. Meanwhile, the globalization of Canadian business continued, often to the detriment of workers. Levi-Strauss closed its Cornwall plant in February as part of its plan to relocate to countries that paid lower wages, and Bell Canada technicians and operators struck in April to protest the transfer of 1,300 operators to a company in Dallas, TX, at about half their salaries. After five weeks, management and the union reached an agreement on a new five-year contract that offered a compensation package to the transferred employees and guaranteed job security to those remaining; however, operators' wages were frozen.

Strike levels in general returned to 1989 levels, with public-sector workers determined to recover from long wage freezes. Illegal nurses' strikes in Saskatchewan and Quebec ended with minimal gains, but public sympathy for the workers increased. In September the Canadian Auto Workers won a pattern settlement for its 13,000 Ford workers; it gave 4.5% increases for each of three years, a $1,000 signing bonus, richer pensions, and retirement after 30 years. Daimler-Chrysler signed a similar deal with the union. In October, after losing a court appeal, Ottawa agreed to a pay-equity settlement estimated at between C$33.5 million ($22.3 million) and C$5 billion ($3.3 billion) to thousands of its female employees.

Nurses in Quebec demonstrated in front of the National Assembly in Quebec City during an illegal walkout in July 1999. The public generally supported the strike.

Environment. Canada suffered from wild weather conditions throughout 1999. Early on New Year's morning, an avalanche swept down on the tiny village of Kangiqsualuijuaq in northern Quebec, crushing the school gymnasium; nine persons were killed, and 25 were injured. In the first few weeks of 1999, Toronto was hit with a succession of blizzards that buried it under more than 47 in (120 cm) of snow; the city had to be dug out by the army. The prairies in British Columbia experienced an unusually wet spring and summer, and eastern Canada had a dry spring and a hot summer.

Culture and Sports. The Canadian Radio-television and Telecommunications Commission (CRTC) required cable operators to provide space for the Aboriginal People's Television Network beginning in September, but the organization decided not to try to regulate the Internet. Perrin Beatty, head of the public-television station CBC, clashed with the Chrétien government over his vision of a full-range, broad-based role for the station. Beatty resigned at the end of September, and after considerable infighting and wrangling over a successor, Bob Rabinovitch took the position in November.

Among Canada's pop divas, Céline Dion retired to have a family; Alanis Morissette embarked on a world tour to promote *Supposed Former Infatuation Junkie*, her less-successful follow-up to the multiplatinum album *Jagged Little Pill*; and Shania Twain continued to produce hits from her album *Come on Over*. Meanwhile, Garth Drabinsky failed to show up in New York to face charges rising from the collapse of his Livent theater company; if convicted, he faced a cumulative 140 years in jail.

Hockey superstar Wayne Gretzky, a Brantford native who broke innumerable National Hockey League (NHL) records in a career spanning Edmonton, Los Angeles, and New York, retired in April.

The 1999 Pan-American Games brought 12,000 competitors, officials, staff, and media personnel from 41 countries to Winnipeg. Canadian athletes had their best results ever, winning 64 gold medals, 52 silver, and 80 bronze.

People. In January, Canadians welcomed drilling-company executive Norbert Reinhart home from Colombia, where he had switched places with one of his employees taken hostage by guerrillas in October 1998....Julie Payette—an engineer, pilot, musician, and linguist from Montreal—served as a crew member of the U.S. shuttle *Discovery* on its May mission to the International Space Station....The case of Tyrell Dueck, a 13-year-old Saskatchewan boy dying of cancer, caused controversy because his parents did not want to give him conventional medical treatment. Instead, they insisted that the boy's fate was in the hands of God and, defying a court order, took him to a clinic in Mexico. Tyrell died in Saskatoon on June 30.

DESMOND MORTON, *Director*
McGill Institute for the Study of Canada

Provinces and Territories

Voters were kept busy marching to the polls in 1999, when provincial general elections were held in six of the ten provinces. Provincial and federal leaders managed to hammer out a new "social union" accord. Many events affected native groups in 1999, particularly the creation of the new Inuit territory of Nunavut (*see* SPECIAL REPORT).

Election Upheavals. When the ballots all had been counted in the various provincial elections, a sharp tilt to the right was evident. In New Brunswick elections on June 7, the Progressive Conservatives (PCs), led by Bernard Lord, soundly thrashed Premier Camille Thériault and his Liberal government, picking up 44 of 55 seats. The PCs also managed to hold their government in Ontario, Canada's most populous province, as Mike Harris was returned to office on June 3 after a bitterly fought campaign against Dalton McGuinty, the Liberal leader, and Howard Hampton, head of the New Democratic Party (NDP). A few weeks later, the Tories ousted the Liberal government in Nova Scotia as well, with Premier Russell MacLellan finishing well behind the PCs' John Hamm.

The Liberals fared better in Newfoundland, as Brian Tobin was reelected to the premiership with a solid majority government on February 9. Meanwhile, the NDP's Gary Doer scored a major triumph in Manitoba on September 21, ending 11 consecutive years of Tory rule by narrowly defeating Premier Gary Filmon. And in Saskatchewan elections, held on September 16, the governing NDP clung to office with a razor-thin majority. Elwin Hermanson, head of the new, surging Saskatchewan Party, actually won the largest share of the vote, but not a majority, so Premier Roy Romanow was able to cobble together a coalition government with the Liberals to stay in power.

With the voting marathon finished, the Conservatives were in power in five provinces, the NDP held three, and the Liberals had only one. The tenth province, Quebec, continued to be governed by the separatist Parti Québécois (PQ). The NDP government of British Columbia was weakened gravely by several scandals, including one involving Premier Glen Clark, who resigned August 21 in the face of allegations that he had helped a friend obtain a lucrative casino contract. Clark proclaimed his innocence in the matter. Deputy Premier Dan Miller was chosen as premier temporarily.

Federal-Provincial Relations. Canada's ten provincial premiers met with Prime Minister Jean Chrétien for a first ministers' conference in Ottawa on February 4, and the result was a "social union" contract that some hailed as a major breakthrough in federal-provincial relations. The contract required that Ottawa obtain the consent of at least six provinces before launching any new joint social programs and give the provinces a say in programs it intended to launch by itself. Nine provinces agreed to the contract, but Quebec Premier Lucien Bouchard opted out, saying the agreement was a recipe for massive federal intervention in provincial affairs. Bouchard, whose PQ government would like predominantly French-speaking Quebec to break away from Canada, went along with the other premiers in agreeing to earmark increased federal health-care grants for the specific purpose of health care and nothing else.

At an August 7 meeting in Quebec City, the premiers—including Bouchard—agreed to a consensus document calling on the federal Liberal government both to reduce taxes and to restore transfer payments to levels that prevailed before the massive cuts of recent years. The pact represented a compromise between Ontario, Alberta, and Quebec, which wanted the federal government in Ottawa to make tax cuts its priority, and Saskatchewan and the Atlantic provinces, which wanted the newfound federal budget surplus to be spent on such things as a national-highways program and child-poverty measures.

© Geoffrey Gammon

Bernard Lord, a 33-year-old bilingual lawyer, became premier of New Brunswick after his Progressive Conservatives scored a victory at the polls on June 7, 1999.

CANADIAN PROVINCES AND TERRITORIES • Information Highlights

Province	Population (in millions)	Area (sq mi)	Area (km²)	Capital	Head of Government
Alberta	2.9	255,286	661 190	Edmonton	H.A. Olson, lieutenant governor Ralph Klein, premier
British Columbia	4.0	365,946	947 800	Victoria	Garde Gardom, lieutenant governor Dan Miller, premier
Manitoba	1.1	250,946	649 950	Winnipeg	Yvon Dumont, lieutenant governor Gary Doer, premier
New Brunswick	.75	28,355	73 440	Fredericton	Marilyn Trenholme Counsell, lieutenant governor Bernard Lord, premier
Newfoundland	.54	156,649	405 720	St. John's	Arthur Maxwell House, lieutenant governor Brian Tobin, premier
Northwest Territories	.04	451,740	1 170 000	Yellowknife	Jim Antoine, premier
Nova Scotia	.94	21,425	55 491	Halifax	J. James Kinley, lieutenant governor John F. Hamm, premier
Nunavut	.03	769,888	1 994 000	Iqaluit	Paul Okalik, government leader
Ontario	11.6	412,580	1 068 580	Toronto	Hilary M. Weston, lieutenant governor Mike Harris, premier
Prince Edward Island	.14	2,185	5 660	Charlottetown	Gilbert R. Clements, lieutenant governor Patrick Binns, premier
Quebec	7.4	594,857	1 540 680	Quebec City	Lise Thibault, lieutenant governor Lucien Bouchard, premier
Saskatchewan	1.0	251,865	652 330	Regina	John N. Wiebe, lieutenant governor Roy Romanow, premier
Yukon	.03	186,660	483 450	Whitehorse	Piers McDonald, government leader

SPECIAL REPORT Nunavut

© Tom Hanson/AP/Wide World Photos

Canada's newest territory, Nunavut, was established officially on April 1, 1999. It is a vast, thinly populated land that sprawls across the mainland portion of the eastern Arctic and the innumerable islands constituting the Canadian northern archipelago. The vast majority of its population of 27,000—about 85%—are Inuit (Eskimo), many of them seminomadic hunters and trappers. With a landmass of 769,888 sq mi (1 994 000 km²)—one fifth of Canada—Nunavut has a population density of roughly 1.3 residents for every 38.6 sq mi (100 km²).

History and Problems. The name, translated from the area's predominant Inuktitut language, means "our land." And Nunavut represents the fulfillment of a generations-old dream of the Inuit to have their own Arctic homeland.

Before becoming a separate territory, Nunavut formed the eastern part of the Northwest Territories, which lost more than half its land and a little less than half its population in the transition. Now 52% of the 40,000 residents in the Northwest Territories are nonindigenous, 10% are Inuit, and the remainder are members of various native groups.

Nunavut was born in an emotional celebration at Iqaluit, the capital, a town of 4,500 situated on Baffin Island, at the extreme eastern end of the territory. The festivities included a giant outdoor festival at which citizens gorged on fish and game delicacies. Prime Minister Jean Chrétien and Governor-General Roméo LeBlanc were on hand for the official, indoor inauguration ceremony.

In mid-December the House of Commons gave first reading to a highly controversial bill, introduced by the Liberal government, that would spell out the terms under which Ottawa would negotiate with Quebec on secession, should Quebecers vote in favor of separation in a future referendum.

Economic Issues. Immersed for years in oceans of budgetary red ink, and then subjected to more years of stern corrective austerity, Canada's provinces confronted a new problem in 1999: how to spend budget surpluses. It was projected that by 2008, given continuing prosperity, the provinces would have surpluses totaling nearly C$28 billion ($18.6 billion) a year. Mirroring what happened federally, the provinces debated heatedly over whether to plow fiscal dividends into new spending programs, use them to pay down accumulated provincial debts, or slash taxes. To help rebuild their battered health-care services, the provinces were given C$11.5 billion ($7.6 billion) from Ottawa over a five-year period beginning in 1999.

Canadian farmers suffered through bleak economic times in 1999. Hurt by a combination of collapsing world markets and declining government subsidies, thousands of producers faced what some said was the worst farm crisis since the 1930s. Responding to the farmers' pleas for help, the federal and provincial governments on February 24 unveiled a joint C$1.5 billion ($1 billion), two-year relief program. The problem lingered, however, and on October 27 the premiers of the grain-producing provinces of Saskatchewan and Manitoba traveled to Ottawa seeking C$1.3 billion ($866 million) more for their farmers. After hesitating and openly accusing the provinces of exaggerating the crisis, Ottawa gave them an additional C$170 million ($113.3 million) in aid.

Native Affairs. After a bitter debate, British Columbia's legislature ratified a

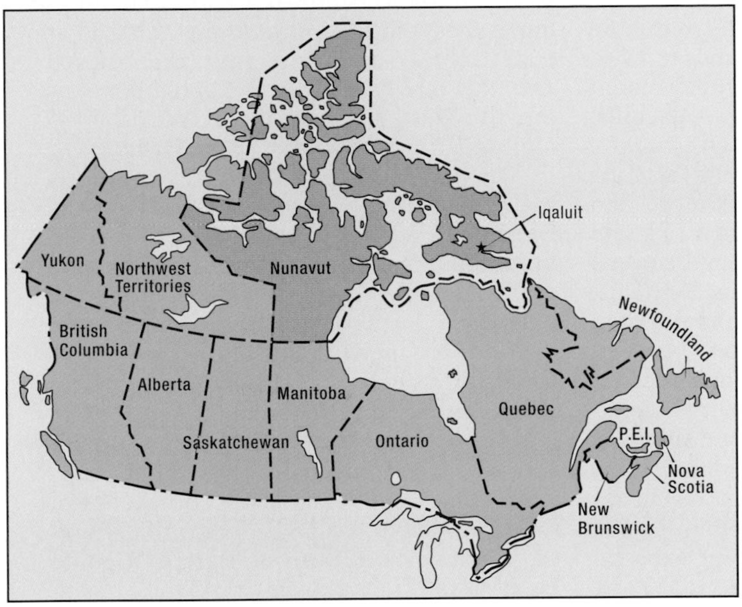

Neither the excitement of the moment, however, nor the rhetoric about the Inuit having "regained control" of their destiny, as newly installed Premier Paul Okalik put it, changed the fact that Nunavut faced enormous economic and social problems. By the late 1990s, there was 20% unemployment; 38% of residents had less than a high-school education; and the rates of teen pregnancy, substance abuse, and suicide were well above the Canadian average.

Government and the Future. There is no official opposition in the 19-member Nunavut legislature, which operates by consensus in all matters, whether it be passing bills or choosing the eight-member cabinet. Some analysts saw a danger of corruption in this close-knit arrangement.

Moreover, the territory depended almost totally on the federal treasury for its finances, a fact underlined when Okalik's government brought down its first budget May 14. Of the C$610 million ($406.6 million) in projected revenues, 90% came in the form of grants from Ottawa, which exercises wide, direct control over Nunavut. Of total program spending, two thirds addressed harrowing deficiencies in the areas of health, education, and social services.

Territorial and federal leaders looked to new investment in mining (particularly a diamond mine that could begin operation by 2002), as well as to a burgeoning worldwide interest in Inuit art, to help Nunavut gain economically.

JOHN BEST

land-rights treaty with the Nisga'a nation that had been signed in 1998 by Minister of Indian Affairs and Northern Development Jane Stewart and the provincial government. The House of Commons approved the treaty in December and sent it to the Senate for consideration in 2000. In September the Supreme Court declared that a 1760 treaty gave the Micmac people and other natives the right to earn a "moderate living" from natural resources by fishing, hunting, and "gathering." Interpreting this decision to mean that they now had permission to fish without licenses and could ignore government hunting and fishing regulations, the Micmac put lobster traps in Miramichi Bay out of season. They planned to log provincial forests too. Nonnative fishermen responded by attacking native lobster traps and boats, and many natives threatened to retaliate. Ottawa set out to negotiate a greater native share of natural resources. The total native claims to Canadian resources were estimated at C$200 billion ($133.3 billion).

Northern Treasures. With several new diamond mines in production or about to go into production in the north, Canada began to emerge as a major player in the world diamond trade in 1999. Two mines in the Northwest Territories—Ekati, opened in 1998, and Diavik, expected to start producing in 2003—were helping drive the development. A third mine, Jericho, in the newly formed territory of Nunavut, could be in operation by 2002. Once all the mines are in full production, Canada will be among the world's top five diamond producers, after South Africa, Botswana, Russia, and the Democratic Republic of the Congo. David Lovell, the mayor of Yellowknife, capital of the Northwest Territories, predicted that the impact would be felt all over the economically depressed north.

JOHN BEST, *"Canada World News"*

Caribbean

Modest recovery characterized the economies of the Caribbean islands in 1999, according to the Caribbean Development Bank. Five islands/island groups—Anguilla, Grenada, St. Vincent and the Grenadines, the Turks and Caicos Islands, and the Cayman Islands—had growth rates of more than 5%. In fact, the Turks and Caicos, with a rate of 13.2%, doubled its growth from the previous year. Five others—Barbados, St. Lucia, Antigua and Barbuda, the Bahamas, and Dominica—posted growth rates between 2% and 4.6%. Trinidad and Tobago's economy, heavily dependent on the energy sector, was dampened in early 1999 by falling oil prices. When the members of the Organization of Petroleum Exporting Countries (OPEC) cut their oil production in the spring, however, prices rose, fueling expectations of economic growth on the islands by the end of the year.

Jamaica eked out only a slender increase in gross domestic product (GDP), while Guyana was the only Caribbean nation to show a contraction of GDP. The economy of Montserrat continued to suffer the effects of the major eruption of the Soufrière Hills volcano in 1995 and smaller eruptions in subsequent years, which rendered the southern two thirds of the island uninhabitable. But during 1999 the volcanic activity seemed to have abated somewhat, parts of the "exclusion zone" (the area surrounding the volcano) reopened, and people began to return to the island.

Hurricanes. In 1999 there were 12 named storms in the Caribbean. Eight qualified as hurricanes, and five of these were classed as Category 4—major storms that posed extreme threats. Floyd, in September, was the strongest, reaching a top speed of 155 mph (249 km/hr) just east of the Bahamas.

The region escaped the hurricane season with relatively light damage. In the Bahamas, Floyd caused damage to houses, uprooted trees, toppled power lines, flooded roads, and killed one person. On October 20, Hurricane José ripped roofs from houses, tore down a newly built church, and scattered debris when it struck Antigua with winds estimated at 100 mph (160 km/hr). In mid-November, Hurricane Lenny's winds, which reached 150 mph (241 km/hr), ravaged homes and boats, stripped beaches of sand, flooded hotels and roads, and disrupted communications from Puerto Rico to Barbados.

Trade. A lengthy trade dispute between the United States and the European Union (EU) that affected the Caribbean inched toward resolution during 1999. The disagreement began in 1993, when the European Commission announced a preferential program for banana imports from the Caribbean. The World Trade Organization (WTO) authorized the United States to impose $191.4 million worth of trade sanctions on EU goods in reprisal for the EU's failure to comply with earlier rulings on bananas. The EU introduced amended arrangements on Jan. 1, 1999, but the United States and five Latin American countries contended that

© Chris Brandis/AP/Wide World Photos

Barbados Prime Minister Owen Arthur and his Barbados Labour Party swept to a landslide victory in January 1999 parliamentary elections, largely on the strength of the island's solid economic performance in recent years.

the new plan remained discriminatory. On April 7 the WTO Disputes Settlement Panel ruled that the EU's regime still was inconsistent with global trade regulations. The EU said that another set of changes could take many months to implement and probably would not be ready until at least January. The banana-producing countries in the Caribbean worried about the impact the changes might have on their trade.

Haiti. More than five years after U.S. forces ousted its military dictatorship and set the stage for democracy, Haiti remained the poorest and most troubled nation in the Western Hemisphere in 1999. Despite $2 billion in U.S. aid over the five-year period, per-capita income in 1999 stood at a meager $250 per year, unemployment hovered at around 60%, and 75% of rural Haitian families lived in poverty. Life expectancy in Haiti was 51 years for men and 56 years for women. In addition, after years of trees being chopped down to meet the demand for construction materials and charcoal, the land was barren, with only 1.5% of the natural forest remaining intact. Officials estimated that 15,000 acres (6 075 ha) of topsoil were being washed away each year because of the lack of natural buffers formerly provided by trees.

Haitian politics was plagued with chaos. Legislative elections, delayed twice already, were pushed back yet again, from December 1999 to March 2000. The voting was delayed due to difficulty in registering voters, setting up the election apparatus, and checking the credentials of the estimated 50,000 candidates for the various offices.

Meanwhile, President René Préval struggled to put together a government. The president had been frustrated repeatedly in his attempts to replace Prime Minister Rosny Smarth, who resigned in June 1997. He had nominated three candidates in succession, but all were rejected by parliament. In January 1999—as his fourth nominee, Jacques-Edouard Alexis, was being considered—the president dissolved parliament and appointed Alexis by decree. This action sparked fears that Préval was trying to establish a dictatorship, and the opposition promptly decried the Alexis administration as illegitimate and called on the United States and the United Nations (UN) not to recognize it. In March, Préval officially installed Alexis as prime minister and set up a new cabinet that consisted of his supporters.

The National Police Force of Haiti, created after the U.S. intervention in 1995, found itself facing charges that its officers were involved in murders, disappearances, drug-running, and other illegal activities. From April through June 1999, 50 killings were attributed to the police, as opposed to only 31 in all of 1998. In one notorious case, several officers commanded by Port-au-Prince Police Commissioner Jean Coles Rameau were implicated in the deaths of 11 prisoners on May 28. Rameau fled to the Dominican Republic, where he was apprehended and brought back to Haiti for prosecution in connection with the incident.

Haiti also was becoming a major drug conduit from Colombia and the Dominican Republic to the United States. U.S. narcotics officers estimated in 1999 that about 59.4 tons of illegal drugs—almost one fifth of the total reaching the United States—passed through Haiti in 1998. This represented an increase of about 18% from the 1997 total.

The White House announced in 1999 that U.S. military personnel in Haiti would be withdrawn by January 2000, ending the five-year occupation. The Pentagon said that the United States would send teams to the Caribbean nation periodically for humanitarian and development projects.

Dominican Republic and Guyana. In the Dominican Republic, Joaquín Balaguer, who had served seven terms as president, appeared to be considering running in the presidential election scheduled for May 2000. Balaguer had been forced to step down in 1996 by a constitutional amendment that barred the president from serving two consecutive terms. Although the former president was 92 years old, blind, in ill health, and housebound, he continued to be a formidable political presence. Balaguer's supporters began organizing a campaign to draft him as a candidate soon after he returned from undergoing medical treatment in Houston in February.

Janet Jagan, Guyana's president, resigned on August 11 because of ill health. Jagan, the 78-year-old widow of former President Cheddi Jagan, was replaced by Finance Minister Bharrat Jagdeo. Opposition leader Desmond Hoyte, who refused to recognize Jagan as president after she defeated him in a bitterly fought contest in December 1997, said he would not recognize Jagdeo either.

Obituary. Sir Vere Cornwall Bird, Sr., who led Antigua and Barbuda to independence from Britain in 1981 and served as prime minister from then until 1994, died at the age of 89 in St. John's on June 28.

RICHARD C. SCHROEDER, *Freelance Writer*

Central America

Millions of Central Americans will remember the year 1999 as a time of figuratively and literally digging out from the destruction caused by Hurricane Mitch in October 1998. Worst hit by the disaster were Honduras and Nicaragua, but the entire region suffered. Nearly 10,000 Central Americans lost their lives; hundreds of thousands were homeless; and damage reached into the billions of dollars. Much infrastructure simply disappeared. Heavy rains late in 1999 badly hampered rebuilding. Tourism and most agricultural exports declined sharply. Rebuilding roads and bridges would take years of effort and vast sums from outside the region. President Bill Clinton spent four days in March discussing the catastrophe with local leaders and determining the extent of U.S. aid—well more than $1 billion by late 1999.

The Inter-American Development Bank found that Central America is most prone to natural catastrophes. In addition to major disasters such as Mitch, hundreds of smaller disturbances—floods, landslides, earthquakes, volcanic eruptions, and tsunamis—strike the region every year. It was clear that greater protection of the forests and the entire environment would be needed to prevent such tragedies in the future.

In May, though strongly opposed by many in the U.S. Congress, President Clinton approved a citizenship process for some 240,000 Guatemalan and Salvadoran illegal aliens who fled civil war at home in the 1980s and now resided in the United States. The plan was similar to the treatment afforded Nicaraguans in 1997.

In March the Central American presidents, minus Panama's, met in Antigua, Guatemala, to discuss freer trade with the United States. They sought arrangements similar to those received by Mexico under the North American Free Trade Agreement (NAFTA). President Clinton promised much aid, but no trade agreement was completed. Then five of the states took first steps toward tariff elimination with Chile. Central American coffee, sugar, and vegetables and Chilean wine, copper, and manufactured goods would get favored treatment.

A new "banana war" broke out in March. The European Union (EU) acted to cut off Central American banana imports in favor of supplies from the Caribbean and other states and colonies more closely tied to Europe. The United States, supporting the major American exporters, threatened to bar certain EU agricultural exports and even landings of the Concorde airplane.

Of great historical importance was the transfer of the Panama Canal from U.S. to

Francisco Flores Pérez, below, *of the Republican National Alliance handily won the presidency of El Salvador in March 1999 elections. The new president vowed to make fighting the nation's crime and poverty problems high priorities.*

Panamanian stewardship on Dec. 31, 1999 (*see* SPECIAL REPORT, page 188).

Belize. A hurricane in 1961 devastated Belize City, the capital of what was then British Honduras. One consequence was the moving in 1970 of the seat of government to Belmopan, a new, planned city 50 mi (80 km) inland. Over the years, Belmopan grew little. Many government officials refused to move there, and most foreign nations failed to build new embassies. But Hurricane Mitch in October 1998 revived memories. The town of 6,000 suddenly had to accommodate 30,000 refugees, and Belizeans remembered why Belmopan was built in the first place. Belize City, however, remained popular as the threat of Mitch subsided.

The republic of Belize relies heavily on tourism and foreign trade for its existence. Natural attractions help augment the former each year, but expanding exports is more difficult. In 1999 the ministry of agriculture inaugurated measures to improve sanitation and eliminate diseases attached to farm exports. The port authority held costs down by giving only 3% raises to workers who had asked for 15%. The Corozal Free Zone investigated the possibility of introducing casinos into the Zone. The United States gave Belize more than $1 million to help cope with illegal drug traffic through the nation. However, budget demands forced a 10% tax on gasoline in the Zone and small increases on everything else. The opposition United Democratic Party claimed it would repeal the taxes whenever it returned to power.

In September, Belize celebrated the 18th anniversary of independence, with publicity extolling to the world its hundreds of species of birds, its jungle ruins, and its great barrier reef. Discussions were under way to increase trade with Guatemala and to build a new road connecting the two nations.

Costa Rica. President Miguel Angel Rodríguez spent much of the year trying to strengthen the nation's stable but fragile economy. In May he visited his old graduate school at Berkeley, making a plea for more U.S. investment similar to that of Intel. That corporation had put more than $300 million into the Costa Rican economy and now was the nation's Number 1 exporter. Stressing his country's skilled labor force, the president met with the executive officers of some 40 high-tech U.S. corporations, seeking their investment in Costa Rica. Currently such manufactures account for more than one fourth of the nation's exports.

One consequence was that, in spite of continuing declines in agricultural sales, preliminary figures indicated a favorable trade balance of about $160 million for 1999, compared with a 1998 deficit of more than $350 million. One repeated threat was rising fuel costs, and President Rodríguez was leading a campaign within the Organization of American States (OAS) to ask the Organization of Petroleum Exporting Countries (OPEC) not to withhold crude oil from the market. Costa Rica lost its banana quota, normally purchased by the EU, as part of the trade war. After a year the government of China still owed Costa Rican growers for 250,000 boxes of bananas. The Costa Ricans had hoped to develop a substantial new market.

Relations with Nicaragua continued to be of major concern, with topics ranging from the Nicaraguan debt to Costa Rica of about $1 billion, to land mines, navigation of the Río San Juan, and the remaining 500,000 or so Nicaraguan refugees still in Costa Rica. Nicaragua feared mass deportation. About one third of the aliens were seeking amnesty and permanent residence.

The nation continued to attract visitors from around the world. In 1999 the total was expected to exceed 1 million, a significant number for a nation whose population is only about 3.5 million. In August several earthquake shocks were felt on the Central Plateau. The worst measured 6.1. No one was killed, and damage was not substantial.

El Salvador. In March 1999 presidential elections, Francisco Flores Pérez contended with Facundo Guardado of the Farabundo Martí National Liberation Party (FMLN)

(Continued on page 190.)

CENTRAL AMERICA • Information Highlights

Nation	Population (in millions)	Area (sq mi)	Area (km²)	Capital	Head of State and Government
Belize	0.2	8,865	22 960	Belmopan	Sir Colville Young, governor-general Said Musa, prime minister
Costa Rica	3.7	19,730	51 100	San José	Miguel Angel Rodríguez, president
El Salvador	5.8	8,124	21 040	San Salvador	Francisco Flores Pérez, president
Guatemala	12.3	42,042	108 890	Guatemala City	Alvaro Arzú Irigoyen, president
Honduras	6.0	43,278	112 090	Tegucigalpa	Carlos Flores Facusse, president
Nicaragua	4.7	49,998	129 494	Managua	Arnoldo Alemán Lacayo, president
Panama	2.8	30,193	78 200	Panama City	Mireya Moscoso de Grubar, president

SPECIAL REPORT

The Panama Canal

"It's yours," said former U.S. President Jimmy Carter to Panama's President Mireya Moscoso de Grubar at ceremonies transferring ownership of the Panama Canal from the United States to the Republic of Panama. The ceremonies, which had been moved up from December 31 to December 14 in order to preclude complications with millennium celebrations, were the final step in carrying out the terms of a 1979 treaty negotiated by President Carter and the late Gen. Omar Torrijos. The consequences of this change in sovereignty for the world's major pathway can be established partly now, but the canal's history is marked by international intrigue and unexpected consequences.

History. The first European to cross the Isthmus of Panama was the Spanish explorer Vasco Nuñez de Balboa in 1513. Within 20 years, Spain had established a muleback trade route across the isthmus to haul the wealth of Peru to Spanish convoys bound for Europe. In Spanish possession, the possibility of a canal rarely was discussed, but after the independence of much of Latin America in the 1820s, several nations—including Russia, France, and the United States—made preliminary and unused surveys of the route. Not until the end of the 19th century did technical skill reach the level where canal construction became feasible.

In 1881 a French company, directed by the diplomat-engineer Ferdinand de Lesseps, made its attack upon the isthmus. De Lesseps had led the building of the Suez Canal and never grasped the degree of difference in the two jobs. Rain, mud slides, malaria, yellow fever, and financial mismanagement permitted only a fraction of the work to be finished. After eight years, thousands of deaths, and millions of dollars in wasted money, the French gave up.

The Spanish-American War of 1898 convinced most Americans, and especially President Theodore Roosevelt, of the necessity for a canal permitting easy access to both oceans for the new, enlarged U.S. fleet. But for defense reasons, Roosevelt wanted the canal to be on American soil. Much of the Isthmus of Panama had been a province of the republic of Colombia since independence and on several occasions unsuccessfully had fought for freedom. Prompted and aided by Roosevelt, Panama rebelled again in 1903, but this time the U.S. Navy prevented Colombian military action. In a matter of days, Panama proclaimed its independence and signed a treaty with the United States creating a Canal Zone through the middle of the young republic. Within the zone, the United States could act "as if sovereign." Washington quickly

In ceremonies on Dec. 14, 1999, former U.S. President Jimmy Carter and Mireya Moscoso (above, left), *who was elected president of Panama in May, exchanged documents transferring ownership of the Panama Canal from the United States to the Republic of Panama. Still a major commercial waterway, the canal,* right, *was under U.S. control for 85 years.*

concluded ongoing negotiations with the French for canal rights. In 1904 the United States paid $40 million for the construction rights still held by the French, and work began.

Learning from the French mistakes, the U.S. engineers, John F. Stevens and Col. George Goethals, approached the massive undertaking differently. Concluding that a sea-level route was impossible, they dammed the raging Chagres River and created the largest man-made lake in the world in the center of the Canal Zone. The waters of Gatún Lake were used to hold back the flooding river and to operate the locks lifting ships over the continental divide. Then, years were spent digging and hauling away soil from the Culebra Cut, which linked the lake to the locks on the Pacific slope. The other great change came in medical procedures. Taking advantage of research done in Havana, Col. William C. Gorgas enforced strict measures to screen homes and offices and to destroy the watery birthplaces of the mosquito types that had killed so many French workers. Deaths from malaria and yellow fever virtually ceased.

In the course of ten years, the U.S. Army engineers moved hundreds of millions of cubic yards of dirt and built the most massive locks and gates ever conceived, at a cost of $352 million. Under estimate on time and cost, the United States completed 51 mi (82 km) of canal, linking the Atlantic and Pacific Oceans into one smooth-running edifice. Opened in 1914, the canal was fully operational by 1916. Methods of moving ships between the seas have changed little in more than 80 years.

Almost immediately, the canal dramatically altered world-trade patterns, as it saved thousands of miles. As ships grew larger and more numerous, much ship construction was determined by the width of those locks. So well designed was the channel that the transit time continued to be about 24 hours, even for ships so large they often scraped the sides of the canal. Operating 24 hours a day, the canal handled thousands of ships every year—an average of 38 a day in the late 1990s.

The canal proved profitable and a matter of great national pride, requiring elaborate defenses and the presence of thousands of U.S. military and civilian personnel. By the 1930s this U.S. presence began to disturb many Panamanians, who looked upon the Canal Zone as a gross violation of their sovereignty and made increasing demands upon the United States for larger annuities and greater responsibility in management. During the 1960s and 1970s, these demands became more insistent and more violent. Matters such as flag flying and commissary usage brought riots, some student deaths, and more pressure upon the United States to ease its control and sovereignty. In addition, many U.S. scholars and political leaders felt that management of the canal properly belonged to Panama, even though most of the American public did not.

Several U.S. presidents had favored a change in ownership but did little about it. However, in 1977, Jimmy Carter concluded a series of agreements, usually called the Carter-Torrijos treaties, with Panama that would lead to the gradual transfer of the canal and other zone properties to Panama. In spite of substantial opposition, the U.S. Senate ratified the treaties in 1978, to begin taking effect in 1979. Most important were the creation of a binational board to operate the canal, 20-year programs to phase out U.S. military and civilian personnel, and the ultimate transfer of all property to Panamanian hands. This was done with no change in the efficiency of transit. By the end of 1999, virtually all canal employees were Panamanian citizens, and no military installations remained in U.S. hands.

The Transfer and Transition. Not everything has been or will be changed smoothly. A number of Panamanians feared that the departure of Americans would impact heavily upon the local economy. The best jobs and property became targets of political favoritism. Some Americans feared that foreign corporations (in particular, Chinese) would threaten security with their business activities. Terrorism always is a threat, and Panama lacks a tradition of political stability.

By late 1999, newly installed President Mireya Moscoso was accusing her predecessor of corruption in the sale of former U.S. property. She issued assurances that the canal revenues would be handled honestly. Still to be settled were matters of unexploded bombs on gunnery ranges and how the changeover would affect the drug war with neighboring Colombia.

Supporters of the transition believed that none of these fears were justified. The canal is too important to Panama and the world to permit mismanagement. Most important, by mutual agreement, the United States retains the right of defense; any threat, military or financial, to the open and neutral operation of the canal certainly would be met by the most prompt and effective U.S. action. Panama's chance to prove to the world that it is a responsible nation that will operate the world's most important waterway efficiently and honestly began on Jan. 1, 2000.

THOMAS L. KARNES

(Continued from page 187.)
and defeated him without need of a runoff. Flores, 39, was inaugurated on June 1 for a five-year term. He is a graduate of Amherst, did some graduate work in the United States, and is a former professor and president of the National Assembly. He calls himself a moderate, but the FMLN worries about his membership in the Republican National Alliance (ARENA), the party of the late hard-liner Roberto D'Aubuisson. ARENA has won the presidency three terms in a row. President Flores announced that his major agenda would be campaigns against the very high rates of poverty and crime. Although his margin of victory was substantial, President Flores had to cope with the fact that his party had only 28 of the 84 seats in the Assembly.

For many decades the boundary between El Salvador and Honduras has been a matter of much contention, and in 1969 the two nations fought a brief and indecisive war over immigration and the border. A clean settlement never has been achieved. In September 1999, however, President Flores and President Carlos Flores of Honduras signed a convention designed to use peaceful means to solve future border issues and to cooperate in economic development. On the Guatemalan border, a new tourist attraction was growing in the form of a joint national park of some 12,000 acres (4 860 ha). There were no roads in the park, which was the last refuge for many wild species.

Possible changes in U.S. immigration policy could have a drastic impact upon El Salvador's economy. In the past few years, remissions home from exiles in the United States had amounted to about $1.2 billion a year. Obviously, if thousands of these migrants were to return home, that source of revenue would disappear.

Guatemala. In November 1999, Guatemalans held their first presidential election since the end of their long civil war in 1996. The two leading candidates were Alfonso Portillo of the Republican Front and Oscar Berger, mayor of Guatemala City, the candidate of the ruling National Advancement Party. The political left put up little opposition. Portillo had bragged of killing two men in Mexico in 1982 and fleeing to avoid trial, and he had the dubious support of former President José Efrain Ríos Montt. Nevertheless, in the November election, Portillo obtained a significant plurality—48% to Berger's 36%—but not the majority he needed to prevent a runoff in December. Portillo easily won the December runoff with 68.3% of the vote.

In a setback to the peace treaty of 1996, a very small number of voters turned out on May 16 and rejected 50 constitutional amendments urged by the United Nations (UN). The changes would have reformed the court system, increased civilian authority over the military, and given official recognition to 24 Indian groups. All future legislation concerning the Indians would require their consultation, and they would be provided with many more services. The reforms had the support of Mayor Berger, but most people seemed to feel the changes were too radical or costly.

Guatemala's human-rights record appeared to be only a little better than during the civil war. The murder of Bishop Juan José Gerardi had not been solved, and judges appeared afraid to prosecute anyone. Indeed, a judge and a prosecutor associated with the case fled the country after receiving death threats. A UN official concluded that the public had no trust in the courts; kidnappings still were common; and murderers were going unpunished. New investigations continued to reveal the extent of the role of the military and the government in past violations of human rights, including 200,000 deaths. While the part played by the U.S. Central Intelligence Agency (CIA) was not totally clear, it was obvious that the agency knew of many atrocities at the time. During his Central American visit in March, President Clinton admitted that the United States had made mistakes in supporting Guatemala's military when it was engaged in violent repression.

Three men charged with the rape and robbery of U.S. college students in January 1998 were convicted and sentenced to 28 years' imprisonment.

Honduras. Few Honduran affairs were untouched by Hurricane Mitch in October 1998 and the torrential rains of late 1999. Thousands of lives were lost; hundreds of thousands of people were made homeless; whole towns were washed away; and the economy was in a shambles. However, with vast multinational help, Hondurans struggled valiantly to restore their nation. Banana and coffee trees were replanted; roads and bridges were opened temporarily. Schools, which had been used as shelters, once again were occupied by teachers and pupils. Even the national map had to be redrawn because of changes brought by the storm. Total damage was estimated at more than $5 billion, while the nation's annual budget was scarcely $1 billion. By mid-1999 the United States had some 5,000 troops in Honduras helping with relief and rebuilding.

On a happier note, Honduras and El Salvador reached agreement on designating their common border, a matter of much trouble since the "soccer war" of 1969. In spite of objections from many officers, the legislature passed a constitutional amendment putting the once-autonomous military under command of civilian authority, the defense minister.

Honduras has the fastest-growing population in Latin America, perhaps explaining severe criticisms of its school system and its very high crime rate. President Flores declared his intention to work on both of those problems immediately. The multinational fruit distributors—Dole, Chiquita, and Del Monte—all reported losses and job layoffs because of the EU quota system, which now gave priority to non–Central American republics. The legislature contemplated changing the constitution to permit foreign investment in certain areas along the Atlantic coast. The plan was popular with developers but strongly opposed by the Garifuna Indians occupying much of the land.

Nicaragua. The brunt of Hurricane Mitch in October 1998 badly bruised northwestern Nicaragua, where much of the horror came from mud slides starting on mountaintops and roaring down to wipe out everything in their paths, including entire towns. Aid came from many nations, especially in the form of medical assistance; the last of about 2,000 U.S. military engineers left Nicaragua in February after rebuilding many miles of highway and dozens of sewer systems. The heavy rains of 1998–99 demonstrated once again the value of conservation. Damage to the countryside was far less in areas where the forests remained uncut. Reforesting and new low-wood-consumption stoves brought some hope for the future. In August a number of earthquakes shook western Nicaragua. No loss of life was reported.

Preoccupied with storm damage, Nicaraguan leaders had other massive problems. The education system, still trapped in the elite methods of the 1960s, needed complete overhaul if the average Nicaraguan was to compete with the world's workers in the new electronic age. The urban dropout rate was 30% by the sixth grade, the rural rate nearly 50%. Another hangover from the civil war was the presence of land mines and the horrors they presented a generation later. An estimated 80,000 had yet to be destroyed, an important project of the OAS.

In August the two major political factions agreed to formalize a pact on constitutional reforms. Hoping to set aside the tradition of too much conflict, the Sandinista Front and the Liberal Constitutional Party of President Arnoldo Alemán agreed upon methods for selecting a fair division of seats in the courts and the electoral commission.

Early in the year the government estimated that the gross domestic product (GDP) would grow more than 6% in 1999. However, in November an outside economist reduced the estimate to about 4.5%, a serious disappointment to the nation's planners. Sugar growers hoped that the new trade agreement with Chile would increase their exports.

Panama. In May, Mireya Moscoso de Grubar of the Arnulfista Party won the presidency from Martín Torrijos of the ruling Democratic Revolutionary Party; the latter is the son of the late Gen. Omar Torrijos. The margin was 45% to 38%. Neither candidate had much political experience for such an important election. The new president, the 53-year-old widow of the late President Arnulfo Arias, studied decorating at Miami's Dade College. She was sworn in September 1, becoming the nation's first woman president. Both candidates had pledged not to interfere with the management of the Panama Canal after its transfer to Panamanian ownership on December 31.

Beside the vast problems attendant to the transfer of the canal, the president promised to attack the 14% unemployment rate and the presence of one third of the nation below the poverty line. Another priority was to reverse changes in the country's judicial system made by the new president's predecessor, Ernesto Pérez Balladares, whom she accused of court-packing. Balladares also was charged with nepotism and favoritism in turning over to cronies some of the military properties of the United States newly transferred to Panama.

Plans were under way for a population and housing census in May 2000. This would be the first thorough census ever made of the entire nation and would give the government important data for future programs in such fields as housing, highways, and education. Activities as diverse as urban renewal and archaeological finds were promising new means of attracting the tourist dollar, somewhat lacking in Panama.

THOMAS L. KARNES, *Arizona State University*

Chemistry

Developments in chemistry in 1999 included efforts to miniaturize devices for studying chemical reactions, an experiment that yielded the first "picture" of an atomic orbital, measurement of the strength of a single chemical bond, and the demonstration of new techniques that capture extremely rapid changes in chemical reactions.

Miniaturization. The downsizing of the central components of a computer onto a single microchip propelled the computer revolution of the 1990s. In 1999 chemists were attempting to achieve a similar revolution in the analysis of chemical reactions by creating extremely tiny devices—so-called "labs on a chip"—that can carry out reactions using very small samples and analyze the results. A key driving force behind this effort has been the pharmaceutical industry's need to test the numerous new compounds created by a popular technique called combinatorial chemistry. The new chemicals produced by this technique are produced in only minute amounts and, for competitive reasons, should be tested quickly as potential drugs and for other applications.

Development of microscale devices to carry out the necessary reactions would generate a number of advantages, including increased speed and accuracy, low cost and low power consumption, ease of automation, reduced waste, and disposability. The miniature devices, which typically are only about 1 inch (2.5 cm) square, can be constructed from glass, quartz, plastic, or silicon and contain tiny channels and chambers where the reactions take place. Beyond their use in drug discovery, the miniature devices have potential uses in areas such as genome DNA sequencing, defense against chemical and biological agents, and clinical analysis.

Two groups of scientists have produced individual molecules that act like "molecular motors" powered by external energy sources. One group, composed of scientists from the Netherlands and Japan, devised a compound that rotates under the influence of ultraviolet light and heat. The compound, which has a corkscrew shape, spins in only one direction; however, a molecule constructed as the compound's mirror image spins in the opposite direction. Another group of scientists, from Boston College in Chestnut Hill, MA, created a compound with a three-bladed fan structure that relies on the energy from a series of chemical reactions to power its rotation.

Orbital Picture. Atomic orbitals are the patterns in space that display where the atom's electrons most likely are to be found. These orbitals have different characteristic shapes familiar even to beginning chemistry students. The problem, however, has been that the orbitals were never "seen"; rather, they were simply mathematical predictions based on abstract theory. In September a team of researchers from Arizona State University reported that it had observed experimentally the shape of an atomic orbital for the first time. The team used a combination of methods called electron and X-ray diffraction to obtain the shape of a so-called "3d" orbital from the copper atom of copper oxide. Reassuringly for the researchers and for science, the experimental orbital looked just like its textbook picture.

Chemical-Bond Strengths. Chemists have several ways to estimate the strengths of the different chemical bonds that occur in molecules, but these methods normally depend on indirect measurements of bulk properties. In March, a team of German and U.S. scientists reported that it had succeeded in directly measuring the minute forces needed to rupture single chemical bonds. The scientists achieved this feat by attaching a single polysaccharide molecule, composed of a long chain, to both a surface and the tip of a device called an atomic force microscope (AFM). They then stretched the chain until either the bond to the surface or that to the AFM tip ruptured. In this way the scientists were able to measure the strengths of both silicon-carbon and sulfur-gold bonds. The values obtained experimentally were in close agreement with values obtained using theoretical calculations based on quantum theory.

Ultrafast Methods. Many chemical reactions are very difficult to study because they occur extremely fast. Accordingly, scientists constantly are developing new methods for these reactions. In January workers from the California Institute of Technology demonstrated the use of an ultrafast electron diffraction method to study the breaking of carbon-iodine bonds in an iodoethylene compound. They found that the second bond ruptured just 17 picoseconds (10^{-12} seconds) after the compound was hit by a pulse of laser light. And in March scientists at the University of California, San Diego, reported that they were able to follow a sound pulse passing through a crystal using ultrafast X-ray pulses.

PAUL G. SEYBOLD, *Wright State University*

Chicago

A mayoral election, political corruption, and frequent power failures made news in Chicago during 1999.

The Mayoral Election. In a nonpartisan mayoral election in February, Mayor Richard M. Daley, 56, won a third full term over Democratic U.S. Rep. Bobby Rush, 52, a former Black Panther leader who had hoped to win back the office for African-Americans. Daley's victory margin was nearly 3 to 1. As he began his tenth year in office, Daley was the city's second-longest-serving mayor after his father, Richard J. Daley, who served for 21 years (1955–76).

The mayor used television ads and a $5.6 million campaign chest to spread his message. He was endorsed by Chicago's major newspapers, including the black *Chicago Defender*, and by influential power groups in the city. "Chicago is cleaner, safer, and more industrious than it was a decade ago," the *Chicago Tribune* said in its endorsement. "Its public schools have begun an extraordinary transformation from national embarrassment to national model."

Daley's victory was tempered by the reelection and subsequent conviction of his city treasurer, Miriam Santos, the first Hispanic to hold citywide office. She was convicted of mail fraud for strong-arming brokerage firms that did business with the city for campaign contributions. Santos was sentenced to 40 months in prison and resigned.

Energy. During a summer heat wave, aging electrical systems brought periodic power failures to neighborhoods and the South Loop area. An angry Mayor Daley told officials of Commonwealth Edison Company, the city's main electrical supplier, to "go to ground zero" to solve the continuing, unexpected outages. A Com Ed executive said the outages were "baffling" and "clearly a string of events we cannot explain."

New Construction Plans. The city that is noted for the high-rise soon could become taller, as the city gave preliminary approval to a new world's tallest building. A developer said he had funding commitments for a proposed $500 million, 1,550-ft (472-m)-high structure in the downtown area. Such a building would eclipse the 1,483-ft (452-m) Petronas Towers in Malaysia, the current world titleholder in regard to height, as well as Chicago's 1,450-ft (442-m) Sears Tower, the U.S. record holder.

Skeptics doubted the 112-story structure would be built, and the developer conceded that a changing real-estate market and other factors could douse his plans.

Other News. Smoke jumpers from the West climbed through trees in Chicago neighborhoods in search of Asian longhorn beetles and their larvae. The tree killing pest first was found in the Ravenswood neighborhood in 1998 and since had spread to other parts of the city and to some suburbs. More than 1,000 trees had been destroyed in an effort to curb the infestation....Chicago mourned the loss of retired Chicago Bears football great Walter Payton, who died at age 45, and of real-estate developer and philanthropist Philip Klutznick, 92.

ROBERT ENSTAD, *Formerly, "Chicago Tribune"*

After an overwhelming reelection victory, Richard M. Daley was sworn in for a third full term as mayor of Chicago on March 1, 1999. Judge Abraham Marovitz administered the oath, as the mayor's children watched.

Chile

Joaquín Lavín, of the right-wing Unión Demócrata Independiente (UDI) party, turned Chile's Dec. 12, 1999, presidential election into an unexpectedly close contest, forcing an early-2000 runoff between him and Ricardo Lagos, the candidate of the Concertation of Parties for Democracy, the governing center-left coalition. The economy took a sharp downturn. Meanwhile, former dictator Gen. Augusto Pinochet continued to face charges of human-rights violations.

Elections. The Concertation of Parties for Democracy—a coalition that included the Socialist Party, the Party for Democracy, and the Christian Democrats (the party of incumbent President Eduardo Frei)—had led the Chilean government since Pinochet's rule ended in 1990. In 1999 the coalition, which always had emphasized its centrism, took a more leftist stance with the nomination of Lagos, the first serious Socialist presidential candidate since former Socialist President Salvador Allende, overthrown by Pinochet in 1973. But Lagos presented himself as a more moderate socialist than the old-line leftist Allende had been.

Lagos' main opponent in the election was Lavín, the popular former mayor of Las Condes, a rich Santiago suburb. Although he was the candidate of the conservative Unión por Chile alliance, Lavín successfully portrayed himself as a nontraditional centrist. He distanced himself from the traditional Chilean hard right and obliquely criticized its leader, Pinochet.

In December, Lavín received 47.52% of the vote, less than half a percentage point behind Lagos' 47.96%. The result was surprising, since Lagos had led throughout the race. Because neither man won more than 50%, a runoff was scheduled for Jan. 16, 2000. It was the first time a presidential race in Chile went to a second round since the new electoral system was instituted in 1990.

Economy. The weakness of the economy in 1999 may have worked against Lagos in the election. The price of copper, Chile's economic backbone, reached an all-time low, and the 1997–98 Asian financial crisis plunged the country into its first recession since 1983. The gross domestic product (GDP), which had grown by 7% annually for 15 years, was expected to shrink by 1% in 1999. Unemployment surged to 11.4%.

In addition, Chile was suffering from the worst drought in 50 years, especially in the nation's southern part. Agricultural losses were estimated at $557 million. Lack of water behind hydroelectric dams triggered months of electrical blackouts, and power rationing was imposed in central Chile.

The poor economic situation forced President Frei to make policy changes that emphasized growth rather than austerity and adjustment. The Central Bank reduced the interest rate to 5%. The government appropriated $400 million to jump-start the flagging economy, with the goal of creating 150,000 new jobs during 1999. Finance Minister Eduardo Aninat said he expected GDP growth of 0.5% as a result of the changes, with a jump to 5.5% growth in 2000.

The Pinochet Case. Several legal developments took place in 1999 in the case of Pinochet, who was in Britain fighting his extradition to Spain, where Judge Baltasar Garzón wanted to try him on charges of torture, murder, and other human-rights abuses against opponents of his 1973–90 regime. In March, Britain's top court ruled that while Pinochet's arrest was lawful, the former dictator could be held accountable only for acts committed after 1988, the year that British law incorporated a United Nations (UN) convention on torture. Garzón later sent an additional 33 charges to British prosecutors that he said took place after 1988.

Chile reacted by asking the Spanish government to allow an international arbitrator to determine whether a Spanish court had the right to try Pinochet. Further, if the two countries were unable to reach an agreement in six months, Chile proposed that the case be referred to the International Court of Justice in the Hague. On October 8 a British magistrate ruled that Pinochet could be extradited to Spain; a few weeks later, Pinochet appealed the ruling.

RICHARD C. SCHROEDER, *Freelance Writer*

CHILE • Information Highlights

Official Name: Republic of Chile.
Location: Southwestern coast of South America.
Area: 292,259 sq mi (756 950 km^2).
Population (July 1999 est.): 14,973,843.
Chief Cities (June 30, 1995 est.): Santiago, the capital, 5,076,808; Concepción, 350,268; Viña del Mar, 322,220.
Government: *Head of state and government,* Eduardo Frei Ruíz-Tagle, president (took office March 1994). *Legislature*—National Congress: Senate and Chamber of Deputies.
Monetary Unit: Peso (536.550 pesos equal U.S.$1, Dec. 20, 1999).
Gross Domestic Product (1998 est. U.S.$): $184,600,000,000 (purchasing power parity).
Economic Indexes: *Consumer Prices* (Santiago, 1998, 1990 = 100): all items, 228.9; food, 230.6. *Industrial Production* (1998, 1990 = 100): 162.6.
Foreign Trade (1998 U.S.$): *Imports,* $18,828,000,000; *exports,* $14,895,000,000.

China

As it prepared to celebrate the 50th anniversary of its founding in 1999, the People's Republic of China faced a number of challenges for the future, including the question of how best to maintain the impressive growth of its economy. The Chinese Communist Party (CCP) government launched a crackdown on Falun Gong, a religious sect whose popularity posed a potential threat to the CCP's dominance in China. Meanwhile, at the end of the year, China welcomed the return of another of its territories, Macao (*see* SIDEBAR, page 197).

Relations with the United States soured during the year for a variety of reasons, including a U.S. congressional report that accused China of stealing U.S. military secrets (*see* SPECIAL REPORT, page 200). Nevertheless, after a 13-year negotiating process, Beijing and Washington worked out an agreement in November that would facilitate China's entry into the World Trade Organization (WTO).

China's 50th Anniversary. On October 1 a 500,000-strong parade in Beijing marked the 50th anniversary of the establishment of the People's Republic of China. For many observers it seemed a throwback in style to a different time and place: Moscow in the 1950s, to be exact. The parade featured 10,000 People's Liberation Army (PLA) troops and 400 pieces of heavy military equipment, including China's newest Dongfeng-31 long-range missile. The parade was organized into three sections: one devoted to the accomplishments of Mao Zedong; one to those of his successor, Deng Xiaoping; and a third to those of Jiang Zemin, the current head of the Chinese state, the CCP, and the PLA.

Although the festivities were heavily stage-managed—onlookers were as carefully selected and rehearsed as the participants were, occupants of buildings along the parade route were prohibited from opening their windows, and factories in the vicinity of Beijing were shut down for several days to clear the air of the usual choking pollution—there was much for the Chinese people to celebrate. Seldom in its history had China been so prosperous and its power so widely recognized by the rest of the world. Although that prosperity was by no means equally shared by all of China's 1.2 billion people—indeed, the gap between rich and poor, rural and urban Chinese was shown in

On Oct. 1, 1999, the 50th anniversary of the proclamation of Communist rule in China was marked elaborately in Beijing. Premier Zhu Rongji addressed various party leaders at a special anniversary banquet, below.

© Chung Chien-min/AP/Wide World Photos

1999 to be even larger than it had been in the notoriously corrupt period before the onset of World War II—the lot of even the poorest citizens was substantially better than at any time in the recent past.

The 61-million-member-strong CCP and its leaders had hoped to capitalize on the anniversary celebrations to consolidate and strengthen their position at the helm of China's remarkable economic development. In retrospect, they appeared to have hoped in vain. As one malicious Chinese pundit put it on the eve of the anniversary, "Communism in China is dead; unfortunately, the Chinese Communist Party is not." For some time now, it has been clear that the Marxist-Leninist values that formed the basis of the CCP and its revolution have become largely irrelevant to the increasingly market-driven lives of most Chinese people.

© Chung Chien-min/AP/Wide World Photos

In April 1999 members of the Falun Gong spiritual movement meditated in the streets of Beijing. The government subsequently staged a crackdown on the organization.

Spiritual Dissidents. Evidence that many Chinese were suspended uncomfortably between two ideological stools was provided by the startling appearance in late April of more than 10,000 demonstrators in the restricted Beijing neighborhood of Zhongnanhai (home to the CCP's most-senior officials). The demonstrators—mostly middle-aged, middle-class men and women—were members of Falun Gong ("Buddhist Law"), an organization built around a belief in *qi gong*, an ancient, very widespread set of beliefs centered on the idea that spiritual forces inside and outside the body can be concentrated and utilized by meditation and exercise. Falun Gong has been propounded in recent years by Li Hongzhi, a former grain-bureau clerk in exile in the United States. Estimates of the size of Falun Gong's membership ranged as high as 100 million, with the vast majority said to be Chinese people not unlike the demonstrators. The protesters said that they were seeking a meeting with senior government officials to clarify the legal status of the organization, which, they insisted, had violated no laws but still was being subjected to surveillance and harassment by local authorities. They insisted that the organization had no political motives, but that its members had experienced achievement of peace of mind and improved health as a result of meditation and exercise.

Although authorities at first ignored the protest, Jiang appeared to have become obsessed with the idea that an organization other than the CCP had grown to the point that it could, unbeknownst to those in power, organize the largest demonstration in Beijing since the student protests of 1989. As June 4, the date of the tenth anniversary of the Tiananmen Square massacre in Beijing, approached (an anniversary that, because of the extraordinary vigilance of the Beijing police, passed uneventfully), Jiang stepped up his attack on the movement. The government asserted that Falun Gong was an "evil cult." In July, Jiang ordered its leaders arrested, called on Washington to extradite Li Hongzhi (Washington refused), and instructed police to break up demonstrations by thousands of Falun Gong supporters in cities throughout the country. Throughout the late summer the government-controlled press was filled with accounts of the dangers of the superstitious cult, which allegedly had caused the deaths of many who had abandoned conventional medicine in favor of its regimens.

CHINA • Information Highlights

Official Name: People's Republic of China.
Location: Central-eastern Asia.
Area: 3,705,809 sq mi (9 598 000 km²).
Population (July 1999 est., including Hong Kong): 1,253,719,076.
Chief Cities (Dec. 31, 1990 est.): Beijing (Peking), the capital, 7,000,000; Shanghai, 7,830,000; Tianjin, 5,770,000.
Government: *Head of state,* Jiang Zemin, president (took office March 1993). *Head of government,* Zhu Rongji, premier (named March 17, 1998). *Legislature* (unicameral)—National People's Congress.
Monetary Unit: Yuan (8.2787 yuan equal U.S.$1, Jan. 2, 2000).
Gross Domestic Product (1998 est. U.S.$): $4,420,000,000,000 (purchasing power parity).
Foreign Trade (1998 U.S.$, including Hong Kong): *Imports,* $184,503,000,000; *exports,* $173,990,000,000.

Macao

On Dec. 20, 1999, sovereignty over the Portuguese colony of Macao passed to the People's Republic of China under a plan modeled after the one that returned Hong Kong to Chinese sovereignty in 1997. First colonized in 1557, Macao has a population of 430,000. It occupies some 7 sq mi (18.1 km^2) of territory consisting of a small peninsula and a series of islands on the southern coast of China, 36 mi (57.9 km) across the Pearl River estuary from Hong Kong. Twice in the recent past, Portugal attempted unsuccessfully to return the colony—once during the tumultuous first months of China's Cultural Revolution in 1966, and again after a leftist revolution in Portugal in 1974. Terms of the 1999 transfer were negotiated successfully in 1987 and formalized in a Joint Declaration signed by the Portuguese and Chinese governments.

The transfer of sovereignty was marked by ceremonies at the stroke of midnight presided over by Portugal's President Jorge Sampãio and China's President Jiang Zemin. Macao then became a special administrative region (SAR) of the People's Republic of China, with substantial autonomy except in the spheres of foreign relations and military affairs. The Basic Law governing the new SAR was passed by China's National People's Congress in 1993.

The new head of government in Macao was 44-year-old banker Edmund Ho, whose appointment was announced by Beijing in May. Ho's first priority was controlling crime, as the territory has been notorious as a haven for criminal gangs. It was decided that a garrison of 1,000 People's Liberation Army (PLA) soldiers would be stationed in Macao to help fight crime; the first 700 soldiers of the garrison arrived the day after the transfer of sovereignty was effected.

While Macao's economy has a gross domestic product (GDP) of slightly less than $6 billion and exports manufactured goods, a very significant portion of its tax revenue derives from tourism and gambling. For many years, Macao has attracted visitors from Hong Kong (and, more recently, from nearby Shenzhen and Guangzhou) to its hotels, bars, and casinos. To facilitate the tourist trade, it opened a new international airport in 1999.

The transfer of sovereignty struck observers as significantly more relaxed than that in Hong Kong in 1997. In general, the Portuguese were not sorry to relinquish control, and most Macanese were not sorry to see them go. The transfer marked the end of what was once a vast European colonial empire in East Asia.

JOHN BRYAN STARR

The government attacked the movement more concretely as well, arresting more than 150 of its members and reportedly sending hundreds of others to labor camps for "reeducation." In late December four CCP members believed to be leaders of Falun Gong were convicted of several charges, including organizing the April demonstration and "using the cult organization to undermine the implementation of laws." They were given prison sentences ranging from seven to 18 years.

Material Dissidents. Spontaneous street demonstrations were of particular concern to the state. As a result of a government program to shore up the perennially unprofitable state-owned sector of the economy, unemployment in China's cities continued to rise during the year. The three-year program, begun in 1998, called for consolidating and strengthening the largest key firms—defined as those with sales and assets exceeding $60 million—slotted to remain under government ownership, selling off those state-owned factories for whom buyers could be found, and closing down the rest.

The principal problem in implementing this plan was the very substantial number of people it would put out of work. In 1999 there were about 105 million workers employed in the state-owned sector, an estimated one third of whom were underemployed. Some 22 million workers had lost their jobs as a result of the plan, and that figure was projected to grow by about 4 million per year. The hope was that these people would find work in collectively or privately owned factories, but lack of growth in these sectors had resulted in there being fewer jobs than anticipated.

The actual number of unemployed people in China's cities was difficult to ascertain. The official figure was set early in 1999 at 11 million, but a Chinese economist writing at about the same time gave the figure as 16.5 million. But neither number included the 3 million to 4 million receiving substantially reduced wages after having been laid off from their jobs.

Throughout the year there were unofficial reports of demonstrations and riots by the unemployed. In the spring, for example, some 500 laid-off cotton-mill workers staged a sit-down strike on a highway bridge in Changde in south-central Hunan province, demanding that they be paid three months' back pay that had been promised to them. And the public expression of dissatisfaction was not confined to China's cities. In Daolin, also in Hunan province, 10,000 took to the streets in February in a violent demonstration protesting excessive taxes and government corruption. The gap between urban and rural economic opportunities continued to widen, and most of the 124 million Chinese who lived below the World Bank's poverty line of $365 per-capita income in 1999 were rural residents.

Relations with the United States. The nearly 30-year relationship between the United States and the People's Republic of China reached a nadir in 1999. The issues that caused tension were not new, but they assumed a particularly virulent form, beginning when Premier Zhu Rongji visited the United States in April. There had been widespread anticipation that a trade agreement would be concluded during Zhu's meetings with President Bill Clinton in Washington, thereby successfully ending nearly 13 years of negotiations and opening the way for China's long-awaited entry into the World Trade Organization (WTO). But Clinton dashed those hopes by rejecting the Chinese side's "last best" bargaining position.

Clinton quickly reversed his position, but two events delayed the resumption of negotiations for more than six months. The first of these was the damage done to Zhu's position at home by Clinton's rejection—damage that was rendered substantially more serious by the administration's making public the previously secret terms of the Chinese offer. Zhu was seen by his colleagues as having failed in his mission to Washington and by many others in China as having been willing to sell out their economic interests in a humiliating eagerness to join the WTO.

Then, scarcely two weeks later, came the bombing by U.S. planes of the Chinese embassy in Belgrade, which killed several persons. The strike, which the United States immediately said was a mistake, came during the North Atlantic Treaty Organization (NATO) campaign against Serbia over Kosovo. The Chinese had opposed NATO bombing of Serb targets from the outset of hostilities in March, to the point that Zhu had come very close to canceling his trip to Washington in protest. Beijing found utterly incredible the U.S. explanation that the bombing was accidental, and the Chinese people agreed, taking to the streets by the thousands to express their anger by attacking the U.S. embassy in Beijing and consulates in other cities. While protesters were hard-pressed to come up with a plausible motivation for such an act on the part of the U.S. government, they could not accept the idea that the world's technologically most sophisticated power could destroy a building and cause the loss of lives by accident. In mid-December the two governments settled the question of compensation for damage to embassies with a payment of $28 million by Washington for damage caused by the bombing in Belgrade (in addition to $4.5 million given to the injured Chinese and the families of those killed), and $2.87 million by Beijing for damage by demonstrators to U.S. diplomatic facilities in China.

It was only with the prospect of a meeting between Clinton and Jiang at the Asia-Pacific Economic Cooperation summit meeting in New Zealand in September that U.S.-China trade talks resumed. After a cliff-hanging final round in Beijing, they were concluded successfully on November 15 with an agreement that, if approved by the U.S. Congress, would pave the way for China to enter the WTO.

But meanwhile, the issue of Taiwan—always a thorn in the side of Beijing-Washington ties—reerupted with Taiwan President Lee Teng-hui's startling announcement in July that relations across the Taiwan Strait henceforth must be conducted only on a "state-to-state" basis. Because Beijing never has acknowledged the separate existence of a Taiwan "state," Lee's comment, during a broadcast on German radio, was taken as a serious provocation, tantamount perhaps to the declaration of Taiwan independence that Beijing has said consistently would be responded to by force.

Washington did all it could to defuse the situation, publicly dissociating itself from the Taiwan position, meeting privately with Taiwan authorities to attempt to persuade them to modify their stance, and actively opposing for the first time Taiwan's annual quest for membership in the United Nations (UN). For its part, Beijing limited its response to verbal threats, remembering, perhaps, that military action against Taiwan under similar circumstances in 1996 only solidified popular support of Lee on the island and may have contributed to his election as president later that year.

As relations between the United States and China degenerated, some thought they saw signs of an emerging anti-American "axis" being constructed among China, Russia, and India. They cited as evidence then-Russian Premier Yevgeny Primakov's call at the end of 1998 for a "strategic partnership" between Russia and China; Zhu Rongji's visit to Moscow in March, during which agreements were signed for the Chinese purchase of Russian arms; and a Beijing–New Delhi agreement in June calling for the opening of a "strategic dialogue" between China and India. While these events may in fact have added up to less than the sum of their parts, it was certainly true that the three nations shared a distaste for a world in which Washington called the shots as the single remaining superpower.

© Vincent Yu/AP/Wide World Photos

After U.S. planes accidentally bombed the Chinese embassy in Belgrade during NATO's campaign against Serbia, anti-U.S. protests were held in Chinese cities.

Economy. Whereas runaway inflation was among the problems that brought people out in support of student demonstrators in 1989, deflation was the issue that the Chinese government had had to contend with for the past two years. The consumer price index continued to drop through most of 1999, despite the government's best efforts at creating incentives for consumers to spend money. Early in the year there was considerable speculation that Beijing would devalue the Chinese currency, the yuan—speculation that the government promptly and consistently denied. Despite the Chinese denials, this possibility aroused concern among China's regional neighbors, since the stability of the yuan was credited with helping to shorten the duration and lighten the effects of the Asian financial crisis in 1997–98.

But late 1999 saw several signs that the Chinese economy was beginning to recover. Both imports and exports were up, beginning in August; there were signs that the consumer price index was becoming stable; and talk of changing the exchange rate ended. In October the Chinese Academy of Social Sciences projected the 1999 economic growth rate at 7.6%, a figure that fell within the 7.5% to 8% guidelines set by the government at the beginning of the year.

However, two major obstacles loomed ahead that must be surmounted before China's economic development could continue. Both were addressed in a serious fashion for the first time during 1999, but neither came close to being resolved fully. The first was the long-standing problem of unprofitable state-owned industries; the second was the weakened Chinese banking system. Dai Xianglong, head of the People's Bank of China, estimated in September that one quarter of the loans in the portfolios of the state commercial banks were unable to be collected. He said asset-management companies were being set up to assume the bad loans and set the reduction of the banks' bad debts by 50% as a goal for 2000.

Hong Kong. As Hong Kong ended its second and began its third year as a Special Administrative Region (SAR) under Chinese sovereignty, the details of what "one state, two systems" actually means in practice continued to be worked out. At issue in 1999 was a court case involving four Chinese citizens whose parents were citizens of Hong Kong. The four sought Hong Kong citizenship, citing a provision of the Basic Law governing the SAR that states that children of Hong Kong citizens born outside Hong Kong have the rights of Hong Kong citizens. The Hong Kong Court of Final Appeal ruled in favor of the four at the end of January. Beijing immediately protested, saying that China's National People's Congress (NPC) and not the Hong Kong court had the sole authority to interpret the Basic Law. The court reviewed the case in February and upheld its decision, noting at the same time that it "[could not] question the authority" of the NPC.

The Hong Kong government, under Chief Executive Tung Chee-hwa, sided with Beijing. Citing the fact that 1.67 million Chi-

SPECIAL REPORT The Espionage Case

As a result of allegations that two U.S. satellite manufacturers—Hughes Space and Communications and Loral Space and Communications—had provided Chinese agencies that launch satellites with information that could improve China's strategic rocket capabilities, the U.S. House of Representatives in spring 1998 established the Select Committee on U.S. National Security and Military/Commercial Concerns with the People's Republic of China, headed by Rep. Christopher Cox (R-CA). While the committee's report gained media and public attention and contributed to several changes in U.S. policy and regulatory procedures, numerous questions remained as to the report's accuracy, the soundness of its findings and recommendations, and the true nature and implications of Chinese technology-acquisition efforts in the United States. Nevertheless, the overall problem of potential Chinese espionage remained serious, and further investigation and tightening of security undoubtedly would follow.

In the course of its investigation, the "Cox Committee" expanded its work beyond the Hughes/Loral case to look into a wide range of alleged espionage and other sensitive technology-acquisition practices by the People's Republic of China (PRC), including in such areas as nuclear-weapons designs, high-performance computers, missile-related information, and other commercial and dual-use technologies.

The Findings. The committee's report was released in a classified version on Jan. 3, 1999, and an 800-plus-page declassified version followed on May 25. Among the most troublesome findings were that China had "stolen design information" of America's most advanced thermonuclear weapons, that these thefts gave China "design information on thermonuclear weapons on a par with" U.S. nuclear weapons, that China's "penetration of [U.S.] nuclear-weapons laboratories" spanned several decades, that China "[had] stolen or otherwise illegally obtained U.S. missile and space technology," and that "United States... export-control policies and practices [had] facilitated [China's] efforts to obtain militarily useful technology."

The Cox Committee noted that in the declassified report, "important factual examples" were omitted, "explicit findings of the Select Committee [were] suppressed," and the classified version of the report remained "the definitive product" of all of the committee's investigations.

Controversy and Contradiction. The classified and declassified findings immediately met with a great deal of criticism from government and nongovernment analysts alike, including members of the Cox Committee itself. While most analysts generally agreed that China, like other nations, was seeking to obtain sensitive technologies from the United States, and that any laxity in security needed tightening, some of them found that the Cox Committee report presented a poorly supported "worst-case" scenario. The critics charged that the lengthy report was put together largely by contracted outside private-intelligence analysts and technical experts with little or no previous knowledge of China, resulting in numerous flaws that undermined its credibility. For example, Rep. John Spratt (D-SC), a committee member, while not formally dissenting to the issuance of the report, released a very damaging assessment of the findings, highlighting the poor evidence behind them; the inaccurate, exaggerated, and misleading conclusions drawn from that evidence; and the committee's refusal to take testimony from witnesses with a broad range of scientific and China-related expertise.

George Tenet, the director of the Central Intelligence Agency (CIA), conducted a classified bipartisan damage assessment by a panel of military-technical specialists at the request of the Cox Committee. Issued in April 1999, this group's findings differed considerably from the Cox Report, concluding that "we do not know whether any weapon design documentation or blueprints were acquired" by China, and that, "to date, the aggressive Chinese collection effort has not resulted in any apparent modernization of

nese citizens were the children of Hong Kong citizens and in theory could move to Hong Kong if the court's ruling stood, the government petitioned the NPC to reverse it. It did so in late June. Although most Hong Kong residents approved the move, opponents criticized it as setting a dangerous precedent with respect to the independence of the Hong Kong judicial system.

The tenth anniversary of the Tiananmen Square massacre was marked in Hong Kong by a candlelit vigil of more than 70,000 people in Victoria Park. Organizers of the event—many of them prominent members their deployed strategic force or any new nuclear weapons deployment." Another study, led by former Sen. Warren Rudman (R-NH), also found no hard evidence that any Chinese thefts of U.S. nuclear-weapons secrets occurred.

A report in July, commissioned by former Rep. Jack Kemp (R-NY) and conducted by an independent nuclear-weapons expert, concluded that while both the administration and Congress were to blame for not properly overseeing security at U.S. national laboratories, "there is no convincing evidence available to the U.S. experts that: (a) the PRC ever 'penetrated' any U.S. weapons lab; (b) the PRC ever 'stole' anything from the labs; (c) any U.S. lab scientist ever 'gave' the PRC any 'classified' information; (d) that the PRC has incorporated any 'secrets' or classified information they may have obtained by 'hook or crook' from the U.S. labs into their weapon designs or into their weapons in stockpile."

Bennett/© "The Christian Science Monitor"

Further Developments. Subsequent revelations further complicated the committee's findings. For example, a central figure in the investigations, Dr. Wen Ho Lee, a naturalized U.S. citizen from Taiwan and a nuclear-weapons scientist at Los Alamos National Laboratories, was not charged formally in 1999 with espionage related to the release of nuclear-weapons secrets to China. Lee was dismissed from his position at Los Alamos for lax security procedures, and at the end of the year, he was indicted for mishandling classified information.

In another wrinkle, it was revealed that what had led the committee to begin its investigations was the report that the CIA had obtained information in 1995 from an unsolicited Chinese "walk-in," who provided information that China had data related to the highly advanced U.S. W-88 thermonuclear weapon. However, it was unclear whether the walk-in was genuine, was engaged in disinformation on China's behalf, or was sent by some third party. Moreover, some analysts argued that simple information would not be enough to fabricate the W-88 in China without far more data on testing, electronics, and other technologies. In addition, experts said that as long as China adhered to its moratorium on nuclear testing, it would remain difficult for it to integrate with confidence any nuclear-weapons information it may have obtained from the United States.

Tightening Security. A number of important new policy, regulatory, and judicial procedures emerged in the wake of the Cox Report. For example, under the National Defense Authorization Act signed into law by President Bill Clinton in October 1998, licensing authority for the export of commercial satellites was transferred back to the U.S. State Department from the Commerce Department. The move was seen as a way to strengthen export controls; the act also included other reporting requirements to assure greater oversight over satellite exports to China.

In spring and summer 1999, the Department of Energy, at the urging of Congress, reorganized its security procedures and its oversight of the national nuclear-weapons laboratories. In addition, a limited program of exchanges and cooperation between U.S. government nuclear-weapons laboratories and their Chinese counterparts was suspended.

BATES GILL

of the Hong Kong Democratic Party—found themselves barred from travel into mainland China. Complaining of their treatment to Tung, they were told that he was likely to be more successful in intervening with Beijing on their behalf if they agreed to end their sponsorship of the annual Tiananmen vigils.

The Hong Kong economy appeared to be on the mend after the adverse effects of the Asian financial crisis. By midyear negative growth figures gave way to positive figures, and 2% growth in the economy was predicted for the second half of 1999.

JOHN BRYAN STARR, *Brown University*

Cities and Urban Affairs

U.S. cities and suburbs were confronting many familiar problems in 1999, as they prepared to enter a new century. Certain central cities faced leadership changes; others contemplated further rebirth in downtowns and neighborhoods; and some began to address the long-festering problem of public schools. In many urban areas, residents in cities and suburbs alike debated how to handle the unplanned and rapid growth of urban development on rural land, a phenomenon known as "urban sprawl."

Changes in Leadership. Who sits at the helm of a city government can have consequences for the locale's redevelopment. Although problems such as scarce resources, a declining middle-class presence, and racial tensions endure, skilled leaders may become innovators or change the tenor of city dialogue. In January 1999 new mayors took the helm in Oakland, CA, and Washington, DC. Former California Gov. Jerry Brown assumed the mayoralty of Oakland, and lost no time asserting his authority and his desire to "shake things up," as he put it. He immediately demanded the resignations of several department heads, as well as of the popular chief of police. Meanwhile, the newly elected mayor of Washington, DC, Anthony A. Williams, hoped to turn things around by returning the District to home rule. His plan to move the University of the District of Columbia from better-off northwest Washington to one of the poorest sections of town derailed, however. Williams, formerly the city's chief financial officer, had to face the thorny problems of race, class, and redevelopment early in his term.

In February, Chicago Mayor Richard M. Daley was reelected to a third full term, defeating U.S. Rep. Bobby Rush, a former Black Panther. Daley picked up a significant portion of the African-American vote, using jobs and contracts to attract support. Daley has fostered redevelopment and beautification downtown and in neighborhoods.

Several other cities selected new mayors in November. In Baltimore city-council member Martin O'Malley (D) trounced Republican David Tufaro to succeed retiring Mayor Kurt Schmoke, becoming the first white mayor since 1986 of the predominantly black city. Like Daley, O'Malley had considerable black support. In Philadelphia many residents would have preferred to see their popular mayor, Edward Rendell, serve a third term. Rendell, who could not run again because of term limits, had fostered development and created enthusiasm for his city. After the primary in Philadelphia, the race boiled down to a choice between African-American John Street, a Democrat and former city-council president, and Sam Katz, a white Republican businessman. Street, a close ally of Rendell, defeated Sam Katz by an exceedingly narrow margin of only 3%.

San Francisco Mayor Willie Brown waged an uphill battle for reelection, as his

U.S. cities have tried to revitalize their downtown areas in recent years. In Portland, OR, below, *for example, condominiums, shops, and restaurants have been built in parklike settings along the Willamette River.*

formerly popular and charismatic image had grown tarnished. Liberals, his former allies, felt he was too close to developers and big business; in addition, his crackdown on the city's homeless hurt his image, as did conflict-of-interest charges against several of his friends and associates. On November 2, Brown led the field of four candidates but failed to win a majority, obligating him to face the runner-up, Board of Supervisors president Tom Ammiano, in a runoff on December 14. Brown easily won the runoff, however.

Central-City Development. Employing various strategies, major U.S. cities tried to bolster their populations, increase the number of businesses in their metropolitan areas, and attract tourist-type venues. Most mayors wanted to add life to the downtown areas, ensuring that there are people on the streets and places to draw them. Detroit embarked on building new baseball and football stadiums downtown, as well as adding casino gambling on the riverfront. Philadelphia launched a plan to erect a magnificent new concert hall for the Philadelphia Orchestra, while Chicago added four new downtown theaters and began constructing two high-rise luxury residential towers to encourage more people to live in the downtown area.

Since the mid-1980s, Denver, CO, has won high marks for creating a vivacious downtown. Its strategies included historic preservation, fostering the arts and entertainment, and creating new shopping areas. Denver's transit mall enables workers and visitors to travel downtown with ease. In Denver many older buildings have become desirable housing stock, and in 1999 the city was contemplating $1 billion in new downtown residential construction. The lure of downtown loft living was evident in St. Louis, Detroit, and Birmingham (AL) as well.

The nation's unprecedented prosperity also stimulated development in lower-income sections of many cities. For instance, New York City's Harlem neighborhood saw a rise in the number of African-American professionals living there, and shopping there increased as well. Chicago's south side saw the construction of a large supermarket and other stores, close to public housing.

Despite some progress, cities continued to grapple with hard-core poverty. Although welfare rolls shrank overall, a higher percentage of recipients resided in cities than in the past. For example, 47% of Pennsylvania's welfare recipients lived in Philadelphia in 1999, up from 39% in 1994. The mayors of Chicago, Boston, and Detroit acted to take over their cities' public schools in order to lessen chronic poverty for future generations and to prevent further middle-class flight to suburbs.

Urban Sprawl. The issue of sprawl took center stage in 1999, as politicians ranging from the mayors of large U.S. cities to Vice-President Al Gore attacked the accelerating spread of urban development into rural areas. Sprawl has become prevalent in many urban areas. U.S. cities have spread outward in virtually unlimited fashion. Critics of sprawl charged that the financial expense of projects caused by it, such as constructing sewer and water lines and building new roads and highways, put an onerous burden on taxpayers. They also said that sprawl promoted pollution (by encouraging long commutes by car); created polarization between outer and inner areas of cities that often had racial and class overtones; and gobbled up farmland.

In January, Vice-President Gore proposed a "Livable Communities Initiative," which would offer grants and tax benefits to communities that preserved green spaces, curbed water pollution, relieved traffic congestion, and revived abandoned industrial sites. Roy Barnes, the governor of Georgia, had made controlling the sprawl of greater Atlanta a top priority. And voters in Alabama, Maryland, Arizona, and other states approved measures that limited peripheral growth. In addition, the designers of new towns and suburbs tried to create a greater feeling of community by incorporating sidewalks and town centers.

Detractors of the ever-widening metropolitan areas continue to decry the environmental and psychic costs involved with commuting, as well as the duplication of basic services. New urbanists lament the design of new communities, and other critics find that the spreading suburbs provide few recreational areas for teenagers. Yet, despite the growing criticisms, large numbers of Americans prefer their single-family, detached dwellings on nice plots of land, separated from their neighbors. The stage is set for a struggle about urban expansion in many metropolitan areas. At the same time, mayors of the core jurisdictions fight to maintain the relevance and viability of the central city. The new century will see if the endless flight continues, or if the inner cities can become more attractive to potential residents.

LANA STEIN
University of Missouri–St. Louis

Coins and Coin Collecting

The year 1999 marked the launch of the U.S. Mint's 50 State Quarters Program. Signed into law on Dec. 1, 1997, the 50 States Commemorative Coin Program Act called for a ten-year series of circulating quarters, featuring a revised portrait of President George Washington on the common obverse and designs emblematic of each of the 50 states on the reverses. The law provided for the release of five issues annually, in the order in which the states ratified the U.S. Constitution or were admitted to the Union. The Delaware quarter debuted first, in mid-January, followed by the release of Pennsylvania's coin in March. New Jersey's quarter was issued in May; pieces representing Georgia entered circulation in July; and Connecticut rounded out the first year's schedule.

Other significant commemorative-coin debuts included the Dolley Madison silver dollar on January 11; the George Washington gold $5 on May 7; and the Yellowstone National Park 125th Anniversary silver dollar on July 16. However, the U.S. Mint's Citizens' Commemorative Coin Advisory Committee voiced concern about the viability of future programs, noting violations of the 1996 Commemorative Coin Reform Act, which limits congressional authorization to no more than two such programs per year.

The United States' new $1 coin, scheduled to replace the Susan B. Anthony dollar in 2000, was unveiled on May 4. The obverse of the gold-colored, 1.04-inch (26.5-mm) coin will display an image representing Sacajawea, the young Shoshone woman who guided Meriwether Lewis and William Clark on their historic expedition beginning in 1804. On her back, she carries her infant son. The design is the work of Glenna Goodacre, acclaimed sculptor of the Vietnam Women's Memorial in Washington, DC. The reverse bears a soaring eagle surrounded by 17 stars, symbolic of the states in the Union at the time of the expedition; it was created by Thomas D. Rogers, Sr., a sculptor/engraver at the Philadelphia Mint.

Consumers reacquainted themselves with the $20 bill, which was revised to incorporate new counterfeiting deterrents. The notes—which feature a large, off-center portrait of the seventh president, Andrew Jackson, and color-shifting ink—withstood the rigors of circulation during their initial months. However, some critics described the new $20 as looking like "Monopoly money" and called for further design changes.

On August 30 the finest known example of a U.S. 1804 dollar (the Class I Childs specimen) sold at auction for $4.14 million, breaking all records for a single coin.

CATHY CLARK
American Numismatic Association

Colombia

Colombia suffered a year of national disintegration in 1999. The economy, which had performed admirably throughout the 1980s and beyond, experienced an almost total collapse. The twin forces of narcotics and guerrilla groups combined to produce a state of national breakdown unprecedented in recent Colombian history. This second-most-populous nation in South America increasingly attracted the attention of outsiders, as it began to appear that Colombia was a nation coming apart. Efforts by President Andrés Pastrana to bring about a truce with the nation's leading guerrilla organization produced no real results, despite the establishment of a demilitarized zone. By late 1999 it appeared that some type of U.S. intervention was inevitable. In late October some 5 million Colombians—members of the "No Más" ("No More") coalition—marched in hundreds of cities to demand an end to the civil conflict and to related human-rights abuses and kidnappings.

Politics. Efforts by President Pastrana to end what has been endemic guerrilla warfare dominated the political agenda. On May 2, Pastrana and the leader of the Revolutionary Armed Forces of Colombia (Fuerzas Armadas Revolucionarias Colombiana, or FARC), Manuel Marulanda Velez (aka Tiro Fijo—"Sure Shot"), met and agreed on a 12-point agenda for peace. No sooner was the agenda accepted than it

COLOMBIA • Information Highlights

Official Name: Republic of Colombia.
Location: Northwest South America.
Area: 439,734 sq mi (1 138 910 km²).
Population (July 1999 est.): 39,309,422.
Chief Cities (mid-1997 est.): Santa Fe de Bogotá, the capital, 6,004,782; Cali, 1,985,906; Medellín, 1,970,691; Barranquilla, 1,157,826.
Government: *Head of state and government,* Andrés Pastrana Arango, president (took office August 1998). *Legislature*—Congress: Senate and House of Representatives.
Monetary Unit: Peso (1,871.5 pesos equal U.S.$1, Dec. 6, 1999).
Gross Domestic Product (1998 est. U.S.$): $254,700,-000,000 (purchasing power parity).
Economic Indexes (1998, 1990 = 100): *Consumer Prices,* all items, 542.5; food, 466.7. *Industrial Production,* 136.5.
Foreign Trade (1997 U.S.$): *Imports,* $15,378,000,000; *exports,* $11,522,000,000.

© Scott Dalton/AP/Wide World Photos

Civil conflict wracked Colombia in 1999. In July soldiers, left, *mourned at the funeral of some of their comrades, killed in one of the continuing clashes between Colombian armed forces and guerrilla groups.*

began to fall apart. Chief among the disagreements was the guerrillas' insistence that the government begin a crackdown on right-wing death squads, which, according to many sources, had close ties to the armed forces. The chief right-wing group, known as the United Self Defenders of Colombia (Autodefensas Unidas de Colombia, or AUC) not only refused to cease operations against suspected guerrilla sympathizers, but also demanded a place at the conference table with the government and the guerrillas. Despite all the false starts, however, by late 1999 it appeared that the FARC was ready to resume talks with the government.

One bright spot in the guerrilla situation was the increased professionalization of the armed forces under the command of newly appointed Gen. Fernando Tapias, resulting in a number of victories in armed clashes with the guerrillas. A guerrilla attack near the capital of Bogotá in July resulted in more than 200 guerrillas being killed and 400 captured. Tapias, a former intelligence officer, appeared to be bringing the war to the guerrillas for the first time.

President Pastrana also suffered a stinging defeat in the Colombian Congress when his political-reform package was voted down. The package, among other things, would have given the president almost unlimited powers in dealing with the rebels, including granting amnesties to guerrilla prisoners. Talk of an imperial presidency—with Pastrana called "Andrés the First"—was a major factor in the defeat of the reform package.

Economy. A conglomeration of factors, some economic and some political, overwhelmed the economy in 1999. Gross domestic product (GDP) declined by an estimated 6%. On June 28 the Colombian peso was devalued by almost 10%. Unemployment neared 20%. Estimates of the decrease in industrial production ranged from 14.3% to 19.6%. Although there was a trade surplus of $468 million for the first half of the year, it was due almost totally to the severe recession. Imports dropped by 36% for the first six months. Colombia's external debt rose to $32 billion, or the equivalent of three years' export earnings. More than 22% of the government's budget went to servicing the nation's domestic debt. The one economic bright spot was a reduction in inflation. A 0.78% increase in April was the lowest in 32 years.

An extremely strong earthquake hit the coffee-growing regions of Quindio and Risaralda on January 25, almost completely destroying the city of Armenia. More than 1,100 people were killed; some 700 were missing and presumed dead; and some 250,000 were left homeless by the quake.

Foreign Affairs. Many U.S. government officials and members of Congress faulted the Pastrana administration for making too many concessions to the guerrillas. Officials from President Bill Clinton on down saw an increasing need for the United States to play a more active role in support of the Colombian government. Late in the year, after a Clinton-Pastrana meeting in Washington, a $3.5 billion loan from the United States and the international community was announced.

ERNEST A. DUFF
Randolph-Macon Woman's College

Computers and Communications

The world breathed a sigh of relief as the year 2000 began with no reports of major computer problems. Widespread fears that the "Y2K bug" would cause havoc proved unfounded, in large part due to massive efforts to avoid such a crisis. Attention again could focus on other trends of 1999, particularly the rapid growth of Internet applications and the convergence of the computer and telecommunications industries.

The Millennium Bug. The Y2K (year 2000) issue demonstrated how dependent the world has become on computers, not only in offices and homes but also in the operation of transportation, communication, and other infrastructure systems. The Y2K problem had its roots in the 1950s and 1960s, when designers of computer operating systems and applications software—in an effort to conserve memory—used only two digits to represent a year. Thus the year 1900 was recorded as 00, 1901 as 01, and so on. As the new century approached, many computers required repairs if they were to deal correctly with the change from 1999 to 2000, rather than misreading the latter year as 1900. Due to the ubiquity of computer chips in today's world, doomsayers predicted malfunctioning of electrical grids and medical equipment, breakdowns in nuclear-power plants, airplanes falling from the sky, and other woes. Instead, problems were minor.

The push to avoid the most dire problems proved to be enormously expensive. In November the U.S. Department of Commerce reported that repairs done to prevent a Y2K crisis cost the United States $100 billion. Estimates of the worldwide cost ranged up to $600 billion. And despite extensive testing of computer systems and the initial absence of major glitches, there remained the possibility that Y2K bugs would manifest themselves during 2000's first months.

National and international networks established to prepare for Y2K proved their worth, and participants were hoping to extend the networks' functions into the future. For example, as part of their Y2K preparations, South American nations had created the first continent-wide map of electricity grids. And the approximately 170 countries that participated in the Internet Worldwide Y2K Watch, a brainchild of the United Nations funded by the World Bank, provided immediate reports to one another as the New Year began in their homelands.

The Internet. The explosive growth of the Internet and its World Wide Web ("the Web") continued in 1999. The Nielsen organization reported that Internet users in the United States spent an average of eight hours and 13 minutes on-line in October. About equal numbers of men and women used the Internet, Nielsen said, but men averaged about 90 minutes more time on-line each month.

At year's end, Zona Research estimated that 90 million Americans used the Internet, compared with 85.3 million who did not use personal computers (PCs) at all. A Harris poll found that 56% of all U.S. adults were on-line. Earlier in the year a Department of Commerce survey found that the number of black and Hispanic households with access to computers and the Internet continued to trail the number of white and Asian households with such access. Also, children in single-parent households had far less access than did those in two-parent households.

The number of on-line shoppers jumped, with the week ending December 5 posting a 44% jump in traffic to e-commerce sites over the same period in 1998, according to Media Metrix. Retail buyers (*see* RETAILING) were but part of the picture; the brokerage firm Goldman Sachs forecast that the value of business-to-business e-commerce would rise from an estimated $114 billion in 1999 to $1.5 trillion in 2004.

Another increasingly popular type of e-commerce is the distribution of music in a digital format known as MP3. Many musicians legally use the format to release songs to generate interest in their music. But copying commercial CDs and giving them away is illegal. The Secure Digital Music Initiative is a coalition of music, electronics, and high-tech companies eager to use the Internet for music sales but also wanting to ensure artists' royalties and prevent piracy. It tentatively agreed to accept MP3 with the addition of a code, or digital watermark, invisibly blended into all copyrighted music that is downloaded. Electronics firms would design CD players that could detect the code and limit the number of copies of a song that could be made.

Instant messaging (IM), which allows people to communicate in real time in both voice and text modes, became a popular use of the Internet in 1999. IM software displays a message in a window on the recipient's computer screen seconds after it is transmitted. The most widely used IM service belonged to America Online (AOL), with some 80 million users. AOL fought to keep its IM user base limited to subscribers and people who downloaded its messaging software. But rivals, including Microsoft and AT&T, released IM software designed to allow users of their services to link to the AOL system. AOL managed to block access, but industry experts believed that it was only a matter of time before open standards prevailed in IM.

Privacy groups moved to counteract new technologies that made it easier to trace communications and gather personal information from Internet users. For example, RealNetworks' RealJukebox software for downloading digital music from the Internet tracked users' listening habits and other activities. Threatened with a lawsuit, RealNetworks took action to stop the program from relaying personal information about users. Similarly, Intel, which had embedded a unique serial number in its Pentium III processor enabling network operators to identify individual computers on the Internet, agreed to changes that would keep the number inactive unless the user switched it on.

Viruses and Worms. The list of known computer viruses grew by about 1,000 a month in 1999. Although most viruses do not spread widely, others proliferate rapidly, often as attachments to E-mail. Once such an attachment is opened, the virus can cause extensive damage.

In March the Melissa virus emerged and spread quickly by automatically sending itself from one recipient's E-mail account to up to 50 names in that person's address book. Melissa disrupted the operations of thousands of companies and some government agencies, but caused no permanent damage. Its author, David L. Smith of Aberdeen Township, NJ, was arrested April 1; in December he pleaded guilty to state and federal charges. Variants of Melissa continued to appear throughout 1999; some were significantly more destructive than their progenitor.

The Chernobyl virus—activated on April 26, the anniversary of the 1986 Chernobyl nuclear disaster—erased hard drives and ROM BIOS (basic input/output systems). It crashed hundreds of thousands of computers worldwide, with damage particularly severe in South Korea and Turkey. It was authored by Chen Inghau, a former computer-engineering student in Taiwan.

ExploreZip, a "worm" spread as an E-mail attachment, appeared in June. It overwrote files and sent out E-mail messages to addresses from newly infected computers. Mini-Zip, a compressed variant in a format unrecognized by security systems, struck in late November. The Mypics worm spread by pretending to be E-mail from an acquaintance, with an attached file of pictures. Opening the attachment infected one's computer with a virus that attacked on New Year's Day.

At least one virus took advantage of computer users' Y2K fears. Disguised as a Y2K software fix, purportedly from Microsoft, it was sent to people as an E-mail attachment that, once opened, stole passwords and destroyed data. (In reality, Microsoft never distributes software by E-mail because the identity of the sender is not guaranteed.)

Security Issues. Many organizations shut down Web sites during the 1999–2000 year change, reflecting concerns not only about Y2K malfunctions but also about security threats. People who use telephone lines or the Internet to break into computers to cause destruction or to gain access to private, often sensitive, data—commonly called hackers or crackers—had become a growing concern. Every day there were 80 to 100 hacking attempts on Pentagon computers, and the Department of Defense said that reported attacks and intrusions on its networks and systems jumped from 5,844 in 1998 to more than 18,000 in the first ten months of 1999. Other governments had similar experiences. A Pakistani hacker changed the front page of the Indian government's Department of Electronics Web site, and Chinese and Taiwanese hackers broke into the Web sites of each other's governments.

"We could wake one morning and find a city, or a sector of the country, or the whole country have an electric power problem, a transportation problem or a telecommunication problem because there was a surprise attack using information warfare," said Richard Clarke, the National Security Council adviser who heads counterterrorism efforts. "Our national security and economy is extremely dependent on [computer] automation. In fact, it's probably too dependent. We are an extremely target-rich environment," stated Alan B. Carroll, an FBI agent at the National Infrastructure Protection Center (NIPC) in Washington, DC. The NIPC, established in 1998, assesses, investigates, and responds to threats and attacks on computer systems and communications networks. Also responding to the problem are security services that evaluate corporate data systems, identifying ways that hackers can break in and then either closing these "back doors" or installing software that prevents unauthorized access.

"Cybercrime" is a broad term covering everything from electronic sabotage to money launderers to cyberstalkers. The extent of on-line crime was unknown, but it was believed to be growing rapidly. Internet criminals "will infest e-commerce and are capable of consuming a great amount of wealth if unchallenged," said Brian Jenkins, an adviser to the International Chamber of Commerce.

Manufacturers of encryption products remained at odds with the U.S. government over export regulations. Firms wanted to sell their security software overseas. However, law-enforcement officials feared that making the software available worldwide would enable criminals and terrorists to better conceal their communications.

Introductions and Advances. Prices of PCs continued to fall in 1999, with the average price of a machine using Microsoft Windows and an Intel microprocessor hovering around $800—down from $1,123 in late 1998. Some PCs were even "free," for consumers who signed up for two- to three-year contracts under which they paid monthly Internet-access fees—and endured a stream of ads running along the monitor's edges.

Apple introduced a lineup of iMacs, including a clamshell-shaped laptop, the iBook, designed as a consumer product. It also presented PowerBook G3, a pricier, more powerful laptop for its core market of graphic artists and multimedia professionals. IBM's latest models included the Thinkpad 240, a portable weighing 3 lb (1.4 kg).

New 1999 personal digital assistants (PDAs) included the Handspring Visor, which uses the same operating system as 3Com's Palm Pilot. In addition to standard PDA software and the ability to synchronize information with a desktop computer, Visor has a data port allowing a user to plug in modules to convert the device into a pager, cell phone, global-positioning device, and so on. Qualcomm introduced the pdQ phone, a digital phone with a built-in Palm Pilot.

Such hybrids may be succeeded by a technology being developed by the Bluetooth Special Interest Group, an industry consortium of about 1,200 companies. Bluetooth promised to use low-cost, low-power radio transmitters to connect PCs, PDAs, and mobile phones over a distance of about 33 ft (10 m), thereby making possible a "personal-area network." In December, Intel demonstrated Bluetooth-based hardware and software, and indicated that retail products should be ready before the end of 2000.

Ever-smaller, more-feature-laden cellular phones appeared, but the percentage of the population using the phones was greater in many parts of Europe and Asia than in the United States. At the end of 1998, 57% of Finns, 48% of Norwegians, 36% of Italians, 30% of South Koreans, and only 26% of Americans used the devices. Europe and Asia also were ahead of the United States in marketing cell phones with Internet access. By mid-1999 some 3 million cell-phone users in Japan subscribed to such services. Part of the problem in the United States was the presence of competing cellular-communications standards; much of the rest of the world used a common standard called GSM.

By the end of 1999 an estimated one third of U.S. households had video-game systems. Sega introduced Dreamcast, the first 128-bit console, with a 200-megahertz processor optimized for 3-D graphics and a built-in modem for on-line game play.

Corporate News. Many on-line companies make little if any profit but nonetheless are attractive to corporate buyers. For example, Excite@Home—an Internet gateway formed early in 1999 by the $6.7 billion merger of Excite and @Home—spent up to

$1 billion to acquire Bluemountain.com, a popular electronic-greeting-card company. Excite@Home predicted that the purchase would increase its audience by 40% and allow both sites to increase their advertising rates.

AT&T, a major owner of Excite@Home, expanded its presence in the cable-television market with the acquisition of MediaOne Group. Microsoft made a $5 billion investment in AT&T in return for a pledge that Microsoft software would be used in as many as 10 million AT&T set-top boxes that would deliver the Internet and other digital services to home TV sets beginning in 2000. Meanwhile, consumer groups and Internet-service providers (ISPs) filed suits and pushed legislation to open cable wires and phone lines to competitors. A coalition led by AOL and GTE wanted AT&T to allow cable customers to use ISPs other than Excite@Home without additional fees. In November the Federal Communications Commission ruled that local telephone carriers had to share their lines with rival high-speed ISPs. Local companies said the order would slow their investment in high-speed services.

Consolidation continued among telecommunications firms. SBC Communications acquired Ameritech, MCI Worldcom agreed to acquire Sprint, and Global Crossing merged with US West. Early in January 2000, AOL announced that it would buy media giant Time Warner for some $165 billion. It would be the largest corporate merger ever; the combined company—to be called AOL Time Warner—would have an estimated market value of $342 billion.

On another front, Bell Atlantic became the first of the "Baby Bells" formed in the 1984 breakup of AT&T to be allowed to compete in the long-distance phone market.

In August, eight months after Iridium began offering phone service via a constellation of 66 low-Earth-orbit satellites, the company filed for bankruptcy protection. Two weeks later, its competitor ICO Global Communications also filed for protection. That left investors in two other fledgling satellite systems, Teledesic and Globalstar, concerned about the industry's future.

In November, Federal District Court Judge Thomas Penfield Jackson issued his "findings of fact" in the government's antitrust lawsuit against industry giant Microsoft. He found that Microsoft was a monopoly and a bully, using "its prodigious market power and immense profits to harm any firm" that challenged it. Jackson also said that Microsoft "could charge a price for Windows substantially above that which could be charged in a competitive market." Microsoft's president, William H. Gates, disagreed with the court's findings, saying, "Microsoft competes vigorously and fairly. Americans should wish that every business was as competitive as the personal computer business." At year's end it was unknown whether Microsoft and the government would reach an out-of-court settlement.

JENNY TESAR, *Author*
"The New Webster's Computer Handbook"

© David Samuel Robbins/Corbis-Sygma

JEFF BEZOS

In 1994 investment-firm employee Jeff Bezos had a sudden vision of the future. He promptly quit his New York City job and headed to Seattle, WA, to fulfill this dream by starting a business; his improbable plan was to sell books over the then-fledgling World Wide Web.

During the next five years, Bezos' unlikely dream exceeded all expectations, and his company, Amazon.com, became the Web's biggest retail store. It sells some 18 million items ranging from books to toys to tools. The 35-year-old Bezos is—on paper, at least—a billionaire. His innovative site's rapid climb to success earned him the accolade of being named *Time*'s 1999 Person of the Year; the magazine dubbed him the "king of cybercommerce."

Retail competition on the Web is growing fiercer, however, and Bezos continues to expand Amazon's reach to keep it in the lead. In 1999 the site added more sales categories and launched a partnership with the auction house Sotheby's. Bezos intends to continue following his dream until Amazon truly is the biggest store on Earth.

Jeffrey Preston Bezos was born Jan. 12, 1964, in Albuquerque, NM. He was graduated from Princeton University. He and his wife, Mackenzie, were expecting their first baby in March 2000.

Congo, Democratic Republic of the

Congo's civil war, which broke out in August 1998, threatened President Laurent Kabila's hold on the government, involved five neighboring states, retarded any significant economic development, and threatened to divide the country permanently, despite a cease-fire agreement reached in August 1999.

The Civil War. The uprising, led at first by Arthur Zahidi Ngoma, spread quickly. From the beginning, the rebels received logistical support from Uganda and Rwanda, and soon troops from those countries were involved directly in the fighting. Within weeks rebel forces occupied the eastern cities of Goma and Bukavu, captured Kisangani, and threatened the capital, Kinshasa, for a brief period. Forced from the capital, Kabila secured military support from Zimbabwe's President Robert Mugabe. By July 1999, 13,000 Zimbabwe troops were active in the Congo. Kabila also had convinced President Eduardo dos Santos of Angola to lend military assistance, and his soldiers played a key role in saving Kinshasa. Backed by Rwandan troops, forces loyal to rebel leader Ernest Wamba dia Wamba drove into the diamond-rich province of Kasai, threatening the provincial capital, Mbuji-Mayi. Overall, the rebels were hampered by a lack of coordination between groups and the presence of large numbers of Hutu troops who had fled Rwanda.

Meanwhile, several African leaders, recognizing that the conflict could destabilize the entire region, made a number of attempts to halt the war. Finally, peace talks held in Lusaka, Zambia, in June led to a complex cease-fire agreement that called for a withdrawal of non-Congolese forces, the disarming of the Hutu, deployment of United Nations (UN) peacekeepers, and a national dialogue among all groups to decide the country's future political structure. The signing of the pact was delayed, however, because of a conflict between Wamba dia Wamba, who had been ousted as the leader of the Congolese Rally for Democracy in May, and his opponents. In August, Kabila's representatives and all of the dissident factions agreed. Nevertheless, violence continued, including fighting in Kisangani between Ugandan and Rwandan troops.

Politics. Soon after taking power, Kabila promised that elections for a democratic government would be held in April 1999, but the civil war ended any chance that this would happen. In January the president promulgated a decree empowering him to govern the country on all matters relating to democratic and electoral progress. In March he appointed a 30-member cabinet charged with the near-impossible task of ending the war. As conditions worsened, many of his previously most ardent supporters were dismissed from the government. A call for a national debate on the future of the Congo that would allow political parties to operate was received coldly by opposition leaders. No political parties were recognized. In May, to mark its second year in power, the government organized a seven-hour parade. Despite such events, the war, unemployment, inflation, and food shortages deeply undercut Kabila's government.

Economy. The war disrupted or destroyed much of the already-primitive communications infrastructure. The road system was almost nonexistent, and river transport above Kisangani was halted by the occupation of much of the east by rebel forces. The Congolese franc, introduced in June 1998, briefly created a relatively stable economic framework, but when the civil war began in August, the economy began to regress. The banking system—the rehabilitation of which formed an integral part of Kabila's recovery plan—barely was functioning, and the franc fell to less than 10% of its initial value. By mid-1999 the official rate of inflation had soared to 240%, and the unofficial rate was more than twice that figure. Businesses throughout the Congo continued to fail, cut off by the war from long-established patterns of trade with the eastern regions. The unemployment rate in the major cities was astronomical. A World Bank study projected that the Congolese economy would have to grow by 6% annually for 46 years for per-capita income to reach $450.

HARRY A. GAILEY, *San Jose State University*

CONGO • Information Highlights

Official Name: Democratic Republic of the Congo.
Location: Central equatorial Africa.
Area: 905,564 sq mi (2 345 410 km²).
Population (July 1999 est.): 50,481,305.
Chief City (1987 est.): Kinshasa, the capital, 2,500,000.
Government: *Head of state and government,* Laurent-Désiré Kabila, president (took office May 1997). *Legislature*—suspended.
Monetary Unit: Congolese franc (2.5 Congolese francs equal U.S.$1, January 1999).
Gross Domestic Product (1998 est. U.S.$): $34,900,000,000 (purchasing power parity).
Foreign Trade (1998 U.S.$): *Imports,* $819,000,000; *exports,* $1,600,000,000.

Consumer Affairs

The Bill Clinton administration and the Congress of the United States maintained a hands-off approach with regard to consumer legislation throughout 1999, a year that saw no new federal consumer-protection laws pass. Various federal agencies, however, did act in numerous ways to guard the interests of consumers.

National Consumer Protection Week. The first annual National Consumer Protection Week (NCPW), featuring a series of consumer-education initiatives, was held in February. NCPW was organized by a broad coalition of federal, state, and private consumer-protection advocates, including the Federal Trade Commission (FTC), the U.S. Postal Inspection Service, the National Consumers League, and the American Association of Retired Persons. The event replaced National Consumers Week, which ended in 1998 after its sponsoring agency, the Office of Consumer Affairs, was eliminated. The theme for 1999, "Credit Fraud—Know the Rules, Use the Tools," focused on helping people detect and avoid credit scams.

In July the FTC started its first toll-free help line, 1-877-FTC-HELP. The service offered a convenient, inexpensive, and expeditious way for consumers to report fraud and obtain consumer information and advice.

Internet. One of the most substantive developments in 1999 was the continued growth of the Internet, which was transforming the way consumers interacted with the marketplace. In 1999, for example, consumers could pay bills on-line, save and invest at a "virtual bank," and purchase almost any product from the convenience of their homes. In addition, the U.S. consumer could find literally thousands of Web sites that provided free, substantive consumer information previously available only through exhaustive study.

The drawbacks to the Internet were highlighted in 1999 as well. According to Internet Fraud Watch, operated by the National Consumers League, complaints regarding the "Net" increased 600% in 1998. "Spamming," the unsolicited mass sending of E-mail that usually was trying to sell something, became a nuisance for most Web surfers.

Privacy issues related to Web-site "profiling" of consumers (both adults and children) became a major source of concern. In March 1998 the FTC presented a survey about Internet privacy to the House Subcommittee on Courts and Intellectual Property. Over three years, the agency had examined more than 1,400 Web sites to determine the information they collected from visitors and to what extent they disclosed their data-gathering and -dissemination practices. The FTC concluded that nearly all commercial sites acquired and distributed personal information, but only a small minority informed visitors that they were doing so. In a follow-up report to Congress in July 1999, however, the agency advised against federal privacy legislation, calling for more industry self-regulation instead. Many Web sites already have launched privacy initiatives, in part to stave off the imposition of federal regulations. Nevertheless, bills were being considered in both the House and Senate that would give consumers increased control over the way Web sites handled their personal information.

Fraudulent and unethical practices on the Internet seemed to be more prevalent in 1999, particularly in the area of on-line auctioning. In the first six months of 1999, auction Web sites accounted for almost 90% of the 6,000-odd complaints filed with Internet Fraud Watch. The FTC received 6,000 complaints of Internet auction fraud in the first half of 1999, compared with only 300 over the same period in 1998.

The federal government continued to have little power to assist consumers in confronting fraud on the Web. Although numerous bills were introduced in Congress in 1999 dealing with Internet-related issues, none passed. Nonetheless, it was clear that this area of consumer protection would be scrutinized closely in the coming years.

Sweepstakes under Fire. In 1999 the U.S. Senate held hearings on widespread deception in the sweepstakes industry. Witnesses testified that some consumers spent thousands of dollars to buy magazines in attempts to win the sweepstakes, while others traveled long distances to pick up prizes they mistakenly believed they had won. In October, American Family Enterprises, whose spokespersons were television celebrities Ed McMahon and Dick Clark, filed for Chapter 11 bankruptcy protection; it blamed its financial woes on dozens of class-action suits that alleged the company had defrauded consumers. Another major sweepstakes operator, Publishers Clearing House, faced suits by nine states over deceptive trade practices.

MEL J. ZELENAK
University of Missouri-Columbia

Crime

For the seventh straight year, crime declined in the United States in 1998, according to 1999 statistics compiled by the Federal Bureau of Investigation (FBI).

The Falling Crime Rate. The latest full-year FBI figures showed that the number of violent crimes and property crimes fell 6%, the largest yearly decline since crime began to decrease in 1992. The Justice Department's Bureau of Justice Statistics, which uses a different method to measure crime, reported that the violent crime rate—excluding murders—fell 7% in 1998 and was 27% lower than in 1993. The property-crime rate fell 12% and was 32% lower than in 1993. The bureau said the rates were at their lowest levels since it began keeping track in 1973. It estimated there were 37 violent victimizations per 1,000 U.S. residents 12 years and older, and 217 property crimes per 1,000 U.S. households.

Experts said a marked decline in robbery—10% as measured by the FBI report—reflects a reduced demand for crack cocaine, a major contributor to rising violent crime in the 1980s. "For people who are heavy drug users, robbery is a favorite way to get drugs," said Alfred Blumstein, a criminologist at Carnegie Mellon University. While outbursts of violence like the school shootings in Littleton, CO, capture headlines and give the impression of rising lawlessness, experts said, the statistics suggest the opposite is true. "For most of our kids, school is the safest place to be," said Professor James Alan Fox, dean of the college of criminal justice at Northeastern University.

The FBI study measured the violent crimes of murder, rape, robbery, and aggravated assault, and property crimes of burglary, larceny, motor-vehicle theft, and arson. The FBI report relies on arrest information provided by local police departments. The Justice Department study is based on a survey of American households and excludes killings, because it asks individuals about their own experiences. The Justice Department survey said attackers used a weapon in about one fourth of violent offenses in 1998. About 40% of robbery victims faced a weapon, as did 9% of rape or sexual-assault victims. About 8% of violent incidents involved an attacker with a firearm.

The FBI said there was a 7% drop in the number of murders in 1998, a 5% decline for rape and aggravated assault, a 7% drop for burglary and arson, and a 10% decrease in motor-vehicle theft. Only larceny, which includes petty theft such as shoplifting and pickpocketing, showed no decrease.

Generally, the reductions were greatest in the nation's largest cities. That trend was attributed by some to additional police and stepped-up law enforcement. Murder declined 11% in cities with a population of more than 1 million, compared with 6% in cities of 50,000 to 100,000 and no change in towns of 10,000 to 25,000. The suburbs reported a 2% increase in homicides.

In a separate study, the Justice Department's Office of Juvenile Justice and Delinquency said young people are at the greatest risk of being the victims of violence during after-school hours—from 3 P.M. to 7 P.M. The study also found a 39% decline in juvenile homicides between 1994 and 1997, due to fewer murders involving firearms. Other findings included: About six juveniles per day were murdered in the United States in 1997, and almost two out of the six were girls; despite the drop in gun-related deaths, more than half the juveniles were killed by firearms, and four out of 10 were killed by a family member.

Attorney General Janet Reno attributed the overall decline in crime to a variety of factors, including "more police officers on the streets, tougher sentences, more prosecutions, better prevention programs, a healthy economy, and a new approach to crime fighting that involves a closer working relationship between communities and federal, state, and local law enforcement." The search for answers to the falling crime rate produced at least one highly controversial thesis propounded by two academics. They theorized that a rise in the number of abortions in the 1970s eliminated many would-be criminals two decades later. A large number of the unwanted pregnancies would have produced children in homes filled with poverty, neglect, and abuse, suggested John Donohue III of Stanford University's Law School in California and Steven Levitt, an economist at the University of Chicago. The theory was questioned by many and condemned by some, who said it had racist overtones because abortion is more common among blacks and other minorities.

Government Action and Reports. The Justice Department inspector general said the Bill Clinton administration would fall short of its goal of adding 100,000 more state and local police on the nation's streets by the end of the year 2000. Inspector General Michael Bromwich estimated the number

© Nick Ut/AP/Wide World Photos

High-profile shootings continued to occur in the United States in 1999. On August 10 a gunman wounded three children and two staff members at a Jewish community center in Los Angeles, CA. Buford Furrow, Jr., a white supremacist, later admitted to committing the crimes and to killing a letter carrier a few miles from the center.

would be closer to 60,000. The additional officers were authorized by a sweeping 1994 law pushed by President Clinton and his administration. In a separate report, Bromwich said lax monitoring of prison telephones enabled federal inmates to arrange for murders, import illegal drugs, and commit fraud from behind bars. Federal policy does not limit the number of phone calls inmates can make, in an effort to promote contact with family members.

The U.S. Education Department reported a decline in the number of students expelled from school for carrying firearms. The agency said that 3,930 students were expelled in the 1997–98 academic year, a 31% decrease from the 5,724 who were forced to leave school for firearms possession the previous school year.

Attorney General Reno appointed former Sen. John C. Danforth (R-MO) to head an investigation into the government's role in the 1993 fire that killed about 80 people at the Branch Davidian complex in Waco, TX. The investigation was prompted by revelations that the FBI had withheld for six years the fact that its agents fired flammable teargas canisters near the compound on April 19, 1993, as the government prepared its assault to end the 51-day standoff.

Gun-control advocates claimed some victories in the aftermath of outbreaks of school violence (*see also* SPECIAL REPORT, page 214). In Congress the Senate approved a juvenile-crime bill in May that included gun-control provisions, such as requiring licensed dealers to sell child-safety devices with each handgun and establishing mandatory background checks on people who buy firearms at gun shows. The stalled House version of the juvenile crime measure did not include the gun controls.

Major Crimes. Among the attacks that spurred calls for stricter gun control was one in July in which Mark Barton, a securities day trader, killed nine people and wounded a dozen more in two office buildings in Atlanta before killing himself in his van. Police said Barton, 44, earlier had killed his wife and children. Recent trading losses were said to have contributed to Barton's violent anger. In Fort Worth, TX, eight people were killed when a man walked into a church service and began shooting before committing suicide. Police said the gunman, Larry Ashbrook, 47, shot a maintenance worker and a woman before going into the church sanctuary and firing on the mostly teenaged crowd. In Honolulu in November, a Xerox-copier repairman shot and killed seven coworkers. The alleged gunman, Byran Uyesugi, was believed to be "a disgruntled employee who snapped." It was the worst mass killing in Hawaii's history.

In California motel handyman Cary Stayner was charged with the beheading of Joie Ruth Armstrong, 26, a Yosemite National Park naturalist whose body was found in July near the western edge of the park. Law-enforcement officials said Stayner, 37, also admitted to killing three sightseers who disappeared in Yosemite months earlier. Stay-

SPECIAL REPORT Gun Control

The term "gun control" is so broad that it encompasses diverse and sometimes competing strategies for the reduction of gun violence. Within the gun-control movement are advocates for many different goals, including setting stiffer penalties for criminals wielding guns; regulating guns as dangerous consumer products that can be redesigned to improve their safety; reforming the firearms-distribution system; expanding the categories of people who cannot purchase or possess guns legally; and banning the manufacture and possession of certain firearms.

Legislation. Changes in gun policy occur infrequently and only with great difficulty in the U.S. Congress, where debate on the issue has been characterized by gridlock and stalemate. Even after events that shocked the nation, such as the mass shooting at Columbine High School in Littleton, CO, in April 1999, Congress has been unable to agree on the appropriate response.

In 1999 congressional attention focused on the acquisition of guns through "secondary sales," transactions between individuals not in the business of selling guns. Secondary sales often occur at gun shows and flea markets. While federal law requires background checks of people buying guns from licensed dealers, this is generally not the case for secondary sales. An estimated 40% of all gun sales in the United States are made in this informal manner, and this is one way that criminals and youths obtain guns. Members of Congress have not yet agreed as to how this issue should be addressed.

In a few states, the ability of individuals to purchase many guns at once has been curtailed by "one-gun-per-month" laws. Research has shown that these laws reduce gun trafficking (buying many guns and selling them on the secondary market for a profit), and therefore some experts advocate for the passage of a federal law of this type.

States also have taken the lead in banning the manufacture and sale of certain types of guns. In 1968 the federal Gun Control Act banned the importation of "Saturday night specials"—cheap, small handguns that frequently are used in crimes—but this had the paradoxical effect of allowing a domestic Saturday-night-special industry to develop and thrive. Several states, including California in August 1999, have passed laws preventing the manufacture and sale of these guns, often called "junk guns." The California law is significant not only because of the large population of that state, but also because most of the current junk-gun makers are located in southern California.

During 1999 several states considered legislation requiring all newly manufactured handguns to be childproofed or personalized, with technology that would allow only authorized users to operate them.

Lawsuits. Perhaps the most significant changes in the way guns are manufactured and sold will occur as a result of litigation. Pending in the courts in late 1999 were lawsuits brought by individuals and 29 cities and counties, alleging the gun industry is liable for damages associated with their products, including the costs of caring for the victims of gunfire. The lawsuits charge that gun manufacturers should have designed their products more safely and distributed them more carefully to reduce the likeli-

---

ner is the brother of Steven Stayner, who was kidnapped in 1972 at age 7 and was missing for seven years before going to police when his abductor kidnapped another boy. Steven Stayner died in 1989 at age 24 in a hit-and-run car accident.

Buford O. Furrow, Jr., a white supremacist, surrendered to the FBI in Nevada and said he had shot five people at a Jewish community center in Los Angeles. Furrow, 37, also admitted to fatally shooting Joseph Ileto, a letter carrier, shortly after the attack at the center, law-enforcement officials said.

Two white supremacists were sentenced to die for the murder of James Byrd, Jr., a black man who was dragged to his death near Jasper, TX, in 1998. Convicted in the attack were Lawrence Brewer, 32, and John W. King, 24. A third defendant, Shawn Berry, 24, also was convicted and sentenced to life in prison. Byrd, 49, had been chained behind a pickup truck and dragged along a back road. Prosecutors said King instigated the attack to draw attention to a white-supremacist group he planned to form in Jasper. The crime was one of the most gruesome since the civil-rights era.

Mexico's former top drug prosecutor, Mario Ruiz Massieu, was charged in Houston with laundering $9.9 million in suspected

© Kevin Moloney/Liaison Agency

Tom Mauser addressed antigun protesters at the Colorado state capitol, following the death of his son in the mass shooting at Columbine High School in Littleton on April 20, 1999. With headquarters in Fairfax, VA, below, the National Rifle Association continued to be a major lobby against gun control.

© Mark Peterson/SABA

hood that guns would fall into the hands of criminals. In early 1999 a jury awarded damages against some gun makers for their negligent distribution practices in the landmark federal-court case *Hamilton v. Accu-Tek*. The cost of defending against this flood of litigation, as well as the threat of substantial jury verdicts such as those that have come from lawsuits against tobacco companies, has caused some gun makers to reorganize their businesses, file for bankruptcy, and alter their relationships with their retailers.

The Future. Significant changes are taking place in U.S. gun policy, fueled by mass shootings that have occurred in recent years. Many of these shootings have happened in places previously believed to be safe havens, such as schools, churches, and day-care centers. These tragedies seem to have galvanized the American public into wanting to decrease the level of gun violence throughout the country. While the overall number of gun-related deaths has decreased in the past few years, the prevalence of guns in American culture has not waned, and the debate between pro- and anti-gun forces remains as loud and unresolved as ever.

STEPHEN TERET and SHANNON FRATTAROLI

drug payoffs through a bank in the city. Ruiz Massieu had been under house arrest in Palisades Park, NJ, since 1995, when he tried to flee to Spain.

In Israel, Samuel Sheinbein of Montgomery county, MD, agreed to plead guilty to murder and receive a 24-year prison sentence in the 1997 killing and dismemberment of Alfredo Enrique Tello, Jr. Sheinbein, 19, had resisted extradition to the United States, where authorities said he could have faced life behind bars if convicted there of the murder.

Mumia Abu-Jamal, a former radio reporter and black political activist, lost a U.S. Supreme Court appeal for a new trial in the 1981 killing of a Philadelphia policeman. Abu-Jamal was sentenced to death for the murder of white police officer Daniel Faulkner. The condemned man's jailhouse writings about the justice system have attracted worldwide attention and support from political leaders and Hollywood celebrities.

Jay Scott Ballinger of Indiana admitted to setting fire to as many as 50 churches in 11 states and said he and two others began the spree as part of a satanic ritual, law-enforcement officials said. Ballinger was arrested with the help of a task force formed by the Justice Department to investigate fires at southern black churches.

In Santa Ana, CA, Charles Ng was convicted of murdering 11 people captured and used as sex slaves in a remote mountain cabin east of San Francisco. Ng, 38, a native of Hong Kong and a former U.S. Marine, had eluded trial for 14 years.

In Chicago the murder convictions of Anthony Porter, who spent 17 years in prison, were overturned, after journalism students at Northwestern University cast doubt on his guilt. Porter, 43, had come within two days of execution in 1998 before the Illinois Supreme Court ordered further inquiry into the shooting deaths of two teenagers. Subsequently, another man was recorded admitting to the killings.

Thomas Capano, a wealthy Delaware lawyer, was sentenced by a judge in Wilmington to die for the murder of his mistress, Anne Marie Fahey, scheduling secretary to Delaware Gov. Thomas Carper. Capano, 49, testified at his trial that he had dumped the woman's body in the Atlantic Ocean but that she was shot accidentally by another mistress who found them together.

Russell Henderson, 21, pleaded guilty to the murder and kidnapping of Matthew Shepard, a gay college student who was lured from a bar in 1998, pistol-whipped, and left for dead, tied to a fence near Laramie, WY. A second accused assailant, Aaron McKinney, 22, was found guilty. Both men received two consecutive life prison sentences.

John A. Gotti, the son of imprisoned Mafia boss John J. Gotti, was sentenced in federal court in White Plains, NY, to six years and five months in prison after pleading guilty to racketeering and extortion. The imprisonment of the younger Gotti, 35, made it unclear who would run the Gambino crime family, law-enforcement officials said. The elder Gotti was convicted of murder and racketeering in 1991 and was sentenced to life in prison without parole.

Amy Fisher, who pleaded guilty in 1992 to assault for shooting her lover's wife, Mary Jo Buttafuoco, was paroled from prison in Albion, NY. Fisher was a 17-year-old high-school senior at the time of the shooting. Mrs. Buttafuoco forgave her attacker and had helped get her prison term reduced.

In New York City a federal appeals court overturned the conviction of Autumn Jackson, who went to prison for threatening to tell a supermarket tabloid that she was Bill Cosby's out-of-wedlock daughter unless he paid her $40 million. Jackson had spent about 14 months in prison. The appeals court said it was an error for the trial judge to bar the jury from considering whether Jackson believed she had a rightful claim to the money, based on her assertion that Cosby was her father. Also in New York City, police officer Justin Volpe pleaded guilty on May 25 in the case involving Haitian immigrant Abner Louima, who charged that he had been assaulted by Volpe and other officers in the New York Police Department as they were arresting him. Volpe pleaded guilty to six federal charges, including assaulting Louima, depriving him of his civil rights, and obstructing justice. The plea came during the trial of Volpe and four other officers, which then continued. In early June the jury in that trial also convicted Officer Charles Schwarz of assault but acquitted the other three policemen.

Marie Noe, 70, was sentenced in Philadelphia to 20 years of probation, including the first five years in home confinement, after pleading guilty to smothering eight of her ten young children in a series of crimes dating back to 1949. Her husband's failing health was cited as a factor in the plea agreement that allowed her to avoid jail time. The eight children, none of whom lived longer than 14 months, were believed to have died of sudden-infant-death syndrome until recent investigation led to Noe's confession.

Computer hacker Kevin Mitnick was sentenced in Los Angeles to 46 months in federal prison and ordered to pay $4,125 in restitution after pleading guilty to breaking into a number of computer systems and stealing the proprietary software of such companies as Motorola Inc, Novell Inc., and Sun Microsystems Inc. Mitnick had been in prison since 1995 awaiting trial and, his lawyer said, could be released early in 2000.

Three former executives of the Archer Daniels Midland Co. (ADM) were sentenced to prison for taking part in a scheme to fix the prices of a feed additive manufactured by the company. Michael Andreas, son of the former chairman of the business, Dwayne Andreas, was sentenced to two years in prison, as was Terrance Wilson, retired chief of ADM's corn-processing division. Mark Whitacre, a government informant in the case, was sentenced to two and one-half years and was ordered to serve 20 months of the sentence on top of a nine-year sentence he was serving for taking millions of dollars illegally from the company.

JIM RUBIN, *"Bloomberg News"*

Croatia

During 1999, Croatia's progress toward democratic rule and membership in international institutions remained stalled by its quasi-authoritarian government. In December, Croatians widely mourned the death of President Franjo Tudjman, who led their country to independence in 1991.

Political Transition. A broad range of domestic reforms—including reform of the election law, an end to persecution of independent media, the rooting out of corruption and political patronage, and the unhindered return of Serbian refugees to their prewar homes—continued to be stalled by the government throughout the year. Tudjman's death from stomach cancer on December 11 plunged Croatia into political uncertainty. Thousands of Croatians turned out to pay their respects to their fallen leader, waiting up to three hours to file past his coffin. But despite this display of devotion, the public seemed unaltered in its desire for political change. The popularity of the ruling Croatian Democratic Union (HDZ) was at an all-time low, and the broad-based opposition coalition had been favored in the upcoming general elections even before the president's death.

Speaker of Parliament Vlatko Pavletic, who had assumed the president's powers upon his incapacitation a few weeks earlier, was named interim president until new elections took place. Such elections were scheduled for January 24. Parliamentary elections, scheduled for late December, were held on Jan. 3, 2000. As expected, the HDZ suffered a decisive defeat. An opposition coalition of the Social Democrats (SDP) and the Social Liberals (HSPL) won the most votes and 71 of 151 parliamentary seats. A second opposition coalition, the Group of Four, captured 24 seats. Together the two coalition groups would be just short of the two-thirds majority required to amend the constitution.

Economic Slowdown. Croatia's gross domestic product (GDP) was projected to shrink by nearly 2% for 1999. Much of the decline was caused by a decrease in trade with the nation's largest trading partners (Germany and Italy), a loss in tourism because of the North Atlantic Treaty Organization (NATO) war with Serbia, and a decline in foreign-investor confidence. Furthermore, corruption scandals implicating top members of the HDZ, as well as the president's family, threatened a general contraction of the financial system.

CROATIA • Information Highlights

Official Name: Republic of Croatia.
Location: Southeastern Europe.
Area: 21,829 sq mi (56 538 km²).
Population (July 1999 est.): 4,676,865.
Chief Cities (1991 census): Zagreb, the capital, 706,770; Split, 189,388; Rijeka, 167,964; Osijek, 104,761.
Government: *Head of state,* Vlatko Pavletic, interim president (took office December 1999). *Head of government,* Zlatko Matesa (took office November 1995). *Legislature*—Assembly: House of Counties and House of Representatives.
Monetary Unit: Kuna (7.3415 kuna equal U.S.$1, Nov. 12, 1999).
Gross Domestic Product (1998 est. U.S.$): $23,600,-000,000 (purchasing power parity).
Economic Indexes (1998, 1990 = 100): *Consumer Prices,* all items, 65,032.2; food, 62,269.5. *Industrial Production,* 64.0.
Foreign Trade (1998 U.S.$): *Imports,* $8,384,000,000; *exports,* $4,546,000,000.

International Issues. Zagreb's obstruction of domestic reform hindered Croatia's progress toward membership in several key international institutions, including NATO and the European Union (EU). In order to move forward, Croatia needed to guarantee full cooperation with the international war-crimes tribunal in The Hague, and revoke all claims to Bosnian territory. It was possible that the new government elected early in 2000 would be more inclined to take such steps. Consistent attacks by Zagreb questioning the legitimacy of the tribunal in The Hague had highlighted the obstructionism of HDZ hard-liners.

JANUSZ BUGAJSKI
Center for Strategic and International Studies

Cuba

During the last year of the 20th century, the Cuban government of President Fidel Castro appeared to be entrenched as firmly as ever. The Cuban people did grumble, but there were few signs of popular opposition to communist rule in Cuba. The economy improved slightly, yet not sufficiently to instill in the apathetic population a hope for better times to come.

The dissident movement was split into minute groups. It also was divided about the issue of the U.S. embargo, which Havana claimed to be the cause of most of its economic and social difficulties. Some opposition leaders, as well as the Catholic Church hierarchy, urged Washington to lift the embargo. Others wanted the United States to adopt a more assertive anti-Castro stance. Dissidents were harassed and routinely detained for questioning, and some were arrested for short periods of time. Some of them were able to meet foreign correspondents and officials visiting Cuba, issue statements to foreign press, and fax news reports and articles to U.S. publications. While many in the West were denouncing Havana for its continuing human-rights violations, dissidents in Cuba had more space to operate than those in China or Vietnam.

The IX Iberoamerican summit was held in Havana on November 15–16. Its final declaration called on Cuba to adopt a democratic system of government (which Castro rejected) and condemned the embargo.

U.S.-Cuba Relations. Even though the 38-year-old embargo has been deemed a failure by a growing number of Americans, there were no signs of a thaw in Washington-Havana relations. Early in 1999, the Bill Clinton administration rejected a proposal by prominent public figures that a bipartisan committee review U.S. policy toward Cuba. Instead, President Clinton allowed additional U.S. charter flights to Cuba, permitted more Americans to send cash to the island, established direct mail service, and sanctioned sales of food and agricultural supplies to charities and privately held farms. The measures, denounced by Havana as "deceptive maneuvers" intended to deflect opposition in many countries to the embargo, were yet to be fully put into effect 12 months later. Cuba's efforts to attract foreign investments to obtain access to new technology and external financing were countered by U.S. diplomats; potential investors were reminded of the punitive actions mandated by the anti-Cuban Helms-Burton Act.

In July, five months after the Cuban National Assembly passed legislation imposing the death penalty on large-scale drug traffickers, Castro offered to cooperate with the United States to fight drug trafficking. The offer was ignored by the White House.

CUBA • Information Highlights

Official Name: Republic of Cuba.
Location: Caribbean.
Area: 42,803 sq mi (110 860 km^2).
Population (July 1999 est.): 11,096,395.
Chief Cities (Dec. 31, 1993 est.): Havana, the capital, 2,175,995; Santiago de Cuba, 440,084; Camagüey, 293,961; Holguín, 242,085.
Government: *Head of state and government,* Fidel Castro Ruz, president (took office under a new constitution, December 1976). *Legislature* (unicameral)—National Assembly of People's Power.
Monetary Unit: Peso (23.0 pesos equal U.S.$1, Nov. 12, 1999).
Gross Domestic Product (1998 est. U.S.$): $17,300,000,000 (purchasing power parity).
Foreign Trade (1998 est. U.S.$): *Imports,* $3,000,000,000; *exports,* $1,400,000,000.

About 100 U.S. jazz and other musicians performed in Cuba, and their equally numerous Cuban counterparts played in various U.S. cities, including Miami. Numerous American executives—an estimated 2,000 in 1998—were visiting Cuba to assess the country's potential for trade. At the end of a five-day October 1999 trip, Illinois Gov. George Ryan, a conservative Republican, said that there was a strong need to end the embargo and that this action would benefit the United States as much as Cuba.

A problem that confronted Washington and Havana was the growing smuggling of Cubans into the United States. Typically, Cuban exiles in Florida would pay local boat owners up to $10,000 per person to bring their family members from Cuba. In September, Cuba sentenced two Florida exiles—one to life imprisonment and the other to 30 years in jail—following an aborted smuggling operation in which one person drowned. When the U.S. Coast Guard intercepts the illegal boaters on high seas, it returns them to Cuba. But if the exiles touch U.S. soil, these Cubans, unlike other nationals, receive parole and are eligible for U.S. permanent-residency status one year later.

The plight of 6-year-old Elián González made the headlines in late 1999. The boy, his mother, and ten other Cubans had taken a small boat from Cuba in an attempt to reach the United States. But the boat sank, and almost everyone on board, including Elián's mother, drowned. On Thanksgiving the boy was found clinging to an inner tube off the coast of Florida and was brought to relatives in Miami. Immediately, he became the center of a tug-of-war between his Cuban-American relatives, who wanted him to stay in the United States, and his father, Juan Miguel González, who was still in Cuba and wanted his son returned to him. The case was unresolved at year's end.

The Economy. The Cuban economy was expected to grow 2.5% in 1999, twice the 1998 rate. The slight improvement was attributed by Havana to a better sugar harvest, an increase in foreign tourism, greater petroleum production and cigar exports, and higher cash remittances from abroad. In 1999, Cuba produced about 4 million tons of sugar, its principal export. Some 1.2 million tourists, mostly from Europe and Canada, vacationed on the island. Money sent home by Cubans abroad—more than $600 million a year—represented the third-largest source of hard currency.

GEORGE VOLSKY, *University of Miami*

Cyprus

The island of Cyprus remained divided into Greek and Turkish sections in 1999, as it had since 1974. However, prospects for resolving the problem looked brighter at the end of the year. Rauf Denktash, president of the Turkish Republic of Northern Cyprus (which has been recognized officially only by Turkey), and Glafkos Clerides, head of the internationally recognized government of the Republic of Cyprus, went to United Nations (UN) headquarters in New York City for talks in December. Turkey continued to keep about 35,000 troops on its part of the island, and Greece maintained a force of about 12,000 on its share. In addition, Great Britain, the former colonial ruler of Cyprus, kept two sovereign bases on the island, and the UN voted in June and December to retain its own peacekeeping force (UNFICYP) in the buffer zone between the two sides. The force had been on the island for 35 years.

Continuing Rivalry. Clerides' major preoccupations during 1999 fell in line with his policies in 1998. He wanted to find some way to end the division of Cyprus, to prevent further encroachments by Turkey on the island, to build up national defense, and to bring Cyprus into the European Union (EU). In pursuing these aims, he kept in close touch with the government of Greece. Conversely, Denktash wanted to see the Turkish Republic of Northern Cyprus recognized as a legal entity, and he wanted the Turkish Cypriots to be equal partners in joining the EU. He maintained close ties with Turkey, which encouraged his efforts to attain these goals. The two leaders had diametrically opposite positions, with Denktash calling for two independent entities on the island and Clerides' attitude more in line with UN efforts to make Cyprus a single sovereign state made up of a bicommunal and bizonal federation. Similarly, they had different opinions about Cyprus' accession to the EU. Clerides remained anxious that entry into the EU not wait for a political solution to the division of the island, but Denktash did not want Cyprus in the EU before the situation was resolved.

During 1998, there nearly had been a confrontation between the Republic of Cyprus and Turkey over Clerides' insistence that his government would deploy Russian S-300 surface-to-air missiles for defense purposes. The crisis was defused only when Clerides backed down in late December 1998. In January 1999 the Clerides government decided to send the missiles to the Greek island of Crete instead. Since Cyprus and Greece have a mutual-defense pact, which was reached in 1993, the arrangement seemed advantageous to both governments. The Greek government said that the missiles would be ready for deployment by the end of 1999.

The bitterness between the Greek and Turkish Cypriots could be seen on July 20, the 25th anniversary of the 1974 Turkish invasion. The Turkish Cypriots gleefully celebrated the day, while the Greek Cypriots mourned and held rallies calling for the end of Turkish control in the north.

Intercommunal Talks. In June the G-8 nations (the seven most industrial nations and Russia) called on UN Secretary-General Kofi Annan to bring the two Cypriot sides together for a meeting. The Greek and Cypriot governments welcomed the G-8 initiative; but Prime Minister Bulent Ecevit of Turkey, who had been in office when Turkey invaded Cyprus in 1974, denounced it as outside intervention.

Turkey and Greece both suffered severe earthquakes during the summer, and each offered humanitarian aid to the other. The resulting rapprochement between the two countries seemed to make the ethnic groups on Cyprus more willing to work with each other. Encouraged by these circumstances, the UN sponsored "proximity talks" between Clerides and Denktash in New York in early December. The two Cypriots never met at the talks directly but carried out discussions through interlocutors, including Annan. In late December it was announced that the talks would resume in Geneva, Switzerland, on January 27.

Meanwhile, the decision in December by the 15 EU members, including Greece, to

CYPRUS • Information Highlights

Official Name: Republic of Cyprus.
Location: Eastern Mediterranean.
Area: 3,571 sq mi (9 250 km²).
Population (July 1999 est.): 754,064.
Chief Cities (Dec. 31, 1997 est.): Nicosia, the capital, 194,100; Limassol, 152,900.
Government: *Head of state and government,* Glafkos Clerides, president (took office March 1, 1993). *Legislature* (unicameral)—House of Representatives.
Monetary Unit: Pound (0.5735 pound equals U.S.$1, Jan. 3, 2000).
Gross Domestic Product (1997 est. U.S.$): $10,000,-000,000 (purchasing power parity).
Economic Indexes (1998, 1990 = 100): *Consumer Prices,* all items, 137.5; food, 144.5. *Industrial Production,* 102.3.
Foreign Trade (1998 U.S.$): *Imports,* $3,687,000,000; *exports,* $1,062,000,000.

accept Turkey as a candidate for membership included probable conditions that could affect Cyprus. One was that Greek-Turkish disputes might be arbitrated through the International Court of Justice at The Hague; another was that the Republic of Cyprus might be allowed to join the EU without the northern territory. The EU also cautioned Turkey that potential members were studied "with particular reference to the issue of human rights." Greek Cypriots felt that that phrase could apply to events on Cyprus and not just those in Turkey itself. Meanwhile, the European Commission of Human Rights of the Council of Europe issued a stinging report in 1999, criticizing Turkey for violations of human rights. The report included references to the unknown fate of persons missing since the Turkish invasion, violations of the property rights of Greek Cypriots who had fled the north, and the poor living conditions of the Greek Cypriots who chose to remain in the Turkish territory.

Foreign Affairs. In February two Israelis suspected of being spies were convicted of encroaching on military zones; each was given a three-year prison sentence. Relations between Israel and Cyprus were affected by the incident. In August, Clerides freed the Israelis in what he called a "gesture towards a friendly neighboring country"; Israeli Prime Minister Ehud Barak responded by expressing his appreciation.

Cyprus saw the resolution of a dispute with Denmark over a kind of cheese known as Halloumi. Denmark had been making cheese of its own with that designation, but Cyprus maintained that Halloumi cheese was a distinctive, indigenous product. In August the U.S. Trademark Trial and Appeal Board agreed, ruling that Cyprus was "the source of Halloumi cheese."

Economy. Cyprus' economy continued to benefit from the fact that the Greek Cypriot area had become a major center of international banking and finance. The three-year-old Cyprus Stock Exchange soared during the year, zooming from 90.3 in December 1998 to 477.17 in late August.

GEORGE J. MARCOPOULOS, *Tufts University*

Czech Republic

In 1999 the Czech Republic continued to deal with serious political and economic problems. The minority Social Democratic government of Prime Minister Miloš Zeman remained in power as the result of its agreement with the opposition Civic Democratic Party of Václav Klaus. Klaus' party abided by the provisions of the agreement, but serious tensions emerged during the year between the two partners.

Domestic Affairs. The leaders of the Social Democratic and Civic Democratic Parties agreed to change the electoral law to benefit larger parties over smaller ones. They also proposed changes that would reduce the already limited powers of the presidency even further by removing the president's right to appoint the prime minister and the board members of the Central Bank. In addition, the new law would give the party that won a parliamentary election the right to form a government.

Political leaders, with the aid of U.S. and Italian experts, launched a new campaign against corruption, a continuing problem. The Freedom Union and the Christian Democratic Party threatened to call for a motion of no confidence in the government in November, but they could not muster enough votes to do so. In November, Parliament voted to create an ombudsman.

The Czech economy continued to experience serious problems in 1999. Parliament approved a budget with a 1-billion-koruna ($33.3 million) deficit in January. Unemployment, which reached 9% in October, led to citizen dissatisfaction and threats of labor unrest. Gross domestic product (GDP) increased by 0.3% in the second quarter of 1999 and by 0.8% in the third quarter, but officials still predicted no overall growth for the year. Inflation averaged 4% in August. Nevertheless, direct foreign investment reached a record high of $1.3 billion in the first half of 1999.

Public dissatisfaction with the political and economic situation was evident in a

CZECH REPUBLIC • Information Highlights

Official Name: Czech Republic.
Location: East-central Europe.
Area: 30,387 sq mi (78 703 km²).
Population (July 1999 est.): 10,280,513.
Chief Cities (Jan. 1, 1998 est.): Prague, the capital, 1,200,455; Brno, 385,866; Ostrava, 323,177.
Government: *Head of state,* Václav Havel, president (took office Jan. 1, 1993). *Head of government,* Miloš Zeman, prime minister (appointed July 17, 1998). *Legislature*—Parliament: Senate and Chamber of Deputies.
Monetary Unit: Koruna (35.5660 koruny equal U.S.$1, Jan. 3, 2000).
Gross Domestic Product (1998 est. U.S.$): $116,700,-000,000.
Economic Indexes (1998, 1990 = 100): *Consumer Prices,* all items, 329.7; food, 273.3. *Industrial Production,* 83.3.
Foreign Trade (1998 U.S.$): *Imports,* $28,917,000,000; *exports,* $26,416,000,000.

© Michal Krumphanzl/AP/Wide World Photos

Czech President Václav Havel (left) *awarded the Order of the White Lion, the nation's highest honor, to former Polish President Lech Walesa* (right) *in recognition of his leadership in the fight against communism in Eastern Europe. The ceremony took place on Nov. 17, 1999, the tenth anniversary of the "Velvet Revolution" that quickly brought down the former Czechoslovakia's communist government.*

proclamation issued in November on the tenth anniversary of the Velvet Revolution of 1989 that toppled the communist regime. The statement, by several people who had been student leaders at the time, called on the heads of all parties to resign in favor of younger leaders. A survey taken in late 1999 showed the Communist Party receiving more support than any of the other parties, another sign of dissension. In December demonstrators in several cities called for an end to the opposition agreement and for the resignation of the government.

The government asked for tougher sentences against those involved in hate crimes against the Roma minority. In October, however, officials in the city of Ústí nad Labem approved the erection of a wall to separate the Roma from the rest of the citizenry. Parliament, along with the European Union (EU) and many Western governments, condemned the action and called for the wall to be removed. Local officials maintained that the government had no jurisdiction over the matter. The wall was taken down in November, after Prague made funds available to the town government to resolve the issue.

Foreign Affairs. In March the Czech Republic became one of the first postcommunist countries to join the North Atlantic Treaty Organization (NATO). Czech leaders were divided in their response to NATO's bombing campaign against Serbia over Kosovo. President Václav Havel supported the action; Prime Minister Zeman and other Social Democratic leaders expressed doubts about it; and Klaus opposed it. However, the government allowed NATO troops to cross Czech territory and made airfields and other facilities available. After the conflict ended, Czech forces participated in the KFOR peacekeeping force in Kosovo. Most citizens of the Czech Republic had opposed NATO's actions in Kosovo.

Czech officials reaffirmed their interest in remaining in the first group of countries to negotiate access to the EU. However, EU officials issued a report in October that sharply criticized Czech preparations for accession. In an attempt to address this criticism, in November the Czech government approved 26 bills to be drafted by the end of 1999, including an environmental plan designed to meet EU standards. Prague also identified several other areas in which new legislation would be necessary. Czech officials agreed to allow free movement of people after January 2000, but indicated that they would ask for a transitional period in which noncitizens would not be allowed to buy real estate in the Czech Republic.

Czech-Slovak relations improved in 1999, as Prague and Bratislava made progress in resolving the remaining issues regarding the division of property after the breakup of Czechoslovakia in 1992. Czech leaders also supported Slovakia's efforts to be admitted to NATO and the EU. Czech-German relations grew warmer after the Czech Constitutional Court ruled to allow Germans expelled from Czechoslovakia after World War II to reclaim their assets and settle in the Czech Republic. But Prague's decision to complete the Temelin nuclear plant near the Austrian border created tensions with Austria.

SHARON WOLCHIK
George Washington University

Dance

Dance in 1999 was filled with celebrations. The New York City Ballet's 50th-birthday festivities included special events and 100 ballets performed over two seasons in New York. Other milestones highlighted during the year were Dance Theatre of Harlem's 30th anniversary and Judith Jamison's decade as artistic director of the Alvin Ailey American Dance Theatre. The Lincoln Center Festival '99 paid tribute to the choreographer Merce Cunningham on his 80th birthday in July.

In ballet, the 19th-century classics dominated the repertory. The Kirov Ballet from Russia presented a four-hour version of *The Sleeping Beauty*, a full-scale spectacle that was a stylistically incoherent attempt to reproduce the 1890 original version. The New York City Ballet's first full-length *Swan Lake* looked too abstract for some tastes but offered a contemporary perspective. Also for the first time, the company performed *The Nutcracker* to taped music during a two-week strike by its orchestra.

Works with a cutting edge came from modern dance. A three-week showcase of experimental choreography was highly successful in the New Europe '99 festival.

Ballet. The New York City Ballet's 50th-anniversary events included revivals and mini-festivals devoted to composers. The winter season featured George Balanchine's most experimental works in "Balanchine Black and White Celebration," as well as Peter Martins' new *Walton Concerto*.

The spring season's mini-festivals were devoted to Igor Stravinsky, Peter Tchaikovsky, and American music. Martins' bold staging of *Swan Lake* stressed formal patterns over overt emotion. But the abstract scenery by Danish painter Per Kirkeby added a psychological resonance. The production was televised nationally on the Public Broadcasting Service (PBS).

New ballets included Christopher Wheeldon's delightful *Scènes de Ballet*, named after its Stravinsky score and performed as a witty classroom vignette by student dancers. Jazz composer Wynton Marsalis wrote a symphonic score for *Them Twos*, Martins' suite of duets about the uneven course of love. *Duke!* consisted of three short works to music by Duke Ellington. In *Rockin' in Rhythm*, Robert La Fosse offered stylized swing dancing, and in *Ellington Elation*, Garth Fagan was more balletic, with dancers suggesting night birds. Susan Stroman's rollicking *Blossom Got Kissed* featured Maria Kowroski as an outsider in a tutu who learned to "swing."

At American Ballet Theatre (ABT), male soloists came to the fore with virtuosity and artistry, especially in the 19th-century classics. Dancing was superior to choreography in the new productions. Kenneth MacMillan's three-act *Anastasia*, last seen in 1972 in New York with Britain's Royal Ballet, proved cheerless and unpersuasive. Viviana Durante, a guest from the Royal Ballet, appeared in the title role as the supposed daughter of Czar Nicholas II of Russia. The premieres by contemporary choreographers were plotless works with emotional subtexts. The best was Lar Lubovitch's *Meadow*; the others were John Neumeier's *Getting Closer* and Robert Hill's *Baroque Game*.

© Carol Pratt/A Kennedy Center Millennium Project

Legendary ballerina Suzanne Farrell assembled a small, ad hoc troupe to perform works by such great modern choreographers as George Balanchine and Jerome Robbins. The show, "Suzanne Farrell Stages the Masters of 20th-Century Ballet," debuted at the Kennedy Center in October 1999. It included Maurice Béjart's "Romeo and Juliet," right, *with Christina Fagundes and Philip Neal.*

Dance Theatre of Harlem had a success with Dwight Rhoden's dazzling *Twist* and also premiered *Return*, by Robert Garland, and *South African Suite*, choreographed by Arthur Mitchell, Augustus Van Heerden, and Laveen Naidu. Eliot Feld created *Felix: The Ballet*, *Cherokee Rose*, and *Mending* for Ballet Tech. Helgi Tomasson staged a major new production of *Giselle*, with dramatic scenery by Michael Melbye, for the San Francisco Ballet.

Former stars of the New York City Ballet toured with permanent or ad hoc troupes during 1999. Suzanne Farrell assembled a chamber company for "Suzanne Farrell Stages the Masters of 20th-Century Ballet," a program sponsored by the John F. Kennedy Center for the Arts; and Edward Villella's Miami City Ballet toured with works by Balanchine and Jimmy Gamonet De Los Heros.

Modern Dance. The Alvin Ailey American Dance Theatre had one of its most brilliant seasons in 1999, with several exuberant premieres: Ronald K. Brown's *Grace*, Donald McKayle's *Danger Run*, and Jawole Willa Jo Zollar's *C-Sharp Street–B-Flat Avenue*. Bill T. Jones, who revised *Fever Swamp* for the Ailey troupe, also created an urban poem, *Out Some Place*, which portrayed life as a cocktail party. The work, choreographed for the Bill T. Jones/Arnie Zane troupe, was a lively collaboration with jazz pianist Fred Hersch as part of a series on jazz and dance presented by the Kennedy Center for the Performing Arts and the American Dance Festival in Durham, NC. Another premiere in that series was Paul Taylor's *Oh, You Kid!* A satire on American life set to ragtime music, the piece was the opposite of another new work by Taylor, the pastoral *Fiddlers Green*.

The tribute to Merce Cunningham at Lincoln Center presented a mini-retrospective of his work as well as *Occasion Piece*, featuring Mikhail Baryshnikov as a guest performer. The piece consisted of Cunningham and Baryshnikov dancing two simultaneous solos. The New York City Ballet appeared in a revival of *Summerspace*, and the New York premiere of *Biped* integrated Cunningham's choreography into computer-animated designs projected in front of and behind the dancers.

The Martha Graham Dance Company marked the premiere of Graham's 1944 masterpiece, *Appalachian Spring*, by returning to the small stage at the Library of Congress, which had commissioned the work and its score by Aaron Copland. The library also commissioned the 1999 premiere of Stroman's *But Not For Me*, set to George Gershwin's music. A piece about youthful hopes, the work looked better during the Graham Company's New York season, which also presented powerfully danced early Graham repertory. A suite of duets included an excerpt from Maurice Béjart's *Nôtre Faust* and the new *Histoire* by Lucinda Childs.

More idiosyncratic productions came from the brilliantly creative tap dancer Herbin (Tamango) Van Cayseele in his *Urban Tap*, and from Martha Clarke in *Vers la Flamme*, inspired by the writings of Anton Chekhov. *The Argument*, by Mark Morris, was performed by Morris' company and Baryshnikov's White Oak Dance Project. Twyla Tharp's new *Diabelli Variations* was seen at Hancher Auditorium in Iowa City.

Non-U.S. Companies. The Next Wave Festival at the Brooklyn Academy of Music featured major attractions, including two parables of life and death—Pina Bausch's *Danzón* and Sankai Juku's *Hiyomeki*—as well as Mats Ek's *Carmen* with the Lyon Opera Ballet.

The New Europe '99 Festival was spread out through three boroughs in New York City. Highly original ideas came from France (Compagnie Kafig, a sophisticated hip-hop group, and José Montalvo's *Paradis*), Belgium (Jan Lauwers' Needcompany), and Germany (Felix Ruckert). In Ruckert's *Hautnah*, the viewer was alone with a dancer in a small space.

Visitors included three companies from Russia: the Moiseyev Dance Company; the Eifman Ballet of St. Petersburg with Boris Eifman's *Requiem*, *My Jerusalem*, and *The Karamazovs*; and the Kirov Ballet. In addition to *The Sleeping Beauty*, the latter company performed *Giselle*, a program of Balanchine works, and *The Fountain of Bakhchisarai*, a Socialist Realist ballet choreographed in 1934 by Rostislav Zakharov.

The Ballets de Monte-Carlo impressed with Jean-Christophe Maillot's *Roméo et Juliette*, with a hoydenish heroine. The revitalized Australian Ballet presented Stanton Welch's *Madame Butterfly* and *Rites*, a version of Stravinsky's *Rite of Spring* inspired by aboriginal customs.

Awards. Judith Jamison was one of the artists recognized at the Kennedy Center Honors in 1999. The Samuel H. Scripps–American Dance Festival Award went to Pina Bausch, and choreographer Bella Lewitzky received the Capezio Award.

ANNA KISSELGOFF, *"The New York Times"*

Denmark

The political focus shifted from the government to the opposition in Denmark in 1999, as the Conservative and right-wing Progress Parties faced crises. Denmark achieved its lowest unemployment in 20 years, while the decision to hold a referendum to join the single currency of the European Union (EU) was delayed. On the Faeroe Islands, public debate began on the issue of independence from Denmark, but no referendum date was set.

Politics and European Affairs. Prime Minister Poul Nyrup Rasmussen's Social Democratic Party (SDP) regained much of the voter confidence lost in opinion polls earlier in the year because of the 1999 budget's reduction of labor-market pensions. During his 1998 election campaign, the prime minister had promised not to make any such cut, and voters reacted strongly against what they saw as a breach of faith and a major assault on the welfare state.

Later in 1999 the difficulties of the Conservative and Progress Parties made headlines. The Conservatives appointed their fourth leader in as many years when Pia Christmas-Moeller resigned in August and was replaced by Bendt Béndtsen after a fierce power struggle between the party's two factions. In the fall the Progress Party was shaken when its four members of parliament decided to become political independents to protest the party's decision to renew the membership of its founder, Mogens Glistrup. Soon after Glistrup established Progress in 1973, he masterminded an antitax campaign that swept it into parliament as the second-largest party; but later he was imprisoned for tax fraud and forced to leave the party. The four defectors objected mainly to Glistrup's strong anti-immigrant views.

The prime minister openly supported Danish membership in the EU's Economic and Monetary Union (EMU), but he postponed deciding the date of a mandatory referendum on that subject until after an SDP caucus in September 2000. In spite of polls that showed a majority of Danes favoring EMU membership, the election of 16 Danish members to the European Parliament in June saw the anti-EU vote rise from 25.5% in 1994 to 29.2% in 1999, with the far-right Danish People's Party—an offshoot of the Progress Party, featuring an anti-EU platform—winning a seat for the first time.

Economy. Unemployment in Denmark fell to 5.6% in August, its lowest level in 20 years and less than half the level it had been five years earlier. The International Monetary Fund (IMF) commended the Danish government for its sustained fiscal discipline and structural reforms but advised further labor-market reforms. Economic growth slowed in 1999 and was expected to remain in the range of 1% to 1.6%.

In June the A.P. Moller group, owner of the Maersk Line, agreed to pay the U.S.-based CSX Corporation $800 million to acquire Sea-Land. The new corporation, Maersk-Sea-Land, was expected to be the world's largest container-transport company, with about 250 vessels. Earlier in the year, Maersk had bought South Africa's Safmarine container line for $240 million.

LEIF BECK FALLESEN, *Editor in Chief*
"Boersen," Copenhagen

DENMARK • Information Highlights

Official Name: Kingdom of Denmark.
Location: Northwest Europe.
Area: 16,638 sq mi (43 094 km^2).
Population (July 1999 est.): 5,356,845.
Chief Cities (Jan. 1, 1998 est.): Copenhagen, the capital, 476,751 (Jan. 1, 1996 est.); Århus, 215,587; Odense, 145,296.
Government: *Head of state,* Margrethe II, queen (acceded Jan. 1972). *Head of government,* Poul Nyrup Rasmussen, prime minister (took office Jan. 1993). *Legislature* (unicameral)—Folketing.
Monetary Unit: Krone (7.1418 kroner equal U.S.$1, Nov. 10, 1999).
Gross Domestic Product (1998 est. U.S.$): $124,400,-000,000 (purchasing power parity).
Economic Indexes (1998, 1990 = 100): *Consumer Prices,* all items, 117.2; food, 116.0. *Industrial Production,* 126.8.
Foreign Trade (1998 U.S.$): *Imports,* $44,847,000,000; *exports,* $46,915,000,000.

Drugs and Alcohol

In 1999 the importation and use of illicit drugs continued to be a significant problem in the United States. Barry R. McCaffrey, director of the White House Office of National Drug Control Policy, said in an April report to Congress that more than 15,000 Americans died each year from drug-related causes and that the number of drug-related hospital emergency-room visits stood at a record-high level, exceeding 500,000 per year. McCaffrey estimated that the use of illegal drugs imposed more than $110 billion in "social costs" on the nation. Drug-related crime, he said, amounted to more than $59 billion per year. The social costs of drug use, he said, accounted for far more than the estimated $57 billion per year spent by Americans to purchase illegal drugs. He added, "Taken as a whole, in any given year, drug use saps over $167 billion from our nation's economic strength."

Surveys indicated that drug use among young people decreased in 1998, while overall drug use remained about the same. The federal government's annual National Household Survey on Drug Abuse reported in August that 9.9% of 12- to 17-year-olds said they had used an illicit drug in the last month, compared with 11.4% in 1997. Among all age groups, the survey found, about 13.6 million Americans were "current users" of illegal drugs in 1998 (down from 13.9 million the year before), accounting for 6.2% of the population aged 12 and over. Those figures, however, were a significant improvement from the highest reported number of drug users—25 million in 1979. According to the survey, marijuana was the most frequently used illegal drug, while about 1.8 million Americans aged 12 and over were current users of cocaine.

The drug-importation fight led by the U.S. Drug Enforcement Agency (DEA) saw some positive results in 1999. In August, after a two-year sting operation, 58 American Airlines baggage handlers, ramp workers, and contract workers at Miami International Airport were arrested and indicted for smuggling heroin, cocaine, and marijuana into the United States from Colombia. DEA agents also were involved in a yearlong investigation that culminated in the October 13 arrests by Colombian police of 31 traffickers believed to be responsible for smuggling as much as 30 tons of cocaine a month from Colombia to the United States.

The U.S. Coast Guard reported in September that, in the previous 12 months, its ships had confiscated a record 56 tons of cocaine destined for the United States. Nearly all of the drugs originated in Colombia; were transported by ship to Mexico, Haiti, and the Dominican Republic; and then were repackaged and taken into the United States along many routes. Drug officials estimated that approximately 400 tons of cocaine were shipped illicitly into the United States in 1998.

A panel of independent experts at the National Academy of Sciences' Institute of Medicine reported in March that the active ingredients in marijuana appeared to be effective in treating several medical problems, primarily pain, nausea, and severe weight loss associated with AIDS. The report, commissioned by the Office of National Drug Control Policy, also found no evidence that smoking marijuana led to the use of harder drugs, such as heroin and cocaine.

The report bolstered the arguments of those who favored legalizing the medical use of marijuana. The results of a November 1998 medical-marijuana referendum in Washington, DC, finally were released on September 20; the measure legalizing the medical use of marijuana was approved by a vote of 69% to 31%. The U.S. Congress had passed an amendment barring election officials from tallying the result, but a federal judge ruled on September 17 that the count could proceed. On November 2, voters in Maine approved a proposal to legalize the possession and use of marijuana for specific medical conditions, including loss of appetite from AIDS or cancer treatment, glaucoma, and seizures.

Alcohol. The abuse of alcohol remained one of the nation's most serious public-health problems, particularly among young people. About 19% of children aged 12 to 17 consumed alcohol in 1998, according to the National Household Survey. The report also said that in 1998, the rate of binge drinking (taking at least five drinks in one night) among those aged 18–25 was 31.7%, and the rate of heavy alcohol use in that same age group was 13.8%—both figures "significantly higher" than those for 1997.

Binge drinking was a particular problem on college campuses, where reports indicated that more than 40% of students engaged in that often-destructive behavior. In 1999 the National Association of State Universities and Land-Grant Colleges funded a nationwide advertising program aimed at curtailing the practice. It featured an advertisement signed by 113 colleges and universities that appeared in 17 large newspapers.

The National Highway Traffic Safety Administration reported in August that alcohol-related traffic fatalities declined in 1998 to about 16,000, or 38.4% of all fatal driving accidents. This figure was the lowest since those statistics first were tabulated in 1975. Meanwhile, arrests for drunken driving declined by about 18% from 1986 to 1997, according to a report issued in June by the U.S. Justice Department's Bureau of Justice Statistics. The report found that about 1.5 million Americans were arrested for drunken driving in 1997, compared with about 1.8 million in 1986. During that time, the number of licensed drivers increased by 15%. Analysts linked the decrease to widely publicized campaigns against drunken driving.

MARC LEEPSON, *Freelance Writer*

Ecuador

In 1999, Ecuador's economy contracted for the first time in a dozen years, the banking system entered into crisis, and Ecuador became the first country to default on the Brady bonds (a portion of its restructured debt to commercial banks). Efforts to reduce the fiscal deficit and reach a new loan agreement with the International Monetary Fund (IMF) were held hostage to political divisions between the governing Popular Democratic Party (DP) and opposition Social Christian Party (PSC), reflecting the historic rivalry between the mountainous area surrounding the capital city of Quito and the coastal regions flanking Ecuador's premier industrial city of Guayaquil.

Fiscal Crisis. President Jamil Mahuad's government, which took office in August 1998, inherited an economy devastated by fallen oil prices, coastal damage from El Niño, and a $16 billion debt burden that consumed more than 40% of government expenditures. After making peace with Peru, Mahuad moved to trim the fiscal deficit by cutting subsidies and abolishing the income tax in favor of a 1% tax on financial transactions.

As 1999 opened, these measures proved unpopular, insufficient, and damaging for investment. Reacting to the 1% tax, capital flight reached $400 million in January alone. Oil production fell 12% in the first quarter of 1999, and the economy shrank by 3.2%. Ecuador was forced to devalue its currency. Government coffers were drained further to cover deposits in insolvent banks. In March the government froze deposits to stop capital flight and prevent a run on the banks. With opposition parties rejecting tax increases, Mahuad sought to raise revenues via a 120% fuel-price hike. That measure provoked a strike in the transportation sector that paralyzed the country, forcing the government to retreat.

Economic Reforms, Legislative Gridlock. The PSC formally ended its flagging legislative alliance with the ruling DP, forcing the government to negotiate each item of legislation with an array of leftist parties. This unstable coalition approved an emergency fiscal package in April, reinstating the income tax, eliminating IVA (the value-added tax) and import-duty exemptions, and contemplating additional taxes on luxury vehicles and corporate assets.

In May the government launched a National Anticorruption Plan and improved its tax collection. And in June, Mahuad instituted an international audit of Ecuador's failing banks. He also proposed a Framework Law to modernize the state that would have facilitated privatization and dedicated resulting revenues to social-development projects.

It was hoped these reforms would persuade the IMF to sign a $400 million agreement that would bring additional credits totaling as much as $1 billion. However, negotiations were delayed by the resignation of the superintendent of banks and the chairman of the Deposit Guarantee Agency (AGD), and by the government's inability to win congressional support for reforms of the AGD. Political tension ran high in July, as, once again, a gasoline-price increase sparked transport strikes that succeeded in halting production, at an estimated cost of $20 million per day. The government called a nationwide state of emergency, but as in March, it ultimately retreated by lowering and freezing gasoline prices and announcing a development fund for indigenous peoples.

IMF Agreement, Brady Bond Default. In August the IMF signed a letter of intent conditioned on Ecuador's passage of a viable budget. The government negotiated in Congress a mix of tax increases that could produce revenues sufficient to satisfy the IMF. That agreement would come too late to save Ecuador from a September default on its $5.6 billion in Brady bonds. In October, Ecuador decided to delay interest payments on par Brady bonds and Eurobonds. Two cabinet ministers resigned in protest over the default and to clear the decks for a budget compromise. A third minister resigned after being accused of mishandling a $3 million contribution to Mahuad's presidential campaign. In November the Congress compromised on a 12% IVA, easing the way for the IMF funds.

SHELLEY MCCONNELL, *The Carter Center*

ECUADOR • Information Highlights

Official Name: Republic of Ecuador.
Location: Northwest South America.
Area: 109,483 sq mi (283 560 km²).
Population (July 1999 est.): 12,562,496.
Chief Cities (mid-1996 est.): Quito, the capital, 1,444,363; Guayaquil, 1,925,479; Cuenca, 247,421.
Government: *Head of state and government,* Jamil Mahuad Witt, president (took office August 1998). *Legislature* (unicameral)—National Congress.
Monetary Unit: Sucre (17,925.00 sucres equal U.S.$1, Dec. 13, 1999).
Gross Domestic Product (1998 est. U.S.$): $58,700,-000,000 (purchasing power parity).
Economic Index (1998, 1990 = 100): *Consumer Prices,* all items, 1,153.1; food, 1,146.4.
Foreign Trade (1998 U.S.$): *Imports,* $5,576,000,000; *exports,* $4,203,000,000.

Education

Tougher accountability policies generated a host of issues for U.S. education in 1999. Behind these controversies were serious concerns about the validity of testing and the use of single tests to make high-stakes decisions about students.

Higher-education institutions, previously above the fray of education policies that demanded results, also began to feel the accountability pinch.

The K–12 accountability push largely was federally induced because of several intertwined pieces of legislation. Goals 2000 required participating states to develop higher content standards and new assessments based on those standards. Even if a state wanted to ignore this legislation, the 1994 Title I legislation required all states to adopt systems for assessing progress in Title I schools; these systems were linked to higher standards and used for all other students. They were to be in place by the year 2000. While these mandates came from the federal level, they also fit with greater accountability demands being made by governors, state legislators, and business leaders.

As policy making regarding accountability began to have dramatic effects on students and schools, the complexities of such policies became more evident. Many districts and states, for example, were relying on a single test score to determine whether students would be promoted and/or graduate from high school, or whether schools would be placed on probationary status. In California results of the SAT-9 test (which had scoring problems with English-as-a-second-language students) were to count for almost two thirds of a school's ranking under the state's new accountability system. Mistakes in scoring on nationally standardized tests tainted the results in at least eight states, including California. In New York City the errors resulted in several thousand students being required to attend summer school and pass another test to be promoted; they would have been eligible for regular promotion, had it not been for the mistake. In several states, such mistakes caused some schools to be put on probation.

The Florida legislature approved a policy proposed by Gov. Jeb Bush that uses test results to grade schools. If a school receives an "F" grade two years in a row, public funds would be available to parents to use as "opportunity scholarships" at successful schools, including nonpublic ones. The idea was picked up by presidential candidate

As educators were pressured to end the policy of social promotion, the use of summer school to bring students up to par expanded greatly; more than half of U.S. urban school districts held remedial summer-school sessions in 1999.

Gov. George W. Bush of Texas as part of his education-policy platform. Civil-rights groups immediately filed suit against the Florida legislation.

In Texas the use of the Texas Assessment of Academic Skills as a high-stakes test that students must pass to graduate from high school was challenged in federal court as discriminatory because of the test-failure rates of minority students. Lawyers for both sides argued the case in October; the decision could have far-reaching effects, especially in the 26 states that had adopted policies requiring students to pass a test for graduation. Early in the year the U.S. Department of Education's Office of Civil Rights (OCR) issued guidelines urging colleges and universities to use "alternative" criteria instead of test scores in making admissions decisions, because tests could have a significant disparate impact on members of a particular race, national origin, or sex. However, objections from the higher-education community, which said tests "are barometers of excellence," forced the OCR to withdraw the guidelines for further work.

While the political community, backed by public opinion, saw little wrong with using high-stakes testing, researchers questioned whether the technical aspects of such testing have kept pace with its use. For example, Kentucky's sophisticated assessment system, which provides rewards and sanctions to schools based on two-year averages of student-score improvement, has skewed the curriculum. According to RAND researchers following the Kentucky results, teachers target their teaching and their own professional development to whatever subject is being tested that year. Another RAND researcher reported that results from Kentucky and other states show that scores on standardized tests rise each year because of teacher coaching, then fall when a new test or version are introduced. Gains on tests tend to be exaggerated, according to the study.

A special committee of the National Research Council, charged with developing guidelines for the use of assessments in the Title I program, called for multiple kinds of assessments. It warned against the use of a single test to cover all the uses of assessment, such as both diagnosing individual students' problems and providing information to the public. Tests should be used primarily to improve instruction, it said, and it recommended that test results help focus aid on schools that need help. The committee was to provide a guide on assessment, but it said that could not be done without also emphasizing the need to improve teachers' skills.

Tests also began to play a larger role in teacher evaluation. The Tennessee Value-Added Assessment System of calculating academic advancements made by K–8 students during a school year began to influence policy elsewhere. In Texas, for example, the performance of all students in a school now was to be taken into account in evaluating teachers.

Denver teachers approved a pilot project to give bonuses to teachers meeting goals for improving student performance. One indicator was to be standardized test scores. Although teacher unions still opposed standardized test scores as a teacher-evaluation tool, they began to show more flexibility on rewards, such as extra compensation for teachers who had proved their competence by obtaining certification from the National Board for Professional Teaching Standards. The Board and other teacher-reform groups have set a goal of 100,000 certified teachers within the decade.

Another aspect of accountability policies was the strong support for ending social promotion among the nation's governors, as well as from President Bill Clinton. This resulted in a greatly expanded use of summer school—more than half of urban districts organized remedial summer schools—and policies whose results often surprised those making them. In Atlanta, GA, for example, district officials estimated that the school board's decision not to promote third graders reading below the norm on the Iowa Test of Basic Skills would mean that half the students would be held back. A majority of students in New York City and Hartford, CT, who were held back at the end of the summer were those who had been expected to enroll in summer school but never showed up. Apparently, the message about tougher standards did not affect students' behavior. Researchers continued to contend that studies overwhelmingly showed retention in grade did not improve student performance beyond the grade that was repeated. They also pointed out that retention already was a well-used strategy in schools, with 20% of a class cohort overage by the middle grades.

Despite reservations about many of the aspects of new accountability systems, the "get tough" attitude of politicians and other policy makers did not seem to falter. In fact, it was reinforced at the third "education summit" of governors and business leaders, who were joined for the first time by education leaders. The summit reaffirmed support for standards-based reforms; it endorsed stiffer certification requirements for teachers, better teacher preparation, extra pay for exemplary teachers, extra help for failing schools and students, and greater attention by employers to high-school records. Two states that had instituted systemic reforms such as those advocated by the summit—Texas and North Carolina—had shown consistent gains in student achievement, according to researchers.

Curriculum Controversy. The Kansas state board of education shocked the science-curriculum field, and even the state's governor, when it deleted most references to evolution in standards recommended by an advisory group. While districts do not have to follow the state's decision, the action set off a national debate—most of it opposing the decision—and a declaration by major science-education groups denying copyright permission to Kansas for their curriculum materials. Meanwhile, a prominent science-education group, the American Association for the Advancement of Science, conducted a study of the most popular middle-school science textbooks; the results found the books contributed to shallow instruction in the middle grades. None of the nine textbooks in the study earned as much as a score of 1.5 on the 0.0–3.0 scale used by the researchers.

In California two lawsuits challenged factors used in admissions decisions by the state's most prestigious state higher-education institutions. The controversy concerned Advanced Placement courses, for which applicants receive extra points. The suits declared that this was discriminatory, since many high schools with a preponderance of minority and low-income students offer few if any Advanced Placement courses.

In a related action, the College Board announced an initiative to study the problem of underachievement by capable minority students and to recommend ways to expand the pool of college-bound minority students. A few months earlier, 15 traditionally high-performing and more-affluent school districts had formed a Minority Achievement Network to collaborate on research and initiatives to improve the academic performance of their minority enrollments.

On the issue of technology in classrooms, *Education Week* reported that "a critical mass" had been reached, with half of the nation's classrooms now connected to the Internet and an average of one instructional computer for every 5.7 students. However, actual use of digital technology was uneven. More than two thirds of teachers with six or more instructional computers in their classrooms relied on digital content to a "very great" or "moderate" extent, compared with 40% of teachers with fewer computers. Nearly four in ten teachers polled said their students did not use classroom computers at all during a typical week. The greatest barrier to use was said to be the lack of time for teacher training.

Teacher Quality. The predicted teacher shortage began to be felt in areas other than the usual shortage of math, science, special-education, and bilingual teachers. Districts also reported an increasing problem in finding school principals, both because of their retirement age and because of the reluctance of educators to assume a difficult job for not much more compensation than an experienced teacher in many areas. However, some observers contended that the teacher-shortage problem is one of poor preparation, inadequate recruitment policies, and a teaching environment that discourages qualified teachers. It cited estimates that colleges produce 30,000 teaching candidates a year beyond the need; however, these potential teachers are thwarted by poor recruitment efforts and a lack of support in their first years of teaching.

It became more obvious that states were willing to tackle the issue of teacher quality through various policies and collaborations. The 1998 Higher Education Act pushed them in this direction, offering grants to states that formed collaborations to improve teaching in high-demand areas and requiring states to collect data on teacher quality. Several states began to require teacher qualifications to be a part of school "report cards" to the public. New York and Maryland decided to phase out emergency certifications, but the number in California jumped from 14,000 to 29,000 in two years because of the state's reduced-class-size initiative. A study by the Education Trust of teacher-candidate examinations found them to require low-level knowledge and skills. Furthermore, it said, states set widely varying cutoff scores.

While many states took on responsibility for improving teacher preparation and certification, districts began to focus on higher-quality professional development and more-structured support for beginning-teacher

The Homework Issue

Teachers blame pressure from parents, and parents blame teachers' demands, but for whatever reason, U.S. students are spending more time on homework than in the past. Moreover, the homework burden is affecting younger and younger children.

According to researchers at the University of Michigan, primary-grade students could expect to spend 44 minutes a week on homework about two decades ago. By 1997 the time had increased to two hours. Similarly, 9- through 11-year-olds were hitting the books at home 40 minutes more than in 1981. Increased loads are not as evident in high schools and seem to be most controversial in suburban schools, where homework often becomes as much an assignment for parents as for students. It appears that—whether to help their children succeed or to ease what they see as an overburden—parents are getting increasingly involved in homework assignments.

Undoubtedly, the push to raise standards for learning has contributed to the increased homework load. However, teachers say that parents often judge their children's education by the amount and quality of homework they receive. The controversy over how much homework and how early is not new. It has been part of the literature on education issues for at least 100 years.

In today's competitive climate, homework is looked upon more favorably than in the past. Some research studies have found that homework contributes significantly to higher student achievement, while others contradict that finding. A study at the University of California/San Diego estimated that students who spent an extra half-hour on math homework beginning in seventh grade would be two grades ahead of their peers in math achievement by 11th grade. However, a study by a University of Missouri psychology professor concluded that the benefits of homework cannot be calculated for younger children. This was disputed by yet another study, which found that students coached daily for an average of 15 minutes more than the regular homework time outperformed others in math and vocabulary.

Another factor in the debate is the influence of technology. Many school districts now post homework assignments on the Internet. Thus, students can be given individualized homework assignments. Students also are becoming expert at using the Internet and CD-ROMs to complete homework assignments or to help each other. This growing use of technology underscores a concern of some educators and student advocates that the homework push puts low-income students at an even greater disadvantage. Often they do not have equal resources, including computers, to help them with homework. Furthermore, part-time work at longer hours is more prevalent among urban high-school students than those in suburban schools, giving them less time to do homework. Many urban districts are establishing after-school programs that include homework help, but these usually target younger students.

Meanwhile, backed by a survey showing that most parents (75%) believe that play is important to children's development, the American Toy Institute, Inc., launched a public-service program in 1999, "The Power of Play," to convince the public that play also is important to children's well-being.

ANNE C. LEWIS

© Liane Enkelis/Stock Boston

programs. Professional-development principles, advocated by researchers working for the National Partnership for Excellence and Accountability in Teaching (NPEAT), stressed the importance of classroom-embedded professional development. NPEAT, a collaboration of more than two dozen groups involved in teacher preparation and teaching standards, reorganized halfway through its five-year, $23 million project funded by the U.S. Department of Education. Its original purpose was to link research and practice, but the mission was too broad, according to participants, and the effort ended as a federal initiative.

Other Controversies. Desegregation, once the dominant policy in U.S. public education, was controversial again, only because it seemed to be fading out as a strategy. A federal judge removed the Charlotte-Mecklenburg, NC, schools from a requirement to use race as a factor in school assignments; Boston voluntarily ended the use of race in assignments; and Milwaukee considered ending busing for desegregation. Black parents in Louisville, KY, filed suit against race-based assignments in that district.

Several states followed the lead of Florida in approving voucher plans. Such plans reached the courts in five states. In Wisconsin the state supreme court ruled that inclusion of religious schools in Milwaukee's program was constitutional; a similar decision in Arizona was appealed to the U.S. Supreme Court. State-court decisions turned down voucher programs in Ohio, Maine, and Vermont. The U.S. Supreme Court agreed to hear a case from Louisiana in which federal funds are used for educational materials in parochial schools. Meanwhile, 36 states now had charter-school laws; California tightened its law to protect teacher-union rights in charter schools. Most of the states without such laws were largely rural, where alternatives to regular public schools are not as much an issue as in urbanized states.

At the federal level, the House and Senate reauthorized the Elementary and Secondary Education Act (ESEA). It was almost certain that Congress would require more accountability for results from federal investments. However, there also was strong support for a block-grant approach to federal K–12 programs, which would negate much of the ESEA's legislation. This idea was approved in the House as a pilot program for ten states. Opponents said block grants would remove responsibility for results from the states. After an 18-month delay, the U.S. Office of Education issued final regulations governing the Individuals with Disabilities Education Act, held up because of educators' concerns over discipline provisions. School districts were handed another problem when the U.S. Supreme Court ruled that they could be sued for damages for failure to respond to student sexual harassment of other students.

Violence. Undoubtedly, the most memorable event in public schooling in 1999 was the violent outburst by two students at Columbine High School in Littleton, CO, in April, which left 14 students and one teacher dead. The killings capped two years of similar, though not as extreme, incidents, most in suburban or semirural settings. The Columbine incident spurred national concern about large schools, lack of attention to troubled youth, and access to firearms. (*See also* FAMILY—*Today's Teenager*.)

Higher Education. The year's headline story about higher education involved the adjustment to the demise of affirmative action, led by California, and attempts to encourage minority students to be better prepared for higher education, an endeavor of campuses as well as education groups such as the College Board and a new federal program linking colleges with middle-school students. Colleges and universities also were under pressure from state policy makers to assess quality of teaching and learning. This requirement became more insistent through direct regulation of teaching loads and, in some states, the adoption of "performance funding systems" tied to indicators of the quality of undergraduate education. Others in the higher-education community, however, insisted that the most successful strategy would be to bolster internal accountability, such as the "academic audit" used in Great Britain.

In one area, however, college administrators agreed on some specific actions—to improve the preparation of teachers, long considered a weak link in building a quality professional culture. Among the recommendations of the American Council of Education, which represents the higher-education community, were to move teacher education to the center of an institution's mission; mandate campus-wide reviews of quality; require that education faculty and courses be coordinated with arts and sciences faculty and courses; and ensure that graduates of teacher-education programs are supported and mentored.

ANNE C. LEWIS, *Education Policy Writer*

Egypt

In October, Egyptian President Hosni Mubarak was sworn in for a fourth six-year term after an overwhelming victory in a referendum. The 71-year-old leader now has served as Egypt's ruler longer than any other person in the 20th century. He was expected to continue his policies of close ties with the United States, active mediation in the conflict between Israel and the Palestinians, and supply-side economics emphasizing privatization.

Domestic Issues. Egypt's parliament—95% of whose members were in Mubarak's National Democratic Party—nominated the president for a fourth term in June. Only 443 of the 454 members participated in the vote, but they all supported the president. No one else was able to muster the one third of the vote required for nomination, so Mubarak was the sole candidate. The opposition agitated for direct multiparty elections in which parties would be free to nominate their own candidates, but the few opposition members in parliament either supported Mubarak or abstained. Meanwhile, attempts by former Islamic militants to form the Sharia party and by former members of the Muslim Brotherhood to form Wasat were not approved by the authorities.

In the September 26 referendum to confirm parliament's choice, 79.2% of the nearly 24 million registered voters turned up at the polls. Of these, 93.79% voted "yes" to a fourth term for Mubarak; the rest were reported either to have voted against him or to have spoiled their ballots. Egypt's opposition factions boycotted the referendum, charging that it was a sham.

In September, a few weeks before the election, Mubarak narrowly escaped assassination when he was wounded slightly by a man who rushed at his car during a visit to Port Said. The attacker was shot dead by the president's bodyguards. Unlike previous attacks by would-be assassins, this attempt was not related to the crackdown on militant Islamic factions. Mubarak continued to refrain from appointing a vice-president or designating a successor, but he scotched rumors that he intended to be replaced by his son, Gamal.

After the election, Mubarak reshuffled his cabinet, replacing 13 of the 32 members. However, the major pillars of the regime—such as the defense, information, and agriculture ministers—remained. Prime Minister Kamal al-Ganzouri was replaced by 67-year-old Atef Ebeid, a U.S.-educated technocrat who had guided Egypt's privatization program.

Libyan leader Muammar el-Qaddafi (below, left) *conferred with President Hosni Mubarak* (right) *during his weeklong visit to Egypt in March 1999. With such diplomacy, Qaddafi sought to rebuild Libya's role on the international scene.*

© Mona Sharaf/Reuters/Archive Photos

Although the war against Islamic militants had diminished greatly the number of terrorist incidents in the country, Egyptian human-rights organizations reported in 1999 an increase in the government's repression of civil liberties. In April, 107 defendants were tried in a military court on charges that they belonged to Islamic Jihad, the group that was responsible for the assassination of President Anwar Sadat in 1981; the trial of Islamists was the largest since the assassination. All but 20 were convicted; nine were sentenced to death, another 11 received life sentences, and the rest received prison terms of up to 15 years. Civil-rights groups said that confessions were obtained under torture, that there was a lack of physical evidence, and that sources of information were not presented at the trial.

In response to a unilateral cease-fire declared in March by members of the largest dissident faction, the Jama al-Islamiya (Islamic Group), the government released several hundred of the thousands suspected of membership in the outlawed Islamic organization. However, the group vowed to continue fighting.

In May parliament passed a new Law on Associations that severely restricted the activities of nongovernmental organizations (NGOs), including human-rights groups, by prohibiting them from working to change government policy. Hafez Abu Saada, head of the Egyptian Organization for Human Rights, charged that the law's main objective was to close down human-rights groups and keep them from monitoring government activities. The law, giving the government control over the composition of the country's 14,000 NGO boards of directors and restricting their funds from abroad, was far more severe than previous legislation, and it was considered vague enough that the government could ban any activity it considered political. The United States observed that this move was "the wrong direction to go. . .if Egypt wants to energize civil society." Prominent Egyptian writers, actors, and artists petitioned the president not to ratify the law. Egyptian authorities responded that any group desiring to engage in political activity should form a political party, despite the fact that all recent applications to form new parties had been rejected.

In April, after debate in parliament, Mubarak decreed an end to a law that allowed rapists to go free if they agreed to marry their victims. The law often had been used by parents to restore family honor and by rapists to escape punishment. Egypt's highest Muslim official commended the "urgently" needed change, observing that a rapist's offer to marry his victim should not erase his punishment—a violation of Islamic law.

EGYPT • Information Highlights

Official Name: Arab Republic of Egypt.
Location: Northeastern Africa.
Area: 386,660 sq mi (1 001 450 km²).
Population (July 1999 est.): 67,273,906.
Chief Cities (December 1996 census): Cairo, the capital, 6,789,479; Giza, 4,779,865; Alexandria, 3,328,196.
Government: *Head of state,* Mohammed Hosni Mubarak, president (took office October 1981). *Head of government,* Atef Ebeid, prime minister (took office October 1999). *Legislature*—People's Assembly.
Monetary Unit: Pound (3.4230 pounds equal U.S.$1, Dec. 16, 1999).
Gross Domestic Product (1998 est. U.S.$): $188,000,000,000 (purchasing power parity).
Economic Index (1998, 1990 = 100): *Consumer Prices,* all items, 207.5; food, 190.9.
Foreign Trade (1998 U.S.$): *Imports,* $16,166,000,000; *exports,* $3,130,000,000.

During 1999, Egypt saw its largest wave of labor unrest since the 1952 revolution, resulting from the privatization of government enterprises, which threatened many workers' jobs. An unprecedented development was the involvement of civil servants who were facing cutbacks in staff. An editor of the opposition *al-Wafd* was charged with encouraging the demonstrators, publishing false reports, and threatening national security when he reported a strike by Central Bank employees. Meanwhile the economy continued to flourish, with projections of 6.9% growth in 1999.

Foreign Affairs. With the election of a new government and prime minister in Israel, relations between the two countries improved. Mubarak praised the new Israeli prime minister, Ehud Barak, for his efforts to achieve a peace settlement with the Palestinians. In late June, Mubarak made a state visit to Washington, DC, where he was received warmly by President Bill Clinton. Egypt's economic ties with Europe were strengthened by a $760 million deal with France to build two new power plants on the bank of the Suez Canal and an agreement with Belgium on economic investment and trade cooperation.

Airline Crash. On October 31 an EgyptAir jetliner flying from New York to Cairo crashed off the coast of Massachusetts, killing all 217 people on board, the majority of whom were Americans. A full investigation into the cause of the crash followed.

DON PERETZ, *Professor Emeritus*
State University of New York, Binghamton

Energy

A two-year slump in world oil prices came to an abrupt halt in 1999, as major oil-exporting countries drove up the price of crude by sticking to production quotas for the first time in recent memory. Concerns about the reliability of the U.S. electricity grid mounted during the summer, after a number of cities experienced power outages caused by heavy use of air-conditioning during seasonal heat waves. Progress continued in the development of renewable-energy sources.

Oil. Because of the efforts of the major oil-exporting countries, the price of crude rose to about $27 a barrel, and many analysts predicted that it soon would exceed $30. By December, regular unleaded gasoline cost about $1.35 a gallon, up from 96 cents in February and the highest level since the 1991 Persian Gulf war.

Oil prices had held fairly steady and at low levels for much of the 1990s, as exporters dependent on oil revenues failed to adhere to rigid export quotas set by the Organization of Petroleum Exporting Countries (OPEC) and flooded the market with crude. Their failure had helped fuel the longest-ever economic expansion in the United States by holding down inflationary pressure related to energy costs. By December 1998, oil prices had fallen below $11 a barrel, the lowest in 12 years.

But in 1999 oil producers held to export quotas set by an unprecedented coalition between the 11 members of OPEC and nonmembers Norway and Mexico. The coalition came into being in early 1998 at the urging of Luis K. Tellez, Mexico's oil minister, in an effort to halt the decline of oil prices that was devastating his country's export-driven economy. By 1999, producers were encouraged to stick to their new quotas by growing demand for oil, especially in Asia, where several countries began pulling out of a severe economic downturn.

The rise in oil prices was bad news for the United States, where petroleum products—56% of them imported—accounted for 44% of total energy consumption. But while analysts predicted that the hike in oil prices eventually would boost inflation, it had little immediate impact on the robust U.S. economy. American consumers also appeared oblivious to the oil-price increase, as they continued to buy gas-guzzling sport-utility vehicles, large houses, and other items with little apparent concern about the commodity's price and future availability.

Oil prices spiked in November, after Iraq halted its exports and called on other producers to refrain from boosting their own oil sales to compensate for the sudden loss of Iraqi oil. Before the cutoff, Iraq had been selling 2.2 million barrels a day, accounting for about 3% of total world supplies. Iraq took this action after the United Nations (UN) extended for only two weeks a program allowing Iraq to sell enough oil to buy humanitarian goods to alleviate the suffering caused by UN economic sanctions imposed on Iraq for its 1990 invasion of Kuwait. The UN previously had extended the oil-for-food program for six-month periods. In early December the UN Security Council voted to renew the program for another six months, paving the way for the resumption of Iraqi exports and a drop in oil prices to $25 a barrel. The impact of Iraq's resumption of oil exports on world markets remained uncertain.

The temporary cutoff had raised concerns that global demand for oil, at around

© P.J. Heller/Reuters/Archive Photos

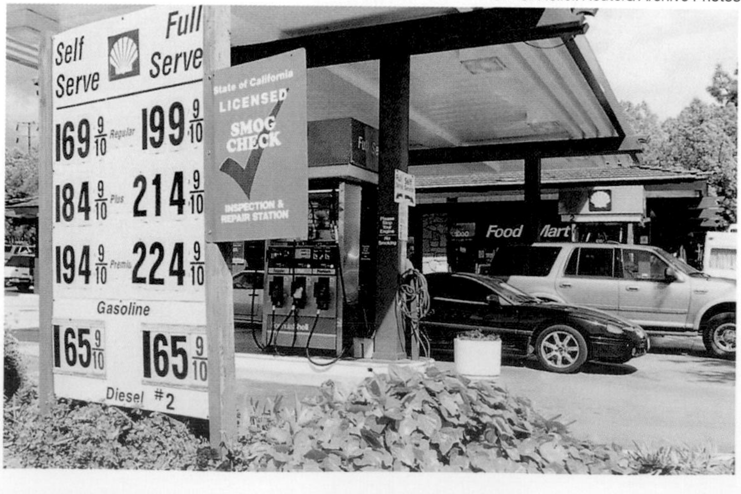

Gasoline prices in the United States soared during 1999, as several of the major oil-producing countries set rigidly restrictive quotas for production and export of crude oil. In some areas, Americans could expect to pay nearly 50% more to fill their gas tanks in December than they had paid at the beginning of the year.

77 million barrels a day, would exceed supplies over the winter, forcing oil prices even higher. Some analysts predicted that an excess of demand over supply could cause oil prices to rise by as much as $10 a barrel and lead to lines at gas stations reminiscent of the energy crises of the 1970s. In an effort to shield American consumers from further price increases during the coming winter heating season, Sens. Charles Schumer (D-NY) and Susan Collins (R-ME) in November introduced legislation to allow the energy secretary to sell oil from the federal Strategic Petroleum Reserve. Set up in 1975 as an emergency oil supply, the 573-million-barrel reserve last was tapped to discourage price hikes during the Gulf war.

Caspian Sea Pipeline. A long-awaited deal to build a pipeline to carry oil from the Caspian Sea to Western markets was announced in November at a European summit meeting in Istanbul, Turkey. The new pipeline would traverse Azerbaijan, Georgia, and Turkey. The Clinton administration long had supported this route for strategic reasons. Oil companies had preferred a less costly route that would have passed through Iran to the Persian Gulf, but continuing U.S. economic sanctions against the Tehran government ruled out that option. Financing of the new pipeline remained uncertain, as was Russia's reaction to the deal.

The administration also had opposed another pipeline, still under construction, terminating at the Black Sea port of Supsa, Georgia, because of the potential threat to the free flow of oil through the region posed by neighboring Russia. The Black Sea route also would require large numbers of oil tankers to pass through the narrow Bosporus, posing an environmental threat to the crowded city of Istanbul, which lies on both sides of the waterway.

U.S. Oil Industry. In November the Federal Trade Commission approved an $81 billion merger of Exxon Corp. and Mobil Corp. that the two domestic oil giants had announced almost a year earlier. The merger, creating the world's largest nongovernment petroleum company, was the latest in a series of industry consolidations sparked by intensifying competition from state-owned oil companies, such as Saudi Aramco and Mexico's Pemex. Only by joining forces could private companies amass the resources needed to conduct the increasingly expensive task of discovering and exploiting the world's dwindling oil deposits. As a condition of the merger, which was expected to save the two companies some $3 billion in operating costs by 2002, the new Exxon Mobil Corp. was required to divest itself of 2,400 service stations in the Mid-Atlantic region, New England, California, and Texas.

Regulatory and court actions posed new financial challenges to the industry. Under a compromise agreement between the Clinton administration and Republican legislators, U.S. oil companies faced the prospect of higher royalties for drilling on public lands beginning March 15, 2000. At the same time, an undisclosed number of the nation's 160 oil refineries came under investigation by the Environmental Protection Agency (EPA) for allegedly "widespread" violations of air-pollution standards set by the 1990 Clean Air Act.

Electric Utilities. In an effort to prevent future power outages, the Energy Department announced it would boost energy-efficiency standards for central air-conditioning, beginning in December 2000. High demand for electricity for air-conditioning was only one factor in the power outages, however. For years utilities had postponed expanding their operations and electrical output, pending congressional action on deregulation of the $220 billion electricity market. Even as many states began the process of dismantling the regional monopolies that have controlled the industry for decades, lawmakers continued to disagree on terms of a federal deregulation bill. Finally, in October the House Energy and Power Subcommittee of the Commerce Committee approved a measure, sponsored by Rep. Joe L. Barton (R-TX), that would both promote competition by allowing utilities to enter new markets and try to improve the reliability of the transmission system. The measure drew intense criticism from House Democrats, however, for leaving most of the responsibility for deregulating the industry to the states, failing to set a deadline for states to complete deregulation, and omitting incentives for utilities to use renewable-energy sources, as called for by the Clinton administration. Consumer advocates also charged that the bill would leave consumers vulnerable to price-gouging. Action on the measure was postponed until Congress reconvened in January.

Coal. Despite concerns about air pollution and global warming linked to its use, coal provided more than half of the fuel consumed for power generation and even widened its lead over other fuels, in part because of deregulation. Forced to compete for customers, utilities with coal-fired power plants enjoyed a price advantage over competitors that relied on nuclear energy, natural gas, and other fuels. It remained to be seen, however, whether low-sulfur coal produced in Wyoming and other western states would be more competitive than the high-sulfur coal produced by suppliers in West Virginia, Kentucky, and Pennsylvania. Although high-sulfur coal produces more pollutants, it was uncertain whether stricter air-quality standards due to take effect Jan. 1, 2000, would prompt generators to install more-efficient scrubbers instead of switching to low-sulfur coal.

The EPA and the Justice Department sued seven major electric utilities and the government-owned Tennessee Valley Authority (TVA) for allegedly failing to add adequate pollution controls to their coal-fired plants as required by the Clean Air Act. The suits alleged that the 32 plants in question, located primarily in the Ohio Valley, spewed pollutants that were carried hundreds of miles and intensified smog conditions in several East Coast cities.

Natural Gas. Natural gas continued barely to outrank coal as the second-most-heavily-used energy source after oil, accounting for almost a quarter of total U.S. consumption. That share was expected to grow when utilities completed scores of natural-gas-fueled power plants under development. But like domestic oil reserves, natural-gas deposits in the United States continued to decline, and Canadian imports accounted for a growing portion of gas consumption. Most remaining domestic gas lay in small, inaccessible deposits that required three-dimensional seismic imaging and other advanced technology to detect and exploit. These technical difficulties, combined with rising demand, helped boost the wellhead price of natural gas by nearly 20% over the year, to $2.30 per thousand cubic feet.

Nuclear Power. Lawmakers once again failed to decide the fate of a federal program to store spent fuel rods and other high-level waste from nuclear-power plants in 34 states. Most proposals called for storing the materials at a temporary site near Yucca Mountain, NV, a deep underground facility still under study as a permanent repository for nuclear waste. But Energy Secretary Bill Richardson, citing the potential dangers of shipping the lethal material to a single facility, proposed that power plants keep reactor waste on-site and hand over responsibility for ensuring its safe management to the federal government. None of the proposals garnered enough support to become law.

Meanwhile, 38 states continued to ship their low-level nuclear wastes to a single disposal site in Barnwell county, SC. But state officials were considering a proposal backed by Gov. Jim Hodges (D) to allow only South Carolina, Connecticut, and New Jersey to dispose of waste at the site, leaving the other states to find alternative facilities.

Renewable Energy. Progress in the development of renewable-energy sources offered hope for a gradual reduction in carbon emissions produced by burning fossil fuels. These emissions are considered the main cause of global warming. Auto manufacturers introduced several new models powered by fuels other than gasoline, a major contributor to carbon emissions. Honda planned to introduce to the U.S. market a "hybrid" car powered by both gasoline and self-generated electricity; it would arrive in California in December and nationwide in February 2000. Toyota had marketed a similar car in Japan.

Fuel cells powered by hydrogen, which emits no carbon and is considered to be the ultimate nonpolluting fuel, also were under development by automakers and industrial designers, who planned to produce workable hydrogen engines and industrial-power plants within the next decade. Signs of hydrogen's promise as an alternative to fossil fuels included oil giant Royal Dutch/Shell's decision to set up a subsidiary to develop hydrogen fuel.

The most widely used renewable-energy source, hydropower, came under growing attack, however, as environmental advocates charged that the damage many dams caused to endangered fish species outweighed the cheap electricity they provided. In July, Maine's Edwards Dam became the first major hydroelectric dam to be dismantled in an effort to save endangered fish. Far more controversial was a proposal to breach four dams on the Lower Snake River in eastern Washington. Interior Secretary Bruce Babbitt supported a plan to breach the dams, which was opposed vigorously by Sen. Slade Gorton (R-WA) and other regional lawmakers. Gorton and other critics charged that removal of the dams, which provided about 5% of the power generated by the federally owned Bonneville Power Administration, would cause area electricity prices to rise.

MARY H. COOPER
"The CQ [Congressional Quarterly] Researcher"

Engineering, Civil

Among civil-engineering highlights of 1999 were the completion of the world's longest bridge, the largest dome, the deepest-water oil-production platform, and the longest elevated expressway. Other significant accomplishments included the continuing work on Berlin's Potsdamer Platz and the relocation of the Cape Hatteras Lighthouse in North Carolina. The Outstanding Civil Engineering Achievement (OCEA) award went to the Los Vaqueros water project in California.

Record-Setting Projects. The longest bridge in the world, the Tatara Bridge in Japan, opened after nine years of construction. Its cable-stayed span of 6,532 ft (1 991 m) just surpasses the previous record holder, the nearby 6,529-ft (1 990-m) Akashi Kaikyo suspension bridge. The bridge was constructed with slim box girders, cables up to 1,509 ft (460 m) long, and steel towers in the shape of inverted Ys.

Shell Oil started to produce oil from its new tension-leg platform in the Gulf of Mexico. The platform sits 3,950 ft (1 204 m) above the floor of the ocean. It is held in place with steel tendons tensioned between the platform's hull and the foundations on the seafloor, allowing the platform to float like a cork.

In the Greenwich district of London, the Millennium Dome, spanning 1,050 ft (320 m) in diameter, was completed in time for the year 2000 celebrations. It is nearly twice the size of the previous record holder, the Georgia Dome. The 164-ft (50-m)-tall roof of the dome is hung from 295-ft (90-m)-tall masts and was built with prefabricated Teflon-coated fiberglass panels clipped to a cable net consisting of 2,600 cables. It covers more than 861,114 sq ft (80 000 m^2) of floor space and will house an ongoing theater piece as well as various shows and exhibits to celebrate the new millennium.

In Bangkok, Thailand, the second, 14-mi (23-km) phase of the $1 billion, 34-mi (54-km) Bang Na-Bang Phli-Bang Pakong Expressway (BBBE) was completed. The entire expressway is built on a viaduct and will support Bangkok's growth to the east. All of the thousands of segmental concrete box girders for the bridge were precast in the world's largest casting facility. The design is similar to the Seven-Mile Bridge in the Florida Keys.

Other Headliners. The crown of the Sony Center, an elliptical roof composed of Teflon-coated fiberglass fabric and glass panels, was completed. The Sony Center is the centerpiece of the redevelopment of the Potsdamer Platz in Berlin, Germany. The development of this area was the largest urban-construction project under way in Europe during 1999.

Design was completed and construction started on a 39-story high-rise in San Francisco. The noteworthy aspect of this project is its use of a precast concrete frame in an earthquake zone. The development of an innovative hybrid moment-resisting column-beam connection combining post-tensioning steel with mild reinforcing steel makes the concrete frame structure more earthquake resistant than cast-in-place frames.

In southern California construction on the Eastern Transportation Corridor project was completed. The 24-mi (38.6-km), two- to four-lane toll road with 72 bridges and tunnels was funded with a $1.5 billion nonrecourse bond. It was one of the largest privately financed transportation projects in recent U.S. history. Up the Pacific coast in Seattle, WA, the geometrically complex structure for the Experience Music Project, designed by Frank Gehry & Associates, was completed. The structure consists of curved steel beams, a shotcrete (blown concrete) shell, and steel panels. Use of three-dimensional computer modeling made the project economical.

On the U.S. east coast, the 129-year-old, 200-ft (61-m)-tall landmark lighthouse at Cape Hatteras, NC, was threatened by the encroaching Atlantic and was moved about 2,953 ft (900 m) to a new foundation. The lighthouse was shored with jacks and mounted on a steel carriage; push jacks then moved it about 350 ft (108 m) per day.

OCEA Award. The American Society of Civil Engineers gave its 1999 OCEA Award to the Los Vaqueros Water Project. Located about 40 mi (65 km) east of San Francisco, the Los Vaqueros reservoir stores 4.34 billion cu ft (123 million m^3) of water collected from the upper section of the Sacramento Delta estuary. The project brings fresh drinking water to a region that often is plagued with high salinity levels because saltwater intrudes from San Francisco Bay. It took the owner, Contra Costa Water District (CCWD), ten years to collect the more than 100 required local, regional, state, and federal permits. The project increased CCWD's emergency water capacity from three days to more than six months.

MARTIN FISCHER, *Stanford University*

Environment

With the U.S. Congress and the Bill Clinton administration still in substantial disagreement over the scope and direction of environmental laws, 1999 was a year that saw few major new initiatives but several incremental steps to protect wilderness areas, regulate pesticides, and address issues such as urban sprawl and nuclear waste. One important unresolved question was whether environmental protection should come via large-scale government programs or through locally crafted initiatives.

Public Lands. In one of the year's most dramatic environmental developments, the Clinton administration in October announced plans to ban logging and road construction on at least 40 million acres (16.2 million ha) of national forests throughout the country. Logging already was permitted on about one quarter of the 192 million acres (77.7 million ha) in the national-forest system; the new protections were aimed primarily at parcels of 5,000 acres (2 025 ha) or more that currently do not have roads. The move reignited the timber disputes that extended back to the early days of the administration. But the White House sidestepped one of the most sensitive potential disagreements by asking for public comment on whether the ban should be extended to the 17-million-acre (6.9-million-ha) Tongass National Forest in Alaska, the nation's largest forest and a longtime source of contention between environmentalists and resource companies.

Some environmental groups hailed the new plan as one of the biggest conservation initiatives since President Theodore Roosevelt created millions of acres of national-forest preserves at the beginning of the 20th century. But Republican members of Congress representing western states, who traditionally have been friendly to resource interests, indicated they would fight the new restrictions, which were set to go into effect in late 2000. The administration said the ban would not affect the nation's timber industry significantly, but resource companies contended it was part of a systematic effort to restrict their activities in public lands, causing the loss of American jobs and a greater reliance on foreign timber.

Endangered Species. In July, President Clinton announced that the American bald eagle would be removed from the endangered species list, because conservation efforts had restored its population sufficiently. The peregrine falcon, Virginia round-leaf birch, and 11 other once-threatened animals and plants also were dropped from the list, but in March nine species of wild salmon in the Pacific Northwest were added.

© Susan Walsh/AP/Wide World Photos

Challenger, a 10-year-old male bald eagle, was a White House guest in July 1999, as the government prepared to remove the species from the endangered list.

Landowners and environmentalists continued to disagree over the merits of the still-controversial Endangered Species Act of 1972. In 1999, Congress considered several proposals that tried to address perceived flaws in the law, but no significant reforms were expected before the presidential elections in 2000. One bill by John Chaffee (R-RI), the late chairman of the Senate Environment and Public Works Committee, would have required the government to identify critical habitats earlier in the process to develop recovery plans for affected species; another measure by Reps. Don Young (R-AK), W.J. "Billy" Tauzin (R-LA), and Richard Pombo (R-CA) would require the government to provide financial compensation to landowners whose property falls within a designated critical habitat. The White House, which preferred regulatory incentives to financial ones, favored other ways of making the act more flexible, such as habitat conservation, which allows landowners to develop or farm parts of their properties if they designate other portions for critical habitats. One such plan, negotiated by nine companies, set aside more than 115,000 acres (6 075 ha) of the North Carolina Sandhills for the endangered red-cockaded woodpecker.

Urban Sprawl. Seeking to address pervasive urban sprawl and address public concerns about the loss of open spaces, the Clinton administration in March announced a "Lands Legacy" initiative, calling for nearly

$1 billion in federal spending to protect battlefields, archaeological sites, historic structures, and other undeveloped areas. In late October, however, Congress dealt the administration a stinging rebuke by providing far less money for the program than the president requested. Opponents depicted Clinton's plan as redundant and said that the accompanying regulations could limit people's ability to live where they wanted.

Although localities continued to regulate most land use through zoning regulations, states recently had become more active in defining urban-growth boundaries. Maryland officials proposed spending $100 million to acquire undeveloped tracts in the suburbs of Washington, DC, while voters in New Jersey, Colorado, and Arizona considered approving new antigrowth measures and open-space laws.

Pesticides. In 1999 the government continued to implement the 1996 Food Quality Protection Act, which overhauled the regulation of pesticides applied to food and other crops. But its efforts to determine precisely what levels of pesticides were safe drew sharp criticism from both environmentalists and agricultural interests. The U.S. Environmental Protection Agency (EPA) in August banned most applications of the widely used methyl parathion on fruits and vegetables, and tightened restrictions on a second pesticide, azinphos methyl. Both agents are organophosphates that kill insects by disrupting their nervous systems, but they have been shown to cause illness in agricultural workers as well. The new regulations, touted as protection for infants and small children, were only part of a broader agency review of nearly 10,000 uses of organophosphates and other chemicals.

Farmers, who use nearly 1 billion lb (453 million kg) of pesticides annually, worried that such restrictions would deprive them of valuable tools with which to fight pests, put them at a competitive disadvantage with foreign growers, and lead to economic losses. They contended the data regarding possible health effects on children were incomplete. Environmentalists, on the other hand, chided the White House for not moving more quickly to use the 1996 act's powers. Meanwhile, the Consumers Union criticized the EPA for not taking action on 125 risky pesticides commonly used on food.

Nuclear Waste. Since 1987 the U.S. Department of Energy has been studying the prospect of burying high-level nuclear waste from commercial power plants under Yucca Mountain, NV, a barren ridge northwest of Las Vegas. The political debate over the disposal plan intensified in 1999, as new questions arose regarding the site's suitability for this purpose. In February a scientific-review panel convened by the Energy Department concluded that the long-term safety of radioactive waste at the site may not be possible to predict. The panel said that over the tens of thousands of years it will take some of the isotopes in the repository to decay, climate changes and the site's possible increased vulnerability to earthquakes could imperil the storage casks. Some opponents of the repository also seized on a newly released scientific analysis that concluded that there were crystals at the site formed by hot water boiling up from under the mountain over the past half-million years. The critics believed hot water

Government officials feared the damage that could be caused to North Carolina's environment as thousands of pigs, chickens, and cattle died during heavy flooding.

© C. Seward/News OBS/Corbis-Sygma

could corrode the storage casks, which then would release contaminated water and radioactive steam.

Despite these questions, the Energy Department released a draft environmental-impact statement saying disposal at Yucca Mountain was safer than leaving the waste where it was, in temporary storage pools at more than 100 reactors in 34 states. By late 1999 the federal government already had invested $3 billion studying the site and contending with geologic challenges, such as water flowing through cracks in the volcanic rock formations. The Energy Department was expected to recommend the site in 2001. If the new president approves the plan, Nevada could object, but Congress could override the state's protest with majority votes in the House and Senate. Even under this scenario, however, the Energy Department conceded that the first containers of waste may not be stored at Yucca Mountain until 2010.

Global Warming. The United States in late 1999 faced charges it was not doing enough to cut emissions of so-called greenhouse gases that many scientists believe contribute to global warming. The European Union (EU) in November announced it wanted to push through an international accord to cut emissions of carbon dioxide and other gases by 2002. But the U.S. delegation to a climate conference sponsored by the United Nations (UN) stated it would not be bound by such mandates.

The urgency on this global-warming issue stemmed from the Kyoto Protocol, a 1997 agreement that committed the industrialized nations as a group to cutting greenhouse-gas emissions by a total of 5.6% from 1990 levels, with a deadline of no later than 2012. Developing countries were given more time to meet the pact's conditions. Many U.S. businesses opposed this treaty, because it may force them to switch to cleaner fuels, which could raise energy prices and reduce profits. Critics also argued that the agreement was not tough enough on developing nations, such as China and India. Opposition to the pact was so intense in the Republican-controlled Congress that President Clinton did not submit it for ratification, although he signed it in November 1998.

The EU, backed by Japan and New Zealand, insisted it wanted the Kyoto Protocol in force by 2002, stating that its target goals were achievable, even without U.S. participation. However, talks were plagued by disagreements over how to implement the agreement. The pact must be ratified by all industrialized countries to become international law, yet few observers expected U.S. action on it before the 2000 elections.

Political Developments. By late 1999 the environment was becoming a key point of contention among the Democratic presidential candidates. Vice-President Al Gore promised in October that, as president, he would bar any offshore oil and gas drilling along the Florida and California coasts, even in areas where leases already had been granted. The move was designed, at least in part, to bolster the vice-president's credentials with environmental groups. Gore enjoyed a strong reputation for environmental advocacy, but so did Bill Bradley, his opponent for the Democratic nomination. Also, environmentalists have criticized the Clinton administration for halfhearted enforcement of some regulations and lack of leadership on the global-warming pact.

But the Gore drilling ban could present a legal challenge to a new administration because of the 36 existing offshore oil and gas leases in California and 146 in Florida. The government might have to buy back leases it had approved before the policy change. For example, in 1995 the Clinton administration agreed to pay $200 million for 73 leases off the Florida coast after they were designated as environmental risks.

Interior Secretary Bruce Babbitt, one of the Clinton administration's top environmental officials, was exonerated in October after a 19-month investigation into whether Babbitt lied to Congress about his department's 1995 rejection of a proposed Indian casino in Wisconsin. Independent counsel Carol Elder Bruce found insufficient evidence to warrant charges. The inquiry had distracted Babbitt and stymied some of his efforts to expand federal protection of fragile lands and wilderness areas. He promptly indicated that he would focus on enlarging the federal estate in the West, which could trigger more battles with Republicans in Congress. At year's end there was speculation that Babbitt would extend new protections for 570,000 acres (230 850 ha) of land on the Shivwits Plateau in Arizona, north of the Grand Canyon. This action would be reminiscent of the administration's 1996 designation of some 2 million acres (810 000 ha) in southwestern Utah as the Grand Staircase Escalante National Monument—a move that angered members of Congress and state officials, who claimed they had not been consulted.

ADRIEL BETTELHEIM, *"CQ Researcher"*

Ethiopia

In 1999 war with Eritrea continued to dominate politics and international affairs in Ethiopia. An uneasy lull that had lasted some eight months was shattered in February, as the armed forces of both countries began months of continuous heavy fighting, with estimates of troop losses on both sides reaching a staggering 50,000–70,000. Multiple peace efforts remained stillborn. With the attention of the world directed to the battlefield's front lines, Ethiopia moved troops into southwestern Somalia, occupying large sections of the region in an effort to secure its border from Somali rebels who claimed parts of southern Ethiopia. The ongoing war between Ethiopia and Eritrea eliminated the possibility of short- and long-term economic growth and development for both nations.

Mortal Combat. A dispute between Ethiopia and Eritrea over a never-formalized 600-mi (966-km) border along the Yiagra Triangle, which had erupted in May 1998, continued to fester until Feb. 6, 1999, when wide-scale shooting again began in the western Badme section of the Triangle. Two days later, Ethiopia launched a ferocious attack further east, near and around Zalambessa. The initial stage of the battles lasted for three weeks, and by the end of the month, Ethiopia had expelled the Eritrean army from the Badme region. Air attacks and ground battles, however, continued to rage in the Triangle.

By mid-May, frustrated by its inability to land a knockout blow, Ethiopia initiated air attacks against the Eritrean seaport of Massawa. Ethiopia claimed that extensive damage was caused to the city as well as to its port, naval base, and oil depots. During May and June furious battles along the Mereb River east of the Badme Plain took thousands of lives. Fighting continued unabated through late 1999, with troops of both sides occupying various sections of the Yiagra Triangle while attempting to dislodge the opposing forces.

U.S. President Bill Clinton estimated that more than 70,000 troops had been killed in the savage fighting; other sources claimed the figure was closer to 50,000. In terms of manpower, this was Africa's largest war, with more than 300,000 soldiers confronting each other. It also was Africa's bloodiest.

Geographically largely shrubland in the highlands between Ethiopia and Eritrea, the Yiagra Triangle had become a cemetery for the economic ambitions and hopes of both countries. Ethiopia was in an economic slump resulting from the war, while Eritrea's economic-growth rate had fallen by 50%. Foreign investment, imports and exports, and tourism were down in both countries. In addition, mass expulsions of Ethiopians from Eritrea and Eritreans from Ethiopia called into question both countries' commitment to democratic reforms.

War Profiteers. The brutality of the 1999 battles was made possible by the fact that both sides had been armed extensively by

The border war between Ethiopia and Eritrea that began in 1998 continued in 1999. Both sides suffered heavy casualties in extremely bloody fighting.

ETHIOPIA • Information Highlights

Official Name: Federal Democratic Republic of Ethiopia.
Location: Eastern Africa.
Area: 435,184 sq mi (1 127 127 km²).
Population (July 1999 est.): 59,680,383.
Chief Cities (October 1994 census): Addis Ababa, the capital, 2,112,737; Dire Dawa, 164,851; Harar, 131,139.
Government: *Head of state,* Negasso Ghidada, president (took office May 1995). *Head of government,* Meles Zenawi, prime minister (took office May 1995). *Legislature*—Parliament: House of Federation and House of People's Representatives.
Monetary Unit: Birr (8.000 birr equal U.S.$1, Nov. 10, 1999).
Gross Domestic Product (1998 est. U.S. $): $32,900,-000,000 (purchasing power parity).
Economic Index (1998, 1997 = 100): *Consumer Prices,* all items, 100.9; food, 101.8.
Foreign Trade (1998 U.S.$): *Imports,* $1,300,000,000; *exports,* $550,000,000.

outside forces. 200 T-55 tanks from Bulgaria (which in 1998 was said to be helping to arm Eritrea) and SU-27 fighter bombers and helicopters from Russia were part of Ethiopia's military arsenal, while container-loads of weapons had been shipped to Ethiopia by both countries via Djibouti. Through 1999, Bulgaria earned $4.4 million in profit from the arms trade, while Russian military sales to Ethiopia totaled $150 million. Eritrea also had been supplied with heavy weaponry from Ukraine.

In June 1999, while Ethiopia and Eritrea were spending massive sums of money to fund their militaries, the Group of Seven (G-7) industrial nations declared both states among the world's poorest and agreed to provide debt relief by reducing their financial obligations. In July the United Nations (UN) Human Development Report indicated that Ethiopia and Eritrea were among the ten least-developed countries in human terms.

Peace Efforts. Attempts at arranging peace were made by individual states, as well as by the UN and the Organization of African Unity (OAU). As of late 1999, all had come to naught. Algerian diplomat Mohammed Sahnoun, the UN special representative for Africa, made numerous abortive trips to the region; meanwhile, Anthony Lake, representing the United States, tried, but failed, to mediate between the two sides. In June the UN Security Council demanded an immediate cease-fire; its call was ignored. Egyptian President Hosni Mubarak met separately in Cairo with Ethiopian Prime Minister Meles Zenawi and Eritrean President Isaias Afewerki in an unsuccessful bid to broker an end to the fighting.

Only the OAU, supported by the UN, made some headway. In August it developed a detailed peace proposal calling for an immediate cease-fire; the withdrawal of both sides from the disputed territory; placement of outside observers to monitor the accord; and demarcation by the UN of the border, based upon treaties signed by Italy and Ethiopia in 1900, 1902, and 1908. The plan also indicated that Eritrea must make the initial withdrawal, in effect admitting it was the first to use military force to resolve the border issue, and that Ethiopia could administer the areas it once held while the new border is drawn up.

Ethiopia agreed to the plan's outlines but refused to sign off on it. It maintained that it would not agree to any redrawing of frontiers that fell outside its own interpretation, and that it needed to clarify what powers it would have in administering sections of Badme and what authority the outside observers would have. Eritrea, which accepted the accord, asserted that Ethiopia, eight times its size, refused to approve the pact because it had an interest in destabilizing Eritrea economically and in securing access to the Eritrean port of Assab—since Ethiopia is landlocked—and believed it could attain these goals by force. Still, it did appear that the OAU peace plan was potentially quite significant and was bringing the two sides nearer to agreeing to a resolution.

Other News. Between June and August, Ethiopia moved forces into southwestern Somalia, occupying the regional capital of Garba Harre and other border towns. Somalia, in a state of anarchy, was unable to control rebels who claimed sovereignty over parts of Ethiopia and who periodically were attacking Ethiopian border villages.

The last group of some 3,500 Ethiopian Jews remaining in the country was flown to Israel in June. Virtually all other Ethiopian Jews (about 22,000) had been flown to Israel between 1984 and 1991.

In March, Human Rights Watch indicated to the UN Human Rights Commission that former President Mengistu Haile Mariam, currently in exile in Zimbabwe, should be tried on charges of murder and torture. In Ethiopia, 3,200 individuals were in prison awaiting trial on charges of torture and murder that occurred during the years Mengistu was in power (1974–91).

Asrat Woldeyes, an Ethiopian physician who was the leader of the opposition All-Amhara People's Organization and a critic of the present government, died in May in Philadelphia. He had been imprisoned for political activity from 1994 until 1998.

PETER SCHWAB, *Purchase College State University of New York*

Ethnic Groups, U.S.

Amid relative U.S. prosperity in 1999, the issues of job discrimination, affirmative action, and unequal access to health care made for a contentious year for the nation's various ethnic groups. Hate-based groups proliferated, and several widely reported hate crimes against African-Americans reminded the nation that racism persisted. Indeed, according to a report by the Federal Bureau of Investigation (FBI) on crime, issued in November, racism motivated more than half the hate crimes reported in 1998, the last full year for which statistics had been compiled. Especially significant were Justice Department figures released in February that showed American Indians as more than twice as likely as any other group to be the victims of violent crime; not all the violence against Indians was hate-based, though, for the same data revealed high levels of rape, child abuse, and neglect among Indian populations. Self-hate, the report and other studies suggested, also was a source of violence. Also disturbing was a Pentagon study, issued in November, that found that almost 75% of blacks and other minorities reported experiencing racially offensive behavior in the military during 1996 and 1997, at a time when the number of minority and women officers had doubled in 20 years.

In a precedent-setting move, the Justice Department, in February, opened an investigation at an Asheville, NC, high school of whether the use of Indian names, logos, and mascots violated the civil rights of Native American students by fostering a hostile racial environment. In July the U.S. Patent and Trade Office began discussions with American Indian groups on a proposed change in federal trademark law to allow Native American tribes to register their insignias as official symbols and thus prevent sacred symbols from being exploited commercially. Also significant was Harvard University's transfer, in May, of the bones of almost 2,000 Native Americans and burial objects to a New Mexico tribe, the largest such transfer under the 1990 federal law requiring the return of Indian artifacts. Also in May, the Makah Indian Nation tested its treaty rights to hunt whales, irrespective of other U.S. international agreements limiting whale hunting, by conducting its first whale hunt in 70 years; the hunt was broadcast on television and evoked mass protests from environmentalists and animal-rights advocates in the Pacific Northwest. The Makah people had argued that a return to whale hunting was essential to maintaining their particular tribal identity.

The Courts. In May the Supreme Court, in *Hunt v. Cromartie*, overturned a three-judge federal court's conclusion that the North Carolina legislature unlawfully had redrawn the 12th District, because the new district diminished minority-voting power; rather, the court stated that federal judges could not invalidate a state-approved redistricting plan simply because it did not enhance minority-voting power. In August, Florida officials agreed to settle a lawsuit involving the boundaries of eight congressional districts in a way that would eliminate three minority-majority districts created in 1992.

© Richard Ellis/Corbis-Sygma

On June 15, 1999, Dennis Hastert (right), *speaker of the U.S. House of Representatives, spoke as Rosa Parks, 86, received the Congressional Gold Medal. The former seamstress had sparked the civil-rights movement by refusing to give up her seat to a white man on a segregated bus in Montgomery, AL, in 1955.*

Also significant for future reapportionment was the court's ruling, in January, that the Census Bureau cannot use statistical sampling for its population count, which city governments and the Bill Clinton administration had wanted to ensure a fuller tally of minorities living in cities. In February the Census Bureau announced that it would do a traditional head count for congressional apportionment and later would provide a "more accurate" count, using sampling, for other purposes.

Job Discrimination and Affirmative Action. In May lawyers for 12,000 black employees of the U.S. Agriculture Department (USDA) filed a class action charging the USDA with a long history of discrimination in hiring, promoting, and training blacks. The suit sought back pay, promotions, and damage awards, as well as the end to a culture of racism that made the USDA "the last plantation." The lawsuit followed the USDA's January settlement of a class-action suit brought by thousands of black farmers who claimed the USDA routinely denied loan and disaster-payment applications submitted by black farmers. By March that deal had soured, as black claimants insisted that the burden of proof of past discrimination was too high and the compensation payment of $50,000 apiece for most claimants too low. In April a U.S. District judge approved a revised settlement that added safeguards to farmers' rights during the settlement process but did not change the scale of payments. More than 18,000 black farmers could be affected by the settlement, which could be worth more than $2 billion. In November, Indian farmers and ranchers filed a $19 billion class-action lawsuit against the USDA, charging the department with discrimination in granting loans over a 20-year period.

In March the Supreme Court let stand a lower-court ruling that refused to allow the Dallas Fire Department to revive an affirmative-action plan to promote more blacks, Hispanics, and women. At the same time, the court let stand a lower-court ruling in a case from Utah, which allowed the federal government to continue to give companies owned by "disadvantaged" people extra help in winning highway-construction projects. In May a U.S. District judge ruled unconstitutional a Memphis Police Department program to promote black officers and set hearings for monetary awards to white officers denied promotions because of the racial-quota system in place for more than two decades. The stage for a major legal and political fight over affirmative action was set in August, when the Southeastern Legal Foundation sued Atlanta for discrimination because its Equal Business Opportunity program sets aside one third of all city contracts for minority-owned businesses. Atlanta Mayor Bill Campbell vowed to fight the challenge.

The U.S. Labor Department announced in February that it was tightening its enforcement of pay-discrimination laws, and several lawmakers proposed legislation to toughen the 1963 Equal Pay Act by permitting victims of wage discrimination to recover compensatory and punitive damages rather than just lost wages, as current law requires.

Conservatives launched an advertising campaign in January to pressure schools to comply with new rules forbidding racial preferences in admissions. In February a coalition of civil-rights groups filed suit against the University of California at Berkeley, charging that its new "color-blind" policies discriminate against blacks, Hispanics, and Filipino Americans by giving undue weight to SAT scores and advanced-placement courses in admissions decisions. The lawsuit reflected a nationwide assault on standardized tests, especially the SAT, as discriminatory because blacks and Hispanics do not score as well as whites and other groups; numerous civil-rights and parents' groups threatened lawsuits against schools using such tests for admission, placement, or graduation, saying the tests violate federal civil-rights laws because they have a disparate racial impact. Discussions over the validity of such tests and calls for more-race-sensitive testing and weighted grading on the basis of race and income filled the airwaves.

In a landmark decision, in September a U.S. district judge ordered an end to race-based busing and school assignments in the Charlotte-Mecklenburg school district in North Carolina. The judge argued that the district's "single-minded focus on racial diversity" undermined educational efforts district-wide. The ruling, in effect, reversed the *Swann v. Charlotte-Mecklenburg* case of three decades earlier.

Economic Issues. A seven-volume survey, "The Multi-City Study of Urban Inequality," released in late September by the Russell Sage Foundation and Harvard University, found that race had a negative and "pervasive influence" in virtually every aspect of economic life in urban America, from housing to hiring patterns. The five-

Racial Profiling

In 1999 the practice by police of stopping and searching suspects on the basis of race—known as "racial profiling"—gained attention. In fact, a late 1999 Gallup poll revealed that a majority of Americans, regardless of race, believed that racial profiling was widespread in the United States. In April the U.S. Justice Department had announced that it was filing a civil-rights lawsuit against the New Jersey State Police, charging that the state police systematically and persistently stopped and searched motorists on the basis of race. The Justice Department action was the largest lawsuit threatened under the 1994 crime bill, which gave Justice the power to investigate police "patterns and practices" and to file lawsuits against entire departments that showed evidence of civil-rights violations. For years minorities had complained that they were subjected to frequent, excessive, and unwarranted stops and searches for illegal drugs, because law-enforcement agencies had drawn a "profile" of likely drug traffickers that targeted minorities, especially young men, for scrutiny.

A U.S. Justice Department–sponsored survey of 12 cities in 1998, released in June 1999, revealed that 24% of blacks were dissatisfied with local police, compared with 10% of whites surveyed, with blacks citing "racial profiling" as the prime reason for such distrust. More damning was the American Civil Liberties Union (ACLU) report, "Driving While Black: Racial Profiling on Our Nation's Highways," issued in June, which charged that the Drug Enforcement Agency (DEA) had trained as many as 27,000 law officers nationwide to identify drug couriers on the highways, and that one mark of such a trafficker was a minority person driving an expensive car. Adding to the public concern was a class-action lawsuit brought by nearly 100 black women against the U.S. Customs Service, charging Customs with racial and sexual profiling. A report to Congress in 1999 stated that black and Hispanic travelers were subjected to 43% of all body searches by Customs officers in 1998.

Controversy had swirled around New Jersey state troopers since April 1998, after two troopers shot into a van carrying four minority men on the New Jersey Turnpike, wounding three of them. The wounded men sued the police for damages and charged they had been stopped because of their race. In February 1999, New Jersey Gov. Christine Todd Whitman forced the state police superintendent from office, following insensitive racial remarks he had made related to the case. In April, New Jersey's attorney general confirmed that some state troopers had engaged in racial profiling of blacks and Hispanics. He later admitted that agency-wide tolerance for police abuse of citizens and stereotyping in the state police existed, and called for significant reforms. In September, Whitman appointed a black Federal Bureau of Investigation (FBI) agent to head the troubled agency. But a new storm broke in September, when two New Jersey state troopers were indicted on charges of attempted murder and aggravated assault for the April 1998 shooting.

In its June report, the ACLU called on police departments nationwide to compile data on traffic stops that included the race of the driver. Several cities, including San Diego, and the state of North Carolina already had approved such data-collection policies. The Traffic Stops Statistics Act was introduced in the U.S. Congress to require police to record racial and other data for all traffic stops, but the bill went nowhere. Meanwhile, in June, President Bill Clinton ordered all federal agencies to develop plans for collecting race and sex data for any stop or arrest by a federal officer. And in December, New Jersey authorities signed a consent decree with the U.S. District Court agreeing to reforms to prevent racial profiling by state troopers, thereby avoiding a federal lawsuit.

RANDALL M. MILLER

year study, based on a sample of 9,000 households and 3,500 employers in four cities, revealed that employers ranked blacks low on their hiring-preference charts, often viewing blacks as the most likely group to commit crimes and cause problems in the workplace, while seeing recent immigrants as better and more reliable workers. The study bore out patterns of employment, income, and poverty reported by the Census Bureau in late September. While the median incomes of white and Hispanic households rose, black median incomes remained unchanged from their all-time high in 1997.

The Urban League's "The State of Black America 1999," issued in November, also reported a mixed picture of progress for minorities. Although general good times benefited blacks overall, they continued to lag behind other groups in education and access to health care, while exceeding them in incarceration rates. Especially troubling, the report concluded, was the underfunding of inner-city and poor rural schools and continued discrimination in bank lending to blacks. The U.S. Civil Rights Commission found that young black men suffered from negative stereotyping in the media as well as from poor schooling, and were represented disproportionately among the nation's un- or underemployed, under-schooled, and incarcerated young men.

According to a Commerce Department survey, "Falling through the Net," issued in July, the "digital divide" between those with access to new technology and those without is a "leading economic and civil-rights issue," as low-income blacks and Hispanics fall farther behind white and Asian households with incomes of $75,000 or above in Internet usage and ownership of a computer. In response, BET Holdings, which owns four cable channels and three magazines largely directed to blacks, announced in August that it was investing $35 million in a partnership with three major media companies to start an Internet portal, BET.com, aimed at blacks, whose Internet use was only half that of whites.

As reported in a major study of investment patterns by Yankelovich Partners Inc. in May, only 57% of black middle-class households (those with incomes of $50,000 or higher) invested in stocks in 1998, compared with 81% of white middle-class households, and blacks were more likely to pull out of the market in a downturn than were whites. Such conservative investment patterns have left blacks behind in wealth accumulation and have made it more difficult for them to fund higher education and save for retirement than for whites. One of the principal reasons blacks invest more in banks than in stocks is that they are more likely to distrust financial advisers.

Health. In January the National Research Council issued a report showing that poor people—and especially African-Americans and other minorities who contracted cancer—received less quality care and were more likely to die from the disease than were whites, with Native Americans the least likely to survive cancer of any group in the nation. The panel of cancer experts attributed the disparities in disease and treatment to culture, poverty, and ignorance and called on the government and research foundations to include more minorities in clinical trials and to collaborate with medical colleges and clinics serving nonwhite groups to get better samples of disease patterns and provide better treatments to a diverse population. In a much-discussed study published in the *New England Journal of Medicine* in February, it was revealed that doctors prescribed less-aggressive treatment for blacks than for whites diagnosed with heart disease and failed to refer black women for heart catheterizations $2\frac{1}{2}$ times more than they did for black or white men. In response, the U.S. surgeon general in February called on medical schools to address racial biases frankly in medical training and identified cardiovascular disease as one of six areas of racial and ethnic disparity that the Department of Health and Human Services had "targeted for elimination by 2010." In October a Census Bureau report estimated that 35% of all Hispanics were without health insurance, compared with 22% of all blacks, 21% of Asians and Pacific Islanders, and 12% of non-Hispanic whites.

Native Americans. In March a U.S. District judge held the secretaries of Interior and Treasury in contempt for refusing to deliver documentation to settle a much-watched land-trust payment suit filed by a Blackfoot in Montana; also in March, an Interior Department lawyer testified that he refused an order to destroy Indian trust records involved in a class-action lawsuit against the government for back-due payments but added that more than half such records were missing. No resolution was in sight by year's end. In March the U.S. Supreme Court upheld the Chippewa tribe's right to hunt and fish on 13 million acres (5.3 million ha) of public land in Minnesota free of state regulation. In April the Justice Department joined the Oneida Indians in a suit demanding compensation for 250,000 acres (101 215 ha) of now much-settled and highly developed land between Syracuse and Utica, NY, that was taken by the state in violation of a 1794 treaty.

And in July members of the Oglala Sioux tribe and American Indian Movement activists marched from the Pine Ridge Reservation in South Dakota into Whiteclay, NE, to protest alleged treaty violations, alcohol sales, and murders. An ensuing clash with police and the evacuation of the town gained national attention for renewed Indian "militancy."

RANDALL M. MILLER
Saint Joseph's University, Philadelphia

Europe

The European Union (EU) began 1999 by introducing a common currency, the euro, which was adopted by 11 of its 15 members. As the year progressed, the EU had intended to focus its attention on several problems that needed to be solved before new members, mostly from Eastern Europe, could be admitted: reforms of the constitutional structure, reduction of the financial burden imposed by the common agricultural policy, and creation of a mechanism for implementing a common foreign and security policy. But action on these issues was delayed, first by the resignation of the entire European Commission in March after charges by the European Parliament of corruption and fraud by its members, then by the North Atlantic Treaty Organization's (NATO's) war with Serbia (*see* THE KOSOVO CRISIS, page 78), and finally by elections to the European Parliament.

The Euro. The creation of an Economic and Monetary Union (EMU) and an EU common currency was laid out in the Maastricht Treaty of December 1991. In March 1998 the European Commission had concluded that 11 of the EU members qualified for the EMU. Britain, Denmark, and Sweden chose not to adopt the new currency (now called the euro), and Greece was found not to have met the stringent fiscal standards required for membership. The European Central Bank (ECB), whose duty was to administer the euro, began work in Frankfurt in July 1998, and the value of the currencies of the 11 EMU participants was fixed as a percentage of the euro in December. The stage was set for the new currency's debut on Jan. 1, 1999.

The introduction of the euro went smoothly. After months of preparation, most banks, stock exchanges, and financial managers were ready to trade in euros. Almost every shop, hotel, and restaurant could draw up its bills in the national currency and the euro. The European Central Bank set up a changeover committee to handle relations with national banks during the transition period. At an exchange rate of $1.17 to the euro on Jan. 1, 1999, the new currency seemed satisfactorily strong. Almost at once, however, the euro began to fall in value. By June it was worth only $1.04, largely due to the very low growth in the German economy and higher deficits in the Italian budget and to slower-than-expected growth in the euro area as a whole. In Britain those who had opposed British adoption of the euro were congratulating themselves on their foresight. But as some economists predicted, the weaker euro stimulated exports by reducing prices without affecting the EU's very low inflation rate. The end of uncertainty over exchange rates was encouraging capital markets. Firms had tripled their bond issues. By October the euro was worth $1.075, although it dropped briefly below parity with the dollar in December.

Expected growth rates for the euro area were being shifted upward, with Germany beginning an export-led recovery and Spain, Portugal, and Ireland achieving dramatic growth. Even France, attempting to solve its high unemployment problem by introducing a costly 35-hour workweek, was maintaining a higher growth rate than the EU average. Moreover, structural reform was being undertaken to attack the EU's 10.3% unemployment rate through company mergers, deregulation, and negotiation of more-flexible work rules with the trade unions.

In view of this success, Greece made firm efforts to cut its deficit and public debt, with the aim of joining in 2001. Public opinion in Sweden and Denmark showed growing support for adoption of the euro, and British Prime Minister Tony Blair declared that he personally supported Britain's entry, given favorable economic conditions, and promised a referendum on the subject.

A New Commission. At the EU summit in Berlin on March 24–25, the organization's leaders had expected to discuss long-postponed changes in the budget and agricultural policy, but only eight days earlier, the whole European Commission had resigned. This drastic turn of events was provoked by the European Parliament, which, after refusing in December 1998 to accept the commission's budget accounts for 1996, ordered in January an independent committee to investigate charges of corruption. The committee found that in at least six cases, commission members had been guilty of fraud, mismanagement, and nepotism. In the most egregious offense, French Commissioner Edith Cresson had paid her dentist for almost nonexistent work. The Berlin summit quickly agreed to ask former Italian Premier Romano Prodi to replace Jacques Santer as the commission's president. Then it went on to issue a brief statement supporting the NATO action in Kosovo and to adopt a compromise on EU finances that unfortunately failed to attack the central question of the wasteful common agricultural policy that was costing $50 billion a year (half of the EU's entire budget).

Prodi was confirmed as president by the European Parliament in May, and his new commission, whose members each had agreed to resign if he requested it, was approved in September. Their tasks for the coming year, Prodi announced, would be to reform the commission's own operations, to prepare the intergovernmental conference that would revise the EU's constitution, and to facilitate early admittance of new members. In October a committee of so-called "wise men" reported to Prodi that among the needed constitutional changes were a greater use of majority voting when national governments were deciding EU matters and increased powers for Prodi himself before EU expansion.

A New European Parliament. The elections to the European Parliament on June 10–13 were more significant than they ever had been, not only because of the new prominence the parliament had taken in forcing out the Santer commission, but because the Amsterdam Treaty of 1997, finally ratified by the 15 member states in 1999, gave the parliament an increased role, not least by giving it the right to approve new commission members, including the president. The political parties attempted to campaign as European rather than national parties. Socialists were grouped in the Party of European Socialists, the strongest party in the outgoing parliament, and moderate conservatives in the European People's Party (EPP); a wide array of other groups were linked in such parties as the Greens, the Liberals, and the rightist Europe of Nations. The elections also offered the opportunity for voters to express their feelings on the performances of their own national governments.

As expected, perhaps because of worries about involvement in the war with Serbia, voters turned against the mostly center-left governments in the EU, giving the EPP 44 seats more than the Socialists. But the most glaring feature of the elections was voter absenteeism. Only 49% of voters went to the polls, compared with 57% in 1994. In Britain, where Conservative criticism of the euro had increased disillusionment with the EU as a whole, only 24% voted.

Common Foreign and Defense Policy. The EU had agreed in the Maastricht Treaty to establish common foreign and defense policies and the means to carry them out, but little had been done since then. At the Cologne summit in June, however, the EU's leaders appointed Javier Solana, the secretary-general of NATO, to be the EU's "high representative" for foreign and defense matters when his term with NATO ended in October 1999. At the same time, Prodi was attempting to increase the commission's role in foreign policy by assigning specific segments of foreign relations (such as trade, EU enlargement, and Third World aid) to individual commissioners and by giving Chris Patten, the British former governor of Hong Kong, the task of supervising the EU's foreign relations as a whole.

Efforts to find a mechanism by which the EU could undertake military operations ran into immediate difficulties. Europe's reliance upon U.S. airpower and logistical support in the Kosovo war led many observers to call for the EU to develop autonomous armed forces, especially for military action in Europe. But the proposal worried neutral members of the EU, such as Austria and Sweden, as well as Poland and Turkey, NATO members that had not been admitted to the EU yet. Moreover, the reactions within NATO countries to the Kosovo war, which varied from the outright opposition of the Greek public to the British willingness to undertake a land war, demonstrated the difficulty of achieving consensus on future military actions.

Speeding Up EU Enlargement. In 1993 the EU had laid down the criteria that future members must meet—a stable democracy, an impartial judiciary, a market economy, and the ability to accept the EU's laws. In 1997 the EU's leaders had divided the 12 applicants for membership into a fast track (Cyprus, Czech Republic, Estonia, Hungary, Poland, Slovenia), with which negotiations on early entry would begin, and a slow track (Bulgaria, Latvia, Lithuania, Romania, Slovakia), which would be helped to overcome the structural weaknesses that made early entry impossible. (Turkey was left out altogether.) In 1999, however, at their summit meeting in Helsinki in December, the EU leaders invited Bulgaria, Latvia, Lithuania, Malta, Romania, and Slovakia to begin negotiations in 2000 for full membership, and even gave Turkey the status of candidate for membership. The EU leaders also agreed to create by 2003 an EU rapid-reaction force of 60,000 troops for use in crisis zones where NATO as a whole was not involved.

F. ROY WILLIS
University of California, Davis

Family

The job of parenting got a closer look in 1999, as questions were asked about parental roles and how well parents know and understand their children, particularly in the wake of the school shooting in Littleton, CO. The latter incident brought new attention to the situation of U.S. teenagers today (*see* SPECIAL REPORT, page 250).

Parenting. Relationships between parents and children were seen as critical to children's future, but survey results did not always match expectations. One study, by child and family expert Ellen Galinsky, found that while 56% of parents think their children want more time with them, most children felt they had enough time. The importance of good child-father relationships was seen in a National Center on Addiction and Substance Abuse study that found that teens who did not get along with their fathers had a 68% greater risk of using drugs than those who did.

Awareness of boys' emotional needs continued to grow. News articles, books, and surveys showed that, following decades of focus on girls' needs, girls had gained in many areas, including academic achievement and self-esteem. Meanwhile, the number of boys in special education or involved in acts of violence had increased.

To improve the quality of parent-child time, educator Lynn McDonald developed the program known as FAST (Families and Schools Together). The FAST program, used in 34 states and four countries, helps parents understand how 15 minutes of daily, undivided attention can have a significant effect on a child's well-being.

Economics. The disparity between rich and poor continued to grow. The Center on Budget and Policy Priorities, a Washington, DC–based nonprofit organization, reported that in 1999 the richest 2.7 million Americans had as many after-tax dollars to spend as the poorest 100 million Americans. The difference had widened considerably since 1977. Then, the poorest one fifth had average after-tax incomes of $10,000 compared to the highest 1%, which had incomes of $234,700. By 1999, income among the poorest, adjusted for inflation, had dropped to $8,800; for the richest, it rose to $515,600.

The middle class lagged in the economic boom. A study by the Conference Board's Consumer Research Center in New York found that the pay of corporate chief executives rose 481% in current dollars between 1990 and 1998, while the average worker's pay rose only 28%. The Economic Policy Institute in Washington, DC, reported that the inflation-adjusted hourly wages of middle-wage men were lower in 1999 than in 1989.

Teenage Births. Both the teen-pregnancy rate and the number of children born to teenage girls dropped in 1998, according to statistics released by the U.S. Department of Health and Human Services. The rate of births was at a 40-year low, declining 5% among girls 15–17 years old, to 30.4 births for every 1,000 teens. This was a 21% drop since 1991. The birthrate among girls 10–14 fell 6%, to its lowest level since 1969. There also was a decline in the teen-pregnancy rate, with an estimated 98.7 pregnancies for every 1,000 teens ages 15–19. This was the lowest rate since figures first were collected in 1976.

Child Care. President Bill Clinton sought to expand the benefits provided by the Family and Medical Leave law. Clinton explored ways that states could use excess unemployment-insurance funds to subsidize parents who take time off to care for a new child. In February a Maryland state trooper was awarded $375,000 when a federal district-court jury agreed that he had been refused extended leave to care for his newborn daughter because he was a male.

A National Institute of Child Health and Human Development study of early child care found that the mother-child bond could be affected negatively during the child's first year when someone other than the mother takes care of the child. The small but statistically significant effect was dependent upon quality and quantity of child care, as well as on the mother's parenting style. Regarding child care for school-age children, a survey of police chiefs conducted by two George Mason University professors found that 86% believed youth crime could be reduced if the government increased after-school and child-care programs.

Adoption. In Tennessee the state Supreme Court upheld a 1995 law allowing adoptees 21 years of age or older to ask to see their records. Birth mothers must be notified of the request and are not required legally to see the child. Birth mothers tried to overturn the law, saying it violated their right to privacy. The verdict could have far-reaching consequences, as similar laws exist or are planned for Oregon, Massachusetts, Connecticut, and New Jersey.

KRISTI VAUGHAN, *Freelance Writer*

SPECIAL REPORT

Today's Teenager

© David Young-Wolff/PhotoEdit

Various shooting rampages at schools across the United States in the last few years not only terrorized students and entire communities but also put the spotlight on American teenagers as they prepare for a new century.

A Capsule View. In an attempt to analyze today's teenagers, the U.S. Department of Education collaborated with Shell Oil Company to survey more than 1,000 high-school students from across the country. The fourth annual Shell Poll— "Teens Talk to America," conducted by Peter D. Hart Research Associates—had some surprising insights into the minds of today's teenagers. In fact, U.S. Secretary of Education Richard Riley noted that the survey shows that most teenagers are "ambitious, striving, and open to the future."

A large majority of the teens reported that their parents' support and guidance are more important to them than that of their friends, and many of them said they were comfortable talking to their parents about their friends and social lives. Seventy-five percent said they were happy "most of the time." A similar percentage felt "pretty confident that things will work out" for them, and 81% expressed the intention to continue their education immediately after high school. Some 67% said that their schools taught good values, and 46% believed that their schools were preparing them "fairly well" for college. Regarding what caption they would like to see under their high-school yearbook photo, 54% responded with "most likely to succeed."

An October 1999 *New York Times*/CBS News nationwide poll of teens aged 13 to 17 offered additional insight into today's teenagers. According to that survey, 83% of today's teens think it is important to be able to stand up for oneself; 60% believe it is important to communicate one's feelings; and only 21% consider it important to be physically attractive. The poll also revealed that 87% of parents of teens establish what time teens come home at night; 30% of parents have guidelines about the amount of television their teenage children can watch; and 21% of parents set rules about whom their teenage children can befriend.

Although relatively small percentages of teens indicated in the Shell Poll that they feel pressures "to use drugs or alcohol" or "to be sexually active," and most respondents believed that their school is a "safe place, without violence," drug and alcohol use, an overemphasis on sex, and school violence are among the pressures facing today's teenagers. Adolescence, always a time of transition, once was made simpler by the many support systems—parents, schools, government programs—in place to help young teens find their way into adulthood. But by the late 1990s, many of those systems were ill-equipped to handle issues that are as unexpected as they are unwelcome.

When looking for causes behind the problems facing today's teenagers, inevitably the media is mentioned as a major source of unwelcome influence on teens. But increasingly, "media" that once consisted of newspapers, radio, and television now encompasses much more, including the Internet. Certainly, teens entering the new millennium are more connected to communication sources than their parents ever imagined. According to the *New York Times*/CBS News poll, 63% of all teenagers regularly use a computer at home, and 48% regularly go on-line. No previous generation had such access to information, or such potential to use it without adult supervision.

Yet today's teenagers seem to see the Internet as a very positive influence. In a survey of U.S. teens, 98% credited technology for making a positive difference in their lives. But other, more negative differences clearly exist. The American Academy of Pediatrics suggests that parents look for often-overlooked "media side effects," such as aggressive speech or fighting, nightmares, unhealthy nutritional habits, and smoking, drinking, or drug use.

While the media is the first target of many observers when discussing the problems of today's teenagers, parents—particularly in families where both parents work—are a close second. Yet three fourths of teens in one study see their mothers, typically the parent who is "blamed" for working, as "raising their children with good values." On the other hand, just more than one third believe their mothers really know what their children are doing.

Violence. Even the best parental supervision cannot protect a teen from violence in society, particularly random violence in the school setting. One newly recognized problem is the ease with which young people may obtain guns—and bring them to school. A national survey of tenth- and eleventh-grade males from 53 high schools nationwide revealed that a few juveniles carried weapons to gain respect from their peers, but most reported carrying firearms for protection.

According to the National Center for Education Statistics, 10% of all public schools experienced one or more serious violent crimes that were reported to law-enforcement officials during the 1996–97 school year. As a result, educators are considering a number of approaches to make campuses safer—measures from metal detectors to peer counseling. Many educators endorse including students in their own safety and safety planning.

Involving teenagers in devising their own solutions to problems is the theory behind another attempt at violence prevention—teen courts. The courts developed partially as a result of complaints that the legal system fails to provide guidance to first-time offenders, who particularly may benefit from a concerted effort to get to the root of their problems. Many juveniles first attract notice through seemingly minor infractions, such as vandalism. Increasingly, the legal system prefers to handle these nonviolent cases more informally; where teen courts exist, they provide another option. By 1999 there were more than 500 teen courts, also called "youth courts" or "peer courts," nationwide. Typical cases include vandalism, shoplifting, truancy, and illegal possession of alcohol. In teen court, teens serve as judge, prosecutor, defense attorney, and jury. Many of the participants are former teen-court defendants. Supporters believe teen courts are effective because they address crime prevention by imposing sentences of victim restitution and remediation.

While such efforts are very important, the serious underlying causes for teenage violence cannot be ignored. One theme often heard is the negative effect of television violence—almost all of it perpetrated onscreen by young males. According to a national poll used in the "Children Now" study, 74% of males in the programs and movies sampled performed antisocial behaviors, ranging from ridiculing others to defiant acts.

Issues among Girls. Perhaps even more serious is the impression among adolescent girls that male violence is directed at them as women. The Association of American University Women (AAUW) published results of a study of the issues that confront girls between the ages of 11 and 17. For 20% of those girls, sexuality issues—violence, pressure to have sex, sexual harassment—were major issues or struggles in their daily lives. Other studies have shown figures as high as 80%. Most striking about the content of the teens' replies are the adult concerns faced by girls as young as 11, and their belief that neither schools nor parents provide the help they need in dealing with worries such as sex and peer pressure.

Also of note is the researchers' finding that there are several cultures that represent today's typical American teen girl. Yet girls of all backgrounds found consensus in blaming "the media for promoting an unattainable body image," and said that they are "forced to grow up too fast as they face concerns of drugs, violence, sex, and pregnancy." Placed in dangerous situations by peer pressure and their belief that they are ready for grown-up responsibilities, teenage girls often discover they are at risk after it is too late. Physical abuse—from date rape to battering—occurs in about 10% of teen dating relationships. Most of the victims are girls, and their plight largely has escaped the notice of teachers, parents, and the legal system.

Health Issues. Yet beyond those dangers teenagers themselves recognize, they ignore

(continues)

many, particularly in the area of health habits. Adolescence brings its own sense of invincibility, and even teens who engage in risky behaviors often believe erroneously that they can focus on a healthy lifestyle after they are adults. For example, most young people who smoke regularly continue to smoke throughout adulthood, according to the Centers for Disease Control and Prevention (CDC). Smoking at an early age can damage the respiratory system and hamper the rate of lung growth. Even more serious is the risk that teens will move from tobacco to other addictive substances. The CDC states that teens who smoke are three times more likely than nonsmokers to use alcohol, eight times more likely to use marijuana, and 22 times more likely to use cocaine.

Such risky behaviors are found today in teens at an earlier age, according to a report from the Santa Clara County Public Health Department in California. The statistics from that report are especially daunting: A higher proportion of middle-school students than high-school students said they have smoked tobacco, used cocaine, and/or had sexual intercourse before age 13. Health officials blamed media images, less parental supervision, and early physical maturation as contributing factors in the rush toward risky or adult behaviors by children.

Approximately 80% of persons who use tobacco begin before age 18. Since tobacco use is the single leading preventable cause of death in the United States, the best way to ensure a longer life for today's teenagers is to educate them about the dangers of tobacco. This is no easy task, since the prevalence of smoking among U.S. high-school students increased 32% during the 1990s. The CDC believes that a number of strategies may be effective in reducing this trend, with emphasis on state-based comprehensive tobacco-control programs.

Teens also face additional risks, both legal and personal, when they drink. In 1997 more than 2,000 youth died in alcohol-related motor-vehicle accidents. More than one third of motor-vehicle fatalities among youth ages 15 to 20 are alcohol-related; the number of impaired drivers in fatal crashes is twice as high as the rate for drivers age 21 and older. One promising federal-government response to this problem is the "Enforcing the Underage Drinking Laws" program, which partially funds states' efforts to prohibit the sale of alcoholic beverages to minors and to prevent the purchase or consumption of alcoholic beverages by minors.

Researchers have associated drinking with early sexual intercourse in some teenagers. The United States has the highest teenage-pregnancy rate among developed countries, and public costs from teenage childbearing cost the nation $120 billion from 1985 to 1990. To receive public aid, most teens who become pregnant must live with a parent, legal guardian, adult relative, or in a group or maternity home. Those without such aid must rely on help from friends or charities—not a sound start for a new life. Yet close to 1 million teenagers become pregnant each year; 95% of those pregnancies are not intended.

Statisticians have identified four types of risk factors associated with teen pregnancy. They include early school failure, early behavior problems, family dysfunction, and poverty. Analysis also shows that, after the birth of a first child to a teen mother, the girl's involvement in outside work or school activities—or the achievement of high-school graduation or a passing score on the general equivalency diploma (GED)—often postpones a second teen birth. Many states have implemented community partnerships to prevent teen pregnancy, and indeed, the teen birthrate has declined slowly since 1991. If each birth could have been postponed just until the mother was at least 20 years old, an estimated $48 billion could have been used for other needs. Researchers also have found that participation in athletics lowers the rates of sexual activity, presumably because participation leads to a rise in self-esteem.

The 14% of teenagers who are not covered by health insurance also present a serious problem. Researchers at the Institute for Health Policy Studies and the Department of Pediatrics, University of California, San Francisco, found that the risk of being uninsured was higher for adolescents who are older, of color, or reside in low-income families and/or in single-parent households. They concluded that uninsured teens were four times as likely to have unmet health needs and twice as likely to go without a physician contact during the course of a year.

Each year, thousands of teenagers in the United States commit suicide, and the numbers increase annually. According to the American Academy of Child and Adolescent Psychiatry, teenagers often experience strong feelings of stress, confusion, self-doubt, pressure to succeed, financial uncertainty, and other fears. Some clinicians advocate a prevention strategy focused on problem solving.

Conclusion. In the Shell Poll, teenagers admitted that their lives are difficult but reported that the future looks promising. Teenagers seem to view the future with a hopefulness that many older adults lack. That is good news for today's teenagers and for society.

MARGARET A. DALTON

Fashion

The fashion industry in 1999 was marked by a continuation of the merger trend and of aggressive marketing of everything from upscale clothing to bedding under designer labels. Meanwhile, clothing designs themselves continued in a casual mode.

The Business. "Mergers" and "acquisitions" were the key words in the fashion business in 1999. For some time, fashion companies had been expanding global distribution, opening retail stores focusing on one designer name, and adding new price lines, cosmetics, accessories, and home furnishings to their collections.

Possibly the most aggressive marketer was the French company LVMH–Moët Hennessey Louis Vuitton, headed by Bernard Arnault. Arnault already owned Paris couture houses Christian Dior and Givenchy. He attempted to take over Gucci, the dominant Italian fashion house, but was repulsed in early 1999. Gucci instead sold a 42% stake to French house Pinault-Printemps-Redoute. In November, Gucci purchased Yves Saint Laurent.

Arnault's aim was to dominate the luxury fashion business. Though he lost Gucci, he had his eye on other prominent Italian fashion houses. He acquired a major interest in Fendi, in a joint venture with Prada. Arnault already had an interest in Michael Kors, who designed for Celine, a ready-to-wear house in Paris owned by Arnault, and for a sportswear collection in New York.

Major U.S. acquisitions included Ralph Lauren's purchase of Club Monaco, a chain of retail fashion stores, and the acquisition of sportswear house Anne Klein by Kasper. Jones Apparel bought Nine West, a shoe company. Estee Lauder, a cosmetics and fragrance house, bought Stila, a smaller company in the same field.

Anthony Horth, Courtesy, Lord & Taylor

© Daniel Simon/Liaison Agency

A dressier look was given to the basics with two of 1999's fashion trends: the use of an elegant cape in place of a traditional coat, far left, *and the embellishment of jeans and pants with embroidery or beading, as in the Versace pantsuit,* near left.

© Daniel Simon-William Stevens/Liaison Agency

Suits continued their tendency to be softer and more fluid, and often consisted of comfortable, sweater-like knits, left. *Meanwhile, the luxurious cashmere shawl or scarf in a warm, pretty shade was a favored accessory.*

© Daniel Simon-William Stevens/Liaison Agency

What was the purpose of all this activity? It was to strengthen the grip of the big names on the market, to help cut costs, and to improve distribution. Fashion was following the pattern set by heavy industry.

Designers. To encourage the development of new fashion talent, an organization called S.O.S. (for South of Seventh) began sponsoring three days of fashion shows in New York City, with about 30 companies participating. While the designers who showed had to pay for their own models, rentals were low, and an audience was provided. Geoffrey Beene presented his fall collection there to add his luster to the young hopefuls. Clothes ranged from cutting-edge to commercial and included tailored suits as well as mad futuristic designs.

Changes also were made in the regular fashion-show format. New York designers—who usually introduced their new collections after a week of showings in London, Milan, and Paris—decided instead to go first. They felt that, after three weeks in Europe, store buyers and journalists generally are too exhausted to give New York designers much attention. So designers showed in mid-September rather than the end of October. The first time the new schedule was tried was in fall 1998; more designers joined the earlier showings in 1999.

Some Europeans (Alexander McQueen and Donatella Versace) joined the throng at the New York shows. The hero of the shows turned out to be Bill Blass, who showed what was purported to be his last collection. He received a standing ovation, as did Ralph Lauren. Both interpreted the casual mode with distinction.

No new leader developed to guide fashion into untrodden paths; still, designers were pleased. At least they would not be accused of copying Europe—one of the reasons they offered for showing first.

Trends. Perhaps the most visible development in fashion in 1999 was the substitution of recognizable personalities—usually movie or pop stars—for the supermodels who had dominated the fashion runways for almost a decade. Kate Moss and Naomi Campbell occasionally appeared in shows, but the news media preferred to use pictures of Gwyneth Paltrow, Minnie Driver, and Nicole Kidman on their covers and in their fashion spreads.

The supermodels had priced themselves out of the market, designers said. Fashion editors believed that young actresses, through their appearances at the Academy Awards and other events, as well as their roles in films, had a wider recognition among their younger readers. In fact, interest in fashion among younger women seemed to have increased. Spurred by television shows, teenagers and even girls in the fifth or sixth grade were aware of the latest hairstyles, makeup, and clothing shapes.

Perhaps as a result of the emphasis on big business, creativity seemed to suffer. No prominent new name emerged, and the same trends that long were recognized as avant-garde continued to dominate. The casual look, derived from American sportswear, continued, but now was slightly more decorated. Jeans, for example, had embroidered legs. Tops often were beaded or embroidered, although the shapes remained simple. After several seasons of emphasis on gray or black, there were more pretty colors. An occasional ruffled hem softened the basic look, but there were still plenty of cargo pants (and now cargo skirts), twin sweater sets, tank tops, and camisoles. Luxury fabrics enhanced the casual feeling; there was much cashmere and silk. The item of the season was the pashmina scarf, made of the very finest cashmere yarn and wrapped around fashionable shoulders day and night.

The ever-popular casual look in fashion was enhanced in 1999 with the use of bright colors and chunky, textured knits for such staples as the turtleneck sweater, below.

© Daniel Simon-William Stevens/Liaison Agency

Because designers figured that the millennium year would give rise to many parties, they focused on evening clothes. Still, these too were in the casual mode, often made of two pieces, like a cashmere sweater with lace pants or a satin skirt. It was the idea of separates carried into evening.

One encouraging aspect of the fashion market was the emerging development of better-fitting, more-adventurous active sports apparel for women, spurred largely by the growing popularity of women's tennis, basketball, and soccer. Some sports figures took an active part in deciding what they would wear, including tennis star Venus Williams, who helped design seven outfits made by Reebok for her to wear in the U.S. Tennis Open tournament; Olympic figure skater Tara Lipinski, who influenced the decorative use of butterflies on a skating dress by Capezio; and tennis player Anna Kournikova, who played in sexy dresses by Adidas.

Fashion's traditional touchstones, like hem length, had less impact. While designers generally endorsed longer, calf-length skirts, they did not expect the mini to disappear. Clothes were expected to be comfortable, and drawstring waistlines on pants and skirts were popular. Stiletto heels still were favored by designers, who liked the look on the runway, but most acknowledged that low-heeled sandals would be worn more widely.

A number of designers presented handbags on the runway. These were usually soft shapes with short leather straps, meant to be worn over the shoulder. Hairstyles were usually not elaborate; long hair flowed gently down the back and was held in place with barrettes. Earrings were not as prominent as they had been, but bracelets occasionally appeared.

The dominant spirit in fashion continued practical and realistic. At the moment, wildly adventurous styles were taking a back seat to clothes that worked. Ponchos and anoraks were important in silk and cashmere for dress-up occasions. There was plenty of glitter in the form of sequins and metallic embroideries, but the underlying shapes were simple. The feeling for casual clothes was dominant. It was not a time for ostentation.

BERNADINE MORRIS
Freelance Fashion Journalist

Finland

FINLAND • Information Highlights
Official Name: Republic of Finland.
Location: Northern Europe.
Area: 130,127 sq mi (337 030 km²).
Population (July 1999 est.): 5,158,372.
Chief Cities (Dec. 31, 1997 est.): Helsinki, the capital, 539,363; Espoo, 200,834; Tampere, 188,726.
Government: *Head of state,* Martti Ahtisaari, president (took office March 1, 1994). *Head of government,* Paavo Lipponen, prime minister (took office April 13, 1995). *Legislature* (unicameral)—Eduskunta.
Monetary Unit: Markka (5.7072 markkaa equal U.S.$1, Nov. 11, 1999).
Gross Domestic Product (1998 est. U.S.$): $103,600,-000,000 (purchasing power parity).
Economic Indexes (1998, 1990 = 100): *Consumer Prices,* all items, 115.6; food, 95.9. *Industrial Production,* 139.5.
Foreign Trade (1998 U.S.$): *Imports,* $32,301,000,000; *exports,* $42,963,000,000.

In 1999, Finnish President Martti Ahtisaari played a key role in helping to engineer the Kosovo peace deal in Serbia (*see* THE KOSOVO CRISIS, page 78). The Finnish Conservatives made headway in the parliamentary elections, but the government of Social Democratic Prime Minister Paavo Lipponen maintained a comfortable majority. Meanwhile, the economy continued its excellent recovery.

Foreign Policy. Capitalizing on Finland's extensive experience in dealing with Russia, President Ahtisaari helped to broker a deal in June that ended the bombing of Serbia by North Atlantic Treaty Organization (NATO) forces in return for the withdrawal of Serbian troops from the province of Kosovo and Russian participation in a NATO peacekeeping force.

Meanwhile, Helsinki remained committed to strengthening integration in the European Union (EU). When Finland assumed the EU presidency during the second half of 1999, its main priority was to introduce a "northern dimension," a program establishing a new northern border region that would include the northwestern provinces of Russia; the Baltic states of Estonia, Latvia, and Lithuania; and Finland itself. The region was intended to be part of the larger Baltic Sea zone and to promote Russian acceptance of enlargement of the EU, with the strategic goal of integrating Russia into Europe as a democracy and a market economy.

Despite the fact that Finland had assumed the EU presidency and had the strongest Nordic voice in the EU, it had the lowest rate of participation of the three Nordic countries in the June elections to the European Parliament, with a voter turnout of only 30%. The Social Democratic Party and the Left coalition lost one seat apiece, while the Greens picked up one seat, doubling their total to two, and the Christian League won a seat for the first time.

Politics. In the March parliamentary elections, the National Coalition Party (also called the Conservatives) gained seats, ending up with 46, while the Social Democratic Party lost 12, slipping to 51 seats. Nevertheless, the so-called Rainbow Coalition—the Social Democrats, the Conservatives, the Greens, the Left-Wing Alliance, and the Swedish People's Party—continued in power with no major policy changes under Lipponen.

Despite Ahtisaari's impressive diplomatic performance abroad, plans continued to

Finnish President and European Union Chairman Martti Ahtisaari (right) *welcomed more than 40 world leaders, including Romanian President Emil Constantinescu* (left), *to the first Stability Pact summit on July 30, 1999. The meeting, convened not long after Ahtisaari helped broker a peace agreement in Serbia, discussed ways to promote democracy and economic prosperity in the Balkan region.*

change the Finnish constitution so that foreign policy no longer would be solely a presidential prerogative. Under a new amendment scheduled to take effect before presidential elections in 2000, foreign policy would be formulated jointly by the president and parliament.

Economy. In 1999 unemployment in Finland dropped to below 10%, its lowest level in eight years. The Finnish economy grew at nearly 4% in 1999, with the same level expected in 2000. This rate was a little slower than in 1997 and 1998, but much higher than the EU average. Inflation was low at about 1%. Much of Finland's economic improvement derived from the explosive growth of the high-tech sector, particularly the mobile-phone company Nokia. More than 25% of Finnish exports were high-tech products, outpacing Finland's traditional staple exports of pulp and paper for the first time.

LEIF BECK FALLESEN, *Editor in Chief*
"Boersen," Copenhagen

Food

Although crops in the eastern and southern United States, Russia, and parts of Africa were affected by adverse weather conditions, most of the world's consumers enjoyed plentiful supplies of affordable, high-quality food in 1999. To offset serious international food shortages, the United States implemented one of the largest food-assistance programs on record, sending aid that included pork, poultry, soy products, and food and feed grains to 41 countries. Total Northern Hemisphere crop production was about steady, while food-grain harvests increased modestly in the Southern Hemisphere. Key issues explored during 1999 included food safety, the routine feeding of antibiotics to livestock, and genetically modified (GM) foods.

Genetically Modified Foods. During the 1990s, genetic modification of food grew increasingly common, as scientists developed the ability to transfer genes from unrelated plants to major food crops. The altered plants often would have a higher resistance to insects and weed killers, as well as improved nutritional quality. By 1999 at least 40 varieties of such plants had cleared government reviews in the United States and Europe.

But in the wake of events such as the outbreak of mad-cow disease in Britain in 1996 and the discovery of dioxin-contaminated animal feed in Belgium in 1999, consumers in the EU began to call for policies to improve food safety. In particular, there were concerns about the possible adverse environmental impact of GM foods. Consumer advocates also argued that consumers had a right to know whether and how a food had been genetically modified. The EU responded by requiring that a food be labeled if at least one of its ingredients contained a minimum of 1% genetically modified DNA or protein. In some countries, the new labeling requirements also applied to restaurants, food caterers, institutional food providers, and school-lunch programs. The EU also considered implementing genetic-origin labeling for livestock- and poultry-feed ingredients. Other nations committed to developing genetic-origin labeling included Japan, Russia, New Zealand, Australia, Thailand, Canada, and the United States.

Fearing negative consumer reaction to GM foods, major supermarket chains in Europe dropped them once the EU food-labeling program was in place. A number of food manufacturers indicated they also would stop producing GM foods. The growing global concern about genetic modification prompted the United States to begin formulating a GM-food labeling plan for discussion at the world trade talks to be held in January 2000.

Food Safety. In September, Tyson Foods, the world's largest producer of chicken products, announced that it would do limited test marketing in 2000 of chicken treated by electronic pasteurization, a type of irradiation designed to reduce the risk of pathogens and improve food safety. Two major beef processors also planned to test electronically pasteurized beef patties. Meanwhile, the U.S. Food Safety Inspection Service (FSIS) announced that a new testing method called immunomagnetic separation (IMS) would be a standard procedure in all of its field-service laboratories. The test, which detects the disease-causing bacterium *Escherichia coli* 0157:H7 (*E. coli*) in uncooked meat, reportedly was four times more sensitive than previous methods.

Researchers at Iowa State University experimented with a virus that might reduce or replace the routine use of antibiotics in pigs, hence reducing the risk that antibiotic-resistant organisms could develop. The virus, bacteriophage, reproduces in bacterial cells and kills them but does not infect animal or human cells.

ROBERT N. WISNER, *Iowa State University*

France

For France, 1999 marked the return of self-confidence after a long period of moroseness and self-doubt. A booming economy accompanied by a significant decline in unemployment resulted in an optimism the French had not known for years. This new mood allowed Prime Minister Lionel Jospin to declare in late 1999 that he foresaw a full-employment economy within a decade, a statement that would have been greeted with incredulity (if not derision) only a year earlier. The reborn optimism also was manifested by the decline of the extreme right-wing National Front. Meanwhile, France strongly supported the bombing campaign by the North Atlantic Treaty Organization (NATO) against Serbia and also dispatched troops to stop the unrest in the Indonesian province of East Timor in September.

Economy. In 1999 the economy dominated the news in France, and the tidings were generally good. On January 1 the euro was introduced in the financial markets of France and ten other countries of the European Union (EU). The euro lost ground to the U.S. dollar during the first few months of the year before partially recovering. In November and December, however, it plummeted, ending 1999 almost even with the dollar. The very fact that the euro was introduced on schedule was a major victory for its proponents, including France, which had been forced to make major financial sacrifices to meet the tough standards set out by the Maastricht Treaty.

More significant for the French, however, was the strong performance their economy registered throughout 1999. A 2.9% growth rate was expected for the year. The International Monetary Fund (IMF) in October praised the French economy and predicted a 3% growth rate in 2000, which was expected to be the highest among the G-7 countries. There was also good news on the inflation rate, which was just 0.6% in 1999 despite strong internal demand.

But the best news by far was the constant decrease in the unemployment rate. The drop began as a steady trickle, but as 1999 progressed, it became a stream and then a near-torrent. In the year ending October 31, the number of unemployed declined by 9.4%, with a 3% decline in the month of September alone. The drop for the months of July, August, and September was greater than for all of 1998, which itself had registered a noticeable decrease in unemployment. The International Labor Organization estimated that the unemployment rate in France fell from 12.6% in June 1997, when the Socialists won the anticipated legislative elections, to 11% at the end of September.

With the economy thriving, French companies frequently launched takeover bids against each other in an effort to create firms large enough to survive in the global marketplace. In February the banks Société

© François Mori/AP/Wide World Photos

Although France made significant progress toward reducing unemployment in 1999, the problem continued to be a focus of attention for both the government and the public. In October thousands of demonstrators, right, *organized by the Communist Party, marched through the streets of Paris to protest the double-digit unemployment rate and demand a more equitable distribution of wealth.*

Générale and Paribas announced they would merge, thereby creating the world's fourth-largest financial institution. But in March, Banque Nationale de Paris (BNP) announced a public-share offering that would result in the merger of all three banks. BNP's action sparked a bruising six-month battle for shareholder votes that resulted in the BNP acquiring 65% of Paribas but less than 37% of Société Générale shares; Société Générale thus was able to remain independent. The battle between Paribas and Société Générale on one side and BNP on the other was an example of the less important role played by the government as the French economy became increasingly market-oriented. Officials had offered discreet support for the three-way merger because it would have created a world-class financial player, but they admitted their unwillingness to influence the outcome directly.

The bank battle was still in full swing when the French-Belgian oil group Total Fina announced in early July an unfriendly bid for its French rival Elf Aquitaine to create the world's fourth-largest oil company. Two weeks later, Philippe Jaffre, Elf's president, put forward a counterbid to form two separate companies. The battle ended in September, when Total Fina and Elf Aquitaine agreed to a friendly merger under terms set by Total Fina.

© Michel Lipchitz/AP/Wide World Photos

Labor unions in France held several strikes and demonstrations during 1999 over such issues as unemployment, high taxes, and worker safety. A work stoppage by transit employees in June caused traffic jams in Paris, above.

Much of 1999 was consumed by the debate on the government's plan to reduce the workweek from 39 hours to 35 without an accompanying drop in pay. In presenting the project, a key element of the Socialist platform, Labor Minister Martine Aubry argued that the new law would create 100,000 jobs a year. But the conservative opposition, the business establishment, and even some members of the left-wing governing coalition countered that half that number of jobs would be created at best. To back up their argument, they pointed to an earlier law, approved in June 1998, that had reduced the workweek for 2.2 million employees but had generated only 30,000 new posts. The project's astronomical cost—about $18 billion a year, due to lower taxes on companies that adopted the reduced workweek—formed the center of the debate.

Leading the charge against the project was France's major business organization, which in an unprecedented show of force brought together about 30,000 executives for a rally against the law in early October. Several weeks later the business group announced it would stop payments into the social-security system if the government insisted on tapping into benefits to finance the program. In the face of this virulent opposition, Aubry dropped her original plan and announced that the law would be underwritten instead from cigarette and alcohol taxes. The legislation—mandating that companies with more than 20 employees must comply by January 2000 and the rest by January 2002—finally was approved, but no one seemed satisfied. The business community and the right charged that it was another example of government interference in business, while the left argued that the government had backtracked to the point of making the law ineffective.

The hero of the year in France was Jose Bove, the head of the independent Farmers Union, who headed a commando raid during the summer against a McDonald's restaurant still under construction. Bove, who was jailed briefly until both French and U.S. farmers paid his bail, came to symbolize farmers' fight against industrial food production. France also led the EU's ban on

U.S. beef treated with hormones, a policy that led Washington to impose 100% tariffs on numerous French products.

Politics. In 1999 the government continued to be shared by a Socialist prime minister and a conservative president, the longest cohabitation between two opposing camps in France since Gen. Charles de Gaulle founded the Fifth Republic in 1958. By midsummer prominent members of the right, led by former President Valéry Giscard d'Estaing, were urging President Jacques Chirac to end the power-sharing and call presidential elections before their scheduled date in 2002. But Chirac, still recovering from his mistake of calling early legislative elections that led to the Socialist victory in 1997 and also aware of Jospin's strong popularity rating, rejected the advice. As a result, the government and the chief executive continued to watch each other closely, with Chirac firing carefully chosen salvos at the government over issues ranging from the reform of the judicial system to the establishment of the 35-hour workweek.

Frequently, however, Jospin's strongest critics came from the ranks of his own governing coalition, especially the Greens and the Communists, who accused him of having become a free-market liberal at the expense of Socialist ideals. The height of discontent within the government came in September, after Jospin said he was powerless to do anything about the decision by the tire manufacturer Michelin to reduce its workforce by 10% over a three-year period despite record profits. The controversy evaporated, however, and the prime minister's popularity continued to be unusually high after two and one-half years in power.

Finance Minister Dominique Strauss-Kahn, a pillar of the Socialist administration who maintained the confidence of the financial markets during the delicate transition to the euro, resigned in November after allegations that he had received about $100,000 in legal fees for fictitious work performed for a student health-insurance fund. Investigating magistrates believed the fund was used illegally to finance the Socialist Party. Although Strauss-Kahn proclaimed his innocence, the revelations were a sharp setback for the government, which prided itself on its honesty after years of scandals.

But the major event of the year in French politics concerned the National Front. In January, after months of infighting, a breakaway faction of the extreme right-wing party led by Bruno Megret held a special congress to create a new party. Megret was furious after Jean Marie Le Pen, the party founder responsible for the meteoric rise of the National Front throughout the 1980s and 1990s, appointed his wife, Jany, to head the National Front's list for the European Parliament elections. The results of the split were quickly evident. In the elections for the European Parliament in June, the two National Front parties together managed to gather only 9% of the vote, compared with 15% in the first round of the 1995 presidential election.

Things were not much better for the traditional conservative parties in the European Parliament elections. The two main components of the right, Chirac's Rally for the Republic Party (RPR) and the Union for French Democracy, together won just 22% of the vote, compared with about 38% for the Socialists, Greens, and Communists, which make up the rest of the ruling coalition. Perhaps most indicative of the malaise on the right was the impressive 13% recorded by a breakaway faction from the RPR led by former Interior Minister Charles Pasqua, who based his campaign on opposition to the EU. The RPR's disastrous showing (just 12.7%) led to the resignation of Nicolas Sarkozy, the party's fourth president in just four years and the second one to leave his post in 1999. A number of political observers proclaimed the death of the RPR, but the right wing's real problems were its internal divisions and failure to provide a clear and coherent alternative to the ruling Socialists.

The most dramatic events in France took place on the Mediterranean island of Corsica, where Prefect Claude Erignac, the highest government official there, had been assassinated in February 1998. A fire in April 1999 that destroyed Chez Francis, one

FRANCE • Information Highlights

Official Name: French Republic.
Location: Western Europe.
Area: 211,208 sq mi (547 030 km^2).
Population (July 1999 est.): 58,978,172.
Chief Cities (1990 census): Paris, the capital, 2,175,200; Marseilles, 807,726; Lyons, 422,444.
Government: *Head of state,* Jacques Chirac, president (took office May 1995). *Head of government,* Lionel Jospin, prime minister (took office June 1997). *Legislature*—Parliament: Senate and National Assembly.
Monetary Unit: Franc (6.4751 francs equal U.S.$1, Dec. 24, 1999).
Gross Domestic Product (1998 est. U.S.$): $1,320,000,-000,000 (purchasing power parity).
Economic Indexes (1998, 1990 = 100): *Consumer Prices,* all items, 116.0; food, 110.7. *Industrial Production,* 108.3.
Foreign Trade (1998 U.S.$): *Imports,* $286,847,000,000; *exports,* $305,493,000,000.

© George de Keerle/Liaison Agency

While on an official visit to the United States in February, French President Jacques Chirac (right) *conferred with Michel Camdessus, managing director of the International Monetary Fund (IMF), in Washington, DC. Among the issues they discussed was the euro, the single European currency that had been introduced a month earlier.*

of the many illegal restaurants that thrive on Corsican beaches, turned out to be a political bomb that badly destabilized the Jospin government, if only briefly. Investigators discovered evidence indicating that the blaze was set by gendarmes acting under the orders of Bernard Bonnet, Erignac's successor. Following the revelations, the prefect was fired and jailed for more than a month. Bonnet, who became something of a media star, insisted that the government in Paris had been kept regularly informed of his actions. The scandal led to one of the periodic flare-ups in the normally placid cohabitation between Chirac and Jospin, but it also unblocked the stalled investigation into Erignac's murder, with five of the six alleged killers quickly arrested. The capture of Erignac's alleged assassins calmed the tensions.

The violence on the island took a new turn in November, when separatists set off two bombs in broad daylight near government offices in the regional capital of Ajaccio. It was the first time that bombs had gone off during the day and with a clear purpose to kill. However, the incident caused only a few minor injuries. But by mid-December, Jospin was able to convince all of the island's political parties, including the separatists, to participate in talks in Paris.

The government also had serious difficulty passing a law giving homosexual couples more rights, which would fulfill a campaign promise by Jospin. In January more than 100,000 people marched through Paris to protest the law, but the government's real problems again came from its heteroclitic coalition. A first vote on the legislation in the National Assembly in October 1998 had been postponed, because large numbers of Socialist deputies, fearing a negative reaction from their constituents, simply did not show up. In an effort to dilute opposition, the law was modified to allow two unmarried persons of any sex living under the same roof to enter into a union and be entitled to the same legal rights as married couples in areas such as housing, inheritance, income taxes, and immigration. The legislation finally was adopted in October 1999.

France also tried to come to terms with its mistakes, both from the distant past and its more recent history. In March a special court acquitted former Prime Minister Laurent Fabius and one of his ministers, Georgina Dufoix, in a case involving the contamination of thousands of people with the HIV virus through blood transfusions. Former Health Minister Edmond Hervé was found guilty of negligence by delaying the testing of donated blood, but he was given no punishment. In October, Maurice Papon, 89—sentenced to ten years in prison in 1998 for deporting more than 1,500 Jews to Nazi concentration camps during World War II—fled the country to escape jail. Before long, however, he was found living under an assumed name in a Swiss hotel, returned to France, and jailed. The fact that he had been allowed to keep his passport and move freely since his condemnation was a poignant reminder of the past complicity of French authorities regarding former war criminals. His quick arrest saved France from international embarrassment.

EDUARDO CUE, *Freelance Writer, Paris*

Gardening and Horticulture

A bounty of blossoms and edibles from the garden were introduced in 1999.

All-America Selections Awards. All-America Selections (AAS), a nonprofit organization that has been evaluating introductions of new, seed-grown varieties for home gardens since 1933, introduced nine award-winning varieties for the year 2000.

Cosmos "Cosmic Orange," an easy-to-grow plant for beginning gardeners, offers a great deal of color on a 12-inch (30.5-cm)-tall, pest- and disease-resistant, plant. "Cosmic Orange" was judged superior for foliage.

Dianthus "Melody Pink," a unique, annual cut flower with stems up to 12 inches (30.5 cm) long topped with sprays of 1-inch (2.5-cm) pink flowers, produces flowers throughout the growing season on cold- and heat-tolerant plants.

Sunflower "Soraya" was the first sunflower in AAS history to earn an award. "Soraya" produces 4- to 6-inch (10.2- to 15.2-cm) orange flowers with chocolate-brown centers on self-supporting plants with a height of 5 to 6 ft (1.52 to 1.83 m).

Tithonia "Fiesta del Sol," the first dwarf Mexican sunflower, thrives on full sun and heat, and reaches a mature height of 2 to 3 ft (0.61 to 0.91 m) with single, 2- to 3-inch (5.1- to 7.6-cm) orange daisy flowers. "Fiesta del Sol" is said to be virtually carefree, is drought tolerant, and may attract butterflies.

Bedding-plant winner *Catharanthus roseus* "Stardust Orchid" is the first vinca with an orchid flower and a large white center. "Stardust Orchid" is both heat- and drought-tolerant and requires minimal care.

Vegetable winners for 2000 included: Cabbage "Savoy Express," with non-bitter, crinkled or waffle-like leaves; "Mr. Big," an improved English or garden pea; "Blushing Beauty," a disease-tolerant bell-pepper plant that produces sweet, 4-inch (10.2-cm) wide and long fruits with a color changing from ivory to pink to red as they mature; and "Indian Summer" sweet corn, featuring festive kernels of yellow, white, red, and purple.

All-America Rose Selections. Ready for the year-2000 planting season were three winners announced by All-America Rose Selections (AARS)—"Knock Out," "Crimson Bouquet," and "Gemini."

"Knock Out," a glowing example of disease resistance at its best, produces a continuous show of cherry-red blossoms, 3 to 3.5 inches (7.6 to 8.9 cm) in diameter, emitting a light tea-rose fragrance. This maintenance-free "flowering shrub" flowers on stems with glossy foliage tinged with eggplant purple with a swirl of burgundy. "Knock Out" was hybridized from a combination of eight roses, including "Carefree Beauty" and "Razzle Dazzle" seedlings.

"Crimson Bouquet" is a vigorous-growing, disease-resistant, hardy grandiflora exhibiting 4-inch (10.2-cm) bright red blossoms on a 4.5-by-3.5-ft (1.37-by-1.07-m) plant with 14- to 18-inch (35.6- to 45.7-cm) stems. It was hybridized from a combination of "Bad Füssing" and "Ingrid Bergman." The deep green, glossy leaves provide a perfect backdrop for the bright red blossoms.

"Gemini," a hybrid tea with large double blossoms in coral pink and rich cream, is a highly disease-resistant plant featuring healthy, dark green foliage. The blossoms slowly spiral open to reveal 4.5-inch (11.4-cm) flowers with 25 to 30 petals on long cutting stems. "Gemini" is a hybrid of "Anne Morrow Lindbergh" and "New Year."

RALPH L. SNODSMITH
Ornamental Horticulturist

Photos, Courtesy, All-America Rose Selections, Inc.

"Crimson Bouquet," extreme right, *and "Gemini,"* right, *were All-America Rose Selections for the year 2000. "Crimson Bouquet," a grandiflora, exhibits bright red blooms, while "Gemini," a hybrid tea rose, has blended shades of coral pink and rich cream.*

Genetics

In 1998–99 it was discovered that the cystic-fibrosis gene protects its carriers from bacterial infection; the production of the various parts of a flower is under separate genetic controls; the genetic determination of organ asymmetry is different in birds and mice; and three specific genes can transform a normal cell into a cancer cell.

A Protective Gene. Cystic fibrosis is a genetic recessive disease. Both parents of the patient are healthy but are carriers (heterozygotes) of the gene. In the past, this disease resulted in the death of affected (homozygote) children by age 1 or 2. Surprisingly, one person in 25 is a carrier of the gene for the disease. One possible explanation for such a high frequency of a recessive deleterious gene is that the gene protects its heterozygote carriers from an otherwise debilitating parasitic infection.

G. Pier and his colleagues at the Harvard Medical School in Boston, MA, investigated the ability of the bacterium *Salmonella typhi* to enter human intestinal epithelial cells that were growing in tissue culture. This bacterium causes typhoid fever. The scientists found that those cells that were heterozygous for the cystic-fibrosis gene were protected from invasion by the *S. typhi* bacteria. This situation resembles that of the sickle-cell-anemia gene, which protects its heterozygote carriers from the protozoan that causes malaria.

Production of Floral Parts. In a flower the reproductive organs (stamens and carpels) are located in the center. Surrounding these parts is a circle of colorful petals that are surrounded by a whorl of leaflike sepals that originally enclosed the floral bud. Although the formation of a flower has been known to be under the control of a gene called leafy, the genetic control of the development of the individual parts of a flower was unknown.

D. Weigel and his associates at The Salk Institute for Biological Studies in La Jolla, CA, reported that the protein product of the leafy gene activates another gene, called agamous, that causes the production of the stamens and carpels. If the agamous gene is nonfunctional, the reproductive organs are replaced by additional petals, making the flower extremely colorful and attractive, but sterile. Other research by E. Meyerowitz and his coworkers at the California Institute of Technology in Pasadena, CA, demonstrated that the leafy gene protein also activates other genes that are responsible for the production of petals and sepals. These findings will help breeders produce ornamental and crop plants with specifically designed flowers.

Genetics of Organ Asymmetry. Although vertebrates such as the chicken and the mouse appear outwardly to be bilaterally symmetrical, many of their internal organs (heart, liver, spleen) are positioned asymmetrically. The developmental pathways that lead to this left-right asymmetry are under genetic control. In the developing chick, internal-organ asymmetry is known to be determined by the action of two genes. One, FGF8 (Fibroblast Growth Factor-8), acts to organize the structures on the right side of the abdominal cavity, whereas a different gene, SHH (Sonic Hedgehog), determines those of the left side. Both FGF8 and SHH genes are found in many organisms, including the mouse.

E. Meyers and G. Martin at the University of California, San Francisco, examined the roles of FGF8 and SHH genes on the development of the mouse. To their surprise, they found that FGF8 is the left-side determinant, whereas SHH controls the right side. Uncovering the full significance of this difference requires similar studies on other organisms, including humans.

Genetics of a Cancer Cell. Most body-cell lines go through a pattern of divisions that are limited in number and result in a final nondividing state. Whether cells are dividing or quiescent depends on the interactive effect of the proteins produced by the division-promoting and division-suppressing genes of the cell. For normal cells to become cancerous, division-promoting genes must be continuously active, and division-suppressing genes must be kept nonfunctional.

W.C. Hahn at the Whitehead Institute for Biomedical Research, Cambridge, MA, and others reported that they were able to transform normal human cells into cancer cells by incorporating three genes into the DNA of normal cells. One of the three genes, ras, is an extremely active cell-division-promoting gene (oncogene). A second gene, large-T, is able to inactivate the normal division-suppressing gene of a cell. The third gene, hTERT, controls the production of the enzyme telomerase, which is essential if cell division is to continue indefinitely. This discovery should lead to early-warning tests that will monitor the genes involved in the formation of a cancer.

Louis Levine, *City College of New York*

Geology

The discovery of a hidden fault below the city of Los Angeles and the unearthing of the oldest complete fossil of a mammal highlighted the field of geology in 1999.

Earth's Core and Mantle. According to a new theory proposed in 1999, there are two distinct layers in Earth's core: a mass of solid iron rotating within an outer layer of molten iron. Previously, scientists thought the planet's hardened nucleus was comprised of a uniform iron crystal, but seismologists studying the data from several historic earthquakes inferred differently. The team noticed that quake-induced seismic waves resonating through Earth from north to south traveled faster than those moving from east to west. By simulating the seismic activity on computers, the scientists discovered that the waves became bogged down in a region 120 mi (193 km) below the surface of the inner core. They concluded that this region must not be a uniform crystal, but rather must contain different material properties than the rest of the core.

For years, scientists have pointed to seismic data indicating that Earth's mantle had two distinct layers that never mix, while others have insisted that geochemical signatures show that the mantle churns like boiling oatmeal. In 1999 geophysicists proposed a new model for the mantle that appeased both sides of this debate. According to the model, slabs of Earth's crust forced to dive into the mantle by tectonic activity encounter a barrier 1,055 mi (1 700 km) below the surface, which prevents the material from mixing with the deep mantle. In a few spots, however, the deep mantle bubbles up through the barrier, carrying its signature to the surface as erupting volcanoes. This theory explains all of the seemingly contradictory data.

Earth's Crust. In March geologists confirmed the presence of a previously unidentified fault system under the city of Los Angeles. Using geological data from oil companies, the scientists determined that a 25-mi (40-km) crustal scar runs from beneath downtown Los Angeles to the Coyote Hills in the north and then turns east to reach Brea. The scientists believe that this fault system was responsible for earthquakes in Whittier Narrows in 1987 and Northridge in 1994.

Scientists at Lehigh University in Bethlehem, PA, made the unusual claim that the Indus River may be causing the Nanga Parbat mountain in the Himalayas to grow taller. They theorized that the river slices a deep gouge through Earth's crust, weakening it. At the same time, the Indian and Asian tectonic plates collide and compress the crust, and the weak spot bulges out in response. The team also said that a mass of hot, buoyant rock lies deep below the crust. As the Indus removes soil during erosion and lightens the load on Earth's crust, this hot rock rebounds, forcing the mountain to swell upward.

© Pata Roque/AP/Wide World Photos

On Sept. 20, 1999, an earthquake of 7.6 magnitude devastated towns and villages, including Dongshi, right, in central Taiwan. More than 2,100 persons lost their lives, and some 100,000 were left homeless in the disaster.

Geologists linked the extinction of 35 kinds of ancient mammals and one species of flightless bird more than 3 million years ago to an asteroid or comet hitting the Earth. The evidence supporting this occurrence was not a crater, but an 18-mi (29-km) scar of green glass and red rock in the ocean cliffs of Argentina, lying just below the layer of hardened dust that contained the now-extinct animals. Chemical signatures in the rock point to the Earth experiencing a devastating impact 3.3 million years ago, and independent atmosphere and water-temperature studies indicate that around that time, the region underwent a climate change that could have killed off the animals.

Paleontology. Paleontologists uncovered the world's oldest complete mammal fossil, dating to 120 million years ago. Named *Jeholodens jenkinsi*, the rodent-sized animal had front legs that looked mammalian, but its back legs were splayed like those of reptiles. A group of prehistoric animals known as monotremes, which evolved into egg-laying mammals, walked with a reptilian gait. All other mammals arose millions of years after the monotremes, from an animal known as a therian. The new discovery, paleontologists claimed, offered two possibilities for how the anatomy of modern mammals developed. According to one theory, modern shoulders and arms evolved twice, once along the monotremes' branch and again along the therians' branch. The other scenario is that shoulders and arms evolved once in an ancestor common to *Jeholodens*, the monotremes, and the therians.

A prehistoric nesting site in Patagonia yielded thousands of eggs belonging to the titanosaur, a kind of sauropod. Not only were the 70-million-year-old fossils the first of their kind, they were also the first to show embryonic bone and fossilized baby dinosaur skin. Titanosaurs typically grew to about 45 in (114 cm) long, but these hatchlings were only 15 in (38 cm) long, revealing a stage in the dinosaur's life never before seen. The fossils also indicated that baby titanosaurs hatched without the bony, armored plates typically embedded in the skin of adults.

Earthquakes. On January 25 a magnitude-6.2 earthquake devastated western Colombia's coffee belt. More than 20 cities and towns suffered damage, while at least 1,185 people lost their lives. At least 100 people died following a magnitude-6.4 quake that rattled northern India on March 28. Officials reported the cataclysm as the strongest event in the area in nearly 100 years. A magnitude-6.9 earthquake destroyed parts of central Mexico on June 15. Hundreds of church towers and many historic buildings toppled. The event claimed 14 lives. On September 30 another quake hit the region, this time a magnitude-7.4 event, killing at least 33 more people.

Perhaps the worst earthquake of 1999 hit northwestern Turkey on August 17. The magnitude-7.4 quake shook an area extending from the city of Eskisehi to the Greek and Bulgarian borders. More than 24,900 people were injured, and at least 15,600 died. Scientists examining the site a couple of weeks later found evidence of tsunamis 66 ft (20.1 m) high. On September 13 a magnitude-5.8 aftershock injured more than 420 people and killed seven. Two months later, northwestern Turkey was struck by another earthquake, which killed more than 300 people.

A magnitude-5.9 quake jarred Athens, Greece, on September 7. Hundreds of buildings turned to rubble, leaving more than 50,000 homeless. At least 135 people died. On September 20 a magnitude-7.6 quake jolted Taiwan, leaving more than 2,100 people dead. Three weeks after the catastrophe, officials announced that the quake had caused considerable alterations to the land.

Volcanoes. Evacuation efforts began April 8, as Mount Cameroon—one of Africa's largest volcanoes—emitted a slow-moving river of lava measuring more than 1 mi (1.6 km) wide and 100 ft (30 m) thick. The volcano had started erupting on March 28. Researchers from the Woods Hole Oceanographic Institution in Massachusetts announced in April that they had found a 14,000-ft (4 270-m) volcano submerged under the Pacific Ocean in the Samoa Islands. They dubbed the hidden peak Fa'afafine, a Samoan word essentially meaning "wolf in sheep's clothing." On June 22 the Mayon volcano in the Philippines spewed a thick cloud of smoke and ash 4 mi (6.4 km) into the sky. Thousands of residents and tourists were evacuated, and one man died while fleeing the eruption. A plume of hot ash shot into the sky on October 7, after Ecuador's Guagua Pichincha volcano erupted three times. The cloud rose 12 mi (19.3 km) high, smudging the skies over the capital city of Quito. Two days earlier, the airport and local schools had closed after both Guagua Pichincha and Tungurahua volcanoes erupted.

TRACY STAEDTER
"Scientific American Explorations"

Georgia

GEORGIA • Information Highlights
Official Name: Georgia.
Location: Western Asia.
Area: 26,911 sq mi (69 700 km²).
Population (July 1999 est.): 5,066,499.
Chief City (1991 est.): Tbilisi, the capital, 1,279,000.
Government: *Head of state and government,* Eduard A. Shevardnadze, president (elected November 1995). *Legislature* (unicameral)—Supreme Council (Parliament).
Monetary Unit: Lari (1.960 lari equal U.S.$1, Jan. 3, 2000).
Gross Domestic Product (1998 est. U.S.$): $11,200,-000,000 (purchasing power parity).
Foreign Trade (1997 est. U.S. $): *Imports,* $931,000,000; *exports,* $230,000,000.

Georgia continued to strengthen its ties with the West in 1999, but relations with Russia remained tense. Parliamentary elections in October reinforced President Eduard Shevardnadze's power. No progress was made on resolving the sovereignty disputes in Abkhazia and South Ossetia. The economy did not repeat the spectacular growth it had enjoyed in 1997 and 1998, but it remained stable.

Domestic Affairs. In January, despite public protests, a law intended to prevent discrimination was passed that removed the description of ethnicity in Georgian passports. In May the government granted a general amnesty to several of Shevardnadze's political opponents. But that same month, a number of people, including a former senior defense-ministry official, were arrested and charged with planning to assassinate Shevardnadze. Two important constitutional changes increased the powers of Georgia's state minister and raised the minimum percentage of votes required for a party to earn proportional representation in Parliament from 5% to 7%.

Georgia's new Parliament, elected under the revised rules on October 31, comprised members of the ruling Citizens' Union of Georgia, which increased its majority; the Union for Democratic Revival; and Industry Will Save Georgia, a new party representing manufacturing interests. Although the election was marred by irregularities, international observers declared the results fair. There also were elections in South Ossetia (May) and Abkhazia (October), but the results were not recognized as legal by either the Georgian government or the international community.

Internationally mediated talks on the return of Georgian IDPs (internally displaced persons) to Abkhazia and the question of Abkhazia's status within Georgia were fruitless. In March the Abkhazian government took unilateral action on the return of IDPs, but very few returned, due to the absence of security guarantees. Georgian guerrillas continued to operate in Abkhazia, and in August the mandate of Russian peacekeeping forces was renewed by Tbilisi.

Georgia's gross domestic product (GDP) grew 1.7% in the first half of 1999, considerably less than in previous years. Service on foreign debt took up 21.4% of the budget, a crushing burden. Real growth was higher, due to the large size of the illegal economy, estimated to be 40% of the total economy. Inflation was in single digits, and unemployment officially stood at 14%. Severe electricity shortages in the fall forced Energy Minister Teimuraz Giorgadze to resign in November. In the spring, however, the Baku-Supsa oil pipeline began operation, and a ferry terminal at Poti opened.

Foreign Policy. Georgia continued its pro-Western direction—entering the Council of Europe, receiving approval for entry into the World Trade Organization (WTO), increasing defense cooperation with Turkey and the United States, and pursuing regional cooperation with Armenia and Azerbaijan. Relations with Russia remained tense over Georgia's withdrawal from the Commonwealth of Independent States (CIS) collective security treaty, the removal of Russian border troops from Georgia's border with Turkey, and Russia's war in Chechnya. But Russia agreed to close the two largest of its four military bases in Georgia by July 1, 2001. President Shevardnadze made trips to the United States, the Netherlands, and Japan to encourage foreign investment.

STEPHEN F. JONES, *Mount Holyoke College*

Germany

The Federal Republic of Germany celebrated its 50th anniversary in 1999. Never before in history has a political order brought more freedom, peace, and prosperity to the Germans and their European neighbors than this democracy so hastily established in 1949 on the ruins of Hitler's Third Reich. The year 1999 also marked the tenth anniversary of the fall of the Berlin Wall and the end of the communist East German regime. The subsequent unification of the divided country meant the fulfillment of West Germany's primary goal. Appropriately, 1999 also saw the German government after 50 years finally leave its provincial and

© Jockel Finck/AP/Wide World Photos

Tens of thousands of Germans gathered at the Brandenburg Gate in Berlin, left, *on Nov. 9, 1999, to celebrate the tenth anniversary of the fall of the Berlin Wall—an event that ultimately led to the reunification of East and West Germany not long afterward.*

provisional capital in Bonn and move once again to Berlin.

The Economy. The German economy in 1999 remained sluggish. Real growth was only about 1.5%, and unemployment held steady at about 11%. Inflation continued to be very low at less than 1%. Unemployment was the major problem facing the government of Chancellor Gerhard Schröder. Among the almost 4 million Germans without work in 1999, more than 35% had been jobless for more than a year.

High wages, cumbersome government regulations, and elaborate and costly social programs continued to deter employers from investing and creating new jobs. German firms increasingly moved jobs to neighboring countries such as Poland and the Czech Republic, where wages were less than a fourth of the German level.

GERMANY • Information Highlights

Official Name: Federal Republic of Germany.
Location: North-central Europe.
Area: 137,931 sq mi (356 910 km²).
Population (July 1999 est.): 82,087,361.
Chief Cities (June 30, 1995 est.): Berlin, the capital, 3,470,200; Hamburg, 1,706,800; Munich, 1,240,600.
Government: *Head of state,* Johannes Rau, president (took office July 1999). *Head of government,* Gerhard Schröder, chancellor (inaugurated November 1998). *Legislature*—parliament: Federal Assembly (Bundestag) and Federal Council (Bundesrat).
Monetary Unit: Deutsche mark (1.9091 D. marks equal U.S.$1, Jan. 3, 2000).
Gross Domestic Product (1998 est. U.S.$): $1,813,000,000,000 (purchasing power parity).
Economic Indexes (1998): *Consumer Prices:* all items (1990 = 100), 118.6; food (1995 = 100), 111.0. *Industrial Production* (1995 = 100): 108.5.
Foreign Trade (1998 U.S.$): *Imports,* $471,478,000,000; *exports,* $543,292,000,000.

The weak economy was cited by some of Germany's European neighbors as a major factor in the sharp decline in the value of the euro, the common European currency, which debuted in January. Originally valued at U.S.$1.17, the euro by year's end had dropped to parity with the greenback. Germany accounts for one third of the 11-nation euro zone's total output.

Politics. The new government of Chancellor Schröder, elected in late 1998, got off to a terrible start. His party, the Social Democrats (SPD), was divided sharply between a traditionalist wing led by Finance Minister Oskar Lafontaine and the modernizers under Schröder. Lafontaine wanted to stimulate consumer demand through tax cuts for lower- and middle-income groups and increases in spending for social programs. Schröder favored a more pro-business policy of reductions in the costs of hiring new employees, tax breaks for investors, and reductions in welfare-state spending. Lafontaine also advocated reforming the international monetary system by returning to fixed currency rates and restraining international capital movements. The conflict between the two men came to a head in March, when Lafontaine—following an emotional cabinet meeting at which Schröder declared that his government must stop antagonizing business interests—resigned as finance minister and leader of the Social Democratic Party. Schröder became SPD chairman, and Hans Eichel was appointed the new head of finance.

This intraparty conflict cost the SPD dearly at a series of local and state elections throughout the year. The SPD faithful were dismayed at Schröder's pro-business approach and stayed home in protest. Longtime strongholds of the party in the Ruhr region fell to the Christian Democrats for the first time in the post–World War II period. By late 1999, however, Schröder had stopped the party's free fall. His intervention to save one of Germany's largest construction companies from bankruptcy—and hence from the loss of thousands of jobs—boosted his popularity. The long-term success of his government, however, would depend on reducing unemployment.

The cornerstone of Schröder's employment program was his "Alliance for Jobs," which consisted of business, labor, and government leaders who were to develop new programs to deal with unemployment. But the work of the Alliance stalled in 1999 over conflicts between business and labor. Labor unions pushed for an earlier retirement age to reduce unemployment, while business and government disagreed, citing higher costs and the already-strapped social-security budget.

Schröder also wanted to stimulate investment by cutting taxes for business. This in turn would require budget cuts, especially in social programs. Ignoring labor-union protests and opposition within his own party, Schröder in late November pushed through $16 billion in cuts, largely in social programs. Further cuts were scheduled in order to reduce the state's share of the national income from the current 49% to 40% by 2003. Labor unions also were upset with the government's plans to phase out sector-by-sector wage bargaining, which had made Germans the best-paid workers in Europe. Schröder wanted the unions to negotiate with individual companies, based on productivity gains.

Johannes Rau, below, *was elected president of Germany by a special federal assembly in May 1999. He took office in July, as the government prepared to move to Berlin.*

© Jockel Finck/AP/Wide World Photos

The major opposition party, the Christian Democrats (CDU), made substantial gains in state and local elections at the expense of the Social Democrats and was able to secure a majority in the upper house of parliament. This gave the CDU the ability to block some of the government's programs. But the Christian Democrats also had their problems in 1999. The party could not offer any alternative to Schröder's budget cuts. Like the Social Democrats, the Christian Democrats were divided between those who wanted to preserve the extensive welfare state and others who wanted to cut taxes and spending to meet the challenges of global competition.

In November the CDU was hit by a major scandal involving former Chancellor Helmut Kohl's fund-raising activities. At a tense press conference in Berlin, Kohl admitted that he indeed had kept secret bank accounts outside of regular party channels to reward favored CDU regional organizations and leaders. He vehemently denied, however, that the funds came from illegal kickbacks. The Social Democrats were not so sure, and in December they convened a special parliamentary investigation committee. They charged that much of Kohl's special funds came from kickbacks by German arms dealers from sales of military vehicles to Saudi Arabia during the 1991 Persian Gulf war. As 1999 ended, German prosecutors announced that a criminal investigation of Kohl would be conducted. The former chancellor, meanwhile, refused to reveal the source of the donations.

Schröder's junior coalition partner, the Greens, paid a heavy price in 1999 for their entrance into the government. Identified since their founding in 1979 above all with the issues of environmental protection and peace, the Greens saw their plans to phase out Germany's remaining nuclear-power plants delayed indefinitely, and they had to

© Ira Schwarz/Reuters/Archive Photos

The Christian Democrats (CDU) did well against the Social Democrats (SPD) in 1999 state elections. In Saarland the CDU's Peter Müller, above, *was elected premier.*

support the North Atlantic Treaty Organization's (NATO's) bombing campaign during the Kosovo crisis. For many traditional supporters, this was too much to endure, and the party lost votes at all local and state elections throughout the year, as well as in the June election to the European Parliament.

The Party of Democratic Socialism (PDS), the successor to the former ruling Communist Party of East Germany, continued to receive the support of more than 20% of voters in the eastern states. The former communists profited from continuing dissatisfaction with the slow pace of unification and, above all, from the 20% unemployment level in a society that had known only full employment under the communists. But in 1999 the PDS also focused much of its efforts on developing a following in West Germany, where the party, a decade after unification, remained insignificant. To succeed in the West, the party must distance itself from its past and reduce the influence of traditional communists in its leadership.

A Decade of Unification. In November, Germans marked the tenth anniversary of the fall of the Berlin Wall and the unification of their country 11 months later. During the ten years, about $900 billion had been spent on the former German Democratic Republic. These payments amounted to about $11,000 for every man, woman, and child in Germany. This money had given the East a state-of-the-art telephone system, new Autobahnen, canals, ultramodern train lines, and much cleaner water and air. Thanks to West German subsidies, East Germany's elderly now received pensions that equaled or exceeded those in the West. East German wages had climbed to about 75% of the West German level, but productivity still lagged well behind that of the West. While comprising about 20% of the total population, easterners contributed only about 10% to the total gross domestic product (GDP) and only 8% of all tax receipts. Thus the improved East German standard of living still was subsidized by West German taxpayers. West German transfers to the East in the past decade accounted for about 80% of the current state debt. Many westerners were asking how much longer they would be expected to transfer such sums to their eastern cousins. Yet 1999 opinion polls found that about two thirds of the public in East and West both supported unification in spite of the costs.

Holocaust Issues. After ten years of sometimes emotional discussion, the parliament in June passed legislation authorizing a Holocaust memorial in Berlin. Designed by the American architect Peter Eisenman, it will be built near the Brandenburg Gate, in the heart of the city where the Nazis planned the extermination of European Jewry. Eisenman's design features a vast field containing 2,700 concrete pillars. A research and study center also will be part of the memorial.

Another legacy of the Nazi era was resolved in late December, when German industry and government officials, after months of bitter negotiations with U.S. government representatives and lawyers, agreed to establish a $5.2 billion fund to compensate surviving slave laborers who had been forced to work at German farms and factories during World War II. Most of the recipients of this money would be non-Jews from Eastern Europe who had not benefited from the more than $60 billion Germany had paid to Holocaust survivors during the previous 50 years.

A New Citizenship Law. In one of its few successes in 1999, the Schröder government in May was able to pass legislation reforming the country's 1913 citizenship and naturalization laws. Based largely on the principle of lineage or blood, the old laws made it difficult for Germany's 7.5 million foreign residents to become naturalized citizens. The new legislation grants automatic citizenship to anyone born in Germany, if at least one parent has lived in the country for at least eight years. Dual citizenship is allowed until the age of 23, when a decision must be made. The new laws also liberalized the naturalization process for foreign residents by reducing the required length of residency and the costs of the process.

German Catholics and the Vatican. The conflict between Germany's Roman Catholic hierarchy and the Vatican over the church's role in abortion counseling continued in 1999. Since 1995, abortions have been allowed in Germany, provided a woman receives counseling at a government-approved center. The centers are required to offer women alternatives to abortion, but the final decision remains with the woman, as long as she has obtained a certificate from a counseling center. The German bishops argued that, in some cases, the counseling efforts prevent abortions and hence should be continued. The Vatican contended that by issuing the counseling certificates, the Catholic clergy was facilitating abortion. In October the bishops accepted the Vatican position and ordered their clergy to stop participating in the work of the counseling centers by early in 2000.

Foreign Policy. A new chapter in post–World War II German foreign policy began in March, when Luftwaffe jets took off from bases in Italy to participate in attacks on Serbia as part of NATO's Kosovo operation. It marked the first time since the 1940s that German military forces, once the most feared on the continent, had engaged in combat. The action was not without controversy. Several members of the SPD-Green government opposed the military deployment. It was one factor in the March resignation of Schröder's finance minister, Oskar Lafontaine. At a stormy Green Party convention, Foreign Minister Joschka Fischer, who once advocated Germany's withdrawal from NATO and the country's unilateral disarmament, was pelted with bags of paint after he argued passionately for Germany's responsibility to stop Serbian aggression in Kosovo. But while participating in the air war, the Schröder government steadfastly argued against the deployment of ground troops to drive out Serbian forces. The cease-fire spared the government from an open conflict with the United States and Britain over this issue. Germany contributed 6,000 troops to the peacekeeping force in the region.

Throughout 1999, Germany also sought to expand its influence in Eastern Europe. It continued to take the lead in sponsoring European Union (EU) membership for Poland, Hungary, and the Czech Republic. The EU's aid package for the Balkans, estimated at about $30 billion, also was largely a German-led project. In its relations with Russia, the Schröder government began to distance itself from President Boris Yeltsin and to cultivate closer ties with his possible successors, above all the mayor of Moscow, Yuri Luzhkov. In September, Luzhkov paid a visit to Berlin and was given an elaborate welcome by Schröder and Foreign Minister Fischer. Like other Western leaders, Schröder was surprised by Yeltsin's resignation as 1999 ended. Official visits to Poland and Hungary also were part of the chancellor's 1999 itinerary.

Berlin's relations with Washington were marred in 1999 by the continuing dispute over the files of East Germany's infamous secret police, the Stasi. Shortly before or after the collapse of East Germany in 1989–90, the U.S. Central Intelligence Agency (CIA), in a major coup (Operation Rosewood), was able to secure the top-secret archives of the Stasi's entire foreign-spy operations. In February during a visit to Washington, Chancellor Schröder expected the Bill Clinton administration to return the archives, which Berlin considers German property. President Clinton, however, at the insistence of the CIA, refused even to discuss the matter. In response, German officials hinted that they might curtail operations of U.S. intelligence agencies in Germany. Later in the year, representatives of Germany's Federal Intelligence Service (BND) were allowed access to some, but by no means all, of the files. It was suspected that the files implicate some Germans and other Westerners who still hold powerful political positions.

In September, Israeli Prime Minister Ehud Barak became the first foreign leader to visit Berlin since it once again became the capital of unified Germany. During the visit, Barak emphasized Germany's special responsibility to combat extremism and urged the Schröder government to compensate World War II slave laborers. The Federal Republic had become Israel's closest European ally, and all postwar governments had given strong political and economic support to the Jewish state.

Culture. On the cultural front, the year's highlight came when Günter Grass was awarded the Nobel Prize in literature. (*See also* LITERATURE—*Overview*.)

DAVID P. CONRADT
East Carolina University

Great Britain

Britain's Labour government continued to remain generally popular in 1999, but lost ground in midyear to the Conservative opposition in elections to the European Parliament. British attitudes toward joining a single European currency became a defining issue in the nation's politics. Prime Minister Tony Blair pursued a policy of constitutional devolution that gave Scotland its own parliament and Wales a legislative assembly. The automatic right of hereditary peers to sit and vote in the House of Lords was abolished. The British economy performed unexpectedly well. By year's end, the long-running Northern Ireland crisis appeared close to resolution.

Domestic Politics. The year opened inauspiciously for Prime Minister Tony Blair. At Christmastime 1998, Peter Mandelson, the trade secretary and a loyal political friend, had resigned from the cabinet after secretly accepting a large housing loan from Geoffrey Robinson, the paymaster general, who also quit the government. The departure of Mandelson, a principal architect of the "new" Labour Party in the early 1990s, the *Economist* magazine reported, left Blair appearing "isolated among senior colleagues," most prominently John Prescott, the deputy prime minister and a leading representative of "old"—i.e., traditional socialist—Labour values. Blair, however, remained highly popular with the voting public, in contrast to William Hague, the leader of the opposition Conservative Party, whose personal ratings remained stubbornly low.

In early 1999, Hague spent much effort berating the Blair government for allegedly failing to fulfill promises that had figured prominently in Labour's successful 1997 general-election campaign. Government statistics confirmed that pledges to cut patients' waiting lists for treatment under the National Health Service had not been redeemed, and that class sizes in most schools were higher than Blair and his ministerial team had promised. The Conservatives also claimed that government-funded schemes designed to put unemployed youngsters back into work were proving only moderately effective.

The Conservatives' comparative failure to make headway on domestic political issues encouraged Hague to put the focus on Britain's relations with the European Union (EU). On January 1 most EU members had joined a single European currency—the euro—but Britain conspicuously retained the pound sterling. The government refused to rule out joining a single currency in the future, and Blair himself made it plain that he favored Britain's doing so, as long as necessary economic criteria could be met. The implication was that Britain might adopt the

Prince Edward, the 35-year-old son of Queen Elizabeth and Prince Philip, and Sophie Rhys-Jones, a 34-year-old commoner, were married before 550 guests in St. George's Chapel at Windsor Castle on June 19, 1999.

euro after the next general election, due in May 2002, if the people voted in a referendum in favor of doing so. Hague, however, committed his party to eschewing membership in the euro for "at least two Parliaments" (effectively a minimum of ten years) and adopted the slogan that Britain should be "part of Europe, but not run by it."

In elections for the European Parliament on June 10, Hague's approach paid off. In a strikingly low voter turnout (fewer than 25% made it to the polls), the Conservatives won 36 seats to Labour's 29. Analyzing the Labour setback, a leading political research group concluded that the government party had done poorly in areas where its performance had been strong in the 1997 general election. Blair commented that Labour had lost support because voters had not understood fully Labour's "yes, but not yet" approach to the euro. Hague and his strategists interpreted the result to mean that the British electorate was unmoved by Blair's enthusiasm for the EU.

At the Tory party's annual conference in October, Hague unveiled a blueprint for a "common sense revolution," including British insistence on the right to opt out of legislation agreed to by other members of the EU—a development that would require amending the Treaty of Rome, the EU's constitution. During the conference, Hague tended to be overshadowed by a series of voluble public appearances by Baroness Margaret Thatcher, the former prime minister, who claimed that Hague was embracing "my" policies on Europe.

Hague's attempts to get a grip on his party's fortunes were not enhanced by the death in September of Alan Clark, a senior Conservative member of Parliament (MP). Michael Portillo, a former Conservative cabinet minister who lost his seat in the 1997 general election and was seen by many as a likely leadership challenger to Hague, won a by-election in Clark's constituency.

Throughout the year debate—much of it rancorous—centered on Blair's earlier promise to outlaw foxhunting with dogs—a pursuit that riles Labour supporters but is defended stoutly by large numbers of Conservatives. Supporters of foxhunting staged rallies in several British cities, insisting that a ban on the activity would cause the loss of thousands of jobs in the countryside. After long hesitation, Blair—apparently concerned that Labour risked losing support in rural areas, where it had done well in the 1997 general election—announced that the government would support a private member's parliamentary bill to ban foxhunting before the next general election. But he also appointed an independent commission to examine the "economic implications" of a ban.

In a sign of continuing confidence in his own leadership, Blair in October reshuffled his cabinet, retiring or demoting "old" Labour members and replacing them with supporters of "new" Labour policies. He appointed former cabinet minister Peter Mandelson as Northern Ireland secretary. Marjorie (Mo) Mowlam, holder of that post since Blair formed his first government, became coordinator of government policy. In January, Paddy Ashdown, leader of the Liberal Democrat Party, announced his resignation. Scottish-born Charles Kennedy was chosen for the party post in August.

Constitutional Affairs. The year witnessed several important constitutional changes that carried forward the Blair government's declared policy of making Britain a more democratic society and bringing the decision-making processes of government closer to the people. On May 6 voters in Scotland elected a devolved national parliament, with headquarters in Edinburgh, and their counterparts in Wales elected a legislative assembly located in Cardiff. The elections, held under proportional representation, produced results sharply different from the party balance in the House of Commons, where an essentially two-party battle between Conservatives and Labour, with the Liberal Democrats in a distant third place, has been the norm for decades.

In Scotland, Labour took 56 parliamentary seats—failing by nine to win an outright

GREAT BRITAIN • Information Highlights

Official Name: United Kingdom of Great Britain and Northern Ireland.
Location: Island, western Europe.
Area: 94,525 sq mi (244 820 km²).
Population (July 1999 est.): 59,113,439.
Chief Cities (mid-1997 est.): London, the capital, 7,122,200; Birmingham, 1,014,400; Leeds, 727,500; Glasgow, 611,700; Sheffield, 530,300.
Government: *Head of state,* Elizabeth II, queen (acceded Feb. 1952). *Head of government,* Tony Blair, prime minister and First Lord of the Treasury (took office May 1997). *Legislature*—Parliament: House of Lords and House of Commons.
Monetary Unit: Pound (0.6108 pound equals U.S.$1, Jan. 3, 2000).
Gross Domestic Product (1998 est. U.S.$): $1,252,000,-000,000 (purchasing power parity).
Economic Indexes (1998, 1990 = 100): *Consumer Prices,* all items, 129.2. *Industrial Production,* 109.1.
Foreign Trade (1998 U.S.$): *Imports,* $314,036,000,000; *exports,* $271,853,000,000.

© Colin McPherson/Corbis-Sygma

On July 1, 1999, Queen Elizabeth and Prince Philip joined Donald Dewar (center), *Scotland's first minister, as the Scottish Parliament, a new 129-seat legislature that had been elected in May, formally opened.*

majority. It was obliged to form an administration with the Liberal Democrats, who won 17 seats. The Scottish National Party, which favors eventual full independence for Scotland, became the official Opposition, with 35 seats. The Conservatives' 18-seat tally put them in third place. Donald Dewar, hitherto Scottish secretary in the London government, became Scotland's first minister. He headed an administration with considerable power over Scottish domestic (though not foreign or defense) policy, and with the right to vary taxes beyond levels set by the Westminster Parliament by up to 3%.

The outcome in Wales was more complex. In voting for a legislative assembly with more-limited powers over spending than the Scottish parliament, Labour won 28 seats, the Conservatives nine, and the Liberal Democrats six. Plaid Cymru, champion of a fully self-governing Wales, unexpectedly notched up 17 seats, including several that Labour had regarded as among its strongholds. Many voters who usually supported Labour appeared to object to Tony Blair's decisive backing for Alun Michael as Labour Party leader in Wales in preference to the more popular—and less predictable—Rhodri Morgan. Michael, lacking an absolute majority in the 60-seat assembly, was obliged to work in an uneasy alliance with Plaid Cymru and with the Conservatives, who were never enthusiastic about devolution; the Liberal Democrats provided most of the opposition.

A common feature of the Scottish and Welsh legislatures was their lack of pomp and ceremony. Members began addressing each other by their first names and kept strict 9-to-5 hours. In the summer it became clear that there was potential for contention between the London government and the two devolved administrations. Dewar found himself in a jurisdictional dispute with his successor as Scottish secretary, and Blair had to step in and warn them of the dangers of public squabbling.

A predictable knock-on effect of devolution for Scotland and Wales was a stirring among some politicians and political groups in England in favor of more clear-cut parliamentary representation for the English themselves. Hague resisted suggestions that there should be an English parliament, distinct from Westminster, to deal with English matters. He did, however, sponsor the view that Scottish and Welsh members of the House of Commons should be denied the right to vote on measures specifically affecting England.

Another aspect of Blair's commitment to devolution—that London, for the first time in its history, should have its own democratically elected executive mayor—created considerable problems for the Labour government. The Conservatives chose the millionaire novelist Lord (Jeffrey) Archer as their candidate, but Labour made heavy weather of its selection. Blair did not disguise his unhappiness with the candidacy of Ken Livingstone, a former leader of the defunct Greater London Council, and seen in 10 Downing Street as an embodiment of "old" Labour values. The prime minister threw his support behind Frank Dobson, who resigned his cabinet post as health secretary to run for the mayoralty in an election scheduled for May 2000. Livingstone, however, remained a popular figure, with opinion polls indicating that he was the preferred choice of most Labour voters in London. In November, Archer was forced to withdraw his mayoral candidacy after allegations that he had lied in connection with a libel case. London's Conservatives had to select a new candidate. Steve Norris, a former transport minister who had a reputation for extramarital affairs, emerged as a possibility.

The Labour government's commitment to end the ancient right of hereditary peers to sit and vote in the House of Lords produced an outcome at variance from what Blair originally had sought. There was never any doubt that, by mobilizing its huge majority in the House of Commons, the government would secure its reform. But in face of stiff resistance from members of the upper chamber, Blair agreed that, as an interim measure, 92 hereditary peers out of a total of about 800 should be allowed to retain their seats alongside "life" peers, whose titles lapse when they die. In early November the "hereditaries" decided among themselves who should be allowed to remain, and on November 11 the peers reluctantly voted for a bill effectively ending centuries of assured aristocratic tenure in the House of Lords. Blair was reported widely to favor a wholly appointed body, but Hague said this would produce an upper house of "Tony's cronies." In October, Lord Wakeham, a former Conservative cabinet minister whom Blair had asked for suggestions, recommended that at least part of a reformed upper chamber should be elected democratically.

Economy. Unemployment continued to fall throughout the year—to about 1.2 million in November—and inflation rates remained below the government's target level of 2.5%. The main surprise was a rapid expansion in the economy that Gordon Brown, chancellor of the exchequer, had failed to forecast the previous year when he said he anticipated growth of 1% to 1.5%. In his March budget, Brown cut the basic rate of income tax from 23% to 22%. In November he estimated future annual growth of 2.5% or better, and consequent budget surpluses, for years ahead. Brown said the government was aiming at closing the "productivity gap" between Britain and the United States by encouraging an "entrepreneurial spirit" throughout the country. He announced tax breaks for small investors, including share-ownership schemes for company employees. He pledged funds to equip all schools with computers and agreed that annual above-inflation increases in the price of motor fuels should end.

© Adil Bradlow/AP/Wide World Photos

Britain's Prime Minister Tony Blair (left) *conferred with Thabo Mbeki, who was elected president of South Africa in June, during his January 1999 visit to Cape Town.*

Blair and his ministers continued their policy of tightening up welfare and social-security payments. Despite heavy criticism from within Labour Party ranks, the government curbed state-paid incapacity payments to handicapped people and intensified its policy of means-testing a range of other social-security benefits. In a further echo of Thatcherite policy, Blair announced plans to privatize partially the London Underground and Britain's air-traffic-control systems.

Foreign Policy. As the seriousness of the crisis in Kosovo became apparent, Blair ordered British aircraft into the bombing campaign and 8,000 troops into neighboring Macedonia. He was reported widely to be in the forefront of those privately urging the Bill Clinton administration to contemplate deploying ground forces in Kosovo against the Slobodan Milosevic regime in Yugoslavia. Blair insisted that the bombing of Serbian targets was a legitimate response to the Belgrade government's policy of "ethnic cleansing" in Kosovo.

When, in September, Indonesia failed to prevent renegade militia in East Timor from challenging the outcome of the territory's independence referendum, Blair and his ministers faced problems. Soon after taking office in 1997, the Labour government had committed itself to an "ethical foreign policy" and ruled out the supply of weapons to governments likely to use them against their own people. At the outset of the conflict in East Timor, however, British-supplied Indonesian air-force trainer aircraft were observed in the skies over the capital, Dili. Downing Street denied newspaper reports that other British-made military equipment was being used by Indonesian forces against the East Timor population.

Gen. Augusto Pinochet, Chile's former dictator, remained under house arrest in Britain, pending extradition moves against him initiated in 1998 by judges in Spain, who alleged that he had been responsible for murder and torture while in power. On March 24 a seven-strong House of Lords legal panel ruled that Pinochet did not enjoy immunity from prosecution as he had claimed, but weakened the case against him by limiting charges to acts of torture allegedly committed after December 1988, when Britain had implemented an antitorture convention. In October, Pinochet's lawyers asked a London magistrate to rule that the 83-year-old general should not be extradited to Spain, but the court rejected the argument. Pinochet's lawyers then filed an appeal.

The government welcomed an autumn ruling by the EU that United Kingdom beef, hitherto considered unmarketable because of fears of "mad cow disease" in British cattle, was safe to be sold on European markets. But France and Germany refused to accept the ruling. The EU decided to take the case to the European Court of Justice.

Northern Ireland. The government, together with the Irish Republic and the Clinton administration, kept up pressure on Northern Ireland political parties to implement the peace agreement transacted on Good Friday 1998. In this it had the help of former U.S. Sen. George Mitchell, who played the role of honest broker between Sinn Fein, the political wing of the Irish Republican Army, and the Ulster Unionist Party (UUP), chief representative of the province's Protestant majority. Throughout most of the year, the key issue of decommissioning paramilitary arms and explosives remained unresolved. David Trimble, the UUP leader who under the Good Friday agreement had become Northern Ireland's first minister–designate in 1998, insisted that the IRA had to begin decommissioning before Sinn Fein joined with him in a devolved Northern Ireland executive. Gerry Adams, president of Sinn Fein, argued that the agreement did not require the IRA to hand over its arms before the executive began work.

In January, Mo Mowlam set March 10 as a "target date" for devolving power to Belfast, but the deadline passed. Only a tiny number of terrorist murders occurred during the year, but vigilante members of the IRA continued to carry out "punishment beatings" of Protestants, as well as of Catholics who, it was claimed, refused to accept the IRA's authority in local areas. Blair and Bertie Ahern, his Republic of Ireland counterpart, called a series of negotiating sessions involving the UUP and Sinn Fein. They told Adams that Sinn Fein and the IRA must give ground over decommissioning for political progress to be possible. Both prime ministers refused to accede to Unionist demands that the early release under the Good Friday agreement of paramilitary prisoners should be halted. They set a revised deadline of June 30 for devolving power to Belfast, but it too passed. Trimble insisted that if guns were not handed over, Sinn Fein must be denied a place in government.

Beginning in early September, Mitchell initiated a virtually nonstop series of closed-door negotiations with the parties. These climaxed on November 16, when Trimble and Adams jointly agreed that a peace settlement was within reach. The two leaders committed themselves to a series of coordinated moves. Adams agreed that weapons decommissioning was "essential" to the furtherance of peace and committed Sinn Fein to work "exclusively" by democratic means. The IRA, in a separate announcement, endorsed Adams' comments. Trimble said Sinn Fein could join a Northern Ireland executive if the IRA agreed to decommissioning by May 2000. This amounted to a reversal of UUP policy and attracted strong criticism from John Taylor, Trimble's deputy, who swore to fight the compromise.

Other News. The British Broadcasting Corporation chose Greg Dyke to succeed Sir John Birt as director general....In June, Prince Edward married Sophie Rhys-Jones and took the title Earl of Wessex....Following a serious train crash in London, Railtrack, the company at the heart of Britain's privatized rail system, came under attack for allegedly putting profit above safety....Work on a giant pleasure dome near Greenwich was completed in time for millennium celebrations....Former Beatle George Harrison was stabbed in the chest at his home on December 30. His assailant was charged with attempted murder.

ALEXANDER MACLEOD
"The Christian Science Monitor"

Greece

In Greece during 1999, the Panhellenic Socialist Movement (PASOK) government under Prime Minister Costas Simitis was involved in the Kosovo conflict between the North Atlantic Treaty Organization (NATO) and Yugoslavia (*see* THE KOSOVO CRISIS, page 78). Greece's relations with its neighbor Turkey improved.

An earthquake registering 5.9 hit the capital, Athens, on September 7. At least 143 persons were killed; another 1,600 were injured; and 53,000 buildings were damaged or destroyed.

Foreign Affairs. As a member of NATO and the European Union (EU), Greece was drawn into the Kosovo crisis, even though the government opposed NATO's bombing campaign against the Serbs. Simitis and his ministers made clear that Greece deplored the "ethnic cleansing" of which the Serbs were accused. The government said that it hoped to see a political settlement to the crisis, the withdrawal of the Serbian army from Kosovo, and the establishment of an international peacekeeping force. At a NATO summit in Washington in April, Simitis cautioned that a continuance of the crisis could lead to further destabilization in southeastern Europe. After the bombing ended and the Serbs accepted a peace plan in June, Greece sent troops to participate in a NATO peacekeeping force in Kosovo.

Within Greece, in general, public opinion and the press tended to feel empathy for the Serbs, who shared Orthodoxy with the Greeks. The lingering anger and resentment felt by the public about the bombing campaign was seen in the demonstrations that greeted U.S. President Bill Clinton when he visited Greece in November.

GREECE • Information Highlights

Official Name: Hellenic Republic.
Location: Southeastern Europe.
Area: 50,942 sq mi (131 940 km²).
Population (July 1999 est.): 10,707,135.
Chief Cities (1991 census): Athens, the capital, 772,072; Salonika, 383,967; Piraeus, 189,671.
Government: *Head of state,* Costis Stephanopoulos, president (took office March 1995). *Head of government,* Costas Simitis, prime minister (took office January 1996). *Legislature* (unicameral)—Parliament.
Monetary Unit: Drachma (325.215 drachmas equal U.S.$1, Jan. 3, 2000).
Gross Domestic Product (1998 est. U.S.$): $143,000,000,000 (purchasing power parity).
Economic Indexes: *Consumer Prices* (1997, 1990 = 100): all items, 218.5; food, 198.0. *Industrial Production* (1998, 1990 = 100): 108.1.
Foreign Trade (1998 est. U.S.$): *Imports,* $27,700,000,000; *exports,* $12,400,000,000.

Relations between Greece and Turkey in 1999 were influenced by politics and natural disasters. The case of Kurdish rebel leader Abdullah Ocalan, arrested in Nairobi by Turkish intelligence in February, exacerbated tensions between the two countries. On the run from the Turkish government, Ocalan reportedly fled to Greece, where officials then transported him to Nairobi and granted him temporary refuge at the Greek embassy. The rebel leader was captured soon after that. Turkey expressed sharp displeasure at what it saw as Greece's attempt to help Ocalan escape. On the other hand, Kurdish exiles in Western Europe mounted protests against Greece, accusing the Greek government of allowing (and possibly even abetting) Ocalan's capture. The crisis led to the resignation of three Greek ministers.

When a major earthquake hit Turkey in August, Greece's humanitarian response led to a general warming between the two countries. Turkey reacted in kind, helping Greece in the aftermath of the Athens quake in September. Greece then reversed its opposition to the entry of Turkey into the EU.

In January 1999 deputies in the European Parliament passed a petition calling for Britain to give the so-called Elgin Marbles back to Greece. Lord Elgin, the British ambassador to the Ottoman Empire, had removed the Marbles from the Parthenon and sold them to the British government in 1816, after which they were housed in the British Museum. In December, British Prime Minister Tony Blair's office stated that Britain had no plans to return the antiquities.

Domestic Affairs. New Democracy, Greece's leading political opposition party, received 36% of the vote in the elections for the European Parliament held on June 13. PASOK's tally, on the other hand, was 32.9%. New Democratic leaders hailed the outcome as indicative of the party's strength.

During 1999 the Athens stock exchange experienced a veritable frenzy of individual stockholder activity. Simitis' government continued with reform measures to strengthen the economy in anticipation of Greece's entry into the Economic and Monetary Union (EMU) by Jan. 1, 2001.

Former King Constantine II had been seeking the return of his private property, confiscated by law in 1994 by the Andreas Papandreou government, or monetary compensation. In November the Council of Europe decided that the case should be tried at the European Court of Human Rights.

GEORGE J. MARCOPOULOS, *Tufts University*

Housing

The U.S. housing market turned in a mixed performance in 1999. Market activity was quite strong early in the year, but rising interest rates took a toll in the second half, as the Federal Reserve tightened monetary policy to slow economic growth and contain inflationary pressures. For the year as a whole, new records were set for sales and production of conventionally built single-family homes, and the total number of new housing units produced in the United States crept above 2 million for the first time since the mid-1980s.

Widespread economic weakness continued to hold down housing-market activity in large parts of Asia, Latin America, and Eastern Europe. Most housing markets in Western Europe performed well in 1999, and Canada saw a substantial rebound following a sharp contraction in 1998.

Market Segments. Mortgage interest rates were at the lowest level in three decades at the beginning of 1999, with 30-year fixed-rate loans available at about 6.75% and one-year adjustable-rate loans at about 5.5%. These financing conditions spurred high rates of home sales and single-family-housing production in early 1999, but market activity slowed during the second half, as fixed-rate mortgages climbed to about 8%, and adjustable-rate loans moved up to about 6.5%. Sales of conventionally built single-family homes rose by about 3% to a record 6.067 million units. In addition, about 400,000 custom homes were built on lots already owned by the occupants. Builders started a total of 1.33 million single-family homes in 1999, the highest number since 1978. In terms of square footage produced, 1999 was easily a record year.

Mobile-home production contracted somewhat in 1999, as shipments from factories to dealers fell by 6.5% to 350,000 units, about the 1997 level. Despite the decline in shipments, dealer inventories rose substantially, climbing to about 120,000 units by late 1999, which put heavy downward pressure on production levels.

The production of apartment units in multifamily structures (containing two or more units) fell by about 3% in 1999, to 332,000 units. Of these units, 80% were built for the rental market (a slightly smaller share than in 1998), and the rest were built for sale as condominium or cooperative units. While the overall rental-vacancy rate in the United States edged up to about 8.2%, the vacancy rate for multifamily structures fell to 8.8%, the lowest rate in more than a decade.

Residential remodeling expenditures rose by about 5% in 1999 to a record $127 billion. About 30% of this total represented maintenance and repair expenditures on single-family and multifamily structures, while the rest were improvements to existing residential units. Owner-occupants accounted for 75% of residential remodeling activity.

New-Housing Characteristics. The average size of conventionally built single-family homes continued to increase in 1999, exceeding 2,200 sq ft (204.6 m^2). About 33% of new homes had at least four bedrooms, more than half had at least 2.5 bathrooms, 80% had garages for two or more cars, and 85% had central air-conditioning.

About 90% of conventionally built new homes in 1999 were constructed from the ground up with traditional "stick-building" techniques, and the remainder (approximately 130,000 units) were assembled from modular components or panelized/precut kits shipped from factories to building sites.

Recent technological advances in the construction of mobile homes have made them less distinguishable from site-built homes when they are placed on permanent foundations rather than in traditional "trailer parks," or are stacked to produce multistory dwellings. In 1999 more than 60% of new mobile homes were double- or triple-wide units, and the average size of new units climbed above 1,500 sq ft (139.5 m^2) for the first time. About 85% of the units had three or more bedrooms, and more than 75% had central air-conditioning. The average price of the units was about $43,000 (excluding site costs), compared with the average of about $190,000 for new, conventionally built single-family homes.

The average size of apartments in conventionally built multifamily structures grew to nearly 1,100 sq ft (102.3 m^2) in 1999, about the same as the previous record set in 1997. More than 66% of the units had at least two bedrooms, and more than half had two or more bathrooms.

The Housing Stock. High housing-production rates in 1999 raised the U.S. housing inventory to about 120 million units by the end of the year. The median age of units remained at about 28 years, and about 15% of all units were less than ten years old. Conventionally built single-family homes accounted for more than 66% of the total housing stock; units in multifamily structures accounted for nearly 25%; and the rest were mobile homes.

About 105.5 million housing units were occupied at the end of 1999. Some of the remaining 14 million were vacant because they were intended for seasonal use (such as vacation homes). Of the occupied units, 67% were owned by their occupants, and the rest were renter-occupied. The number of owner-occupied housing units rose substantially during 1999, while the number of renter-occupied units contracted by about 300,000 units, the second consecutive annual decline. This pattern reflected an ongoing shift from renting to owning property.

Home-Ownership Patterns. The U.S. home-ownership rate rose to a record 67% by the third quarter of 1999, up from about 64% in 1994. The rate rose for all four geographic regions (Northeast, Midwest, South, and West), all major racial divisions of the population, and most age groups. The increase was most dramatic for households having heads younger than 25 years old; for this group, the home-ownership rate climbed by more than two percentage points, exceeding 20% for the first time since 1980.

Despite improvements in 1999, the home-ownership rates for racial and ethnic minorities remained well below the rate for white households. The home-ownership rate for whites rose to 73.5%, while the rates for blacks and Hispanics were only 47% and 45.5%, respectively. Striking differences in home-ownership rates also persisted at different income levels. Households with family income greater than or equal to the median family income in their geographic area had a home-ownership rate of 81.7%, while households with below-median family income had a rate of only 51.4%.

The relatively low home-ownership rates for blacks and Hispanics, lower-income households, and households in central cities remained a challenge for policy makers in the United States at the end of 1999. The Bill Clinton administration set a target of 67.5% for the U.S. home-ownership rate in 2000 and expressed a commitment to increase home ownership in central cities.

Rental-Housing Needs. Shortages of decent, affordable rental units for low-income people remained America's biggest housing problem in 1999, as government studies showed that roughly 5 million low-income renter households still faced a crisis of unaffordable rents and substandard living conditions despite the expanding U.S. economy. In response, the U.S. Congress approved a significant increase in the budget for the U.S. Department of Housing and Urban Development (HUD), giving HUD more resources to deal with the rental-housing problem in 2000. The additional funding was targeted primarily to preservation of the stock of public and federally assisted rental housing, the provision of rental-housing vouchers to an additional 60,000 households, and increased aid for the homeless. HUD also was authorized to fight housing discrimination in the markets for both home ownership and rental housing.

International Comparisons. In the United States the real (inflation-adjusted) value of residential fixed investment in the national economic accounts—including the production of new housing units (single-family, multifamily, and mobile homes), improvements to the existing stock of housing, and commissions on home sales—grew by 7% in 1999 to a record level. This performance lifted the ratio of housing investment to gross domestic product (GDP) to 4.2%, the highest since the late 1980s.

Large parts of the developing world were in economic recession in 1999, and housing production naturally was depressed in these areas. Much of Latin America—including Venezuela, Argentina, Colombia, Chile, and Brazil—had weak economies. In Eastern Europe, Russia, the Ukraine, and Romania were in desperate economic straits, and the Czech Republic also struggled. In Asia, Indonesia was in recession, while Japan and Hong Kong remained in economic trouble.

In Japan, where housing production plunged dramatically in 1997–98, the number of new housing units produced recovered a bit in 1999, reaching about 1.2 million. In the process, the real value of residential construction grew by about 3%, following double-digit contractions in 1997 and 1998.

Economic growth was sluggish, but positive, in Western Europe in 1999, providing a reasonably positive environment for housing markets. The ratio of housing production to GDP remained relatively high in Germany and Great Britain and relatively low in France and Italy.

Housing-market activity picked up in Canada during 1999, following a sharp contraction in 1998 caused by the global economic crisis. The number of new housing units rose to about 146,000, and the real value of residential construction expanded by about 10% during 1999.

DAVID F. SEIDERS
National Association of Home Builders

Human Rights

In 1999 human rights resonated in world affairs, especially because of the North Atlantic Treaty Organization's (NATO's) decision to confront Serbia militarily for its mounting atrocities against its Muslim citizens in Kosovo. Doctors without Borders, a human-rights group founded in 1971 by French doctors that works in some 80 countries, won the 1999 Nobel Peace Prize.

Sovereignty v. Human Rights. The Kosovo crisis brought to a head the fundamental policy question of whether human rights ever should trump sovereignty. The answer that prevailed, at least in this case, was capsulized in June by Peter Van Walsum, the Netherlands' representative to the United Nations, addressing the Security Council: "Today no sovereign state has the right to terrorize its own citizens." Fourteen out of the 15 Security Council members agreed by voting to approve a NATO-led peacekeeping force for Kosovo and to bestow legitimacy on the NATO-led military operations there. China abstained. (*See also* FEATURE SECTION, pages 78–90.)

By early September a new round of the debate flared up as a result of mass killings by local militias backed by the Indonesian military in East Timor, whose people had voted overwhelmingly in favor of independence from Indonesia. At the United Nations (UN) General Assembly that month, China's Foreign Minister Tang Jiaxuan called national sovereignty and noninterference in another country's affairs "the basic principles governing international affairs," any deviation from which would "wreak havoc" in the world. Under international pressure, Indonesia's President B.J. Habibie soon agreed to a UN peacekeeping force in East Timor.

Mary Robinson, UN High Commissioner for Human Rights, broke new ground by addressing the mid-September meeting of the Security Council, the first human-rights commissioner to do so. Robinson, who just had visited Indonesia and East Timor, stressed that gross human-rights violations are often early warning signs of grave threats to security and stability.

The Pinochet Case. Another 1999 human-rights debate with international repercussions centered on whether Gen. Augusto Pinochet, the former Chilean leader, was immune from prosecution outside of Chile itself for crimes committed during his 1973–90 dictatorship. Britain had been wrestling with this case since Pinochet's October 1998 arrest in London, at the request of Spain, to face prosecution in a Spanish court for committing crimes against Spanish citizens in Chile. In March the Law Lords, Britain's highest court, held that Pinochet must remain in Britain and face possible extradition. The court also said that he could not be prosecuted for crimes allegedly committed before 1988, when Britain signed the International Convention against Torture. In April, Britain's Home Secretary Jack Straw said that he was allowing the case to go forward. In October a London magistrate followed up with a technical decision that Pinochet could be extradited to Spain under British law.

Capital Punishment. In April the 53-member UN Commission on Human Rights adopted a European Union (EU) resolution calling on states to "progressively restrict the number of offenses for which the death penalty may be imposed and to establish a moratorium on executions, with a view to completely abolishing the death penalty." It was the third time the commission had adopted such a resolution. The vote was 30 in favor, 11—including the United States and China—against, and 12 abstentions.

China. A U.S. resolution before the UN Commission on Human Rights to condemn China for human-rights violations did not come up for a vote, or even for discussion, during the commission's six-week session. China blocked any complaints against it by winning passage of a procedural "no action" resolution. The vote on the motion was 22 in favor, 17 against, and 14 abstentions.

The U.S. State Department's annual report on the full range of human-rights practices worldwide, issued in February, was of record size—2,000 pages, in two volumes. Of the 194 countries surveyed, China received the lengthiest treatment, nearly 50 pages. The report noted that the status of human rights in China had "deteriorated sharply" toward the end of 1998 with a crackdown on organized political dissent.

Religious Freedom. Complying with the International Religious Freedom Act passed in 1998, the U.S. State Department in September released its first annual report assessing the status of religious freedom in 194 countries. In October, China, Iran, Iraq, Myanmar, and Sudan were designated as nations of special concern for "particularly severe violations of religious freedom."

ROBERT A. SENSER
Editor, "Human Rights for Workers"

Hungary

In 1999, Hungary became a full North Atlantic Treaty Organization (NATO) member and made progress on its aspirations for inclusion in the European Union (EU). The country remained politically and economically stable, and the government was supportive of NATO's war in neighboring Yugoslavia, even though it feared the impact on the large Hungarian minority in the Serbian province of Vojvodina.

Political Stability. The government of the Young Democrats was stable and did not face any serious political opposition. However, the year was marred by financial scandals and the resignations of several top officials. More than 100 leading politicians allegedly had received interest payments at 10%–15% above the market rate on their Postabank accounts. Laszlo Gal, a senior interior-ministry official, resigned in October over allegations of illegal transactions. Socialist Party Deputy Chairman Sandor Nagy and Democratic Forum official Judit Csiha announced their resignations in June, in response to reports that they had received preferential loans from a Hungarian bank. Hungary also was shaken by terrorist attacks linked with competing criminal networks active in the country. A number of car bombings were reported in Budapest in apparent assassination attempts on gang leaders.

Economic Progress. Hungary's economic performance proved positive. The country enjoyed one of the highest growth rates in Eastern Europe, with gross domestic product (GDP) projected to grow by about 4% for 1999. The inflation rate fell to under 10% for the year. Although the authorities pushed forward with their market-reform program, they postponed the planned tax reforms for 2001. Prime Minister Viktor Orban stated that, because of the economic difficulties associated with the Yugoslav war, no one was prepared to see large-scale tax and social-insurance reforms at present.

International Affairs. In February the national parliament approved Hungary's accession to NATO. The country's membership was approved formally by the Atlantic Alliance in March. Budapest supported the NATO military operation against neighboring Serbia in response to Belgrade's brutal policies in Kosovo. Parliament approved NATO's use of Hungarian military airfields for strikes against Yugoslavia. The decision was supported by all parliamentary groups except the xenophobic Justice and Life Party. However, serious concerns were voiced over the fate of the large Hungarian population in Serbia's province of Vojvodina. The number of Hungarians in Vojvodina was estimated at some 350,000, or about 17.5% of the province's total population. Hungary favored autonomy for Vojvodina but feared a crackdown by the Serbian regime of Slobodan Milosevic.

Hungary's relations with Slovakia remained steady, even though the government claimed that the new Slovak minority-language law hindered the development of Hungarian-Slovak relations. Hungary hoped that the Slovak government would make amendments to the law so that it would meet the provisions of the 1995 Hungarian-Slovak basic treaty.

Relations with Romania continued to develop, but the dispute over a Hungarian-language university in the Transylvanian region continued. Premier Orban stated that the Romanian leadership lacked the political will to set up a Hungarian-language university. He also promised the Transylvanian Hungarians that they will have Hungarian-language education from nursery to university level by 2002. On the positive side, the Hungarian and Romanian defense ministers agreed on plans to allow troops to transit each other's territories without prior parliamentary approval. They also agreed that the planned joint Hungarian-Romanian peacekeeping battalion will be set up in 2000.

The European Union (EU) concluded that Hungary remained on track for membership and was a well-functioning market economy. Nevertheless, problems remained in the areas of corruption, the treatment of the Roma (Gypsy) population, press freedoms, and protection of the environment. The head of the European Commission's

HUNGARY • Information Highlights

Official Name: Republic of Hungary.
Location: East-central Europe.
Area: 35,919 sq mi (93 030 km^2).
Population (July 1999 est.): 10,186,372.
Chief Cities (Jan. 1, 1998 est.): Budapest, the capital, 1,861,383; Debrecen, 206,882; Miskolc, 175,744.
Government: *Head of state,* Arpád Goncz, president (elected August 1990). *Head of government,* Viktor Orban, prime minister (took office July 1998). *Legislature* (unicameral)—National Assembly.
Monetary Unit: Forint (252.0150 forints equal U.S.$1, Dec. 16, 1999).
Gross Domestic Product (1998 est. U.S.$): $75,400,-000,000 (purchasing power parity).
Economic Indexes (1998, 1990 = 100): *Consumer Prices,* all items, 517.7; food, 479.8. *Industrial Production,* 113.4.
Foreign Trade (1997 U.S.$): *Imports,* $20,652,000,000; *exports,* $18,613,000,000.

working group for EU expansion stated in October that Hungary and Poland were the economic leaders among the 13 countries aspiring to the EU. Hungary fulfilled the political criteria for membership. In terms of minority protection, the government launched a Roma "action plan" but needed to make available adequate budgetary resources. According to the EU, the government's struggle against corruption also needed to be reinforced. Budapest's strategic goal was to complete its preparedness for EU membership by December 2001.

JANUSZ BUGAJSKI
Center for Strategic and International Studies

ICELAND • Information Highlights

Official Name: Republic of Iceland.
Location: North Atlantic Ocean.
Area: 39,768 sq mi (103 000 km²).
Population (July 1999 est.): 272,512.
Chief City (December 1998 est.): Reykjavík, the capital, 107,764.
Government: *Head of state,* Ólafur Ragnar Grímsson, president (took office August 1996). *Head of government,* David Oddsson, prime minister (took office April 1991). *Legislature* (unicameral)—Althing.
Monetary Unit: Króna (72.445 krónur equal U.S.$1, Dec. 16, 1999).
Gross Domestic Product (1998 est. U.S.$): $6,060,000,000.
Economic Index (1998, 1990 = 100): *Consumer Prices,* all items, 125.9; food, 116.7.
Foreign Trade (1998 U.S.$): *Imports,* $2,489,000,000; *exports,* $2,050,000,000.

Iceland

The Icelandic economy continued to grow briskly in the first half of 1999. Growth was led by investment, private consumption, and exports. Inflation was rising slowly, while unemployment declined to a low level, well below 3%. The prospects for economic progress for the second half of 1999 and in the year 2000 were favorable. The ruling conservative Independence Party was returned to power in a general election.

Economy. Iceland's economy had enjoyed growth of 5% or more since 1996. The National Economic Institute forecast a 1999 growth rate in the gross domestic product (GDP) close to the 1998 rate—5.1%. Economic growth in 1998 was driven by an expansion in gross fixed investment and private consumption, while exports and public consumption grew slowly. In 1999 exports were expected to increase by 8.2%, and investment was expected to be at a high level, although not as high as in 1998.

The upturn in the economy and increased purchasing power was reflected in a rapid increase of imports in 1998—22.1% over the previous year. Imports were expected to grow by 2.7% in 1999. To prevent "overheating" of the economy, the Central Bank of Iceland increased its interest rates three times during the first half of 1999. The trade balance was negative, of the same order as in 1998, and terms of trade deteriorated from 1998, mainly because of rising oil prices.

Fishing, Iceland's leading industry, continued to enjoy success. Catches of cod in the first seven months of 1999 increased 11% over the same period in 1998, while total fish catch was almost the same in tons. Prices of marine products fell in the first half of 1999 after a substantial rise in 1998. The outlook for an increase in marine-export prices was favorable, as the supply conditions of demersal fish deteriorated worldwide.

The tourism sector had been one of the fastest-growing industries in recent years. Foreign visitors in 1998 numbered 232,000, compared with 129,000 in 1987. The foreign-exchange revenues generated by tourism in 1998 amounted to approximately 12% of the total foreign-exchange revenues of the economy. Whale watching had been growing rapidly as a tourist activity in recent years.

Politics. In the May election the ruling conservative Independence Party secured 26 seats and 40.7% of the vote, an increase of one seat and 3.6% of the vote from the 1995 election. The coalition partner, the centrist Progressive Party, saw a 4.9% drop in support and lost four seats compared with 1995. Davíd Oddsson, who had been in power since April 1991, entered the history books as the nation's longest-sitting premier. The Independence Party victory was overshadowed by an upsurge of the Left-Green Alliance, and the Liberals unexpectedly gained two seats in the Althing.

European Union. In a report to the Althing in October, Foreign Minister Halldór Ásgrímsson revealed plans to commission an independent study to evaluate the benefits of Iceland's membership in the European Union (EU). The minister made it clear that no decision had been made regarding possible membership.

Anniversaries. At the end of 1999, Iceland was preparing for two major anniversaries in 2000: the discovery of North America by Leif "the Lucky" Eriksson in A.D. 1000 and the Christianization of the country, also in 1000. Reykjavík was selected as one of the European Cities of Culture in the Year 2000.

RICHARD MIDDLETON
Freelance Writer, Reykjavík

India

Another parliamentary election, missile launchings, war with Pakistan, and a devastating cyclone dominated events in India in 1999.

Politics. The Bharatiya Janata Party (BJP)–led coalition lost a vote of no confidence on April 17 by one vote. Precipitated by the withdrawal of the All India Anna Dravida Munnetra Kazhagam (AIADMK) party from the ruling coalition and the Congress Party's refusal to back it on the confidence motion, the vote sent India's electorate to its third election for the Lok Sabha (lower house of Parliament) in as many years in September–October, resulting in another BJP-led coalition win.

Jayalalitha Jayaram, leader of the AIADMK party, had been asking for three instead of two cabinet appointees and for the government to drop corruption investigations against her. When Prime Minister Atal Bihari Vajpayee refused, the AIADMK formally withdrew from the coalition. Unable to get support from either the Congress or other smaller parties, Vajpayee tendered his government's resignation.

The Congress Party tried to win the support of smaller parties and the left. When this failed, Parliament was dissolved on April 26. Under Indian law, elections must be held within six months. The BJP and its allies pushed the Election Commission to schedule polls for July, hoping for a voter backlash against the Congress Party and its allies for bringing down the government. This was turned down on the grounds that north India was experiencing one of the hottest summers ever, with temperatures reaching 118°F (48°C). Further, the commission noted, it would take until July simply to update voters' lists, to which would be added 15 million people, and to find the 4 million workers needed to man about 800,000 polling stations. Thus elections were held in five stages between September 5 and October 3.

As parties geared up to campaign, the Congress found itself in initial disarray. Three top leaders—including Sharad Pawar, a strongman from Maharashtra state—challenged party president Sonia Gandhi, the Italian-born widow of former Prime Minister Rajiv Gandhi. They said that her foreign birth was a legitimate electoral concern and asked her commitment to a law requiring Indian birth for the president, vice-president, and prime minister of the country. Gandhi, a naturalized citizen, refused and resigned as party president. After much internal turmoil, Pawar and his two colleagues were expelled from the party, and Gandhi returned to the presidency. The "anti-foreign-born" theme was echoed by the BJP and its allies.

There were few policy differences between parties. All promised more-equitable development, social justice, and eradication of corruption. Observers noted this was the most issueless campaign in India's history and was distinguished only for personal attacks by all. The Congress ran by itself, with electoral "understandings" reached

© Baldev/Corbis-Sygma

After its coalition government lost a no-confidence vote earlier in the year, India's Bharatiya Janata Party (BJP) rebounded to lead another coalition to victory in parliamentary elections in September and October 1999. BJP leader Atal Bihari Vajpayee (center, second from left) *continued as prime minister.*

with the leftist parties. The BJP forged an electoral coalition with primarily regional parties, called the National Democratic Alliance (NDA).

The BJP-led NDA won a comfortable majority of 298 (out of 543) seats. Of these, the BJP itself got 182, with the rest divided among its 20 allies. Congress came next, with 113 for itself and an additional 23 for its allies—its worst record since independence. Ironically, its popular vote was higher than that of the BJP: 28.42% versus 23.07%. This was due to India's "winner takes all" rule and to the fact that the BJP contested fewer seats: 339 to Congress' 453. Of the remaining 103 Lok Sabha seats, the left—including the Communist Party of India (Marxist) and the Communist Party of India—won 42, with other parties and independents splitting the rest. The success of the expanded NDA coalition of 21 parties showed a decided swing in favor of the regional parties that made up the bulk of the alliance. Despite calls over the past several years for a 33% representation for women in Parliament, only 47 women out of 277 candidates won.

The NDA government was sworn in on October 13, with Atal Bihari Vajpayee as prime minister. Sonia Gandhi was named opposition leader. She had won handily in both constituencies in which she ran, but decided to represent Amethi in Uttar Pradesh state, the traditional Gandhi base. The Union Council of Ministers was expanded to 70 to accommodate coalition members (25 cabinet ministers, 37 ministers of state, and seven without portfolio or with "independent charges"). However, due to the large number of partners, the BJP retained a majority of positions (46). Though this, along with the NDA parliamentary majority, gave the party a strong base for policy enactment and implementation, divisions within the more radical and moderate wings of the BJP itself, as well as the need to satisfy its partners, led some to question whether the government would be effective.

Several controversial issues faced the new Parliament immediately. A bill to open up the banking and insurance industries more fully to the private sector was opposed strongly by the left, which viewed it as a sellout of the economy. The measure passed relatively easily in December, although many leftist members of Parliament staged a walkout during the vote. Other aims of the government might be equally controversial. It proposed a review of the constitution, including measures to ensure full five-year terms for the Lok Sabha and states' assemblies. Electoral laws were to be revised further to prevent fraud. Tax reforms were expected to be hotly debated, as was the reintroduction of 1998's bill guaranteeing women 33% of Lok Sabha seats immediately.

INDIA • Information Highlights

Official Name: Republic of India.
Location: South Asia.
Area: 1,269,340 sq mi (3 287 590 km²).
Population (July 1999 est.): 1,000,848,550.
Chief Cities (1991 census): New Delhi, the capital, 301,297; Mumbai (Bombay), 9,925,891; Delhi, 7,206,704; Calcutta, 4,399,819.
Government: *Head of state,* Kocheril Raman Narayanan, president (elected July 1997). *Head of government,* Atal Bihari Vajpayee, prime minister (sworn in on March 19, 1998). *Legislature*—Sansad (Parliament): Rajya Sabha (Council of States) and Lok Sabha (People's Assembly).
Monetary Unit: Rupee (43.4238 rupees equal U.S.$1, Dec. 6, 1999).
Gross Domestic Product (1998 est. U.S.$): $1,689,000,-000,000 (purchasing power parity).
Economic Indexes (1998, 1990 = 100): *Consumer Prices,* all items, 217.7; food, 228.8. *Industrial Production,* 156.0.
Foreign Trade (1998 U.S.$): *Imports,* $42,765,000,000; *exports,* $33,656,000,000.

Missiles, Nuclear Policy, and Kashmiri Insurgents. Contributing to the NDA win were undoubtedly India's missile and nuclear policies and renewed hostilities with Pakistan (*see* SPECIAL REPORT, page 285). In December 1998, Prime Minister Vajpayee had stated his government's intention to continue development of the Agni missile program. Between January and March, peace talks with Pakistan looked hopeful, and a new bus route linking Amritsar city to Lahore in Pakistan became symbolic of better relations. However, on April 11, India test-fired an Agni missile, raising consternation in Pakistan and the West. Vajpayee argued that the missile program was vital to India's national security and should not be seen as a threat directed toward Pakistan. To many in India, its missile technology has been a source of pride.

In August, with the election campaign in full swing, the government unveiled a policy that would start equipping missiles with nuclear warheads. Some observers noted the impropriety of a "lame duck" government undertaking such major actions without any public debate or parliamentary consideration. However, there were indications that many in the public were supportive.

In mid-May renewed hostilities with Pakistan over its support of "insurgents" in Kashmir garnered the most support for Vajpayee's coalition. India used its air and land power effectively in the mountainous Kargil and Dras regions of Kashmir to eradicate rebels and their bases, which it maintained were trained and armed by Pakistan. As the action escalated over the next two months, India accused Pakistan of actually having its own armed forces involved within Indian territory—a claim denied by Pakistan. Pakistan in turn accused India of killing Pakistani soldiers and shooting down aircraft inside Pakistan, which was denied by India. International pressure on Pakistan from the United States and members of the British Commonwealth ultimately made Prime Minister Nawaz Sharif agree to a staged withdrawal of troops and insurgents from the Indian side of the border in July. Despite the withdrawal, sporadic incidents of violence continued in Kashmir for the rest of the year. During the electoral campaign, Congress raised the issue of why so many insurgents had been able to infiltrate Indian territory without the government knowing and accused the BJP of ineptness in dealing with Kashmir in general.

The Kashmir issue resurfaced with the December 24 hijacking of an Indian Airlines flight from Nepal to New Delhi. The hijackers, who took the 190 people aboard the plane hostage, made brief stops in India, Pakistan, and the United Arab Emirates before finally landing in Afghanistan. They killed one of the hostages shortly after the hijacking began, and they said they would kill the rest unless India released 36 militants jailed for fighting Indian rule in Kashmir. They also demanded a $200 million ransom. After initial reluctance, the Indian government began to negotiate with the hijackers with the help of Afghanistan's Taliban government. After a weeklong standoff, India agreed to release three of the militants. Indian Foreign Minister Jaswant Singh delivered the three prisoners to the plane on December 31, and the hijackers drove away with them. The hostages were freed.

Other Domestic Issues and Events. Two state elections, held along with the national ones, saw BJP fortunes decline. In Maharashtra the Hindu-nationalist coalition government of the BJP and the Shiv Sena was defeated by Sharad Pawar's new National Congress Party (NCP). The NCP joined with the Congress to form a new government. In Uttar Pradesh the BJP barely held a majority of seats. Chief Minister Kalyan Singh refused to take responsibility for the election setback and instead again promised radical BJP supporters that a Hindu temple would be built on the site of the destroyed Muslim mosque at Ayodhya. He was removed from office in November.

Violence against Christian communities escalated alarmingly. In January an Australian missionary and his two sons were burned to death as they slept in their van in Orissa state. In March, 157 Christian homes were burned; in September a Catholic priest was killed—also in Orissa. A nun was attacked savagely in Bihar province. Gujerat also experienced anti-Christian violence. Radical elements of the Rashtriya Swayamsevak Sangh (RSS) wing of the BJP were suspected of instigating these activities. Radical Hindus accused Christians of "preying" on poor communities by offering food and jobs in return for conversion. While many converts come from such communities, there was no evidence to back such claims. The new NDA government stated that it would not tolerate such violence and would work toward greater religious harmony. Pope John Paul visited India in October, and, while he condemned any sectarian violence, he indicated that Asia should be the next major push for Christian evangelization.

Indian courts handed down two important decisions. In August the Supreme Court struck down the use of special standards for entrance into "super specialty" graduate fields of study, such as medicine and engineering, by low and backward caste students. Many institutions had required lower marks for these communities. The court argued that in the national interest, all those working in such fields must be fully competent practitioners. In September the court struck down a ban on publication of exit polls enacted by the Elections Commission. Citing freedom of expression as vital to democracy, the court said the Elections Commission had no jurisdiction to restrict such freedoms.

On October 29 a devastating cyclone hit the eastern coast. Most severely hit was the state of Orissa, with lesser damage in parts of Andhra Pradesh. Casualty and damage reports showed that more than 10,000 people perished; thousands of livestock died; roads, power lines, telecommunications, and port facilities were destroyed; and fields were submerged under seawater. Government assistance was unable to reach many people for up to a week after the storm, which was the worst one since 1977. Critics said the government should have realized the vulnerability of the entire seacoast, updated its early-warning system, and built storm-proof shelters. As relief supplies became available, there were also indications of black marketing.

SPECIAL REPORT

India-Pakistan Relations

The ancient Indian statesman Kautilya noted more than 2,000 years ago that neighbors are natural enemies. India and Pakistan have demonstrated this clearly. In the half-century since they became independent in August 1947, they have fought three full-scale wars. But the Indo-Pakistani rivalry assumed new dimensions in 1998, when both countries tested nuclear devices. New fears of the nuclearization of regional conflicts and further nuclear proliferation were raised around the world, and economic sanctions were applied to both countries.

In early 1999 the two rivals appeared to be seeking to improve relations. In February, Indian Prime Minister Atal Bihari Vajpayee traveled to Pakistan to meet with Prime Minister Mohammad Nawaz Sharif. Vajpayee declared that he and his fellow Indians sought "abiding peace and harmony with Pakistan," and Sharif suggested that the time was not far off when the relationship between India and Pakistan might be as peaceful as the one between the United States and Canada. By midyear, however, the two armies were in their most intense confrontation since 1971. The undeclared war lasted only a couple of months, but its impact had longer-term repercussions for both Indo-Pakistani relations and the internal politics of both countries.

The 1999 Kashmir Conflict. Uncertainty over the disposition of the former princely state of Jammu and Kashmir, ruled by a Hindu maharaja but with a largely Muslim population, led to the first Kashmir war in 1947–48. India agreed at the time to hold a plebiscite in the disputed territory, but subsequently has refused to do so. The second Kashmir war erupted in August 1965, after the Indian constitution was modified to integrate the state more closely into India. Kashmir was also a battleground in the 1971 war, which resulted in the creation of Bangladesh (formerly East Pakistan). The 1972 Simla Agreement, concluded by Indian Prime Minister Indira Gandhi and Pakistan's Zulfikar Ali Bhutto, pledged that the two countries would settle their differences bilaterally.

Since 1984, Indian and Pakistani troops have jockeyed for position on the massive Siachen Glacier, the undemarcated and high-altitude wasteland at the far northeastern terminus of the boundary between Indian and Pakistani Kashmir. Indo-Pakistani relations continued to be strained throughout the 1990s, but in 1999 the hostilities escalated.

In the spring about 700 Pakistani forces moved across the line of control at Kargil to occupy the heights in the Indian-held territory. Initially, Pakistan claimed that none of its troops were involved, but it later gave up that pretense. Then it was rumored that the army had acted without the government's knowledge; however, after Sharif was deposed in October, Pakistan's new military ruler, Gen. Pervez Musharraf, claimed that the prime minister had been involved fully in the matter.

Beginning May 8, India sent about 30,000 troops to the area. On May 26, India began using aircraft to bomb Pakistani positions. The next day, Pakistan shot down two Indian MiG fighters, claiming that they had violated Pakistani territory. U.S. President Bill Clinton, among other leaders, urged both countries to exercise restraint, and the U.S. Congress postponed its planned lifting of the 1998 economic sanctions. After meeting with Clinton in Washington, DC, on July 4, Sharif pledged to effect the withdrawal of the Pakistani forces, which took place two weeks later. Even then, tensions remained high. On August 10, India shot down a Pakistani naval observer aircraft, killing all 16 people aboard.

A Rocky Future. The undeclared warfare in Kashmir in mid-1999 set back attempts to normalize Indo-Pakistani relations. It also undermined two opposing assumptions that had emerged after the 1998 Indian and Pakistani nuclear tests. In one scenario, any conflict between the two countries might escalate into nuclear warfare; in the other, the acknowledged possession of nuclear weapons by both sides might create a "balance of terror" that would reduce the probability of armed conflict, since neither would want to provoke nuclear war. The Kargil conflict of 1999 was not thwarted by the nuclear threat, nor did it escalate beyond conventional warfare.

One assumption that was supported by the events of 1999 was the close link between domestic politics and foreign relations in South Asia. For Pakistan, the Kargil conflict appeared both to have grown out of Sharif's hope to shore up his shaky political support and to have contributed to his ouster by Musharraf. As for India, the country was governed during the conflict by a caretaker Bharitiya Janata Party (BJP) government pending national elections, which then returned the BJP to power.

Kashmir has dominated Indo-Pakistani relations for the last half of the 20th century. As the century ended, it appeared destined to remain an intractable challenge, perhaps for decades.

WILLIAM L. RICHTER

The Economy. Despite political instability, economic growth measured a respectable 5.5%. The industrial sector contributed substantially to this. Although foreign-exchange reserves fell, India's external debt remained at the low end of all emerging nations, at just above 20% of the gross domestic product (GDP). That compared with 80% for Indonesia and almost 70% for Thailand. Inflation was not a major factor during 1999.

Observers questioned increases in defense spending, which were allocated primarily to missile and nuclear development. It was felt more should be given to salaries of military personnel and updating of conventional weapons. Some felt that social services and infrastructure would be affected adversely by the emphasis on defense spending. Power generation continued to lag behind demand during the summer.

While states such as Tamil Nadu showed entrepreneurship in attracting investment, most states ran large deficits. Some, such as Bihar, faced virtual bankruptcy. With the central government trying to cut back on its deficits, funding for the states under India's revenue-sharing agreements would be a major problem for the NDA government.

Foreign Relations. Early in the year, Washington continued to pressure both India and Pakistan to sign the Comprehensive Test Ban Treaty (CTBT). Such pressure escalated as India test-fired the Agni missile. Although India hinted that it might be persuaded to sign, the issue was pushed aside with the armed action in Kashmir. After the U.S. Congress refused to ratify the treaty late in the year, the Indian government stated that it saw no reason why it should sign it.

India's efforts to open markets among the South Asian Association for Regional Cooperation (SAARC) countries made little headway, as its smaller neighbors continued to be wary of its comparatively stronger advantage in trade. India also made little headway in improving relations or being accepted into the Association of Southeast Asian Nations (ASEAN). ASEAN members were not convinced of India's own willingness to open its markets, and they also resented India's lack of help during the 1997–98 economic crisis. Additionally, India's nuclear-development program—which strained relations with China, Japan, and the United States—and its hostilities with Pakistan meant few states wanted close relationships with it.

ARUNA NAYYAR MICHIE
Kansas State University

Indonesia

In June 1999, Indonesia held its first free election since 1955, resulting in a new parliament. A democratic government headed by President Abdurrahman Wahid (who was chosen by parliament in October) confronted daunting economic problems and challenges to the country's integrity. Meanwhile, the province of East Timor voted overwhelmingly for independence from Indonesia, sparking a wave of violence (*see* SPECIAL REPORT, page 288).

Politics. On June 7, 112 million Indonesians chose 462 members of a new parliament. After the Suharto regime collapsed in 1998, transitional President B.J. Habibie promised fair elections as the first step in establishing a legitimate post-Suharto government. There were 48 parties on the ballot, but only 21 won legislative seats, and only five of those were major political players. The Indonesian Democratic Party-Struggle (PDI-P), a party of secular nationalists, won 33.7% of the popular vote and obtained 154 parliamentary seats in the proportional-representation system. The PDI-P was headed by Megawati Sukarnoputri, the daughter of Sukarno, Indonesia's first president. President Habibie's governing party, Golkar, garnered 22.4% of the votes and 120 seats. The National Awakening Party (PKB) came in third (12.6%) and earned 51 seats. Its constituency was Indonesia's largest traditional Islamic social movement, the 30-million-member Nahdlatul Ulama (NU), led by Wahid, one of Indonesia's most respected advocates of democracy. The PPP (United Development Party), the Muslim umbrella party during the Suharto years, won 10.7% of the vote; however, because of proportional representation, it won 58 seats, seven

INDONESIA • Information Highlights

Official Name: Republic of Indonesia.
Location: Southeast Asia.
Area: 741,097 sq mi (1 919 440 km^2).
Population (July 1999 est.): 216,108,345.
Chief Cities (Dec. 31, 1996, est.): Jakarta, the capital, 9,341,400; Surabaya, 2,743,400; Bandung, 2,429,000; Medan, 1,942,000.
Government: *Head of state and government,* Abdurrahman Wahid, president (appointed October 1999). *Legislature* (unicameral)—People's Consultative Assembly.
Monetary Unit: Rupiah (7,195.00 rupiahs equal U.S.$1, Dec. 6, 1999).
Gross Domestic Product (1998 est. U.S.$): $602,000,000,000 (purchasing power parity).
Economic Indexes (1997, 1990 = 100): *Consumer Prices* all items, 176.2; food, 186.2. *Industrial Production* (1998, 1990 = 100): 112.8.
Foreign Trade (1998 U.S.$): *Imports,* $27,337,000,000; *exports,* $48,847,000,000.

ABDURRAHMAN WAHID

© Bullit Marquez/AP/Wide World Photos

Muslim scholar Abdurrahman Wahid, elected by parliament as Indonesia's president in October 1999, was born Aug. 4, 1940, in Jombang, East Java, to a family of leading Muslim teachers and leaders. He is known popularly as Gus Dur—"Gus" being an East Javanese term of respect. Following the family tradition, Gus Dur was educated in traditional Islamic boarding schools (*pesantren*) and later studied literature and social studies in Baghdad and Cairo. Returning to Indonesia in 1974, he quickly established a reputation as a leading scholar and commentator on cultural and social affairs. In 1984 he was named chairman of Nahdlatul Ulama (NU), a 30-million-member traditionalist Muslim social and cultural movement. He and his supporters established the National Awakening Party (PKB) after Suharto left office in 1998. A trenchant critic of the authoritarian policies of the Suharto government, he is a strong defender of a nonsectarian democratic pluralist society. Serious health problems, including two strokes, have made him nearly blind. He is married to Sinta Nuriyah and has four daughters.

MEGAWATI SUKARNOPUTRI

© Paula Bronstein/Liaison Agency

Megawati Sukarnoputri, chosen by parliament in October 1999 as Indonesia's vice-president, was born on Jan. 23, 1947, in Jakarta. She was the second child and eldest daughter of Indonesia's first president, Sukarno, and Fatmawati, his third wife. Megawati studied at two different universities but dropped out of both. She emerged as a political actor in 1987, when she was recruited by the Indonesian Democratic Party (PDI). She brought to the PDI the Sukarno legacy and an animosity against the Suharto regime that had toppled her father. In 1993, over government objections, she was elected to head the PDI; three years later, the government masterminded a party coup that stripped her from office. She continued opposition politics under the banner of the PDI-Struggle (PDI-P), becoming a leader of the 1997–98 struggle for democracy that resulted in Suharto's ouster. Her first husband, a pilot in the Indonesian air force, disappeared when his plane went down in midflight, leaving her with two small children. Her second husband, Mohammad Taufik Kiemas, is a successful businessman and her behind-the-scenes political broker.

DONALD E. WEATHERBEE

more than the PKB. The National Mandate Party (PAN) finished fifth, with only 7.1% of the vote and 34 seats.

The parliament, known as the People's Consultative Assembly (MPR), consisted of the 462 elected members plus 238 appointed ones—a group that included 38 representatives from the military, 135 representatives from provincial parliaments, and 65 nominated members of various social, cultural, and religious groups. The MPR met in October and named PAN's Amien Rais its presiding officer.

One of the parliament's duties was to select Indonesia's president. In the interval between the June elections and the convening of the MPR, Amien had led a campaign to unite all Muslim political parties behind Wahid. There were several reasons for the antipathy toward Megawati: She represented secular, not Muslim, interests; she had too many non-Muslim advisers; she refused to bargain; and she was a woman. Habibie's hopes for election were dashed when the MPR rejected his report on his temporary stewardship of the country by a vote of 355 to 322. He then withdrew from the race. His handling of the East Timor referendum that led to its withdrawal from Indonesian sovereignty, and the subsequent violence and international intervention, had wounded him. He also was tarnished by a financial scandal involving his Golkar party.

On October 20, in a secret ballot, Wahid defeated Megawati by a vote of 373 to 313. Megawati supporters felt cheated of their June electoral victory and took to the streets in a night of rioting. They were mollified by her election as vice-president the next day.

President Wahid unveiled a 35-member "Cabinet of National Unity" on October 26. It was a compromise cabinet reflecting the interests of the five major parties as well as the armed forces. Democratic activists felt that the cabinet, with its six army generals and four Habibie holdovers, represented business as usual rather than a new beginning. Within a month, Wahid stated that three members of his cabinet would be ousted because of corruption. The issue of corruption also dogged the new government because of the slow pace of proceedings

SPECIAL REPORT East Timor

The violent and tragic events surrounding the transfer of the territory of East Timor from Indonesian sovereignty to international stewardship overshadowed Indonesia's emergence in 1999 as the world's third-largest democracy. East Timor, sharing an island with Indonesia's West Timor province, had been integrated forcibly into the republic as its 27th province in 1976, after the collapse of Portuguese colonial rule, a Timorese civil war, and an Indonesian invasion. The global community never accepted East Timor as a part of Indonesia and demanded that the province be allowed to decide its own status in an internationally supervised forum. In East Timor more than two decades of guerrilla resistance prompted excesses by the Indonesian military and human-rights abuses, which in turn further fueled domestic and international opposition to Indonesian rule.

During the transition from the Suharto regime to a democratic government, interim President B.J. Habibie, without consulting his senior advisers and military, announced in January 1999 that a referendum would be held in East Timor. The Timorese would be offered autonomy within Indonesia. If they rejected this, they

© Reuters/Newmedia Inc./Corbis

would be set free. The referendum took place on August 30 after four months of preparation by a United Nations Mission in East Timor (UNAMET). Nearly 99% of the eligible voters in East Timor cast their ballots, and 78.5% decisively rejected autonomy in Indonesia in favor of independence.

The climate leading up to the referendum was largely peaceful, but when the results were confirmed and announced, pro-Indonesian militia groups went on a violent rampage. The Indone-

against former President Suharto, his family, and his cronies. Wahid sparked student anger when he said if Suharto were found guilty, he would pardon him.

Meanwhile, other ethnic and regional movements, taking their cue from East Timor, challenged the integrity of the united Indonesian state. A major issue was revenue, because most of Indonesia's natural-resource wealth comes from the outer islands. The most critical problem was the future of Aceh, the northernmost province on Sumatra and an area rich in natural gas. The site of a guerrilla war by the Free Aceh Movement for the last three decades, its population, brutalized by military repression, was inspired to mass protests by the East Timor model. In November, Wahid agreed to a mid-2000 referendum on Aceh's future status. For the Free Aceh Movement, the only acceptable outcome was independence. Jakarta, however, feared that independence for Aceh would be the first step in national disintegration. The government had had similar concerns about East Timor, but unlike that province, which had been integrated into the country only in 1976, Aceh had been a part of Indonesia from the republic's birth in 1945. By late 1999, the problem of Aceh was spurring new ideas about federalism for Indonesia.

Economy. The flow of investment capital and foreign assistance to Indonesia slowed in 1999, as uncertainty about the outcome of the elections, chaos in East Timor, and concerns about corruption shook confidence in the government's capability to carry its recovery program forward. Year-end projections calculated growth of –1% to –0.1%.

The Indonesian Bank Restructuring Agency (IBRA), the main agency for the overhaul of the financial system sponsored by the International Monetary Fund (IMF), was paralyzed in the third quarter by a banking scandal. Bank Bali, operating under IBRA, was charged with funneling illegally nearly $70 million to President Habibie's Golkar party. There was also evidence of a government cover-up and suppression of a damning audit by the U.S. firm PricewaterhouseCoopers. On September 15 the IMF and the World Bank suspended aid prosian military watched (and, according to some observers, even aided) the militias as they sacked the East Timorese capital of Dili, murdered leading independence advocates, and uprooted more than a quarter of the population. UNAMET came under siege as well. Thousands of refugees fled to the mountains or into West Timor. It was as though the militias wanted to leave a legacy in independent East Timor of nothing but scorched earth.

With its own security forces unable or unwilling to restore order, the Indonesian government was pressured into accepting outside intervention by strong international sanctions that included a cutoff of aid from the International Monetary Fund (IMF). An International Force for East Timor (INTERFET), consisting of 7,000 troops under Australian command, was deployed on September 20. Its task was to restore immediate security, so that the refugees could return and the rebuilding of East Timor could begin. At times, the relationship between INTERFET and the Indonesian army was tense, particularly on the border between East Timor and West Timor, where the militias continued to terrorize refugees to impede their return.

On October 26 the United Nations (UN) Security Council authorized a UN Transitional Authority in East Timor (UNTAET) to establish an effective administration. The plan called for UNTAET to have a peacekeeping contingent of more than 10,000, plus a civilian component with total legislative and executive authority. UN Secretary-General Kofi Annan named Undersecretary-General Sergio Vieira de Mello, a Brazilian, as the UNTAET civilian administrator. Meanwhile, a UN human-rights investigation began. As INTERFET and the UN assumed control of East Timor, the last few hundred Indonesian troops quietly pulled out of the former province on October 30, hauling down the Indonesian flag that had flown there for 24 years.

UNTAET's mandate runs to Jan. 31, 2001, but it is renewable. The job of reconstruction and rehabilitation of East Timor will be long, difficult, and expensive. The goal is an independent East Timor. The possible leader of the new state is guerrilla leader José Alexandre "Xanana" Gusmão, who was released in August from a Jakarta prison after seven years and returned in October to a hero's welcome in East Timor. Gusmão and José Ramos-Horta, leader of the exiled East Timorese, met with new Indonesian President Abdurrahman Wahid on November 29 to begin to establish a new political relationship.

DONALD E. WEATHERBEE

grams to Indonesia to add to the pressure to end the violence in East Timor and to clean up what was being called "Bali-gate."

As president, Wahid began to repair Indonesia's relations with the World Bank and the IMF. He met the senior management of both institutions in Washington, DC, on November 12, and his government released the Bank Bali audit and promised to root out corruption. Detailed negotiations with an IMF mission for a resumption of financial assistance was expected to lead to the new government's first letter of intent to the IMF in December. The IMF aid was important in filling an expected budget gap of about 8%. The deficit budget was designed to spur 2% real growth in 2000, but some believed that estimate to be optimistic.

Foreign Affairs. During the last months of the Habibie government, foreign relations were dominated by international concerns over East Timor. President Wahid's first task was to reassure anxious friends and neighbors about his country's stability and commitment to democracy. In early November he made a whirlwind tour of Indonesia's fellow nations in the Association of Southeast Asian Nations (ASEAN). This was followed by a quick trip to the United States, where he had a hurriedly arranged meeting with President Bill Clinton on November 13. Clinton stated the great U.S. interest in a partnership to help build a strong, stable, prosperous, and democratic Indonesia. Wahid underlined the importance of the Indonesian-U.S. relationship. Finally, Wahid stopped in Tokyo to establish face-to-face relations with Japanese Prime Minister Keizo Obuchi, who pledged full backing for Indonesia's recovery.

Wahid's November travels were working meetings, not official state visits. He planned for his first state visits to be to China and India, underlining his government's desire to balance politically its reliance on the United States and Japan. In a bold initiative, Wahid announced that he would seek to open trade relations with Israel. This raised a storm of fundamentalist Muslim protest and denunciation, including public demonstrations.

DONALD E. WEATHERBEE
University of South Carolina

Industrial Production

Led by strength in manufacturing, especially in the output of motor vehicles, office equipment, and electrical machinery, production of U.S. factories and utilities rose strongly throughout 1999. In some categories the pace quickened late in the year.

The strong performance was enhanced by gains in output per worker that kept production well within operating capacity and avoided strains on plant equipment and personnel. Still, there were weaknesses in some areas, such as mining, lumbering, apparel products, and printing and publishing. Defense- and space-equipment production in 1999 was less than 65% of the size it was in the late 1980s, and year-to-year declines continued through 1999. The steel industry argued that it was being hurt by low-priced imports and dumping, but it nevertheless ended the year strongly. In fact, the demand for steel rose as some contractors complained of an inability to obtain fabricated steel items, and some construction projects were said to be behind schedule.

Production's strength had become a continuing story. In every year since 1992, annual gains of at least 3.1% were on record, and growth continued uninterrupted on a monthly basis throughout 1999. According to the Federal Reserve, total industrial output rose an average of 4.5% a year from 1995 through 1999, with output of computers, semiconductors, and communications equipment accounting for more than half the increase. Industry analysts added that a similar level of growth was likely to continue for several years. Examining the data in December, Robert Parry, president of the Federal Reserve Bank of San Francisco, observed that many businesses had yet to embrace computers, the Internet, and other technologies. "You could make the case that some of the developments in high-tech areas are going to have significant impact on all industries," he said. High-tech had become the most vital part of the economy, not just in size and speed of growth but in its contributions to other industries. According to a report in late 1999 by Macroeconomic Advisers, a forecasting firm, improvements in technology have raised the level of U.S. productivity so sharply that the nation's economy could grow up to 3% a year in the next decade without adding to inflation.

The Impact of Technology. Among industries already benefiting, automotives were at the forefront, and they illustrated clearly the powerful impact of the new techniques. Computer-assisted assembly lines helped produce vehicles with longer life spans and fewer maintenance problems, and vehicle performance was directed and measured by tiny chips. This in turn raised buyer confidence in the product, and sales of cars and trucks rose to almost 16 million units for 1999. Citing suppliers to the automotive industry, *The Wall Street Journal* reported that hereafter, a "normal" year might be sales of between 15.7 million and 16.2 million units—as much as 1 million more than automotive executives had believed. If so, the newspaper continued, the newer norm would amount to a huge conceptual change and would affect future investments in a sector accounting for 4% of the U.S. economy. Moreover, Internet sales of vehicles, though embryonic, were rising. And in moves that hardly could have been imagined just a few years earlier, both Ford and General Motors made plans to allow other companies to utilize on-line their computerized supply software, in effect becoming e-commerce companies themselves.

Technology's impact also was clear in the production of energy and electrical machinery. In late 1999 the annual rate of manufactures of electrical machinery was nearly 20% higher than in 1998. The 1999 total was

INDUSTRIAL PRODUCTION—MAJOR MARKET GROUPS

(1992 = 100; monthly data seasonally adjusted)

	1989	1994	1999*
Consumer Goods			
Total	97.7	107.1	116.1
Durable	101.3	119.5	146.5
Nondurable	96.7	104.0	108.9
Equipment			
Total	103.7	108.3	148.9
Business	98.8	112.8	172.9
Defense and space equipment	117.4	87.0	72.5
Intermediate Products			
Total	102.9	106.3	119.7
Construction	105.5	110.6	132.1
Business supplies	101.3	103.7	112.4
Materials			
Total	97.0	111.9	150.3
Energy	99.5	101.2	102.2
Primary Metals			
Total	104.9	113.4	128.2
Iron and steel	106.2	113.7	126.9
Fabricated Metal Products	104.8	112.2	128.1
Industrial Machinery and Equipment	103.0	124.9	225.0
Electrical Machinery	85.8	131.4	352.2
Transportation Equipment			
Total	105.1	107.4	121.5
Motor vehicles and parts	101.2	130.4	150.2
Lumber and Products	104.3	105.9	118.2
Nondurable Manufactures			
Apparel products	100.3	106.3	88.4
Printing and publishing	103.5	100.7	103.3
Chemicals and products	95.1	104.7	116.9
Food	95.9	103.7	109.0

*September preliminary

Source: Board of Governors of the Federal Reserve System

about double that of 1995, and three and one-half times the level at the beginning of the expansion in 1991. The production of electricity had become highly reliant on computerization; the industry said it had spent $2 billion just to check and fix its computers to prevent problems that could result from the Y2K bug.

It was another story in the production of defense and space equipment, an industry whose research and technology had helped spur the expansion in other industries. Continuing a long, steady downturn, output in this sector in 1999 reached less than 75% of what it had been in 1992. This decrease was attributed to reduced international tensions, budget battles, and, according to some newspaper accounts, a degree of disenchantment with space exploration. Other experts theorized that in the midst of an economic boom, Americans had transferred their efforts to more earthly areas, such as homes, factories, and offices.

Other Basic Industries. In consumer goods, the greatest growth during the expansion was in durables. The broad category of consumer durables, including furniture and appliances, rose 7% in 1999, bringing the total gain for the expansion to more than 45%. Consumer nondurables, meanwhile, rose less than 10% in nearly nine years, and fell in 1999, as it had in 1998. Greater growth was achieved in business equipment, a consequence of the changing economy and the emphasis on more-efficient production of goods and services. In some economists' view, these statistics told a story of people and industries increasingly concerned with substance and permanence.

New-construction expenditures had gained added strength in 1997 and 1998, and the momentum continued through 1999. The total for the year topped $700 billion for the first time—a gain of nearly $35 billion over 1998. The largest share, more than $320 billion, was for residential construction, with government projects (about $156 billion) and commercial and industrial efforts ($144 billion) making up the bulk of the remainder. But the strength in this and other categories was not shared by the mining industry, where output shrank for the second year in a row, falling to near 1992 levels.

Electronic Items. While Americans plunged into business with an intensity that seemed to feed on itself, they still had time for games and gadgets. Office managers became accustomed to the sight of employees playing electronic games on their computer screens; few factory foremen were without interactive paging devices; and cell telephones (production of which was estimated at 150 million units in 1999) became common. Penny-pinching tourists increasingly were accompanied by $9.95 throwaway cameras, while the more affluent purchased digital photographic devices costing at least ten times that much. Creators and producers did not forget younger consumers. Pokémon, a Japanese electronic video game that pitted cute monsters against each other, became an expensive rage among children, expanding into trading cards, stuffed toys, and other playthings. Its success spawned scores of domestic competitors.

Every aspect of American life, from prebirth to old age, was infused by electronics, and—if one believed those in the midst of changing the industrial world—a great deal more was to come. While production of consumer items was in itself big business, most of the money invested in electronics was going deep down in the industrial system, in durable goods, machinery, and systems used in making other items—and, based on recent evidence, in making those items more productively.

JOHN CUNNIFF, *The Associated Press*

INDUSTRIAL PRODUCTION

Major Industrial Countries
1992 = 100 (seasonally adjusted)

	Canada	France	Germany	Great Britain	Italy	Japan	United States
1989	105.8	100.9	95.1	103.4	95.7r	99.9	99.1
1990	102.9	102.4	99.9	103.1	101.7r	104.1	98.9
1991	98.9	101.2	102.3	99.7	101.3	106.1	97.0
1992	100.0	100.0	100.0	100.0	100.0	100.0	100.0
1993	104.5	96.1	92.4	102.2	97.9r	96.5	103.5
1994	111.3	100.0	95.6	107.7	103.9r	97.7	109.1
1995	116.3	102.0	96.8	109.5	109.2r	100.9	114.4
1996	118.3	102.2	97.4	110.7	107.1r	103.2	119.5
1997	124.8	106.2	100.8	111.8	111.2r	107.0	126.8
1998*	127.7	111.0	105.0	112.6	112.3r	99.9	131.3
1999**	134.8	114.1	106.3	113.4	113.9	103.6	135.5r

*Preliminary
**August preliminary
rRevised

Source: National data as reported by U.S. Department of Commerce

Interior Design

In 1999 the worlds of fashion and interior design continued to converge. During the year, interior design discovered branding. From Michael Graves for Target to Martha Stewart for KMart, the concept of the "name brand" seeped across the household-goods market from the high end to the low. Recognizable fashion brands continued to extend their reach into the home. Following fashion designers Ralph Lauren and Calvin Klein into the brave new world of furnishings and accessories were Donna Karan, Coach Leather, Banana Republic, Club Monaco, Fendi, Gucci, and even Spa Perrier, the bottled-water company.

Interior designers also were rediscovering name brands from earlier in the 20th century. In the process, they reinvented a modernism that—while it took its cue from such masters as Frank Lloyd Wright, Mies van der Rohe, and Le Corbusier—revered such post–World War II American design influences as Florence Knoll, George Nelson, and Charles and Ray Eames. In vogue again were the Danes, Finns, and Swedes, whose clean-lined, blond, moderately priced designs once filled middle-American homes with what was called Scandinavian Modern. Even more fashionable were designs from the 20th century's Italian renaissance, the era after the war when Italy's greatest contemporary designers experimented with plastics and industrial processes to create now-iconic and highly collectible furniture, lighting, and accessories.

The infatuation with the mid-20th century created a fashion for interiors with strictly edited elements from the 1940s, 1950s, 1960s, and even the 1970s. The spaces, often modeled after artists' lofts, were spare in respect to furniture, open in plan, deliberate in choice of objects, subdued (if not entirely neutral) in color palette, rich with texture, but generally lacking in surface pattern. This influence—whether American, Italian, French, or Nordic—could be seen in everything from magazines to music videos. It also expanded beyond those architect-designed pieces now considered iconic to include previously unsung designers whose work captures the paradoxical blend of simplicity and voluptuousness currently popular with designers. Among prominent names were T.H. Robsjohn-Gibbings, Warren McArthur, Donald Desky, and Ed Wormley. And—apart from the ubiquity of the late Jean-Michel Frank and his omnipresent reinterpreter Christian Liaigre—French furniture and interior designers from the 1940s were in vogue as well. The Hollywood of the 1940s injected a certain glamour into the world of interiors via the rediscovery of the work of the late silent-screen-star-turned-decorator Billy Haines.

Versions of these designs could be found everywhere from flea markets to antique shops, as well as in the new product brought to market twice a year by American manufacturers. The home-furnishing world's infatuation with mid-century modern led to the year's most surprising collection, named for author Ernest Hemingway, a mid-century icon if there ever was one. The 96-piece collection was produced by Thomasville and 11 other companies.

JUDITH NASATIR, *Interior Design Writer*

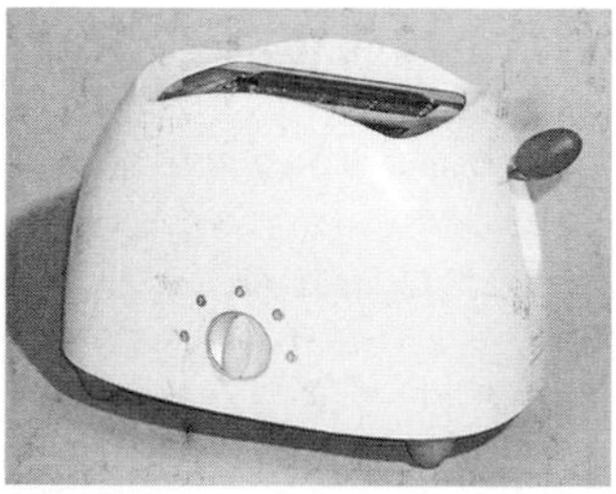

As the desire for the "brand name" became a trend in interior design, architect Michael Graves introduced more than 200 "innovative and contemporary" products for the home. Target Stores began selling the Graves Design Collection in 1999.

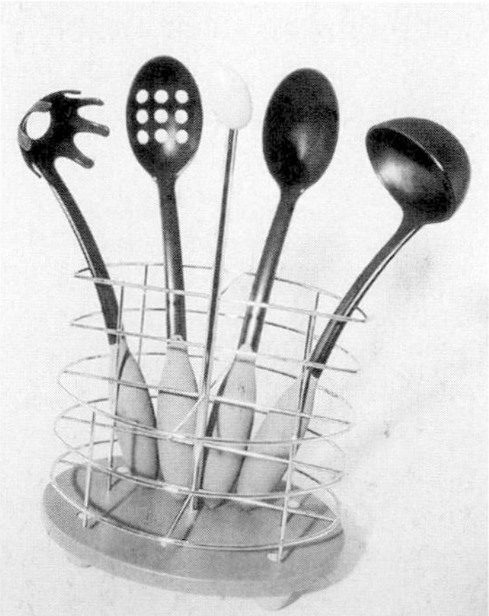

© Photos, Courtesy, Tunheim Santrizos Co. for Target

International Trade and Finance

For many of the world's nations, 1999 was a year of economic healing. "The global economy has passed through a great ordeal," Michel Camdessus, managing director of the International Monetary Fund (IMF), told the world's assembled finance ministers and central bankers at the joint annual meeting of the Fund and the World Bank in late September in Washington. "Now, the storm is abating and the horizon is brightening," Camdessus noted.

Decline and Growth. Somewhat beaten by that storm, Camdessus several weeks later announced his plan to resign as the top executive of the 182-nation institution after nearly 13 years in the job. The last years may well have been his toughest. The Asian financial crisis began with trouble in Thailand in the summer of 1997, ending two decades of spectacular growth. It was followed in August 1998 by Russia's floating of the ruble and default on about $15 billion of domestic debt, one third held by foreigners. Then Brazil got into trouble. In the United States the Federal Reserve organized a rescue of Long-Term Capital Management (LTCM), a huge and prominent hedge fund, from failure.

By the end of 1999, the world looked a lot cheerier economically. The 14 financial institutions that bailed out LTCM with a $3.625 billion capital infusion had been repaid 72% of that capital by the end of September. The Brazilian economy had fallen far less than anticipated after a sharp devaluation in January of its currency, the real. The IMF counted on 1% growth in the economy after inflation in 1999. Four other key Latin American nations saw production fall about 5%. Even Russia was doing better. Boosted by the 75% devaluation of the ruble, which encouraged domestic production of goods, and a near doubling of oil prices, the economy built up some steam. National output rose more than 1% in 1999. Russian industry, though, remained only half as productive as it was in 1982, according to the American consulting firm McKinsey & Co. And gross domestic product (GDP), after inflation, was down 40% from the 1992 level. Nonetheless, the IMF reckoned real growth would bounce back 2% in 2000. Moreover, the postcommunist nations of Eastern Europe shrugged off the Russian storm after an initial shock. Poland and Hungary, for example—two nations that embraced free enterprise more enthusiastically than Russia—enjoyed 4% growth.

In the crisis nations of Asia, the rebound from the financial crisis was faster than anticipated. Thailand's GDP was up about 4% in 1999. South Korea doubled that rate of growth. Malaysia, which had caused some consternation in the Western industrialized world by imposing foreign-exchange controls on its currency, the ringgit, and on trading in its stocks, saw growth of about 4% after inflation. Indonesia was hit hardest by the crisis. Economic output fell a huge 13.2% in after-inflation terms. But the severe troubles did bring about the overturn of the government of President Suharto in 1998. And his successor, B.J. Habibie, was replaced after a democratic election on June 7, 1999, with a new president, Abdurrahman Wahid. There was considerable hope that the frail Muslim cleric would reduce governmental corruption. In any case, the rupiah recovered nicely after the election. The Asian Development Bank (ADB) reckoned on 2% real growth in Indonesia in 1999 and twice that in 2000. For the 14 developing nations of Asia, which include China and India, the ADB saw 5.7% real growth in 1999. China's growth was down to about 7.2%, less than Beijing would have liked, with millions of peasants leaving the farms. Prices in China were falling sharply. India enjoyed about 6% growth. "Asia has made great strides recovering from the worst economic crisis in a generation," said an ADB official. Japan, the world's second-largest economy, surprised most everyone with an economic rebound after what amounted to a ten-year pause. The recovery was driven by massive pump-priming of government expenditures, mostly in the construction area. A new package of $171 billion in government spending was announced in November. Further, the Bank of Japan pressed interest rates down to near zero and was under almost constant pressure to pump ever more yen into the economy.

When the finance ministers and central bankers of the Group of Seven (G-7) industrial nations met in Washington on September 25, just prior to the IMF–World Bank meeting, they talked about what could be done to put more vigor into the Japanese revival. It was seen as crucial to the rest of Asia and key to trimming Japan's huge trade surplus with the rest of the world, especially the United States. In November economists at the Paris-based club of the 29 world's richest nations, the Organization for Economic Cooperation and Development (OECD), called for Japan to maintain its easy monetary stance and work against any contractionary impact from the strengthening of the yen on foreign-exchange markets. It figured on Japan's economy growing 1.4% in 1999 and 2000.

Western Europe too was showing more economic pep. The OECD expected 2.1% real growth in the 11 countries that joined in forming a common currency, the euro, at the start of 1999. These nations were Ireland, Portugal, Spain, France, Italy, Germany, Luxembourg, Belgium, the Netherlands, Finland, and Austria. Britain chose to stay out of the currency union, at least for the time being. With the U.S. economy growing at nearly a 4% pace, the OECD economists were able to note that "the outlook for world and OECD-wide output growth has improved substantially over the past few months." They anticipated real growth in GDP of 2.9% in 1999 for the OECD nations, about the same as foreseen by IMF economists in September. The IMF economists expected 3% growth for the world in 1999, up from 2.5% in 1998. "The slowdown which occurred late in 1998 has ended," the OECD stated. The bulwark of that growth was the United States, which entered its ninth year of economic recovery in March 1999.

But all was not hunky-dory in 1999. During the year, net private-capital flows to the leading emerging market economies amounted to a subdued $136 billion, estimated the Washington-based Institute for International Finance. That was far below the record $335 billion in 1996, prior to the Asian financial crisis. That shock made private money more hesitant to invest in the emerging nations of Asia and Eastern Europe. The Institute estimated that, indeed, $20 billion of money fled Russia—and since the end of 1991, cumulative capital flight had reached more than $140 billion from that troubled nation. The greatest volume of net private flows of capital was attracted by Latin America. It got about $60.1 billion to use in economic development, down from $83.7 billion in 1998. Asia got $39 billion, which was at least an improvement from the $8.6 billion in crisis year 1998.

World Poverty. Further, the divisions in the world between rich and poor were worsened by the economic crisis. The World Bank reckoned that the number of people living on less than $1 a day appeared to be rising. It would reach 1.5 billion by the end of 1999, up 200 million from 1993. "Countries that until recently believed they were turning the tide in the fight against poverty are witnessing its reemergence," lamented bank president James D. Wolfensohn. Indonesia was among the worst hit, with 30 million newly poor. Poverty was rising again in India, with 340 million poor in 1997, up from 300 million in the 1980s. It was up in Africa and sharply worsening across Eastern Europe and Central Asia. China was an exception. The number of absolute poor in China was believed to have declined from 280 million in 1990 to 120 million in 1997, and possibly further since then. Part of the poverty story was the world's continued population growth, especially in Asia and Africa. The world passed the 6 billion mark in October, the United Nations (UN) estimated. The UN, in a mid-1999 look at the world economy, complained that about one person in four in the developing world, roughly 1.2 billion people, lived in countries that suffered a decline in per-capita output in 1998. It estimated that in 1999 only 13 countries, including China, grew fast enough to raise the living standards of their people. That compares with 39 developing countries that met that criterion in 1996, prior to the Asian crisis. UN officials urged Western nations to let in more manufactured goods from the poor nations to help remedy this problem. Though private-capital flows to poorer countries were weak in 1999, the worldwide flow of foreign direct investment, a driving force behind economic growth, continued to grow. This investment in plant, equipment, and offices rose 8.7% to $700 billion in 1999, according to an estimate by the United Nations Conference on Trade and Development (UNCTAD). It had risen 39% to $644 billion in 1998.

Debt. Some progress was made in an international effort to reduce the debts of the most-indebted poor countries. At the Group of Eight (G-8) summit in June in Cologne, Germany, the G-7 leaders agreed on more relief. The overall costs under the new plan would double to $27.5 billion in "net present value," the IMF estimated. That was carried forward to the IMF–World Bank session in September, when the policy-making committees pledged "deeper, broader, and faster debt relief" for 36 of the world's poorest countries. They approved a plan for the IMF to revalue up to 14 million ounces of its gold reserves in transactions with central banks to partly finance the debt initiative. U.S. President Bill Clinton announced the United States would forgive all the debt owed to Washington of 36 poor countries, as long as they use the money saved on debt payments for health care, education, and other basic human needs. Most of these countries are in sub-Saharan Africa. It would cost the United States about $450 million, since most of the $5.7 billion in total debts already had been written off. Subsequently, congressional leaders agreed to appropriate $123 million for relief of debt owed to the United States. And Congress also allowed the IMF to carry out its plan to use some of its own resources, mainly the revaluation of its gold reserves in transactions not involving the gold market, to free up $2.3 billion for debt relief. The World Bank will use some of its profits to reduce debts. Other nations will contribute also to the $14.2 billion of bilateral debt relief.

Trade Developments. The volume of world trade in goods and services grew about 3.7% in 1999, well below the nearly 10% level that prevailed prior to the Asian financial crisis. Two hot trade disputes got considerable press attention. One was a surge in steel imports into the United States that was restrained when U.S. steel companies moved forward with a host of antidumping suits. Another involved what the United States considered to be unfair restriction by the EU on banana imports from Latin America. The United States took this issue to the Dispute Settlement Body of the World Trade Organization (WTO) on behalf of those Latin American nations. The banana battle still was festering as the year approached an end.

One major accomplishment was the move to get China into the WTO. After lengthy negotiations, the United States and China agreed on November 15 on a deal for China's admission into the 135-nation body, climaxing a 13-year quest by China. The deal will open China's markets considerably to U.S. exports and investment, if properly implemented. China still had to complete arrangements with the EU, Canada, and other developing countries before its application to join WTO would be considered by all of the member states.

A meeting of WTO trade ministers in Seattle, WA, starting in late November, made news for the wrong reason. Some 30,000 demonstrators blocked many of the delegates from 135 nations from reaching the opening of the conference, which had the main purpose of launching a round of trade negotiations for the 21st century. The police imposed a curfew in the downtown area and used tear gas to help disperse the protesters. Dozens of protesters were arrested.

© Donald Stampfli/AP/Wide World Photos

In July 1999, Mike Moore, a 50-year-old economist and former prime minister of New Zealand, was appointed director general of the World Trade Organization (WTO).

The majority of the demonstrators, however, were peaceful. They had diverse objectives. A large group of trade-union members maintained that the expansion of free trade was hurting working Americans and especially protested an influx of foreign steel. Some environmentalist groups claimed the WTO, in effect, was allowing shrimpers to take sea turtles, an endangered species, into their nets along with the shrimp. Some other nongovernment bodies protested the WTO's support of the U.S. desire to export hormone-treated beef. Others held that the WTO was too secretive and powerful.

Despite efforts by President Clinton to get results from the conference he had sought, the delegates were unable to agree on an agenda for a new round. Some trade gurus held that the talks were premature and that more time was needed to get adequate domestic and international support for negotiating a new trade deal. In any case, the experts noted, trade negotiators can continue with unfinished business from the last major trade agreement, dubbed the Uruguay Round. Progress toward freer trade perhaps was slowed, but was not stopped. Meanwhile, the protesters may have aroused more suspicion of "globalization"—a rapid merging of national economies through commerce and finance.

See also STOCKS AND BONDS.

DAVID R. FRANCIS
"The Christian Science Monitor"

Iran

Developments in Iran in 1999, the 20th anniversary of the Islamic revolution, had, even more than in recent years, a clearly defined theme: the ongoing conflict between two visions for the future of the country. One saw the future in terms of the continuance of an Islamic theocracy, with Western values, ideas, and contacts kept to a bare minimum, if not excluded altogether. The other, although accepting Islam, looked for a loosening of the country's rigid outlook, especially in such matters as censorship of publications and contacts with the West. President Mohammed Khatami was the standard-bearer for the reformists, and the Ayatollah Ali Khamenei presented the conservative, or traditionalist, point of view.

This struggle was actually less clear-cut than it appeared, however. On both sides, there was a general, fundamental acceptance of Shia Islam as the basis of law and society; the differences arose with regard to interpretation and application. As events in 1999 showed, Khatami and Khamenei were capable of forming a harmonious working partnership and agreeing on some issues. Institutionally, the traditionalists held all the high cards, as they continued to dominate the Assembly of Experts (the Iranian equivalent of the Supreme Court), the Majlis (parliament), and the judiciary. Khamenei, the supreme spiritual leader, was superior to Khatami in status and power and controlled the armed forces. But demographics favored the reformers. In the 20 years since the revolution, Iran's population had doubled in size and become increasingly youthful. The support of younger voters brought Khatami his election victory in 1997. The country's dire financial straits, which most experts believed could be improved only by more external links to the global economy, also favored the reformers.

The tug-of-war between old and new continued throughout 1999, with each side scoring victories. On the whole, though, it appeared that the conservatives' behavior had the flavor of desperation.

Domestic Affairs. The preferred strategy of the conservatives appeared to be physical or legal attacks on prominent individuals on the opposing side. A leading Khatami supporter, Abdullah Nouri, had been ousted from his post of minister of the interior in June 1998, and the traditionalists continued their attack on him in 1999. In November, Nouri was tried on charges of having published sacrilegious articles in his popular newspaper, *Khordad*. After a four-week trial, during which Nouri roundly denounced the clerical establishment for having betrayed the ideals of the 1979 revolution, he was found guilty and sentenced to five years' imprisonment. In addition, *Khordad* was shut down, and Nouri was fined $5,000 and forbidden to run in parliamentary elections for five years. But an attempt by some members of the Majlis to impeach Ataollah Mohajerani, another Khatami ally who had provided political and financial support to several independent newspapers, failed to gain a majority.

Another newspaper, *Zan* (Woman), was shut down when its editor, Faezeh Hashemi,

© Corbis

The closing of a pro-reform newspaper in Iran in early July 1999 sparked several weeks of angry demonstrations and rioting by students in Tehran and other cities. Supporters of the conservative regime, some carrying pictures of supreme spiritual leader Ayatollah Ali Khamenei, countered by holding their own rallies, right.

daughter of former President Hashemi Rafsanjani and a member of the Majlis, published a New Year's message from former Empress Farah Diba, as well as a cartoon deemed offensive to Islam. Despite such victories, the conservatives were finding it increasingly difficult to quash press freedom, as new reformist media kept appearing and attracting wide readership.

A graver matter, however, was the murder in December 1998 of four middle-rank dissidents. The killings were condemned by President Khatami—and also, emphatically, by Khamenei, who pressed for a vigorous investigation. Not long after the murders occurred, the intelligence ministry announced that some of its agents had been arrested for the crime, and in June one of them, former Deputy Intelligence Minister Said Emami, died in jail, reportedly by his own hand.

The banning of *Salam*, a long-established pro-reform newspaper, under a new press law in early July sparked several days of student unrest and riots against the government—events without parallel in the regime's 20-year history. Hundreds of Tehran University students staged a protest demonstration, and, in reaction, a mixed band of far-right extremists and police broke into dormitories on the campus, beating students and destroying property. Several students died during the violence. Days of rioting in Tehran and other major cities followed. Both Khatami and Khamenei condemned the violence on both sides. By July 21 order had been restored. Later, Tehran Police Chief Hossein Lotfian apologized for his role in the violent incidents.

The first municipal elections in 20 years, held on February 26, marked a significant advance for the reformists, with overwhelming victories in Tehran and other major cities. The real revelation of public opinion, however, was expected to come with the elections to the Majlis, to be held in February 2000. On April 28 several of the newly elected Tehran City Council members were disqualified by the conservative electoral supervisory committee; however, the Interior Ministry overturned the decision the next day. Khamenei, in another instance where he seemed to be distancing himself from the hard-line conservatives, sided with the reformers in the dispute.

In March the United Nations' human-rights observer for Iran reported that the government was becoming more respectful of human rights, including freedom of expression. On March 21, *Nowruz*, a traditional holiday to celebrate the beginning of spring, took place with full official approval for the first time in 20 years. On April 28 the U.S. State Department announced that U.S. firms would be permitted to sell food, medicine, and medical equipment to Iran; however, the country remained on the U.S. list of nations involved in terrorist acts.

IRAN • Information Highlights

Official Name: Islamic Republic of Iran.
Location: Southwest Asia.
Area: 636,293 sq mi (1 648 000 km²).
Population (July 1999 est.): 65,179,752.
Chief Cities (1996 census): Tehran, the capital, 6,758,845; Mashad, 1,887,405; Esfahan, 1,266,072; Tabriz, 1,191,043.
Government: *Head of state and government,* Mohammed Khatami, president (elected May 1997). *Legislature* (unicameral)—Islamic Consultative Assembly (Majlis).
Monetary Unit: Rial (1,752.50 rials equal U.S.$1, Jan. 3, 2000).
Gross Domestic Product (1998 est. U.S.$): $339,700,000,000 (purchasing power parity).
Economic Index (1998, 1990 = 100): *Consumer Prices,* all items, 616.0; food, 669.2.
Foreign Trade (1998 est. U.S.$): *Imports,* $13,800,000,000; *exports,* $12,200,000,000.

Khatami made two important démarches in economic policy that did not appear to be entirely compatible with each other. On September 15 he presented his first five-year economic plan, calling for a "total restructuring" of the economy, with major steps toward privatization. The plan would privatize the communications, postal, railroad, and tobacco sectors, thereby doubling the portion of the economy that was privatized from the current 10% to 15% to about 30%. But in a basically anti-U.S. speech in Paris on October 29, Khatami denounced the globalization of the economy, calling it a "destructive force" that resembled a kind of "neo-colonialism."

Foreign Relations. The president continued his policy of reestablishing ties with Iran's Arab neighbors. In May, Khatami and his foreign minister went to Saudi Arabia in an attempt to mend relations, which had been no better than cool since the 1979 revolution. The visit seemed to have positive results, and indeed the two countries already had begun cooperating to push for higher oil prices. From Saudi Arabia, the president went on to Qatar. He also visited several European countries, including Italy, where he met with Italian leaders and Pope John Paul II; and France, where he talked with President Jacques Chirac. Khatami was the first Iranian leader to visit either country since the revolution.

In September, Khatami welcomed Austrian President Thomas Klestil, the first head of state from the European Union (EU) to visit Iran. Iran and Britain restored ambassadorial relations in May, a move facilitated by Tehran's announcement in September 1998 distancing itself from the *fatwa* (death edict) against British-Indian author Salman Rushdie. But Tehran rebuffed several tentative U.S. attempts to make contact.

In late May, 13 Jews from Fars province in southern Iran were arrested on charges of spying for Israel; if found guilty, they would face the death penalty. The United States, France, and other Western countries called for the prisoners' release, a request that Iran refused.

ARTHUR CAMPBELL TURNER
University of California, Riverside

Iraq

Saddam Hussein, the dictatorial president of Iraq for the past two decades, remained in power in 1999—more than eight years after the Gulf war of early 1991. His domestic situation was probably more secure than ever. In late 1998 he got rid of the handicap of United Nations (UN) inspectors whose function had been to make sure his government was destroying its chemical, nuclear, and biological weapons and was not researching or manufacturing any more. Few observers believed that Iraq was failing to take advantage of these more favorable circumstances to advance its weapons programs. Meanwhile, three of the five permanent members of the UN Security Council—France, Russia, and China—were edging closer to supporting Iraq in its demand for an end to the trade sanctions that had been imposed on it. These three powers were more interested in the economic possibilities of relations with Iraq than in maintaining the sanctions.

To a remarkable extent, the question of Iraq had become a duel between Hussein and the United States, with Britain as the only reliable U.S. ally. And U.S. policy, on the whole, had failed. Hussein was still in power, with only negligible, extremely weak opposition. Overwhelming U.S.-British airpower and the imposition of "no-fly zones" in the north and south had not made the Kurds and other dissidents in the north secure, nor had it protected the marsh peoples of the south from a draconian reordering of their historic way of life. While the inspections had led to the destruction of many of the prohibited weapons, adroit concealment no doubt had kept many other stores and facilities from discovery.

The plight of most Iraqis remained bad, however. Infant mortality rose, and all indexes of public health indicated severe and continuing deterioration.

Ineffective Opposition. Hussein's firm grip on power was due not only to his demonstrated readiness to repress savagely any dissent or revolt, but also to the ineptitude and disunity of the opposition. There simply was no plausible legatee of Hussein's power, and no alternative government in sight.

The Iraqi opposition consisted of about 100 mostly small groups with widely divergent aims. The most convincing umbrella organization uniting a number of opposition groups, the Iraqi National Congress (INC), had been hamstrung ever since most of its leaders had been killed, imprisoned, or exiled after an Iraqi raid into the north in 1996. In the Kurdish north, an agreement engineered by the United States in September 1998 between two rival leaders, Massoud Barzani and Jalal Talabani, seemed to be holding; but the two men also had an informal understanding with the government in Baghdad not to disturb the status quo. Although the U.S. Congress and President Bill Clinton had approved an allotment of $97 million for military aid to democratic forces in Iraq in October 1998, it appeared at the end of 1999 that none of this money actually was disbursed.

Sporadic Unrest. Every now and then, however, incidents occurred that suggested the existence of a good deal of seething unrest among the Iraqi people. One such event happened in February, when Grand Ayatollah Mohammed Sadeq al-Sadr, the most prominent Shiite Muslim cleric in Iraq, was assassinated along with his two sons. This was one of several attacks on Shiite clergy in recent years. In 1998, for example, two ayatollahs in Najaf were shot dead, and

IRAQ • Information Highlights

Official Name: Republic of Iraq.
Location: Southwest Asia.
Area: 168,754 sq mi (437 072 km²).
Population (July 1999 est.): 22,427,150.
Chief City (1987 census): Baghdad, the capital, 3,844,608.
Government: *Head of state and government,* Saddam Hussein, president (took office July 1979). *Legislature* (unicameral)—National Assembly.
Monetary Unit: Dinar (0.3231 dinar equals U.S.$1, Jan. 3, 2000).
Gross Domestic Product (1998 est. U.S. $): $52,300,000,000 (purchasing power parity).

© Jassim Mohammed/AP/Wide World Photos

Saddamiat Al-Thirthar, a new lakeside resort west of Baghdad, opened in May 1999. Like most public places in Iraq, the complex was filled with elaborate tributes to President Saddam Hussein, from a huge statue of the Iraqi leader at the entrance, left, *to the buildings themselves, constructed of bricks engraved with his initials. But the grandeur of the resort stood in stark contrast to the dire poverty faced by most ordinary Iraqis.*

others were harassed or assaulted. Hussein and his ruling clique, who are Sunni Muslims, are outnumbered somewhat by Shiite Muslims, especially south of Baghdad, and there was some suspicion of government involvement in these attacks. The killing of the Grand Ayatollah sparked demonstrations in Baghdad, Najaf, and Nasiriyah, all of which were suppressed ruthlessly by the government. Many protesters in Baghdad were killed, but the exact number was unknown. The government denied that there had been any unrest.

The official Iraqi gazette reported on March 14 that eight Iraqis had been executed for the murders of the two Shiite clerics in 1998. A few days later, four men confessed on television to killing the Grand Ayatollah. They were executed on April 6.

Continuing Air Strikes. After the end of "Operation Desert Fox," the severe four-day bombing campaign launched by the United States and Britain against Iraq in December 1998, low-intensity warfare continued throughout 1999. U.S. and British planes made almost daily attacks on Iraqi antiaircraft installations and other targets. In February, Iraqi media said that three days of bombing in the southern no-fly zone had caused civilian casualties, and similar reports were released throughout the year.

Meanwhile, a British newspaper published an unconfirmed report, based on Moscow sources, that Russia had signed a $160 million deal with Iraq to upgrade its air defenses, which would be a breach of the UN embargo. The Russian government denied the report.

Dealings with the UN. From the late spring through the end of the year, much diplomatic effort went into devising a new proposal that would be mild enough to be acceptable to Iraq (as well as to China, Russia, and France), and yet would allow some form of inspection on Iraqi soil to resume. On December 17 such a resolution finally cleared the Security Council by a vote of 11–0. (China, Russia, France, and Malaysia abstained.) The agreement said that sanctions against Iraq would end if the country accepted a new inspections system that would be much less independent than UNSCOM had been. Iraqi Foreign Minister Tariq Aziz rudely rejected the proposal the next day.

In November, Iraq abruptly cut off its oil exports after the UN extended for only two weeks a deal that permitted Iraq to sell $5.2 billion worth of oil every six months to buy food, medical supplies, and humanitarian goods for its people. The UN previously had extended the oil-for-food program for six-month periods. Iraq's action led to a brief spike in oil prices, which already had been rising during the year. Three weeks later, the Security Council voted to extend the program by the normal six months, and Iraq resumed its oil sales.

ARTHUR CAMPBELL TURNER
University of California, Riverside

Ireland

Official investigations into political corruption captured headlines in Ireland in 1999.

Political Corruption. Driving the corruption inquiries were charges of bribes paid by property developers and the misuse of funds by leaders of the Fianna Fail party. In addition, several banks had loaned thousands of pounds to leading politicians without charging interest or expecting repayment.

One of the chief recipients of money from property developers was Ray Burke, the former minister for foreign affairs, who allegedly had pocketed at least 40,000 Irish pounds ($51,000). According to Burke, these payments were donations to Fianna Fail, without any strings attached. Another Fianna Fail politician, European Commissioner Padraig Flynn, allegedly had received 50,000 Irish pounds ($64,000) on behalf of the party in 1989, when he was minister for the environment, from London-based developer Tom Gilmartin. But this donation went unrecorded in the party's ledgers.

Former prime minister and former Fianna Fail leader Charles J. Haughey suffered further embarrassment from disclosures that he had spent many thousands of pounds from private loans or gifts and party funds on luxury items. Meanwhile, the Dail Committee of Public Accounts uncovered the names of wealthy Irish who had set up accounts in the Cayman Islands.

Although the allegations did not end in any indictments, their cumulative weight damaged Fianna Fail and forced Prime Minister Bertie Ahern to defend the bruised reputation of his government.

Northern Ireland and European Union. Ahern did not allow these domestic concerns to distract him from promoting reconciliation in Northern Ireland. In addition to private talks with British Prime Minister Tony Blair, he joined Northern Irish leaders at the White House on St. Patrick's Day to hear U.S. President Bill Clinton's plea for a break in the impasse over the decommissioning of weapons. Ahern welcomed a late-in-the-year agreement on the weapons issue that paved the way for devolution, or the creation of a power-sharing government in the North.

On the European front, Ireland officially became a member of the European Monetary Commission on January 1. Elections to the European Parliament were held June 10–13. Fianna Fail lost one seat, going from seven to six. Fine Gael retained four seats, and Labour held onto its one seat. The Green Party returned two members. Only half the electorate voted.

During the summer, Italy's Prime Minister Romano Prodi, president of the European Commission, appointed David Byrne as commissioner for consumer affairs and food safety. And Pat Cox, leader of the Liberal Democrat and Reform Party, was named to succeed Nicole Fontaine as president of the European Parliament after two and one half years.

The Economy. The Irish economy showed signs of robust growth in 1999, as employment figures and consumer spending rose impressively. House prices and the value of many Irish stocks and shares also climbed. Finance Minister Charlie McCreevy's budget speech on December 1 promised a tax cut of almost 1 billion Irish pounds ($1.28 billion) that would benefit the wealthy and working couples. The budget also increased old-age pensions as well as expenditures on roads, transportation, and housing.

A mid-October strike by some 28,000 nurses—the largest strike in Ireland's history—was resolved after nine days, when a majority of Nursing Alliance members voted in favor of a wage package increase of some 125 million Irish pounds ($159.75 million).

Other News. In July drug dealer and gang member Brian Meehan was found guilty of conspiring to murder journalist Veronica Guerin in 1996. And on October 20 police discovered an underground bunker full of weapons at Stamullen and arrested seven members of the Real Irish Republican Army (IRA).

The country mourned the passing of Jack Lynch, 82, who had served as Taoiseach (1966–73; 1977–79). He died on October 20.

L. PERRY CURTIS, JR., *Brown University*

IRELAND • Information Highlights

Official Name: Ireland.
Location: Island in the eastern North Atlantic Ocean.
Area: 27,135 sq mi (70 280 km²).
Population (July 1999 est.): 3,632,944.
Chief Cities (1996 census [incl. suburbs]): Dublin, the capital, 952,716; Cork, 180,000; Limerick, 79,100.
Government: *Head of state,* Mary McAleese, president (took office Nov. 11, 1997). *Head of government,* Bertie Ahern, prime minister (elected June 26, 1997). *Legislature*—Parliament (Oireachtas): Senate (Seanad Eireann) and House of Representatives (Dail Eireann).
Monetary Unit: Pound (1.2779 pounds equal U.S.$1, Dec. 1, 1999).
Gross Domestic Product (1998 est. U.S.$): $67,100,000,000 (purchasing power parity).
Economic Indexes (1998, 1990 = 100): *Consumer Prices,* all items, 119.6; food, 119.2. *Industrial Production,* 228.2.
Foreign Trade (1998 U.S.$): *Imports,* $44,226,000,000; *exports,* $63,962,000,000.

Israel

With the collapse of Israel's government in December 1998, the Knesset (parliament) called for national elections in 1999, a year ahead of schedule. In the May 17 election, Labor's Ehud Barak (*see* BIOGRAPHY) decisively defeated incumbent Prime Minister Benjamin Netanyahu, leader of the Likud Party. Barak immediately focused on concluding peace agreements with Syria and the Palestinians.

Domestic Affairs. According to Israel's electoral law, voters can cast two ballots—one for prime minister, the other for the party of their choice. At one point, there were six candidates for prime minister, but by election eve in May, only two remained: Netanyahu and Barak. More than 30 parties represented the three traditional large blocs: labor, religious-orthodox, and the nationalist-right. Other parties represented a host of special interests, including women; various ethnic groups such as Russian, Romanian, and Sephardic Jews; and several Israeli Arab factions.

Prior to the election, the party system was transformed by a series of new amalgamations and factionalizations. Of the Knesset's 120 members, 29 switched to rival parties or formed new factions of their own. Likud, the largest party until the election, saw half a dozen of its leading members leave to join new parties, including the middle-of-the-road Center and the anti-peace-agreement faction National Unity. The Center Party was led by former Likud Defense Minister Yitzhak Mordechai, a former army chief of staff fired by Netanyahu.

Under Barak the Labor Party joined with Gesher, led by former Likud Foreign Minister David Levy, and Meimad, a moderate Orthodox religious group, to form One Israel. Although electioneering focused on the peace process, Barak also promised to expand free education, to lower Israel's 8% unemployment rate by creating 300,000 new jobs, and to invest $1 billion in new infrastructure. One of his most controversial promises was to withdraw Israeli forces from Lebanon by midyear 2000.

Both Barak and Netanyahu sought to win through the use of American-style election tactics. One Israel and Likud employed American consultants, including Stan Greenberg, Bob Schrum, and James Carville, one of U.S. President Bill Clinton's advisers.

Predictions of a close race for prime minister were confounded when Barak won 56.1% of the vote to Netanyahu's 43.7%, the largest victory in any election for prime minister. Within an hour after exit-poll results were published, Netanyahu conceded defeat and announced that he would resign from the Knesset and from the leadership of Likud. He was replaced by former general Ariel Sharon.

The outcome of Knesset voting was a different matter, producing a more factionalized parliament than in the last several elections. A total of 15 parties were chosen, the largest number represented in any Knesset. Among the most surprising results were the decline of the two major parties, Labor and Likud, and the rise to third place of Shas, the party of ultra-Orthodox Sephardic Jews. Barak's One Israel fell from 34 seats to

© Reuters/Archive Photos

In June 1999, a few weeks after winning Israel's premiership by an overwhelming margin, Ehud Barak (left) *met with the man he defeated, incumbent Prime Minister Benjamin Netanyahu of the Likud Party. The meeting took place as Barak was considering including Likud in his new coalition. Ultimately, Likud became the main opposition party.*

ISRAEL • Information Highlights

Official Name: State of Israel.
Location: Southwest Asia.
Area: 8,019 sq mi (20 770 km^2).
Population (July 1999 est.): 5,749,760.
Chief Cities (Dec. 31, 1996, est.): Jerusalem, the capital, 613,600 (including East Jerusalem); Tel Aviv–Jaffa, 349,200; Haifa, 262,600.
Government: *Head of state,* Ezer Weizman, president (took office March 1993). *Head of government,* Ehud Barak, prime minister (sworn in July 6, 1999). *Legislature* (unicameral)—Knesset.
Monetary Unit: Shekel (4.2334 shekels equal U.S.$1, Nov. 29, 1999).
Gross Domestic Product (1998 est. U.S.$): $101,900,-000,000 (purchasing power parity).
Economic Indexes (1998, 1990 = 100): *Consumer Prices,* all items, 233.7; food, 203.9. *Industrial Production,* 158.4.
Foreign Trade (1998 U.S.$): *Imports,* $29,342,000,000; *exports,* $23,286,000,000.

27; Likud from 32 seats to 19. The three Orthodox religious parties—Shas (17 seats), National Religious Party (NRP; five seats), and United Torah Judaism (UTJ; five seats)—emerged as a powerful bloc, with more seats than in any previous Knesset. Three Arab parties—the United Arab List, Hadash, and Balad—together won ten seats, an increase of one since the last Knesset. The new Knesset also included the first Arab member of the prestigious committee on foreign and security affairs.

Polarization on religious issues was evident in the increase of votes for parties strongly emphasizing secularization of government and society: Meretz, a leftist party, held onto its nine seats; and Shinui, a new militantly anti-Orthodox faction formerly associated with Meretz, won six additional seats. The conflict between the Orthodox and the secular was intensified by the conviction for corruption and bribery of Shas leader Aryeh Deri.

As in previous elections, no party won a majority, necessitating the formation of a coalition government. After extensive bargaining with several political groups, including Likud, Barak formed a government of seven parties holding 75 of the 120 Knesset seats. They were One Israel, Shas, Meretz, Yisrael B'aliya (a Russian immigrant party), Center, NRP, and UTJ. The new coalition represented a diverse array of interests—hawks and doves, socialists and free-enterprisers, fervently Orthodox religious practitioners and secularists. More than half of the new government had been members of Netanyahu's coalition and had supported his bid for reelection.

An initial cabinet crisis arose when Barak backed transporting a huge piece of electrical machinery from one region of the country to another on the Sabbath, a move considered essential to avoid weekday road congestion. Ultra-Orthodox parties in the coalition threatened to quit over the issue, but a compromise was worked out whereby the machinery was loaded before sundown, unloaded after sundown, and driven by a non-Jewish truck driver. Shas also threatened several times to quit the coalition over budget matters; it demanded increased government support for its network of religious schools and social-welfare institutions. A conflict with NRP was avoided when Barak agreed to remove only a dozen of the more than 40 unauthorized Jewish hilltop outposts recently established in the occupied West Bank.

Clashes between Israeli Arab Christians and Muslims came to a head in a dispute over land fronting the Church of the Annunciation in Nazareth. The Christian community planned to use the half acre for a large plaza. However, the plot—containing the tomb of a 12th-century Muslim hero who fought the Crusaders—was claimed by Muslims for construction of a large mosque. The government proposed a plan calling for a small mosque to be erected near the church, leaving room for a plaza to accommodate Christian pilgrims expected for the millennium. But some Roman Catholic and Orthodox Christian leaders resisted the idea, and in November several churches across the Holy Land, including the Church of the Annunciation, closed for two days in protest.

The Peace Process and Foreign Affairs. Although Barak appointed David Levy minister of foreign affairs, the prime minister himself took charge of peace negotiations with the Palestinians. He announced that the framework for a final settlement would be drafted by February 2000 and that, by September, a treaty with the Palestinians would be achieved. Shortly after taking office, Barak invited Palestine Authority President Yasir Arafat to a secret meeting at the prime minister's residence to discuss peace plans. He also visited Cairo and Washington for strategy conferences with Egyptian President Hosni Mubarak and U.S. President Clinton. Barak and Syrian President Hafiz al-Assad exchanged compliments in June, raising the possibility that peace negotiations between Syria and Israel, which broke off in 1996, could be renewed. That hope was realized on December 8, when Clinton announced that talks would begin again between the two countries. On December 15–

16, Barak and Syrian Foreign Minister Farouk al-Shara (acting as Assad's proxy) met in Washington, DC, to open negotiations. In January the two men went to Shepherdstown, WV, to continue trying to work out a peace accord.

In September, Barak and Arafat signed a new broad agreement at the Egyptian town of Sharm el-Sheikh; the agreement renewed many of the terms previously agreed on between Israel and the Palestinians but unfulfilled during Netanyahu's tenure. The agreement envisaged settlement within a year of many difficult issues, including the boundaries between Israel and the Palestinians, the status of Jerusalem, the future of more than 3 million Palestinian refugees, and an equitable distribution of scarce water resources. Short-term arrangements called for full implementation of the October 1998 Wye River Memorandum, providing for the transfer in September of 7% of the West Bank from total Israeli to joint Israeli-Palestinian control. In November another 2% would be transferred to the Palestinians and 3% placed under joint control. In January 2000 a third transfer of land would result in 40% of the West Bank being in partial or full control by the Palestinians. Other terms provided for Israel's release of several hundred Palestinian political prisoners and the opening of a "safe passage" through Israel between the Palestinian-controlled areas in Gaza and the West Bank. The main street in the Arab town of Hebron, which had been under Israeli army control to separate the few Jewish residents from the Arab majority, also was to be opened.

Even after the new agreement, difficulties remained in opening final-status talks, principally Arafat's objection to continued Jewish settlement in the West Bank. However, after Clinton, Barak, and Arafat met in Washington, DC, and Oslo, talks began in Ramallah in November between lower-level Israeli and Palestinian representatives.

Although Barak stated his intention to withdraw troops from Lebanon by mid-2000, border conflict in the north intensified beginning in June, when the Israel Air Force launched the most extensive raids against guerrilla targets since the 1996 Grapes of Wrath operation. Striking deep inside Lebanon, the assaults knocked out electricity plants, causing power outages in Beirut. The attacks continued into November.

In October, Mauritania became the third Arab country (after Egypt and Jordan) to establish full diplomatic ties with Israel. Despite the efforts of Mubarak and Jordan's King Abdullah II to speed up peace negotiations, Israel's relations with both countries were strained. In March, Jordan charged that Israel violated the peace treaty by withholding the agreed-upon quantities of water. Egypt attempted to pressure Mauritania to withhold recognition and to block meetings of the multilateral peace negotiations until Israel reached peace with Syria.

Israel's sale of a sophisticated airborne radar system and other advanced military technology to China during 1999 strained its close relations with the United States. The Clinton administration feared that China's acquisition of such weaponry would endanger another U.S. ally, Taiwan.

See also MIDDLE EAST.

DON PERETZ
Professor Emeritus, Binghamton University

Italy

According to Carlo Azeglio Ciampi, who was elected president of Italy by Parliament in May 1999, the nation made notable progress during the year toward what he called a "culture of stability." He went on to predict that the country would reduce its deficit to 1% of gross domestic product (GDP) in 2000, and also cited Italy's political stability. But Prime Minister Massimo D'Alema faced numerous difficulties in 1999, including tension among members of his ruling coalition over Italy's participation in the bombing of Serbia by the North Atlantic Treaty Organization (NATO).

Foreign Affairs. Foreign-policy issues dominated 1999, an unusual situation for Italy. The country was involved intimately in the conflict between Serbia and NATO over the province of Kosovo (*see* THE KOSOVO CRISIS, page 78). The airbase at Aviano served as the principal launching area for NATO's bombing raids. But the participation of Italian warplanes in the raids, painful memories of the country's military involvement in the Balkans during both world wars, and the constitution's prohibition against wars except for defense purposes fomented a divisive debate within the ruling coalition.

The principal criticism of the bombing came from Armando Cossutta's hard-line Party of Italian Communists (PCI), whose participation was essential to maintain the coalition. Cossutta demanded that the bombing stop and that negotiations with Yugoslav President Slobodan Milosevic be

In May 1999 the Italian Parliament elected Treasury Minister Carlo Azeglio Ciampi, right, as the country's tenth president. A longtime civil servant, Ciampi most recently had distinguished himself by skillfully preparing Italy for the introduction of the euro, the common European currency, as the year began.

© Plinio Lepri/AP/Wide World Photos

opened immediately. The disaffection rapidly spread to the coalition's various Catholic groups, influenced by the Vatican's hostility to the raids. Most seriously for D'Alema, his own party, Democrats of the Left (DS), was torn between its traditional pacifism and its leader's support for NATO's action.

The growing opposition forced D'Alema to shift gears. On a visit to Berlin on March 25, the Italian premier shrugged off Cossutta's criticism. An hour later, he stated that a political solution now appeared possible, because the NATO bombing had achieved significant results. This declaration irritated President Bill Clinton and British Prime Minister Tony Blair, who quickly contradicted him. D'Alema's about-face, however, bolstered his position in Italy.

Meanwhile, members of the coalition undertook delicate negotiations to keep the D'Alema cabinet in power despite their statements criticizing it. As the factions worked on a parliamentary motion acceptable to all, Cossutta demanded that the motion state that the bombing must end. The final motion approved by Parliament sanctioned the government's actions "within the context of Italy's alliances," but it instructed the cabinet to work with NATO to find a way to open negotiations and halt the bombing. D'Alema attempted to adhere to this agreement, even though it created embarrassment for him. Following reports that Milosevic had stepped up his military operations and that 500,000 refugees were streaming out of Kosovo, D'Alema spoke with Clinton and agreed that the bombing must be intensified. At the same time, he telephoned the heads of the French and German governments encouraging negotiations. Italian diplomats also were working with the Russians to seek a solution to the crisis.

In a brief, nationally televised address on March 30, D'Alema said that Italy supported the bombing because of Serb atrocities and because all possible attempts at negotiation had failed. The speech provoked Cossutta's ire once again and resulted in new infighting among the coalition members. Throughout the remainder of the Kosovo crisis, D'Alema had to maintain a delicate balance between placating the detractors within his own coalition and keeping Italy loyal to NATO.

Another important aspect of Italy's Kosovo involvement was the aid the country extended to the refugees in "Operation Rainbow." The government declared a state of emergency, giving full powers to relief agencies to provide shelter and food. The Italians also patrolled their own military zone in Kosovo, contributing more than 5,000 troops to the peacekeeping force.

In other international news, Italy was outraged in March when a U.S. military court acquitted Marine Capt. Richard Ashby of 20 counts of negligent manslaughter after his plane cut a ski-gondola cable in 1998. Informed of the court's decision after a speech at the Massachusetts Institute of Technology (MIT) in Cambridge, MA, D'Alema protested directly to Clinton in Washington, DC. After the verdict, anti-American feeling among Italians rose dramatically. The disclosure that U.S. atomic weapons had been stored in Italy during the Cold War and that Italian Tornado warplanes had been modified to carry them also sparked debate.

In a continuation of startling revelations from the East, newspapers quoted Czech documents in the hands of the Italian secret services as proof that the Soviet KGB had conspired to murder Pope John Paul II and to destabilize the Catholic Church.

Politics. As 1999 ended, support for D'Alema's government slipped badly. After former Prime Minister Romano Prodi was appointed president of the European Commission in March, his new duties frequently took him out of the country; however, this did not lessen the ability of the Democrats—a new party established by Prodi—to pressure the government from within the coalition.

In June elections to the European Parliament, Silvio Berlusconi's Forza Italia (25.2%) and D'Alema's DS (17.4%) finished in first and second place, but both parties lost seats. The Communists (6.3%), meanwhile, gained one seat, to hold a total of six. One of the big winners, however, was the Democrats, who earned 7% of the vote and seven seats.

The murder of governmental adviser Massimo D'Antona in June by a "new" incarnation of the Red Brigades, the Italian group that assassinated former Prime Minister Aldo Moro, raised the specter of a fresh onslaught of terrorism in Italy.

Concerned about the country's low birthrate, Parliament passed a subsidy program to encourage families to have more children. For each child born after July 1, 1999, the state pledged a $536 cash payment. Families with three minor children would receive about $1,395 yearly. The plan also provided subsidies for new mothers not covered by social insurance. In addition, legislation to regulate Italy's fertility services was set to pass. Critics charged that the Vatican unduly influenced this program, that it did not meet European standards, and that it served as an excuse to revisit the country's abortion laws, which were opposed by the Catholic parties.

The country was scandalized in October by revelations that documents smuggled out of Russia in 1992 named 261 Italians as KGB informants, including Cossutta. Cossutta denied the charge, but former President Francesco Cossiga demanded that Parliament investigate the Italian Communist Party's (PCI's) links with the former Soviet Union. Such an investigation could prove embarrassing, because the PCI was the forerunner of both the PDCI and the DS and counted Cossutta and D'Alema among its most influential members. Cossiga, who wielded important influence on coalition members, published an open letter to the prime minister intimating that D'Alema did not want the truth to come out. Fearing his cabinet's fall, D'Alema denied the charge in abject terms. At the same time, opposition to D'Alema in his own party strengthened. Polls suggested that the center-right opposition might win new elections.

On December 18, D'Alema resigned in order to reshuffle his cabinet. The new government was sworn in and received a vote of confidence in the Senate on December 22. The next day, the Chamber of Deputies gave the government a bare majority, thanks to the abstention of 18 former members of the coalition. Because these deputies made clear that they could vote against it at any time, however, D'Alema's second government appeared much weaker than his first.

Economy. In December 1998 the Bank of Italy lowered its prime rate to 3%, bringing the country in line with the rest of the euro bloc. In 1999 two major economic issues concerned the country—high taxes and the high cost of social programs. In July, Wim Duisenberg, president of the European Central Bank (ECB), cautioned Italy to get its welfare costs into line, and especially to cut public spending as soon as possible. This intervention focused the Italian debate on the bloated pension system. Experts suggested that the retirement age might have to be raised or that Italians might have to contribute to the system for a longer time before drawing benefits.

The government faced two main obstacles to cutting pension costs—Cossutta's PDCI and the unions. In July unemployed Neapolitans humiliated the formerly Communist D'Alema by staging demonstrations against him, further strengthening the case of his coalition partners who wished to delay pension reductions. At the end of the month, Parliament approved a four-year economic program designed to cut the deficit by $8.2 billion for the 2000 fiscal year. There was talk of a funding crisis if the state did not reform the swollen pension system by 2005, but D'Alema's union allies warned him that they would strike and end political collaboration should he support drastic economic measures. The government countered by suggesting that it could abolish abuses first and then reform the system.

In September, Labor Minister Antonio Bassolino met with the heads of the country's three major unions. The participants agreed to changes in the nature of some labor contracts, the abolition of early retirement, and the increase and extension of unemployment benefits to sectors that previously had not enjoyed full coverage. But the unions themselves could not agree on how to reform the way pension benefits were calculated. Nevertheless, the prime minister applauded these talks as a good start and denied that the country faced a crisis. D'Alema also insisted that a million new jobs could be added to the economy, and announced a plan to reduce the income tax for lower- to middle-income Italians from 27% to 26%.

Although there had been early signs of an economic recovery, signals remained mixed in late 1999. A rise in oil prices hit energy-poor Italy especially hard, as the cost of gasoline, heating oil, and other commodities dependent on petroleum increased. By the end of 1999, inflation was estimated to be 2.1%. The rate of production in the first ten months of 1999 slipped 0.7% compared with the same period in 1998. Despite this ominous note, however, the government reported good news in its ongoing efforts to privatize important economic sectors. ENEL, the giant state electric monopoly, reported that its first offer of shares to the public had been oversubscribed, bringing much more money to the Treasury than had been anticipated. As a result of the huge demand, ENEL could fulfill only half the requests for shares.

Justice. Developments in 1999 held out promise that progress would be made in halting the widespread misuse of informants by Italian prosecutors. Giving renewed impetus to the demand for reform were two acquittals of seven-time Prime Minister Giulio Andreotti: first, on September 24, of complicity in the 1979 murder of a journalist; and then, on October 23, of being the Mafia front man in Rome. Because both cases had rested on the testimony of Mafia turncoats, Andreotti's acquittals intensified the debate about prosecutors' mishandling of informers and their testimony. The leftist vice-president of the national magistrates' association said that the ability of the courts to acquit Andreotti proved that the system was fundamentally sound. But the moderate president of the organization insisted that the law governing informant testimony required urgent revision. He also reiterated that the current practice of allowing the same magistrate to conduct the investigation and the prosecution of defendants should be eliminated.

Parliament considered legislation to reform the handling of informant testimony, but it ran into difficulties. The center-left majority insisted that the law be applied only to future trials, but the right-center demanded that it apply to trials that already were under way. At last, the ruling coalition and the opposition compromised by agreeing that new legislation would apply to current trials only if informers refused to confirm their statements to the police in open court. On November 10, Parliament ratified this agreement and amended the constitution. The new amendment stated that trials should take place before an impartial judge, with defense and prosecution lawyers on an equal footing; that the defense had the right to cross-examine witnesses; that a guilty verdict could not be based on the declarations of witnesses who refused to be cross-examined openly in court by the defense; and that the defendant must be informed of the nature of any accusation against him or her and be given the time and opportunity to organize a defense. The new law also barred prosecutors from exploiting the media in their attempts to convict public figures.

A major issue, however, remained the acceptance of hearsay testimony. Senate-proposed legislation would abolish the use of such testimony unless a witness had "directly and personally" been part of the proceedings about which he or she testified, and unless the testimony was corroborated by a second independent witness who had direct knowledge of the events in question.

Spencer M. Di Scala
University of Massachusetts, Boston

ITALY • Information Highlights

Official Name: Italian Republic.
Location: Southern Europe.
Area: 116,305 sq mi (301 230 km²).
Population (July 1999 est.): 56,735,130.
Chief Cities (Dec. 31, 1996): Rome, the capital, 2,645,322; Milan, 1,303,925; Naples, 1,045,874.
Government: *Head of state,* Carlo Azeglio Ciampi, president (sworn in May 18, 1999). *Head of government,* Massimo D'Alema, prime minister (sworn in Oct. 21, 1998). *Legislature*—Parliament: Senate and Chamber of Deputies.
Monetary Unit: Lira (1,919.19 lire equal U.S.$1, Nov. 29, 1999).
Gross Domestic Product (1998 est. U.S.$): $1,181,000,-000,000.
Economic Indexes: *Consumer Prices* (1998, 1990 = 100): all items, 138.0; food, 132.4. *Industrial Production* 111.6.
Foreign Trade (1998 U.S.$): *Imports,* $215,721,000,000; *exports,* $242,147,000,000.

Japan

Prime Minister Keizo Obuchi opened the Diet (parliament) in January 1999 by noting that Japan was entering an era of the "third reform." The first reform, he said, was during the Meiji Restoration (late 19th century), when modernization transformed the nation. The second (1945–52) came after defeat in the Pacific War and was marked by democratization, significant economic change, and rapid growth. The third, on the way to the millennium, would involve the need for a revived economy after seven years of recession.

Domestic Affairs

The new year saw the prime minister struggling with political coalitions to manage economic problems. His Liberal Democratic Party (LDP) held a slim majority in the (lower) House of Representatives, but in 1998 it had lost its hold on the upper House of Councillors. On January 14, Obuchi recognized the need for allies and formed a coalition cabinet.

Party Politics. The prime minister entered into an agreement with a former LDP member, Ichiro Ozawa, now leader of the Liberal Party. Obuchi added a liberal to his cabinet and began moving toward creating a tripartite bloc. The third party was to be the New Komeito, backed by Japan's largest lay Buddhist organization, the Soka Gakkai. In a July 24 party convention, the Komeito agreed to join the coalition but indicated that sharp differences with the liberals remained.

Another former LDP member led the main opposition party. Naoto Kan, known in the press as "the destroyer," headed the Democratic Party of Japan (DPJ), which had engineered the defeat of the LDP in the 1998 upper-house election. Kan had been nominated that year by the House of Councillors to be prime minister, but the lower house's choice of Obuchi legally prevailed. On occasion the Democrats could count on support from two groups to the left, the Social Democratic Party and the Japan Communist Party. The combination accounted for 131 seats in the lower house and led to the hope for a no-confidence vote and a general election to bring down the Obuchi regime.

Kan failed to form a united opposition, however, and in a September election for party president, the DPJ chose still another former member of the rival LDP, Yukio Hatoyama. The latter, the grandson of late Prime Minister Ichiro Hatoyama, had worked with Kan in 1996 to found the DPJ. He was expected to follow a more moderate policy path.

In February, Gov. Yukio Aoshima announced that he would not seek reelection as head of Tokyo Metropolitan Prefecture. Six candidates, including two members of the LDP, declared their intention to run. The April 11 election was won by independent Shintaro Ishihara, a former LDP transport minister who was more famous as a prizewinning author and as an outspoken critic of U.S. trade pressure. Ishihara quickly showed his right-wing inclinations by referring repeatedly to China as Shina, an imperialistic term from World War II.

© Katsumi Kasahara/AP/Wide World Photos

Japanese Prime Minister Keizo Obuchi (front row, center left) reshuffled his cabinet in 1999 to include ministers from the Liberal Party and the Buddhist-backed New Komeito, as well as his own Liberal Democratic Party (LDP). He was forced to put together a coalition government to bolster the LDP's weak position in parliament.

An even more important election, for the Liberal Democratic Party president, was held on September 21. Three leaders filed for candidacy in August. Prime Minister Obuchi was the clear favorite, having the largest personal faction in the party and support pledged by two thirds of LDP Diet members. The other candidates, Koichi Kato and Taku Yamasaki, were running to position themselves for future leadership. Although Obuchi won with a comfortable majority, it was clear that in the LDP ranks, and in the public mind as well, there still were doubts about his coalition strategy. The prime minister formed a three-party coalition government on October 5. The new cabinet had one member each from the Liberal Party and the New Komeito, and accurately reflected the strengths of competing LDP factions.

Meanwhile, a quiet but significant step was taken to review the constitution for the first time since the document took effect on May 3, 1947. In a speech to the second convention of the Liberal Party in June, Ozawa proposed procedures for constitutional revision. On July 29 the Diet passed a bill setting up panels in the two chambers to analyze the constitution "widely and comprehensively." The legislation was supported by the LDP, the Liberal Party, the New Komeito, and, surprisingly, the opposition DPJ. It was opposed by the Social Democratic and Japan Communist Parties. Any reevaluation of Article 9 of the organic law (the so-called no-war clause) was certain to cause future controversy.

Economy. In general, the Japanese were less interested in politics and more concerned about their stubborn recession. In fiscal 1998, according to the International Monetary Fund (IMF), inflation-adjusted gross domestic product (GDP) shrank 1.7%. One in four companies listed on the Tokyo Stock Exchange, excluding banks and financial firms, posted losses. Although the IMF expected a continued decline in 1999, the year ended with a modest 1.4% growth. Nevertheless, the head of the Economic Planning Agency (EPA), Taichi Sakaiya, found it difficult to believe that the recession had bottomed out. The banking community offered a striking example of why the recession remained so tenacious. Earnings reports as of the end of fiscal 1998 revealed that the nation's 17 top banks held a total of $173.5 billion in loan losses. By injections of public funds in March, they already had disposed of $86.8 billion more in bad loans.

Compared with other advanced industrial nations, Japan still enjoyed a relatively low rate of unemployment, but for the Japanese it was frighteningly high. According to the Management & Coordination Agency, in 1998 the jobless rate reached a monthly average of 4.1%, representing more than 3 million unemployed. This was the highest unemployment rate since checks began in 1953. The February 1999 average reached 4.6%, and the July rate hit a peak of 4.9%. By September the level eased off slightly to 4.6%. Nevertheless, many Japanese, raised on the myth of lifetime employment in one firm, were dismayed.

The government moved promptly into a pump-priming mode. In March the upper house had rejected legislation providing economic stimulus, but, with lack of compromise, by the constitution the $682 billion budget proposed by the lower chamber became law. In July the Diet adopted a supplementary budget of $4.5 billion, designed to create 700,000 jobs. On November 11 a further package of economic stimulants, worth $171.4 billion, was passed to increase public works and aid small businesses.

Society. In January, only six months after an application was filed, the Health Ministry approved the import of the impotence drug Viagra. Family-planning experts and women's-rights activists immediately pointed out that for ten years the ministry had refused to approve the low-dose birth-control pill for women, although the much more dangerous high-dose pill was available. Bowing to pressure, the health bureaucracy finally legalized the low-dose pill in the fall.

Another subject of widespread debate concerned symbols. After vigorous debate, on August 9 the Diet legally recognized the rising-sun flag (Hinomaru) as the country's

JAPAN • Information Highlights

Official Name: Japan.
Location: East Asia.
Area: 145,882 sq mi (377 835 km²).
Population (July 1999 est.): 126,182,077.
Chief Cities (Oct. 1, 1995 census, metropolitan areas): Tokyo, the capital (city proper), 7,967,614; Yokohama, 3,307,136; Osaka, 2,602,421; Nagoya, 2,152,184.
Government: *Head of state,* Akihito, emperor (acceded Jan. 9, 1989). *Head of government,* Keizo Obuchi, prime minister (took office July 30, 1998). *Legislature*—Diet: House of Councillors and House of Representatives.
Monetary Unit: Yen (101.5050 yen equal U.S.$1, Dec. 22, 1999).
Gross Domestic Product (1998 est. U.S.$): $2,903,000,-000,000 (purchasing power parity).
Economic Indexes (1998, 1990 = 100): *Consumer Prices,* all items, 109.7; food, 109.4. *Industrial Production,* 94.4.
Foreign Trade (1998 U.S.$): *Imports,* $280,618,000,000; *exports,* $388,117,000,000.

national flag and the Kimigayo melody as its national anthem. Both were associated with wartime militarism. Japan had been without an official flag or anthem since 1945.

In October, Japan suffered the worst nuclear accident since the 1986 Chernobyl incident, when a uranium-processing plant 85 mi (137 km) northeast of Tokyo leaked a flash of radiation from a chain reaction that had gotten out of control. Plant workers caused the accident by mixing nuclear fuel without proper certification, using the wrong procedure. Police evacuated some 200 people from homes near the plant and issued warnings to more than 300,000 in the general area; at least 49 persons were hospitalized.

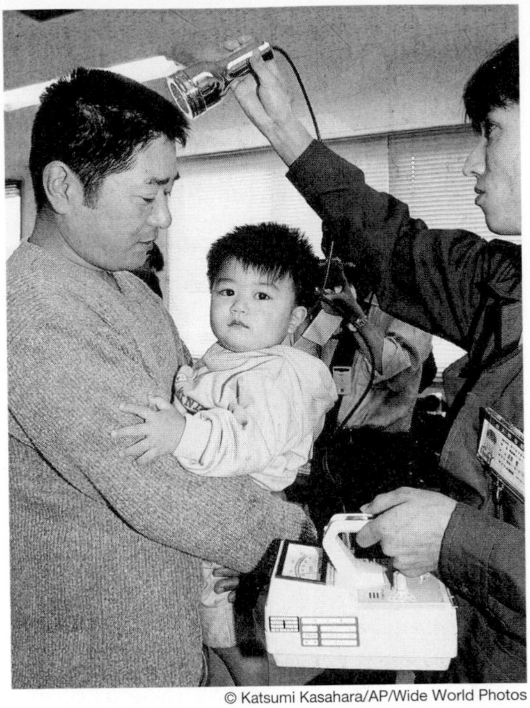

© Katsumi Kasahara/AP/Wide World Photos

In 1999 an accident at the Tokaimura nuclear plant in Japan released high levels of radiation into the air. Area residents had to be tested for radiation exposure.

Foreign Affairs

Despite recession at home, abroad Japan continued to be among the most advanced industrial nations in the world. The Finance Ministry announced that at the end of March, Japan held $222.2 billion in foreign reserves, leading the world for the 65th straight month. In fiscal 1998 the Japanese rang up a surplus in merchandise trade of $128 billion. Japan's politically sensitive surplus with the United States rose 24.3% to $4.6 billion in August and, as usual, created a trade issue in Washington.

U.S. Relations. When Prime Minister Obuchi was in the United States in May, U.S. President Bill Clinton used an approach to trade that was milder than usual, encouraging Japan to rebuild its economy and become "another engine" in world growth. On July 7, however, a U.S. trade commission said that Japan had exported steel sheets at prices below cost of production, and retaliatory tariffs were imposed on major Japanese firms, retroactive to January 4.

The main theme of the Obuchi-Clinton summit of May 3 revolved around security relations. The two leaders reaffirmed the Japan-U.S. alliance and noted the passage through the Japanese lower house of legislation updating the Guidelines for Japan-U.S. Defense Cooperation. In Japan, though, the revised guidelines remained contentious. For example, one clause provided for bilateral defense cooperation in "areas surrounding Japan." The geography was deliberately imprecise, but critics immediately assumed that "areas" might include Taiwan. Many Japanese believed that the revisions violated the no-war constitution.

Security issues were important in Okinawa prefecture, the nation's southernmost islands and home to about 75% of U.S. military installations in Japan. In 1996, in response to antibase protests among residents, the United States signed a joint security declaration with Japan designed to consolidate and reduce the American military presence in the prefecture. The agreement foresaw the closing of the U.S. Marine Corps air station at Futenma and the transfer of other facilities, providing Japan cooperated in finding alternative areas in the near future. In 1997, Tokyo proposed a sea-based heliport in northern Okinawa, off the coastal city of Nago. In a local plebiscite, however, residents opposed the project. Then, on April 29, Prime Minister Obuchi announced that the July 2000 conference of the Group of 8 (G-8) major industrial democracies would be convened in Nago; it would be the first summit held outside Tokyo. It was apparent that the decision was made to assuage Okinawan unrest. President Clinton indicated that he would be reluctant to attend the G-8 meeting in 2000 if the issue were not resolved.

China. In May during the Washington summit, both the prime minister and the U.S. president publicly had declared that their defense guidelines were not aimed at China. The prime minister was in Beijing July 8–11 to meet President Jiang Zemin and Premier Zhu Rongji. The aim was to carry on a theme from the Chinese president's visit to Japan the previous November—to "build a partnership toward the 21st century." Instead, Obuchi heard echoes of the Chinese demand for a formal apology for Japan's wartime record. Premier Zhu was more specific: He urged the Japanese to exclude Taiwan explicitly from the Japan-U.S. security agreement. Later the Chinese did receive an indirect reply. In Tokyo on August 15, at the regular memorial ceremony marking the 54th anniversary of Japan's surrender, the prime minister expressed "deep remorse" for the pain and sorrow imposed on many people during the Pacific War, particularly "those in neighboring Asian countries."

The Two Koreas. Although Japan had no formal contact with the Democratic People's Republic of (North) Korea, it did offer technical assistance through a consortium. Japan had joined the Republic of (South) Korea and the United States to form the Korean Peninsula Energy Development Corporation (KEDO). In May, while Prime Minister Obuchi was in the United States, the Foreign Ministry announced a contract to provide to the North Koreans $1 billion for light-water nuclear reactors. The grant was made in exchange for Pyongyang's promise to freeze its nuclear program. The arrangement was delayed, because in August 1998, North Korea had fired a test missile over Japan into the Pacific east of Tokyo.

In the 1999 white paper released July 27, the Defense Agency urged Japan to expand coordination with South Korea and the United States to meet North Korean threats. On August 5, Japanese and South Korean naval units carried out a joint exercise in waters between Kyushu and the Korean peninsula. The maneuver was limited to search and rescue operations, because bitter anti-Japanese war memories remained among South Koreans.

Russian Relations. In September 1998 former Prime Minister Ryutaro Hashimoto, acting as a foreign-policy adviser, was in Moscow. Meeting with President Boris Yeltsin, Hashimoto carried on an interminable dialogue toward a peace treaty. Although diplomatic relations between Tokyo and Moscow had been reestablished, a pact formally ending the war had not been signed after 54 years. The unresolved issue involved four tiny islands at the southern tip of the Kuril Island chain, recognized as Japanese territory but occupied by the Russians since 1945.

In November 1998 in Moscow, Prime Minister Obuchi and President Yeltsin hopefully had agreed on 2000 as the target date for a treaty. In May, Foreign Minister Masahiko Komura, while in Moscow, confirmed that the Russian president would visit Japan in the autumn. Yeltsin's recurring illness, however, postponed the visit.

United Nations. Most Japanese believe that it would be unconstitutional to send Self-Defense Force (SDF) units overseas. Thus the world's second-largest economy has tended to use financial resources to implement foreign policy. In 1998, Japan provided $10.7 billion in what was called ODA (Official Development Assistance), and thus it became the leading donor-nation in the world.

In February a consortium of nations met in Tokyo and offered $470 million in aid to Cambodia. Japan, Cambodia's largest aid donor, contributed $100 million. Then in May, Tokyo pledged $200 million to nations receiving refugees from Kosovo. Although a UN member, Japan still declined to send personnel to the region.

In an accurate forecast, Japan's representative to the Security Council identified the next UN priority as the situation in East Timor. In May, Japan contributed $10.1 million to UN operations designed to guarantee a fair referendum on the fate of East Timor, a former Portuguese colony annexed by Indonesia in 1975. The East Timorese voted overwhelmingly for independence in August, but violence derailed a settlement. On September 16, Foreign Minister Komura announced that Japan would offer $2 million for aid to victims of the turmoil. Again Japan would contribute financial aid but could not assign personnel until stability was restored.

ARDATH W. BURKS, *Rutgers University*

Jordan

There was one great change of overwhelming importance in Jordan in 1999—that of the monarch. The courageous, strong-willed, and beloved King Hussein succumbed to cancer in February after 46 years on the throne, leaving his people bereft of his accustomed leadership and uncertain of the future. Moreover, in another unsettling development, shortly before his death he unexpectedly chose to remove his younger brother Hassan as crown prince, replacing him with his own eldest son, Abdullah (*see* BIOGRAPHY).

© Marc Deville, Noel Quidu, Jean-Michel Turpin/Liaison Agency

Thousands of Jordanians took to the streets to mourn the death of King Hussein from cancer on Feb. 7, 1999. Many of them clutched photographs of the beloved monarch, who had ruled for 46 years.

Succession. On January 16 in London, King Hussein said that he planned a "comprehensive review" of Jordan's future. In a decree issued a few days later, he designated Abdullah as his heir, replacing Hassan, who had been crown prince for 34 years. Before he departed again for the Mayo Clinic in Minnesota, Hussein named Abdullah as regent. The king also sent a letter to Hassan giving the reasons why he was being replaced. In this letter, which was made public, Hussein said that he had differed with his brother over succession questions since 1991 and criticized him for the way in which he had behaved during his regency in the latter half of 1998. He accused Hassan of "meddling" in the armed forces, of trying to make changes in the foreign ministry, and of unjust transfer of ambassadors.

However, despite the king's surprising nomination of a successor, and despite rumored dissensions within the royal family, everything went smoothly when King Hussein died on February 7, almost immediately after he returned again from the United States. Abdullah succeeded to the throne; no family dissensions surfaced; and the public welcomed the new king hopefully. This stability in the Jordanian state and monarchy also provided evidence of the formidable achievements of King Hussein (*see* OBITUARIES) in his 46-year reign.

King Abdullah demonstrated from the beginning every indication that he would deal with the many problems facing him and his country with energy and competence. He began by appointing as crown prince his 18-year-old half-brother, Prince Hamzeh, son of Queen Noor—a move that was received with general approval. In the opening months of his reign, Abdullah also won some surprised, if amused, favor from the public through several forays in which, in disguise, he sought to observe for himself how life was lived in his kingdom.

In March, Abdullah dismissed Prime Minister Fayez Tarawnah, who had been appointed by Prince Hassan in August 1998. The new prime minister was Abdel Rauf Rawabdeh, a former mayor of Amman and a known conservative. Although some ministers from the former cabinet were retained in the new one, the appointment of Rawabdeh clearly distanced Abdullah from Hassan; this was underlined by the exclusion from the new cabinet of Hassan's son-in-law, Nasser Juda, who had been information minister. Abdullah also replaced Jawad Anani as chief of the royal court—a post of considerable importance in Jordan—with Abdul-Karim Kabariti.

JORDAN • Information Highlights

Official Name: Hashemite Kingdom of Jordan.
Location: Southwest Asia.
Area: 34,445 sq mi (89 213 km^2).
Population (July 1999 est.): 4,561,147.
Chief Cities (Dec. 31, 1991 est.): Amman, the capital, 965,000; Zarqa, 359,000; Irbid, 216,000.
Government: *Head of state,* Abdullah II, king (acceded Feb. 7, 1999). *Head of government,* Abdel Rauf Rawabdeh, prime minister (took office March 1999). *Legislature*—National Assembly: Senate and House of Representatives.
Monetary Unit: Dinar (0.7040 dinar equals U.S.$1, Dec. 22, 1999).
Gross Domestic Product (1998 est. U.S.$): $15,500,-000,000 (purchasing power parity).
Economic Indexes (1998, 1990 = 100): *Consumer Prices,* all items, 139.3; food, 149.8. *Industrial Production,* 136.1.
Foreign Trade (1998 U.S.$): *Imports,* $3,829,000,000; *exports,* $1,749,000,000.

Abdullah indicated that he expected the new government to proceed with "fundamental reforms" in fighting corruption and unemployment, as well as in broadening democratic freedoms. However, not much progress could be seen on these points in 1999. It was only with some difficulty that the king, in a special second session of parliament in the summer, achieved the passing of a slight softening of the press law, which restrained the media's freedom to report and publish information. At the same time, though, several editors of papers critical of the government were imprisoned or physically assaulted by unknown assailants. Some observers professed to see in such incidents evidence of conflict between the conservatism of Rawabdeh and the supposedly more liberal tendencies of Kabariti.

However, municipal elections held July 14–15 were acknowledged, even by the Islamic Action Front (IAF), the political wing of the Muslim Brotherhood and the most important opposition group, to have been conducted democratically. The IAF, which had boycotted previous municipal elections, participated this time and had considerable if not overwhelming success.

Peripatetic Diplomacy. Much in his father's style, the new king spent much of his time making diplomatic trips to cement or reestablish good relations with many countries. Early in his reign, Abdullah expressed his intention to have friendly relations with all Arab countries. (Later, he also said that his Arab policies would not impair his very good relations with Israel.) There was certainly a good deal of bridge-building to be done between Jordan and the Arab world: Jordan's siding with Iraq rather than with Kuwait in the 1991 Persian Gulf war had not been forgotten, despite the efforts of King Hussein to achieve reconciliation in the subsequent years.

Abdullah's first destination, in early April, was Saudi Arabia, where he was received cordially by King Fahd and Crown Prince Abdullah. From there he went to Oman and then to Abu Dhabi in the United Arab Emirates (UAE), where he also met with President Hosni Mubarak of Egypt. Moving on to Libya, King Abdullah congratulated Muammar el-Qaddafi on the fact that the UN sanctions against Libya had been lifted, and announced the resumption of direct air passenger service between Jordan and Libya. While he was in Libya, the king also had a friendly visit with Palestinian leader Yasir Arafat.

Most significant of all, probably, was Abdullah's visit on April 21–22 to Damascus to confer with Syrian President Hafiz al-Assad. The leaders of the two countries had not met since 1994, when Jordan and Israel signed a peace treaty. But Assad had come unexpectedly to King Hussein's funeral and had been the first to offer good wishes to Abdullah. The visit was reckoned a great success. Syria undertook to supplement Jordan's deficient water supply. The year had been (and continued to be) exceptionally arid, and Israel had reneged on its water-supply commitment under the peace treaty. A joint Syrian-Jordanian committee on water cooperation began working on May 2, and the Jordanian-Syrian Higher Committee, dormant for five years, was reactivated in June.

In financial matters—an ever-present worry in Jordan—no immediate resumption of subsidies, ended in 1991, from Saudi Arabia and other oil-rich states was expected, but it was quite likely that Jordanian workers might be welcomed again in the Gulf area, and other steps of economic cooperation implemented. Meanwhile, in June, Jordan put a series of austerity measures in place, and all ministries and government departments were asked to reduce their annual budgets by 5%.

The king's other diplomatic travels took him to the West. In May he visited Germany, Britain, Canada, and the United States. Abdullah hoped these and other creditor nations would cancel or scale down repayments on nearly $7 billion of Jordan's debts—a burden that took up one third of the country's budget. The immediate financial aid promised was much more modest than Abdullah had wished, but the king was received warmly everywhere he went, as he was on two return trips to Washington, DC, later in the year.

From August onward, Jordan carried on a very firm campaign against the Palestine-based group Hamas, which opposed the 1994 peace treaty and indeed the very existence of Israel. This crackdown was a reversal of Jordan's earlier tolerant attitude toward the group. The activities of Hamas in Jordan were ended and many of its leaders exiled or imprisoned. These actions had the enthusiastic support of Israel, the United States, and Arafat. Also, in mid-December, Jordan arrested 13 supposed members of Osama bin Laden's terrorist network, who were accused of planning an attack on American tourists.

ARTHUR CAMPBELL TURNER
University of California, Riverside

Kenya

Kenya's politics in 1999 were dominated by the question of succession to President Daniel arap Moi, whose final term of office ends in 2002, and the constitution that the country would have afterward. The economy continued to struggle with many problems, including food shortages caused by drought, inefficient management, and loss of resources through corruption. In October, Kenya was ranked one of the world's ten most corrupt countries.

Politics. The ruling Kenya African National Union (KANU) continued to be divided, as factions jockeyed to succeed President Moi. In January several young KANU members of parliament, led by Kipruto arap Kirwa, joined with non-KANU figures to form the United Democratic Movement (UDM). Moi promptly directed Attorney General Amos Wako to stop the registration of political parties associated with sitting members of parliament, so the UDM could not be registered. In February reform-minded Finance Minister Simeon Nyachae, leader of the so-called KANU-A faction, resigned rather than accept demotion to another ministry. In April, President Moi filled the position of vice-president, vacant since 1997, with the former occupant of the office, Professor George Saitoti, leader of the KANU-B faction.

The country's severe economic difficulties caused significant governmental changes in mid-1999. In late July, Moi appointed paleoanthropologist and former opposition member of parliament Richard Leakey as head of the civil service and secretary to the cabinet. Leakey vowed to fight corruption, restore services, and streamline the bureaucracy. At the same time, technocrats were recruited from the private sector and international organizations to head the treasury and the agriculture ministry. Further changes came in September, when Moi announced he would reduce the number of ministries from 27 to 15. Some observers criticized the move, noting that while several ministers changed portfolios in the transition, none lost their positions altogether.

Despite strong pressure from religious and civic groups for constitutional reform, little progress was made. KANU maintained that parliament was the only acceptable forum for defining a constitution for the post-Moi era, while opposition parties and religious organizations contended that civil society must be involved in the process.

KENYA • Information Highlights

Official Name: Republic of Kenya.
Location: East coast of Africa.
Area: 224,961 sq mi (582 650 km²).
Population (July 1999 est.): 28,808,658.
Chief Cities (1990 est.): Nairobi, the capital, 1,505,000; Mombasa, 537,000.
Government: *Head of state and government,* Daniel T. arap Moi, president (took office Oct. 1978). *Legislature* (unicameral)—National Assembly.
Monetary Unit: Kenya shilling (72.880 shillings equal U.S.$1, Dec. 24, 1999).
Gross Domestic Product (1998 est. U.S.$): $43,900,-000,000 (purchasing power parity).
Economic Index (1998, 1990 = 100): *Consumer Prices,* all items, 377.8; food, 401.6.
Foreign Trade (1998 U.S.$): *Imports,* $3,194,000,000; *exports,* $2,007,000,000.

The Economy. During 1999 the Kenyan economy was marked by weak growth, increased domestic debt, donor refusal to provide additional aid, and rampant high-level corruption. Economic growth during 1998 slowed to 1.8%, and unemployment had risen to 25% by October. The output of tea, Kenya's most important export, declined in 1999 from the 1998 level. Production of coffee, the country's second leading export, rose slightly, but worldwide coffee prices fell, and many growers expressed extreme dissatisfaction with marketing arrangements.

The shilling depreciated as well, dropping to about 74 to $1 by November. In late 1999 northern and eastern Kenya faced the likelihood of famine due to extended drought. Rationing of electricity also placed constraints on industrial production. The negative economic impact of the rapid spread of HIV/AIDS in Kenya continued to be felt, with some analysts predicting that AIDS would reduce Kenya's per-capita income by 10% and its gross domestic product (GDP) by 14.5% by 2005.

The government sought to convince international donors, particularly the International Monetary Fund (IMF), that it was serious about achieving effective management and fighting corruption. In March, Aaron Ringera, a former judge, was chosen to head the Anti-Corruption Authority. Encouraged by Ringera's appointment, the IMF said in May that Kenya appeared to have lifted all of the barriers to negotiating the resumption of a $205 million aid package that had been frozen in 1997, although the IMF set no firm date for talks to begin.

On November 30, President Moi, with the presidents of Tanzania and Uganda, signed a treaty establishing an East African Community that encompassed a common market.

ROBERT M. MAXON, *West Virginia University*

Korea

Both South and North Korea showed signs of economic recovery in 1999, but no significant changes in domestic politics or external affairs. South Korean President Kim Dae Jung (DJ) resisted pressure from his coalition partners for a constitutional revision to establish a parliamentary form of government, but reports of corruption at high levels of his administration diminished his political effectiveness. Kim Jong Il, the "supreme leader" of North Korea, remained inaccessible to foreign visitors, but succeeded in winning some concessions from the United States in return for a temporary halt to a test of a long-range missile. In inter-Korean relations, economic and cultural exchanges and tourism in North Korea grew steadily, despite the absence of any breakthrough in official contacts.

Republic of Korea (South Korea)

Politics. In the first half of 1999, the question of revising South Korea's constitution to replace the presidential form of government with a parliamentary system occupied the center stage of political debate. DJ had promised such a change as part of a political deal with Prime Minister Kim Jong Pil (JP), his coalition partner, whose support was crucial for DJ's 1997 election to the presidency. After much inconclusive discussion—and angry outbursts by JP's supporters—the two Kims agreed to shelve the issue indefinitely until the nation's economy recovered.

In the aftermath of the temporary truce, and also in preparation for the next National Assembly election in April 2000, DJ began to take steps to disband his National Congress for New Politics (NCNP) and create a new, broader-based political party that could assure him a comfortable majority in the Assembly without a coalition partner. Another advantage to this new party would be that it might weaken the opposition Grand National Party (GNP) by attracting some of its members. There also was speculation that the NCNP and the United Liberal Democrats (ULD), the two coalition parties, were considering a merger, although the prime minister declared his firm opposition to the union. Meanwhile, JP announced in late November that he would resign from his post and return to the ULD; a few days later, however, he said he would delay the move until early 2000.

The GNP's decisive victory in two Assembly by-elections in June caused concern within the ruling coalition. Partisan rivalry grew intense throughout 1999, as the normal functions of the National Assembly were obstructed by angry physical confrontations and occasional boycotts of Assembly sessions by the opposition. Prolonged behind-the-scenes negotiations took place on an NCNP-sponsored change in election laws that would have replaced single-member electoral districts with plural-member districts. In December the two sides appeared to have reached a compromise whereby the single-member districts would remain, but a new proportional-representation system would be introduced. The details

A news story published by The Associated Press in September 1999 said that in 1950, during the Korean War, U.S. troops had opened fire on South Korean civilians hiding under a bridge at the small village of No Gun Ri, right. *The report estimated that up to 300 Koreans had been killed in the incident. The Pentagon promptly launched an investigation into the allegation.*

of how to implement this scheme remained unresolved at the end of the year.

To help weather the partisan tensions, President Kim reshuffled the senior leadership of the NCNP and the cabinet in April and May, but a string of scandals tainted key members of his government and party. "Furgate" involved bribes of expensive clothes and furs that allegedly were given to the wives of a few present and past cabinet ministers. Kim Tae-joung, former prosecutor general and then justice minister, was imprisoned for leaking a secret justice report to the accused bribe-giver; by year's end, a former senior member of the presidential secretariat was facing arrest on the same charge. Lim Chang-yuel, the NCNP governor of the populous Kyonggi province, and his wife were jailed in July for accepting bribes; he continued to perform his gubernatorial duties from prison for two months. In October a written blueprint for muzzling the press was made public, to the discomfort of a high-ranking NCNP leader who was suspected of having asked for such a plan. In addition, the arrest of Hong Seok-hyun, the publisher of the daily newspaper *Joongang Ilbo*, at about the same time on charges of embezzlement and tax evasion was thought to be politically motivated.

Economy and Society. South Korea's economy recovered from its 1997 financial crisis faster than anticipated. The Bank of Korea estimated that the gross domestic product (GDP) for 1999 would grow 9% or more—a sharp contrast to the 1998 rate of –5.8%. The foreign-exchange reserve stood at $68 billion, inflation was kept to a low 1%, and unemployment fell 40% from what it had been in January. On the strength of such remarkable statistics and similarly encouraging export surpluses, President Kim announced in mid-November that his country had overcome the foreign-exchange crisis completely in only 18 months.

The surprising rebound did not benefit everyone, however. The Daewoo Group, the second-largest *chaebol* (business conglomerate) in the country, encountered in July a crippling financial crisis—a $47 billion debt. Unable to meet the creditors' claims, the corporate leadership (including founder Kim Woo-choong) resigned, and the future of the business empire was murky at best in late 1999.

The government, which had been pressing for basic *chaebol* reforms, partly in response to recommendations by the International Monetary Fund (IMF), showed little inclination to save Daewoo from ruin. In fact, considerable heat reportedly was applied on other big businesses to stop their dilatory tactics in carrying out structural and financial reforms that they had promised. The tax probe of Cho Choong-hoon, head of the Hanjin Group and owner of Korean Air (KAL), was seen by some as a warning to uncooperative business leaders. The government-business nexus, a target for much foreign criticism, appeared to be undergoing considerable change.

SOUTH KOREA • Information Highlights

Official Name: Republic of Korea.
Location: Northeastern Asia.
Area: 38,023 sq mi (98 480 km^2).
Population (July 1999 est.): 46,884,800.
Chief Cities (1995 census, preliminary): Seoul, the capital, 10,229,262; Pusan, 3,813,814; Taegu, 2,449,139; Inchon, 2,307,618.
Government: *Head of state,* Kim Dae Jung, president (formally inaugurated Feb. 25, 1998). *Head of government,* Kim Jong Pil, prime minister (appointed March 3, 1998). *Legislature* (unicameral)—National Assembly.
Monetary Unit: Won (1,128.25 won equal U.S.$1, Dec. 13, 1999).
Gross Domestic Product (1998 est. U.S.$): $584,700,000,000.
Economic Indexes (1998, 1990 = 100): *Consumer Prices,* all items, 159.2; food, 164.3. *Industrial Production,* 159.8.
Foreign Trade (1998 U.S.$): *Imports,* $93,282,000,000; *exports,* $132,313,000,000.

Foreign Affairs. The central issue in South Korean–U.S. relations remained focused on North Korea's nuclear and missile development. Former Defense Secretary William Perry, appointed as an envoy to the Koreas by President Bill Clinton in 1998, visited Seoul frequently to consult with South Korean leaders, who reportedly advocated a policy of "engagement"—a new name for DJ's "sunshine" policy. Perry's report to the president, made public in October, reflected Seoul's conciliatory approach.

In late September a report by the Associated Press about an alleged attack on South Korean civilians by U.S. troops at No Gun Ri in July 1950 took both Seoul and Washington by surprise. Based on the testimonies of the surviving victims and some of the U.S. soldiers involved in the incident, the printed account produced sorrowful reactions but no serious explosion of anti-American hatred in Korea. The Pentagon promised an investigation and appropriate follow-up measures. The disclosure in November that Agent Orange, a chemical defoliant, was used in the Demilitarized Zone (DMZ) between the two Koreas in 1968–69 was followed initially by bureaucratic finger-pointing between the U.S. and South Korean militaries. In late November the South Kore-

© Dennis Cook/AP/Wide World Photos

Secretary of State Madeleine Albright (left) *and William Perry, U.S. envoy to the Koreas, announced in September that the United States was relaxing some trade, travel, and banking restrictions against North Korea.*

an government announced plans to compensate civilian victims of the spraying with benefits such as medical treatment.

South Korea's relations with Japan passed an important threshold in 1999. Since October 1998, imports of Japanese popular culture had grown slowly, and pop-music groups from Japan had public performances in Seoul in November for the first time. Japanese Prime Minister Keizo Obuchi's formal visit to Seoul in March was followed by the first-ever joint naval exercise and the establishment of a military hot line in August, after rumors that North Korea was testing a long-range missile. When Prime Minister Kim made a reciprocal visit to Japan in September, Emperor Akihito hosted a formal dinner for him, an event usually reserved for a visiting head of state.

North Korea was on President Kim's agenda when he visited Russia and Mongolia in May and June, and also when he hosted Egyptian President Hosni Mubarak in April. Several other foreign heads of state, including Queen Elizabeth II of Britain, visited South Korea in 1999.

In early October, South Korea sent about 400 combat troops to East Timor as part of the United Nations (UN) peacekeeping force—the first instance of Korean participation in such an international operation.

Democratic People's Republic of Korea (North Korea)

Politics and Foreign Affairs. In March, 29,442 deputies to provincial, city, and county people's assemblies were chosen in a nationwide election in North Korea, with the customary 99% voter turnout and 100% affirmative votes. The elections, which were long overdue, seemed to signal an attempt to return to the normal governance procedures that had been disrupted by the 1994 death of "the eternal president," Kim Il Sung, Kim Jong Il's father.

Although the doctrine of placing "the military first as the ideology of revolution" remained in official propaganda, signs pointing to possible changes in North Korea's attitude surfaced in 1999. Pyongyang's reaction to the sinking of one of its torpedo boats by the South Korean navy in June was limited to verbal threats of retaliation. Much-publicized plans for test-firing a long-range missile were suspended through negotiations with the United States. At the same time, there were reports of North Korean doctors receiving training at Johns Hopkins University Hospital in Maryland, 30 North Koreans undergoing "management training" by the UN Development Program, and a computer college being created at Kim Il Sung University.

North Korea concluded in March a new treaty of friendship and cooperation with Russia to replace the 1961 treaty with the old Soviet Union. Military-alliance provisions were conspicuously absent in the new agreement. Pyongyang dispatched in June a large, high-level delegation to China headed by Kim Yong-nam, the nominal head of state, who was received by top Chinese leaders, including President Jiang Zemin.

A few months later, North Korean Foreign Minister Paek Nam Sun requested meetings with his counterparts in European Union (EU) nations. Meanwhile, after 16 Japanese politicians visited North Korea in late November, Pyongyang and Tokyo agreed to resume their often-stalled talks on normalization of relations, launching preliminary discussions in late December and full-fledged negotiations early in 2000.

Nuclear and Missile Development. Pyongyang agreed in March to allow an inspection of a vast, empty cave at Kumchangri, located in the western part of the country, which Washington suspected to be a new underground nuclear site. In May a group of U.S. experts visited the site and verified that no nuclear program was in progress. Washington did not pay the hundreds of millions of dollars Pyongyang had demanded in return, but instead promised a shipment of 600,000 tons of grain.

Washington's negotiations with Pyongyang over the development and export of North Korean weapons technology ran their customary tortuous course. The United

States, along with Japan and South Korea, offered a carrot-and-stick deal in which North Korea would be rewarded for not pursuing or exporting missile technology. The U.S. plan to develop an advanced theater missile defense (TMD) system against the North Korean threat provoked not only Pyongyang but Beijing as well. But the threatened firing of a Taepo Dong 2 missile, whose estimated range of 5,000 mi (8 045 km) could reach Hawaii or parts of Alaska, did not take place. Instead, a tentative agreement to suspend the test-firing was reached on September 11.

In response, President Clinton announced on September 17 the partial lifting of economic sanctions that had been imposed on North Korea since the Korean War. Pyongyang followed, on September 25, with an official announcement of a test moratorium "while talks are under way." At a subsequent meeting in November, North Korea reportedly asked for a total dismantling of economic sanctions.

Pyongyang gave a warm welcome to U.S. envoy William Perry, although he was denied a hoped-for meeting with Kim Jong Il. Pyongyang also returned, as it had done before, ten sets of what were believed to be remains of U.S. soldiers from the Korean War.

But reactions to North Korea in Washington were diverse. The Perry report spoke of the need for improving bilateral relations by offering measured doses of inducement, but "at a faster rate," while maintaining a vigilant deterrent posture. The report apparently struck a sympathetic chord with the White House, the State Department, and most Democrats in the U.S. Congress. But Republican hard-liners, including Rep. Benjamin Gilman, chairman of the House International Relations Committee, reacted strongly against any conciliatory moves from the United States toward North Korea. Gilman introduced the "North Korea Threat Reduction Act," which made any U.S. aid contingent on verification of North Korea's complete cessation of nuclear and missile development. North Korea responded by maintaining that it had the right to develop missiles and that, at any rate, the United States had not complied completely with the terms of a 1994 agreement to construct a light-water nuclear-power plant and deliver oil in return for North Korea's not developing its technology.

In December the Korean Peninsula Energy Organization, a U.S.-led consortium, signed a $4.6 billion deal to build two nuclear reactors in North Korea, a reward for Pyongyang's promise to freeze and eventually dismantle its nuclear program. South

NORTH KOREA • Information Highlights

Official Name: Democratic People's Republic of Korea.
Location: Northeastern Asia.
Area: 46,540 sq mi (120 540 km²).
Population (July 1999 est.): 21,386,109.
Chief Cities (1986 est.): Pyongyang, the capital, 2,000,000; Hamhung, 670,000.
Government: *Supreme leader,* Kim Jong Il, chairman of the National Defense Commission and General Secretary of the Workers' Party of Korea (Communist Party). *Nominal head of state,* Kim Yong-nam, chairman of the Presidium of the Supreme People's Assembly. *Legislature* (unicameral)—Supreme People's Assembly.
Gross Domestic Product (1998 est. U.S.$): $21,800,-000,000.
Foreign Trade (1997 est. U.S.$): *Imports,* $1,830,000,000; *exports,* $743,000,000.

© Greg Baker/AP/Wide World Photos

Pak Yong Su (center), *deputy director of the Committee for the Peaceful Reunion of Fatherland, led a North Korean delegation to meet with South Korean officials in Beijing in late June. The talks, however, concluded without results. A tense naval clash between the two sides had occurred several days earlier.*

Korea, Japan, and the EU also will contribute to the financing of the project.

Economy. In 1999, according to a South Korean source, North Korea achieved a small gain in GDP for the first time in years. However, per-capita income was only $126 in 1998, or about 8% that of South Korea's. Even with a slight increase, therefore, North Korea continued to be one of the poorest nations in the world in 1999. North Korea's trade in 1998 was valued at only $1.66 billion, one third less than in 1997. The decline continued in the first half of 1999, showing two-way trade of only $580 million.

The 1999 budget approved in April showed the impact of the stagnant economy. It totaled 20.4 billion won ($9.4 billion), or less than half the budget in 1994, the last time the country had announced its expenditures. Despite such budgetary cutbacks, the finance minister reportedly declared that North Korea would increase its investment in agriculture by 11% to relieve the chronic food shortage, while the expenditures for another critical sector, the power industry, also would grow, by 15%.

Famine. South Korean sources estimated that North Korea's food production grew by 20% in 1998, but the harvest of 3.6 million tons still fell far short of the minimum requirement of 6.6 million tons. Thus, despite the larger budgetary investment and mostly favorable weather conditions in 1998 and 1999, North Korea still required external food assistance.

The cumulative effect of the prolonged famine produced a significant rise in the mortality rate, from 6.8 per 1,000 people in 1995 to 9.3 in 1998, or 55,000 more deaths per year, according to official North Korean statistics. Equally distressing was a report in December 1998 that 62% of North Korea's children were suffering from stunted growth.

Inter-Korean Relations

In February, Pyongyang sent letters to South Korea calling for a pan-national conference to achieve peaceful unification, a reprise of similar propaganda moves in the past. Days later, South Korean President Kim offered a package deal promising economic and food aid as well as support for North Korea's normalization of its relations with Japan and the United States, in return for cessation of Pyongyang's nuclear and missile programs. Nothing came of either proposal.

Equally unproductive were the four-party political conferences that included China and the United States as well as the two Koreas. The fourth, fifth, and sixth plenary sessions met in January, April, and August, but they were totally fruitless, and the last meeting adjourned without setting a date for the next one. While North Korea continued to demand the withdrawal of U.S. troops from South Korea as a precondition for any substantive discussions, the other three conferees chose to establish a control and coordination group to meet quarterly to map out joint strategies. South Korea, acting on its own, sent 50,000 tons of fertilizer to North Korea in March to reopen the government-level discussions between the two nations.

On June 10, only days before the vice-ministers from the two Koreas were to meet in Beijing, a naval battle broke out near the demarcation line off the west coast of the peninsula. In a brief exchange of gunfire, a North Korean torpedo boat was sunk, with the loss of about 40 lives. The hostile encounter was the result of a long-standing dispute on the exact location of the sea boundary. Pyongyang issued angry warnings of retaliation and also renounced any recognition of the existing line, but refrained from going beyond the verbal blast. The vice-ministerial conference met on June 21 but produced no results.

At about the same time, a South Korean woman on a group tour of scenic Mount Kumgang, on the east coast of North Korea, was detained and accused of trying to persuade a Northern guide to defect. Frantic intervention by Hyundai, the South Korean business group that ran the tour, secured the tourist's release after six days, but the project was suspended for 45 days until detailed rules to prevent a similar incident in the future had been worked out. The Mount Kumgang tour scheme provided a glimpse of North Korea for 140,000 visitors (mostly South Koreans) between its launch in November 1998 and November 1999. It also provided $190 million to North Korea. Hyundai founder Chung Ju-yung reportedly was planning to invest in a large industrial park on the west coast, as well as to other tour sites in North Korea.

Inter-Korean trade recovered well from the setback caused by the sharp downturn in South Korea's economy in 1998. In the first half of 1999, the value of trade more than doubled to $165 million, and it grew even more as the year progressed.

HAN-KYO KIM, *University of Cincinnati*

Labor

The United States continued its economic expansion in 1999 with little sign of inflation and modest wage increases. Unemployment declined from the already low 1998 rate, and worker productivity made significant increases. Despite some notable organizing victories and an increase in membership numbers, unionized workers decreased as a percentage of the labor force.

Most other countries also experienced falling unemployment and only modest increases in inflation. The largest decreases in unemployment occurred in Spain, Ireland, Australia, and Canada. Only Japan showed an increase in the rate of unemployment.

United States

Employment and Unemployment. Civilian employment rose by 1.1% in November 1999 from 12 months earlier, while unemployment declined to 4.1% from 4.4% in November 1998. The number of unemployed remained steady at about 5.7 million. The greatest improvement occurred among Hispanic workers, whose unemployment percentage declined to 6% from 6.7%. The rates for adult women (3.6%) and teenagers (14.1%) also were down from 1998, while the rates for adult men (3.3%), white workers (3.5%), and African-Americans (8.1%) registered little or no change.

Worker productivity in the United States rose strongly by 4.9% in the third quarter of 1999—the largest increase since the fourth quarter of 1992. The percentage of unionized workers in the labor force declined to 13.9% in 1998 from 14.1% in 1997, although the overall number of union members increased by 100,000.

The lowest rate of unemployment in Europe was in Switzerland, at 2.4%. Spain, Belgium, Italy, France, and Germany reported more than 10% unemployment.

Labor Negotiations. Daimler-Chrysler and the United Auto Workers (UAW) reached a four-year agreement in September, awarding some of the biggest raises obtained in a union contract in years. The contract provided for annual wage increases of 3%, on top of cost-of-living adjustments. The contract served as a model for contracts negotiated with General Motors and Ford Motor Company, with allowances for special conditions peculiar to those companies. In all, some 400,000 auto workers were affected by the settlements.

A six-month lockout of professional basketball players ended in January, when the National Basketball Association (NBA) and the players' union agreed to a six-year contract, thus ending the most costly labor dispute in professional-basketball history. Estimates placed the players' salary losses at $400 million and the owners' revenue losses at hundreds of millions of dollars. The crux of the dispute was how to divide up the $2 billion in annual revenues generated during the season. The settlement provided that players would receive 55% of revenues during the last three years of the contract, with no fixed percentage during the first three

© Le Segretain Pascal/Corbis-Sygma

Thousands of protesters disrupted the opening of a World Trade Organization (WTO) summit in Seattle on Nov. 30, 1999, left. *The angry demonstrators, who included many union members, accused the WTO of allowing its member countries to engage in unfair labor practices.*

years. The NBA won its main goal of containing the contracts of high-salaried players and putting a limit on individual salaries. The union achieved its stated priority of bettering the economic position of its middle-level players. Most sports experts believed that the owners came off better than the players in the final agreement.

The professional umpires' union had less success in its dealings with major-league baseball later in the year. In an attempt to force the league into early negotiations, Richie Phillips, the union head, led a mass resignation of more than 50 major-league umpires that took effect in September, just before the play-offs began. The negotiating strategy backfired, as the league owners accepted 22 of the resignations and hired 25 replacements. The union was forced to accept a settlement in which those 22 umpires would receive their salaries for the three months remaining under their existing agreement, but would not be rehired. The union also agreed not to strike in support of its 22 affected members. Phillips' miscalculation wound up costing him his job. In December, 62% of the umpires decertified the union and ended his 21-year stint as chief negotiator. At the same time, a new union, the Major League Umpires Independent Organizing Committee, was formed to represent umpires in collective bargaining with the league owners. Phillips' union filed an objection to the decertification vote, and a hearing on the issue was set for early 2000. Meanwhile, one of the new union's top priorities was getting the 22 dismissed umpires their jobs back; the issue was to be decided in arbitration.

American Airlines, the nation's second-largest airline, was forced to cancel one third of its flights after 2,000 of its pilots called in sick during the busy Presidents' Day holiday period. The Allied Pilots Association, an independent union representing 9,200 pilots, began the sick-out on February 5 after negotiations broke down over how American Airlines would integrate a small airline, Reno Air, into its network and when the airline would raise the salaries of the lower-paid Reno pilots. On February 10 a federal judge ruled that the sick-out was illegal and ordered the pilots to return to work. When the pilots defied the judge's order, he imposed a fine of $10 million on the union, plus a $10,000 fine on its president. The pilots finally went back to work on February 14. In April the judge increased the penalty against the union to $45.5 million. Meanwhile, the dispute was settled in October. The settlement provided that American could not furlough 300 pilots—matching the number of Reno pilots who joined American. Also, Reno pilots received a 45% raise retroactive to March 1, 1999.

Unionizing Activities. Efforts to unionize doctors accelerated in 1999. Even the American Medical Association (AMA), long opposed to doctors' forming unions, voted in May to set up a unit to do collective bargaining. About 35,000 doctors, or 5% of the nation's physicians, belonged to unions in 1999, up from 25,000 in 1996. Health-maintenance organizations (HMOs) opposed unionization of doctors, asserting that they were independent contractors and therefore were not allowed to unionize. Hospitals also fought the unionization movement, fearing that their profits would go down.

Most of the union activity was among salaried staff doctors at public and private hospitals, who were bargaining over wages, hours, and working conditions. Many doctors in private practice also were joining unions to give themselves more power in negotiations with HMOs. With more than 90% of the nation's physicians having at least one contract with a managed-care company, many doctors cited a loss in their decision-making authority and a drop in reimbursements as reasons for joining unions. Other doctors, however, opposed unionization because they believed unions were for blue-collar workers, not professionals. They also felt that going on strike would violate the Hippocratic oath by denying care to patients. The AMA also openly opposed strikes or other tactics that would interfere with patient care.

Several large nonmedical unions moved aggressively to persuade doctors' unions to merge with them, and several small doctors' unions agreed to do so. For instance, the 10,000-member Committee of Interns and Residents merged with the 1.3-million-member Service Employees International Union.

U.S. EMPLOYMENT AND UNEMPLOYMENT

(Armed forces excluded)

	Nov. 1998	Nov. 1999
Labor Force	138,288,000	139,827,000
Participation Rate	67.1%	67.0%
Employed	132,577,000	134,085,000
Unemployed	5,711,000	5,743,000
Unemployment Rate	4.4%	4.1%
Adult Men	3.2%	3.3%
Adult Women	3.8%	3.6%
Teenagers	14.6%	14.1%
White	3.6%	3.5%
Black	8.1%	8.1%
Hispanic	6.7%	6.0%

Source: U.S. Bureau of Labor Statistics

And the Union of American Physicians and Dentists, with 5,000 members, joined with the 1.3-million-member American Federation of State, County, and Municipal Employees. The AMA, whose membership includes 34% of the nation's doctors, stated that it preferred physicians to form independent bargaining units that were not affiliated with traditional trade unions. In November the National Labor Relations Board (NLRB) ruled that interns and residents at privately owned hospitals had the right to form unions. Hospital officials criticized the decision, which involved the Boston Medical Center in Massachusetts, saying it would fuel tensions and interfere with the educational mission of teaching hospitals.

In another breakthrough in organizing professionals, the 3,200-member New York State Psychological Association (NYSPA), whose members mostly were therapists with doctorates in psychology, agreed to join the American Federation of Teachers (AFT). The motive for joining the AFT, according to NYSPA officials, was to gain more clout in lobbying for legislation in New York state and in Washington, DC, and to force managed-care organizations to provide better mental-health coverage.

Dissatisfaction among teaching assistants, Ph.D. candidates who do much of the teaching of undergraduates at the nation's major research universities, had led to union organizing at 18 public universities. The University of California at Los Angeles (UCLA) fought unionization of its 9,000 graduate assistants for 16 years, arguing that they were primarily students, not employees. But in March the California Public Employment Relations Board ordered the state's universities to allow union elections at seven campuses. Teaching assistants at UCLA and the University of California at Berkeley voted overwhelmingly to join a UAW affiliate. California's other state universities soon followed suit. The union was seeking improvement in health benefits, an effective grievance procedure, better workload distribution, and higher salaries.

Union Fraud. In the wake of evidence that the ratification of the 1996 contract between District Council 37 of the American Federation of State, County, and Municipal Employees (AFSCME) and New York City was secured by fraud, Stanley Hill was forced to resign his post as executive director of the 120,000-member union. The council was placed under trusteeship by the parent federation. Manhattan District Attorney Robert Morgenthau was investigating the union and its 56 constituent locals not only for the vote fraud, but also for allegations of embezzlement, falsification of records, and receipt of kickbacks from caterers, insurance companies, law firms, and travel agencies.

International

France. In 1998, France passed a law calling for a 35-hour workweek with no reduction in hourly pay. Companies with more than 20 employees were to achieve this goal by Jan. 1, 2000, while those with fewer than 20 employees had until Jan. 1, 2002. As of mid-1999, only about 1% of employers had concluded agreements for a 35-hour workweek. The plan was aimed at creating 1 million new jobs and alleviating France's double-digit unemployment rate.

While labor initially supported the idea, many unions began to have second thoughts, fearing that the plan would freeze salary levels and reverse benefits. Employers also protested, claiming that the 35-hour week would cost too much and would destroy France's competitiveness in world markets.

France's unemployment rate dropped to 11.1% in August, from 11.7% in the third quarter of 1998. However, unemployment was still higher than in Great Britain and Germany. One of the reasons for French noncompetitiveness, according to employers, was the high cost of social insurance and labor taxes, which amounted to 45.4% of hourly production costs per manufacturing worker in France, as compared with 35.1% in Germany and 14.8% in Britain.

Germany. Collective bargaining in Germany in 1999 was characterized by sectoral pay agreements considerably above inflation, ending the pay moderation of previous years. Settlements were generally for a period of 14 or 15 months, providing increases of 3.1% to 3.3%. Typically, a flat-rate payment to cover the first two or three months also was awarded. Many agreements included employees in both East and West Germany, which had not been true in the past.

The key settlement was made by the IG Metall union, covering about 3.2 million employees in metalworking industries. It provided for a flat-rate payment in January and February, followed by an increase of 3.2%. The total deal amounted to an increase of 4.2% over 14 months. The next major agreement was concluded in the public sector, also covering about 3.2 million workers. It generally followed the precedent set in metalworking and was estimated to be worth about 2.5%. Employers maintained that the agreement would place an unacceptable burden upon central and local governments, possibly resulting in job losses. Other significant settlements were reached in construction, where 800,000 workers in the West got a 2.9% raise, but construction workers in the East received no increase; and in the chemical industry, where 600,000 workers received a 3% raise over 13 months.

Japan. The 1999 spring wage negotiations in 223 major companies in Japan resulted in wage increases of up to 2.14% from 1998. The 1999 increase was the lowest since the annual wage survey was instituted in 1956.

The 1999 negotiations were influenced by several factors. As corporate performance worsened, many companies settled for an annual increment only, without raising the average wage base. Some companies cut wages, extended working hours, and lowered overtime pay. More and more companies abolished uniform wage raises in favor of tailoring increases to each company's ability to pay and to worker productivity. An increasing number of companies introduced a new bonus system based on performance. And finally, more and more employers departed from guaranteeing workers lifetime employment in favor of offering opportunities for workers to receive the education and training necessary to allow them to change employers.

Israel. About 400,000 unionized state workers in Israel engaged in a strike in March over wage negotiations with the government. The government had proposed a 3.85% raise, about equal to the projected rate of inflation. Workers, however, countered that their last wage increase, in 1997, had been undercut by an inflation rate of 8.6% in 1998. The walkout failed, as it did not halt most essential public services, nor did it force the government to accept the union's wage proposals. Mail deliveries and garbage collection stopped, and passport offices closed, but a court order kept skeleton crews running state utilities and bus and train lines, minimizing economic disruption.

The failure of the strike underscored the weakness of an organized labor movement that was rooted in government jobs, while high-tech business was providing most new employment, and the government was privatizing state industries. As its economic power declined, the Histadrut labor federation, once the organizational and ideological backbone of the Labor Party, found itself becoming politically marginal. Israelis had become accustomed to national and municipal work stoppages that disrupted telephone service, school schedules, or welfare programs on an almost monthly basis. In 1999 strikes shut down airports, universities, the state water company, the weather service, Social Security offices, and even Histadrut itself.

Romania. In the worst crisis that the Romanian government had faced since coming to power in 1996, 10,000 coal miners struck for 15 days in January. They were seeking a 35% raise and $10,000 in severance pay in case of layoffs. They also wanted the government to rescind the planned closing of two mines that employed 2,000 workers. Although they were supported by impoverished Romanians in their march toward Bucharest, the strikers met with hostility from residents of the capital, who felt that their demands were excessive, given that miners' earnings were twice the average monthly wage of $100.

The miners headed back to work when the government agreed not to close two pit mines that were among 140 scheduled to be shut down in 1999 as part of a restructuring plan.

Mexico. A seven-month-long student strike led to the resignation of Francisco Barnes de Castro, president of the 268,000-student National Autonomous University of Mexico. Students took over the university buildings in April, after President Barnes proposed the first tuition increase in 50 years—from a few cents to $140 a year, which would apply only to students who could afford to pay. The strikers demanded elimination of all fees, as well as the elimination of recently instituted admission and graduation examinations, the lifting of limits on the time students could remain enrolled before graduating, and the reinstatement of automatic admission for students from a network of high schools linked to the university. They also wanted students to have equal power in decisions with the administration and faculty. Many of Mexico's most prominent scholars turned against the shutdown and warned that it could cripple the university permanently. University officials estimated that, despite the strike, about 65% of the undergraduates were able to complete their work for the semester by continuing their studies off campus.

See also OBITUARIES—*Lane Kirkland.*

JACK STIEBER, *Michigan State University*

Laos

While failing to develop effective economic policies in 1999, Laos reaffirmed key foreign ties. Leadership changes reflected frustration over the economic crisis.

Politics. After Lao leaders were unable to cooperate in addressing the country's economic woes, President Khamtai Siphandon in August removed Finance Minister Khamphoui Keoboualapha and the Central Bank governor. Their replacements followed the Lao People's Revolutionary Party's pattern of placing security and political stability before consideration of major economic changes. The 99-member Lao National Assembly played a more activist role, as members met with counterparts from Israel, Vietnam, the United States, India, and Belgium. Press reports suggested that a planned political protest was stopped in Laos on October 26. It would have been the first such organized protest since 1975.

Economy. Laotian inflation was high, and revenues were insufficient to meet rising costs. The Lao kip had lost more than 50% of its value since 1997 and failed to recover despite stabilization of the closely linked Thai baht. Foreign investment remained low, forcing the government to abandon some projects. Lao leaders lobbied Bangkok to buy more electricity—one of Laos' top foreign-exchange earners—and raised import taxes to address the growing trade deficit.

The dependence of 85% of workers on subsistence agriculture meant many Lao still met basic needs. A Japanese delegation promised to visit in 2000 to aid in formulating macroeconomic policies.

Foreign Policy. Highlighting growing relations with China, Prime Minister Sisavath Keobounphan met with China's President Jiang Zemin in Beijing in January. In March, Sisavath reaffirmed cooperative ties with Thailand during his first official visit to that nation. Relations with Vietnam were strengthened during an exchange of presidential visits.

The speech of Foreign Minister Somsavat Lengsavat at the July meeting of the Association of Southeast Asian Nations (ASEAN) reiterated Vientiane's policy of broadening foreign relations to maintain regional stability and attract foreign assistance. The visit of a U.S. congressional delegation highlighted bilateral U.S.-Laotian cooperation despite tension over human-rights issues.

CHRISTINE VAN ZANDT
U.S. Government Analyst on East Asian Affairs

LAOS • Information Highlights

Official Name: Lao People's Democratic Republic.
Location: Southeast Asia.
Area: 91,430 sq mi (236 800 km²).
Population (July 1999 est.): 5,407,453.
Chief City (March 1995 census): Vientiane, the capital, 528,109.
Government: *Head of state,* Khamtai Siphandon, president (appointed Feb. 24, 1998). *Head of government,* Sisavath Keobounphan, prime minister (named Feb. 24, 1998). *Legislature* (unicameral)—National Assembly.
Monetary Unit: New kip (9,350.0 new kips equal U.S.$1, Dec. 2, 1999).
Gross Domestic Product (1998 est. U.S.$): $6,600,-000,000.
Foreign Trade (1998 est. U.S.$): *Imports,* $553,000,000; *exports,* $370,000,000.

Latin America

In 1999, Latin America was undergoing its deepest economic slump since the debt crisis of the early 1980s. Throughout much of the year, nearly all Latin American countries were experiencing sharp slowdowns in growth or full-fledged recessions. The United Nations Economic Commission for Latin America and the Caribbean (UNECLAC) predicted that the regional gross domestic product (GDP) would shrink slightly in 1999, for the first time in the 1990s; however, it was expected to start to grow again in 2000. The hemisphere-wide recession marked a disappointing turn in a decade noted for Latin America's robust economy, with high growth rates fueled by the widespread adoption of free-market practices.

The economic falloff was related partly to the financial crises in East Asia and Russia, but also to older, recurring problems, such as low commodity prices, soaring public debt, unemployment, currency destabilization, and the lack of foreign investment. While the value of exports fell in 1998 for the first time in more than a decade, imports continued to expand. Consequently, the region's current-account deficit grew from an average of 3.4% of GDP in 1997 to 4.5% in 1998.

Faced with the possibility of significant external imbalances, many Latin governments and central banks decided to restrict fiscal expenditures and raise interest rates. At first, there was a tendency to avoid using devaluation to alter relative prices; later, however, governments began to opt for more-active exchange-rate management. The combination of slower growth and currency depreciation was expected to pare the current-account deficit to about 3.5% of GDP by the end of 1999.

Brazil fared better than most countries in the hemisphere. Financial analysts welcomed the country's fiscal restructuring, and the Brazilian economy was projected to contract just 3% in 1999, rather than the earlier estimate of 5%. Peru and Mexico were the only significant Latin economies that were expected to grow in 1999. Argentina, Chile, and Venezuela performed worse than predicted in 1999, and Colombia and Ecuador saw their most serious recessions in the last 50 years. Overall, experts were forecasting a 0.5% reduction in growth for 1999.

Despite the continuing crisis, inflows of foreign direct investment rose 5% in 1998, to $72 billion, according to preliminary figures from the United Nations Conference on Trade and Development (UNCTAD). Southern Cone countries received 70% of the investment capital, with Brazil attracting the largest part, $28.7 billion. The United States accounted for the bulk of the investment. Of the 100 largest companies investing in the hemisphere, 44 were owned by U.S. interests, and 37 were European-owned. Spain was the major European investor.

Commodity Prices. In the first quarter of 1999, commodity prices continued to slide. The price of oil, on the other hand, rose sharply as a result of the renewal of an agreement by the Organization of Petroleum Exporting Countries (OPEC) to limit supplies. In most of the region's larger economies, the slowdown in exports that began in 1998 intensified, and merchandise export values in Argentina, Brazil, Ecuador, Paraguay, and Uruguay plunged by between 15% and 25%. Paraguay and Uruguay, in particular, also were affected by the sharp reduction in value of Brazil's currency, the real, in early 1999.

Colombia and Chile also saw their merchandise exports slip, but to a lesser extent. The damage to exports by the hurricanes in Central America became more evident, as coffee sales by Central American countries fell sharply in the October 1998–May 1999 harvest period. On the other hand, Costa Rica saw a new increase in total export earnings, as did Mexico, and this had a decisive effect on the regional aggregate.

The poor performance lasted into the first half of 1999, so that only slight growth was expected for the year. Since most countries of the region had high population-growth rates, per-capita GDP was expected to contract in 1999. As a result, the overall improvement in per-capita GDP for the 1990s was expected to be barely 15%.

San José Pact. Presidents Ernesto Zedillo of Mexico and Hugo Chávez of Venezuela officially renewed the Program of Energy Cooperation with the Countries of Central America and the Caribbean—the so-called San José Pact—early in August. The agreement mandated that Mexico and Venezuela each sell 160,000 barrels of oil a day at reduced rates to Barbados, Belize, Costa Rica, El Salvador, Guatemala, Haiti, Honduras, Jamaica, Nicaragua, Panama, and the Dominican Republic. Venezuela had proposed expanding the pact to include Cuba, but Mexico objected.

Free Trade. The drive to create a free-trade zone in the Western Hemisphere by 2005—first proposed in June 1990 by U.S. President George Bush as the "Enterprise for the Americas Initiative"—gained new momentum in 1999. Trade ministers from 34 countries in the hemisphere agreed to play down their differences and move immediately to ease the passage of goods across borders. The large countries of the hemisphere agreed to allow the smaller and less-developed countries more time to reduce tariffs and open their economies to foreign investment, while the smaller countries agreed to accept the inclusion of labor and environmental standards in the next round of negotiations.

Meanwhile, the leaders of nearly 50 countries—including members of the European Union (EU), Argentina, and Chile—met in June in Rio de Janeiro, Brazil, to discuss plans to create a free-trade zone between Europe and Latin America. At the summit, they signed the Declaration of Rio, a statement of their intention to liberalize trade and reduce tariffs and other trade barriers.

Drugs. U.S. law-enforcement officials reported an "alarming" increase in the quantity of marijuana and cocaine reaching the United States from Latin America and the Caribbean in 1998 and 1999. Seizures of marijuana by U.S. drug interdiction agencies jumped from 113 tons to 720 tons between 1991 and 1998, while cocaine loads also appeared to have increased dramatically. In 1999 the U.S. Coast Guard made the largest cocaine hauls in history in both the Pacific Ocean and the Caribbean.

According to statistics reported in 1999, the increase in illicit drugs flowing into the United States from Latin America was accompanied by a relatively new phenomenon: a significant jump in drug use and abuse by Latin Americans themselves.

RICHARD C. SCHROEDER, *Freelance Writer*

Law

The relative powers of the states and the U.S. Congress dominated the 1998–99 term of the U.S. Supreme Court as much as any issue, and in three cases the sharply divided court again reaffirmed its support of states' rights. Many observers said the 5–4 rulings in all three cases underscored a deepening rift between the justices that could have sweeping significance. By granting the states broad immunity from congressional interference, the narrow conservative majority again signaled a willingness to circumscribe federal authority. Important rulings on police authority, citizenship, and the rights of the disabled also were highlights of the term.

The justices continued their trend of limiting their review by handing down 75 signed opinions, about half the number of opinions in the mid-1980s. Justices Sandra Day O'Connor and Anthony M. Kennedy had the fewest dissents—eight. By contrast, Justice John Paul Stevens dissented 19 times, the highest number for anyone on the court. Justices O'Connor and Kennedy joined with Chief Justice William H. Rehnquist and Justices Antonin Scalia and Clarence Thomas in forming the pro–states' rights alliance. The four dissenters, generally regarded as the liberal wing on ideological issues, were Justices Stevens, David H. Souter, Ruth Bader Ginsburg, and Stephen G. Breyer. Also of note, the high court ended its term on June 23, the earliest it had done so in 30 years.

The sharp divisions on the high court and the advancing years of some members suggested to commentators that the winner of the 2000 presidential election could have a big say in the court's direction.

In the lower courts, the rising importance of the Internet spurred some important rulings. Federal judges reaffirmed constitutional protections for freedom of expression on the World Wide Web. An analysis of civil litigation showed that plaintiffs stood a better chance of winning in trials before judges than juries—though juries were more generous in awarding damages.

In early November, in preliminary findings in an antitrust lawsuit against Microsoft, Judge Thomas Penfield Jackson found that the computer-software manufacturer enjoyed "monopoly power" that it used to the disadvantage of its competitors and customers. Delivering the "finding of facts" before the verdict gave the government and Microsoft a chance to reach an out-of-court settlement in the case.

In international law, prosecutors for the International Criminal Tribunal for the Former Yugoslavia handed down a four-count indictment against Yugoslav President Slobodan Milosevic and four of his top deputies in May.

United States

Supreme Court. The justices, voting 5–4, issued three decisions that held that the principle of sovereign immunity shielded states from lawsuits alleging violations of federal law. In an opinion by Justice Kennedy, the court said that states could not be sued in their own courts by state employees for violations of the Fair Labor Standards Act (*Alden v. Maine*). The court previously had barred similar suits in federal court, meaning employees were left without legal recourse to sue for alleged violations of federal labor law. The federal government still may sue on behalf of a state employee.

In a pair of companion decisions, the justices ruled that states are immune from patent-infringement and trademark suits. In the disputes, the College Savings Bank of Princeton, NJ, said Florida officials falsely advertised a competing state program that violated federal law (*Florida Prepaid v. College Savings Bank* and *College Savings Bank v. Florida Prepaid*). The high court was no more deferential to presidential power, as it ruled, 5–4, that statistical sampling may not be used in the 2000 census to determine how many members of Congress should be apportioned to each state (*Department of Commerce v. U.S. House of Representatives*). The Bill Clinton administration had proposed the plan to alleviate what officials said was the traditional undercounting of racial minorities.

A series of three cases yielded a restrictive view of who is covered by the Americans with Disabilities Act. All three were decided by 7–2 votes, as the justices said the law does not apply to people with conditions that can be corrected with medication, eyeglasses, or other devices. The justices held that two nearsighted sisters with correctable vision were not disabled and thus could not sue an airline that refused to hire them because of their impairments (*Sutton v. United Air Lines*). The court rejected a bias claim by a truck driver who was fired because he was functionally blind in one eye (*Albertsons Inc. v. Kirkinburg*). And the justices ruled that it was not discrimination for a company to dismiss a truck driver whose high blood pressure prevented him from obtaining federal certification to drive a truck (*Murphy v. United Parcel Service*).

Decisions involving police powers presented a mixed picture. The court, voting 6–3, struck down an ordinance in Chicago that barred loitering and was intended to be a weapon against street gangs (*Chicago v. Morales*). Justice Stevens, writing for the court, said the ordinance gave too much discretion to police by letting the authorities target anyone "in one place with no apparent purpose." The court ruled unanimously that a successful prosecution under a federal law barring illegal gratuities to officials requires a showing that the gift had a bearing on the official's actions (*United States v. Sun-Diamond*). The justices, rejecting the independent counsel's view of the law, ruled in a case in which Mike Espy, former secretary of agriculture in the Clinton cabinet, was investigated for allegedly accepting illegal gratuities.

In a unanimous ruling, the court said police may not permit journalists and photographers to enter people's homes when the news media accompany authorities in residential searches and arrests (*Wilson v. Layne*). The raids violate constitutional assurances of privacy, the justices held. By a 5–4 vote, the justices said people temporarily in a private home to conduct business there may not challenge a police search of the home (*Minnesota v. Carter*). The ruling left open the possibility that a social guest might be able to contest a search. Police do not have authority to search a car automatically when they issue a speeding ticket (*Knowles v. Iowa*), the court ruled unanimously. But once they have probable cause to search a car, the justices ruled , 6–3, they can search personal belongings—such as a pocketbook—of passengers who themselves are not suspected of criminal activity (*Wyoming v. Houghton*).

The justices divided, 5–4, in ruling that school districts may be sued for damages when one student accuses another of sexual harassment (*Davis v. Monroe County*). In another decision that strengthened individual rights, the court said, voting 7–2, that states may not restrict new residents to welfare benefits they would have received in their home states (*Saenz v. Roe*). The ruling overturned part of a new federal law that let states set up two-tiered welfare-benefit systems.

In a voting-rights case from North Carolina, the high court unanimously held that congressional district lines drawn primarily for political reasons are not invalid merely because they take into account the racial composition of the district (*Hunt v. Cromartie*). The ruling reinstated a heavily Democratic district that is almost half black in population. The court, in a 6–3 decision, struck down restrictive provisions of Colorado's system for placing initiatives on the ballot on grounds that they violated 1st Amendment free-expression protections (*Buckley v. American Constitutional Law Foundation*). States cannot require people who circulate initiative petitions to be registered voters or wear identification badges, the ruling held.

The court issued a number of notable rulings affecting businesses. Voting 6–3, the justices overturned a 65-year-old federal ban on broadcast advertising of casino gambling (*Greater New Orleans Broadcasting Assoc. v. United States*). Companies that make good-faith efforts to comply with federal antidiscrimination laws cannot be sued for punitive damages, even if a senior official deliberately violates company policy and the law, the justices held in a 5–4 decision (*Kolstad v. American Dental Association*). The court, in a 5–3 ruling, restricted the Federal Communications Commission's authority to oversee telephone deregulation under the Telecommunications Act of 1996 (*AT&T Corp. v. Iowa Utilities Board*).

The justices were unanimous in granting federal judges expanded authority to exclude testimony from experts of questionable reliability when companies are sued in product-liability cases (*Kumho Tire v. Carmichael*). The decision was a victory for businesses. The court, in a 7–2 ruling, overturned a $1.5 billion settlement in an asbestos class-action suit, ruling it was unfair to victims excluded from the settlement and may have been the result of a conflict of interest on the part of lawyers who forged the settlement (*Ortiz v. Fibreboard Corp.*).

The justices unanimously ruled that foreigners who have committed serious crimes in their home countries are not entitled to refugee status in the United States, even if there is a risk they could be persecuted if deported and forced to return to their homeland (*Immigration and Naturalization Service v. Aguirre*). The court ruled, 6–3, that people from foreign lands may be deported based on their political views and associations (*Reno v. American-Arab Anti-Discrimination Committee*).

Local Law. U.S. District Judge Nancy G. Edmunds in Detroit refused to bar the gadfly operator of an Internet site from publishing confidential documents obtained from the Ford Motor Co. The judge rejected arguments that the site disclosed trade secrets that should be protected. Experts said the ruling, and others like it, suggested the courts view the Internet in much the same way they treat newspapers and books, granting broad free-expression protection.

The 9th U.S. Circuit Court of Appeals, based in San Francisco, ruled against the Clinton administration's effort to restrict posting of encryption codes on the Internet. By a 2–1 vote, the appeals-court panel said the material is protected by the 1st Amendment. Soon after, however, a majority of the full court granted a new hearing. Encryption software scrambles communications to protect privacy, and officials fear the technology will be used to conceal criminal activity.

In a ruling that limited Internet expression, a jury in Oregon penalized antiabortion activists $107 million for using a Web site called the Nuremberg Files to target physicians who ran abortion clinics. However, the verdict—which was appealed—seemed to apply only to statements threatening assault or bodily harm.

The 8th U.S. Circuit Court of Appeals, based in St. Louis, ruled that three states' laws banning late-term abortions were unconstitutional. The three-judge panel said laws in Nebraska, Arkansas, and Iowa were so vague that they could be interpreted to ban all abortions. The 7th U.S. Circuit Court of Appeals, based in Chicago, voting 5–4, subsequently upheld bans on late-term abortions enacted by Wisconsin and Illinois. The conflict in rulings increased the likelihood that the U.S. Supreme Court would agree to resolve the issue. Some 30 states had adopted laws since 1995 that prohibit what opponents of the procedure call partial-birth abortions.

An analysis of 15,000 civil cases by the U.S. Bureau of Justice Statistics found that judges are more likely than juries to rule for the plaintiff in civil lawsuits, but that juries generally award larger damages than do judges. The study looked at personal injury, contract, and real-property cases that went to trial in state courts in the nation's 75 largest counties in 1996. The study found that 52% of the plaintiffs won their cases. In cases tried before a jury—two out of three—the plaintiffs won 49% of the time, while plaintiffs prevailed in 62% of the cases when a judge decided the outcome. Half of jury awards to plaintiffs were for at least $35,000 each, compared with $28,000 when a judge determined the amount.

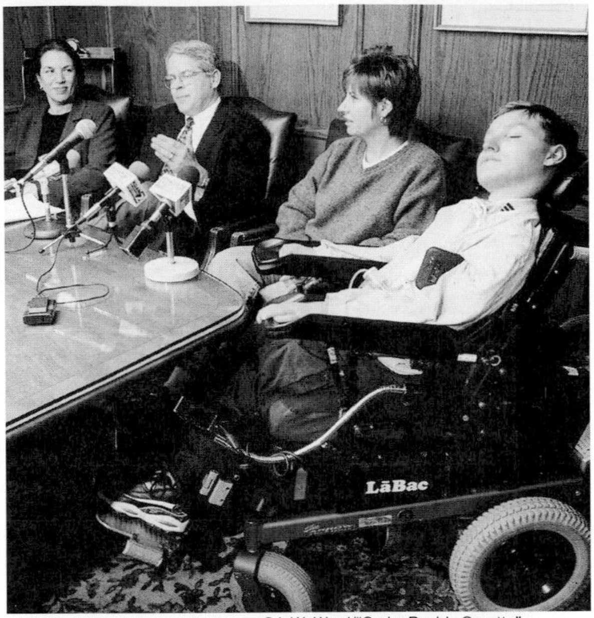

© L.W. Ward/"Cedar Rapids Gazette"

In a case brought by the parents of Garret Frey (right), *the U.S. Supreme Court ruled in March 1999 that public schools must accommodate disabled students who need special assistance during the day, as long as that aid can be provided by a person who is not a physician.*

A federal judge briefly blocked a Cleveland program that uses taxpayer money for vouchers to send several thousand children to private and parochial schools. U.S. District Judge Solomon Oliver, Jr., in Cleveland changed his decision days later to permit most of the children to stay in the program for the time being. His reversal affected students who had been in the program in 1998, letting them receive tuition money for the first semester of the 1999–2000 academic year. The ruling stirred discussion on the merits of school vouchers.

U.S. District Judge Royce Lamberth in Washington, DC, said drug companies may inform doctors about off-label uses of prescription drugs, as he struck down a 1997 federal law as a violation of free-speech guarantees. The law was aimed at limiting dissemination of scientific articles on the uses of medication not approved by the FDA.

JIM RUBIN, *"Bloomberg News"*

International Law

During 1999 the International Criminal Tribunal for Rwanda and the International Criminal Tribunal for the former Yugoslavia issued a number of indictments and judicial decisions relating to the commission of war crimes in Rwanda and the former Yugoslavia. These decisions greatly affected the development of international law.

Rwanda Tribunal. In April three members of the 1994 interim government of Rwanda were arrested in Cameroon and transferred to the Rwanda Tribunal Detention Facility in Arusha, Tanzania. Jerome Bicamumpaka, the former foreign minister; Justin Mugenzi, the former commerce minister; and Prosper Mugiraneza, the former minister of the civil service, joined former Health Minister Casimir Bizimungu, who was already in custody. The four were charged with genocide, conspiracy to commit genocide, and crimes against humanity. All pleaded not guilty.

Former Rwandan Minister for the Family and Women's Affairs Pauline Nyiramasuhuko, along with her son Arsene Shalom Ntahobali, were indicted in August for genocide, conspiracy to commit genocide, crimes against humanity, encouraging mass rape campaigns, and "outrages upon personal dignity, in particular humiliating and degrading treatment, rape, enforced prostitution, and indecent assault" against Tutsi women. Mikaeli Muhimana, formerly a councillor in the Kibuye prefecture, was arrested on November 8 in Tanzania and indicted on 25 counts of conspiracy to commit genocide, crimes of genocide, crimes against humanity, and violations of the Geneva Convention. By late November, 39 individuals had been detained and charged with genocide and other crimes against humanity.

Omar Serushago, a businessman, was found guilty of genocide and crimes against humanity and sentenced to a 15-year prison term on February 5. On May 21, Clement Kayishema, a medical doctor and prefect of Kibuye, was judged responsible for crimes of genocide and sentenced to life in prison; on the same day, Obed Ruzindana, a businessman, was convicted of genocide and sentenced to 25 years in prison. Georges Anderson Nderubumwe Rutaganda, leader of the Interahamwe militia, was convicted of genocide and crimes against humanity and sentenced to life imprisonment in December.

Yugoslav Tribunal. On May 27 the Yugoslav Tribunal indicted Yugoslavian President Slobodan Milosevic, Serbian President Milan Milutinovic, Yugoslavian Deputy Prime Minister Nikola Sainovic, Yugoslavian Army Chief of Staff Dragoljub Ojdanic, and Serbian Minister of Internal Affairs Vlajko Stojiljkovic for persecution of Kosovar Albanians on political, racial, or religious grounds between January 1 and late May 1999. The specific charges brought against the three included murder, a crime against humanity, and also a violation of the laws or customs of war, punishable under the 1949 Geneva Conventions; persecutions on political, racial, or religious grounds, a crime against humanity; and deportation, a crime against humanity.

In another important action, the tribunal detained Gen. Momir Talic on August 25, while he was on an official visit to Vienna. Talic, who was the chief of staff of the Republika Srpska, had been charged with crimes against humanity and persecutions of individuals based on political, racial, and religious grounds in a sealed indictment on March 14. In addition, Dragan Kolundzija was detained by international peacekeeping forces in northwest Bosnia on June 7. Kolundzija had been indicted in July 1995 for unlawful detainment and cruel treatment of 3,000 Bosnian Muslims and Croats. Also, on August 9, Croatia surrendered to the tribunal Vinko Martinovic, who had been indicted in December 1998 for ethnic cleansing.

In October the Yugoslav Tribunal acquitted Goran Jelisic of genocide but found him guilty of 31 counts of crimes against humanity and violations of laws or customs of war. Jelisic was sentenced to 40 years in prison. The Appeals Chamber in 1999 reviewed the case of Dusko Tadic, who was found guilty in May 1997 of 11 counts of crimes against humanity but acquitted on other counts, on the grounds that the victims in those cases were not "protected persons" under the Geneva Convention. On reconsideration, the court found in July that the victims were indeed protected persons, and then went on to convict Tadic of those additional counts of crimes against humanity. On November 11, Tadic was given nine more sentences, ranging from six to 25 years, for these crimes.

Leadership Change. Louise Arbour, chief war-crimes prosecutor for the Yugoslav and Rwanda Tribunals since 1996, left her position in the fall to join the Supreme Court of Canada. Her replacement was Swiss prosecutor Carla Del Ponte, who was known for waging tough battles against money laundering and organized crime.

PAUL R. WILLIAMS, *American University*

Lebanon

Lebanon's anomalous international position remained unchanged in 1999. Nominally, it was a sovereign state, but since 1990 it effectively had been under Syrian control. Major policy decisions often were decided in Damascus rather than in Beirut. However, Syrian domination had been the price for not having a civil war, a fact wryly accepted by most Lebanese.

The year was an interesting one, as newly appointed Prime Minister Salim al-Hoss, a U.S.-trained economist, served his first full year in office. He had begun his tenure in December 1998. Hoss twice had been prime minister for brief periods during the time of the civil war.

Political Affairs. Announcing his main policy objectives on Dec. 2, 1998, Hoss made his first priority the reduction of public expenditure. Lebanese finances are chronically in deficit, with about 40% of spending not met by income. He also pledged to bring to an end the "security zone" in southern Lebanon maintained by Israel and Israel's allies the South Lebanon Army (SLA).

Several cabinet members appointed by Hoss had been conspicuous critics of the administration of former Prime Minister Rafik al-Hariri, but two members were carried over from the Hariri cabinet. The new cabinet was largely technocratic in character.

The new government generally was welcomed by public opinion, with some exaggerated heralding of a new era dawning for Lebanon. There was predictable dissent on this point from Hariri and from Druze leader Walid Jumblatt. Public approval increased as a vigorous campaign against corruption was launched in January 1999. More than 20 high-ranking officials were dismissed, and the purge continued throughout the year. The Lebanese diplomatic corps also was reshuffled.

Israeli Security Zone. The chronic problem of the Israeli security zone continued. On February 18, Israeli troops and allied Lebanese militia seized the village of Arnoun, slightly beyond the zone's northern edge. On February 28 an Israeli general and three soldiers were killed by a car bomb planted by the anti-Israeli guerrilla group Hezbollah. In retaliation, Israeli planes the next day hit Hezbollah bases deep in Lebanon. Israel gave up Arnoun, then retook it on April 15.

June 24–25 saw the heaviest battles in Lebanon since 1996. Hezbollah rockets were fired into northern Israel, and Israeli planes struck targets in Lebanon, damaging the coast road and interrupting Beirut's electricity. Each side blamed the other for the flare-up. Several civilians perished, and scores were wounded.

Things became quieter when Ehud Barak succeeded Benjamin Netanyahu as Israel's premier in early July. Barak favored an Israeli withdrawal from Lebanon, as did an increasing number of Israeli leaders. Israel unsuccessfully was attempting to tie a withdrawal to concessions by either Lebanon or Syria. The violence resumed on August 16, however, when Hezbollah commander Ali Hassan Deeb (better known as Abu Hassan) was killed near Sidon. The next day the guerrillas launched a raid against Israeli forces, killing two Israeli soldiers.

Internal Affairs. Amin Kayed, a high official of the Fatah movement headed by Palestine Liberation Organization (PLO) leader Yasir Arafat, and his wife were killed in a drive-by shooting in Sidon on May 19. Two days later, Kayed's assistant Jamal ad-Dayekh lost both legs in a car-bomb explosion. Also in Sidon, on June 8 gunmen invaded a courtroom, killing three judges and a prosecutor. The assailants escaped.

Foreign Relations. U.S. Secretary of State Madeleine Albright paid a surprise visit to Beirut on September 4 and conferred with Prime Minister Hoss. President Emile Lahoud visited Jordan in May, becoming the highest-ranked Lebanese official to go to Amman in 25 years. And Abdullah II, Jordan's new king, went to Beirut in September; he was the first Jordanian head of state to visit Lebanon since 1969. Abdullah met with both Lahoud and Hoss. He was believed to be eager to bolster economic ties among Jordan, Syria, and Lebanon.

ARTHUR CAMPBELL TURNER
University of California, Riverside

LEBANON • Information Highlights

Official Name: Lebanese Republic.
Location: Southwest Asia.
Area: 4,015 sq mi (10 400 km²).
Population (July 1999 est.): 3,562,699.
Chief Cities (1982 est.): Beirut, the capital, 509,000; Tripoli, 198,000.
Government: *Head of state,* Emile Lahoud, president (took office November 1998). *Head of government,* Salim al-Hoss, premier (appointed December 1998). *Legislature* (unicameral)—National Assembly.
Monetary Unit: Lebanese pound (1,506.00 pounds equal U.S.$1, Dec. 10, 1999).
Gross Domestic Product (1998 est. U.S.$): $15,800,-000,000 (purchasing power parity).
Foreign Trade (1998 est. U.S.$): *Imports,* $7,063,000,000; *exports,* $716,000,000.

Libraries

By 1999 it was obvious that U.S. libraries had become essential service centers for Internet access. A 1998 survey by the U.S. National Commission on Libraries and Information Science found that 83.6% of libraries had Internet connectivity, 73.3% provided public Internet access, and 68.6% offered graphical public Internet access. In addition, a 1998 U.S. National Center for Education Statistics survey of public schools revealed that 51% of "instructional rooms" (classrooms, computer labs, library media centers) were connected to the Internet.

Internet Filtering. The U.S. Congress attempted several times during the year to require public libraries to install software filters on Internet computers to prevent children from accessing pornographic Web sites. In June the House of Representatives approved an amendment to the Juvenile Justice Bill that requires schools and libraries receiving federal telecommunications subsidies to install filtering software. In August, Sen. Rick Santorum (R-PA) introduced the Neighborhood Children's Internet Protection Act. Seen as an alternative to more-restrictive legislation proposed in January by Sen. John McCain, the bill would require schools and libraries receiving E-rate discounts "to install systems or implement policies for blocking or filtering Internet access to matter inappropriate for minors." None of the measures were enacted in 1999.

Meanwhile, many public libraries were embroiled in controversies about whether to filter Internet-access workstations. In November 1998 a federal judge ruled unconstitutional the Loudoun county (VA) library board's decision to install blocking software on all of its computers. In May the St. Tammany (LA) parish library board voted unanimously to have Internet filters installed on some public-access machines and to require parents to choose whether their children can use the unblocked workstations. In August, Plano (TX) Public Library compromised with the city's demand that all computers be filtered by offering unfiltered access on one computer in each of its four branches.

INTERNET LINKS

American Library Association: http://www.ala.org
Canadian Library Association: http://www.cla.ca
Special Libraries Association: http://www.sla.org
Library of Congress: http://www.loc.gov
700+ Great Sites for Kids:
http://www.ala.org/parentspage/greatsites
Teen Hoopla: An Internet Guide for Teens:
http://www.ala.org/teenhoopla

LIBRARY AWARDS IN 1999

Beta Phi Mu Award for distinguished service to education for librarianship: D. W. Krummel, Graduate School of Library and Information Science, University of Illinois at Urbana-Champaign
Caldecott Medal for the most distinguished picture book for children: Mary Azarian (illustrator), for *Snowflake Bentley*, written by Jacqueline Briggs Martin; published by Houghton Mifflin
Melvil Dewey Medal for recent creative professional achievement in the tools and techniques of librarianship: Helen Moeller, director, LeRoy Collins Leon County Public Library, Tallahassee, FL
Grolier Foundation Award for unique contributions to the stimulation and guidance of reading by children and young people: Elizabeth Huntoon, director of children's and young adult services, Chicago Public Library
Joseph W. Lippincott Award for distinguished service to the profession of librarianship: Peggy Barber, associate executive director of communications, American Library Association
Newbery Medal for the most distinguished contribution to literature for children: Louis Sachar, for *Holes*, published by Farrar Straus and Giroux

Filtering opponents contend that the software frequently blocks child-appropriate sites that may be essential to a youngster's research.

Taking the "Library" Out of Library School. In May the University of California–Los Angeles (UCLA) Department of Library and Information Science was renamed the UCLA Department of Information Studies, making it the tenth library school to drop the word from its title in recent years. Some worried that this trend could lead educators to focus too much on information management rather than on traditional librarianship—especially services to children and young adults. Prompted by these concerns, the American Library Association (ALA) convened a Congress on Professional Education in Washington, DC, held April 30–May 1. The 116 delegates did not agree on all the issues, but they called for renewed efforts in recruitment and professional development.

Associations. The ALA's 118th annual conference, held June 25–30 in New Orleans, LA, drew 22,598 librarians and library supporters. Presiding over the event was ALA President Ann Symons. The conference's theme, "Celebrating the Freedom to Read! Learn! Connect!," focused on intellectual-freedom issues. Sarah Ann Long, director of the North Suburban Library System, Wheeling, IL, was inaugurated as the ALA's new president.

The Special Libraries Association, the second-largest library association in North America, held its 90th annual conference June 5–10 in Minneapolis.

The Canadian Library Association's 54th annual conference, held June 16–20 in Toronto, Ont., had as its theme "Facing the Challenges."

GEORGE M. EBERHART
"American Libraries" magazine, Chicago, IL

Libya

LIBYA • Information Highlights

Official Name: Socialist People's Libyan Arab Jamahiriya ("state of the masses").
Location: North Africa.
Area: 679,359 sq mi (1 759 540 km²).
Population (July 1999 est.): 4,992,838.
Chief Cities (1988 est.): Tripoli, the capital, 591,062; Benghazi, 446,250.
Government: *Head of state and government,* Muammar el-Qaddafi (took office 1969). *Legislature* (unicameral)—General People's Congress.
Monetary Unit: Dinar (0.46 dinar equals U.S. $1, July 1999).
Gross Domestic Product (1998 est. U.S.$): $38,000,-000,000 (purchasing power parity).
Foreign Trade (1998 est. U.S.$): *Imports,* $6,900,000,000; *exports,* $6,800,000,000.

President Muammar el-Qaddafi took several steps to rebuild Libya's relations with the rest of the world in 1999, the 30th anniversary of his rise to power. After Libya agreed in April to settle a prolonged international dispute concerning terrorists alleged to have destroyed a U.S. plane, the United Nations (UN) suspended sanctions. Qaddafi then sought to revive the weakened economy through foreign investments and to play a major role in African politics.

Terrorism Issues. In April, after more than a year of intense negotiations, Libya surrendered two of its citizens accused of blowing up a Pan Am airliner over Lockerbie, Scotland, in 1988. The suspects were scheduled to be tried in early 2000 in the Netherlands, with Scottish judges presiding in accordance with Scottish law. In return, the UN suspended sanctions imposed in 1992 that prohibited the sale of weapons and oil-industry equipment, banned air travel to and from Libya, and froze Libyan assets overseas. The United States, however, blocked Libya's request in July that the UN Security Council permanently lift the sanctions, arguing that Libya had not met the necessary requirements, including cooperating with the Lockerbie investigation, ending support for terrorism, and compensating victims' families. In addition, the United States continued unilateral economic sanctions dating from 1986, although some relaxation occurred in July, when sales of food and medicine were authorized, and oil executives were permitted to travel to Libya to inspect abandoned assets there.

A French court in March convicted in absentia six Libyans of conspiring to sabotage a French airliner in 1989. As with the Lockerbie case, Libya had refused to extradite the suspects. In July, however, it agreed to pay more than $30 million in compensation, although Qaddafi insisted that this was not an admission of guilt. A few months later, Libya took responsibility for the 1984 murder of a British policewoman during demonstrations at the Libyan embassy in London, restoring diplomatic relations with Britain, which had been broken by the incident.

Foreign Relations. Soon after the UN suspended its sanctions, Qaddafi visited Zambia and South Africa, underscoring his intention of focusing on Africa rather than the Middle East. In July he attended the Organization of African Unity (OAU) summit for the first time since 1977, and at a meeting of African heads of state in Tripoli in September, he proposed the creation of "the United States of Africa," an African union and parliament based on the European model. Qaddafi also participated in attempts to mediate the civil wars in Sierra Leone and the Sudan, as well as the conflicts between Eritrea and Ethiopia, and the Congo and Uganda. Libyan diplomats worked with their counterparts from Algeria, Tunisia, Morocco, and Mauritania to revive the Arab Maghreb Union, which in November held its first summit meeting since 1995.

Economy. A decline in oil production, caused by a dramatic slump in crude-oil prices and shortages of spare parts due to the sanctions, reduced Libya's oil revenues during early 1999, prompting a devaluation of the dinar. The short-term economic outlook improved when crude prices rose in the summer, while long-term prospects brightened with a surge of international interest in investing in Libya. The Italian natural-gas supplier ENI was among the first and largest investors, announcing in July that it would launch a five-year, $5.5 billion project to tap gas fields in the Sahara and offshore. ENI also planned to export 10.5 billion cubic yds (8 billion m³) of natural gas annually through a pipeline it would build between Libya and Sicily, with another 2.6 billion cubic yds (2 billion m³) remaining in the Libyan market. Libya announced in September its intention to secure $35 billion in investments to develop industry, agriculture, and infrastructure between 2001 and 2005. The national petroleum law also was amended to attract investment in the oil industry. In October, Russia and Libya signed a $182 million contract for the construction of a 72-mi (117-km) gas pipeline between Khums and Tripoli.

KENNETH J. PERKINS
University of South Carolina

Literature

Overview

In 1999, Günter Grass became the first German-language author to win the Nobel Prize for literature since Heinrich Böll in 1972....The 100th anniversary of Ernest Hemingway's birth in July was celebrated throughout the United States....The Modern Library published a list of the best nonfiction books written in English over the past 100 years.

Nobel Prize. Günter Grass' vivid prose, evocative style, and passionate politics were epitomized by his epic 1959 novel *The Tin Drum*, an incisively critical look at Nazism through the eyes of a small boy. In its presentation of the Nobel Prize to Grass, the Swedish Academy cited the writer's gift "for reviewing contemporary history by recalling the disavowed and the forgotten: the victims, losers, and lies that most people wanted to forget because they had once believed in them...[Grass] unearths the intertwined roots of good and evil."

© Michael Probst/AP/Wide World Photos

Günter Grass

Born in Danzig (now Gdansk), Poland, on Oct. 16, 1927, Grass served a brief stint in the German army, beginning in 1944. After World War II, he worked as a journalist and also began writing plays and poems. *The Tin Drum* was his first major work; in this and other books such as *Cat and Mouse* (1961), *Dog Years* (1963), and, more recently, *A Broad Field* (1995) and *My Century: A Novel of Stories* (1999), he explored the nature of 20th-century German society, often castigating its complacency and racism.

Hemingway at 100. The centennial of Ernest Hemingway's birth on July 21, 1899, was marked by many special events, including a symposium at the John F. Kennedy Library in Boston, MA; an eight-day festival of readings, exhibits, and movies based on his works, held in his birthplace of Oak Park, IL; and a Hemingway exhibit at the National Portrait Gallery in Washington, DC. But the publication of *True at First Light*, Hemingway's unfinished fictional treatment of an African safari he took with his wife in 1953, garnered the most attention—and controversy. The book, produced from a manuscript that had been cut nearly in half and extensively edited by the writer's son, Patrick, received decidedly mixed notices, and many critics attacked the entire concept of the project, saying that Hemingway would not have wanted his unfinished work to be published at all.

The Century's Best. In the spring the editorial board of Modern Library, an imprint of Random House, announced its choices for the 100 best English-language nonfiction books of the past 100 years, a follow-up to its 1998 list of the century's outstanding novels. Heading the list was Henry Adams' autobiography, *The Education of Henry Adams*; *The Varieties of Religious Experience* by William James, *Up From Slavery* by Booker T. Washington, *A Room of One's Own* by Virginia Woolf, and *Silent Spring* by Rachel Carson rounded out the top five. James Joyce's *Ulysses*, F. Scott Fitzgerald's *The Great Gatsby*, Joyce's *Portrait of the Artist as a Young Man*, Vladimir Nabokov's *Lolita*, and Aldous Huxley's *Brave New World* had led the earlier fiction list.

Later in the year, *The Best American Short Stories of the Century*, co-edited by John Updike and Katrina Kenison, featured Updike's choices for the top 55 of the 2,000-odd stories that have appeared in the annual *Best American Short Stories* anthology since its launch in 1915. The compilation included works by Hemingway, William Faulkner, Joyce Carol Oates, Willa Cather, Flannery O'Connor, John Cheever, and Saul Bellow.

SUSAN H. MCCLUNG

American Literature

American literature in 1999 reflected the mingled feelings of the nation as it perched on the brink of a new century. The literary community looked back not only to established authors but to writers long dead, who were exhumed and reexamined through collections and posthumous publications. At the same time, a bevy of new authors battled the old guard for acceptance and acclaim. Poets and science writers alike wrestled with the mysteries of the universe, while others dealt with the host of superstitions promulgated by the approach of the millennium. Other media continued to exert pressure upon the literature produced, as perhaps best shown by the influence that television talk-show host Oprah Winfrey's book club had on sales. Winfrey even was chosen to receive an honorary prize at the 1999 National Book Awards ceremony.

Novels. The two most anticipated and controversial novels of 1999 were written by deceased authors. Ernest Hemingway's novel *True at First Light* was edited and patched together by the author's son Patrick from a far larger, unfinished manuscript; it was released in 1999 as part of the Hemingway centenary. This "fictional memoir" tells of an African safari by a middle-aged writer much like Hemingway; it intermingles the story of the narrator's desire for a young African woman with his wife's need to shoot a lion. Ralph Ellison's novel *Juneteenth* was published under similar circumstances; it too was excerpted and edited from a far larger and incomplete draft. *Juneteenth* is about a young man of mixed race who sheds the African-American culture of his upbringing to pass as a white man; he becomes a successful politician, known for his disdain for the black community. Critics argued that each novel falls far short of the standards the two authors maintained in their lifetimes and that posthumous publication of such works usurps an author's control over his or her own writing.

Another past writer is examined in Frederick Busch's *The Night Inspector*, about a disfigured Civil War veteran who befriends an unnamed but easily identified Herman Melville. The Civil War also plays a large part in Stewart O'Nan's *A Prayer for the Dying*; this novel employs magical realism in its examination of a veteran's attempts to hold together his cursed town. The lingering effects of a far more modern war are portrayed in Beverly Gologorsky's *The Things We Do to Make It Home*, a novel that asks about the war's attrition on veterans and on their families.

Andre Dubus III discusses the dark side of the American dream in *House of Sand and Fog*, the story of a former colonel in the Iranian military and his attempts to enter into American life. Rural America in the form of Holt, CO, provides the setting for Kent Haruf's *Plainsong*. David Guterson's *East of the Mountains* is about the last days and reminiscences of a man who has led a full and long life. Janet Fitch's *White Oleander* offers a complex portrayal of a daughter's relationship with her mother.

Two long-term trilogies were completed in 1999. Larry McMurtry's novel *Duane's Depressed* ends the Texas trilogy of small-town life that began with *The Last Picture*

© Jean-Marc Giboux/Liaison Agency

© American Stock/Archive Photos

The centennial of the birth of Ernest Hemingway, above, *was marked throughout 1999—at such places as the Hemingway Museum in Oak Park, IL,* left.

AMERICAN LITERATURE MAJOR WORKS • 1999

NOVELS

Andersen, Kurt, *Turn of the Century*
Arensberg, Ann, *Incubus*
Baker, Kevin, *Dreamland*
Belfer, Lauren, *City of Light*
Canty, Kevin, *Nine Below Zero*
Egolf, Tristan, *Lord of the Barnyard*
Ellis, Trey, *Right Here, Right Now*
Gay, William, *The Long Home*
Grand, David, *Louse*
Graver, Elizabeth, *The Honey Thief*
Ha Jin, *Waiting*
Henley, Patricia, *Hummingbird House*
McNamer, Deirdre, *My Russian*
Offill, Jenny, *Last Things*
Rosenbaum, Thane, *Second Hand Smoke*
Russell, Josh, *Yellow Jack*
See, Carolyn, *The Handyman*
Silko, Leslie Marmon, *Gardens in the Dunes*
Strout, Elizabeth, *Amy and Isabelle*
Tarloff, Erik, *Face-Time*
Whitehead, Colson, *The Intuitionist*
Wolitzer, Meg, *Surrender, Dorothy*

SHORT FICTION

Bausch, Richard, *Someone to Watch over Me*
Braverman, Kate, *Small Craft Warnings*
Chabon, Michael, *Werewolves in Their Youth*
Clyde, Mary, *Survival Rates*
Davis, Amanda, *Circling the Drain*
Englander, Nathan, *For the Relief of Unbearable Urges*
Gautreaux, Tim, *Welding with Children*
Jenkins, Greg, *Night Game*
Miller, Alyce, *Stopping for Green Lights*
Mueller, Daniel, *How Animals Mate*
Polansky, Steven, *Dating Miss Universe*
Reid, Elwood, *What Salmon Know*

MEMOIR, CRITICISM, AND LITERARY BIOGRAPHY

Anderson, Edith, *Love in Exile*
Honan, Park, *Shakespeare: A Life*
Podhoretz, Norman, *Ex-Friends: Falling out with Allen Ginsberg, Lionel and Diana Trilling, Lillian Hellman, Hannah Arendt, and Norman Mailer*
Powers, Ron, *Dangerous Water: A Biography of the Boy Who Became Mark Twain*
Schiff, Stacy, *Véra: Mrs. Vladimir Nabokov*
Vidal, Gore, *The Essential Gore Vidal*

SOCIETY, HISTORY, AND BIOGRAPHY

Angier, Natalie, *Woman: An Intimate Geography*
Brookhiser, Richard, *Alexander Hamilton, American*
Cantrell, Gregg, *Stephen F. Austin: Empresario of Texas*
Cook, Blanche Wiesen, *Eleanor Roosevelt, Volume 2: 1933–1938*
Crittenden, Danielle, *What Our Mothers Didn't Tell Us*
Dahl, Robert A., *On Democracy*
Dower, John W., *Embracing Defeat: Japan in the Wake of World War II*
Guralnick, Peter, *Careless Love: The Unmaking of Elvis Presley*
Kenan, Randall, *Walking on Water: Black American Lives at the Turn of the Twenty-First Century*
Kissinger, Henry, *Years of Renewal*
Lydon, Michael, *Ray Charles: Man and Music*
Malcolm, Janet, *The Crime of Sheila McGough*
McMurtry, Larry, *Crazy Horse*
Orlean, Susan, *The Orchid Thief*
Rehnquist, William H., *All the Laws but One: Civil Liberties in Wartime*
Santos, John Phillip, *Places Left Unfinished at the Time of Creation*
Scanlon, T.M., *What We Owe to Each Other*
Thurman, Judith, *Secrets of the Flesh: A Life of Colette*
Underhill, Paco, *Why We Buy: The Science of Shopping*

POETRY

Ai, *Vice: New and Selected Poems*
Anderson, Jack, *Traffic: New and Selected Prose Poems*
Berman, David, *Actual Air*
Calbert, Cathleen, *Bad Judgment*
Halladay, Mark, *Selfwolf*
Kinsolving, Susan, *Dailies & Rushes*
Major, Clarence, *Configurations: New and Selected Poems 1958–1998*
Santos, Sherod, *The Pilot Star Elegies*
Swenson, Karen, *A Daughter's Latitude*
Williams, C.K., *Repair*

Show. Similarly, Peter Matthiessen's *Bone by Bone* concludes his three-volume examination of race and imperialism.

Experimental novels were strong in 1999, as best exemplified by Steve Erickson's postmodern *The Sea Came in at Midnight*, about a young woman who sells the memories of her life in the years following the millennium. Former science-fiction writer Neal Stephenson creates a dense, picaresque tale that interweaves computer lore of today and tomorrow with World War II code-breaking in *Cryptonomicon*.

Short Fiction. One of the most important occurrences in 1999 in short fiction was another tribute to the literary past; John Updike and Katrina Kenison edited *The Best American Short Stories of the Century*, as chosen from *The Best American Short Stories of the Year* series. The collection contains writers as diverse as F. Scott Fitzgerald, John Cheever, E. Annie Proulx, Philip Roth, and Eudora Welty.

© Ceasar Maragni/AP/Wide World Photos

Kent Haruf, a 56-year-old teacher at Southern Illinois University, has the town of Holt on the Colorado plains as the setting for his third novel, "Plainsong."

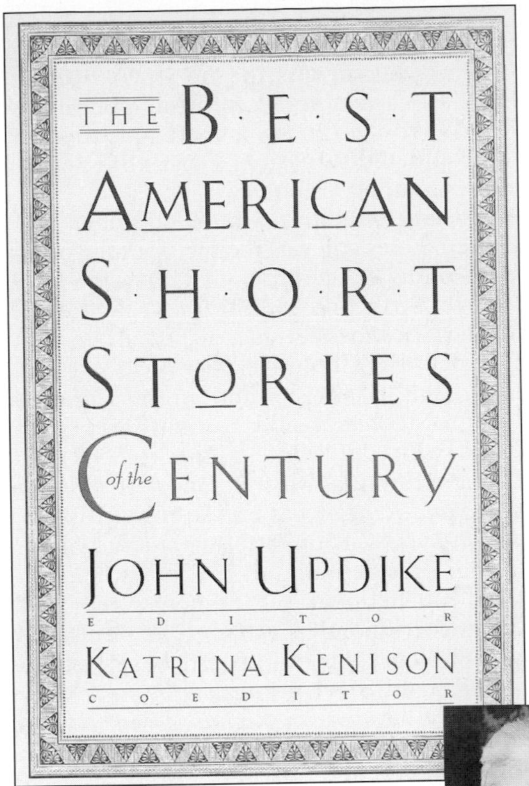

Courtesy, Houghton Mifflin Company

A number of established writers produced new collections in 1999. Chris Offutt once again distills the essence of rural Kentucky in his *Out of the Woods*; Jean Thompson makes stories of unrequited love seem fresh and new in her *Who Do You Love*. Thom Jones tackles the demons of modern life in *Sonny Liston Was a Friend of Mine*, and David Foster Wallace places a relentless microscope upon American masculinity in *Brief Interviews with Hideous Men*. Annie Proulx shows the West is not quite as tamed as one might think in *Close Range: Wyoming Stories*.

© Martha Updike, Courtesy, Houghton Mifflin Company

© Anne Parker, Courtesy, Houghton Mifflin Company

More important in 1999, however, were the number of excellent first collections. Dale Ray Phillips' *My People's Waltz* is a gathering of optimistic stories centered around the affairs of a family. Joseph Clark's *Jungle Wedding* points out the vain shortcomings of suburban American life. Women writers were particularly impressive in their debuts; Melissa Bank's *The Girls' Guide to Hunting and Fishing* considers the problems of being a young and single woman in today's society; Jane Mullen shows how relationships can spiral out of control in *A Complicated Situation*. Tales of the eccentric and grotesque proved to be alive and well in Julia Slavin's *The Woman Who Cut off Her Leg at the Maidstone Club and Other Stories* and in Stacey Richter's *My Date with Satan*.

Poetry. Poetry proved to be as haunted as fiction in 1999 when R.W. Franklin released *The Poems of Emily Dickinson*, a collection condensed from his previous variorum edition. Living poets continued to search for meaning and to add to their legacies as well. W.S. Merwin's *The River Sound* deals with the day-to-day problem of living when so much of life is about loss. In a similar vein, Charles Wright's *Appalachia* is a collection of poems about simple people and the yearning for religious transcendence. Charles Simic's *Jackstraws* examines life in its most minute detail to tackle the mysteries of the universe. Louise Glück considers resignation to life's vagaries in a book-length work of verse, *Vita Nova*.

Barbara Hamby's *The Alphabet of Desire*, her second collection, offers energetic meditations on life's more casual and common lessons. Mary Jo Salter examines similar questions through consideration of our famous predecessors, including Helen Keller and Alexander Graham Bell, in her *A Kiss in Space*. Philip Levine's *The Mercy* is a compilation of his attempts to recapture his blue-collar heritage through poetry; in *On the Bus with Rosa Parks*, Rita Dove attempts to understand the private side of public lives. Language poet John Ashbery stays true to form in *Girls on the Run*, a dense, complicated collection based on a graphic novel.

Memoir, Criticism, and Literary Biography. Memoirs seemed again to lose ground to fiction in 1999, although the year did mark the publication of Irish emigré Frank McCourt's *'Tis*, the sequel to his best-seller *Angela's Ashes*. Bobbie Ann Mason contributed a loving work to the genre and showed where much of her fiction is born in her memoir *Clear Springs*. Ellen Douglas told of traumatic events from her life never presented fictionally in *Truth: Four Stories I Am Finally Old Enough to Tell*. Annie Dillard ponders the existence of an ultimately good God in a world where evil exists in *For the Time Being*. Novelist Bob Shacochis turned war correspondent for *The Immaculate Invasion*, his account of the mishandled 1994 U.S. mili-

Courtesy, Little Brown & Company

tary intervention in Haiti. The secrets of journalism are laid bare by Max Frankel, who covers his years with *The New York Times* in *The Times of My Life*, and Susan E. Tifft and Alex S. Jones take a look at the private and powerful family behind the *Times* in *The Trust*. Michael Korda reveals the ins and outs of the publishing world in *Another Life: A Memoir of Other People*.

© George Bennett, Courtesy, Little Brown & Company

Several important literary biographies were published in 1999; Hemingway's last years are disclosed in wonderful narrative form in Michael Reynolds' *Hemingway: The Final Years*. Walt Whitman is revealed in a new light in *Walt Whitman: The Song of Himself*, by Jerome Loving. Henry James is reexamined through focusing on two women who had profound influence on his life in Lyndall Gordon's *A Private Life of Henry James: Two Women and His Art*.

John Updike published *More Matter: Essays and Criticism*, a collection of works previously presented in periodicals and magazines. A collection of Randall Jarrell's essays, *No Other Book*, was released contemporaneously with his wife Mary von Schrader Jarrell's recollection of their life together, *Remembering Randall: A Memoir of Poet, Critic, and Teacher Randall Jarrell*. Jay Parini confronts the notion of Robert Frost as a sweet and comforting poet in his *Robert Frost, a Life*, which attempts to show the conflicted turmoil of Frost's life and its influence upon his poetry.

Society, History, and Biography. The United States still was reeling from the political scandal of the previous year when 1999 brought forth Andrew Morton's rendition of Monica Lewinsky's side of her affair with President Bill Clinton in *Monica's Story*; former Clinton adviser and press secretary George Stephanopoulos recounts his experiences with the White House in *All Too Human*. Edmund Morris' *Dutch: A Memoir of Ronald Reagan* was met with controversy, due in part to its unflattering portrait of the former president and in part to its employment of fictional techniques. *New York Times* correspondent Adam Clymer offered a new biography of Edward M. Kennedy, and Ronald Steel presented *In Love with Night: The American Romance with Robert Kennedy*.

Science writers in 1999 focused on uncovering the mysteries of the universe and of human life itself in response to the superstitions and paranoia surrounding the approach of the millennium. Brian Greene (*The Elegant Universe: Superstrings, Hidden Dimensions, and the Quest for the Ultimate Theory*) and John Maddox (*What Remains to Be Discovered*) attempt to explain the possibility of a universal plan governing the scientific laws of the physical world; in *The Fifth Miracle: The Search for the Origin and Meaning of Life*, Paul Davies not only questions the point of life but wonders whether it is of an extraterrestrial origin. Richard Dawkins attempts to debunk millennial pseudoscience and superstition in *Unweaving the Rainbow: Science, Delusion, and the Appetite for Wonder*; Alex Heard tackles a similar project in his *Apocalypse Pretty Soon: Travels in End-Time America*.

Scott Ritter, a former United Nations arms inspector, discusses U.S. concern with the Persian Gulf and Middle East in *Endgame: Solving the Iraq Problem—Once and for All*. Mark Bowden's *Black Hawk Down: A Story of Modern War* depicts a botched military operation in Somalia in 1993.

SCOTT YARBROUGH
Charleston Southern University

Children's Literature

Even as the Harry Potter phenomenon heated up (*see* SIDEBAR), old favorites made a comeback in 1999 in children's literature. Brand-name publishing continued as an important part of marketing strategy, as publishers tried to find new ways to make their presence felt in the all-important bookstore market. Consequently, new life was breathed into many old favorites, not always with justification. There was a relaunch of the four Eloise books by Kay Thompson, illustrated by Hilary Knight, with Knight providing some new pictures. A manuscript and sketches for another Madeline story were found in the files of Ludwig Bemelmans. His grandson, John Bemelmans Marciano, completed the art in color, and the book was published as *Madeline in America*. More controversial was a new edition, meant for a younger audience, of Rachel Fields' *Hitty: Her First Hundred Years*, the Newbery Award winner for 1930. Newly titled *Rachel Fields' Hitty*, the handsome oversize volume was illustrated by Susan Jeffers. The text, which was abridged and rewritten by Rosemary Wells, annoyed some purists, who felt Wells was tampering with a classic. Among other books reintroduced were new versions of the Raggedy Ann and Andy stories and a picture-book version of Felix Salten's *Bambi*.

As it had for the past several years, Holocaust literature continued to add strong, stirring selections to the children's literary canon, as survivors grew old and wished to record their memories. *In My Hands* by Irene Gut Opdyke describes how a young Polish girl hides Jews in the home of her employer—a high-ranking Nazi. *Eleanor's Story* by Eleanor Ramrath Garner tells what it is like for an American girl living in Germany as World War II rages. Fiction titles such as *The Good Liar* by Gregory Maguire, in which two French brothers befriend a young German soldier, were also in evidence.

In award news, Louis Sachar was awarded the Newbery Award for his thought-provoking fantasy *Holes*, and Mary Azarian received the Caldecott Medal for her woodcut illustrations in *Snowflake Bentley*, the true story of a Vermont photographer who was the first person to take pictures of snowflakes.

Children's literature suffered a loss in May with the death of poet, cartoonist, and musician Shel Silverstein, 66. He was the much-admired author and illustrator of four best-selling children's books: *The Giving Tree* (1964), *Where the Sidewalk Ends* (1974), *A Light in the Attic* (1981), and *Falling Up* (1996).

Picture Books. The year 1999 was not a distinguished one for picture books. The best work was done by experienced authors and artists, often working with familiar subjects. For instance, *Off to School, Baby Duck* was the fourth in a series written by Amy Hest and illustrated by Jill Barton. Maurice Sendak illustrated the manuscript of *Swine Lake*, by the late James Marshall, and Rosemary Wells illustrated a second Mother Goose compilation collected by Iona Opie, *Here Comes Mother Goose*.

Middle-Grade Books. With the exception of the Animorphs series, no paperback series had appeared to replace such perennial favorites as Goosebumps and The Babysitters Club. In hardcover, readers were treated

SELECTED BOOKS FOR CHILDREN

Picture Books

Anholt, Laurence, *Stone Girl, Bone Girl*
Aylesworth, Jim, *The Full Belly Bowl*
Cowley, Joy, *Red-Eyed Tree Frog*
Frazee, Marla, *Hush Little Baby*
Grimes, Nikki, *My Man Blue*
Henkes, Kevin, *Oh*
High, Linda Oatman, *Barn Savers*
Howe, James, *Horace and Morris but Mostly Dolores*
Monks, Lydia, *The Cat Barked?*
Say, Allen, *Tea With Milk*
Shannon, Mark, *The Acrobat and the Angel*
Stevenson, James, *Mud Flat Spring*

The Middle Grades

Aliki, *William Shakespeare and the Globe*
Almond, David, *Skellig*
Bridges, Ruby, *Through My Eyes*
Butler, Susan, *The Hermit Thrush Sings*
Calabro, Marian, *The Perilous Journey of the Donner Party*
Cooper, Susan, *King of Shadows*
Earle, Sylvia A., *Dive!*
Horvath, Polly, *The Trolls*
Krull, Kathleen, *They Saw the Future*
Levine, Gail Carson, *Dave at Night*
McKay, Hilary, *Dolphin Luck*
Perkins, Lynne Rae, *All Alone in the Universe*
Prelutsky, Jack, *The Gargoyle on the Roof*
Rylant, Cynthia, *The Heavenly Village*
Senn, J.A., *Quotations for Kids*

Young Adults

Abelove, Joan, *Saying It Out Loud*
Alexander, Lloyd, *Gypsy Rizka*
Book, Rick, *Necking with Louise*
Calhoun, Dia, *Firegold*
Gaskins, Pearl Fuyo, *What Are You?*
Lally, Soinbhe, *A Hive for the Honeybee*
Lester, Julius, *When the Beginning Began*
Marchetta, Melina, *Looking for Alibrandi*
Paterson, Katherine, *Preacher's Boy*
Stanley, Diane, *A Time Apart*
Wittlinger, Ellen, *Hard Love*
Wood, Nancy, *Thunderwoman*

Harry Potter

Two words sum up all that was fresh and exciting about the children's-literature scene in 1999—Harry Potter. During the year, the three books about the young wizard in training became a publishing phenomenon. Newspaper articles, television features, and interviews with the British author, J.K. Rowling, permeated the media. Harry even made the cover of *Time.* Late in the year, the Harry Potter titles were in the top three slots on the *New York Times* bestseller list.

In a refreshing twist, instead of standing in line for the latest toy, parents waited to get copies of the two new entries in the series—*Harry Potter and the Chamber of Secrets* and *Harry Potter and the Prisoner of Azkaban.* These books followed the first in the series, 1998's *Harry Potter and the Sorcerer's Stone*, which introduced the orphan Harry, who is called away from the home of his cruel aunt and uncle to Hogwarts School of Witchcraft and Wizardry. Until his summons to Hogwarts, Harry is unaware that his parents were killed by an evil wizard, Lord Voldemort. Somehow, baby Harry escaped, destroying Voldemort's dark power and making an enemy for life. Harry has brushes with Voldemort or his minions in each volume, and the final showdown is much anticipated by readers.

Above: © Douglas Mason/Woodfin Camp & Assoc.; left: © Murdo Macleod/Woodfin Camp & Assoc.

Readers of all ages were captivated in 1999 by the Harry Potter books, authored by J.K. Rowling, left. *The fantasy novels detail the adventures of a young wizard in training.*

The books, which author Rowling says she considers one long story that for practicality she must divide into seven parts, create a world that combines elements of traditional English boarding-school stories and fantasy tales in the tradition of C.S. Lewis' *The Chronicles of Narnia*. Unlike other recent series phenomena such as the Sweet Valley High and Babysitters Club books, the Harry Potter books are literate and complex as well as highly entertaining. Despite the critical acclaim and popularity enjoyed by the series, several U.S. school districts were urged by parents to ban the books due to their supernatural subject matter as well as to claims that they are violent. Harry Potter's tremendous popularity continued, however, and the fourth book in the series was expected in the summer of 2000.

ILENE COOPER

to the return of several favorite characters, including Beverly Cleary's Ramona in *Ramona's World*; there also was another entry in the Anastasia series by Lois Lowry—*Zooman Sam*, featuring Anastasia's younger brother.

Junior-High and High-School Books. Although not quite as bleak as in recent years, books for older readers continued to deal with serious subjects in ways that were both provocative and appealing to the audience. *Monster* by Walter Dean Myers is written in the form of a film script; it details the trial of an African-American teen who may have been an accessory to a murder. *Hard Love* by Ellen Wittlinger incorporates the writing style of the "'zines" (individually published magazines) to tell the story of one young writer who has trouble getting close to people. *When Zachary Beaver Came to Town* by Kimberly Willis Holt is set in 1971 and describes what happens to two young residents when their small Texas town is visited by "the world's fattest boy." Holt's book won the 1999 National Book Award for young people's literature.

ILENE COOPER, *Editor, Children's Books "Booklist" Magazine*

English Literature

The naming of a new poet laureate for England, Andrew Motion, on the eve of a new calendar era signaled more than literary transition; with one eye on tradition and one tenuously on the future, the year 1999 concluded a century of momentous change with a fulsome literary range in English fiction as well as poetry.

Fiction. Salman Rushdie, in *The Ground Beneath Her Feet*, tells a musical tale of an international rock band, with rich use of the symbolics of the Orpheus-Eurydice myth. But in his latest novel, Barry Unsworth creates in *Losing Nelson* not only a new look at the heroic Lord Nelson but at the possibility of heroism itself. Through the devoted eyes of the narrator, Charles Cleasby, the reader is able to approach the complex subjects of this, Unsworth's 14th novel. In *Ladysmith*, another British historical novel, Giles Foden's prose illustrates how difficult it is to re-create what otherwise might be regarded as epical when one gets so close to the subjects—including chance encounters with the young Winston Churchill and Mohandas Gandhi—in this retelling of a famous battle of the Boer War. Creating an imaginary tale of tribute from the realm of the actual, Peter Everett's novel *The Voyages of Alfred Wallis* amplifies with resonance the life of a St. Ives mariner-painter. In *An Equal Music*, Vikram Seth structures a musician's poignant tale around the life and tropes of a string quartet in a highly charged, well-written novel of variations on a theme.

In fiction of a more local or regional cast, Andrew O'Hagan's novel *Our Fathers* tells the stories of three generations to achieve its impact; it is a tale of Scottish political life of the 20th century, with a focus more on a family than an individual character. The book, O'Hagan's first novel, was shortlisted for the Booker Prize. *Evening*, a novel by Susan Minot, is told in the voice of an old woman dying, whose reflections verge on the poetic as she pieces together the particulars of her transitory condition. Stanley Middleton's 38th novel, *Necessary Ends*, relies on conversations to generate interest in his characters, drawn from the English Midlands. *The Harvest*, Christopher Hart's well-crafted first novel, is set in the borderlands of Dorset. In *The Haunt*, A.L. Barker, best known for her short stories, gives intimate portraits of old people on holiday in a hotel, "The Belle Chasse," in Cornwall. The chase motif, curtailed of necessity by age, results in a poignancy made more vivid by the finely etched detail of Barker's prose. Helen Dunmore's new novel, *With Your Crooked Heart*, charts what seems a scope of narrower choice, but the residual pain of familial secrets coming to light is told with an intense simplicity.

The lure of the exotic intensifies many tales, with no place better than the Orient to satisfy romance; Ahdaf Soueif's novel *The Map of Love*, set in Egypt of the late 19th century, proves this rule. However romantic, the tale provides an excuse for a stern critique of then-contemporary British political interests and actions. It, too, was on the Booker Prize shortlist. Tim Parks' novel *Destiny* focuses more on character and material concerns than on its action, which is set in Italy and told in a voice attuned to much suffering. Claire Keegan reveals intense actions through an evenhanded prose style in a collection of short stories, *Antarctica*. *Disgrace*, a new novel by 1983 Booker Prize winner J.M. Coetzee, explores figures undergoing compelling transitions within the complex cultural strata of urban Cape Town, South Africa; it was awarded the 1999 Booker Prize. The other books that were honored by being named to the shortlist for the prestigious prize were *Fasting, Feasting* by Anita Desai, *Headlong* by Michael Frayn, and *The Blackwater Lightship* by Colm Toibin.

Poetry. Despite the reach implied in the title, Peter Fallon's *News of the World (Selected and New Poems)* gives focus to life on the farm, where the risk of grief and happiness are often in the journey of a single day. Breaking a long silence, poet J.H. Prynne offers a generous array of modernist glimpses of many moods in *Poems*. *Tribute*, Stephen Romer's third book of lyric poems, asks probing questions of a lasting nature, rooted in language of an immediate consequence. In her latest book of poems, *Five Fields*, Gillian Clarke hones her eye on the Welsh rural scene, always with a hint of the larger social scene as backdrop. In this vein, one should not overlook a collection of prose, posthumously published, of Orkney island poet George Mackay Brown: *Northern Lights, A Poet's Sources*. Edited by Archie Brown and Brian Murray, it contains memoirs and travel accounts, and comments on the strong link between the land, seasonal and ritual cycles, and living a creative, communal life.

DONALD L. JENNERMANN
Indiana State University

World Literature

New works from Asia and Africa dominated world literature in 1999.

Asia. Leading the Asian charge was Salman Rushdie with his new novel *The Ground beneath Her Feet*, an exuberant and elegiac work spanning several continents and several decades to tell its sometimes hilarious, sometimes tragic tale of two musical celebrities, the captivating but ill-fated rock singer Vina Aspara and her husband and partner, composer Ormus Cama.

A Matter of Time, the first novel by India's Shashi Deshpande to reach North America, uses a skillful blend of first- and third-person narration and an effective amalgam of dialogue, memories, and meditations to follow the travails of an abandoned professional-class Indian wife and her three daughters, who are forced to move back into her family's large and somewhat dysfunctional household in Bangalore. In *Freedom Song*, Amit Chaudhuri links three short novels that move effortlessly and with wondrously observed detail from teeming Calcutta, to bustling Bombay, to refined distant Oxford and back. And in *When Dreams Travel*, Githa Hariharan recasts the classical Arabic story of Shahrzad (Scheherazade) and the Sultan through the lens of Shahrzad's sister Dunyazad, focusing more on what preceded and what followed the 1,001 nights of storytelling than on those "Arabian nights" themselves.

From China in 1999 came major works by two younger fiction writers. *Waiting*, the second novel (after *In the Pond*) by Ha Jin, who left his mainland home in 1985 for study and eventual resettlement in the United States, tracks the poignant course of an ordinary man so bound by a strong sense of duty—to tradition, to family, to the party—that he misses out on most of the opportunities life offers him. And in *Notes of a Desolate Man*, the Taiwanese novelist Chu T'ien-wen presents the story of a gay man reflecting on his life, loves, and intellectual influences.

With *South of the Border, West of the Sun*, Japan's immensely popular novelist Haruki Murakami produced one of his most humane and pleasurable works yet, a compact (barely more than 200 pages) and lyrical tale of long-separated childhood friends overwhelmed by longing for an unreclaimable past and the chaste yet consuming passion they once knew. Murakami's countryman Hikaru Okuizumi made his English-language debut in 1999 with *The Stones Cry Out*, an absorbing study of obsession, family disintegration, and the dehumanizing effects of war. And from the pen of Kenji Nakagami, who died in 1992, came two new (to the West) collections of short fiction, *Snakelust* and *The Cape and Other Stories from the Japanese Ghetto*. Nakagami is a revelation to readers familiar with Japanese fiction only through the refined prose of Kawabata, the samurai mentality of Mishima, or the largely westernized fabulations of Murakami; for his world is that of Burakumin, Japan's untouchable caste. Though Nakagami occasionally draws on his rural background for tales of mountain bandits and woodland demons, the focus of his spare, rough-hewn, Hemingwayesque prose mainly is the violent lives of his urban contemporaries—drunks, day laborers, gamblers, and battered wives.

Africa. Perhaps the single most powerful book released in Africa in late 1998 and early 1999 was *Country of My Skull*, South African poet Antjie Krog's collected reports on the work of the Truth and Reconciliation Commission, charged with bringing to light the horrors of the apartheid years in a process of national confession and catharsis. Poignancy and tenderness alternate with unspeakable cruelty in the testimony of victims and perpetrators alike from every segment of the South African spectrum. An Afrikaner herself, Krog feels a particular need to try and find some access to the minds and hearts of those who perpetuated a system such as apartheid. That goal ultimately eludes her, but the cumulative effect of her book is nonetheless powerful.

More-conventional fiction appeared in 1999 from the pens of Krog's fellow South African writers André Brink and J. M. Coetzee. With *Devil's Valley*, Brink essentially presents South African history writ large and mythically in his story of an isolated settlement whose inhabitants have been cut off almost entirely from the outside world for more than 150 years—a physical metaphor for the "apartness" that so dominated the South African psyche from the mid-19th century until about 1990, and a close, unblinking look at the past that may convey some sense of whether and how a new beginning may be made for the present and the immediate future. The brutal politics of contemporary South Africa also are evident in Coetzee's novel, *Disgrace*, as generational and ideological fault lines separate fallen academic David Lurie from his daughter Lucy both before and after a vicious attack on their remote farmstead. Although that cleft never is bridged, a gradual transformation of a much more fundamental and personal kind is effected in Lurie.

From the prizewinning Algerian-born novelist and filmmaker Assia Djebar in 1999 came the autobiographical novel *These Voices Which Importune Me*, wherein she recounts in fictional form the course of her life and career as a female Berber-Arabic-French intellectual. She evokes all the constituencies for which she has become a de facto spokesperson during the last 30 years of political, social, and religious turmoil in her homeland and in the diaspora. The young Cameroonian novelist Calixthe Beyala continued her meteoric rise on the literary horizon—begun in 1987 but now in full ascent with seven acclaimed novels and several major literary awards. Beyala's *Savage Loves* is a ribald and often politically incorrect tale of yet another young refugee from the slums of the African metropolis now married to a Westerner and attempting to refashion her life in an extremely color- and race-conscious modern-day France.

In a related work of note from the French-African Caribbean, *The Rum Producer*, the Martinican creolist Raphaël Confiant completed his depiction (begun in 1994's *Canefield Commander*) of the West Indian sugarcane plantation as a brutally exploitative feudal institution dependent on racial inequality and resistant to any form of social change. Characters from the earlier work appear briefly, but the story focuses on the next generation as it attempts vainly to maintain absolute control of its plantations and distilleries while the world lurches toward the outbreak of World War II.

Europe. Three émigré authors highlighted the French literary year in 1999. The Russian-born Andreï Makine followed up his award-winning *Dreams of My Russian Summer* with *The Crime of Olga Arbyelina*, another sumptuously lyrical novel involving the displaced and disintegrating Russian aristocracy in pre– and post–World War II France, but this time with a potentially scandalous admixture of incest and abortion to complicate matters considerably and create a suitably tragic aura about its tormented, mysterious heroine. J.M.G. Le Clézio, originally from the Indian Ocean island of Mauritius, issued two complementary novelettes—*Hazard* and *Angoli Mala*—in a single volume, tracking at 15-year intervals the fates of a youthful seaman and the beautiful young runaway he discovers hiding belowdecks. And in *The Gardens of Light*, the Lebanese-born Amin Maalouf ingeniously blends history, fiction, and mythology to create a saga of the life and times of the third-century Mesopotamian mystic and artist Mani, whose name eventually was attached to the doctrine of Manicheism.

From the acclaimed Italian novelist Alessandro Baricco in 1999 came *Ocean Sea*, a sweeping and enchanting book of extraordinary power that ranges from harrowing shipwrecks at sea, to the restorative powers of love and faith, to the artistic and scientific contemplation of the boundaries where ocean and shore begin and end. In *The Clay Machine-Gun*, a wonderfully witty if sometimes too-glib tale, Victor Pelevin, the best of the post-*glasnost* generation of Russian writers, ponders which way Russia now should look for its cultural direction. No clear answers are forthcoming.

The perennial Dutch Nobel nominee Hugo Claus brought out *Past Imperfect* in early 1999, concluding his fictional retelling (begun in 1998 with *Rumors*) of the horrific Dutroux kidnappings and murders through the voice and eyes of Noël Catrijsse, the dim-witted brother of the mercenary mastermind, René. Another perpetual Nobel candidate—the grand old man of Estonian letters, Jaan Kross—produced a new novel in 1998 with the enigmatic title *Hovering*. Yet another installment in Kross' "nation-building" series of historical narratives and monologues, this new work chronicles the fate of a fictional Estonian Everyman named Ullo from the collapse of the short-lived free republic in the late 1930s through the Nazi and Soviet occupations of wartime, and into the first decades of Sovietization. And from former Swedish Academy member Kerstin Ekman came *The Wolfskin*, a richly detailed and evocative novel about humankind's need for tradition and the role of art and culture in recovering and preserving the past.

Middle East. And lastly, two noteworthy works came from Israel and Egypt. In *Four Mothers*, talented young Hebrew novelist Shifra Horn celebrates the strength, fortitude, determination, and mutual support of several generations of Jewish women from the late 19th century to the era of statehood. And in *A Daughter of Isis*, the almost larger-than-life Egyptian novelist Nawal El Saadawi presents a similarly nonlinear, poetic, and very literary autobiographical account covering her childhood and adolescence in a rigidly traditional society.

WILLIAM RIGGAN, *"World Literature Today"*

Los Angeles

Many have called the second-largest U.S. city the nation's most diversified. In 1999, "Thai Town" was added to the many other ethnic area designations in Los Angeles.

Politics. City voters approved sweeping changes in the local government in June, adopting a new city charter to replace the one in force since 1925. The new document, which increased the powers of both city hall and local communities, was seen as a victory for Mayor Richard Riordan.

Schools. A serious shortage of classrooms in the Unified School District created demand for new construction, but problems abounded. Work was halted on the partially completed Belmont Learning Complex because of the high level of toxins found at the site, a former oil field. It remained to be seen if the area could be cleaned or if the city would have to abandon the $200 million facility.

Much of the blame for such mishaps fell on district superintendent Ruben Zacarias, a career official who had worked his way up within the district as a teacher and administrator for 33 years. A number of his supporters on the school board were voted out in a spring election—another victory for Mayor Riordan—and the new board promptly stripped Zacarias of much of his power by creating the office of chief operating officer. In November, Zacarias accepted a $750,000 retirement package, and the board quickly appointed Ramon Cortines, who had headed school systems in three other California cities, as interim superintendent.

Police. A major law-enforcement scandal, involving personnel from the Ramparts station house, unfolded during the fall. The police department fired or suspended 13 officers on charges that included the "framing" of accused persons by planting evidence on them; the use of prostitutes to sell confiscated narcotics; and the operation of an apartment for rendezvous with prostitutes. Investigators also looked into a number of questionable police shootings.

In spite of the scandal, it generally was acknowledged that the operation of the police department had improved under the leadership of Chief Bernard C. Parks, who took over in 1997. In one important 1999 operation, police evicted some 150 drug dealers from rental property.

Transportation. A new section of the Red Line of the Los Angeles Metro opened in June, with a final section scheduled to be completed in mid-2000. However, officials suspended planning for future subway development due to its extremely high cost, although interest in light-rail surface lines remained. The city continued to struggle to comply with a federal-court order that directed the Metropolitan Transit Authority to buy 481 new buses, Los Angeles' most important form of public transportation.

Water. The Metropolitan Water District completed the Eastside Reservoir Project in 1999, which nearly doubled the surface-storage capacity for the Los Angeles vicinity and provided six months of emergency storage against a major earthquake. The development included a storage lake near Hemet, about 65 mi (105 km) east of downtown.

In October 1999 the Staples Center, right, a $375 million sports and entertainment facility, opened in Los Angeles. The sleek, state-of-the-art venue—the home turf for the city's professional basketball, hockey, and arena-football teams—was expected to help revitalize the downtown area.

Sports. The city endured another year without a professional-football team. The public was not prepared to underwrite a for-profit team with taxes. No plan for an elaborate stadium was considered suitable, and a possible expansion team did not generate enthusiasm. The Staples Center, an elaborate sports facility, was completed and would serve as the home site for professional basketball and hockey. It also could be used for other public performances.

CHARLES R. ADRIAN
University of California, Riverside

MACEDONIA • Information Highlights

Official Name: The Former Yugoslav Republic of Macedonia.
Location: Southeastern Europe.
Area: 9,781 sq mi (25 333 km²).
Population (July 1999 est.): 2,022,604.
Chief City (1994 census): Skopje, the capital, 444,299.
Government: *Head of state,* Boris Trajkovski, president (took office Dec. 15, 1999). *Head of government,* Ljupco Georgievski, prime minister (took office November 1998). *Legislature* (unicameral)—Assembly.
Monetary Unit: Denar (57.99 denars equal U.S.$1, August 1999).
Gross Domestic Product (1998 est. U.S.$): $2,100,000,000 (purchasing power parity).
Economic Index (1997, 1993 = 100): *Consumer Prices,* all items, 277.2; food, 252.1.
Foreign Trade (1997 est. U.S.$): *Imports,* $1,600,000,000; *exports,* $1,200,000,000.

Macedonia

During 1999, Macedonia held presidential elections, which brought to a close the era of President Kiro Gligorov. Macedonia also survived a major crisis stemming from the inflow of Albanian refugees fleeing the war in neighboring Kosovo. The government welcomed a larger North Atlantic Treaty Organization (NATO) presence in the country and took a number of initiatives to enhance regional security in the Balkans.

Domestic Turmoil. Boris Trajkovski won the Macedonian presidential elections in the fall, defeating his nearest challenger, Tito Petkovski of the oppositionist Social Democratic Party. Trajkovski was the candidate of the ruling party, the Internal Macedonian Revolutionary Organization (VMRO). In the first round of the ballot at the end of October, Petkovski gained 33% of the vote, while Trajkovski registered 21%. Petkovski deliberately whipped up the specter of Albanian separatism to frighten and mobilize Macedonian voters. In stark contrast, Trajkovski and VMRO Prime Minister Ljupco Georgievski focused on pressing economic issues in their campaign and rejected nationalism and ethnic division. Since neither candidate won a majority, a runoff was held on November 14 and was won by Trajkovski. After Petkovski's Social Democrats complained of vote fraud in western Macedonia in the second round of balloting, a partial rerun was held in early December. The state-run electoral commission declared Trajkovski the winner of the rerun.

The government coalition—comprising the former nationalist VMRO organization and the largest Albanian party, the DPA (Democratic Party of Albanians)—weathered a series of domestic and regional storms. To defuse tensions, the Albanians were offered positions in various government organs; several high-ranking Albanian political prisoners were released; and concessions were made regarding Albanian-language higher education.

The Macedonian economy was unsettled severely by the war in neighboring Serbia. Macedonia estimated that its losses from the war—including trade, investment, and refugee assistance—totaled some $1.5 billion by the end of the year. Foreign investments dropped off dramatically, and many contracts with European and U.S. companies were canceled. As a result, the gross domestic product (GDP) was projected to drop by up to 15% for the year.

Foreign Policy. One of Macedonia's most significant foreign-policy developments during 1999 was the breakthrough in relations with Bulgaria. This was symbolized by the signing in February of a declaration settling the language dispute and stating that the two countries harbored no territorial claims on each other. The declaration was signed in the official languages of the two countries, ending a conflict that arose when Bulgaria refused to recognize Macedonian as a language separate from Bulgarian. Several other agreements also were initialed, in the areas of trade and investment.

In March, Macedonian Defense Minister Nikola Kljusev and his Bulgarian counterpart, Georgi Ananiev, signed a framework accord on military cooperation between armies of the two countries. Macedonia received from Bulgaria a delivery of decommissioned military equipment, including 150 tanks and an equal number of artillery pieces. Among other agreements, the two countries negotiated the creation of a free-trade area, expected to enter into force in January 2000.

Macedonia's relations with Serbia remained strained. Belgrade refused to recognize the current border between the two states, despite years of negotiations. Skopje believed that Serbian delays were designed deliberately to keep Macedonia off balance and to maintain some leverage over the government. Belgrade also tried to blackmail Macedonia by threatening to provoke interethnic incidents inside the country through the use of militant members of the Serbian minority. During the NATO-Serb war, Yugoslav President Slobodan Milosevic tried to destabilize Macedonia by pushing Kosovar refugees into the country and by promoting anti-Albanian and anti-NATO unrest among the Serb minority. The early return of Albanians to Kosovo took pressure off Macedonia that could have been exploited by Belgrade. (*See also* THE KOSOVO CRISIS—*The Spotlight Turns to the Refugees*, page 82.)

The name dispute between Macedonia and Greece remained unresolved. Talks were held periodically at the United Nations (UN) between government representatives, without any results. The name issue aside, relations between Athens and Skopje at most levels developed well. There was increasing Greek economic investment, while the Macedonian authorities viewed Greece as a potential gateway to the European Union (EU).

In July the foreign ministers of Greece, Albania, and Macedonia reached an agreement on issues of tripartite cooperation. They agreed to hold regular meetings every six months. Macedonia also participated in the Balkan ministerial meetings and was highly supportive of the EU-sponsored Stability Pact for South East Europe.

JANUSZ BUGAJSKI
Center for Strategic and International Studies

Malaysia

Malaysia underwent a political crisis in 1999 as it held its tenth national election on November 29.

Political Crisis. In the November voting, Prime Minister Mahathir Mohamad and his Malay-based United Malay National Organization (UMNO) led the 14-party Barisan Nasional, or BN (national front), to victory, winning 148 of 193 seats in Parliament. The BN kept the two-thirds majority needed to amend the federal constitution and to protect special Malay privileges imbedded in the document. Politics in the multiethnic state—composed of 60% Malays, 25% Chinese, and 12% Indians—have been dominated by the BN since 1971. UMNO and its primary partners in the BN, the Malaysian Chinese Association (MCA) and the Malaysian Indian Congress (MIC), have led Malaysia along a moderate political course, carefully balancing the interests of the three ethnic communities.

The BN's November 29 victory was actually a significant setback. The opposition Alternative Front's (AF's) Islamic party, Parti Islam Se Malaysia (PAS), won 27 parliamentary seats and now controlled two states in northern Malaysia—Kelantan and oil-rich Terengganu. PAS, which wants to turn Malaysia into an Islamic state, succeeded by taking a large number of Malay votes away from UMNO. Of PAS' AF partners, the Chinese-based Democratic Action Party (DAP) won ten seats, and the National Justice Party won five.

The success of PAS could be blamed on Prime Minister Mahathir. In 1998 he sacked his popular deputy prime minister and minister of finance, Anwar Ibrahim. He then had Anwar arrested on charges of corruption. In April 1999 the former deputy prime minister was convicted and sentenced to six years in prison by a judiciary, which has little to no independence from the prime minister. Anwar openly had criticized Mahathir's handling of Malaysia's economic crisis.

While in detention, Anwar was beaten by Malaysian police. His wife, Wan Aziazh Ismail, launched the National Justice Party and called on the opposition to unite and unseat the prime minister. She won a seat in Parliament in the November election. Anwar's persecution stirred substantial unrest among both rural Malays and young, educated Malays, whose numbers continue to grow as a result of the country's policy of sending large numbers of students abroad for their education. In April more than 10,000 people marched in Kuala Lumpur, Malaysia's capital, to protest Anwar's treatment. Political unrest continued up to the election.

Election results suggested that it was in fact the Chinese vote that saved the BN from an even more serious defeat. Chinese voters feared the more radical PAS and were willing to put up with Mahathir's authoritarian ways. It also must be noted that the prime minister ran a strong campaign, visiting each of Malaysia's 13 states. The opposition was hurt by the government-controlled press, which refused to run its ads. And, while the AF cooperated to oppose the BN in straight fights for 152 parliamentary seats, strained relations between the Islamic party, PAS, and the Chinese DAP made full cooperation difficult. The UMNO's Malay base of support was split over the treatment of Anwar, thus giving PAS the opportunity to expand. However, while many Malays want to live in an Islamic state, time is on the side of the moderate and youthful Malay middle class, which recognizes the need for tolerance of the country's minorities.

On December 23, Mahathir designated his deputy, Abdullah Badawi, to succeed him as president of the UMNO if he chose to retire. The statement also was an indication that Abdullah would be Malaysia's next prime minister in the not-too-distant future.

Economy. The government's imposition of capital controls brought strong criticism from the International Monetary Fund (IMF). However, even the IMF admitted that Prime Minister Mahathir's brainchild of such controls had worked. In 1999 the gross domestic product (GDP) was projected to grow by at least 4.5%, compared with a 7.5% contraction in 1998; inflation and unemployment each were down to about 3%. By the end of the year, interest rates had fallen to the 6% range, and domestic consumption was on the rise. The economy benefited from a large increase in exports, supported by a controlled and undervalued ringgit, and from a large budget deficit equaling 6% of GDP.

The political implications of economic policy were made clear in October, when, in order to win support from the Chinese financial community, the prime minister backed away from merging 58 small banks—many of them Chinese—into six more-competitive mega-institutions under Malay direction. In September the government rescinded exit taxes on the principal of portfolio investments. However, in spite of this calculated easing of controls, foreign direct investment was down for the year, and full economic recovery could be delayed. Mahathir stated that controls would not disappear totally until curbs were placed on international money speculators.

© David Loh/Reuters/Archive Photos

Malaysia's coalition, led by Prime Minister Mahathir Mohamad, above, *enjoyed a decisive victory in November 1999 elections, but political turmoil continued.*

Foreign Relations. The five-day November visit of Chinese Premier Zhu Rongji to Kuala Lumpur to discuss several large joint-venture projects was aimed at Malaysia's 5.6 million ethnic Chinese and especially the powerful Chinese business community. The election put Malaysia's regional relations on the back burner, when the prime minister pulled out of the Association of Southeast Asian Nations (ASEAN) summit in Manila. Relations were ruffled with Britain, Australia, Canada, and the United States when these nations' embassies were accused of funding the Alternative Front and supporting ousted Deputy Prime Minister Anwar.

Mahathir's most serious foreign-affairs flap surfaced when informal contacts between Israel and Malaysia were revealed. To demonstrate his pro-Arab stance, the prime minister publicly stated that terrorism by Muslims was justified in a hegemonic world.

PATRICK M. MAYERCHAK
Virginia Military Institute

MALAYSIA • Information Highlights

Official Name: Malaysia.
Location: Southeast Asia.
Area: 127,317 sq mi (329 750 km²).
Population (July 1999 est.): 21,376,066.
Chief Cities (1991 census): Kuala Lumpur, the capital, 1,145,342; Ipoh, 382,853; Johor Baharu, 328,436.
Government: *Head of state,* Sultan Salahuddin Abdul Aziz Shah, king (installed September 1999). *Head of government,* Mahathir bin Mohamad, prime minister (took office July 1981). *Legislature*—Parliament: Senate and House of Representatives.
Monetary Unit: Ringgit (Malaysian dollar) (3.7997 ringgits equal U.S.$1, Dec. 22, 1999).
Gross Domestic Product (1998 est. U.S.$): $215,400,000,000 (purchasing power parity).
Economic Indexes: *Consumer Prices* (1998, 1990 = 100): all items, 135.8; food, 151.4. *Industrial Production* 191.9.
Foreign Trade (1998 U.S.$): *Imports,* $58,326,000,000; *exports,* $73,304,000,000.

Medicine and Health

During the 20th century, the life expectancy of a U.S. infant increased dramatically, from approximately 47 years to more than 76 years. Improved nutrition, better sanitation, and the development of a broad array of drugs and medical procedures to combat disease played critical roles in enabling Americans to live longer, healthier lives. But as the century drew to a close, numerous health problems continued to bedevil humanity, and, as an outbreak of West Nile fever in New York demonstrated (*see* SIDEBAR), such problems often were not contained by national boundaries.

Ethical and political issues were as significant as medical news. Stem-cell research and the method used to allocate organs to people awaiting transplants were debated fiercely, as were proposals to help people with insufficient or no health insurance.

On June 7 the first-ever White House Conference on Mental Health took place at Howard University in Washington, DC. It focused on issues such as treatment options, lack of health-insurance coverage for mental illnesses, and the need to lift the stigma associated with psychological disorders. The event was spearheaded by Tipper Gore, wife of Vice-President Al Gore, who revealed that she herself had been treated medically for depression in the early 1990s. About 400 people participated. President Bill Clinton announced several initiatives to address mental-health issues, including a new requirement that the Federal Employees Health Benefits Plan provide the same coverage for mental illnesses and substance-abuse problems as it did for physical ailments; a $7.3 million study by the National Institute of Mental Health (NIMH) to explore the nature of mental illness; and programs to detect, prevent, and treat mental illnesses among vulnerable groups such as the homeless, children, and the elderly.

Overview

Healthy People 2000. In 1979 the U.S. Department of Health and Human Services (HHS) launched *Healthy People 2000*, a program that set 319 goals to improve the health of the American people significantly by 2000. The plan focused on increasing the span of healthy life, reducing health disparities, and providing preventive services for everyone. A 1999 report, however, indicated that progress toward these goals was mixed. Although movement toward the targets had been made for most of the objectives, only 15% of them had been met, including reductions in infant and child mortality and breast-cancer deaths. For 18% of the objectives—including level of physical activity and number of overweight people—movement away from the targets had occurred. Furthermore, racial and ethnic disparities showed little change. For instance, the death rate among black infants remained about twice that for whites, and Hispanics were twice as likely as whites to be diabetic.

Cancer. The American Cancer Society reported that U.S. cancer incidence fell 2.2% annually from 1992 through 1996, largely because of a decline in smoking. Health officials feared, however, that high smoking rates among teenagers could reverse the trend. Cigarette smoking by high-school students increased 32% during the 1990s.

Research by scientists from the University of California at San Francisco School of Medicine and the Harvard School of Public Health suggested that smoking during childhood or adolescence caused genetic damage that increased the risk of cancer even if people soon quit smoking. An analysis of tissue from 143 lung-cancer patients showed that DNA changes were lowest among patients who never had smoked and highest in people who smoked. Among the former smokers, DNA changes were greatest in patients who began smoking as children or teenagers, regardless of when they quit.

Swedish researchers reported that chronic heartburn, or gastroesophageal reflux disease, increased by nearly eight times a person's risk of a particularly deadly cancer of the esophagus called esophageal adenocarcinoma. Approximately 15 million Americans have heartburn daily, and at least twice that number experience it at least once a week. In recent decades the incidence of esophageal adenocarcinoma in the United States rose faster than that of any other cancer, though it remained comparatively rare, with an estimated 12,500 diagnosed cases and 12,200 deaths in 1999.

Liver cancer also increased in the United States, with some 14,500 new cases in 1999. The most common form, hepatocellular car-

© Rusty Kennedy/AP/Wide World Photos

Matthew Scott, who in January 1999 became the first person in the United States to receive a hand transplant, was thrilled to throw out the first pitch at the Philadelphia Phillies' home opener 11 weeks later.

cinoma, rose 71% from the mid-1970s to the mid-1990s. It often is caused by hepatitis B and C. Effective treatments and a vaccine have slowed hepatitis B infections, but there is no effective treatment or vaccine for hepatitis C.

In May 1997 a Harvard University research team headed by Judah Folkman reported that cancerous tumors in mice could be destroyed by giving the mice a protein called endostatin, which blocked the tumors' ability to grow new blood vessels. In early 1999, for the first time, scientists at the National Cancer Institute announced that they had been able to duplicate Folkman's work. The first human trials of endostatin, in volunteers with solid tumors who had not benefited from other treatments, began later in the year.

AIDS. In 1999, AIDS became the leading cause of death in sub-Saharan Africa, where 22.3 million adults were infected with HIV (the virus that causes the disease), primarily through heterosexual sex. The United Nations reported that in sub-Saharan Africa, more women than men were HIV-positive. Until recently, most African political leaders were reluctant to admit that AIDS was a problem in their countries, and thus failed to set up effective prevention programs. But with the social and economic impact of the disease stunningly apparent, attitudes began to change.

U.S. health officials continued to stress the importance of prevention. They worried that improved treatments had made people complacent about AIDS, noting that new HIV infections were dangerously high in some areas among young gay men and heterosexual women. AIDS deaths in the United States continued a decline that had begun in 1997, though at a much slower rate.

Antibiotic Resistance. Evidence reported in 1999 highlighted how the misuse and overuse of antibiotics has resulted in the development and spread of resistant bacteria. For example, some strains of *Staphylococcus aureus*, a common cause of infection, were found to be resistant to the most-available antimicrobial drugs, including vancomycin, the last line of treatment for staph infections. In August the Centers for Disease Control and Prevention (CDC) announced that more than 200 people in North Dakota and Minnesota had become sick, and four children had died, from a drug-resistant strain of staph. In September the U.S. Food and Drug Administration (FDA) approved Synercid, an antibiotic that appeared to be effective in some cases in which vancomycin failed. Meanwhile, a vaccine that researchers hoped would prove effective in preventing staph infections began testing in mid-1999.

It was reported that multidrug-resistant strains of the tuberculosis (TB) bacterium were spreading faster than anticipated, with especially high numbers of cases in China and Russia. To combat the spread of resistant TB, the recommended approach had been directly observed therapy (DOT), consisting of daily observation of patients for six to eight months to ensure they took up to four different medications. But physicians at Harvard Medical School said a more intensive—and more expensive—strategy was needed. Called DOTS Plus, this approach involved taking up to seven drugs daily, with patients remaining under direct observation for 18 to 24 months.

Medications Introduced... and Withdrawn. Celebrex, an arthritis painkiller introduced in January, became the fastest-selling new drug ever in the United States, selling 6.86 million prescriptions during its first six months on the market. Celebrex was the first in a new class of painkillers called cyclooxygenase-2 (COX-2) inhibitors, which target the enzyme that causes inflammation.

Ramipril, in the class of drugs called ACE inhibitors, has been marketed since 1991 to treat high blood pressure and chronic heart failure. In 1999 it was reported that ramipril also significantly cut the risk of heart attacks, strokes, and diabetes in people with heart disease, and also lowered the need for bypass surgery.

The West Nile Virus—A Deadly Visitor

In August 1999, New York City officials announced that dozens of people were believed to have contracted St. Louis encephalitis, a viral illness never before identified in the area. Concurrently, wildlife scientists, birders, and other people in New York City and its environs noticed that unusually large numbers of birds were dying. The coincidence led to the discovery that the real culprit in both cases was not the St. Louis virus but a closely related strain, the West Nile virus, first discovered in Uganda in 1937. Usually found in Africa, West Nile virus also has caused epidemics in Europe and Asia. But it never had been seen in the Western Hemisphere.

Like the St. Louis virus, the West Nile virus spreads from one organism to another via mosquitoes. For example, a mosquito might bite an infected bird and then bite a human; as the mosquito gorges, the virus travels from the mosquito's gut into the person's blood. Within three to six days of exposure, the person suffers symptoms, including fever, muscle weakness, and headache. Usually, the symptoms are mild. But in some cases—particularly among the elderly, children under age 5, and people with weakened immune systems—the virus causes neurological disorders and death. By the time cold weather reached the New York City area, killing mosquitoes and effectively ending the outbreak, there were 37 confirmed cases of West Nile virus, including seven deaths, plus another 25 probable cases.

By late 1999 it was not known how the West Nile virus reached New York. It may have been carried in the blood of someone who had been in Africa or southern Russia. Someone may have smuggled in an infected bird. It is even possible that a mosquito carrying the virus traveled aboard an airplane across the Atlantic.

Municipalities in the region responded with mosquito sprayings (*photo, page 349*) and other measures. Residents were advised to remain indoors at dawn and dusk, when mosquitoes are most active. Meanwhile, birds had begun their fall migrations, and health officials expressed concern that infected birds might be carrying the West Nile virus southward. Such fears were strengthened when a dead bird found near Baltimore Harbor in mid-October

LYMErix, the first vaccine against Lyme disease, became available for people aged 15 through 70 in January. The vaccine is made from a genetically engineered protein found on the outer surface of *Borrelia burgdorferi*, the bacterium that causes Lyme disease. A series of three injections of LYMErix over a period of one year was shown to provide 78% protection against the disease.

Orlistat, the first in a new class of antiobesity drugs, was approved for people who were at least 30% overweight but were otherwise healthy, and for those who were 20% overweight and had high blood pressure, high cholesterol, or diabetes. Orlistat blocks an enzyme needed to digest fat; about one third of the fat eaten by a person taking the drug is excreted instead of absorbed.

A number of drugs were pulled off the market in 1999. Following FDA warnings that the antihistamine Hismanal could cause fatal heart-rhythm disturbances, either in high doses or in combination with other drugs, the manufacturer, Janssen Pharmaceutica, stopped selling the medicine. The next month, American Home Products withdrew RotaShield, the only vaccine to prevent infant diarrhea caused by rotaviruses, after a CDC report linked the drug with more than 100 cases of intussusception, a painful and potentially fatal bowel obstruction.

Transplants and Implants. Even though the number of organ donors increased substantially, thanks to strong procurement efforts, the need for organs remained greater than the supply. An estimated 4,000 people die each year waiting for transplants. The criteria dictating who should receive an organ were the subject of bitter arguments. Under the existing system, donated organs were offered first locally, then regionally, and then (rarely) nationally. Clinton-administration efforts to change the system so that the sickest patients would be given priority, regardless of where they lived, were unsuccessful.

In January surgeons at Jewish Hospital in Louisville, KY, performed the first hand transplant in the United States, attaching a cadaver's left hand to Matthew Scott, a 37-year-old New Jersey man who had lost his hand in a fireworks accident in 1985. It was the world's second such operation, following a similar procedure performed in France in 1998 on Clive Hallam, a 48-year-old Australian. Both men recuperated faster than tested positive for the virus. Health officials also worried about the possibility of a renewed outbreak in the New York City area in spring 2000.

The advent of West Nile virus in the New World was the latest in a string of menacing diseases unleashed as a result of increased international travel, climatic changes, the destruction of rain forests, growing resistance to antibiotics, and other factors. It joins the greater incidence of malaria around the world, the emergence of AIDS, and the spread of drug-resistant tuberculosis as a formidable opponent of human health.

JENNY TESAR

© Jonathan Elderfield/Liaison Agency

had been expected. Scott, for example, wiggled a finger two days after his operation.

To prevent a person's body from rejecting the "foreign" tissue of a transplant, antirejection drugs that suppress the immune system generally must be taken for the rest of the person's life. But these drugs can have drawbacks. For instance, researchers with Cornell University, New York University, and the Tokyo University School of Medicine reported in February that cyclosporine, an antirejection drug, appeared to enhance cancer growth in people who had cancerous tumors. Meanwhile, physicians at Massachusetts General Hospital in Boston announced that they had used a bone-marrow transplant instead of antirejection drugs in a woman with cancer who also had received a kidney transplant. The transplanted bone marrow made it easier for her body to accept the new organ, the doctors said. Because of the invasiveness of the procedure, bone-marrow transplants would not be done solely to prevent rejection, but the doctors believed that the same result could be achieved by giving transplant patients stem cells, which are contained in blood and marrow.

Confirming earlier findings, an independent scientific panel convened by the Institute of Medicine of the National Academy of Scientists found no credible evidence that silicone breast implants caused rheumatoid arthritis, lupus, or other serious diseases. This finding contradicted several jury verdicts that had resulted in more than $7 billion in settlements to women who claimed that their implants had caused such problems.

Nutrition. A study of 88,795 women contradicted conventional wisdom when it found no evidence that a high-fat diet promotes breast cancer—or that a low-fat diet prevents the disease. Analysis of fiber and colon-cancer data from the study suggested that a high-fiber diet does not lower the risk of colon cancer, although it does appear to protect against coronary heart disease. In another surprising finding, researchers at Harvard Medical School reported in June that eating an egg a day does not appear to increase the risk of heart attacks and strokes in people who do not have diabetes or cholesterol problems already, as had been thought. This backed up previous studies saying that dietary cholesterol does not necessarily increase blood cholesterol.

At the University of Wisconsin Medical School, researchers found that people with atherosclerosis, or narrowing of the arteries, benefited from drinking purple grape juice. The elasticity of their blood vessels increased, and the rate at which they oxidized LDL ("bad") cholesterol significantly decreased. Meanwhile, researchers at the Karmanos Cancer Institute in Detroit reported that lycopene, the carotenoid that gives tomatoes their red color, appeared to protect men against prostate cancer by shrinking tumors and slowing their spread. And a study that analyzed 72 past experiments found that high consumption of tomatoes and tomato products also reduced the risk of lung, stomach, and other cancers.

Managing Pain. Although physicians long have recognized that untreated pain slows patients' recovery and increases health-care costs, they frequently undermedicate pain because they fear criminal prosecution, particularly on charges of supplying narcotics or participating in assisted suicide. A University of Iowa survey in 1999 found that physicians often withheld pain medication from patients in emergency situations, either because the doctors feared the drugs might affect the accuracy of their diagnoses or because of informed-consent issues. The Joint Commission on Accreditation of Healthcare Organizations, the accrediting body for most U.S. hospitals and other health-care facilities, adopted standards in August saying that the organizations must "recognize the right of patients to appropriate assessment and management of pain."

JENNY TESAR, *Freelance Science Writer*

Health Care

For the first time since the crash and burn of President Bill Clinton's plan to overhaul the U.S. health-care system in 1994, the health-care issue returned to center stage of the national agenda in 1999. But by year's end, Congress and the president had failed to agree on three major health-policy issues: how to shore up the finances of the Medicare program, how to protect patients from the alleged abuses of health-maintenance organizations (HMOs) and other managed-care insurance plans, and how to help the estimated 44 million Americans who lacked insurance coverage.

Medicare. The fate of the nation's health-insurance program for 39 million elderly and disabled Americans was a key concern for the public, judging from opinion polls. Its future also occupied Congress and President Clinton. The problem was a demographic one: The aging of the massive baby-boom generation was threatening to swamp the program, as the oldest boomers would become eligible in 2011. Obviously, Medicare either would require more money—from taxes or from beneficiaries themselves—or would have to be revised to provide fewer benefits if it was to be sustained. Diagnosing the problem, however, proved considerably easier than finding a politically acceptable solution.

Hopes early in 1999 were pinned on the 17-member National Bipartisan Commission on the Future of Medicare. The commission was created by the 1997 Balanced Budget Act, after lawmakers were unable to settle on a long-term strategy for shoring up the program's troubled finances. To ensure that any solution the commission would propose would have broad support, the law required the affirmative votes of 11 panel members in order to forward a formal recommendation to Congress.

The commission, cochaired by Sen. John Breaux (D-LA) and Rep. Bill Thomas (R-CA), put together a proposal it called "premium support." Under this plan, Medicare no longer would be run directly by the federal government, but would consist of private plans competing under the supervision of a quasi-independent Medicare board. Breaux and Thomas hoped the savings gleaned from introducing competition—along with some other changes, including raising the program's eligibility age from 65 to 67—would keep the program solvent.

The plan did win a majority of votes from the commission, but the 10–7 tally left the proposal one vote short of formal adoption. The chief complaint of those who voted against the proposal was that it failed to make outpatient prescription drugs universally available to beneficiaries. Medicare's lack of a drug benefit long had been a frustration to those who followed the program. Indeed, Democrats and President Clinton pounced on the drug issue, and several proposals were introduced that would add a drug benefit to Medicare. Clinton's plan, unveiled in June, would have provided up to half the cost of prescription drugs—up to a limit of $5,000—when fully implemented.

But no action was taken. Republicans in Congress resisted efforts to add a drug benefit without a more comprehensive reform of the program. And the prescription-drug

© Terry Ashe/Liaison Agency

President Bill Clinton lobbied in 1999 for his version of a Patients' Bill of Rights. Although both houses of Congress passed legislation giving patients new rights in managed-care plans, there was no final action on the issue.

industry fought most of the proposals, fearing that if the federal government began paying more directly for drugs, price control could follow quickly.

But it was not merely Medicare's future that commanded legislative attention in 1999. Ironically, while most attention was focused on how much Medicare would cost in the future, at present, spending on the program actually was falling. For the fiscal year ending Oct. 1, 1999, Medicare spending fell for the first time in the program's history, from $213.6 billion to $212 billion.

Analysts disagreed on the reasons for the spending slowdown, but health-care providers insisted that it was because the cuts imposed by the 1997 law went too far. In response, Congress and President Clinton did agree to a bill late in the session that would restore an estimated $12 billion in payments over the next five years. Congress also passed legislation allowing individuals receiving Social Security Disability (SSDI) or Supplemental Security Insurance (SSI) to return to work without losing their Medicare or Medicaid health insurance.

Managed Care. Both the U.S. House and Senate in 1999 managed to pass legislation aimed at providing new rights to patients in managed-care plans, but the bills were so different, and the House passed its bill so late in the year, that no final act emerged.

The Senate acted first, passing its "Patients' Bill of Rights" on July 15 by a vote of 53–47. But all those voting for the measure were Republicans, with Democrats and President Clinton arguing that it would provide too few protections for too few patients. Most of the new protections—such as requiring plans to pay for emergency-room care if a "prudent layperson" deemed such care necessary—would cover only 48 million of the 161 million Americans with private health coverage. The bill also included no right for patients to sue their health plans if care denials resulted in injury or death. A glitch in federal law prohibits such suits for virtually all 125 million Americans who get insurance through their jobs.

Passage of the House bill on October 7 by a vote of 275–151 came over the objections of the chamber's Republican leaders. Democrats joined with renegade GOP health professionals, led by former dentist Charlie Norwood (GA) and plastic surgeon Greg Ganske (IA), to draft a bill that resembled the version of the "Patients' Bill of Rights" backed by Clinton. Unlike the Senate bill, the House-passed measure would give patients injured by care denials access to the courts. Congress was expected to continue the managed-care debate in 2000.

The Uninsured. In October the Census Bureau reported that in 1998, an estimated 44.3 million people in the United States lacked health insurance. That was up only slightly from 1997, but the fact that the number of uninsured rose at all during a period of low unemployment and strong economic growth concerned policy analysts.

Still, policy makers could not agree on what to do. President Clinton focused on "incremental" steps to expand insurance coverage, such as allowing those over age 55 but under 65 to "buy into" Medicare. Republicans in Congress advanced a series of tax proposals they said could help make insurance more affordable. But the issue of the uninsured looked increasingly as though it next would be debated in the context of the 2000 presidential campaign.

JULIE ROVNER, *Health-Policy Writer*

Bioethics

The health and science issues debated in 1999 in many ways brought bioethical issues into the lives of many Americans.

Genetic Code. Celera Genomics, a biotechnology company launched in 1998 by Maryland geneticist J. Craig Venter, changed the shape of human genetics and ignited a debate about how genetics will and should proceed. The U.S. National Human Genome Research Institute, led by geneticist Francis Collins, has labored since 1989 through an allotment of funds from Congress. At a number of universities, tax dollars have financed the discovery of a number of genes associated with diseases. Some of these have been patented, a few by the National Institutes of Health itself. However, in 1999, Venter's creation of Celera Genomics demonstrated its ability to map the human genome with much greater rapidity. In 1999, using a new technology that maps single nucleotide polymorphisms, or "SNPs," Venter's group rapidly gathered information about much of the human genome, causing commentators and scientists to note that there may be dangers in a single company racing, and defeating, the U.S. government's program. Moreover, the company filed in October a preliminary application for more than 6,000 patents on genes it had identified in its efforts to date, causing a debate about whether or not it is ethical and commercially profitable to patent human genetic information.

Embryology and Surgery. The November 1998 isolation of special cells in the early human embryo called human embryonic pluripotent stem cells created a major flurry of debate. The cells, which will be isolated predominantly from frozen human embryos or embryos made through cloning, seem to have almost unlimited power to produce new human cells of almost any type. Scientists hope that stem-cell therapies may revolutionize treatment of degenerative disease, including Parkinson's disease, Alzheimer's disease, and diabetes. Stem-cell transplants would create new cells and tissues that patients would assimilate into their own organs, such as brain, liver, kidneys, or muscle. The use of human embryos, which would involve destroying the shell of the embryo while keeping its DNA coding intact, caused many in the antiabortion movement to refer to the development as a potential holocaust of human embryos. On the other side, patients'-rights groups pointed out that more than 130 million Americans might be aided by stem cells, and researchers at the University of Pennsylvania noted that the embryos are not destroyed but rather are rendered dormant, stored inside the recipient's body rather than a freezer.

A roiling debate continued over surgery on fetuses still in the womb, a procedure conducted at only three institutions in the United States. When one program chose to develop a surgical intervention for fetuses whose spina bifida defects were not lethal, much attention was focused on the difficulty of developing fetal surgery and on its ethical implications. Specifically, many wondered who the patient of fetal surgery should be, the fetus or the mother, since the fetus has no standing under U.S. abortion law. Others were concerned that innovation of this radical kind is not regulated by federal laws. Still others argued that there is no room for this kind of surgery on humans who cannot give consent, as a fetus cannot. Development of fetal surgery promises to increase the pressure on policy makers and ethicists to define the difference between responsibilities to women and to future children.

Reproductive Medicine. Debate about reproductive medicine has heated up in the United States since the birth of the cloned sheep, Dolly, in Scotland in 1996. In 1999 two events further ignited controversy. First, in March a child was born from sperm harvested from a dead man. This raised anew questions about what it means to parent a child. Many wondered whether or not children from posthumous gametes might be harmed by the technology that gives them life, and about what sorts of goals reasonably might be realized by such technology. Second, in late October an on-line auction was sponsored, in which egg donations from young models were offered to the highest bidder through a Web site. The offer prompted many in reproductive medicine to complain of the ethical wrong associated with the search for eggs from the beautiful, and cries of outrage from geneticists about the false advertising associated with a promise of beauty from 50% of a baby's genes.

End-of-Life Care. Ethical issues involved in end-of-life care continued in the spotlight. Texas Gov. George W. Bush signed into law a bill making it illegal to withdraw treatment from terminally ill patients without the approval of a special committee. Similarly, the U.S. House of Representatives approved a measure that makes it illegal to provide lethal doses of drugs to patients. The latter bill, which was not approved by the Senate, would disable a 1994 Oregon law permitting assisted suicide, involving the use of lethal doses of drugs under certain conditions.

GLENN MCGEE, *Center for Bioethics University of Pennsylvania*

Mental Health

In 1999 researchers worked with genetically engineered mice to learn more about how to treat anxiety, and studies found that stress from various sources can increase susceptibility to infectious illness. An investigation revealed that depressed women seem able to understand the ramifications of treatment choices, despite their illness. And new research suggests that as people age, they experience fewer negative emotions.

Anxiety Model. Scientists suspect that they will gain valuable insights about anxiety-prone people by studying mice deprived of a gene that encourages the transmission of specific chemical messages in the brain. Experimental removal of the gene results in a large drop in the number of molecular receptors, or gateways, for a neurotransmitter called GABA, reported Florence Crestani and Hanns Mohler of the University of Zurich. GABA lowers the activity of brain regions involved in fear and anxiety. Antianxiety drugs prod GABA receptors into working harder. An inherited shortage of these receptors on brain cells may predispose a person to develop an anxiety disorder in response to stressful or traumatic experiences, the researchers suggested.

Crestani and Mohler first determined that mice missing one of the two copies of the GABA-receptor gene had many fewer GABA receptors in key brain areas than did mice retaining both copies of the gene. They then found that gene-deprived mice exhibited greater anxiety on several laboratory tests. Such mice may prove useful in testing new antianxiety drugs.

Schizophrenia Caregivers. People caring for a family member suffering from schizophrenia may catch more than their fair share of colds and other infectious illnesses, at least in certain cases. High numbers of infectious ailments occurred in adults caring for a relative with pronounced hallucinations and delusions, the so-called positive symptoms of schizophrenia, according to a team led by Dennis G. Dyck of Washington State University in Spokane. Far fewer infectious ills appeared in caregivers who dealt mainly with negative symptoms of schizophrenia, such as apathy and social withdrawal, the researchers noted. However, negative symptoms appear to create a greater burden on the caregivers. The scientists measured caregivers' burden by having them rate their care-related money problems, worries about the mentally ill relative, self-blame for the situation, and any stigma that they felt about having a mentally ill family member.

A nurse interviewed 70 people caring for relatives with schizophrenia about their own physical problems and physician visits in the past six months. A second interview probed for each caregiver's perceived burden, depression, anger, support from others, and style of coping with stress. Caregivers whose coping style consisted of wishful thinking, avoiding their problems, self-blame, and formulating specific problem-solving plans found their situations most burdensome. Although citing moderate burdens, caregivers who relied on religious faith or had strong support from friends and family reported the lowest rates of infectious illness.

Decisions. In 1998 and 1999 a federal bioethics panel and a number of media reports suggested that scientists often do not properly inform patients with mental disorders about the risks and benefits of participating in drug trials or other research. Two new studies, however, suggested that many people diagnosed with severe mental disorders retain plenty of judgmental insight and require no special protection beyond that granted to medical patients taking part in research.

One investigation, directed by Paul Appelbaum of the University of Massachusetts Medical School in Worcester, found that women suffering from major depression of at least moderate intensity understand the pros and cons of participating in a psychotherapy research project. A total of 26 women enrolled in a study of different courses of psychotherapy for depression completed a short interview assessing their competence to consent to treatment. The interview focused on each woman's understanding of the project, appreciation of the effects of research participation on her own situation, and ability to compare participation with other treatment options. Nearly all the women exhibited a comprehensive understanding of the study.

In the second study, led by William Gardner of the University of Pittsburgh School of Medicine, about half of a group of people involuntarily committed to a psychiatric hospital later agreed that they had needed the treatment. Gardner's group interviewed 267 patients within two days of their admission to a psychiatric hospital and again one to two months after discharge. Of 64 patients who initially had objected to commitment, 33 later said that they had needed it. It was unclear, however, how many of the coerced patients who later insisted that they had not needed treatment were hospitalized due to clinical error.

Stress and Immunity. People who feel unable to deal with daily stresses exhibit an immune reaction that may worsen their physical symptoms once they have contracted a virus. Sheldon Cohen of Carnegie Mellon University in Pittsburgh and his colleagues have yet to determine whether this immune reaction—elevated production of a chemical messenger known as interleukin-6 (IL-6)—intensifies viral symptoms or develops in response to them. In previous research, Cohen's group had reported that the risk of becoming infected by respiratory viruses and developing cold symptoms rises sharply among people who experience high levels of mental stress.

Their latest study linked stress to both a specific immune-system change and resulting physical illness. The researchers recruited 55 healthy, infection-free adults, each of whom spent eight consecutive days quarantined in a hotel room. On the second day, volunteers received nasal drops containing an infectious dose of an influenza A virus. All developed verified infections from the virus during their hotel stays. At the end of each day, participants described their symptoms. Their used tissues were collected to assess mucus production and IL-6 levels. Those people reporting the highest daily stress levels just prior to entering the study produced the most mucus, displayed the largest IL-6 increases, and cited the most severe infectious symptoms. Psychological stress may weaken physiological controls on IL-6 release, helping to trigger a process that results in cold symptoms, Cohen proposed.

Emotional Maturity. Despite evidence of mounting memory and intellectual losses as people age, the elderly regulate emotional states much better than do younger folks, according to research directed by Laura Carstensen of Stanford University. As individuals age, they experience a fairly constant rate of positive emotions and a declining number of negative emotions, Carstensen's team found. Emotions of all kinds retain their full intensity among the elderly, the researchers said.

After reaching a low point at around age 60, the amount of sadness, anger, and other types of negative emotion experienced daily slowly rises, but it remains well below the peak level cited by people in their early 20s. In addition, positive emotions last longer, and negative emotions appear for briefer periods as adults age. Older people also describe experiencing richer mixes of feelings, such as feeling simultaneous anger at and affection for a close friend.

Carstensen and her colleagues studied 184 adults ranging in age from 18 to 84 years. Each volunteer carried an electronic pager for a week. At randomly chosen times of the day and night, the pagers beeped, signaling the volunteers to fill out a brief questionnaire on the nature and intensity of current emotions. The participants mailed their responses to the researchers daily. Carstensen suspects that as people age, a growing sense of having limited time left in life boosts interest in cultivating the emotional quality of established relationships.

Depressed Smokers. Men suffering from major depression who smoke up to a pack of cigarettes daily experience immune-cell disturbances thought to promote cancer development. The same declines in immune function do not show up either in depressed nonsmokers or in mentally healthy men who smoke up to a pack of cigarettes daily.

These findings support long-term community studies in which cigarette smokers with major depression exhibit elevated cancer rates, even for cancers not linked to cigarette use. Researchers long have known that rates of cigarette smoking rise sharply among people with major depression.

Waymond Jung and Michael Irwin, both of the San Diego Veterans Affairs Medical Center, collected blood samples from 127 nonsmokers who had no psychiatric disorders, 11 moderate smokers in good mental health, 46 nonsmokers with major depression, and 61 moderate smokers suffering from major depression. All participants were male. Only depressed men who smoked cigarettes displayed large numbers of white blood cells—a general sign of a weakened immune system—and a sluggish response of natural killer cells to foreign cells introduced in laboratory tests. Natural killer cells destroy any cells in a person's body that exhibit early stages of cancerous growth. Similar immune changes previously have been noted in mental healthy men who smoke two or more packs of cigarettes daily.

BRUCE BOWER, *"Science News"*

Meteorology

Hurricanes, tornadoes, and concerns about long-term climate changes focused the world's attention on the weather in 1999.

Stormy Weather. The United States experienced intense bouts of both hurricanes and tornadoes in 1999. The Atlantic hurricane season yielded 12 named storms; eight of these became hurricanes, and four of those were intense (category 4 or 5). These numbers were somewhat above average, but the big news was the destruction they brought to the mainland. In late August, Hurricane Dennis caused massive beach erosion as it meandered off the North Carolina coast for days before coming onshore. Then, in mid-September, Hurricane Floyd tracked over eastern North Carolina, the Mid-Atlantic beaches, and southern Maine, bringing a record number of evacuations (exceeding 3 million), wind damage, power outages, and flooding. The worst damage overall was centered in North Carolina, where rainfall from Hurricanes Dennis, Floyd, and Irene (in October) produced an estimated $2 billion in damage.

Tornado activity was above average in both occurrence (about 1,200) and fatalities (92), although the numbers for 1999 were lower than for 1998. January saw 163 twisters—three times the previous record—largely due to an outbreak across the Mississippi Valley and Gulf coast. In early May, 70 tornadoes swept across Oklahoma and Kansas, causing more than 45 deaths, more than 900 injuries, and damage in excess of $1 billion. Strong tornadoes seemed to hit metropolitan areas—including Oklahoma City and Wichita, KS, in May; Cincinnati, OH, in April; and Salt Lake City, UT, in August—more often than in previous years.

Extreme drought conditions gripped the eastern United States for much of 1999. In many areas, precipitation during the winter was below average, and an expanse of the eastern seaboard saw no concentrated rainfall during the summer. Maryland instituted mandatory statewide water restrictions in early August, and the levels of the Great Lakes were reported to be at a 32-year low. The areas affected by the hurricanes saw partial or total reversal of the drought, but the remaining areas finished the year with a deficit. Temperatures across the nation tended to be above normal, although a notable late-season snowstorm blanketed the Ohio Valley and Northeast in March. A heat wave in July was blamed for 285 deaths in 22 states, particularly Illinois, Missouri, and Ohio.

Tropical Cyclone Vance brought 165-mph (265-km/hr) winds to Exmouth, Western Australia, in March, setting a new record for winds on the Australian mainland, but no deaths resulted. In contrast, the worst tropical cyclone to hit eastern India since the 1970s produced thousands of fatalities in November, mostly as the result of flooding.

Meanwhile, the heavy snows that fed the avalanches in the Alps (*see* SIDEBAR) melted through the spring and summer and augmented unusually heavy rains to cause flooding throughout the Danube, Loisach, and Rhine River valleys in Austria, France, Germany, and Switzerland. Heavy flooding also occurred in central and southern China, where evacuations were estimated at 2 million, and the level of the Yangtze River broke a 50-year record in July. Southeast Asia in general suffered drought through midyear, when heavy rains and flooding set in. The Middle East saw an extended drought through much of the year.

La Niña. The beginning of 1999 saw a moderately strong La Niña, the "negative phase" of El Niño featuring cooler-than-normal sea-surface temperatures and a westward shift of deep convection across the equatorial Pacific Ocean. La Niña faded in the boreal summer but strengthened again by year's end. The occurrence of El Niño and La Niña through 1997–99 provided a windfall of data for researchers, since there is usually a gap of two to five years between such events. On the other hand, areas suffering anomalous weather events caused by these patterns were eager to return to normal.

Global Climate Changes. In late December 1998 a comprehensive study of temperature data for the last 1,200 years showed that the "medieval warm period," an apparent warming between the 9th and 14th centuries, was weaker and less widespread than previously thought—implying that the current warming trend was actually more unusual than scientists believed. Another study of drought in North America over the past 2,000 years showed two "megadroughts" that dwarfed the Dust Bowl of the 1930s.

A study published in January found that increases in nighttime temperatures, possibly caused by global warming, were allowing new plants to displace native grasses on grasslands in Colorado. These nonnative plants tended to lack grazing and drought tolerance, weakening the ecosystem. Night-

Avalanches

© Rudi Blaha/AP/Wide World Photos

A snow-covered slope appears glistening, quiet, and still, but under the surface, the snowpack is stressed. Old, wind-packed layers do not bond well to newly fallen snow, and layers that have gone through cycles of freezing and thawing sometimes convert to crumbly "corn snow." Wind-fashioned drifts and overhanging shelves strain the cohesion of the grains of snow. When a small section of the snowpack is disturbed, whether by wind pressure, a falling cornice, or the slice of a ski or snowboard, the surrounding snow usually absorbs the load, but occasionally more and more of the snowpack starts to break loose.

Once in motion, the smooth layers become a turbulent jumble of air, snow, and debris rushing downhill like an express train—an avalanche! The avalanche continues until the mountain's slope flattens enough that the drag of intervening obstacles and the surface absorbs the forward momentum.

Techniques for preventing and coping with these events include avoiding avalanche-prone areas and building protective structures such as avalanche fences, made of heavy steel, and avalanche sheds, reinforced concrete covers for roads and railroad lines. In some high-value and high-traffic areas, such as ski slopes or mountain passes, avalanches are provoked intentionally, using explosives or trained skiers, to dissipate the threat before it causes an unfortunate catastrophe.

Unfortunately, these techniques can fail in unusual circumstances, such as the winter of 1998–99, when snowfall in the Alps was the heaviest in 40 years. Accumulations of 20 ft (6 m) in six weeks, and sometimes up to 6 ft (2 m) in a single day, were reported. On February 23 and 24, the ski towns of Galtür and Valzur—located in an area of Austria that had not seen a major avalanche since at least the 17th century, according to historical records—experienced massive snowslides that killed 38. Helicopters had to ferry in supplies and remove some 10,000 stranded tourists. At the same time, 100,000 people were snowed into homes and resorts in Switzerland. Across the entire Alps, more than 70 people died during avalanche season. Statistics show that there is an 86% chance of finding avalanche victims alive if they can be dug out within the first 15 minutes, but transportation problems hampered rescue efforts. In the case of Galtür, for instance, no outside help could reach the village until the next day.

George J. Huffman

time temperature increases also may be lengthening the growing season.

In another development blamed on increasing temperatures, the Larsen B and Wilkins ice shelves in the Antarctic together lost almost 1,100 sq mi (2 850 km^2) in one year, compared with 2,300 sq mi (5 960 km^2) over the previous 50 years. The remaining 6,600 sq mi (17 100 km^2) of the ice shelves were considered at significant risk of a similar fate. In southern Greenland aircraft-borne surveys showed significant thinning of ice near the coast, as much as 3 ft (1 m) per year since 1993. The decreases were attributed to more-rapid outflow to the Atlantic Ocean rather than decreased snowfall or increased melting.

According to a report released in July, the world's coral reefs could be eliminated almost totally as early as 2100 by rising ocean temperatures, which in turn were caused by global warming. Another danger to coral was the increasing level of carbon dioxide in seawater, which scientists believed was inhibiting coral growth by altering the chemistry of the oceans.

Chemicals that deplete ozone in the stratosphere declined about 3% between 1994 and 1997, evidence that the Montreal Protocol, an international agreement passed in 1987 to restore the ozone layer over about 50 years, was having some success. Methyl chloroform, a cleaning solvent, was nearly gone; however, concentrations of longer-lived chemicals continued to increase. Meanwhile, the Antarctic ozone hole shrank slightly from 1998's record size—the first decline in several years—but scientists warned that progress would be slow.

Technology. In June the National Aeronautics and Space Administration (NASA) launched QuickSCAT, a quickly launched scatterometer that replaced one lost in June 1997. Built in just 12 months, QuickSCAT provided vital near-surface wind data for oceanic areas under all weather and cloud conditions. In November, NASA launched the first major Earth Observing System satellite, named Terra (Latin for "Earth"). It carried five instruments that collectively covered more of the electromagnetic spectrum than any previous satellite. The United States and the European Organization for the Exploration of Meteorological Satellites (EUMETSAT) agreed to coordinate polar-orbit meteorological satellites in the future. Previously, the United States provided two such satellites, but EUMETSAT agreed to provide one starting in 2003.

The National Weather Service (NWS) modernization program was completed in July, 12 years and $4.5 billion after it began. The project included total replacement of the antiquated radar system, introduction of automated systems for collecting routine meteorological data, significant upgrades to communications links, and total integration of meteorological-data display at weather-forecast offices. The NWS organization also was revamped and streamlined. Officials pointed to the fact that tornado and flash-flood warnings were being created further in advance of events as evidence of the modernized system's success. At the same time, however, they cautioned that future improvements should be done incrementally to avoid the high risks of making such massive changes. In September a fire destroyed the main supercomputer used for forecasting, and long-standing backup arrangements with other NWS computers and U.S. Air Force and Navy meteorological centers were activated, pending delivery of a previously ordered replacement.

Field Experiments. Two observational studies were carried out to monitor how clouds behave: the Large-area Biosphere-Atmosphere Experiment during January and February in the tropical rain forest of western Brazil, and the Kwajalein Experiment during August and September in the tropical ocean environment around Kwajalein Atoll in the Marshall Islands. Both experiments established additional weather-balloon, meteorological-instrument-tower, rain-gauge, and radar sites to conduct coordinated observations with cloud-physics-research aircraft.

The Indian Ocean Experiment collected observations of atmospheric aerosols, tiny particles (about 1 micron in diameter) whose net effect on climate is highly uncertain. Researchers based in the Republic of Maldives used ships, aircraft, and land stations to collect data on aerosol numbers and chemistry, atmospheric gases, and standard meteorological parameters.

In the same vein, two aircraft crisscrossed the South Pacific Ocean between the Cooke Islands and South America to measure air chemistry in the second Pacific Exploratory Mission to the Tropics. The air in the region encompassed by the study is the cleanest in the world, and scientists wanted to measure how efficient the cleansing processes are.

GEORGE J. HUFFMAN
Science Systems and Applications, Inc.

Mexico

Candidates began positioning themselves for the mid-2000 national elections in which Mexican voters would select a president, a 500-seat Chamber of Deputies, and half of the 128-member Senate. The ruling Institutional Revolutionary Party (PRI) made history by choosing its nominee in a national primary. Mindful of the economic emergencies that have marred the last four presidential transitions, chief executive Ernesto Zedillo sought to "armor" his country against a similar crisis when he completes his six-year term.

Politics. The PRI has controlled the presidency since the party's founding in 1929. Traditionally, the outgoing president "fingered" his successor in a maneuver known as the *dedazo*, after the Spanish word for "finger," *dedo*. A positive experiment with primaries or *consultas* in gubernatorial contests in 1998 and early 1999 convinced Zedillo—an advocate of democratic reform—to renounce the time-honored *dedazo* in favor of an open nominating procedure, which culminated in a November 7 primary.

Zedillo did not remain indifferent to the selection process. He handpicked the PRI's president and secretary-general, and named former Government Secretary Fernando Gutiérrez Barrios, a tough-as-nails traditionalist renowned for his loyalty to the PRI, to referee the intramural contest. President Zedillo also turned thumbs down on two prospective contenders—the billionaire governor of Veracruz and son of a former president, Miguel Alemán Velasco, and Social Development Secretary Esteban Moctezuma Barragán, a Zedillo confidant whose political skills did not match his ambitions. As a result, only four veteran PRI members vied for the party's nomination—former Government Secretary Francisco Labastida Ochoa, who had held three key cabinet posts and served as governor of Sinaloa; Roberto Madrazo, who had held seats in the Chamber of Deputies and the Senate before winning the governorship of Tabasco in 1994; Manuel Bartlett, the former governor of Puebla, who—as government interior minister—had ensured the PRI's triumph in the fraud-ridden 1988 presidential race; and Humberto Roque, a former legislator and erstwhile party president.

Party traditionalists or "dinosaurs" groused that throwing open this critical choice would wreak havoc on the party. They warned darkly of the possibility of an embarrassingly low turnout, the inability to recruit militants to staff 64,000 voting places nationwide, and the possibility that a bare-knuckled internecine battle would rupture the faction-ridden party. The upshot, naysayers insisted, would be a victory by the center-right National Action Party (PAN) or the leftist-nationalist Democratic Revolutionary Party (PRD). The wisdom of the president's rejecting such advice became evident on November 7. Despite cold weather and rain in many areas, nearly 10 million Mexicans went to the polls, awarding the lion's share of their votes to Labastida. So few serious irregularities marred the balloting that even Zedillo's nemesis Madrazo, whom PRD insiders had urged to jump ship, vowed to stick with the PRI.

© Heriberto Rodriguez/Reuters/Archive Photos

Francisco Labastida Ochoa emerged the winner as Mexico's Institutional Revolutionary Party (PRI) held its first-ever presidential primary on Nov. 7, 1999.

The *consulta* not only boosted the 57-year-old Labastida's credibility, it also ensured that future presidential aspirants would stress issues, popular appeal, and organizational prowess rather than skill at toadying to the incumbent. The *consulta* also furnished the PRI evidence of its strength and weakness in 300 districts from which members of Congress would be elected in July 2000, and buried forever the authoritarian *dedazo* as a selection device for chief executives.

Zedillo's entourage, it must be noted, unmistakably signaled its preference for Labastida, deemed most likely to continue the nation's market-oriented reforms. These cues emboldened a majority of governors to weigh in on behalf of the president's favorite. Nonetheless, Zedillo snatched the PRI from underdog status by involving almost one fifth of the electorate in a decision that used to be made by one man. Provided the party's postprimary unity endures, the process also endowed Labastida with a solid advantage.

Officials from these two parties devoted months to exploring the possibility of a joint candidate to oust the PRI from the presidency. After protracted, highly publicized parleys, the negotiations collapsed in September 1999, because neither former Mexico City Mayor and PRD candidate Cuauhtémoc Cárdenas nor PAN standard-bearer Vicente Fox would step aside for the other. Cárdenas, 65, had been battling for the presidency since he bolted the PRI in 1987, and seemed to believe he was destined to become chief executive like his father, Lázaro. Militating against Cárdenas' presidential prospects was his poor performance as Mexico City's mayor. Further diminishing his chances were venomous attacks from his former ally, Porfirio Muñoz Ledo, who accepted the presidential bid of the small Authentic Party of the Mexican Revolution. Insiders viewed this move as a means to divide the electorate further and enhance the electoral prospects of Fox, who—it was alleged—would bring the wily Muñoz Ledo into a top cabinet post.

Fox, the 57-year-old former president of Coca-Cola in Mexico and Guanajuato state governor since 1995, had been barnstorming the country for two years in pursuit of "PANista" support. He had to launch his campaign early, because party traditionalists looked askance at the Guanajuato native, who formed part of National Action's "Northern Barbarian" wing, composed largely of hard-charging entrepreneurs turned politicians.

As Zedillo entered the last year of his tenure, he boasted the approval of more than 60% of citizens interviewed by public-opinion firms. Reasons for his remarkable popularity sprang from his perceived honesty, as well as his promptness in responding to victims of natural disasters. When, in October, storm-driven floods devastated Mexico's southern states, the chief executive made nine trips to affected areas and offered assistance to the 300,000 people driven from their homes by mud slides and torrential rains.

Economics. Zedillo made good on campaign promises to keep a lid on official spending, limiting public debt to 1.25% of gross domestic product (GDP). Two measures attested to the confidence in his no-nonsense economic management: Foreign investment rose from $7.6 billion in 1996 to $10 billion in 1999; during the same period, hard-currency reserves nearly doubled, from $17.5 billion to $30 billion. Meanwhile, GDP expanded 3.5% amid declining prices—with growth of 4.5% and an inflation rate of 10% predicted for 2000.

President Zedillo left several institutional legacies to fortify Mexico's economy. To begin with, he placed the central bank on a quasi-independent status to militate against the politically motivated expansion of the monetary supply that took place during Carlos Salinas' last year in office, precipitating the 1995–96 crisis. Zedillo also sought to increase woefully low domestic savings, expand bank deposits, and provide retirement income for workers. Thus, he devised the Pension Fund Administrators program (Afores), permitting more than 12 million workers to establish individual retirement accounts. By mid-1998, one year after the creation of Afores, 96% of eligible participants had affiliated with the program, to which employers also contributed.

Moreover, Zedillo established the Bank Savings Protection Institute (IPAB) to supervise and rehabilitate private banks that the government had rescued during the 1995–96 financial crisis. Although critics

MEXICO • Information Highlights

Official Name: United Mexican States.
Location: Southern North America.
Area: 761,602 sq mi (1 972 550 km²).
Population (July 1999 est.): 100,294,036.
Chief Cities (November 1995 census): Mexico City (Federal District and surrounding municipalities), the capital, 15,012,848; Guadalajara, 1,633,216; Nezahualcóyotl, 1,233,868; Puebla, 1,122,569; Monterrey, 1,088,143; León, 1,042,132; Ciudad Juárez, 1,011,786.
Government: *Head of state and government,* Ernesto Zedillo Ponce de León, president (took office Dec. 1, 1994). *Legislature*—National Congress: Senate and Chamber of Deputies.
Monetary Unit: Peso (9.4075 pesos equal U.S.$1, Dec. 13, 1999).
Gross Domestic Product (1998 est. U.S.$): $815,300,-000,000 (purchasing power parity).
Economic Indexes (1998, 1990 = 100): *Consumer Prices,* all items, 422.0; food, 408.9. *Industrial Production,* 132.2.
Foreign Trade (1998 est. U.S.$): *Imports,* $111,500,000,000; *exports,* $117,500,000,000.

attacked the extremely costly bailout, Zedillo's failure to act might have delivered the coup de grâce to the country's wobbly banking system. Finally, in mid-1999, Zedillo's regime, which benefited from a brisk upturn in oil earnings, negotiated a standby credit of $4.12 billion with the International Monetary Fund (IMF) to support the government's 1999–2000 economic program. Even though Mexico did not plan to draw on these funds, Zedillo wanted to immunize the nation against the financial distress associated with past changes in administrations.

Prospects. Zedillo deserves credit for preparing the country for sustained growth and for changing the PRI's nominating procedure. Yet, Zedillo's reforms proceeded without the agreement of key political actors on either new rules of the game or institutions for resolving disputes. Three examples illustrate this threat to the country's stability.

First, even though three successive administrations had endorsed and advanced the nation's economic opening, in 1999 the PRD savaged neoliberalism, while the PAN gave only qualified support for much-needed private investment in the electricity industry. Three of the four PRI primary candidates, moreover, lambasted free-market economic policies.

Second, the presence of a half-dozen parties in Congress meant representation for many more interests than when the San Lázaro legislative palace constituted a virtual PRI clubhouse. Rather than striving to strengthen their branch vis-à-vis the executive, the various groups of lawmakers too often eschewed building coalitions for booing speakers, engaging in fistfights, and shouting insults at one another. According to respected analyst Luis Rubio, these tactics reveal that "not all politicians and parties appear satisfied with existing mechanisms of representation or, even more serious and worrisome, they are not disposed to accept electoral results." For example, instead of working to resolve a strike that closed the 260,000-student National Autonomous University of Mexico (UNAM) for more than eight months in 1999, leftist leaders in the capital's city council aligned with the demonstrators against the courageous rector who had sought to raise tuition from pennies to $140 per year. The strike raged even after UNAM's governing body agreed that increased payments could be voluntary.

Third, despite PRI-PAN agreements over budgets in 1997 and 1998, the rescue of the banking system, and some privatization measures, intolerance pervaded the system. This fact manifested itself during the negotiations between the PAN and the PRD over a possible joint presidential candidate in 2000. Fox's overwhelming advantage in public-opinion polls aside, Cárdenas' allies insisted on selecting the nominee in a national primary. They favored this method not because it would produce the strongest standard-bearer, but because they hoped to manipulate the voting to defeat the PAN front-runner.

The inchoate political process militated against officials being able to combat corruption, curb drug trafficking, and eradicate poverty. Failure of Mexico's leaders to resolve problems that concern average citizens could discredit the major parties.

Foreign Affairs. Although President Zedillo developed a constructive personal relationship with U.S. President Bill Clinton, the run-up to presidential elections sharpened nationalist sensibilities in Mexico. Evidence of tensions surfaced in September, when the Mexican army returned 72 Vietnam war–vintage helicopters that the Pentagon had provided in 1996 to assist in drug interdiction. Even before two Mexican pilots perished in a March 1998 Huey crash, the army was having problems keeping the choppers in service.

In early November, U.S. Secretary of State Madeleine Albright stated that drug trafficking and organized crime along the U.S. frontier with Mexico constitute "a major threat to U.S. national security." Noting that Mexico was enjoying increased economic and political stability, Albright urged the Zedillo administration to upgrade its law-enforcement agencies, long deemed infused with corruption. This comment, which raised hackles in Mexico City, came on the heels of U.S. drug czar Barry McCaffrey's report that 55% of cocaine entering the United States came across the Mexican border. As for other matters, Secretary Albright stressed that the neighboring countries had signed an agreement in February, calling for cooperation to decrease the number of deaths at the border. Late in the year, Mexican authorities worked closely with their U.S. counterparts to investigate an alleged "mass grave" on a farm just below the border city of Ciudad Juárez.

Zedillo postponed an early-December U.S. visit when opposition lawmakers demanded budgetary concessions before authorizing a presidential trip.

George W. Grayson
College of William & Mary

Microbiology

The year 1999 was noted for discoveries of fossils of early life and a hitherto unknown bacterial lithotroph, a double-pronged attack on the influenza virus, and an early warning of a possible epidemic of a flesh-eating bacterium.

Fossils. In studying the fossil record of early life-forms, paleontologists work with chemical compounds called biomarkers. These are geologically stable molecules known to be derived from specific groups of microorganisms. Until 1999, no biomarkers had been found in sedimentary rocks that were formed more than 1,700 million years ago (Ma).

In August 1999, J.J. Brocks of the University of Sydney, Australia, and his coworkers reported on their study of an exceptionally well-preserved deposit of shale (fine-grained sedimentary rock formed of hardened clay) located in northwestern Australia. The shale has been dated 2,700 Ma and was found to contain two very different types of biomarkers. One group of biomarkers consisted of 2-methylhopanes (chemical compounds that are found only in the cyanobacteria). These are prokaryotic (without nucleus) microorganisms that contain chlorophyll and carry on photosynthesis. The other group of biomarkers consisted of steranes (chemical compounds that are found only in eukaryotic—with nucleus—microorganisms.)

These discoveries extended the molecular fossil record by 1 billion years and demonstrated that complex microorganisms had evolved close to 3 billion years ago.

Bacterial Lithotroph. All organisms, humans included, must obtain energy in order to carry on their activities. Most do so through the breakdown of organic compounds and, because of this, are called organotrophs. Certain bacteria, called lithotrophs, are able to obtain the needed energy from chemical reactions involving inorganic compounds. Although a number of such chemical reactions and the bacteria that can perform them are well known, until recently, no bacterium had been discovered that can obtain energy from combining ammonium and nitrite (anammox reaction), which results in the formation of water and the release of the gas nitrogen.

M. Strous and his colleagues at the Delft University of Technology, the Netherlands, discovered a bacterium that can perform the anammox reaction. The importance of this discovery lies in the fact that the increased use of fertilizers in agriculture has resulted in an increased deposit of both nitrites and ammonium in wastewater from farms. This water eventually pollutes rivers. This newly discovered bacterium eventually may be used to clean up the pollution.

Influenza. After an influenza (flu) virus invades a cell and multiplies, the new virus particles that emerge are bound together in a bundle by the chemical compound neuraminic acid. Before they can infect other cells, the viruses must separate from each other. This is accomplished by the enzyme neuraminidase, which the viral particles have on their surfaces. Among the drugs used to combat a flu infection, zanamivir appears to be most effective. It binds to neuraminidase, preventing it from acting, with the result that the virus particles remain in a bundle and are unable to infect new cells.

A.S. Monto and his coworkers at the University of Michigan, Ann Arbor, investigated whether zanamivir also can act as a vaccine, protecting people from infection by the flu virus. The scientists found that when the drug, in powdered form, was inhaled once a day for four weeks during the height of the flu season, it effectively cut the rate of infection by 67% and also reduced the severity of the disease in those who did contract it. The discovery of a drug that can treat as well as prevent a disease represents a major advance.

Flesh-Eating Bacteria. Most bacterial infections of the skin are restricted to relatively small areas and result in limited cell destruction. Unfortunately, there are virulent bacteria that tend to spread to underlying cells, killing large numbers of them and causing a wasting away of the soft tissues (flesh) of the body.

One flesh-eating bacterium, *Mycobacterium ulcerans*, occurs worldwide and periodically affects large numbers of people in a particular area. This occurred recently in Ghana. The bacterium infects and destroys both skin cells and the underlying fat tissue, resulting in open lesions that may spread. The lesion is referred to as a Buruli ulcer, after a region in Uganda where many cases occurred. No one knows where the microbe usually lives or how it is transmitted. Outbreaks of the disease appear to be associated with regions containing stagnant or slow-moving bodies of water. World Health Organization scientists fear the emergence of a disease with possible epidemic consequences.

LOUIS LEVINE, *City College of New York*

Middle East

The deaths of the kings of Jordan and Morocco, as well as a change of leadership in Israel, made the Middle East a very different place at the end of 1999 than it had been at the beginning of the year. Events, as well as long-term factors, offered many reasons for feeling either pessimistic or optimistic about the region. On the whole, however, perhaps a guarded optimism would be justified.

On the negative side, in a number of countries there were still many extremists, fanatics, and terrorist groups ready to do their worst to destroy whatever attempts countries might be making to repair breaches. There was no guarantee that any of the many negotiations in progress at the end of 1999 would reach a successful conclusion. And there were some situations where there was no goodwill observable at all. For example, Iran continued its unremitting hostility toward Israel, with its supreme religious leader, Ayatollah Ali Khamenei, calling for Israel's total destruction in a December 31 speech. Iraq continued on its maverick way throughout 1999, with no kind of supervision or inspection of its arms program in place. Also, the Middle East had to grapple with other major problems, such as water scarcity, soil erosion, and increasing drug usage in some states.

But there was a large number of positive developments as well. Broken links were being reestablished, and solutions at least were being attempted. The diplomacy of Abdullah II, the new king of Jordan, who was seeking to create good relations with all Arab states "without exceptions," was a good example of this. Indeed, Jordan managed to restore normal diplomatic relations with Kuwait, which had been ruptured, understandably, by Jordan's moral support of Iraq in the Persian Gulf war of 1991. Similarly, Iranian President Mohammed Khatami actively attempted to create better relations with at least some neighboring states—though not with Iraq. In late October, Mauritania established full diplomatic ties with Israel, to the consternation of Arab League officials and the Palestinians. It thus became the third Arab nation (after Egypt and Jordan) to have such relations.

The greatest examples of auspicious ongoing developments that seemed to point in the direction of peace were Israel's separate dealings with the Palestinians and Syria. Third, but less important, was the newly cooperative spirit evinced by Libyan leader Muammar el-Qaddafi.

Israeli-Palestinian Relations. Under the Wye Agreement of October 1998, Israel had committed itself to a timetable of ceding to the PLO control, or joint control, of certain percentages of West Bank territory. Implementation of the agreement, however, had ground to a virtual halt because of Israeli Premier Benjamin Netanyahu's not-

Thousands of cheering Moroccans turned out to greet their new king, Mohamed VI, as he visited the northern part of the country in October 1999. Mohamed succeeded to the throne when his father, King Hassan II, died on July 23 after a 38-year reign.

unfounded concerns about the security of Israel. Palestinian leader Yasir Arafat had threatened to declare the areas under Palestinian control an independent sovereign state on May 4, but, under heavy pressure from the United States and other countries, he did not do so.

In May elections for prime minister, Netanyahu was defeated by Ehud Barak. With Barak's assumption of office in July, a new spirit of conciliation seemed to inform the situation, especially when the new prime minister set a goal to achieve a final treaty with the Palestinians by September 2000. From mid-1999 on, Israel and the Palestinians made progress toward settling some issues, although the process was bumpy, and sometimes it stalled altogether. And at the end of the year, the major and most difficult questions still were unresolved.

Soon after taking office, Barak met with President Hosni Mubarak of Egypt, King Abdullah II of Jordan, and Arafat. From July 14–20 he was in Washington, DC, where he appeared to establish warm personal relations with U.S. President Bill Clinton. Among other points agreed to in the Washington meetings was that the United States and Britain should play less prominent roles in the peace process—a program that again proved unrealistic, as later it took U.S. prodding on several occasions to push the stalled talks back in motion.

Israeli and Palestinian negotiators met more than a dozen times in August, but it was only in September, at the end of a five-day visit to the region by U.S. Secretary of State Madeleine Albright, that a new accord was signed. The agreement set February 2000 as the date for laying out a broad agenda for a permanent peace accord, to be achieved in time to meet Barak's September 2000 deadline. The formidable agenda to be addressed included the final Palestinian-Israeli borders, the question of Palestinian refugees, and the status of Jerusalem, seen by each side as its capital. The pact also set a schedule for progressive withdrawals by Israel: one installment in September, another in November, and a third in January 2000, by which time 40% of the West Bank would be under full Palestinian or joint control. An agreement also was reached on the return of some Palestinian prisoners from Israeli jails. Clinton, Barak, and Arafat met in Oslo, Norway, on November 2.

A major step in ameliorating life for the Palestinians took place on October 25, with the opening by Israel of a "safe passage," a 28-mi (45-km) route between the Gaza Strip and the West Bank, promised in 1995. But the Palestinians held up a scheduled transfer of 5% of West Bank land in November, because they were unhappy with the actual areas proffered. On December 22, Barak and Arafat met in Ramallah on the West Bank to bridge their differences on this question and on that of Israeli settlements, but the deadlock ended on Jan. 4, 2000, only with an agreement on the choice of parcels of land to be allocated. The Israeli pullout took place the next day. A further 6.1% was set to be transferred in late January.

Israel and Syria. Barak's election as prime minister also created a more cordial atmosphere in Syrian-Israeli relations, but little happened from July through November. The sticking point was Syrian President Hafiz al-Assad's adamant insistence that discussion of any other issues must be preceded by Israel's total withdrawal from the Golan Heights, which it had held since 1967. It was thus a surprise when President Clinton, after another Middle East trip by Secretary Albright, announced on December 8 that Syria and Israel had decided to resume peace talks, in abeyance since 1996.

Speculation was rife as to motives, particularly Assad's. It was thought that Assad, 69 and ailing, wanted to conclude a peace himself and not leave the issue to his heir, presumably his son Bashar. Economic issues may have played a part as well: Syria's hardly robust economy needed foreign capital and technology, which only good relations with the United States could facilitate.

Barak certainly appeared to have no pressing reason to give up the Golan Heights, a tremendous asset. Being only 40 mi (64 km) from Damascus, the Heights possess strategic dominance. They also have ample water, rich arable land—and a large number of Israeli settlers who had been led by their government to believe they were secure there permanently. For Israel, a tiny country with oddly shaped borders, the whole idea of "land for peace" was a tremendous gamble. But successful talks with Syria could lead to a resolution of the continuing military conflict between Israel and Lebanon, which was unobtainable without Syrian cooperation.

Preliminary talks began in mid-December. On January 3 more-substantive discussions began between Barak and Syrian Foreign Minister Farouk Shareh in the small town of Shepherdstown, WV. President Clinton went there occasionally to spur on the participants. Meanwhile, Arafat and the Palestinians worried that their less weighty talks would be put on the back burner.

Libya. After years of delays, a breakthrough occurred in the case of two Libyan nationals accused of the terrorist bombing of Pan Am Flight 103 over Lockerbie, Scotland, in December 1988. For years, Libya had refused to surrender the suspects because of U.S.-British insistence that their trial take place in either the United States or Britain.

In July 1998 the British and U.S. governments had suggested an ingenious compromise: that the suspects should be extradited to The Hague, Netherlands, to be tried under Scots Law. After many months of evasion by Libya—and protracted mediation by the United Nations (UN), Egypt, and Saudi Arabia—Qaddafi agreed to the proposal, and the suspects were flown to The Hague on April 5. The trial was set for May 2000.

Libya immediately began to reap the fruits of its long-delayed cooperation. Economic sanctions, in place since 1991, were lifted by the UN; Libyan oil began to reach markets normally; and international flights to and from Libya resumed.

Deaths of Three Kings. The deaths of King Hussein of Jordan on February 7 and of King Hassan of Morocco on July 23 signaled the end of an era not only in their countries, but in the region as a whole. There were some similarities. Both had reigned for a long time: Hussein for 46 years, Hassan for 38. Both were voices for moderation in a region where that was relatively uncommon. Morocco, of course, did not have to face the dilemmas imposed on Jordan by its geographic location, but it had to deal with radical Algeria on its eastern border and the still-unresolved matter of the Polisarios and Western Sahara to the southwest. They were succeeded by their sons, Mohamed VI in Morocco and Abdullah II in Jordan.

The emir of Bahrain, Sheikh Isa bin Salman Al Khalifa, died of a heart attack at the age of 65 on March 6. He had become ruler of Bahrain after his father's death in 1961 and took the title of emir upon his country's independence from Britain in 1971. Under his leadership, Bahrain developed relatively liberal domestic and foreign policies, compared to other Middle Eastern countries. The emir was popular among his people and well regarded by the West, particularly the United States, which has military bases in Bahrain. His son, Sheikh Hamad bin Isa Al Khalifa, assumed the throne.

Bin Laden and Ocalan. A great deal of the world's attention in 1999 focused on two non-royal figures—Osama bin Laden and Abdullah Ocalan. The former, an Islamic extremist, was wanted in the United States to be tried on charges of plotting the bombings in 1998 of the U.S. embassies in Kenya and Tanzania, which killed 224 people. Bin Laden took refuge in Afghanistan, and the Taliban regime there refused to extradite him. The United States and later the United Nations responded by imposing international sanctions on Afghanistan.

Ocalan, the leader of Kurdish guerrillas rebelling against the Turkish government, was arrested in Kenya in February by Turkish special agents. In May he was put on trial. During the proceedings, he urged reconciliation on the Kurdish nationalists he formerly led. Nevertheless, he was found guilty of treason and of causing as many as 20,000 deaths, and he was sentenced to death. It was uncertain whether the sentence ever would be carried out, however, as doing so would jeopardize Turkey's bid for membership in the European Union (EU).

Other Developments. Two natural products, water and oil, were important in 1999. The region endured the most arid year in three decades or more, and this triggered serious contentions about water between Syria and Iraq on one side, and Turkey (where both the Tigris and Euphrates Rivers originate) on the other, as well as between Jordan and Israel....Oil prices surged upward dramatically during 1999, mainly because the members of the Organization of Petroleum Exporting Countries (OPEC) and several other oil-producing nations adhered to strict production quotas they had set in the spring. The price per barrel, as low as $11 in late 1998, by year's end was around $27, a level not seen since the time of the Gulf war in 1991. This relieved the financial stringency that the oil-producing countries had been suffering since 1997....With regard to the great new source of oil, the Caspian region, the United States decided in November to lend full support to a route that would bring oil from Baku, the capital of Azerbaijan, through Georgia to Ceyhan, a Turkish port on the Mediterranean. The route would avoid Russia entirely and had an estimated cost of $2.4 billion....In Kuwait a newly elected parliament faced a reform agenda but voted down the most significant item on it, a proposal to give the vote to women.

ARTHUR CAMPBELL TURNER
University of California, Riverside

Military Affairs

As was often the case during the Cold War, and more recently in the post–Cold War era, the world's major military powers pondered questions of arming and disarming as the 20th century drew to an end. In Washington the Senate refused to ratify the Comprehensive Test Ban Treaty (CTBT) that was to have been the final step in stopping the proliferation of nuclear weapons. The United States suggested to Russia that the Antiballistic Missile (ABM) Treaty be modified so as to permit Washington to deploy a scaled-down missile-defense system. The Chinese celebrated their nation's 50th birthday with a massive military parade that signaled Beijing's drive to attain modern military status, possibly with the help of secret information stolen from U.S. laboratories and businesses. For its part, the United States moved ahead with the testing of an antiballistic-missile system, and a deal was struck in Congress to commence building a limited number of F-22 jet fighters to provide air superiority in the 21st century. Even as it looked to the future, the United States had to contend with the consequences of past conflicts in Korea, the Persian Gulf, and Kosovo.

Comprehensive Test Ban Treaty. On October 13 the Senate rejected the CTBT, 51 to 48. The vote was generally along party lines, with all of the 51 "nay" votes coming from Republicans. Four Republicans crossed over to vote, with 44 Democrats, in favor; one Democratic senator, Robert C. Byrd of West Virginia, voted "present."

The CTBT dates from 1996, when all five of the declared nuclear-weapon states at that time—Britain, China, France, Russia, and the United States—signed the agreement. Since then, 154 nations had signed; however, China and Russia, now joined by the United States, have not ratified the agreement. For the treaty to take effect, the 44 nations with nuclear weapons, or the capability to develop them, must ratify it. By late 1999, 26 nations had done so.

The treaty contains four major provisions. It permanently prohibits all testing of nuclear weapons. It establishes a global network of stations to monitor and verify compliance. There is a procedure whereby inspectors can investigate potential test sites that appear to be suspicious. Experiments may be conducted to prove the safety and reliability of existing nuclear warheads, provided no nuclear detonations are involved.

Advocates of nuclear-arms control and disarmament viewed the CTBT as the capstone for a series of treaties negotiated by the United States and the Soviet Union that were designed to stop the proliferation of nuclear weapons. The process began in 1963 with the Partial Nuclear Test Ban Treaty, which prohibited nuclear-weapon testing in the atmosphere, in space, or underwater. Underground testing was permitted, as both Washington and Moscow sought to develop a greater spectrum of nuclear weapons. In 1968 came the Non-Proliferation of Nuclear Weapons Treaty, in which the nuclear-weapon states agreed not to assist nonnuclear-weapon states in developing nuclear weapons, and the nonnuclear-weapon states

© Chuck Robinson/AP/Wide World Photos

In April the Pentagon called up reservists, including members of the U.S. Air Force Reserve, left, *to "fill critical support positions" in the air campaign being waged by the North Atlantic Treaty Organization (NATO) against Yugoslavia. To help alleviate difficulties in recruiting and retraining, a 4.8% pay raise for U.S. military personnel was enacted in 1999.*

agreed not to do so. This treaty also contained a commitment by the nuclear-weapon states to move toward nuclear disarmament. The Threshold Test Ban Treaty of 1974 prohibited nuclear tests above 150 kilotons (equivalent to 150,000 tons of TNT), which was the detectable level at that time.

Senate Majority Leader Trent Lott (R-MS) explained why his party opposed the CTBT with references to its flawed character. His concern focused on the belief that low-level nuclear tests could not be verified with existing technology; that the United States needed to test warheads in its active arsenal to verify their safety and reliability; and that nations such as Iraq and North Korea probably would not be constrained by the treaty. For his part, President Bill Clinton angrily denounced the Senate Republicans in a press conference the day after the CTBT defeat when he said, "By this vote, the Senate majority has turned its back on 50 years of American leadership against the spread of weapons of mass destruction. They are saying America does not need to lead either by effort or by example." He also accused the Republicans of engaging in a "new isolationism" that endangers U.S. security. Despite the defeat of the CTBT, the president pledged that the United States would continue its moratorium on all testing and asked the other nuclear nations to follow suit.

Antiballistic Missile (ABM) Treaty. In the fall the Clinton administration suggested that changing times warranted that consideration be given to altering the ABM Treaty of 1972. In that treaty the United States and the Soviet Union agreed to limit severely the testing and deployment of antiballistic missiles. Since the treaty was ratified, the United States has made technological advances that some claim may make it possible to shoot down one or a few incoming nuclear warheads; and there has developed a growing threat to the United States from a number of nuclear-capable nations—particularly those termed rogue nations, such as Iraq, Iran, and North Korea. The amendments in the ABM Treaty sought by the Clinton administration would allow the United States to construct a battle-management radar complex in Alaska, together with 100 ballistic missile interceptors, to be completed about 2005; and a similar deployment in North Dakota with an operational date of 2010.

U.S. negotiators approached the Russians with the proposal that the United States would help Moscow complete an advanced radar installation in Siberia, near the city of Irkutsk, and might share information gathered on missile launches by American early-warning radars, and possibly satellites, in return for the requested modifications in the ABM Treaty. What Washington wanted was to change the treaty so that the United States could deploy a limited ABM force as a response to the threat of a small number of warheads being launched by accident from China or Russia, or the more likely possibility of a small number of warheads being launched intentionally by minor nuclear powers.

The problem in persuading the Russians to accept changes in the ABM Treaty was to convince Moscow that the deployment of the U.S. ABM system, which the Russians probably could not duplicate because of fiscal constraints and technological problems, would not jeopardize Moscow's security by undercutting the Russian nuclear deterrent. Since China was not a signatory to the ABM Treaty, there was no need to obtain Beijing's concurrence in the changes. However, there was a different problem in regard to China. The Chinese already had announced that they would object strongly should the United States deploy an ABM system in Asia, particularly on the island of Taiwan, which Beijing regards as a renegade province that ultimately should be returned to Chinese control.

Although Washington officials claimed their plan posed little threat to Russian nuclear-deterrent forces, because Moscow's large number of warheads and decoys easily could overwhelm it, the Russians rejected the U.S. proposal. Russian spokesmen said any effort to alter the ABM Treaty would destroy the entire system of arms-control and disarmament treaties that have led in recent years to dramatic scaling back in the number of nuclear weapons maintained by both nations. They feared that the modifications in the treaty sought by the United States might provide a basis for constructing what could become the building blocks for a much more robust defense system that seriously would threaten Russia's deterrent capability. Both Russia and China submitted a resolution to the United Nations Security Council calling for "strict compliance" with the ABM Treaty.

Ballistic Missiles and Antiballistic-Missile Defenses. In September the Central Intelligence Agency (CIA) released a report that described as "most likely" the possibility

© Pablo Martinez Monsivais/AP/Wide World Photos

On July 28, 1999, U.S. Secretary of Defense William Cohen announced that Gen. Joseph Ralston, left, *vice-chairman of the Joint Chiefs of Staff, would succeed Gen. Wesley Clark as supreme commander of NATO.*

that North Korea would obtain a long-range-missile capability by 2015; "probable" in the case of Iran; and "possible" in regard to Iraq. In midsummer it was expected widely that North Korea would test its Taepodong 2 long-range missile, which is thought capable of carrying a nuclear warhead. However, in September the Clinton administration reached a tentative deal with North Korea under which Washington would relax the trade embargo imposed during the Korean War if North Korea would postpone the missile test.

In response to the growing threat of missile attack from small states, the United States moved forward in testing one component of a new national missile-defense system that is a much-downsized version of the Strategic Defense Initiative (SDI) suggested by President Ronald Reagan in 1983. That plan called for building a multilayered defense to protect the entire nation against a full-scale Soviet attack. Technical difficulties had prevented the development of the SDI. In October a Minuteman ICBM was launched from Vandenberg Air Force Base in California that subsequently released a dummy warhead and decoy balloon over the Pacific. The mock warhead was intercepted and destroyed upon impact by a "kill vehicle" carried aloft by another Minuteman launched from the U.S. test site on Kwajalein in the Marshall Islands. Additional tests were planned early in 2000, with President Clinton expected to make a decision on deployment of the system in June.

In November a report by an independent panel appointed by the Pentagon to assess the technical viability of the proposed system was released. The 40-page document was critical of the work done so far and noted that the program contained a "high risk of failure." Cited among the chief problems were inadequate testing, management fragmentation, and the imposition of deadlines based more upon political expediency than technical capability. Despite the gloomy findings in the report, Republicans in the capital, led by Sen. Thad Cochran (MS), continued to support the missile-defense plan because of their concern about the risks from ballistic-missile attack.

The U.S. Defense Budget. Despite Clinton's criticism of congressional Republicans for including "pork-barrel" projects of dubious military value in the 1999 national defense-spending bill, the president signed the $268 billion bill into law. It had as its centerpiece a 4.8% pay raise for the nation's military personnel. It was hoped that the pay increase would help to alleviate the problems the services, except for the Marines, were encountering with recruiting and retaining military personnel. The president's criticism focused upon his allegation that the Republicans had added unnecessary big-ticket items, such as planes and ships, to the bill that were not requested by the Department of Defense, but that would provide jobs to workers in the home districts of powerful politicians.

One of the most controversial aspects of the defense-budget debate concerned whether the request by the air force for a new jet fighter should be funded fully. The plane in question was the F-22 Raptor, described by Secretary of Defense William Cohen as "the cornerstone of our national global airpower in the 21st century." In a deal negotiated between the Senate and House of Representatives, up to six of the $200 million jets would be built and tested before a final decision was made on combat deployment in the next year to 18 months. Part of the reservations about the plane involved the question of whether the United States could afford the F-22, as well as two other aircraft: the Joint Strike Fighter—intended for the air force, navy, Marines, plus a number of allies—and an updated version of the navy's F/A-18, termed the F/A-18E/F Super Hornet. The estimated cost over the next decade for all three jets was $350 billion.

Combat Readiness. A report in November that two of the army's ten divisions were rated as unprepared for battle after a routine inspection raised concerns about the combat readiness of the U.S. military. In particular, some experts doubted whether the armed forces would be able to fight two wars simultaneously. Republicans in Congress blamed the Clinton administration for not allotting enough of the federal budget to defense. Others disputed that argument, saying that Pentagon spending per soldier was higher in 1999 than it was in 1991 during the Persian Gulf war. Part of the problem was attributed to the difficulty the military was having in recruiting soldiers; for instance, in the year ending September 30, the army had enlisted 6,300 fewer recruits than it had deemed necessary.

The China Threat. Although the major successor state to the Soviet Union, Russia, retained the strategic nuclear capability to devastate the United States, some American politicians and pundits were voicing more concern over the threat from Beijing than from Moscow. There were several reasons for this:

• On October 1, National Day, when the Chinese celebrated the 50th anniversary of the founding of the People's Republic of China, Beijing's Tiananmen Square was used to showcase China's growing military might. As jets roared overhead, President Jiang Zemin reviewed waves of goose-stepping troops and row upon row of tanks and various kinds of missiles. The scene reminded observers of the annual military parades in Moscow's Red Square during the height of the Cold War. Those involved with national-security matters argued whether China was on its way to replace the Soviet Union as the primary external threat to the United States.

• In Congress the Select Committee on U.S. National Security and Military/Commercial Concerns with the People's Republic of China issued what was called the Cox Report, named after the committee's chairman, Rep. Christopher Cox (R-CA). The basic findings of the Cox Report were: "The People's Republic of China (PRC) has stolen design information on the United States' most advanced thermonuclear weapons"; "The Select Committee judges that the PRC's next generation of thermonuclear weapons, currently under development, will exploit elements of stolen U.S. design information"; and "PRC penetration of our national weapons laboratories spans at least the past several decades and almost certainly continues today." (*See also* CHINA—*Special Report.*)

• The continued tough rhetoric from Beijing that Taiwan is a "renegade province" of China, and thus subject to being incorporated physically into China, raised a question that did not receive a definitive answer from the Clinton administration: Would the United States defend Taiwan and attack China, should Beijing attempt an invasion of the island?

The Aftermaths of Three Wars. Forty-nine years after an alleged massacre of South Korean civilians under a railroad bridge at No Gun Ri, President Clinton ordered the Pentagon to begin an investigation. According to the recollections of survivors and U.S. infantrymen, members of the 2d Battalion, 7th Cavalry, shot Korean civilians upon orders of their officers, who were concerned the refugees had been infiltrated by North Korean soldiers.

Eight years after the expulsion of Saddam Hussein's forces from Kuwait by a coalition of forces led by the United States, American and British jets continued to patrol northern and southern "no-fly zones" over Iraq. Pilots frequently attacked Iraqi radar and antiaircraft sites, which they claimed acted in a hostile fashion. According to Baghdad, such attacks killed civilians as well as soldiers.

Seven months after forces of the North Atlantic Treaty Organization (NATO) expelled Serb troops from the Yugoslav province of Kosovo, both NATO and U.S. military experts were debating the lessons to be drawn from what some called the "first humanitarian war," a reference to NATO's goal of protecting Kosovars from ethnic cleansing ordered by Yugoslav President Slobodan Milosevic. The aspect of the conflict that attracted the most analysis was that only airpower was used. (*See also* THE KOSOVO CRISIS, page 78.)

ROBERT M. LAWRENCE
Colorado State University

Morocco

King Hassan II of Morocco died in Rabat on July 23, 1999, after 38 years of rule; he was 70 years old. After the announcement of the king's death, the nation began a 40-day mourning period. Hassan's son, Crown Prince Sidi Mohamed, was enthroned immediately as King Mohamed VI. Scores of foreign dignitaries paid tribute to King Hassan, recognizing his efforts to improve Morocco's future. In November the new king dismissed the powerful interior minister, Driss Basri.

MOROCCO • Information Highlights

Official Name: Kingdom of Morocco.
Location: Northwest Africa.
Area: 172,413 sq mi (446 550 km^2).
Population (July 1999 est.): 29,661,636.
Chief Cities (1994 census): Rabat, the capital (incl. Salé), 1,385,872; Casablanca, 2,940,623; Fez, 774,754; Marrakech, 745,541.
Government: *Head of state,* Mohamed VI, king (acceded 1999). *Head of government,* Abderrahmane Youssoufi, prime minister (appointed November 1997). *Legislature* (bicameral)—Chamber of Councillors and House of Representatives.
Monetary Unit: Dirham (10.0525 dirhams equal U.S.$1, Dec. 2, 1999).
Gross Domestic Product (1998 est. U.S.$): $107,000,000,000 (purchasing power parity).
Economic Indexes (1998): *Consumer Prices* (1991 = 100): all items, 143.3; food, 146.4. *Industrial Production* (1990 = 100): 124.1.
Foreign Trade (1998 U.S.$): *Imports,* $10,276,000,000; *exports,* $12,480,000,000.

The Economy. The implementation of the Morocco–European Union (EU) free-trade zone got final approval on July 28. The association agreement between Morocco and the EU came into effect in October 1999. Trade barriers between Morocco and the EU would be lifted slowly to allow for competition. Morocco established a corporate-upgrade system to modernize its businesses and industrial units in preparation for opening its markets to Europe.

The partnership agreement entails the progressive dismantling of custom duties for EU products and would culminate in a complete exoneration of custom taxes. Agricultural tariffs would be the subject of separate negotiations, due to start in 2000. Thus far, the agricultural market had been blocked out of the agreement by the EU.

As Morocco prepared to link its economy with that of Europe, it faced major economic and social problems. The country's heavy reliance on its agricultural sector was a hindrance to economic performance. The vulnerability of this sector to changes in the weather dampened the economy particularly in 1999, as it was a drought year. The cereal harvest dropped by approximately 41%, to 3.76 million tons, in 1998–99 in comparison to the previous season, due to the dry weather. The import of soft wheat during the same time frame rose to 2.5 million tons from 2 million tons.

Morocco responded to its economic problems by maintaining fiscal discipline and speeding up privatization, which generated much-needed revenue. The opening of the telecommunications sector to foreign investment provided balance-of-payments relief. The new king endorsed the sale of the second GSM mobile-phone license to a Spanish-Portuguese consortium. The projected proceeds initially were estimated at $450 million, but the actual revenue generated was $1.1 billion. The extra revenue was earmarked for major infrastructure projects and job-creation programs. This was expected to waylay criticisms that the government had made no progress in relieving unemployment and rural poverty.

The second quarter of 1999 revealed a jobless rate of 12.9%, with at least 1.328 million out of work. Moroccan urban areas faced the brunt of this problem, with an average unemployment rate of 21.3%. A three-year government plan calling for the creation of 180,000 new jobs was approved. The government introduced initiatives aimed at boosting job creation. However, labor unions and an employer confederation forecast a worsening labor market.

Human Rights. Morocco made improvements in the area of human rights but was criticized for its slow progress. On July 30, King Mohamed VI stated his intent to hasten reforms. The return of communist opposition figure Abraham Serfaty on September 30 marked a major turning point. The new king also hinted that he would allow the return of the exiled Ben Barka family. This stood in contrast to the continued house arrest of Islamist opposition figure Sheikh Abdessalam Yassine, who had been imprisoned since 1989.

Regional Affairs. The regional conflict over the Western Sahara continued. Morocco insists on the area's annexation, while the Algeria-backed Polisario Front seeks its independence. In 1999 the United Nations (UN) led an effort to identify participants for a 2000 referendum on the territory's future. The process was a subject of contention between Morocco and the Polisario Front, forcing the UN Security Council to extend the mandate of the Mission for the Referendum (Minurso) by three months.

ROSE RYAN, *"The North Africa Journal"*

Motion Pictures

The film industry had its share of blockbusters in 1999 whose success seemed to have nothing to do with critical approval. The most prominent example of this was *Star Wars: Episode I—The Phantom Menace*, the latest release in the renowned series. Although George Lucas' highly touted film had its admirers, the critical response was cool, particularly when measured against the hype; nevertheless, the film achieved a U.S. box-office gross of more than $425 million. *The Mummy*, a remake of the 1932 horror film, was trounced roundly in reviews but grossed some $155 million. M. Night Shyamalan's mysterious *The Sixth Sense*, starring Bruce Willis and featuring a mesmerizing performance by Haley Joel Osment as a psychic young boy, proved popular with both audiences and critics, bringing in $240 million.

The most talked-about phenomenon of 1999 was *The Blair Witch Project*, directed by Eduardo Sánchez and Daniel Myrick. The offbeat make-believe documentary followed the fate of three young filmmakers who vanish while making a movie about a series of mysterious disappearances in a wooded area of Maryland. *Blair Witch* was made on a minuscule budget of only about $40,000, but clever promotion on the Internet and a buzz creating the impression that it was a true story awakened enormous interest, and the film reached a surprising box-office total of more than $138 million.

American Beauty, a searing if sometimes amusing look at the gnawing, potentially explosive problems beneath the surface of overtly normal lives, drew considerable praise, and many critics speculated that it could be a leading candidate for awards. Kevin Spacey and Annette Bening were hailed for their performances, and Sam Mendes, until now best known as a stage director, was lauded for his first screen effort. Another powerful drama was *Boys Don't Cry*, based on the true story of a young woman who felt she really should be a man, masqueraded as one, and was raped and murdered after her ruse was exposed. Directed by Kimberly Peirce, the film was a hit at the New York Film Festival, with Hilary Swank giving an exceptionally gripping performance in the lead.

One of the year's late releases, *The Hurricane*, directed by veteran filmmaker Norman Jewison, featured Denzel Washington's shattering portrayal of boxer Rubin "Hurricane" Carter, who was framed and sent to prison for a murder he did not commit. Washington also starred as a paralyzed cop in *The Bone Collector*.

A distinguished performance of a different sort was given in *The Straight Story* by Richard Farnsworth, playing an elderly Midwesterner who—upon learning that his brother, from whom he has been estranged, has had a stroke—drives his tractor-lawnmower from Iowa to Wisconsin to see him. The film was a gentle, moving answer to those who complain about the lack of posi-

George Lucas' much-anticipated "Star Wars: Episode I—The Phantom Menace" opened with much hoopla in the spring of 1999 and rapidly became a blockbuster. The critics were cool in their praise, however.

tive family entertainment—and it reflected a surprising change of pace for its director, David Lynch, best known for cynical, violent films such as *Blue Velvet* and *Wild at Heart*.

Other Films of Substance. *Eyes Wide Shut*, the last film directed by Stanley Kubrick before he died suddenly in England, starred Tom Cruise and Nicole Kidman in a story dealing with the potential explosiveness of sex, whether real or fantasized. It was based on Arthur Schnitzler's 1926 novella *Traumnovelle*, but Kubrick gave it a modern New York setting and, as usual, made it his own unique creation. Also as usual with a Kubrick film, it drew diametrically opposed reviews.

Another major film that sought to deliver a serious message as well as to entertain was director Ang Lee's *Ride with the Devil*, a Civil War epic that focused on the marauding fighters involved in battles away from the front lines, with the emphasis on Southern men who continued fighting even though their cause seemed lost. The film featured a fine performance by Tobey Maguire. The actor earned further attention from his work in *The Cider House Rules*, portraying a young man who receives informal training in medicine and must face ethical decisions and personal choices.

Three Kings, directed by David O. Russell, mixed wartime adventure with irreverent comedy in a critical and surrealistic depiction of events during the Persian Gulf war. George Clooney, Mark Wahlberg, and Ice Cube starred as Special Forces fighters who decide to steal some of Saddam Hussein's gold. *Snow Falling on Cedars*, directed by Scott Hicks, involved reflection on the imprisonment of Japanese-Americans during World War II. *The Insider*, directed by Michael Mann and starring Al Pacino and Russell Crowe, dramatized the situation surrounding the initial reluctance of the CBS newsmagazine *60 Minutes* to broadcast an exposé of the tobacco industry by a whistleblower.

Dick, an imaginative political satire directed by Andrew Fleming in which two ditsy teenage girls turn out to be responsible for the downfall of President Richard Nixon, featured a wickedly funny impression of Nixon by Dan Hedaya. Michelle Williams and Kirsten Dunst played the girls. There was also sharp satire in *Election*, director Alexander Payne's film that ostensibly was about an election of a high-school class president but was really a microcosm of larger issues concerning values in the country as a whole.

One of the year's most charming and sumptuous motion pictures was Mike Leigh's *Topsy-Turvy*, a look at the lives of Gilbert and Sullivan and the backstage maneuvers as they rehearsed their production of *The Mikado*. Jim Broadbent gave a striking performance as William Schwenk Gilbert, as did Allan Corduner as Arthur Sullivan. Other highbrow dramas included an adaptation of Jane Austen's 1814 novel *Mansfield Park*; Oliver Parker's film of the Oscar Wilde play *An Ideal Husband*, starring Rupert Everett; and *Miss Julie*, directed by Mike Figgis.

Trend toward Grossness. A number of films raised the ire of those who are appalled by the extent of vulgarity, anything-goes language, explicit violence, and overt sexuality in contemporary entertainment. Conversely, many delighted in the results of such freedom. But given some of the violent events that engulfed youth, particularly in the United States, movies and television became targets of disapproval.

American Pie, which topped $101 million at the box office, concerned a group of male high-school students determined to have sex before they graduate; the movie contained its share of gross scenes. Based on the cable television series, the animated *South Park: Bigger, Longer & Uncut* not only was full of profanity and raunchy humor, but the plot itself comically thumbed its nose at overzealous parents trying to keep children from seeing taboo movies. *Austin Powers: The Spy Who Shagged Me*, written by and starring Canadian comic Mike Myers, had audiences lining up in droves to see its outrageous blend of slapstick, scatological humor, and double entendres. Many viewers were upset by the graphic violence in David Fincher's *Fight Club*, starring Edward Norton and Brad Pitt in a story about men who engage in bloody, bare-knuckled boxing that leads eventually to terrorism.

There was also controversy concerning religion. Kevin Smith's satire *Dogma* reflected on Catholicism in a broad, comic parable that really was about saving the world but contained ideas and situations that provoked outrage and opposition. Miramax, owned by the Disney Company, had intended to distribute the film but decided to sell it to Lions Gate, which then released it.

Wide Variety of Choices. Albert Brooks spoofed Hollywood with *The Muse*, starring himself as a frustrated writer and Sharon Stone in a funny performance as a Muse he

(Continued on page 376.)

© Laurie Sparham/Photofest

Shakespeare—From Stage to Screen

William Shakespeare may have thought he was writing only for the theater, but it turned out that he also provided the basis for an art form of the future. His work has been a fruitful source for scores of films, especially in recent years. *Shakespeare in Love*, starring Gwyneth Paltrow and Joseph Fiennes (*photo above*), netted seven Oscars in 1999. It demonstrated that the Bard's popularity has become so entrenched that even a fanciful film speculating on the inspiration for his creativity could be considered a serious work of art.

Titus Andronicus, one of Shakespeare's most difficult (and most violent) plays, so fascinated Julie Taymor, the renowned director of the innovative Broadway hit *The Lion King*, that she decided to direct a film version, *Titus*, with Anthony Hopkins in the title role. Her vision was to do the production in modern dress, with all of the play's bloody events intact.

In 1996, Baz Luhrmann's version of *Romeo + Juliet* featured gang members in contemporary Los Angeles reciting Shakespeare's dialogue; the film was popular with young audiences, largely due to teen favorites Leonardo DiCaprio and Claire Danes. On the heels of that success, another effort was made to reach the youth market by updating *The Taming of the Shrew*. The result was Gil Junger's 1999 film *10 Things I Hate About You*, set in a high school and replete with the sexual humor and dialogue typical of contemporary youth films.

Michael Hoffman wrote and directed a new production of *A Midsummer Night's Dream* (1999) with a cast that included Kevin Kline as Bottom, Michelle Pfeiffer as Titania, Rupert Everett as Oberon, Stanley Tucci as Puck, and Calista Flockhart as Helena. Unfortunately, the result was something of a hodgepodge. The great play *Hamlet* has been adapted to the screen more than 20 times, featuring such distinguished actors as Laurence Olivier, Kenneth Branagh, and Mel Gibson; the latest version, directed by Michael Almereyda, stars Ethan Hawke.

What is it about Shakespeare's playwriting that lends itself so well to the screen, apart from the lure of adopting classics? His writing begs for visual illustration and lends itself to a wide variety of imaginative interpretations, not only for directors, but also for actors, cinematographers, and designers. Moreover, the Bard provided all of the ingredients that filmmakers hope to find in screenplays: the sweep of history; abundant action; great, deeply explored characters; passionate emotions; humor; well-structured plots; stirring climaxes; and fatal flaws that are as recognizable today as they were in Shakespeare's time.

William Wolf

MOTION PICTURES • 1999

AGNES BROWNE. Director, Anjelica Huston; screenplay by John Goldsmith and Brendan O'Carroll, based on O'Carroll's novel *The Mammy*. With Anjelica Huston.
ALL ABOUT MY MOTHER. Written and directed by Pedro Almodóvar. With Cecilia Roth, Marisa Paredes, Antonia San Juan, Candela Peña, and Penélope Cruz.
AMERICAN BEAUTY. Director, Sam Mendes; screenplay by Alan Ball. With Kevin Spacey, Annette Bening, Thora Birch, and Mena Suvari.
AMERICAN PIE. Director, Paul Weitz; screenplay by Adam Herz. With Jason Biggs, Shannon Elizabeth, Alyson Hannigan, and Chris Klein.
ANALYZE THIS. Director, Harold Ramis; screenplay by Peter Tolan, Ramis, and Kenneth Lonergan, based on a story by Lonergan and Tolan. With Robert De Niro, Billy Crystal, Lisa Kudrow, and Joe Viterelli.
ANGELA'S ASHES. Director, Alan Parker; screenplay by Laura Jones and Parker, based on Frank McCourt's novel. With Robert Carlyle and Emily Watson.
ANNA AND THE KING. Director, Andy Tennant; screenplay by Steve Meerson and Peter Krikes, based on the diaries of Anna Leonowens. With Jodie Foster, Chow Yun-Fat, and Bai Ling.
ANY GIVEN SUNDAY. Director, Oliver Stone; screenplay by John Logan, Stone, and Pat Toomay, based on the novel by Rob Huizenga. With Al Pacino, Dennis Quaid, James Woods, and Edward Burns.
ANYWHERE BUT HERE. Director, Wayne Wang; screenplay by Alvin Sargent, adapted from Mona Simpson's novel. With Susan Sarandon and Natalie Portman.
ARLINGTON ROAD. Director, Mark Pellington; screenplay by Ehren Kruger. With Jeff Bridges, Tim Robbins, Joan Cusack, Hope Davis, and Robert Gossett.
AUSTIN POWERS: THE SPY WHO SHAGGED ME. Director, M. Jay Roach; screenplay by Mike Myers and Michael McCullers. With Mike Myers, Heather Graham, Michael York, Robert Wagner, and Elizabeth Hurley.
AUTUMN TALE. Written and directed by Eric Rohmer. With Marie Rivière, Béatrice Romand, Alain Libolt, Didier Sandre, and Alexia Portal.
BEING JOHN MALKOVICH. Director, Spike Jonze; screenplay by Charlie Kaufman. With John Cusack, Cameron Diaz, Catherine Keener, and John Malkovich.
BESIEGED. Director, Bernardo Bertolucci; screenplay by Bertolucci and Clare Peploe, based on a story by James Lasdun. With Thandie Newton, David Thewlis, and Claudio Santamaria.
BICENTENNIAL MAN. Director, Chris Columbus; screenplay by Nicholas Kazan, based on a story by Isaac Asimov. With Robin Williams.
BIG DADDY. Director, Dennis Dugan; screenplay by Steve Franks, Tim Herlihy, and Adam Sandler, based on a story by Franks. With Adam Sandler, Joey Lauren Adams, Jon Stewart, and Josh Mostel.
THE BLAIR WITCH PROJECT. Written and directed by Daniel Myrick and Eduardo Sánchez. With Heather Donahue, Michael C. Williams, and Joshua Leonard.
THE BONE COLLECTOR. Director, Phillip Noyce; screenplay by Jeremy Iacone, based on a novel by Jeffery Deaver. With Denzel Washington, Angelina Jolie, Queen Latifah, and Ed O'Neill.
BOYS DON'T CRY. Director, Kimberly Peirce; screenplay by Peirce and Andy Bienen. With Hilary Swank, Alison Folland, Alicia Goranson, and Chloë Sevigny.
BREAKFAST OF CHAMPIONS. Written and directed by Alan Rudolph, adapted from the novel by Kurt Vonnegut, Jr.. With Bruce Willis, Albert Finney, Nick Nolte, and Barbara Hershey.
BRINGING OUT THE DEAD. Director, Martin Scorsese; screenplay by Paul Schrader, from *Taxi Driver* by Joe Connelly. With Nicolas Cage, Patricia Arquette, John Goodman, Ving Rhames, and Tom Sizemore.
BUENA VISTA SOCIAL CLUB. Director, Wim Wenders. Documentary on reunion of Cuban musicians.
THE CIDER HOUSE RULES. Director, Lasse Hallström; screenplay by John Irving, based on his novel. With Tobey Maguire, Charlize Theron, Delroy Lindo, Paul Rudd, and Michael Caine.
COOKIE'S FORTUNE. Director, Robert Altman; screenplay by Anne Rapp. With Glenn Close, Julianne Moore, Liv Tyler, Chris O'Donnell, and Charles S. Dutton.
CRADLE WILL ROCK. Written and directed by Tim Robbins. With Susan Sarandon, Vanessa Redgrave, Emily Watson, Hank Azaria, John Cusack, Joan Cusack, Bill Murray, and John Turturro.
CRAZY IN ALABAMA. Director, Antonio Banderas; screenplay by Mark Childress, based on his novel. With Melanie Griffith, David Morse, Lucas Black, and Rod Steiger.
THE DINNER GAME. Written and directed by Francis Veber. With Jacques Villeret, Thierry Lhermitte, and Daniel Prévost.
DOGMA. Written and directed by Kevin Smith. With Ben Affleck, Matt Damon, Linda Fiorentino, Salma Hayek, Jason Lee, Alan Rickman, and Chris Rock.
DOUBLE JEOPARDY. Director, Bruce Beresford; screenplay by David Weisberg and Douglas S. Cook. With Ashley Judd, Tommy Lee Jones, Bruce Greenwood, and Annabeth Gish.
DREAMLIFE OF ANGELS. Director, Erick Zonca; screenplay by Zonca and Roger Bohbot. With Elodie Bouchez and Natacha Régnier.
EDTV. Director, Ron Howard; screenplay by Lowell Ganz and Babaloo Mandel, based on the motion picture *Louis XIX: le roi des ondes*, written by Emile Gaudreault and Sylvie Bouchard. With Matthew McConaughey, Jenna Elfman, Woody Harrelson, and Sally Kirkland.
ELECTION. Director, Alexander Payne; screenplay by Payne and Tom Perrotta. With Reese Witherspoon and Matthew Broderick.
THE END OF THE AFFAIR. Written and directed by Neil Jordan, based on the novel by Graham Greene. With Julianne Moore, Ralph Fiennes, and Stephen Rea.
ENTRAPMENT. Director, Jon Amiel; screenplay by Ron Bass and William Broyles, based on a story by Bass and Michael Hertzberg. With Sean Connery, Catherine Zeta-Jones, Ving Rhames, and Will Patton.
EYES WIDE SHUT. Director, Stanley Kubrick; screenplay by Kubrick and Frederic Raphael, inspired by *Traumnovelle* by Arthur Schnitzler. With Tom Cruise, Nicole Kidman, Sydney Pollack, and Todd Field.
FELICIA'S JOURNEY. Written and directed by Atom Egoyan, based on the novel by William Trevor. With Elaine Cassidy and Bob Hoskins.
FIGHT CLUB. Director, David Fincher; screenplay by Jim Uhls, based on the novel by Chuck Palahniuk. With Brad Pitt, Edward Norton, Helena Bonham Carter, and Jared Leto.
FLAWLESS. Written and directed by Joel Schumacher. With Robert De Niro, Philip Seymour Hoffman, Barry Miller, Chris Bauer, and Skipp Sudduth.

Lorey Sebastian © Dreamworks LLC/Kobal Collection

Kevin Spacey and Annette Bening won much critical acclaim for their portrayals of a disillusioned suburban husband and his frustrated wife in the Dreamworks film "American Beauty."

In "All About My Mother," Spanish director Pedro Almodóvar brought his signature visual style to the tale of a woman (played by Cecilia Roth, right*) who searches for her son's father after the son is killed in an accident.*

Teresa Isais © Sony Pictures Enterprises Inc./Kobal Collection

THE GENERAL'S DAUGHTER. Director, Simon West; screenplay by Christopher Bertolini and William Goldman, based on a novel by Nelson DeMille. With John Travolta, Madeleine Stowe, James Cromwell, and Timothy Hutton.

GIRL, INTERRUPTED. Written and directed by James Mangold, based on the book by Susanna Kaysen. With Winona Ryder, Angelina Jolie, and Whoopi Goldberg.

THE GREEN MILE. Written and directed by Frank Darabont, adapted from Stephen King's novel. With Tom Hanks and Michael Clarke Duncan.

HIDEOUS KINKY. Director, Gilles MacKinnon; screenplay by Billy MacKinnon, from the novel by Esther Freud. With Kate Winslet and Saïd Taghmaoui.

HOLY SMOKE. Director, Jane Campion; screenplay by Anna Campion and Jane Campion. With Kate Winslet, Harvey Keitel, Paul Goddard, Pam Grier, and Julie Hamilton.

THE HURRICANE. Director, Norman Jewison; screenplay by Armyan Bernstein and Dan Gordon, based on books by Rubin "Hurricane" Carter and by Sam Chaiton and Terry Swinton. With Denzel Washington, Clancy Brown, Dan Hedaya, David Sparrow, and Rod Steiger.

AN IDEAL HUSBAND. Written and directed by Oliver Parker, based on the play by Oscar Wilde. With Cate Blanchett, Minnie Driver, Rupert Everett, Julianne Moore, and Jeremy Northam.

THE INSIDER. Director, Michael Mann; screenplay by Mann and Eric Roth, based on a *Vanity Fair* article by Marie Brenner. With Al Pacino, Russell Crowe, and Christopher Plummer.

THE IRON GIANT. Written and directed by Brad Bird, based on Ted Hughes' book *The Iron Man*. With the voices of Jennifer Aniston, Eli Marienthal, and Harry Connick, Jr.

JAKOB THE LIAR. Director, Peter Kassovitz; screenplay by Kassovitz and Didier Decoin, based on the book by Jurek Becker. With Robin Williams, Hannah Taylor-Gordon, Bob Balaban, and Alan Arkin.

JOE THE KING. Written and directed by Frank Whaley. With Noah Fleiss, Val Kilmer, Karen Young, Camryn Manheim, and Ethan Hawke.

LIBERTY HEIGHTS. Written and directed by Barry Levinson. With Adrien Brody, Bebe Neuwirth, and Joe Mantegna.

THE LIMEY. Director, Stephen Soderbergh; screenplay by Lem Dobbs. With Terence Stamp and Peter Fonda.

MAGNOLIA. Written and directed by Paul Thomas Anderson. With William H. Macy, Julianne Moore, Philip Baker Hall, John C. Reilly, Jason Robards, Felicity Huffman, and Tom Cruise.

MAN ON THE MOON. Director, Milos Forman; screenplay by Scott Alexander and Larry Karaszewski. With Jim Carrey, Courtney Love, and Danny DeVito.

MANSFIELD PARK. Written and directed by Patricia Rozema, based on the novel by Jane Austen and her early letters and journals. With Frances O'Connor, Embeth Davidtz, Jonny Lee Miller, Alessandro Nivola, and Harold Pinter.

A MAP OF THE WORLD. Director, Scott Elliott; screenplay by Peter Hedges and Polly Platt, based on the novel by Jane Hamilton. With Sigourney Weaver and Julianne Moore.

THE MESSENGER: THE STORY OF JOAN OF ARC. Director, Luc Besson; screenplay by Besson and Andrew Birkin. With Milla Jovovich, John Malkovich, Faye Dunaway, and Dustin Hoffman.

MICKEY BLUE EYES. Director, Kelly Makin; screenplay by Adam Scheinman and Robert Kuhn. With Hugh Grant, James Caan, Jeanne Tripplehorn, and Burt Young.

A MIDSUMMER NIGHT'S DREAM. Director, Michael Hoffman; screenplay by Hoffman, based on the play by William Shakespeare. With Kevin Kline, Michelle Pfeiffer, Rupert Everett, Stanley Tucci, and Calista Flockhart.

MISS JULIE. Director, Mike Figgis; screenplay by Helen Cooper, from the play by August Strindberg. With Saffron Burrows, Peter Mullan, and Maria Doyle Kennedy.

MUMFORD. Written and directed by Lawrence Kasdan. With Loren Dean, Alfre Woodard, Hope Davis, David Paymer, Ted Danson, Jason Lee, and Martin Short.

THE MUMMY. Written and directed by Stephen Sommers. With Brendan Fraser, Rachel Weisz, John Hannah, and Kevin J. O'Connor.

Courtesy, The Everett Collection

Michael Caine (left) *played a Maine doctor who adopts a young orphan (Tobey Maguire) and grooms him as his protégé in "The Cider House Rules," based on the John Irving novel.*

George Kraychyk © Beacon Comm. Corp. A Universal Release/Kobal Collection

In the docudrama "The Hurricane," Denzel Washington (right) gave one of the best performances of his career as Rubin "Hurricane" Carter, a boxer wrongly convicted of murder who languished in prison nearly 20 years before being exonerated.

THE MUSE. Director, Albert Brooks; screenplay by Brooks and Monica Johnson. With Brooks, Sharon Stone, Andie MacDowell, and Jeff Bridges.

MUSIC OF THE HEART. Director, Wes Craven; screenplay by Pamela Gray, adapted from the documentary *Small Wonders*. With Meryl Streep, Aidan Quinn, Angela Bassett, and Gloria Estefan.

MY LIFE SO FAR. Director, Hugh Hudson; screenplay by Simon Donald, based on the book *Son of Adam* by Sir Denis Forman. With Elaine Ellis, Colin Firth, Rosemary Harris, Irène Jacob, and Mary Elizabeth Mastrantonio.

NOTTING HILL. Director, Roger Michell; screenplay by Richard Curtis. With Julia Roberts, Hugh Grant, Hugh Bonneville, and Emma Chambers.

OCTOBER SKY. Director, Joe Johnston; screenplay by Lewis Colick, based on the book *Rocket Boys* by Homer H. Hickam, Jr. With Jake Gyllenhaal, Chris Cooper, William Lee Scott, and Laura Dern.

ONEGIN. Director, Martha Fiennes; written by Peter Ettedgui and Michael Ignatieff, based on a work by Alexander Pushkin. With Ralph Fiennes and Liv Tyler.

OUTSIDE PROVIDENCE. Director, Michael Corrente; screenplay by Peter Farrelly, Corrente, and Bobby Farrelly, based on the novel by Peter Farrelly. With Shawn Hatosy, Jon Abrahams, Tim Crowe, and Alec Baldwin.

PLAYING BY HEART. Written and directed by Willard Carroll. With Gillian Anderson, Ellen Burstyn, Sean Connery, and Anthony Edwards.

PRIVATE CONFESSIONS. Director, Liv Ullmann; screenplay by Ingmar Bergman. With Pernilla August, Max von Sydow, Samuel Fröler, and Kristina Adolphson.

PUSHING TIN. Director, Mike Newell. Screenplay by Glen Charles and Les Charles, based on a *New York Times Magazine* article by Darcy Frey. With John Cusack, Billy Bob Thornton, Cate Blanchett, and Angelina Jolie.

RANDOM HEARTS. Director, Sydney Pollack; screenplay by Kurt Luedtke and adapted by Darryl Ponicsan, based on the novel by Warren Adler. With Harrison Ford, Kristin Scott Thomas, Charles Dutton, and Bonnie Hunt.

RIDE WITH THE DEVIL. Director, Ang Lee; screenplay by James Schamus, based on the novel *Woe to Live On* by Daniel Woodrell. With Tobey McGuire, Skeet Ulrich, Jeffrey Wright, and Jewel.

ROSETTA. Written and directed by Luc and Jean-Pierre Dardenne. With Emilie Dequenne, Anne Yernaux, Fabrizio Rongione, and Olivier Gourmet.

RUNAWAY BRIDE. Director, Garry Marshall; screenplay by Josann McGibbon and Sara Parriott. With Julia Roberts and Richard Gere.

SHE'S ALL THAT. Director, Robert Iscove; screenplay by R. Lee Fleming, Jr. With Freddie Prinze, Jr., Rachael Leigh Cook, Matthew Lillard, and Paul Walker.

THE SIXTH SENSE. Written and directed by M. Night Shyamalan. With Bruce Willis, Toni Collette, Olivia Williams, Haley Joel Osment, and Donnie Wahlberg.

SLEEPY HOLLOW. Director, Tim Burton; screenplay by Kevin Yagher, adapted from Washington Irving's story. With Johnny Depp and Christina Ricci.

SNOW FALLING ON CEDARS. Director, Scott Hicks; screenplay by Ron Bass and Hicks, based on the novel by David Guterson. With Ethan Hawke, James Cromwell, Max von Sydow, Youki Kudoh, and Rick Yune.

SOUTH PARK: BIGGER, LONGER & UNCUT. Director, Trey Parker; screenplay by Parker, Matt Stone, and Pam Brady. With the voices of Trey Parker, Isaac Hayes, and George Clooney.

STAR WARS: EPISODE I—THE PHANTOM MENACE. Written and directed by George Lucas. With Liam Neeson, Ewan McGregor, Natalie Portman, Jake Lloyd, Ian McDiarmid, and the voice of Frank Oz.

STIGMATA. Director, Rupert Wainwright; screenplay by Tom Lazarus and Rick Ramage, based on a story by Lazarus. With Patricia Arquette, Gabriel Byrne, Jonathan Pryce, Nia Long, and Enrico Colantoni.

THE STORY OF US. Director, Rob Reiner; screenplay by Alan Zweibel and Jessie Nelson. With Bruce Willis, Michelle Pfeiffer, Tim Matheson, Rob Reiner, and Julie Hagerty.

THE STRAIGHT STORY. Director, David Lynch; screenplay by John Roach and Mary Sweeney. With Sissy Spacek, Richard Farnsworth, Harry Dean Stanton, and Wiley Harker.

STUART LITTLE. Director, Rob Minkoff; screenplay by Gregory J. Brooker, based on E.B. White's book. With Geena Davis, Hugh Laurie, Jonathan Lipnicki, and the voices of Michael J. Fox, Jennifer Tilly, Nathan Lane, and Chazz Palminteri.

SUMMER OF SAM. Director, Spike Lee; screenplay by Victor Colicchio and Michael Imperioli. With John Leguizamo, Adrien Brody, and Mira Sorvino.

SWEET AND LOWDOWN. Written and directed by Woody Allen. With Sean Penn, Uma Thurman, and Samantha Morton.

THE TALENTED MR. RIPLEY. Written and directed by Anthony Minghella, adapted from the novel by Patricia Highsmith. With Matt Damon, Gwyneth Paltrow, Cate Blanchett, and Philip Seymour Hoffman.

TARZAN. Directors, Chris Buck and Kevin Lima; written by Tab Murphy, Bob Tzudiker, and Noni White, based on the story by Edgar Rice Burroughs. With the voices of Brian Blessed, Glenn Close, Minnie Driver, Tony Goldwyn, Nigel Hawthorne, and Rosie O'Donnell.

TEA WITH MUSSOLINI. Director, Franco Zeffirelli; screenplay by John Mortimer and Zeffirelli. With Cher, Judi Dench, Joan Plowright, Maggie Smith, and Lily Tomlin.

THE THOMAS CROWN AFFAIR. Director, John McTiernan; screenplay by Leslie Dixon and Kurt Wimmer, based on a story by Alan R. Trustman. With Pierce Brosnan, Rene Russo, Denis Leary, and Ben Gazzara.

THREE KINGS. Written and directed by David O. Russell, based on a story by John Ridley. With George Clooney, Mark Wahlberg, Ice Cube, and Spike Jonze.

TITUS. Director, Julie Taymor; screenplay by Taymor, based on William Shakespeare's play *Titus Andronicus*. With Anthony Hopkins, Jessica Lange, and Alan Cumming.

TOPSY-TURVY. Written and directed by Mike Leigh. With Jim Broadbent and Allan Corduner.

TOY STORY 2. Director, John Lasseter with Ash Brannon and Lee Unkrich; screenplay by Andrew Stanton, Rita Hsiao, Doug Chamberlain, and Chris Webb. With the voices of Tom Hanks, Tim Allen, Joan Cusack, Kelsey Grammer, Don Rickles, Jim Varney, Wallace Shawn, John Ratzenberger, and Annie Potts.

TRUE CRIME. Director, Clint Eastwood; screenplay by Larry Gross, Paul Brickman, and Stephen Schiff, based on the novel by Andrew Klavan. With Clint Eastwood, Isaiah Washington, Denis Leary, and James Woods.

TUMBLEWEEDS. Director, Gavin O'Connor; screenplay by O'Connor and Angela Shelton, adapted from her memoirs. With Janet McTeer, Kimberly Brown, Gavin O'Connor, Jay O. Sanders, and Michael J. Pollard.

A WALK ON THE MOON. Director, Tony Goldwyn; screenplay by Pamela Gray. With Diane Lane, Viggo Mortensen, Liev Schreiber, and Anna Paquin.

THE WAR ZONE. Director, Tim Roth; screenplay by Alexander Stuart, based on his book. With Ray Winstone, Kate Ashfield, and Aisling O'Sullivan.

THE WINSLOW BOY. Written and directed by David Mamet, based on the play by Terence Rattigan. With Nigel Hawthorne, Jeremy Northam, and Rebecca Pidgeon.

THE WORLD IS NOT ENOUGH. Director, Michael Apted; screenplay by Neal Purvis, Robert Wade, and Bruce Feirstein, based on a story by Purvis and Wade. With Pierce Brosnan, Denise Richards, Sophie Marceau, and Judi Dench.

hires to help get his edge back. Martin Scorsese directed *Bringing Out the Dead*, starring Nicolas Cage as a paramedic fighting burnout. Susan Sarandon played the single mother of Natalie Portman in Wayne Wang's *Anywhere But Here*. Tony-winning stage actress Janet McTeer starred in the mother-daughter story *Tumbleweeds*.

Robert Altman returned with *Cookie's Fortune*, an amusingly odd comedy about life in a Mississippi town with a strange assortment of characters played by a cast that included Glenn Close, Julienne Moore, Patricia Neal, and Charles S. Dutton. A Washington Irving classic provided the basis for *Sleepy Hollow*, directed by Tim Burton and starring Johnny Depp. Tim Robbins, best known as an actor, directed *The Cradle Will Rock*, the 1930s saga of a government attempt to thwart the militant staging of a Marc Blitzstein work. *The Matrix*, starring Keanu Reeves and Laurence Fishburne, excited video-game enthusiasts but befuddled many others with a plot that skidded in and out of reality.

David Mamet effectively remade *The Winslow Boy*, a classic British film based on the Terence Rattigan play depicting a real-life drama about a father's determination to clear the name of his son, a cadet accused of theft. Spike Lee's *Summer of Sam* attempted to capture the atmosphere in New York during the summer of 1977, when the murderer known as Son of Sam held the city in terror. In a more literary vein, *Angela's Ashes* brought Frank McCourt's best-seller to the screen. One of the year's most imaginative films was Spike Jonze's *Being John Malkovich*, in which a file clerk discovers a secret passageway that allows him to become film star John Malkovich (who plays himself). Disney scored with the animated *Tarzan*, which charmingly gave yet another life to the ever-popular jungle tale.

Colorful performances highlighted an assortment of films. *Tea with Mussolini*, which director Franco Zeffirelli based on his childhood wartime memories, offered showy star turns by Maggie Smith, Joan Plowright, Judi Dench, and Cher. Sean Penn gave a particularly charismatic performance as a jazz-guitar player in Woody Allen's documentary-style comedy *Sweet and Lowdown*. Meryl Streep played Roberta Guaspari in *Music of the Heart*, an upbeat true story about a violinist's struggles to save her music program for East Harlem schoolchildren.

The public still responds to star power, as evidenced by the popularity of Julia Roberts (*see* BIOGRAPHY) and Hugh Grant in the romantic *Notting Hill* ($116 million at the U.S. box office) and the reteaming of Roberts with her *Pretty Woman* costar Richard Gere in *Runaway Bride* ($147 million).

The Hollywood star tradition was echoed by the American Film Institute, which polled the film community and came up with a list of the top 50 movie stars of all time. Humphrey Bogart, Cary Grant, and James Stewart led the male contingent, with Katharine Hepburn, Bette Davis, and Audrey Hepburn the top three among women. By 1999 the most bankable stars in Hollywood were Tom Hanks, Mel Gibson, Tom Cruise, Harrison Ford, and Jim Carrey, according to a poll by the trade paper *Hollywood Reporter*. The top actress on the list was Roberts, who was eighth.

Among foreign films, *The Dinner Game*, a French import written and directed by Francis Veber, was a hilarious farce about a wealthy man who challenges several friends to invite the biggest fool they can find to a dinner party. Also from France, the charmer *Autumn Tale*, about adults trying to find happiness, showed why Eric Rohmer is still one of the world's best directors. Iranian director Majid Majidi captivated critics with two films, *Children of Heaven* and *The Color of Heaven*, both sensitively told stories about life in his country. The Cannes Film Festival gave its top award, the Palme d'Or, to the Belgian film *Rosetta*, directed by the brothers Jean-Pierre and Luc Dardenne.

Business. After earning only $315.71 million gross box-office business in 1998, Universal Studios bounced back in 1999, taking in $773.38 million as a result of such hits as *The Mummy*, *Patch Adams* (starring Robin Williams), *Notting Hill*, *American Pie*, and *Bowfinger*.

A study conducted on behalf of the Directors Guild of America and the Screen Actors Guild revealed that 27% of U.S. movies and television series made in 1998 were filmed abroad, attributing the desire to save money as the prime motivation. According to the study, some 23,000 full-time jobs were lost as a result.

Controversy. The decision to give an honorary Oscar to elderly director Elia Kazan stirred debate and protests as a result of lingering anger in the film community over his naming several of his colleagues as Communists to the House Committee on Un-American Activities in the 1950s.

See also PRIZES AND AWARDS.

WILLIAM WOLF, *New York University*

Music

Overview

During 1999 the business of making and creating music continued to flourish, even as the recording industry still found itself threatened and floundering. The news throughout the year was dominated by an unprecedented number of searches for music directors, as well as by the premieres of an impressive number of American operas that came into the world kicking, screaming, and full of life.

The 1999 Pulitzer Prize for music went to Melinda Wagner for her *Concerto for Flute, Strings and Percussion*, which was written for the Westchester Philharmonic. The Grawemeyer Award was given to the 28-year-old British composer Thomas Ades for his *Asyla*.

The 100th anniversary of the birth of jazz great Duke Ellington led to celebrations at New York City's Lincoln Center and elsewhere. The festivities were indicative of the current interest in jazz. The popularity of Ricky Martin illustrated the growing influence of the Latin beat, and swing music continued to enjoy a renewal. Lauryn Hill was a dominant winner at the Grammy Awards.

Classical

Conductors. The Atlanta Symphony, the Boston Symphony, the Cincinnati Symphony, the New York Philharmonic, the Philadelphia Orchestra, the Houston Symphony, the Indiana Symphony, and the Minnesota Orchestra began or continued to search for new music directors during 1999. The Cleveland Orchestra staked out a minority by finding one, Franz Welser-Möst. The most unexpected development was Seiji Ozawa's June announcement, after 25 seasons, that he was leaving the Boston Symphony in 2002 to become music director of the Vienna State Opera. One possible leading contender for Ozawa's job, Sir Simon Rattle, accepted the music directorship of the Berlin Philharmonic that same weekend.

The game of musical chairs focused attention on two points: the small number of major conductors around today and the important question of what a real music director of a major institution ought to be. Old-style music directorships marked by a long-term, committed symbiotic relationship between conductor and ensemble barely exist anymore. When such a relationship does occur, as it has with James Levine at the Metropolitan Opera, the artistic results speak for themselves.

Opera. The most prominent new entry into the operatic repertory was John Harbison's *The Great Gatsby*, based on F. Scott Fitzgerald's novel, which opened at the Metropolitan Opera in December and which the company chose as the first work it would perform in the year 2000. Most American operas that hold the stage are built on a folk-music model. Harbison's *Gatsby* is an urban creation. At the center of the score are several pop songs and dance tunes written without condescension in the style of the 1920s. The complex yearnings of the characters are expressed in deconstructions of those melodies and harmonies, the dialogue

The Boston Symphony Orchestra announced in June 1999 that Seiji Ozawa, left, *would resign as the company's music director and conductor in 2002. Ozawa, who has been the Boston Symphony's music director since 1973, has been credited with maintaining its status as one of the world's leading orchestras.*

John Harbison's opera "The Great Gatsby," based on the F. Scott Fitzgerald novel, premiered at the New York Metropolitan Opera in December 1999. Soprano Dawn Upshaw (left) *created the role of Daisy; Jerry Hadley was Gatsby.*

© StageImage

bouncing off jazz rhythms. The opera proved controversial, but the quality of the workmanship and the dimensions of heart in the piece promised staying power. Dawn Upshaw and Jerry Hadley were Daisy and Gatsby, and Lorraine Hunt Lieberson made a powerhouse debut as Myrtle.

The Lyric Opera of Chicago's premiere of William Bolcom's *A View from the Bridge*, with a libretto by the composer's longtime associate Arnold Weinstein in collaboration with playwright Arthur Miller, was also an international event and was accompanied by an almost unprecedented amount of publicity for a new opera. The work itself proved to be a musically and theatrically striking adventure in the post-verismo style, with an eclectic and attractive score that may need some minor adjustments before its next outing at the Metropolitan. Chicago, which had premiered Bolcom's *McTeague*, seemed pleased enough to commission two additional operas from him; the first of them, *A Wedding*, based on the film by Robert Altman, is scheduled for 2004–05.

Renowned American composer Elliott Carter lengthened the list of his contributions to musical history by writing his first opera at the age of 90. *What Next?* premiered at the Berlin Staatsoper under the direction of Daniel Barenboim in September. The 45-minute opera, on a text by critic/novelist Paul Griffiths, presents six people, one of them a child, who regain consciousness after a car accident and try to remember who they are and what they mean to each other.

Resurrection, based on the Leo Tolstoy novel, surprised admirers of Tod Machover when it was premiered by the Houston Grand Opera—but admirers of Machover have learned to prepare themselves for the unexpected, because this composer's music has mediated among Boulezian complexity, envelope-pushing electronic adventures, and a lifelong love of rock music. *Resurrection* was an attempt to write a contemporary opera in the great romantic style; in idiom it was not more advanced than the opera the Italian composer Franco Alfano had fashioned from the same source in 1904, but most of the way, Machover kept the new rendition interesting.

Other new operas included Jack Beeson's *Sorry, Wrong Number*, Paul Schoenfield's *The Merchant and the Pauper* (both at the Opera Theatre of St. Louis), *Belladonna* by Bernard Rands (in Aspen, CO), and *The Golden Ass* by the Canadian composer Randolph Peters, based on an unset libretto by the late eminent Canadian novelist Robertson Davies (Toronto). Lowell Liebermann's *The Picture of Dorian Gray*, introduced at Monte Carlo in 1996, had a successful U.S. premiere in Milwaukee.

Central Park, a trilogy of one-act operas presented by Glimmerglass Opera and the New York City Opera and also seen on television, paired prominent playwrights with somewhat less prominent composers (Robert Beaser with Terrence McNally, Deborah Drattell with Wendy Wasserstein, and Michael Torke with A.R. Gurney). Afterward, the consensus seemed to be that music took second place. Composer Tan Dun and stage director Peter Sellars created an unusual evening of music-theater based on the ancient Chinese epic drama *The*

Peony Pavilion that enthralled audiences in the United States and Europe.

The Metropolitan Opera belatedly took two 20th-century works into its repertory—Arnold Schoenberg's *Moses und Aron*, begun in 1930 and left incomplete after his immigration to the United States a few years later, and Carlisle Floyd's *Susannah*, which had become one of the most widely performed American operas. At the Met it proved as effective a vehicle for Renée Fleming and Samuel Ramey as it had been for several earlier generations of singers. Other revivals of American operas were the City Opera's version of Beeson's *Lizzie Borden* and Washington Opera's investigation of Robert Ward's *The Crucible*, which, like *A View from the Bridge*, was an operatic version of an Arthur Miller play. Unfamiliar operas of the past also reappeared—from the Boston Early Music Festival's staging of Francesco Cavalli's 1662 *Ercole Amante* (Hercules in Love), to Washington's attempt to revive Ermanno Wolf-Ferrari's *Sly* for José Carreras, to the Spoleto Festival USA's American premiere of Kurt Weill's *Die Bürgschaft*, a work that only now was recovering from Nazi-generated controversy at the time of its premiere in Berlin in 1932.

Jane Eaglen and Ben Heppner brought their historic characterizations of Richard Wagner's *Tristan and Isolde* to the Met, and Cecilia Bartoli stirred up controversy by singing some alternate arias Mozart had created for *Le Nozze di Figaro* in Vienna. José Cura, a protégé of Plácido Domingo's, made a loud and only partially successful attempt to join the inner circle of top tenors, and there were now at least three countertenors—David Daniels, Andreas Scholl, and Bejun Mehta—vying for the superstar status none of their predecessors achieved.

The New York City Opera generated nonmusical controversy by introducing a "sound enhancement system" to the acoustically challenged New York State Theater, undermining, in the view of many, the essential nature of operatic singing.

Orchestras. Mstislav Rostropovich and the Chicago Symphony performed a Dmitry Shostakovich festival organized according to suggestions by the composer himself; Michael Tilson Thomas mounted an Igor Stravinsky festival with the San Francisco Symphony; and the New York Philharmonic celebrated the centennial of the birth of Aaron Copland with a program featuring the composer's complete orchestral music.

Judith Weir's *Natural History* (Boston Symphony) and Christopher Rouse's *Kabir Padavali* (Minnesota Orchestra) were written for soprano Dawn Upshaw. The individual pieces of John Corigliano's *Dylan Thomas Trilogy* came together for the first time in a performance at Carnegie Hall by the National Symphony Orchestra and the

William Bolcom used an Arthur Miller play as the basis of his new opera "A View from the Bridge." The Lyric Opera of Chicago presented the new work in the fall. Gregory Turay (below right) *sang the part of Rodolpho.*

© Chris Hardy/Courtesy, San Francisco Symphony

Michael Tilson Thomas and the San Francisco Symphony staged an Igor Stravinsky Festival at San Francisco's Davies Symphony Hall and Grace Cathedral in June. The festival offered a complete exploration of Stravinsky's music.

Choral Arts Society of Washington. Other new orchestral works of merit included Harbison's *Four Psalms* for chorus, soloists, and orchestra, commissioned to commemorate Israel's 50th anniversary and premiered by the Chicago Symphony; the *Piano Concerto* of Wolfgang Rihm (also by Chicago); John Adams' *Naive and Sentimental Music* (San Francisco Symphony); Roberto Sierra's *Percussion Concerto* (Los Angeles Philharmonic); and Peter Lieberson's *Red Garuda* (performed by the Boston Symphony with pianist Peter Serkin).

Recordings. In general, 1999 was not a good year for the recording industry, but there were a few major projects. Nonesuch Records celebrated a 15-year collaboration with Adams, which was unrivaled on the contemporary American scene, by issuing a ten-CD retrospective set containing most of his music, *The John Adams Earbox*. Philips Classics finished its 200-CD series devoted to the great pianists of the century. RCA/BMG commemorated one of its greatest artists, pianist Arthur Rubinstein, with a massive 94-CD collection featuring 706 performances of more than 347 works. The company planned to release the discs individually in the future. Garrick Ohlsson completed his distinguished survey of the complete piano music of Chopin for Arabesque, and Naxos released a box set of discs by the remarkable Turkish pianist Idil Biret.

British pianist Leslie Howard arrived at the end of his staggering, 94-disc survey of the complete piano music of Liszt for Hyperion, and Graham Johnson came closer to finishing his 37-CD survey of the complete songs of Schubert (also from Hyperion). The year's major attempt to tie music to a film, Corigliano's score to *The Red Violin*, met an equivocal response. The music, played in the film and in concert by violinist Joshua Bell, was more successful than the movie. Another film, *Hilary and Jackie*, made cellist Jacqueline du Pre's recording of the Elgar *Concerto* a best-seller again.

Van Cliburn Competition. The Van Cliburn Foundation in Fort Worth, TX, sponsored a competition for amateur pianists based on a similar contest in Paris that proved very popular and attracted a lot of publicity—as well as controversy, because defining an "amateur" turned out to be a slippery matter. One of the contestants in the Van Cliburn competition was *The New York Times*' art critic, Michael Kimmelman, who chronicled his experiences in the newspaper's magazine. The winner was Alexandre Bodak, a 62-year-old French physician.

RICHARD DYER, *Classical Music Critic*
"The Boston Globe"

Popular and Jazz

As popular music was poised to move into the 21st century, the music business was on the brink of a host of changes, spurred on by digital technology and the Internet. Meanwhile, the commercial story of 1999 was the success achieved by performers in a rather old-fashioned category—the teen idol. Young male groups like the Backstreet Boys and 'N Sync scored major hits alongside teen queens like Britney Spears and Christina Aguilera. The fact that Spears, Aguilera, and some members of 'N Sync got their start in the cast of *The New Mickey Mouse Club* before becoming video stars on MTV underscores the importance of television in promoting teenage stars.

Teenage tastes tend to be fickle, suggesting that few teen idols will have long-lasting singing careers, though they should have no trouble paying for college. The Backstreet Boys' self-titled debut album was a hit in Europe before selling 10 million copies in the United States, and 1999's *Millennium* started at full steam, debuting at the top of the charts. 'N Sync's eponymous debut sold more than 6 million copies, while albums by Spears (*...baby one more time*) and Aguilera (*Genie in a Bottle*) also sold in the millions.

At September's MTV Video Music Awards, 'N Sync, Backstreet Boys, and Britney Spears all performed, with Backstreet Boys winning a viewers' choice award.

The biggest trend in rock was to combine the hard beats of hip-hop with the screaming guitars of heavy metal, a noisy combination that made popular bands out of Korn and Limp Bizkit. Kid Rock also merged hard rock and rap on his popular *Devil Without a Cause* album. Other acts succeeded with punk rock (Offspring), blues-tinged rap (Everlast), ska-rock (Smash Mouth), and industrial rock (Nine Inch Nails).

Madonna's dance-oriented *Ray of Light* was a hit on the charts and at the Grammy Awards, where it was named best pop album. Madonna, always a shrewd trendmonger, contributed a song to the second Austin Powers film, *The Spy Who Shagged Me,* and performed a duet with Ricky Martin on his English-language debut.

Ricky Martin (*see* BIOGRAPHY) led the Latin-music invasion of the pop charts (*see* FEATURE ARTICLE), but his self-titled album quickly was joined on the pop charts and video channels by high-profile releases from Jennifer Lopez and Marc Anthony. Whereas Lopez' recording career came after film success, Anthony was already a singing star in the Spanish-language community, and some critics complained that his English-language record favored familiar pop styles at the expense of the fiery salsa that had made his reputation. For artists crossing the divides of language and musical styles, credibility is a precious commodity.

The fragmented rock audience still includes fans weaned on Elvis Presley and the Beatles. A hugely successful concert tour by the Rolling Stones underscored the box-office clout of this older demographic. In less than two years of touring, the venerable English rock band performed 147 concerts, many in outdoor stadiums, and generated $337.28 million. The latest Stones tour came in the wake of profitable concert swings by bands such as the Eagles and Fleetwood Mac. In all three cases, a catalog of vintage hits proved to be a successful draw for acts that no longer have much clout on the contemporary charts. Similarly, a tour that reunited Bruce Springsteen with his E Street Band sold out arenas across the United States.

No wonder such acts as Blondie and the Eurythmics reunited for new albums and tours in 1999. Crosby, Stills, Nash & Young released *Looking Forward,* their first album since 1988, and announced plans for an ambitious tour. Carlos Santana scored his first Number 1 album since 1971 with *Supernatural*, which shrewdly paired the guitarist with young singers such as Rob Thomas of Matchbox 20. Cher had her biggest hit in years with "Believe," a dance tune (from an album with the same title) that was Number 1 in 22 countries. The summer's most intriguing tour paired two of the era's most acclaimed songwriters, Bob Dylan and Paul Simon. Faded rock stars are often the subject of *Behind the Music,* a popular musical biography series on the cable-music channel VH-1 that has given new life to the careers of performers ranging from Meatloaf to Poison.

Rap and Rhythm and Blues. Gangsta rap, produced and promoted by rapper and entrepreneur Master P, continued to be popular. DMX followed up his 3-million-selling *It's Dark and Hell is Hot* with a new collection that debuted at Number 1: *Flesh of My Flesh... Blood of My Blood.* Jay-Z's *Vol 2...Hard Knock Life* made tough times sound like a party, while Eminem's *The Slim Shady LP* confirmed that a white rapper can make music every bit as violent and sexist as that of his black peers.

Female artists countered by putting a feminine spin on both rap and rhythm and blues. The solo-star status of Lauryn Hill (*see* BIOGRAPHY) of the Fugees was underscored when her album *The Miseducation of Lauryn Hill* won five Grammy Awards. The female rap trio TLC had a hit with *Fan Mail* on the strength of songs that mocked unworthy suitors ("No Scrubs") and questioned such man-pleasing pursuits as cosmetic surgery ("Unpretty"). Singer Mary J. Blige's latest album, *Mary*, solidified her reputation as one of her generation's preeminent vocalists. Female fans were also integral to the appeal of such popular male balladeers as Usher, R. Kelly, and the duo of K-Ci and JoJo.

Jazz. The Pat Metheny Group's *Imaginary Day* won the Grammy for best contemporary jazz album, and guitarist Metheny got splendid reviews for a duet album with another influential jazz guitarist, Jim Hall. Another guitar player, Bill Frissell, continued to record in a wide variety of musical styles. On the heels of such albums as the country-tinged *Nashville* and the bluesy *Gone, Just Like a Train,* Frissell released *The Sweetest Punch,* a collection that reinterpreted songs from a recent collaboration between Elvis Costello and Burt Bacharach. The mostly instrumental album included vocal cameos by Costello and Cassandra Wilson, who consolidated her own position as one of the day's top jazz vocalists with *Traveling Miles*, an album that explored the music of Miles Davis.

The centennial of the birth of Duke Ellington was celebrated with extensive reissues documenting his remarkable catalogue of compositions. Many artists celebrated his legacy, including Tony Bennett—who released *Bennett Sings Ellington Hot & Cool*—and the Lincoln Center Jazz Orchestra.

Among young jazz players debuting in 1999, few drew as much notice as Richard Bona; jazz insiders predicted Bona could become the first star of the bass since the late Jaco Pastorius. His debut album, *Scenes from My Life*, also revealed him to be a dulcet singer with an appreciation for international styles.

Country. It was the year of the woman in Nashville, with Shania Twain and the Dixie Chicks spending virtually the entire year at the top of the charts. Twain's *Come On Over* reached sales of 13 million, with the Grammy-winning single "You're Still the One" cementing her prominence in both the country and pop fields. The Dixie Chicks—a trio that embraces traditional instruments, contemporary fashions, and feminist notions—won the Grammy Award for best country album for their multimillion-selling *Wide Open Spaces*. The win, plus the inclusion of a Dixie Chicks tune on the sound track to *The Runaway Bride*, helped the group debut at the top of the pop charts with its latest album, *Fly*.

Emmylou Harris and Linda Ronstadt collaborated on a critically acclaimed album called *Western Wall* that drew upon their affection for country as well as the work of contemporary singer-songwriters. Steve Earle, whose celebrated songs frequently roam the borders between country and rock, released *The Mountain*, a collection of original bluegrass songs recorded with the Del McCoury Band. But the oddest musical switch of all was executed by the best-selling country artist of all time, Garth Brooks, who released a pop-rock album under the alias "Chris Gaines." The so-called greatest-hits collection—entitled *In...The Life of Chris Gaines*—was released, said Brooks, to lay the groundwork for a future film about the fictional pop star.

Business Trends. Sales of recorded music were robust during 1999, though competing interests also suggested a music business in transition. Sales of music from on-line stores and record-label Web sites continued to expand, as did speculation about a future in which digital music would be sold to consumers via downloads from the Internet. Record labels worked to curb the spread of MP3, a relatively primitive technology through which consumers were downloading music files, and sought to reach an industry consensus on a digital format that would prevent piracy while producing revenue for the artist and the record label. At the same time, some artists continued to see a digital future in which they could market their music without being signed to a major label.

Obituaries. Among notable musicians who passed away during 1999 were Milt Jackson, a master of the vibraphone and member of the Modern Jazz Quartet; the influential jazz and pop singer Mel Torme; blues pianist and singer Charles Brown; British pop singer Dusty Springfield; jazz and blues singer Joe Williams; trumpeter Al Hirt; British pop singer Anthony Newley; funk musician Roger Troutman; cowboy singer Eddie Dean; and World War II–era pop singer Helen Forrest. *See also* OBITUARIES.

JOHN MILWARD, *Freelance Writer and Critic*

Myanmar

Myanmar continued to be a pariah state in 1999. The United Nations General Assembly Commission on Human Rights issued a report in March that once again deplored the human-rights violations perpetrated by the governing State Peace and Development Council (SPDC). Freedom House, which monitors adherence to civil liberties around the globe, placed Myanmar in its lowest category.

Politics. Throughout the year, Aung San Suu Kyi—leader of the opposition National League for Democracy (NLD) and winner of the 1991 Nobel Peace Prize—was under house arrest, as she had been since 1990, when the NLD overwhelmingly won a national election that was annulled by the regime. In early 1999 the SPDC refused to allow Suu Kyi's cancer-stricken husband, Michael Aris, to visit her from England; Suu Kyi was permitted to leave Myanmar to visit him, but she did not, because she feared she would not be allowed to return. Rhetoric against Suu Kyi in the official press grew more shrill. Aris died in March.

During 1999 some cracks appeared in the NLD strategy of pushing the government to allow more political freedom. For instance, a group of 25 within the NLD signaled a willingness to negotiate with the government, but Suu Kyi and most of the membership resisted any such attempts. The government claimed to have crushed a mass uprising scheduled to be held within the country on September 9, but several demonstrations against the regime took place in Thailand on that date.

The universities remained closed, since the government considered students to be even more of a threat than the NLD. Six students were arrested and charged with subversion in 1999; if convicted, they could be sentenced to seven years of hard labor. A burgeoning opposition movement among high-schoolers began to gain momentum.

In October an activist group calling itself the Vigorous Burmese Student Warriors took 38 people hostage at the Myanmar embassy in Thailand, in an attempt to focus attention on the political conditions in Myanmar. Thai officials negotiated the release of the hostages about a day later. They also guaranteed the kidnappers safe passage, calling them freedom fighters. Angered, Myanmar promptly closed its border with Thailand and canceled Thai fishing commissions in its waters.

MYANMAR • Information Highlights

Official Name: Union of Myanmar.
Location: Southeast Asia.
Area: 261,969 sq mi (678 500 km^2).
Population (July 1999 est.): 48,081,302.
Chief Cities (1983 census): Yangon (Rangoon), the capital, 2,513,023; Mandalay, 532,949.
Government: *Head of state and government,* Gen. Than Shwe (took power April 23, 1992). *Legislature* (unicameral)—People's Assembly.
Monetary Unit: Kyat (6.2200 kyats equal U.S.$1, Nov. 3, 1999).
Gross Domestic Product (1998 est. U.S.$): $56,100,000,000 (purchasing power parity).
Economic Index (1998, 1990 = 100): *Consumer Prices,* all items, 703.5; food, 834.6.
Foreign Trade (1998 U.S.$): *Imports,* $2,667,000,000; *exports,* $1,067,000,000.

The Economy. Economic conditions remained grim throughout 1999. Reports in August noted that foreign investment was at a five-year low. Many foreign companies—including Levi Strauss, Pepsi, and Liz Claiborne—left Myanmar. Official commentaries blamed the Asian financial crisis for the country's economic troubles. By late 1999 the government had privatized more than 36,000 state-run enterprises, part of a program that critics called "military capitalism." However, the Union of Myanmar Economic Holding Company remained wholly owned and operated by defense officials, veterans, and military regiments undertaking joint ventures with foreign investors. Tourism facilities that had been built with forced labor had low occupancy rates.

Britain and Germany charged the regime with drug trafficking, and the United States and many European nations continued to support economic sanctions against Myanmar. A proposed $1 billion in aid from the World Bank was shelved when the SPDC rejected all reform measures.

Foreign Affairs. Relations with Europe and the United States remained frayed. SPDC chairman Than Shwe denounced Western criticism as neocolonialist. The Association of Southeast Asian Nations (ASEAN), which admitted Myanmar in 1997, continued to be disappointed and embarrassed by the regime's human-rights abuses.

Thailand favored collaboration with Yangon on antidrug initiatives but was concerned about the spillover of insurgents' activities into Thailand. Japan continued to give substantial aid, and China continued to lend support to Myanmar's naval buildup—a development that led to rumors that China could be viewing these naval bases as potential future sites for its own military.

LINDA KAY RICHTER, *Kansas State University*

Netherlands

Despite a brief political spat and mild disaffection from the governing coalition, in 1999 the Netherlands maintained its tradition of quiet consensus and economic growth. On the international scene, more than 2,000 Dutch troops were assigned to participate in the United Nations peacekeeping force in Kosovo.

Politics. The left-libertarian Democrats 66 (D'66) was the smallest of the three parties in Prime Minister Wim Kok's ruling coalition. Yet it played a key role in holding together the two larger but more divergent parties of the ministry: Kok's left-of-center Labor (Social Democratic) Party and the right-leaning, free-market Liberal Party. One issue dear to D'66 was that of popular referenda—the possibility that, by popular vote, citizens could overrule parliament on a given issue. When, on May 19, the upper house defeated by one vote a bill expanding the use of referenda, with a Liberal member of the government coalition failing to support the bill, D'66 resigned from the ministry. The remaining parties failed to find common ground to overcome the crisis and resigned as well. The cabinet stayed on in a caretaker capacity. Compromise arrived in three weeks; more referenda would be held, but they would be consultative, not binding. D'66 came back to the fold, and Kok's government retracted its resignation; all but one member returned.

June elections to the European Parliament reflected some disaffection with the government coalition parties. Labor's representation fell two seats to six, the same number that the Liberals retained, while D'66 representation was halved to two. The big winner was Green Left, gaining three seats for a total of four. The Christian Democrats lost a seat; their share of the vote fell from 30.8% in the previous European election to 26.9%. Yet this percentage was significantly higher than the 18.4% they had won in the previous national election; it once again made them the most popular party (with 6.8% more votes than Labor) in the country.

Economics. According to the Central Bureau of Statistics, the average purchasing power of the Dutch citizen rose by about 5.8% from 1994 to 1996, to 34,350 guilders (about $16,400) per year. The provinces of Groningen and Friesland experienced lower-than-average disposable incomes, while towns in the province of Utrecht generally had higher-than-average levels. Cities with populations of more than 100,000—like Amsterdam, Rotterdam, and Groningen—were the poorest, while smaller cities fared much better.

The government was investing in Amsterdam to make it a center of new-media technology, with the equivalent of tens of millions of dollars flowing into information infrastructure and technology-research institutes. Rotterdam still was being expanded as a port, as the government decided to use all available space there before expanding Vlissingen and Terneuzen to handle excess shipping. This decision came as a major disappointment to the Zeeland ports.

Other News. The Netherlands experienced two major food scares in 1999, first over dioxin-tainted Belgian farm products and then over Coca-Cola–produced beverages that had caused illness in some Belgian children. In both cases, the Dutch government banned sale of the items within the Netherlands for several weeks.

Teacher shortages continued. An appeal to retirees to return to the classroom failed, so the government authorized schools to hire teachers lacking certification. The shortage was blamed on demanding workloads and poor pay.

Euthanasia long had been technically illegal but was permitted if doctors acted within approved guidelines. Kok's cabinet proposed to end this paradox with a bill approving euthanasia if certain guidelines are followed; failure to adhere to them would be a criminal offense....One billion guilders were allocated to the National Purchase Fund for art....The 40-volume *Dictionary of the Dutch Language* was completed after 150 years of work.

JONATHAN E. HELMREICH, *Allegheny College*

NETHERLANDS • Information Highlights

Official Name: Kingdom of the Netherlands.
Location: Northwestern Europe.
Area: 16,036 sq mi (41 532 km²).
Population (July 1999 est.): 15,807,641.
Chief Cities (Jan. 1, 1997 est.): Amsterdam, the capital, 715,148; Rotterdam, 589,987; The Hague, the seat of government, 442,159.
Government: *Head of state,* Beatrix, queen (acceded April 30, 1980). *Head of government,* Willem Kok, prime minister (took office Aug. 22, 1994). *Legislature*—States General: First Chamber and Second Chamber.
Monetary Unit: Guilder (2.1383 guilders equal U.S.$1, Nov. 19, 1999).
Gross Domestic Product (1998 est. U.S.$): $348,600,000,000 (purchasing power parity).
Economic Indexes (1998, 1990 = 100): *Consumer Prices,* all items, 121.6; food, 114.3. *Industrial Production,* 116.8.
Foreign Trade (1998 U.S.$): *Imports,* $185,111,000,000; *exports,* $199,631,000,000.

New York City

Education, crime, and welfare dominated the headlines in New York City in 1999, and, as usual, the city's combative mayor, Rudolph W. Giuliani, was on center stage in nearly every case. Giuliani proclaimed success in his efforts to end welfare in the city by shifting recipients into work, job training, or drug and mental-health treatment. The mayor said that by the end of 1999, all able-bodied welfare recipients without infant children were either in jobs or on the road to getting them, though some City Council members disputed his numbers.

Giuliani suffered a number of legal setbacks. An appeals court ruled that his administration had been overly aggressive in its bid to shut down pornography businesses; a judge found that the mayor had retaliated improperly against an AIDS organization that had been critical of his policies by blocking it from receiving $2.4 million in federal money; and he lost a referendum that would have revised the city charter to prevent a longtime critic, Public Advocate Mark Green, from succeeding him as mayor. Giuliani also failed in his attempt to cut public financing to the Brooklyn Museum of Art for mounting an exhibit that he found offensive and was rebuked in his effort to deny a permit for a youth rally in Harlem. But Giuliani, who was expected to run as the Republican candidate for the U.S. Senate in 2000, seemed to shrug it all off, emphasizing instead his victories. These included his homeless policies and the city's swift response in containing an outbreak of West Nile virus—a mosquito-borne illness that killed seven people and sickened dozens of others in the region during the summer.

© Jeff Christensen/Reuters/Corbis

"Sensation," a controversial exhibit at the Brooklyn Museum of Art, above, led New York Mayor Rudolph Giuliani to try to cut off city subsidies to the institution.

Education. Capping a tumultuous year in education, the Board of Education voted in December not to renew the contract of Schools Chancellor Rudy Crew, maintaining that he had lost his grip on the nation's largest public-school system, with 1.1 million children. Three of the votes against Crew were cast by allies of Giuliani, who had become disenchanted with the chancellor's behavior. Earlier, a state study found that not only did the city have a disproportionate number of uncertified teachers, but those who were certified performed much more poorly than their counterparts elsewhere in the state. Also, new data showed that a large majority of the city's eighth graders failed to meet tough new state standards in mathematics and English.

Crime. Despite an 8% overall decline in crime and a 9% decline in violent crime in the city in 1999, murders rose nearly 7%, a rebound that puzzled criminal-justice experts and city officials. Four police officers were charged with murdering Amadou Diallo, an unarmed immigrant from Guinea, in a barrage of 41 bullets outside his Bronx apartment; a court ordered the trial moved to Albany because the public outcry over the case had made a fair trial in the Bronx impossible. Justin A. Volpe—an officer who pleaded guilty in May to brutalizing a Haitian immigrant, Abner Louima, in a Brooklyn police station in 1997—was sentenced to 30 years in prison. A second officer, Charles Schwarz, was convicted in the case.

Other News. A public-transportation strike was averted after a last-minute deal was reached between the transit employees' union and the city that would increase the pay of subway and bus workers by more than 18% over three years....One of the city's most famous residents, John F. Kennedy, Jr., was killed with his wife and her sister when his small plane crashed over the Atlantic Ocean near Nantucket; hundreds of mourners paid their respects at a memorial service in Manhattan and outside his Tribeca apartment....For the third time in four years, the New York Yankees basked in a ticker-tape parade along lower Broadway, having swept the Atlanta Braves in the World Series.

SCOTT VEALE
"The New York Times"

New Zealand

A general election in November 1999 saw New Zealand's conservative National Party government defeated after nine years in office and replaced by a minority Labour-Alliance coalition, headed by Helen Clark.

Politics. The National government, led by Prime Minister Jenny Shipley, struggled to rejuvenate itself via strategic actions, such as promoting young ministers to key portfolios. However, polls consistently revealed that the government's popularity had slid substantially. During a protracted but lackluster election campaign, National hoped that the record 2.5-million electorate would choose stability, while Clark's Labour Party conducted a restrained, safe course—emphasizing education, welfare, and responsibility in government.

The results of the proportional voting system gave only the center-left Labour (38.7% and 49 seats) and its partner, the Alliance (7.7%, ten seats), the prospect of forming a viable government. However, in order to pass legislation, the government would need to rely on the Greens (5.2%, seven seats). National recorded its lowest-ever level of support (30.5%, 39 seats). The new 20-member cabinet, headed by Prime Minister Clark, faced the task of devising a compromise policy program, the top priority being a 6% increase in income tax on yearly earnings above $60,000.

In addition, two nonbinding referenda passed by a wide margin. One, which called for the reduction of Parliament from 120 members to 99, received 82% backing, while another wanting tougher penalties for violent crime attracted some 92% support.

Foreign Relations. Shipley took several trips to the United States and Europe, as well as to the South Pacific Forum, principally to discuss trade access for New Zealand. The Asia-Pacific Economic Cooperation (APEC) summit, held in Auckland in September, brought together 21 leaders, including U.S. President Bill Clinton and Chinese President Jiang Zemin. The official communiqué heralded further trade and economic reform. Immediately afterward, Clinton announced a qualified resumption of joint U.S.–New Zealand military exercises. Also in September, former Labour Prime Minister Mike Moore accepted the post of director-general of the World Trade Organization (WTO) for a three-year term.

In November, Don McKinnon, minister of foreign affairs since 1990, secured the position of secretary-general of the Commonwealth Secretariat. The decision to send more than 800 troops to participate in the United Nations (UN) peacekeeping force during East Timor's transition to independence from Indonesia received approval from all of New Zealand's political parties.

Economy. The final budget, presented by Treasurer Bill Birch in May, was notable for its lack of major tax-cut, education, or employment initiatives. Coming into sharper focus, however, were forecasts of a marginal budget deficit and a 3.5% rate of growth of gross domestic product (GDP) in 2000–01. Creating considerable anxiety were the high unemployment rate (7.7% in February) and the climbing current-account deficit of 8.3%. Predictions of a 2.7% inflation rate and 3.2% export growth in 2000 encouraged the Treasury to anticipate a solid recovery, but other observers were more pessimistic.

GRAHAM BUSH, *University of Auckland*

NEW ZEALAND • Information Highlights

Official Name: New Zealand.
Location: Southwest Pacific Ocean.
Area: 103,737 sq mi (268 680 km^2).
Population (July 1999 est.): 3,662,265.
Chief Cities (March 1996 est.): Wellington, the capital, 335,468; Auckland, 997,940; Christchurch, 331,443.
Government: *Head of state,* Elizabeth II, queen, represented by Sir Michael Hardie-Boys, governor-general (sworn in March 21, 1996). *Head of government,* Helen Clark, prime minister (took office Dec. 10, 1999). *Legislature* (unicameral)—House of Representatives (Parliament).
Monetary Unit: New Zealand dollar (1.9286 N.Z. dollars equal U.S.$1, Jan. 5, 2000).
Gross Domestic Product (1998 est. U.S.$): $61,100,-000,000 (purchasing power parity).
Economic Indexes (1998, 1990 = 100): *Consumer Prices,* all items, 116.2; food, 110.2. *Industrial Production,* 116.4.
Foreign Trade (1998 U.S.$): *Imports,* $12,496,000,000; *exports,* $12,071,000,000.

Nigeria

Local, parliamentary, and presidential elections held in late 1998 and early 1999 brought Nigeria its first elected civilian government in 20 years. The new president, Olusegun Obasanjo, promised to improve Nigeria's depressed economic situation and its place in the international community.

Politics. Gen. Abdulsalam Abubakar, who had assumed power after the June 1998 death of strongman Gen. Sani Abacha, delivered on his promise of a prompt return to democracy. All old political parties were dissolved, and five new ones were created, the most important of which were Obasanjo's People's Democratic Party (PDP), the Alliance for Democracy (AD), and the All People's Party (APP). Local elections took place in early December 1998, followed by balloting for government and state assemblies on January 9, for the National Assembly on February 20, and for president on February 27. The clear victor in the major parliamentary elections was the PDP, which gained more than half of the 469 seats in the Senate and House of Representatives.

The chief candidate for president was Obasanjo, who had ruled Nigeria after the assassination of Gen. Murtala Muhammad in 1976 and returned the state to civilian rule in 1979. His opponent was Olu Falae, the nominee of the APP and AD, who had been finance minister during the regime of Gen. Ibrahim Babangida. Monitored by more than 10,000 observers, including former President Jimmy Carter and Gen. Colin Powell from the United States, the elections were generally peaceful. Obasanjo won easily, gaining more than 60% of the vote. Falae briefly questioned the results, citing fraud, but an appeals court dismissed his claim.

Obasanjo was sworn in as president on May 29, and Abubakar formally handed over power and resigned from military service. The new president immediately pledged to fight corruption at all levels, improve the communications infrastructure, and end the bloody fighting in the petroleum-rich but desperately poor Delta region. He also promised to take firm action against the drug lords who had made Nigeria one of the key players in the international drug trade. Many of his cabinet appointees were members of the Nigerian political establishment.

The change in government did not end the ethnic violence that has been endemic throughout the country, and particularly in the Delta region. For example, 100 people died in a clash between Muslims and Christians in Kafanchan, northeast of Abuja, in April; and in June about 200 people were killed in fighting among three ethnic groups near the town of Warri in the Delta, which led the Shell Oil Company to threaten to close down production.

In mid-November, Evan Enwerem, an Obasanjo loyalist, was removed as Senate president. He was accused of perjury.

NIGERIA • Information Highlights

Official Name: Federal Republic of Nigeria.
Location: West Africa.
Area: 356,668 sq mi (923 770 km²).
Population (July 1999 est.): 113,828,587.
Chief City (1993 unofficial est.): Abuja, the capital, 250,000.
Government: *Head of state and government,* Olusegun Obasanjo, president (sworn in May 29, 1999). *Legislature*—National Assembly: Senate and House of Representatives.
Monetary Unit: Naira (97.700 naira equal U.S.$1, Dec. 13, 1999).
Gross Domestic Product (1998 est. U.S.$): $106,200,-000,000 (purchasing power parity).
Economic Index (1998, 1990 = 100): *Consumer Prices,* all items, 1,075.5; food, 984.6.
Foreign Trade (1998 U.S.$): *Imports,* $13,624,000,000; *exports,* $11,519,000,000.

The Economy. Despite the movement from dictatorship to democracy in Nigeria, the economy continued to decline. A decision in January to allow market forces to dictate the value of the naira (N) caused it to drop precipitously. Falling international prices for crude oil, which provides 80% of the country's revenue, dragged the economy lower, and the disturbances in the Delta also reduced the amount of petroleum exports. The government was forced to import gasoline to meet domestic needs. The 1999 budget projected a deficit of N34.1 billion ($396.5 million), with only N1.5 billion ($17.4 million) set aside for paying Nigeria's $30 billion international debt. The minimum wage was reduced 45% from its earlier announced level, and unemployment in the major cities rose dramatically, as did the crime rate.

Foreign Policy. Most Western states applauded Nigeria's transition to democracy and moved to restore friendly relations. The Commonwealth readmitted Nigeria shortly after Obasanjo took office, and Britain lifted trade sanctions and began bilateral talks on economic cooperation. U.S. Secretary of State Madeleine Albright visited Nigeria in early October and communicated strong approval of Obasanjo's government; in addition, reflecting the U.S. economic interest in Nigeria's petroleum industry, she proposed raising U.S. aid fourfold from its level of $27 million a year. Mindful of the need to reduce the annual payments on Nigeria's huge international debt, Obasanjo challenged Albright to help provide a "democracy dividend" in debt relief. During a visit to Washington a few weeks later, he enlisted President Bill Clinton's aid in rescheduling Nigeria's heavy external debts. Nigeria's premier position in West Africa was bolstered by the settlement of the bloody civil war in Sierra Leone, made possible largely by Nigeria's leadership in the Economic Community of West African States (ECOWAS) and the dispatch of its troops to contain the rebels there.

HARRY A. GAILEY, *San Jose State University*

Norway

Norway's economy slowed in 1999 despite rising oil prices, and growth was expected to remain low in 2000. The main opposition party, Labour, lost ground in local elections, while the Christian People's Party of Prime Minister Kjell Magne Bondevik advanced, and his minority government strengthened its power base.

Politics. The three-party coalition government led by Bondevik, holding only 42 of the 165 seats in the Norwegian parliament, consolidated its weak base in 1999 by accommodating the majority view on several issues. At 55.5%, turnout for Norway's municipal elections in September was lower than usual, but national political interest in the outcome was above average, as the vote was seen as a test of the government's strength in preparation for parliamentary elections in 2001. Two coalition members, the Liberals and the Centre Party, lost support compared with 1995 results, but the Christian People's Party rose from 8.6% to 10.1%. The major opposition party, Labour, dropped more than three points to 28.1%, fostering rumors that its leader, former prime minister Thorbjørn Jagland, would be forced out in favor of the more popular Jens Stoltenberg. But Jagland, who commanded strong support from party stalwarts and the trade unions, was not challenged openly.

Oil prices rose by almost 250% in 1999, reaching $24 a barrel, and the resulting increase in revenues helped balance the budget. The 13.3-billion-kroner ($1.7 billion) deficit was eliminated, leaving a surplus of 71.8 billion kroner ($9.1 billion) in the government oil fund, which accumulates wealth in anticipation of oil shortfalls.

Political controversy was sparked by foreign interest in merging with or acquiring Norwegian companies in all sectors. Norsk Hydro, which is 51% government-controlled, took over publicly held Saga Petroleum, outbidding the French company Elf Aquitaine. The government planned a partial privatization of the entire oil industry but recoiled when state-run Statoil proposed taking over the core government assets in the State Direct Financial Interest (SDFI), which controls 40% of Norwegian oil reserves and production. Statoil argued that the merger would make it the world's fourth-largest oil company. Parliament planned to debate the restructuring of Norway's oil industry in 2000.

Merita-Nordbanken, a Finnish-Swedish bank, launched a bid for Christiania Bank, Norway's second-largest, which would create the largest bank in the Nordic countries. Even though the government was expected to sell its 35% stake, the success of the transaction remained uncertain in late 1999. In September, after tough negotiations, the state-owned telecommunications companies Telenor of Norway and Telia of Sweden merged. The rancorous tone of the discussions was epitomized by a comment by Sweden's Trade and Industry Minister Björn Rosengren in which he called Norway "the last Soviet state"; he later apologized.

Economy. As the world's second-largest exporter of oil, Norway experienced a boost in its economy from the rise in oil prices in 1999, which averted a recession. Investment in the oil sector slowed down, however, and the country's other industries performed dreadfully. Economic growth was expected to be below 1% in both 1999 and 2000.

LEIF BECK FALLESEN, *Editor in Chief "Boersen," Copenhagen*

NORWAY • Information Highlights

Official Name: Kingdom of Norway.
Location: Northern Europe.
Area: 125,182 sq mi (324 220 km²).
Population (July 1999 est.): 4,438,547.
Chief Cities (Jan. 1, 1997 est.): Oslo, the capital, 741,621; Bergen, 198,627; Trondheim, 137,123; Stavanger, 107,570.
Government: *Head of state,* Harald V, king (acceded January 1991). *Head of government,* Kjell Magne Bondevik, prime minister (took office October 1997). *Legislature*—Storting.
Monetary Unit: Krone (8.0096 kroner equal U.S.$1, Dec. 13, 1999).
Gross Domestic Product (1998 est. U.S.$): $109,000,000,000 (purchasing power parity).
Economic Indexes (1998, 1990 = 100): *Consumer Prices,* all items, 119.5; food, 115.5. *Industrial Production,* 137.9.
Foreign Trade (1998 U.S.$): *Imports,* $36,196,000,000; *exports,* $39,649,000,000.

Obituaries

HUSSEIN, King

Monarch of the Hashemite Kingdom of Jordan from 1952: b. Amman, Jordan, Nov. 14, 1935; d. Amman, Feb. 7, 1999.

One of the most remarkable careers in recent Middle East history ended when King Hussein of Jordan died on Feb. 7, 1999.

King Hussein's heritage as a descendant of the Prophet Muhammad and as a Hashemite, a member of a family formerly prominent in the Hejaz in western Arabia, pulled him toward the strong pro-Arab feelings of the large Palestinian presence in Jordan, while his culture and education pulled him toward moderate pro-Western policies. Yet Hussein succeeded in the 46 years of his reign in not merely maintaining Jordan's independent existence. His kingdom developed economically; traditions of civility were maintained; and a considerable degree of political liberty existed in a firm monarchy. Also, geographical conditions demanded of him a cautious, tightrope-walking policy, for Jordan has limited access to the sea through its one port, Aqaba. It has frontiers with Syria, Iraq, Saudi Arabia, and Israel.

Background. Hussein Ibn Talal el-Hasimi was British-educated—at Harrow and at the Royal Military College, Sandhurst. Hussein was present when his grandfather, King Abdullah, was assassinated in 1951. Hussein's father's brief reign ended on Aug. 11, 1952, when the king was deemed mentally unfit to rule. Hussein, 17, was enthroned formally on May 2, 1953. Hastening to dispel an image as a British puppet—for Jordan, like Iraq, was a British creation—the king refrained in 1955 from joining the pro-Western Baghdad Pact. In 1956 he dismissed Gen. John Bagot Glubb as the British commander of the Arab Legion—the best-trained Arab army in the Middle East. In the joint Arab attack on fledgling Israel in 1948, the Arab Legion had been able to take over East Jerusalem and the West Bank, enabling Transjordan to be renamed Jordan.

Although no friend of President Gamal Abdel Nasser of Egypt, Hussein joined in the 1967 attack on Israel known as the Six-Day War. In consequence, Jordan lost all the West Bank territories it had gained in 1948. Hussein never again offered a serious military challenge to Israel, participating only limitedly in the 1973 war. In 1970 he disposed successfully of the threat to Jordanian sovereignty created by the Palestine Liberation Organization's (PLO's) base in Jordan, which was becoming a state within a state. The PLO was driven out of Jordan after heavy fighting; but Hussein in 1974 had to suffer the humiliation of having the other Arab states recognize the PLO as "the sole legitimate representative of the Palestinian people." In 1988 he ceased to oppose this dictum and relinquished all responsibility for the West Bank territories.

© Corbis-Sygma

In the 1990–91 Kuwait crisis, Hussein strove fruitlessly to exert a calming, neutral influence and avert war. His seeming sympathy for Iraq cost him large subsidies from Saudi Arabia and other states, but played well at home. From the 1960s on, he met secretly with Israeli leaders. In 1994 he concluded a formal peace treaty with Israel.

Hussein survived many attempts on his life. He underwent a serious operation for cancer of the urinary tract in 1992. In 1998 he began to suffer from an unrelated form of cancer—non-Hodgkin's lymphoma. But in October he made the effort to intervene in the Wye summit talks in Maryland, urging the Palestinian and Israeli parties to accept the 1998 agreement.

In 1978 the king married his fourth wife, Lisa Halaby, an American, who was given the title of Queen Noor. He had 11 children by his four marriages. In the very last weeks of his life, he ousted his brother Hassan from the succession and nominated his eldest son, Abdullah, as heir.

ARTHUR CAMPBELL TURNER

DiMAGGIO, Joe

U.S. professional-baseball player and celebrity: b. Martinez, CA, Nov. 25, 1914; d. Hollywood, FL, March 8, 1999.

"For several generations of baseball fans, Joe was the personification of grace, class, and dignity on the diamond." With those few words, baseball commissioner Allan H. (Bud) Selig expressed the sentiments of millions after lung cancer claimed the life of former New York Yankees star Joe DiMaggio in Hollywood, FL, on March 8, 1999.

DiMaggio paced the Yankees to ten pennants and nine world championships during his 13-year tenure with the team. Between his rookie year of 1936 and his final campaign in 1951, the star center fielder took batting crowns in 1939 and 1940, won home-run titles in 1937 and 1948, and knocked in the most runs in 1941 and 1948. He was an all-star every year of his career.

From May 15 to July 17, 1941, the 6′3″ (1.9-m), 195-lb (88-kg) right-handed batter hit safely in 56 consecutive games—a record widely considered unbreakable. During the 56 games, he had 16 doubles, four triples, 15 home runs, 21 walks, seven strikeouts, and 55 runs batted in (RBIs) in 223 at-bats. He had four four-hit games and a .408 batting average during the streak. DiMaggio was rewarded after that season with his second of three most-valuable-player (MVP) awards. He also was American League MVP in 1939 and 1947. "The Yankee Clipper" had a .325 lifetime batting average, 361 home runs, and 1,537 runs batted in (an average of 118 RBIs per season). His numbers might have been better without the interference of military service (1943–45) and a painful heel injury that forced him to retire at age 36.

During his prime, DiMaggio glided gracefully across acres of outfield, pounded prodigious long hits when his team needed them most, and proved it possible for a power hitter to put the ball in play. (He averaged just more than one strikeout per home run during his career.) The owner of a powerful throwing arm, DiMaggio always threw to the right base, never missed the cutoff man, and rarely made errors.

Like Babe Ruth before him and Mickey Mantle after him, DiMaggio was the Yankees. Even though Mantle surfaced before he left, DiMaggio's retirement left a gaping void not only in the Yankee lineup but also in the national psyche. More than 30 years later, Simon & Garfunkel's soulful song "Mrs. Robinson" dared ask, "Where have you gone, Joe DiMaggio? The nation turns its lonely eyes to you."

© Archive Photos/PNI

After retiring from the game, DiMaggio was married briefly to movie star Marilyn Monroe. He served as pitchman for Mr. Coffee and a savings bank and worked as a spring-training coach for both the Yankees and the Oakland Athletics. The Yankee Clipper was elected to Baseball's Hall of Fame in 1955. In 1969, when professional baseball celebrated its centennial, fans voted him "the greatest living player." Six years later, DiMaggio's 56-game hitting streak was voted the most memorable moment in American League history.

Background. The eighth of nine children born to Italian immigrants who settled in San Francisco, DiMaggio had two siblings, Dom and Vince, who also became major-league outfielders. During the Depression, the teenage DiMaggio sold newspapers and worked in a cannery to help his family. In 1932 he served as backup shortstop for the San Francisco Seals of the old Pacific Coast League. The Yankees got him for five players and $25,000.

The first $100,000 ballplayer later would command $100,000 per appearance at baseball-card shows. DiMaggio's legacy lives at the Joe DiMaggio Children's Hospital in Hollywood, FL, which is funded primarily through a DiMaggio endowment. In 1939 the future baseball star had married actress Dorothy Arnold. They were divorced in 1944. Their son, and Joe's only child, Joe, Jr., died in August 1999.

DAN SCHLOSSBERG

© Paul Gero/Corbis-Sygma

Lane Kirkland

KIRKLAND, Lane

U.S. labor leader: b. Camden, SC, March 12, 1922; d. Washington, DC, Aug. 14, 1999.

Lane Kirkland, the only president in the American Federation of Labor to be forced to resign in the 20th century, died on Aug. 14, 1999, at the age of 77. Kirkland, president of the AFL-CIO from 1979 to 1995, resigned in the face of opposition from some 20 unions, which believed that he was not sufficiently active in organizing new members and that he spent too much time and effort on international affairs. Kirkland was succeeded by John J. Sweeney, president of the Service Employees International Union.

Background. Lane Kirkland served in World War II in the merchant marine, spending much of that time as chief mate aboard ships transporting war materiel to the Allies. He joined the International Organization of Masters, Mates, and Pilots. After the war he studied at the School of Foreign Service at Georgetown University. Upon graduating in 1948, he worked as a researcher in the American Federation of Labor and then went on to serve as director of research and education for the International Union of Operating Engineers from 1958 to 1960. In 1960 he returned to the AFL-CIO as executive assistant to President George Meany. Kirkland was elected secretary-treasurer of the AFL-CIO in May 1969, a position he held until he succeeded Meany as president in 1979.

Kirkland was a strong supporter of U.S. involvement in the Vietnam war in the 1960s and 1970s, despite the opposition of many unions. In the 1980s he assisted Lech Walesa's Solidarity movement in bringing democracy to Poland. In recognition of his many achievements, he was awarded the Presidential Medal of Freedom by President Bill Clinton in 1994. Kirkland was well-known for his commitment to civil rights. Under his leadership, the AFL-CIO placed the first woman on the executive council and increased the participation of blacks and Hispanics.

Survivors included his wife, Irena Neumann, a German concentration-camp survivor; five children from his first marriage; five grandchildren; and two great-grandchildren.

JACK STIEBER

SCOTT, George C.

U.S. screen, stage, and television actor: b. Wise, VA, Oct. 18, 1927; d. Westlake Village, CA, Sept. 22, 1999.

History has played a trick on renowned World War II Gen. George S. Patton, Jr. Future generations may not visualize him as he really was, but rather may tend to picture him as actor George C. Scott, so indelible was Scott's performance in the 1970 film *Patton*.

Scott played a broad spectrum of parts during his lengthy career, encompassing some 50 films, 150 plays, and countless television shows. He was showered with film, stage, and television awards, most of which he refused, denouncing such honors as mere popularity contests. Scott declined to accept either his nomination or his best-actor Oscar

George C. Scott

© Lookout/Camera Press

for *Patton*, as he previously had rejected Oscar nominations for *Anatomy of a Murder* (1959) and *The Hustler* (1961). In his private life, which often was also very public, he earned a reputation for hard drinking, hard living, and a furious temper.

Background. Although born in the coal town of Wise, VA, George Campbell Scott spent most of his youth in Detroit, MI. His mother died when he was 8. His father worked on an auto-assembly line. After high school, Scott joined the U.S. Marines and was assigned the duty of burying World War II dead at Arlington National Cemetery, a task that caused him a great deal of anguish. While attending the University of Missouri School of Journalism after the war, he played the role of barrister Sir Robert Morton in Terence Rattigan's play *The Winslow Boy*. From then on, Scott was hooked on acting.

Scott received his training in stock productions, then tried to make his living in New York City as an actor, while supporting himself with odd jobs. His break came in 1957, thanks to theatrical producer Joseph Papp, who risked casting the unknown actor in the title role of a Central Park production of Shakespeare's *Richard III*. Favorable critical reviews of that performance provided the career leap Scott coveted, and he had enjoyed considerable success ever since, despite periods when his drinking and marital problems conflicted with his work.

Besides Patton, Scott's most memorable film roles include those of Buck Turgidson, the hawkish, pro–nuclear war general in Stanley Kubrick's satirical *Dr. Strangelove* (1964), and Bert Gordon, the poolroom promoter in *The Hustler*. His other movies include *Petulia* (1968), *They Might Be Giants* (1972), *Hardcore* (1979), and *Gloria* (1999).

His triumphs in the theater, where Scott felt most at home, included *The Andersonville Trial* (1959), *The Merchant of Venice* (1962), and *Death of a Salesman* (1975). When he starred in a revival of *Inherit the Wind* on Broadway in 1996, he suffered an aortic aneurysm and had to withdraw. His extensive television work included *The Last Days of Patton* (1986). He appeared in two TV series, *East Side/West Side* (1963–64) and *Mr. President* (1987–88). He also directed several films and theatrical productions.

Scott twice was married to and divorced from actress Colleen Dewhurst, with whom he sometimes costarred. The actor was survived by his wife, actress Trish Van Devere, to whom he was married in 1972; by their two sons; and by three children from two other marriages.

WILLIAM WOLF

CHAMBERLAIN, Wilt

U.S. basketball player: b. Philadelphia, PA, Aug. 21, 1936; d. Los Angeles, CA, Oct. 12, 1999.

Wilt Chamberlain made it acceptable to be a very big man in basketball. Before Chamberlain, big men were viewed as gawky freaks who were dominant only because of their unfair size advantage. But Chamberlain, who stood a regal 7′ 1″ (2.3 m) tall and weighed 275 lb (125 kg), changed all that. He was a superb athlete who happened to be encased in a huge body. His agility, quickness, and natural skills, coupled with his imposing height, made him virtually unstoppable. And his success changed the way professional basketball was played. The National Basketball Association (NBA), starting in the 1960s, became a league dominated by big men with skills nearly comparable to Chamberlain's—players like Boston's Bill Russell. Chamberlain was so good that he even had two nicknames, "Wilt the Stilt" and the "Big Dipper." His accomplishments were as impressive as his physique, with the

Wilt Chamberlain

© George Long/"Sports Illustrated"

most astonishing being his 100-point game against the New York Knicks in 1962.

Background. Wilton Norman Chamberlain was born Aug. 21, 1936, in Philadelphia, PA. A versatile athlete who also ran cross-country in high school, he did not begin playing basketball until he was in seventh grade. At Overbrook High School, he became the most highly recruited high-school basketball player in history. He signed with the University of Kansas, where his team lost the 1957 National Collegiate Athletic Association (NCAA) basketball championship to North Carolina, falling in triple overtime. He left college after his junior year and played a season with the Harlem Globetrotters before joining the Philadelphia Warriors of the NBA. In 14 seasons, which also included stops in San Francisco and Los Angeles, he averaged 30.1 points per game and scored 31,419 points—a record at the time. His teams won two NBA titles.

He averaged an astonishing 50.4 points per game in the 1961–62 season and once led the NBA in assists, just to prove he could do more than score. He also never fouled out of any of his 1,205 pro games. He led the league in scoring for seven straight seasons and in rebounding 11 times, and was the most valuable player four times (1960, 1966, 1967, and 1968). He still holds the NBA record for career rebounds (23,924). He was so good that the league even widened the free-throw lane to push him further from the basket. His only flaw was an inability to shoot free throws. He established a great rivalry with Russell, whose teams kept Chamberlain from winning more championships. But he always felt he was the villain in the rivalry with the shorter, thinner Russell.

A moody man with a good sense of humor who once said, "No one loves Goliath," Chamberlain loved to debate a wide range of topics, from politics to his own achievements. Despite his size and enormous strength, he was considered a gentle man who purposely tried not to be a bully on the court. After retiring in 1973, Chamberlain ran marathons, played professional volleyball, sponsored a women's track team, and briefly coached in the old American Basketball League. He was elected to the Basketball Hall of Fame in 1978. He never married.

PAUL ATTNER

Adhikary, Man Mohan (78), prime minister of Nepal (1994–95); was the nation's first communist prime minister: d. Katmandu, Nepal, April 26.

Agronsky, Martin Z. (84), broadcast news correspondent; helped develop one of television's first discussion news programs. *Agronsky & Company* was syndicated nationally (1969–87). He won a Peabody Award in 1952 for his radio coverage of Sen. Joseph McCarthy, and an Alfred I. duPont Award in 1961 for covering Nazi war criminal Adolf Eichmann's trial: d. Washington, DC, July 25.

Aigner, Lucien (born Ladislaz Aigner) (97), Hungarian-born photographer; a pioneer in photojournalism, he was famed for his pictures of historical events and famous figures such as Albert Einstein, Benito Mussolini, and Haile Selassie: d. Waltham, MA, March 29.

Allen, Rex, Sr. (78), country-western singer and actor; one of the last of the early 1950s' "singing cowboys." His best-known song was "Crying in the Chapel" (1953). He later served as narrator for many films, most notably *The Incredible Journey* (1963) and *Charlotte's Web* (1973): d. Tucson, AZ, Dec. 17.

Alyn, Kirk (born John Feggo, Jr.) (88), dancer and actor; was the first to play the role of Superman in a film, in the serials *Superman* (1948) and *Atom Man vs. Superman* (1950): d. Woodlands, TX, March 14.

Armstrong, William H. (87), teacher and author; best known for his children's novel *Sounder* (1969). The story won the Newbery Medal in 1970 and was made into a 1972 feature film: d. Kent, CT, April 11.

Axton, Hoyt (61), singer, songwriter, and actor; best known for writing "Joy to the World," a 1971 hit for Three Dog Night. He wrote hits for many pop stars, including Elvis Presley, Joan Baez, John Denver, Linda Ronstadt, and Ringo Starr ("No No Song," 1975). He also appeared in several films: d. Victor, MT, Oct. 26.

© Arthur Grace/Corbis-Sygma

Harry Blackmun

Bart, Lionel (born Lionel Begleiter) (68), English musical composer, lyricist, and playwright; best known for creating the hit musical *Oliver!*, based on the Charles Dickens novel. It was a hit in London in 1960 and on Broadway in 1963. He won a Tony for the show's music and lyrics, and *Oliver!* was made into a 1968 film that won several Oscars: d. London, England, April 3.

Bate, Walter J. (81), author and English professor at Harvard University; won Pulitzer Prizes for his biographies *John Keats* (1963) and *Samuel Johnson* (1977). The latter work also won a National Book Award and a National Book Critics Circle Award: d. Boston, MA, July 26.

Bates, Daisy (84), civil-rights leader; in 1956, worked to desegregate the Little Rock, AR, bus system. The following year, she gained nationwide frame as she helped nine black students break the color barrier at Little Rock Central High School. She received more than 200 awards and citations, and her book *The Long Shadow of Little Rock* won a 1988 American Book Award: d. Little Rock, AR, Nov. 4.

Belloni, Robert C. (80), U.S. judge for the District Court of Oregon; in 1969 he upheld the fishing rights of American Indians in the Pacific Northwest. He was appointed to the federal bench by President Lyndon Johnson in 1967, serving as chief judge from 1971–76 and retiring in 1995: d. San Mateo, CA, Nov. 3.

Bernstein, Morey (79), businessman and author; his 1956 book *The Quest for Bridey Murphy*, an account of his hypnotizing a woman into allegedly remembering a previous life, was a best-seller that triggered a fad for hypnotism and a new interest in reincarnation: d. Pueblo, CO, April 2.

Berriault, Gina (born Arline Shandling) (73), author of novels and short stories; her 1996 short-story collection *Women in Their Beds* won the National Book Critics Circle Award and other prizes: d. Greenbrae, CA, July 15.

Bird, Vere C. (89), prime minister of Antigua (1981–94); before Antigua achieved full independence in 1984, he had been a labor leader and leader in the colonial legislature. Despite widespread international accusations of corruption and involvement with the drug trade, Bird remained in power until he retired in 1994: d. St. Johns, Antigua, June 28.

Blackmun, Harry A. (90), U.S. Supreme Court justice (1970–94); appointed to the court by President Richard Nixon. A Republican with a reputation as a noncontroversial moderate, he nonetheless became one of the Supreme Court's most controversial justices with his authorship of the 1973 *Roe v. Wade* decision, legalizing abortion. He forever after was linked with the issue and defended the legality of abortion in later Supreme Court cases: d. Arlington, VA, March 4.

Bogarde, Dirk (born Derek van den Bogaerde) (78), English actor; with roles in such films as *The Servant* (1963) and *Death in Venice* (1973), he became one of the few British film actors to reach international stardom. He also wrote several best-selling novels and seven volumes of autobiography. He was knighted in 1992: d. London, England, May 8.

Bowles, Paul (88), writer and musical composer; became known as an author with the publication of his novel *The Shelter-*

ing Sky (1949), which was a best-seller. He wrote several more novels and many musical works, including scores for plays, operas, songs, and concertos: d. Tangier, Morocco, Nov. 18.

Boxcar Willie (born Lecil Travis Martin) (67), country-music singer and songwriter; fascinated by trains and hobos, he fashioned a professional image for himself as a hobo, naming himself after a song he wrote in the mid-1960s. He joined the Grand Ole Opry in 1981 and was a regular on the series *Hee Haw* in the early 1980s. He established the Boxcar Willie Theater in Branson, MO, in 1986, and became one of the city's main tourist attractions: d. Branson, MO, April 12.

Bresson, Robert (98), French film director; his 13 films were marked by spiritual themes and an austere, abstract visual impression. His 1950 film *Diary of a Country Priest* won the Grand Prix at the 1951 Venice Film Festival. *A Man Escaped* (1956) won him the best-director award at the Cannes International Film Festival in 1957, and *Money* (1983) was named best film at Cannes: d. Droué-sur-Drouette, France, Dec. 18.

© AP/Wide World Photos

Pete Conrad

Brown, George E., Jr. (79), member of the U.S. House of Representatives (D-CA); was serving his 18th term and was the oldest member of the current House. He served as chairman of the House Science, Space, and Technology Committee (1991–95): d. Bethesda, MD, July 15.

Cabral de Melo Neto, João (79), Brazilian poet; considered one of the greatest Portuguese-language poets of the 20th century. His "The Death and Life of Severino" became a popular success: d. Rio de Janeiro, Brazil, Oct. 9.

Cadmus, Paul (94), artist; best known as a figurative painter, he also produced many drawings and photographs. His unique style—which tended toward grotesque caricature—fell out of favor in the 1940s. In 1934 his painting "The Fleet's In," depicting uniformed sailors associating with prostitutes and homosexuals, caused controversy; U.S. Navy officials had it removed from a Washington, DC, exhibit, and it was not shown publicly again until 1981: d. Weston, CT, Dec. 12.

Calhoun, Rory (born Francis Timothy Durgin) (76), actor; played the hero in many Western films of the 1940s and 1950s, and starred in the television series *The Texan* (1958–60): d. Burbank, CA, April 28.

Callahan, Harry (86), photographer; especially known for dramatic photos of his wife, and of the streets of Chicago. In 1978 he became the first U.S. photographer to present his work at the Venice Biennale. He was awarded the National Medal of the Arts in 1997: d. Atlanta, GA, March 15.

Campbell, Jack M. (82), two-term Democratic governor of New Mexico (1963–67); he worked to reduce partisanship and improve services for the mentally ill. His work to further science education in rural areas earned him a public-service award from the National Aeronautics and Space Administration (NASA): d. Santa Fe, NM, June 14.

Carr, Allan (62), theatrical and film producer; produced the movie musical *Grease* (1978) and the Broadway hit *La Cage aux Folles* (1984), which won six Tony Awards, including one for best musical: d. Beverly Hills, CA, June 29.

Carter, Anita (66), country singer; best known as a member of the country-music group the Carter Family, which was a regular member of the Grand Ole Opry beginning in 1950. She had two Top 5 duets with singer Hank Snow: "Bluebird Island" and "Down the Trail of Achin' Hearts": d. Nashville, TN, July 29.

Cass, Peggy (74), actress; won a Tony as best supporting actress for her portrayal of a secretary in the 1957 Broadway play *Auntie Mame*. She reprised her role in the 1958 film version of the show and was nominated for an Oscar: d. New York City, March 8.

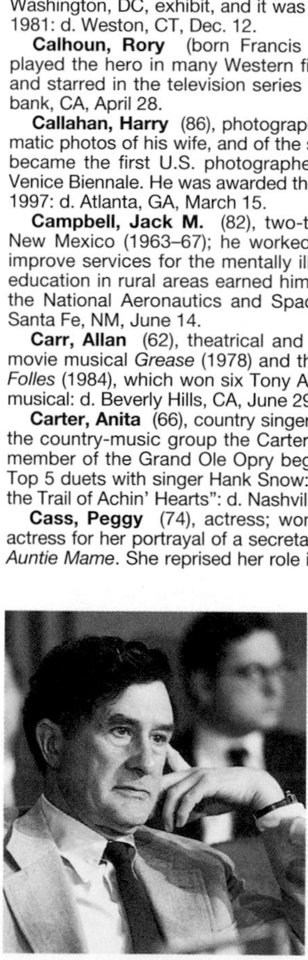
© Roddey E. Mims/Corbis-Sygma

John Chafee

Castelli, Leo (born Leo Krause) (91), art dealer; wielded extraordinary influence in the development of modern art through his choice of which artists he fostered; these included Robert Rauschenberg, Jasper Johns, Roy Lichtenstein, Frank Stella, and Andy Warhol. Born in Trieste, then part of Austria-Hungary, he moved to the United States in 1941 and was given U.S. citizenship following his service in World War II: d. New York City, Aug. 21.

Cato, Bob (75), graphic designer; his work helped turn record-album covers into contemporary works of art during the 1960s. He won two Grammys for his designs—for Barbra Streisand's *People* (1964) and *Bob Dylan's Greatest Hits* (1967); the National Academy of Recording Arts and Sciences presented him its President's Merit Award in 1997: d. New York City, March 19.

Chafee, John H. (77), U.S. senator (R-RI, 1976–99) and governor of Rhode Island (1963–69); also served as secretary of the U.S. Navy (1969–72). As governor, he pushed for antidiscrimination laws and for the construction of an interstate highway, I-95. As a senator, he worked with Democrats on bills to protect the environment and to expand Medicaid. He was chairman of the Senate's Republican Conference (1984–90) and of the Senate Committee on Environment and Public Works (1995): d. Bethesda, MD, Oct. 24.

Chebrikov, Viktor (76), chief of the Soviet Union's Committee for State Security (KGB) (1982–88); a hard-line Communist, he headed the KGB during one of the Cold War's most infamous incidents—the shooting down by the USSR of Korean Airlines Flight 007, which the KGB claimed was on a U.S.-sponsored spy mission: d. Moscow, Russia, July 1.

Cherne, Leo (86), chairman of the International Rescue Committee (1951–91); the organization became the world's largest agency for refugee resettlement. He was awarded the Presidential Medal of Freedom in 1984: d. New York City, Jan. 12.

Cockerell, Sir Christopher (88), English engineer and inventor; known best as the creator of the hovercraft. His work with the Marconi Company during World War II led to several inventions invaluable to the Allied war effort. He unveiled the first hovercraft publicly in 1959, and it went into commercial production shortly thereafter. He was knighted in 1969: d. Hythe, Hampshire, England, June 1.

© Bridges/Corbis-Sygma

Gertrude Elion

Cody, Iron Eyes (94), actor; appeared in some 100 films, but was best known for his appearance in a 1971 antilittering commercial first aired on Earth Day in 1971, showing him shedding a tear over the polluted U.S. environment: d. Los Angeles, CA, Jan. 4.

Cohelan, Jeffery (84), member of the U.S. House of Representatives (D-CA, 1959–71); advocated civil-rights legislation and was a sponsor of the Civil Rights Act of 1964 and floor leader for the Voting Rights Act of 1965. He also favored the causes of labor and the environment, cosponsoring 1968 legislation establishing Redwood National Park and Point Reyes National Seashore, both in California: d. Washington, DC, Feb. 15.

Conrad, (Charles) Pete, Jr. (69), aeronautical engineer and former astronaut; commanded the *Apollo 12* mission in 1969 and became the third person to walk on the Moon. He also flew in 1973 on the first Skylab mission, remaining in space an unprecedented 28 days: d. Ojai, CA, July 8.

Corby, Ellen (born Ellen Hansen) (87), actress; best known for her role as the grandmother in the television series *The Waltons* (1972–81). She also appeared in more than 100 films and was nominated for an Oscar for her role in *I Remember Mama* (1948): d. Woodland Hills, CA, April 14.

Couve de Murville, Maurice (92), French prime minister (1968–69); the last prime minister to serve under President Charles de Gaulle. As foreign minister from 1958 to 1968, he had advocated the need for greater European unity. He was known as a skilled diplomat and had held several ambassadorial posts, as well as briefly serving as French representative to the North Atlantic Treaty Organization (NATO): d. Paris, France, Dec. 24.

Cox, Robert (72), journalist; won a Pulitzer Prize for general news reporting in 1967 for his report on the hunt for a sniper, written for *The Public Opinion* of Chambersburg, PA. He later wrote two books: d. Chambersburg, PA, April 12.

Crane, Harry (85), comedy writer; best known for creating and writing the classic television series *The Honeymooners* (1955–56). He wrote several films and scripted material for many renowned comedians of his day, including Abbott and Costello, Jimmy Durante, Laurel and Hardy, and the Marx Brothers. He also worked on TV specials for such stars as Milton Berle and Dinah Shore, and scripted major awards shows: d. Beverly Hills, CA, Sept. 13.

Dance, Stanley (88), jazz critic; won a Grammy Award in 1963 for his liner notes for the album *The Ellington Era*. He coined the term "mainstream" to describe a certain jazz style, and cowrote Duke Ellington's autobiography, as well as other jazz-related books: d. San Diego, CA, Feb. 23.

© Corbis-Bettmann

James Farmer

Darrow, Whitney, Jr. (89), cartoonist; more than 1,500 of his witty cartoons were published in *The New Yorker* magazine. He published four collections and illustrated books by other authors: d. Shelburne, VT, Aug. 10.

Delany, Sarah (Sadie) (109), retired teacher and coauthor of *Having Our Say: The Delany Sisters' First 100 Years* (1993); the book, a best-seller, received much publicity and was made into a play, which ran on Broadway in 1995. The sisters later wrote a second book, and in 1997, after the death of her sister Bessie, Sadie published *On My Own at 107*: d. Mount Vernon, NY, Jan. 25.

Dezza, Cardinal Paolo (98), Italian Roman Catholic cardinal; named to lead the Jesuit order in 1981, as the order suffered from political division and conflicts with the Vatican. He had served as confessor to Popes Paul VI and John Paul I. He was elevated to cardinal in 1991 by Pope John Paul II: d. Rome, Italy, Dec. 17.

DiCarlo, Dominick L. (71), U.S. judge; was appointed by President Ronald Reagan to the U.S. Court of International Trade in 1982. He became chief judge in 1991 and left the post in 1996, but continued to hear cases as a senior judge: d. New York City, April 27.

Dmytryk, Edward (90), film director; among his films were *Crossfire* (1947), for which he received an Oscar nomination, and the classic *The Caine Mutiny* (1954). During the 1940s he served more than four months in prison after refusing to testify before the House Committee on Un-American Activities (he briefly had been a member of the Communist Party). He later returned to the committee and gave it information: d. Encino, CA, July 1.

Dolanc, Stane (74), one of the joint presidents of Yugoslavia (1984–89); served as second in command to Yugoslav leader Josip Tito during the 1970s: d. Ljubljana, Slovenia, Dec. 13.

Drapeau, Jean (83), mayor of Montreal, Quebec (1954–57; 1960–86); during his tenure, helped reshape Montreal into a grand international city. He worked to draw such projects as a world's fair, the 1970 Olympics, and a major-league-baseball team, and instigated high-profile construction projects, including a modern subway system. In later years, he was criticized for his autocratic governing style and extravagant projects: d. Montreal, Que., Canada, Aug. 12.

Dubus, Andre (62), author; known particularly for his short stories. He won a MacArthur Award in 1988 following the publication of *Selected Stories*, and received the Rea Award for short fiction in 1996: d. Haverhill, MA, Feb. 24.

Dudley, Jimmy (89), sports broadcaster; from 1948 to 1967, was known as the "voice" of the Cleveland Indians major-league-baseball team on radio. He was inducted into the broadcasters' wing of the Baseball Hall of Fame in 1997: d. Tucson, AZ, Feb. 12.

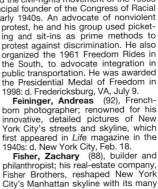

© Archive Photos

Allen Funt

Duquette, Tony (85), interior and theatrical designer; won a Tony Award for his costume designs for *Camelot* (1961). He designed furniture, interiors, and jewelry for such luminaries as the Duchess of Windsor, Elizabeth Arden, Doris Duke, and Mary Pickford: d. Los Angeles, CA, Sept. 9.

Edwards, Ben (82), theatrical-set designer; his striking interiors for many Broadway productions were much admired. He was presented with a lifetime-achievement Tony Award in 1998. He also had designed sets for television shows and films: d. New York City, Feb. 12.

Ehrlichman, John D. (73), domestic-affairs adviser in the administration of President Richard M. Nixon; served 18 months in prison and was disbarred permanently after being convicted in 1975 of obstruction of justice, conspiracy, and perjury in connection with the Watergate break-in scandal: d. Atlanta, GA, Feb. 14.

Elion, Gertrude B. (81), medical researcher; shared the 1988 Nobel Prize in physiology or medicine for her pioneering work in drug research. She developed or helped develop drugs for use in treating such disorders as herpes, malaria, leukemia, and AIDS, as well as immune suppressants for organ-transplant recipients. She was awarded the National Medal of Science in 1991: d. Chapel Hill, NC, Feb. 21.

Elliott, Carl (85), member of the U.S. House of Representatives (D-AL, 1949–65); was committed to legislation that assisted the poor in obtaining education and health care, as well as to the advancement of civil rights. Among important pieces of legislation he championed were the National Defense Education Act (1958) and the Library Assistance Act (1956). He received the first Profiles in Courage Award from the John F. Kennedy Library Foundation in 1990: d. Jasper, AL, Jan. 9.

© Derek Hudson/Corbis-Sygma

Raisa Gorbachev

Ervin, Samuel J. 3d (73), U.S. judge; served as chief judge of the U.S. Court of Appeals for the Fourth Circuit in North Carolina (1989–96). He was named to the federal bench in 1980 by President Jimmy Carter: d. Morganton, NC, Sept. 18.

Exner, Judith (65), socialite and reputed mistress of President John F. Kennedy; gained the spotlight in 1975, when she testified before the U.S. Senate intelligence committee that she had had an 18-month affair with Kennedy, but denied knowing of any ties between him and Mafia figures. In her 1977 autobiography *My Story*, however, she claimed that she had delivered messages between the president and Mafia boss Sam Giancana: d. Duarte, CA, Sept. 21.

Fanfani, Amintore (91), Italian politician; served as premier six times between 1954 and 1987. He also served as president of the United Nations General Assembly (1965–68): d. Rome, Italy, Nov. 20.

Farmer, James L. (79), civil-rights activist; considered one of the "Big Four" who shaped the civil-rights movement of the 1950s and 1960s. He was a principal founder of the Congress of Racial Equality (CORE) in the early 1940s. An advocate of nonviolent protest, he and his group used picketing and sit-ins as prime methods to protest against discrimination. He also organized the 1961 Freedom Rides in the South, to advocate integration in public transportation. He was awarded the Presidential Medal of Freedom in 1998: d. Fredericksburg, VA, July 9.

Feininger, Andreas (92), French-born photographer; renowned for his innovative, detailed pictures of New York City's streets and skyline, which first appeared in *Life* magazine in the 1940s: d. New York City, Feb. 18.

Fisher, Zachary (88), builder and philanthropist; his real-estate company, Fisher Brothers, reshaped New York City's Manhattan skyline with its many high-rise office towers and apartment buildings. Beginning in the 1970s, he championed the founding of the Intrepid Sea-Air-Space Museum on the Hudson River, and gave more than $25 million toward its establishment. He was awarded the Presidential Medal of Freedom in 1988. He also set up several foundations to give various types of financial aid to military personnel and their families: d. New York City, June 4.

Fuchs, Sir Vivian Ernest (91), British explorer and geologist; led the team that made the first surface crossing of Antarctica, in 1957–58. He was knighted in 1958: d. Cambridge, England, Nov. 11.

Funt, Allen (84), creator and original host of the television program *Candid Camera*; the show, which began on radio in 1947 as

Candid Microphone, was so popular that it appeared on all three TV networks. It still continues as a CBS series: d. Pebble Beach, CA, Sept. 5.

Garrity, W(endell) Arthur, Jr. (79), U.S. judge in Massachusetts; known for his controversial 1974 decision to mandate busing in Boston to desegregate the schools there. The decision triggered several years of sometimes-violent protests in the city: d. Wellesley, MA, Sept. 16.

Gizikis, Phaidon (82), Greek army general and president of Greece (1973–74); took power following a coup that overturned a military dictatorship. In 1974 he asked former civilian Prime Minister Constantine Caramanlis to return as government leader; Caramanlis was sworn in in July, and Gizikis stepped down in December, paving the way for a return to democracy. Treason and mutiny charges later were dropped against him: d. Athens, Greece, July 26.

© Laurent Maous/Liaison Agency

King Hassan II

Godwin, Mills E., Jr. (84), governor of Virginia (1966–70; 1974–78); elected first as a Democrat, he overhauled the state's infrastructure and constitution, introduced a sales tax, and established a system of community colleges. He switched to the Republican Party before being elected a second time: d. Newport News, VA, Jan. 30.

© Sue Ogrocki/Reuters/Corbis

Joseph Heller

Gold, Ernest (77), musical composer; won an Oscar for the score of the 1960 film *Exodus*. His scores for *On the Beach* (1959), *It's a Mad, Mad, Mad, Mad World* (1963), and *The Secret of Santa Vittoria* (1969) also were Oscar-nominated: d. Santa Monica, CA, March 17.

Gorbachev, Raisa (67), wife of former Soviet President Mikhail Gorbachev, the USSR's final leader; a college professor, she was considered by far the most sophisticated and elegant Soviet first lady. She maintained a high profile, advising her husband and accompanying him on international visits: d. Münster, Germany, Sept. 20.

Greenfield, Meg (born Mary Ellen Greenfield) (68), journalist; editor of the *Washington Post*'s editorial page and a regular contributor to *Newsweek*. She was known especially for her shrewd, knowledgeable, and influential political commentary. She was awarded a Pulitzer Prize for commentary in 1978: d. Washington, DC, May 13.

Gross, Ludwik (94), Austro-Hungarian–born cancer researcher; in the 1950s, discovered a virus that induces cancer in mice. He was awarded an Albert and Mary Lasker Foundation Award in 1974 for his work: d. New York City, Aug. 12.

Hassan II, King (born Moulay Hassan ben Mohammed) (70), king of Morocco since 1961; more Western-oriented than other Middle East leaders, he often served as an intermediary in regional diplomacy and aided in rapprochement with Israel. He authored Morocco's first constitution but nonetheless was often an autocratic ruler: d. Rabat, Morocco, July 23.

Hegedus, Andras (76), prime minister of Hungary (1955–56); a Communist stalwart until the late 1950s, he gradually became an outspoken dissident, calling for an end to the powers of the secret police and denouncing the USSR-led invasion of Czechoslovakia in 1968. He was ejected from the Communist Party in 1973: d. Budapest, Hungary, Oct. 23.

Heller, Joseph (76), author; best known for his popular 1961 World War II novel *Catch-22*. The book was made into a critically praised film in 1970: d. East Hampton, NY, Dec. 12.

Helstoski, Henry (75), member of the U.S. House of Representatives (D-NJ, 1965–77); was indicted in 1976 for allegedly accepting a bribe to introduce legislation that would allow several Chileans to immigrate to the United States. He never was tried on the charges, which were dropped in 1980, and maintained that he was framed: d. Wayne, NJ, Dec. 16.

© Corbis-Bettmann

Frank Johnson

Herzberg, Gerhard (94), German-born Canadian physicist; won the 1971 Nobel Prize in chemistry for his research on the structure of molecules. He pioneered the field of modern molecular spectroscopy, the study of light emitted by molecules: d. Ottawa, Ont., Canada, March 3.

Higgins, George V. (59), author; originally a journalist for The Associated Press, he became an attorney and turned to writing crime fiction. His *The Friends of Eddie Coyle* (1972) became a surprise best-seller and was made into a movie the following year. Its heavy use of realistic dialogue influenced other writers: d. Boston, MA, Nov. 6.

Hirt, Al(ois) M. (76), jazz trumpeter; won a Grammy Award in 1964 for the instrumental song "Java." He recorded more than 50 albums, four of which went gold and one platinum, and was one of the United States' best-known musical performers in the 1960s, nicknamed "the king of the trumpet": d. New Orleans, LA, April 27.

Horst, Horst P. (born Horst P.A. Bohrmann) (93), German-born photographer; best known for his stylized, classically elegant photos of celebrities and models. Among his subjects were Harry S. Truman, Maria Callas, Gertrude Stein, and Andy Warhol: d. Palm Beach Gardens, FL, Nov. 18.

Hruska, Roman L. (94), member of the U.S. House of Representatives (R-NE, 1953–54) and U.S. senator (1954–76); was an influential member of the Senate Judiciary Committee. A conservative, he strongly opposed violence and excessive sexual content in films and on television. He was a leader in the fight to restore the death penalty and also led opposition to gun control: d. Omaha, NE, April 25.

Al Hirt

Hume, Cardinal Basil (born George Haliburton Hume) (76), British Roman Catholic cardinal; leader of the church in England and Wales since he was elevated to cardinal in 1976. He helped renew the public role of the church in England; he was presented with an Order of Merit by Queen Elizabeth II in early June 1999: d. London, England, June 17.

Hunter, Catfish (born James A. Hunter) (53), professional baseball player (1965–79); a pitcher for the Oakland A's (1965–74) and New York Yankees (1975–79), he pitched in six World Series and was an eight-time All-Star. He threw one perfect game, in 1968, and won the Cy Young Award in 1974. He was inducted into the Baseball Hall of Fame in 1987: d. Hertford, NC, Sept. 9.

Jakobovits, Lord (Rabbi Immanuel) (78), German-born English rabbi; served as chief rabbi of the United Hebrew Congregations of the British Commonwealth (1967–91). Although conservative on social issues such as abortion rights and homosexuality, he supported more-liberal stands on political issues, including civil rights for Palestinian Arabs. He was knighted by Queen Elizabeth II in 1981 and was made a peer in 1988: d. London, England, Oct. 31.

Joelson, Charles S. (83), member of the U.S. House of Representatives (D-NJ, 1961–69); best known for his work to push through an amendment that added $1 billion to the 1969 federal education budget, allowing thousands of school libraries nationwide to remain open, as well as permitting the continued operation of vocational, remedial, and guidance programs: d. Freehold Township, NJ, Aug. 17.

Johnson, Frank M., Jr. (80), U.S. judge; served in the district court of Alabama (1955–79) and on the U.S. 5th Circuit Court of Appeals (1979–92). His decisions helped the move toward integration in the South and advanced the U.S. civil-rights movement. Among his controversial rulings was one allowing the 1965 march from Selma, AL, to Montgomery, AL, led by Martin

Luther King, Jr., to support blacks' voting rights. He was awarded the Presidential Medal of Freedom in 1995: d. Montgomery, AL, July 23.

Jones, Henry (86), actor; won a Tony Award in 1958 for his role in the Broadway play *Sunrise at Campobello*. He also appeared in films—most notably Alfred Hitchcock's *Vertigo* (1958)—and on television: d. Los Angeles, CA, May 17.

Kahn, Madeline (57), actress; best known for her comic roles in several films directed by Mel Brooks, including *Young Frankenstein* (1974) and *Blazing Saddles* (1974); she was nominated for an Academy Award for her work in the latter. She also received an Oscar nomination for her role in *Paper Moon* (1973), and won a Tony Award as best actress for *The Sisters Rosensweig* (1993): d. New York City, Dec. 3.

© Laura Luongo/Liaison Agency

Madeline Kahn

Kanin, Garson (86), playwright, screenwriter, and director; with his wife, Ruth Gordon, wrote five films, including three nominated for Academy Awards—*A Double Life* (1948), *Adam's Rib* (1949), and *Pat and Mike* (1952). He wrote or directed more than 30 plays, including *Born Yesterday* (1946), *The Diary of Anne Frank* (1955), and *Funny Girl* (1964): d. New York City, March 13.

Karekin I, Catholicos (born Neshan Sarkissian) (66), Syrian-born head of the Armenian Apostolic Church; became worldwide leader of the 6-million-member church in 1995: d. Echmiadzin, Armenia, June 29.

Karmin, Monroe (69), journalist; in 1967, while an investigative reporter for *The Wall Street Journal*, won a Pulitzer Prize for an article discussing links between U.S. organized crime and businesses located in the Bahamas: d. Bethesda, MD, Jan. 15.

Kelley, DeForest (79), actor; appeared in some 150 films and television programs, including several Western series, but was best known for his role as Dr. Leonard McCoy on the 1960s television series *Star Trek* and the movies it spawned: d. Woodland Hills, CA, June 11.

Kendall, Henry W. (72), physicist; shared the 1990 Nobel Prize in physics for research in the 1960s and 1970s confirming the existence of quarks, the fundamental particles of matter: d. Wakulla Springs State Park, FL, Feb. 15.

Kennedy, John F., Jr. (38), son of U.S. President John F. Kennedy and editor of *George* magazine: d. near Martha's Vineyard, MA, July 16. (*See also* SIDEBAR, page 565.)

Khalifa, Sheikh Isa bin Salman Al (65), leader of Bahrain since 1961; worked for independence for Bahrain, which was a British protectorate when he took power. He took the title of emir upon independence in 1971. He established an elective legislature in 1973 but dissolved it in 1975. Under his leadership, Bahrain's oil wealth was used to make the nation a financial center and to establish heavy industry: d. Manama, Bahrain, March 6.

Kiley, Richard (76), actor; won Tony Awards for his roles in the Broadway musicals *Redhead* (1959) and *Man of La Mancha* (1965). He appeared in many other musicals and plays, and in films and on television as well, winning three Emmys and two Golden Globe Awards for his performances in the TV programs *The Thorn Birds*, *A Year in the Life*, and *Picket Fences*. He was inducted into the Theater Hall of Fame in January 1999: d. Warwick, NY, March 5.

Kilgore, Joe M. (80), member of the U.S. House of Representatives (D-TX, 1955–65): d. Austin, TX, Feb. 10.

Kubrick, Stanley (70), film director; among his films—which won eight Academy Awards—were *Dr. Strangelove* (1964), *2001: A Space Odyssey* (1968), *A Clockwork Orange* (1971), *The Shining* (1980), and *Full Metal Jacket* (1987). His last film, *Eyes Wide Shut*, was released posthumously in July 1999. His films are known for their originality and biting wit, although some have been criticized as glorifying violence: d. Hertfordshire, England, March 7.

© Sunset Boulevard/Corbis-Sygma

Stanley Kubrick

Lakas, Demetrio (74), president of Panama (1972–78); his authority was limited, since Gen. Omar Torrijos Herrera, leader of the National Guard, held the final power in the nation. He did play a role, however, in the establishment of treaties between Panama and the United States regarding the turnover of the Panama Canal to Panama: d. Panama City, Panama, Nov. 2.

Lang, Serge (79), French journalist, skier, and bicycle racer; founder of alpine skiing's World Cup competition. He established the World Cup in 1966, knitting together several unrelated races into a popular international circuit and bringing new publicity to the sport: d. Paris, France, Nov. 21.

Leontief, Wassily (93), Russian-born economist; won the 1973 Nobel Prize in economics for his development of the input-output analysis method, which became an important tool for economic planning and predictions: d. New York City, Feb. 5.

Lillehei, Walton (80), surgeon; regarded as the father of open-heart surgery. He performed the first successful open-heart surgery in 1952 at the University of Minnesota, and trained hundreds of surgeons, including Dr. Christiaan Barnard, who performed the first successful heart transplant in 1967. He led in the development in 1955 of a machine that pumped oxygenated blood through a patient's body—eventually making heart transplants possible—and in the creation of the first wearable pacemaker in 1957, and contributed to the design of artificial heart valves: d. St. Paul, MN, July 5.

Lini, Walter (57), Anglican priest and former leader of Vanuatu; as the newly independent nation's first prime minister (1980–91), sought to maintain a steady but slow developmental pace: d. Port Vila, Vanuatu, Feb. 21.

© AP/Wide World Photos

DeForest Kelley

Litwack, Harry (91), college-basketball coach; served as Temple University's head coach from 1952 to 1973. During that time, his team twice went to the National Collegiate Athletic Association (NCAA) Final Four and once won the National Invitational Tournament (1969). He was elected to the Basketball Hall of Fame in 1975: d. Huntingdon Valley, PA, Aug. 7.

Llewelyn, Desmond (85), British actor; known for his portrayal of Q, the technical-equipment expert, in 17 James Bond films between 1963 and 1999: d. East Sussex, England, Dec. 19.

Lortel, Lucille (98), philanthropist and patron of New York theater; her theater in Greenwich Village bears her name. She produced or coproduced some 500 plays, five of which were nominated for Tony Awards. Among the many honors she received were the Lee Strasberg Lifetime Achievement Award (1985) and induction into the Theater Hall of Fame (1990): d. New York City, April 4.

Lowe, Mary J. (74), U.S. district-court judge; appointed in 1978 to New York's Southern District by President Jimmy Carter, she was only the second African-American woman appointed to the federal judiciary. She acquired senior status in 1991. Her most-noted action probably was her ruling barring New York City from preventing homeless people from voting: d. Las Vegas, NV, Feb. 27.

Luckman, Charles (89), architect; among the buildings he designed are New York City's Madison Square Garden and Lever House, Boston's Prudential Center, and Houston's Johnson Space Center. He was both praised and criticized for his modernist, pragmatic style: d. Los Angeles, CA, Jan. 25.

Lumbard, J(oseph) Edward (97), U.S. appeals-court judge; appointed to the Second Circuit in 1955 by President Dwight D. Eisenhower. He be-

© Fabian/Corbis-Sygma
Yehudi Menuhin

came chief judge in 1959 and took senior status in 1971. He also served on the U.S. Special Court of Appeals, responsible for appointing independent counsels (1974–80). In 1968 he was awarded the Gold Medal of the American Bar Association for his contributions to justice administration: d. Fairfield, CT, June 3.

Lynch, Jack (John) M. (82), prime minister of Ireland (1966–73; 1977–79); among important decisions made under his leadership was one not to intervene militarily in Northern Ireland when sectarian violence broke out in 1969. He also urged the nation toward membership in the European Economic Community, which it joined in 1973: d. Dublin, Ireland, Oct. 20.

Mainassara, Gen. Ibrahim Bare (49), president of Niger since 1996; was assassinated, apparently by members of his security team: d. Niamey, Niger, April 9.

Mature, Victor (86), actor; best known for his good looks and physique, often shown off in scanty attire. Among his films were *One Million B.C.* (1940), *My Darling Clementine* (1946), and *Samson and Delilah* (1949). He also starred on Broadway in *Lady in the Dark* (1941): d. San Diego, CA, Aug. 4.

Mayfield, Curtis (57), soul singer and songwriter; as leader of the soul group the Impressions, his songs—such as the 1964 hit "Keep on Pushing"—brought civil-rights themes to public attention. He began producing solo albums in 1971; his best-known song from that era is the funk hit "Superfly." He was inducted twice into the Rock and Roll Hall of Fame—in 1991 as a member of the Impressions and in 1999 as a solo artist: d. Roswell, GA, Dec. 26.

McCarty, Oseola (91), washerwoman and philanthropist; gave away her life savings—some $150,000—to endow a scholarship fund for poor students at the University of Southern Mississippi. Her gift brought her worldwide fame; she received the Presidential Citizen's Medal and hundreds of other honors and awards: d. Hattiesburg, MS, Sept. 26.

© Archive Photos
Clayton Moore

McKeithen, John J. (81), governor of Louisiana (1964–72); a Democrat, he proved so popular during his first term that the state's law banning governors from serving two consecutive terms was overruled. He worked to solve racial tensions through moderate policies. He was a strong backer of the building of New Orleans' Superdome in the early 1970s: d. Columbia, LA, June 3.

Mellon, Paul (91), philanthropist; made enormous contributions to U.S. cultural life, most notably through his presentation of the National Gallery of Art in Washington, DC, in 1941, and his continuing patronage of the gallery. He served as its president (1938–39, 1963–75) and board chairman (1979–85). He also used his family's wealth to establish the Yale Center for British Art and to fund the Bollingen Prize for poetry, as well as to help save U.S. seashores: d. Upperville, VA, Feb. 1.

Menuhin, Yehudi (82), violinist and musical conductor; a child-prodigy violinist in the 1920s, he was admired for the intensity and virtuosity of his playing. He began a second career in conducting in the 1940s. He founded Switzerland's Gstaad Festival in 1956 and served as music director of England's Bath Festival (1958–68). He founded two schools for music students and wrote several books. Among the honors he received were an honorary British knighthood, Kennedy Center honors, and awards from France, Germany, Belgium, and Greece: d. Berlin, Germany, March 12.

Mizell, Wilmer David (68), member of the U.S. House of Representatives (R-NC, 1969–75) and former professional baseball player; known as "Vinegar Bend" during his baseball career, he pitched for three major-league teams in the 1950s and early 1960s. In his congressional career, he strongly defended North Carolina's tobacco interests: d. Kerrville, TX, Feb. 21.

Mokhehle, Ntsu (80), prime minister of Lesotho (1993–98); was a leader in the movement toward independence, which was achieved in 1966. During the days of apartheid in South Africa, he directed a guerrilla campaign against South African–influenced politicians in Lesotho: d. Bloemfontein, South Africa, Jan. 6.

Moore, Clayton (born Jack Carlton Moore) (85), actor; gained fame with his portrayal of the Lone Ranger on television and in films. He appeared in 169 episodes of the television series *The Lone Ranger* (1949–57), and in two Lone Ranger films, in 1956 and 1958. He continued making public appearances as the character for many years: d. West Hills, CA, Dec. 28.

Morris, Willie (64), writer; as the youngest editor in chief ever of *Harper's* magazine (1967–71), he revitalized it by bringing in the stories of some of the finest U.S. writers. His own writings were known for their evocation of the rhythms of life in the South, especially in his native Mississippi. His best-known book was probably the critically praised memoir *North Toward Home* (1967): d. Jackson, MS, Aug. 2.

Morton, Gary (born Morton Goldaper) (74), comedian and film and television producer; the husband of comedian Lucille Ball from 1961 until her death in 1989. He produced Ball's solo TV series, *The Lucy Show* and *Here's Lucy* (1962–74), and *Life with Lucy* (1986). He also produced film and television specials, as well as the film *All the Right Moves* (1983). He appeared in supporting roles in several films: d. Palm Springs, March 30.

Moser, Jürgen (71), German-born U.S. mathematician; best known for his work on the Kolmogorov-Arnold-Moser theory, which deals with celestial mechanics. He was awarded the Wolf Prize for mathematics in 1995: d. Schwerzenbach, Switzerland, Dec. 17.

Motley, Marion (79), professional football player; a fullback for the Cleveland Browns (1946–53). One of the National Football League's (NFL's) first black players, he is considered one of the best fullbacks ever. He was elected to the Pro Football Hall of Fame in 1968: d. Cleveland, OH, June 27.

Murdoch, Iris (born Jean Iris Murdoch) (79), Irish-born British author; her 26 novels were much admired and received many honors. *The Sea, the Sea* (1978) won the Booker Prize, and *The Sacred and Profane Love Machine* (1974) was awarded the Whitbread Literary Award for Fiction. She also wrote several plays as well as criticisms and philosophical works. She was made a Dame of the British Empire in 1987: d. Oxford, England, Feb. 8.

Nathans, Daniel (71), molecular biologist; his advanced technique for analyzing DNA led to his sharing the 1978 Nobel Prize for medicine. He was awarded the National Medal of Science in 1993: d. Baltimore, MD, Nov. 16.

Nkomo, Joshua (82), Zimbabwean political figure; considered the father of Zimbabwe's fight for independence from white colonial rule. He founded the African National Congress in 1952 and served as its leader. The black nationalist movement in what was then Rhodesia fought a guerrilla war against white rule for almost 30 years, finally achieving independence in 1980: d. Harare, Zimbabwe, July 1.

Nyerere, Julius K. (born Kambarage Nyerere) (77?), president of Tanzania (1964–85); cofounder in 1954 of the Tanganyika African National Union, which worked to gain Tanganyika's independence from Great Britain. At independence in 1961, he served briefly as the new nation's prime minister. He was elected in 1962 as president of Tanganyika, and oversaw the unification of that nation with Zanzibar and Pemba to form Tanzania in 1964. He instituted a largely unsuccessful policy of agrarian socialism and worked to improve education and form a sense of national identity. He continued to serve as chairman of the ruling Chama Cha Mapinduzi party until 1990: d. London, England, Oct. 14.

Ogilvy, David (88); English-born advertising executive; founder of the international ad agency Ogilvy & Mather. Among his innovations in advertising were the eye patch on the Hathaway

© Corbis-Bettmann
Walter Payton

Shirt man and "Schweppervescent" mixers: d. Bonnes, France, July 21.

Opoku Ware II, Otumfuo (79), king of the Asante people of Ghana; during his 29-year reign, had influence throughout the Asante-dominated southern half of the country and helped maintain the Asante's relationship with Ghana's government: d. Kumasi, Ghana, Feb. 25.

Papadopoulos, George (80), leader of a military dictatorship that headed Greece from 1967–73; took power following a bloodless coup. Following his fall from power, he was tried and sentenced to death in 1975; the sentence was commuted to life imprisonment: d. Athens, Greece, June 27.

Paredes, Americo (83), writer; one of the founders of the Chicano-studies movement during the 1960s. His best-known book, *With His Pistol in His Hand* (1958)—his doctoral dissertation—was hailed as a scholarly piece of revisionist history. He won the Charles Frankel Prize from the National Endowment for the Humanities in 1989, and was awarded Mexico's highest honor given a foreigner—the Águila Azteca—in 1991: d. Austin, TX, May 5.

© Archive Photos

Elliot Richardson

Paterson, Jennifer (71), British television personality; cohosted, with Clarissa Dickson Wright, the eccentric and internationally popular cooking program *Two Fat Ladies* since its debut in 1996: d. London, England, Aug. 10.

Payton, Walter (45), professional football player for the NFL's Chicago Bears (1975–87); the league's all-time leading rusher (more than 16,700 yards). He also held career records for rushing attempts and seasons with 1,000 or more rushing yards. He led the Bears to a 1985 Super Bowl victory and was inducted into the NFL Hall of Fame in 1993 and the College Football Hall of Fame in 1996: d. Barrington, IL, Nov. 1.

Perrot, Kim (32), professional-basketball player; a point guard with the Houston Comets of the Women's National Basketball League (WNBA), she helped the team to back-to-back WNBA championships in 1997 and 1998. She was a standout for the University of Southwestern Louisiana (1986–90), then played on women's professional-basketball teams in Europe before joining the Comets in 1997: d. Houston, TX, Aug. 19.

Polhill, Robert (65), business professor; along with three fellow faculty members at Beirut University College in Lebanon, was taken hostage by militiamen in January 1987. Their capture was the largest single kidnapping of Americans in Beirut. He was released in April 1990 in an effort to improve U.S.-Iranian relations: d. Washington, DC, July 1.

Potter, Clare (95), fashion designer; during the 1930s and 1940s, was one of the designers credited with the invention of American sportswear. Known for her simple, sophisticated designs, she received numerous awards. In 1939 she designed a dress for U.S. first lady Eleanor Roosevelt to wear while meeting the king and queen of England: d. Fort Ann, NY, Jan. 5.

Powers, J(ames) F. (81), author; won a National Book Award in 1963 for his first novel, *Morte d'Urban*. His fiction generally dealt with Roman Catholic priests of the U.S. Midwest: d. Collegeville, MN, June 12.

Pritzker, Jay A. (76), businessman; founder of the Hyatt hotel chain. In 1979 he endowed the Pritzker Architecture Prize, now the most coveted prize in the field of architecture: d. Chicago, IL, Jan. 23.

© Archive Photos

Glenn Seaborg

Pulliam, Eugene (84), newspaper publisher; known for his work to defend the 1st Amendment during Sen. Joseph McCarthy's anticommunist crusade in the 1950s. He served on a committee of newspaper editors investigating McCarthy's attacks on James Wechsler, editor of the *New York Post*; the committee found McCarthy's methods to be "a peril to American freedom." He was publisher of the *Indianapolis Star* and the *Indianapolis News* for many years: d. Indianapolis, IN, Jan. 20.

Puzo, Mario (78), novelist and screenwriter; best known for his 1969 best-selling novel *The Godfather*. The book sold more than 21 million copies and became the number-one-selling novel in many countries. The 1972 Francis Ford Coppola film based on the novel, with a screenplay by Puzo and Coppola, won several Oscars and became one of the most popular films of its time. Two sequels, in 1974 and 1990, also were popular and highly praised by critics. Puzo won two Academy Awards for his screenwriting for the films: d. Bay Shore, NY, July 2.

Quintero, José (74), Panama-born theatrical director; his stagings of the plays of Eugene O'Neill renewed the popularity of O'Neill's works. He won a 1974 Tony Award for his direction of *A Moon for the Misbegotten* (1973): d. New York City, Feb. 26.

Radziwill, Anthony S. (40), television producer; won three Emmy Awards—in 1988 for his work with NBC Sports on the 1988 Summer Olympics, in 1990 for producing a report on the Menendez double-homicide case, and in 1997 for an HBO documentary entitled *Taxicab Confessions*. He also won a Peabody Award in 1990 for his investigation into neo-Nazism in the United States: d. New York City, Aug. 10.

Rayburn, Gene (81), television game-show host and actor; best known as host of *The Match Game* (1962–69; 1973–79; 1983–84). He was nominated for five daytime Emmy Awards and received a lifetime-achievement award from the National Academy of Television Arts and Sciences in 1999. He acted in live television dramas in the 1950s and appeared on Broadway in the early 1960s in *Bye Bye Birdie*: d. Gloucester, MA, Nov. 29.

Reed, Oliver (61), English actor; appeared in some 53 films, including three films based on Alexandre Dumas' novel *The Three Musketeers* as well as the musical film *Oliver!* (1968): d. Valletta, Malta, May 2.

Reese, Pee Wee (born Harold Henry Reese) (81), former major-league-baseball player for the Brooklyn (later Los Angeles) Dodgers (1940–42; 1946–58); as a shortstop and the team's captain, led the Dodgers to seven league pennants and one World Series victory, in 1955. A nine-time All-Star, he retired with more than 2,000 hits and more than 200 stolen bases. He was inducted into the Baseball Hall of Fame in 1984: d. Louisville, KY, Aug. 14.

Rich, Giles S. (95), U.S. judge and patent-law expert; appointed to the federal bench by President Dwight D. Eisenhower in 1956. He served on the U.S. Court of Appeals for the Federal Circuit, the court of last resort before the Supreme Court for cases involving patent law. Earlier in his career, he helped draft the Patent Act of 1952, the basis of U.S. patent law. He was the nation's oldest practicing judge, carrying a full caseload until a month before his death: d. Washington, DC, June 9.

Richardson, Elliot L. (79), prominent government figure; served in four U.S. cabinet positions. He was head of the Department of Health, Education, and Welfare (1970–73); secretary of defense (1973); U.S. attorney general (1973); and secretary of commerce (1976–81). He was best known for his 1973 refusal, as U.S. attorney general, to fire special prosecutor Archibald Cox at President Richard Nixon's behest; Nixon was attempting to limit the investigation into the Watergate scandal. Instead, Richardson resigned his position and was praised widely for his integrity. He was awarded the Presidential Medal of Freedom in 1998: d. Boston, MA, Dec. 31.

Ripken, Cal (Calvin E.), Sr. (63), professional-baseball player, coach, and manager; was the father of two major-leaguers—Cal Ripken, Jr., and Billy Ripken. In 1987, as manager of the Baltimore Orioles, he became the only person to manage two of his sons on the same team: d. Baltimore, MD, March 25.

Ritter, Rev. Bruce (born John Ritter) (72), Roman Catholic cleric and founder of the Covenant House shelter for runaways. The shelter, established in New York City in 1969, became a hugely successful international program, serving as many as 25,000 youths. Ritter resigned early in 1990 following accusations of financial and sexual misconduct: d. Decatur, NY, Oct. 7.

Robinson, Betty (87), Olympic athlete; in 1928, only four months after beginning her track-and-field career at age 16, she won the first Olympic gold medal awarded to a woman in the sport. She made a comeback following a 1931 plane crash and won a gold medal in the 4x100-m relay in the 1936 Olympics. She set four world records and was inducted into the National Track and Field and U.S. Track and Field Halls of Fame: d. Colorado, May 18.

Rogers, Buddy (born Charles E. Rogers) (94), actor and bandleader; starred in *Wings* (1927), which won the award for best film at the first Academy Awards. He was married to legendary star Mary Pickford (1937–79): d. Rancho Mirage, CA, April 21.

Rountree, Martha (87), radio and television producer; was the cocreator and first moderator of the long-running news program *Meet the Press*; the show premiered on radio in 1945 and on tele-

Dusty Springfield

vision two years later. In 1997, Rountree was honored as the only woman moderator in the program's history: d. Washington, DC, Aug. 23.

Sabines Gutiérrez, Jaime (72), Mexican poet; much admired for his plainspoken but powerful and intensely personal poetry. He was awarded the National Prize for Letters in 1983: d. Mexico City, Mexico, March 19.

Sarazen, Gene (born Eugene Saraceni) (97), champion professional golfer during the 1920s and 1930s; in 1935 he won the Masters with a 235-yard shot that became famous. He was one of only four golfers ever to win all four major championships, and invented the sand wedge, first using it in 1932. He was inducted into the World Golf Hall of Fame in 1974: d. Naples, FL, May 13.

Sarett, Lewis Hastings (81), organic chemist; his work in the chemical synthesis of cortisone and other therapeutic substances led to his being awarded the National Medal of Science in 1975: d. Viola, ID, Nov. 29.

Sarkisian, Vazgen (40), premier of Armenia; appointed to the post in June 1999, he earlier had served as defense minister. He was shot by assassins during a session of Armenia's parliament: d. Yerevan, Armenia, Oct. 27.

Schawlow, Arthur L. (77), physicist; shared the 1981 Nobel Prize in physics for his pioneering work in the development of lasers and laser spectroscopy: d. Palo Alto, CA, April 28.

Seaborg, Glenn (86), chemist and nuclear physicist; led the research team that created plutonium, the fuel used in the first atomic bombs, as well as eight other artificial elements. He shared the 1951 Nobel Prize in chemistry. From 1961 to 1971 he served as chairman of the Atomic Energy Commission. He was awarded the National Medal of Science in 1991, and in 1997 became the first living person to have a newly discovered natural element named after him—Element 106, called seaborgium: d. Lafayette, CA, Feb. 25.

Seidner, David (42), fashion photographer; combined the influences of various artists in his fashion shots. He wrote several books dealing with photography. He received the Eisenstaedt Award for Portrait Photography from *Life* magazine and Columbia University in 1998: d. Miami Beach, FL, June 6.

Semon, Waldo L. (100), chemist and inventor; invented vinyl in 1928, while employed with B.F. Goodrich. He also helped develop Ameripol, a synthetic rubber; later versions of the substance replaced natural rubber in automobile tires. He was inducted into the National Inventors Hall of Fame in 1995: d. Hudson, OH, May 26.

Shannon, Anthony F. (69), journalist; a reporter at *The New York World-Telegram and Sun*, he shared a 1963 Pulitzer Prize in reporting for a story about a plane crash at Idlewild Airport: d. Warren Township, NJ, Feb. 16.

Shaw, Robert (82), musical conductor; considered widely to be one of the United States' greatest choral conductors. He served as director of the Atlanta Symphony Orchestra from 1967 to 1988. He received Kennedy Center Honors in 1991 and was presented with the National Medal of Arts in 1992. He won 14 Grammys for his conducting: d. New Haven, CT, Jan. 25.

Shepherd, Jean (77), radio storyteller; his easy, folksy style inspired comparisons to Mark Twain. He wrote several books, and wrote and narrated the film *A Christmas Story* (1983): d. Sanibel Island, FL, Oct. 16.

Silva Henríquez, Cardinal Raúl (91), Chilean Roman Catholic cardinal; was elevated to cardinal by Pope John XXIII in 1962. He was known as a champion of human rights and campaigned for reforms throughout Latin America to improve the lives of the poor. During the years when Chile was ruled by dictator Gen. Augusto Pinochet, he demanded the restoration of democracy and documented human-rights abuses. He also was instrumental in preventing a 1978 war between Chile and Argentina: d. Santiago, Chile, April 9.

Silverstein, Shel(by) (66), children's writer; his poetry, which he illustrated with cartoons, was notable for silliness mixed with occasional touches of the macabre. His collections *Where the Sidewalk Ends* (1974) and *A Light in the Attic* (1981) both were best-sellers, and his *The Giving Tree* (1964) became a children's classic. Also a songwriter, he wrote "A Boy Named Sue," which was a hit for singer Johnny Cash in 1969: d. Key West, FL, May 10.

Siskel, Gene (53), film reviewer; with colleague Roger Ebert, became half of one of the most influential film-review teams in the United States. The two—Siskel was a reviewer for *The Chicago Tribune* and Ebert for *The Chicago Sun-Times*—had their own nationally syndicated television program, premiering in 1982: d. Evanston, IL, Feb. 20.

Smith, David H. (67), medical researcher; shared the Lasker Award for clinical medical research in 1996 for his work in finding an effective vaccine against a bacterium, *Haemophilus influenzae* type B, that causes meningitis in young children: d. New York City, Feb. 23.

Snow, Hank (born Clarence Eugene Snow) (85), Canadian-born country singer and songwriter; one of country music's most popular stars of the 1950s. Among his hits were "I'm Movin' On," "Golden Rocket," and "Rhumba Boogie," which all reached Number 1. He was inducted into the Country Music Hall of Fame in 1979: d. Madison, TN, Dec. 20.

Spence, Skip (born Alexander Spence) (52), rock musician; a founding member of the legendary 1960s psychedelic-rock band Jefferson Airplane, as well as of the band Moby Grape: d. Santa Cruz, CA, April 16.

Springfield, Dusty (born Mary Isabel O'Brien) (59), English pop singer; most of her major international hits came during the 1960s; they included "I Only Want to Be With You" (1964) and "The Look of Love" (1967). She was awarded the Order of the British Empire in December 1998: d. Henley-on-Thames, England, March 2.

Stears, John (64), English creator of special effects for films; won a 1965 Oscar for his work on the James Bond film *Thunderball*, and shared one in 1977 for *Star Wars*; for the latter film, he created the robots R2-D2 and C-3PO. He created many of the impressive gadgets used in the James Bond movies: d. Los Angeles, CA, June 28.

Payne Stewart

Stein, Herbert (83), economist; served as a member (1969–74) and chairman (1972–74) of the Council of Economic Advisers during the administration of President Richard Nixon. He was a key figure in the development of the administration's inflation-fighting wage- and price-control policies: d. Washington, DC, Sept. 8.

Steinberg, Saul (84), Romanian-born artist and cartoonist; best known for his many drawings—among them 85 covers—for *The New Yorker* magazine. He also published several books; his work was exhibited in galleries in the United States and abroad: d. New York City, May 12.

Stewart, Donald (69), screenwriter; with cowriter Constantin Costa-Gavras, won an Oscar for the 1982 film *Missing*. He also wrote the screenplays for the film adaptations of Tom Clancy's books *Hunt for Red October*, *Patriot Games*, and *Clear and Present Danger*: d. Los Angeles, CA, April 28.

Stewart, (William) Payne (42), professional golfer; won 18 professional tournaments during his 19-year career, including three majors: the Professional Golfers' Association (PGA) in 1989 and the U.S. Open in 1991 and 1999: d. near Mina, SD, Oct. 25.

Stoph, Willi (84), premier of East Germany (1964–73; 1976–89); after the reunification of Germany, he was tried in 1993 along with other East German officials on charges of manslaughter, related to the standing government order that anyone trying to flee the country should be shot. The case against him was dropped due to his illness: d. Berlin, Germany, April 13.

Strasberg, Susan (60), actress; best known for her first Broadway performance, in the title role of *The Diary of Anne Frank* (1955). Daughter of famed acting coach Lee Strasberg, she was admired for her natural acting talent and appeared in several other Broadway plays and films: d. New York City, Jan. 21.

© Hrvoje Knez/AP/Wide World Photos

Franjo Tudjman

Strax, Philip (90), radiologist; an early and influential advocate of mammograms for breast-cancer detection. In 1988 he shared a prize from the General Motors Cancer Research Foundation for his work on a 1963–66 study proving the efficacy of mammograms: d. Bethesda, MD, March 9.

Sunthorn Kongsompong (68), military leader of Thailand (1991–92); took power in a bloodless military coup overthrowing the country's democratic government. Pro-democracy demonstrations—leading to a military crackdown in which dozens were killed—eventually led to the intervention of King Bhumibol Adulyadej and the downfall of Sunthorn's regime: d. Bangkok, Thailand, Aug. 2.

Tannenwald, Theodore, Jr. (82), U.S. tax-court judge; appointed by President Lyndon Johnson in 1965 to the Washington, DC, tax court. He was elected to a two-year term as chief judge in 1981 and took senior status in 1983. He served as an adviser in the presidential administrations of Harry Truman, John F. Kennedy, and Johnson: d. Washington, DC, Jan. 17.

Thorp, Roderick (62), novelist; wrote two best-selling crime novels: *The Detective* (1966), which was made into a 1968 film; and *Nothing Lasts Forever* (1979), which was made into the 1988 hit film *Die Hard*: d. Oxnard, CA, April 28.

Tilberis, Liz (born Elizabeth Kelly) (51), English fashion-magazine editor; served as editor in chief of *British Vogue* (1987–92) and of *Harper's Bazaar* (1992–99). *Vogue* won numerous awards and increased its circulation under her leadership, and she was instrumental in reversing a long decline at *Harper's Bazaar* and helping it regain prestige. Her 1998 autobiography *No Time to Die* described her long fight against ovarian cancer: d. New York City, April 21.

Torme, Mel(vin) H. (73), pop and jazz singer and actor; known as the "Velvet Fog" for his smooth voice. In a career spanning almost 70 years, he had several enduring hits, including "Blue Moon" and "The Christmas Song," which he also cowrote with lyricist Robert Wells. He received a Grammy Award for lifetime achievement in February 1999. He also wrote several books: d. Los Angeles, CA, June 5.

Tretick, (Aaron) Stanley (77), news photographer; became known for the memorable photographs he took for *Look* magazine of President John F. Kennedy and his young family: d. Gaithersburg, MD, July 19.

Tudjman, Franjo (77), president of Croatia (1990–99); in 1991, led Croatia in its secession from Yugoslavia, contributing to the collapse of the Yugoslav Federation and to a crushing war in the region. His harsh rule was criticized strongly by international groups: d. Zagreb, Croatia, Dec. 10.

Washington, Grover, Jr. (56), jazz saxophonist and composer; won a 1981 Grammy Award for best fusion jazz performance for his album *Winelight*: d. New York City, Dec. 17.

Wazzan, Shafik al- (74), prime minister of Lebanon (1980–84); during his tenure, the nation was wracked by civil war, an Israeli invasion, and the massacre of almost 900 people in a Palestinian refugee camp, as well as the 1983 truck-bomb attack that killed 241 U.S. Marines in Beirut: d. Beirut, Lebanon, July 8.

Weigel, Stanley A. (93), U.S. judge; a Republican who had served on the national committee of the American Civil Liberties Union, he was appointed to the U.S. District Court for the Northern District of California in 1962 by President John F. Kennedy: d. San Francisco, CA, Sept. 1.

Wences, Señor (born Wenceslao Moreno) (103), Spanish-born ventriloquist; famed for his television performances—mainly on *The Ed Sullivan Show*—during the 1950s and 1960s with his puppets Pedro and Johnny: d. New York City, April 20.

Wexler, Norman (73); screenwriter and playwright; twice nominated for an Oscar, for his scripts for *Joe* (1970) and *Saturday Night Fever* (1977). His screenplay for 1973's *Serpico* also was much praised: d. Washington, DC, Aug. 23.

Whitney, Ruth (70), fashion-magazine editor; served as editor in chief of *Glamour* for 31 years. She widened the magazine's focus to include topical subjects and helped its circulation more than double. *Glamour* became the only women's publication to win two National Magazine Awards for general excellence (in 1981 and 1991): d. Irvington, NY, June 4.

Whyte, William H. (81), journalist, author, and urbanologist; his book *The Organization Man* (1956) was a best-seller that became a classic. His observations about urban life were used in planning by many city leaders. He published several books on the environment as well as a study, *Conservation Easement* (1959), that helped spur open-space legislation in several U.S. states: d. New York City, Jan. 12.

Williams, Joe (born Joseph Goreed) (80), jazz singer; first gained attention as a singer with the Count Basie Orchestra (1954–61). He won a Grammy Award as best jazz vocalist in 1984 for his album *Nothin' but the Blues*. His signature song, "Every Day (I Have the Blues)," was added to the Grammy Awards Hall of Fame for recordings in 1992: d. Las Vegas, NV, March 29.

Williams, Sherley Anne (54), novelist, poet, and playwright; won a Caldecott Award and a Coretta Scott King Book Award for her 1992 children's book *Working Cotton*. A television performance of poems from her 1982 poetry collection *Some One Sweet Angel Chile* won an Emmy Award: d. San Diego, CA, July 6.

Wisdom, John Minor (93), U.S. appeals-court judge for the 5th Circuit; was named to the federal bench in 1957 by President Dwight Eisenhower. His jurisdiction comprised several southern states; his opinions helped end segregation and led to the establishment of the civil-rights laws of the 1950s and 1960s. He was presented with the Presidential Medal of Freedom in 1993: d. New Orleans, LA, May 15.

Woodward, C. Vann (91), historian and writer; known for his respected and readable histories of the U.S. South. His best-known work was *The Strange Career of Jim Crow* (1955), which became a best-seller. He won the Pulitzer Prize for history in 1982 for his editing of *Mary Chesnut's Civil War*: d. Hamden, CT, Dec. 17.

Woolf, Sir John (86), British film producer; won 13 Academy Awards for his films, which included *African Queen* (1951), *Richard III* (1956), and *Oliver!* (1968). He was knighted in 1975 by Queen Elizabeth II: d. London, England, June 28.

Wynn, Early (79), professional-baseball player from 1939–63; a pitcher for the Washington Senators, Cleveland Indians, and Chicago White Sox. He was a 20-game winner five times and won the Cy Young Award in 1959, and is one of only 20 pitchers to have achieved 300 career victories. He was inducted into the Baseball Hall of Fame in 1972: d. Venice, FL, April 4.

Zipprodt, Patricia (74), costume designer for stage, film, and television productions; won Tony Awards for her costumes for the Broadway shows *Fiddler on the Roof* (1964), *Cabaret* (1966), and *Sweet Charity* (1985). She was inducted into the Theatrical Hall of Fame in 1992: d. New York City, July 17.

Zoll, Paul M. (87), cardiologist and medical researcher; worked on the development of many medical devices, including heart monitors, pacemakers, and defibrillators. He won the Albert Lasker Clinical Medical Research Award in 1973: d. Chestnut Hill, MA, Jan. 5.

Zubrod, Charles G. (84), physician; pioneered the use of chemotherapy as a cancer treatment. He served as clinical director of the National Institutes of Health (1954–61) and was awarded the Albert Lasker Clinical Medical Research Award in 1972: d. Washington, DC, Jan. 19.

© CBS Television/AP/Wide World Photos

Mel Torme

Oceanography

While 1998 was dominated by the phenomenon El Niño, 1999 played host to La Niña—characterized by a cooling of the Eastern Tropical Pacific Ocean and, essentially, a reversal of the temperature and precipitation patterns seen the year before. The cooling of the ocean was particularly impressive. Consider a swimming pool some 2,000 mi (3 200 km) long, 1,000 mi (1 600 km) wide, and 100 ft (30 m) deep. Nature cooled this body of ocean from an average sea-surface temperature (SST) of 5° C (9° F) above normal to 5° below, and it did this in little more than one month!

La Niña's effects in the United States ranged from wildfires in California to record precipitation in the Northwest. Mount Baker in the Cascade Mountains of Washington received 1,100 inches (28 m) of snow—a record for the United States and probably the world.

Observations. Great strides were made in the extension of the global-climate-observing system for the world's oceans. With international cooperation involving the United States, France, and Brazil, the Pilot Research Moored Array in the Tropical Atlantic (PIRATA) was established. These moorings will provide time-series measurements of surface fluxes (momentum, heat, moisture), surface and upper-ocean temperature, and surface and upper-ocean salinity. Also, the Atlantic Drifter Array, ultimately comprising 140 drifting buoys deployed between 20° S and 30° N latitude, will provide systematic, basin-scale measurements of upper-ocean circulation and SST.

Again in the Atlantic, the U.S. National Science Foundation—in cooperation with Canada, France, Germany, Portugal, Spain, and Great Britain—deployed an array of nearly 200 autonomous profiling floats across the equatorial South Atlantic to study the evolution of the regional near-surface temperature field.

On May 13, 1999, U.S. federal agencies involved in oceanography released the report "Toward a U.S. Plan for an Integrated, Sustained Ocean Observing System." This report was a tangible accomplishment of the National Ocean Research Leadership Council, which was created by Congress as an oversight body for the National Oceanographic Partnership Program.

The year 1999 also saw the formation of the ARGO program—a global array of profiling floats. This program will deploy a global array of 3,000 profiling floats to observe the ocean's upper layer in real time. Along with satellites, the ARGO array will initiate the oceanic equivalent of today's operational observing system for the global atmosphere.

Sustainable Seas Expeditions. On Earth Day, April 22, 1999, U.S. Commerce Secretary William Daley launched a first-of-its-kind exploration of the nation's 12 marine sanctuaries. The Sustainable Seas Expeditions (SSE) is a project of the National Geographic Society in partnership with the National Oceanic and Atmospheric Administration (NOAA), made possible by an initial grant of $5 million from the Richard & Rhoda Goldman Fund. The three fundamental goals of the expeditions are undersea exploration, scientific research, and education. The SSE will explore the deep space of the oceans using the innovative Deep Worker submersible.

Antarctic Circumpolar Wave. Although discovered in 1996, the Antarctic Circumpolar Wave now is known to affect climate by switching between warm and cool phases. These phases change sea-surface temperatures. Colder sea temperatures mean less evaporation, less cloud formation, and, hence, less rain. The wave, which moves under the ocean's surface, is as big as the Australian continent and 0.6 mi (1 km) deep. It endlessly circles Antarctica and takes eight to nine years to complete a rotation. The wave is believed to interact with other large climate effects such as the El Niño–La Niña, enhancing or reducing the impact depending on the circumstances. A huge part of the southern world, from about 25° S latitude, is in the weather domain of the wave. This includes most of southern Australia; much of Argentina, Brazil, Uruguay, and Chile; all of New Zealand; part of Madagascar; and most of South Africa and Namibia.

Ocean Policy. A report was presented to U.S. Vice-President Al Gore on Sept. 2, 1999, outlining nearly 150 actions to protect, restore, and explore America's ocean resources. Titled "Turning to the Sea: America's Ocean Future," the cabinet-level report stemmed from the National Ocean Conference held in Monterey, CA, in June 1998. The vice-president, in accepting the report, launched a high-level task force to oversee implementation of its most important recommendations.

JOHN KERMOND, *National Oceanic and Atmospheric Administration*

Pakistan

Pakistan began 1999 facing severe political, economic, and foreign-policy challenges, but with some hope of finding solutions on all three fronts. By October, however, everything had deteriorated to the point where the civilian government of Prime Minister Mohammad Nawaz Sharif was overthrown by Gen. Pervez Musharraf, head of the army.

Politics. On January 3 a bomb exploded under a bridge on a road outside Lahore, killing three persons and wounding several others. The attack was interpreted as an assassination attempt on the prime minister by the Muttahida Qaumi Movement (MQM), an opposition party based in Karachi. A few weeks later, Sharif announced a decree that permitted the establishment of military courts anywhere in the country. The military also was given responsibility for the management of major social and economic administrative systems, including the massive Water and Power Development Authority (WAPDA).

In April, Benazir Bhutto, leader of the Pakistan People's Party (PPP) and prime minister from 1988 to 1990 and 1993 to 1996, was found guilty in absentia on charges of corruption while in office. She and her husband, Asif Ali Zardari, were sentenced to five years in prison and a fine of $8.6 million, plus disqualification from holding political office. Zardari, in jail in Karachi on murder-conspiracy charges, was hospitalized a month later under unclear circumstances. Police alleged he had tried to commit suicide, but Zardari, Bhutto, and PPP supporters claimed he had been tortured.

As Sharif tightened his grip on governmental institutions and overwhelmed his political opposition, he also undertook to silence dissent within the press. The most prominent target of repression in 1999 was Najam Sethi, editor of *The Friday Times*, a Lahore-based English-language weekly. Soon after Sethi returned to Pakistan after speaking at the Indian International Center in New Delhi, he was beaten, arrested, and detained for several weeks. A government spokesman said Sethi was being held for making critical comments about Pakistan in India and being linked with Indian intelligence. Some observers speculated that the true reason for Sethi's arrest was that he had given an interview to a team from the British Broadcasting Corporation (BBC) that was making a documentary about corruption in Pakistan. Several other journalists, some of whom also cooperated with the BBC team, were subjected to detention or harassment during the same period. In addition, nongovernmental organizations (NGOs) came under attack. On May 9 the government banned 1,940 NGOs, froze their bank accounts, and seized their assets.

Antigovernment protests erupted in the fall, following a military clash between Pakistan and India over the long-disputed territory of Kashmir. Islamic groups, angered when Sharif withdrew Pakistani troops from Kashmir, and PPP supporters together called for an end to the prime minister's repressive rule. On September 1 a large

The overthrow of Pakistan's civilian government by army head Gen. Pervez Musharraf in October 1999 received public approval. In Lahore, the hometown of deposed Prime Minister Mohammad Nawaz Sharif, Pakistanis demonstrated in support of their new leader, left.

PAKISTAN • Information Highlights

Official Name: Islamic Republic of Pakistan.
Location: South Asia.
Area: 310,402 sq mi (803 940 km²).
Population (July 1999 est.): 138,123,359.
Chief Cities (1981 census): Islamabad, the capital, 204,364; Karachi, 5,180,562.
Government: *Head of state and government,* Gen. Pervez Musharraf, leader under martial law (took power October 1999). *Legislature*—suspended.
Monetary Unit: Rupee (51.8925 rupees equal U.S.$1, Dec. 14, 1999).
Gross Domestic Product (1998 est. U.S.$): $270,000,-000,000 (purchasing power parity).
Economic Index (1998, 1990 = 100): *Consumer Prices,* all items, 221.9; food, 229.0.
Foreign Trade (1998 U.S.$): *Imports,* $9,315,000,000; *exports,* $8,501,000,000.

protest rally was held in Lahore. On the eve of an opposition strike scheduled for September 4, the government arrested thousands of activists and outlawed strikes. In mid-September, 19 opposition parties formed a Grand Democratic Alliance to demand Sharif's removal. Even within the prime minister's Pakistan Muslim League (PML), voices of concern and dissent were raised.

The Sharif government was dismissed on October 12, shortly after the prime minister attempted to fire General Musharraf. Relations between the two had grown increasingly tense as the year progressed. Sharif announced Musharraf's removal while the general was flying home from a visit to Sri Lanka. Musharraf's plane also was refused landing rights at the airport in Karachi. When the general's firing was announced, the army seized the cabinet building and media outlets in Islamabad and took over all of the major airports. Musharraf's plane then was allowed to land. Sharif and several government ministers were placed under house arrest, and Musharraf announced that he was heading the government.

The military initially called its action an "emergency," but three days later it imposed martial law. The new regime arrested key leaders of the former government, dismissed Parliament, suspended the constitution, and appointed new provincial governors and a new cabinet. Musharraf gave no timetable for a return to representative government, but promised stabilization of the economy and a thorough cleanup of corruption so that "true democracy" might be established. In November, Sharif was charged with hijacking, kidnapping, and conspiracy connected with the decision not to let the general's plane land, which military officials ascribed to the prime minister. He also was accused of corruption and stealing.

Economy. The State Bank of Pakistan's rosy predictions for the economy, issued in December 1998, were not fulfilled, largely because of the unanticipated military conflict with India and interruptions in financial assistance from the World Bank and the International Monetary Fund (IMF) because of the coup. Economic growth, originally projected at 6%, turned out to be approximately 3%. Still under sanctions imposed following its 1998 nuclear tests, Pakistan suffered a 10.5% decline in exports in 1998–99. At the same time, imports declined by 8.2%, widening the trade gap to $1.5 billion, 5.3% more than in 1997–98. Inflation also rose to more than 10%, up from about 6% in 1997–98.

Even before the coup occurred, foreign donors were put off by Pakistan's pervasive corruption and its failure to implement reforms. In May the IMF released $51 million to Pakistan, the third installment of a loan pledged during the 1997–98 Asian economic crisis, but the World Bank in July postponed a rural-development loan of $110 million. In late 1999 the United States, Germany, and other donors rescheduled Pakistan's foreign debt.

One of Musharraf's first acts in October was to demand repayment of approximately $4 billion in bad loans, largely held by politicians and wealthy businessmen. Defaulters were forbidden to leave the country, their names were published in the press, their bank accounts were frozen, and those who failed to repay the loans in a timely fashion were arrested.

Adding to Pakistan's economic stress was a major cyclone that devastated the coast east of Karachi in late May. The storm killed more than 175 persons, flooded towns throughout the area, and destroyed thousands of houses and other buildings.

Foreign Affairs. Relations with India dominated Pakistan's foreign policy (*see* INDIA—*India-Pakistan Relations*). After the coup, Musharraf sought to renew a diplomatic dialogue, but India was reluctant to lend legitimacy to his regime. Similarly, the Commonwealth reacted to the coup by quickly suspending Pakistan's membership.

The prominent U.S. role during the Kashmir conflict, highlighted by President Bill Clinton's extraction of Sharif's commitment to withdraw troops, made the United States a target of protests. In the weeks before the coup, Clinton had issued warnings to Pakistanis not to use extraconstitutional means to effect governmental change. Afterward, the United States urged Pakistan to establish a timetable for a return to democratic government.

Rocket attacks took place against U.S. facilities (including the embassy) in Islamabad on November 11, resulting in a few injuries. The motivation behind the incident was believed to be imminent United Nations (UN) sanctions against the Taliban regime in Afghanistan for its protection of alleged terrorist Osama bin Laden.

WILLIAM L. RICHTER, *Kansas State University*

Paraguay

A struggle involving separation of powers in Paraguay led in 1999 to a high-level assassination, a new government, and tense relations with Argentina and Uruguay. A chaotic trend in the economy deepened.

Politics. In late 1998 the Supreme Court ruled that President Raúl Cubas, in defying a court order to return retired Gen. Lino Oviedo to prison to serve a ten-year term for an attempted coup in 1996, was not fulfilling his constitutional duties. Congress scheduled an impeachment process on the matter for April. In March, Vice-President Luis María Argaña was assassinated. Head of the dominant Colorado Party, he stood in the way of a determined Oviedo's path to the presidency by ballot. Both Oviedo and Cubas were accused of complicity in his murder. Congress reacted by launching Cubas' impeachment trial ahead of schedule. Belatedly, Cubas detained Oviedo, assigning him to a barracks. A general strike was called, and large crowds gathered outside Congress demanding Cubas' resignation. Supporters of Oviedo were believed to have fired on the demonstrators (reportedly on the general's orders), killing eight and injuring nearly 200. Rather than appear before the impeachment proceeding, Cubas resigned and sought exile in Brazil on March 28. Oviedo fled to Argentina (where he continued to meddle in Paraguay's internal affairs), while Defense Minister José Segovia Boltes sought refuge in Uruguay.

The incoming chief executive was Senate President Luis González Macchi. Hoping to avoid calls for a presidential election, González Macchi formed a "unity" cabinet, the first in Paraguay since 1946, which contained several members of opposition parties. The Supreme Court ruled in April that the new president could finish out Cubas' term, which was set to end in 2003.

The coalition began to crumble almost immediately; internal divisions surfaced in its main partner, the Authentic Liberal Radical Party, forcing replacements. The slowness of the government in scheduling an election for the vacant vice-presidency, revitalizing the economy, and returning Oviedo to prison contributed to a steep decline in popular support of González' administration.

Economy. The economy continued to struggle throughout 1999. The Cubas administration devalued the guaraní by 2.5% in February. In mid-1999 it was revealed that the gross domestic product (GDP) would not reach its goal of 2% growth for the year. In May the González government authorized a $400 million bond issue to assist the banking sector. After the first seven months of 1999, export earnings from the Mercosur trade pact were down by 30% from the same period in 1998, in part because Brazil, the top market for Paraguayan goods, devalued its currency in January by 40%. Overall, export earnings fell by 22%. Industry and Commerce Secretary Guillermo Vargas threatened in August that Paraguay might withdraw from Mercosur if Argentina implemented its plan to open a free-trade zone at Clorinda, on the border between the two countries.

Foreign Affairs. Paraguay's relations with Argentina and Uruguay deteriorated badly when the latter two nations refused to extradite General Oviedo and Segovia Boltes (who was wanted for misuse of public funds). Paraguay withdrew its ambassadors from both countries in September. Cooperation did continue, however, in the terrorist-dominated tri-border area with Argentina and Brazil, where targets were mostly Muslim activists.

LARRY L. PIPPIN, *University of the Pacific*

PARAGUAY • Information Highlights

Official Name: Republic of Paraguay.
Location: Central South America.
Area: 157,046 sq mi (406 750 km²).
Population (July 1999 est.): 5,434,095.
Chief Cities (1992 census): Asunción, the capital, 502,426; Ciudad del Este, 133,896; San Lorenzo, 133,311.
Government: *Head of state and government,* Luis González Macchi, president (sworn in March 28, 1999). *Legislature*—Congress: Chamber of Senators and Chamber of Deputies.
Monetary Unit: Guaraní (3,317.00 guaraníes equal U.S.$1, Dec. 14, 1999).
Gross Domestic Product (1998 est. U.S.$): $19,800,000,000 (purchasing power parity).
Economic Index (Asunción, 1998, 1990 = 100): *Consumer Prices,* all items, 303.1; food, 275.1.
Foreign Trade (1997 U.S.$): *Imports,* $3,403,000,000; *exports,* $1,089,000,000.

People, Places, and Things

The following four pages recount the stories behind a selection of people, places, and things that may not have made the headlines in 1999 but that drew attention and created interest.

© Stan Godlewski/Liaison Agency

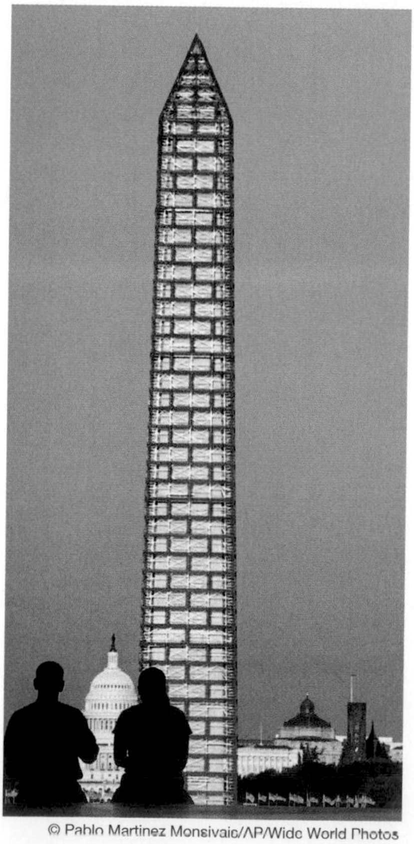

© Pablo Martinez Monsivais/AP/Wide World Photos

© Paul Connors/AP/Wide World Photos

The war of the amusement parks in Orlando, FL, heated up a bit more in May with the opening of Universal Studios' 100-acre Islands of Adventure, top, *featuring thrill rides and such themed areas as Toon Lagoon, Marvel Super Hero Island, and Jurassic Park. Universal hoped that its $2.5 billion extravaganza would present a formidable challenge to its main rival, Disney. After undergoing four months of exterior restoration, the Washington Monument,* left, *reopened to the public on February 22, its namesake's 267th birthday. Sergei Khrushchev,* above, *the 64-year-old son of the late Soviet premier Nikita Khrushchev, and his wife, Valentina Garlenka, were sworn in as U.S. citizens in July. His action culminated a gradual political and philosophical evolution from communism to capitalism.*

© Mary Ann Chastain/AP/Wide World Photos

© U.S. Navy Photo by Michael W. Prendergrass

© Dushko Despotovic/Corbis-Sygma

In May, Nancy Mace, above left, *became the first female cadet to graduate from the Citadel, a military college in Charleston, SC. She accepted her diploma from her father, J. Emory Mace, the Citadel's commandant of cadets. Women continued to play a bigger role in the U.S. military. For example, U.S. Navy Lt. Kendra Williams,* above right, *had flown a mission over Iraq on Dec. 16, 1998, as part of Operation Desert Fox, marking the first time a woman pilot bombed enemy targets in combat. Cristina Sanchez,* left, *made history in May 1998 by becoming the first female matador to perform in Spain's Las Ventas ring, a feat considered to be the pinnacle of bullfighting. But barely a year later, she announced her retirement, saying that "the bullfight world is made by and for men."*

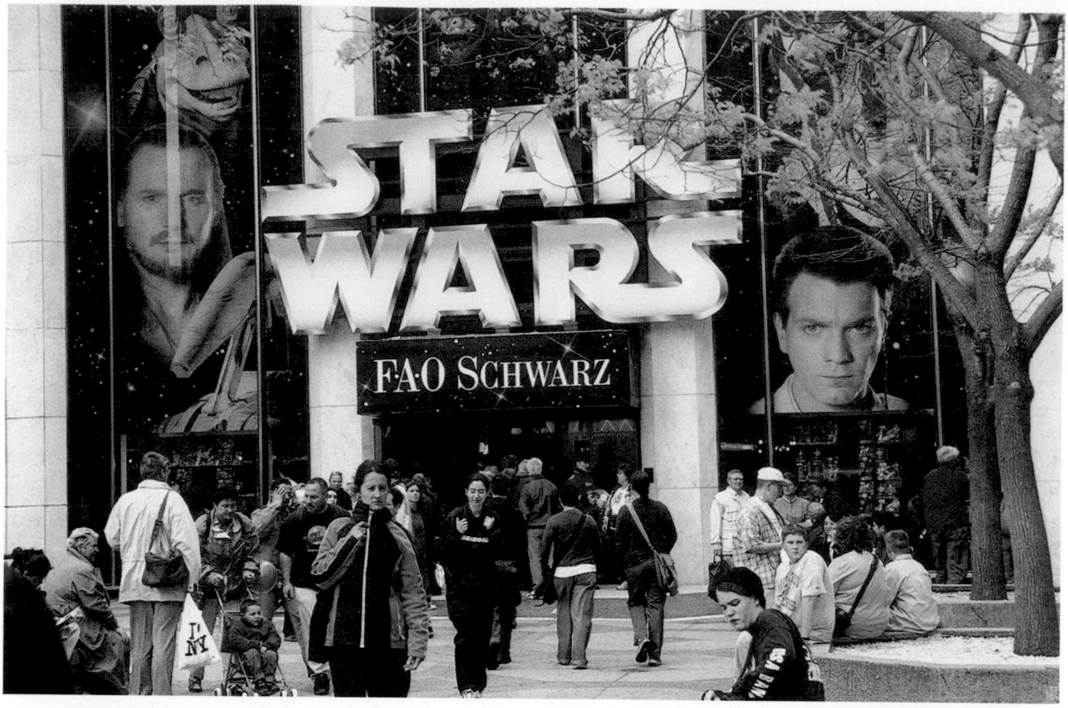

© Ed Bailey/AP/Wide World Photos

© Charles Krupa/AP/Wide World Photos

Fans of the hit "Star Wars" series of films rejoiced at the release of the long-awaited next installment, "Star Wars Episode I: The Phantom Menace," in spring 1999. The movie's success could be measured not only by box-office receipts (more than $400 million), but also by the booming sales of toys and other related merchandise, often featured in special displays in stores such as New York City's FAO Schwarz, top. *Another hugely popular phenomenon that swept the United States in 1999 was Pokémon, a Japanese game that encouraged children to "capture" cute little monsters. Originally just a video game, it quickly spread to include trading cards,* above, *a TV cartoon series, and even an animated feature film. In late 1996 former Chrysler head Lee Iacocca came out of retirement to launch a company called EV Global Motors. A little more than two years later, in February 1999, he triumphantly unveiled its first product: a Taiwan-produced electric bicycle, the E-Bike,* right, *which he hoped would revolutionize the electric-vehicle industry.*

© Richard Sheinwald/AP/Wide World Photos

© Antonio Calanni/AP/Wide World Photos

© Eric Vanderville/Liaison Agency

© Bebeto Matthews/AP/Wide World Photos

A major archaeological find—possibly a fossilized Homo erectus *skull that could shed further light on the process of human evolution—turned up in March in a Manhattan specialty shop run by Henry Galiano,* above. *Galiano donated his discovery, which he had received in a shipment of items from Indonesia, to paleoarchaeologists in Indonesia. Engineers excavated land around the Leaning Tower of Pisa,* left, *as part of an effort to prevent it from collapsing. The tower has been closed to tourists since the project began in 1990. Farther north, in Milan, a 24-foot-high silicon bronze horse,* top, *based on an unfinished work by Leonardo da Vinci that had been destroyed by French soldiers 500 years ago, was unveiled in September.*

Peru

The year 1999 was a calm one for Peru. As presidential and legislative elections approached in April 2000, however, this calm could prove to come before the storm.

Politics. The most divisive political issue was the likely candidacy of President Alberto Fujimori for the 2000–05 term. Fujimori first had been elected in 1990 and was reelected in 1995. Most legal experts believed that the 1993 constitution prohibited Fujimori's candidacy in 2000. However, every indication was that, via questionable laws passed by his party's legislative majority, the president would run. Many Peruvians worried that the electoral playing field was too skewed in Fujimori's favor to produce an electoral outcome that would be considered legitimate. The Fujimori government had established a powerful National Intelligence Service that was used for the president's political ends; it had achieved an unprecedented hegemony in the nation's broadcast media; and it allocated public resources for partisan purposes.

Nevertheless, in most polls, either or both of the two leading opposition aspirants—Alberto Andrade, the mayor of Lima, and Luís Castañeda Lossio, director of Peru's Social Security Institute (1990–96)—usually defeated Fujimori in a runoff contest. The political parties that had been dominant during the 1980s but had performed poorly continued to be scorned by most Peruvians, and both leading opposition aspirants were independents who had founded their own political vehicles. Andrade, the founder of *Somos Perú* (We Are Peru), was elected mayor of Lima in 1995 and reelected in 1998; he was viewed widely as a competent manager and shrewd politician, but his political base was solely in Lima. Castañeda Lossio, the founder of *Solidaridad Nacional* (National Solidarity), had been praised widely for his direction of the Social Security Institute and was working to build political support in the provinces; however, his abilities as a politician were largely untested.

By late 1999 the opposition's policy positions were vague, and strategic questions, including a possible alliance between the two front-runners, remained unanswered. There also was time for a dark horse to rise from among the more than ten opposition candidates.

The Economy. Peruvians' primary concern was the national economy. Peru's annual average economic-growth rate was about 3% in 1996–98, and the forecast for 1999 was approximately 2.4%. Most of this growth was in mining, a sector with scant labor requirements. Unemployment remained severe; real wages were stagnant. The sluggish economy was attributed to high taxes and interest rates, slower privatization, bad weather, and the 1998 financial crisis in Russia, Asia, and Brazil. It was not clear how much economic concerns would hurt a Fujimori candidacy.

Internal and External Peace. In July 1999 the government captured Oscar Ramírez Durand. Known as "Feliciano," he had succeeded Abimael Guzmán as the leader of the Shining Path guerrillas after Guzmán's capture in 1992. Although this guerrilla group wielded a mere fraction of its former strength, Feliciano's capture was a reminder to many Peruvians of the government's favorable counterinsurgency record.

Peru's October 1998 peace agreement with Ecuador at first had rankled many Peruvians. They had been dismayed by Peru's concessions to Ecuador, in particular the ownership of 0.4 sq mi (1 km^2) inside Peruvian territory at Tiwintza (where Ecuadoran troops had fared well against Peruvian soldiers in February 1995), and free navigation and trade rights along the Amazon border. Increasingly, however, most Peruvians seemed to agree that the end of the most intense border dispute in Latin America was worth those concessions.

U.S. and most Latin American leaders were aware of Fujimori's authoritarian proclivities. In July 1999 he withdrew Peru from the jurisdiction of the Inter-American Human Rights Court, an arm of the Organization of American States (OAS), after the court had ruled that four Chilean members

PERU • Information Highlights

Official Name: Republic of Peru.
Location: West coast of South America.
Area: 496,224 sq mi (1 285 220 km^2).
Population (July 1999 est.): 26,624,582.
Chief Cities (1993 census): Lima, the capital, 6,321,173 (metropolitan area); Arequipa, 642,478; Trujillo, 588,638; Chiclayo, 566,027.
Government: *Head of state,* Alberto Fujimori, president (took office July 28, 1990). *Head of government,* Victor Joy Way, prime minister (appointed Jan. 5, 1999). *Legislature* (unicameral)—Democratic Constituent Congress.
Monetary Unit: New sol (3.4645 new sols equal U.S.$1, Nov. 15, 1999).
Gross Domestic Product (1998 est. U.S.$): $111,800,-000,000 (purchasing power parity).
Economic Indexes: *Consumer Prices* (Lima, 1997; 1990 = 100): all items, 2,187.9; food, 1,784.3. *Industrial Production* (1998, 1990 = 100): 144.5.
Foreign Trade (1997 U.S.$): *Imports,* $10,263,000,000; *exports,* $6,814,000,000.

of a guerrilla group had been denied a fair trial. On the other hand, the U.S. government was pleased with the Fujimori government's antinarcotics and economic policies.

CYNTHIA MCCLINTOCK
The George Washington University

Philippines

In 1999—one year into the six-year term of Philippine President Joseph Estrada—the reviews were mixed. The former movie actor and former vice-president was credited with some good cabinet appointees, adroit foreign-policy moves, and a sweeping identification of his policies with the more than 50% of Filipinos below the poverty line. Critics charged that the president's social agenda was mostly rhetoric and "gimmicks." One plan, for example, targeted the 100 poorest families in every province and major city. That would distribute the largesse politically but scarcely would make a dent in the poverty of the 37 million poor.

The Presidency, Constitutional Change, and Controversy. President Estrada also launched a controversial campaign to amend the 1987 constitution, passed in the aftermath of the Ferdinand Marcos dictatorship. Both Estrada's predecessor, Fidel Ramos, and Estrada supporters wanted to see the single six-year presidential term changed to one that would permit reelection. Estrada himself claimed no interest in changing that provision, but argued that the constitution's protectionist elements must go if foreign investment was to be accelerated. Critics questioned his sincerity, since he took no moves to liberalize the economy in ways not dependent on the constitution. Estrada argued that there should be no restriction on foreign ownership of land, utilities, and other properties. Opponents said the real obstacles were corruption and the continuance of the president's links to Marcos "cronies."

Chief among the opponents of constitutional change were Cardinal Jaime Sin, the head of the dominant Roman Catholic Church, and former President Corazon Aquino, who argued that tinkering with the constitution could open the floodgates to changing other provisions. There also was concern about the way the president dealt with criticism. The *Manila Times* closed down rather than be sold to an Estrada loyalist. The *Philippine Inquirer* saw most of its entertainment advertising pulled by those close to the president.

Estrada was enjoying a 74% approval rating from the public late in 1999, but that same public was 80% in favor of leaving the constitution alone. More controversy also emerged, with the Catholic Church opposed to population planning and the reemergence of the death penalty. President Estrada favored both. He became the first president since President Marcos in 1975 to permit executions.

The president enjoyed a commanding influence over Congress. In August the coalition of three parties that had elected him was dissolved, and he formed the new Party of the Filipino Masses (LAMP), which immediately became the majority party in the House of Representatives and the Senate. Philippine politicians never were known for fidelity to particular parties, but until the martial-law era of President Marcos, power had fluctuated between two nonideological parties. Defections to the party of the president were common. In 1999, however, the

A Manila business district was the site of an Aug. 20, 1999, rally against Philippine President Joseph Estrada. Although Estrada enjoyed a high approval rating during his first full year in office, there was major opposition to his plan to amend the nation's 1987 constitution.

parties were numerous and resembled little more than opportunistic groups linked to powerful personalities.

The Economy. The Philippines did not suffer the drastic swings in economic fortune that many neighbor nations endured during the 1997–98 crisis, because it had not enjoyed earlier prosperity and had fewer outstanding loans. The Philippines' earnings growth was low, though employment growth was up 4.3% over 1998, with the agricultural sector up 6.8%. The balance of trade improved in 1999. Estrada's budget promised a 51% increase for agriculture, most of which was directed at modernization. Only half the land needing it was irrigated, and soil conditions had been compromised severely by years of excessive logging.

Though international aid agencies applauded the president's agenda and rhetoric, they were concerned about his ability to control and target assistance. On the positive side, the administration was active on the housing front, and more than 25,000 low-cost homes were built in Manila alone. Still, more than 1 million persons remained homeless in the capital. Developers were unhappy about the requirement that 80% of construction be in low-cost housing, up from 19% in the previous five years.

Estrada showed less influence over congressional spending, which included an unprecedented amount of pork-barrel spending projects ($700,000) for every member of Congress. Another concern impacting the economy was the skyrocketing epidemic of tuberculosis. By 1999, TB was the country's fourth-largest killer. More than 63% of the nation's 75 million people were infected, with about 10% of those expected to develop the disease. Compounding the disaster was the doubling of costs for health care, which put treatment out of the reach of those who needed it most.

Insurgencies. The Philippines continued to be plagued with a small communist insurgency, the New People's Army. In July talks between the government and the rebel leadership broke down over the government's decision to ratify new U.S. ties. More serious was the chronic struggle for Muslim autonomy in the southern Philippines. Though there now was an Autonomous Region in Muslim Mindanao (ARMM), violence continued. The Muslims were split into several factions, so that successful negotiations with the once-dominant Moro National Liberation Front did not end the problem of the others. Christian teachers in Basilan were kidnapped and threatened with being fed to the crocodiles.

PHILIPPINES • Information Highlights

Official Name: Republic of the Philippines.
Location: Southeast Asia.
Area: 115,830 sq mi (300 000 km²).
Population (July 1999 est.): 79,345,812.
Chief Cities (1995 census): Manila, the capital, 1,654,761; Quezon, 1,989,419; Caloocan, 1,023,159; Davao, 1,006,840.
Government: *Head of state and government,* Joseph Estrada, president (sworn in June 30, 1998). *Legislature*—Congress: Senate and House of Representatives.
Monetary Unit: Peso (40.15 pesos equal U.S. $1, Nov. 15, 1999).
Gross Domestic Product (1998 est. U.S.$): $270,500,-000,000 (purchasing power parity).
Economic Index: *Consumer Prices* (1998, 1990 = 100): all items, 203.4; food, 187.1.
Foreign Trade (1998 U.S.$): *Imports,* $30,705,000,000; *exports,* $27,783,000,000.

In December 1998 the leader of the Abu Sayyaf Muslim group was killed in a gun battle with police. Bombings, kidnappings, and clashes with the military followed in Mindanao and Sulu. While some of the terrorism was the work of ordinary criminals, the Abu Sayyaf group tried to set up a protection racket among the besieged teachers. In August 1999, 18 members of the Moro Islamic Liberation Front, a group demanding complete independence for the region, were killed by soldiers. President Estrada resisted demands for martial law but was criticized for his lack of attention to conditions in the southern Philippines.

Foreign Policy. Scarcely seven years after the U.S. military was forced out of its bases after being denied an extension of its lease, a new era of military cooperation began. On May 27 the Philippine Senate ratified the Visiting Forces Agreement, which provides for joint U.S.-Philippine military exercises and fleet visits, and U.S. aid in the modernization of the badly neglected Philippine armed forces. The change of heart reflected new Philippine and U.S. concerns that the Chinese military was taking advantage of the turmoil in the Association of Southeast Asian Nations (ASEAN) and the Asian financial crisis.

President Estrada specifically cited Chinese incursions on the Spratly Islands. The disputed islands are claimed not only by China and the Philippines but also by Vietnam, Taiwan, Malaysia, and Brunei. The islands are thought to have significant oil and mineral wealth and also are important strategically.

LINDA KAY RICHTER
Kansas State University

Photography

The main topic of conversation among photographers, whether amateur or professional, in 1999 remained the progress of digital imaging.

Digital Imaging. Consumers watched the quality of digital "point-and-shoot" cameras increase steadily, while prices edged downward. Professionals, meanwhile, pondered the proper point at which to take the plunge. Photographers who cover events—such as proms, award ceremonies, and sports tournaments—where quick turnaround is the difference between success or failure were beginning to embrace the digital medium with open arms. Several companies were offering various turnkey hardware/software packages (digital camera, computer, dye-sublimation printer, and proprietary special-effects software) that let photographers generate finished prints on the spot, in a matter of minutes, in any quantity the customer desired. Sales increased, as customers tended to place larger, in-hand orders at the event, rather than later.

As an illustration of the current digital price-versus-quality curve, a one-megapixel (1 million pixels) consumer camera in 1998 was rare and cost well more than $1,000; in 1999 they were the rule rather than the exception and were priced at less than $1,000. Indeed, new consumer cameras of 1.5 or even 2+ megapixel capability were appearing almost weekly. One Japanese camera company, Ricoh, stopped making film cameras altogether in order to concentrate on digital models.

A main limitation of digital-camera potential has been the difficulty of manufacturing larger CCD sensors. A major electronics giant now was pursuing the feasibility of "stitching" several CCDs together to, in effect, produce a large one. If this effort succeeds, it could revolutionize the industry.

Reminiscent of the VHS/Beta wars when VCRs were in their infancy, standardization of storage media for digital cameras remained somewhere over the horizon. Most current cameras used either CompactFlash or SmartMedia "flash memory" cards. New contenders included Sony's Memory Stick, Iomega's Clik!, and IBM's MicroDrive. As usual, confusion reigned supreme.

Another factor that has enhanced the appeal of digital cameras is the amazingly rapid evolution of high-resolution inkjet printers. Printers with 1,440-dpi resolution now could be purchased for a few hundred dollars, producing photo-quality prints with ease. Fading of color with inkjet inks has been a major weakness, but great strides were being made on this front, too.

The Advanced Photo System and New Cameras. Three years after its introduction, the Advanced Photo System (APS) slowly was beginning to win some converts from 35mm. The APS benefits of foolproof, drop-in loading; three switchable picture formats; and an index print (showing small images of every picture on the roll) included with film processing were attracting potential buyers as their aging 35s needed replacement.

The most notable development in new cameras was the appearance of several medium-format autofocus models, all with a 6x4.5cm image size and motor-driven film transport. Fuji fielded its GA645Zi viewfinder camera, with a noninterchangeable 55–90mm zoom lens (equivalent to 34–56mm in 35mm format). With Fuji's Easy-Load, Barcode-film system, the camera automatically senses the film speed and adjusts the film pressure plate for 120- or 220-size films. Pentax introduced the 645N, featuring interchangeable lenses and a fixed, 90° prism finder; film "holders" are quick-change inserts, but not mid-roll changeable. Contax surprised everyone with its first medium-format camera, the Contax 645. It sports Zeiss optics and interchangeable lenses, finders, and film backs; an optional vacuum back assures maximum flatness for 220 film. The latest 1999 entry was the Mamiya 645AF. The finder is a fixed, 90° prism, while lenses and film backs are interchangeable; the backs are designed for eventual adaptation to digital imaging.

Yet another surprise was the Hasselblad XPan, a collaboration between Hasselblad and Fuji. It is a 35mm, dual-format, rangefinder camera, capable of switching at any point in a roll of film between standard 24x36mm format and a panoramic 24x65mm format. The XPan accepts two Hasselblad lenses, a 45mm and a 90mm.

The venerable German Voightländer name was appearing on a Japanese-made, dedicated wide-angle (not panoramic) 35mm camera, the Bessa-L, with interchangeable 15mm and 25mm lenses. Interestingly, the lenses are Leica screw-mount; they also can be used on vintage screw-mount Leicas (with the Bessa-L's separate viewfinders), or, with an adapter, on bayonet-mount M-series Leicas.

Lens Technology and Film Advances. Canon continued to wow its legions of followers with its Image Stabilizer (IS) lens technology. Eight autofocus IS lenses, including a 100–400mm zoom, a 300mm and 400mm f/2.8, and 500mm and 600mm f/4, were available. A pair of gyroscopic sensors and a 16-bit microprocessor in the lens detect camera/lens shake and compensate by shifting a group of lens elements in a counteractive manner. This lets the photographer take handheld pictures at up to two shutter-speed steps slower than usual.

On the film front, APS users finally got a black-and-white film, Kodak Advantix Black & White + 400. It is a chromogenic film, which means that it is developed in the same C-41 chemistry as color negative films, making processing available practically anywhere. The long-awaited APS slide film still did not materialize. The frenzy for supersaturated color films was upped a notch with Kodak's Ektachrome E100VS. This color slide film produces brilliant, strong colors but does so while maintaining a quite neutral gray scale.

Photo-Cultural Undertaking. Perhaps the most significant photo-cultural undertaking of 1999 was the National Gallery of Art/Eastman Kodak collaboration in the presentation of the world's largest collection of photographs by Alfred Stieglitz (1864–1946). One has merely to scratch the surface of photographic history to encounter this influential photographer. His contributions to the medium were numerous, but most photography students' indelible impression of him was as the dynamic leader of the Photo-Secessionist movement during the early years of the 20th century. Stieglitz' equally famous wife was artist Georgia O'Keeffe, who donated 1,600 of her husband's photographs to the gallery.

The multiyear endeavor, entitled "Stieglitz," kicked off in August with the release of a new edition of the gallery's long-out-of-print book, *Alfred Stieglitz: Photographs & Writings*. In September the first of a series of seven thematic presentations went up on the gallery's Web site (www.nga.gov). Images shown will span work from the 1890s through the late 1930s, encompassing early studies in Europe, views of New York City, and portraits of luminaries, including his wife, in 20th-century art and culture. In 2002 all 1,600 photographs will be published in a 600-page catalog. Finally, in the spring of 2002, curator of photography Sarah Greenough will mount an exhibition of 70 of Stieglitz' famous and little-known photographs.

© Arnold Newman

Arnold Newman's portrait of pop artist Claes Oldenberg, above, was part of the 1999 Newman retrospective at New York City's International Center of Photography.

Those who have followed the career of Arnold Newman had the opportunity to view an updated retrospective of his work, "Newman's Gift: 60 Years of Photography," held at the International Center of Photography (ICP) in New York City. Newman, 81, developed and perfected the concept of environmental portraiture; his images of the greatest personalities of the last six decades, incorporating his subjects' cherished surroundings and implements of their professions, have become visual icons.

DAVE HOWARD
Freelance Writer and Photographer

Physics

The field of physics in 1999 was marked by breakthroughs in quantum computing and quantum mechanics, as well as by the supercooling of fermions and the creation of several new elements.

Creating the Qubit. Quantum computing replaces the conventional binary bit, valued at either 1 or 0, with a "qubit," a unit that represents an indeterminate blending of 1 and 0 called a superposition. This indeterminacy would allow a quantum computer to solve a calculation for many different input values simultaneously, using the same number of qubits as a regular computer would need to carry out a single computation. In mid-1999 physicist Yasunobu Nakamura and his colleagues at the NEC Fundamental Research Laboratory in Tsukuba, Japan, announced the creation of the first qubit, with the 1 and 0 of the digital system represented by superconducting electron pairs oscillating back and forth. One problem with the design, however, is that the qubit's electron pairs quickly are torn apart by interaction with a probe electrode, which is needed to measure their position. The next step will be finding a method to keep the qubits stable while stringing an array of them together to build an actual quantum computer.

Broken Symmetry Strikes Again. The Standard Model in quantum mechanics is based on the idea that each particle has an antiparticle, a mirror image with the opposite charge and parity. For example, an electron's antiparticle, the positron, has the same mass as the electron but carries a positive rather than a negative charge; this is known as charge (C) symmetry. Likewise, if a particle has a clockwise spin, its corresponding antiparticle spins in the opposite direction; this is parity (P) symmetry.

Experiments conducted in 1964 by James Cronin at the University of Chicago and Val Fitch at Brookhaven National Accelerator Laboratory showed that long-lived K-mesons (or kaons) called K-longs did not always follow CP symmetry when they decayed. To explain the findings, theorists postulated the existence of a "superweak" force. In 1999, Bruce Winstein and colleagues at Fermi National Accelerator Laboratory in Batavia, IL, reported that the flaw Cronin and Fitch found in the mirror of symmetry is even larger than previously thought. Winstein's group exploited advances in particle-detector technology to record and analyze millions of particle decays, and they found that CP violations occurred much more often than expected. These results not only rule out the "superweak" force theory but also suggest that the Standard Model either is flawed or still incomplete.

Fermions Evade Exclusion. In 1995 physicists at the University of Colorado in Boulder created a new kind of matter called a Bose-Einstein condensate (BEC). The atoms in BECs are supercooled until they become locked into a single quantum state, behaving as a kind of "superatom." Particles come in two types, however—bosons (such as photons) and fermions (such as electrons, neutrons, and protons)—and it had appeared that BECs could be made only from bosons. In September 1999 physicist Deborah Jin and graduate student Brian DeMarco at the University of Colorado showed that fermions indeed can be cooled to the point of quantum condensing.

Unlike boson behavior, fermion behavior is governed by the "exclusion principle": Two fermions cannot share the same space at the same time if they have the same "spin," a property that treats particles like miniature magnets. Jin and DeMarco cooled a gas of potassium-40 atoms to just above absolute zero, circumventing the exclusion principle by preparing the atoms in two different spin states.

A Bevy of New Elements. In January 1999 physicists Yuri Oganessian and Vladimir Utyonkov at the Joint Institute for Nuclear Research in Dubna, near Moscow, bombarded a plutonium film with calcium atoms to forge element 114, an atom with 114 protons and 175 neutrons in its nucleus. Scientists at Lawrence Livermore National Laboratory in Livermore, CA, confirmed that element 114 lasted a startling 30 seconds before decaying—an extraordinary length of time in the world of experimental particle physics. Element 114's durability supports a 30-year-old theory predicting an "island of stability" where superheavy atoms remain stable for long periods.

Elements 116 and 118 were created a few months later, when a team led by physicist Victor Ninov at Lawrence Berkeley National Laboratory bashed a lead target with a krypton beam. Although the two elements lasted only about 1.2 milliseconds and 200 microseconds respectively, those times were still long enough to hint that physicists are beginning to explore the edges of the fabled island of stability.

CHARLENE BRUSSO, *Freelance Science Writer*

Poland

Poland experienced continuing economic development and political consolidation in 1999, although not without some underlying disparities, tensions, and divisions. A major highlight of the year was Pope John Paul II's visit in June.

Politics. The first two months of the year began with several acute political and economic conflicts related to income disparities between rural and urban sectors. In the last week of January and first week of February, Polish farmers angered over declining food prices held numerous protests and demonstrations, erecting barricades at various road and border crossings throughout the country. The government responded on February 8 by agreeing to subsidize pork and dairy products, but some of the more militant farm protesters, led by Andrzej Lepper, demanded not only substantial subsidies but also steep increases in tariffs on imported foods. Eager to gain entry into the European Union (EU), the government was reluctant to raise tariffs, but in May it offered to give direct subsidies to grain producers. While overt acts of agricultural protest gradually diminished, the farmers remained widely discontented despite these concessions. The government was also hard-pressed by new wage claims in the health industry, as doctors picketed hospitals, and nurses staged a protest at the parliament over low wages. In September, 30,000 farmers and union workers marched through Warsaw to protest Poland's austerity program.

Prime Minister Jerzy Buzek undertook a number of internal government changes in March, reducing the cabinet from 24 to 17 members and cutting the number of secretaries and undersecretaries of state. Agriculture Minister Jacek Janiszewski resigned on March 15, following disclosures in the press of alleged conflict-of-interest actions taken by the Farm Property Agency, which he had managed from 1992 to 1995; Artur Balasz took his place. Other new appointments included that of Franciszka Cegielska, the third woman to serve in the cabinet, as minister of health. Poland's most influential free-market reformer, Deputy Prime Minister and Finance Minister Leszek Balcerowicz, survived a no-confidence vote in the Sejm (lower house of parliament) by 228 to 180 on March 18. He had been accused by left-wingers of increasing unemployment and poverty levels with his hard-line, antideficit budgetary policies.

On January 17, Buzek was elected chairman of the Electoral Committee of Solidarity. But although his leadership position seemed stronger, he faced a number of potentially damaging recriminations early in the year, including the question of whether he had acted as a spy for the secret police during Poland's communist years. In May the nation's public-interest ombudsman, Boguslaw Nizienski, announced that he would not inquire further into those allega-

Customers at a Warsaw café, below, *appear to be oblivious to the antigovernment protest that is occurring in the heart of the city on Sept. 24, 1999. Polish farmers and workers were demanding higher wages and job security.*

© Czarak Sokolowski/AP/Wide World Photos

tions, but Adam Slomka, the leader of the conservative KPN-O (Confederation for an Independent Poland-Fatherland), denounced the decision as a political cover-up and claimed that at least 11 witnesses from the old secret police could identify Buzek as a former police spy. One KPN-O deputy filed an appeal with Nizienski on May 19 seeking a reversal of his decision.

More controversies were generated by the judicial actions of Polish authorities. In early January, Sergei Stankevich, a former aide to Russian President Boris Yeltsin, was granted political asylum in Poland. Stankevich had been accused of bribery at home. That decision increased tensions between Russia and Poland, as Moscow argued that Stankevich did not meet the criteria for asylum. On May 20 a 79-year-old former Gestapo officer, Alfons Goetzfried, was sentenced to ten years in prison for the murders of some 17,000 Jews in the Majdanek execution camp in 1943, but the court ruled that he did not have to serve any of that time, because he already had spent 13 years in a Soviet labor camp.

Economy. In January the Sejm passed the 1999 budget, which set revenues at 129.3 billion zlotys (about $37 billion) and expenditures at 142.1 billion zlotys (about $41 billion). While the deficit in 1998 had amounted to 2.8% of gross domestic product (GDP), the 1999 deficit was estimated at only 2.18%. Economic growth was forecast at 5.1%, with a decline in the annual rate of inflation from 9.5% in 1998 to 7.5% in 1999. A drastic drop in purchases of Polish produce by Russia contributed to falling food prices. In November it was reported that unemployment was at its 1989 level, 10%.

By the end of the first quarter, Poland's labor unrest, both agricultural and urban, appeared to be largely over. The economy continued its relatively vigorous aggregate growth, and both foreign investment and privatization proceeded apace. In January the government announced the privatization of the country's national airline, LOT, and telecom giant TPSA was expected to sell up to 35% of its shares to a foreign strategic investor in 1999. Overall, the Polish economy once again outperformed those of most of the other postcommunist states. Fiscal prudence and a favorable business climate prevailed. The tourist industry was an outstanding achievement, as Poland was one of Europe's top destinations in 1999.

Religious Issues. Pope John Paul II visited his native land for the eighth time since 1978, arriving in Gdansk on June 5. For the next 12 days he traveled to 21 cities and towns and was greeted by an estimated total of 10 million people, roughly one quarter of Poland's population. In what many feared might be his last visit to Poland, the pope energized the Roman Catholic Church and its followers. On June 11 he addressed the Sejm, expressing support for Poland's bid for entry into the EU and calling for a balance between rapid economic development and respect for moral and spiritual values. The pope also made a symbolic visit to Victory Square in Warsaw, where in 1979 he first had expressed public support for Solidarity's struggle against communism. The pope prayed at the Warsaw site from which hundreds of thousands of Jews had been shipped to gas chambers in 1942 and 1943, and called for increased respect and appreciation of the immense sufferings endured by Jews in the Holocaust. In addition, he announced the beatification of 108 Polish Roman Catholics who had died in concentration camps during Nazi rule in Poland.

Meanwhile, the controversy between Catholic and Jewish communities in Poland over the placing of crosses at the site of the Auschwitz concentration camp continued. On May 8, President Aleksander Kwasniewski signed a law limiting development and public access at or in the vicinity of former Nazi concentration camps. The law was an attempt to curb the demands of Polish Catholics who had planted commemorative crosses in these areas and wanted to plant still more, and to address the desire of Jewish groups in Poland, Israel, and elsewhere to preserve places where millions of Jews had been murdered. On May 28 police and military contingents removed 300 crosses erected near Auschwitz.

POLAND • Information Highlights

Official Name: Republic of Poland.
Location: Eastern Europe.
Area: 120,728 sq mi (312 683 km^2).
Population (July 1999 est.): 38,608,929.
Chief Cities (Dec. 31, 1996, est.): Warsaw, the capital, 1,628,500; Lodz, 818,000; Kraków, 740,700; Wroclaw, 640,600; Poznań 580,800.
Government: *Head of state,* Aleksander Kwasniewski, president (took office December 1995). *Head of government,* Jerzy Buzek, prime minister (named Oct. 17, 1997). *Legislature*—National Assembly: Senat and Sejm.
Monetary Unit: Zloty (4.275 zlotys equal U.S.$1, Nov. 5, 1999).
Gross Domestic Product (1998 est. U.S.$): $263,000,000,000 (purchasing power parity).
Economic Indexes (1998, 1990 = 100): *Consumer Prices,* all items, 857.5; food, 677.0. *Industrial Production,* 157.7.
Foreign Trade (1998 U.S.$): *Imports,* $46,494,000,000; *exports,* $27,191,000,000.

Foreign Affairs. Trade issues and Poland's integration into Western security and economic institutions, especially the North Atlantic Treaty Organization (NATO) and the EU, continued to dominate foreign policy. In late January, Canadian Prime Minister Jean Chrétien visited Poland, where he discussed Polish-Canadian trade relations with Kwasniewski and Buzek. On March 12, Poland officially joined NATO, along with the Czech Republic and Hungary—the first former members of the communist bloc and its Warsaw Pact to do so.

Poland gave political support to NATO's bombing operations over Serbia, but it did not provide any military assets or personnel. However, Poland did contribute approximately 800 soldiers to the peacekeeping force that began its mission on June 12.

At the beginning of May, Kwasniewski met in Nancy, France, with President Jacques Chirac of France and Chancellor Gerhard Schröder of Germany for talks on Poland's prospective entry into the EU, anticipated to occur in 2002. In August, both Germany and France openly backed Poland's membership bid.

In late December, Poland and Israel agreed to allow their citizens reciprocal rights of up to three months for tourist residence without a visa.

ALEXANDER J. GROTH, *Professor Emeritus*
University of California, Davis

Polar Research

The polar regions continued to attract the interest of politicians and the public as well as the scientific community during 1999, as their importance in understanding global problems became more evident. Chief among these issues were the various aspects of global climate change. The pressure for commercial development and the expansion of polar tourism raised concerns about environmental management and conservation.

Antarctic. In a major speech during his state visit to New Zealand in September, U.S. President Bill Clinton dwelt at length on the international importance of Antarctica. He also announced that the National Imagery and Mapping Agency (NIMA) would provide surveillance-satellite images of Antarctica to scientists, making these products of the Cold War era available for research on a continent reserved by treaty for peaceful scientific study.

In February the U.S. Navy made its final flight in support of the U.S. Antarctic Program run by the National Science Foundation (NSF), concluding an important 44-year era in naval aviation. Logistical support was assumed by the New York Air National Guard's 109th Airlift Wing, based in Schenectady, NY.

A personal story received attention when Dr. Jerri Nielsen, working at a research station at the South Pole, discovered a lump in her breast. The isolation of the station, as well as the fact that Nielsen was the only doctor there, limited her treatment options, but an airdrop of drugs and equipment in July allowed her to perform chemotherapy on herself until a U.S. military plane arrived on October 16 to fly her to a hospital.

A researcher at Ohio University in Athens, OH, who discovered four previously unknown species of fish in the Antarctic seas suggested that the continent's frigid seas are a natural evolutionary laboratory comparable to the Hawaiian Islands or Lake Baikal in Russia. Several countries increased fisheries patrols and launched diplomatic activities in an attempt to control the aggressive poaching of Patagonian toothfish throughout the Southern Ocean before it caused the species to become extinct.

Arctic. Fossilized bones from several crocodile-like beasts known as champsosaurs found on Axel Heiberg Island in December 1998 provided evidence of Arctic warming during the late Cretaceous period, about 90 million years ago. The fossils indicated that at least at one time in the past, high levels of carbon dioxide warmed Earth to much higher temperatures than now. The researchers theorized that, as a result of carbon dioxide spewed out by massive volcanic eruptions, Arctic temperatures were as warm as present-day Florida. Such findings could help scientists predict how Earth might react to future increased levels of carbon dioxide in the atmosphere from the burning of fossil fuels.

Despite protests from environmental groups, U.S. Secretary of the Interior Bruce Babbitt agreed to allow exploitation leases for $105 million over an area of 4 million acres (1.62 million ha) of the National Petroleum Reserve in Alaska. Set aside in 1923 as a strategic reserve, it had become a major wildlife refuge. The oil and gas companies then were faced with the challenge of proving they could develop the area without damaging its wildlife.

DAVID W.H. WALTON, *British Antarctic Survey*

Portugal

Electoral gains by Prime Minister António Guterres' Socialist Party (PS) in general elections held in October 1999 reflected public approval of Portugal's robust economy. Portugal was rewarded for its economic improvement with membership in the European Economic and Monetary Union (EMU) in January. Guterres earned admiration by helping to mobilize international efforts against Indonesia's crackdown on East Timor. Portugal prepared to assume the presidency of the European Union (EU) in January 2000.

Politics. During 1999, Guterres continued to work toward improving Portugal's economy. Ever since he took office in 1995, he had benefited from support on key issues from the center-right Social Democratic Party (PSD), as well as from the PSD's general internal disarray. The latter was highlighted in 1999 by the troubles of its leader, Rebelo de Sousa. His idea of joining with the conservative, anti-EU Popular Party (PP) in a "Democratic Alliance," which would craft a shared platform for both the European Parliament elections and the general election, alienated some supporters. The pact never crystallized, and de Sousa was forced to resign in March. His replacement, former Foreign Minister José Manuel Durão Barroso, had little time to prepare for the upcoming campaigns. This factor, combined with Guterres' popularity and a booming economy, enabled the PS to capture 43.1% of the European Parliament vote (up from 34.7% in 1994) and increase its number of seats from ten to 12. Meanwhile, the PSD slipped to 31.1% (from 34.3% in 1994) and lost a seat, winding up with eight. Voter turnout was low, however.

Durão Barroso urged President Jorge Sampãio to postpone the national elections—ostensibly because of the East Timor conflict, but more likely due to polls projecting Socialist gains—but Sampãio refused. In the October 10 balloting, the Socialists did increase their number of seats—to 115—while the PSD declined from 83 seats to 81. Still lacking a majority in the 230-member parliament, Guterres would need to continue to work with opposition parties to further his goals of revamping the nation's social-security, health-care, and justice systems.

Economy. October reports showed the Portuguese economy growing by 3.3%, which was down from 3.5% in 1998, but higher growth was projected for 2000, as exports expand to core European economies. Although the government kept energy rates artificially low, inflation remained unchanged from 1998's rate of 2%. Portugal preserved its 10.4% share of EU structural-aid funds for 2000–06, and it will continue to receive "cohesion" monies allocated to countries that have a gross domestic product (GDP) below 90% of the EU average. Lisbon's still-prickly relationship with Madrid soured a major business deal in June, when, in spite of Guterres' best efforts, the government vetoed a proposal for Spain's Banco Santander Central Hispano (BSCH) to acquire 40% ownership of Mundial Confianca in return for 1.6% of BSCH. The Spanish bank complained to the European Commission, which launched two procedures against Portugal for violating European legislation on cross-border alliances and freedom of capital movement.

Foreign Policy. After 78.5% of East Timorese opted for independence from Indonesia in an August 30 referendum—whose conditions had been negotiated by Guterres' administration—Indonesian forces and ad-hoc militia groups rampaged through the small island, killing hundreds. Portugal rallied international support for ending the bloodshed in its former territory and helped to convince Jakarta to accept the vote.

In late October, Chinese President Jiang Zemin met with Guterres and other parliamentary leaders in Lisbon to discuss trade, investment, and the future of Macao, Portugal's last colony, scheduled to be handed back to China on December 20. At the mid-November Ibero-American Summit in Havana, Sampãio criticized the antidemocratic character of the Cuban regime.

GEORGE W. GRAYSON
College of William & Mary

PORTUGAL • Information Highlights

Official Name: Portuguese Republic.
Location: Southwestern Europe.
Area: 35,672 sq mi (92 391 km²).
Population (July 1999 est.): 9,918,040.
Chief Cities (1991 census): Lisbon, the capital, 681,063; Oporto, 309,485; Vila Nova de Gaia, 247,499.
Government: *Head of state,* Jorge Sampãio, president (took office March 1996). *Head of government,* António Guterres, prime minister (took office October 1995). *Legislature* (unicameral)—Assembly of the Republic.
Monetary Unit: Escudo (193.4688 escudos equal U.S.$1, Nov. 8, 1999).
Gross Domestic Product (1998 est. U.S.$): $144,800,000,000 (purchasing power parity).
Economic Indexes (1998): *Consumer Prices* (1991 = 100): all items, 137.6; food, 128.0. *Industrial Production* (1990 = 100): 107.4.
Foreign Trade (1998 U.S.$): *Imports,* $37,046,000,000; *exports,* $24,218,000,000.

Prisons

Statistics released in 1999 showed that the U.S. prison population increased once again in 1998; this trend, which has continued over the past two decades, even though the overall crime rate has decreased in recent years, suggested a consistent policy of tougher treatment of offenders. Corrections funding took up an even greater share of state budgets in 1999, with no relief in sight; and a study highlighted the growing problem of mentally ill people serving time in U.S. jails.

Increasing Prison Population. According to a report issued in August by the U.S. Bureau of Justice Statistics, the incarceration rate for those people under national and state jurisdictions was 461 per 100,000 at the end of 1998—an increase of more than 300% from the 1980 level of 139. The survey indicated that by 2000 the rate would exceed 700 per 100,000—higher than in any other country in the world at any time, past or present. (The general rate of incarceration among other industrialized societies in 1999 ranged from 50 to 135 per 100,000.)

A state-by-state breakdown of incarceration rates, also included in the report, provided evidence that the "get tough on crime" stance encouraged over the past three decades in the United States was harsher in some states than in others. Louisiana had the highest incarceration rate (736 per 100,000), followed by Texas (724) and Oklahoma (622), while the states with the lowest rates were Minnesota (117), Maine (125), and North Dakota (128). Statistics also showed an even greater disparity between races, with the incarceration rate for African-Americans (3,253) almost seven times the rate for whites (491). Out of the total population of African-American men between the ages of 20 and 40 in the United States, 7% of them were in prison in 1999. At the beginning of the year, the combined federal, state, and local adult correctional population exceeded 5.9 million—a record high—with some 1.8 million in prison and another 4.1 million on parole.

Skyrocketing Budgets. The economic strain of building and staffing correctional systems to contain the constantly growing prison population became more apparent. State corrections budgets as a whole exceeded $25 billion, with California ($3.88 billion), New York ($2.35 billion), and Texas ($1.86 billion) heading the list. During the 1990s, corrections appropriations grew faster than those for education and Medicaid; these three areas make up two thirds of all state spending. According to a report issued by the National Conference of State Legislatures in April, initial corrections appropriations by state legislatures for 1998 and 1999 no longer were growing faster than the other major areas. But while the planned appropriations were held to a 5% increase, actual spending reported at the end of the year grew by more than 10.5%, a larger increase than in any other category. A total of 48 states reported increases in actual spending, and the two states reporting decreases, New Jersey and Texas, acknowledged that overestimates in savings would have to be made up through additional appropriations. Recreational, training, and other programs behind bars were reduced drastically, thereby increasing the time prisoners spent locked in their cells. In almost every prison and jail, the bulk of the day-to-day, non-security-related work—such as custodial duties and food preparation and distribution—was done by the prisoners. Efforts to constrain corrections budgets were not successful.

Jailing the Mentally Ill. In the 1960s and 1970s, public mental hospitals were closed wholesale throughout the United States, often without local provisions for the discharged patients. The number of patients in state hospitals dropped from a high of 559,000 in 1955 to less than 70,000 in 1999. An increasing number of these people have wound up in prison facilities, a fact highlighted in 1999 by the release in July of a study on the subject by the Justice Department. The report said that 16% of the imprisoned population (an estimated 283,800) suffered from mental illnesses. In addition, it noted that mentally ill convicts in state prisons were more likely than other prisoners to have been convicted for a violent crime, to have been in prison before, and to serve longer sentences. Many other mentally ill people would be caught in a revolving-door system in which they would be arrested for petty crimes such as loitering or public intoxication, jailed for a brief period, then released to the streets, where they often would be rearrested for a similar offense. In some states more mentally ill persons were housed in correctional facilities than in psychiatric hospitals. In recent years, many newly built state prisons have included psychiatric units to meet the needs of this growing segment of their population.

DONALD GOODMAN
John Jay College of Criminal Justice

Prizes and Awards

NOBEL PRIZES [1]

Chemistry: Ahmed Zewail, California Institute of Technology at Pasadena; "for showing that it is possible with rapid laser technique to see how atoms in a molecule move during a chemical reaction"; this led to the use of femtochemistry, the use of high-speed cameras to monitor chemical reactions

Economics: Robert A. Mundell, Columbia University; his work "established the foundation for the theory that dominates practical policy considerations of monetary and fiscal policy in open economies." (*See* BIOGRAPHY—*Mundell, Robert A.*)

Literature: Günter Grass, Germany; "his writing constitutes a dialogue with the great traditions of German culture, conducted with punctilious affection." (*See* LITERATURE—*Overview.*)

Peace: Doctors Without Borders, for its "pioneering humanitarian work on several continents"

Physics (shared): Gerardus 't Hooft, University of Utrecht; and Martinus J.G. Veltman, Bilthoven, the Netherlands; for their research on the quantum structure of electroweak interactions, which has "given researchers a well-functioning theoretical machinery" and has "placed particle physics theory on a firmer mathematical foundation"

Physiology or Medicine: Guenter Blobel, The Rockefeller University, New York; his research on proteins has "contributed to the development of a more effective use of cells as 'protein factories' for the production of important drugs"

[1]approx. $960,000 in each category

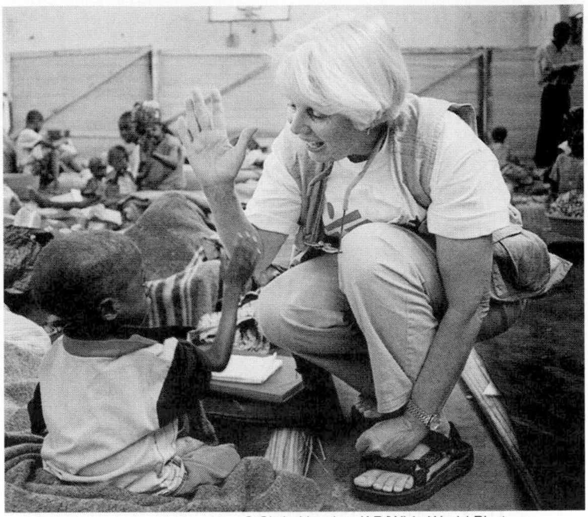

© Chris Hondros/AP/Wide World Photos

The 1999 Nobel Peace Prize was won by Doctors Without Borders, an organization that sends medical personnel to the world's troubled areas, such as Angola, above.

ART

American Academy and Institute of Arts and Letters Awards
- Academy-Institute Awards: architecture—Eric Owen Moss; art—George Condo, Frank Moore, Thomas Nozkowski, Altoon Sultan, Joe Zucker; music—Nathan Currier, Michael Gordon, Erica Muhl, Julia Wolfe
- Award for Distinguished Service to the Arts: Harvey Lichtenstein
- Arnold W. Brunner Memorial Prize in Architecture: Fumihiko Maki
- Jimmy Ernst Award in Art: Dorothea Rockburne
- Gold Medal for Painting: Robert Rauschenberg
- Walter Hinrichsen Award: Edmund Campion
- Charles Ives Fellowship in Music: Steven Burke
- Charles Ives Scholarships in Music: Roshanne Etezady, Paul Yeon Lee, David Mallamud, Carter Pann, Jason Roth, Robert Zimmerman
- Wladimir and Rhoda Lakond Award in Music: David Stock
- Goddard Lieberson Fellowships in Music: Tamar Diesendruck, David Sampson
- Medal for Spoken Language: Mario Cuomo
- Willard L. Metcalf Award in Art: Desirée Alvarez
- Richard and Hinda Rosenthal Foundation Award: Karen Davie

Canada Council Molson Prize for the Arts ($50,000)**:** Jeanne Lamon

Capezio Dance Award ($10,000)**:** Bella Lewitzsky

George and Ira Gershwin Award for outstanding musical achievement: Diane Warren

Dorothy and Lillian Gish Prize for outstanding contribution to the arts ($200,000)**:** Arthur Miller

Grawemeyer Award for musical composition ($200,000)**:** Thomas Ades, *Asyla*

John F. Kennedy Center Honors for career achievement in the performing arts: Victor Borge, Sean Connery, Judith Jamison, Jason Robards, Stevie Wonder

National Academy of Recording Arts and Sciences Grammy Awards for excellence in phonograph records
- Album of the year: Lauryn Hill, *The Miseducation of Lauryn Hill*
- Classical album: Robert Shaw, *Barber: Prayers of Kierkegaard/Vaughan Williams: Dona Nobis Pacem/Bartok: Cantata Profana*
- Classical vocalist: Renee Fleming, *The Beautiful Voice*
- Country album: Dixie Chicks, *Wide Open Spaces*
- Country song (songwriter's award): Robert John "Mutt" Lange and Shania Twain, "You're Still the One"
- Country vocal performance: (female)—Shania Twain, "You're Still the One"; (male)—Vince Gill, "If You Ever Have Forever in Mind"; (group or duo)—Dixie Chicks, "There's Your Trouble"
- Jazz instrumental performance: Herbie Hancock, "Gershwin's World"
- Jazz instrumental solo: Chick Corea and Gary Burton, "Rhumbata"
- Jazz vocal performance: Shirley Horn, "I Remember Miles"
- Lifetime achievement awards: Johnny Cash, Mel Torme, Smokey Robinson, Sam Cooke (posthumous), Otis Redding (posthumous)
- New artist: Lauryn Hill
- Pop album: Madonna, *Ray of Light*
- Pop vocal performance: (female)—Celine Dion, "My Heart Will Go On"; (male)—Eric Clapton, "My Father's Eyes"; (group or duo)—Brian Setzer Orchestra, "Jump Jive an' Wail"
- Rap album: Jay-Z, *Vol. 2... Hard Knock Life*
- Rap duo or group performance: Beastie Boys, "Intergalactic"
- Rap solo performance: Will Smith, "Gettin' Jiggy Wit It"
- Record of the year: Celine Dion, "My Heart Will Go On"
- Rhythm-and-blues album: Lauryn Hill, *The Miseducation of Lauryn Hill*
- Rhythm-and-blues song (songwriter's award): Lauryn Hill, "Doo Wop (That Thing)"
- Rhythm-and-blues vocal performance: (female)—Lauryn Hill, "Doo Wop (That Thing)"; (male)—Stevie Wonder, "St. Louis Blues"; (group or duo)—Brandy & Monica, "The Boy Is Mine"
- Rock album: Sheryl Crow, *The Globe Sessions*
- Rock song (songwriters' award): Alanis Morissette, "Uninvited"
- Rock vocal performance: (female)—Alanis Morissette, "Uninvited"; (male)—Lenny Kravitz, "Fly Away"; (group or duo)—Aerosmith, "Pink"
- Song of the year (songwriters' award): James Horner and Will Jennings, "My Heart Will Go On"

National Humanities Medal (presented by President Bill Clinton on Sept. 29, 1999)**:** Patricia M. Battin, Taylor Branch, Jacquelyn Dowd Hall, Garrison Keillor, Jim Lehrer, John Rawls, Steven Spielberg, August Wilson

National Medal of Arts (presented by President Clinton on Sept. 29, 1999)**:** Irene Diamond, Aretha Franklin, Michael Graves, The Juilliard School, Norman Lear, Rosetta LeNoire, Harvey Lichtenstein, Lydia Mendoza, Odetta, George Segal, Maria Tallchief

Praemium Imperiale for lifetime achievement in the arts ($150,000 ea.)**:** Fumihiko Maki, Japan (architecture); Oscar Peterson, Canada (music); Anselm Kiefer, Germany (painting); Louise Bourgeois, United States (sculpture); Pina Bausch, Germany (theater and film)

Pritzker Architecture Prize ($100,000)**:** Sir Norman Foster, England

Pulitzer Prize for Music: Melinda Wagner, *Concerto for Flute, Strings and Percussion*

Samuel H. Scripps/American Dance Festival Award ($25,000)**:** Pina Bausch, Germany

JOURNALISM

Maria Moors Cabot Prizes ($1,500 ea.)**:** Jorge Zepeda Patterson, editor in chief and founder, *Público*, Guadalajara, Mexico; Linda Robinson, Latin America bureau chief, *U.S. News and World Report*; Juan Tamayo, Latin America correspondent, *The Miami Herald*; **special citations:** James McClatchy, publisher, McClatchy Newspapers; Raul Rivero, founder and president, Cuba Press news agency, Havana, Cuba

International Press Freedom Awards (for journalists who have suffered personally and professionally in their pursuit of journalism and free expression)**:** Mark Chavunduka and Raymond Choto, *Sunday Standard* (Zimbabwe); Zafaryab Ahmed, freelance journalist living in United States (Pakistan); Jesús Barraza Zavala, *Pulso* (Mexico)

National Magazine Awards
- Design: *ESPN The Magazine*
- Essays and criticism: *The Atlantic Monthly*
- Feature writing: *The American Scholar*
- Fiction: *Harper's Magazine*
- General excellence: *Vanity Fair, Condé Nast Traveler, Fast Company, I.D. Magazine*
- General excellence in new media: *Cigar Aficionado*
- Personal service: *Good Housekeeping*
- Photography: *Martha Stewart Living*
- Public interest: *Time*
- Reporting: *Newsweek*
- Single-topic issue: *The Oxford American*
- Special interest: *PC Computing*

Overseas Press Club Awards
- Whitman Bassow Award (for best foreign environmental reporting in any medium): Anne Garrels and Loren Jenkins, National Public Radio
- Robert Spears Benjamin Award (for best reporting in any medium from Latin America): Edwin Garcia, Michelle Levander, and Ricardo Sandoval, *San Jose [CA] Mercury News*

Hal Boyle Award (for best newspaper or wire service reporting from abroad): Ken Guggenheim and Niko Price, The Associated Press
Eric and Amy Burger Award (for best foreign reporting on human rights for broadcast): Cynthia McFadden and Beth Osisek, *Primetime Live*, ABC News
Robert Capa Gold Medal (for photographic reporting from abroad requiring exceptional courage and enterprise): James Nachtwey, Magnum for *Time*
Bob Considine Award (for best newspaper or wire service interpretation of foreign affairs): Barton Gellman, *The Washington Post*
Ed Cunningham Memorial Award (for best magazine reporting from abroad): Mark Danner, *The New York Review of Books*
Joe and Laurie Dine Award (for best reporting in a print medium dealing with human rights): Mark O'Keefe, *The Oregonian*
John Faber Award (for best photographic reporting from abroad in newspapers or wire services): Eric Mencher, *The Philadelphia Inquirer*
Malcolm Forbes Award (for best business reporting from abroad in newspapers or wire services): Richard Read, *The Oregonian*
Morton Frank Award (for best business reporting from abroad in magazines): Michael Shari, Joyce Barnathan, Pete Engardio, Dean Foust, Jonathan Moore, Sheri Prasso, and Christopher Power, *Business Week*
David Kaplan Award (for best TV spot news reporting from abroad): CNN, "Strikes Against Iraq and the Impeachment Hearings"
Edward R. Murrow Award (for best interpretation or documentary on foreign affairs): William Cran, Stephanie Tepper, David Fanning, Michael Sullivan, *Frontline*/WGBH Boston
Thomas Nast Award (for best cartoons on foreign affairs): Kevin Kallaugher, *The Baltimore Sun*
President's Award for lifetime achievement: Maynard Parker, *Newsweek* (posthumous)
Olivier Rebbot Award (for best photographic reporting from abroad for magazines or books): Ettore Malanca, Sipa Press/*The New York Times Magazine*
Madeline Dane Ross Award (for best foreign reporting in any medium showing a concern for the human condition): Kevin Sullivan, Mary Jordan, and Keith Richburg, *The Washington Post*
Cornelius Ryan Award (for best nonfiction book on foreign affairs): Philip Gourevitch, *We Wish to Inform You That Tomorrow We Will Be Killed with Our Families: Stories from Rwanda*
Carl Spielvogel Award (for best foreign business reporting for broadcast): Breanda Breslauer and Brian Ross, ABC News
Lowell Thomas Award (for best radio news or interpretation of foreign affairs): Sandy Tolan, Homelands Productions for Fresh Air

George Polk Memorial Awards
Book award: Philip Gourevitch, *We Wish to Inform You That Tomorrow We Will Be Killed with Our Families*
Career award: Russell Baker, *The New York Times* (retired)
Commentary: Juan Gonzalez, *The New York Daily News*
Economic reporting: Mary Jordan, Keith Richburg, and Kevin Sullivan, *The Washington Post*, for "Shattered Lives"
Environmental reporting: Gardiner Harris and R.G. Dunlop, *Louisville Courier-Journal*
Foreign reporting: Tracy Wilkinson, *Los Angeles Times*
International reporting: Alix M. Freedman, *The Wall Street Journal*, for "Population Bomb"
Legal reporting: Joe Stephens, *The Kansas City Star*, for "On Their Honor"
Local reporting: Clifford J. Levy, *The New York Times*
Medical reporting: Robert Whitaker and Dolores Kong, *The Boston Globe*, for "Doing Harm: Research on the Mentally Ill"
National reporting: Donald L. Barlett and James B. Steele, *Time*
Radio reporting: Amy Goodman and Jeremy Scahill, Democracy Now/Pacifica Radio, for "Drilling and Killing: Chevron and Nigeria's Oil Dictatorship"
Television reporting: Brian Ross and Rhonda Schwartz, *ABC News/20-20*, for "Made in America?"

Pulitzer Prizes
Beat reporting: Chuck Philips and Michael Hiltzik, *The Los Angeles Times*
Breaking news reporting: Staff of *The Hartford Courant*
Commentary: Maureen Dowd, *The New York Times*
Criticism: Blair Kamin, *The Chicago Tribune*
Editorial cartooning: David Horsey, *The Seattle Post-Intelligencer*
Editorial writing: *The New York Daily News* editorial board
Explanatory reporting: Richard Read, *The Oregonian*
Feature photography: Susan Walsh, The Associated Press
Feature writing: Angelo B. Henderson, *The Wall Street Journal*
International reporting: Staff of *The Wall Street Journal*
Investigative reporting: Staff of *The Miami Herald*
National reporting: Staff of *The New York Times*
Public service: *The Washington Post*
Spot news photography: John McConnico, The Associated Press

LITERATURE

American Academy and Institute of Arts and Letters Awards
Academy-Institute Awards: Edmund Keeley, Jon Krakauer, Susanna Moore, Ron Padgett, Richard Price, Sherod Santos, Lee Smith, C.K. Williams
Michael Braude Award for Light Verse: Thomas M. Disch
Witter Bynner Prize for Poetry: Brigit Pegeen Kelly
E.M. Forster Award in Literature: Nick Hornby
Gold Medal for Belles Lettres and Criticism: Harold Bloom
Sue Kaufman Prize for First Fiction: Michael Byers, *The Coast of Good Intentions*
Addison M. Metcalf Award in Literature: Reginald McKnight
Arthur Rense Poetry Prize: James McMichael
Rome Fellowship in Literature: Tom Andrews
Richard and Hinda Rosenthal Foundation Award: Sigrid Nunez, *Mitz: The Marmoset of Bloomsbury*
Harold D. Vursell Memorial Award: Dava Sobel, *Longitude*
Morton Dauwen Zabel Award: Kathryn Davis

Bancroft Prize in American history ($4,000): Ira Berlin, *Many Thousands Gone: The First Two Centuries of Slavery in North America*
Bollingen Prize for Poetry: Robert White Creeley
Booker Prize: J.M. Coetzee, *Disgrace*
Canada's Governor-General Literary Awards ($10,000 ea.)
English-language awards
Drama: Michael Healey, *The Drawer Boy*
Fiction: Matt Cohen, *Elizabeth and After*
Nonfiction: Marq de Villiers, *Water*
Poetry: Jan Zwicky, *Songs for Relinquishing the Earth*
French-language awards
Drama: Jean Marc Dalpé, *Il n'y a que l'amour*
Fiction: Lise Tremblay, *La danse juive*
Nonfiction: Pierre Perrault, *Le Mal du Nord* (posthumous)
Poetry: Herménégilde Chiasson, *Conversations*

Lannan Foundation Prizes for Distinctive Literary Merit
Fiction ($75,000 ea.): Gish Jen, Jamaica Kincaid, Richard Powers, Joanna Scott
Lifetime achievement ($100,000): Adrienne Rich
Nonfiction ($75,000 ea.): Jared Diamond, Gary Paul Nabhan, Jonathan Schell
Poetry ($75,000 ea.): Louise Glück, Dennis O'Driscoll, C.D. Wright

Mystery Writers of America/Edgar Allan Poe Awards
Critical or biographical work: Robin Winks and Maureen Corrigan, *Mystery and Suspense Writers*
Fact crime: Carlton Stowers, *To the Last Breath*
First novel: Steve Hamilton, *A Cold Day in Paradise*
Grandmaster award: P.D. James
Novel: Robert Clark, *Mr. White's Confession*
Original paperback: Rick Riordan, *The Widower's Two-Step*
Short story: Tom Franklin, *Poachers*

National Book Awards ($10,000 ea.)
Medal for distinguished contribution to American letters: Oprah Winfrey
Fiction: Ha Jin, *Waiting*
Nonfiction: John W. Dower, *Embracing Defeat: Japan in the Wake of World War II*
Poetry: Ai, *Vice: New and Selected Poems*
Young people's literature: Kimberly Willis Holt, *When Zachary Beaver Came to Town*

National Book Critics Circle Awards
Biography/autobiography: Sylvia Nasar, *A Beautiful Mind*
Criticism: Gary Giddins, *Visions of Jazz: The First Century*
Fiction: Alice Munro, *The Love of a Good Woman*
Nonfiction: Philip Gourevitch, *We Wish to Inform You That Tomorrow We Will Be Killed with Our Families*
Poetry: Marie Ponsot, *The Bird Catcher*
Nona Balakian Citation for Excellence in Reviewing: Albert Mobilio

PEN Literary Awards
Emerging writer awards: Nick Flynn (poetry), Valerie Hobbs (children's books), Kim Todd (nonfiction by a woman writer)
Essay: Marilynne Robinson, *The Death of Adam*
Memoir: Ted Solotaroff, *Truth Comes in Blows*
Nonfiction: Philip Gourevitch, *We Wish to Inform You That Tomorrow We Will Be Killed With Our Families*
Translation: Michael Hofmann, translation of *The Tale of the 1002nd Night* by Joseph Roth; Richard Zenith, poetry translation of *Fernando Pessoa & Co.*
Hemingway Foundation/PEN Award for first fiction ($7,500): Rosina Lippi, *Homestead*
PEN/Faulkner Award for fiction ($15,000): Michael Cunningham, *The Hours*
L.L. Winship/PEN New England Award: Donald Hall, *Without*

Pulitzer Prizes
Biography: A. Scott Berg, *Lindbergh*
Fiction: Michael Cunningham, *The Hours*
General nonfiction: John McPhee, *Annals of the Former World*
History: Edwin G. Burrows and Mike Wallace, *Gotham: A History of New York to 1898*
Poetry: Mark Strand, *Blizzard of One*

Tanning Prize for Poetry ($100,000): Jackson Mac Low
Kingsley Tufts Poetry Award ($50,000): B.H. Fairchild, *The Art of the Lathe*
Whitbread Book of the Year Award: Ted Hughes, *Birthday Letters*

MOTION PICTURES

Academy of Motion Pictures Arts and Sciences ("Oscar") Awards
Actor—leading: Roberto Benigni, *Life Is Beautiful*
Actor—supporting: James Coburn, *Affliction*
Actress—leading: Gwyneth Paltrow, *Shakespeare in Love*
Actress—supporting: Judi Dench, *Shakespeare in Love*
Cinematography: Janusz Kaminski, *Saving Private Ryan*

Costume design: Sandy Powell, *Shakespeare in Love*
Director: Steven Spielberg, *Saving Private Ryan*
Documentary feature: *The Last Days*
Film: *Shakespeare in Love*
Foreign-language film: *Life Is Beautiful* (Italy)
Original dramatic score: Nicola Piovani, *Life Is Beautiful*
Original musical or comedy score: Stephen Warbeck, *Shakespeare in Love*
Original song: "When You Believe," *Prince of Egypt* (music and lyrics by Stephen Schwartz)
Screenplay—original: Marc Norman and Tom Stoppard, *Shakespeare in Love*
Screenplay—adaptation: Bill Condon, *Gods and Monsters*

American Film Institute's Life Achievement Award: Dustin Hoffman

Cannes Film Festival Awards
Palme d'Or (best film): Jean-Pierre and Luc Dardenne, *Rosetta* (Belgium)
Caméra d'Or (first-time feature direction): Murali Nair, *Marana Simhasanam* (India)
Grand Prize: Bruno Dumont, *L'Humanité* (Humanity) (France)
Jury Prize: Manoel de Oliveira, *The Letter* (Portugal)
Best actor: Emmanuel Schotté, *L'Humanité* (Humanity) (France)
Best actress (shared): Séverine Caneele, *L'Humanité* (Humanity) (France); Emilie Dequenne, *Rosetta* (Belgium)
Best director: Pedro Almodóvar, *All About My Mother* (Spain)
Best screenplay: Youri Arabov and Marina Koreneva, *Moloch* (Germany and Russia)

Directors Guild of America Awards
Documentary: Jerry Blumenthal, Peter Gilbert, and Gordon Quinn, *Vietnam: Long Time Coming*
Feature film: Steven Spielberg, *Saving Private Ryan*

Golden Globe Awards
Actor—drama: Jim Carrey, *The Truman Show*
Actress—drama: Cate Blanchett, *Elizabeth*
Actor—musical or comedy: Michael Caine, *Little Voice*
Actress—musical or comedy: Gwyneth Paltrow, *Shakespeare in Love*
Director: Steven Spielberg, *Saving Private Ryan*
Drama: *Saving Private Ryan*
Musical or comedy: *Shakespeare in Love*

National Society of Film Critics Awards
Actor: Nick Nolte, *Affliction*
Actress: Ally Sheedy, *High Art*
Cinematography: John Toll, *The Thin Red Line*
Director: Steven Soderbergh, *Out of Sight*
Documentary: *The Farm*
Film: *Out of Sight*
Foreign film: *Taste of Cherry* (Iran)
Screenplay: Scott Frank, *Out of Sight*
Special citation: *Mother and Son*
Supporting actor: Bill Murray, *Rushmore*
Supporting actress: Judi Dench, *Shakespeare in Love*

PUBLIC SERVICE

Africa Prize for Leadership for the sustainable end of hunger: The African woman food farmer ($100,000 initiative to invest in income-earning skills of the African woman)

Charles A. Dana Foundation Distinguished Achievement Award: Barbara Bush, Rosalynn Carter, Betty Ford, Lady Bird Johnson, Nancy Reagan

Heinz Awards:
Arts and Humanities: Walter Turnbull
Environment: Lois Gibbs and Florence Robinson
Human Condition: Luis Garden Acosta and Frances Lucerna
Public Policy: U.S. Sen. Daniel P. Moynihan
Technology, the Economy, and Employment: Dean Kamen

Sidney Hillman Foundation Awards for pursuit of social justice and public policy for the common good:
General awards ($2,000 ea.): (book)—Taylor Branch, *Pillar of Fire: America in the King Years, 1963–65*; (newspaper reporting)—Jerry Mitchell, "The Preacher and the Klansman" and other articles, *The Clarion-Ledger*, Jackson, MS; (magazine feature)—Donald Barlett and James Steele, "Corporate Welfare" series, *Time*
Officers' UNITE Award for Public Service: Rev. Jesse Jackson; Students Against Sweatshops

American Institute for Public Service Jefferson Awards
Benefiting the Disadvantaged: Millard Fuller
Elected or Appointed Official: U.S. Sen. Daniel P. Moynihan
Private Citizen: Elizabeth Dole
Citizen 35 or Younger: Anthony K. Shriver

John F. Kennedy Profile in Courage Award ($25,000)**:** U.S. Sen. John McCain, U.S. Sen. Russell Feingold, for bipartisan efforts to pass campaign-finance legislation

Robert F. Kennedy Human Rights Award: Archbishop Michael Kpakala Francis, Liberia

Lannan Foundation Prize for Cultural Freedom ($250,000)**:** Eduardo Galeano, Uruguay

Eleanor Roosevelt Human Rights Award (presented by President Bill Clinton on Dec. 6, 1999)**:** Sister Jean Marshall, founder, St. Rita's Center for Immigrant and Refugee Services, Bronx, NY

Franklin D. Roosevelt Four Freedoms Medal:
Freedom of Speech and Expression: U.S. Rep. John Lewis
Freedom of Worship: Corinne C. Boggs, U.S. ambassador to the Holy See
Freedom from Want: George McGovern, U.S. Mission to the United Nations—Agencies for Food and Agriculture
Freedom from Fear: Robert O. Muller and Solange MacArthur, Vietnam Veterans of America Foundation
Franklin D. Roosevelt Medal: U.S. Sen. Edward M. Kennedy

Templeton Prize for Progress in Religion ($1,240,000)**:** Ian Barbour, author, physicist, and theologian

U.S. Congressional Gold Medal (presented by President Clinton on June 15, 1999)**:** Rosa Parks; (presented by President Clinton on Oct. 27, 1999): Gerald and Betty Ford; (presented by President Clinton on Nov. 9, 1999): Melba Patillo Beals, Elizabeth Eckford, Ernest Green, Gloria Ray Karlmark, Carlotta Walls Lanier, Terrence Roberts, Jefferson Thomas, Minnijean Brown Trickey, Thelma Mothershead Wair

U.S. Department of Defense Public Service Award (presented by Defense Secretary William Cohen on Aug. 11, 1999)**:** Steven Spielberg

U.S. Presidential Medal of Freedom (presented by President Clinton on April 20, 1999)**:** Helmut Kohl; (presented by President Clinton on Aug. 9, 1999): Jimmy and Rosalyn Carter; (presented by President Clinton on Aug. 11, 1999): Lloyd M. Bentsen, Edgar Bronfman, Sr., Evelyn Dubrow, Sr. Isolina Ferre, Gerald Ford, Oliver White Hill, Max Kampelman, Edgar Wayburn

SCIENCE

John Bates Clark Medal (for the best U.S. economist under age 40)**:** Andrei Shleifer, Harvard University

King Faisal International Prize for Medicine ($200,000 shared)**:** Patrick G. Holt, National Health and Medical Research Council of Australia; Stephen T. Holgate, University of Southampton, England

King Faisal International Prize for Science ($200,000 shared)**:** Ryoji Noyori, Nagoya University, Japan; Dieter Seebach, Laboratory of Organic Chemistry, Federal Polytechnic School ETH, Zurich, Switzerland

Albert Lasker Medical Research Awards
Basic Research ($10,000 ea.): Clay M. Armstrong, University of Pennsylvania School of Medicine; Bertil Hille, University of Washington; Roderick MacKinnon, Rockefeller University and the Howard Hughes Medical Institute
Clinical Research ($25,000 shared): David W. Cushman and Miguel A. Ondetti, formerly, Bristol-Myers Squibb Pharmaceutical Research Institute
Special Achievement in Medical Science ($25,000): Seymour S. Kety, McLean Hospital and Harvard Medical School

National Medal of Science (presented by President Bill Clinton on April 27, 1999)**:** Bruce N. Ames, National Institute of Environmental Health Sciences, University of California at Berkeley; Don L. Anderson, California Institute of Technology Seismological Laboratory, Pasadena, CA; John N. Bahcall, Institute for Advanced Study, Princeton University; John W. Cahn, National Institute of Standards and Technology, Gaithersburg, MD; Cathleen S. Morawetz, Courant Institute of Mathematical Sciences, New York University; Janet D. Rowley, University of Chicago; Eli Ruckenstein, State University of New York; George M. Whitesides, Harvard University; William Julius Wilson, John F. Kennedy School of Government, Harvard University

National Medal of Technology (presented by President Clinton on April 27, 1999)**:** Denton A. Cooley, Texas Heart Institute, Texas Medical Center, Houston; Robert T. Fraley, Robert B. Horsch, Ernest G. Jaworski, and Stephen G. Rogers, Monsanto Company; Kenneth L. Thompson and Dennis M. Ritchie, Bell Laboratories, Lucent Technologies; Biogen, Inc., Cambridge, MA; Bristol-Myers Squibb Co., New York City

Tyler Prize for Environmental Achievement ($200,000 shared)**:** Te-Tzu Chang (Taiwan), International Rice Research Institute, Philippines (retired); Joel E. Cohen (United States), Rockefeller University and Columbia University, New York City

Wolf Prizes ($100,000 ea.)
Chemistry: Raymond U. Lemieux, University of Alberta
Mathematics (shared): Laszlo Lovasz, Yale University, and Elias M. Stein, Princeton University
Medicine: Eric Kandel, Columbia University
Physics: Dan Shechtman, Technion

World Food Prize ($250,000)**:** Dr. Walter Plowright, discoverer of rinderpest vaccine for cattle

TELEVISION AND RADIO

Academy of Television Arts and Sciences ("Emmy") Awards
Actor—comedy series: John Lithgow, *3rd Rock From the Sun* (NBC)
Actor—drama series: Dennis Franz, *NYPD Blue* (ABC)
Actor—miniseries or movie: Stanley Tucci, *Winchell* (HBO)
Actress—comedy series: Helen Hunt, *Mad About You* (NBC)
Actress—drama series: Edie Falco, *The Sopranos* (HBO)
Actress—miniseries or movie: Helen Mirren, *The Passion of Ayn Rand* (Showtime)
Comedy series: *Ally McBeal* (Fox)
Directing—comedy series: Thomas Schlamme, "Pilot," *Sports Night* (ABC)
Directing—drama series: Paris Barclay, "Hearts and Souls," *NYPD Blue* (ABC)
Directing—miniseries or movie: Allan Arkush, *The Temptations* (NBC)
Directing—variety or music program: Paul Miller, *1998 Tony Awards* (CBS)
Drama series: *The Practice* (ABC)
Individual performance—variety or music program: John Leguizamo, *John Leguizamo's Freak* (HBO)
Miniseries or a special: *Horatio Hornblower* (A&E)

Bernadette Peters, right, received a Tony Award and an Outer Critics Circle Award as best actress in a musical for her portrayal of the title character in "Annie Get Your Gun".

© Karl Feile/Archive Photos

Movie made for television: *A Lesson Before Dying* (HBO)
Supporting actor—comedy series: David Hyde Pierce, *Frasier* (NBC)
Supporting actor—drama series: Michael Badalucco, *The Practice* (ABC)
Supporting actor—miniseries or movie: Peter O'Toole, *Joan of Arc* (CBS)
Supporting actress—comedy series: Kristen Johnston, *3rd Rock From the Sun* (NBC)
Supporting actress—drama series: Holland Taylor, *The Practice* (ABC)
Supporting actress—miniseries or movie: Anne Bancroft, *Deep in My Heart* (CBS)
Variety, music, or comedy series: *Late Show with David Letterman* (CBS)
Variety, music, or comedy special: *1998 Tony Awards* (CBS)
Writing—comedy series: Jay Kogen, "Merry Christmas, Mrs. Moskowitz," *Frasier* (NBC)
Writing—drama series: James Manos, Jr., and David Chase, "College," *The Sopranos* (HBO)
Writing—miniseries or movie: Ann Peacock, *A Lesson Before Dying* (HBO)
Writing—variety or music program: Tom Agna, Vernon Chatman, Louis CK, Lance Crouther, Gregory Greenberg, Ali LeRoi, Steve O'Donnell, Chris Rock, Frank Sebastiano, Chuck Sklar, Jeff Stilson, Wanda Sykes-Hall, and Mike Upchurch, *The Chris Rock Show* (HBO)

Directors Guild of America Awards
Comedy series: Thomas Schlamme, "Pilot," *Sports Night* (ABC)
Movie for television: Michael Cristofer, *Gia* (HBO)
Nighttime dramatic series: Paris Barclay, "Hearts and Souls," *NYPD Blue* (ABC)

Golden Globe Awards
Drama series: *The Practice* (ABC)
Musical or comedy series: *Ally McBeal* (Fox)

Humanitas Prizes
Feature film ($25,000): Lewis Colick, *October Sky*
Cable- or public-television production ($25,000): John Sacret Young, *Thanks of a Grateful Nation* (Showtime)
Children's animated television production ($10,000): Richard Gitelson, *Rugrats* (Nickelodeon)
Children's live-action television production ($10,000): Heather Conkie, *The Artists' Specials* (HBO)
Network television production (90-minute or longer) ($25,000): Nicholas Wootton, Steven Bochco, David Milch, Bill Clark, *NYPD Blue* (ABC)
Network television production (60-minute) ($15,000): T.J. English, Julie Martin, David Simon, *Homicide: Life on the Street* (NBC)
Network television production (30-minute) ($15,000): Aaron Sorkin, Matt Tarses, David Walpert, Bill Wrubel

George Foster Peabody Awards
Radio: National Public Radio and correspondent Charlayne Hunter-Gault, for coverage of Africa; WHAS Radio, Louisville, KY, *Sisterhood of Hope*; National Public Radio, *I Must Keep Fightin': The Art of Paul Robeson*; National Public Radio, *Performance Today*
Television: CBS, *Public Eye with Bryant Gumbel*, "The Reckoning"; Christiane Amanpour, for international reporting for CNN and for CBS' *60 Minutes*; KTVX-TV, Salt Lake City, UT, *The Olympic Bribery Scandal*; WGBH/Frontline, Washington Media Associates, and Public Affairs Television, *Frontline*, "Washington's Other Scandal"; KRON-TV, San Francisco, *About Race*; BBC and the Learning Channel, *The Human Body*; WGBH-TV, Boston, *Africans in America: America's Journey through Slavery*; ITVS and City People Productions, *Travis*; Florentine Films and WETA-TV, Washington, *Frank Lloyd Wright*; BBC and WGBH-TV, Boston, *When Good Men Do Nothing*; Thirteen/WNET, New York, and Florentine Films/Sherman Pictures, *American Masters*, "Alexander Calder"; Jeremy Isaacs Productions and CNN Productions, *Cold War*; The American Experience, the American History Project, Out of the Blue Productions, and WGBH Educational Foundation, *The American Experience*, "Riding the Rails"; *Dateline NBC*, "Checks and Balances"; The American Experience, David Grubin Productions, and WGBH Educational Foundation, *The American Experience*, "America 1900"; WANE-TV, Fort Wayne, IN, *Christopher*; TVC and Channel 4, London, *The Bear*; HBO Sports Documentaries; Comedy Central, Tom Snyder Productions, and Popular Arts Entertainment, in association with HBO Downtown Productions, *Dr. Katz: Professional Therapist*; Chestermead Productions for the BBC and WGBH-TV, *Mobil Masterpiece Theater*, "King Lear"; HBO, *Shot Through the Heart*; Showtime, Egg Pictures, and Pacific Motion Pictures, *The Baby Dance*; ABC and David E. Kelley Productions, *The Practice*; ABC and Steven Bochco Productions, *NYPD Blue*, "Raging Bulls"; Fox and David E. Kelley Productions, *Ally McBeal*; HBO and Brillstein-Grey Entertainment, *The Larry Sanders Show*, "Flip"; Linda Ellerbee, Nickelodeon; Jac Venza, for presenting arts programming such as *Great Performances* and *American Masters*; Robert Halmi, Sr., for television dramas

THEATER

American Academy and Institute of Arts and Letters Awards
Award of Merit for Drama: Romulus Linney
Richard Rodgers Development Awards for Musical Theater: Lenora Champagne and Daniel Levy, *The Singing*; Kirsten Childs, *The Bubbly Black Girl Sheds Her Chameleon Skin*; Keythe Farley, Brian Flemming, and Laurence O'Keefe, *Bat Boy*; Rickyian Gordon and Tina Landau, *Dream True: My Life with Vernon Dexter*; Jonathan Sheffer, *Blood on the Dining Room Floor*

New York Drama Critics Circle Awards
Best foreign play: *Closer*
Best musical: *Parade*
Best new play: *Wit*
Special citation: David Hare

Outer Critics Circle Awards
Actor—play: Kevin Spacey, *The Iceman Cometh*
Actor—musical: Martin Short, *Little Me*
Actress—play: Kathleen Chalfant, *Wit*
Actress—musical: Bernadette Peters, *Annie Get Your Gun*
Choreography: Matthew Bourne, *Swan Lake*
Director—play: Howard Davies, *The Iceman Cometh*
Director—musical: Matthew Bourne, *Swan Lake*
Musical: *Fosse*
Play: *Not About Nightingales*
Revival—play: *The Iceman Cometh*
Revival—musical: *Annie Get Your Gun*

Antoinette Perry ("Tony") Awards
Actor—play: Brian Dennehy, *Death of a Salesman*
Actor—musical: Martin Short, *Little Me*
Actress—play: Judi Dench, *Amy's View*
Actress—musical: Bernadette Peters, *Annie Get Your Gun*
Choreography: Matthew Bourne, *Swan Lake*
Director—play: Robert Falls, *Death of a Salesman*
Director—musical: Matthew Bourne, *Swan Lake*
Featured actor—play: Frank Wood, *Side Man*
Featured actor—musical: Roger Bart, *You're a Good Man, Charlie Brown*
Featured actress—play: Elizabeth Franz, *Death of a Salesman*
Featured actress—musical: Kristin Chenoweth, *You're a Good Man, Charlie Brown*
Musical: *Fosse*
Musical—book: Alfred Uhry, *Parade*
Musical—score: Jason Robert Brown, *Parade*
Play: *Side Man*
Reproduction of a musical: *Annie Get Your Gun*
Reproduction of a play: *Death of a Salesman*

Pulitzer Prize for Drama: Margaret Edson, *Wit*

Publishing

Guarded optimism gave way to signs of continued health in the U.S. publishing industry as 1999 unfolded. Advertising sales grew encouragingly, paper prices fell, and active acquisition developments continued.

Books. The U.S. Commerce Department predicted book sales would rise about 4.3% in 1999, to some $24 billion. U.S. trade units sold rose 6% in 1998, the first increase in four years, according to the Book Industry Study Group. Internet sales grew by 300%. Adult trade unit sales were expected to grow modestly, by more than 2% annually, through 2003, the group said. Those figures suggested that on-line stores may not increase the market for popular books.

Signs emerged that the growth of bookstore chains, largely fueled by new superstores, was moderating. For the year ended in January, sales at the four largest chains grew by 8.6% to $6.17 billion, the slowest in six years. From February through July, such sales increased about 10% in comparison with the same time in 1998. One of the four chains, Crown Books, appeared close to emerging from bankruptcy. Overall 1998 bookstore sales grew by just 2.6%.

Meanwhile, on-line sellers continued both their rapid expansion and financial losses. For example, giant Amazon.com reported that its revenues grew by 312% and its operating losses by 243% during 1998. In September the company announced plans to remake itself into an Internet shopping bazaar. It would allow a wide variety of merchants to use its Web site for a small fee. Partly as a result of Amazon's growth, mail-order book sales continued to decline, falling by 8.2% during 1998. On-line retailing expanded rapidly into the college-textbook market, following the founding of VarsityBooks.com in December 1997. For example, Follet and Barnes & Noble College Bookstores created Internet textbook sellers.

Merger and acquisition activity continued, although the pace appeared to slow from the unprecedented levels of 1998. News Corp. acquired the Hearst Book Group from the Hearst Corp. for almost $180 million. It then integrated its new assets, William Morrow and Avon Books, into HarperCollins, forming the second-largest U.S. trade publisher. IDG Books purchased most of the Macmillan General Reference Group for $83 million from Pearson plc. In June, however, the planned Barnes & Noble acquisition of the nation's largest wholesaler, Ingram Book Group, fell through. Federal Trade Commission (FTC) staff had recommended that the FTC block the deal. Concerns existed that the deal could slow delivery of books to independent sellers and hamper the growth of Internet selling.

Among the books drawing widespread interest was Edmund Morris' *Dutch: A Memoir of Ronald Reagan*. In the authorized biography of the former president, Morris created a controversial fictional character to help with the narrative. NBC news anchor Tom Brokaw's *The Greatest Generation* spent months on best-seller lists. It features stories about the generation that came of age during the Great Depression and World War II. ABC anchor Peter Jennings also penned a best-seller, *The Century*, coau-

© Kamenko Pajic/AP/Wide World Photos

Edmund Morris' authorized biography of the 40th president of the United States, "Dutch: A Memoir of Ronald Reagan," created a stir in publishing circles in 1999. Although critics questioned Morris' use of fictional characters to enhance his story, the bio became a best-seller.

thored with Todd Brewster. *Monica's Story*, the life of Monica Lewinsky as chronicled by Andrew Morton—the biographer of Britain's Princess Diana—briefly topped best-seller charts in March. Interest died quickly, however. After receiving threats of legal action, Little, Brown canceled Christopher Mason's *Undressed: The Life of Gianni Versace*, an unauthorized biography of the late fashion designer.

A number of legal issues arose. Independent booksellers continued to charge that publishers and bookstore chains made deals in violation of antitrust laws. For example, bankrupt independent Taylors Ltd. filed separate suits against Barnes & Noble and 17 publishers.

Magazines. Early indications suggested that 1999 would be a strong year for magazines. For the first nine months, magazine advertising grew by about 11%, according to the Publishers Information Bureau. Pages rose 3%. Investment bankers Veronis, Suhler & Associates projected that overall spending on consumer titles would grow at an estimated 5.5% compound annual rate, from $18.1 billion to $23.7 billion, from 1998 to 2003. For 1998, consumer-magazine advertising grew by 7.1%.

During early 1999, *Modern Maturity*—received by members of the American Association of Retired Persons (AARP)—remained the paid circulation leader, with more than 20 million. *Reader's Digest* and *TV Guide* followed, according to the Audit Bureau of Circulations. The latter two experienced circulation declines in the previous year of about 9%, however. In October, Gemstar International Group announced that it was purchasing *TV Guide* from Robert Murdoch.

Other merger and acquisition activity continued. In January 1999, British publisher EMAP plc bought Petersen Cos. Inc. for $1.2 billion, plus $300 million in debt. Petersen publishes *Teen*, *Motor Trend*, and a number of extreme-sports titles. The deal made EMAP one of the world's largest magazine publishers. A group of investors, including feminist writer Gloria Steinem, bought *Ms.* from MacDonald Communications Corp. MacDonald had folded the title during the fall of 1998. *Ms.* reappeared with a March–April issue. In July, BPI Communications, Inc. agreed to purchase Editor and Publisher Co. BPI then included a redesigned version of the 115-year-old *Editor & Publisher*, a highly visible newspaper-industry weekly, in its Adweek Magazines group. During August, Condé Nast Chairman S.I. Newhouse, Jr., agreed to purchase Walt Disney Co.'s Fairchild Publications for $650 million. The deal gave Condé Nast control of most of the U.S. fashion press. The acquisition included *Women's Wear Daily*, *W*, and *Jane* magazines. Condé Nast already published *Vogue*, *Vanity Fair*, and *Mademoiselle*. In September, *National Journal* owner David Bradley purchased *The Atlantic Monthly* from Mortimer Zuckerman.

In August the debut issue of *Talk* featured a widely discussed, exclusive interview with First Lady Hillary Rodham Clinton. Tina Brown, former editor of *Vanity Fair* and *The New Yorker*, is the new magazine's editor in chief. *Talk* is a joint venture of Miramax Films and Hearst Magazines, which handles printing and circulation. In July, Hearst launched *CosmoGirl!*, the most recent in a flurry of titles designed for teenage girls. Among the other, more-successful new titles was Arthur Frommer's *Budget Travel*.

In March, 650,000-circulation *Eating Well* magazine closed, due to insufficient advertising and sales. Also in March, computer-oriented *Byte* reappeared, but only on the Internet. The title had folded during 1998. In the wake of the July death of John F. Kennedy, Jr., some observers expressed doubt as to whether *George*, his four-year-old political lifestyle magazine, would continue. In October, French firm Hachette Filipacchi announced plans to purchase the remaining half of *George* from the Kennedy family.

Significant legal issues continued to arise. In January a judge awarded $1.5 million in punitive damages to actor Dustin Hoffman, doubling what *Los Angeles* magazine must pay for using a digitally altered photo of him in a 1997 fashion article. Some U.S. magazine publishers won a victory during May. Canada agreed eventually to allow split-run issues of U.S. titles without strings, if the editions contain no more than 18% Canadian ads. Split-runs contain small amounts of additional Canadian content and feature inexpensive rates for Canadian ads. Canadian publishers had lobbied to keep them out, and the U.S. government had threatened to unleash a trade war. During the early fall, the U.S. Second Circuit Court of Appeals reversed a ruling giving publishers the right to reproduce freelance work on on-line databases or CD-ROMs without explicit permission from authors. The decision could affect significantly the digital repackaging of printed materials.

Newspapers. As 1999 developed, falling newsprint prices helped offset somewhat slower increases in ad spending. Publishers especially worried about the existence of free on-line classified ads, which threaten a particularly lucrative revenue source.

During the first six months of 1999, U.S. newspaper advertising spending grew by 5.1% versus the same period in 1998. For all of 1998, it grew 6.3% to $43.9 billion, according to the Newspaper Association of America. In late 1998, Veronis, Suhler & Associates projected 7.2% compound annual increases in newspaper ad spending through 2002. The investment-banking firm also predicted a reversal of declining newspaper circulations.

Allegations of fictionalized or otherwise unethical journalism continued, although they did not involve the high-profile personnel of 1998. In one case, the *Owensboro* (KY) *Messenger-Inquirer* fired reporter Kim Stacy, who fabricated columns about a fictitious bout with cancer. In July, Mike Gallagher, lead reporter on a repudiated 1998 *Cincinnati Enquirer* series criticizing Chiquita Brands' business practices, received five years of probation. He pleaded guilty to two counts of illegally gaining access to Chiquita's voice-mail system. The *New York Daily News* hired Mike Barnicle, who had resigned in 1998 from *The Boston Globe* following an accusation of plagiarism, which he denied.

The number of dailies continued to fall during 1998, to 1,489, in part due to newspaper mergers. Total circulation decreased somewhat, from about 56.7 million in 1997 to about 56.2 million in 1998. Sunday circulation declined as well, from about 60.5 million to about 60.1 million. *The Wall Street Journal* remained the daily circulation leader, with about 1.74 million copies, followed by *USA Today*, *The Los Angeles Times*, and *The New York Times*. According to the Newspaper Association of America, about 8,193 weeklies, with a total circulation of about 74.3 million, were being published.

A number of merger and acquisition deals involved Community Newspaper Holdings, Inc. (CNHI), which is bankrolled by Alabama's retirement system. It owned more dailies than any other U.S. firm. In the first months of 1999, it bought 45 dailies from Hollinger International for almost $475 million. In late 1998, 120 years of family ownership at *The Chattanooga Times* ended when Walter E. Hussman, Jr., purchased it. In January 1999 a merged *Times* and *Chattanooga Free-Press*, which Hussman's WEHCO Media had purchased earlier, appeared. During February, Evercore Capital Partners LLC bought American Media, the parent company of the *National Enquirer* and *Star* magazine, for $767 million—including the assumption of $473 million in debt. The new owners pledged that the *Enquirer*, which had lost about half of its circulation during the previous 14 years, would concentrate on accurate celebrity features. In August, Hearst Corp. agreed to buy the family-owned *San Francisco Chronicle* for a reported $660 million. Observers expected Hearst to try to sell its smaller *San Francisco Examiner*. Failing this, the afternoon *Examiner* might join with the *Chronicle*. The deal would leave intact about 12 newspaper joint-operating agreements. These agreements, legalized by the controversial 1970 Newspaper Preservation Act, involve separately owned papers that share advertising and printing operations. A number of San Francisco officials urged the U.S. Justice Department, which must approve the deal, to hold hearings before doing so. During October the 130-year-old *Indianapolis News* folded.

In late September the owners of the *Honolulu Star-Bulletin* announced plans to close the afternoon daily, which began in 1882, on October 30. The Gannett Pacific Corp., owner of the morning *Honolulu Advertiser*, planned to pay the *Star-Bulletin* owners $26.5 million to end their joint operating agreement. The state of Hawaii argued that the payment violated antitrust law. In mid-November a federal appeals court ruled that the paper must remain operating while courts consider Hawaii's antitrust lawsuit.

A number of noteworthy content innovations occurred. Several newspapers, including *The New York Times*, banned advertisements for tobacco products. *The Miami Herald*, the *National Enquirer*, and the *Philadelphia Inquirer* unveiled new designs. *The Washington Post* introduced color photos to its front page. The *Journal of Commerce*, a daily newspaper devoted to international trade and transportation, became a tabloid.

Readers reacted favorably to some unusual news practices. In April the *Chicago Sun-Times* kept the Littleton, CO, school shooting off its front page. The paper cited the possibility that publicity could contribute to more such tragedies. In June the *St. Petersburg Times* printed a photo of a man dying from lung cancer. The man had requested the publicity in hopes of dissuading others from smoking.

DAVID K. PERRY
The University of Alabama

Refugees and Immigration

During 1999 the world was shocked by the barbarism and atrocities carried out in Kosovo (*see* THE KOSOVO CRISIS—*The Spotlight Turns to the Refugees*), East Timor (*see* INDONESIA—*East Timor*), Chechnya, Sierra Leone, Angola, and other African countries. The abuses and violence included deliberate targeting of civilian populations, ethnic cleansing, the use of rape as a weapon of war, the mutilation and amputation of limbs, the use of civilians as human shields, genocide, and the seizure of relief supplies intended for noncombatants by warring factions. In addition to attacks on civilians and refugees, there was a further marked erosion of the respect accorded to humanitarian-aid personnel from the United Nations (UN) and nongovernmental organizations, who were attacked, kidnapped, and killed by criminal gangs and warring factions.

African Refugee Problems Neglected. While the international community focused attention and resources on the crises in Kosovo and East Timor, it virtually ignored conflict and displacement in Africa. Humanitarian disasters continued to dominate Africa, and tens of thousands of new refugees took flight throughout that continent. An estimated 600,000 Angolans were in acute need during 1999, and there were up to 3 million more whose condition could not be ascertained because they lived beyond the operating range of UN agencies. In Sudan hundreds of thousands of southern Sudanese became uprooted—adding to the nearly 4 million people already displaced from their homes—and chronic malnutrition deteriorated into full-scale famine. In Somalia 300,000 people faced starvation, and another 1 million faced a rapidly deteriorating condition. Cease-fire agreements sought to bring peace to Sierra Leone and the Democratic Republic of the Congo, but 500,000 refugees in Sierra Leone remained in camps in Guinea and Liberia. Burundi, Congo-Brazzaville, Ethiopia, Eritrea, Guinea-Bissau, Rwanda, Tanzania, and Uganda also faced serious humanitarian need.

International organizations criticized governments for neglecting refugee problems in Africa while allotting generous resources to the refugee crisis in Kosovo. Faced with a severe cutback in funds for humanitarian relief, the UN cut food aid and other essentials to millions of refugees. In August the UN High Commissioner for Refugees, Sadako Ogata, complained that her office had received only a little more than half of its funding requests for refugee programs in sub-Saharan Africa. In October the World Food Program had to cut emergency aid to more than 1.8 million refugees in Sierra Leone, Liberia, and Guinea, because donors provided less than one fifth of the $106 million needed to feed refugees and displaced people in those countries.

Refugee Crisis in the Caucasus. New refugee crises emerged on the southern border of the Russian Federation. Russia invaded Chechnya after Chechnya-based rebels invaded neighboring Dagestan, displacing some 33,000 people, and after a series of bombings in Moscow and other cities that the Russian government attributed to the rebels. Russian planes and artillery fired wave after wave of strikes on Chechnya, causing mass displacement and widespread misery and hunger among civilians. More than 200,000 Chechens fled to neighboring Ingushetia. Tens of thousands of others were trapped in a war zone in their own country and forced to live in the open, often without food or water, as the temperatures plummeted. In a particularly brutal move, Russian troops sealed the border with Ingushetia, causing tens of thousands of women, children, and the elderly to be stranded for weeks on the Chechen side of the border. Criminal gangs made the work of international humanitarian agencies very difficult.

U.S. Immigration Policy. The issue of immigration, both legal and illegal, as well as efforts to reform the Immigration and Naturalization Service (INS), captured the attention of many U.S. legislators during 1999. According to statistics reported in May, two thirds of U.S. population growth stemmed from immigration, and the foreign-born segment of the population grew from 4.4% in 1965 to 9.7% in 1998, not counting illegal immigrants. Rep. Lamar Smith (R-TX), chairman of the House Immigration Subcommittee, proposed limiting the number of immigrants allowed into the United States to 550,000 per year and having admission requirements focus more on prospective immigrants' education level to make sure they can get jobs and care for their families without government assistance. Meanwhile, Smith cosponsored a bill in the House that would split the INS into two units—one that would process applications for visas, U.S. citizenship, asylum, and refugee status, and another that would oversee the Border Patrol and investigate and deport illegals.

GIL LOESCHER, *University of Notre Dame*

Religion

Overview

The year 1999 marked the foundation of the U.S. Commission on International Religious Freedom and the appointment of Robert Seiple as U.S. ambassador at large for international religious freedom. Seiple, an evangelical Christian and former head of the World Vision relief agency, would be the main adviser to the president and secretary of state on the promotion and protection of international religious freedom. He also would serve as an ex-officio member of the commission. That body issued its first annual Report on International Religious Freedom in September 1999. It found that, worldwide, many people still faced harassment, imprisonment, or death for practicing their faith. Among the most religiously repressive countries were said to be China, Iran, Iraq, Myanmar, and Sudan. The 1,000-page report, covering 194 countries, was intended to aid the U.S. government in shaping foreign policy.

The Evangelical Lutheran Church in America voted to enter an agreement for full communion with the Episcopal Church....In a historic first, Pope John Paul II in May traveled to Romania, attending an Orthodox cathedral in Bucharest and meeting with Patriarch Teoctist...Archbishop Spyridon, the highest-ranking cleric of the U.S. Greek Orthodox Church, resigned in August and was replaced by Archbishop Demetrios, in a move aimed at calming internal conflict in the church....Leaders of U.S. Reform Judaism adopted a document encouraging its members to consider adopting some of the traditional rituals of Judaism, which the Reform movement long has rejected.

Templeton Prize. In March physicist and theologian Ian Barbour, 75, was announced as the winner of the $1.24 million Templeton Prize for Progress in religion. Barbour—a professor of religion and physics at Carleton College in Northfield, MN, and author of 12 books—is known for his exploration of the religious implications of scientific theories and his application of Christian ethics to technological advances. In 1965 he wrote the groundbreaking book *Issues in Science and Religion*, which the Templeton nomination said "literally created the current field of science and religion."

Far Eastern

Among the biggest news in far Eastern religion during 1999 was the forceful suppression by the Chinese government of a popular meditation sect.

Falun Gong Sect. China banned the Falun Gong (Wheel of Law) meditation sect in July 1999, in the wake of arrests of dozens of its leaders and public protests by tens of thousands of its adherents against the government crackdown. Founded in 1992 in Changchun by Li Hongzhi, the movement blends Buddhist and Taoist beliefs. Its tens of millions of followers, whose numbers rival those of the Communist Party, assembled in parks to meditate and do yogalike exercises designed to promote health. The govern-

© Marty Lederhandler/AP/Wide World Photos

Physicist and theologian Ian Barbour (right), *the recipient of the 1999 Templeton Prize for Progress in Religion, is congratulated by Sir John Templeton, founder of the prestigious prize.*

© Evan Agostini/Liaison Agency

During a summer 1999 visit to the United States, the Dalai Lama, above, *leader of Tibetan Buddhism, addressed some 40,000 in New York City's Central Park.*

ment claimed the sect practiced "evil thinking" and posed a threat to social stability.

An April gathering in which more than 10,000 Falun Gong members massed near Tiananmen Square in Beijing to demand official recognition was the largest demonstration in China since the pro-democracy protests of 1989. The crackdown later, in which more than 4,000 people were detained in Beijing alone, was also the largest of its kind in ten years.

At least a dozen Falun Gong members were taken into custody in early November during a peaceful protest in Tiananmen Square, days after the Chinese government designated the movement as an illegal cult. Some of the detainees were sentenced to labor camps.

Buddhism. The Dalai Lama continued to give Tibetan Buddhism a high profile in the West in 1999. His books *Ethics for the New Millennium* and *The Art of Happiness* were on *The New York Times* best-seller list at the same time. The Dalai Lama drew a crowd of 40,000 for an appearance in New York's Central Park in August. Later in the month, he spent 12 days in Bloomington, IN, for a Kalachakra ritual of enlightenment that involved leaders of all four Tibetan Buddhist sects.

In April a jewel-encrusted golden umbrella known as a *htidaw* was installed atop the Shwedagon Pagoda in Yangon, Myanmar. According to tradition, the temple was built 2,500 years ago to enshrine eight hairs of the Buddha. The replacement of the *htidaw* was part of a restoration of the temple.

Hinduism. In Lanham, MD, in August, 11 Hindu priests from India conducted a Satha Chandi Homam prayer ceremony for the first time in the United States. The ten-day ceremony involves chanting the 700 verses of the ancient Sanskrit text Devi Mahatmyam and burning gifts to the goddess Devi.

Hindu radicals were blamed widely for the burning alive in January of Australian Baptist missionary Graham Staines and his two sons outside a village in eastern India. Dara Singh, an activist with the radical Hindu group Bajrang Dal, was charged with the murders, along with 18 other suspects. A panel headed by Indian Supreme Court Justice D.P. Wadhwa concluded that the killing was "an act of hatred" by Singh but was not planned by the Hindu movement.

Sikh Celebration. An estimated 2 million Sikhs celebrated the 300th anniversary of the religion's Khalsa movement in April in Anandpur Sahib, India. The celebration was peaceful, despite a contest for the loyalty of the country's 20 million Sikhs between Prakash Singh Badal, Punjab state's highest elected official, and Gurcharan Singh Tohra, an ousted leader of a committee that controls Sikh places of worship. The Khalsa, or Sikh Brotherhood, was launched by Guru Gobind Singh to persuade the traditionally pacifist Sikhs to take up arms to counter persecution by Mogul and Afghan invaders.

DARRELL J. TURNER, *Freelance Religion Writer*

Islam

Debate between Muslims who believed that Islam should provide the framework for all aspects of public life and those who wished to limit its role to the personal sphere created problems in several countries in 1999. In areas with Muslim minorities, efforts to secure autonomy or guarantee Muslims' fundamental rights resulted in some confrontations.

Algerian Insurgency Ends. In June, Islamic Salvation Army guerrillas ended their seven-year insurgency against the Algerian government. President Abdelaziz Bouteflika responded by pardoning thousands of rebels and releasing 2,500 prisoners. His formulation of a "civil concord" law setting a maximum prison sentence of 20 years for guerrillas who laid down their arms (except for those convicted of rape, murder, or planting bombs) prompted other insurgents to surrender during the summer. Bouteflika further sought to promote national reconciliation through his commitment to opening the political process to all responsible viewpoints, including those of Islamist groups. The civil-concord law's overwhelming endorsement by 98% of the voters in a September referendum augured well for ending a conflict that had claimed some 100,000 lives.

Secularism and Islamism in Turkey. In Turkey the Virtue Party and other Islamist parties opposed to the government's insistence on secularism fared poorly in parliamentary elections in April. Islamist activists continued to criticize government policies. When a catastrophic earthquake struck northwestern Turkey in August, Islamist leaders accused the government of constraining the work of Muslim charitable and relief agencies to prevent their acquiring additional popular support.

Indonesian Elections. In June the world's largest Muslim country, Indonesia, held its first democratic elections since 1955. During those decades, the country's rulers had striven successfully to minimize Islam's influence on national politics. Many of the parties that contested the 1999 elections, however, stressed the importance of Islamic values. The three largest Muslim-based parties garnered some 35% of the vote, placing their leaders in a strong position to affect the composition and policies of the new government.

Conflicts. On the Philippine island of Mindanao, the Moro Islamic Liberation Front revived a guerrilla movement whose goal was the establishment of an independent Islamic state. Its leaders maintained that the government had failed to fulfill the terms of a 1996 accord reached with an older organization, the Moro National Liberation Front, that envisioned semiautonomy for the region's Muslims and an effort to promote economic development.

The year's most serious clashes between Muslims and non-Muslims occurred in Serbia's Kosovo province. Efforts by Muslim Kosovars to loosen Serbian control triggered a campaign of ethnic cleansing directed against Muslims. The North Atlantic Treaty Organization (NATO) responded with air strikes intended to force Serbian troops out of Kosovo. After almost three months of bombing that created a serious refugee problem and destroyed much of Serbia's infrastructure, President Slobodan Milosevic complied with NATO's demands but refused to relinquish Serbian sovereignty over Kosovo. Despite the presence of a multinational peacekeeping force, the return of the refugees to Kosovo kept tensions between Muslims and non-Muslims at dangerous levels.

Muslim guerrillas based in Chechnya raided the predominantly Islamic neighboring Russian republic of Dagestan in August, mounting a larger invasion in September. The goal of the rebels, whose ranks included foreign volunteers, was to spread the influence of Wahhabism, a conservative interpretation of Islam whose adherents already controlled portions of Dagestan.

Mecca Pilgrimage Difficulties. Two million Muslims participated in the annual pilgrimage to the Saudi Arabian city of Mecca in March. Libya and Iraq, both under United Nations (UN) embargoes on air travel, nonetheless sent pilgrim flights to Saudi Arabia, but the UN opted not to pursue the violations. A more serious difficulty developed when 18,000 Iraqi pilgrims illegally entered Saudi Arabia. The Saudi government agreed to finance their journey, but Iraq ordered them to return when Saudi authorities refused to use Iraqi funds frozen since its invasion of Kuwait to cover the pilgrims' expenses.

Muslims in the United States. In an indication of the growing influence of Muslims in the United States, now estimated to number 6 million, the Dow Jones Islamic Market Index was created in February. By tracking hundreds of companies whose products conform with the requirements of Islamic law, the index provided crucial data to Muslims wishing to make investments in accordance with the principles of their faith. Other signs that Islam was creating a place for itself in mainstream American life included the appointment of the first Muslim to serve as a U.S. ambassador and the designation of space in the U.S. Capitol building for Muslim employees to hold prayer services.

Kenneth J. Perkins
University of South Carolina

Judaism

There were several important developments within Judaism in 1999 that reflected both increased interest in returning to tradition and making the elements of tradition relevant to contemporary concerns. These efforts to reinvigorate Judaism came, in large part, out of the fear of demographic erosion, as a low Jewish birthrate and a high percentage of Jews marrying non-Jews raised the specter of a much-diminished world Jewish community in the 21st century.

Ritual. In May the Reform movement's Central Conference of American Rabbis approved a historic new statement of principles stressing the performance of *mitzvot*, the sacred obligations mandated by the classic Jewish texts. This ran counter to older, "classical" Reform ideology, which had placed prophetic, universalistic ethics at the center of Judaism and dismissed ritual as a relic of the past. To be sure, the final version of the document, ratified by a vote of 324 to 68, only suggested but did not require the performance of *mitzvot*, and it specifically mentioned, as examples of important obligations, only the study of Hebrew and Torah and the observance of the Sabbath. This was a considerably weakened version of earlier drafts. Nevertheless, the new statement elicited vocal opposition from those rabbis and laypeople who feared that emphasis on *mitzvot* threatened to render Reform indistinguishable from traditional Judaism.

For Conservative Judaism, which officially upholds the ritual requirements, the challenge was implementing them among the lay leadership. In the face of some criticism, the United Synagogue of Conservative Judaism, the movement's congregational body, announced that members of its governing boards would be expected to study Jewish texts for at least an hour a week, to resolve to be guided by Jewish tradition even when it conflicted with personal desires, and to pledge to fulfill three new *mitzvot* each year. And the United Synagogue announced a movement-wide program to study a chapter of the Bible daily, starting with the Book of Joshua on October 3.

Edah Conference. In Orthodox circles, the first conference of the two-year-old organization Edah, held in February in New York City, attracted 1,500 Orthodox Jews and considerable media attention. Attempting to reinvigorate modern Orthodoxy, which had been put on the defensive in recent years, Edah's conference theme was

© Marc Asnin/Saba

In May 1999 the Reform movement's Central Conference of American Rabbis approved a new statement of principles stressing traditional Jewish ritual.

"Orthodoxy Encounters a Changing World." The sessions sought to address the challenges of modernity to Jewish tradition—such as historical approaches to Scripture and Talmud, the impact of secular culture in an open society, and the claims of feminism—from a perspective rooted in Orthodoxy but sensitive to changing conditions. Orthodox critics, however, charged that modern values were so corrosive to Judaism that a policy of isolation was preferable to accommodation.

Spirituality and Continuity. All sectors of Judaism were affected by the growing interest, within Western religions as a whole, in "spirituality," the individual's sense of communion with God. The media abounded with stories about Jewish and non-Jewish celebrities who had found inner peace through study of Kabbala—Jewish mysticism. Hoping to attract more young people, congregations of all types instituted sessions of meditation in addition to, or even in place of, standard prayer, and neo-Hasidic melodies found their way into the liturgy. This tendency, however, aroused fears that the individualistic stress upon intense religious experience was coming at the price of Jewish ethnicity and group cohesion.

Indeed, Jewish communal organizations in the United States continued to search for ways of ensuring Jewish continuity in succeeding generations. One plan was to get local Jewish federations to fund Jewish all-day schools by convincing all Jews to leave 5% of their assets, in their wills, to a special fund. Another initiative, called Birthright Israel and initiated by a handful of philanthropists, sought to guarantee young Jewish adults a free ten-day trip to Israel, on the assumption that even a brief exposure to the Jewish state would have a positive impact on Jewish identity. Gary Tobin, president of the Institute for Jewish and Community Research, was convinced that the existing Jewish community could not sustain itself and proposed the "proactive conversion" of Christians to Judaism.

LAWRENCE GROSSMAN
"The American Jewish Year Book"

Orthodox Eastern

Yielding to the request of the five metropolitans who comprise the Holy Synod of the Greek Orthodox Archdiocese in America (GOA), Ecumenical Patriarch Bartholomew of Constantinople called for the resignation of GOA primate Archbishop Spyridon in 1999. The resignation, characterized by the archbishop as "totally independent of and unrelated to my personal intentions," became effective on August 30. The new archbishop, Demetrios Trakatellis, 71, from Greece, a graduate of and former professor at Harvard Divinity School, was installed as GOA primate in New York on September 18.

Visits and Disputes. Ecumenical Patriarch Bartholomew visited the Church of Greece, where he met with Archbishop Christodoulos of Athens. Efforts were made to smooth relations between the two churches stemming from long-standing jurisdictional disputes about territories in northern Greece. Patriarch Ignatius of Antioch visited the Antiochian Archdiocese in North America, headed by Metropolitan Philip.

Pope John Paul II met with Patriarch Teoctist, the leader of Romania's Orthodox Church, in Romania in May. It was the first visit of a Roman Catholic pope to a predominantly Orthodox country in 1,000 years.

Disputes between the Moscow Patriarchate and the Church of Romania over territories in Moldova continued, as did disputes among several Orthodox groups in Ukraine. Schism between two opposing Orthodox patriarchs in Bulgaria also persisted, and the Orthodox Church in Macedonia remained unrecognized by all other churches.

World Council of Churches and Other Meetings. The Orthodox Church of Bulgaria followed the Church of Georgia in withdrawing from the World Council of Churches (WCC) before its 8th Assembly in Harare, Zimbabwe, in December 1998. The Harare assembly appointed a special commission to review the participation of the Orthodox churches in the WCC. The Russian Orthodox Church ceased all activities in the council until the commission concluded its work. The Standing Conference of Orthodox Bishops in America affirmed Orthodox participation in ecumenical activities, while reiterating familiar criticisms of liberal Christian views on such issues as biblical interpretation, church authority, sexual conduct, and abortion.

The Orthodox Church in America (OCA), headed by Metropolitan Theodosius, held its 12th All-American Council since becoming an autocephalous church in 1970. Meeting in Pittsburgh in July, the council hosted two workers of International

© Louis Lanzano/AP/Wide World Photos

U.S. First Lady Hillary Rodham Clinton applauded as 71-year-old Demetrios Trakatellis was installed as primate of the Greek Orthodox Archdiocese in America (GOA) on Sept. 18, 1999.

Orthodox Christian Charities who had been held captive in Chechnya and were freed through efforts led by OCA archpriest Leonid Kishkovsky.

Balkans Conflict. Kishkovsky also participated in the peacemaking mission of U.S. church leaders to Belgrade in early May, which met with Serbian President Milosevic and gained the release of three American POWs in the Balkan war. All Orthodox churches in America and abroad condemned the bombing of Serbia by the North Atlantic Treaty Organization (NATO), while supporting the Serbian Orthodox Church's call for Milosevic's resignation and the establishment of multiethnic democracies in the Balkans. Serbian Patriarch Pavle went to Kosovo, the cradle of Serbian Christianity, where he urged Serbs to remain at peace with their neighbors. In Pec, Pavle witnessed the destruction of hundreds of Serbian Orthodox churches and monasteries. The Orthodox Church in Albania, led by Archbishop Anastasios, welcomed thousands of refugees from the Kosovo war.

Obituaries. Serbian-American Metropolitan Iriney Kovacevic died in February at the age of 84. He had led a schismatic Serbian church group outside Yugoslavia until being reconciled with the Belgrade patriarchate in 1992. American-educated Metropolitan Theodosius of Tokyo, primate of the Orthodox Church of Japan, died in May.

THOMAS HOPKO
St. Vladimir's Orthodox Theological Seminary

Protestantism

Protestants experienced both successes and setbacks in ecumenical relations during 1999. The year also was marked by continuing controversy over homosexuality. Several Protestant groups saw changes in leadership, including a painful transition for the National Baptist Convention, the largest black Baptist denomination.

Ecumenical Relations. The Evangelical Lutheran Church in America (ELCA) approved full communion with the Episcopal Church at its churchwide assembly in Denver, CO, in August, culminating 30 years of dialogue. In so doing, the ELCA agreed to accept the historic episcopate, requiring new clergy to be ordained by bishops and bishops to be ordained by three others in a line believed to extend back to the early years of Christianity. Such steps had been taken by other Lutheran bodies, but the 5.2-million-member ELCA was the first U.S.-based church to do so. The 2.4-million-member Episcopal Church was expected to ratify the proposal at its convention in 2000. The ELCA convention also approved full communion with the 49,000-member Moravian Church in America, whose Northern and Southern provinces had endorsed the move in 1998. These ecumenical initiatives drew criticism from the 2.6-million-member Lutheran Church–Missouri Synod, whose president, the Rev. Alvin Barry, said they would "inevitably lead to an even more seri-

At a churchwide assembly in Denver, CO, in August 1999, the 5.2-million-member Evangelical Lutheran Church in America ended 30 years of dialogue and voted in favor of full communion with the Episcopal Church.

ous erosion of a genuine Lutheran identity" in the ELCA.

Representatives of nine Protestant denominations with a combined membership of 17 million proposed recognition of each other's membership and ministries by 2002, in a relationship to be known as Churches Uniting in Christ. The proposal, which resulted from 39 years of talks, would have to be approved by the governing body of each denomination. It faced some resistance from the Episcopal Church, whose representatives said questions about the historic episcopate still needed to be resolved before they could forward it for approval.

Controversial Issues. In January, 68 United Methodist ministers blessed the union of two women in Sacramento, CA, defying a church law against same-sex marriages. In March the Rev. Gregory Dell of Chicago was found guilty of disobeying church law by performing such a ceremony for two men in 1998. He was suspended from the ministry.

In the Presbyterian Church (U.S.A.), the Presbytery of the Hudson River voted in January to permit clergy to perform same-sex unions if they are not called marriages. In March a tribunal upheld the right of the First Presbyterian Church in Stamford, CT, to elect an openly gay elder to its governing board. The executive committee of the General Assembly Council reversed an action of another national agency and permitted the Rev. Jane Spahr of Rochester, NY, an activist lesbian cleric, to receive a Women of Faith award at the General Assembly of the 2.6-million-member denomination in June in Fort Worth, TX.

In July delegates to the national meeting of the Reformed Church in America in Sioux Falls, SD, defeated proposals to sever ties with the United Church of Christ (UCC) over the latter's acceptance of homosexuality. The General Board of American Baptist Churches, USA, voted in June to deny the appeals of four California congregations that were removed from their region over their "welcoming and affirming" stance toward homosexuals. However, six regions in the 1.5-million-member denomination requested adjudication of the matter, and the expulsion was postponed.

The Rev. Jimmy Allen, a past president of the Southern Baptist Convention, addressed the international convention of the 42,000-member predominantly gay Universal Fellowship of Metropolitan Community Churches in July in Los Angeles and called for a dialogue to reach out across differences. In October the Rev. Jerry Falwell hosted a meeting at his Thomas Road Baptist Church in Lynchburg, VA, with about 200 gay Christians—including the Rev. Mel White, who was Falwell's ghostwriter before revealing his homosexuality. The two men apologized for statements they had made against each other, and Falwell called on Christian ministries "to halt any rhetoric that might engender violence against the homosexual community, and vice versa."

© Chris O'Meara/AP/Wide World Photos

The Rev. Stewart Cureton *(left), acting president of the National Baptist Convention, congratulates the convention's new president, the Rev.* William Shaw.

In contrast to these developments, at least 27 of the 120 clergy in the state Lutheran church in Norway said they no longer could accept the guidance of Bishop Rosamarie Kohn, after she reinstated the Rev. Siri Sunde, an openly lesbian clergywoman who had been barred in 1997 for marrying another woman.

Protestant groups found themselves receiving criticism on other issues as well. In July the Rev. Choan-Seng Song, president of the 214-denomination World Alliance of Reformed Churches, declared at the alliance's Executive Committee meeting in Taipei, Taiwan, that the "ecumenical mind-set" was far removed from both authentic spirituality and the everyday lives of millions of Christians. Initiatives launched in the fall by the Southern Baptist Convention to evangelize Jews during their high holy days in September and to pray for Hindus during their Festival of Lights in November were denounced by leaders of both faiths.

Leadership Appointments. The Rev. William Shaw of Philadelphia was elected president of the National Baptist Convention, USA, in September in Tampa, FL, succeeding the Rev. Henry J. Lyons, who had resigned in March after being convicted in a state court of grand theft and racketeering. Later, Lyons was ordered to pay $5.2 million in restitution for tax evasion and bank fraud and was given a federal prison sentence of four years and three months, to be served concurrently with the state sentence of five and one-half years.

The Rev. Setri Nyomi, a pastor of the Evangelical Presbyterian Church of Ghana, was appointed general secretary of the World Alliance of Reformed Churches in July, becoming the first non-European to hold the post. The Rev. John H. Thomas, ecumenical officer of the UCC, was elected president of the 1.4-million-member denomination at its General Synod meeting in July in Providence, RI, where the UCC also adopted a restructuring plan to reduce its number of national officers from more than a dozen to five. Jan Paulsen of Norway, a vice-president of the General Conference of Seventh-day Adventists, became the first European to be elected president of the 10-million-member denomination. He was chosen in March to replace Robert S. Folkenberg, who resigned amid allegations that he was involved in fraudulent business dealings.

The National Council of Churches (NCC), which includes 35 Protestant and Orthodox denominations with 52 million members, celebrated its 50th anniversary in November in Cleveland, OH, and installed the Rev. Andrew Young—a minister of the UCC and a former ambassador, congressman, and mayor of Atlanta, GA—as its 20th president. The Rev. Robert Edgar, a United Methodist minister, was chosen to succeed the Rev. Joan Brown Campbell as general secretary. A budget deficit estimated at $3.5 million plagued the NCC.

The Rev. Paige Patterson was reelected president of the Southern Baptist Convention at its annual meeting in June in Atlanta. He urged the nation's largest Protestant denomination to reach out to urban areas and establish 160 new congregations in six cities over a three-year period.

Other News. In addition to Lyons, other Protestant leaders facing legal difficulties during 1999 included Allan Boesak, former president of the World Alliance of Reformed Churches, and the Rev. Canaan Banana, former president of Zimbabwe. In March, Boesak was sentenced in Cape Town, South Africa, to six years in prison for taking $400,000 from a foundation organized to help victims of apartheid. That same month, Banana, 63, was defrocked by the Methodist Church of Zimbabwe after being convicted of sexually assaulting men whom he employed while he was president. Meanwhile, leaders of the 328,000-member Christian and Missionary Alliance apologized in May to 80 alumni of one of its boarding schools in Guinea for the emotional, physical, and sexual abuse they had suffered at the school between 1950 and its closing in 1971.

The two largest Protestant denominations in the United States reported contrasting membership trends during 1999. The Southern Baptist Convention's membership decreased 1.02% to 15.7 million, its first decline since 1926. The United Methodist Church also suffered a decline, losing 38,477 members to reach a total of 8.4 million, but this was the smallest decrease it had seen since its establishment in 1968.

DARRELL J. TURNER

Roman Catholicism

For the Roman Catholic Church, 1999 was a time of anticipation for the coming Jubilee Year 2000. At Christmas 1998, Pope John Paul II said he was thinking ahead to Christmas 1999, when he would open the Holy Door at St. Peter's Basilica to usher in the millennium year. The pope—now 79 and physically failing—remained mentally agile and kept a full schedule for the year.

Papal Travels. January 23–26 saw a papal visit to Mexico, followed by a two-day stop in St. Louis, MO, where John Paul's impassioned plea against the death penalty moved Missouri Gov. Mel Carnahan to commute the sentence of death-row inmate Darrell Mease to life in prison.

The pope traveled to Romania May 7–9, the first-ever papal visit to a predominantly Orthodox country. Other destinations included the pope's native Poland in June; Slovenia in September; and India and the Republic of Georgia early in November.

John Paul, who had declared more saints than any other pope in history, put Mother Teresa of Calcutta on a fast track to sainthood in March by waiving the rule requiring a candidate to have been dead for five years before his or her cause can be opened. Mother Teresa died in September 1997. Another cause that was advancing was that of Pope Pius XII, who died in 1958. Questions regarding whether Pius did enough to save Jews from the Nazis in World War II have made him controversial. Meanwhile, a

© Massimo Sambucetti/AP/Wide World Photos

During a historic visit to Romania in May 1999, Pope John Paul II conferred with Patriarch Teoctist (right)*, the leader of Romania's Orthodox Church.*

second miracle attributed to Mother Katharine Drexel (1858–1955), an American heiress who chose the life of a nun, was approved by a board of Rome physicians.

Interfaith News. Friction developed in Indonesia between Catholics in East Timor and the country's Muslim majority during the summer. Catholic-Muslim relations had taken an upswing in March, however, when Iranian President Mohammed Khatami visited Pope John Paul II at the Vatican.

Catholic and Lutheran representatives, meeting in Augsburg, Germany, on October 31, signed a long-awaited document on the Lutheran doctrine that believers are justified and saved by faith alone. The joint document said justification comes through faith alone, but good works are an essential sign of true faith. Earlier, the Anglican–Roman Catholic International Commission announced that it had deepened and extended its agreement on the primacy of the pope. However, it was clear the two communions are still far apart on the issue of just how that primacy should be exercised.

Issues. A Maryland priest and nun—Father Robert Nugent and Sister Jeannine Gramick—were notified by the Vatican in July they must discontinue any "pastoral work involving homosexual persons." The two headed New Ways Ministry, which they had founded in 1977. The Vatican Congregation for the Doctrine of the Faith said their ministry "advanced doctrinally unacceptable positions."

An August report by the U.S. bishops called attention to the fact that half of all U.S. couples, including Catholics, cohabit before marriage. The report suggested that by "supporting the couple's plans for the future rather than chastising them for the past," the church could cause them to "be drawn more deeply into the Church community." On November 17 the U.S. bishops approved new norms that would require teachers of theology at Catholic colleges and universities to have official church approval, usually from the local bishop.

American Catholics were angered by what they considered a deliberate mockery of their faith when, in October, the Brooklyn Museum of Art showed an exhibit including a likeness of the Virgin Mary by artist Chris Ofili; the artwork was smeared with elephant dung and included cutouts of body parts from pornographic magazines. New York City Mayor Rudolph W. Giuliani tried to cut off the museum's funding but was blocked by the courts.

Other News. There were 62 million U.S. Catholics in 1999, up from 61.5 million in 1998, according to official Church census figures. Catholics comprise 23% of the U.S. population. There was a slight increase in the number of U.S. men studying for the priesthood—4,826, compared with 4,588 in 1998.

England's Cardinal George Basil Hume died June 17. New York's Cardinal John O'Connor underwent surgery for a brain tumor in late summer.

A Vatican synod of the bishops of Europe was held October 1–23.

LOU BALDWIN
Reporter, "Catholic Standard and Times"

Retailing

"Stores welcome shopping frenzy: Economic good news brings hordes of happy consumers eager to spend extra cash" was the headline in *USA Today* during the Christmas 1999 buying season. In fact, the headline could have appeared virtually anytime during the year. It was a robust year for almost all retailers. Signs of economic strength included a thriving stock market, low inflation, unemployment at 29-year lows, and unparalleled consumer confidence in the economy. Retailing's boom was felt in nearly every segment of the industry. According to the U.S. Commerce Department, overall retail sales increased by 8.9% in 1999—the largest gain since 1984, when sales rose by 10%.

Consumer Confidence. When consumer confidence in the economy is high, consumer spending—approximately two thirds of the U.S. economy—is usually vigorous. The consumer-confidence index, measured by the Conference Board based on a comparison to the 1985 level of 100, surged in June to 138.4, the highest reading in more than 30 years. The index fell nearly ten points by October, but then rebounded to 135.8 in November. The substantive increase in the index in November was particularly important because consumer exhilaration is critical for retail sales, specifically late in the year, when many retailers obtain up to half of their annual sales during the holiday season. Projections for final retail sales for Christmas 1999 indicated that consumers would spend about $184 billion over the 30-day holiday shopping period, up from $174 billion in 1998.

Two other important indexes that survey consumer perceptions of the economy also grew in 1999. The present-situation index, which summarizes consumers' current perspectives on the economy, rose into record territory, reaching 179.2 (its highest level since 1969) in July. The expectation index, which measures consumers' anticipation of where the economy is moving, reached a high of 114.9 in June. By November this index dropped slightly, but it was still a full ten points higher than in November 1998.

E-Commerce (Internet Shopping). The strong economy also encouraged shoppers to venture into cyberspace in unprecedented numbers. Projected on-line sales for the fourth quarter were expected to exceed $8 billion, more than double 1998's sales revenues for the same period. The Christmas-sales volume alone was expected to equal total Internet sales revenues for all of 1998. A poll by *The New York Times* and CBS News found that 17% of their respondents had bought or were planning to buy holiday gifts on-line in 1999, compared with only 7% in 1998. In late December, Boston Consulting Group, a management consulting firm, and Shop.org, an industry association, reported that during the 1999 holiday shopping season, on-line orders by consumers increased 270%, and Internet sales revenues rose 300%, compared with the same period of 1998. In fact, the fastest-growing sector in retailing as a whole was e-commerce. Although e-commerce constituted only about 1% of retail sales, the growth rate of sales from the Internet was expected to rise to 25% within five years, reported Mary Tolan of Andersen Consulting.

Internet shopping registered enormous gains in sales, generating revenues of approximately $20 billion in 1999. Approximately 7 million shoppers purchased a product over the Internet during the year. The Internet economy grew an astounding 68% in 12 months, far outpacing the 6% growth rate of the overall U.S. economy. Because of the growing popularity of the Internet, the U.S. Commerce Department announced in September that the nation's retailers soon would begin reporting e-commerce sales.

The phenomenal growth in cyberspace shopping notwithstanding, business-to-business electronic transactions were expected to be even more impressive. For example, Internet sales to consumers were expected to exceed $100 billion by 2003, but business-to-business sales over the Internet were projected to top $1.3 trillion by that time.

Despite the optimism noted above about e-commerce, customer doubts about credit-

© Jeff Stahler; reprinted by permission of Newspaper Enterprise Association

card security, prices on the Internet, privacy concerns, return policies, and poor customer service continued to plague the industry. In the opinion of most analysts, the e-commerce industry still had a lot of improvements to make before it could compete effectively with more-traditional retail outlets. During the holiday season, for example, a number of on-line sellers, including Toys "R" Us, found themselves unable to guarantee on time delivery because they could not handle the unexpectedly high volume of orders. The e-commerce industry lost approximately $7 billion in revenues in 1999 when potential customers did not buy because of technical glitches, poor customer service, or a combination of the two. Internet retailers were working to solve these problems.

During 1999 it became evident that some shopping malls were concerned about the unprecedented growth of on-line commerce. For example, The Galleria, the most popular mall in the St. Louis, MO, area, sent letters to its 170 retail stores in November informing them of a new policy that banned in-store signs, decals, advertising, or displays promoting the purchase of merchandise over the Internet. Some of the stores protested or simply ignored the policy.

The changes e-commerce was bringing to the retail industry may be the most dramatic in retail in all of the 20th century. In fact, most large and medium-sized retail companies had established an Internet presence by late 1999. Most of them entered the new retail milieu reluctantly, but triple-digit growth in e-commerce left them little choice.

Credit-Card Spending and Debt. Even in the exceptional economic times in recent years, personal bankruptcies were increasing at an alarming rate, reaching a record 1.4 million in 1998. The trend started to turn around in 1999, as consumers appeared to have spending and debt under control for the first time in nearly a decade. In the three-month period ending Sept. 30, 1999, filings fell 10% from the same period in 1998. Furthermore, credit-card delinquencies reached a four-year low, and the proportion of credit-card accounts paid in full each month increased from 29% in 1991 to 43% in 1999, according to CardWeb.com, a credit-card-tracking Web site.

Retail Leader. Wal-Mart continued to dominate and expand its lead in the retail industry in 1999, reporting record sales for the third quarter of more than $40 billion, an increase of 21% over the same period in 1998. As of November 15, the company had 1,803 Wal-Mart stores, 682 Supercenters, and 456 Sam's Clubs in the United States. Internationally, Wal-Mart operated a total of 985 units in Argentina, Brazil, Canada, Germany, Mexico, Puerto Rico, Great Britain, China, and South Korea.

The Most Popular Toy of 1999. The "must-have" toy of the moment in 1999 was actually a wide range of items, all related to a Japanese game called Pokémon. Developed by Nintendo and introduced in the United States in fall 1998, Pokémon involved a collection of little "pocket monsters" with various powers and abilities. It quickly became a marketing phenomenon, with sales of Pokémon-related merchandise estimated at $6 billion worldwide by the end of 1999. Pokémon was different from most other fashionable toys because of the many types of products available—everything from video games to trading cards to toys—and because these products were marketed successfully to both boys and girls.

MEL ZELENAK
University of Missouri-Columbia

Romania

Romania's coalition government held together in 1999 despite periodic conflicts between its members, but the economy remained a cause for concern, and significant social protests were held against the government's reform program. Romania supported the air campaign against Serbia by the North Atlantic Treaty Organization (NATO).

Political Conflicts. Disagreements were evident among the parties within the governing coalition, led by the Democratic Convention of Romania (CDR), centering on issues such as the allocation of ministries and the pace and scope of economic reform. The most persistent disputes were with the Democratic Union of Hungarians (UDMR). UDMR representatives participated in the government but voiced disappointment with the pace of administrative decentralization, the continuing restrictions on Hungarian education, and the delay in opening a Hungarian-language university in Transylvania. The popularity of the opposition parties increased because of frustrations with economic austerity and rising unemployment. In late November some 5,000 demonstrators in Bucharest demanded the government's resignation. By late 1999 former President Ion Iliescu, leader of the Social Democratic Party, was well ahead of President Emil Constantinescu in the polls. Presidential elections were scheduled for the fall of 2000.

On December 13, Constantinescu dismissed Premier Radu Vasile after all seven ministers from Vasile's Christian Democratic National Peasants' Party, as well as three Liberal Party members, resigned. Vasile initially vowed to fight for his job, but backed down. The president appointed Mugur Isarescu, governor of the central bank, as prime minister on December 16.

Economic Slowdown. Romania's economy continued to stagnate, largely because of bureaucratic interference in structural reform, insufficient foreign investment, and pervasive corruption and inefficiency. The war in Serbia also negatively affected the economy (causing losses of $500,000 per week, according to some estimates), especially as blockages along the Danube River that continued even after the conflict ended led to a loss of trade with Western Europe.

Romania's gross domestic product (GDP) for 1999 was expected to fall by about 4.8%; inflation was projected at about 50.2%; and unemployment rose to more than 11%. Several of the state-owned banks and some private institutions also neared collapse. The International Monetary Fund (IMF) provided standby credits to assist in the government's stabilization plan.

The closure of unprofitable state-subsidized enterprises led to major protests by Romanian workers, including miners.

International Relations. Romania's relations with most of its neighbors (except Serbia) continued to improve, and Bucharest participated in several multilateral regional initiatives in such areas as fighting organized crime, trade promotion, and infrastructural development. Bucharest supported NATO's war against Serbia despite the serious economic costs it entailed and overwhelming public opposition. Romania continued to press for inclusion in NATO as well.

Romania was included in plans for aid under the South East European Stability Pact, sponsored by the EU to promote democratic reform and economic development in the Balkans. In October the EU Commission recommended including Romania with several "first-tier" central European countries in starting negotiations for EU membership in 2000, but EU officials pointed out that the country still did not meet the economic requirements.

In May, Pope John Paul II traveled to Romania for the first papal visit to a predominantly Orthodox Christian country in more than 1,000 years. His main purpose was to improve relations between the Greek Catholic (Uniate) and Orthodox Churches, whose disputes over church property heightened social tensions in parts of the country. Many Roman Catholics from Transylvania went to Bucharest to see the pontiff.

JANUSZ BUGAJSKI
Center for Strategic and International Studies

ROMANIA • Information Highlights

Official Name: Romania.
Location: Southeastern Europe.
Area: 91,699 sq mi (237 500 km²).
Population (July 1999 est.): 22,334,312.
Chief Cities (July 1, 1997 est.): Bucharest, the capital, 2,027,512; Iaşi, 348,399; Constanţa, 344,876.
Government: *Head of state,* Emil Constantinescu, president (elected November 1996). *Head of government,* Mugur Isarescu, prime minister (named December 1999). *Legislature*—Parliament: Senate and Chamber of Deputies.
Monetary Unit: Leu (17,965.00 lei equal U.S.$1, Dec. 9, 1999).
Gross Domestic Product (1998 est. U.S.$): $90,600,000,000 (purchasing power parity).
Economic Indexes: *Consumer Prices* (1998, 1991 = 100): all items, 19,474.4; food, 18,607.2. *Industrial Production* (1998, 1990 = 100): 53.6.
Foreign Trade (1998 U.S.$): *Imports,* $11,821,000,000; *exports,* $8,300,000,000.

Russia

The last year of the 20th century was anything but tranquil for Russia, but the country made further progress in its transition to democracy and free markets. While the government again experienced much turnover as President Boris Yeltsin repeatedly shuffled his prime ministers, Russia's third parliamentary elections since the end of the Soviet Union were conducted successfully. Other major events in 1999 included the attempted impeachment of the president by his Communist opponents in the State Duma (the lower house of parliament), and the resumption of fighting in the Chechen Republic. The second half of the year saw the economy begin to recover from the financial crisis of summer 1998 and ended with Yeltsin's dramatic resignation as president.

In foreign affairs, Russia continued to oppose Western multilateral initiatives such as the bombing of Serbia (*see* THE KOSOVO CRISIS, page 78) and the military confrontation with Iraq, while remaining tethered to the goodwill of international lending institutions. In a sad footnote to 1999, Raisa Gorbachev, 67, the spouse of former Soviet President Mikhail Gorbachev, died in September after a long illness. Gorbachev's devotion to his wife in her last days struck a responsive chord among Russians.

A group of supporters of Boris Yeltsin demonstrated outside the State Duma in mid-May 1999 as the Russian president faced impeachment. The proceedings failed.

© Viktor Korotayev/Reuters/Archive Photos

Political Developments. The Duma's special commission on the impeachment of the president, which had been at work for many months, presented multiple charges against President Yeltsin to the full body in May. This was not the first time that Yeltsin had been at risk of impeachment at the hands of the large Communist faction and its allies in the Duma, but it was the most extensive effort, resulting from years of friction. Russian impeachment procedures were modeled generally after the U.S. Constitution (requiring approval by a two-thirds majority of the Duma), but with the additional step of judicial confirmation by both the Supreme Court and the Constitutional Court. The politically inspired charges had intended to hold Yeltsin accountable for the dissolution of the USSR in 1991, the forcible disbanding of parliament in 1993, and Russia's 1994–96 war against its Chechen province. The president also was accused of destroying Russia's military and committing genocide against the people by allowing the nation's living standards to plummet. After extensive floor debate, only the Chechen charge attracted broad support, but even that fell short of the required two-thirds majority.

On the eve of impeachment, President Yeltsin dismissed his prime minister, Yevgeny Primakov. Appointed by Yeltsin in the wake of the August 1998 financial crisis, Primakov had been charged with the task of restabilizing Russia politically and economically. A calm, steady person, he soon achieved the former goal, but the latter eluded him. Primakov's failure in the economic arena was the public reason Yeltsin gave for his dismissal, but the actual reason was probably the prime minister's rising popularity, along with his close ties with the Communists and speculation that he might enter the race to succeed Yeltsin as president in 2000.

Primakov was followed in office by Sergei Stepashin, a deputy prime minister. Much younger than his predecessor, the 47-year-old Stepashin had an extensive résumé and was considered an unquestioning Yeltsin loyalist. He had served the president as domestic-intelligence chief, justice minister, and minister of internal affairs. During the summer, the new prime minister successfully conducted crucial financial diplomacy with Russia's creditors, but he failed to dissuade Yuri Luzhkov, the powerful mayor of Moscow and a critic of the president, from forming the Fatherland–All Russia political alliance with a bloc of regional leaders. However, it was the outbreak of fighting in the North Caucasus that sealed Stepashin's political fate. In August a large Chechen guerrilla force attacked the neighboring republic of Dagestan, reopening hostilities in the region, and Yeltsin, apparently believing that Stepashin was not tough enough to deal with the crisis, quickly fired him.

Enter Vladimir Putin, the president's replacement for Stepashin and the fifth Russian prime minister in 18 months. Yet another turnover in the office—this one after less than three months—led to widespread criticism of Yeltsin and a renewed call to amend the constitution to reduce the scope of presidential power. Nonetheless, Putin was confirmed as prime minister surprisingly easily. The 46-year-old Putin, a lawyer like his predecessor, had been a career intelligence officer in the Soviet Union and, since 1991, in Russia. He served for many years in Germany as an officer of the KGB, followed by a stint in St. Petersburg politics from 1990 until his appointment to the president's staff in 1996. Then, in quick succession, Yeltsin selected Putin as head of the Federal Security Service (the domestic-intelligence agency that replaced the KGB), secretary of the powerful Security Council, and, finally, first deputy prime minister.

Upon taking office, Prime Minister Putin boldly predicted that the Chechen incursion into Dagestan would be dealt with within two weeks. Initially, nearly 1,000 guerrilla fighters led by Shamil Basayev, one of the most successful Chechen commanders of the earlier war with Russia, had linked up with the Wahhabis, a radical Muslim sect living along the Dagestan-Chechnya border. The Wahhabis hoped to create an Islamic state in Dagestan, a region about half the size of Austria with a population of 2 million people in 30 different ethnic groups. However, they found little support among the Dagestanis, and after a brief engagement, the Chechens were driven back across the border by Russian military units. A low-intensity conflict continued in the area, which the Russians were content to contain until September, when a series of bloody bombings took place in apartment houses and other buildings in Moscow and elsewhere. More than 300 people were killed in the blasts.

This violence, attributed to Chechen terrorists, escalated the conflict. At that point, the Yeltsin administration, with public support, decided to conduct a large-scale campaign in Chechnya that it dubbed an "antiterrorist operation." Unlike the previous Chechen war, in which Russia suffered defeat and political humiliation, this time the military was deployed with much greater skill, proficiency, and success. One by one, the major Chechen towns and strongholds were taken, and by early December, Russian forces were closing in on the capital, Grozny.

© Mikhail Metzel/AP/Wide World Photos

In August 1999, Vladimir Putin (center), *46, who had served with the Soviet-era KGB, took office as premier of Russia. He became acting president on December 31.*

Russia's new campaign in Chechnya was not without costs. A large number of civilians were killed or wounded in the fighting. In addition, more than 200,000 civilians, caught between the Chechen Islamic warriors and the Russian army, fled to neighboring provinces. The Republic of Ingushetia was overwhelmed by the arrival of more than 150,000 refugees from Chechnya. In addition, Russia received much criticism from abroad for the human toll of its campaign. The one clear beneficiary of the Chechen conflict was the prime minister. Putin's popularity rose rapidly in public-opinion polls, and he became the front-runner in the shadow presidential race being conducted within the framework of the fall parliamentary election campaign.

By the close of registration for the Duma elections scheduled for December 19, a total of 26 parties and electoral alliances had been registered, down from the 43 groups that participated in the 1995 elections. More than 3,500 candidates were running for the 225 party seats in the 450-member Duma. Under the proportional-representation rules, a party must win at least 5% of the vote to earn any seats. Another 2,300 candidates were contesting the remaining single-mandate seats.

Only a handful of the parties and alliances stood a chance of getting past the 5% barrier. One of these was the Communist Party, the largest faction in the outgoing Duma. The party's leading candidates were its leader and former presidential candidate, Gennady Zyuganov, and Duma Speaker Gennady Seleznev. Another major contender was the Fatherland–All Russia alliance, created during the summer as a coalition of Mayor Luzhkov's Fatherland party and All Russia, a party led by influential regional leaders. Its leading contender was former Prime Minister Primakov.

Other parties in the running included Yabloko—a liberal, pro-reform party—and Our Home Is Russia, a center-right party. Leading candidates for the former were Grigory Yavlinsky and former Prime Minister Stepashin, while the latter was led by former Prime Minister Viktor Chernomyrdin and Deputy Duma Speaker Vladimir Ryzkov. Rounding out the major contenders were the Union of Right Forces, a coalition of young reformers led by former Prime Minister Sergei Kiriyenko and former Deputy Prime Minister Anatoly Chubais; and Unity, led by Sergei Shoigu, Yeltsin's minister for emergency situations. Unity had been created with the support of a number of governors, principally to draw votes away from Fatherland–All Russia, whose coleader, Primakov, was considered by the Kremlin to be Putin's most serious competition for president. A few weeks before the election, the strategy appeared to be working. Throughout the campaign, the Communists had led the polls with support ranging from 20% to 29%, followed by Fatherland–All Russia at 10% to 14%, Yabloko at 8% to 9%, and Unity at 7%–8%. Just before the balloting, however, polling showed Unity moving into second place behind the Communists.

© Misha Japaridze/AP/Wide World Photos

A series of bloody bombing attacks at apartments, above, *and other buildings in Moscow in September 1999 was attributed to Chechen terrorists. With support from an outraged public, Russia escalated its military campaign against the republic. In mid-November demonstrators,* right, *were assembling in Red Square to demand an end to the war in Chechnya.*

© Viktor Korotayev/Reuters/Archive Photos

The results of the parliamentary voting on December 19 proved to be a realigning election for post-Soviet Russia. Six parties cleared the 5% hurdle, compared with only four in the 1995 elections, and while turnout was down, it still was very good at more than 60%. Although the Communist Party won the party vote by a narrow margin and gained nearly one quarter of the seats in the new Duma, it no longer dominated the lower house as it had since 1993. Centrist parties loyal to or at least friendly toward the Kremlin enjoyed broad support. Foremost was the latecomer Unity, which came in just behind the Communists and won the second-largest bloc of seats. Unity's success was attributed largely to Prime Minister Putin's endorsement late in the campaign, since the party had no organization, platform, or generally well-known candidates. Also riding Putin's political coattails was the Union of Right Forces, which won 8.60% of the vote. In addition, Yabloko was returned to the Duma, although with considerably less support, due to its leader's criticism of the Chechnya campaign. The remaining two winning groups were Zhirinovsky's Bloc, the reincarnation of the nationalist Liberal Democratic Party from the outgoing Duma, and Fatherland–All Russia, which came in third and drew fewer votes than anticipated.

As 1999 ended, Yeltsin surprisingly resigned the presidency six months before the conclusion of his term. Yeltsin named Prime Minister Putin, whom he had favored as his successor, acting president. Presidential elections were scheduled for March 2000, three months ahead of schedule. The new acting president granted Yeltsin immunity from criminal or administrative investigations.

RUSSIA • Information Highlights

Official Name: Russian Federation.
Location: Eastern Europe and northern Asia.
Area: 6,592,772 sq mi (17 075 200 km^2).
Population (July 1999 est.): 146,393,569.
Chief Cities (July 1, 1995, est.): Moscow, the capital, 8,368,449; St. Petersburg, 4,232,105; Nizhniy Novgorod (Gorky), 1,375,570; Novosibirsk, 1,367,596; Yekaterinburg (Sverdlovsk), 1,276,659.
Government: *Head of state,* Vladimir Putin, acting president (appointed Dec. 31, 1999). *Head of government,* Vladimir Putin, prime minister (confirmed in August 1999). *Legislature*—Federal Assembly: Federation Council and State Duma.
Monetary Unit: Ruble (26.900 rubles equal U.S.$1, Dec. 10, 1999).
Gross Domestic Product (1998 est. U.S.$): $593,400,-000,000 (purchasing power parity).
Economic Indexes: *Consumer Prices* (1998, 1991 = 100): all items, 416,814.0; food, 412,044.0. *Industrial Production* (1998, 1990 = 100): 45.4.
Foreign Trade (1998 U.S.$): *Imports,* $58,996,000,000; *exports,* $74,160,000,000.

Economy. By the end of 1998, due to the financial crisis in August, the Russian economy was in a severe downturn. The gross domestic product (GDP) had fallen 4.6%, inflation had climbed to 84.4%, and the International Labor Organization estimated unemployment at 22%. Foreign investment had fallen nearly by half, the foreign-trade surplus was down 25%, disposable income had shrunk by 16%, and nearly 40 million people were living below the subsistence level. Complicating the situation, in 1999, Russia was facing $17.5 billion in debt service, and Standard and Poor's (S&P) had cut the country's long-term-debt credit rating to CCC–, the world's lowest for sovereign debt.

During the first two quarters of 1999, the economy continued to struggle, but by the second half of the year, the situation began to brighten. Whether the partial recovery was real or "virtual" was the subject of debate among economists from both East and West. They all agreed, however, on the two relevant variables—the devalued ruble, which made imports more expensive and thus favored domestic goods, and the higher price of oil, Russia's main export, which created an unexpected revenue windfall. By late 1999 a number of economic indicators had turned moderately positive. The GDP had stopped falling and was expected to show a positive growth rate of 1.5% to 2%. By fall, inflation had leveled off at 31.4%, while the foreign-investment decline slowed, even showing a 60% year-to-year increase in the second quarter. The foreign-trade surplus, thanks to oil prices that reached $24 a barrel, was headed for a record total for the previous five years. Industrial production rose by 7.5% in the first ten months, tax collections had soared by 72% by the end of the third quarter, and the country was paying overdue pensions and reducing wage arrears. Rail-freight traffic increased in the Far East, labor markets were tightening in Siberia, and more than 1,000 banks had regained solvency after nearly failing in 1998. Finally, most of the debt service owed abroad had been rescheduled, or negotiations toward that end were under way.

Still, there remained bad economic news that could not be ignored. Central Bank reserves remained low, capital investment was down, and the number of people living in poverty jumped appreciably. Agriculture was hit hard by a cold snap in May, followed by drought, a heat wave, and locust infestations. As a result, the harvest, while better than in 1998, was not enough to meet the

© Roland Weihrauch/AP/Wide World Photos

Russia's President Boris Yeltsin met with German Chancellor Gerhard Schröder (right) *at the Group of 8 (G-8) industrialized nations summit in Cologne, Germany, on June 20, 1999. Following Yeltsin's sudden resignation as 1999 came to an end, Schröder noted that the departing Russian president had "played a crucial role in helping the country develop democracy and a free-market economy."*

country's demands. Millions of tons of feed grain had to be imported. In addition, the driest summer since 1956 led to 20,000 forest fires, an increase of 25% over summer 1998. Fuel shortages hampered both harvesting and fire-fighting efforts. Crime rose by 18% in the first 11 months of 1999, which continued to sap the economy.

Meanwhile, the country's efforts to obtain more international financial aid were complicated by a money-laundering scandal. It was reported in August that U.S., British, and Russian law-enforcement officials were looking into allegations that Russian organized-crime figures had funneled billions of dollars through U.S. banks over several years. The officials said that some of the laundered money might have come from loans to Russia from the International Monetary Fund (IMF). The investigation included several current or former members of Yeltsin's government, including his daughter and adviser Tatyana Dyachenko. The Kremlin denied any wrongdoing.

By the end of 1999, S&P had classified Russia as SD (selective default), meaning that the economy was technically bankrupt. The IMF held up a $640 million tranche as it tried to determine for certain whether its funds were involved in the money-laundering scandal.

Foreign Affairs. Russia's foreign relations developed in 1999 much as expected, although the Chechnya operation caused unexpected complications abroad. Except for its unavoidable financial dependence on the West, Russia continued to reorient its foreign policy toward the east and south. Actions to this end included Yeltsin's participation in the Shanghai Five talks with the leaders of China, Kyrgyzstan, Kazakhstan, and Tajikistan in August; special cooperative agreements with China; and the signing in December of a treaty to form an economic and political confederation with Belarus. Conversely, Russia boycotted the 50th-anniversary celebration of the North Atlantic Treaty Organization (NATO), held in April in Washington, DC; opposed NATO's bombing of Serbia; and continued to condemn U.S. and British bombing attacks on Iraq. Especially irksome to the United States was Russia's refusal to renegotiate the 1972 Antiballistic Missile (ABM) treaty, which restricted the testing and deployment of antimissile defense systems.

Meanwhile, evidence surfaced that Russia was embarking on a strategic modernization program, including the building of a new mobile intercontinental ballistic missile (ICBM) and the refitting of its largest missile-firing nuclear submarines. Russia's latest military operations in Chechnya further complicated its ambivalent relations with the West. At a summit meeting of the Organization for Security and Cooperation in Europe (OSCE) in Istanbul in November, Russia was criticized by U.S. President Bill Clinton and other world leaders. Yeltsin and his ministers reacted with outrage, arguing that it was hypocritical for the West to launch bombing strikes against sovereign states such as Yugoslavia, and then object to Russia's military action against insurrection and terrorism within its own borders.

ROBERT SHARLET, *Union College*

Saudi Arabia

Fluctuations in oil prices affected most aspects of Saudi Arabia during 1999. Crown Prince Abdullah ibn Abd al-Aziz consolidated his leading position in the government of the kingdom.

Economy. Saudi Arabia continued to dominate oil-policy issues in the Organization of Petroleum Exporting Countries (OPEC) in 1999, while also strongly influencing worldwide petroleum developments. By late 1998, Saudi crude-oil prices averaged between $10 and $11 a barrel, a historic low. Production was about 8 million barrels per day. On Nov. 26, 1998, the Saudis called for strict enforcement of OPEC oil-production quotas, a clear reference to the overproduction by some member states. Then, on December 9, Saudi Arabia and the other Gulf Cooperation Council (GCC) members asked that OPEC quotas begun the previous June be extended through 1999 to stabilize the market. At a meeting on March 11, 1999, Saudi Arabia persuaded Iran, Venezuela, Algeria, and Mexico to call for reduced oil production. This policy was adopted at an OPEC meeting in Vienna, Austria, on March 23, when the organization called for a yearlong, 7% (1.7 million barrels per day) cut in production beginning April 1, to overcome the 40% fall in oil revenues during 1998. Saudi Arabia then reduced its own production by 585,000 barrels per day. Oil Minister Ali al-Naimi encouraged foreign oil companies to invest in exploration and production activities inside Saudi Arabia, thereby reversing the trend toward exclusive Saudi control of this vital natural resource.

World prices for oil steadily rose, climbing to $24 per barrel by late September. OPEC supported this process by extending the March 1999 quotas to March 2000, even though some nations began to break the agreement and increase production in response to rising prices.

Domestic Affairs. The country's finances changed considerably during 1999 in reaction to the fluctuation in oil prices. In November 1998, falling revenues forced Saudi Arabia to ask the United Arab Emirates for a loan of $5 billion to close out the fiscal year's budget. The new Saudi budget, announced on December 28, predicted an income of $32 billion and expenditures of $44 billion, even though spending was to be slashed by 13%. In May 1999 the government increased the cost of gasoline by 50% to help meet the budget deficit. Foreign tourists also provided a new source of income, as tour groups sponsored by the Smithsonian Institution began to visit Saudi Arabia in the fall.

Crown Prince Abdullah took on more of the day-to-day running of government business, as his brother King Fahd went to the hospital various times during the year for treatment of his prolonged illnesses. When the king took a lengthy holiday in Spain during the summer, Crown Prince Abdullah exercised nearly complete authority.

Several domestic changes showed both the strength of conservatism and a desire for reforms. The death on May 13 of the 87-year-old Sheikh Abdul Aziz bin Baz, the Grand Mufti (chief religious official) since 1993, opened the way for a younger generation when King Fahd named the 56-year-old Abdel Aziz bin Abdullah al-Asheikh as the new Grand Mufti. As the four-year terms of office of the Saudi cabinet expired, King Fahd on June 16 reappointed most of the officials, while creating a new Ministry of Civil Service. And even though the country more than tripled the number of executions in 1999 compared with 1998, Crown Prince Abdullah showed clemency to four radical Islamic fundamentalists on June 25, freeing them after almost five years in prison. The prince also appealed in a July speech for Saudi women to make a full contribution to the nation, indirectly suggesting that the extremely limited role of women in public issues might expand.

International Relations. Even though U.S. policy in Iraq seemed unlikely to bring about the removal of President Saddam Hussein, Saudi Arabia continued to support most U.S. actions, even while remaining open to diplomatic ties with Iran. King Fahd and Crown Prince Abdullah welcomed Iranian President Mohammad Khatami to Jidda for a state visit on May 15.

SAUDI ARABIA • Information Highlights

Official Name: Kingdom of Saudi Arabia.
Location: Arabian peninsula in southwest Asia.
Area: 756,981 sq mi (1 960 582 km²).
Population (July 1999 est.): 21,504,613.
Chief City (1993 est.): Riyadh, the capital, 3,000,000.
Government: *Head of state and government,* Fahd bin Abd al-Aziz Al Sa'ud, king and prime minister (acceded June 1982). *Legislature*—consultative council.
Monetary Unit: Riyal (3.750 riyals equal U.S.$1, Dec. 28, 1999).
Gross Domestic Product (1998 est. U.S.$): $186,000,000,000 (purchasing power parity).
Economic Index (1998, 1990 = 100): *Consumer Prices,* all items, 111.3; food, 117.0.
Foreign Trade (1997 U.S.$): *Imports,* $28,742,000,000; *exports,* $62,381,000,000.

Saudi Arabia provided limited backing to the United States and Great Britain when they attacked Iraq in December 1998 for refusing to cooperate with United Nations (UN) weapons inspections. Refueling of aircraft was permitted, but flight missions were not allowed to operate directly from the kingdom. Nevertheless, by March, U.S. military aircraft based in Saudi Arabia had flown 511 missions over southern Iraq to enforce the "no-fly" zone, after the full-scale hostilities ended. In response, Iraq threatened to bomb Saudi Arabia, but did not.

Saudi-U.S. relations were strained when the U.S. State Department issued its annual report on human relations on February 26 and a new International Report on Religious Freedom on September 9, both of which alleged Saudi discrimination. But a long-running dispute between Washington and Riyadh concerning Hani al-Sayegh, a Saudi citizen suspected of the June 1996 killing of Americans at al-Khobar, Saudi Arabia, was resolved in October. Al-Sayegh was sent from the United States to Saudi Arabia, after officials there promised that he would be interrogated and tried fairly.

Crown Prince Abdullah continued to establish himself with world leaders as the chief figure forming both foreign and domestic policy in Saudi Arabia. The prince visited Italy in May, meeting with Italian Prime Minister Massimo D'Alema and other government officials, as well as with European Commission President Romano Prodi. He then visited several Middle Eastern countries, including Syria. In October, Chinese Premier Jiang Zemin visited Riyadh, and the two countries agreed to work toward increasing their political and economic ties. Crown Prince Abdullah also met with new Pakistani ruler Gen. Pervez Musharraf in October, not long after the general assumed power.

The Internet. In the past, the estimated 500,000 Saudi computer users who wanted to gain access to worldwide computer systems had to make an expensive long-distance phone call, as Saudi Arabia had no local Internet provider. That situation changed in early 1999, as the country established direct-dial access to the Internet for the first time. However, the interior ministry announced that it would attempt to filter out sites deemed to be immoral or seditious.

William Ochsenwald
Virginia Polytechnic Institute and State University

Singapore

In 1999, Singapore enjoyed political stability and made real progress in recovering

Singapore's Prime Minister Goh Chok Tong, below, *spoke at the East Asia Economic Summit, held in Singapore City in October 1999. Politicians, economists, and businesspeople met for three days to discuss Asia's financial prospects.*

from the Asian economic crisis of 1997–98. The government expressed concern about several social issues, however, including the declining birthrate.

Politics and Society. In early 1999, after surveys indicated that only about half of Singaporeans believed they had any say in government decisions, the island nation launched the "Singapore 21" campaign, aimed at convincing its citizens to take a greater role in shaping the country's future. The country's three opposition members of Parliament, with uncharacteristic frankness, accused the government of creating a climate of fear among those who would challenge the ruling People's Action Party (PAP). For example, in February two opposition politicians were jailed briefly and barred from taking part in elections for five years for violating a law requiring police permits for political speeches.

In August, S.R. Nathan, director of Singapore's Institute of Defense and Strategic Studies, was declared the nation's next president. He replaced Ong Teng Cheong, who chose not to run for reelection. The government-backed Nathan was deemed the only eligible candidate, so elections scheduled for August 28 were canceled.

The government worried about the decline in Singapore's birthrate, reflected in 1998 statistics showing that the total fertility rate was 1.5, as opposed to 2.1, the rate necessary to sustain a stable population. The country also struggled with a shortage of native-born talent for its increasingly technology-driven society. Foreign-born corporate executives and research scientists were being recruited to fill key positions, and as many as one third of Singapore's information-technology specialists were foreigners. In addition, the government was concerned that "Singlish"—a mix of English, Malay, and several Chinese dialects—was superseding English as the language of the people. The Ministry of Education initiated remedial training for 8,000 English teachers, contending that the country could not compete globally if it could not be understood.

Economy. Growth in gross domestic product (GDP) was projected to be 5.2% for 1999, compared with only 0.3% in 1998. Inflation was estimated to be about 1.6%, and unemployment about 3.4%, down from 4.1% in 1998. Singapore's per-capita GDP (about $21,000) was the third highest in Asia, behind Hong Kong and Japan. In October exports hit a record-high $9.2 billion. The government committed $5.1 billion of its budget for economic development and offered ten-year tax exemptions for corporations locating their global headquarters on the island. It also launched a skills-redevelopment program to help companies retrain their workers in English, mathematics, and other basic skills.

SINGAPORE • Information Highlights

Official Name: Republic of Singapore.
Location: Southeast Asia.
Area: 250 sq mi (647.5 km²).
Population (July 1999 est.): 3,531,600.
Chief City: Singapore City, the capital.
Government: *Head of state,* S.R. Nathan, president (took office Sept. 1, 1999). *Head of government,* Goh Chok Tong, prime minister (took office November 1990). *Legislature* (unicameral)—Parliament.
Monetary Unit: Singapore dollar (1.6662 S. dollars equal U.S. $1, Dec. 28, 1999).
Gross Domestic Product (1998 est. U.S.$): $91,700,-000,000 (purchasing power parity).
Economic Index (1998, 1990 = 100): *Consumer Prices,* all items, 117.1; food, 114.7.
Foreign Trade (1998 U.S.$): *Imports,* $104,728,000,000; *exports,* $109,905,000,000.

Singapore suffered a blow to its image as a model for economic development, and possibly to its global economic strategy as well, when its Suzhou Industrial Park in southern China earned low profits due to stiff competition from the municipally backed Suzhou New District. In July, Singapore and China agreed to swap their respective stakes in the project, so that Singapore's share would be cut from 65% to 35% by the end of 2000.

Foreign Relations. Singapore's foreign relations were dominated by unresolved issues with Malaysia. An agreement with Malaysia to provide water to Singapore through the 21st century was delayed, owing to more inflammatory issues. In March, for example, Singapore's decision to redevelop the historic Istana Kampong Glam into a Malay cultural-heritage center brought denunciations from the Malaysian press. Singapore's plan was portrayed as an attempt to wipe out all evidence of former Malay rule, as the Istana was the home of Sultan Hussain, the Malay royal who ceded Singapore to the British in 1824.

Singapore maintained good working relations with its largest neighbor, Indonesia, in spite of that country's turmoil. In January, Singapore signed an $8 billion agreement to receive natural gas from an Indonesian company and hinted that a similar pact to receive water from Indonesia in the future might be possible.

PATRICK M. MAYERCHAK
Virginia Military Institute

Slovakia

In 1999, Slovakia's coalition government, headed by Prime Minister Mikulás Dzurinda, continued its efforts to reverse many of the policies of the previous government, led by Vladimir Mečiar. There were tensions over a number of policy issues. However, party leaders were able to overcome these difficulties and maintain the four-party coalition. Rudolf Schuster, the mayor of Košice, became Slovakia's first directly elected president on May 29.

Domestic Affairs. The Dzurinda government took steps to restart stalled economic reforms. In October a plan was approved to deal with banks' bad debts and to privatize three banks. Unemployment continued to increase, reaching 18% in October. Inflation was expected to be at 10%, and the gross domestic product (GDP) was projected to increase by 2%. Direct foreign investment rose.

The National Parliament lifted the immunity of Ivan Lexa, former head of the state security service, allowing him to be tried on charges that he participated in the 1995 abduction of former President Michal Kovač's son. He had become immune from prosecution upon securing a seat in Parliament following the September 1998 election.

In July the Parliament passed a law allowing citizens in areas with at least a 20% minority population to use their own language in official dealings.

Foreign Affairs. In October the European Commission (EC) recognized Slovakia's efforts to meet the European Union's (EU's) admission criteria. The EC's evaluation called for Slovakia to be among the 12 countries with which the EU would conduct accession talks in 2000. The evaluation called for greater efforts to create a well-functioning market economy and to speed up the harmonization of Slovak laws with EU standards. It also called for improvement in the status of the Roma minority. The EU agreed to allocate $5 million in Phare funds for programs to assist Roma. The World Bank agreed to provide a $200 million loan in 2000 to help restructure Slovak industry and banking.

Slovak officials continued to work toward North Atlantic Treaty Organization (NATO) membership as well. The government allowed NATO forces to use Slovak airspace during the Kosovo crisis early in the year, despite protest from the opposition and the disapproval of many citizens. In October, Slovakia's National Program of Preparations for NATO Membership was presented to NATO officials. Slovak leaders, including Prime Minister Dzurinda, reaffirmed Slovakia's interest in NATO membership during visits to the United States and several European capitals.

Slovak relations with the Czech Republic improved. Czech and Slovak leaders reached agreement concerning the final

Rudolf Schuster, above, the mayor of Košice, won Slovakia's first direct election for president in May 1999, beating former Prime Minister Vladimir Mečiar in a runoff.

SLOVAKIA • Information Highlights

Official Name: Slovak Republic.
Location: East-central Europe.
Area: 18,859 sq mi (48 845 km²).
Population (July 1999 est.): 5,396,193.
Chief Cities (Dec. 31, 1997 est.): Bratislava, the capital, 451,395; Košice, 242,170.
Government: *Head of state,* Rudolf Schuster, president (elected May 29, 1999). *Head of government,* Mikulás Dzurinda, prime minister (sworn in October 1998). *Legislature* (unicameral)—National Parliament.
Monetary Unit: Koruna (39.965 koruny equal U.S.$1, Dec. 20, 1999).
Gross Domestic Product (1998 est. U.S.$): $44,500,000,000 (purchasing power parity).
Economic Indexes (1998): *Consumer Prices* (December 1995 = 100): all items, 116.3; food, 113.5. *Industrial Production* (1990 = 100): 86.7.
Foreign Trade (1998 U.S.$): *Imports,* $13,032,000,000; *exports,* $10,667,000,000.

SLOVENIA • Information Highlights

Official Name: Republic of Slovenia.
Location: Southeastern Europe.
Area: 7,821 sq mi (20 256 km^2).
Population (July 1999 est.): 1,970,570.
Chief Cities (Dec. 31, 1994 est.): Ljubljana, the capital, 269,972; Maribor, 103,113.
Government: *Head of state,* Milan Kucan, president (took office April 22, 1990). *Head of government,* Janez Drnovsek, prime minister (took office May 14, 1992). *Legislature* (unicameral)—National Assembly.
Monetary Unit: Tolar (197.235 tolars equal U.S.$1, Dec. 20, 1999).
Gross Domestic Product (1998 est. U.S.$): $20,400,-000,000 (purchasing power parity).
Economic Indexes (1998, 1990 = 100): *Consumer Prices,* all items, 1,547.6; food, 1,499.7. *Industrial Production,* 84.8.
Foreign Trade (1998 U.S. $): *Imports,* $10,110,000,000; *exports,* $9,048,000,000.

aspects of dividing property from their former federation. Slovak-Hungarian relations also brightened, as the result of the new Slovak language law and the resolution of the long-festering disagreement over the Gabčikovo-Nagymaros dam. However, relations with Austria were complicated by differences concerning the timing of the closure of nuclear reactors at Mochovce and Bohunice. In October leaders of the Visegrad Four (the Czech Republic, Poland, Hungary, and Slovakia) met in Slovakia and agreed to cooperate in a wide range of areas.

SHARON WOLCHIK
George Washington University

Slovenia

During 1999, Slovenia maintained a sufficient degree of political stability to keep its reform programs on track and to continue its progress toward membership in the major pan-European institutions.

Political Stability. Slovenia's center-left coalition government in Ljublana remained reasonably united. The two major parties—the Liberal Democratic Party and the People's Party—agreed to changes in the ministries of defense, interior, and economics, following negative press reports about corruption and poor performance.

On the domestic front, the government was preoccupied with economic questions, particularly reforms in the welfare and pension systems. Unlike the situation in Poland or the Czech Republic, however, the authorities faced little public resistance to their reform programs, and the political opposition remained largely fragmented. The next National Assembly elections were scheduled for the fall of 2000.

Economic Performance. The country's economic development remained steady in 1999. The government estimated gross-domestic-product (GDP) growth at about 3.5%, matching the figure for 1998. Some Western analysts, however, put growth at 1.9%. Nonetheless, Slovenia claimed the highest living standard of any former communist state. The inflation rate was projected at about 6.8% for the year, down from 7.9% in 1998. Unemployment, also slightly down, stood at about 13% by mid-1999.

Slovenia made strides in encouraging foreign investment. Provisions of the New Banking Act that went into effect in February allowed foreign banks to open branches in the country, rather than costlier subsidiaries, thus inviting investment and competition. Slovenia was given a favorable foreign-investment risk rating by several international institutions. Nearly 70% of the country's trade was with the European Union (EU).

International Issues. Slovenia supported the North Atlantic Treaty Organization (NATO) in the alliance's air war against Serbia over the province of Kosovo in the spring. In the aftermath of the war, the government endorsed the South East European Stability Pact and Slovenia's participation in this major initiative promoting democracy and economic reconstruction in the Balkans.

The government's primary foreign-policy goal was accession to the EU. Slovenia, an associate member of the EU, remained among the six countries slated for full EU membership between 2002 and 2004. The authorities claimed that about 70% of the national program for adopting EU laws and regulations had been completed by fall 1999. Nonetheless, according to the EU's annual report on candidate countries, Slovenia still needed to improve its economic competitiveness and to bring its legislation fully in line with EU standards.

Slovenia continued to press for NATO membership, although the April 1999 Washington summit made no further commitments to NATO enlargement. The government adopted a Membership Action Plan (MAP) outlining the steps to be taken toward achieving NATO membership. Slovenia was unlikely to receive an official invitation before the next NATO summit but would continue to enhance its participation in NATO's Partnership for Peace (PfP) program.

JANUSZ BUGAJSKI
Center for Strategic and International Studies

Social Welfare

With abundant jobs, low unemployment, and low inflation, the U.S. economy enjoyed a healthy year in 1999. Despite the robust economy, though, millions of American families continued to experience severe economic difficulties.

"Even though this is a blessed time for America, not all Americans have been blessed by it," President Bill Clinton said on July 5 in Hazard, KY, the first stop of a heavily publicized four-day, six-stop tour he took of economically disadvantaged areas of the country. The president went on to visit Clarksdale, MS; East St. Louis, IL; Pine Ridge, SD; a barrio in Phoenix, AZ; and south central Los Angeles. The purpose of his trip was to stimulate private investment as a means of overcoming poverty. The president made a similar-type trip to Newark, NJ, and Hartford, CT, in early November.

The U.S. Poverty Outlook. Economic statistics released during 1999 shed light on the American poverty situation. The annual Census Bureau survey of family income and poverty, released on September 30, reported that some 34.5 million Americans lived below the poverty line in 1998—defined as a total income of $16,655 for a family of four. The national poverty rate was 12.7%, according to the report, compared with 13.3% in 1997.

Some 26.1% of African-Americans—about 9.1 million people—lived below the poverty line in 1998, about the same number as in 1997, a year that marked the lowest African-American poverty percentage since the government began tabulating such data in 1959. Some 8.1 million Hispanic Americans lived below the poverty line in 1998, the survey found. At 25.6%, Hispanic Americans had the highest poverty rate among ethnic groups. The poverty rate for non-Hispanic whites stood at 8.1% (15.8 million people). The survey found that 13.5 million children, just less than 19% of U.S. children, were living in poverty in 1998. That compared with 14.1 million children (or some 19.9%) living in poverty in 1997.

The survey also reported that in 1998 the median household income rose for the fourth consecutive year to a record high of $38,885, a 3.5% increase over 1997. The only group of Americans that experienced statistically significant growth in median income in 1998 compared with 1997, however, was non-Hispanic white Americans, whose household incomes increased 3%, from $41,209 to $42,439.

A report issued on September 4 by the nonprofit Center on Budget and Policy Pri-

Hazard, KY, below, *was President Bill Clinton's first stop during a July 1999, six-stop tour of economically disadvantaged regions of the United States. The president sought to encourage private investment in such areas.*

© J. Scott Applewhite/AP/Wide World Photos

SPECIAL REPORT Defining the Disabled

The U.S. Supreme Court made a series of decisions in 1999 that had a significant impact on the future of the legal rights of the nation's disabled. Some of the most important decisions dealt with the sweeping 1990 Americans with Disabilities Act (ADA). The ADA made it illegal to discriminate against the nation's physically and mentally disabled in the workplace, housing, retail stores, and other public facilities. The law's regulations were promulgated in the mid-1990s and, among other things, mandated employers to take steps to accommodate physically and mentally disabled employees.

U.S. Supreme Court Rulings. In a March 3 decision seen as a victory for disabled children, the Supreme Court, in a 7–2 vote, ruled that public schools must accommodate the needs of the nation's disabled schoolchildren at public expense, provided that the services can be supplied without a doctor. The ruling held that such care was mandated under the 1975 federal Individuals with Disabilities Education Act. In another ruling that was seen as a victory for the disabled, the court, in a 6–3 vote, decided on June 23 that states must allow some mentally disabled persons to be treated in community homes rather than in psychiatric hospitals. The court ruled that confining mentally disabled persons who could benefit from community-home treatment in large state institutions was a violation of the ADA.

Three other Supreme Court rulings on June 23, on the other hand, were viewed as significant curtailments of the ADA. In those cases the court ruled, in separate 7–2 votes, that the law did not apply to disabled persons who were able to function normally when their maladies were corrected with medicine, eyeglasses, or other measures. In what observers called the more far-reaching of the cases, *Sutton v. United Airlines*, the court ruled that correctable extreme nearsightedness was not considered a disability under ADA. Therefore, job applicants with that condition could not claim discrimination under ADA if they were denied employment because of that condition. "It is apparent that if a person

---

orities examined the difference between the incomes of the richest and poorest Americans from 1977 to 1999. The report, based on Congressional Budget Office data, found that the average after-tax income of the richest one fifth of American households increased some 38% in that 22-year period; that the average after-tax income for all middle-income households rose 8%; and that the average income of the poorest fifth of Americans declined 12%. The report used data that included some types of income, such as capital gains, that Census Bureau income data do not use. The report calculated that the average after-tax income of the richest 1% of the population more than doubled in the 22-year span, rising 115% after adjusting for inflation. The richest 2.7 million Americans (the top 1%) had as much after-tax income to spend in 1999 as did the 100 million poorest Americans combined.

One reason the income figures were lower among the lower-income households was the fact that that group is made up of many elderly and retired persons. Social Security benefits, a Center on Budget and Policy Priorities report released in April found, kept about one third of the nation's elderly from falling into poverty. Without Social Security income, some 47.6% of elderly Americans—about 15.3 million people—would have had incomes below the poverty level in 1997, the report said.

Welfare Reform. Aug. 22, 1999, marked the third anniversary of President Clinton's signing into law a far-reaching welfare-reform measure that turned the national welfare program over to the states, thereby ending the federal government's six-decade guarantee of assistance to needy families. That law went into effect on Oct. 1, 1996. It was designed to encourage welfare recipients to find jobs by restricting how long families could receive benefits—most often to two years—and by creating a lifetime five-year limit on benefits.

The federal government reported that in March some 7.3 million Americans were receiving welfare benefits. That compared with some 12.2 million welfare recipients in August 1996, when the sweeping reform law was passed, and to 14.1 million people who were on welfare in January 1993, when President Clinton took office pledging to "end welfare as we know it." Welfare rolls, President Clinton said in an August speech, "have been cut in half. They're at their lowest level in 32 years."

is taking measures to correct for, or mitigate, a physical or mental impairment, the effects of those measures—both positive and negative—must be taken into account when judging whether that person is 'substantially limited' in a major life activity," said Justice Sandra Day O'Connor.

Advocates for the disabled were particularly dismayed with the Sutton ruling; business groups applauded the action. The decision "will send a shock wave through the disability community," said Sen. Tom Harkin (D-IA), a sponsor of the ADA. The ruling "cut the heart out of the ADA," added Chai Feldblum, a Georgetown University law professor who helped write the law. Corporate representatives said the rulings provided much-needed clarity about the types of disabilities covered by the ADA's provisions.

Other Actions. Two other 1999 actions were seen as positive signs for the disabled-rights movement: a July 14 Federal Communications Commission order implementing rules—set up with the help of the communications industry—to make new telecommunications products easier for the disabled to use, and President Bill Clinton's October 16 announcement directing all federal agencies to recruit, hire, promote, and help people with disabilities.

On the other hand, studies by advocates for the disabled in suburban Chicago, Baltimore, Tucson, and Phoenix found that large percentages of apartments and condominiums in those areas built since the ADA went into effect were not in compliance with the regulations. That included requirements that common areas and first-floor units be accessible to those who use wheelchairs. The National Federation for the Blind announced on July 2 that 70% of blind Americans who wanted jobs were unable to find them. The main reasons, the organization said, were job discrimination, a decline in Braille literacy, and computer manufacturers' widespread reliance on software that required users to work with a mouse to click on screen icons. The ADA, a federation spokeswoman said, "seems to have had no impact on this." The National Council on Disability, a federal agency, reported March 30 that the disabled often were mistreated by airline personnel and, in many cases, denied special accommodations such as wheelchairs and escorts in airports.

MARC LEEPSON

The president and others praised the drop in welfare recipients, citing examples of many former recipients who were working in well-paying jobs and who had become economically independent. However, others pointed out that many of those who left welfare still lived in poverty. Large numbers of former female welfare recipients in particular, analysts said, were working in low-paying service jobs. Some of those jobs paid wages so low that workers could not afford to provide adequate food for their families or to pay rent. A study of the impact of the 1996 welfare-reform law released in August by the Urban Institute found that more than 25% of women who left welfare since 1996 work night schedules, and that more than half are struggling with coordinating work schedules and child care. Some two thirds of that group, the study said, do not have health insurance from their employers.

The biggest drops in the welfare rolls were in rural states and suburban areas. Rolls were trimmed significantly, but much less slowly, in the nation's large cities. "The largest American cities are becoming home to a larger and larger share of the nation's welfare recipients," said Bruce Katz, director of the nonprofit Center on Urban and Metropolitan Policy, which completed a two-year study of welfare rolls in June. The study found that the nation's 30 largest cities had 39% of all welfare recipients in 1998, compared with 33% in 1994. The number of welfare recipients in large cities declined 35% from 1994 to 1998, the report found, while nationwide the number declined by 44%. The federal Department of Health and Human Services estimated that 75% of all welfare recipients lived in the nation's inner cities.

Food Stamps. The 1996 welfare-reform law also ended eligibility for food stamps for most legal immigrants who were not U.S. citizens and restricted childless adults aged 18 to 50 to three months of food stamps over three years. The result was a large drop in the number of Americans receiving food stamps. Some 18 million Americans received food stamps in April 1999, according to U.S. Department of Agriculture statistics. That compared with an average of more than 25 million Americans who had received food stamps in 1996.

Government statistics showed that more than 90% of the households that received food stamps had gross incomes at or below the poverty line; some 40% of the food-stamp families had incomes below half the poverty line. More than 60% of food-stamp benefits went to households with children. More than half of the food-stamp recipients were children aged 17 and under; about one third were under age 5. Some 20% of food-stamp households contained at least one disabled person. About 2 million senior citizens received food stamps.

Secretary of Agriculture Dan Glickman, whose department's Food and Nutrition Service administers the food-stamp program, said the decreasing number of recipients "was first thought to be a major success story." However, Glickman said in an April 6 speech, "food stamp rolls were declining at five times the rate of poverty, which meant that there were many eligible people out there, including children, needlessly going without food." Evidence of that fact, Glickman said, included a "dramatic rise in people seeking help from food pantries and other voluntary feeding efforts around the country." That situation was confirmed by officials at Second Harvest, a nationwide nonprofit group that oversees the distribution of some $1 billion worth of donated food annually to some 26 million Americans through soup kitchens and food pantries. Because of greater demand for their services, Second Harvest officials said, many soup kitchens and food banks around the nation were forced to cut hours, ration some items, and—in some cases—turn people away.

Other federal food programs continued to provide assistance to millions of Americans. The Special Supplemental Nutrition Program for Women, Infants and Children (WIC), for example, provided supplemental foods, nutrition education, and health-care referrals to low-income, pregnant, postpartum, and breast-feeding women, and to nutritionally at-risk infants and children up to age 5. The number of WIC participants was 7.3 million in 1999, compared with 5.9 million in 1993. That increase, Agriculture Secretary Glickman said, showed that "there are still people who need the help that the federal food safety net provides."

International Social Conditions. The scope of social problems in the United States was dwarfed once again in 1999 by the severe poverty, malnutrition, and social dislocation faced by hundreds of millions of people in developing countries around the world. In many of those areas, social conditions worsened in recent years, according to a report on worldwide poverty issued by the World Bank in June.

That report predicted that if present trends continued, some 1.5 billion people worldwide would be living on less than $1 a day at the end of 1999. That compared with 1.2 billion people living at that level in 1987 and 1.3 billion in 1993. The financial crisis in Asia, the bank reported, had a significant impact on a surge in poverty in the late 1990s in East Asia and in other areas. "The financial turmoil of the last two years has dealt a blow to the expectations we had for reducing poverty," said James D. Wolfenson, the bank's president. "Today, countries that until recently believed they were turning the tide in the fight against poverty are witnessing its reemergence along with hunger and the human suffering it brings."

The report said that the East Asian nations of Indonesia, Malaysia, and Thailand experienced "significant" increases in poverty, and that recent progress in the fight against poverty in the Philippines was "likely to slow but not reverse itself." Poverty remained widespread in India—where an estimated 340 million people were living in poverty—in flood-ravaged Bangladesh, and in Pakistan. The situation in Africa was termed "worrisome" because of deteriorating economic conditions throughout the continent, which were exacerbated by continuing civil and tribal wars and political upheaval in several countries.

Natural disasters, including several hurricanes, caused severe social dislocation in Latin America and the Caribbean in 1999. The World Bank report predicted "sharp declines in growth and increase in poverty" in Russia, Ukraine, and Romania, and an increase in the poverty rate in the Middle East and North Africa.

In 1999 the people of North Korea continued to face one of the world's worst social crises, brought about by severe food shortages caused by a drought and the policies of that nation's isolated, repressive government. However, fears of a full-scale famine in North Korea eased, following a sharp increase in international food aid. The effort was led by the United Nations World Food Program (WFP), which had six offices in North Korea distributing food to some 8 million people, most of them children. About 80% of the food the agency distributed consisted of wheat donated by the United States. North Korea also received substantial food aid from the governments of China and South Korea and from private aid groups, such as the Red Cross.

MARC LEEPSON, *Freelance Writer*

South Africa

The single most significant event in South Africa in 1999 was the smooth transfer of political power from the country's first democratically elected president, Nelson R. Mandela, to its second, Thabo Mbeki (*see* BIOGRAPHY). The country's second multiracial election was considered to be free and fair by all observers. President Mbeki's first cabinet had few surprises, and his reappointment of key ministers inspired confidence from the business sector.

Politics. In opening the South African Parliament on February 5, President Mandela made his last state-of-the-nation address. He listed many of the achievements of the government since 1994, including the delivery of running water, electricity, and telephones to millions of black South Africans. At the same time, he was remarkably candid about the problems facing the country, such as corruption, violent crime, and widespread unemployment. While opposition leaders paid tribute to the 80-year-old Mandela, they also criticized the speech because it did not present concrete measures for job creation or propose policies to deal with the country's crime problem.

On June 2, 41 registered political parties participated in South Africa's second multiracial election. Eight of them—the African National Congress (ANC), the African Christian Democratic Party (ACDP), the Democratic Party (DP), the Freedom Front (FF), the Inkatha Freedom Party (IFP), the New National Party (NNP), the Pan African Congress (PAC), and the United Democratic Movement (UDM)—were considered to be the primary contenders. Nearly 16 million of the 18 million eligible voters went to the polls. With 65% of the vote, the ANC won 266 seats in Parliament, an improvement over the 252 it won in 1994 but one shy of the two-thirds majority it had hoped to achieve. During the campaign, opposition parties had emphasized that a two-thirds majority for the ANC would be dangerous and could lead to abuse of power, because it would give the ruling party enough votes to amend the constitution over all objections. Mbeki responded that the ANC had no intention of amending the constitution.

Ultimately, the ANC succeeded in creating a two-thirds majority by entering into a coalition with the Minority Front, which had obtained one seat in the national election. The DP won 38 seats, becoming the official opposition in Parliament. The IFP took 34 seats, and the NNP (the former National Party, which had ruled South Africa until 1994) had 28. The DP, led by Tony Leon,

South Africa's President Nelson Mandela (left) *and Deputy President Thabo Mbeki* (right) *joined together to launch the African National Congress' (ANC's) 1999 electoral campaign. As a result of national voting in June, Mbeki, 56, succeeded Mandela as the nation's president.*

SOUTH AFRICA • Information Highlights

Official Name: Republic of South Africa.
Location: Southern tip of Africa.
Area: 471,008 sq mi (1 219 912 km²).
Population (July 1999 est.): 43,426,386.
Chief Cities (1991 census, city proper): Pretoria, the administrative capital, 525,583; Cape Town, the legislative capital, 854,616; Durban, 715,669; Johannesburg, 712,507.
Government: *Head of state and government,* Thabo Mbeki, president (took office June 16, 1999). *Legislature*—Parliament: National Assembly and National Council of Provinces.
Monetary Unit: Rand (6.1253 rands equal U.S.$1, Jan. 3, 2000).
Gross Domestic Product (1998 est. U.S.$): $290,600,000,000 (purchasing power parity).
Economic Indexes (1998, 1990 = 100): *Consumer Prices,* all items, 212.6; food, 244.2. *Industrial Production,* 104.7.
Foreign Trade (1998 U.S.$): *Imports,* $28,277,000,000; *exports,* excluding exports of gold, $25,396,000,000.

appealed primarily to white voters, many of whom had shifted from the NNP, which they felt had become ineffective. The DP's backers believed Leon would present a more aggressive opposition to the ANC than the NNP had done. The UDM, a new party led by Gen. Bantu Holomisa, who had been expelled from the ANC in 1996 because he accused it of corruption, won 14 seats.

Responding to the election results, Mbeki maintained, "In a very clear voice the people have said that democracy is alive and well in South Africa. The people of South Africa have entrusted us not only with their emancipation, but also with improving the safety and security of everyone." Some saw the landslide victory as a clear indication of the confidence and support of the majority of black South Africans for the ANC. The results also indicated that both right-wing white parties and more-radical black parties were unappealing to the electorate. The Pan Africanist Congress, the Azanian People's Organization, and the Socialist Party of Azania—as well as two separatist white parties, the Freedom Front and the Eenheidsbeweging—received less than 2% of the vote.

The ANC won all of the nine provincial elections except for KwaZulu/Natal province, a stronghold of the IFP, and Western Cape province. In the latter, it earned a majority of the vote but was not able to take power because the NNP, the DP, and the ACDP formed a coalition to govern the province. The coalition had offered the ANC one of its 12 cabinet posts, but the ANC refused. The ANC was angered by the outcome because it believed it should have been able to form the government of Western Cape province, since it received a majority of the popular vote.

Mbeki was sworn in as South Africa's second president on June 16 at a ceremony in Pretoria. The inauguration was attended by more than 30 foreign leaders and representatives from 130 countries, as well as thousands of South Africans. As soon as Mbeki finished taking the oath of office, Mandela stood up and escorted the new president to the Presidential Chair, where Mandela had been sitting. The 56-year-old Mbeki, who had been educated as an economist in Britain, had served as deputy president and was Nelson Mandela's designated heir. Indeed, for the past few years many believed he essentially had been running the country on a day-to-day basis. Mbeki's inaugural speech and his cabinet appointees indicated continuity rather than a sharp break with the past, although it generally was thought that the party would intensify its efforts to address African aspirations and needs over the next five years.

President Mbeki expanded the cabinet from 24 to 27 members. He left key economic ministries unchanged, with Trevor Manuel continuing in the ministry of finance and Alex Erwin in the ministry of trade and industry. The reappointments of Manuel and Erwin immediately received strong approval from the business sector. Jacob Zuma was appointed deputy president, although it had been thought that Chief Mangosuthu Buthelezi of the IFP might be chosen for that position. Buthelezi retained the key ministry of home affairs, which put him second in line for the presidency after Zuma. Two other IFP members were given cabinet appointments as well, in a clear effort by Mbeki to keep the party within the government so as to avoid bloody clashes in the deeply divided KwaZulu/Natal province. Nkosazana Zuma, formerly minister of health, was appointed foreign minister, and Steve Tshwete was made minister of safety and security, with the responsibility to deal with the country's rampant crime and corruption problems. Overall, the new cabinet reflected a balance between political considerations, such as the IFP alliance, and the need for strong leaders to tackle the issues of unemployment, corruption, the economy, foreign investment, and violent crime.

In the new Parliament, the ANC made a conscious effort to marginalize the DP by excluding it from positions on key committees. In the previous Parliament, five opposition-party members had chaired committees, but in the new one, the IFP (which really was not considered to be in opposition) was the only other party given committee chairmanships. Since parliamentary-committee leaders are selected by the ruling party, all the DP could do was express its anger and dismay at the process.

In October new legislation was introduced to address illegal discrimination beyond race, sex, religion, and physical disability. The proposed Promotion of Equality and Prevention of Unfair Discrimination Bill would outlaw discrimination on many additional grounds, such as education, socioeconomic background, and marital status. Denial of insurance or a loan based on unemployment, for example, would be considered discrimination. As part of the bill, new "Equality Courts" would review cases, award damages, and settle disputes. Organizations and businesses might have their licenses revoked if they had unacceptable antidiscrimination records. The DP strongly opposed the bill, which would become law in February if ratified by Parliament.

In November, President Mbeki announced that the South African government would not approve the anti-AIDS drug zidovudine (better known as AZT) for pregnant women, because it was toxic. The decision was a departure from the government's previous policy, which tried to find ways to reduce the cost of AZT but never condemned it based on its toxicity. The move surprised many medical specialists because of research showing that AZT could cut the transmission of HIV, the virus that causes AIDS, from mother to child by as much as 50%. Mbeki's position was said to be in part the result of a dispute with the manufacturer of AZT, Glaxo Wellcome, over the high cost of the drug. The government also was backing the manufacture of Virodene, a locally produced anti-AIDS drug, which was considered ineffective by many medical experts. Some argued that Mbeki was trying to find an African, rather than a Western, solution to the continent's major medical epidemic.

Economy. Two major credit-rating agencies, Duff and Phelps Credit and Moody's Investor Service, gave the South African economy a high rating. While there was concern with the continuing high unemployment and inequality of living standards, they found the smooth transition from Mandela to Mbeki to be positive and reassuring, and they anticipated that South Africa's policy of gradual fiscal consolidation and low inflation would remain in place. Duff and Phelps said that it expected the 1999–2000 budget deficit to be contained to 2.8% of gross domestic product (GDP), down from initial projections of 3.5%. Inflation was projected to fall in 1999 to approximately 5% and could decline further in 2000, to approximately 3.5%. Both agencies were concerned about the very high unemployment rate of 33% (due in part to limited labor reforms and the slow pace of privatization), but felt that an increase in foreign investment could lead to higher growth and savings rates.

For 1999, GDP was expected to increase by only 1.2%. Cumbersome labor regulations approved in 1999 were unlikely to improve the situation of the labor market and could damage opportunities for employment. A further threat to South African employment was Britain's decision to sell half of its gold reserves in a series of auctions during 1999 and 2000. The sales threatened to close some of South Africa's gold mines.

Cape Town Bombing. In November a bomb exploded in a pizzeria in Camps Bay, a suburb of Cape Town, injuring 48 persons. Safety and Security Minister Tshwete indicated that the blast was part of an unsuccessful effort to disrupt a major international meeting, the Parliament of the World's Religions, which brought 600 delegates and religious leaders—such as the Dalai Lama—to Cape Town on December 1–8. There was speculation that People Against Gangsterism and Drugs (PAGAD), a militant Islamic vigilante group based in Cape Town, might have been responsible for the attack. PAGAD had been linked to a series of similar incidents in and around Cape Town, including the bombing of a Planet Hollywood restaurant in August 1998 and explosions at several police stations. Key police officials investigating PAGAD were said to have been killed by the organization, and in February a former key investigator was shot and wounded by an unknown assailant. In his February opening address to Parliament, then-President Mandela condemned the bombings and shootings.

Commonwealth Meeting. On November 12, Queen Elizabeth II of Britain, accompanied by Prince Philip, arrived in South Africa to open the Commonwealth Heads of Government meeting. Delegates from the 54 member countries assembled in Durban for the meeting, hosted by President Mbeki. The four-day summit marked the 50th anniversary of the Commonwealth, whose total population of 1.7 billion people generated more than 25% of world trade.

PATRICK O'MEARA and N. BRIAN WINCHESTER
Indiana University

Space Exploration

Space exploration in 1999 was marked more by mishaps, technical snags, and outright failures than by major successes. The exploration of Mars suffered a setback when two U.S. spacecraft were lost as they entered the Martian atmosphere. A string of U.S. launch failures occurred in the Delta, Titan, and Athena boosters—the greatest number of booster failures within a single year in more than a decade. Russia's Proton booster, Japan's H2 launcher, and Brazil's VLS rocket also experienced launch failures.

The year did encompass several bright spots, however, such as the deployment of the Chandra X-ray Observatory by the National Aeronautics and Space Administration (NASA) and the orbiting of the European Space Agency's (ESA's) X-ray Multimirror Mission (XMM). Europe's Ariane booster chalked up ten out of ten flights, including the orbiting of the largest commercial telecommunications satellite ever launched. And at the end of 1999, China launched and recovered an unpiloted test craft, signaling that nation's expected entry into the human-spaceflight arena, perhaps as early as 2000.

Human Spaceflight. NASA's entire shuttle fleet was grounded for one quarter of the year, so that wiring problems in all four space planes could be fixed. As a result, the agency conducted only three space-shuttle missions in 1999, instead of the six that were planned.

In May the *Discovery* shuttle rendezvoused with the existing components of the International Space Station (ISS), a complex of modules and hardware to be assembled over the next several years. This mission was the first shuttle docking to the ISS. Astronauts delivered more than 3,600 lb (1 633 kg) of supplies to the linked Russian Zarya and U.S. Unity modules. During the mission, a small free-flying sphere named Starshine, coated with 878 tiny mirrors, was ejected from *Discovery* into space. Starshine would be tracked by some 25,000 students worldwide.

After a delay of several months, *Columbia*—with a crew led by U.S. Air Force Col. Eileen Collins (*see* BIOGRAPHY), the first woman to command a shuttle mission—roared skyward in July. On the five-day flight, the $1.6 billion Chandra X-ray Observatory, the latest device from NASA's "Great Observatories" program, was deployed. After initial checkout, Chandra began its work of capturing images in the universe, including one of the Crab Nebula that revealed a never-before-seen ring around the nebula's heart.

© NASA

NASA's Chandra X-ray Observatory, above, *a high-tech device designed to photograph objects in space that ordinary telescopes cannot detect, was sent into orbit in 1999.*

In December, after a record nine launch delays, the *Discovery* shuttle set out on a service call to the Hubble Space Telescope, which had stopped operations in November due to failing gyroscopes. Over the eight-day flight, the astronauts outfitted the $3 billion Hubble with $70 million worth of new equipment and replaced all six of its gyroscopes. It was the Hubble's third in-space tune-up.

Russia's *Mir* space station was abandoned by its crew in late August. The cash-strapped Russian Aviation and Space Agency had insufficient funds to maintain the aging outpost, now more than 13 years old. The possibility of using private investment to save the facility were under way in late 1999, and Energia, *Mir*'s operating agency, hoped to launch another crew in early 2000. If the necessary financial support were not found, however, *Mir* would be deorbited in 2000.

Russia's financial woes also confounded its work on the ISS, a key element of which was the Russian-built Zvezda service module, capable of housing station personnel. A Russian Proton launcher, similar to the one set to launch Zvezda, suffered a failure October 27. In late 1999 the Zvezda liftoff seemed likely to be postponed until at least March 2000.

On November 19, China sent the Shenzhou unpiloted capsule into space using its Long March 2F rocket from Jiquan, its launch center. Returning to Earth after orbiting 21 hours, the recovered capsule was considered a forerunner to a piloted space vehicle. Plans called for the same model capsule to carry one or more taikongauts (*tai kong* means "cosmos" in Chinese) into orbit, perhaps in 2000.

Applications Satellites. The remote sensing satellite Ikonos 2, owned by Space Imaging of Denver, CO, was launched on September 24 atop an Athena 2 booster. The private firm began marketing 1-m-resolution imagery from the Ikonos to commercial customers. On April 27 the company lost its first Ikonos satellite when the Athena 2's payload fairing failed to separate, tossing the satellite into the South Pacific Ocean.

Placed into Earth orbit via a Delta 2 rocket on April 15, the $666 million U.S. Landsat 7 began its imaging of Earth's land and coastal areas. The satellite was able to map the planet in 15-m or 30-m resolution. Landsat 7 will be used for such functions as charting population densities of cities and forecasting agricultural crop yields.

On June 20 the U.S. Quick Scatterometer (QuikSCAT) was launched by a Titan 2 rocket from Vandenberg Air Force Base in California. This $71 million oceanographic satellite was designed, built, and flown very quickly after Japan's Adeos spacecraft failed in orbit in June 1997. QuikSCAT carried a similar microwave scatterometer designed to measure ocean winds and directions by monitoring wind-induced ripples near the ocean surface. The satellite would explore how winds distribute heat absorbed by Earth and how that heat travels through ocean movements.

NASA's Terra satellite, the flagship in a new series of satellites for the U.S. Global Change Research Program, rode into orbit on an Atlas IIAS rocket on December 18. Despite initial computer and antenna problems, the $1.3 billion Terra was headed for full operation in early 2000. Scientists planned to use the spacecraft, equipped with five state-of-the-art instruments, to collect data and study the interaction among the oceans, lands, atmosphere, and biosphere of Earth.

The Okean-O Russian-Ukrainian remote sensing satellite—which monitors ocean

In December 1999 the shuttle "Discovery" was dispatched on a repair mission to the Hubble Space Telescope, left, *which had stopped functioning a few weeks earlier due to a mechanical breakdown. Over several days, the shuttle crew installed $70 million worth of new equipment, restoring the telescope to working order. This was the third time the trouble-prone device had required in-space adjustments since its launch in 1990.*

salinity, waves, and ice conditions—was launched by a Zenit 2 booster on July 17. A Resurs F-1M Russian satellite, loaded with cameras to capture images of natural resources on Russian territory, was launched September 28. After a three-week mission, the Resurs spacecraft parachuted to Earth on October 22. On May 26 a Polar Satellite Launch Vehicle (PSLV-C2) rocket orbited India's IRS-P4, a remote sensing satellite with instruments to scan potential fishery locales, ocean currents, and pollution and sediment inputs in coastal zones. The rocket also carried India's first foreign satellites: the German remote sensing microsatellite Tubsat and a South Korean remote sensing minisatellite called Kitsat 3.

Getting a boost from China's Long March 4B rocket on October 14 was the China-Brazil Earth Resources Satellite (CBERS-1). Toting three high-resolution cameras, CBERS-1 was built for monitoring environmental and vegetation conditions in China, Brazil, and other countries. On December 21 a Taurus rocket shot into space NASA's Active Cavity Radiometer Irradiance Monitor satellite (ACRIMSAT). During its five-year mission, the spacecraft would measure the amount of sunlight reaching Earth. Also on board the Taurus was the Korea Multi-Purpose Satellite (KOMPSAT) from South Korea, which would create digital elevation maps of the country.

Communications Satellites. Several telecommunications-satellite companies met severe financial obstacles in 1999 that pushed them into bankruptcy. Iridium LLC, a U.S. firm operating a 66-satellite network, filed for Chapter 11 bankruptcy in August, after the high prices for its service kept it from building a profitable customer base. The London-based ICO Global Communications Ltd. sought Chapter 11 bankruptcy protection soon afterward. Both companies were looking for new business models in an attempt to sustain their operations. Meanwhile, the industry as a whole wrestled with tightened export-control laws invoked by the U.S. State Department and the U.S. Congress because of heightened worry over the transfer of U.S. technology to other nations, particularly China.

Globalstar, another low-altitude-satellite system, continued to put its 48-satellite fleet in place during the year. More than three quarters of the constellation were launched in 1999. Space Systems/Loral of Palo Alto, CA, the company financing the system's installation, began offering first-phase Globalstar service in October.

France-based Arianespace had a successful run of ten flights, despite a four-month hiatus caused by delays in assembly of satellites by its customers. Twice during the year, the private company was able to make deals with customers requiring only three months from signing to actual launch.

Other successful deployments included those of Hong Kong's AsiaSat 3S using a Russian Proton K rocket on March 21; ASTRA 1H for the SES consortium in Luxembourg on June 18; a U.S. DirecTV 1-R satellite on October 10 (the first commercial launch by the Sea Launch consortium owned by U.S., Russian, and Ukrainian companies); and the LMI-1 (Lockheed-Martin Intersputnik), a U.S.-Russian geosynchronous satellite, on September 26. But the launch of a South Korean Orion 3 satellite went awry on May 5, when its U.S. Delta 3 rocket's upper stage failed to sustain thrust, placing the satellite into a useless orbit.

Space Science. NASA's Mars Polar Lander, launched on January 3, featured equipment to collect information on the terrain of Mars and to look for subsurface water. The mission promised to open a new chapter in exploration of the Red Planet. But that hope was dashed by the Polar Lander's mysterious disappearance. On December 3 scientists lost contact with the $165 million spacecraft as it was preparing to land at the south pole of Mars. The final whereabouts of the spacecraft and the reason for its disappearance remained unknown in late 1999. Just a few months earlier, NASA had experienced a similar failure with its Mars Climate Orbiter. The $125 million vehicle, launched in late 1998 to gather data on the atmosphere and weather conditions of Mars, was destroyed on September 23 upon entry into the Martian atmosphere. The mishap occurred because the craft had been programmed into a much lower trajectory than intended, due to a failure to convert British units of measure into metric units.

These setbacks were offset somewhat by the continuing success of the Mars Global Surveyor, which relayed detailed images of Mars throughout the year, including the first three-dimensional map of the planet. The map delineated an impact basin deep enough to swallow Mount Everest and surprising slopes in Valles Marineris, a huge canyon system.

On February 7 the U.S. Stardust mission headed for a rendezvous in 2004 with the

© NASA/JPL/AP/Wide World Photos

NASA's Mars Polar Lander, illustrated at left, *vanished without a trace after it entered the Martian atmosphere in December 1999. That mishap, coupled with the failure a few months earlier of a similar probe, the Mars Climate Orbiter, forced the space agency to reassess its entire Mars exploration program.*

comet Wild 2. The spacecraft carried special traps to snag interstellar- and cometary-dust samples to be returned to Earth in 2006 for chemical and isotopic analysis.

The Wide-field InfraRed Explorer (WIRE), a U.S. research spacecraft, was launched on March 5. Shortly after reaching orbit, however, WIRE's telescope cover opened prematurely, exposing the instrument to direct sunlight. Solid hydrogen surrounding the infrared detectors boiled away, and the payload became inoperable, allowing the device to perform only a limited amount of research. Another mission gone wrong was the Tomographic Experiment, using Radiative Recombinative Ionospheric EUV and Radio Sources (TERRIERS), which was sent into space May 18. The spacecraft was to profile Earth's ionosphere, but efforts to orient the solar panels failed, and contact was lost with TERRIERS after its battery discharged.

On June 24 a Delta 2 rocket hurled the Far Ultraviolet Spectroscopic Explorer (FUSE) into space. FUSE was designed to study intergalactic and interstellar clouds, which, presumably, carry deuterium undepleted by the voracious consumption of stellar cores. Assessing deuterium and hydrogen ratios may help approximate the status of the universe shortly after the Big Bang.

After completing its mission, NASA's Lunar Prospector was sent on a controlled crash into the Moon's southern pole on July 31. Scientists hoped that the impact would kick up a sample of water ice believed to be deposited there, but none was detected. The Galileo spacecraft, which has been circling Jupiter since December 1995, took several photographs of the planet's volcano-laden moon, Io, on close flybys in October and November. The spacecraft continued to operate despite being exposed to high amounts of radiation.

NASA's Deep Space One (DS1) continued on its trek, testing a set of various high-tech devices, including an ion-propulsion engine. Due to a control problem, DS1 failed in July to capture an image of an asteroid at close range. In November the probe went into safe mode due to a star-tracker failure. Scientists hoped to regain control of DS1 to carry out a close encounter with two comets, Wilson-Harrington and Borrelly, scheduled to occur in 2001.

The ESA's X-ray Multimirror Mission (XMM) telescope was delivered into space on December 10 by the powerful Ariane 5 booster. The $710 million observatory, the biggest spacecraft built in Western Europe, uses huge mirrors to scan X rays churned out by remote stars, allowing scientists to chart the edges of black holes and measure extreme sources of heat and energy.

LEONARD DAVID
Space Data Resources & Information

Spain

During 1999, Spanish Prime Minister José María Aznar witnessed his Popular Party (PP) lose ground in elections for the European Parliament, as well as in a regional election in Catalonia. These reverses set the stage for a hard-fought battle over elections to the nation's Chamber of Deputies (Cortés) in early 2000, even as the nation's economy continued to improve. Meanwhile, Chile and Spain continued to feud over Madrid's efforts to try former Chilean dictator Augusto Pinochet on charges of human-rights abuses.

Politics. Although conservative politicians did well in most of Europe in June's elections for the European Parliament, the Spanish Workers Socialist Party (PSOE) gained in the vote tally by more than 5% and went from 22 to 24 seats. Meanwhile, the PP lost a seat. The results of the mid-October election for Catalonia's regional parliament also dismayed Aznar and the PP. His parliamentary ally, Jordi Pujol, managed to eke out an unprecedented sixth consecutive term as president of the region, but the Socialists actually won more total votes than the PP and gained 18 seats. The PSOE's surge indicated that the PP would have to rally its forces in the March national election to maintain its working majority in the 350-member Cortés.

As part of its strategy to wrest power from the PP, the PSOE replaced José Borrell, who resigned as leader in May, with party secretary-general Joaquín Almunia. Borrell stated that he was stepping down because the allegations of corruption that swirled around several of his subordinates when he was a cabinet minister could hurt Socialist candidates in the national election.

Both the PP and the PSOE worried about the potential political threat posed by Jesús Gil, the populist right-wing mayor of the upscale Andalusian resort of Marbella and founder of the upstart Independent Liberal Group (known by the Spanish acronym GIL). Aznar in particular was concerned that the GIL could siphon votes from the PP in the upcoming national elections. In January, Gil was arrested and charged with illegally diverting Marbella city-council funds to the soccer team he owned in Madrid; both the PP and the PSOE hoped that the investigation would curb Gil's political aspirations. Gil was

© Arnaberri/AP/Wide World Photos

A young boy plays in front of ETA graffiti in a Basque town in Spain. In June 1999, Spain's Prime Minister José María Aznar confirmed that representatives of his government had conferred with members of the ETA (the main Basque separatist group) for the first time since the ETA had called a cease-fire in September 1998.

jailed briefly on the charge, but he posted bail and steered the GIL to victory in elections in Ceuta and Melilla, Spanish enclaves on Morocco's north coast. Politicians in Madrid were concerned that those successes signaled that Spain was losing its hold on the North African outposts, annexed in 1497.

Economy. In November the government predicted that Spain's economy would grow by 3.7% in both 1999 and 2000 (down from 4% in 1998), with the service and manufacturing sectors recording the most improvement. Meanwhile, inflation climbed to 2.4% and the public deficit in relation to gross domestic product (GDP) fell from 1.8% to 1.4%—with 0.8% forecast for 2000. This financial probity sprang in part from Spain's January entry into the European Union's (EU's) Economic and Monetary Union (EMU), which buoyed the confidence of the nation's business leaders. The Aznar government also enjoyed a relatively peaceful relationship with Spain's often-rambunctious trade unions.

The unemployment rate fell to 15.9%, a 2.2% drop from 1998 but still above the EU average. Aznar's efforts to move people off the unemployment rolls were hampered by Spain's still-generous benefits, as well as by a new "guest worker" program, in which up to 1 million people from Africa, Latin America, and Eastern Europe will enter the country over the next three years to work nine-month stints in construction and agriculture. The initiative came in response to complaints from business executives that Spanish workers refused to take the low-salaried jobs in these industries.

Aznar announced that his government would launch a 5.8% increase in investment in research and infrastructure, to attain at least 3.5% growth in 2000. He also reported that he would eliminate the $1.4 billion deficit afflicting the social-security fund by raising taxes rather than by increasing contributions.

Foreign Policy. The Aznar administration endorsed the North Atlantic Treaty Organization (NATO) bombing of Serbia, although it supplied only a tiny fraction of the aircraft involved in the operation. Spain's Javier Solana, NATO secretary-general during the attacks on the Slobodan Milosevic regime, played a key role in maintaining unity within the alliance. Solana's subsequent appointment as the EU's military and foreign-policy czar opened up the possibility that he would work with his successor at NATO, Britain's George Robertson, in devising a European "defense identity" that would preserve the organization's transatlantic character.

SPAIN • Information Highlights

Official Name: Kingdom of Spain.
Location: Iberian Peninsula in southwestern Europe.
Area: 194,884 sq mi (504 750 km²).
Population (July 1999 est.): 39,167,744.
Chief Cities (May 1, 1996 est., metropolitan areas): Madrid, the capital, 2,866,850; Barcelona, 1,508,805; Valencia, 746,683; Zaragoza, 601,674; Málaga, 549,135.
Government: *Head of state,* Juan Carlos I, king (took office Nov. 1975). *Head of government,* José María Aznar, prime minister (took office May 5, 1996). *Legislature*—Cortés Generales: Senate and Chamber of Deputies.
Monetary Unit: Peseta (162.9239 pesetas equal U.S.$1, Dec. 9, 1999).
Gross Domestic Product (1998 est. U.S.$): $645,600,000,000 (purchasing power parity).
Economic Indexes (1998, 1990 = 100): *Consumer Prices,* all items, 138.3; food, 127.9. *Industrial Production,* 115.1.
Foreign Trade (1998 U.S.$): *Imports,* $133,153,000,000; *exports,* $109,231,000,000.

The ultimate fate of former Chilean dictator Pinochet remained a bone of contention between Spain and Chile during 1999. In July, Chile appealed to Spain have an international arbitration panel decide who had thc jurisdiction to prosecute Pinochet. The Spanish government refused, saying it could not interfere with extradition proceedings that were under way in Britain. In October, Chile asked the British courts to release the ailing Pinochet on humanitarian grounds, and Spanish Foreign Minister Abel Matutes responded that, should the court decide to grant that request, Spain would not appeal. (*See also* CHILE.)

Left unspoken was the Aznar government's concern that Pinochet's standing trial in Spain could impede the financial dealings of Spanish businesses in Chile and other Latin American countries. In September, Elena Pisonero, Spain's secretary for trade and tourism, said at an international conference in Santiago that "no [bilateral] economic deals [had] been aborted" because of Pinochet's arrest. Nevertheless, Aznar worked hard to curry favor in the Western Hemisphere. In July he visited Caracas, where he gave a vote of confidence (and $805 million in aid) to Venezuela's populist President Hugo Chávez. The Spanish leader also promoted Spanish commerce in Ecuador and the Caribbean.

At the November Ibero-American Summit in Havana, King Juan Carlos called for "authentic democracy" and "scrupulous respect" for human rights—a clear condemnation of Cuba's authoritarian regime.

GEORGE W. GRAYSON
College of William & Mary

Sports

Overview

For the major U.S. sports, 1999 began and ended with repeats. In January the Denver Broncos under quarterback John Elway won their second straight National Football League (NFL) championship, beating the Atlanta Falcons, 34–19, in Super Bowl XXXIII. Nine months later the New York Yankees repeated as baseball champions, sweeping the Atlanta Braves in four games to win a record 25th World Series.

Headline Winners. Due to a labor dispute between players and owners, the 1998–99 men's pro-basketball season did not start until February. The National Basketball Association (NBA) championship was taken by the San Antonio Spurs, who defeated a plucky but injury-ridden New York Knicks team in five games. The Houston Comets won the Women's NBA title, their third straight, by beating the New York Liberty.

In the hockey play-off finals, the Dallas Stars squeaked past the Buffalo Sabres on a controversial goal in the third overtime of the sixth game to give the Stanley Cup a new home down south. Tennis star Andre Agassi (*see also* BIOGRAPHY), rated only 141st in 1997, had a wonderful year, reaching the finals at Wimbledon, winning the French and U.S. Opens, and in September gaining the world Number 1 ranking. After playing two hours of scoreless soccer before a crowd of 90,185 at the Rose Bowl, the U.S. women's team won the Women's World Cup, beating China, 5–4, in an exciting penalty-kick shootout.

Good-byes. The year saw a surprising number of retirements of big stars. Michael Jordan, by all estimates the best player in basketball history, stepped down in January. He had led the Chicago Bulls to six championships in eight years and set a bushel basket's worth of records. In April, hockey's greatest player retired. Wayne Gretzky, nicknamed the "Great One," had starred on four Stanley Cup–winning teams and set or tied records in 61 different categories during a 21-year pro career. A few weeks later, Denver's signal caller, John Elway, announced that he was "graduating from pro football." Elway spent 16 years with the Broncos, winning the most games in NFL history. He had suffered Super Bowl losses in 1987, 1988, and 1990 before going out a two-time champion.

Tennis' Steffi Graf ended her career in August. She won a Grand Slam in 1988 and a total of seven Wimbledon singles titles, six French Opens, five U.S. Opens, and four

© Barry Gossager/NBA Photos

Michael Jordan

Australian Opens. She spent more time ranked Number 1 in the world—377 weeks—than any other player, man or woman; and she earned nearly $22 million in prize money, more than any other woman athlete in any sport.

Wrestling and Roller Derby. Professional wrestling, always controversial, became even more so with the death of Owen Hart in the spring. Hart, performing for the World Wrestling Federation (WWF) as a becaped, bemasked character called the Blue Blazer, fell 90 ft (27 m) to the ring in front of 16,300 fans when a cable that was to lower him from a catwalk accidentally released. In spite of Hart's death, the WWF refused to cancel the rest of the matches that night and, after holding a tribute to Hart the next night, seemed to act as if the whole thing never had happened.

What many call wrestling on wheels—roller derby, which was very popular in the 1950s—made a surprising comeback early in 1999, with RollerJam, a six-team league sponsored by cable-television station TNN. Each team has male and female squads. All the matches initially were held on a TV sound stage in Florida. Other roller-derby ventures began to spring up as the year developed.

Pan-American Games. At the Pan-American Games, held during the summer in the Canadian city of Winnipeg, Cuba beat the United States to win the baseball title, and Brazil overwhelmed the Americans in basketball, but the U.S. delegation still won 106 gold medals and 296 medals total; Canada came in second in the medal count. Five gold medalists from Cuba, Canada, and the Dominican Republic tested positive for drugs and were stripped of their medals.

Other Champions. Chamique Holdsclaw became the first woman basketball player to win the James E. Sullivan Memorial Trophy as the nation's top amateur athlete. The University of Virginia Cavaliers beat Syracuse for the national championship in men's lacrosse. Brigham Young won its first national championship in men's volleyball.

© Paul Chiasson/AP/Wide World Photos

Wayne Gretzky

© Focus on Sports

Steffi Graf

© John Gaps III/AP/Wide World Photos

John Elway

Just two years after undergoing two operations and four rounds of chemotherapy for testicular cancer, Lance Armstrong (*see also* BIOGRAPHY) awed the sporting world by winning the grueling 2,290-mi (3 685-km) Tour de France bicycle race in July. Armstrong, 27, riding for the U.S. Postal Service Team, was only the second American to win cycling's prestigious race. Doug Swingley of Lincoln, MT, won his second Iditarod Trail Sled Dog Race. At nearly 46 years of age, he was the oldest winner, and the only non-Alaskan to take the 1,100-mi (1 770-km) Anchorage-to-Nome endurance contest. He had taken the 1995 Iditarod in record time.

For the first time, a papillon, Ch. Loteki Supernatural Being, won the best-in-show title from the Westminster Kennel Club. The Cat Fanciers' Association best cat of 1999 was GC, NW PaJean's Bougalie, a cream and white bicolor Persian.

A major tragedy hit the world of golf in October, when Payne Stewart, the winner of the 1999 U.S. Open and a member of the U.S. team that took the Ryder Cup in September, lost his life in a plane accident.

JIM ANDERSON

Auto Racing

Finland's Mika Hakkinen successfully defended his Formula One world auto-racing championship in 1999. Hakkinen became the seventh driver to win consecutive season titles. He won six races and 11 poles to finish with 76 points.

Sweden's Kenny Brack won the 83d running of the Indianapolis 500 when leader Robby Gordon ran out of fuel with just more than a lap remaining. Gordon finished fourth, behind Jeff Ward and Billy Boat. The winning speed was 153.176 mph (246.5 km/hr).

Dale Jarrett won his first Winston Cup stock car championship, clinching the title in the season's next-to-last race at Homestead, FL. Jarrett finished with 5,262 points, to 5,061 for runner-up Bobby Labonte. Tony Stewart won three races; he was the first rookie to win a Winston Cup event since the late Davey Allison in 1987.

Jeff Gordon outdueled defending champion Dale Earnhardt to win the Daytona 500 stock-car race and $2.1 million—the biggest auto-racing payday ever.

Greg Moore, a 24-year-old CART driver, was killed October 31 at Fontana, CA, and CART rookie Gonzalo Rodriguez died in a September 11 crash at Monterey, CA. Three spectators at an Indy Racing League event in Charlotte, NC, were killed May 1 when accident debris went into the grandstands.

A 2.61-mi (4.2-km) road course was constructed at the Indianapolis Motor Speedway, after Formula One announced it would hold the U.S. Grand Prix there in 2000.

STAN SUTTON, *Freelance Sportswriter*

Auto Racing

Major Race Winners, 1999

Indianapolis 500: Kenny Brack, Sweden
Daytona 500: Jeff Gordon, United States
U.S. 500: Tony Kanaan, Brazil
Brickyard 400: Dale Jarrett, United States

1999 Champions

Formula One: Mika Hakkinen, Finland
Winston Cup: Dale Jarrett, United States
CART: Juan Montoya, Colombia
Indy Racing League: Greg Ray, United States

Grand Prix for Formula One Cars, 1999

Australian: Eddie Irvine, Great Britain
Brazilian: Mika Hakkinen, Finland
San Marino: Michael Schumacher, Germany
Monaco: Schumacher
Spanish: Hakkinen
Canadian: Hakkinen
French: Heinz-Harald Frentzen, Germany
British: David Coulthard, Scotland
Austrian: Irvine
German: Irvine
Hungarian: Hakkinen
Belgian: Coulthard
Italian: Frentzen
European: Johnny Herbert, Great Britain
Malaysian: Hakkinen
Japanese: Hakkinen

Baseball

In 1999, for the second year in a row, two baseball players hit more than 60 home runs, a New York Yankee pitched a perfect game, and an American Leaguer won the Triple Crown of pitching. It was also the second straight season that the National League (NL) needed a sudden-death play-off to determine its wild-card participant, and that the New York Yankees swept the World Series in four straight games. After three years of increases, attendance dropped 0.3% in 1999, averaging 29,210 fans per game.

Play-offs and World Series. For 162 games at least, the most valuable team was the Atlanta Braves. Although they lost five players to season-ending injuries or illnesses, the Braves won 103 games, the most in the big leagues. The New York Mets, rebuilt with improved speed and defense, challenged the Braves all summer and even moved ahead briefly in August. When the Mets went to Atlanta for the first of six late-season games on September 21, they trailed by only a single game. But the Braves, powered primarily by Chipper Jones, swept the Turner Field matches, starting the Mets on a seven-game losing streak that almost proved fatal. With three games left, New York stood two games behind Cincinnati and Houston in a wild wild-card race.

The Astros won two out of three to clinch the NL Central crown, but the Reds dropped two out of three at Milwaukee, allowing the Mets to tie for the wild-card slot. New York then won a sudden-death play-off game, 5–0, behind Al Leiter's two-hitter at Cincinnati's Cinergy Field on October 4. As a result, the Mets flew to Phoenix to meet the free-spending Arizona Diamondbacks, a 1998 expansion team that lavished huge contracts on veteran free agents, in the best-of-five Division Series. Arizona's only postseason win was a 7–1 verdict in Game 2. The Mets won by scores of 8–4 and 9–2 before Todd Pratt's tenth-inning homer in Game 4 ended the game, 4–3, and the series. The other NL Division Series paired the Braves with the Astros. After losing a 6–1 opener at home, the Braves won three straight, 5–1, 5–3, and 7–5.

In the American League (AL), the New York Yankees swept the Texas Rangers, champions of the AL West, in the Division Series, 8–0, 3–1, and 3–0. The Cleveland Indians blew a 2–0 Division Series lead against the Boston Red Sox, the league's wild-card winner, and failed to reach the final round of

© John Bazemore/AP/Wide World Photos

The Atlanta Braves' Chipper Jones, left, *hits a two-run homer in a late-season game against the New York Mets. Jones later helped the Braves to victory over the wild-card Mets in the NL Championship Series, leading his team to the World Series. He was named the NL's most valuable player (MVP).*

the play-offs. Boston used six hitless innings of relief pitching by Game 1 starter Pedro Martinez to win the finale. But the Yankees beat the Red Sox handily in five games in the AL Championship Series (ALCS), winning 4–3 and 3–2 in the first two games and 9–2 and 6–1 in the last two. The Red Sox won only Game 3, when Martinez fanned 12 in seven innings of a 13–1 laugher. Orlando (El Duque) Hernandez, who made strong starts in the first and last games, was voted most valuable player (MVP) of the ALCS.

There was more excitement in the National League play-offs. After taking the first three games, 4–2, 4–3, and 1–0, Atlanta had trouble closing the deal. The Mets won Game 4, 3–2, and Game 5, 4–3 in 15 innings. That sent the series back to Atlanta, where the Braves outlasted the Mets, 10–9 in 11 innings. Eddie Perez, a backup catcher, hit .500 with two homers—one of them a game-winner—to win NLCS MVP honors.

Exhausted by the feisty Mets, the Braves had trouble during the World Series against the Yankees. Atlanta blew leads in the eighth innings of the first and third games, and fell in four straight, 4–1, 7–2, 6–5 in ten innings, and 4–1. Closer Mariano Rivera, who saved two games and won one, extended his postseason shutout streak to 25$^{2}/_{3}$ innings and was voted the World Series MVP. The victory gave the Yankees their third World Series in four seasons and their 25th overall. For Atlanta, which won more pennants (five) than any team during the 1990s, it was a forgettable finish.

Regular Season. The season opened in Mexico's Monterrey Stadium—the first time

New York Yankees pitcher Mariano Rivera was voted World Series MVP. The closer saved two games and won one in New York's four-game sweep over Atlanta.

© Ron Frehm/AP/Wide World Photos

BASEBALL

Professional—Major Leagues

Final Standings, 1999

AMERICAN LEAGUE

Eastern Division

	W	L	Pct.
New York	98	64	.605
Boston*	94	68	.580
Toronto	84	78	.519
Baltimore	78	84	.481
Tampa Bay	69	93	.426

Central Division

	W	L	Pct.
Cleveland	97	65	.599
Chicago	75	86	.466
Detroit	69	92	.429
Kansas City	64	97	.398
Minnesota	63	97	.394

Western Division

	W	L	Pct.
Texas	95	67	.586
Oakland	87	75	.537
Seattle	79	83	.488
Anaheim	70	92	.432

NATIONAL LEAGUE

Eastern Division

	W	L	Pct.
Atlanta	103	59	.636
New York*	97	66	.595
Philadelphia	77	85	.475
Montreal	68	94	.420
Florida	64	98	.395

Central Division

	W	L	Pct.
Houston	97	65	.599
Cincinnati	96	67	.589
Pittsburgh	78	83	.484
St. Louis	75	86	.466
Milwaukee	74	87	.460
Chicago	67	95	.414

Western Division

	W	L	Pct.
Arizona	100	62	.617
San Francisco	86	76	.531
Los Angeles	77	85	.475
San Diego	74	88	.457
Colorado	72	90	.444

*Play-off wild-card team

Play-offs—American League: Division Series—New York Yankees defeated Texas, 3 games to 0; Boston defeated Cleveland, 3 games to 2. Championship Series—New York defeated Boston, 4 games to 1. National League: Division Series—Atlanta defeated Houston, 3 games to 1; New York Mets defeated Arizona, 3 games to 1. Championship Series—Atlanta defeated New York, 4 games to 2.

World Series—New York defeated Atlanta, 4 games to 0. First Game (Turner Field, Atlanta, Oct. 23, attendance 51,342): New York 4, Atlanta 1; Second Game (Turner Field, Oct. 24, attendance 51,226): New York 7, Atlanta 2; Third Game (Yankee Stadium, New York, Oct. 26, attendance 56,794): New York 6, Atlanta 5; Fourth Game (Yankee Stadium, Oct. 27, attendance 56,752): New York 4, Atlanta 1.

All-Star Game— (Fenway Park, Boston, July 13, attendance 34,187): American League 4, National League 1.

Most Valuable Players—American League: Ivan Rodriguez, Texas; National League: Chipper Jones, Atlanta.

Cy Young Memorial Awards (outstanding pitchers)—American League: Pedro Martinez, Boston; National League: Randy Johnson, Arizona.

Managers of the Year—American League: Jimy Williams, Boston; National League: Jack McKeon, Cincinnati.

Rookies of the Year—American League: Carlos Beltran, Kansas City; National League: Scott Williamson, Cincinnati.

Leading Hitters—(Percentage) American League: Nomar Garciaparra, Boston, .357; National League: Larry Walker, Colorado, .379. (Runs Batted In) American League: Manny Ramirez, Cleveland, 165; National League: Mark McGwire, St. Louis, 147. (Home Runs) American League: Ken Griffey, Jr., Seattle, 48; National League: Mark McGwire, St. Louis, 65. (Hits) American League: Derek Jeter, New York, 219; National League: Luis Gonzalez, Arizona, 206. (Runs) American League: Roberto Alomar, Cleveland, 138; National League: Jeff Bagwell, Houston, 143. (Slugging Percentage) American League: Manny Ramirez, .663; National League: Larry Walker, Colorado, .710.

Leading Pitchers—(Earned Run Average) American League: Pedro Martinez, Boston, 2.07; National League: Randy Johnson, Arizona, 2.48. (Victories) American League: Pedro Martinez, 23; National League: Mike Hampton, Houston, 22. (Strikeouts) American League: Pedro Martinez, 313; National League: Randy Johnson, 364. (Shutouts) American League: Scott Erickson, Baltimore, 3; National League: Andy Ashby, San Diego, 3. (Saves) American League: Mariano Rivera, New York, 45; National League: Ugueth Urbina, Montreal, 41. (Innings) American League: David Wells, Toronto, 231.2; National League: Randy Johnson, 271.2.

Professional—Minor Leagues, Class AAA

International League: Charlotte
Mexican League: Mexico City Red Devils
Pacific Coast League: Vancouver

Amateur

NCAA: Miami
Little League World Series: Osaka, Japan

it started outside the United States or Canada—when the Colorado Rockies defeated the San Diego Padres, 8–2, on April 4. By the time the season ended, Mark McGwire and Sammy Sosa had become the first two players to top 60 home runs in consecutive campaigns.

McGwire, who had hit 70 in 1998, finished with 65 after clearing the fences six times in his last seven games. The St. Louis slugger averaged one home run every 8.02 at-bats and finished the season with 522 career homers, one ahead of Ted Williams and Willie McCovey on the lifetime list. McGwire also led the league with a career-best 147 runs batted in (RBIs). He also was the first man to produce more RBIs than hits (145) and the first with four straight 50-homer campaigns. Although the Chicago Cubs' Sammy Sosa led the homer chase, 59–54, on September 9, a late-season slide held his final total to 63.

Chipper Jones of the Atlanta Braves was the National League's most valuable player after becoming the first player ever to hit .300 (.319) with 100 runs scored (116), 100 runs batted in (110), 40 doubles (41), 40 homers (45), and 20 stolen bases (25). His 45 home runs were the most ever produced by a National League switch-hitter and second only to Mickey Mantle's 54 in 1961.

In a major upset, Texas Rangers catcher Ivan (Pudge) Rodriguez won AL MVP honors over Red Sox pitcher Pedro Martinez (*see* BIOGRAPHY). Rodriguez—the first catcher to be voted MVP since the Yankees' Thurman Munson in 1976—hit .332, the best for an AL backstop since 1937. He had 35 homers, a record for an AL receiver, and 199 hits, the second-highest total ever collected by a catcher. Nonetheless, fans were amazed that Martinez, Boston's star pitcher, had not won. Martinez took the AL's Cy Young Award after leading the league with 23 wins, 313 strikeouts, a 2.07 earned run average (ERA), and an opponents' batting average of .205. It was the third straight year an AL pitcher won the Triple Crown of pitching.

Randy Johnson won the NL's Cy Young Award. In his first year with the Arizona Diamondbacks, Johnson led the majors in strikeouts for the sixth time (364), helped by 23 double-digit performances. The left-hander also led the National League with a 2.48 ERA. Atlanta's Kevin Millwood held hitters to the lowest average (.202) of any starter in the majors. Mike Hampton—with José Lima one of two 20-game winners in Houston—led the NL with 22 wins, while Montreal's Ugueth Urbina had the league's most saves (41). Mariano Rivera of the New York Yankees led the majors with 45 games saved.

On July 18, David Cone needed no relief, as the Yankee veteran threw a 6–0 perfect

All-Century Team

A highlight of the 1999 baseball season was the selection of the All-Century team by the fans. Members of the team were introduced prior to the start of Game 2 of the World Series in Atlanta. Those selected were:

Pitchers	Sandy Koufax, Nolan Ryan, Cy Young, Bob Gibson, Warren Spahn, Walter Johnson, Lefty Grove, Roger Clemens, Christy Mathewson.
Catchers	Johnny Bench, Yogi Berra.
First Basemen	Lou Gehrig, Mark McGwire.
Second Basemen	Jackie Robinson, Rogers Hornsby.
Shortstops	Cal Ripken, Jr., Honus Wagner, Ernie Banks.
Third Basemen	Mike Schmidt, Brooks Robinson.
Outfielders	Babe Ruth, Ted Williams, Willie Mays, Hank Aaron, Joe DiMaggio, Mickey Mantle, Pete Rose, Ty Cobb, Ken Griffey, Jr., Stan Musial.

game against the Montreal Expos, an interleague opponent. Cone's 88-pitch gem was one of three no-hitters in 1999. Rookie José Jimenez of the St. Louis Cardinals held Arizona hitless during a 1–0 win in Phoenix on June 25, and Eric Milton of the Minnesota Twins had a 7–0 September 11 shutout against the Anaheim Angels.

On August 6 eight-time batting king Tony Gwynn of the San Diego Padres became the 22d player to reach the 3,000-hit plateau. The next night, Wade Boggs of the Tampa Bay Devil Rays reached 3,000 hits with a home run. Only late-September back surgery kept Cal Ripken, Jr., from joining them. The Baltimore Orioles star finished the season nine hits short of 3,000.

Colorado's Larry Walker, en route to his second consecutive batting crown, hit .379, the NL's best full-season mark since Arky Vaughn hit .385 for the 1935 Pittsburgh Pirates. (Tony Gwynn's .394 of 1994 occurred in a strike-shortened season.) Playing half his schedule in Denver's Coors Field also helped Walker become the first man to hit .360 three years in a row since Hall of Fame outfielder Al Simmons did it for the 1929–31 Philadelphia Athletics. A pair of shortstops, Nomar Garciaparra of the Boston Red Sox and Derek Jeter of the New York Yankees, waged a yearlong battle for the AL batting crown. The Bosox star finally prevailed, finishing at .357, eight points ahead of his rival. Cleveland outfielder Manny Ramirez collected 165 RBIs, the most in the majors since Jimmie Foxx had 175 for the 1938 Red Sox.

Arizona's Tony Womack led the National League in stolen bases for the third straight season, swiping 72. AL leader Brian Hunter of Seattle had the league's lowest total (44) since Luis Aparicio led with 40 in 1963.

The American League had more than its fair share of hitting heroes. Cleveland second baseman Roberto Alomar compiled impressive numbers (.323 average, 24 homers, and 120 RBIs), topped the league with 138 runs scored, and stole 37 bases. Like Texas' Rodriguez, he also supplied stellar defense. Jeter topped Alomar in on-base percentage (.438), slugging (.552), total bases (346), and hits. He also hit 26 points higher and had the same number of home runs.

The American League won the All-Star Game at Boston's Fenway Park, 4–1, on July 13, with Martinez the starting and winning pitcher as well as the MVP. He fanned the first four hitters, an All-Star record.

Honors and Labor War. The Hall of Fame opened its doors to seven new members—pitcher Nolan Ryan, third baseman George Brett, shortstop-outfielder Robin Yount, first baseman Orlando Cepeda, umpire Nestor Chylak, manager Frank Selee, and Negro-leagues pitcher Smokey Joe Williams. Ryan, Brett, and Yount all were elected in their first year of eligibility.

Umpires-union chief Richie Phillips announced July 14 that the umpires would resign en masse on September 2 if their soon-to-expire contract was not settled. When the commissioner's office announced it would accept the resignations, many umpires raced to rescind, but 22 lost their jobs. On November 30 the umpires voted to replace the existing union with a new association—effectively ousting Phillips.

DAN SCHLOSSBERG, *Baseball Writer*

Basketball

The San Antonio Spurs won their first National Basketball Association (NBA) title by defeating the New York Knicks in the final round of the league play-offs. The Spurs, who were led by the stellar play of forward Tim Duncan, became the first former American Basketball Association (ABA) team to win an NBA title.

In women's professional basketball, the Houston Comets beat the New York Liberty in the championship round to win their third straight Women's National Basketball Association (WNBA) title.

In men's college basketball, the University of Connecticut won its first National Collegiate Athletic Association (NCAA) basketball championship. The Huskies took the title by defeating heavily favored Duke in the final game. The women's NCAA title went to Purdue University, which beat Duke in the championship contest.

San Antonio forward Tim Duncan (21) led the Spurs to their first NBA championship. He averaged 27.4 points and 14 rebounds against the New York Knicks in the championship round of the play-offs to capture the MVP award.

Professional

NBA Regular Season. The main questions surrounding the 1998–99 season were supposed to be: Will Chicago Bulls star Michael Jordan retire, and, if so, how will the league survive without him? But the possible absence of the man considered to be the greatest basketball player ever was overshadowed when the league and its players' association became entangled in a volatile labor dispute that resulted in the NBA locking out its players. As a result, the start of the season was postponed. Commissioner David Stern even threatened to cancel the entire schedule. A settlement was not signed until Jan. 20, 1999. It allowed the season to begin in early February. The labor dispute had revolved around the league's desire to put a cap on the tremendous salary growth. The players' association finally agreed to substantial restrictions, which enabled the season to start. However, teams played only a 50-game schedule—32 games shorter than normal. Since teams had been forced to rush through training camp, and players spent the opening weeks of the schedule working their way into top condition, the quality of play suffered. A lot of low-scoring games and inconsistent performances resulted. In the interim, Jordan had announced his retirement on Jan. 13, 1999.

Some coaching changes also attracted attention. George Karl, who had been very successful with the Seattle SuperSonics before being fired following the 1997–98 season, took over in Milwaukee. Taking over in Chicago for Phil Jackson, who quit after winning the 1998 title, was Tim Floyd, the former coach at Iowa State. Floyd presided over a weakened Bulls team. Not only was Jordan gone, but Scottie Pippen now was in Houston, and Dennis Rodman was a free agent who later signed with the Los Angeles Lakers. Latrell Sprewell, who had been suspended the previous season for choking coach P.J. Carlesimo, served out his suspension with the Golden State Warriors and wound up with the New York Knicks.

Without Karl, the Sonics slumped badly in the Pacific Division. Instead, the Portland Trail Blazers and Los Angeles Lakers vied for first place. The young Trail Blazers, led by emerging star forward Brian Grant, finished strongly to nose out the Lakers. The veteran Utah Jazz managed to finish in a tie for first place with the San Antonio Spurs in the Midwest Division. The Jazz still got strong seasons from aging stars Karl Malone and

John Stockton. But the Spurs got an even better season from forward Tim Duncan.

The Indiana Pacers, who had played a great play-off series against the Bulls in 1998, were expected to dominate the Eastern Conference and the Central Division. But the veteran Pacers never found consistency. They wound up tying the Miami Heat and the Orlando Magic for the conference's best record (33–17). Orlando proved the most surprising team in the conference behind the fine coaching of Chuck Daly, who earlier had guided the Detroit Pistons to two titles. Philadelphia, which had not been in the play-offs since the early 1990s, had a superior season to qualify for the postseason. Other play-off teams included Atlanta, Detroit, Milwaukee, and New York in the East, and, in the West, Houston, Sacramento, Phoenix, and Minnesota.

Without Jordan, the way was opened for Philadelphia 76er guard Allen Iverson to take the scoring title, with an average of 26.8 points per game. He nosed out Laker center Shaquille O'Neal, who had a 26.3 average. Rodman, Jordan's former Bull teammate, had won seven rebounding titles. But he was released by the Lakers before season's end and lost his championship. Instead, the top rebounder was Sacramento forward Chris Webber, averaging 13.0 rebounds per game. There was also a new leader in assists: Jason Kidd of Phoenix averaged 10.8 assists per game.

Karl Malone of Utah became the ninth player in NBA history to win the most-valuable-player (MVP) award twice. Malone also won it after the 1996–97 season. Miami's Alonzo Mourning was second to Malone, and Tim Duncan of San Antonio was third. Malone made the all-league team along with Duncan, Mourning, Iverson, and Kidd. Second-team honors went to Webber, Grant Hill of Detroit, Shaquille O'Neal, Gary Payton of Seattle, and Tim Hardaway of Miami.

There were a number of coaching changes during the season. John Calipari of the New Jersey Nets, Bernie Bickerstaff of the Washington Wizards, Del Harris of the Lakers, and Dave Cowens of the Charlotte Hornets either were fired or resigned. After the season, Chuck Daly retired from the Magic. New coaches for the 1999–2000 season included Phil Jackson, who was lured out of retirement by the Lakers; Glenn (Doc) Rivers, who was hired by Orlando to replace Daly; and Gar Heard, who succeed-

MEN'S PROFESSIONAL BASKETBALL

National Basketball Association
(Final Standings, 1999)

Eastern Conference

Atlantic Division	W	L	Pct.	Games Behind
*Miami	33	17	.660	—
*Orlando	33	17	.660	—
*Philadelphia	28	22	.560	5
*New York	27	23	.540	6
Boston	19	31	.380	14
Washington	18	32	.360	15
New Jersey	16	34	.320	17
Central Division				
*Indiana	33	17	.660	—
*Atlanta	31	19	.620	2
*Detroit	29	21	.580	4
*Milwaukee	28	22	.560	5
Charlotte	26	24	.520	7
Toronto	23	27	.460	10
Cleveland	22	28	.440	11
Chicago	13	37	.260	20

Western Conference

Midwest Division	W	L	Pct.	Games Behind
*San Antonio	37	13	.740	—
*Utah	37	13	.740	—
*Houston	31	19	.620	6
*Minnesota	25	25	.500	12
Dallas	19	31	.380	18
Denver	14	36	.280	23
Vancouver	8	42	.160	29
Pacific Division				
*Portland	35	15	.700	—
*Los Angeles Lakers	31	19	.620	4
*Phoenix	27	23	.540	8
*Sacramento	27	23	.540	8
Seattle	25	25	.500	10
Golden State	21	29	.420	14
Los Angeles Clippers	9	41	.180	26

*In play-offs

Play-offs

Eastern Conference

First Round	Atlanta	3 games	Detroit	2
	Indiana	3 games	Milwaukee	0
	New York	3 games	Miami	2
	Philadelphia	3 games	Orlando	1
Second Round	Indiana	4 games	Philadelphia	0
	New York	4 games	Atlanta	0
Finals	New York	4 games	Indiana	2

Western Conference

First Round	L.A. Lakers	3 games	Houston	1
	Portland	3 games	Phoenix	0
	San Antonio	3 games	Minnesota	1
	Utah	3 games	Sacramento	2
Second Round	Portland	4 games	Utah	2
	San Antonio	4 games	L.A. Lakers	0
Finals	San Antonio	4 games	Portland	0
Championship	San Antonio	4 games	New York	1
All-Star Game	canceled			

Individual Honors

Most Valuable Player: Karl Malone, Utah
Most Valuable Player (championship): Tim Duncan, San Antonio
Rookie of the Year: Vince Carter, Toronto
Coach of the Year: Mike Dunleavy, Portland
Defensive Player of the Year: Alonzo Mourning, Miami
Sixth-Man Award: Darrell Armstrong, Orlando
Most Improved Player: Darrell Armstrong
Executive of the Year: Geoff Petrie, Sacramento
J. Walter Kennedy Citizenship Award: Brian Grant, Portland
Leader in Scoring: Allen Iverson, Philadelphia
Leader in Assists: Jason Kidd, Phoenix
Leader in Rebounds: Chris Webber, Sacramento
Leader in Field-Goal Percentage: Shaquille O'Neal, Los Angeles Lakers
Leader in Three-Point-Shooting Percentage: Dell Curry, Milwaukee
Leader in Free-Throw Percentage: Reggie Miller, Indiana
Leader in Steals: Kendall Gill, New Jersey
Leader in Blocked Shots: Alonzo Mourning, Miami

ed Bickerstaff with the Wizards. In addition, two interim coaches—Don Casey of the Nets and Paul Silas of the Hornets—signed contracts to become those teams' head coaches. Mike Fratello was dismissed as coach of the Cleveland Cavaliers and was replaced by Randy Wittman.

The NBA Play-offs. The San Antonio Spurs began the play-offs as the league's hottest team, having won 31 of their final 36 games. And they did not cool off during the play-offs. They wound up crushing the Minnesota Timberwolves and the Los Angeles Lakers in the early rounds before taking on Portland. The latter could not handle the size of the Spurs, who featured twin big men Tim Duncan and David Robinson. The Spurs beat Portland in four games.

The Knicks were the Eastern Conference's eighth-seeded team and were expected to lose early in the play-offs. But it did not turn out that way. They began by eliminating top-seeded Miami and Atlanta in the opening round. They then continued their unexpected run by overcoming the Indiana Pacers, a team considered by many to be the heir apparent to the Bulls in the East. What was more, the Knicks' veteran center, Patrick Ewing, could not play after injuring an Achilles tendon early in the Pacers series.

In the championship round between the Spurs and the underdog Knicks, New York had a considerable height disadvantage but was hoping that its quickness could neutralize Duncan and Robinson. But Duncan was emerging as the league's Number 1 player. He had been overpowering during the early rounds of the play-offs and became even better against the Knicks. He averaged 27.4 points and 14 rebounds in the series, which the Spurs won in five games, 4–1. He also teamed with Robinson to hold the Knicks to 39.2% shooting. He was the unanimous choice as the most valuable player of the championship round. The Knicks relied mostly on the scoring of guards Latrell Sprewell and Allan Houston.

In Game 1, Spurs guard Jaren Jackson helped out Duncan and Robinson by making five three-point shots and finished with 17 points as San Antonio won, 89–77. In Game 2, guard Mario Elie of San Antonio stepped up with 15 points to complement Duncan's 25 and Robinson's 16, and the Spurs won, 80–67. The Knicks were heartened in Game 3 as New York overcame another strong performance by Duncan with an 89–81 win. The Knicks, however, were thwarted, 96–89, in Game 4 by a fine defensive effort from San Antonio. They then lost for the second time on their home court in Game 5, as the Spurs wrapped up the championship, 78–77. San Antonio ended with a 15–2 play-off record, tying the second-best play-off winning percentage in league history. Duncan, who scored a total of 59 points in the last two games, was named most valuable player of the final series. The Spurs also became the only team other than the Bulls, Rockets, and Pistons to win an NBA title in the 1990s.

WOMEN'S PROFESSIONAL BASKETBALL

Women's National Basketball Association

Eastern Conference	**W**	**L**	**Pct.**	**Games Behind**
*New York	18	14	.563	—
*Detroit	15	17	.469	3
*Charlotte	15	17	.469	3
Orlando	15	17	.469	3
Washington	12	20	.375	6
Cleveland	7	25	.219	11
Western Conference				
*Houston	26	6	.813	—
*Los Angeles	20	12	.625	6
*Sacramento	19	13	.594	7
Minnesota	15	17	.469	11
Phoenix	15	17	.469	11
Utah	15	17	.469	11

*In play-offs

Play-offs

	Eastern Conference	
First Round	Charlotte 60	Detroit 54
Final	New York 2 games	Charlotte 1
	Western Conference	
First Round	Los Angeles 71	Sacramento 58
Final	Houston 2 games	Los Angeles 1
Championship	Houston 2 games	New York 1
All-Star Game	West 79	East 61

The WNBA. The WNBA entered its third season strengthened by the addition of players from the rival American Basketball League (ABL), which folded after two seasons. But the new players did not change the WNBA's balance of power. The Houston Comets lived up to the preseason hype and wound up winning the Western Conference title by six games. The Eastern Conference title went to the New York Liberty.

Houston and New York were favored to make it to the championship round of the play-offs. The Comets received a scare in the second round, when they lost to Los Angeles in the first game. However, Cynthia Cooper scored a total of 45 points in the next two games to pull out the series. The Comets then were saddened by the death of star guard Kim Perrot, who died of lung cancer on August 19.

In the championship series, Teresa Weatherspoon made a 50-ft (15-m) shot at the buzzer to win Game 2 for New York and tie the series. Houston took the title for a third consecutive time, however, behind Cooper's 24 points in Game 3.

Sacramento's Yolanda Griffith, who played the previous season in the ABL, won MVP, newcomer-of-the-year, and defensive-player honors. She was the leading rebounder (11.3). Cooper led in scoring (22.1), and Ticha Penicheiro of Sacramento led in assists (7.1). Chamique Holdsclaw of Washington was rookie of the year. Sheryl Swoopes of Houston, Natalie Williams of Utah, Cooper, Penicheiro, and Griffith were first-team all-league.

College

Regular Season and Star Performers. At the start of the 1998–99 college-basketball season, the unquestioned favorites for the national championship were the Duke Blue Devils, who had most of the players back from a strong team that had advanced deep into the 1997–98 NCAA basketball tournament. Duke was led by All-Americans Elton Brand and Trajan Langdon, plus a very talented supporting cast.

But Duke was not the only strong team. Connecticut had two scorers, Richard Hamilton and Khalid El-Amin. Cincinnati had a powerful frontcourt. Michigan State had great quickness. Utah had many of its stars back from the previous season's Final Four team. Stanford returned virtually its entire squad from its 1997–98 NCAA team. Kentucky had impressive depth, and Arizona was blending talented newcomers with a core of veterans. Maryland had its best talent in years, and North Carolina, as usual, was expected to contend for top honors.

Very few of these strong teams wound up disappointing during the regular season. Duke finished its regular schedule with only one loss, to Cincinnati. The Blue Devils ran up impressive numbers by overpowering most of their opponents. On many nights, they appeared invincible with their combination of speed, good defense, rebounding, and outside shooting. Connecticut improved as the season went on, and upstart Miami (FL) became a contender in the Big East. Auburn emerged as one of the surprising clubs, bolting to an impressive record. Kentucky and Kansas were not as strong as in previous years but still easily made the NCAA tournament. Arizona, which developed quickly in the west, joined Stanford and UCLA as the best in that region. Michigan State led the Big 10, and Maryland was the Atlantic Coast Conference's (ACC's) second-best team, behind Duke. St. John's came out of the Big East as a team to respect, as did Utah in the mountain region.

Elton Brand of Duke was named the nation's best player by most of the selecting organizations. He made All-American, as did Richard Hamilton of Connecticut, Andre Miller of Utah, Jason Terry of Arizona, and Mateen Cleaves of Michigan State. Other standout players included Evan Eschmeyer of Northwestern, Chris Porter of

Manny Millan/"Sports Illustrated"/© Time Inc.

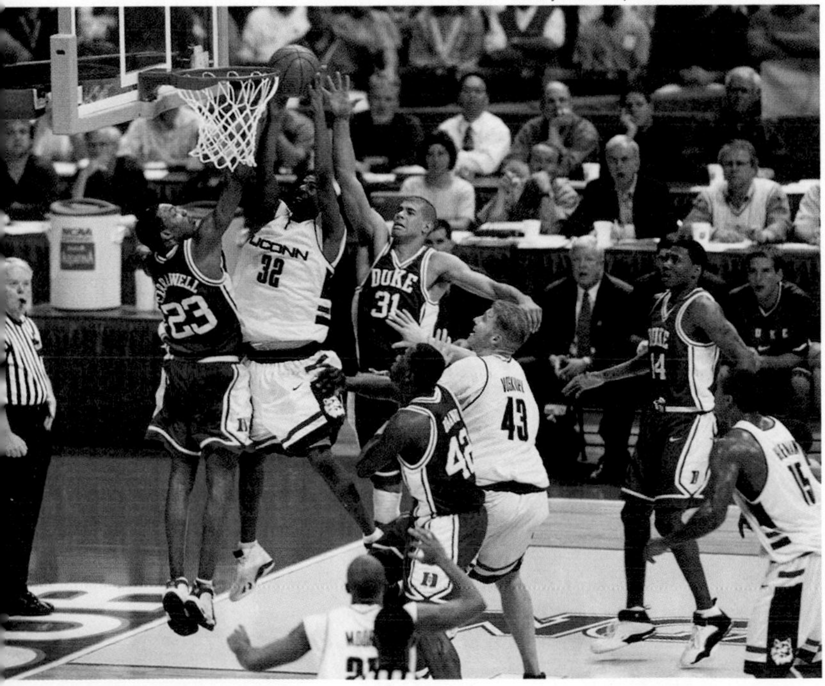

The University of Connecticut took its first NCAA Division I men's basketball title by defeating favored Duke University, 77–74, in the tournament final. UConn's All-American forward Richard Hamilton (32) scored 27 points in the "big" game.

Auburn, Wally Szczerbiak of Miami (OH), Steve Francis of Maryland, Trajan Langdon of Duke, Baron Davis of UCLA, and Scoonie Penn of Ohio State.

Two notable coaches left the game. Tom Davis of Iowa did not have his contract renewed, and John Thompson of Georgetown retired during the season.

The NCAA Tournament. The top seeds entering the NCAA tournament were Duke, Connecticut, Auburn, and Michigan State. Auburn proved to be overrated, losing in the South Region semifinals to Ohio State. Otherwise, the rankings were very accurate. Duke, playing very impressively, coasted through the East Region, defeating Temple in the final. Michigan State outran Kentucky in the Midwest final. And Connecticut outlasted unheralded Gonzaga in the West Region final. That set up a Final Four of Duke, Connecticut, Michigan State, and Ohio State, which had won in the South Region by beating St. John's in the final.

COLLEGE BASKETBALL

Men's Division I Conference Champions

America East: Delaware and Drexel[r]; Delaware[t]
Atlantic Coast: Duke[r,t]
Atlantic 10: Temple (East)[r], George Washington (West)[r]; Rhode Island[t]
Big East: Connecticut[r,t]
Big Sky: Weber State[r,t]
Big South: Winthrop[r,t]
Big 12: Texas[r]; Kansas[t]
Big Ten: Michigan State[r,t]
Big West: Boise State (East)[r], University of California, Santa Barbara (West)[r]; New Mexico State[t]
Colonial Athletic: George Mason[r,t]
Conference USA: Cincinnati (American)[r], Alabama Birmingham (National)[r]; UNC Charlotte[t]
Ivy League: Pennsylvania
Metro Atlantic Athletic: Siena and Niagara (tied)[r]; Siena[t]
Mid-American: Miami (Ohio) (East)[r], Toledo (West)[r]; Kent[t]
Mid-Continent: Valparaiso and Oral Roberts (tied)[r]; Valparaiso[t]
Mid-Eastern Athletic: South Carolina State and Coppin State (tied)[r]; Florida A&M[t]
Midwestern Collegiate: Detroit[r,t]
Missouri Valley: Evansville[r]; Creighton[t]
Northeast: Maryland Baltimore County[r]; Mount St. Mary's[t]
Ohio Valley: Murray State[r,t]
Pacific 10: Stanford
Patriot: Lafayette[r,t]
Southeastern: Tennessee (East)[r], Auburn (West)[r]; Kentucky[t]
Southern: Appalachian State (North)[r], College of Charleston (South)[r]; College of Charleston[t]
Southland: Southwest Texas[r]; Texas–San Antonio[t]
Southwestern Athletic: Alcorn State[r,t]
Sun Belt: Louisiana Tech and Arkansas State (tied)[r]; Arkansas State[t]
Trans America: Samford[r,t]
West Coast: Gonzaga[r,t]
Western Athletic: Tulsa and UNLV (tied) (Mountain)[r], Utah (Pacific)[r]; Utah[t]

[r]regular-season winner
[t]conference-tournament winner

Men's Tournaments

NCAA Division I: Connecticut
NCAA Division II: Kentucky Wesleyan
NCAA Division III: Wisconsin-Platteville
NAIA Division I: Life University
NIT: California

Women's Tournaments

NCAA Division I: Purdue
NCAA Division II: North Dakota
NCAA Division III: Washington, MO
NAIA Division I: Shawnee State

In the Final Four, held at Tropicana Field in St. Petersburg, FL, Ohio State faced Connecticut in one semifinal, while Duke played Michigan State in the other. Ohio State gave away too much quickness and experience to the Huskies, who relied on the steady performance of Richard Hamilton and the playmaking of Khalid El-Amin. Hamilton scored 24 points, and Connecticut pulled away to a 64–58 victory. Michigan State, behind the gutsy play of guard Mateen Cleaves, stayed with Duke longer than expected. But the Blue Devils had too much depth and scoring balance, and the Spartans also could not find a way to stop center Elton Brand. The result was a 68–62 Duke victory.

That set up a Duke-Connecticut final. Connecticut coach Jim Calhoun had established one of the nation's most successful basketball programs, but his teams never had made it into the Final Four before, much less won a national title. This time, it would be different. The Huskies were not intimidated by Duke's reputation or talent. Even with El-Amin in foul trouble, they parlayed good defense and the scoring of Hamilton to stay ahead of Duke in the second half and not allow the Blue Devils to unleash a typical scoring spurt. Hamilton finished with 27 points, and Connecticut celebrated its first title, 77–74. It was only the second loss of the season for Duke and ended a 32-game winning streak.

The Women. Tennessee began the season heavily favored to win its fourth straight national championship in women's basketball. But the Lady Vols found the road to another title to be harder than expected. They slipped from the Number 1 ranking during the regular season and saw Purdue finish as the top-rated team. Then, in the women's NCAA tournament, Tennessee lost to underdog Duke in the final of the East Region. Connecticut, another highly regarded team, was stunned by Iowa State in the first round of the Mideast Region. Purdue breezed through the Midwest, while Louisiana Tech, Number 1 in the West Region, also made it to the Final Four.

In the Final Four, which was held in San Jose, CA, Duke beat Georgia, 81–69, in one semifinal, while Purdue rolled over Louisiana Tech, 77–63. In the final, the veteran Boilermakers parlayed 18 points from guard Ukari Figgs and tough defense to subdue Duke easily, 62–45. It was the last game for Purdue coach Carolyn Peck, who moved to the WNBA.

PAUL ATTNER, *"The Sporting News"*

Boxing

Lennox Lewis became the undisputed heavyweight boxing champion in 1999.

Heavyweights. Lewis, the World Boxing Council (WBC) champion, apparently outpointed Evander Holyfield, the World Boxing Association (WBA) and International Boxing Federation (IBF) champion, in March. He, however, had to wait until he scored a unanimous decision over Holyfield in November before being recognized as the first undisputed champion since the early 1990s. The WBC, WBA, and IBF are considered the major organizations in an era of numerous sanctioning bodies, and a fighter who holds those three titles generally is considered undisputed champion.

Many observers thought Lewis of Britain was the clear winner in his March bout against Holyfield in New York City, but the decision was a majority draw that touched off legislative hearings and a Manhattan grand-jury investigation. A focal point of the controversy was the scoring of IBF judge Eugenia Williams, who favored Holyfield. No indictments resulted, but in November a federal grand jury in Newark, NJ, indicted IBF president Robert W. Lee, Sr., and three other IBF officials for soliciting and accepting bribes to fix rankings.

Tyson fought in January for the first time since he was disqualified for biting Holyfield's ears in June 1997. Trailing on all three cards, he knocked out François Botha of South Africa with a single right to the head in the fifth round. A planned busy schedule for the former champion fell apart when he served 3½ months in a Maryland jail for assaulting two motorists after a minor traffic accident. When he did fight again in October, his match against Orlin Norris was declared a no-contest after one round. Tyson knocked down Norris with a left to the jaw after the bell rang, and Norris injured his right knee in falling and could not continue. The blow was ruled an accidental foul.

Lighter Divisions. Unbeaten IBF welterweight champion Felix Trinidad of Puerto Rico won the WBC title in September by handing Oscar De La Hoya his first loss as a pro. De La Hoya thought he had it won after nine rounds. Roy Jones, Jr., became boxing's second undisputed champion by adding the IBF title with a one-sided decision over Reggie Johnson in June. Prince Naseem Hamed of Britain won the WBC featherweight title on a unanimous decision in a rough-and-tumble match with Cesar Soto of Mexico in September. Hamed, who held the fringe WBO title, gave up the WBC crown early in 2000. Paulie Ayala became the WBA bantamweight champion by outpointing previously unbeaten Johnny Tapia in June.

While De La Hoya, the only U.S. boxing gold-medal winner in the 1992 Olympics, was losing a title, David Reid, the only U.S. Olympic boxing champion in 1996, was winning one. Reid did it by outpointing Laurent Boudouani of France for the WBA junior-middleweight championship in March.

Although Julio Cesar Chavez of Mexico had not announced his retirement at the end of the year, he apparently was finished as a major player in boxing. The former junior-lightweight, lightweight, and junior-welterweight champion lost a lopsided decision to journeyman Willie Wise. On the same October card, Ricardo Lopez of Mexico, who had been WBC strawweight champion since 1990, moved up and won the IBF junior-flyweight title on a decision over Will Grigsby.

ED SCHUYLER, JR., *Boxing Writer*

WORLD BOXING CHAMPIONS*

Heavyweight: World Boxing Council (WBC)—Lennox Lewis, Britain, 1997; World Boxing Association (WBA)—Lewis, 1999; International Boxing Federation (IBF)—Lewis, 1999.

Cruiserweight: WBC—Juan Carlos Gomez, Cuba-Germany, 1998; WBA—Fabrice Tiozzo, France, 1998; IBF—Vassily Jirov, Kazakhstan-United States, 1999.

Light Heavyweight: WBC—Roy Jones, Jr., United States, 1996; WBA—Jones, 1998; IBF—Jones, 1999.

Super Middleweight: WBC—Markus Beyer, Germany, 1999; WBA—Byron Mitchell, United States, 1999; IBF—Sven Ottke, Germany, 1998.

Middleweight: WBC—Keith Holmes, United States, 1999; WBA—William Joppy, United States, 1996; IBF—Bernard Hopkins, United States, 1995.

Junior Middleweight: WBC—Francisco J. Castillejo, Spain, 1999; WBA—David Reid, United States, 1999; IBF—Fernando Vargas, United States, 1998.

Welterweight: WBC—Felix Trinidad, Puerto Rico, 1999; WBA—James Page, United States, 1998; IBF—Trinidad, 1993.

Junior Welterweight: WBC—Konstantin Tszyu, Russia-Australia, 1999; WBA—Sharmba Mitchell, United States, 1998; IBF—vacant.

Lightweight: WBC—Steve Johnston, United States, 1999; WBA—Gilbert Serrano, Venezuela, 1999; IBF—Paul Spadafora, United States, 1999.

Junior Lightweight: WBC—Floyd Mayweather, United States, 1998; WBA—Jong Kwon Baek, South Korea, 1999; IBF—Diego Corrales, United States, 1999.

Featherweight: WBC—vacant; WBA—Freddy Norwood, United States, 1999; IBF—Paul Ingle, England, 1999.

Junior Featherweight: WBC—Erik Morales, Mexico, 1998; WBA—Nestor Garza, Mexico, 1998; IBF—Benedict Ledwaba, South Africa, 1999.

Bantamweight: WBC—Veerapohl Sahaprom, Thailand, 1999; WBA—Paulie Ayala, United States, 1999; IBF—Tim Austin, United States, 1998.

Junior Bantamweight: WBC—Injoo Cho, South Korea, 1998; WBA—Hideki Todaka, Japan, 1999; IBF—Marc Johnson, United States, 1999.

Flyweight: WBC—Medgoem Singsurat, Thailand, 1999; WBA—Sornipinchai Kratchingdaeng, Thailand, 1999; IBF—Irene Pacheco, Colombia, 1999.

Junior Flyweight: WBC—Yosam Choi, South Korea, 1999; WBA—Pitchinoi Chor Siriwat, Thailand, 1998; IBF—Ricardo Lopez, Mexico, 1999.

Strawweight: WBC—Wandee Chor Chareon, Thailand, 1999; WBA—Noel Arambulet, Venezuela, 1999; IBF—Zolani Petelo, South Africa, 1998.

*As of Jan. 10, 2000. Date indicates year title was won.

Football

© Tom Hauck/Allsport

Wisconsin's running back Ron Dayne, above, *broke college football's career rushing record and was awarded the 1999 Heisman Trophy as the top college player.*

The championship game of the 1999–2000 National Football League (NFL) season paired the Tennessee Titans against the St. Louis Rams. It was the first time either franchise had played in the Super Bowl, although the Rams—then based in Los Angeles—were defeated by the Pittsburgh Steelers in Super Bowl XIV. The Rams featured one of the most prolific offenses in the league, led by quarterback Kurt Warner. The Titans, who had moved to Nashville, TN, from Houston in 1997, had one of the league's best defenses. In Super Bowl XXXIV, which was played in Atlanta on Jan. 30, 2000, before 72,625 fans, the Rams defeated the Titans, 23–16.

In college football, undefeated Florida State beat surprising Virginia Tech, 46–29, in the Sugar Bowl to win the national championship. The game was the second under a system designed to produce a more legitimate national winner than in the past, although the college game still resisted calls for a formal play-off setup. Running back Ron Dayne of Wisconsin won the Heisman Trophy as the best player in college football.

The Professional Season

The 1999 season was filled with surprises. Teams that had been expected to excel turned out to be disappointments, while franchises that had been mediocre in the past turned out to be dominant. It was also a season in which such stars as John Elway of the Denver Broncos and Barry Sanders of the Detroit Lions did not play. Elway announced his retirement soon after the Broncos had won a second straight Super Bowl in January 1999, and then Sanders shocked the Lions by announcing he no longer felt excited enough to continue playing, even though he was within range of breaking the league's all-time rushing record. Walter Payton, the former Chicago Bear who holds that record, died in November.

A number of teams started with new coaches—Brian Billick in Baltimore, Gunther Cunningham in Kansas City, Mike Riley in San Diego, Mike Holmgren in Seattle, George Seifert in Carolina, Ray Rhodes in Green Bay, and Andy Reid in Philadelphia. The most intriguing hiring was that of Holmgren by the Seahawks. He had led the Packers to one Super Bowl triumph, but the Seahawks offered him more power and money. Daniel Snyder bought the Redskins and their stadium for a record price ($800 million), and the Jets were put up for sale after the death of their owner, Leon Hess. They eventually were bought by Robert Wood Johnson. The city of Cleveland, which had seen its franchise move to Baltimore after the 1995 season, welcomed the restart of football when the expansion Browns returned to the league. The Browns played in a new stadium. The NFL also decided to add a 32d team, awarding an expansion franchise to the city of Houston. The Houston team will start play in the 2002 season. In that year the league also will realign itself to include eight four-team divisions. New England, which had announced plans to build a new stadium in Hartford, CT, decided to remain in Massachusetts. The Patriots will build a stadium near their present facility in Foxboro, MA.

The season began with the Jacksonville Jaguars and New York Jets favored to compete for the American Football Conference (AFC) title, and the Minnesota Vikings and Atlanta Falcons favored to fight for the National Football Conference (NFC) crown. The Jaguars lived up to expectations, winning 14 of 16 games to win the AFC Central title despite a tough challenge from the Tennessee Titans. The Titans beat the Jags twice in the regular season but still lost the division championship by a game.

The Jets, however, were a major disappointment. In the opening game, Vinny Testaverde, their starting quarterback, was injured for the season. His injury, combined with others, combined to knock the team out of play-off contention. The AFC East crown went to the Colts of Indianapolis, one of the real surprise teams of the season. The Colts were coming off a 3–13 record in 1998 and were not supposed to be title contenders. But behind the play of quarterback Peyton Manning, running back Edgerrin James, and receiver Marvin Harrison, they had a wonderful season, winning 13 of 16 games and making history for their ten-victory turnaround from the previous year. They outperformed the Miami Dolphins, another strong preseason pick. The Dolphins did squeeze into the play-offs despite the disappointing play of quarterback Dan Marino.

Without Elway, the Broncos got off to a slow start and then lost star running back Terrell Davis to a knee injury. They quickly fell out of postseason contention after winning two straight Super Bowls. The void they left in the AFC West was filled by the Seattle Seahawks, who managed to hold off the Kansas City Chiefs, the Oakland Raiders, and the San Diego Chargers.

The St. Louis Rams became the talk of the league. The Rams, usually downtrodden, rode the passing of quarterback Warner and the running of Marshall Faulk to a 13–3 season and their first NFC West title since moving to St. Louis. The San Francisco 49ers, who had dominated the division for years, fell off once quarterback Steve Young was sidelined with the aftereffects of a fourth concussion in three years. The Atlanta Falcons, who won the division in 1998 before advancing to the Super Bowl, lost star runner Jamal Anderson to a knee injury and did not make the play-offs.

In the NFC Central, the defensive-minded Tampa Bay Bucs pulled out a close race against the Minnesota Vikings. The Bucs won despite having to play a rookie quarterback, Shaun King. The Washington Redskins rode the passing of quarterback Brad Johnson and the running of Stephen Davis to outplay the Dallas Cowboys in the NFC East. The Arizona Cardinals, who were rated a strong contender, never could get on track.

Play-offs. In the early play-offs, the most entertaining game was played by Buffalo and Tennessee. The Titans won the AFC wild-card contest when Kevin Dyson returned a kickoff 75 yards off a trick play in the final seconds. The Titans then went into Indianapolis and upset the Colts, 19–16. The Dolphins surprised by beating the Seahawks in Seattle, but Miami then was overwhelmed, 62–7, by the Jaguars.

In the NFC, the Redskins dominated the Detroit Lions in one wild-card game, while the Cowboys ended a mediocre season by falling to the Vikings in Minnesota. The Redskins then played the Bucs closely before losing, 14–13, when they botched a field-goal try in the final minutes. Minnesota had hoped to slow down the high-scoring

PROFESSIONAL FOOTBALL

Final Standings, 1999

AMERICAN CONFERENCE

					Points	
Eastern Division	**W**	**L**	**T**	**Pct.**	**For**	**Against**
Indianapolis	13	3	0	.813	423	333
Buffalo	11	5	0	.688	320	229
Miami	9	7	0	.563	326	336
N.Y. Jets	8	8	0	.500	308	309
New England	8	8	0	.500	299	284
Central Division						
Jacksonville	14	2	0	.875	396	217
Tennessee	13	3	0	.813	392	324
Baltimore	8	8	0	.500	324	277
Pittsburgh	6	10	0	.375	317	320
Cincinnati	4	12	0	.250	283	460
Cleveland	2	14	0	.125	217	437
Western Division						
Seattle	9	7	0	.563	338	298
Kansas City	9	7	0	.563	390	322
San Diego	8	8	0	.500	269	316
Oakland	8	8	0	.500	390	329
Denver	6	10	0	.375	314	318

PLAY-OFFS

Miami 20, Seattle 17
Tennessee 22, Buffalo 16

Jacksonville 62, Miami 7
Tennessee 19, Indianapolis 16

Tennessee 33, Jacksonville 14

NATIONAL CONFERENCE

					Points	
Eastern Division	**W**	**L**	**T**	**Pct.**	**For**	**Against**
Washington	10	6	0	.625	443	377
Dallas	8	8	0	.500	352	276
N.Y. Giants	7	9	0	.438	299	358
Arizona	6	10	0	.375	245	382
Philadelphia	5	11	0	.313	272	357
Central Division						
Tampa Bay	11	5	0	.688	270	235
Minnesota	10	6	0	.625	399	335
Detroit	8	8	0	.500	322	323
Green Bay	8	8	0	.500	357	341
Chicago	6	10	0	.375	272	341
Western Division						
St. Louis	13	3	0	.813	526	242
Carolina	8	8	0	.500	421	381
Atlanta	5	11	0	.313	285	380
San Francisco	4	12	0	.250	295	453
New Orleans	3	13	0	.188	260	434

PLAY-OFFS

Minnesota 27, Dallas 10
Washington 27, Detroit 13

St. Louis 49, Minnesota 37
Tampa Bay 14, Washington 13

St. Louis 11, Tampa Bay 6

Super Bowl XXXIV: St. Louis 23, Tennessee 16

Rams, but instead the Vikings were defeated, 49–37.

The Jaguars were favored to beat the Titans in the AFC final, but Tennessee defeated Jacksonville for the third time in the season, 33–14, in good part because of six Jaguar turnovers. The Rams were favored heavily to down Tampa Bay in the NFC final, and they did so, but only after scoring a touchdown in the final four minutes for an 11–6 triumph.

Super Bowl. In a game that was decided on the very last play, the St. Louis Rams defeated the Tennessee Titans, 23–16, in Super Bowl XXXIV. Titans receiver Kevin Dyson was tackled by the Rams' Mike Jones at the 1-yard line as time ran out. The Titans had overcome a 16–0 third-quarter deficit to tie the score. With less than two minutes remaining, however, Rams quarterback Kurt Warner threw a 73-yard touchdown pass to Isaac Brown for what would be the winning score. In all, Warner passed for a Super Bowl record of 414 yards and was named the game's most valuable player.

Individual Performances. The Rams' Warner became only the second quarterback in NFL history to throw for at least 40 touchdowns in a season. Warner, who was a backup in 1998 and played in 1999 only because starter Trent Green was hurt in the preseason, had 41 touchdown passes. Earlier in his career, he had played in the Arena League and had been a store clerk in between football jobs. Dan Marino twice had thrown more than 40 touchdown passes. Warner, the most unlikely hero of the season, was the league's most valuable player. Warner also was the highest-rated quarterback in the league. Another surprise was Minnesota quarterback Jeff George, who took over at midseason from Randall Cunningham and guided the Vikings into the play-offs.

Edgerrin James of the Colts led the league in rushing with 1,553; he was also rookie of the year. Jimmy Smith of Jacksonville had the most receptions (116), and Marvin Harrison of the Colts the most receiving yards (1,663). Defensive end Jevon Kearse of the Titans, another rookie, became one of the league's best pass rushers, as did the Rams' end Kevin Carter. Tampa defensive tackle Warren Sapp was selected by some organizations as defensive player of the year. Dick Vermeil of the Rams was the coach of the year.

Grey Cup. The Hamilton Tiger-Cats defeated the Calgary Stampeders, 32–21, to win the Canadian Football League's (CFL's) Grey Cup. Danny McManus, the league's leading passer, threw two touchdown passes.

COLLEGE FOOTBALL

Conference Champions
Atlantic Coast—Florida State
Big Ten—Wisconsin
Big 12—Nebraska and Kansas State (tied, North); Texas (South)
Big West—Boise State
Pacific Ten—Stanford
Southeastern—Florida (East); Alabama (West)
Western Athletic Conference—Fresno State, Hawaii, Texas Christian (tied)

NCAA Champions
Division I-AA—Georgia Southern
Division II—Northwest Missouri State
Division III—Pacific Lutheran

NAIA Champion: Northwestern Oklahoma State University

Individual Honors
Heisman Trophy—Ron Dayne, Wisconsin
Lombardi Award—Corey Moore, Virginia Tech
Outland Trophy—Chris Samuels, Alabama

MAJOR BOWL GAMES
Alamo Bowl (San Antonio, TX, Dec. 28)—Penn State 24, Texas A&M 0
Aloha Bowl (Honolulu, HI, Dec. 25)—Wake Forest 23, Arizona State 3
Blue-Gray Classic (Montgomery, AL, Dec. 25)—Gray 22, Blue 22
Citrus Bowl (Orlando, FL, Jan. 1)—Michigan State 37, Florida 34
Cotton Bowl (Dallas, TX, Jan. 1)—Arkansas 27, Texas 6
Fiesta Bowl (Tempe, AZ, Jan. 2)—Nebraska 31, Tennessee 21
Gator Bowl (Jacksonville, FL, Jan. 1)—Miami 28, Georgia Tech 13
Heritage Bowl (Atlanta, GA, Dec. 18)—Hampton 24, Southern 3
Holiday Bowl (San Diego, CA, Dec. 29)—Kansas State 24, Washington 20
Humanitarian Bowl (Boise, ID, Dec. 30)—Boise State 34, Louisville 31
Independence Bowl (Shreveport, LA, Dec. 31)—Mississippi 27, Oklahoma 25
Insight.com Bowl (Tucson, AZ, Dec. 31)—Colorado 62, Boston College 28
Las Vegas Bowl (Las Vegas, NV, Dec. 18)—Utah 17, Fresno State 16
Liberty Bowl (Memphis, TN, Dec. 31)—Southern Mississippi 23, Colorado State 17
Micron PC Bowl (Miami, FL, Dec. 30)—Illinois 63, Virginia 21
Mobile Alabama (Mobile, AL, Dec. 26)—Texas Christian 28, East Carolina 14
Motor City Bowl (Pontiac, MI, Dec. 27)—Marshall 21, Brigham Young 3
Music City Bowl (Nashville, TN, Dec. 29)—Syracuse 20, Kentucky 13
Oahu Bowl (Honolulu, HI, Dec. 25)—Hawaii 23, Oregon State 17
Orange Bowl (Miami, FL, Jan. 1)—Michigan 35, Alabama 34
Outback Bowl (Tampa, FL, Jan. 1)—Georgia 28, Purdue 25
Peach Bowl (Atlanta, GA, Dec. 30)—Mississippi State 17, Clemson 7
Rose Bowl (Pasadena, CA, Jan. 1)—Wisconsin 17, Stanford 9
Sugar Bowl (New Orleans, LA, Jan. 4)—Florida State 46, Virginia Tech 29
Sun Bowl (El Paso, TX, Dec. 31)—Oregon 24, Minnesota 20

The College Season

Under the Bowl Championship Series (BSC) format, undefeated Florida State and undefeated Virginia Tech met in the Sugar Bowl, the game chosen to host the title contest at the end of the 1999 season. The BSC format relies on a combination of newspaper and coach polls, computer rankings, and strength of schedule determinations.

Entering the season, both Florida State and Penn State were considered the nation's strongest teams. Other quality schools were defending national titlist Tennessee, Arizona, Florida, Nebraska, Michigan, Texas A&M, Ohio State, and Wisconsin.

© AP/Wide World Photos

Florida State, led by Peter Warrick (8), defeated Virginia Tech, 46–29, in the Sugar Bowl to capture college football's national championship. The Seminoles were undefeated in 1999.

Florida State had lost to Tennessee in the previous national title game, but the Seminoles had most of their starters returning and were led by star receiver Peter Warrick. They survived a couple of close midseason games to finish atop the final major regular-season polls. Behind sensational freshman quarterback Michael Vick, Virginia Tech slowly climbed the polls until it stood in second place behind Florida State.

But before the two teams were matched up for the national title game, other schools had to fall out of the running. Penn State had an inside track for the championship before collapsing over the final weeks of the season. Nebraska lost only once, to Texas, but that was enough for it to lose out. Florida fell to Florida State late in the season to end its hopes. Tennessee, Arizona, and Ohio State were disappointments.

Bowl Games. In the Sugar Bowl matchup between Florida State and Virginia Tech, much of the spotlight focused on the quarterbacks, Vick of Tech and veteran Chris Weinke of State. Vick was much more mobile, while Weinke was the better passer. Both played very well. Vick especially was dazzling. He rallied the Hokies from a slow start, and they led midway through the second half before Weinke combined with Warrick to rally the Seminoles. Warrick, who already had run a punt back for a touchdown, caught the pivotal scoring pass in the fourth period to put away the victory for coach Bobby Bowden, who won his second national title and had his first undefeated season. Florida State had the highest winning percentage (.890) of any college team during the 1990s. Despite the loss, Virginia Tech remained second in the final polls.

Nebraska used the Fiesta Bowl to finish the season strongly, beating a very good Tennessee team, 31–21. Wisconsin continued its run as a dominant team in the Big Ten by downing Stanford, 17–9, in the Rose Bowl. Michigan rallied against Alabama in the Orange Bowl and wound up winning, 35–34, in overtime. Michigan State helped its standing in the polls by defeating Florida in the Citrus Bowl, even though its coach, Nick Saban, had left to become coach at Louisiana State. Marshall finished as the only other undefeated team, besides Florida State, with a win in the Motor City Bowl.

The Best Players. Ron Dayne, a running back from Wisconsin, emerged as the best player in the country. He broke the National Collegiate Athletic Association (NCAA) all-time career rushing record set the previous season by Ricky Williams of Texas and was the most valuable player in the Rose Bowl. Florida State's Peter Warrick cost himself any chance at the player-of-the-year award when he was arrested for shoplifting during midseason. He was suspended for two games. Joe Hamilton of Georgia Tech and Virginia Tech's Vick were the best quarterbacks. Other standouts included receiver Troy Walters of Stanford; placekicker Sebastian Janikowski of Florida State; defensive linemen Courtney Brown of Penn State, Corey Moore of Virginia Tech, and Corey Simon of Florida State; and linebackers LaVar Arrington of Penn State and Raynoch Thompson of Tennessee.

PAUL ATTNER, *"The Sporting News"*

Golf

The year 1999 began with David Duval staking his claim as the best golfer in the world. It ended as definitely the year of the Tiger—Tiger Woods—with other triumphs and tragedies mixed in. France's Jean Van de Velde tossed away the British Open with some silly decision-making; the United States snatched the Ryder Cup away from Europe with some last-day heroics; a new Spanish sensation, Sergio Garcia, emerged; and Payne Stewart died in a mysterious plane crash just four months after winning his second U.S. Open. Young Karrie Webb and veteran Julie Inkster dueled for honors on the LPGA Tour, and a couple of 50-year-old rookies—Bruce Fleisher and Allen Doyle—stole much of Hale Irwin's thunder on the Senior PGA Tour.

PGA Tour. Duval won the season-opening Mercedes Championships and three more tournaments by the first week in April. That included a come-from-behind victory in the Bob Hope Chrysler Classic on the wings of a final-round 59. It was just the third 59 in PGA Tour history and the first in the last round to win a tournament. But Duval was not to win again, and Tiger Woods took over in midseason. He rolled to eight victories on the Tour—including four in a row, becoming the first man to do that since Ben Hogan in 1953. He won his second major championship at the PGA in August, banked a record $6.6 million in winnings on the PGA Tour, and established himself as clearly the dominant player in the game.

In the other major championships, José María Olazábal won his second Masters title, and Paul Lawrie of Scotland won the British Open in a play-off against Justin Leonard and Van de Velde. Needing only a play-it-safe double-bogey on the long 72d hole at tricked-up Carnoustie, the Frenchman hit an errant driver off the tee and an errant 2-iron out of the rough, flubbed a pitch shot into the burn, and made a triple-bogey 7 to force the play-off.

Stewart made a 15-ft (4.6-m) par putt on the 72d hole at historic Pinehurst Number 2 to beat Phil Mickelson by a stroke. In the PGA at Medinah, the 19-year-old Garcia made a series of spectacular shots to come within a stroke of Woods and win the hearts of the world.

At year's end, Woods was named player of the year, of course, and won the Vardon Trophy with a record adjusted stroke average of 68.43. Paraguay's Carlos Franco, a two-time winner, was rookie of the year, and Steve Pate, recovering from a number of injuries, was the year's comeback player.

Senior PGA Tour. Fleisher, who had won only once during his PGA Tour career, did it seven times in his first year as a senior, earning $2,515,705 and player and rookie-of-the-year honors. He also won the Byron Nelson Award for low scoring average at 69.19.

Irwin won five times, including the FORD SENIOR PLAYERS Championship, and finished second on the money list with $2,025,232.

LPGA Tour. Webb, in her fourth season, and Inkster, in her 17th, ran off with most of the honors. Webb won six times, including her first major at the du Maurier Classic; won the money title with a record $1,591,959; won the Vare Trophy with a

In Ryder Cup competition at The Country Club in Brookline, MA, players from the United States, right, *won eight of 12 singles matches on the final day, including the first six, to overcome a four-point deficit and win back the trophy from Europe, 14½–13½.*

GOLF

PGA Tour

Mercedes Championships: David Duval (266)
Sony Open in Hawaii: Jeff Sluman (271)
Bob Hope Chrysler Classic: David Duval (334)
Phoenix Open: Rocco Mediate (273)
AT&T Pebble Beach National Pro-Am: Payne Stewart (206)
Buick Invitational: Tiger Woods (266)
Nissan Open: Ernie Els (270)
World Golf Championships (Andersen Consulting Match Play): Jeff Maggert
PGA Grand Slam: Tiger Woods
Touchstone Energy Tucson Open: Gabriel Hjertstedt (276)
Doral-Ryder Open: Steve Elkington (275)
Honda Classic: Vijay Singh (277)
Bay Hill Invitational: Tim Herron (274)
THE PLAYERS Championship: David Duval (285)
BellSouth Classic: David Duval (270)
Masters Tournament: José María Olazábal (280)
MCI Classic (The Heritage of Golf): Glen Day (274)
Greater Greensboro Chrysler Classic: Jesper Parnevik (265)
Shell Houston Open: Stuart Appleby (279)
Compaq Classic of New Orleans: Carlos Franco (269)
GTE Byron Nelson Classic: Loren Roberts (262)
MasterCard Colonial: Olin Browne (272)
Kemper Open: Rich Beem (274)
Memorial Tournament: Tiger Woods (273)
FedEx St. Jude Classic: Ted Tryba (265)
U.S. Open: Payne Stewart (279)
Buick Classic: Duffy Waldorf (276)
Motorola Western Open: Tiger Woods (273)
Greater Milwaukee Open: Carlos Franco (264)
John Deere Classic: J.L. Lewis (261)
Canon Greater Hartford Open: Brent Geiberger (262)
Buick Open: Tom Pernice, Jr. (270)
PGA Championship: Tiger Woods (277)
Sprint International: David Toms (47 points)
World Golf Championships (NEC Invitational): Tiger Woods (270)
Reno-Tahoe Open: Notah Begay (274)
Air Canada Championship: Mike Weir (266)
Bell Canadian Open: Hal Sutton (275)
B.C. Open: Brad Faxon (273)
Westin Texas Open at LaCantera: Duffy Waldorf (270)
Buick Challenge: David Toms (271)
Michelob Championship at Kingsmill: Notah Begay (274)
Las Vegas Invitational: Jim Furyk (331)
National Car Rental Golf Classic at Walt Disney World Resort: Tiger Woods (271)
THE TOUR Championship presented by Southern Company: Tiger Woods (269)
Southern Farm Bureau Classic: Brian Henninger (202)
World Golf Championships—American Express Championship: Tiger Woods (278)

Senior PGA Tour

MasterCard Championship: John Jacobs (203)
Royal Caribbean Classic: Bruce Fleisher (205)
American Express Invitational: Bruce Fleisher (203)
GTE Classic: Larry Nelson (205)
ACE Group Classic: Allen Doyle (203)
Toshiba Senior Classic: Gary McCord (204)
Liberty Mutual Legends of Golf: Hubert Green/Gil Morgan (194)
Emerald Coast Classic: Bob Duval (200)
The Tradition Presented by Countrywide: Graham Marsh (136)
PGA Seniors' Championship: Allen Doyle (274)
Home Depot Invitational: Bruce Fleisher (205)
Bruno's Memorial Classic: Larry Nelson (205)
Nationwide Championship: Hale Irwin (206)
Las Vegas Senior Classic by Tru-Green-Chemlawn: Vicente Fernandez (274)
Bell Atlantic Classic: Tom Jenkins (206)
Boone Valley Classic: Hale Irwin (203)
Cadillac NFL Golf Classic: Allen Doyle (204)
BellSouth Senior Classic at Opryland: Bruce Fleisher (200)
Southwestern Bell Dominion: John Mahaffey (204)
FORD SENIOR PLAYERS Championship: Hale Irwin (267)
State Farm Senior Classic: Christy O'Connor (198)
U.S. Senior Open: Dave Eichelberger (281)
Ameritech Senior Open: Hale Irwin (206)
Coldwell Banker Burnet Classic: Hale Irwin (201)
Novell Utah Showdown: Dave Eichelberger (197)
Lightpath Long Island Classic: Bruce Fleisher (206)
Foremost Insurance Championship: Christy O'Connor (205)
FleetBoston Classic: Tom McGinnis (205)
AT&T Canada Senior Open: Jim Ahern (272)
TD Waterhouse Championship: Allen Doyle (198)
Comfort Classic: Gil Morgan (201)
Bank One Championship: Tom Watson (196)
Kroger Senior Classic: Gil Morgan (198)
Vantage Championship: Fred Gibson (195)
The Transamerica: Bruce Fleisher (199)
Raley's Gold Rush Classic: David Graham (199)
EMC² Kaanapali Classic: Bruce Fleisher (199)
Pacific Bell Senior Classic: Joe Inman (199)
Ingersoll-Rand SENIOR TOUR Championship: Gary McCord (276)
Qualifying Tournament: Mark Hayes (277)

LPGA Tour

The HEALTHSOUTH Inaugural: Kelly Robbins (205)
Subaru Memorial of Naples: Meg Mallon (272)
The Office Depot: Karrie Webb (278)
Valley of the Stars Championship Presented by Yamaha: Catrin Nilsmark (204)
Sunrise Hawaiian Ladies Open: Alison Nicholas (209)
Australian Ladies Masters: Karrie Webb (262)
Welch's/Circle K Championship: Juli Inkster (273)
Standard Register PING: Karrie Webb (274)
Nabisco Dinah Shore: Dottie Pepper (269)
Longs Drugs Challenge: Juli Inkster (280)
Chick-fil-A Charity Championship: Rachel Hetherington (204)
City of Hope Myrtle Beach Classic: Rachel Hetherington (137)
The Titleholders presented by Mercury: Karrie Webb (271)
Sara Lee Classic: Meg Mallon (199)
The Philips Invitational Honoring Harvey Penick: Akiko Fukushima (267)
LPGA Corning Classic: Kelli Kuehne (278)
U.S. Women's Open: Juli Inkster (272)
Wegmans Rochester International: Karrie Webb (280)
ShopRite LPGA Classic: Se Ri Pak (198)
McDonald's LPGA Championship: Juli Inkster (268)
Jamie Farr Kroger Classic: Se Ri Pak (276)
Michelob Light Classic: Annika Sorenstam (278)
Japan Airlines Big Apple Classic: Sherri Steinhauer (273)
Giant Eagle LPGA Classic: Jackie Gallagher-Smith (199)
du Maurier Classic: Karrie Webb (277)
areaWEB.COM Challenge: Mardi Lunn (275)
Weetabix Women's British Open: Sherri Steinhauer (283)
Firstar LPGA Classic: Rosie Jones (207)
Oldsmobile Classic: Dottie Pepper (270)
State Farm Rail Classic: Mi Hyun Kim (204)
Samsung World Championship of Women's Golf: Se Ri Pak (280)
SAFECO Classic: Maria Hjorth (271)
The Safeway LPGA Golf Championship: Juli Inkster (207)
New Albany Golf Classic: Annika Sorenstam (269)
First Union Betsy King Classic: Mi Hyun Kim (280)
AFLAC Champions presented by Southern Living: Akiko Fukushima (279)
Nichirei International: United States
Mizuno Classic: Maria Hjorth (201)
PageNet Championship: Se Ri Pak (276)

Other Tournaments

British Open: Paul Lawrie (290)
Ryder Cup: United States 14½, Europe 13½
Walker Cup: Great Britain/Ireland 15, United States 9
U.S. Women's Amateur Public Links: Jody Niemann
U.S. Amateur Public Links: Hunter Haas
U.S. Girls' Junior: Aree Wongluekiet
U.S. Junior Amateur: Hunter Mahan
U.S. Women's Amateur: Dorothy Delasin
U.S. Amateur: David Gossett
U.S. Women's Mid-Amateur: Corey Weworski
U.S. Mid-Amateur: Danny Green
U.S. Senior Women's Amateur: Carole Semple Thompson
U.S. Senior Amateur: Bill Ploeger
NCAA Women: Team—Duke (895); Individual—Grace Park, Arizona State (212)
NCAA Men: Team—Georgia (1,180); Individual—Luke Donald, Northwestern (284)
British Seniors Open: Christy O'Connor (282)
British Amateur: Graeme Storm
World Cup of Golf: Team—United States (545); Individual—Tiger Woods (263)
Cisco World Match Play Championship: Colin Montgomerie
JC Penney Classic: Laura Davies/John Daly (260)
PGA Grand Slam of Golf: Tiger Woods
Senior Slam: Gil Morgan (132)
Dunhill Cup: Spain
Sun City Million Dollar Challenge: Ernie Els (263)
Franklin Templeton Shark Shootout: Fred Couples/David Duval
Senior Skins Game: Hale Irwin
Skins Game: Fred Couples
Senior Match Play Challenge: Larry Nelson
Office Depot Father/Son Challenge: Jack and Gary Nicklaus
Wendy's Three-Tour Challenge: Senior PGA Tour—Tom Watson/Jack Nicklaus/Hale Irwin

---

record 69.43 stroke average; and was named Rolex Player of the Year. Inkster won the U.S. Women's Open, the McDonald's LPGA Championship, and three other tournaments to earn $1,337,253. She became just the third player in LPGA history to achieve the career Grand Slam by winning all the major championships. Inkster earned her way into the LPGA Tour Hall of Fame, as did Amy Alcott and Beth Daniels, after the LPGA revised its criteria for entrance.

Mi Hyun Kim won twice and was named Rolex Rookie of the Year.

LARRY DENNIS
Creative Communications

Horse Racing

Cat Thief, a 19–1 long shot, won the $4 million Breeders' Cup Classic at Hallandale, FL, on Nov. 6, 1999, in the most unique race in the Cup's 16-year history. Cat Thief went to the post with one victory in 11 starts and was followed to the finish line by 26–1 choice Budroyale, 75–1 long shot Golden Missile, and 63–1 pick Chester House. Ridden by Pat Day, Cat Thief covered the 1.25 mi (2 km) at Gulfstream Park in 1:59.52 and paid $41.20 on a $2 wager. The Classic winner was trained by D. Wayne Lukas, who climaxed a spectacular season in which he also won the Kentucky Derby and Preakness Stakes with Charismatic.

The $2 million Breeders' Cup Turf was won by Daylami, which outran Royal Anthem and Buck's Bay to the finish under the ride of Frankie Dettori.

Lukas saddled another Breeders' Cup victor, Cash Run, which paid $67 as a 32–1 choice in the Juvenile Fillies. Lukas ran his string of Breeders' Cup victories to 15, while upstaging rival Bob Baffert. The latter came up winless despite having the favorite in three races. Baffert's brilliant filly, Silverbulletday, was sixth in the $2 million Distaff, which was won by Beautiful Pleasure. Silverbulletday won the Juvenile Fillies in 1998 and was trying to become the first horse to win two different Breeders' Cup races.

Anees, a 30–1 shot, overcame a strong 14-horse field to win the Juvenile. Anees, which was last after a half mile (.8 km), ran the $1\frac{1}{16}$ miles (1.7 km) in 1:42.29 to beat runner-up Chief Seattle. The Breeders' Cup Sprint winner was Artax, which tied a 26-year-old track record of 1:07.89 for a mile.

General Challenge and Prime Timber, both Baffert horses, were one-two in the Santa Anita Derby, and, with Excellent Meeting, Baffert had three strong horses in the 125th Kentucky Derby. But Chris Antley rode 31–1 long shot Charismatic to victory for Lukas. Menifee finished second, and Cat Thief was third. Charismatic's winning time was 2:03.29 over 1.25 mi (2 km). Charismatic followed up by beating Menifee by 1.5 lengths in the 124th Preakness, as Badge finished third. But Charismatic's bid to win the Triple Crown saw the former claimer finish third at the Belmont Stakes. Lemon Drop Kid won with Vision and Verse second. Sixty yards (55 m) past the finish line, Charismatic pulled up lame with an injured left leg. Antley's quick jump from the saddle may have prevented further injury.

Valhol's victory in the Arkansas Derby was disallowed following an investigation into alleged use of a battery by jockey Billy Patin, who was suspended for five years.

Harness Racing. Blissfull Hall, a 3-year-old, became the ninth triple-crown winner in pacing history, sweeping the Cane Pace, the Little Brown Jug, and the Messenger Stakes.

The Hambletonian, for 3-year-old trotters, saw Michael Lachance drive Self Possessed to victory and a world record for the fastest trotting mile—1:51.3.

STAN SUTTON

HORSE RACING

Major U.S. Thoroughbred Races

Arkansas Derby: Valhol*, $500,000 (total purse)
Belmont Stakes: Lemon Drop Kid, $1 million
Blue Grass Stakes: Menifee, $750,000
Breeders' Cup Classic: Cat Thief, $4 million
Breeders' Cup Filly & Mare Turf: Soaring Softly, $1 million
Breeders' Cup Juvenile: Anees, $1 million
Breeders' Cup Juvenile Fillies: Cash Run, $1 million
Breeders' Cup Mile: Silic, $1 million
Breeders' Cup Distaff: Beautiful Pleasure, $2 million
Breeders' Cup Sprint: Artax, $1 million
Breeders' Cup Turf: Daylami, $2 million
Donn Handicap: Puerto Madero, $500,000
Florida Derby: Vicar, $750,000
Haskell Invitational Handicap: Menifee, $1 million
Hollywood Gold Cup: Real Quiet, $1 million
Illinois Derby: Vision and Verse, $500,000
Kentucky Derby: Charismatic, $1,186,200
Kentucky Oaks: Silverbulletday, $551,000
Louisiana Derby: Kimberlite Pipe, $640,000
Metropolitan Handicap: Sir Bear, $500,000
Pacific Classic: General Challenge, $1 million
Preakness Stakes: Charismatic, $1 million
Santa Anita Derby: General Challenge, $750,000
Santa Anita Handicap: Free House, $1 million
Suburban Handicap: Behrens, $400,000
Swaps Stakes: Cat Thief, $500,000
Travers Stakes: Lemon Drop Kid, $1 million
Wood Memorial: Adonis, $600,000
Woodward Stakes: River Keen, $500,000
*Valhol later was disqualified.

Major North American Harness Races

Breeders Crown Open Pace: Red Bow Tie, $380,000
Breeders Crown Open Trot: Supergrit, $580,000
Breeders Crown Mare Pace: Shore By Five, $282,500
Breeders Crown 2-year-old Filly Pace: Eternal Camnation, $637,833
Breeders Crown 2-year-old Colt Pace: Tyberwood, $823,347
Breeders Crown 2-year-old Filly Trot: Dream of Joy, $652,092
Breeders Crown 2-year-old Colt Trot: Master Lavec, $662,529
Breeders Crown 3-year-old Filly Pace: Odies Fame, $764,400
Breeders Crown 3-year-old Colt Pace: Grinfromeartoear, $588,000
Breeders Crown 3-year-old Filly Trot: Oolong, $588,000
Breeders Crown 3-year-old Colt Trot: C R Renegade, $588,000
Hambletonian: Self Possessed, $1 million
Hambletonian Oaks: Oolong, $500,000
Little Brown Jug: Blissfull Hall, $489,580
Meadowlands Pace: The Panderosa, $1 million
Peter Haughton Memorial: Smok'n Lantern, $509,400
Sweetheart Pace: Panything Goes, $461,400
Woodrow Wilson Pace: Richess Hanover, $600,000

Ice Hockey

While the Dallas Stars won their first Stanley Cup in 1999, the feat was dwarfed by the retirement of Wayne Gretzky, hockey's 38-year-old "Great One."

Gretzky decided to quit after his 20th National Hockey League (NHL) season, leaving in his wake a trail of records that likely never will be broken. Gretzky—who won four Stanley Cup championships with the Edmonton Oilers, took ten scoring titles, and was the league's most valuable player nine times—set or shared 61 NHL records. The most impressive were scoring 50 goals in the fewest number of games (39), getting at least one point in 51 consecutive games, and eclipsing 200 points in four seasons. No other player ever has had 200 points in a single season. During a seven-year span in the 1980s, Gretzky averaged a staggering 192 points per season for the Oilers. He finished with 2,857 points—more than 1,000 ahead of his closest pursuer, Gordie Howe, who had 1,850. The "Great One" had 894 goals—93 more than Howe—and 1,963 assists. At the time of Gretzky's retirement from the New York Rangers—his fourth NHL club, after the Oilers, the Los Angeles Kings, and the St. Louis Blues—he still was averaging close to a point per game (62 points in 70 games). His legacy was so great that league commissioner Gary Bettman announced that no other player would wear his number, 99.

NHL Regular Season. Jaromir Jagr, carrying the torch since his Pittsburgh Penguins teammate Mario Lemieux retired two years before, repeated as the scoring champion, with 127 points—20 points clear of the league's highest goal-scorer, Teemu Selanne of the Anaheim Mighty Ducks, who had 47 goals and 107 points. It was Jagr's third scoring crown in five years. Only one other player, Selanne's Anaheim teammate Paul Kariya, had more than 100 points in the 1998–99 season. He finished with 101. No player scored 50 goals, and only nine players scored 40 or more. Jagr, Tony Amonte of the Chicago Blackhawks, and Alexei Yashin of the Ottawa Senators were tied for second behind Selanne, each with 44 goals.

While Colorado Avalanche goalie Patrick Roy became the all-time leader in wins, including play-off games, with his 506th victory, Vancouver Canucks captain Mark Messier became the tenth player to score 600 goals. He also moved past Howe into third place in the all-time assist list, behind Gretzky and Paul Coffey. Calgary defenseman Phil Housley also surpassed Joe Mullen as the highest-scoring U.S.-born player in history. In a blockbuster trade, Theoren Fleury, the Calgary Flames' all-time leading scorer, and Chris Dingman were dealt to Colorado for three young players—Rene Corbet, Robyn Regehr, and Wade Belak. What once had been one of the game's greatest buildings, Toronto's Maple Leaf Gardens, closed its doors after 68 years, as the Air Canada Centre became the new home of the Maple Leafs. The league also added one new team, the Nashville Predators, giving it 27 franchises.

In the Eastern Conference, Ottawa won its first regular-season title in the most competitive division, the Northeast, with 103 points. The New Jersey Devils took the Atlantic Division with 105 points, and the Carolina Hurricanes finished first in the weakest division, the Southeast, with 86 points. In the

Dallas center Joe Nieuwendyk (25) scored 11 goals, including six game-winners, in 23 play-off games and was awarded the Conn Smythe Trophy as the most valuable player of the play-offs.

Western Conference, the reigning two-time Stanley Cup champion Detroit Red Wings won the Central with 93 points. The Dallas Stars rolled to the Pacific crown with 114 points, and Colorado won the Northwest Division, with 98 points.

Play-offs. There was one huge upset in the first round of the play-offs, when the Devils blew a 3–2 series lead and fell in seven games to Pittsburgh, a team 15 points worse in the regular season. Jagr, playing with a painful groin injury, rallied the Penguins. Ottawa also was bounced in four straight by Buffalo, after being 12 points better over the 82 games. Yashin had no points in the series. Toronto got great goaltending from Curtis Joseph to beat the Philadelphia Flyers in six games. The Flyers played without captain Eric Lindros, who had a collapsed lung. The Boston Bruins beat Carolina in six games in the other Eastern round. Carolina then mourned the loss of defenseman Steve Chiasson, who died in a car crash.

In the Western Conference, Dallas got a slight scare but disposed of an old nemesis, the Edmonton Oilers, in four straight one-goal decisions. The clinching game was not decided until late in the third overtime, when Joe Nieuwendyk scored. The Detroit Red Wings whipped Anaheim in four; Colorado won two overtime games in a 4–2 series win over the San Jose Sharks; and Pierre Turgeon scored in overtime in Game 7, as St. Louis rallied from a 3–1 series deficit to beat the Phoenix Coyotes.

In round two, the Maple Leafs knocked off Pittsburgh in six—winning the last three games of the series, two of those in overtime. Buffalo continued its hot roll, squeezing by the Bruins in six games, even though the team played without its 40-goal scorer, Miroslav Satan, for the entire series because of a badly bruised foot. In the West, Dallas got by St. Louis in six games, with Mike Modano getting the winner early in the first overtime of the last game. In a great battle, Colorado ended Detroit's reign as Stanley Cup champs, beating the Wings in six games. Detroit had won the first two games behind backup goalie Bill Ranford but dropped the next four games.

In the conference finals, Buffalo rolled over Toronto in five games, even though its goalie Dominik Hasek did not play the first two games because of a slight hernia. The Sabres scored 21 goals in the series. In the West, Dallas rallied from a 3–2 series deficit to sneak past the Avalanche in seven games. Coming off a lackluster 7–5 performance in Game 5, Stars goalie Eddie Belfour only allowed two goals the last two games, as the Stars registered 4–1 wins.

ICE HOCKEY

National Hockey League
(Final Standings, 1998–99)

Eastern Conference

					Goals	
Atlantic Division	**W**	**L**	**T**	**Pts.**	**For**	**Against**
*New Jersey	47	24	11	105	248	196
*Philadelphia	37	26	19	93	231	196
*Pittsburgh	38	30	14	90	242	225
N.Y. Rangers	33	38	11	77	217	227
N.Y. Islanders	24	48	10	58	194	244
Northeast Division						
*Ottawa	44	23	15	103	239	179
*Toronto	45	30	7	97	268	231
*Boston	39	30	13	91	214	181
*Buffalo	37	28	17	91	207	175
Montreal	32	39	11	75	184	209
Southeast Division						
*Carolina	34	30	18	86	210	202
Florida	30	34	18	78	210	228
Washington	31	45	6	68	200	218
Tampa Bay	19	54	9	47	179	292

Western Conference

					Goals	
Central Division	**W**	**L**	**T**	**Pts.**	**For**	**Against**
*Detroit	43	32	7	93	245	202
*St. Louis	37	32	13	87	237	209
Chicago	29	41	12	70	202	248
Nashville	28	47	7	63	190	261
Northwest Division						
*Colorado	44	28	10	98	239	205
*Edmonton	33	37	12	78	230	226
Calgary	30	40	12	72	211	234
Vancouver	23	47	12	58	192	258
Pacific Division						
*Dallas	51	19	12	114	236	168
*Phoenix	39	31	12	90	205	197
*Anaheim	35	34	13	83	215	206
*San Jose	31	33	18	80	196	191
Los Angeles	32	45	5	69	189	222

*In play-offs

Stanley Cup Play-offs

Eastern Conference

Quarterfinals	Boston	4 games	Carolina	2
	Buffalo	4 games	Ottawa	0
	Pittsburgh	4 games	New Jersey	3
	Toronto	4 games	Philadelphia	2
Semifinals	Buffalo	4 games	Boston	2
	Toronto	4 games	Pittsburgh	2
Finals	Buffalo	4 games	Toronto	1

Western Conference

Quarterfinals	Colorado	4 games	San Jose	2
	Dallas	4 games	Edmonton	0
	Detroit	4 games	Anaheim	0
	St. Louis	4 games	Phoenix	3
Semifinals	Colorado	4 games	Detroit	2
	Dallas	4 games	St. Louis	2
Finals	Dallas	4 games	Colorado	3

Stanley Cup Finals

Dallas 4 games Buffalo 2

Individual Honors

Hart Trophy (most valuable player): Jaromir Jagr, Pittsburgh
Ross Trophy (leading scorer): Jaromir Jagr
Maurice Richard Trophy (most goals): Teemu Selanne, Anaheim
Vezina Trophy (top goaltender): Dominik Hasek, Buffalo
Jennings Trophy (fewest goals allowed): Ed Belfour and Roman Turek, Dallas
Norris Trophy (best defenseman): Al MacInnis, St. Louis
Selke Trophy (best defensive forward): Jere Lehtinen, Dallas
Calder Trophy (rookie of the year): Chris Drury, Colorado
Lady Byng Trophy (most gentlemanly player): Wayne Gretzky, New York Rangers
Conn Smythe Trophy (most valuable in play-offs): Joe Nieuwendyk, Dallas
Adams Award (coach of the year): Jacques Martin, Ottawa
King Clancy Trophy (leadership and humanitarian service): Roy Ray, Buffalo
Bill Masterton Trophy (perseverance, sportsmanship, and dedication): John Cullen, Tampa Bay
Lester B. Pearson Award (outstanding player, voted by the players): Jaromir Jagr

Stanley Cup Finals. The final series was a matchup of two teams who never had had much success. The Stars had reached the finals only twice before—in 1981 and 1991, when they were known as the North Stars and based in Minnesota. Buffalo had been there once—in 1975, losing to Philadelphia. In the 1999 finals, the Sabres drew first blood when defenseman Jason Woolley beat Belfour late in the first overtime in Dallas for a 3–2 win in Game 1. The Stars came back in Game 2, with Brett Hull blasting a shot by Hasek in the final three minutes for the game-winner in a 4–2 victory.

The Stars held the Sabres to 12 shots in a 2–1 win in Game 3 in Buffalo. The 12 shots equaled the record for the lowest shot total in a Stanley Cup final. Dixon Ward of the Sabres swept a shot by Belfour in the second period in Game 4, and Buffalo held on to take a 2–1 victory to tie the series, 2–2. Belfour blanked the Sabres, 2–0, in Dallas in a stiflingly defensive Game 5. Hull ended Game 6, 2–1, with a controversial goal five minutes before a fourth overtime period. Hull's foot was in the crease when he scored on Hasek, a violation of the rules, but the league counted the goal after a short debate.

Personnel Changes. Early in the season, Mike Keenan was fired by the Vancouver Canucks and replaced by former Colorado coach Marc Crawford, who had been working as a broadcaster. In Chicago, Dirk Graham was dismissed, and assistant coach Lorne Molleken took over. New York Islander general manager–coach Mike Milbury fired himself as coach during the year, named his assistant Bill Stewart as coach, and then hired onetime Islander Butch Goring as coach when the season ended. Los Angeles let Larry Robinson go after four years and replaced him with onetime NHL assistant Andy Murray. In Edmonton, Ron Low left, and longtime Oiler defenseman Kevin Lowe took his place. Phoenix fired Jim Schoenfeld after its play-off ouster, and Boston assistant Bobby Francis was the surprise pick as head coach.

Other Winners. For the second time in four years, the Czech Republic won the Ice Hockey World Championships. It defeated Finland in the finals. The University of Maine scored an overtime victory over the University of New Hampshire to capture the National Collegiate Athletic Association (NCAA) Division I hockey title. Jason Krog of the University of New Hampshire was named college player of the year.

JIM MATHESON, *"The Edmonton Journal"*

Ice Skating

The 1999 figure-skating season belonged to Russia.

Figure Skating. At the World Figure Skating Championships in Helsinki, Finland, in March, Russian skaters captured all four events—a feat they had accomplished earlier at the 1999 European championships in Prague, Czech Republic. At both competitions, Alexei Yagudin, 19, took the men's title for a second consecutive year; Maria Butyrskaya captured the women's crown; and Anjelika Krylova and Oleg Ovsyannikov were the champions in dance. Yelena Berezhnaya and Anton Sikharulidze repeated as world's pairs winners, and Maria Petrova and Alexei Tikhonov won the pairs title in Prague. In Helsinki, Butyrskaya—who was nearing her 27th birthday—became the oldest women's world champion in history and the first Russian woman to take the crown. She defeated the defending champion, Michelle Kwan of the United States.

Earlier, at the U.S. championships in Salt Lake City, UT, Kwan, 18, won the women's title for a third time. Michael Weiss, 22, the men's runner-up in 1997 and 1998, finished first among the men's skaters.

Speed Skating. Gunda Niemann-Stirnemann took the all-around world speed-skating title for an eighth time. The 32-year-old German also repeated as winner of the World Cup 1,500-meter and 3,000/5,000-meter events. The men's all-around world speed-skating crown went to Rintje Ritsma of the Netherlands.

ICE SKATING

World Figure Skating Championships
Men: Alexei Yagudin, Russia
Women: Maria Butyrskaya, Russia
Pairs: Yelena Berezhnaya and Anton Sikharulidze, Russia
Dance: Anjelika Krylova and Oleg Ovsyannikov, Russia

U.S. National Figure Skating Championships
Men: Michael Weiss
Women: Michelle Kwan
Pairs: Danielle and Steve Hartsell
Dance: Naomi Lang and Peter Tchernyshev

European Figure Skating Championships
Men: Alexei Yagudin, Russia
Women: Maria Butyrskaya, Russia
Pairs: Maria Petrova and Alexei Tikhonov, Russia
Dance: Anjelika Krylova and Oleg Ovsyannikov, Russia

Speed Skating World Cup—Final Points
Men's 500 meters: Jeremy Wotherspoon, Canada
Men's 1,000 meters: Jeremy Wotherspoon
Men's 1,500 meters: Adne Sondral, Norway
Men's 5,000 meters/10,000 meters: Bart Veldkamp, Belgium
Women's 500 meters: Catriona LeMay Doan, Canada
Women's 1,000 meters: Monique Garbrecht, Germany
Women's 1,500 meters: Gunda Niemann-Stirnemann, Germany
Women's 3,000 meters/5,000 meters: Gunda Niemann-Stirnemann

World Speed Skating Championships
Men's Overall: Rintje Ritsma, Netherlands
Women's Overall: Gunda Niemann-Stirnemann

SPECIAL REPORT The 2002 Salt Lake City Olympics Come under Fire

In the 100-plus years since Baron Pierre de Coubertin of France founded the modern Olympic Games, the movement has survived political boycotts, terrorist attacks, and drug scandals. As troubling as those various episodes were, nothing prepared the 107-member International Olympic Committee (IOC) for the worldwide condemnation it received when allegations of bribery and vote buying surfaced in the selection of Salt Lake City, UT, for the 2002 Winter Olympics.

Investigations and Findings. The resulting outcry prompted investigations by the U.S. Justice Department and the state of Utah, as well as the U.S. Olympic Committee (USOC). The IOC also launched its own internal investigation. Eventually, ten IOC members lost their positions; a Salt Lake City businessman pleaded guilty to a tax violation in connection with the case; and the son of IOC Vice-President Un-Yong Kim was indicted on criminal charges.

Worse, it was discovered that the vote-buying efforts of Salt Lake City's bidders were not isolated incidents. Evidence came to light showing that similar tactics were used by organizers of the 1998 Winter Games in Nagano, Japan; the 1996 Summer Olympics in Atlanta, GA; and the 2000 Summer Games in Sydney, Australia. In fact, some Olympic critics said that the IOC for decades had turned a blind eye to the practice of bid-city officials making under-the-table payments to its members in an effort to influence their votes. IOC members, promoted as the guardians of the Olympic ideal, regularly enjoyed first-class airfare around the globe, stayed in five-star hotels, partook of opulent meals, and received expensive gifts courtesy of bid-city committees.

The sudden downfall of the 2002 Games began in November 1998, when a Salt Lake City television station first reported that the Salt Lake City Organizing Committee paid for a "scholarship" for Sonia Essomba, daughter of late IOC member René Essomba of Cameroon, to attend American University in Washington. As the scandal mushroomed, organizing-committee chairman Frank Joklik revealed in December 1998 that Salt Lake organizers had given 13 individuals a total of $393,871 in financial aid or scholarships. Six of those individuals were relatives of IOC members, Joklik said. Later, it was learned that three Africans connected to the IOC were given nearly $28,000 in free health care at a Salt Lake City–area hospital. Another revelation implicated IOC member Jean-Claude Ganga of the Republic of Congo, who earned a $60,000 profit on a land deal arranged through a member of the Salt Lake City bid committee.

The roots of Salt Lake City's vote-buying efforts could be traced to 1991, when the city, despite being heavily favored, lost its bid to host the 1998 Winter Games. Salt Lake City bidders had not given lavish gifts in that effort, believing the merits of their city would win out. They painfully learned that merit was not enough when Nagano won the IOC vote after spending an average of $22,000 on each visiting IOC member—a total well in excess of IOC limits.

Results. No individual received more criticism as a result of the scandal than Juan Antonio Samaranch of Spain, president of the IOC since 1980. Samaranch had been credited with the enormous financial growth of the Olympic Games. Yet, when the Salt Lake City bribery scandal erupted, Samaranch was accused of accepting lavish gifts that cost far more than the $200 limit imposed by the IOC. There were numerous calls for Samaranch's resignation or ouster. Samaranch survived, however, receiving a near-unanimous vote of confidence from IOC members at the start of an emergency general assembly to address the scandal. But the IOC suffered a severe blow to its once lofty image. The organization voted in December to implement a number of reforms, including prohibiting members from visiting bid-city sites; setting term limits for the presidency; subjecting delegates, who formerly were appointed for life, to reelection every eight years; and appointing active athletes to the IOC.

There were other casualties, too. Organizing-committee chairman Joklik and Vice-President Dave Johnson were ousted. Former committee chairman Tom Welch, who had resigned under fire in an unrelated incident before the scandal broke, was stripped of his $1 million pension. Wary corporate sponsors backed away from the 2002 Games, leaving Salt Lake City fund-raisers $90 million short of revenue. That forced new organizing-committee boss Mitt Romney to trim costs to ensure that the Games would be able to repay $59 million to Utah taxpayers, who had approved upfront money to get the Games started.

Before the scandal, the 2002 Winter Games were expected to create a financial windfall for Utah and the USOC. By late 1999, Salt Lake City officials were not sure the Games would break even.

MIKE SPENCE

Skiing

In the 1999 Alpine World Cup, the men's overall championship went to Lasse Kjus of Norway; Alexandra Meissnitzer of Austria won the women's overall title easily. Both of the overall winners at the Nordic World Cup, Bjorn Dahlie and Bente Martinsen, came from Norway. At the U.S. Alpine Championships, all of the winners on both the men's and women's sides were Americans, with the exception of Slovenia's Uro Pavlovcic, who won the giant slalom in one of the last races of his career.

At the Nordic World Championships, Finland dominated the men's competition, with Mika Myllyla winning the 10-km, 30-km, and 50-km events, and the Finnish team earning the combined trophy. On the women's side, Stefania Belmondo of Italy won the 10-km and 15-km events, Martinsen finished first in the 5-km, and Larissa Lazutina of Russia won the 30-km.

The University of Colorado successfully defended its title at the 1999 National Collegiate Men's and Women's Skiing Championships, defeating Denver University by a net point score of 650 to 636.

SKIING

Alpine World Cup

Men's Downhill: Lasse Kjus, Norway
Men's Slalom: Thomas Stangassinger, Austria
Men's Giant Slalom: Michael Von Gruenigen, Switzerland
Men's Super-Giant Slalom: Hermann Maier, Austria
Men's Overall: Lasse Kjus
Women's Downhill: Renate Goetschl, Austria
Women's Slalom: Sabine Egger, Austria
Women's Giant Slalom: Alexandra Meissnitzer, Austria
Women's Super-Giant Slalom: Alexandra Meissnitzer
Women's Overall: Alexandra Meissnitzer

U.S. Alpine Championships

Men's Downhill: Chad Fleischer, United States
Men's Slalom: Sacha Gros, United States
Men's Giant Slalom: Uros Pavlovcic, Slovenia
Men's Super-Giant Slalom: Jakub Fiala, United States
Women's Downhill: Kirsten L. Clark, United States
Women's Slalom: Alexandra Shaffer, United States
Women's Giant Slalom: Alexandra Shaffer
Women's Super-Giant Slalom: Kathleen Monahan, United States

Alpine World Championships

Men's Downhill: Hermann Maier
Men's Slalom: Kalle Palander, Finland
Men's Giant Slalom: Lasse Kjus
Men's Super-Giant Slalom: Hermann Maier and Lasse Kjus (tied)
Men's Combined: Kjetil Andre Aamadt, Norway
Women's Downhill: Renate Goetschl
Women's Slalom: Zali Stegall, Australia
Women's Giant Slalom: Alexandra Meissnitzer
Women's Super-Giant Slalom: Alexandra Meissnitzer
Women's Combined: Pernilla Wiberg, Sweden

NCAA Alpine Championships

Men's and Women's Team: University of Colorado

Nordic World Championships

Men's 10 kilometers: Mika Myllyla, Finland
Men's 15 kilometers: Thomas Alsgaard, Norway
Men's 30 kilometers: Mika Myllyla
Men's 50 kilometers: Mika Myllyla
Men's Relay: Austria
Women's 5 kilometers: Bente Martinsen, Norway
Women's 10 kilometers: Stefania Belmondo, Italy
Women's 15 kilometers: Stefania Belmondo
Women's 30 kilometers: Larissa Lazutina, Russia
Women's Relay: Russia
Jumping—90-m Hill: Kazuyoshi Funaki, Japan
Jumping—120-m Hill: Martin Schmitt, Germany
Jumping—Team: Germany
Combined Individual: Bjarte Engen Vik, Norway
Combined Team: Finland

Nordic World Cup

Men's Overall: Bjorn Dahlie, Norway
Women's Overall: Bente Martinsen

Soccer

The English team Manchester United steamrollered its competition in 1999, winning three major world tournaments. Meanwhile, skyrocketing player salaries prompted leaders from both the International Federation of Association Football (FIFA), world soccer's governing body, and the Union of European Football Associations (UEFA), which controls European soccer, to broach the previously taboo subject of salary caps; neither, however, took any action. The victory of the U.S. team in the third Women's World Cup in July was most impressive (*see* SIDEBAR).

Europe and South America. Manchester United of England, the world's wealthiest soccer club, swept away everything before it in 1999, becoming the first English team to complete the "treble"—winning the English Premier League championship, the Football Association (F.A.) Cup, and, in an astonishing finale, the European Champions Cup. The latter victory, over Bayern Munich of Germany in Barcelona, Spain, on May 26 was perhaps the most improbable. Trailing, 1–0, with less than a minute to play, Manchester scored twice to claim the trophy for the first time in 31 years. The win came in front of 90,000 incredulous fans at the Camp Nou stadium and an estimated worldwide television audience of 500 million.

Europe's other major trophies were taken by Italian clubs. Parma of Italy earned the UEFA Cup with a 3–0 victory over Olympique Marseille of France on May 12 at Luzhniki Stadium in Moscow; and Lazio of Rome won the 39th and last Cup Winners' Cup, defeating Mallorca of Spain, 2–1, in the May 19 final at Villa Park in Birmingham, England. The tournament will be incorporated into the UEFA Cup beginning in

The 1999 Women's World Cup— A Milestone for Women's Sports

Among the success stories in U.S. sports in 1999, one stood out. The third International Federation of Association Football (FIFA) Women's World Cup, played in eight U.S. cities between June 19 and July 10, turned out to be the biggest women's sports event in history. Not only did the U.S. team reclaim the world title it had lost four years earlier in Sweden, but its players captured the imagination in a way that no one had thought possible. More than 650,000 fans—a record for the tournament—bought tickets to attend the 32 matches, and millions watched at least some of them on television. By the time coach Tony DiCicco's 20-member squad (*photo, page 489*) had edged China, 5–4, on penalty kicks, in the final in front of a sellout crowd of 90,185 at the Rose Bowl in Pasadena, CA, there were few Americans who did not know the team's stars by name.

Some, such as Mia Hamm, the world's all-time leading goal scorer, and Michelle Akers, the top overall scorer in the first Women's World Cup in 1991, already were well known. But the summer of 1999 brought the rest of the players into the spotlight—particularly after the championship, when the team was featured on the covers of major national magazines and made the customary visit to the White House. But even before the victory, some of the team members had done television commercials and appeared on talk shows.

The Americans' path to the final was marked by sellout crowds all the way; a total of 412,486 fans attended their six games. In the early rounds they easily defeated Denmark (3–0), Nigeria (7–1), and North Korea (3–0). In the quarterfinals against Germany, the U.S. team had to come from behind to win, 3–2, thrilling a capacity crowd at Jack Kent Cooke Stadium in Landover, MD, that included President Bill Clinton and his family. In the semifinal round against Brazil, the U.S. team triumphed again, winning 2–0 to face a formidable Chinese team in the last round. China had beaten the United States twice earlier in the year, and it had blazed an equally impressive path to the final, but this time the Americans would not be denied. After 90 scoreless, nail-biting minutes of regulation and another scoreless and equally tense 30 minutes of overtime, the game went to penalty kicks. China went first and scored on four out of five attempts. All five Americans then made their penalty kicks, seizing the victory.

The American team's phenomenal success—not just in 1999, but throughout the 1990s—awakened the country's interest in women's soccer, and in women's sports in general. Over the past decade, the United States had seen an exponential growth in the number of soccer leagues, many oriented toward girls. Of 18 million registered soccer players in the United

2000. Three weeks after Lazio's victory, it sold its striker Christian Vieri to Internazionale Milan for a world-record $50 million, an act that outraged some onlookers.

In a surprising result, Mexico won the eight-nation FIFA Confederations Cup, defeating Brazil, 4–3, in a thrilling final on August 4 in front of 115,000 at Azteca Stadium in Mexico City. Brazil had retained its South American title the month before by shutting out Uruguay, 3–0, in the final of the Copa America tournament on July 18 in Asunción, Paraguay.

Manchester United was victorious in the Toyota/Intercontinental Cup final in Tokyo, Japan, on November 30 in the 38th edition of the annual game between the reigning European and South American club champions. Manchester United beat Palmeiras of Brazil, 1–0.

In late December, Rivaldo, a Brazilian midfielder who played for both Brazil and Barcelona, was named European player of the year by the French magazine *France-Football*, which has given the award since 1956. Until 1994, the award was open only to Europeans, but since then it has been given to the best player of any nationality who plays in a European league. The Brazilian, who was Barcelona's top scorer in 1999, narrowly beat Manchester United's David Beckham. The honor made Rivaldo a leading contender to win FIFA's top player of 1999 award, to be given out in Brussels in January.

U.S. Developments. The U.S. men's national team continued its resurgence under coach Bruce Arena, compiling a 7-3-2 record in 1999, including victories over international powers Germany and Argentina, and a

© Peter Read Miller/"Sports Illustrated"

States, 7.5 million were women and girls, according to the Soccer Industry Council of America. Membership in the American Youth Soccer Organization had more than doubled since the late 1980s, to 607,000, and the percentage of female members had jumped from 25% to 40%. Some observers hoped that the U.S. World Cup triumph in 1999—and perhaps another medal finish at the 2000 Olympics in Sydney—would lead to the formation of a professional U.S. women's soccer league in 2001.

GRAHAME L. JONES

third-place finish in the FIFA Confederations Cup.

Major League Soccer got a new commissioner in 1999, as Doug Logan stepped aside and was replaced by former National Football League (NFL) executive Don Garber. Attendance in the 12-team league dipped slightly, to an average of 14,282 per game. Washington DC United won the championship, defeating the Los Angeles Galaxy, 2–0, in front of 44,910 spectators at Foxboro (MA) Stadium on November 21.

The U.S. Open Cup was renamed the Lamar Hunt U.S. Open Cup in honor of the man who invested $28.5 million in 1999 to build a 22,500-seat, soccer-specific venue in Columbus, OH. The stadium, which opened May 15, is the first of its kind in the United States. On September 14 the Rochester Raging Rhinos of the A-League won the Open Cup, which dates from 1914, by defeating the Colorado Rapids of MLS, 2–0, in the final at Hunt's new stadium.

On the college level, the National Collegiate Athletic Association (NCAA) men's championship was won by Indiana, which defeated Santa Clara, 1–0, in the final in Charlotte, NC. It was the second straight men's soccer championship for Indiana. North Carolina won the women's NCAA title for the 15th time in 18 years, beating Notre Dame, 2–0, in the championship game in Santa Clara, CA, in front of 14,410—a record crowd for an NCAA women's soccer final.

Obituary. The soccer world lost one of its legends in April with the death of 79-year-old Sir Alf Ramsey, the coach who guided England to its World Cup victory in 1966.

GRAHAME L. JONES, *"Los Angeles Times"*

Swimming

The 1999 swimming year was an extraordinary one. It started out fast in January and reached a crescendo in the summer with the heroics of Ian Thorpe, Jenny Thompson, and Lenny Krayzelburg at the Pan Pacific Championships. Even at year's end, records seemingly were falling almost every time the starter's horn was sounded. There were plenty of high-level meets in 1999, with four swimmers providing most of the fireworks.

Thorpe, Heyns, Krayzelburg, and Thompson. Australian Ian Thorpe, a 16-year-old phenomenon known as "The Thorpedo," set two individual world marks. At the Pan Pacs in Sydney, he clocked 1:46.00 for the 200-m freestyle, taking the record away from his teammate Grant Hackett, who earlier in the year had broken Giorgio Lamberti's ten-year-old mark. Thorpe's performance in the 400-m freestyle at the Pan Pacs, however, left experts speculating as to whether they had seen the swim of the century. The teen sensation kicked his size-17 feet into high gear and swam a mind-boggling 3:41.83, slashing two full seconds from what many believed to be the toughest record in the book.

Thorpe took part in a third world mark when he led off Australia's 4 x 200-m freestyle relay that clocked 7:08.79, more than three seconds faster than the old mark, set by another Aussie team in 1998. At year's end, Thorpe was named *Swimming World* magazine's male "world swimmer of the year" for the second year in a row.

Penny Heyns, a double gold medalist at the 1996 Olympics, was equally impressive as she broke world records in the women's breaststroke events 11 times over the course of just six weeks. When Heyns was done, she had set world marks in the 50-m (30.83), 100-m (1:06.52), and 200-m breaststroke (2:23.64). The South African captured *Swimming World*'s female "world swimmer of the year" award for the second time.

Americans Lenny Krayzelburg and Jenny Thompson provided some fireworks of their own. Krayzelburg destroyed all three world records in the men's backstroke events at the Pan Pacs, posting times of 24.99 for the 50-m, 53.60 for the 100-m, and 1:55.87 for the 200-m. Thompson broke the oldest record in the books when she swam 57.88 for the women's 100-m butterfly. The old mark, 57.93, had been set more than 18 years earlier by Mary T. Meagher.

Other Records, NCAA, and Drug Front. In December, Australia's Michael Klim twice lowered his own world standard in the 100-m butterfly, with his 51.81 making him the first man under 52 seconds in the event. Other world long-course records were set by Sandra Volker of Germany (women's 50-m backstroke, 28.71) and Anna-Karin Kammerling of Sweden (women's 50-m butterfly, 26.29). No fewer than 20 short-course (25-m course) world marks were set in 1999, with seven coming at the World Short Course Championships in Hong Kong in April and five at the European Short Course Championships in Lisbon in December.

In National Collegiate Athletic Association (NCAA) competition, the University of Georgia won its first-ever women's title; Auburn reigned supreme among the men.

Six more Chinese swimmers tested positive for illegal performance-enhancing substances in 1999. They, along with four coaches, were suspended for terms of up to four years. Michelle Smith-DeBruin, Ireland's triple Olympic gold medalist in 1996, lost her appeal for adulterating her urine sample. Her four-year ban from the sport was upheld.

PHILLIP WHITTEN
"Swimming World" Magazine

WORLD SWIMMING RECORDS SET IN 1999

Men—50-m Pool
50-m backstroke: Lenny Krayzelburg, United States, 0:24.99
100-m backstroke: Lenny Krayzelburg, 0:53.60
200-m backstroke: Lenny Krayzelburg, 1:55.87
100-m butterfly: Michael Klim, Australia, 0:51.81
200-m freestyle: Ian Thorpe, Australia, 1:46.00
400-m freestyle: Ian Thorpe, 3:41.83
800-m freestyle relay: Australian National Team, 7:08.79

Women—50-m Pool
50-m backstroke: Sandra Volker, Germany, 0:28.71
50-m breaststroke: Penny Heyns, South Africa, 0:30.83
100-m breaststroke: Penny Heyns, 1:06.52
200-m breaststroke: Penny Heyns, 2:23.64
50-m butterfly: Anna-Karin Kammerling, Sweden, 0:26.29
100-m butterfly: Jenny Thompson, United States, 0:57.88

Men—25-m Pool
50-m backstroke: Neil Walker, United States, 0:24.12
200-m backstroke: Lenny Krayzelburg, 1:52.47
50-m butterfly: Michael Klim, 0:23.21
100-m butterfly: Michael Klim, 0:50.99
200-m freestyle: Ian Thorpe, 1:43.28
400-m freestyle: Grant Hackett, Australia, 3:35.01
800-m freestyle relay: Australian National Team, 7:01.60
400-m medley relay: Australian National Team, 3:29.88

Women—25-m Pool
50-m breaststroke: Penny Heyns, 0:30.60
100-m breaststroke: Penny Heyns, 1:05.40
200-m breaststroke: Masami Tanaka, Japan, 2:20.22
50-m butterfly: Anna-Karin Kammerling, 0:25.64
200-m butterfly: Susan O'Neill, Australia, 2:04.43
50-m freestyle: Therese Alshammar, Sweden, 0:24.09
100-m freestyle: Therese Alshammar, 0:52.80
200-m freestyle relay: Swedish National Team, 1:38.45
800-m freestyle relay: Swedish National Team, 7:51.70
100-m individual medley: Jenny Thompson, 0:59.30
200-m medley relay: Swedish National Team, 1:49.47
400-m medley relay: Japanese National Team, 3:57.62

Tennis

At 29, Andre Agassi (*see* BIOGRAPHY) was the tennis player of the year in 1999. Agassi seized two major titles (the French and U.S. Opens); wrested the Number 1 ranking from Pete Sampras, who had held it for six years; and rounded out a select quintet of men who have won all four majors. Agassi's come-from-behind win (1–6, 2–6, 6–4, 6–3, 6–4) over Ukrainian Andrei Medvedev at the French enabled him to join four other Big Four titleists: American Don Budge, Briton Fred Perry, and Australians Roy Emerson and Rod Laver. He won a second U.S. Open title over compatriot Todd Martin in another comeback, 6–4, 6–7 (5–7), 6–7 (2–7), 6–3, 6–2. In addition, Agassi finished first in prize money in 1999, earning $4,269,265.

Although the injury-plagued Sampras slipped to Number 3 in the rankings, he became the man of the century at Wimbledon with his record sixth title (6–3, 6–4, 7–5, over Agassi). It was his 12th major, pulling him abreast of male record holder Emerson. Sampras also won the year-end ATP Championship, his fifth, again beating Agassi, 6–1, 7–5, 6–4. It was his fifth title in 1999, lifting his career total to 61, the high among current players. The other major, the Australian Open, went to Russian Yevgeny Kafelnikov, over Swede Thomas Enqvist, 4–6, 6–0, 6–3, 7–6 (7–1).

© Ron Angle/Liaison Agency

Serena Williams, 17, above, captured the women's singles title at the 1999 U.S. Open. She and her sister, Venus, also took the tournament's doubles crown.

The Women. Lindsay Davenport was the woman of the year, despite giving the Number 1 ranking back to 19-year-old Swiss Martina Hingis. Davenport, who ended the year at Number 2, won Wimbledon over seven-time victor Steffi Graf of Germany, 6–4, 7–5; led the United States to a 15th Federation Cup (4–1 over Russia in the final); and capsized Hingis, 6–4, 6–2, in the climactic Chase Championships at Madison Square Garden. She was 3–0 against Hingis during the year, winning seven titles. Hingis also won seven titles, including her third straight Australian Open, where she beat French 19-year-old Amélie Mauresmo, 6–2, 6–3.

The most startling results were 17-year-old Serena Williams' historic U.S. Open triumph and 30-year-old Graf's sixth French, both victimizing Hingis. Not only was the powerful Serena the longest shot ever to win the Open, bounding from the seventh seed to take the title, 6–3, 7–6 (7–4), but she was also the first African-American woman to take a major since Althea Gibson in 1958.

TENNIS

Davis Cup: Australia
Federation Cup: United States

Major Tournaments

Australian Open—men's singles: Yevgeny Kafelnikov (Russia); men's doubles: Jonas Bjorkman (Sweden) and Patrick Rafter (Australia); women's singles: Martina Hingis (Switzerland); women's doubles: Martina Hingis (Switzerland) and Anna Kournikova (Russia); mixed doubles: David Adams (South Africa) and Mariaan De Swardt (South Africa).

French Open—men's singles: Andre Agassi; men's doubles: Leander Paes (India) and Mahesh Bhupathi (India); women's singles: Steffi Graf (Germany); women's doubles: Venus Williams and Serena Williams; mixed doubles: Katarina Srebotnik (Slovenia) and Piet Norval (South Africa).

Wimbledon—men's singles: Pete Sampras; men's doubles: Leander Paes (India) and Mahesh Bhupathi (India); women's singles: Lindsay Davenport; women's doubles: Lindsay Davenport and Corina Morariu; mixed doubles: Leander Paes (India) and Lisa Raymond.

U.S. Open—men's singles: Andre Agassi; men's doubles: Sebastien Lareau (Canada) and Alex O'Brien; women's singles: Serena Williams; women's doubles: Venus Williams and Serena Williams; mixed doubles: Ai Sugiyama (Japan) and Mahesh Bhupathi (India).

Other Tournaments

Lipton International Players Championships—men's singles: Richard Krajicek (Netherlands); men's doubles: Boris Becker (Germany) and Jan-Michael Gambill; women's singles: Venus Williams; women's doubles: Martina Hingis (Switzerland) and Jana Novotna (Czech Republic).

Italian Open—men's singles: Gustavo Kuerten (Brazil); men's doubles: Ellis Ferrreira (South Africa) and Rick Leach; women's singles: Venus Willliams; women's doubles: Martina Hingis (Switzerland) and Anna Kournikova (Russia).

Chase Championship—singles: Lindsay Davenport; doubles: Anna Kournikova (Russia) and Martina Hingis (Switzerland).

ATP World Tour Championships—singles: Pete Sampras; doubles: Sebastien Lareau (Canada) and Alex O'Brien.

NCAA (Division I)—men's singles: Jeff Morrison, Florida; men's doubles: Ryan Wolters and K.J. Hippensteel, Stanford; men's team: Georgia; women's singles: Zuzana Lesenarova, San Diego; women's doubles: Amanda Augustus and Amy Jensen, California; women's team: Stanford.

N.B. All players are from the United States unless otherwise noted.

Close to defeat as Hingis served for the French Open title at 5–4 in the second set, Graf revived, 4–6, 7–5, 6–2. It was her last of 107 singles titles and her 22d major. Hingis' emotional outbursts and unsportsmanlike behavior during the final cost her both penalty points in the match and the sympathy of the crowd, who began to root against her.

Graf, the great "Fraulein Forehand," the only player in history to win each major at least four times, retired shortly after Wimbledon. She was ranked Number 3. Also withdrawing was the 1998 Wimbledon champ, Czech Jana Novotna, 31.

Davis Cup. A worldwide celebration of the 100th year of the Davis Cup culminated in Australia's 27th triumph, a 3–2 victory over France. Mark Philippoussis' two singles wins led Australia. The United States got as far as the quarterfinals, where—in a return to the Cup's baptismal site, the Longwood Cricket Club in Brookline, MA—Aussie Pat Rafter's wins over Jim Courier and Martin carried the weekend, 4–1.

BUD COLLINS, *"The Boston Globe"/NBC*

Track and Field

The buildup to the 2000 Olympics came early, as track and field athletes in 1999 attacked the record books while making the campaign one of the most memorable ever.

New Records. One of the most important standards fell to American Maurice Greene, whose 9.79 seconds in the 100-m in Athens shattered the old best of 9.84 seconds. Greene went on to become the first man ever to win golds in the 100-m, 200-m, and 4x100-m relay at the World Championships.

The middle distances also thrilled, thanks to Morocco's Hicham El Guerrouj and Kenya's Noah Ngeny. In an epic battle in Rome, the two shattered the mile record, with El Guerrouj winning in 3:43.13. At the Worlds, El Guerrouj again won, running the fastest 1,500-m championship race ever, 3:27.65, as Ngeny grabbed silver. Following the Worlds, both broke records. Ngeny nipped the 18-year-old mark in the 1,000-m with a 2:11.96, while El Guerrouj crushed the 2,000-m record with his 4:44.79.

Decathlete Tomas Dvorak of the Czech Republic took American Dan O'Brien out of the record books, tallying 8,994 points in July to just miss being the first man with more than 9,000 points in the grueling two-day, ten-event contest.

Pole vaulter Emma George of Australia flew over 15′1″ (4.60 m), but failed to win at the World Championships. That honor went to America's Stacy Dragila, who matched that record to capture gold. In the hammer throw, Miheala Melinte of Romania notched three records, topped by a 249′7″ (76.07 m).

The World Championships and Grand Prix Titles. The World Championships in Seville, Spain, claimed center stage as the most stirring meet of the year. Michael Johnson of the United States sprinted 43.18 seconds to capture 400-m gold and the world record. Haile Gebrselassie of Ethiopia, undefeated all year, decisively won the 10,000-m (27:57.27). Abel Anton of Spain became the first man to win two gold medals in the marathon with his 2:13:36.

American Marion Jones, expected by many to dominate, captured gold in the 100-m with a stunning 10.80-second dash, and then earned bronze in the long jump. An injury in the semifinals of the 200-m ended her season, however. The 10,000-m went to

In a thrilling mile race in July 1999, Morocco's Hicham El Guerrouj, below, outpaced Kenya's Noah Ngeny. El Guerrouj's time of 3:43.13 set a new world record.

© Ferdinando Mezzelani/AP/Wide World Photos

© Photo News/Liaison Agency

In the men's 400-m race at the 1999 World Championships in Spain, Michael Johnson of the United States, above, *established a new world record of 43.18 seconds.*

Ethiopia's Gete Wami, the world cross-country champion, in 30:24.56. In hot-weather conditions, Song-Ok Jong produced an amazing 2:26:59 marathon to win North Korea's first-ever medal. Gail Devers of the United States won the 100-m hurdles in a U.S.-record 12.37 seconds, marking her fifth world title.

At season's end, overall Grand Prix titles went to Kenyan Bernard Barmasai and Romanian distance runner Gabriela Szabo. Barmasai dominated the steeplechase all year, despite finishing only fifth in Seville. Szabo, undefeated in 1999, won two indoor world titles as well as the gold in the 5,000-m in Seville. She became the first woman track star ever to earn more than $1 million in prize money in one season.

Notable Marathons. Standards continued to be raised, as more and more athletes ran marathons in times that were unimaginable not long ago. Romania's Lydia Simon took the early-season Osaka women's race in 2:23:24. South African Gert Thys won its counterpart, Tokyo's men's race, in 2:06:33, the second-fastest time ever. April saw Kenyans dominate at Rotterdam, with Japeth Kosgei (2:07:09) and Tegla Loroupe (2:22:48) winning. In London, Morocco's Abdelkadir El Mouaziz ran 2:07:57, while Kenyan Joyce Chepchumba won in 2:23:22. Joseph Chebet of Kenya won Boston in 2:09:52; 1996 Olympic champion Fatuma Roba of Ethiopia took the women's crown in 2:23:25.

In Berlin in September, Loroupe broke her own world best in the marathon by clocking 2:20:43. In October's Amsterdam contest, Kenyan Fred Kiprop won in 2:06:47, as an amazing four men broke 2:07. Lorna Kiplagat of Kenya led the women in 2:25:29. Khalid Khannouchi of Morocco set a new record of 2:05:42 in Chicago on October 24, with Chepchumba finishing first among the women. Chebet (2:09:14) and Adriana Fernandez of Mexico (2:25:06) won in New York City.

JEFF HOLLOBAUGH
Track and Field Correspondent

Yachting

The main highlight in yachting in 1999 was the Louis Vuitton Cup, a four-month-long series of round-robins to determine the yacht that would challenge Team New Zealand in the America's Cup final in February 2000.

A total of 11 contestants from seven countries squared off against one another beginning in mid-October; by the end of the year, five had been eliminated. The remaining six entries—Prada Challenge (Italy), Nippon Challenge (Japan), Le Défi (France), and three American teams: America True, AmericaOne, and Team DC—went on to the semifinals, which were scheduled to start on January 2.

In May, Giovanni Soldini and his 60-ft (18-m) sailboat *Fila* cruised to victory in the Around Alone competition, a 27,000-mi (43 443-km) around-the-world solo race beginning and ending in Charleston, SC. Not only was he the first Italian to win the Around Alone, but he did it in record time—just under 116 days—beating the previous mark by more than four days. Earlier in the race, Soldini had gone out of his way to rescue a fellow competitor, Frenchwoman Isabelle Autissier, whose boat had gotten swamped in the southern Pacific.

Sports Summaries[1]

ARCHERY—U.S. Target Champions: men's Olympic bow: Vic Wunderle, Mason City, IL; women's Olympic bow: Denise Parker, Salt Lake City; men's compound bow: Dave Cousins, Westbrooke, ME; women's compound bow: Sally Wunderle, Mason City, IL. **U.S. Intercollegiate Champions:** team: Texas A&M.

BEACH VOLLEYBALL—Association of Volleyball Professionals (AVP) Championship: King of the Beach: David Swatik, Manhattan Beach, CA; Men's Team (overall ranking): Karch Kiraly and Adam Johnson, San Clemente, CA; Queen of the Beach: Holly McPeak, Manhattan Beach, CA.

BIATHLON—World Champions: men: 10k: Frank Luck, Germany; 20k: Sven Fischer, Germany; 4x7.5k relay: Belarus; women: 7.5k: Martina Zellner, Germany; 15k: Olena Zubrilova, Ukraine; 4x7.5k relay: Germany.

BILLIARDS—U.S Champions: Camel Pro Billiards Series (Top Ranking): Earl Strickland, Greensboro, NC.

BOWLING—Professional Bowlers Association (PBA) Tour: Tournament of Champions: Jason Couch, Clermont, FL; PBA National Championship: Tim Criss, Bel Air, MD; PBA Senior Championship: Steve Neff, Homosassa Springs, FL. **Professional Women's Bowlers Association (PWBA):** Sam's Town Invitational: Wendy Macpherson, Henderson, NV; Women's International Bowling Congress Queens: Leanne Barrette, Pleasanton, CA; Hammer Players Championship: Lisa Bishop, Belleville, MI; AMF Gold Cup: Dana Miller-Mackie, Albuquerque, NM; Brunswick Women's World Open: Cara Honeychurch, Australia. **American Bowling Congress (ABC):** singles: Dan Winter, Rockford, IL; doubles: Ryan Lever, Waterford, WI, and Dale Traber, Cedarburg, WI; all events: Thomas Jones, Greenville, SC; regular team: Zawadzki Jewelers, Lackawana, NY; team all events: Ottman Enterprises, Troy, MI; Masters Tournament: Brian Boghosian, Middletown, CT; Brunswick/ABC World Team Challenge, open division: Storm, Buffalo; senior masters: Darrell Storkson, Everett, WA. **Women's International Bowling Congress (WIBC):** classic division: singles: Nikki Gianulias, Vallejo, CA; doubles: Timi McCorvey, Huntsville, AL, and Marianne DiRupo, Succasunna, NJ; team: Cascade Beauty College, Renton, WA; all events: Hidemi Mizobuchi, Japan; Queen's Tournament: Leanne Barrette.

EQUESTRIAN—U.S. Champions: State Line Tack United States Equestrian Team (USET) Grand Prix Dressage Champion: G Tudor, Cherri Reiber, Toronto; Rolex USET Show Jumping Champion (tie): Macanudo DeNiro, Peter Wylde, Dover Plains, NY, and Moonstar, Francie Steinwedell Carvin, La Cañada, CA; State Line Tack USET Intermediate Dressage Champion: Brentina, Debbie McDonald, Hailey, ID; Rolex USET Three-Day Event Spring Champion: Over the Limit, Kim Vinoski, Scottsville, VA.

FENCING—U.S. Championships: men: foil: Jon Tiomkin, Hewlett, NY; épée: Tamir Bloom, New York City; saber: Akhnaten Spencer-El, New York City. women: foil: Felicia Zimmermann, Rochester, NY; épée: Arlene Stevens, Fairport, NY; saber: Nicole Mustilli, South Orange, NJ; **World Championships:** men: foil: Sergei Golubitsky, Ukraine; épée: Arnd Schmitt, Germany; saber: Damien Touya, France; women: foil: Valentina Vezzali, Italy; épée: Laura Flessel-Colovic, France; saber: Elena Jemaeva, Azerbaijan. **National Collegiate Athletic Association (NCAA):** team: Penn State.

FIELD HOCKEY—NCAA: women: Division I: Maryland. **World:** Men's Champions Trophy: Australia; Women's Champions Trophy: Australia.

GYMNASTICS—U.S. Men's Championships: all-around: Blaine Wilson, Columbus, OH; floor: Jason Gatson, Mesa, AZ; pommel horse: John Roethlisberger, Falcon Heights, MN; still rings: Blaine Wilson; vault: Guard Young, Oklahoma City; parallel bars: Jason Gatson; high bar: Jamie Natalie, Hockessin, DE. **U.S. Women's Championships:** all-around: Kristen Maloney, Pen Argyl, PA; vault: Vanessa Atler, Canyon Country, CA; uneven bars: Jennie Thompson, Cincinnati, OH; balance beam: Vanessa Atler; floor: Elise Ray, Columbia, MD. **NCAA Men:** all-around: Jason Hardabura, Nebraska; team: Michigan. **NCAA Women:** all-around: Theresa Kulikowski, Utah; team: Georgia.

JUDO—U.S. International: 56 kg: Hiram Cruz, Jacksonville, FL; 60 kg: Brandon Greczkowski, Colorado Springs; 66 kg: David Somerville, Britain; 73 kg: Ryan Reser, Colorado Springs; 81 kg: Jason Morris, Scotia, NY; 90 kg: Brian Olson, Colorado Springs; 100 kg: Marius Paskevicius, Lithuania; 100 kg plus: Martin Boonzaayer, Palatine, IL; Men's Open: Sung Hoon Choo, South Korea. **Women's International:** 45 kg: Margaret Zubek, Des Plaines, IL; 48 kg: Asami Kurmochi, Japan; 52 kg: Hye Suk Kim, Korea; 57 kg: Ellen Wilson, Colorado Springs; 63 kg: Carly Dixon, Australia; 70 kg: Liliko Ogasawara, Montvale, NJ; 78 kg: Chika Teshima, Japan; 78 kg plus: Hyun Kyung Lee, South Korea; Open: Hyun Kyung Lee.

LUGE—World Championships: men's singles: Armin Zoeggeler, Italy; doubles: Patrick Leitner and Alexander Resch, Germany; women's singles: Sonja Weidemann, Germany. **World Cup:** men's singles: Markus Prock, Austria; women's singles: Silke Kraushaar, Germany; doubles: Mark Grimmette, Muskegon, MI, and Brian Martin, Palo Alto, CA.

RODEO—Professional Rodeo Cowboys Association: World Champion All-Around Cowboy: Fred Whitfield, Hockley, TX.

ROWING—Men's World Championships: single sculls: New Zealand; lightweight single sculls: Denmark; double sculls: Slovenia; lightweight double sculls: Italy; pair: Australia; pair with coxswain: United States; lightweight pair: Italy; quadruple sculls: Germany; lightweight quadruple sculls: Italy; four: Britain; coxed four: United States; lightweight four: Denmark; eight: United States; lightweight eight: United States. **Women's World Championships:** single sculls: Belarus; lightweight single sculls: Switzerland; double sculls: Germany; lightweight double sculls: Romania; pair: Canada; lightweight pair: United States; quadruple sculls: Germany; lightweight quadruple sculls: United States; four: Belarus; eight: Romania. **International Rowing Association (IRA) Regatta:** men's varsity eight: California; men's lightweight varsity eight: Harvard; women's lightweight varsity eight: Princeton.

SHOOTING—U.S. Champions: Running Target: running target 30 plus 30: Armando Ayala, El Paso, TX; running target 20 plus 20: Kelly Miltner, Pueblo, CO; running target mixed: Armando Ayala. **Rifle:** women's air rifle: Nancy Johnson, Downer's Grove, IL; 3x20 rifle: Jean Foster, Bozeman, MT; men's air rifle: Jason Parker, Omaha, NE; 3x40 rifle: Glenn Dubis, Bethel Park, PA; men's prone: Tom Tomas, Columbus, GA; women's prone: Jean Foster. **Pistol:** men's rapid fire pistol: John McNally, Heath, TX; men's standard pistol: Eric Weeldreyer, Kalamazoo, MI; men's center fire pistol: Eric Weeldreyer; men's free pistol: Daryl Szarenski, Saginaw, MI; men's air pistol: Bill Demarest, Mission Viejo, CA; women's air pistol: Beki Snyder, Grand Junction, CO; women's sport pistol: Beki Snyder. **Shotgun:** men's double trap: Glenn Eller, Katy, TX; men's trap: Matt Depuydt, Houghton, MI; women's double trap: Theresa DeWitt, Cincinnati, OH; men's skeet: Shawn Dulohery, Lee's Summit, MO; women's skeet: Lauryn Ogilvie, San Jose, CA; women's trap: Cindy Gentry, Stone Mountain, GA.

SOFTBALL—Amateur Softball Association (ASA): men's major fast pitch: Decatur Pride, Decatur, IL; super slow pitch: Team Easton, North Carolina; major slow pitch: Gasoline Heaven/Worth, Commack, NY; women's major fast pitch: California Commotion, Woodland Hills, CA; women's major slow pitch: Lakerettes, Conneaut Lake, PA. **Collegiate (women):** NCAA Division I: UCLA.

SUMO—New Year Grand Sumo: Chiyotaikai; Spring Grand Sumo: Musashimaru; Summer Grand Sumo: Musashimaru; Autumn Grand Sumo: Musashimaru.

TRIATHLON—World Champions: men: Dimitry Gaag, Kazakhstan; women: Loretta Harrop, Australia. **U.S. Champions:** men's elite: Hunter Kemper, Orlando, FL; women: Barb Lindquist, Jackson Hole, WY.

VOLLEYBALL—International Champions: Men's World League: Italy; Women's World Cup: Cuba; Women's Grand Prix: Russia; **U.S. Open champions:** men: L.A. Athletic Club; women: Dominican Dream Team. **NCAA:** Division I men: Brigham Young; Division I women: Penn State.

WEIGHT LIFTING—Men's World Champions: 56 kg: Halil Mutlu, Turkey; 62 kg: Le Maosheng, China; 69 kg: Galabin Boevski, Bulgaria; 77 kg: Saelem Nayef Badr, Qatar; 85 kg: Shahin Nasirinia; 94 kg: Akakios Kakiasvilis, Greece; 105 kg: Denys Gotfrids, Ukraine; 105 kg plus: Andrei Chemerkine, Russia. **Women's World Champions:** 48 kg: Donka Mincheva, Bulgaria; 53 kg: Li Feng-Ying, Taipei, Taiwan; 58 kg: Yanqing Chen, China; 63 kg: Yui-Lien Chen, Taipei, Taiwan; 69 kg: Tianni Sun, China; 75 kg: Jaio Xu, China; 75 kg plus: Meiyuan Ding, China.

WRESTLING—Men's World Championships: freestyle: 127.75 lb: Harun Dogan, Turkey; 152 lb: Daniel Igali, Canada; 187.25 lb: Yoel Romero, Cuba; 286 lb: Stephen Neal, United States; Greco-Roman: 119 lb: Lazaro Rivas, Cuba; 127.75 lb: Kim In-Sub, South Korea; 138.75 lb: Makhtar Manoukyan, Kazakhstan; 152 lb: Son Sang-Pil, South Korea; 167.5 lb: Nazmi Avluca, Turkey; 187.25 lb: Luis Mendez, Cuba; 213.75 lb: Gogi Koguachvili, Russia; 286 lb: Alexander Karelin, Russia. **Women's World Championships:** 101.25 lb: Tricia Saunders, U.S.; 112.25 lb: Seiko Yamamoto, Japan; 123.25 lb: Anna Gomis, France; 136.5 lb: Ayako Shoda, Japan; 149.75 lb: Sandra Bacher, U.S.; 165.25 lb: Kyoko Hamaguchi, Japan.

[1]Sports for which articles do not appear in pages 464–93.

Sri Lanka

SRI LANKA • Information Highlights

Official Name: Democratic Socialist Republic of Sri Lanka.
Location: South Asia.
Area: 25,332 sq mi (65 610 km²).
Population (July 1999 est.): 19,144,875.
Chief Cities (mid-1990 est.): Colombo, the capital, 615,000; Dehiwala–Mount Lavinia, 196,000; Moratuwa, 170,000.
Government: *Head of state,* C.B. Kumaratunga, president (took office November 1994). *Head of government,* S. Bandaranaike, prime minister (appointed November 1994). *Legislature* (unicameral)—Parliament.
Monetary Unit: Rupee (71.7500 rupees equal U.S.$1, Nov. 12, 1999).
Gross Domestic Product (1998 est. U.S.$): $48,100,-000,000 (purchasing power parity).
Economic Index (Colombo, 1998; 1990 = 100): *Consumer Prices,* all items, 226.5; food, 237.6.
Foreign Trade (1998 U.S.$): *Imports,* $5,917,000,000; *exports,* $4,734,000,000.

After the ruling People's Alliance did well in elections for Sri Lanka's Provincial Council in January and April 1999, President C.B. Kumaratunga called for early presidential elections to be held at the end of the year. After a campaign marked by violence, Kumaratunga was reelected. Despite the continuing civil war, Sri Lanka's economy showed reasonable growth.

Politics. In elections held in the North-Western Province in January, the People's Alliance won 30 of 52 council seats, while the main opposition, the United National Party (UNP), took only 19. According to observers, the polling was the most corrupt in Sri Lanka's history, as armed gangs intimidated voters and stole and stuffed ballot boxes. Subsequently, leaders of the country's major parties met to ensure that the rest of the provincial elections, held in April, would be conducted peacefully and fairly. This appeared to be the case, despite sporadic incidents of violence, and the People's Alliance won in all five provinces.

Perhaps because of her party's strong showing, Kumaratunga called for presidential elections to be held a year early, on December 21. The main campaign issue for the presidential election was Kumaratunga's plan to devolve powers to the provinces to ensure minority participation in government as a way of ending the civil war.

President Kumaratunga continued her call for a negotiated settlement with the Liberation Tigers of Tamil Eelam (LTTE). While the government held out the negotiation carrot, the LTTE escalated the war. Several moderate Tamil leaders—including Neelan Tiruchelvam, who had tried to negotiate with both the Tamil and Sinhala communities, and Ramesh Nadarajah, a member of Parliament—were assassinated. In early November the LTTE overran two army camps in Oddusuddan, northeast of Colombo, and shortly afterward the rebels took another 460 sq mi (1 191 km²) of territory in the north, handing the government its worst defeat since the conflict began in 1983.

A few days before the election, bombs exploded at separate rallies for the People's Alliance and the UNP. A total of 33 persons were killed, and several others were hurt, including Kumaratunga, who suffered facial and eye injuries. The bombings were thought to be the work of the LTTE. The attack on the president may have helped bolster her campaign, which had been faltering badly, by arousing the sympathy of the electorate. In the December 21 balloting, Kumaratunga won reelection with 51% of the vote.

With the pressures of the war and an increased crime rate, Colombo revived the death penalty for murder and drug-trafficking cases in March. The last time capital punishment had been carried out in Sri Lanka was in 1977.

Economy. In spite of the war, Sri Lanka's economy grew by 4.7% during 1998–99. In addition, foreign investments rose from about $129 million in 1997–98 to $137 million in 1998–99. In August the International Finance Corporation predicted it would triple its investments in Sri Lanka and expand them beyond the traditional tourism, financial-services, and power sectors to health care, information technology, and education. Declines in oil prices and strong tea prices helped maintain a surplus balance of payments of $37 million. Sri Lanka continued to rank highly among all developing countries—especially its South Asian neighbors—on the Human Development Index, partly because of its consistently fine investments in education and health. The war may affect this ranking adversely, however.

Foreign Affairs. Sri Lanka signed a trade pact with India in December 1998 that promised freer trade between the two countries, but implementation, scheduled for March, was delayed by a disagreement over products that India wanted excluded from the free-trade list. Sri Lanka asked Thailand to investigate allegations that the LTTE was smuggling weapons and ammunition along the Thai coast. Thailand said that it would crack down on any such activity.

Aruna Nayyar Michie
Kansas State University

Stamps and Stamp Collecting

In 1999 the United States Postal Service (USPS) issued more than 200 different postage stamps, the most ever in one year. The first postage-rate increase in four years went into effect on Jan. 10, 1999. The cost for first-class mail weighing up to 1 oz (28 g) rose by 1¢, to 33¢.

USPS Stamp Issues. The continuation of the "Celebrate the Century" commemorative series that began in 1998 helped boost the total. Four sheets of 15 stamps each honored the events, personalities, and culture of the 1940s, 1950s, 1960s, and 1970s. The series was slated to end in 2000 with sheets for the 1980s and 1990s.

As usual, the USPS chose many stamp subjects for their appeal to young people. Twenty different creepy bugs and spiders were depicted on a single sheet. Another sheet showed a scene from the Sonoran Desert, with ten wildlife stamps that could be punched out. Four "Xtreme Sports" stamps featured snowboarding, skateboarding, in-line skating, and BMX biking (bicycle motocross). A stamp for Daffy Duck continued the series picturing Warner Bros. Studios' Looney Tunes characters.

In other ongoing series, the 1999 Black Heritage and Legends of Hollywood stamps honored Malcolm X and James Cagney, respectively. A 45¢ commemorative marking the 125th anniversary of the Universal Postal Union (UPU) had its first-day sale at a world postal congress in Beijing, China.

SELECTED U.S. STAMPS FOR 1999

Subject	Denomination	Date
Year of the Hare	33¢	Jan. 5
Malcolm X	33¢	Jan. 20
Victorian Love	33¢, 55¢	Jan. 28
Hospice Care	33¢	Feb. 9
Celebrate the Century 1940s	33¢	Feb. 18
Irish Immigration	33¢	Feb. 26
Alfred Lunt and Lynn Fontanne	33¢	March 2
Arctic Animals	33¢	March 12
Sonoran Desert	33¢	April 6
Daffy Duck	33¢	April 16
Ayn Rand	33¢	April 22
Cinco de Mayo	33¢	April 27
Tropical Flowers	33¢	May 1
Niagara Falls	48¢	May 12
John and William Bartram	33¢	May 18
Celebrate the Century 1950s	33¢	May 26
Prostate-Cancer Awareness	33¢	May 28
California Gold Rush	33¢	June 18
Aquarium Fish	33¢	June 24
Xtreme Sports	33¢	June 25
American Glass	33¢	June 29
James Cagney	33¢	July 22
Rio Grande	40¢	July 30
General William "Billy" Mitchell	55¢	July 30
Honoring Those Who Served	33¢	Aug. 16
Universal Postal Union	45¢	Aug. 25
All Aboard!	33¢	Aug. 26
Frederick Law Olmsted	33¢	Sept. 12
Hollywood Composers	33¢	Sept. 16
Celebrate the Century 1960s	33¢	Sept. 17
Broadway Songwriters	33¢	Sept. 21
Insects and Spiders	33¢	Oct. 1
Hanukkah	33¢	Oct. 8
Christmas Madonna and Child	33¢	Oct. 20
Christmas Deer	33¢	Oct. 20
Kwanzaa	33¢	Oct. 29
Celebrate the Century 1970s	33¢	Nov. 18

U.S. Postal Service

The USPS postponed a 33¢ commemorative for the 50th anniversary of the North Atlantic Treaty Organization (NATO) until October, rather than issuing the stamp during NATO's bombing campaign against Serbia. And plans to issue a 60¢ airmail stamp picturing Arizona's Grand Canyon were called off after it was noticed that the stamp's caption mistakenly placed the canyon in Colorado. The USPS destroyed the 100.75 million stamps already printed and announced that a corrected version would be issued in 2000.

International Stamp Issues. Abroad, Brazil issued a stamp that smelled of burnt wood and publicized forest-fire prevention. Sweden and Singapore jointly issued blocks of four stamps depicting butterflies.

Canada marked the end of the millennium with a set of 68 stamps; a similar set from Great Britain numbered 48 stamps. Sweden, New Zealand, and other countries released more-limited millennium series.

Canada also issued stamps depicting historic planes of the Royal Canadian Air Force, while Great Britain postally commemorated the wedding of Prince Edward and Sophie Rhys-Jones.

GEORGE AMICK
Author, "Linn's U.S. Stamp Yearbook"

States, U.S.

Gubernatorial elections were held in three U.S. states—Kentucky, Louisiana, and Mississippi—and mayors were selected in such cities as Baltimore, Chicago, Houston, Philadelphia, and San Francisco during 1999, an off year for voting. Education issues, the allocation of funds from the tobacco settlement, and other budgetary matters were high on the legislative agendas of the states. Random shootings at such unlikely places as schools and churches drew national attention and concern. Hurricane Floyd and related flooding did extensive damage, especially in New Jersey and North Carolina. Tornadoes and other weather phenomena caused havoc elsewhere.

ALABAMA. Alabama voters defeated a proposal for a lottery in a special election held on Oct. 12, 1999. The lottery was to have funded college scholarships for Alabama high-school seniors with a B average, technology upgrades in schools, and preschool programs. Gov. Don Siegelman, who was elected in November 1998 on a pro-lottery platform, said the state would have to find other alternatives to fund education reforms.

In November 2 elections, City Councilman Bernard Kincaid defeated Birmingham Mayor William Bell, and Bobby Bright defeated Montgomery Mayor Emory Folmar.

Government. A group of 18 Democratic senators boycotted the Alabama Senate from the first day of its session, March 2, until April 6; as a result, the Senate was unable to conduct any business during that period. The senators were protesting newly elected Republican Lt. Gov. Steve Windom's move to restore the lieutenant governor as presiding officer of the Senate. The Democratic Senate had changed its rules in January to take away powers allowed the lieutenant governor as presiding officer. The paralysis endangered Governor Siegelman's legislative agenda, as state law limited the legislature's session to only 30 working days. At last, the Democratic senators reached an agreement that restored some of Windom's powers.

Once the dispute was resolved, the Senate joined the House in passing the lottery proposal and education measures. The legislature also enacted changes in tort law that limited jury awards to injured parties. Several large jury awards in Alabama had captured national attention. For instance, in a 1999 case, a Hale county jury awarded $581 million to a couple who sued a finance company for overcharging them $612. In other action, the legislature allowed consumers to sue sweepstakes sponsors or promoters when they are tricked and suffer damages as a result. The legislature set aside at least $60 million a year from the monies Alabama was due to receive in the 1998 national tobacco settlement for programs serving at-risk children.

ELAINE STUART

ALASKA. In 1999, ten years after the *Exxon Valdez* oil spill, controversy continued to surround the incident.

Lingering Damage. A report issued in early 1999 by the joint federal-state council monitoring the continuing environmental effects of the 1989 *Exxon Valdez* tanker spill said that out of 28 species in the area, only two (the bald eagle and the river otter) were "fully recovered," and another five were described as "not recovering." The accident, which dumped at least 10.8 million gal (40.9 million l) of oil into the water off the Gulf of Alaska's coastline, was one of the nation's worst environmental disasters. In 1994 a federal jury ordered Exxon Corporation to pay $5 billion in punitive damages to thousands of native villagers and commercial fishermen affected by the spill, but due to ongoing appeals, Exxon had yet to comply. Exxon—which

© Ray Stubblebine/Reuters/Corbis

Hurricane Floyd wreaked havoc on East Coast states in September 1999. Particularly hard hit was North Carolina, where up to 20 inches of rain flooded more than 70 towns, turning the streets into brackish rivers, left.

spent \$2.3 billion on cleanup activities, \$1 billion in a settlement with the federal government, and approximately \$300 million in compensatory pay to people in the area—viewed the \$5 billion award as "grossly excessive" in light of all the company had done to mitigate the effects of the accident.

Trans-Alaska Class-Action Suit. The Alaska Electrical Pension Fund settled a class-action lawsuit brought on behalf of current and former plan participants who worked on the Trans-Alaska pipeline project in the late 1970s. Three former participants in the plan filed the suit in 1990, seeking to recover retirement benefits for workers with less than ten years of service who were laid off and ceased to be plan participants during 1978–79 or 1984–88. Under the terms of the \$18 million settlement, individual class members who were terminated from active-participant status prior to 1980 and who filed a claim form prior to Dec. 31, 1999, may be eligible to receive a distribution.

Legislation. A law was passed on May 12, without Gov. Tony Knowles' signature, prohibiting civil action against a person who manufactures or sells firearms or ammunition if the action is based on the lawful sale, manufacture, or design of firearms or ammunition. In an advisory election on September 14, 83% of Alaska voters rejected a proposal to spend a portion of Permanent Fund earnings to help balance the budget. The proposal, set forth by Knowles and the legislature, would have offset the state's \$1 billion deficit. It also would have reduced Permanent Fund dividends paid to Alaska residents by about \$500 each in 2001, to \$1,340.

LYNDI SCHRECENGOST

ARIZONA. For the first time in any state, women held all of the top elected state offices in Arizona in 1999. Voters in November 1998 had elected women as governor, attorney general, treasurer, and superintendent of public instruction.

Government. Arizona adopted a \$12.1 billion budget for fiscal years 2000 and 2001. The budget increased education and prison funding, provided tax cuts, accelerated highway construction, and funded health care. New legislation set out provisions, including local voter approval, for public financing of stadiums, multipurpose facilities, and theme parks. A new law allowed local governments to force slumlords to clean up their properties and stop illegal activities. Other new laws protected consumers against telemarketing fraud and gave students in home, private, and charter schools standing in seeking college scholarships in the state.

Arizona in 1999 distributed \$375 million in state funds to school districts statewide for building new schools and repairing old ones. The funds were authorized by a 1998 state law passed to meet a state Supreme Court mandate for more-equitable school funding. In November 2 elections, Tucson selected Republican Bob Walkup as its mayor and voted not to ban the use of Central Arizona Project water for city homes. In September, Tucson passed an ordinance placing requirements on stores of 100,000 sq ft (9 300 m^2) or more. Wal-Mart promptly began circulating petitions for a ballot measure opposing the new law.

Crime and the Courts. Scott Falater, a Phoenix engineer, was convicted June 25 of murder in a case that attracted international attention because of his defense strategy: He claimed that he was sleepwalking when he stabbed his wife, Yarmila, 44 times in 1997. Arizona attracted national attention in August, when a county superior court allowed a 14-year-old ward of the court, who was in her 24th week of pregnancy after being raped, to have an out-of-state abortion. Although state law permits late-term abortions, doctors in Arizona generally do not perform the procedure after the 20th week.

Other News. The Arizona Department of Economic Security reported in October that an estimated 900,000 people in the state were "hungry or are at risk of hunger."

ELAINE STUART

ARKANSAS. On March 12, 1999, President Bill Clinton's boyhood home in Hope was dedicated as a historic site. Approximately 200 Clinton supporters attended the event. The restored house had been opened to the public on June 1, 1997.

Rising Hispanic Population. According to Census Bureau estimates reported in 1999, the Hispanic population was growing at a faster rate in Arkansas than in any other state, rising from 19,988 in 1990 to 49,473 in 1998. But Hispanics still constituted less than 2% of the total population in the state.

Tornadoes. A storm system that hit the Little Rock area in January caused a number of tornadoes that killed seven persons, flattened buildings, and cut off electricity to more than 70,000 Arkansas homes and businesses. Gov. Mike Huckabee declared two thirds of the state's 75 counties to be disaster areas.

Whitewater. In April a jury in Little Rock acquitted Susan H. McDougal on charges of obstructing justice because she refused to testify before a grand jury about the financial dealings of President Clinton and First Lady Hillary Rodham Clinton, but it deadlocked on two other charges of criminal contempt. McDougal and her former husband, James B. McDougal, had been partners with the Clintons in the failed Whitewater land-development deal, and both were convicted of fraud in May 1996 in connection with an illegally attained \$300,000 loan. After completing an 18-month jail term for civil contempt for her refusal to testify before Starr's grand jury, McDougal just barely had begun to serve an additional two-year sentence for fraud conviction in the Whitewater trial when Federal District Court judge George Howard, Jr., who had sentenced her, released her because of her health problems. Starr then charged McDougal with criminal contempt and obstruction of justice.

Later, in July, Webster Hubbell, formerly the third-ranking official in the Clinton Justice Department, pleaded guilty to a felony count of concealing information from Whitewater investigators and a misdemeanor count of failing to pay federal income taxes.

Former Gov. Jim Guy Tucker was ordered to pay \$1 million for setting up a sham bankruptcy to avoid taxes. Tucker served 18 months of home detention after being convicted of fraud and conspiracy with the McDougals in the Whitewater development deal. Prosecutors had charged Tucker with lying in order to obtain nearly \$3 million in fraudulent loans. Tucker vowed to fight to have the conviction overturned.

LYNDI SCHRECENGOST

CALIFORNIA. In 1999, California passed tough gun-control and health-care laws and coped with extensive fire damage in the northern part of the state.

Fires. Fires sparked by lightning strikes tore through northern California in August and September. Gov. Gray Davis asked President Clinton to declare a state of emergency in a number of counties, and a red-flag warning (the highest level of alert) was put into effect for the entire northern part of the state, except the coastline. A series of fires in December destroyed more than 5,550 acres (2 247 ha) of land in southern California, including parts of the San Gabriel Mountains, the Angeles National Forest, the Los Padres National Forest, and the Santa Anita and Trabuco Canyons.

© Eric O'Connell

In 1999, Arizona became the first state in the country to have all of its top elected officials be women. The new government was led by Gov. Jane Hull (second from left).

Senior Citizens. Since 1987, fatal crashes in the United States involving drivers 70 and older had risen 42%. State Representative Tom Hayden introduced a bill that would make it more difficult for people 75 and older to renew their California driver's license. He introduced the bill after the death in 1998 of Brandi Mitock, 15, who was run over by 96-year-old Byron Cox, who suffered from dementia.

The residents of Leisure World, a retirement community in Laguna Hills, voted to make their community the state's newest city, Laguna Woods. The average age of the 18,000 residents of the city was 77, making it one of the few U.S. towns where more than 90% of the population was aged 55 or older.

Legislation. In October, Governor Davis signed into law the nation's most stringent ban on military-type guns and a measure to limit buyers to one handgun per month. Under the old law, the sale, manufacture, import, and, often, possession of more than 50 military-style weapons was prohibited, but gun makers got around the regulation by modifying their guns and selling them under different names. The new law spelled out the physical characteristics of banned guns, making "copycatting" weapons more difficult.

The governor signed a bill making California the first state to require hospitals to meet fixed nurse-to-patient ratios. He also approved a number of bills that broaden the rights of patients of health-maintenance organizations (HMOs), including allowing them to sue HMOs for punitive damages and solicit outside reviews of decisions denying them coverage.

Proposition 187, the landmark 1994 referendum that barred illegal immigrants and their children from receiving government services such as public education, was weakened greatly when Davis agreed to drop a state appeal of a federal court ruling that found the law unconstitutional. The agreement essentially voided Proposition 187's core provisions permanently. In exchange, opponents of the referendum agreed to stop their lawsuits against the state.

Crime. Elmer Pratt, a former Black Panther who spent 27 years in prison for the 1968 robbery and murder of Caroline Olsen, was released after a state court of appeals upheld the decision not to retry the case. Pratt, now 51 and a decorated Vietnam war veteran, always has maintained his innocence. Another Vietnam veteran, Manuel Piña Babbitt, was executed on May 4 for the 1980 murder of Leah Schendel, a 78-year-old Sacramento woman. Babbitt was denied clemency, in spite of the efforts of thousands of veterans who believed he had suffered from post-traumatic stress syndrome and had been having a flashback when he attacked Schendel.

At a Jewish community center in Granada Hills, five people, including three young boys, were shot by a man who then fled. A few hours later, Buford Furrow turned himself in to police in Las Vegas and confessed to the shooting at the center, as well as to killing a Filipino-American mail carrier shortly afterward. Two weeks later, another gunman walked into Robotek, an auto-parts store in Garden Grove, and opened fire, killing two people and wounding four others. The gunman remained at large in late 1999.

LYNDI SCHRECENGOST

COLORADO. The worst school shooting in U.S. history occurred in April 1999 at Columbine High School in Littleton, when two teenage boys shot and killed 12 other students, a teacher, and themselves.

School Shooting. On April 20 two students armed with guns and explosives went on a rampage through Columbine High School in Littleton. The gunmen, 18-year-old Eric Harris and 17-year-old Dylan Klebold, shot 12 of their fellow students and a teacher to death and wounded dozens of other people before finally killing themselves. In addition, law-enforcement officers found more than 30 bombs in the school that they suspected were planted by the two gunmen for the purpose of destroying the building. Harris and Klebold, who previously had been arrested on a charge of breaking into a van and stealing electronic equipment, appeared to be targeting minorities and athletes.

Legislation. Prior to the shootings, the Colorado legislature had been moving on a package of gun bills backed by the National Rifle Association (NRA), which held its annual meeting in Denver in May. After the shootings, the proposals were scuttled. In August, Republican Gov. Bill Owens, a previous opponent of gun control, announced a package of gun restrictions to present to the 2000 legislative session.

The legislature finished its 1999 session in May after enacting a permanent reduction in the state income tax from 5% to 4.75%, a temporary tax break for the working poor, and various tax breaks for businesses. In addition, the state will return $565.1 million in excess revenues in tax refunds calculated against returns filed in 2000. A 1992 constitutional amendment required the refunds. Other new laws included one that guaranteed patients in HMOs the right to an external review of the HMO's decisions. The state switched its presidential-primary date for 2000 to March 10—a Friday—in what turned out to be a failed attempt to form a regional primary for the Western states. In a November 2 ballot referendum, voters approved issuing $2.3 billion in revenue-anticipation bonds for highway projects. The highway borrowing would be the state's first since 1963.

Ramsey Case. In October, after a three-year investigation, a Boulder grand jury did not indict anyone in the 1996 slaying of 6-year-old JonBenet Ramsey, but both Governor Owens and Boulder law-enforcement officials said the investigation would continue.

ELAINE STUART

CONNECTICUT. Paul J. Silvester, who was Connecticut's youngest state treasurer when he was elected in 1998, pleaded guilty in September 1999 to racketeering and money laundering in office. He admitted to illegal activity concerning the investment of state pension funds, but by the end of the year, investigators had expanded their work to include political fund-raising. Gov. John Rowland, who was sworn in to his second term in January, said he knew nothing of the wrongdoing.

Economy. Boom times continued in Connecticut, as demonstrated by the state's low jobless rate and a record $551.9 million budget surplus. The jobless rate, which dipped to 2.1% in August, was the lowest in the nation at the time and the lowest for the state in more than 20 years. A summer drought hit farmers hard, however, with the state declared a federal disaster area in August.

Crime. National attention focused on Bridgeport when 8-year-old Leroy "B.J." Brown, Jr., and his mother, Karen Clarke, were found shot to death. The boy was to be a witness in an upcoming murder trial.

F. Mac Buckley—a lawyer, former federal prosecutor, and boxing promoter who had vanished on his way to a March 1 hearing—turned himself in to police in mid-April. Shortly after his disappearance he had been charged with first-degree larceny and second-degree forgery and declared a fugitive from justice.

Greenwich financier Martin Frankel was arrested in Germany in September, four months after he fled the country with what was alleged to be millions of dollars that he had embezzled from insurance companies.

Other News. Connecticut sports fans were disappointed when the New England Patriots football team decided not to move to Hartford, as had been announced in November 1998. Patriots owner Robert Kraft backed out of the agreement, which would have included the construction of a $350 million stadium for the team, in May, because the venue would not be ready by 2002.

KRISTI VAUGHAN

DELAWARE. The state was devastated in 1999 by a summer drought, followed by fall floods.

Government. The Delaware legislature passed a $2 billion budget for fiscal 2000, with one third of the funds going to education. In its 1999 session, the legislature passed laws to use monies from the 1998 tobacco settlement for smoking-cessation programs; to deregulate electricity; and to ban firearms for people under domestic-abuse orders. Tax breaks included reducing the top state-tax rate from 6.4% to 5.95%, eliminating the marriage penalty, and increasing personal tax credits. A new law increased the state's minimum wage in phases from $5.15 to $6.15 per hour by Oct. 1, 2000. The state expanded a program to aid senior citizens with prescription-drug costs. Other legislation aimed to curb aggressive driving. The state legislature met in October in a special session on educational accountability.

Crime. Thomas J. Capano received the death penalty in March for the June 1996 murder of Anne Marie Fahey, Gov. Thomas Carper's scheduling secretary and Capano's former lover. Capano, the eldest son of a wealthy Delaware family and a former prosecutor, had been convicted of the crime in January.

Disasters. Delaware operated under mandatory water-conservation restrictions in August in the wake of a statewide drought. The U.S. Department of Agriculture declared a crop disaster in Delaware as a result of the dry conditions. The state suffered the opposite problem in September, as Hurricane Floyd caused storm-related flooding and other damage.

ELAINE STUART

FLORIDA. As part of the largest evacuation in U.S. history, more than 1 million people left Florida's Atlantic coast in September 1999 for safer ground inland when the area was threatened by Hurricane Floyd. However, the giant storm turned north while still out at sea. A few weeks later, Hurricane Irene hit parts of Florida, causing scattered flooding and killing five persons.

Education. A statewide school-voucher program, the first in the nation, took effect in August, allowing students in schools ranked F because of poor test results to use state funds to attend private schools. The plan had been a keynote of Republican Gov. Jeb Bush's election campaign in 1998.

In November, Governor Bush signed an executive order eliminating race and ethnicity as factors for admission to state universities, and guaranteeing entry to the top 20% of the graduating classes of all Florida high schools.

Crime. In August federal agents arrested dozens of baggage and food handlers at Miami International Airport. The suspects, most of whom worked for American Airlines, were charged with using their security clearances and flight privileges to help smuggle drugs and weapons from Latin America.

Tobacco. In the first class-action case against the tobacco industry to reach a verdict, a jury in a Miami state court found in July that the four largest tobacco producers and two tobacco trade groups conspired to hide the addictive nature of cigarettes. In October the U.S. Court of Appeals for the Third Circuit ruled that damages in the case could be awarded in one lump sum rather than in individual payments. An appeal of that ruling by the tobacco industry to the state Supreme Court was rejected in December. At year's end the jurors still were reviewing damage claims filed by the nine lead plaintiffs.

JIM ANDERSON

GEORGIA. In a special election in February, Republican Johnny Isakson won the seat of U.S. House Speaker Newt Gingrich, who had resigned in November 1998.

Crime. Several large-scale shootings took place in Georgia during the year. In Conyers, 15-year-old T.J. Solomon walked into his high school on May 20 and opened fire on his fellow students, wounding six of them. Occurring exactly a month after the massive school shooting at Columbine High School in Littleton, CO, the incident served to raise concerns further about implementing gun control and improving the safety of

Florida Gov. Jeb Bush, below, *launched a statewide voucher program that allowed students in failing schools to receive scholarships to attend private institutions.*

© Wilfredo Lee/AP/Wide World Photos

schools. On July 29, Mark Barton shot to death nine people and wounded 13 others in two Atlanta office buildings before committing suicide a few hours later. He also allegedly had bludgeoned his wife and two children to death a couple of days earlier. Barton had lost heavily in day trading—an activity that involves trying to make money on the stock market by doing extremely short-term buying and selling of stocks—and his victims included some of his colleagues. Less publicity had been given to a July 12 mass shooting by another Atlanta resident, Cyrano Marks, who shot and killed six family members and then himself.

Government. Gov. Roy Barnes signed a measure allowing disgruntled patients to sue HMOs for refusing to cover treatment. Under the new legislation, patients also were allowed to go outside HMO networks (for an additional premium) as long as their doctor abided by the HMO's conditions. Another health-related measure required insurers to cover prescribed contraceptives. A transportation proposal backed by the governor passed as well, with the result of providing more mass-transportation projects in the metropolitan Atlanta area. In other action, the legislature gave home owners a tax credit; teachers were empowered to remove disruptive students from classes; and state police were allowed to take away radar-operating permits from local police departments deemed to be setting up "speed traps."

Other News. Georgia suffered a drought throughout 1999, with rainfall levels up to 20 in (50.8 cm) below normal in parts of the state as of October. A U.S. Navy Blue Angels jet crashed on a training flight near Moody Air Force Base in October, killing two pilots.

ELAINE STUART

HAWAII. Hawaii, which became a state on Aug. 21, 1959, marked its 40th anniversary in 1999. The Hawaii Visitors and Convention Bureau launched an advertising campaign around the occasion, and Gov. Ben Cayetano appeared at a celebration held at Candlestick Park on August 29.

Legislation. The Hawaii legislature attempted to revive the sluggish economy by enacting business-tax relief. New laws reduced the excise tax on wholesale services and exempted professional-service firms from the general excise tax on services performed outside the state. The legislature also passed a $12 billion, two-year budget that included retroactive pay raises for state workers. However, state-employee unions filed a lawsuit in October challenging a two-year wage freeze that the legislature enacted. Other legislation promoted development of high-technology industries, allocated funds from the 1998 tobacco settlement toward preventive health, protected consumers from telemarketing fraud, and established charter public schools.

Other News. A federal judge in October granted the state's motion to stop the planned shutdown of the *Honolulu Star-Bulletin*, the island's 117-year-old afternoon daily newspaper. In April, Hawaii announced that it had secured a deal to relocate the television series *Baywatch* to the islands, a move that government officials and local businesspeople hoped would help the economy. On November 2, Byran Uyesugi shot and killed seven of his coworkers at a Xerox engineering office in Honolulu.

ELAINE STUART

IDAHO. During 1999 lawmakers tried to improve health care throughout the state, with particular emphasis on improving Idaho's low immunization rate. In the one referendum on the November ballot, voters in Ketchum strongly endorsed a traditional mock shoot-out held during Labor Day celebrations.

Controversy. About 90 members of the white-supremacist group Aryan Nations paraded through downtown Coeur d'Alene in July, but more than 1,000 protesters gathered to demonstrate against the march. The organization canceled plans for a second march in Coeur d'Alene on Labor Day weekend, after a former member, Buford Furrow, admitted opening fire on a Jewish community center in Los Angeles, injuring five persons.

In November atheists in Idaho launched a campaign to remove a 60-ft (18.3-m) lighted cross that stood on a bluff overlooking Boise, saying that it was built on public land and thus violated the separation of church and state. The Jaycees, who erected the cross in 1956, countered that they had bought the site of the cross from the state in 1972, and therefore it was private property. On November 27 more than 10,000 people marched to the statehouse in Boise to show their opposition to the anti-cross movement.

Environment. Federal officials announced that the experimental restoration of the gray wolf into the Northern Rockies area had worked so well that at least 12 wolf packs, comprising about 115 adults and 60 to 65 pups, now called the wilderness of central Idaho home. Canadian wolves were introduced into the area in 1995 and 1996.

Health. State officials attempting to pass a bill to raise the immunization rate among children (in 1999 Idaho ranked 49th in the nation for immunization against preventable diseases) ran into opposition from a conservative religious group. The Idaho Christian Coalition opposed legislation setting up a statewide immunization registry to help parents keep track of vaccination records, arguing that it was an invasion of privacy. A modified bill was passed after legislators reached a compromise with coalition leaders.

JIM ANDERSON

ILLINOIS. In 1999 more than ten people in several areas of Illinois were killed or wounded by a violent racist; meanwhile, four prisoners sentenced to death were released on the basis of new evidence, causing many people to take a fresh look at the fairness and efficacy of capital punishment.

Hate Crimes. Over the July 4 weekend, a white-supremacist gunman went on a shooting rampage throughout the state, targeting blacks, Asians, and Jews. Benjamin Smith killed two people and wounded nine others before committing suicide during a police chase. Smith was a member of the Peoria-based World Church of the Creator, a hate group that preached "racial holy war." Just before Smith's killing frenzy began, the group's leader, Matthew Hale, a law-school graduate, had been denied a license by the Illinois Bar Association. The state Supreme Court upheld the denial in November; Hale said he would appeal to the U.S. Supreme Court.

Capital Punishment. A scant two days before his scheduled execution, death-row inmate Anthony Porter was released, after journalism students at Northwestern University found evidence to clear him of a double murder in Chicago during a 1982 robbery attempt. Soon afterward, DNA tests showed that death-row prisoner Ronald Jones was not guilty of the rape and murder of a Chicago woman in 1989. All told, Illinois courts in 1999 exonerated four inmates awaiting execution. Also, in a major investigation, the *Chicago Tribune* found that Illinois death-penalty cases over the past 22 years had been marked by faulty evidence, incompetent lawyering, and unscrupulous trial tactics.

Other News. The Rev. Jesse Jackson led thousands of people in several protest marches through the blue-

© Glenn Oakley for "The New York Times"

Questions arose in November about the constitutionality of a lighted, 60-ft cross, right, *that had been erected in 1956 by the Jaycees on a hill overlooking Boise, ID. One of the issues being debated was whether the cross, a Christian symbol, stood on public property, which would violate the separation of church and state.*

collar town of Decatur after the local high school used its "zero tolerance" policy toward student violence to expel six black students for brawling during a football game. About a dozen Ku Klux Klan members held a counterdemonstration.

JIM ANDERSON

INDIANA. Prosecutors were kept busy in 1999 by cases involving mass arson, serial murder, and the killing of an infant.

Crime. In April an Indiana drifter named Jay Scott Ballinger was charged in federal court with setting ten church fires in Indiana and Georgia, including one that killed a fireman. According to federal agents, Ballinger had confessed in February that he had set up to 50 church fires between 1994 and 1998. He was scheduled to stand trial early in 2000.

In a case that shocked the country, Ronald L. Shanabarger confessed to police that, to get revenge on his then-girlfriend for an emotional slight in 1996, he married her, fathered a child, and then smothered the infant seven months later.

In another notorious criminal case, a jury in the small town of Peru found former nurse Orville Lynn Majors guilty of murdering six elderly patients at a rural hospital. Police suspected he may have killed up to 100 people between 1993 and 1995.

Politics. In November, Bart Peterson took 52% of the vote in a four-way race to become the first Democrat to be elected mayor of Indianapolis in 36 years. It was the most expensive mayoral race in the city's history. Peterson and his main opponent, Indiana Secretary of State Sue Anne Gilroy (R), combined to spend more than $5 million.

JIM ANDERSON

IOWA. During 1999 state political leaders dealt with such issues as drug addiction, a budget surplus, and gay rights. Incumbents did well in mayoral elections.

Government. During his first year as governor, Democrat Tom Vilsack signed a law-enforcement package that levied penalties of up to 99 years in prison for anyone caught making or selling methamphetamine, a prevalent drug in the Midwest. The legislation included extra funding for antidrug education and for treatment of methamphetamine addicts.

Despite the fact that Iowa began 1999 with a $900 million budget surplus, Vilsack vetoed most of the $150 million tax-cut plan proposed by the Republican-controlled legislature. He did approve a $42 million property-tax cut.

Vilsack came under fire in October for signing Executive Order No. 7, prohibiting discrimination based on sexual orientation and gender identity. Opponents accused the governor of damaging the institution of marriage and attempting to establish a quota system for homosexuals and transsexuals as payback for their support in his 1998 election. Vilsack said the order, which had no enforcement provisions, was meant as a statement of philosophy to administration officials.

In November elections, incumbent Preston Daniels beat back a challenge from city-council member Tim Urban for the mayoralty of Des Moines. Cedar Rapids Mayor Lee Clancey won a third term after taking heat for backing a gay-rights ordinance earlier in the year. She defeated Larry Johnson, a local minister well known for organizing antiabortion protests. None of these candidates ran as members of a political party.

JIM ANDERSON

KANSAS. Tornadoes struck portions of Kansas and Oklahoma in May, killing 49 people.

Education. In a decision that received nationwide attention, the Kansas State Board of Education adopted new science standards in August that de-emphasized the teaching of evolution in public schools. While it was not forbidden to teach evolution, the topic was removed from the state curriculum and state assessment tests, thus making it less likely that teachers would spend time explaining the subject to their students. The new standards left the choice of how to handle evolution and creationism in the classroom to local school boards.

Government. Democrats and Republicans formed a coalition to pass most of the legislation approved by the 1999 session, giving the Democrats a greater impact than in previous years. The legislature established a children's trust fund to accept the state's $1.6 billion share of the 1998 national tobacco settlement over the next 25 years. However, almost $80 million of the money will go into the general fund in fiscal 2001 and 2002. For the first time, the legislature passed a multiyear funding of the school finance formula. The plan mandated that school budgets would increase by $50 per pupil for the next two fiscal years.

The $8.9 billion budget, passed in April, also provided millions of additional dollars for programs for mentally ill, retarded, and physically disabled people. The session approved a ten-year, $12.6 billion transportation program advocated by Gov. Bill Graves. The measure called for the transfer of nearly $91 million in sales-tax revenues from the general fund to the state-highway fund in fiscal 2001. The session also restructured the management of higher education and approved an additional $21 million for higher education in fiscal 2001 to bring community colleges and vocational schools under a new State Board of Regents. However, in August lawmakers found that the state had collected $73 million less than expected in the fiscal year ending June 30, 1999. Budget analysts attributed the deficit largely to tax cuts enacted from 1995 to 1998.

Under another new piece of legislation, teens who bring a gun or drugs to school will have their driver's license taken away for one year. The 1999 legislature also established a hot line to allow students to report weapons and threats in their schools.

ELAINE STUART

KENTUCKY. Democrat Paul Patton became the first Kentucky governor to win a second consecutive term in nearly two centuries when he was reelected in November. (Governors were not allowed to succeed themselves in Kentucky until 1992, when voters approved an amendment to the constitution.) In September, Heather Renee French won the Miss America contest, the first Kentuckian to do so.

Politics. Patton easily outdistanced Republican Peppy Martin and Reform Party candidate Gatewood Galbraith in the November 2 election. Republicans took majority control of the Kentucky Senate for the first time in the state's history when two Democratic senators switched parties. With Republicans gaining a 20–18 majority, Senate President Larry Saunders, a Democrat, announced he would not fight to retain his leadership position when the legislature met in 2000.

Environment. The U.S. Department of Energy began looking into allegations made in a federal lawsuit filed in June charging that former operators of the Paducah Gaseous Diffusion Plant covered up environmental contamination at the plant. The plant had been used to enrich uranium for nuclear weapons. In a report issued in October, the Energy Department acknowledged past problems at the plant. The Nuclear Regulatory Commission found no current problems at the plant in an October inspection. Kentucky suffered a drought in the summer, with the governor declaring a water emergency for all or part of 53 counties.

ELAINE STUART

LOUISIANA. Voters chose a new U.S. congressman in spring 1999 and reelected Republican Gov. Mike Foster in the fall. In a tragic reflection of events in other states during the year, a gunman opened fire at a church gathering.

Politics. In a special open election on May 1, nine candidates vied for the U.S. House of Representatives seat vacated by Robert Livingston in February. Livingston had resigned when he was forced to acknowledge that he had had extramarital affairs. Because no candidate received a majority, a runoff election was held between the two top finishers—former Gov. David Treen (winning 25% of the vote) and state legislator David Vitter (with 22%). White supremacist and former Ku Klux Klan leader David Duke came in third, with 19%. In the runoff between the two Republicans on May 29, Vitter won with 51% of the vote.

Governor Foster won reelection in October against a field of ten challengers. Foster took more than 60% of the vote—twice that of his closest rival, state Rep. William Jefferson (D) of New Orleans.

Other News. In March a homeless man, Shon Miller, Sr., burst into a Bible class being held in a Baptist church in the small town of Gonzales and opened fire with a semiautomatic handgun, killing three people and wounding four. Among the dead were Miller's estranged wife, Carla, who was seeking a divorce, and their 2-year-old son, Shon, Jr. Police also charged that Miller had shot and killed his mother-in-law before going to the church. Miller was arrested after he was wounded by a police officer.

A chartered bus carrying members of a gambling club to New Orleans crashed on Mother's Day after being forced off the road by a car. The accident killed 21 of the 46 passengers; 16 others were hospitalized.

On December 13 a group of inmates, mostly Cubans, in the St. Martinville parish jail took several people hostage, including the warden, and demanded to be permitted to leave the country. The Cubans, illegal immigrants who had completed prison sentences for crimes committed in the United States, were being held indefinitely because the Cuban government was blocking their deportation. On December 16 two of the inmates surrendered and released four of the hostages. Finally, on December 19 the inmates released the other hostages, after the U.S. State Department agreed to send the remaining seven Cubans to Cuba. Six of them were deported the next day. The other remained in the United States while federal officials investigated charges that he had raped one of the hostages. Not long after the St. Martinville incident, six convicts at the Louisiana State Penitentiary took three guards hostage, killing one of them. The brief standoff ended when the warden and several guards overcame the inmates, fatally shooting one of them in the process.

JIM ANDERSON

MAINE. The best place to raise a child in 1999, according to the Children's Rights Council, a national child-advocacy group, was Maine. The state was ranked first based on statistical criteria that included the percentage of child-abuse and -neglect reports, immunizations, high-school dropout rate, child death rate, infant mortality, health care for pregnant mothers, juvenile arrests, teen births, and percentage of divorces.

Education. The constitutionality of school choice came into question when five families in the state sought to use publicly financed school vouchers for payment to a church-affiliated school. In April the Maine Supreme Court upheld the state's policy of restricting the use of such vouchers to nonreligious schools.

At his second-term inauguration in January, Independent Gov. Angus King made education a top priority, calling for the creation of a community-college system and more spending on education.

Health. The state's subsidized drug program grew in enrollment when the Department of Human Services announced that it had issued 10,000 new cards to low-income elderly or disabled people who previously were not eligible. In 1999 about 40,000 of the state's elderly residents qualified to participate in the program.

KRISTI VAUGHAN

MARYLAND. A summer hot spell resulted in drought conditions in Maryland, as it did elsewhere in the East in 1999. By the end of July, Gov. Parris N. Glendening had declared the first statewide drought emergency in Maryland's history. The federal government in August declared counties bordering West Virginia, including parts of Maryland, disaster areas.

Politics. In November 2 elections, Baltimore voters overwhelmingly chose former prosecutor Martin O'Malley (D) as mayor over Republican David Tufaro.

Environment. In 1999 a plan was announced for Maryland, Virginia, and Delaware to purchase 76,000 acres (30 780 ha) of the Delmarva Peninsula from the Chesapeake Forest Products Company in order to preserve the land. Maryland's part of the acquisition—58,000 acres (23 490 ha)—was the largest.

Schools. Maryland was one of ten states joining in an effort to improve middle-school students' math performance through the creation of a common curriculum. The standards were to be developed by Achieve, Inc., a group jointly headed by Louis Gerstner, Jr., chairman of the International Business Machines Corp. (IBM), and Wisconsin Gov. Tommy Thompson.

Business. The four largest tobacco companies agreed to establish a $5.15 billion relief fund for farmers in Maryland and elsewhere who would be hurt by market declines expected as the result of a settlement reached in 1998 in nationwide tobacco-related suits.

KRISTI VAUGHAN

MASSACHUSETTS. The days of using busing as a means of accomplishing school desegregation were declared officially over when the Boston School Committee voted in July to drop race as a factor in deciding which school children should attend. Boston had been the site of boycotts and violence in the early 1970s as protesters objected to the busing.

Sports. After considering a move to Hartford, CT, the New England Patriots football team decided in early May to stay in Massachusetts. A few weeks later, the state legislature approved a plan for the construction of a new $225 million stadium.

Economy. The Progressive Policy Institute rated Massachusetts' economy as the nation's best. The state legislature approved an increase in the minimum wage from $5.25 to $6.75, to be phased in over two years.

Politics. Massachusetts had the dubious honor of being the last state to pass its budget for the 1999 fiscal year. The budget was approved in October, more than three months after the fiscal year began. At his January inaugural, Gov. Paul Celucci, a Republican, promised improvements in education and health care.

Crime. Stephen Fagan, a Massachusetts man who had kidnapped his two daughters in 1979 and raised then in Palm Beach, FL, pleaded guilty in May to the kidnapping. In exchange for the plea, he received no jail time but agreed to serve 2,000 hours of community service and to pay $100,000 in his former wife's name to a home for at-risk children.

Tragedy. In December in Worcester, six firemen were killed in a fire in an abandoned warehouse. Two squatters who allegedly knocked over a candle during an argument were charged with involuntary manslaughter in connection with the blaze.

See also UNITED STATES—*The Kennedy Family: Another Tragedy.*

KRISTI VAUGHAN

MICHIGAN. A number of events in 1999 focused Michigan's attention on youth violence.

Crime. Four teenagers were arrested in May after their classmates at Holland Woods Middle School in Port Huron heard them plotting to kill students and teachers. Shortly after the plot was revealed and the boys were taken into custody, a bomb was found outside the school. Justin Schnepp, 14, Jedaiah Zinzo, 15, and Daniel Fick, 13, were charged with conspiracy to commit murder. The fourth boy, whose name was not revealed, was released after a judge ruled that a statement he had made to police was inadmissible as evidence. In a televised interview in November, Schnepp claimed that the whole thing was just idle talk because he and his friends were bored. However, just before his trial was due to begin a week later, Schnepp pleaded guilty to a juvenile charge of conspiracy to commit assault with intent to commit great bodily harm. Zinzo pleaded guilty to the same charge, and Fick was to be tried in juvenile court in January 2000.

In November, Nathaniel Abraham, a 13-year-old boy from Pontiac, was convicted of second-degree murder for shooting 18-year-old Ronald Greene, Jr., outside a convenience store in 1997. Abraham, one of the youngest murder defendants ever in the United States, had been charged with first-degree murder and tried as an adult under a strict juvenile-justice law passed in Michigan in 1997. In January 2000, Judge Eugene Moore sentenced Abraham to seven years in a maximum-security juvenile-detention center.

Other News. Using money from the state's share of the 1998 tobacco settlement, lawmakers announced plans to spend about $1 billion over 20 years to create or improve medical-research facilities. Reacting to poor test scores, the state legislature voted in March to transfer control of Detroit's schools from the elected school board to the mayor and governor. After a six-day strike at the start of the school year, Detroit teachers ratified a new contract offering a 2% raise each year for three years. Three new casinos opened in Detroit, adding more than 7,000 new jobs in a city where the unemployment rate was 7%. Michigan launched a pilot program in October that required welfare applicants to pass a drug test in order to receive benefits, but a few weeks later a federal judge temporarily halted the program.

JIM ANDERSON

MINNESOTA. Taking office in 1999, newly elected Minnesota Gov. Jesse Ventura continued to attract attention from the national news media.

Politics. In his inaugural speech, Ventura promised to promote "citizen-friendly government" and said that honesty would be the hallmark of his administration. In an interview in the November issue of *Playboy*, the U.S. Navy SEAL-turned-pro wrestler-turned-politician ruffled more feathers with provocative comments, saying that religion is a crutch for the weak-minded and that overweight people lack willpower. His approval rating quickly dropped 19 points to 35%.

Ventura emerged as a leader of the national Reform Party in 1999. He briefly considered running for the Reform presidential nomination, but announced at the party's convention in July that he would finish out his term as Minnesota's governor instead. At the convention, however, he solidified his influence within the party by successfully backing the selection of Jack Gargan as chairman. Ventura then encouraged real-estate tycoon Donald Trump to seek the Reform presidential nomination.

Ventura's most bitter critic was not a rival politician but a humorist. Minnesota native Garrison Keillor mocked Ventura in a book, *Me, by Jimmy (Big Boy) Valente*, and in unusually barbed skits on his weekly radio show, *A Prairie Home Companion*. Ventura's own book, *I Ain't Got Time to Bleed*, was a best-seller.

During the 1999 legislative session, state lawmakers dipped into a huge budget surplus to return a record $2.7 billion to taxpayers through tax cuts and rebates. The amount worked out to $575 for each Minnesotan.

Lawsuit. In January, 16 women miners settled a groundbreaking sexual-harassment case that dated from 1988. The legal action against Eveleth Mines was the first sexual-harassment lawsuit to be granted federal class-action status. Details of the settlement were confidential.

Other News. Members of the Animal Liberation Front (ALF) raided two laboratories at the University of Minnesota in the spring, releasing animals, destroying $700,000 worth of equipment, and delaying work on a cancer vaccine to treat brain tumors. A probe by the Federal Bureau of Investigation (FBI) produced no arrests by the end of 1999.

Voters in St. Paul turned out in record numbers in November to reject a referendum that would have increased the sales tax in order to help fund a new stadium for the Minnesota Twins baseball franchise.

Farrah Slad, a Minnesota woman, was the sole claimant of a $150 million Powerball jackpot in July. It was the third-biggest prize ever in the multistate lottery.

JIM ANDERSON

MISSISSIPPI. After the closest governor's race in Mississippi history, the November 1999 elections resulted in a standoff, with neither candidate earning enough votes to win.

Elections. Democratic Lt. Gov. Ronnie Musgrove got 6,642 more votes in the November 2 gubernatorial election than his Republican opponent, former U.S. Rep. Mike Parker. Musgrove declared victory after receiving 49.5% of the popular vote to Parker's 48.6% in the four-candidate race. According to the state's 1890 constitution, a winning candidate for governor must receive a majority of the popular vote as well as a majority of electoral votes, which are based on House districts. Since Musgrove did neither, and Parker refused to concede, the state constitution mandated that House members would choose between the two top candidates. This provision in the constitution never has been used in Mississippi, although a similar clause, since repealed, in the Georgia constitution resulted in Lester Maddox becoming governor there in 1967. In January the Democratic-controlled House approved Musgrove by a large margin.

Also in the November elections, a constitutional amendment to limit legislators to two consecutive terms was defeated. It was the first time in the country that voters rejected such a referendum proposal.

Government. Gov. Kirk Fordice, a Republican, was ineligible to run for a third term because of term limits. Fordice's popularity suffered when he announced he would divorce his wife, Pat, to be with a longtime woman friend. The 1999 legislature created a trust fund dedicated to health care and funded by the state's 1998 tobacco settlement, which would bring in $4 billion over the next 25 years. Lawmakers also used $10.6 million in tobacco funds to get $56 million in federal monies for health insurance for low-income children. Tobacco funds also were tapped for other health needs. Teachers and state workers received pay raises. Welfare benefits were increased for the first time since 1986. The state's welfare rolls had declined from 60,000 to 17,000 in the six years since 1993.

Other News. Attorney General Mike Moore announced in August that fewer minors were buying tobacco products at stores in Mississippi since retailers and law officers began enforcing laws banning sales to children. The effort was funded by part of Mississippi's tobacco settlement, which Moore won in June 1997.

ELAINE STUART

MISSOURI. Democratic Gov. Mel Carnahan aroused controversy in 1999 by commuting one murderer's death sentence while allowing other executions.

Death Penalty. Following a personal appeal in January from Pope John Paul II, who was visiting St. Louis, Governor Carnahan, a supporter of capital punishment, commuted the death sentence of convicted murderer Darrell J. Mease, who was scheduled to die in February. The gesture aroused criticism from all sides, however, when Carnahan allowed the executions of two other prisoners to take place in February and March.

Political and Legal Developments. Voters in April rejected an attempt to lift the state's ban on concealed weapons, with the main opposition coming from the St. Louis and Kansas City areas. The National Rifle Association and other pro-gun groups had spent $3.7 million to support the measure. Governor Carnahan had promised to veto any bill to overturn the ban.

Federal District Court Judge Scott Wright put an antiabortion law on hold in September, because it was drawn too broadly. The Infant's Protection Act, which had passed the Missouri House and Senate over Governor Carnahan's veto only a day earlier, was aimed at outlawing the procedure called partial-birth or late-term abortion, but abortion-rights advocates said it could be interpreted so as to criminalize all forms of abortion. A trial to determine the constitutionality of the law was planned.

Casino. New York developer Donald Trump brought his brand name to the state, opening the Trump Casino Kansas City in a make-believe riverboat.

JIM ANDERSON

MONTANA. Range fires devastated 33,000 acres (13 365 ha) north of Billings and came within 1 mi (1.6 km) of the town of Musselshell in 1999. The Forest Service marked the 50th anniversary of the Mann Gulch fire, which killed 13 smoke jumpers in a single day.

Freemen Trial. Ending three years of legal proceedings, a federal judge in Billings sentenced LeRoy Schweitzer, the leader of the antigovernment Montana Freemen group, to 22½ years in prison. Six other Freemen received terms of up to 15 years; the wives of two members were released with time served. The Freemen, who claimed they were not subject to federal or state laws, had been convicted of bank and mail fraud in 1998 for issuing thousands of bogus checks.

Harassment Charges. Democratic Sen. Max Baucus was accused of sexual harassment by his former chief of staff, Christine Niedermeier. She filed a complaint to Congress, claiming that the married senator had made sexually related comments to her and suggested they have a relationship. Baucus denied the charges, noting that he had fired Niedermeier after receiving a signed petition from 36 staff members complaining about her abrasive behavior to them.

Legislation. Gov. Marc Racicot signed a bill to prohibit local governments from filing suit against firearms or ammunition makers, reserving that right for the state. State authorities rolled back the speed limit from the ambiguous "reasonable and proper judgment" to 75 mph (121 km/hr) on interstates and 70 mph (113 km/hr) on other highways.

JIM ANDERSON

NEBRASKA. The Nebraska legislature passed a large number of laws in 1999 in the areas of health care, tax relief, social issues, and commerce.

Politics. The Nebraska legislature passed a law adopting a two-year pause in executions to allow for a study on the fairness of the death penalty. However, the legislation was vetoed by first-year Republican Gov. Mike Johanns, who said that capital punishment was the law of Nebraska and that the state had a duty to enforce the law. The legislature did not try to override Johanns' veto, but it did enact the study.

In the area of crime control, new laws toughened penalties for methamphetamine and amphetamine abuses, and made enticing children under 14 into vehicles for the purpose of kidnapping a separate crime. Health measures required insurers to treat mental and physical ailments equally in coverage and gave patients access to their medical records. The session also allocated funds to provide a relief program to aid people who look after elderly parents, disabled children, or others with special health needs.

Another piece of new legislation shielded governmental agencies and financial institutions from lawsuits

THE U.S. STATES

	Population* (in millions)	Area (sq mi)	(km²)	Capital	Governor**
Alabama	4.4	52,423	135 776	Montgomery	Donald Siegelman (D)
Alaska	.6	656,424	1 700 130	Juneau	Tony Knowles (D)
Arizona	4.8	114,006	295 276	Phoenix	Jane Dee Hull (R)
Arkansas	2.5	53,182	137 741	Little Rock	Mike Huckabee (R)
California	33.1	163,707	424 001	Sacramento	Gray Davis (D)
Colorado	4.1	104,100	269 619	Denver	Bill Owens (R)
Connecticut	3.3	5,544	14 359	Hartford	John Rowland (R)
Delaware	.7	2,489	6 447	Dover	Tom Carper (D)
Florida	15.1	65,758	170 313	Tallahassee	Jeb Bush (R)
Georgia	7.8	59,441	153 952	Atlanta	Roy Barnes (D)
Hawaii	1.2	10,932	28 314	Honolulu	Benjamin J. Cayetano (D)
Idaho	1.2	83,574	216 457	Boise	Dirk Kempthorne (R)
Illinois	12.1	57,918	150 008	Springfield	George Ryan (R)
Indiana	5.9	36,420	94 328	Indianapolis	Frank O'Bannon (D)
Iowa	2.9	56,276	145 755	Des Moines	Tom Vilsack (D)
Kansas	2.6	82,282	213 110	Topeka	Bill Graves (R)
Kentucky	4.0	40,411	104 664	Frankfort	Paul Patton (D)
Louisiana	4.4	51,843	134 273	Baton Rouge	Mike Foster (R)
Maine	1.2	35,387	91 652	Augusta	Angus King, Jr. (I)
Maryland	5.2	12,407	32 134	Annapolis	Parris N. Glendening (D)
Massachusetts	6.2	10,555	27 337	Boston	Paul Cellucci (R)
Michigan	9.9	96,705	250 466	Lansing	John Engler (R)
Minnesota	4.8	86,943	225 182	St. Paul	Jesse Ventura (Reform)
Mississippi	2.8	48,434	125 444	Jackson	Kirk Fordice (R)
Missouri	5.5	69,709	180 546	Jefferson City	Mel Carnahan (D)
Montana	.9	147,046	380 849	Helena	Marc Racicot (R)
Nebraska	1.7	77,358	200 357	Lincoln	Mike Johanns (R)
Nevada	1.8	110,567	286 369	Carson City	Kenny Guinn (R)
New Hampshire	1.2	9,351	24 219	Concord	Jeanne Shaheen (D)
New Jersey	8.1	8,722	22 590	Trenton	Christine Todd Whitman (R)
New Mexico	1.7	121,598	314 939	Santa Fe	Gary Johnson (R)
New York	18.2	54,556	141 300	Albany	George Pataki (R)
North Carolina	7.6	53,821	139 396	Raleigh	James B. Hunt, Jr. (D)
North Dakota	.6	70,704	183 123	Bismarck	Edward Schafer (R)
Ohio	11.2	44,828	116 105	Columbus	Bob Taft (R)
Oklahoma	3.4	69,903	181 049	Oklahoma City	Frank Keating (R)
Oregon	3.3	98,386	254 820	Salem	John Kitzhaber (D)
Pennsylvania	12.0	46,058	119 290	Harrisburg	Tom Ridge (R)
Rhode Island	1.0	1,545	4 002	Providence	Lincoln Almond (R)
South Carolina	3.9	32,008	82 901	Columbia	Jim Hodges (D)
South Dakota	.7	77,121	199 743	Pierre	William Janklow (R)
Tennessee	5.5	42,146	109 158	Nashville	Don Sundquist (R)
Texas	20.0	268,601	695 673	Austin	George W. Bush (R)
Utah	2.1	84,904	219 901	Salt Lake City	Michael O. Leavitt (R)
Vermont	.6	9,615	24,903	Montpelier	Howard Dean (D)
Virginia	6.9	42,777	110 792	Richmond	James S. Gilmore III (R)
Washington	5.8	71,302	184 672	Olympia	Gary Locke (D)
West Virginia	1.8	24,231	62 758	Charleston	Cecil Underwood (R)
Wisconsin	5.2	65,499	169 642	Madison	Tommy G. Thompson (R)
Wyoming	.5	97,818	253 349	Cheyenne	Jim Geringer (R)

*July 1, 1999, estimate **As of Jan. 1, 2000

over problems attributed to Y2K computer glitches. In addition, laws were passed to protect consumers from phone companies switching their services without permission (a practice known as "slamming") and from fraudulent telemarketers. The session revisited its restrictions on large livestock operations. The budget for 2000 contained property-tax relief and increased aid for schools.

In a primary held in May, former state Sen. Don Wesely, a Democrat, was elected mayor of Lincoln. He replaced Johanns, whose election as governor in 1998 had left the post vacant.

ELAINE STUART

NEVADA. During the summer of 1999, wildfires blazed through Nevada, destroying an area larger than the state of Delaware. A massive project to reseed the barren ground with native grasses and shrubs was planned, at an estimated cost of at least $50 million. Meanwhile, the federal government declared Clark county a disaster area, after flooding in Las Vegas on July 8 caused millions of dollars in damage. The disaster declaration cleared the way for federal aid and loans to the city.

Elections. Las Vegas held an election in May to replace retiring Mayor Jan Jones, who ran an unsuccessful campaign for governor in 1998. Oscar Goodman, a colorful, controversial defense attorney whose clients included alleged mobsters, won the three-candidate race with 49% of the vote. But because no one won a clear majority, a runoff took place in June between Goodman and the second-place finisher, city-council member Arnie Adamsen. Goodman beat Adamsen easily, garnering 64% of the vote.

Legislation. The state legislature ended its session in June, within the 120 days mandated by a 1998 constitutional amendment, and first-term Gov. Kenny Guinn got much of the legislation he wanted. Guinn, the first Republican governor of the state in 16 years, faced a Republican Senate and a Democratic Assembly. The session established the governor's proposal for giving scholarships to every Nevada high-school graduate with a B average or better, beginning in the 2000–01 school year. Funds for the scholarships were to come partly from the state's share of the 1998 national tobacco settlement. Money from the settlement also was slated to fund health programs for the state's senior citizens.

In other action, the legislature provided a cost-of-living increase for state workers, passed an ethics-reform measure, equalized health benefits for male and female employees, and prohibited discrimination against homosexuals in the workplace. Health-related measures included requiring insurance companies to cover prescription contraceptives and establishing a health-care ombudsman in the governor's office. In response to a case in which a man raped and killed a 7-year-old in a Las Vegas hotel in 1997, the state passed a law requiring onlookers to report suspected sexual abuse or violence against children. After entertainer Jerry Lewis testified before the state Assembly that he feared for his life because of a stalker, the legislature increased the penalty for stalking.

Crime. Zane Floyd was charged with shooting to death four employees at a supermarket in Las Vegas on June 3.

ELAINE STUART

NEW HAMPSHIRE. The Granite State struggled with tax issues during 1999 as it tried to find a way to fund its schools.

School Funding. After the state Supreme Court ruled in 1997 that New Hampshire unfairly relied on local property taxes (which varied widely by town) to fund its schools, it gave the state until April 1, 1999, to remedy the situation. That date came and went, as the legislature struggled with the problem of finding another way to fund education. In March the Senate passed a bill that would tax residents' income for the first time. However, the legislation died in the House, ensuring that New Hampshire would remain one of only two states without either a general sales tax or an income tax. (The other was Alaska.)

Martin Luther King Holiday. Until 1999, New Hampshire had been the only state not to have a holiday commemorating slain civil-rights leader Dr. Martin Luther King, Jr. Ever since the U.S. Congress created a federal holiday to honor King in 1983, the state had debated whether to follow suit. Finally, in May 1999 the legislature approved a permanent Martin Luther King holiday to be observed at the same time as the federal holiday.

Politics. U.S. Sen. Robert C. Smith announced in July that he would leave the Republican Party and run for president as a third-party candidate. He was the first sitting Republican senator in nearly 50 years to make such a move. He said he was leaving the party because it had abandoned its core conservative principles. Within a few months, however, he gave up his presidential campaign and returned to the GOP. State Senate president Clesson "Junie" Blaisdell died in August at the age of 72. Sen. Beverly Hollingsworth filled his seat, becoming the third woman to hold a top state position in 1999 (joining Gov. Jeanne Shaheen and House Speaker Donna Sytek).

Meanwhile, presidential aspirants began to campaign in the state in anticipation of the New Hampshire primary in early February 2000.

KRISTI VAUGHAN

NEW JERSEY. Reversing an earlier announcement, Gov. Christine Todd Whitman, a Republican, decided in September not to run for the U.S. Senate seat being vacated by Democrat Frank Lautenberg. Senator Lautenberg had announced in February that he would not run for reelection. Whitman cited money and her gubernatorial work as her reasons for declining. Attorney General Peter G. Verniero was appointed to the state Supreme Court, despite objections that he was too inexperienced and had been too slow to investigate allegations of racial profiling.

Water Problems. Governor Whitman declared a drought emergency in August, as much of the East Coast suffered through the worst dry spell in decades. A month later, New Jersey had more water than it could handle, as Hurricane Floyd dumped nearly 2 ft (0.6 m) of rain on parts of the state. A number of towns were under floodwaters for days and had to be evacuated. Electricity, phone, and water service were knocked out for as many as 650,000 people.

Crime. A police officer from Orange was shot to death during an encounter with a robbery suspect in April, and one death-row inmate killed another during a fistfight in a fenced recreation area at the New Jersey State Prison in September. The death penalty was upheld in the case of Jesse K. Timmendequas, the man convicted of killing 7-year-old Megan Kanka in 1994. In May, Judge Reginald Stanton imposed a death sentence on Thomas J. Koskovich, a 21-year-old man convicted in the 1997 ambush and murder of two pizza deliverymen.

Governor Whitman signed a law in October that made New Jersey the fourth state in the nation to prohibit the sale of handguns without trigger locks.

See also ETHNIC GROUPS—*Racial Profiling.*

KRISTI VAUGHAN

NEW MEXICO. In an October 1999 speech to a group of college students in Washington, DC, Gov. Gary Johnson called the country's war on drugs a multibillion-dollar failure. He also said that the tough crackdown on drug users has resulted only in courts and prisons becoming overwhelmed by people arrested for possessing small amounts of illegal substances. He suggested that if drugs were legalized, they could be regulated, and people could be held accountable for what they did under their influence. But he added that he had no plans to push for a change in his state's drug policy. Johnson, a Republican, had admitted to using marijuana and cocaine while in college. The state's top law-enforcement official resigned in November over Johnson's stand on drugs. Darren White, secretary of the Department of Public Safety, said the governor's position had lowered morale in New Mexico's law-enforcement community.

Native American Remains. Some 200 Pueblo Indians gathered in the Pecos Valley in May to receive the bones of their ancestors when Harvard's Peabody Museum returned nearly 2,000 skeletons kept in storage in Massachusetts since an excavation more than 70 years ago. The bones were returned in compliance with the Native American Graves Protection and Repatriation Act, passed in 1990. It was believed to be the largest single restoration of Native American remains ever.

Crime. Police arrested David Parker Ray and Cynthia Lea Hendy after a chained woman escaped from their trailer compound in Elephant Butte and accused them of kidnapping, raping, and torturing her. The case expanded as another woman came forward with a similar story, and FBI agents searched the area around the trailer for the remains of other victims. The investigation spread into Texas and Arizona as well. A third suspect, Dennis Roy Yancy, later was charged in the kidnapping and murder of a woman who disappeared near Ray's trailer in 1997. Ray's daughter also was arrested. Investigators, however, had not found any bodies by the end of 1999. In September a guard at a private prison was stabbed to death in an inmate riot.

JIM ANDERSON

NEW YORK. New York lawmakers weathered a contentious legislative session in 1999. In November elections, Republicans lost control of the Nassau-county legislature on Long Island for the first time in 100 years, as voters gave Democrats a slim majority.

Legislation. The New York legislature passed a budget in August, 126 days into the fiscal year. The budget nearly doubled spending on child-care subsidies for the poor and raised aid to local school districts by more than $900 million. About $400 million a year in tax cuts also was included, but cuts in Medicaid and education proposed by Gov. George Pataki were defeated. In a long and generally contentious session, New York lawmakers also passed legislation that stiffened penalties for stalking and for blocking abortion clinics, expanded the state's database of DNA specimens from criminals, and eliminated New York City's income tax on commuters who worked in the city but lived elsewhere.

Education. Grade-school students throughout the state did badly on standardized math tests, apparently because many teachers were ignoring the curriculum. The state's fourth graders also did poorly on a new type of English test, according to a May report. The test replaced multiple-choice questions with essay questions; the new design was intended to set higher standards for reading and writing. But fewer than half the students scored well enough to meet the state's standards for fourth graders, and 11% fell into the lowest category.

Mrs. Clinton's Listening Tour. In July, First Lady Hillary Clinton took a trip through New York state to present herself as a potential candidate to replace U.S. Sen. Daniel Patrick Moynihan. She held several forums at which she said she was gathering information about state residents' concerns. Speculation continued on whether she would commit to entering the race, particularly after she and President Clinton bought a $1.7 million house in the upscale town of Chappaqua. Finally, in November she stated that she did intend to run for the Senate from New York as a Democrat in 2000. New York City Mayor Rudolph Giuliani was considering entering the race as well, as the Republican candidate.

JIM ANDERSON

NORTH CAROLINA. Widespread flooding from Hurricane Floyd in September 1999 devastated North Carolina, causing billions of dollars in damages, wiping out entire towns, and causing at least 51 deaths.

Natural Disasters. Hurricane Floyd's floodwaters caused unprecedented human suffering and damage throughout the state. Tens of thousands of people were left homeless as water covered more than 70 towns, and hundreds of roads were closed. Environmental problems mounted from flooded sewage plants; the flooding deaths of hundreds of thousands of chickens, turkeys, and hogs; and pollution from overflowing hog-waste lagoons. Power and telephone service were cut off to hundreds of thousands of people. Gov. Jim Hunt asked the U.S. Congress for $1.76 billion to compensate farmers for lost crops, to provide new housing, and to repair bridges and roads. Hunt estimated the state would need at least $5 billion in federal aid. Federal disaster officials and other states aided North Carolina with recovery efforts. Floyd's onslaught was the third major natural disaster in the state in 1999. Two weeks earlier, eastern North Carolina was hit by high winds and heavy rains from Hurricane Dennis, and in August all 100 counties in the state were allocated federal disaster relief because of drought and agricultural losses. Just as the state was recovering from Floyd, Hurricane Irene hit in October, dumping up to 11 in (27.9 cm) of rain in some areas.

Government. In the regular 1999 session, which ended in July, the legislature expanded Smart Start—a comprehensive system to help communities with child care, early education, preventive health care, and parent and teacher education—to all the state's 100 counties. The session also funded a measure designed to raise teacher-salary levels. Juvenile-justice measures included community prevention efforts and mentoring programs. Another law made it a felony to bring a firearm to school, suspended the driver's license of anyone who commits violence at a school or makes bomb threats at a school, and fined parents of students who make bomb threats.

New environmental-protection laws cracked down on water pollution, banned new hog-waste lagoons, reduced sulfur in motor fuel sold in the state, and tightened vehicle-emissions inspections. North Carolina also halted plans to build a landfill in rural Wake county to dispose of low-level nuclear waste and passed a law to withdraw from the Southeast Compact Commission, a group of seven states that had been formed in 1983 to share the responsibility of handling low-level radioactive waste.

ELAINE STUART

NORTH DAKOTA. In April 1999, North Dakota became the first state to remove criminal penalties for the cultivation of industrial hemp, a crop grown legally in other countries (but not the United States) for its fiber, seed, and oil. The bill was supported strongly by the state's wheat farmers, who had been hurt economically by falling prices and rising costs. However, the federal-government prohibition against growing hemp (because its leaves and flowers can be smoked as marijuana) continued to be in force, so the practice remained illegal for North Dakota farmers.

Health. After a 1-year-old North Dakota boy died from a lung infection that rapidly developed into pneumonia, federal health officials warned of the spread of a lethal form of staphylococcus in the northern Midwest. The disease was caused by *Staphylococcus aureus*, a germ that is resistant to the two antibiotic families most commonly used to combat it. Although this form of staph had been seen only in hospitals and nursing homes in the past, the officials said more than 200 people in North Dakota and neighboring Minnesota had become sick from the germ, and that it was probably at large in the wider environment.

Rising Tides. Since 1993 a gradually rising lake had threatened to engulf the town of Devil's Lake, northeast of Bismarck. By late 1999 the lake, which has no natural outlet, had quadrupled in size to swallow up 80,000 acres (32 400 ha) of farmland, three state parks, and more than 450 homes. The cause was a prolonged wet-weather cycle that brought heavier-than-usual snow and rain to the area. One proposed solution was to have the U.S. Army Corps of Engineers build a pumping system to funnel the water into the nearby Sheyenne River, but some feared that doing that would cause flooding elsewhere in the state and in Canada.

JIM ANDERSON

OHIO. Ohio carried out its first death sentence since 1963 when convicted murderer Wilford Berry was executed by lethal injection in February. Berry had insisted his sentence not be appealed, although groups opposing capital punishment claimed he was mentally ill.

Four white students at South High School in Cleveland were arrested for plotting a massacre of students and teachers, similar to the incident that occurred at Columbine High School in Colorado, on the school's Homecoming Day in October. Police found guns in the houses of two of the accused. In December, Andy Napier and Benjamin Balducci, both 15, pleaded guilty to conspiracy to commit aggravated murder, and Adam Gruber, 14, and John Borowski, 15, pleaded guilty to inducing panic. Officials had thought the plot might be racially motivated—about 70% of the school's students were black—but prosecutors said there was no evidence of that.

Education. On the day before the start of the school year in Cleveland, Federal Judge Solomon Oliver, Jr., blocked the city's voucher program on the grounds that it violated the separation of church and state. The four-year-old system allowed some 3,000 children to attend

56 mostly parochial schools at taxpayer expense. Three days later, Oliver reversed his decision, allowing the program to continue temporarily. In November the U.S. Supreme Court allowed the program to continue until its constitutionality could be determined. In December, Oliver ruled that the program was unconstitutional, and the state vowed to appeal to the Sixth Circuit Court. Children were to be allowed to continue using the vouchers during the appeal.

Politics. In line with the nationwide movement to set health-care standards for health-maintenance organizations (HMOs), Gov. Bob Taft signed the Ohio Patient Protection Act in July. Columbus voters elected Michael Coleman as the city's first black mayor in November. In defeating County Commissioner Dorothy Teater, Coleman also became the first Democrat to hold the post since 1971.

JIM ANDERSON

OKLAHOMA. In May 1999 more than 40 tornadoes tore a path through Oklahoma. The largest, which began near Chickasha, made the record books for both its size—nearly 1 mi (1.6 km) in width—and the peak speed of its wind, which reached 318 mph (511.6 km/hr). It was the deadliest tornado to hit the state in 52 years. Oklahoma City, the capital, was hit especially hard, with huge sections destroyed. A total of 44 people died, and nearly 7,000 homes were destroyed or damaged. President Clinton declared 16 counties disaster areas, and the Oklahoma legislature voted to reallocate money that had been set aside for a state trial of Terry Nichols, the federally convicted Oklahoma City bombing conspirator, to helping tornado victims.

Native American Affairs. Chad Smith, a Tulsa attorney, was elected chief of the 200,000-member Cherokee Nation, the second-largest Indian tribe in the United States. He defeated incumbent Joe Byrd in a runoff election held in July. Byrd was accused by other tribal leaders of financial wrongdoing, which he denied.

Crime. In December a seventh grader opened fire on his fellow students outside the Fort Gibson Middle School in Fort Gibson, a small town in eastern Oklahoma. The boy, who was described as being either 13 or 14 by police officials, used a semiautomatic pistol. Five people were wounded in the attack.

Other News. A dozen Oklahoma farmers living in the tiny town of Gould won $23 million in a Texas lottery in August.

KRISTI VAUGHAN

OREGON. In March 1999 an Oregon jury awarded $81 million to the family of a man who smoked for about 40 years before he died of lung cancer. It was the largest award made in a tobacco-related lawsuit by an individual. The suit charged that the Philip Morris Companies knew of the dangers of cigarette smoking but misrepresented that information; the company planned to appeal.

Health and Medicine. Oregon officials released a report in February showing that during 1998, the first year of a legally sanctioned assisted-suicide program, 15 terminally ill patients ended their lives using pain medication prescribed by their doctors. Proponents of right-to-die laws said that the relatively low number showed that the law was not abused.

Meanwhile, Paul Bilder, a Roseburg doctor, became the first physician to be disciplined for failing to prescribe enough pain medication to his patents. The Oregon Board of Medical Examiners found six cases between 1993 and 1998 when Dr. Bilder should have taken stronger steps to alleviate pain. The doctor signed a statement admitting that his treatment showed "unprofessional or dishonorable conduct," and he had to take a course on doctor-patient communication.

Crime. In September, only days before his trial was to begin, Kipland Kinkel, 17, pleaded guilty to murdering his parents and going on a shooting rampage at his Springfield high school that killed two students and left 22 others wounded in May 1998. He was sentenced to 112 years in prison with no chance of parole.

Environment. Oregon joined several other states in prohibiting "canned hunting," the keeping of exotic animals in enclosed areas so that they can be hunted.

The radioactive reactor of the Trojan Nuclear Plant in Ranier, which closed in 1993, was barged down the Columbia River to the Hanford Nuclear Reservation in Washington state, where it was buried. The *New Carissa* cargo ship, which ran aground off the Oregon coast in February, spilled about 70,000 gal (264 980 l) of fuel and bunker oil, resulting in an estimated $14 million in cleanup costs.

KRISTI VAUGHAN

PENNSYLVANIA. Like much of the East, Pennsylvania suffered through drought, followed by torrential hurricane-induced rains, in the summer of 1999. A February explosion at a chemical-processing plant in Hanover Township killed five persons and injured 13 others.

A new 79,500-seat stadium opened in 1999 in Cleveland, OH, to house the second coming of the Browns, the city's football franchise. When the team moved to Baltimore in 1995, Cleveland lobbied the NFL for an expansion team.

© Tom Hauck/Allsport

© Anthony Bolante/Reuters/Archive Photos

The "New Carissa" freighter ran aground off the coast of Oregon in February. The ship broke in two, above, *and thousands of gallons of fuel spilled into the Pacific Ocean.*

Health. In May, Pennsylvania officials said that they would begin offering stipends of about $300 to help families of organ donors cover the donors' funeral costs, hence breaking the long-held taboo in the United States against paying for organ donations. Under the three-year pilot project, the payments would be made to funeral homes rather than directly to the relatives.

Crime. A man whose crime had formed the basis for the 1986 Sean Penn film *At Close Range* was captured almost three weeks after he escaped from a maximum-security prison. Norman Johnston had been convicted of killing four teenagers in the late 1970s to cover up a multimillion-dollar burglary ring he ran with his two older brothers.

A Philadelphia grand jury in July ordered 1960s antiwar activist Ira Einhorn to pay $907 million to the family of Holly Maddux, a woman he was convicted in absentia of killing. The family said that they filed the suit to prevent Einhorn from making any money from telling his story. When the verdict was handed down, Einhorn was in France fighting extradition.

Marie Noe, 70, was sentenced to 20 years' probation for killing eight of her young children between 1949 and 1968. She also was ordered to undergo psychiatric treatment in an attempt to find out the reason she committed the crimes. The deaths previously had been believed to be the result of sudden-infant-death syndrome (SIDS), but the case was reopened in 1990, and Noe was charged in 1998.

In early December the city of Philadelphia was shocked by the killing of W. Russell G. Byers, a journalist at *The Philadelphia Daily News* for ten years. Byers, a popular columnist on urban affairs, was stabbed to death by a mugger outside a convenience store in an affluent section of town. Two days later, police arrested a suspect in the killing, 20-year-old Javier Goode.

Economics. Four years after it was closed down during a wave of military-base closings, the Philadelphia Naval Shipyard was put on the market as a commercial site. The marketing began under an agreement between the city of Philadelphia and the U.S. Navy.

KRISTI VAUGHAN

RHODE ISLAND. Rhode Island's attorney general sued eight paint manufacturers and an industry trade group in 1999. The suit seeks payment for treating children poisoned by lead paint and for the costs of removing lead paint from buildings. At least a dozen other states, counties, and cities were considering filing similar suits.

Politics and Scandal. U.S. Sen. John H. Chafee, 77, a moderate Republican who had served as Rhode Island's governor from 1963 to 1969, died in October. Earlier in the year, Chafee—who first was elected to the U.S. Senate in 1976—had said he would not seek reelection in 2000. His son, Lincoln Chafee, 46, Republican mayor of Warwick, was appointed by Gov. Lincoln Almond to complete his father's Senate term.

Former Gov. Edward DiPrete was sentenced in December 1998 to a three-year prison term (two years of which were suspended), after pleading guilty to 18 counts of perjury, bribery, extortion and racketeering. Early in 1999, DiPrete waged a court battle to retain his $50,000-per-year state pension; in April a judge ruled that the former governor's crimes while in office disqualified him from receiving the pension. DiPrete's wife, Patricia, requested that, as an innocent party, she be allowed to keep all or part of the pension, but the request was denied.

In late April, Federal Bureau of Investigation (FBI) agents raided Providence's city hall and arrested two top tax officials in a wide-ranging probe into alleged corruption in the state capital's government. Four officials later were indicted by a federal grand jury on charges of conspiracy, attempted extortion, and mail fraud; all four pleaded not guilty.

KRISTI VAUGHAN

SOUTH CAROLINA. After failing in negotiations to end the flying of the "Stars and Bars," the Confederate battle flag, atop the state capitol in Columbia, the National Association for the Advancement of Colored People (NAACP) announced in the summer of 1999 that it would launch an economic boycott of South Carolina beginning in January 2000. South Carolina was the only state that still displayed the flag, which was put up in 1962 as a gesture of defiance to the civil-rights movement. Gov. Jim Hodges worked to find a graceful way to take down the flag, and a number of organizations called for its removal. But several legislators said that even if they had been inclined to compromise before, they would not do it under the duress of the threatened boycott. Governor Hodges asked the NAACP to forego the boycott, but the organization refused.

A mass of Confederate flags flew in Charleston in November, as 300 members of the Confederate Heritage Trust staged a funeral at Magnolia Cemetery and reinterred the remains of 22 rebel soldiers and one child who died during the Civil War. The remains had been found during an archaeological dig at The Citadel, a military school in the city.

Gambling. In a complex case, the South Carolina Supreme Court ruled in October that the state's 34,000 video poker machines must be shut down by July 1, 2000. The court said that a scheduled November referendum on the legality of the machines was unconstitutional under state law. Because the bill authorizing the referendum stated that video poker could continue only if the voters approved, the court decreed that the machines must be banned.

Religion. South Carolina became the seventh state to enact a religious-freedom law when Governor Hodges signed a bill in June to prevent officials from intruding on religious expression by residents except in cases of "compelling public interest."

JIM ANDERSON

SOUTH DAKOTA. Although South Dakota is not part of the section of the country known as "Tornado Alley," several tornadoes struck the state in 1999.

Tornadoes. One person was killed and about 80 homes were damaged or destroyed in June, when a tornado struck the small town of Ogala, on the Pine Ridge Indian Reservation. A month earlier the state had been hit by two tornadoes spawned by the same massive storm system that created killer tornadoes in Oklahoma, Kansas, and Tennessee.

Legislation. After being approved by the legislature and signed by Gov. William Janklow, a law took effect on July 1 that absolved firearms and ammunition manufacturers from liability for the use or misuse of their products.

Indian Affairs. President Clinton traveled to the Pine Ridge Indian Reservation in July to announce federal initiatives to help Native Americans buy homes. The reservation, the nation's second largest, was one of the most poverty-stricken U.S. communities in 1999, with an unemployment rate of more than 70%. Clinton's visit was the first by a sitting president to an Indian reservation since Franklin D. Roosevelt in 1936.

KRISTI VAUGHAN

TENNESSEE. In 1999 one of the state's best-known political figures, U.S. Vice-President Al Gore, came back to Carthage, near the family farm where he had spent boyhood summers, to announce his candidacy for U.S. president. In December a jury in Memphis hearing a wrongful-death suit brought by the family of Martin Luther King, Jr., found that the civil-rights leader was the victim of a vast murder conspiracy and not of a single assassin.

Politics. Willie Herenton, who in 1991 became Memphis' first black mayor, was reelected to a third term in October. He won with 45.7% of the vote in a field of 15 candidates.

A budget crisis late in the year led Republican Gov. Don Sundquist to call a special legislative session to consider enacting a state income tax—a step he long had opposed. The legislature adjourned without passing a new tax, however.

Adoption Rights. The state Supreme Court upheld a law, passed in 1995, that allows adoptees who are 21 years or older to ask to see their records. Birth mothers must be notified of the request and are not required legally to see the child. Birth mothers tried to overturn the law, saying it violated their right to privacy.

Business. The entrepreneurial spirit was alive and well in Memphis, where a $75 million minor-league baseball stadium was being built, contemporary-art galleries were opening, and new malls were replacing those built in the 1970s and 1980s.

Disaster. Two chains of tornadoes struck the state in mid-January, killing ten persons. The state also was affected by the massive storm system and killer tornadoes that devastated Oklahoma in early May.

KRISTI VAUGHAN

TEXAS. During 1999, Texas Gov. George W. Bush emerged as the front-runner in the race for the Republican presidential nomination in 2000.

Government. The Texas legislature passed a $98.1 billion two-year budget. The session put most of the state's budget surplus into education, for a total of $6.4 billion over two years that would give teachers a $3,000 pay raise each and expand Head Start for preschoolers and kindergarten programs. A new law aimed to stop the practice of social promotion, in which schools move failing students to a higher grade. The legislature denied the governor's request for private-school vouchers, however. The legislature enacted $1.35 billion in property-tax relief for home owners and $506 million in sales- and business-tax cuts. Other measures required parental notification for minors to obtain abortions, lowered the blood-alcohol threshold for drunken driving, and helped welfare recipients entering the workforce. Lawmakers established a health-insurance program to cover children. Other new legislation allowed doctors to negotiate collectively with health plans and prevented cities and other local governments from filing suits against legal manufacturers or sellers of guns. Texas prison officials took over operations of a state jail in Austin, which had been contracted out to private operators to run.

In November 2 elections, Houston voters rejected spending $80 million for a new basketball-hockey arena and elected Lee P. Brown to a second term as mayor. San Antonio voted for a new $175 million arena for the Spurs of the National Basketball Association (NBA). Statewide on November 2, voters approved a measure to clarify gubernatorial succession and authorized $400 million in bonds for student loans.

In May, Dallas' Mayor Ron Kirk, San Antonio's Mayor Howard Peak, and El Paso's Mayor Carlos Ramirez were reelected.

Crime. In separate trials, Texas tried three white men charged with killing James Byrd, Jr., who was black, in 1998 by dragging him to his death from the back of a pickup. The three defendants—John William King, Lawrence Brewer, and Shawn Allen Berry—were convicted. King and Brewer were sentenced to death; Berry was sentenced to life in prison. As a result of the crime, the legislature considered, but did not pass, a hate-crimes bill.

In another case of mass violence, Larry Gene Ashbrook on September 15 fatally shot seven people during a service for young people and then killed himself in the sanctuary of Wedgwood Baptist Church in Fort Worth. Police in Texas and West Virginia arrested four suspects in October in the slayings of four teenage girls at an Austin yogurt shop in 1991. Texas took into custody suspected serial killer Angel Maturino Reséndez, a migrant laborer accused of a rape and nine slayings in Texas, Kentucky, and Illinois. His trial in Houston was scheduled to begin in 2000.

Disasters. In November, 11 students at Texas A&M University and a recent graduate were killed when the tower for a bonfire collapsed. The bonfire had been a 90-year-old tradition at the school on the eve of its football game against arch rival the University of Texas. In August, President Clinton declared a seven-county region a disaster area as a result of Hurricane Bret, which struck Corpus Christi and surrounding regions.

ELAINE STUART

UTAH. Various shootings in Salt Lake City and an Olympic bidding scandal occurred in Utah in 1999.

Government. Utah passed a growth act as a move toward managing urban sprawl. The law sought to promote affordable housing and preserve green space. It created a commission to study growth issues. A new state office would answer consumers' health-care questions. The legislature adopted a record $6.5 billion budget. New laws placed additional requirements on teen drivers and further punished drunk drivers. A consumer-protection law banned long-distance carriers from switching users' service without approval. The minimum marriage age was raised from 14 to 16 years old. Gov. Mike Leavitt and Attorney General Jan Graham settled a dispute over the attorney general's powers, after Graham threatened to sue over a law restricting her authority. Rocky Anderson, a Democrat, won the Salt Lake City mayor's race on November 2.

Other. A freak tornado on August 11 in Salt Lake City caused millions of dollars in damage, prompting the governor to seek federal disaster aid. A man described as mentally ill shot up a library owned by the Mormon Church in downtown Salt Lake City in April, killing two people and injuring others before being shot by police. In January a woman, also believed to be mentally ill, shot and killed a person at the Triad Center in Salt Lake City. Another former mental patient was shot by police in April after robbing two banks. The shootings resulted in calls for more gun control, but no action was taken.

The spotlight settled on Utah, due to the tradition of polygamy in the Mormon Church. John Daniel Kingston was sentenced to seven months in prison for abusing his daughter after she fled an arranged polygamous marriage with her uncle, David Ortell Kingston. The latter was convicted of incest and unlawful sexual conduct with a minor. He received a prison term of up to ten years.

See also SPORTS—*The 2002 Salt Lake City Olympics Come under Fire.*

ELAINE STUART

VERMONT. Educational issues were noteworthy in Vermont in 1999.

Schools. The Vermont Supreme Court upheld a lower-court ruling that public money cannot be used to pay tuition for religious schools. The issue arose when the Chittenden school district, which does not have its own high school and must pay for its students to attend schools in other towns, agreed in 1995 to pay tuition for students attending a Roman Catholic school in nearby Rutland.

Vermont was one of ten states joining in an effort to improve middle-school students' math performance through development of a common curriculum. The standards were to be developed by Achieve, Inc., a group chaired jointly by Louis Gerstner, Jr., chairman of the International Business Machines Corporation (IBM), and Wisconsin Gov. Tommy Thompson.

Other. In a controversial decision that made national front-page headlines, the Vermont Supreme Court ruled in December that under the state constitution, Vermont must guarantee the same protections and benefits to gay and lesbian couples that it does to heterosexual spouses. The court left it to the legislature to decide whether to legalize gay marriage or to adopt a domestic-partnership law.

Abortion clinics and Planned Parenthood Federation of America centers in several Vermont cities were among those nationwide that received letters claiming to contain the deadly anthrax bacteria. Tests showed that there were no bacteria.

Stargazing lost out in June, when voters in Springfield approved construction of a 350-bed state prison. Astronomers said the prison's lights—which, unlike town lights, will remain on all night—will ruin viewing from an 80-year-old nearby observatory.

KRISTI VAUGHAN

VIRGINIA. In November 1999 elections, Republicans won majorities in both houses of Virginia's General Assembly for the first time in the state's history.

Schools. The quality of public education in Virginia came into question in early 1999, when 98% of the state's 1,800 schools failed to measure up in at least one core subject area on new standardized tests. The tests, which had been administered in 1998, examined learning in English, math, science, and social studies. Beginning in 2006, 70% of students in a school must pass the exams, or the school may lose its certification. Similarly, by 2004, students must pass six of the high-school exams to graduate.

Melissa Graham and Chih-Yuan Ho became the first women to graduate from Virginia Military Institute, on May 15.

Crime and Law. A Ku Klux Klan leader was convicted of trying to intimidate others by burning a cross. Barry Black had maintained that he was exercising his right to free speech. Gov. James S. Gilmore commuted the death sentence of Calvin Swann, a mentally ill man who was convicted of robbing and shooting a 62-year-old man in 1992.

Paula Johnson—whose baby was switched at birth with another baby in a 1995 case that attracted national attention—was denied custody of her biological child. Johnson was granted visitation rights, however.

Environment. A bill restricting where landfills can be built, where trash-carrying barges can travel, and how much refuse can be imported from other states was signed into law by Governor Gilmore in March. The state, like others on the East Coast, was affected severely by a summer heat wave and drought. In late July, 500,000 dead fish were found in Bullbegger Creek, a tributary of Maryland's Pocomoke River. Their death was attributed to oxygen depletion cased by the drought, among other causes.

Hurricane Floyd came up the East Coast in September, dumping nearly 2 ft (0.6 m) of rain on much of the mid-Atlantic region. As many as 500,000 people in Virginia lost electricity. Floyd arrived little more than two weeks after Hurricane Dennis had spawned tornadoes and caused two deaths in the state.

Business. The four largest tobacco companies agreed to establish a $5.15 billion relief fund for farmers in Virginia and elsewhere who could be hurt by market declines expected as the result of a settlement reached in nationwide tobacco-related suits.

KRISTI VAUGHAN

WASHINGTON. Washington state news was highlighted in 1999 by protests and rioting at the conference of the World Trade Organization (WTO), held November 30–December 3 in Seattle.

The WTO Uproar. As the trade conference was set to begin, thousands of demonstrators converged on Seattle to protest the WTO's policies and its existence. Violence soon broke out; store windows were smashed and businesses looted. Some $2 million of damage resulted. Police subdued the crowds with tear gas, pepper spray, and rubber bullets, and the National Guard was called in to help restore order. More than 500 persons were arrested. The uproar trapped WTO delegates in their hotels and forced the cancellation of the opening ceremonies. The conference proceeded the next day as planned, and included a visit by President Clinton.

Peaceful demonstrators claimed police unnecessarily had used violent tactics on them and had attacked some innocent parties. Police Chief Norm Stamper resigned a few days after the conference; many officers had criticized his handling of the crisis and failure to anticipate it. Meanwhile, several groups were slated to investigate police actions during the rioting.

Initiative 695. On November 2, Washington voters approved Initiative 695, which made major changes to the state's tax code. The state vehicle tax—which had been set at 2.2% of a vehicle's value—was replaced with a flat annual fee of $30 per vehicle. In addition, the legislature now would be required to hold a referendum to approve or reject any proposed tax or fee increase. Washington was the only state to have approved such an initiative.

Other News. Women made up 41% of Washington's state legislature in 1999; this was the highest proportion in any U.S. state at any time in the nation's history. A

© Adress Latif/Liaison Agency

In a tragic accident, 11 Texas A&M students and a recent graduate were killed when a tower of logs they were building for the annual Aggie Bonfire toppled onto them. In the aftermath of the incident, students and faculty debated whether to discontinue the bonfire, a long-standing tradition used to rally support for the school's football team, the Aggies.

series of one-day strikes by public-school teachers were held across the state to protest inadequate pay raises. Major League Baseball's Seattle Mariners moved in July from the Kingdome, their home for more than 22 years, to the new $517 million Safeco Field.

THE EDITORS

WEST VIRGINIA. A federal judge's ruling on pollution from strip mining caused a furor in the state in 1999. In August the state was declared a federal agricultural disaster area, due to drought.

Mining. On October 20, U.S. District Judge Charles Haden banned coal companies from dumping rock and dirt from mountaintop-removal strip-mining sites within 100 ft (30.5 m) of any stream that flows at least six months per year. Haden later put his ruling on hold, pending an appeal, and the state's Division of Environmental Protection allowed mining operations affected by the ruling to resume November 1, also pending the appeal. Gov. Cecil Underwood had said the ruling would devastate West Virginia's economy.

Thousands of miners from West Virginia and other states rallied in Washington, DC, on November 8 to protest the decision. In addition, U.S. Sen. Robert Byrd (D-WV) attempted unsuccessfully to attach legislation to a federal appropriations bill to nullify the ruling.

Government. In an effort to raise more revenue, the legislature in 1999 permitted video lottery machines at racetracks to pay out in cash rather than in paper slips redeemable for cash. Racetracks began converting the lottery machines in November. The legislature also permitted a casino at The Greenbrier, a historic resort, if local voters approved.

Lawmakers also passed the governor's $2.66 billion budget and authorized the sale of $110 million in road bonds. Other new laws called for parent education and mediation in divorce and child-custody cases, regulated mountaintop-removal mining, restored some cuts in workers' compensation passed in 1995, and prohibited cities from restricting gun owners' rights. The legislature created a special fund to hold part of the state's share of the national tobacco settlement.

ELAINE STUART

WISCONSIN. In January, Wisconsin officials released a report on the state's welfare program, Wisconsin Works or W-2, which began in 1997. The survey indicated that while a high percentage of the state's welfare recipients had found employment, economic difficulties remained common and grew even worse for some recipients.

Achieve Inc., a nonprofit organization chaired jointly by Louis Gerstner, Jr., chairman of the International Business Machines Corp. (IBM), and Wisconsin Gov. Tommy Thompson, was to establish a common curriculum and standardized tests in mathematics for middle-school students. Ten states, including Wisconsin, agreed to participate in the project.

Legal Developments. State legislation calling for telemarketers to disclose whom they work for and what they are selling, as well as limiting the hours during which they may call, became effective on August 1. In October a Wisconsin prosecutor filed rape and kidnapping charges against a defendant without a name, only a DNA code. The charges were filed against "John Doe, unknown male with matching deoxyribonucleic acid (DNA)," after tests matched the DNA contained in semen samples from three 1993 rape cases. A backlog of cases had prevented the samples from being tested, and it was believed the prosecutor wished to avoid the state's six-year statute of limitations.

THE EDITORS

WYOMING. In a Laramie courtroom in early November, Aaron J. McKinney, a 22-year-old former roofer, was given two consecutive life sentences in prison after being convicted of the second-degree murder, robbery, and kidnapping of Matthew Shepard, a 21-year-old gay student at the University of Wyoming, in October 1998. Shepard's parents had requested that McKinney be spared the death penalty. In April, Russell A. Henderson, 21, had pleaded guilty to the crime and also was sentenced to two consecutive life terms. During the year, Judy Shepard, the victim's mother, had campaigned for federal and state legislation that would include the sexual orientation of a crime victim as a basis for designating a crime as a hate crime.

Other News. As a result of a July 1995 incident in which Wyoming state troopers stopped a car for speeding and a faulty brake light and then proceeded to search the car and the purse of a passenger, the U.S. Supreme Court ruled in April that law-enforcement officers have the authority to search the belongings of automobile passengers, even if the officers suspect only the car driver of illegal activity.

On March 4, Gov. Jim Geringer signed legislation allowing Wyoming's attorney general to intervene on behalf of gun manufacturers and dealers in liability lawsuits brought by local governments and individuals, if the suits are considered frivolous.

THE EDITORS

Stocks and Bonds

The U.S. stock market closed out the 1990s in fitting style, recording its fifth consecutive two-digit gain in 1999. Many overseas stock markets also prospered. The bond market struggled, however, as the Federal Reserve Board tightened credit conditions with three moves to nudge short-term interest rates higher. The Fed's actions, reversing a series of three reductions in 1998, were intended to restrain inflation—and also speculative enthusiasm among stock investors—in the midst of a technology boom.

The Dow Jones average of 30 industrial stocks surpassed 10,000 for the first time early in the year and closed December 31 at 11,497.12, up 2,315.69 points, or 25.2%, from the end of 1998. The composite index of the Nasdaq market, home to some of the most popular computer and telecommunications stocks, soared 1,876.62 points, or 85.6%, to 4,069.31 at year's end. Standard & Poor's (S&P's) 500-stock composite index gained 240 points, or 19.5%, to 1,469.25.

In bonds, by contrast, the interest rate on long-term Treasury bonds climbed to above 6% from about 5% as 1999 began. The Lehman Brothers Long-Term Treasury-Bond Index showed a loss of about 7.5% heading into the final weeks of the year.

A Continuing Bull Market. At the end of the 1990s, the fruits of a historic bull market were everywhere to see. The Dow Jones industrial average stood at more than ten times where it had been less than 20 years earlier. A survey sponsored jointly by the Securities Industry Association, a brokers' group, and the mutual funds' Investment Company Institute reported that the number of Americans owning stocks had grown to an estimated 78.7 million from 42.4 million in 1983. As of 1998, the survey said, stocks owned either directly or through intermediaries such as mutual funds accounted for a record 35% of all U.S. household financial assets, up from 17% in 1980. The big question for 2000 and beyond was how much further increase was likely, or even possible. In 1999, at least, the growth continued.

Technology. The uncontested stars of the stock market were companies with links to the Internet and World Wide Web. Stocks in the "technology" group, which a few years before had accounted for less than 5% of the S&P 500's market value, had grown to more than 25% of the index by year's end.

High-tech change was happening fast in the securities business itself. On-line brokers, offering automated trading systems at bargain-basement commission rates of $10

Designed by George Stewart

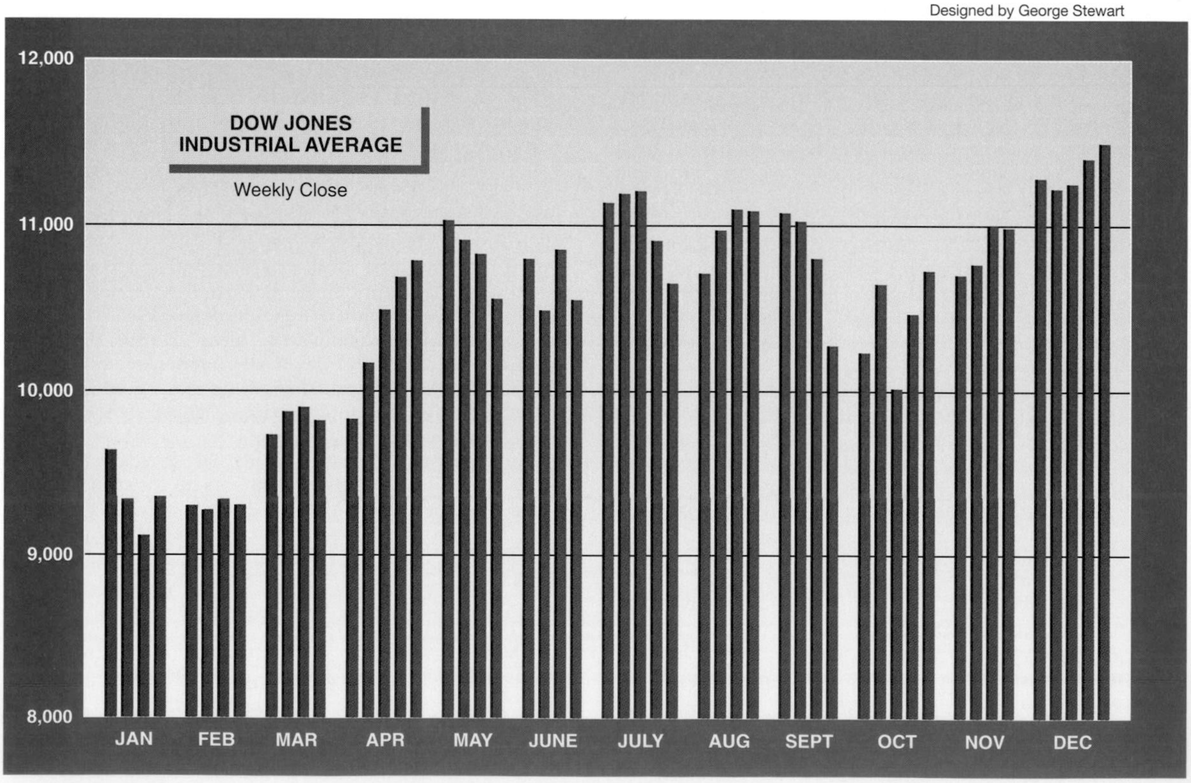

or less per trade, put pressure on full-line and discount brokerage firms to adapt. One of the great mythic cultural figures of 1999 was the freewheeling "day trader." In truth, most regulators and Wall Street officials said, there was more story than substance to this trend. Experts agreed that almost everybody who tried day-trading was bound to lose. Nevertheless, day traders served as a representative image of a heady era.

Change loomed as well for Wall Street insiders. Corporate-finance departments at investment firms, while enjoying a banner year for new stock offerings, faced the possibility of losing some of their franchise to the Internet. In a moment of symbolic impact in November, the city of Pittsburgh sold tax-free municipal bonds over the Internet directly to investing institutions, rather than through an investment banker.

At the New York Stock Exchange (NYSE), the "specialists" on the exchange floor worried that their roles also might be diminished severely in the future by automated trading systems. Near year's end, the exchange repealed a decades-old rule that effectively shielded the specialists from automated competitors trading in Big Board–listed stocks.

Exchange officials also debated, and experimented with, ways to extend the daily trading schedule beyond the 9:30 A.M. to 4 P.M. routine. In an increasingly global marketplace, some investors clamored for 24-hour markets. Many investment firms resisted any expansion of the trading day, though, complaining of added costs and questioning whether investors could expect liquid markets with reasonable prices in the middle of the night. It seemed inevitable, however, that the length of the trading day would increase in future years. To compete on a global scale, both the NYSE and Nasdaq proposed turning themselves into public companies via sales of shares to the public. While that seemed a worthy idea in many ways, it raised questions for government agencies about whether these market operators could function effectively as self-regulatory organizations while also working on behalf of shareholders.

As a further nod to progress, Dow Jones & Co. shook up the roster of its 30 industrial-average components on November 1. It added Microsoft and Intel—two Nasdaq high-tech giants that became the first non-NYSE issues ever in the Dow—as well as SBC Communications and Home Depot. These companies replaced Sears Roebuck, Goodyear Tire, Chevron, and Union Carbide on the index.

Mutual Funds. One of the great financial successes of the 20th century, the U.S. mutual-fund industry, faced new uncertainties. In the 1990s its assets under management soared from $1 trillion to $6 trillion, but growth in 1999 showed signs of slowing. Analysts warned that fund investors risked almost certain disappointment at some point if they came to see double-digit market gains as routine.

Inflows of new money into stock funds in 1999 were concentrated in a few "hot" fund families, most notably the Janus Funds in Denver, the Vanguard Group in Valley Forge, PA, and Fidelity Investments in Boston. The largest of all stock funds, the Fidelity Magellan Fund, became the first to surpass $100 billion in assets.

Bond funds, which showed slightly negative total returns late in the year, along with the bond market generally, continued to see their share of the business shrink—to about 13% of all fund assets, from almost 30% just six years earlier.

Money-market funds, however, enjoyed a second consecutive year of strong growth, as their yields climbed from an average of about 4.6% to above 5%. Assets of these funds, which invest in short-term securities such as Treasury bills and commercial paper issued by corporations, climbed past $1.5 trillion—50% above where they had stood just two years earlier.

World Markets. International funds also had a good year, in many cases outperforming U.S. stock funds for the first time since 1993. Stock markets in Asia and Latin America, in particular, staged a sharp rally as the world economy bounced back vigorously from the financial crises of 1997–98 in Asian currency markets and of 1998 in Russia. European markets settled for more-modest gains, however. The euro, an 11-nation currency that debuted at the start of 1999 at about 1.18 to the U.S. dollar, fell to parity with the dollar by early December.

As of early December, indexes compiled by the investment firm Morgan Stanley Dean Witter & Co. of nine stock markets around the world showed nary a loser on the lists. Hong Kong led the parade, up 46%, and was followed by Japan, up 36%. France was up 35%; Canada, up 29%; Germany, up 19%; and the United States, up 14%. In smaller gains, Britain was up 10%; Switzerland, up 6%; and Australia, up 5%.

CHET CURRIER, *"Bloomberg News"*

Sudan

In 1999 the government of Lt. Gen. Omar Hassan Ahmed al-Bashir and the National Islamic Front (NIF) celebrated the tenth anniversary of the military coup that brought it to power. The continuing civil war dominated Sudanese affairs.

Domestic Affairs. At the end of 1998, Bashir signed the Political Associations Act, which allowed for the beginnings of a multiparty system. The older opposition parties rejected this measure, but some chose to form groups. One, the Alliance for the Working Forces, was established by Jaafar al-Nemery, who had come to power in Sudan through a coup in 1969 and ruled until he was overthrown in 1985. He returned to Sudan from exile in May as part of the government's reconciliation campaign but had limited political impact.

The Sudanese National Congress reorganized, emerging as a major political force. In early 1999, Bashir was elected to head the party, while Hassan al-Turabi was reelected speaker of the parliament and the party's executive director. The party overwhelmingly won an election in Khartoum state in June, taking 62 of 65 seats in the local parliament. In October a restructuring of the Congress reduced the president's powers and strengthened the role of the executive director. At the same time, the party nominated Bashir for reelection in 2001. Outside observers saw these events as signaling Turabi's victory in a power struggle with Bashir.

Bashir struck back on December 12, dissolving the legislature and declaring a three-month state of emergency. The National Congress then urged all senior executives to quit, so that Bashir could have "a free hand to reshape the government," and on December 31 the entire cabinet did so. The president accepted the resignations but asked the officials to stay on until he could form a new government. Turabi and his supporters, meanwhile, opposed Bashir's action, and the year ended with public debates.

Sudan continued to face major economic problems, including a large foreign debt and economic sanctions imposed by the United States. In the fall, however, a pipeline from oil fields in southwestern Sudan to Red Sea terminals was completed, initially transporting 120,000 barrels per day. Observers estimated that Sudan soon could be earning $200 million annually from oil sales.

Civil War. The military conflict between the government and various opposition forces continued during 1999. The conflict was marked by stalemate on every front, as in previous years. The Sudan People's Liberation Army (SPLA) continued to control significant territories in the south, and various armed forces representing northern opposition groups in the National Democratic Alliance (NDA) scored symbolic successes; but the government's military position was not changed significantly. Fighting was interrupted sometimes by cease-fire agreements to allow humanitarian operations, but all of the combatants accused each other of violations.

Negotiations to end the war also continued, with the Inter-Governmental Authority on Development (IGAD), a trade group of African states, mediating. The negotiation process was augmented with special diplomatic initiatives by Egypt and Libya. There was general consensus on all sides on the basic measures needed for peace, including acceptance of the right of self-determination as provided in the Declaration of Principles developed by IGAD, but high levels of mutual mistrust and a lingering hope within the opposition that a military victory might be possible stood in the way.

International Affairs. Relations with the United States were dominated by the issues of U.S. sanctions, the aftermath of the American bombing of a pharmaceutical plant in Khartoum in 1998, and the human-rights situation in Sudan. The United States released the assets of Salih Idris, the owner of the plant, which had been frozen at the time of the bombing. This act was perceived in Sudan as a strong indication that the bombing had been in error, although the U.S. government maintained officially that it had been justified. Some members of the U.S. Congress led efforts for international condemnation of human-rights violations by the Sudanese government. Diplomatic relations

SUDAN • Information Highlights

Official Name: Republic of the Sudan.
Location: Northeast Africa.
Area: 967,494 sq mi (2 505 810 km^2).
Population (July 1999 est.): 34,475,690.
Chief Cities (1993 census): Khartoum, the capital, 947,483; Omdurman, 1,271,403; Khartoum North, 700,887; Port Sudan, 308,195.
Government: *Head of state and government,* Omar Hassan Ahmed al-Bashir, president (took power June 30, 1989). *Legislature* (unicameral)—National Assembly.
Monetary Unit: Pound (1,540.0 pounds equal U.S.$1, Nov. 10, 1999).
Gross Domestic Product (1998 est. U.S.$): $31,200,-000,000 (purchasing power parity).
Foreign Trade (1998 est. U.S.$): *Imports,* $1,915,000,000; *exports,* $596,000,000.

were reestablished with Egypt and Great Britain during the year, and agreements signed with Eritrea and other previously hostile neighbors further lessened tensions.

JOHN O. VOLL, *Georgetown University*

Sweden

SWEDEN • Information Highlights

Official Name: Kingdom of Sweden.
Location: Northern Europe.
Area: 173,732 sq mi (449 964 km²).
Population (July 1999 est.): 8,911,296.
Chief Cities (Dec. 31, 1997 est.): Stockholm, the capital, 727,339; Göteborg, 456,661; Malmö, 251,408.
Government: *Head of state,* Carl XVI Gustaf, king (acceded Sept. 1973). *Head of government,* Göran Persson, prime minister (took office March 1996). *Legislature* (unicameral)—Riksdag.
Monetary Unit: Krona (8.3217 kronor equal U.S.$1, Nov. 10, 1999).
Gross Domestic Product (1998 est. U.S.$): $175,000,-000,000 (purchasing power parity).
Economic Indexes (1998, 1990 = 100): *Consumer Prices,* all items, 123.8; food, 97.4. *Industrial Production,* 127.9.
Foreign Trade (1998 U.S.$): *Imports,* $68,420,000,000; *exports,* $84,739,000,000.

Bolstered by the strength of the Swedish economy, the Social Democratic government in 1999 cut income taxes in the 2000 budget (the first such reduction in almost ten years), but major defense cuts could herald a significant change in Sweden's status as a nonaligned country. Sweden also moved forward on closing the first of its 12 nuclear reactors, confirming a radical change in energy policy.

Politics and European Affairs. The major opposition party, the conservative Moderates, chose a new leader, former tax minister Bo Lundgren, to replace Carl Bildt. In June's European Parliament elections (in which only 38% of Swedish voters participated), the big losers were the Greens, who almost halved their support; they earned only 9.4% of the vote and two of Sweden's 22 seats. The big winner was the strongly pro–European Union (EU) Liberals, who almost trebled their segment of the vote (13.8%) and won three seats. Support for Swedish membership in the EU's Economic and Monetary Union (EMU) weakened in 1999. In January, 51% of Swedes declared that they favored joining, but by October the support had dropped to 38%.

Finance Minister Erik Asbrink, considered a fiscal conservative, resigned in April and was replaced by Bosse Ringholm after a power struggle with Prime Minister Göran Persson. On September 20, Ringholm presented a budget for 2000 that included the first significant cut in income taxes in almost a decade, as well as a reduction in corporate taxes. Overall, fiscal balance was preserved by the sharp increase in government revenues in the wake of the unexpected strength of the economy.

A plan to cut defense spending by 12 billion Swedish krona ($1.5 billion) and eliminate more than 6,500 jobs was presented to parliament in November. Senior officers argued that if the proposal—which must be finalized by parliament in early 2000—were enacted, Sweden no longer would be strong enough to sustain its credibility as a nonaligned nation and might have to join the North Atlantic Treaty Organization (NATO). Production of the JAS advanced jet fighter would continue despite the cuts.

In June the Supreme Administrative Court of Sweden supported the government's decision to close the nuclear reactor at Barsebäck in southern Sweden; it was the first of the country's 12 nuclear facilities to be shut down. The court rejected a claim by the owner, Sydkraft, that the action was illegal under both Swedish and EU law. Sydkraft appealed the decision to the EU Commission.

Economy. The Swedish economy was expected to maintain a growth rate above 3% in 2000, only slightly less than the predicted outcome for 1999. Unemployment was projected to drop to 4.5% in 2000 (from 5.3% in 1999), although those figures exclude participants in publicly funded work programs. Both the International Monetary Fund (IMF) and the Organization for Economic Cooperation and Development (OECD) praised Sweden for its economic achievements but stressed that continued structural changes of the welfare state were needed to sustain long-term growth.

In March, Volvo sold its car division to the U.S.-based Ford Motor Company for $6.3 billion. Later in the year it acquired a majority share of fellow Swedish automaker Scania, the world's second-largest producer of heavy trucks, for $7.4 billion.

Foreign Policy. Chinese Foreign Minister Tang Jiaxuan made an official visit to Stockholm in March, during which he clashed with his Swedish counterpart, Anna Lindh, over Sweden's criticism of China's human-rights policies. Also visiting in March was South African President Nelson Mandela, who praised Sweden as his staunchest ally during apartheid.

LEIF BECK FALLESEN, *Editor in Chief "Boersen," Copenhagen*

Switzerland

In 1999 the multiyear banking crisis involving victims of the Nazi Holocaust receded into the background in Switzerland.

Economic Issues. On January 23 two Swiss Banks, UBS and Credit Suisse, formally signed the agreement negotiated in 1998 to create a $1.25 billion account to compensate Holocaust victims and their families. One week later, Swiss President Ruth Dreifuss and U.S. Vice-President Albert Gore announced that the dispute between the U.S. government and Swiss banks regarding this issue was considered closed. A December report by an international committee, headed by former U.S. Federal Reserve Chairman Paul Volcker, concluded that the $1.25 billion would be sufficient to cover claims resulting from the more than 54,000 undisclosed bank accounts uncovered by the committee's investigation.

On June 23, at the request of the International War Crimes Tribunal, Swiss officials froze all Swiss bank accounts held by indicted Yugoslav President Slobodan Milosevic. However, on July 16 the Swiss Supreme Court overturned the government's 1998 seizure of $90 million in assets of Raúl Salinas, brother of former Mexican President Carlos Salinas, although the funds remained frozen pending new legal action. And on July 29 the license of the Japanese subsidiary bank of Credit Suisse was revoked because of its role in helping hide losses incurred by Japanese commercial companies.

Swiss authorities froze 59 accounts and agreed to provide information regarding 24 Russians who were alleged to have engaged in money-laundering activities. This was part of a larger scandal involving the movement of moneys out of Russia through both Swiss and New York–based banks. It was asserted in late August that the "Russian Mafia" had moved some $27 million in funds through 300 Swiss-based companies it allegedly controlled. In September, Swiss authorities moved against two companies, Andava SA and Forus Service SA, which were charged with setting up accounts through which revenues of the Russian firm Aeroflot could be diverted out of Russia. Auxiliary to this were charges that the Swiss firm Mabetex, which had large construction contracts in Russia, had paid more than $10 million in kickbacks to Russian officials, including open-ended credit cards to fund expenses for the family of President Boris Yeltsin.

Politics. On April 18, 59% of Swiss voters ratified the first major revision of the Swiss constitution since 1874. While it included new provisions such as the right to strike and equal opportunity for handicapped persons, the major change involved dropping the gold standard. This allows Swiss banks and the government to sell much of their gold reserves, thereby raising funds to shore up the national pension system and fund the $1.25 billion Holocaust Victims Fund.

On June 13, in what was seen as a reaction against the influx of 240,000 Kosovo refugees into Switzerland, voters approved a referendum proposal that tightened rules for granting political asylum. They also rejected a plan for a nationally mandated 14 weeks of maternity leave at 80% of pay.

Federal elections on October 24 resulted in the ultraconservative Swiss People's Party receiving almost 23% of the vote, up from 14.9% in 1995, ranking it second behind the Social Democrats. Its success threatened the long-standing four-party balance of seats on the seven-member Federal Council, in which the People's Party traditionally held only one. Led by industrialist Christoph Blocher, the People's Party espoused an anti-immigrant, antitax, anti–United Nations and anti–European Union (EU) platform.

Other Events. In August, Swiss police arrested Dino Bellasi, a former accountant in the Swiss military, and charged him with embezzling $5.6 million from the defense ministry....A flash flood on July 27 at Saxeten Brook near Interlaken resulted in the deaths of 21 persons who were engaged in the sport of canyoning, which involves rappelling into gorges and free-floating down narrow mountain-canyon streams.

PAUL C. HELMREICH, *Wheaton College (MA)*

SWITZERLAND • Information Highlights

Official Name: Swiss Confederation.
Location: Central Europe.
Area: 15,942 sq mi (41 290 km²).
Population (July 1999 est.): 7,275,467.
Chief Cities (Dec. 31, 1997 est.): Bern, the capital, 124,412; Zurich, 338,594; Geneva, 172,586; Basel, 171,170.
Government: *Head of state and government,* Ruth Dreifuss, president (took office January 1999); Adolf Ogi, vice-president (took office January 1999). *Legislature*—Federal Assembly: Council of States and National Council.
Monetary Unit: Franc (1.5885 francs equal U.S.$1, Dec. 15, 1999).
Gross Domestic Product (1998 est. U.S.$): $191,800,-000,000 (purchasing power parity).
Economic Indexes (1998, 1990 = 100): *Consumer Prices,* all items, 118.4; food, 108.0. *Industrial Production,* 111.8.
Foreign Trade (1998 U.S.$): *Imports,* $73,885,000,000; *exports,* $75,439,000,000.

Syria

The year in Syria suggested the likelihood of great changes in the near future in both domestic affairs and foreign relations; but it was through hints and anticipations rather than actual, concrete events. During 1999 the country continued to be ruled in authoritarian fashion, but skillfully, by President Hafiz al-Assad.

SYRIA • Information Highlights

Official Name: Syrian Arab Republic.
Location: Southwest Asia.
Area: 71,498 sq mi (185 180 km^2).
Population (July 1999 est.): 17,213,871.
Chief Cities (September 1994 census): Damascus, the capital, 1,394,322; Aleppo, 1,582,930; Homs, 540,133.
Government: *Head of state,* Gen. Hafiz al-Assad, president (took office officially March 1971). *Head of government,* Mahmoud Zubi, prime minister (took office November 1987). *Legislature* (unicameral)—People's Council.
Monetary Unit: Pound (43.00 pounds equal U.S.$1, Jan. 3, 2000).
Gross Domestic Product (1998 est. U.S.$): $41,700,-000,000 (purchasing power parity).
Economic Index (Damascus, 1998; 1990 = 100): *Consumer Prices,* all items, 177.0; food, 163.0.
Foreign Trade (1998 U.S.$): *Imports,* $3,895,000,000; *exports,* $2,890,000,000.

Domestic Affairs. On February 10, Assad was elected to a fifth seven-year term as president. Assad, the sole candidate, officially was reported to have received endorsement by 99.98% of the voters. While the almost unanimous approval might invite skepticism, it was undoubtedly true that the president enjoyed general respect and support from the Syrian people.

As in recent years, there were reports that Assad, who turned 69 in 1999, was in poor health. But the tone of the 1999 reports was more somber and suggested some real decline in the president's condition. Some confirmation of the pessimistic attitude perhaps could be seen in the assignment of various duties of middle-rank importance to Assad's son Bashar, the presumed, if not formally designated, heir. The other obvious possible candidate to succeed Assad (but a very unlikely one) was his not-much-younger brother Rifaat, 62. Although Rifaat has been mostly in exile after being deprived of his nominal vice-presidency in February 1998, he continued to be an influence in Syria through a London-based satellite-television station owned by his son Sawmar. Continued suspicion of Rifaat's activities and influence was shown in a roundup of about 1,000 of his followers by government agents in September; and in a raid by government forces on a residential compound owned by Rifaat near the city of Latakia. On

Posters of Syrian leader Hafiz al-Assad (right) *and Jordan's new king, Abdullah II, decorated a train linking Damascus and Amman. This train service, launched in July 1999, indicated warmer relations between the two nations.*

his son's television station, Rifaat denounced the raid as a "massacre," involving hundreds of deaths, but the government countered that the facility was an illegal port used for smuggling.

As it had been for many years, the Syrian government was condemned by the United States for its policies on two issues: human rights and terrorism. In two annual reports released during 1999, the U.S. State Department cited Syria for human-rights abuses and listed Syria as a sponsor of international terrorism.

Foreign Relations. Several events in 1999 opened up the lines of communication between Syria and Jordan, which had been closed for many years. Assad attended the funeral of Jordan's King Hussein in Amman on February 8, and indeed was first in line to offer his condolences to the new king, Abdullah. Bashar, Assad's son, met with Abdullah in Amman a few weeks later, and Abdullah visited Damascus and met with Assad himself in late April. The last previous meeting between the rulers of Syria and Jordan was in 1994. The Jordanian king went to Syria again on July 26. The Syrian and Jordanian prime ministers held talks in Amman on August 2–3, and a trade agreement, reducing customs duties on 100 products, was signed. Also, express train service between Amman and Damascus was inaugurated on July 29.

Perhaps the most hopeful development was progress toward a peace treaty between Syria and Israel, which technically were still at war. Peace talks with Israel had broken off in 1996. The defeat of Israeli Prime Minister Benjamin Netanyahu by Ehud Barak in May elections was viewed positively in Syria, as Barak seemed more likely to be willing to make concessions than Netanyahu had been. Assad surprisingly called Barak "a sincere and honest man," and while on a visit to Moscow in July, he said that with Barak as Israel's leader, there were "specific opportunities for constructive efforts towards a comprehensive and just peace." The United States made several attempts, including a number of visits to Damascus by Secretary of State Madeleine Albright, to bring both sides to the table. As a result, in mid-December, Israel and Syria resumed peace negotiations in Washington, DC. A follow-up round of talks began in early January between Barak and Foreign Minister Farouk al-Shara, acting as Assad's proxy, in Shepherdstown, WV. Those talks finished inconclusively, and another round, scheduled to begin in mid-January, was postponed due to Syria's insistence that Israel withdraw from the Golan Heights, which it has occupied since 1967, before negotiations could continue.

ARTHUR CAMPBELL TURNER
University of California, Riverside

Taiwan

A devastating earthquake of a 7.6 magnitude struck Taiwan on Sept. 21, 1999, killing 2,100, injuring 8,000, and leaving more than 100,000 homeless. In addition to the damage to lives and property, there was also political fallout. Many people blamed the Nationalist Party government for tardy and insufficient relief efforts, as well as for the failure to enforce stringent building codes. The government rejected an offer of relief assistance from the People's Republic of China and bristled at a message of condolence from the United Nations (UN) addressed to the "Taiwan Province of China."

Taiwan also prepared for its second presidential election, to be held in March 2000. The Nationalist Party nominated Vice-President Lien Chan, President Lee Teng-hui's chosen successor, over James Soong, who had been the popular governor of the Taiwan provincial government until it was dissolved in 1997. Shortly after his defeat, Soong left the Nationalist Party, mounting a campaign as an independent candidate. The opposition Democratic Progressive Party (DPP) chose Taipei Mayor Chen Shui-bien as its nominee.

Cross-Strait Relations. The ambiguities of Taiwan's international status and its relationship to the government in Beijing were at the forefront of Taiwan's domestic and international politics during 1999. During a German interview in early July, President Lee made the startling assertion that any further discourse across the Taiwan Strait must be conducted on a "state-to-state" basis. This statement clarified and altered the ambiguous fictions that had characterized the dialogue in recent years.

For decades, China has asserted that there is only one Chinese state, the People's Republic of China, and that Taiwan is a province of that state. Beijing has proposed reunification with Taiwan under a formula ("one state, two systems") similar to the one that was used to return Hong Kong to Chinese sovereignty. It also has vowed that any attempt by Taiwan to assert its independence would be resisted with force. Until July, the position of the Nationalist Party mirrored Beijing's, except that it questioned the legitimacy of the Communist government's sovereignty over Taiwan. Even the DPP, which repeatedly called for Taiwan's independence in its early years, gradually muted its position in recent elections.

Lee's confrontational move initially was interpreted as being motivated by an interest in bolstering Lien's flagging candidacy by moving the Nationalist Party's position closer to that of the DPP. As time passed, however, another possible explanation emerged, having to do with the triangular relationship shared by Taipei, Beijing, and Washington, DC. The U.S. position on the relationship between Taiwan and the mainland was laid out in the Shanghai Communiqué of February 1972, in which Washington "acknowledge[d] that all Chinese on either side of the Taiwan Strait maintain there is but one China and that Taiwan is a part of China." After a serious glitch in U.S.-China relations that followed Lee's visit to Cornell University in 1995, President Bill Clinton subtly but importantly modified the 1972 policy by saying publicly that "we don't support independence for Taiwan, or two Chinas, or one Taiwan/one China." What had been "acknowledged" in 1972 as the Chinese and Taiwanese position had evolved into the U.S. position.

This "three no's" policy, as Taiwanese authorities called it, was followed in the spring of 1999 by Assistant Secretary of State Stanley Roth's calling for "interim agreements... on any number of topics" between China and Taiwan. Taipei interpreted this statement as pressure from Washington to enter into negotiations with Beijing, and found it disturbingly reminiscent of an earlier proposal put forward by Kenneth Lieberthal, director of East Asia policy at the UN National Security Council. Lieberthal's proposal, calling for an "interim arrangement" in which Taipei and Beijing would agree to the concept of "one China" but would delay actual reunification for 50 years, had been interpreted by Taiwan as tantamount to an endorsement for Beijing's "one state, two systems" solution. In June, Roth reiterated his call for "technical agreements" on "significant issues." Two weeks later, Lee put forward his "state-to-state" proviso. Some observers theorized that through this action, Lee was responding to what he perceived as U.S. pressure to accept reunification on China's terms.

TAIWAN • Information Highlights

Official Name: Taiwan.
Location: Island off the southeastern coast of mainland China.
Area: 13,892 sq mi (35 980 km²).
Population (July 1999 est.): 22,113,250.
Chief Cities (Dec. 31, 1996 est.): Taipei, the capital, 2,605,374; Kaohsiung, 1,433,621; Taichung, 876,384; Tainan, 710,954; Panchiaio, 524,323.
Government: *Head of state,* Lee Teng-hui, president (took office January 1988). *Head of government,* Vincent Siew, prime minister (appointed August 1997). *Legislature* (unicameral)—Legislative Yuan; (unicameral)—National Assembly.
Monetary Unit: New Taiwan dollar (31.388 NT dollars equal U.S.$1, Jan. 3, 2000).
Gross Domestic Product (1998 est. U.S.$): $362,000,000,000 (purchasing power parity).

Whatever Taiwan's motivation, China's response was immediate and angry. It seemed as though there would be a repeat of the saber rattling that preceded Taiwan's first presidential election in 1996, when China undertook military exercises in the Strait. In an attempt to forestall such a response, Clinton, in a half-hour telephone conversation with Chinese President Jiang Zemin, dissociated himself and his government from Lee's formulation and reiterated U.S. backing for "one China." Perhaps influenced by this gesture from Washington and by the fact that its earlier bellicose response had succeeded only in increasing Lee's margin of victory in 1996, Beijing confined itself to a barrage of angry prose.

Meanwhile, Taiwan's friends in the U.S. Congress used the summer events as an opportunity to fish in troubled waters. They renewed the call for a theater missile-defense system in East Asia that would protect Taiwan, as well as Japan and South Korea, from attack and put forward a "Taiwan Security Enhancement Act" that would create a relationship tantamount to an alliance between the U.S. and Taiwanese military establishments, while upgrading and expanding U.S. arms sales to Taiwan. The bill was tabled in early November.

Economy. Despite the aftereffects of the earthquake and President Lee's radical change of policy, Taiwan's economy performed well in 1999. The earthquake was estimated to have cost the economy about $11 billion. Deteriorating relations with the mainland caused Taiwanese investment there to drop by some 41%, and trade with the mainland peaked at $2 billion in May, dropping off in subsequent months. Nevertheless, overall economic growth was projected at a healthy 5.3% for 1999.

JOHN BRYAN STARR, *Brown University*

Tajikistan

The fragile peace between the government of Tajikistan and the United Tajik Opposition (UTO) held in 1999, as they continued to implement the 1997 accord that ended the civil war.

Domestic Affairs. In 1999 the government took several steps to relax political restrictions on the UTO. UTO supporters were appointed to positions in the central and local governments, charges filed against opposition figures in 1993 were dropped, and the Supreme Court ordered an end to the ban on four opposition parties and coalitions. However, the regime hampered the activities of several other political parties not affiliated with the UTO. The UTO ordered its armed units to disband and turn in weapons, although the extent of their compliance was uncertain. Former UTO fighters were assigned to the police or the armed forces or returned to civilian life.

In September a majority of voters in a referendum endorsed revisions to Tajikistan's constitution. Changes included permitting political parties based on religion and changing the president's term of office from a five-year period that could be repeated once, to a single period of seven years. Presidential elections were held on November 6, and the incumbent, Imomali Rahmonov, ran for the newly created seven-year term. Parties that tried to run candidates against him found their efforts hampered by the regime. In the end, one other candidate, Davlat Usmon, of the Islamic Rebirth Party, was put on the ballot after having been excluded initially. He denounced this as a ploy to disguise a rigged election. The UTO halted its participation in the National Reconciliation Commission to protest the conduct of the election and called for a boycott of the vote. It reversed this stance on the eve of the election, after the government promised to release 93 imprisoned UTO supporters and conduct free legislative elections in 2000.

According to official figures, President Rahmonov was reelected with 96.9% of the vote. Human Rights Watch, the Organization for Security and Cooperation in Europe (OSCE), the European Union (EU), and the U.S. government criticized the way the election was handled. Russia, however, praised the election as a step in the peace process.

Although the civil war was over, political violence remained a problem in Tajikistan, with clashes among armed bands, bombings, and assassinations. A number of people were killed by such violence in 1999, the most prominent of whom was Safarali Kenjaev, head of the Socialist Party.

TAJIKISTAN • Information Highlights

Official Name: Republic of Tajikistan.
Location: Central Asia.
Area: 55,251 sq mi (143 100 km²).
Population (July 1999 est.): 6,102,854.
Chief Cities (July 1, 1993, est.): Dushanbe, the capital, 528,600; Khojand, 161,500.
Government: *Head of state,* Imomali Rahmonov, president (took office November 1992). *Head of government,* Yahyo Azimov, prime minister (took office February 1996). *Legislature* (unicameral)—Supreme Assembly.
Monetary Unit: Tajikistani ruble (1,436.00 Tajikistani rubles equal U.S.$1, Dec. 27, 1999).
Gross Domestic Product (1998 est. U.S.$): $6,000,-000,000 (purchasing power parity).
Foreign Trade (1998 U.S.$): *Imports,* $771,000,000; *exports,* $602,000,000.

Foreign Relations. Tajikistan's relations with neighboring Uzbekistan deteriorated during 1999. Uzbekistan accused Tajikistan of insufficient efforts to curb terrorism, in connection with bombings in Tashkent and an incursion by armed opponents of the Uzbekistani government into Kyrgyzstan from adjoining Tajikistani territory. Dushanbe, meanwhile, charged Uzbekistan with backing a rebel attack on northern Tajikistan in November 1998 and accused it of aerial attacks on parts of Tajikistan near the border with Kyrgyzstan. Uzbekistani President Islam Karimov claimed a right to attack terrorist camps in Tajikistan, comparing the situation to the Russian attack on Chechnya. Tajikistan also alleged that Uzbekistan seized 1,977 acres (800 ha) of Tajikistani territory by putting border-defense installations on the land.

MURIEL ATKIN
George Washington University

Tanzania

As its economy suffered from the effects of continued drought and limited prospects for growth, Tanzania experienced the resolution of the long-running political impasse in the self-governing territory of Zanzibar during 1999. However, for many Tanzanians, the most significant event of the year was the death in October of the nation's founder and former president, Julius K. Nyerere.

Domestic Affairs. The political conflict in Zanzibar, which originated in the disputed election of 1995 on the island, was ended formally in June, when both the ruling Chama Cha Mapinduzi (CCM) and Civic United Front (CUF) parties accepted an

© Jean-Marc Bouju/AP/Wide World Photos

The funeral of Julius Nyerere, former president and founder of Tanzania, was held October 21 in Dar es Salaam. The ceremonies were attended by many foreign dignitaries, including South African President Thabo Mbeki (left, with his wife) *and Nigerian President Olusegun Obasanjo* (far right).

agreement brokered by the Commonwealth secretariat. The pact opened the way for new elections scheduled for 2000.

On the mainland, religiously inspired disputes continued. Muslim activists clashed with police in Dar es Salaam in April and September. Realignment of the political opposition marked the year as well. Augustine Mrema, the former leader of the National Convention for Construction and Reform–Change (NCCR-Mageuzi) and likely a major opponent for President Benjamin Mkapa in the 2000 elections, joined the Tanzania Labour Party (TLP).

Nyerere's death in London plunged Tanzania into mourning, and dignitaries from all over the world attended his funeral. Although Nyerere retired from the presidency in 1985, he had continued to play a significant part in Tanzania's politics; it remained to be seen how the CCM and Tanzania would fare without his guidance.

Economy. Drought caused localized food shortages and necessitated grain imports during 1999. Partly as a result of a less-than-favorable environment, earnings from Tanzania's largely agricultural exports (particularly coffee, cotton, and sisal) dropped to $562 million for 1998–99, a decline of almost 13% from 1997–98. By mid-1999, Tanzania's external debt had grown to $8 billion.

But 1999 also produced positive indicators for the Tanzanian economy. The growth rate rebounded to approximately 4%, and inflation fell to single digits, reaching 7.5% by the start of August. This represented a dramatic decline from the rate of nearly 30% in 1995. The value of Tanzania's mineral exports continued to rise as well. Praising Tanzania's implementation of financial reforms, the International Monetary Fund (IMF) promised to release additional support in July, and the World Bank announced that Tanzania would receive debt relief in September. The political settlement in Zanzibar paved the way for international economic assistance to the island to be resumed, and rising world prices for cloves—combined with expectations of a bumper crop on Zanzibar and its sister island, Pemba—were good news for the islands' economies.

Tanzania's decision to leave the Common Market for Eastern and Southern Africa (Comesa) in mid-1999, while remaining in the Southern African Development Community (SADC), raised questions regarding future trade relations. The reduction and eventual elimination of tariffs were a particular concern, since Tanzania's partners in the revived East African Community, Kenya and Uganda, were members of Comesa but not of SADC. During 1999, Tanzania imported three times more from Comesa states than it exported to them.

ROBERT M. MAXON, *West Virginia University*

TANZANIA • Information Highlights

Official Name: United Republic of Tanzania.
Location: East coast of Africa.
Area: 364,900 sq mi (945 090 km²).
Population (July 1999 est.): 31,270,820.
Chief Cities (1985 est.): Dar es Salaam, the capital, 1,096,000; Mwanza, 252,000; Tabora, 214,000.
Government: *Head of state,* Benjamin Mkapa, president (took office Nov. 23, 1995). *Head of government,* Frederick Sumaye, prime minister (appointed November 1995). *Legislature* (unicameral)—National Assembly.
Monetary Unit: Tanzanian shilling (792.00 shillings equal U.S.$1, Dec. 27, 1999).
Gross Domestic Product (1998 est. U.S.$): $22,100,000,000 (purchasing power parity).
Economic Index (Tanganyika, 1998; 1990 = 100): *Consumer Prices,* all items, 36,111.2; food, 42,146.4.
Foreign Trade (1998 U.S.$): *Imports,* $1,452,000,000; *exports,* $675,000,000.

Taxation

In 1999 the booming U.S. economy generated tax receipts in excess of government expenditures, fueling a debate over what to do with the projected federal budget surplus. Many Republicans in the U.S. Congress called for returning the windfall to taxpayers in the form of income-tax cuts, while the Bill Clinton administration and other Democrats favored using it to pay off the national debt, shore up the Social Security Trust Fund, and improve Americans' access to health care before radically altering the current tax code. Republican lawmakers failed to transform their tax-cut proposals into law. However, tax cuts and tax reform played a prominent role in the political debate, especially as the campaign for the November 2000 presidential election began to take shape. At the state level, calls to eliminate transportation taxes continued to build, while governors were divided on the question of whether to impose sales taxes on the burgeoning sector of Internet commerce.

© Dennis Cook/AP/Wide World Photos

A GOP tax-cut bill, touted by Speaker of the House J. Dennis Hastert, above, *was passed by Congress but was vetoed by President Bill Clinton in 1999.*

Congressional Action. Although President Clinton opposed using up the budget surplus on massive tax cuts, in February he proposed a package of limited and targeted tax breaks. Congressional Republicans, led by House Budget Committee Chairman John R. Kasich of Ohio, responded with a sweeping tax-cut proposal of their own that would have reduced taxes across the board by 10%. In midsummer, after reports that the budget surplus would be even higher than expected, both chambers passed versions of that measure. In addition to the 10% tax cut, the House bill would have reduced capital-gains taxes (levied on profits taken from the sale of securities and other capital assets); reduced the "marriage penalty," which forces some married couples to pay higher taxes than they would if they were single; and phased out estate taxes. As a lure to moderate lawmakers, the House measure called for reductions in the interest paid on the national debt after 2001. The Senate tax bill was less sweeping than the House version. It would have cut income taxes only for individuals in the lowest tax bracket (15%) and lowered but not eliminated inheritance taxes.

The compromise bill that emerged from the House-Senate conference committee reduced the tax cut from 10% to just 1% for each of the five tax brackets. It also reduced the marriage penalty by $117 billion over ten years. Despite the measure's failure to address tax simplification, a long-standing Republican priority, GOP lawmakers supported the tax bill, which was approved on August 5. As he had promised earlier, President Clinton vetoed the measure on September 23. As a result of Clinton's tax veto and congressional rejection of many of the president's spending proposals, Congress adjourned without making major changes in federal taxation and spending policies. House Speaker J. Dennis Hastert (R-IL) placed tax relief at the top of the agenda for 2000.

Among the last measures to clear Congress in 1999 was a bill that extended a dozen tax breaks that otherwise would have expired at the end of the year. The provisions, worth $21 billion over ten years, included a five-year extension of the research and development credit, a top priority for high-tech companies. All of the other credits were extended for one year. One provision allowed the nation's 1 million high-income taxpayers who were subject to the alternative minimum tax (which prevents individuals with high deductions and credits from erasing their tax liability altogether) to continue using personal tax credits, such as the $500 credit for each child. Another gave employers who hire disabled workers and other hard-to-place individuals an extension of the work-opportunity and welfare-to-work tax credits. The bill also extended a tax credit offered to companies that use wind and other renewable resources to generate electricity, and expanded the list of eligible fuels to include poultry waste.

IRS Actions. For most of the 1990s, the booming economy translated into higher corporate profits. To protect their rising profits, U.S. companies took increasing advantage of such tax loopholes as foreign tax credits, interest deductions, and depreciation allowances. As a result, the increase in corporate-tax receipts, which rose almost 100% over the decade, lagged behind the growth in corporate profits. In fiscal 1999, which ended September 30, corporate-tax receipts actually declined by 2%, or $4 billion. The discrepancy prompted the Clinton administration to close a number of tax loopholes by administrative action. Challenged by such companies as Winn-Dixie Stores Inc. and Compaq Computer Corp., these actions were upheld by the courts.

Following enactment of major Internal Revenue Service (IRS) reform legislation in 1998, the agency embarked on an internal review aimed largely at ending abuse of taxpayers targeted for audits by its agents. David C. Williams, the Treasury Department inspector general for tax administration (a position created by the 1998 law), established goals that included greatly expanded investigations of IRS workers accused by taxpayers of misconduct. But Williams was forced to withdraw his plan of investigating some 3,400 IRS agents after employees charged that this action amounted to an unfair quota that would disrupt their work and make it harder to investigate legitimate cases of tax fraud.

In late October, IRS Chief Technology Officer Paul J. Cosgrave assured lawmakers at a House hearing that the agency did "not anticipate a major failure" of its computers related to the millennial changeover. He acknowledged, however, that the agency still had trouble tracking its computer inventory, a problem that the IRS reform law had been designed to correct.

State Trends. When Virginia's Republican Gov. James S. Gilmore III swept to victory in 1997 after promising to abolish the state's hated car tax, critics in other states called for the elimination of similar transportation taxes. On November 2, voters in Washington state approved Initiative 695, which abolished the state car-registration tax and made any future tax increases by state government agencies subject to approval by voters.

The volume of goods sold over the Internet boomed in 1999, more than doubling to an estimated $20 billion. As e-commerce grew, so too did a debate over whether to extend state sales taxes, imposed on retail sales in stores and on catalog purchases, to include Internet purchases as well. Because many states depend heavily on sales-tax revenues, the debate was especially heated among the nation's governors.

Supporters of the Internet sales tax—including Republican Gov. Michael Leavitt of Utah, chairman of the National Governors' Association—argued that failure to extend existing sales taxes to e-stores not only would reduce tax revenues but also would be unfair to owners of walk-in stores, whose business already was being eroded by Internet retailers. The association also warned that failure to tax Internet sales would deplete sales-tax revenues and would force states to cut education and public-safety budgets. Acknowledging the difficulty of imposing a mandatory tax on Internet sales, Governor Leavitt proposed a "voluntary" e-tax plan in which a bank or credit-card company would calculate, collect, and distribute sales-tax revenues based on the tax in the buyer's home state.

Gilmore and other opponents of this proposal predicted that taxing Internet sales would impede the growth of e-commerce and argued that any revenues lost by e-stores' exemption from taxation would be more than compensated for by overall economic growth. Gilmore's position won support among a number of Republican members of Congress. On November 10, Kasich and fellow Ohio Republican Rep. John Boehner introduced a bill that would put a permanent ban on states' taxing Internet sales. John McCain (R-AZ), chairman of the Senate Commerce, Science, and Transportation Committee and a leading contender for the Republican presidential nomination, introduced a similar bill.

Candidates' Tax Proposals. Taxation was catapulted to the top of the political agenda again in December, when Texas Gov. George W. Bush, the front-runner for the Republican presidential nomination, declared that tax cuts were his first priority and presented a detailed plan to reduce taxes by $483 billion over five years. In addition to an across-the-board tax cut for all income brackets, Bush's proposal would double the existing $500 child tax credit and expand the deduction for charitable donations. The plan would include a much bigger tax cut than the Republican tax proposal vetoed earlier by President Clinton. Despite Bush's claim that across-the-board tax cuts would help lower-income taxpayers enter the middle class, Democrats charged the plan would benefit upper-income taxpayers at the expense of the poor. Some of Bush's Republican challengers also criticized the proposal because it would not simplify the tax code.

Several presidential candidates targeted the federal estate tax for change or abolition. The tax, which can claim up to 55% of an estate, had come under fire from a growing number of critics, including business groups, who claimed it prevented many younger Americans from carrying on family farms and other businesses. Among Republican candidates, Senator McCain and millionaire publisher Steve Forbes called for abolishing the tax, while Governor Bush proposed phasing it out over eight years. For his part, Vice-President Al Gore proposed increasing estate-tax deductions for conservation easements (land permanently withheld from development).

Another feature of the current tax code that came under mounting criticism was the marriage penalty. Bush's plan would reduce the marriage penalty, while Gore would eliminate it altogether. McCain also promised to eliminate the marriage penalty as part of his plan to cut taxes for lower- to middle-income families by applying the lowest tax rate of 15% to incomes of up to $70,000, an increase from the current limit of $43,050.

Radical reform of current tax law, a prominent issue in the 1996 campaign, continued to be championed only by the most conservative Republican candidates. Forbes and social activist Gary Bauer endorsed replacing the progressive tax code with a flat rate of 17% and 16%, respectively.

The Democratic candidates downplayed the need for major changes in the tax code and said the current budget surplus should be used to pay down the national debt and improve access to health care. Gore called for modest tax cuts but said the bulk of the surplus should be used to pay off the national debt by 2015. Gore's challenger for the Democratic nomination, former New Jersey Sen. Bill Bradley, opposed major tax cuts as long as the economy remained healthy and called instead for spending the surplus to reduce the national debt and to finance universal health insurance and programs to reduce child poverty.

International Tax Issues. The United States was not the only country where tax issues dominated the political debate. U.S. and Mexican negotiators had struggled for years over which country should derive tax revenues from the thriving manufacturing enterprises along the U.S.-Mexican border known as *maquiladoras*. In November the IRS announced that the United States and Mexico had agreed on a system that was expected to eliminate double taxation of these businesses and remove a major source of friction between the two countries.

Members of the European Union (EU) continued long-standing negotiations in an effort to create a unified tax code. Agreement was held up, however, following the release of a finance ministers' report that singled out the Netherlands for infringing on a voluntary code adopted to discourage member states from unfairly encouraging businesses to locate in one state at the expense of others. Another obstacle to the unified tax code was Britain's objection to a proposal for a 20% withholding tax on nonresident savings.

Since his election in 1996, Australian Prime Minister John Howard had made tax reform one of his legislative priorities. In 1999 he gained approval of his proposal to cut the income tax, to be paid for with a new 10% tax on goods and services due to take effect in July 2000. But another series of tax reforms supported by Prime Minister Howard ran into trouble after a parliamentary investigation found that the changes would create a national budget deficit. The proposed reforms, which would cut Australia's capital-gains tax and reform the business-tax regime, were considered vital to attracting international investment.

The desire to attract foreign investment also fueled efforts by President Fernando Henrique Cardoso to reform Brazil's tax code. The world's eighth-largest economy had been threatened by a financial crisis that had thrown the economies of other Latin American nations into recession, and Cardoso's plan was designed to shore up investor confidence. In November, however, he announced that the effort had failed because of state and local officials' opposition to the proposed transfer to the federal government of all power to raise taxes.

MARY H. COOPER
"The CQ [Congressional Quarterly] Researcher"

Television and Radio

One of the most compelling television sequences of 1999 was Katie Couric's interview on the National Broadcasting Company's (NBC's) *Today* show with Colorado teenager Craig Scott, tearfully recounting the April 20 killing of his friend, Isaiah Shoals, at Columbine High School, while clutching the arm of Isaiah's father, Michael. The interview tore at the nation's heart and yet stirred up an already-ferocious debate: Is TV the objective observer, healer, or exploiter of violence? Does even its well-meaning coverage of violence beget more?

If the social role of TV news was complex and ambiguous, one thing was clear in entertainment programming: Violence sells. Sex and sensation of all kinds also filled ever-greater hours of the TV universe. In response to the post-Columbine criticism of violent entertainment that reached to the halls of Congress, the Warner Brothers (WB) Network delayed the showing of an episode of *Buffy the Vampire Slayer* that included high-school violence, and the Columbia Broadcasting System (CBS) canceled an upcoming Mafia series.

But for the most part, it was business as usual in television. To illustrate, let us consider the following events:

• The most dramatic improvement in prime-time cable viewership was on the USA Network, due to the fierce popularity of its lurid, outrageously violent World Wrestling Federation shows, *WWF Raw* and *WWF War Zone.* The latter show toned down its content after the Coca-Cola Co. canceled its ads during the program.

• *The Man Show* tapped into the same market of men under 35, scoring the highest-rated premiere in Comedy Central history. The show celebrated what once was known as "male chauvinist pig" behavior.

NBC's drama series "The West Wing," featuring Martin Sheen (center) *as a U.S. president, was a fall ratings hit.*

• During the ratings sweeps month of February, Fox grabbed a 67% higher rating over its regularly scheduled shows with such "shockumentaries" (*Variety*'s term) as *World's Most Shocking Medical Videos* and *When Good Times Go Bad 2*.

• The return of roller derby—which one critic described as "a tough and tawdry spectacle from the 1950s"—boosted ratings on the Nashville Network, which featured the sport on its show *RollerJam*.

• Fox's *Action*, an exposé of the Hollywood scene, was said by some critics to be exactly the kind of crass product it purported to satirize.

• Barbara Walters' interview with Monica Lewinsky on the American Broadcasting Companies' (ABC's) *20/20* capped a year and a half in which President Bill Clinton's affair with Lewinsky dominated the news. The episode featuring Lewinsky's interview was the most-watched newsmagazine show in television history, with 70 million viewers.

• A 1999 study by the Annenberg Public Policy Center found that the average American child spent more time—four and one half hours—in front of a TV, computer, or video screen than he or she did in school. It also reported that teens were better able to name the characters on *The Simpsons* than the vice-president of the United States, Al Gore.

The 1998–99 Network Season. *The Washington Post*'s Tom Shales summed up 1998 as "a 12-month dark ages of TV—the big broadcast networks have reason to be terrified." Indeed, with little improvement in quality in 1999, there was an accelerating loss of viewers to cable; the WB was the only broadcast network to gain audience.

Even though *ER* (NBC) lost 16% of its audience from 1997–98, it still repeated as the highest-rated show for the season ending May 23. NBC came in first among the broadcast networks for the season, with the three top-rated shows. The top 15 programs, and their average ratings points, were: *ER*, NBC (17.8); *Friends*, NBC (15.7); *Frasier*, NBC (15.6); *Monday Night Football*, ABC (13.9); tie: *Jesse*, NBC (13.7), and *Veronica's Closet*, NBC (13.7); *60 Minutes*, CBS (13.2); *Touched by an Angel*, CBS (13.1); *CBS Sunday Movie*, CBS (12.1); *20/20–Wednesday*, ABC (11.2); *Everybody Loves Raymond*, CBS (10.6); *NYPD Blue*, ABC (10.4); *Home Improvement*, ABC (10.1); tie: *The Drew Carey Show*, ABC (10), and *Law and Order*, NBC (10). Each ratings point represents 994,000 households. *Sports Night* (ABC), the look behind the scenes at a TV sports show that critics felt was the season's freshest new show, finished almost halfway down the list of shows at Number 65.

Among made-for-TV films, *Joan of Arc* (CBS) was, in *Variety*'s words, "a classy and straightforward telling" of the medieval epic, starring Leelee Sobieski and featuring Peter O'Toole and Jacqueline Bisset in supporting roles. *Noah's Ark* (NBC) with Jon Voight was described by critics as laughable, but it had good ratings. *The '60s* (NBC) was also a hit, although the *Post*'s Shales called it "simplistic and ridiculous."

The New York Times saluted the ever-fresh satirical wit of *The Simpsons* (Fox) after ten seasons, calling it "the only laugh-out-loud show on television." The ratings strength of that show and the crude *South Park* (Comedy Central)—along with the lack of new ideas for live-action sitcoms—spurred the creation of more animated Fox series, including *The PJs*, with the voice of Eddie Murphy; *Family Guy*; and *Futurama*, by *Simpsons* creator Matt Groening. UPN's new animated entry was *Home Movies*, featuring the voice of Paula Poundstone.

PBS. The Public Broadcasting Service (PBS), already suffering from eroding support for its congressional subsidy and long suspected of liberal bias, took another blow in July when it was discovered that network affiliates WGBH (Boston) and WETA (Washington, DC) had traded mailing lists with the Democratic National Committee.

The highly praised, lavishly produced HBO series "The Sopranos" won two Emmys, including one for Edie Falco, below, as best actress in a drama.

© HBO, Anthony Neste/AP/Wide World Photos

But as always, PBS shows (such as *Nova*, *Frontline*, and *The American Experience*) commanded critics' respect. *New York: A Documentary Film,* a ten-hour miniseries, was "nothing short of gripping," according to *Variety*. Although producer Ric Burns lacked the humorous and lyrical touch of brother Ken (of *The Civil War* and other well-received miniseries), he matched the elder Burns for capturing history with big-name interviews and stunning archive photographs.

Cable. A rare phenomenon—a series with both high quality and popular appeal—was *The Sopranos*, on Home Box Office (HBO). The comedy-drama series by David Chase (*Northern Exposure*) portrayed New Jersey mobsters with real-life problems (requiring, in one case, psychiatric care). *The Sopranos* led all series in Emmy nominations with 16, and at $2 million per episode, it cost 25% to 40% more than a standard series.

HBO's *RKO 281*—the studio code name for *Citizen Kane*—colorfully retold the making of that significant film. The excellent cast included Liev Schreiber as 25-year-old filmmaker Orson Welles; James Cromwell as press lord William Randolph Hearst, trying to quash the movie modeled on his life; Melanie Griffith as Hearst's mistress, Marion Davies; and John Malkovich as bilious screenwriter Herman Mankiewicz. Showtime's *Strange Justice* was a praised dramatization of the 1991 Anita Hill–Clarence Thomas sexual-harassment case. Turner Network Television (TNT) and Fox had bought the rights to the book of the same title but backed away from filming the controversial material. TNT's *Animal Farm*, a live-action version of George Orwell's novel, drew high praise. It featured footage of real animals mixed in with realistic animatronic animals, and a distinguished British-American cast voiced the barnyard characters.

The aforementioned shows were part of a movement toward made-for-cable films, which expanded from HBO, Showtime, TNT, and USA to establish a new presence on the Disney Channel, Arts and Entertainment (A&E), Fox Family Channel, and Lifetime.

Another cable trend was biographical shows. Among these were *Bravo Profiles* (Bravo), *E! True Hollywood Story* (E!), and *Intimate Portrait* (Lifetime), joining the well-established *Biography* (A&E). VH1's *Behind the Music* revealed the life experiences (and especially the travails) of such rock stars as Madonna, Cher, David Cassidy, and Donna Summer.

© ABC, Maria Melin/AP/Wide World Photos

"Who Wants to Be a Millionaire?," a quiz program hosted by Regis Philbin, above right, *was a surprise ratings powerhouse for ABC in the summer and fall of 1999.*

The Cartoon Network, owned by Ted Turner, was one of the big success stories of 1999, regularly challenging Nickelodeon, the perennial leader in children's programming, in the ratings. Another Turner creation was Turner South, which presented a new geographic wrinkle in theme programming with its Dixie-flavored shows and Atlanta sports events. The opening slate was called "E Day! 28 Hours of Elvis."

News. *Time* magazine reported a shift in the types of stories on local TV news shows, with the percentage of stories on crime decreasing for the first time in several years from 28% to 22%. Human-interest stories jumped from 1% to 5% of broadcast time.

Emblematic of the increasingly combative attitude of business toward investigative journalism was the campaign of Metabolife International, a diet-pill maker, against *20/20*. Anticipating the show's unflattering report on its product, Metabolife set up a Web site and published its own transcript of the *20/20* interview with its chief executive before the show even aired. ABC received good news in October, when an appeals court overturned a jury finding that the network had committed fraud in its reporting for a 1992 *Prime Time Live* exposé of unsanitary conditions at the Food Lion supermarket chain.

In May, *The Jenny Jones Show*, a syndicated talk show, was found negligent and ordered to pay $25 million in damages to the family of Scott Amedure, a gay man who was shot to death after revealing on the show that he was attracted to another guest,

TELEVISION • 1999

Some sample programs

The American Experience: New York: A Documentary Film—Ten-hour look at New York City history from 1609–1931. PBS, Nov. 14–18.

The American Experience: Race for the Superbomb—Documentary covering the period 1945–60. PBS, Jan. 11.

An American Love Story—Documentary on the interracial family of black blues musician Bill Sims and Karen Wilson, a white corporate manager. PBS, Sept. 12–16.

American Masters: Robert Rauschenberg—A one-hour look at the artist. PBS, April 7.

Animal Farm—Adaptation of George Orwell's anti-Stalinist allegory using animatronic puppetry. TNT, Oct. 3.

Behind the Mask—Drama based on the true story of a developmental workshop for the mentally handicapped. With Donald Sutherland and Matthew Fox. CBS, Feb. 28.

Black and Blue—Drama based on Anna Quindlen's book about a wife abused by her policeman husband. With Mary Stuart Masterson and Will Rothhaar. CBS, Nov. 17.

Cleopatra—Four-hour miniseries extravaganza on the historic figure. With Leonor Varela, Timothy Dalton, and Billy Zane. ABC, May 23 and 24.

The Color of Courage—Fact-based drama about an African-American couple buying a house in an all-white Detroit neighborhood in 1944. With Lynn Whitfield and Roger Guenveur Smith. USA, Feb. 10.

Confronting the Crisis: Childcare in America—Special on the state of child care, hosted by Kyra Sedgwick. Lifetime, April 20.

Dare to Compete: The Struggle of Women in Sports—Documentary about female athletes. Narrated by Lauren Hutton. HBO, March 8.

Dash and Lilly—Drama on the mystery novelist Dashiell Hammett and the playwright Lillian Hellman. With Sam Shepard and Judy Davis. A&E, May 31.

Dean Koontz's Mr. Murder—Two-part miniseries about a mystery novelist battling his killer clone. With Stephen Baldwin. ABC, April 26 and 29.

Deep in My Heart—Drama about a black girl's search for her white birth mother. With Anne Bancroft, Gloria Reuben, and Lynn Whitfield. CBS, Feb. 14.

The Devil's Arithmetic—Drama about a jaded Jewish teen's *Twilight Zone*-like transportation to 1941 Poland. With Kirsten Dunst and Louise Fletcher. Showtime, March 28.

Durango—Hallmark Hall of Fame tale of a 40-mi (64-km) cattle drive in 1939 Ireland. With Brenda Fricker, Matt Keeslar, and Patrick Bergin. CBS, April 25.

The 50 Years War—Documentary on the Arab-Israeli conflict. Interviewees include former Presidents Jimmy Carter and George Bush and Jordan's King Hussein. PBS, Jan. 24 and 25.

Fists of Freedom—Documentary on black athletic protest at the 1968 Summer Olympics in Mexico City. HBO, Aug. 12.

Frontline: John Paul II: The Millennial Pope—Special on John Paul II. PBS, Sept. 28.

Great Expectations—ExxonMobil Masterpiece Theatre adaptation of the Charles Dickens classic. With Ioan Gruffudd, Charlotte Rampling, and Bernard Hill. PBS, May 9 and 10.

Great Performances: Long Day's Journey into Night—Eugene O'Neill's play. With William Hutt, Martha Henry, and Peter Donaldson. PBS, Sept. 19.

© Everett Collection

"Annie," ABC's warmhearted adaptation of the Broadway musical, starred Victor Garber and Alicia Morton, above, *as Daddy Warbucks and Annie.*

Great Performances: Turandot at the Forbidden City—Multinational cast performs opera in Beijing's Forbidden City. PBS, June 9.

Having Our Say—Drama based on the lives of Sadie and Bessie Delaney. With Diahann Carroll and Ruby Dee. CBS, April 18.

Holy Joe—Drama about an Episcopalian priest's return to faith. With John Ritter and Meredith Baxter. CBS, March 28.

Howard Cosell: Telling It Like It Is—Profile of the legendary sportscaster. HBO, Nov. 1.

The Hunt for the Unicorn Killer—Miniseries based on the true story of Ira Einhorn, who was convicted in absentia for the murder of his girlfriend. With Kevin Anderson and Tom Skerritt. NBC, May 9 and 10.

I'll Make Me a World: A Century of African-American Arts—Six-hour documentary on the 20th-century African-American arts scene. Narrated by Vanessa L. Williams. PBS, Feb. 1–3.

Introducing Dorothy Dandridge—The story of the first African-American to be nominated for the best-actress Oscar. With Halle Berry. HBO, Aug. 21.

Joan of Arc—Two-part miniseries on the French teen who was backed by God on the battlefield. With Leelee Sobieski and Patrick Harris. CBS, May 16 and 18.

A Lesson before Dying—Drama based on Ernest J. Gaines' novel about a teacher who visits a man awaiting execution for a murder he did not commit. With Cicely Tyson, Don Cheadle, and Mekhi Phifer. HBO, May 22.

Love Letters—Adaptation of A.R. Gurney's 1988 play. With Laura Linney and Steven Weber. ABC, April 12.

Diana Rigg, host of the PBS detective series "Mystery!," helped celebrate the program's 20th season by starring as a detective in "The Mrs. Bradley Mysteries," right.

© Photofest

Michael Landon: The Father I Knew—TV movie based on a son's unflattering look at his famous actor father. With John Schneider, Cheryl Ladd, Trevor O'Brien, and Joel Berti. CBS, May 23.
Murder in a Small Town—Murder mystery. With Gene Wilder and Mike Starr. A&E, Jan. 10.
Mutiny—Fact-based drama about a group of inadequately trained African-American seamen who were court-martialed for refusing to load munitions at a U.S. Navy base in 1944. With Michael Jai White, Duane Martin, and David Ramsey. NBC, March 28.
Noah's Ark—Four-hour miniseries with comedic overtones on the Old Testament story. With F. Murray Abraham, Carol Kane, Mary Steenburgen, and Jon Voight. NBC, May 2 and 3.
Not for Ourselves Alone: The Story of Elizabeth Cady Stanton and Susan B. Anthony—Ken Burns' documentary on the leaders of the women's suffragette movement. PBS, Nov. 7 and 8.
Nova: To the Moon—Two-hour look at lunar exploration. PBS, July 13.
One Special Night—TV movie about two strangers who strike up a friendship while stranded in a cabin during a snowstorm. With Julie Andrews and James Garner. CBS, Nov. 28.
Our Guys—Drama based on the real-life sexual assault by high-school athletes of a 17-year-old mentally retarded girl. With Heather Matarazzo, Ally Sheedy, and Eric Stoltz. ABC, May 10.
Passing Glory—True-life story of a black high school taking on a white high school for the unofficial city championship in 1965 New Orleans. With Andre Braugher and Rip Torn. TNT, Feb. 21.
The Passion of Ayn Rand—Dramatization of Rand's relationship with the much-younger Nathaniel Branden. With Helen Mirren, Peter Fonda, and Eric Stoltz. Showtime, May 30.
Passion's Way—Adaptation of Edith Wharton's 1912 novel *The Reef*. With Sela Ward, Timothy Dalton, and Jamie Glover. CBS, July 25.
Pete Peterson: Assignment Hanoi—One-hour documentary on former U.S. Rep. Douglas "Pete" Peterson's tenure as the first postwar ambassador to Vietnam. PBS, Sept. 7.
Pirates of Silicon Valley—Irreverent look at Microsoft chairman Bill Gates and Apple cofounder Steve Jobs. TNT, June 20.
Purgatory—Western with a *Twilight Zone*–like twist. With Eric Roberts, Randy Quaid, and Sam Shepard. TNT, Jan. 10.
Rabbit in the Moon—P.O.V. documentary on Japanese-Americans forced into internment camps during World War II. PBS, July 6.
A Rather English Marriage—ExxonMobil Masterpiece Theatre presentation about a friendship between two men who meet when their wives die in the same hospital on the same day. PBS, Oct. 3.
A Saintly Switch—Fantasy in which a dad and a mom trade personalities. With David Alan Grier, Vivica A. Fox, Shadia Simmons, and Scott Owen Cumberbatch. ABC, Jan. 24.
A Season for Miracles—Hallmark Hall of Fame Christmas offering in which a woman runs away with her drug-addicted sister's children to save them from foster care. With Carla Gugino and David Conrad. CBS, Dec. 12.
Seasons of Love—Two-part miniseries on the family saga of Thomas Linthorne, a post–Civil War Ohio farmer, and his wife. With Rachel Ward and Peter Strauss. CBS, March 7 and 9.
Shake, Rattle & Roll—Four-hour miniseries on the early history of rock. With Dana Delany, Brad Hawkins, Bonnie Somerville, and Terence Trent D'Arby. CBS, Nov. 7 and 10.
The '60s—Four-hour miniseries on the turbulent era. With Josh Hamilton, Jerry O'Connell, Jordana Brewster, and Julia Stiles. NBC, Feb. 7 and 8.

© Photofest

Welsh actor Ioan Gruffudd, above, *played young British sailor Horatio Hornblower in A&E's series of four movies set during the Napoleonic War of the 1790s.*

Small Vices—Adaptation of Robert Parker's 24th Spenser mystery. With Joe Mantegna and Marcia Gay Harden. A&E, July 18.
The Story of Fathers & Sons—Interviews with 40 men and boys exploring what it means to be a father, son, and grandfather. ABC, June 17.
Strange Justice—Adaptation of Jane Mayer and Jill Abramson's book about Anita Hill and Clarence Thomas. With Regina Taylor, Delroy Lindo, and Mandy Patinkin. Showtime, Aug. 29.
Summer's End—Drama about a retired black physician's return to his hometown in Georgia. With James Earl Jones. Showtime, Feb. 28.
Swing Vote—Supreme Court drama occurring in the fictional future after *Roe v. Wade* has been overturned. With Lisa Gay Hamilton and Andy Garcia. ABC, April 19.
36 Hours to Die—Thriller about brewery owner battling to prevent a crime syndicate from using his business as a front. With Saul Rubinek and Treat Williams. TNT, April 11.
Tobacco Wars—Three-hour documentary on the tobacco industry. Narrated by Walter Cronkite. TLC, Oct. 21 and 22.
The Vietnam War: A Descent into Hell—Documentary on the origins of U.S. involvement in Vietnam. Narrated by Martin Sheen. Discovery Channel, Aug. 7.

Jonathan Schmitz; Schmitz later was convicted of the crime. Some legal experts worried that the decision, with the implication that a show was responsible for the future actions of people who appear on it, might have a chilling effect on all media.

60 Minutes 2 came nowhere near matching its distinguished parent, finishing 43d in the broadcast-program rankings.

As part of the overall growth in cable viewership, Cable News Network (CNN) improved its overall season ratings—but so did its cable rivals. MSNBC topped CNN for the first time with its coverage of the royal wedding of Prince Edward and Sophie Rhys-Jones. CNBC's *BusinessCenter* cut into the audience of CNN's *Moneyline*. Fox News Channel (FNC) also grew steadily.

The 1999–2000 Season. For the first time in a decade, there were more new dramas than comedies introduced on the broadcast networks. One WB executive explained that compared to comedy fans, 50% less of the drama audience had abandoned the networks.

The producers of these new dramas were among the most seasoned and respected in the industry. Dick Wolf introduced *Law & Order: Special Victims Unit* (NBC), a companion piece to his current NBC hit *Law & Order*; and *DC* (WB), about new college graduates on the make in the nation's capital. Marshall Herskovitz and Ed Zwick (*thirtysomething*) brought forth *Once and Again* (ABC), focusing on the burgeoning relationship between two divorced parents. John Wells (*ER*) launched *The West Wing*, set in the White House, and *Third Watch*, about New York paramedics; both were on NBC. David Kelley (*Ally McBeal, The*

© Everett Collection

One of fall 1999's unexpected hits was "Judging Amy," starring Amy Brenneman, above, *as a recently divorced woman starting a new life as a juvenile-court judge.*

Practice) featured private eyes in *Snoops* (ABC).

Surprising critics with their fast ratings starts (especially among women) were CBS' *Judging Amy*, about a female judge restarting her life after a divorce; and *Family Law*, about a lawyer dumped by her husband who starts an idealistic new law firm.

Inspired by the popularity of WB's *Buffy the Vampire Slayer* and *Dawson's Creek*, a slew of teen comedy-dramas appeared, centering on the quest for acceptance and other issues of adolescence. They included *Manchester Prep* and *The Opposite Sex* on Fox; *Freaks and Geeks* on NBC; and the aliens-at-school *Roswell* and *Popular* on WB.

At the start of the season, leaders of the African-American community chastised TV producers for the complete lack of major black characters on the new fall shows. The networks responded by adding African-American and other minority characters to some of their shows, but the protesters were only somewhat mollified.

ABC, drawing upon the Broadway expertise of its corporate parent, Disney, triumphed in November with the family musical *Annie*, featuring stage veterans Audra McDonald, Alan Cumming, and Kathy Bates as Miss Hannigan.

The new and surprising fall-ratings king was ABC's *Who Wants to Be a Millionaire?*, with Regis Philbin. Modeled on a wildly popular British series, *Millionaire* dumbfounded critics who believed that evening quiz shows—a 1950s staple—never could be resuscitated. After its first two-week run in August scored sky-high ratings, ABC brought it back for another short stint in November, with similar results. The network announced in December that *Millionaire* would become a regular prime-time series beginning in January 2000.

Bryant Gumbel returned to morning television in November with the premiere of *The Early Show* on CBS, which replaced the moribund *CBS This Morning*. Gumbel was cohosting the show with Jane Clayson, a former reporter with ABC News.

Radio. A survey found that radio stations featuring songs by African-American artists—R&B, rap, hip-hop, and oldies—were the most popular music stations in the nation's major cities for the first time. Black music moved ahead of adult contemporary targeted mainly to whites, while news/talk remained the top overall format nationwide.

Included in the black-music category was "Jammin' Oldies," a biracial mix of rock, funk, disco, and alternative music from the 1970s and early 1980s, described as "the hottest format since the birth of alternative rock" by the *Dallas Morning News*. It was adopted by 13 stations after being introduced in 1997 by KISQ-FM in San Francisco and being picked up by KCMG-FM in Los Angeles, which gave the format its name. Many of the stations doubled their revenue after reaching a new audience of Generation-Xers and young baby boomers.

The New York Times reported that the Catholic Family Radio network began broadcasting in January with 14 flagship stations. One mission was to counter the influence of Protestant evangelical stations in the United States, estimated to number more than 1,600.

On National Public Radio (NPR), *This American Life* sparked the kind of popular excitement and critical acclaim not heard since the early days of *A Prairie Home Companion* two decades before. The Chicago-based program—hosted by Ira Glass and showcasing quirky, sometimes poetic writing; probing interviews; and humor—was deemed "on the vanguard of a journalistic revolution" by *The American Journalism Review*. In October radio mourned the passing of Jean Shepherd, 78, a cult star of the airwaves and pioneer of offbeat raconteurship who paved the way for NPR's Glass.

DAN HULBERT
"The Atlanta Journal & Constitution"

Terrorism

The United States experienced a variety of types of terrorism in 1999. Incidents ranged from hate crimes by individuals associated with white-supremacist groups to a rocket attack against the U.S. embassy in Pakistan. The most significant legal development was the turning over by Libya of two of its citizens for trial in the Netherlands for the 1988 bombing of Pan Am Flight 103 over Lockerbie, Scotland.

Domestic Terrorism. Hate crimes dominated terrorism within U.S. borders during 1999. In August, Buford Furrow, a mentally unstable man who was a former member of the neo-Nazi group Aryan Nations, admitted that he had walked into a Jewish community center in the Los Angeles area and opened fire, wounding five people. He then left the center and allegedly shot to death a Filipino-American mail carrier. After eluding police in Los Angeles, Furrow surrendered to the Federal Bureau of Investigation (FBI) in Las Vegas a day later. In another incident, Benjamin Smith, an Indiana University student associated with the World Church of the Creator, an antiblack and anti-Jewish organization, killed two persons and wounded nine others in a Fourth of July weekend of violence that spanned across Illinois and Indiana. Smith—who targeted blacks, Jews, and Asians in his attacks—killed himself in southern Indiana during a police chase.

In western North Carolina a bomb exploded at an abortion clinic on March 13. No one was injured in the blast. On May 5 federal law-enforcement officials issued an arrest warrant for James Kopp, an antiabortion militant, for the October 1998 killing of Dr. Barnett Slepian, an abortion-clinic doctor in Buffalo, NY. On June 7, Kopp was added to the FBI's Ten Most Wanted List.

President Bill Clinton offered clemency in August to 16 members of a Puerto Rican nationalist group, the Armed Forces for National Liberation (FALN). The FALN was responsible for 130 bombings in the United States that killed six people and wounded dozens of others between 1974 and 1983. The prisoners were serving sentences for seditious conspiracy and possession of weapons and explosives, but not in connection with any of the bombings. The offer required the prisoners to renounce violence and accept restrictions on their travel and their right of free association. Of the 16 prisoners, 12 accepted the conditions. One was scheduled for parole in 2004, and 11 were released from prison on September 10. Several law-enforcement officers and members of the U.S. Congress criticized President Clinton's decision, saying that it constituted leniency toward terrorism.

In March, Terry Nichols was charged in an Oklahoma court with 160 counts of first-degree murder for the bombing of the Alfred P. Murrah Federal Building in Oklahoma City in 1995. Nichols was given a life sentence in prison after being convicted in December 1997 of federal charges of conspiracy and involuntary manslaughter for the deaths of eight federal law-enforcement officers who died in the blast. If convicted of

© Ricardo Figueroa/AP/Wide World Photos

Several members of a Puerto Rican terrorist group, including Dylcia Pagan (center), were released from prison in September 1999 in a controversial clemency deal offered by President Bill Clinton.

the state charges, Nichols could face the death penalty.

Meanwhile, a federal appeals court agreed on October 22 to hear a request by Theodore Kaczynski to withdraw his 1998 guilty plea for the "Unabomber" mail bombings that killed three persons and injured 23 others. Kaczynski said he wanted to be tried in court on the charges. The FBI on June 16 arrested Kathleen Ann Soliah, a fugitive member of the Symbionese Liberation Army, a 1970s radical group, on charges of building bombs intended to kill Los Angeles Police Department officers in 1975.

Ahmed Ressam, an Algerian with ties to the Algerian terrorist group GIA (Armed Islamic Group), was arrested at the U.S. border crossing in Port Angeles, WA, in December, when customs officials found bomb-making materials in his car. Later in the month, several other people associated with Ressam were taken into custody. The arrests sparked fears that terrorists might commit violence against Americans as the new millennium arrived. However, the United States saw no major terrorist incidents over the New Year's holiday.

International Terrorism. The repercussions from the August 1998 bombings of the U.S. embassies in Kenya and Tanzania, which killed more than 200 persons and injured more than 5,000, continued to be felt during 1999. In January a commission appointed by the U.S. government to investigate the bombings issued a report that criticized the inadequate resources allocated to providing security against terrorism.

Meanwhile, on June 7 the FBI placed Osama bin Laden, the alleged mastermind of the two embassy bombings and the leader of Al-Qaeda, an international organization of Islamic militants, on its Ten Most Wanted List. Bin Laden was indicted in November 1998 by a federal grand jury for murder and conspiracy to murder U.S. nationals outside the United States, and for attacks on a federal facility resulting in death.

In a related development, President Clinton signed an executive order on July 6 imposing financial and other commercial sanctions on Afghanistan, because its rulers, the Taliban group, allegedly allowed bin Laden and Al-Qaeda to use the territory under its control as a safe haven and base of operations. In October the United Nations (UN) Security Council voted to impose sanctions against Afghanistan by November 14 unless Taliban handed over bin Laden to stand trial on terrorism charges. Two days before the deadline, several rockets were fired in Islamabad, Pakistan, at the U.S. embassy, a U.S.-run library and cultural center, and an office tower housing several UN agencies. Six persons were injured.

Meanwhile, a Tanzanian man, Khalfan Khamis Mohamed, was arrested in Cape Town, South Africa, and flown to New York, where he was arraigned on October 8 in federal court on charges of murder and conspiracy connected with the bombing of the U.S. embassy in Tanzania. In addition, a former U.S. Army sergeant, Ali Mohamed, was indicted on May 19 on charges of collaborating with bin Laden in a conspiracy to kill Americans abroad.

One of the most significant developments in international terrorism in 1999 was the handing over by Libya on April 5 of two of its intelligence agents to stand trial in the Netherlands for the 1988 bombing of Pan Am Flight 103 over Lockerbie, Scotland, that killed 270 persons. Abdel Basset al-Megrahi and Al-Amin Khalifa Fahima, who had been on the FBI's Ten Most Wanted List until their surrender, will be tried under Scottish law. On April 6 they were charged formally with murder, conspiracy to commit murder, and violations of international aviation-security laws. In a related development, the UN suspended sanctions that it had imposed on Libya since 1992 for failing to turn over the suspects.

On October 31, Egyptair Flight 990 crashed into the Atlantic shortly after taking off from New York. All 217 passengers and crew were killed. Investigators were looking into the possibility that a relief copilot deliberately crashed the plane by sending it into a dive; however, by late 1999 the cause of the crash had not been determined, and no evidence had emerged that linked the incident to terrorism.

On December 24 an Indian Airlines jet with 190 people aboard, including an American woman, was hijacked during a flight from Nepal to India. After an odyssey spanning several countries—during which one of the hostages was killed and several others were released—the plane landed in Kandahar, Afghanistan. There, the five terrorists kept the more than 150 remaining hostages on the plane for more than eight days, until the Indian government agreed to free three Kashmiri militants and deliver them to Kandahar. The terrorists and freed militants then fled together, and the hostages were released.

JEFFREY SIMON, *Author, "The Terrorist Trap"*

Thailand

THAILAND • Information Highlights

Official Name: Kingdom of Thailand.
Location: Southeast Asia.
Area: 198,456 sq mi (514 000 km^2).
Population (July 1999 est.): 60,609,046.
Chief City (1990 census): Bangkok, the capital (metropolitan area), 5,876,000.
Government: *Head of state,* Bhumibol Adulyadej, king (acceded June 1946). *Head of government,* Chuan Leekpai, prime minister (took office November 1997). *Legislature*—National Assembly: Senate and House of Representatives.
Monetary Unit: Baht (38.78 baht equal U.S.$1, Nov. 12, 1999).
Gross Domestic Product (1998 est. U.S.$): $369,000,000,000 (purchasing power parity).
Economic Index (Bangkok, 1998; 1990 = 100): *Consumer Prices,* all items, 152.7; food, 168.4.
Foreign Trade (1998 U.S.$): *Imports,* $42,971,000,000; *exports,* $54,455,000,000.

The Thai government of Prime Minister Chuan Leekpai completed two full years in office in November 1999. Slow recovery from the 1997–98 economic crisis and scandal continued to fuel political opposition.

Politics. A divided opposition was unable to mount a major challenge to the stability of the coalition government of Prime Minister Chuan Leekpai, but public-opinion polls indicated a steady decline in Chuan's popularity. A parliamentary no-confidence motion in January raised serious questions about the integrity and competence of three senior cabinet ministers. It was defeated handily, 251–125. The coalition majority became smaller in July, when the Social Action Party withdrew its 20 legislators. An independent audit documented a history of bad loans and dubious practices at the state-controlled Krung Thai Bank. Finance Minister Tarrin Nimmanahaeminda was accused of trying to cover up Krung Thai's poor record to protect his brother, who was bank president until late in 1998.

Chuan also came under attack for lack of leadership in attacking problems of corruption, for signing off on honors for former military dictator Field Marshal Thanom Kittiikachorn, and for inactivity in resolving the controversy over the Phra Dhammakaya Buddhist temple. Its abbot was accused of massive financial irregularities but refused to cooperate with either ecclesiastical or secular criminal investigators. Meanwhile, Chuan remained determined to be in office for the celebration of the king's 72d birthday on December 5. This birthday was of particular significance, because it was the sixth-cycle birthday in Thai-Buddhist tradition. Elections must be held by November 2000, however.

Economics. The Thai economy continued its slow road to recovery within the framework of its letters of intent to the International Monetary Fund (IMF). In March the government launched an ambitious new $3.5 billion stimulus package of tax cuts and injection of new funds to boost liquidity. The goal was to create domestic demand, establish new jobs, and provide social supports. Some measure of success was the government's increase in its forecast of real growth in 1999 from an early figure of only 1% to a third-quarter projection of 3.5%. It also decided to forgo drawing on the final $3.7 billion of the IMF's $17.2 billion rescue package.

The task of restructuring the financial system was daunting. Nearly half of the loans in the financial system were classified as nonperforming. Normal lending slowed to a crawl, creating a lending black market. The effectiveness of new bankruptcy and foreclosure laws had yet to be tested. The international financial circle's concern was that a return to real growth would temper any sense of urgency in attacking structural problems.

Foreign Policy. Thailand concentrated great effort on securing the post of director general of the World Trade Organization for its deputy prime minister, Supachai Panitchpakdi. Supachai was locked in a bitterly contested diplomatic contest with former New Zealand Prime Minister Mike Moore. A compromise was struck that each candidate, beginning with Moore, would have a three-year term.

On October 1 five gunmen favoring democracy for Myanmar took over the Myanmar embassy in Bangkok for 25 hours, holding 38 hostages. Thai negotiators ended the siege by allowing the five activists, accompanied by the Thai deputy foreign minister as surrogate hostage, to escape by helicopter to the border areas. The Myanmar junta closed the entire border and interrupted all normal relations with Thailand. In November, despite the closed border, the Thai government began the forcible expulsion of illegal Burmese workers in Thailand. The border reopened late in the month.

Thailand's 1,500-man military contingent in the multinational intervention in the former Indonesian province of East Timor was the second largest in the 7,000-strong force. (*See also* INDONESIA—*East Timor.*)

DONALD E. WEATHERBEE
University of South Carolina

© Joan Marcus

Marin Mazzie and Brian Stokes Mitchell, above, *starred in a highly acclaimed staging of "Kiss Me, Kate," which opened on Broadway in November. It was the first revival ever of the 1948 Cole Porter musical.*

Theater

Broadway maintained its phenomenal success at the box office in the 1998–99 season, posting record-high attendance figures for the second consecutive year. A large number of dramas—both revivals and original plays—received critical acclaim. But Broadway continued to have trouble producing high-quality original musicals, although a few bright prospects showed up at the end of 1999.

The 1998–99 New York Season. Rarely have two worthier contenders faced off in the Tony Awards competition than the 1999 Broadway productions of *Death of a Salesman* and *The Iceman Cometh*. Although the commercial success of two such dark, heavyweight plays ran promisingly against the conventional wisdom of Broadway in the 1990s, the news on the musical side of "The Street" was less encouraging. Despite these mixed artistic results, however, the season was an unqualified box-office success. Broadway productions had an all-time-high attendance of 11.7 million, and 39 new shows opened, compared with 33 the previous season.

The 50th-anniversary production of *Salesman*, Arthur Miller's shattering portrait of a small man's misguided chase after the American Dream, had originated at Chicago's Goodman Theatre. It won Tonys for best revival of a play, best director (Robert Falls), best actor (Brian Dennehy), and best featured actress (Elizabeth Franz). The London-bred revival of Eugene O'Neill's *Iceman*, an even more improbable hit with its four-hour running time, just as well could have won the trophies for best revival and actor (Kevin Spacey).

The third of the "Big Three" American playwrights, Tennessee Williams, also was represented on Broadway and in the Tony Award nominations. Although Williams' *Not About Nightingales*—a long-lost prison melodrama written in 1938—was a hardly a classic, Trevor Nunn's production from London still was deemed powerful. It garnered six Tony nominations, including ones for best play, best director (Nunn), and best actor (Corin Redgrave).

With all the emphasis on vintage plays, *Side Man*, a quiet, poignant drama by Broadway novice playwright Warren Leight, won the Tony for best play. It was Leight's bittersweet profile of his jazzman father.

Dame Judi Dench (*see* BIOGRAPHY), fresh from her Oscar win for *Shakespeare in Love*, repeated her triumphant London role in David Hare's *Amy's View*, winning the Tony for best actress in a play. Meanwhile, fellow Britisher Claire Bloom made a striking return as Clytemnestra in *Electra*.

The late choreographer-director Bob Fosse, having proven himself to be a stylist ahead of his time in the continuing 1996 revival of *Chicago*, was saluted further in *Fosse*, which won the best-musical Tony. Conceived, codirected, and co-choreographed by Ann Reinking, Chet Walker, and Richard Maltby, Jr., the well-received revue was scenically spare but visually dazzling, thanks to the wry, erotic, ironic, and sometimes explosive dance of Fosse. And yet some critics argued that, as a bookless compilation of previously produced material, *Fosse* qualified for the best-new-musical category only because the Tony nominating committee had so few decent choices.

This controversy pointed up the dearth of popular, high-quality new musicals on Broadway. For instance, *Parade*, a musical telling of the tale of Leo Frank—a murder suspect lynched by an anti-Semitic mob in Georgia in 1915—drew respectful but sharply mixed reviews and was short-lived. Lacking competition, it earned Tonys for Alfred Uhry (book) and Jason Robert Brown (score).

The notices also were mixed for the Tony-winning revival of *Annie Get Your Gun*, featuring Irving Berlin's greatest score. Bernadette Peters, playing Annie Oakley, won the Tony for best actress in a musical, holding her own against the legend of Ethel Merman in the 1946 original. But the production showed the strain of adapter Peter Stone's attempts to make the script politically correct (less sexist and offensive to Native Americans), while Graciela Daniele's direction was lackluster.

You're a Good Man, Charlie Brown, in its first Broadway revival since the 1960s original, got mostly positive reviews. Among the most enthusiastic was that of *The New York Times* critic Vincent Canby, who wrote that Charles Schulz—whose *Peanuts* comic strip was the show's inspiration—deserved to be grouped with John Cheever and John Updike for his astute chronicling of suburban life. Charlie Brown's bratty little sister, Sally, was a star-making role for diminutive Kristin Chenoweth, who won the Tony for best featured actress in a musical.

1998–99 Off-Broadway. A highly anticipated London import, *Ashes to Ashes*, was a disappointment from one of the greatest living English-language playwrights, Harold Pinter. Cryptic even by Pinter's standards, the 40-minute enigma seemed to deal with a rich couple's denial of totalitarian atrocities. Lindsay Duncan perfectly embodied the haunted wife. But one critic said of David Strathairn, who played the husband, "His British accent and mannerisms seem as much an assumed costume as his baggy tweeds."

Film star Uma Thurman made a rare New York stage appearance in the Classic Stage Company's production of Molière's *The Misanthrope*, an updated version set in 20th-century London. A Manhattan Theatre Club musical version of Rudyard Kipling's *Captains Courageous* with Treat Williams swiftly sank beneath a critical stoning. A similar fate befell a musical adaptation of the hip 1984 novel *Bright Lights, Big City*, the New York Theater Workshop's attempt to recapture the hard-edged excitement of its 1996 *Rent*.

Playwright Christopher Durang broke a decade-long dry spell with the Playwrights Horizons' riotous *Betty's Summer Vacation*. One critic wrote that the play shows how "life imitates and blurs into television in a country where attention deficit disorder is the Number 1 disease."

Margaret Edson's *Wit*, an uncompromising but philosophical look at mortality

Brian Dennehy won the Tony Award for best actor for his portrayal of Willy Loman in Arthur Miller's "Death of a Salesman." The drama had its 50th anniversary in 1999.

© Joan Marcus

BROADWAY OPENINGS • 1999

MUSICALS

Annie Get Your Gun, book by Herbert and Dorothy Fields, newly revised by Peter Stone; music and lyrics by Irving Berlin; directed by Graciela Daniele; co-choreographed by Daniele and Jeff Calhoun; with Bernadette Peters; March 4– .

The Civil War, lyrics by Frank Wildhorn, Gregory Boyd, and Jack Murphy; music by Wildhorn; directed by Jerry Zaks; with Michael Lanning, Gilles Chiasson, Irene Malloy, Keith Byron Kirk; April 22–June 13.

It Ain't Nothin' But the Blues, by Charles Bevel, Lita Gaithers, Randal Myler, Ron Taylor, and Dan Wheetman; directed by Myler; with Charles Bevel, Gretha Boston, Carter Calvert, Eloise Laws, Gregory Porter, Ron Taylor, Dan Wheetman; April 26– .

James Joyce's The Dead, book by Richard Nelson; lyrics by Shaun Davey and Nelson; music by Davey; directed by Jack Hofsiss and Nelson; with Christopher Walken, Blair Brown; Dec. 14– .

Kat and the Kings, by David Kramer and Taliep Petersen; directed by Kramer; with Terry Hector, Kim Louis, Jody J. Abrahams, Luqmaan Adams, Junaid Booysen, Alistair Izobell; Aug. 19– .

Kiss Me, Kate, music and lyrics by Cole Porter; directed by Michael Blakemore; choreographed by Kathleen Marshall; with Brian Stokes Mitchell, Marin Mazzie, Michael Berresse, Amy Spanger; Nov. 18– .

Marie Christine, music and lyrics by Michael John LaChiusa; directed and choreographed by Graciela Daniele; with Audra McDonald; Dec. 2– .

Saturday Night Fever, adapted by Nan Knighton, in collaboration with Arlene Phillips, Paul Nicholas, and Robert Stigwood; featuring the music of the BeeGees; directed and choreographed by Phillips; with James Carpinello, Paige Price, Orfeh, Paul Castree, Bryan Batt, Richard H. Blake, Andy Blankenbuehler, Sean Palmer; Oct. 21– .

The Scarlet Pimpernel, book and lyrics by Nan Knighton; music by Frank Wildman; directed by Robert Longbottom; with Ron Bohmer, Carolee Carmello, Marc Kudisch; Sept. 10– .

You're a Good Man, Charlie Brown, based on "Peanuts," by Charles M. Schulz; music, book, and lyrics by Clark Gesner; additional music by Andrew Lippa; directed by Michael Mayer; with Kristin Chenoweth, Roger Bart, Anthony Rapp, B.D. Wong, Stanley Wayne Mathis; Feb. 4–June 13.

PLAYS

Amadeus, by Peter Shaffer; directed by Sir Peter Hall; with David Suchet, Michael Sheen; Dec. 16– .

Amy's View, by David Hare; directed by Richard Eyre; with Judi Dench; April 15–July 16.

Death of a Salesman, by Arthur Miller; directed by Robert Falls; with Brian Dennehy; Feb. 10–Nov. 7.

Epic Proportions, by Larry Coen and David Crane; directed by Jerry Zaks; with Kristin Chenoweth; Sept. 30–Dec. 19.

The Iceman Cometh, by Eugene O'Neill; directed by Howard Davies; with Kevin Spacey, Tony Danza; April 8–July 16.

The Lion in Winter, by James Goldman; directed by Michael Mayer; with Laurence Fishburne, Stockard Channing, Emily Bergi; March 11–May 30.

The Lonesome West, by Martin McDonagh; directed by Garry Hynes; with Maeliosa Stafford, Brian F. O'Byrne, Dawn Bradfield, David Ganly; April 27–June 13.

Night Must Fall, by Emlyn Williams; directed by John Tillinger; with Matthew Broderick, Judy Parfitt, J. Smith Cameron; March 8–June 27.

Not About Nightingales, by Tennessee Williams; directed by Trevor Nunn; with Corin Redgrave, Finbar Lynch, James Black, Sherri Parker Lee, J.P. Linton; Feb. 25–June 13.

The Price, by Arthur Miller; directed by James Naughton; with Harris Yulin, Jeffrey DeMunn, Bob Dishy, Lizbeth Mackay; Nov. 9– .

The Rainmaker, by N. Richard Nash; directed by Scott Ellis; with Woody Harrelson and Jayne Atkinson; Nov. 11– .

Voices in the Dark, by John Pielmeier; directed by Christopher Ashley; with Judith Ivey; Aug. 12–Oct. 10.

Waiting in the Wings, by Noel Coward; directed by Michael Langham; with Lauren Bacall, Rosemary Harris, Dana Ivey, Barnard Hughes; Dec. 16– .

The Weir, by Conor McPherson; directed by Ian Rickson; with Jim Norton, Brendan Coyle, Kieran Ahern, Dermot Crowley, Michelle Fairley; April 1–Nov. 28.

OTHER ENTERTAINMENT

Contact, a dance play; devised by Susan Stroman and James Weidman; directed and choreographed by Stroman; with Karen Ziemba, Boyd Gaines, Deborah Yates; Oct. 7– .

Dame Edna: The Regal Tour, conceived and performed by Barry Humphries; Oct. 17– .

Fosse, a revue; conceived by Richard Maltby, Ann Reinking, and Chet Walker; codirected by Maltby and Reinking; co-choreographed by Reinking and Walker; Jan. 14– .

Jackie Mason: Much Ado about Everything, a comedy show; directed and performed by Jackie Mason; Dec. 30– .

Minnelli on Minnelli, a concert; with Liza Minnelli; Dec. 8– .

Morning, Noon and Night, written and performed by Spalding Gray; Nov. 8– .

Putting It Together, a musical revue; music and lyrics by Stephen Sondheim; directed by Eric D. Schaeffer; with Carol Burnett, Ruthie Henshall, George Hearn, John Barrowman, Bronson Pinchot; Nov. 21– .

Swing!, directed and choreographed by Lynne Taylor-Corbett; supervised by Jerry Zaks; with Ann Hampton Callaway; Dec. 9– .

Tango Argentino, a dance revue; created and directed by Claudio Segovia and Hector Orezzoli; Nov. 17– .

---

through the eyes of a cancer patient, continued its run at the Union Square Theatre and won the 1999 Pulitzer Prize for drama.

Regional Theater. At the 23d annual Humana Festival of New American Plays at the Actors Theatre of Louisville (KY), the best-received script was *Y2K*, by Arthur Kopit (*Wings*), the story of a couple terrorized by a computer hacker that loomed as a cautionary tale for the digital age.

The Shakespeare Theatre of Washington, DC, mounted a production of Euripides' *The Trojan Women* by the noted avant-garde director JoAnne Akalaitis, in which contemporary costumes and wreckage clearly evoked the ongoing strife in the Balkans. At the same theater, Hal Holbrook was praised for his Shylock in the ever-ambiguous *Merchant of Venice*.

In a departure from its usual fare of musical revivals, the Signature Theatre of Arlington, VA (not to be confused with its New York namesake), presented the world premiere of *Over & Over*, a musical based on Thornton Wilder's *The Skin of Our Teeth* with a score by John Kander and Fred Ebb (*Cabaret*, *Chicago*). Gwyneth Paltrow was a well-received Rosalind in the Williamstown (MA) Theatre Festival's *As You Like It*.

The Alley Theatre of Houston proudly noted that two of its 1998 premieres—*Not About Nightingales* and the critically

© M. Le Poer Trench/Courtesy, Guthrie Theater

Cameron Mackintosh's production of "Martin Guerre"—a musical retelling of a 16th-century legend—made its U.S. debut at the Guthrie Theater in Minneapolis in 1999.

drubbed musical *The Civil War*—received a total of eight 1999 Tony nominations for their New York transfers. *Love, Janis*, a rock musical based on Laura Joplin's memoir of her fiery sister, was a hit premiere at the Cleveland Play House.

Emmy Award winner Rip Torn (*The Larry Sanders Show*) and Broadway diva Betty Buckley (*Cats*) headlined the Hartford Stage production of Tennessee Williams' *Camino Real*. Also at the Hartford was Lanford Wilson's *Book of Days*, voted best play of 1999 by the American Theatre Critics Association.

The newest London hit by Tom Stoppard, *The Invention of Love*, about closeted gay poet A.E. Houseman, had its U.S. premiere at San Francisco's American Repertory Theatre. At the American Repertory Theatre in Cambridge, MA, playwright David Mamet made a startling—and not very successful—departure from his stark, bristling style with *Boston Marriage*, a comedy of manners about two lesbian lovers set at the turn of the 20th century. ART also presented, in cooperation with Harvard University's Institute of the Arts and Civic Dialogue, the U.S. premiere of *Disremember Me*, playwright Arben Kumbaro's exposé of mayhem in his native Albania. *Martin Guerre*, a musical by Alain Boublil and Claude-Michel Schonberg, premiered in Minneapolis after a successful London run.

Actor's Express of Atlanta mounted a searing, sprawling adaptation of Fyodor Dostoyevsky's *The Devils* (often translated as *The Possessed*) in which the Russian revolutionaries mirrored the directionless rage of America's Generation X.

A 40-year-old musical from the bottom of Stephen Sondheim's trunk, *Saturday Night*, finally got its U.S. premiere in Chicago. The witty snapshot of big-city romance was mounted by the tiny, non-Equity Pegasus Players but earned a respectful notice from *Time* magazine. A little-known 1931 stage comedy by Preston Sturges, *A Cup of Coffee*, set aside and forgotten when the director achieved his film success, enjoyed a rare mounting at Yale Repertory Theatre of New Haven, CT, in late 1999.

Anne Hamburger was named artistic director of the La Jolla (CA) Playhouse, but with the unfortunate result that her daring off-Broadway troupe, En Garde Arts, disbanded. *Aida*, the Disney Company musical by Elton John and Tim Rice that debuted to mixed reviews in Atlanta in 1998, got a new

Lanford Wilson's "Book of Days," a new play about a murder in a Missouri town, opened the 1999–2000 Mainstage season of The Repertory Theatre of St. Louis.

© Judy Andrews/Courtesy, The Repertory Theatre of St. Louis

© Joan Marcus

Television and film actor Woody Harrelson (left) made his Broadway debut—to mixed reviews—in a revival of N. Richard Nash's "The Rainmaker," costarring Jayne Atkinson.

director, Robert Falls (Broadway's *Death of a Salesman*), and a new design team. The revamped, pre-Broadway rock treatment of Verdi's Egyptian opera opened in December 1999 at Chicago's Palace Theatre; it was scheduled to move to New York in 2000.

The New Fall Season in New York. *Kiss Me, Kate* was acclaimed widely as the most exciting and enjoyable musical revival since *Cabaret* in March 1998. Cole Porter's 1948 backstage musical featured a feuding married couple (modeled on Alfred Lunt and Lynn Fontanne) at the center of a production of Shakespeare's *The Taming of the Shrew*. The buoyant Michael Blakemore production confirmed Brian Stokes Mitchell and Marin Mazzie (who both appeared in *Ragtime*) as Broadway romantic leads of the first rank.

Expectations were just as high for *Putting It Together*, the London revue of Stephen Sondheim songs starring Carol Burnett (with Kathie Lee Gifford subbing on selected shows). The reviews, however, were generally cool. *The New York Times* critic Ben Brantley observed that the chilly intellect and muted emotions of Sondheim were mismatched with the "warm, friendly, and vulnerable" Burnett.

Saturday Night Fever, the Broadway-musical version of the hit 1977 movie that launched John Travolta to stardom, opened in October to reviews ranging from mediocre to awful, but set a blistering pace at the box office. Critical raves were garnered by *Contact*, a dance play directed and choreographed by Susan Stroman that debuted at Manhattan's Lincoln Center in October. The show—consisting of three one-act set pieces punctuated with dance and a bit of dialogue, but no singing—was described as "a sustained endorphin rush of an evening, that rare entertainment that has you floating all the way home." *Marie Christine*, a new Lincoln Center musical featuring three-time Tony winner Audra McDonald in her first leading role, was deemed a disappointment in its effort to update *Medea* to 19th-century New Orleans.

Waiting in the Wings was clobbered by *Variety* in its pre-Broadway Boston tryout. Despite the glittering pairing of Rosemary Harris and Lauren Bacall, Noel Coward's late, rarely revived backstage comedy was deemed too weak a vehicle for them. The play started a run at the Walter Kerr Theatre in New York in December.

Movie and television star Woody Harrelson made his Broadway debut in November in the revival of N. Richard Nash's *The Rainmaker* at the Brooks Atkinson Theater. Harrelson received some good notices for his performance as Starbuck, a smooth-talking salesman who promises to bring rain to a drought-plagued town in the West, but critics dismissed the play itself as outdated and overly sentimental.

Fall 1999 Off-Broadway. The Signature Theatre Company dedicated its new theater, named for company benefactor Peter Norton, and, in accordance with its acclaimed one-playwright-per-season policy, named Maria Irene Fornes its featured dramatist for 1999–2000.

Marsha Norman, whose *'night, Mother* made her a star playwright in the 1980s but who was long overdue for a hit, offered the MCC Theater *Trudy Blue*. She described the play, which debuted in late 1999, as "the story of a quintessentially modern Manhattan woman and how she manages the thousand voices in her head."

DAN HULBERT
"The Atlanta Journal & Constitution"

Transportation

Many changes and transitions took place in the various sectors of the transportation industry during 1999. High-profile problems with commercial-airline flights led to calls for airlines to pay more attention to customer service. But the airlines enjoyed another year of growth in spite of their many difficulties. Late in the year the United States formally transferred control of the Panama Canal to Panama, even as the canal was becoming less important to commercial and military shipping. Several major mergers and acquisitions took place in both the rail and shipping industries, and the U.S. bus industry disappeared almost completely, as American companies were purchased by foreign firms.

Aviation. The airline industry got off to a rocky start in 1999, as a January 2 snowstorm in Detroit, MI, snarled air traffic and created worse-than-normal delays for hundreds of passengers. Some Northwest Airlines planes were stranded on the runways for more than eight hours, without food, beverages, or even toilet facilities for the passengers for much of that time. The incident prompted the U.S. Congress to introduce bills calling for improved service to airline passengers. None of the legislation passed, but the industry's attempt to defeat the efforts led members of the Airline Transport Association (ATA) to issue new customer-service plans that included increased liability for lost luggage, faster payment of refunds, and better access to information on the lowest possible fares and regarding delays and cancellations.

Not long after the Detroit snowstorm, airline passengers dealt with another serious service problem—a sick-out by pilots of American Airlines, the nation's second-largest carrier, during the busy Presidents' Day holiday period. The action, which started February 5, was sparked by the Allied Pilots Association's objections to the airline's plan to merge the lower-paid pilots of recently purchased Reno Air into its roster of pilots. In response to a complaint from the airline, U.S. District Judge Joe Kendall ordered the 9,000 pilots back to work on February 10, but the job action continued until February 14. The airline and the union agreed to arbitration of the dispute, and while the union achieved many of its goals, it still had to fight a compensatory-damage award of $45.5 million that Judge Kendall ordered it to pay the airline in April, along with a class-action suit filed by passengers. The sick-out forced the cancellation of more than 6,600 flights, and American Airlines management estimated losses of more than $200 million.

American faced another problem in May, when the U.S. Justice Department filed an antitrust action against it, charging it illegally sought to keep low-cost carriers out of its Dallas–Fort Worth hub by saturating any market served by the new competitors—such as Vanguard, Sunjet, and Western Pacific—with low-priced service of its own. Each of those three either exited the Dallas mar-

© Paul David Mozell/Stock Market

As airline passengers grew increasingly irritated by recurrent problems such as lengthy flight delays and lost luggage, the U.S. Congress in 1999 introduced, but failed to enact, legislation that called for improved airline service—a so-called "passengers' bill of rights."

ket or severely curtailed service. American denied the charge. The case, which had not been resolved by the end of 1999, was seen as an important test of a policy proposed by the U.S. Department of Transportation that called for greater opportunities for competition by upstart carriers.

On June 1, American Airlines Flight 1420 crashed while landing in bad weather in Little Rock, AR, killing 11 of the 145 persons aboard, including the pilot. The crash caused the first fatalities on a U.S. carrier since 1997. Investigators were trying to determine whether pilot fatigue due to excessive hours of flying on the day of the crash was a factor in the accident.

Several of the highest-profile air crashes in the United States in 1999 did not involve U.S. commercial carriers. EgyptAir Flight 990 crashed in the Atlantic Ocean shortly after taking off from New York City's John F. Kennedy International Airport on October 31, killing all 217 on board. The initial investigation suggested that there was no mechanical problem with the plane and that perhaps a copilot on the flight intentionally sent the plane into the ocean in a suicide–mass murder. Egyptian officials argued against that theory, and the investigation was continuing as 1999 ended.

On July 16 a single-engine, six-seat Piper Saratoga plane piloted by John F. Kennedy, Jr., went down in the Atlantic Ocean off of Martha's Vineyard, killing him, his wife, and his sister-in-law. Besides spurring national grief (*see* UNITED STATES—*The Kennedy Family: Another Tragedy*), the crash focused attention on the safety of general-service aircraft. In another high-profile air fatality, a private jet carrying professional golfer Payne Stewart crashed October 25, killing all six people aboard. The plane flew off course from Florida to North Dakota, apparently without anyone at the controls, before it ran out of fuel. Investigators were considering the possibility that loss of cabin pressure had caused the accident.

The year ended with increasing fuel prices dampening airline profits. To reduce costs, the airlines cut the commissions they paid to travel agents to 5% from 8%, as the industry continued to see an increasing percentage of tickets being booked via the Internet rather than through agents.

Despite all the problems and bad publicity faced by aviation in 1999, it was generally a good year for the industry. Among ATA carriers, revenue passenger miles (a measure of carrying a passenger 1 mi/1.6 km) increased 4.4% in the first 11 months of 1999 to 567.4 billion, twice the rate of increase as in the same period of 1998. The number of passengers increased 3% to 525.6 million, while the percentage of available seats filled was 71.8%, slightly higher than in 1998.

Railroads. The biggest news in the railroad industry took place at the very end of the year, as Canadian National (CN), Canada's largest rail company, and Burlington Northern Santa Fe Corp., the second-largest U.S. railroad, announced plans for the largest merger in industry history on December 20. The $19 billion deal would give a western U.S. railroad direct access to the Atlantic for the first time. The combined railroad, to be known as North American Railway, Inc., would have 50,000 mi (80 450 km) of track, stretching from Halifax, Nova Scotia, to Los Angeles, and from Port Rupert, British Columbia, to Mobile, AL.

© Kevin Moloney/Liaison Agency

Delays in equipment deliveries caused Amtrak to postpone the introduction of a new high-speed train, the Acela, right, *along the Northeast Corridor until 2000. The train, whose sleek, innovative design will allow it to travel at speeds up to 150 mph, continued to be tested in 1999.*

The regulatory hurdles of the merger were expected to take at least 18 months to clear, as some rail customers expressed concerns about further service disruptions from such a large combination. While CN's merger with Illinois Central was completed in 1999 with relatively few disruptions in service, rail customers in the East saw problems with the integration of the former Conrail into CSX Corp. and Norfolk Southern Corp., which took place June 1. Despite more than a year of planning, the two railroads struggled with delays and reduced profits after the switch was completed. And memories of the two years of service problems caused by Union Pacific Corp.'s 1997 merger with Southern Pacific were still fresh in rail customers' minds.

There was also the belief that the CN-Burlington deal might be the start of a final round of mergers that could leave North America with just two major railroads that each would cover virtually all of the United States and Canada.

Passenger rail carrier Amtrak had its own service setbacks in 1999, as it had to delay plans for its Acela high-speed service along its profitable Northeast Corridor line due to problems in getting the necessary equipment. The service, with trains reaching 150 mph (241 km/hr) running between Boston, MA, and Washington, DC, was set to launch in 2000. Still, even without the new higher-priced service, the railroad saw its passenger count and revenue rise and began to carry more mail and small freight shipments during the year as well.

Ocean Shipping. Ocean shipping was deregulated greatly in 1999, as the Ocean Shipping Reform Act took effect on May 1. Under this U.S. legislation, importers and exporters were allowed to negotiate private contracts with ship lines rather than pay tariffs on file with the federal government. The move led to the end of some of the shipping cartels (known as conferences) that had set rates in the past. But as the change was taking place, an increase in trade rates for shipping containers rebounded on several major lanes, notably for transpacific shipments, where some rates were up as much as 18% in the third quarter, compared to the same period of 1998.

Sea-Land Service, the largest U.S. carrier and the company that helped create container shipping, saw much of its operations sold to its foreign partner, Maersk Line, for $800 million in July. Before that deal was announced, the two shipping lines made another agreement that appeared to determine the hub of shipping on the East Coast for decades to come: They decided to keep their operations at the Port of New York/New Jersey. The arrival of larger container ships has created the need for mega-ports that send containers to other areas on the coast by rail or feeder ship.

At the end of 1999, the United States officially turned over control of the Panama Canal, one of the 20th century's engineering marvels and a link between the Atlantic and Pacific Oceans, to the country of Panama. While the change remained the subject of some criticism in the United States, changes in both commercial and military shipping have limited the canal's importance since the treaty was negotiated in 1977. The current generation of container ships, which carry the highest-value ocean-borne cargo, are known as "post-Panamax," because they are too large to fit through the canal locks. The growth of containerization in recent years has meant that it can be as quick and inexpensive to carry freight across the country via the railroad as it formerly was to sail through the canal to the opposite coast. Key military ships, such as aircraft carriers, also no longer fit through the canal.

In late 1999, Carnival Corp., the world's largest cruise operator, made an unsolicited $1.7 billion bid for NCL Holdings ASA, operator of Norwegian Cruise Lines (NCL). The hostile bid was rejected by NCL's board. Instead, Singapore's Star Cruises PLC, which was not subject to the same restrictions as Carnival on the purchase of NCL stock, ended up buying a majority of the company without the NCL board's knowledge.

Trucking. A familiar name returned to trucking in late 1998, as James P. Hoffa assumed the presidency of the International Brotherhood of Teamsters, the union his famous father, James R. Hoffa, once headed. Hoffa's election had been a three-year process that included federal authorities throwing out results of a 1996 vote he narrowly lost to Ron Carey, a former UPS driver who had been elected as a reformer in 1991. Carey was barred from running in the new election when it was discovered that union funds were channeled illegally into his 1996 campaign.

Hoffa's union has far less clout than it did in his father's day. The union's strength in 1999 lay primarily in three sectors of trucking—at UPS, the world's largest package-distribution company and the largest Team-

In response to a recent rise in fatalities caused by trucking accidents, Congress passed a bill creating a new agency within the U.S. Transportation Department to monitor and improve truck safety. President Bill Clinton signed the bill into law in late 1999.

ster employer, with more than 200,000 union members on the payroll; at the carriers delivering new cars to dealer showrooms; and at the carriers consolidating pallet-sized shipments of freight through a labor-intensive series of warehouses. The latter sector, known as less-than-truckload (LTL), saw the trend of declining union membership continue in 1999, however, as two major Teamster carriers, Preston Trucking Company and NationsWay Transport, halted operations due to losses. Another, ANR Advance, went out of business in the last days of 1998 in the midst of a Teamsters strike.

As 1999 drew to a close, the Teamsters were waging a strike against Overnite Trucking Co., a division of Union Pacific Corp., which the union had been trying to organize since late 1994. The union charged that the company engaged in a series of unfair labor practices to defeat the union, and it took the unusual step of picketing outside the carrier's customers as well as at Overnite's terminals. The company insisted that the strike, which started in October, did not hurt its operations seriously.

Union membership did not seem to hurt UPS in 1999, judging from its successful initial public offering (IPO) of stock on November 10. The company, which had been owned by about 126,000 employees, retirees, and descendants of former employees, had the largest IPO ever by a U.S. firm, raising $5.47 billion by allowing investors to buy shares representing 10% of the company. UPS' strong balance sheet, combined with its large lead in the growing business of delivering goods purchased on the Internet to customers' homes, attracted investors both large and small. Demand for the stock led to the IPO price being set at almost double the value of the stock when it was being traded privately. The price then jumped another 30% on its first day of trading.

Buses. The U.S. bus industry virtually vanished in 1999 as domestic companies were being purchased by foreign firms. Canadian holding company Laidlaw Inc. bought Greyhound, the leading intercity bus company, in March for $650 million. In June the largest U.S. bus company, Coach USA, was purchased by British transportation holding company Stagecoach Holdings for $1.8 billion. Coach USA, which had used acquisition to consolidate the diverse charter, tour, and commuter segments of the bus industry, had seen its revenue climb from $184.7 million in 1996 to $803.6 million in 1998, topping Greyhound in the two companies' final year as independent operators.

The purchases left the United States without any major domestically owned bus companies. Even the major school-bus operators were being purchased by foreign companies. British firm FirstGroup PLC bought the public-transportation-services division of Ryder System Inc. in September for $650 million. This transaction made Laidlaw and FirstGroup the two largest school-bus operators in the country. Another British company, National Express, became the nation's third-largest school-bus company by buying Durham Transportation for about $178.7 million in August.

CHRIS ISIDORE
Freelance Transportation Writer

Travel

The tourism industry ended the 1990s with another booming year. Despite global climatic disasters, isolated area violence, and advisories about the possible Y2K computer problem, international travel was on target to grow 3% in 1999, according to the Travel Industry Association of America. The Kosovo crisis in Serbia did not affect tourism numbers as much as the Persian Gulf war did in 1991.

The U.S. travel industry, with a projected 50.4 million visitors in 1999, grew even faster than experts had predicted, ranking third (after France and Spain) in inbound arrivals. International visitors spent $74.5 billion on lodging, meals, and entertainment, plus $20 billion on transportation. International Trade Commission figures showed 55.9 million U.S. citizens vacationed abroad, a slight increase over 1998. Tourism was the largest services export industry, the third-largest retail-sales industry, and one of the largest employers in the United States.

Domestic Travel. Seeing the United States remained a popular pastime for Americans in 1999, with domestic travel rising 4%, to 271 million. Short vacations structured around weekends were popular with families, but young adults without families were the most active travelers. According to estimates by the American Automobile Association (AAA), the average expenditure for meals and lodging for a family of four was $213 a day, $3 a day more than in 1998. Thanks to a strong economy, the leisure market dominated U.S. travel, with total person-trips—defined as traveling 100 mi (160 km) or more away from home—jumping to 1.3 billion, and total expenditures increasing 5.2% to $446.2 billion. Business travel also increased, for the first time in several years. Both domestic and international travelers continued to gravitate to California and Florida, with Texas ranking third. The addition of three dramatic and luxurious resorts—the $950 million Mandalay Bay Hotel and Casino (which itself contained another hotel, the Four Seasons), the $1.4 billion Venetian, and the $765 million Paris Las Vegas—helped Las Vegas overtake Orlando as the top U.S. city destination in 1999.

International Travel. Travel to Europe, the favorite destination for the U.S. market, increased, with 11.5 million Americans projected to visit Britain and Western Europe in 1999. Germany and the Netherlands posted double-digit increases, and Austria saw the largest improvement since 1992. The continued strength of the U.S. dollar also made travel to Australia and the South Pacific popular. Travel to New Zealand jumped significantly, largely because of the America's Cup yacht race, which began in the fall outside Auckland. Thanks to a good exchange rate, U.S. travelers spent record amounts in Canada—17.5% over 1998. Travel to the Caribbean slowed slightly, due to fewer flights and competitive transatlantic fares.

Canada and Mexico accounted for the most foreign travelers to the United States in 1999, with 13.4 million and 9.3 million visitors, respectively. U.S. travel suppliers anticipated a 12% rise in European arrivals, with increases from Britain, Germany, France, Italy, the Netherlands, the Czech Republic, Hungary, and Poland. Increases also were noted for Japan, Brazil, Venezuela, and Argentina. South Africa's international arrivals rose, thanks to a solid increase in nature-based tourism, while tourism was down in Turkey, Greece, and parts of Asia.

Cruising. Cruising continued to be the fastest-growing segment of the travel industry, with 1999 seeing an increase of 6% to 10% in passengers from North American ports. Ships introduced during the year included the world's largest luxury liner, the 142,000-gross-ton, 3,100-passenger *Voyage of the Seas,* from Royal Caribbean; the 385-cabin *Ocean Explorer*, from a new line, World Cruise Co.; and the *Columbia Queen* riverboat, from the American Classic Voyages Co., scheduled to begin service in the Pacific Northwest in late 1999.

Trends. Electronic tickets (abbreviated "E-tickets") increasingly replaced conventional paper tickets for commercial airline flights, accounting for more than 40% of all travel-agent transactions in 1999. In addition, a growing number of Americans used the Internet to make travel plans without professional assistance; according to the Travel Industry Association, 16.5 million adults booked travel reservations on-line in 1999, a 146% increase from 1998.

In addition to cruising, growth markets included adventure trips (*see* SIDEBAR), ecotourism, cultural and educational travel, and spa vacations. High-end travelers sought out remote, exotic locations such as Guatemala's Petén region, Patagonia, Spain's Basque country, the Baltic countries, Russia's Kamchatka peninsula, the Marquesa Islands, Vanuatu, and Bhutan.

BARBARA J. BRAASCH
Freelance Travel Writer

SPECIAL REPORT Adventure Travel

Floating down the Amazon River, cycling along Britain's byways, dogsledding on Minnesota's frozen Boundary Waters, viewing wildlife from atop an elephant on the African savanna—all are forms of adventure travel, the travel industry's hottest new trend. The Adventure Travel Society defines these excursions as "exciting participatory travel that takes place in unusual outdoor settings." Outings may include everything from hiking, fishing, and snorkeling to ballooning, mountaineering, and jungle trekking.

Surge in Popularity. According to a 1998 Travel Industry Association study, 98 million Americans had participated in a form of adventure travel in the previous five years. When combined with expedition cruising, this market now accounts for 35% of all upscale travel. Such trips are most popular with young, affluent adults looking to test their physical ability and gain a sense of accomplishment. Although travelers 55 and older spend twice as much for such adventures, they account for only 23% of the market.

Tour companies have responded to this rapidly growing market by offering a new crop of programs geared to active and adventurous baby boomers. Even standard sight-seeing packages have been retooled. For example, MaupinTrek's Greenland and Iceland tours now incorporate more free time and a variety of physical activity. In addition to hiking, horseback riding, and swimming, itineraries may add volcano-climbing and white-water-rafting excursions.

Many innovative adventure tours take place in some of the globe's most pristine—and fragile—destinations: Central and South America, Africa, Mongolia, Papua New Guinea, and the Antarctic. International Expeditions' riverboats probe Peru's remote rain forest. On Trinidad and Tobago, treks through nature reserves focus on spotting birds, bees, and butterflies. Responsible tour operators help these developing regions realize the economic importance of protecting, rather than destroying, fragile environments to create sustainable tourism. Costa Rica was en-

Adventure tourism—be it rafting along the U.S.-Canadian border, below left, *or hiking in Lake Tahoe, CA,* below right*—is the latest travel-industry trend. Such adventures are divided into two categories: "hard" and "soft."*

couraged to place more than 25% of its land in designated Conservation Areas, and Brazil was assisted in protecting nests of five of the world's species of migrating marine turtles along its coastline.

Categories of Adventure Travel. Most travel falls into the "soft adventure" category, which requires only that participants be in reasonably good health and fitness. These adventurers need not sacrifice creature comforts. Typical outings range from tracing the tides on walking tours along the beaches of Washington state's Olympic National Park and camping on Hawaii's Big Island to barging through France's wine country and skin-diving off the Cayman Islands in the Caribbean.

More than 31 million people have engaged in "hard adventures" since the mid-1990s. These are more-physical exertions, such as rock climbing, parasailing, and spelunking (cave exploring). Participants must be in top shape and accustomed to fairly demanding regimens. Creature comforts are apt to be scarce. Sample itineraries feature back-to-back climbs of Africa's Mounts Kenya and Kilimanjaro, kayaking off New Zealand's South Island, or clambering around Alaska's glacial ice formations.

Mountain Travel Sobek, one of the oldest and most prominent U.S. adventure-tour operators, has been offering strenuous programs for 30 years. The company notes that today's clients prefer shorter, more frequent trips. It also has discovered that young clients want a variety of activities rather than a single adventure. Two-week tours to the Galápagos Islands and Antarctica sell much faster than does the 29-day Ultimate Everest Trek, once the company's most popular offering.

Expedition cruises highlighting natural history, culture, light adventure, and water sports also fall under the adventure-travel umbrella. Tour operators use small ships to visit remote regions, such as the ice fields of the Strait of Magellan and the islands in Baja's Sea of Cortés. Hallmarks of such ship travel are an informal lifestyle and an accent on learning and ability. These not-so-luxurious voyages incorporate many of the factors that drove early explorers, such as flexibility of scheduling and a premium on learning. They appeal primarily to well-educated, well-traveled clients. While travelers need not be in top physical shape, a sense of adventure helps. Society Expeditions has been taking people on far-flung adventures for 25 years on their 138-passenger *World Discovery*. Recent demand has been so large that the company plans to add two additional ships.

© Philippe Blondel/Allsport USA/Vandystadt

Bungee jumping—a sport in which a physically fit person harnessed to an elastic bungee cord flings himself or herself off a bridge, platform, or other high place—was developed in New Zealand in the late 1980s.

Another type of adventure travel, termed "extreme sports," involves various high-risk activities like bungee jumping, tandem skydiving, and "catarafting." The target audience for these activities is the young, bold, and physically fit traveler. Zegrahm DeepSea Voyages, a firm specializing in extreme adventure tourism to remote locations, offers inquisitive nonscientists the opportunity to travel in minisubmarines to underwater volcanoes and hydrothermal vents in the mid-Atlantic Ocean near the Azores archipelago.

New Horizons. And, for those looking to "push the envelope," the future is literally out of this world. Several travel operators now offer space adventures at Russia's Star City, including a few minutes of weightless flight. Longer suborbital flights will be launched in several locations between 2002 and 2005.

BARBARA J. BRAASCH

Tunisia

While under heavy criticism from international human-rights organizations, Tunisia held its first pluralist presidential elections in 1999. It continued to boast the best economy in North Africa.

Politics. On Oct. 24, 1999, Tunisia held its first pluralist presidential elections since achieving independence in 1956. The process reaffirmed the incumbent leader, 63-year-old Zine El Abidine Ben Ali, who was facing his final term. Tunisians also went to the polls to choose their representatives in parliament. The presidential election marked the first time opposition parties were allowed to run legally against the incumbent president. Two moderate opponents, Mohamed Belhaj Amor, secretary-general of the Parti de l'Unité Populaire, and Abderrahman Tlili, head of the Union Démocratique Unioniste, ran in the general elections. Official results showed that Ben Ali won the election with 99.44% of the total votes cast, while Abderrahman Tlili received only 0.23%, and Mohamed Belhaj Amor only 0.31%. Voter turnout was 91.4%.

In response to strong criticism that his party had an unfair monopoly in parliament, President Ben Ali made constitutional changes introducing a presidential term limit and reserving a minimum of 20% of seats in parliament for opposition parties. These changes were met with skepticism by his opponents, as Ben Ali's party, the Rassemblement Constitutionnel Démocratique (RCD), maintained a parliamentary majority. The party won 148 of the 182 available seats. The remaining 34 seats, reserved by law for minority parties, were shared by five opposition parties. The Socialist Democrats Movement, a supporter of Ben Ali, won 13 seats. Tlili's and Belhaj Amor's parties each won seven seats, while a former communist party that also campaigned for Ben Ali, the Attajdid, won five seats, and the Social Liberal Party won two.

In November, President Ben Ali named Mohamed Ghannouchi, former international cooperation minister, as premier. He succeeded Hamed Karoui.

Human Rights. Although officially the elections were reported to be free and fair, the government's commitment to political pluralism was questioned. Tunisia has a negative track record in the areas of human rights and democratization. Amnesty International reported that the targeting of human-rights activists dramatically increased in 1999. Human-rights defenders and lawyers increasingly were being harassed and imprisoned. Similarly, the Paris-based Journalists without Borders (RSF) reported that freedom of the press in Tunisia was virtually nonexistent.

In response to this criticism and shortly before the elections, Ben Ali released a number of jailed human-rights activists. Among them was the vice-president of the Tunisian Human Rights League, Khemais Ksila, who had been detained for 14 months on charges of inciting rebellion. Raouf Chammari, the brother of prominent human-rights activist Khemais Chammari, also was released. Chammari had been condemned to a one-year jail term for defamation of a former government official.

Economy. Tunisia was on its way to becoming an open-market economy. Despite having no significant natural resources, Tunisia had recorded an average growth rate of 5% since the beginning of the decade. Tunisia boasted one of the highest growth rates in the region and an inflation rate of approximately 3.5%.

Tunisia was the first south Mediterranean country to sign a free-trade agreement with the European Union (EU), in 1995. As a result, it was engaging in a major economic-liberalization program. The privatization of dozens of state-owned companies was encouraged by the World Bank and the EU, which were funding the country's modernization of industry. Tourism is the major source of revenue. Each year more than 4 million visitors travel to Tunisia, generating nearly 47% of GDP. While foreign investment continued to flow into the country, unemployment was on the rise. Official data reported an unemployment rate of 15.6%.

ROSE RYAN, *"The North Africa Journal"*

TUNISIA • Information Highlights

Official Name: Republic of Tunisia.
Location: North Africa.
Area: 63,170 sq mi (163 610 km^2).
Population (July 1999 est.): 9,513,603.
Chief Cities (1994 census): Tunis, the capital, 674,100; Sfax, 230,900.
Government: *Head of state,* Zine El Abidine Ben Ali, president (took office Nov. 7, 1987). *Head of government,* Mohamed Ghannouchi, prime minister (appointed November 1999). *Legislature* (unicameral)—Chamber of Deputies.
Monetary Unit: Dinar (1.1775 dinars equal U.S.$1, Nov. 9, 1999).
Gross Domestic Product (1998 est. U.S.$): $49,000,-000,000 (purchasing power parity).
Economic Indexes (1998, 1990 = 100): *Consumer Prices,* all items, 146.8; food, 146.6. *Industrial Production,* 139.2.
Foreign Trade (1998 U.S.$): *Imports,* $8,338,000,000; *exports,* $5,750,000,000.

Turkey

Disastrous earthquakes battered Turkey in 1999, while the dramatic capture of Kurdish leader Abdullah Ocalan seemed to weaken the long-lasting Kurdish uprising.

Earthquakes. In the early hours of August 17, an earthquake with a magnitude of 7.5 struck northwestern Anatolia, with its epicenter near Izmit, a city of almost 1 million. The earthquake caused widespread death and destruction in a heavily populated and industrialized zone around the Sea of Marmara and reaching to the outer suburbs of Istanbul.

Thirty-two countries, including the United States and Greece, sent rescue squads and assistance to help Turkish authorities in freeing the living from collapsed buildings. Most often the squad found bodies, with a final death toll of 15,600. The injured numbered 25,000, and those forced out of their homes exceeded the staggering total of 250,000. Frequent aftershocks hampered rescue efforts and made people fear moving back into what usable housing had survived.

Government response to the earthquake was slow, with the army joining rescue missions on August 21. Widespread criticism of the country's political leadership centered on the government's delayed response and on allegations that corrupt contractors had bribed inspectors to allow the construction of shoddy housing. In September the World Bank estimated direct damage at about $6.5 billion, with an additional $2 billion in indirect costs. The Turkish government gave a higher damage estimate of between $9 billion and $13 billion.

A 5.9-magnitude aftershock on September 13 caused substantial additional damage. A more severe November 12 earthquake measuring 7.1 hit a wide zone stretching from Istanbul to Ankara, resulting in at least 705 deaths.

Kurdish Developments. On February 15, Turkish commandos—probably acting on the basis of U.S. intelligence information—seized Abdullah Ocalan, head of the Kurdistan Workers Party (PKK), in Nairobi, Kenya, under mysterious circumstances. He was flown to Turkey and imprisoned on the island of Imrali in the Sea of Marmara. Ocalan was charged with treason and separatism for his role in directing the PKK's 15-year-old insurgency against the Turkish government. On May 31, at the beginning of his monthlong trial on these charges, Ocalan presented a conciliatory stand. He said that he would dedicate his life to bringing Turks and Kurds together. On June 29 the court convicted Ocalan and sentenced him to death.

Kurdish groups reacted to Ocalan's conviction with several bombings and suicide attacks. In a July letter, Ocalan appeared to call for an end to the conflict. Turkish Prime Minister Bulent Ecevit responded on August 3, stating that "the separatist terror in Turkey has come to the end of a dead-end street." Ocalan's appeal for a retrial was rejected in November; his sentence had to be approved by parliament and the presidency to be carried out.

When a severe earthquake hit northwestern Turkey in mid-August 1999, Greece sent rescue squads, supplies, and financial aid—a gesture that began to thaw the icy relations between the two countries. In October, Greek Foreign Minister George Papandreou (center right) toured the stricken areas and met with some of the victims.

TURKEY • Information Highlights

Official Name: Republic of Turkey.
Location: Southeastern Europe and southwestern Asia.
Area: 301,382 sq mi (780 580 km²).
Population (July 1999 est.): 65,599,206.
Chief Cities (mid-1995 est.): Ankara, the capital, 2,837,937; Istanbul, 7,774,169; Izmir, 2,017,699; Adana, 1,066,544.
Government: *Head of state,* Suleyman Demirel, president (took office May 16, 1993). *Head of government,* Bulent Ecevit, prime minister (took office December 1998). *Legislature*—Grand National Assembly.
Monetary Unit: Lira (527,210.0 liras equal U.S. $1, Dec. 13, 1999).
Gross Domestic Product (1998 est. U.S.$): $425,400,-000,000 (purchasing power parity).
Economic Indexes: *Consumer Prices* (1998, 1994 = 100): all items, 1,163.0; food, 1,162.0. *Industrial Production* (1998, 1990 = 100): 138.4.
Foreign Trade (1998 U.S.$): *Imports,* $45,369,000,000; *exports,* $25,938,000,000.

During the Ocalan trial, Turkey continued to press its counterinsurgency campaign. On July 7 the European Court of Human Rights criticized Turkey, saying that the government denied its Kurdish citizens freedom of speech and equal justice under the law.

Politics. National elections on April 18 saw a turnout of 87% of the 37 million eligible voters. In order to qualify to sit in the 550-seat parliament, a party had to get a minimum of 10% of the vote; only five parties met that standard. The Democratic Left Party of Bulent Ecevit, since December 1998 the leader of a caretaker government, won 22% of the vote and 136 of the 550 seats. The Nationalist Action Party, a small far-right organization, surprisingly came in second with 18% and 129 seats. The Islamic fundamentalist Virtue Party was reduced to third place, with 15% of the vote and 111 seats. Two long-established centrist parties—the Motherland and True Path groups—gained a total of 171 seats. Ecevit became prime minister of a three-party coalition—the Democratic Left, Nationalist Action, and Motherland parties—and passed a vote of confidence on June 9 by a margin of 354 to 182. Suleyman Demirel continued as the country's president.

The two political issues of Kurdish rights and Islamic fundamentalism appeared in the April national elections. Courts rejected the February request of prosecutors to ban the mostly Kurdish People's Democracy Party from the election on the grounds that the party favored secession and violence, though the party did not gain enough votes for parliamentary seats. An elected Islamist female deputy, Merve Kavakci, was prevented from taking the oath of office when she would not take off a head scarf, the symbol of Islamist identity. The influential Turkish National Security Council on October 28 accused extremist Islamic groups of trying to push Turkey into chaos through bombings and assassinations.

Economy. Politicians attempting to deal with the Turkish economy faced daunting challenges—a 1999 inflation rate of about 50% and a government deficit exceeding $20 billion. Some 40% of the national budget was pledged to paying interest on foreign debt. On July 2 the International Monetary Fund (IMF) promised aid if Turkey reduced its inflation rate and cut the deficit through reductions in farm subsidies and social-security retirement payments. As a result, parliament on August 13 approved several measures aiming at privatization, international mediation of foreign-investment disputes, and reductions in subsidies. At this point, the August 17 earthquake seriously disrupted the general economy as well as reform plans.

Foreign Affairs. Before the earthquakes, Turkish foreign policy continued along a path established in earlier years. Turkey allowed the United States to operate air surveillance over northern Iraq from Turkish territory, maintained cold relations with Greece and Syria, strengthened a military alliance with Israel, and bargained over oil-pipeline routes in the Caucasus region.

Greek assistance during the August earthquake became a symbol indicating that a new stage in Turkish-Greek diplomacy might be possible. On September 5, Greek Foreign Minister George Papandreou accelerated this new development by saying that "it is in Greece's interests to see a European Turkey" that could become a member of the European Union (EU), although only after a resolution of the dispute over Cyprus. When an earthquake struck Greece on September 7, Turkey sent aid.

President Bill Clinton, the third U.S. president ever to visit Turkey, toured the earthquake zone. Clinton went through a tent city of refugees, sharing coffee with the victims and extending his personal sympathy to them. In a speech to parliament on November 15, President Clinton first praised the 50 years of alliance between the United States and Turkey, including recent Turkish assistance in Kosovo, before urging improvements in Turkish-Greek relations and in the treatment of the Kurdish minority in Turkey.

WILLIAM OCHSENWALD
Virginia Polytechnic Institute and State University

Uganda

Despite economic growth, Ugandan security continued to be threatened by several rebel groups during 1999. The Ugandan military provided support to rebels in the Democratic Republic of the Congo.

Politics and Security Issues. President Yoweri Museveni made major cabinet changes in April—dropping eight ministers and replacing Prime Minister Kintu Musoke with Apollo Nsibambi. Vice-President Specioza Wandira Kazibwe retained office, but the ministry of agriculture, animal industry, and fisheries was taken from her. During the second half of 1999, parliament passed a bill to provide for a referendum in June 2000 to decide whether to continue with the "movement system" of government advocated by Museveni or to allow political parties to operate again. Proponents of a multiparty system saw the legislation, and the way it was approved by parliament, as paving the way for continuation of the current government.

Guerrilla actions by two rebel groups, the Allied Democratic Front (ADF) in the west and the Lord's Resistance Army (LRA) in the north, continued in 1999. The ADF was blamed for bombings in the capital, Kampala, during February. Further bombings rocked the capital in April. At the start of March, eight foreign tourists and four Uganda game wardens were kidnapped and killed in Bwindi Impenetrable Forest National Park. Rwandan Hutu rebels operating from the Congo were blamed for the attack, which drew much adverse publicity to Uganda's security situation. While Museveni ordered troops to hunt down those responsible, he altered his previous stand of seeking to defeat the LRA militarily, offering amnesty to the rebel leader, Joseph Kony, and his followers. Uganda and Sudan concluded a peace agreement on December 8; the latter promised to end its support for the LRA, while Uganda promised to stop supporting rebel groups in southern Sudan.

Economy. The Ugandan economy continued to enjoy the highest growth rate—in excess of 7%—in the region. Coffee, Uganda's leading export, experienced a growth of 20% in value for 1998–99. Nevertheless, the year also brought several economic setbacks. A banking crisis, which began in late 1998, continued with the closure of Greenland Bank and the government takeover of the Uganda Commercial Bank. The Uganda shilling fell to an all-time low against the dollar, and the March attack on foreign tourists set back the tourist industry.

UGANDA • Information Highlights

Official Name: Republic of Uganda.
Location: Interior of East Africa.
Area: 91,135 sq mi (236 040 km^2).
Population (July 1999 est.): 22,804,973.
Chief Cities (1991 census): Kampala, the capital, 773,463; Jinja, 60,979; Mbale, 53,634.
Government: *Head of state,* Yoweri Museveni, president (took office Jan. 29, 1986). *Head of government,* Apollo Nsibambi, prime minister (took office April 1999). *Legislature* (unicameral)—National Assembly.
Monetary Unit: Uganda shilling (1,505.00 shillings equal U.S.$1, Dec. 27, 1999).
Gross Domestic Product (1998 est. U.S.$): $22,700,-000,000 (purchasing power parity).
Economic Index (1996, 1990 = 100): *Consumer Prices,* all items, 260.5; food, 226.6.
Foreign Trade (1998 U.S.$): *Imports,* $1,413,000,000; *exports,* $500,000,000.

While promising continued economic assistance, the International Monetary Fund (IMF) and other donors showed reluctance to release such aid to Uganda. They expressed concern about high levels of corruption and the drain on resources caused by Uganda's participation in the civil war in the Democratic Republic of the Congo.

On November 30, Museveni, with the presidents of Kenya and Tanzania, signed a treaty establishing an East African Community that would include a common market.

Foreign Affairs. Uganda continued to be involved in the civil war in the Congo, as its soldiers, and those of Rwanda, supported rebel forces seeking the ouster of President Laurent Kabila. This caused strained relations with Zimbabwe and Angola, whose troops supported Kabila, and with the United States and European countries, which wished to see an end to the conflict.

ROBERT M. MAXON, *West Virginia University*

Ukraine

Presidential elections dominated 1999 in Ukraine. In foreign affairs, Ukraine continued its balancing act of trying to lean toward the West without offending Russia.

Politics. Ukraine's second post-Soviet presidential-election campaign ran from midspring to late fall. President Leonid Kuchma won reelection to a second term, but not easily. Since Kuchma was elected in 1994, his pro-market policies had not really taken hold but had left a legacy of public discontent. By the time the formal presidential campaign was under way, the Central Election Commission had registered 15 candidates. When voters went to the polls for the first round of voting on October 31, there were only 13 candidates, but this multiplicity created an advantage for Kuchma.

Recognizing that the various anti-Kuchma candidates would divide the vote, four of the candidates attempted to form a last-minute alliance, but in the end they could not agree on who would represent the alliance on the ballot. Kuchma went on to win the first round with 36.5% of the vote, but because he did not win a plurality, a runoff election was required. His opponent in the runoff was Communist Party leader Petro Symonenko, who had garnered 22.2% of the vote. While foreign observers judged the balloting to have been fair, the campaign had been rough, marred by forged newspapers, a leaflet claiming Kuchma had died, a grenade attack on another candidate, and an attempted parliamentary maneuver to remove the president from the ballot.

In the November 14 runoff, Symonenko's hope for support from the other leftist candidates fell short, while Kuchma gained the support of the fifth-place finisher as well as of the right-wing candidates. Kuchma won reelection in a landslide, 56.5% to 37.5%, but the numbers alone did not tell the full story. Kuchma converted the second-round voting into a plebiscite on the most unsavory aspects of Ukraine's communist past, gaining his second term as the lesser of two evils.

The issue of power-sharing also roiled Ukrainian politics during 1999. Early in the year, Kuchma survived the parliamentary opposition's attempt to revise the constitution to abolish the presidency and transform Ukraine into a parliamentary republic. In the fall, Kuchma retaliated by initiating a signature-gathering campaign for a referendum on constitutional amendments that would convert the Verkhovna Rada (parliament) into a bicameral legislature, with a new upper house representing the 25 regions that would be filled by the governors, who are appointed by the president. Kuchma's election victory enhanced the referendum campaign's prospects for success.

In December, Prime Minister Valeriy Pustovoytenko resigned. Kuchma named central-bank chairman Viktor Yushchenko to replace him, and the parliament approved the appointment later in the month.

Economy. Ukraine began 1999 reeling from the Russian financial crisis of 1998, which had driven Ukrainian inflation to 20%. By election time, the indicators continued to reflect economic problems. Some $2.5 billion was owed in unpaid wages and pensions to the population, the majority of whom lived below the poverty line. Unemployment stood at 25%, and 17% of those who worked were employed in the "shadow economy"—businesses that had gone underground to avoid paying taxes. Meanwhile, vast numbers of Ukrainians traveled to the Czech Republic and Poland in search of work as manual laborers. By fall the gross domestic product (GDP) was predicted to decrease by 1.7%. A bright spot was the harvest, which was projected to be a little ahead of that of 1998. However, foreign trade was down by a quarter, foreign investment fell by nearly one half, and inflation was expected to run at about 20% again. The legislative-executive stalemate over economic policy also hampered the situation. While parliament thwarted the president's efforts at tax reform and privatization, Kuchma in turn consistently vetoed parliament's budget-busting spending bills.

Foreign Affairs. Kuchma continued to maintain a foreign-policy course based on Ukraine's aspiration to join the European Union (EU), while at the same time cooperating with Russia. Most important was the final conclusion in early 1999 of the Treaty on Friendship with Russia, along with several agreements between the countries on the Black Sea naval fleet. The International Monetary Fund (IMF) approved the release of another tranche of its three-year, $2.5 billion loan, while Ukraine expanded its contacts with the North Atlantic Treaty Organization (NATO). The leftist parliamentary majority attempted unsuccessfully to derail these pro-Western moves. Finally, Ukraine was faced with the threat of suspension from the Council of Europe if it did not improve its human-rights record by 2000.

ROBERT SHARLET, *Union College*

UKRAINE • Information Highlights

Official Name: Ukraine.
Location: Eastern Europe.
Area: 233,090 sq mi (603 700 km^2).
Population (July 1999 est.): 49,811,174.
Chief Cities (Jan. 1, 1995 est.): Kiev, the capital, 2,635,000; Kharkov, 1,576,000; Dnepropetrovsk, 1,162,000; Donetsk, 1,102,000; Odessa, 1,060,000.
Government: *Head of state,* Leonid Kuchma, president (took office July 1994). *Head of government,* Viktor Yushchenko, prime minister (took office December 1999). *Legislature* (unicameral)—Supreme Council (Verkhovna Rada).
Monetary Unit: Hryvnia (5.2600 hryvnias equal U.S.$1, Dec. 27, 1999).
Gross Domestic Product (1998 est. U.S.$): $108,500,000,000 (purchasing power parity).
Foreign Trade (1998 est. U.S.$): *Imports,* $13,100,000,000; *exports,* $11,300,000,000.

United Nations

The last year of the millennium saw the United Nations (UN) once more at the center of the world community's international activities. UN Secretary-General Kofi Annan was given some of the credit for restoring the organization to its predominant role in the world. Annan had won the trust and confidence of the UN's member nations with his doctrine of pragmatism, mixed with his long experience at the world body. As a result, the UN was undertaking some of the most complex responsibilities in its history. It was administering two territories thousands of miles from each other and from UN headquarters in New York City—the Yugoslavian province of Kosovo in the Balkans and the Indonesian territory of East Timor in Asia. The UN moved into both areas after violent conflicts decimated the people, their property, their cities, and the very structure of their lives. Being mandated by the international community to rebuild these territories represented a rebirth for the UN after a period in which it seemed marginalized from world events. After the end of the Cold War, great emphasis was placed on using the UN to correct the world's ills. But an anti-UN Congress in the United States blocked the move until it became apparent that, unless the United States wanted to be the world's policeman, it must turn to the UN.

The year 1999 also was marked by UN accountability and lessons learned from sometimes-deadly past mistakes in Srebrenica, Bosnia, and in Rwanda—another two areas thousands of miles apart, but where the UN and the international community had ignored warnings of genocides and had failed to act in time to save thousands of people. Annan was given reports on each of the genocides and said that "the tragedy of Srebrenica will haunt our history forever." According to Annan, the lesson taught by these episodes was to address issues such as the difficulty the UN faces when it is given a mandate without the means to back it up. The secretary-general emphasized that "when the international community makes a solemn promise to safeguard and protect innocent civilians from massacre, then it must be willing to back its promise with the necessary means."

Commenting on the report on the UN role in the genocide in Rwanda, Annan said that approximately 800,000 Rwandans were slaughtered by their fellow countrymen and -women, for no other reason than that they belonged to a particular ethnic group. "That is genocide in its purest and most evil form," he said, adding that "all of us must regret that we did not do more to prevent it." He went further, saying: "On behalf of the United Nations, I acknowledge this failure and express my deep remorse."

With the UN's revived role in the world, its officials promised in 1999 to put the lessons they had learned to good use.

Security Council. Until the fall of the Berlin Wall in 1989, the Security Council, the UN's main organ, met only for sudden emergencies. Since then, however, the council has

© Jeff Christensen/Reuters/Archive Photos

Richard Holbrooke (left), whose appointment as U.S. ambassador to the United Nations was confirmed by the U.S. Senate on Aug. 5, 1999, after a long delay, conferred with UN Secretary-General Kofi Annan at UN headquarters after taking office.

held consultations behind closed doors, sometimes several times a day, to discuss crisis areas. In cases in which it needs to act on the outcome of those discussions, it then holds an open meeting. During the Cold War, council members fought out their differences in open meetings for all the world to hear and see.

Because so much of the council's activity is controlled by its five permanent members (China, Russia, France, the United States, and the United Kingdom) and carried out in secrecy, other UN members have been demanding in recent years that the council be reformed. But even though a working group has been set up to discuss reform, there is little agreement about how it should be carried out. Some want the permanent members to give up their vetoes—but the five would be sure to veto any move in that direction. Yet others merely want to exercise veto power themselves. Some believe the council should have 20 or so members instead of the 15 currently at the table, while others say that to increase membership only would make decisions more difficult. Most delegates agree, however, that the Security Council is undemocratic in its current form and should be changed—but real change would be blocked by the very members that make the body undemocratic in the first place.

In 1999 the Security Council had one of the busiest years in its history. The council was mandated by the UN Charter to authorize the use of force. Early in the year, however, divisions over state sovereignty prevented it from playing a role in the use of force against Yugoslavia over the issue of Kosovo (*see* THE KOSOVO CRISIS, page 78). One side insisted that the sovereignty of a nation must not be breached; the other side said there could be exceptions when people were in need. In response to the council's inaction, the North Atlantic Treaty Organization (NATO) bypassed it, launching a bombing campaign on its own. But after the military action ended, the UN was called upon to administer Kosovo for the next few years. When East Timor exploded in violence after a UN-organized referendum in August favored Timorese independence from Indonesia, and local militias reacted by attacking civilians (reportedly with the support of the Indonesian military), the UN authorized an Australian-led force to pacify the situation. It also set up a plan to send its own troops and civilian staff to administer East Timor until independence.

Much of the council's work in 1999 was in Africa, as it tried to end civil wars in Angola, Sierra Leone, the Democratic Republic of the Congo, and other crisis zones. But most of its time was spent trying to come up with a new policy toward Iraq. After Iraq was bombed in December 1998 by the United States and Britain in strikes that were not authorized by the UN, Iraq refused to permit UN weapons inspectors to return unless sanctions against it (put in place following Iraq's 1990 invasion of Kuwait) were lifted. Finally, after months of negotiations that mainly involved the five permanent members of the council, a resolution was adopted on December 17 that would suspend the sanctions temporarily if the new disarmament inspectors and the International Atomic Energy Agency (IAEA) report that Iraq has cooperated with them for at least 21 months. The council vote was 11 in favor, but four members—France, China, Russia, and Malaysia—abstained, weakening the resolution in the eyes of Iraq. The Iraqi government rejected it.

General Assembly. The 54th session of the General Assembly, which opened in mid-September, had as its elected president Namibian Foreign Minister Theo-Ben Gurirab. The new session of the UN General Assembly "is heralding in a new millennium," Gurirab told delegates on the opening day. He added that the organization was ready "to craft workable solutions and institutions for the problems of our planet." Gurirab said that this upcoming session of the General Assembly was the first ever to straddle two millennia. The people of the world, he said, were yearning for a peaceful, humane, and prosperous world—and without the UN, this could not come about. At the "Millennium Summit" in September 2000, world leaders will be asked to present their views on the role the UN should play in the 21st century.

The session began with the admittance of three new members—Kiribati, the Republic of Nauru, and the Kingdom of Tonga—increasing UN membership to 188. The annual request for Taiwan to be part of the organization was rejected.

The General Assembly had a full agenda, with more than 163 items ranging from discussions concerning the protection of child soldiers to the meaning of globalization for poorer countries, which considered themselves marginalized from its advantages.

Peacekeeping. At the opening of the General Assembly, Annan surprised dele-

ORGANIZATION OF THE UNITED NATIONS

THE SECRETARIAT *Secretary-General:* Kofi Annan (until Dec. 31, 2001)
THE GENERAL ASSEMBLY (1999) *President:* Theo-Ben Gurirab, Namibia

The 188 member nations were as follows:

Afghanistan
Albania
Algeria
Andorra
Angola
Antigua and Barbuda
Argentina
Armenia
Australia
Austria
Azerbaijan
Bahamas
Bahrain
Bangladesh
Barbados
Belarus
Belgium
Belize
Benin
Bhutan
Bolivia
Bosnia and Herzegovina
Botswana
Brazil
Brunei Darussalam
Bulgaria
Burkina Faso
Burundi
Cambodia
Cameroon
Canada
Cape Verde
Central African Republic
Chad
Chile
China, People's Republic of
Colombia
Comoros
Congo
Congo, Democratic Republic of the
Costa Rica
Croatia
Cuba
Cyprus
Czech Republic
Denmark
Djibouti
Dominica
Dominican Republic
Ecuador
Egypt
El Salvador
Equatorial Guinea
Eritrea
Estonia
Ethiopia
Fiji
Finland
France
Gabon
Gambia
Georgia
Germany
Ghana
Greece
Grenada
Guatemala
Guinea
Guinea-Bissau
Guyana
Haiti
Honduras
Hungary
Iceland
India
Indonesia
Iran
Iraq
Ireland
Israel
Italy
Ivory Coast
Jamaica
Japan
Jordan
Kazakhstan
Kenya
Kiribati
Korea, Democratic People's Republic of
Korea, Republic of
Kuwait
Kyrgyzstan
Laos
Latvia
Lebanon
Lesotho
Liberia
Libya
Liechtenstein
Lithuania
Luxembourg
Macedonia, The Former Yugoslav Republic of
Madagascar
Malawi
Malaysia
Maldives
Mali
Malta
Marshall Islands
Mauritania
Mauritius
Mexico
Micronesia
Moldova
Monaco
Mongolia
Morocco
Mozambique
Myanmar
Namibia
Nauru
Nepal
Netherlands
New Zealand
Nicaragua
Niger
Nigeria
Norway
Oman
Pakistan
Palau
Panama
Papua New Guinea
Paraguay
Peru
Philippines
Poland
Portugal
Qatar
Romania
Russia
Rwanda
Saint Kitts and Nevis
Saint Lucia
Saint Vincent and The Grenadines
Samoa
San Marino
São Tomé and Príncipe
Saudi Arabia
Senegal
Seychelles
Sierra Leone
Singapore
Slovak Republic
Slovenia
Solomon Islands
Somalia
South Africa
Spain
Sri Lanka
Sudan
Suriname
Swaziland
Sweden
Syria
Tajikistan
Tanzania
Thailand
Togo
Tonga
Trinidad and Tobago
Tunisia
Turkey
Turkmenistan
Uganda
Ukraine
United Arab Emirates
United Kingdom
United States
Uruguay
Uzbekistan
Vanuatu
Venezuela
Vietnam
Yemen
Yugoslavia
Zambia
Zimbabwe

COMMITTEES

General. Composed of 28 members as follows: The General Assembly president; the 21 General Assembly vice-presidents (heads of delegations or their deputies of Algeria, Bolivia, China, Congo, Cuba, France, Grenada, Iceland, Iran, Iraq, Ivory Coast, North Korea, Lithuania, Monaco, Nigeria, Russia, Seychelles, Tajikistan, Thailand, United Kingdom, United States) and the chairmen of the main committees below, which are composed of all 188 member countries.

First (Disarmament and International Security): Raimundo Gonzalez (Chile)

Second (Economic and Financial): Roble Olhaye (Djibouti)

Third (Social, Humanitarian and Cultural): Vladimir Galuska (Czech Republic)

Fourth (Special Political and Decolonization): Sotirios Zackheos (Cyprus)

Fifth (Administrative and Budgetary): Penny Wensley (Australia)

Sixth (Legal): Phakiso Mochochoko (Lesotho)

THE ECONOMIC AND SOCIAL COUNCIL

President: Francesco Paolo Fulci (Italy)
Membership ends on December 31 of the year noted.

Algeria (2000)
Angola (2002)
Austria (2002)
Bahrain (2002)
Belarus (2000)
Belgium (2000)
Benin (2002)
Bolivia (2001)
Brazil (2000)
Bulgaria (2001)
Burkina Faso (2002)
Cameroon (2002)
Canada (2001)
China (2001)
Colombia (2000)
Comoros (2000)
Congo, Democratic Republic of the (2001)
Costa Rica (2002)
Croatia (2002)
Cuba (2002)
Czech Republic (2001)
Denmark (2001)
Fiji (2002)
France (2002)
Germany (2002)
Greece (2002)
Guinea-Bissau (2001)
Honduras (2001)
India (2000)
Indonesia (2001)
Italy (2000)
Japan (2002)
Lesotho (2000)
Mauritius (2000)
Mexico (2002)
Morocco (2001)
New Zealand (2000)
Norway (2001)
Oman (2000)
Pakistan (2000)
Poland (2000)
Portugal (2002)
Russia (2001)
Rwanda (2001)
Saint Lucia (2000)
Saudi Arabia (2001)
Sierra Leone (2000)
Sudan (2002)
Suriname (2002)
Syria (2001)
United Kingdom (2001)
United States (2000)
Venezuela (2001)
Vietnam (2000)

THE SECURITY COUNCIL

Membership ends on December 31 of the year noted; asterisks indicate permanent membership.

Argentina (2000)
Bangladesh (2001)
Canada (2000)
China*
France*
Jamaica (2001)
Malaysia (2000)
Mali (2001)
Namibia (2000)
Netherlands (2000)
Russia*
Tunisia (2001)
Ukraine (2001)
United Kingdom*
United States*

THE TRUSTEESHIP COUNCIL

Composed of the five permanent members of the Security Council: China, France, Russia, United Kingdom, United States. The Council meets as occasion requires.

THE INTERNATIONAL COURT OF JUSTICE

President: Stephen M. Schwebel (United States, 2006)
Vice-President: Christopher G. Weeramantry (Sri Lanka, 2000)
Membership ends on February 5 of the year noted.

Mohammed Bedjaoui (Algeria, 2006)
Carl-August Fleischhauer (Germany, 2003)
Gilbert Guillaume (France, 2000)
Géza Herczegh (Hungary, 2003)
Rosalyn Higgins (United Kingdom, 2000)
Pieter H. Kooijmans (Netherlands, 2006)
Abdul G. Koroma (Sierra Leone, 2003)
Shigeru Oda (Japan, 2003)
Gonzalo Parra-Aranguren (Venezuela, 2000)
Raymond Ranjeva (Madagascar, 2000)
José Francisco Rezek (Brazil, 2006)
Shi Jiuyong (China, 2003)
Vladen S. Vereshchetin (Russia, 2006)
Christopher G. Weeramantry (Sri Lanka, 2000)

INTERGOVERNMENTAL AGENCIES

Food and Agricultural Organization (FAO); International Atomic Energy Agency (IAEA); International Bank for Reconstruction and Development (World Bank); International Civil Aviation Organization (ICAO); International Fund for Agricultural Development (IFAD); International Labor Organization (ILO); International Maritime Organization (IMO); International Monetary Fund (IMF); International Telecommunication Union (ITU); United Nations Educational, Scientific and Cultural Organization (UNESCO); United Nations Industrial Development Organization (UNIDO); Universal Postal Union (UPU); World Health Organization (WHO); World Intellectual Property Organization (WIPO); World Meteorological Organization (WMO); World Trade Organization (WTO).

gates by introducing the concept of "humanitarian intervention." He said that the international community should intervene in cases of human suffering. Annan further explained that, while the Security Council was still the ultimate authority in peacekeeping matters, it always should be able to form a consensus to aid people who are suffering. The concept caused intense debate, with numerous governments denouncing it as a violation of sovereignty, and it was likely to continue to be a controversial topic in the future.

UN peacekeeping expanded greatly in 1999. Its operations in Kosovo called for approximately 5,000 personnel, and its mandated duties in administering East Timor were expected to employ another 10,000. In October a new operation was established in Sierra Leone, and the authorized military strength was expected to reach at least 6,000. By December the UN was carrying out 17 peacekeeping activities, using 14,615 military personnel and civilian police as well as some 9,284 civilians.

In addition, by late 1999 the organization had 59 military observers in the Democratic Republic of the Congo. Once peace was established firmly there, that operation could be expanded to thousands of peacekeepers. And the UN also was considering assisting in the border dispute between Eritrea and Ethiopia.

The cost of operations from July 1999 to June 2000 was estimated to be almost $2 billion. Yet by December 1, about $1.76 billion was owed the UN by member nations that had not paid their peacekeeping bills. Another problem was that the staffing of the UN peacekeeping office had been reduced by 20% as part of an overall reform program that included personnel cuts throughout the organization. The UN was preparing to hire additional experts to compensate for the loss of staff.

The UN was working to ready its standby system so that it could answer an urgent call far more quickly than it had in the past. It also appealed to governments to have trained troops on hand, should they prove necessary.

Financing. The UN's financial picture improved during 1999 for the first time in years. In previous years the UN was so poor that it had to borrow from peacekeeping funds to support its regular budget. But in 1999 the UN had a $100 million budget surplus. That good news was due mainly to a U.S. payment of approximately $726 million between January 1 and the end of December. In mid-November the U.S. Congress passed legislation authorizing repayment over three years of $819 million of the approximately $1.2 billion in back dues the United States owed the UN. In return for making this payment, the legislation required that the UN make several changes, including reducing the U.S. share of the UN budget from 25% to 20%, and decreasing the U.S. share of peacekeeping funds from 31% to 25%.

Meanwhile, 122 other governments paid their regular UN dues in full and in some cases paid what they owed from previous years. In contrast, only 117 governments had paid in full by late 1998. But the many governments that contributed troops and equipment for UN peacekeeping had gone for years without being reimbursed for their costs. In 1999 a large number of governments paid their peacekeeping assessments, but the UN still owed approximately $729 million to those that contributed troops and equipment.

Treaties. In June the International Labor Organization, an agency of the UN, adopted a treaty to abolish many of the worst forms of child labor. The pact was intended to end the exploitation of millions of children throughout the world who were involved in such activities as pornography, slavery, hazardous work, and forced recruitment into military service. The treaty prohibited persons under 18 from being conscripted as soldiers against their will, but it did not ban voluntary enlistment, a compromise adopted at the urging of the United States, which allows 17-year-olds to enlist.

The UN also modified a 20-year-old treaty on women's rights to create an international committee to rule on claims of discrimination against women. A protocol was added to the 1979 Convention on the Elimination of All Forms of Discrimination Against Women that would allow a woman suffering discrimination to appeal to the committee once she had exhausted all means of redress in her own country. The committee also was given the power to investigate complaints if it received "reliable information indicating grave or systematic violations" of women's rights. The new protocol was scheduled to come before the 54th session of the General Assembly; it must be ratified by at least ten nations to come into force.

See also LAW—*International*.

RUTH PEARSON
Freelance United Nations Correspondent

United States

For Americans the final year of the 20th century began ominously, with a constitutional crisis at home because of the impeachment of President Bill Clinton, and a war abroad as a result of the effort by the United States to prevent the purging of ethnic Albanians from the province of Kosovo, their homeland in Yugoslavia. But the impeachment ended quickly, with Clinton's acquittal; and the war concluded in ten weeks, on terms dictated by the United States and its North Atlantic Treaty Organization (NATO) allies, without any American combat casualties.

That left the country free to luxuriate in the continued economic boom and in the benign social climate, reflected by declines in such troublesome phenomena as teenage pregnancy, divorce, and violent crime. No wonder then that a year-end survey by the Pew Center on the Peoples and the Press indicated that citizens were feeling less angry at their government and more compassionate toward the needy than they had been in years. Certainly there was no lack of optimism about material goals. Another survey showed that nearly four out of five college students expected to be millionaires. But such statistics begged a critical question: Would affluence merely create smugness and acquisitiveness, or would it provide Americans with the confidence to face the challenges the new century would bring?

Domestic Affairs

The Presidency. "America is working again," President Clinton declared in his State of the Union address on Jan. 19, 1999. Striving to behave as if his impeachment trial going forward in the Senate was not really taking place (*see* SPECIAL REPORT, pages 559–60), the president set a confident and lofty tone for his seventh year in the White House. "The promise of our future is limitless. But we cannot realize that promise if we allow the hum of our prosperity to lull us into complacency. How we fare as a nation far into the 21st century depends upon what we do as a nation today."

Many analysts applauded the president's rhetoric but questioned whether he was up to the task of moving the country ahead that he himself had outlined. "You have to have a leader who has what President [George] Bush once called the 'vision thing,'" said historian Michael Beschloss, "a leader who says, 'here we are with a surplus. This is a time we can really attack basic problems of poverty and health care and education.'"

In his State of the Union address, the main problem Clinton targeted was Social Security. Rather than raising taxes or cutting benefits, Clinton urged the Congress to "make the historic decision to invest the surplus to save Social Security," which by some projections would run into financial trouble

© David Hume Kennerly/Corbis-Sygma

The new speaker of the House of Representatives, J. Dennis Hastert (right), *and Vice-President Al Gore joined in the applause as President Bill Clinton delivered his State of the Union address on Jan. 19, 1999. The president's talk focused on such programs as Social Security and ignored his impeachment trial, which was occurring in the Senate at the time.*

in about 30 years. The president proposed using about 60% of the budget surplus—projected to reach $4.4 trillion in the next 15 years—to bolster Social Security, while using about 15% to bolster Medicare. He also called for expanding Medicare to help pay for prescription drugs, which he labeled "the greatest growing need" for senior citizens.

Liberal critics complained that the president should have proposed using the budget surplus to fund domestic programs. Fiscal conservatives argued that by failing to propose tax increases or benefit reductions for Social Security, Clinton merely was delaying the day of reckoning for the program. And they added that his proposal to help pay for prescription drugs would increase the financial problems of Medicare.

While the debate over his proposals raged on Capitol Hill, Clinton turned his attention to another national problem, youth violence, as a result of an outbreak of shooting at a high school in Littleton, CO. The violence took the lives of 12 students, a teacher, and the two student attackers, who shot themselves; and it came in the wake of a rash of shootings in schools over the previous two years. "We must do more to reach out to our children and teach them to express their anger and to resolve their conflicts with words, not weapons," the president declared. In addition to pressing for new gun-control measures, President Clinton called a White House conference on violence. He used that occasion to decry pointedly the "coarsening of the culture," and to urge the entertainment industry to stop marketing to children products that glorify violence, as key lawmakers renewed warnings that Hollywood faced a federal investigation. The president followed up that rhetoric by announcing a two-pronged federal probe by the Federal Trade Commission and the Justice Department of the entertainment industry's marketing of violent movies, music, and video games to children. "We can no longer ignore the well-documented connection between violence in the media and the effects that it has on children's behavior," Clinton said.

Even as the president tried to put his impeachment behind him, his actions provoked a new congressional inquiry in August, due to his making a conditional offer of clemency to 16 members of a Puerto Rican nationalist group called FALN, the Spanish initials for Armed Forces of National Liberation. This organization, dedicated to bringing about the independence of Puerto Rico, was involved in more than 100 bombings of political and military installations in the United States from 1974 to 1983. Twelve of the 16 ultimately accepted the offer, which was conditioned on their renouncing the use of terrorism to achieve their goal.

Clinton's action regarding the nationalists came under fire immediately from Republicans, who claimed that the president had acted to help First Lady Hillary Rodham Clinton's candidacy for the Senate in New York state, which has a substantial Puerto Rican population, and that he had undercut his own administration's efforts to combat terrorism. Mrs. Clinton herself then called on her husband to withdraw the offer, because the Puerto Ricans were slow to reject terrorism as a tactic. It also was disclosed that Louis J. Freeh, director of the Federal Bureau of Investigation, had opposed the clemency, claiming that the move would spur the ultranationalist movement. Responding to the criticism, the president denied that he had consulted his wife before making the offer, and claimed he had not taken political considerations into account. Clinton said that he was influenced by the lengthy sentences the imprisoned men already had served and by the lobbying of former President Jimmy Carter and South African Archbishop Desmond Tutu. Nevertheless, the House Government Reform Committee, chaired by Republican Rep. Dan Burton (IN), launched an investigation into his decision.

In the midst of this controversy, Clinton was forced to deal with yet another potentially damaging investigation, this one arising out of the FBI's 1993 assault by federal officers on the Branch Davidian compound near Waco, TX, that took the lives of 75 Branch Davidian members, including cult

UNITED STATES • Information Highlights

Official Name: United States of America.
Location: Central North America.
Area: 3,717,813 sq mi (9 629 091 km^2).
Population (July 1999 est.): 272,639,608.
Chief Cities (July 1, 1998, est.): Washington, DC, the capital, 523,124; New York, 7,420,166; Los Angeles, 3,597,556; Chicago, 2,802,079; Houston, 1,786,691; Philadelphia, 1,436,287; San Diego, 1,220,666.
Government: *Head of state and government,* Bill Clinton, president (took office Jan. 20, 1993). *Legislature*—Congress: Senate and House of Representatives.
Monetary Unit: Dollar.
Gross Domestic Product (1998 est.): $8,511,000,000,000 (purchasing power parity).
Economic Indexes (1998, 1990 = 100): *Consumer Prices,* all items, 124.8; food, 122.0. *Industrial Production,* 132.8.
Foreign Trade (1998): *Imports,* $944,353,000,000; *exports,* $682,497,000,000.

SPECIAL REPORT

The Bill Clinton Impeachment Trial

When the U.S. House of Representatives closed out the 105th Congress in December 1998 by impeaching President Bill Clinton on two counts—perjury and the obstruction of justice—the stage was set for high drama in the Senate. Both articles of impeachment had been adopted by largely party-line votes after bitter and divisive debate. This rancorous prelude raised concerns as 1999 began that Clinton's trial, only the second presidential-impeachment trial in American history, would turn into a prolonged and polarizing confrontation.

The Trial. But as it turned out, the Senate proceedings were far blander and calmer than the turbulent debate in the House. The main reason for this was simple arithmetic. Though Senate Republicans outnumbered Democrats, 55 to 45, for conviction on impeachment charges, the Constitution requires a two-thirds majority of 67. This would force advocates of conviction to get 12 more votes than there were Republican senators, a highly unlikely prospect. That reality was made clear in a key test roll call on January 27, when the Republican majority, with the addition of one Democratic senator, voted solidly to defeat a Democratic motion to dismiss the charges. On its face, the 56–44 vote was a victory for the GOP. With all but one Democrat voting for dismissal, however, even the GOP House managers who determinedly argued the case against Clinton realized that the president ultimately would be acquitted.

With the outcome all but assured, it became easier for both sides to compromise, as they did on the issue of witnesses. Impeachment advocates wanted to hear from witnesses, while Clinton's defenders said they were unnecessary. The Senate solved the impasse by voting to call Monica Lewinsky—the former White House intern whose involvement with the president had led to the charges against him—and two presidential confidantes, White House aide Sidney Blumenthal and Washington lawyer Vernon Jordan. But instead of having these witnesses appear at public sessions of the trial, the Senate agreed to limit their testimony to videotaped excerpts of depositions each gave behind closed doors. None of their testimony appeared to alter the outlook of senators on either side of the issue.

While there was much talk about President Clinton's legacy, White House counsel Charles Ruff, who defended the president, was fighting not just for Clinton's place in history, but, more

With U.S. Chief Justice William H. Rehnquist presiding, the U.S. Senate acquitted William Jefferson Clinton of two articles of impeachment on Feb. 12, 1999. It was the second such trial of a U.S. president in history.

U.S. Senate Photo Studio

(continues)

urgently, to preserve enough of his reputation so that he could govern effectively in the two years that remained of his term. Accordingly, Ruff set a high and limited standard for determining guilt. "There is only one question before you," Ruff told the senators. "Would it put at risk the liberty of the people to retain the president in office? Putting aside partisan animus, if you can honestly say that it would not, that those liberties are safely in his hands, then you must vote to acquit."

On the prosecution's side, House Judiciary Chairman Henry Hyde, who had overseen the impeachment inquiry in the House, was fighting for the future of his party—to avoid having Republicanism being equated with intolerance and extremism. And to judge the president, Hyde proposed a different standard than Ruff's—not the imminent threat of tyranny but, instead, the threat to the presidency as an institution. "A failure to convict will make a statement that lying under oath, while unpleasant and to be avoided, is not all that serious," Hyde said.

On February 12 came the Senate verdict. The vote to impeach on the count of perjury was 45 to 55, with ten Republicans joining the solid phalanx of Democrats for acquittal. On the charge of obstruction of justice, the vote split 50 to 50, with five Republicans deserting their party. The White House could take some satisfaction in the failure of Republicans to get a majority on either count. But no one on Clinton's side could take much solace from the day's reckoning. Although a bipartisan group of senators failed to obtain a vote on a motion censuring President Clinton for bringing "shame and dishonor" to himself and to his office, Sen. Dianne Feinstein (D-CA) entered a censure statement, signed by 29 Democrats and nine Republicans, into *The Congressional Record*. All told, 82 senators went on record as denouncing the president's conduct, even though they could not summon a majority to support either censure or removal from office.

The Aftermath. In anticipating the president's acquittal, some of Clinton's defenders worried that he might gloat over the result. Instead, the president sought to convey a feeling of humility. "I want to say again to the American people how profoundly sorry I am for what I said and did to trigger these events and the great burden they have imposed on the Congress and the American people." Asked whether he could "forgive and forget," Clinton replied in the same tone, "I believe any person who asks for forgiveness has to be prepared to give it." Later, though, he made plain he was not embarrassed by his impeachment. "I do not regard this impeachment vote as some great badge of shame," he told Dan Rather of CBS News. "I do not. Because, I do not believe it was warranted, and I don't think it was right." To the contrary, Clinton said, "...I am honored that something that was indefensible was pursued and that I had the opportunity to defend the Constitution."

The end of the struggle over Clinton's impeachment did not end the controversy over his behavior. Less than two weeks after his acquittal, the media aired a new charge against him that was unprovable but that many thought credible. The accuser was Juanita Broaddrick, an Arkansas nursing-home operator, who claimed that Clinton had forced her to submit to his sexual advances in a convention hotel room more than 20 years earlier. And on April 12, Federal Judge Susan Webber Wright, who in 1998 had dismissed the Paula Jones sexual-harassment suit against Clinton, found the president in contempt of court for lying about his affair with Monica Lewinsky in the Jones case. The judge later ordered Clinton to pay nearly $90,000 to Paula Jones' lawyers for extra work they performed because of his false testimony.

Some scholars worried that the prolonged legal battle over impeachment might harm the institution of the presidency. But others argued that image of the presidency would be shaped by the conduct of Clinton's successors. There was one institutional casualty of the Clinton scandal—the office of independent counsel, whose current occupant, Kenneth Starr, was blamed by many for causing extra confusion and bitterness during the controversy. After even Starr himself, in Senate testimony, said the 21-year-old law creating the office he held tries to "cram a fourth branch of government into our three-branch system," Congress let the statute expire. Starr, meanwhile, resigned as independent counsel in mid-October. Former federal prosecutor Robert Ray was appointed as his successor and was to supervise the drafting of a final report.

On the political front, though, it appeared that the character issue, which was at the heart of Clinton's impeachment, would remain a potent factor. This was demonstrated by the early rhetoric of the presidential candidates for 2000. Other evidence of the lingering political impact of the scandal came from First Lady Hillary Rodham Clinton, who suggested in a magazine interview that her husband's sexual behavior may have resulted from his troubled childhood. In response to criticism, she denied that she was trying to make excuses for the president.

ROBERT SHOGAN

leader David Koresh. The tragic end to this standoff between the government and religious separatists, among other things, reportedly inspired Timothy J. McVeigh two years later to blow up the federal building in Oklahoma City.

The renewal of the Waco controversy stemmed from the disclosure by the FBI that its agents may have fired some potentially flammable tear-gas canisters on the final day of the siege of the compound. This admission, which reversed six years of denials by the bureau that it had used flammable munitions in the last hours of the Branch Davidian siege, resulted from efforts at discovery by lawyers for Waco families and survivors who had been pressing a wrongful-death suit against the government. Attorney General Janet Reno immediately vowed to find out why the FBI had suppressed the truth for so long. But she and other federal law-enforcement officials faced serious credibility problems, which were magnified by tension between Reno and FBI Director Freeh. Their mutual mistrust was underlined when Reno ordered U.S. marshals to FBI headquarters to seize a previously undisclosed tape recording of conversations between bureau commanders and field agents during the assault on the compound. Shrugging off demands that she resign, Reno named former U.S. Sen. John C. Danforth (R-MO) as special counsel to investigate the battle at Waco and the allegations of a cover-up.

The president could take some comfort in the fact that prolonged controversies involving two of his appointees finally were put to rest. In September, Clinton's former Housing Secretary Henry G. Cisneros resolved 18 felony charges on the eve of his trial by pleading guilty to a single misdemeanor count of lying to the FBI about money he paid to a former mistress. The plea bargain ended a wide-ranging independent-counsel investigation that lasted more than four years. The following month, Interior Secretary Bruce Babbitt was cleared by an independent counsel of allegations that he lied to a Senate committee about his role in rejecting an Indian casino in Wisconsin four years earlier.

Clinton suffered a jolt in the international-policy arena late in the year, when vigorous and sometimes violent demonstrations by antitrade groups delayed the opening of a global meeting of the World Trade Organization (WTO) in Seattle. On a visit to that city, Clinton condemned the violence and defended his open-trade agenda, which set off the demonstrations, by claiming that, over the long run, it would benefit most Americans.

© Doug Mills/AP/Wide World Photos

Attorney General Janet Reno named John Danforth (right) *to conduct an investigation of the 1993 federal assault against the Branch Davidian compound.*

Congress. From the start, it was clear that the first session of the 106th Congress would have a hard time accomplishing much. The usual partisan tensions symptomatic of divided government were exacerbated by the bitter struggle over impeachment. And the Republicans, nominally in control on Capitol Hill, were handicapped in the House of Representatives by their narrow majority and by the inexperience of their rookie speaker, J. Dennis Hastert of Illinois (*see* BIOGRAPHY), who took over after two months of extraordinary leadership turmoil.

Seeking traction on this uncertain ground, Republicans rallied around an old standby— tax cuts. They put forward a $792 billion tax-relief package over ten years but were unable to stir much enthusiasm for their proposal in the hustings. And when the president kept his promise to veto the measure, no one even tried to negotiate a follow-up compromise. Instead the Republicans shifted ground, and—seeking to steal some of President Clinton's thunder—sought to present themselves as the true defenders of Social Security. Denouncing Clinton's various spending proposals as raids on the Social Security surplus, the Republicans promised—and won Democratic backing—to end the long-standing budgetary practice of using Social Security revenues to finance other parts of government. Indeed, the GOP claimed that the massive compromise spending bill negotiated with President Clinton, which brought to a close a year of congressional wrangling with the White House, contained a "lockbox" preventing Social Security's surplus funds from being looted to finance other government programs. In fact, though, the nonpartisan Congressional Budget Office in its own analysis predicted that spending in fiscal year 2000 would draw about $19 billion from Social Security surpluses, though that figure could shrink if tax revenues should grow.

The $385 billion spending bill, containing appropriations for seven cabinet departments, provided money to finance centerpiece proposals of both political parties, from President Clinton's plan to hire more teachers to a GOP-sponsored boost for medical research. It was the last piece of a $1.7 trillion federal budget for fiscal 2000 that included a $17.3 billion increase in defense spending and money to begin paying almost $1 billion in dues to the United Nations.

In its closing hours the Congress also renewed a number of expiring tax breaks, extended for five years a tax credit for research and development, and passed legislation to permit disabled workers to take jobs without losing their federal health benefits. Probably the Congress' most significant accomplishment was a major rewrite of the nation's banking laws, the first such change since the Great Depression. Administration officials and other supporters in both parties said the measure—which makes it easier and cheaper for commercial banks, securities houses, and insurers to enter one another's businesses—would save consumers billions of dollars and was necessary to keep up with trends in both domestic and international banking.

Among other accomplishments, Republicans persuaded Clinton to sign a bill endorsing their defense priority—a national missile-defense system. Also passed was a bill to give states more flexibility in administering federal education money. But for the most part, the two parties seemed more concerned with defining their differences for the 2000 campaign than with bridging their disagreements over legislation. The result was a year riddled with false starts and dashed hopes, frustrating both sides' efforts to get their priorities into law. A bill backed by the president to give patients more rights in their dealings with managed health plans passed the House but ran into conflict with a

© Joe Marquette/AP/Wide World Photos

U.S. Sen. Kay Bailey Hutchison joined Senate Majority Leader Trent Lott (center) *and House Speaker J. Dennis Hastert in pushing the GOP program in Congress in 1999.*

Senate bill dealing with the same issue, and was referred to a conference committee for action in 2000. The Senate passed a $1-an-hour increase in the minimum wage, but Clinton threatened to veto it because it included business-tax cuts that he opposed. House and Senate negotiators spent months seeking a compromise on modest gun-control measures but failed to produce a new law. Campaign-finance reform also was discussed but not enacted.

Partisan squabbling spilled over into the foreign-policy arena. Many Republicans openly challenged Clinton on the war in Kosovo, ignoring the tradition of deference to the presidency on matters of war and peace. Then, in October, the Senate rejected the Comprehensive Test Ban Treaty—the first major international pact to suffer such a fate since the Treaty of Versailles after World War I.

Politics. Although President Clinton's impeachment trial ended early in the year, the impact of the prolonged controversy over his behavior lingered with the electorate. A *Washington Post* survey, taken a year before Election Day 2000, indicated that, while voters wanted a Congress that would deal effectively with the problems of health care, education, and other family issues, they also wanted a strong president with personal values and convictions worthy of respect. The *Post* survey, like the year-end poll by the Pew research center, found the anger that had pervaded the electorate for most of the past decade had subsided, largely because of good news on the economic front. But the *Post* warned that voters still were deeply skeptical about the political system because of the influence of big campaign contributors and of excessive partisanship within both parties. Moreover, while the issues that seemed to dominate the public's agenda were those that normally favored the Democrats, *Post* correspondent David Broder wrote: "The Number 1 Democrat, Bill Clinton, has seeded the atmosphere with so many doubts about his presidential character that the hunger for a trustworthy successor could trump any issues on which the rival nominees choose to run."

Against this backdrop, the contest to succeed Clinton got off to a notably early start in both parties. One reason was that Clinton's constitutional inability to run again stimulated competition. Another factor was the front-loading of primaries on the 2000 campaign calendar, which made it likely that the nomination contests in both parties would be decided by mid-March. This compression forced presidential candidates to raise vast amounts of money in a great hurry.

When it came to fund-raising, Texas Gov. George W. Bush, eldest son of former President Bush and the early Republican front-runner, seemed to have an advantage over everyone else in the race. By October, Bush, helped by wealthy backers in his own state and by a national network of GOP fat cats, had raised a record $57 million. This was more than any of his rivals in either party, and three times as much as 1996 Republican nominee Robert Dole had raised at the same stage of the presidential campaign four years earlier.

This fat treasury allowed Bush to eschew federal financing, leaving him free to spend as much as he wanted to get the nomination. His fund-raising success also drained away money that might have gone to his rivals and forced no fewer than six of them to quit the race before the year ended. The dropouts included such prominent figures as Elizabeth Dole, wife of the former senator; former Vice-President Dan Quayle; former Tennessee Gov. Lamar Alexander; and former presidential contender Pat Buchanan, who launched a campaign for the Reform Party nomination, as well as Ohio Rep. John Kasich and New Hampshire Sen. Bob Smith.

Even with his financial advantage, Bush faced problems. Rivals charged he lacked experience, particularly in foreign policy—a weakness they claimed was underlined by Bush's failure to name the heads of several foreign governments during an impromptu quiz on a radio talk show. The character issue dogged him, too, because of his past reputation as a hard-drinking young hellion. Bush claimed that he had turned over a new leaf and become a teetotaler, but he still was forced to face persistent questions about allegations he had used illegal drugs as a young man.

Character was also a problem for Republican Sen. John McCain of Arizona, a former Vietnam prisoner of war and crusader for campaign reform, who emerged as Bush's most formidable challenger. McCain was said to have a bad temper, a charge he sought to fend off with humor. Asked about his alleged hotheadedness during a televised campaign debate in New Hampshire, McCain replied facetiously: "You know a question like that really makes me mad." The other former Republican candidates were Sen. Orrin Hatch of Utah, magazine publisher Steve Forbes, conservative activist Gary Bauer, and former talk-show host and State Department official Alan Keyes—the only African-American in the 2000 presidential campaign.

The campaign for the Democratic presidential nomination also started out with a highly favored front-runner, Vice-President Al Gore. But Gore's campaign soon ran into unexpected problems. The character issue was a factor here, too. Though Gore tried hard to separate himself from President Clinton's unsavory conduct and to promise moral leadership, critics pointed out that he steadfastly had supported and praised Clinton at the height of the White House sex scandal. Another and more tangible problem for Gore was his challenger, former New Jersey Sen. Bill Bradley, who waged an

With the backing of U.S. Rep. Charles Rangel (center), *First Lady Hillary Rodham Clinton* (right) *"explored" the possibility of a U.S. Senate run from New York in 2000.*

On Nov. 2, 1999, Democrat Paul Patton, right, *became the first governor of Kentucky to win reelection in some 200 years.*

© Ed Reinke/AP/Wide World Photos

aggressive campaign for the nomination, raising nearly as much money as Gore and spending significantly less. To better stave off Bradley, and to underline his separation from Clinton, Gore announced in September that he would move his campaign "lock, stock, and barrel" to Nashville, in his home state of Tennessee. The move was part of a campaign overhaul that included an updated wardrobe and a livelier stump speech for the candidate. Gore did receive some good news in October, when he won the coveted endorsement of the AFL-CIO, the most politically potent of Democratic interest groups. (*See also* BIOGRAPHY—*Election 2000—The Candidates*.)

Attracting about as much attention as the presidential race was First Lady Hillary Clinton's prospective candidacy for the New York Senate seat to be vacated by retiring Sen. Pat Moynihan. New York City's Republican Mayor Rudolph Giuliani was expected to be the GOP candidate in the race. Each candidate faced potential problems. The first lady, who never before had lived in New York, was certain to be labeled a carpetbagger, while critics said that Giuliani's aggressive personality would hurt him with upstate voters.

On Jan. 4, 2000, the Mississippi House of Representatives elected Lt. Gov. Ronnie Musgrove (D), below, *the state's governor after he and his opponent, Mike Parker, failed to capture a majority of the popular vote in November.*

© Rogelio Solis/AP/Wide World Photos

In state and local November elections, Democrats retained the governorship of Kentucky, where incumbent Paul Patton easily won a second term. In Mississippi the Democratic candidate, Lt. Gov. Ronnie Musgrove, finished barely ahead of his Republican opponent, former Congressman Mike Palmer; but since neither candidate got a majority of the popular vote, the contest was to be decided in January in the Mississippi House of Representatives. The Democratic-controlled House chose Musgrove on January 4.

In the most important mayoralty races of the day, in Philadelphia, Democratic City Council President John F. Street narrowly preserved his party's hold on city hall in that traditionally Democratic stronghold. Democrats also took back two Midwest mayor's chairs from Republicans. In Indianapolis they elected developer Bart Peterson, and in Columbus they elected City Council President Michael Coleman, who became the Ohio capital's first black mayor. For Republicans, the biggest success of the day was in Virginia, where they won a majority in both chambers of the House of Delegates, giving them total control of the state legislature for the first time in the 20th century. Earlier in October, Louisiana Gov. Mike Foster (R) captured a second term.

ROBERT SHOGAN
Washington Bureau, "The Los Angeles Times"

The Kennedy Family: Another Tragedy

© Mike Segar/Reuters/Archive Photos

In the evening hours of Friday, July 16, 1999, at the Essex County Airport in Fairfield, NJ, 38-year-old John F. Kennedy, Jr. (*photo above*), climbed into the cockpit of his single-engine Piper Saratoga. With him were his wife of three years, Carolyn Bessette Kennedy (*photo above*), 33, and his sister-in-law, Lauren Bessette, 34. Kennedy and his wife were flying to Hyannis Port, MA, where his cousin Rory Kennedy was getting married. But first they were going to drop off Lauren Bessette, an investment banker, at Martha's Vineyard, a Massachusetts resort island. The plane left at 8:38 P.M. and was expected to land at Martha's Vineyard at around 10:30 P.M. It never arrived.

The next day, debris from the plane was found in the surf off Martha's Vineyard, indicating that the plane had crashed into the Atlantic Ocean. On July 21 the wreckage of the plane and the bodies of John, Carolyn, and Lauren were found and brought to the surface. The next day, with family members aboard the U.S. Navy destroyer *Briscoe*, their ashes were scattered at sea. The nation mourned. Thousands of mourners created a monument of flowers and candles outside the Kennedys' apartment in New York City. The coverage by the news media was intensive—some claimed excessive. And newsstands were flooded with commemorative issues of magazines about Kennedy and the Kennedy family.

This emotional response to the tragedy was partly a result of the tremendous interest the nation has had in the Kennedy family, as well as of the special affection Americans had had for John F. Kennedy, Jr., ever since he was a child. He was just three days away from his third birthday when his father, President John F. Kennedy, was assassinated in 1963, and the photograph of John, Jr., saluting his father's coffin captured the hearts of people around the world. The response also was partly the result of the man John, Jr., had become. He led a decent and purposeful life, becoming a lawyer, a crusader who helped impoverished children and the mentally disabled, and the founder and publisher of *George*, a political magazine.

The death of John F. Kennedy, Jr., was the latest tragedy to strike the Kennedy family. Five years after his father's assassination, his uncle, Sen. Robert Kennedy, met the same fate. Another uncle, Joseph Kennedy, Jr., was killed in World War II, and an aunt, Kathleen Kennedy, died in a plane crash in 1948. His mother, Jacqueline Kennedy Onassis, died of cancer at the relatively young age of 64 in 1994. And there were other Kennedy deaths, too—most recently that of John, Jr.'s cousin Michael, one of Robert Kennedy's sons, in a 1997 skiing accident.

The Kennedys long have been considered one of the country's most prominent political families. And through these tragedies they have continued in public service. Kathleen Kennedy Townsend, Robert Kennedy's eldest daughter, is lieutenant governor of Maryland. Her brother Joseph had served in the U.S. House (1987–99). Patrick Kennedy, the son of Sen. Edward M. (Ted) Kennedy, is a U.S. congressman from Rhode Island. Another Kennedy cousin, Mark Shriver, is a Maryland state legislator. And Ted Kennedy himself has served in the U.S. Senate since 1962.

William E. Shapiro

The Economy

The 1999 U.S. economy was one not just to remember, but to study as well. It seemed to defy old rules of economic behavior—strengthening into a record peacetime expansion when it was expected to tire, keeping inflation at bay, producing the biggest budget surplus (as a percentage of the economy) in nearly half a century, spurring the most explosive stock-market growth in U.S. history, creating enormous new wealth, and spawning ingenious companies that, it was said, would produce even bigger changes as they became the giants of tomorrow.

The expansion, already 105 months old in December, quickened its pace as the year ended and seemed certain to surpass in February 2000 the longest uninterrupted period of economic growth ever. It was a stunning performance, "an exceptional year," in the words of an oft-doubting Alan Greenspan, the Federal Reserve Board chairman, who remained alert for evidence of inflation and raised interest rates three times. But every brief indication of imbalance, including inflation, was countered quickly by later statistics, and the year ended with most guidelines remarkably strong and coordinated.

"An Exceptional Year." Gross domestic product (GDP) soared at an annual rate of 5.7% in the third quarter; inflation settled to under 2.5% for the year; unemployment stood at a rate of 4.1% in December; household income rose to close to $40,000; and poverty fell to its lowest in two decades. While doubters looked for weaknesses and remained convinced they would appear, believers contended that a new economic paradigm, based in technology and enhanced productivity, had evolved. Comparing its power to that of the Industrial Revolution of the 19th century, they repeatedly irritated skeptical old hands. But, as if to underscore the economy's strength, the Commerce Department completed its benchmark revisions of GDP to show that annual gains in the long expansion were even higher than at first measured.

Impressive as the rate of expansion was, the changed makeup of GDP was perhaps more so. For the first time, business investment in equipment and in computer software, growing at an average annual rate of nearly 10% a year for a decade, exceeded consumer spending as the major contributor to growth. Reflecting this, manufacturing employment continued to fall, but the category maintained its position as a percentage of total output.

Gross Domestic Product
Percent Change*

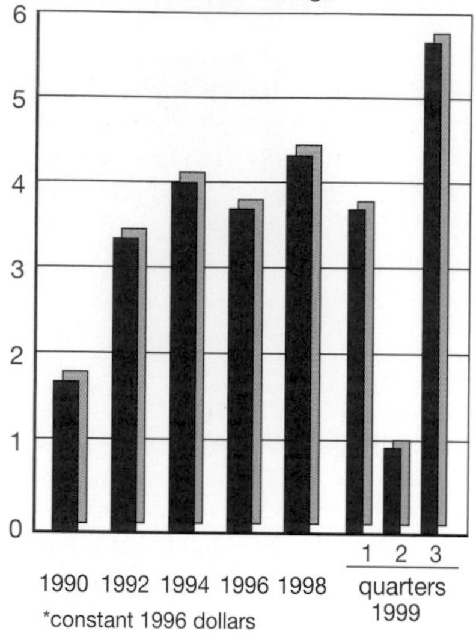

*constant 1996 dollars

On the surface at least, American consumers seldom had had it better. The number of households at or below the poverty level—for a family of four, an annual income of $16,655, not counting food stamps or other benefits—fell below 1998's 12.7%. With inflation checked, even scant increases in average hourly earnings—0.1% to $13.41 in November, for example—resulted in real buying power. But wages told only part of the story. Extrapolating from official government and industry figures, the libertarian Cato Institute issued a report estimating that 79 million Americans owned stocks directly or through mutual funds. "The most significant demographic shift of this century," said the Cato paper, "is the rise of history's first mass class of worker capitalists—men and women whose wealth-seeking activities include both wage earnings and capital ownership." New York Stock Exchange figures indicated more than half of all shareholders had incomes of $60,000 or less. Indicative of the mood, conservative economic professors Dwight Lee and Richard McKenzie wrote a popular book, *Getting Rich in America.* Its theme is that "becoming rich is a matter of choice." Despite earning academic salaries, they said they had become millionaires.

Strong and rising housing prices and easy access to home equity added to the buying power of consumers. Some of that money too went to purchase stocks, contributing to market values and adding even more to the "wealth effect," a term used to describe the high level of consumer confidence. It unnerved some. "Is the U.S. Building a Debt Bomb?" asked *Business Week* magazine. It asked readers to consider that "total household debt is now perilously close, at 98%, to disposable annual income." The savings rate actually fell below zero before regaining plus territory when consumers began paying down high-interest credit-card debts. The Financial Markets Center, a liberal think tank, noted that broker loans, or margin debt, had ballooned from $97.4 billion in December 1996 to $177 billion in June 1999, putting it at the highest level relative to GDP in at least 63 years. A falling stock market, it suggested, could have a domino effect.

Real Strengths. Still, economists found evidence of real strength in the basic statistics. These were among the most notable numerical measurements:

• GDP, the total output of goods and services, exceeded $8.85 trillion in real terms (1996 dollars), but grew at an annual rate of more than $9 trillion late in the year. This compared with $8.52 trillion in 1998 and $6.68 trillion in 1990.

• The Consumer Price Index (CPI) late in the year was just 2.6% above its year-earlier level. The core increase, which excluded the more volatile oil and energy categories, was under 2%.

• Gains in productivity, the output per hour of work and the most meaningful indication of production efficiency, averaged close to 3% for the year. Second-half gains were especially strong.

• In the 12 months from October to October, the number of civilian jobs rose more than 2 million to a total of 133.9 million, suggesting that even the least skilled were employed. The jobless rate fell to an annual rate of just 4.1% late in the year. Long-term unemployment shrank to less than 1.5 million workers, nearly 2 million fewer than in 1992.

• Wages remained relatively steady, averaging $14.08 hourly in manufacturing early in the fourth quarter, compared with $13.57 a year earlier. However, upward pressure rose late in the year.

• Corporate profits before taxes rose at an annual rate of close to $850 billion late in the year, bringing the yearly total to near $840 billion, or double that of 1991.

• Stock prices reached new highs. The Dow Jones industrial index of 30 large stocks exceeded 11,400 points just before Christmas, 22% and more than 2,000 points higher for the year. However, that performance was overshadowed by the technology-heavy Nasdaq composite, which leaped close to 80% and flirted with 4,000 points. Some Internet-related stocks rose tenfold, and a few initial public offerings leaped several hundred percent on their first day of trading. Companies without earnings but gilded with expectations were among those deemed most attractive. Meanwhile, dividends in the total marketplace fell to just more than 1% (1.21% in November), compared with 3.61% in 1990.

• After three one-quarter-point increases by the Federal Reserve, the Federal Funds rate, at which banks lend to each other overnight, reached 5.50%. The prime lending rate, at which banks lend to the most creditworthy customers, rose to 8.50%. Rates on the 30-year Treasury bond, sometimes used as a guide in setting long-term borrowing rates, such as on home mortgages, rose above 6% early in the year and then fluctuated between 6.10% and 6.50%.

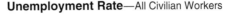

Unemployment Rate—All Civilian Workers

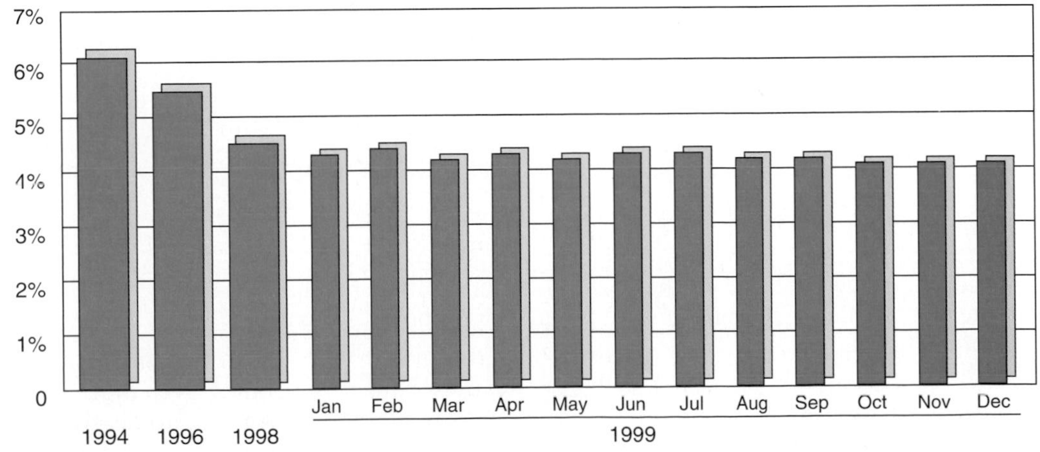

• To the surprise even of some industry officials, sales of cars and light trucks had the biggest year ever, exceeding 16.7 million units. The figure was more than 5 million units higher than in 1990.

• Housing too had another excellent year. Although the pace weakened as the year went on, the industry began construction on more than 1.6 million units, comparable to the strong 1998 performance. Sales also were strong; the National Association of Realtors reported that sales of existing homes were at an annual rate of more than 5 million units, 9% higher than in 1998. The $137,700 median price for a house in August was more than 5% higher than in the like month a year earlier. With mortgages generally stable at just under 8% and money plentiful, the desire to own prevailed over renting. The vacancy rate for housing units exceeded 8% throughout the year, highest in more than a decade.

News from Washington. In general, but not totally, the news from Washington also was good. Most impressive was the budget surplus, which the federal government estimated at $122.7 billion for fiscal year 1999. It exceeded the fiscal 1998 surplus of $69.2 billion, and in terms of size, it was the largest since 1951. Still, the surplus could not have been achieved without Medicare cuts and borrowing from a temporary surplus in the Social Security trust fund. And the total was tiny in relation to the national debt, which stood at $5.5 trillion.

There were other concerns too. Throughout the year, Congress discussed a tax cut, but little of lasting significance developed. And President Bill Clinton and Congress discussed a major restructuring of Social Security, the centerpiece of which would have been the diversion of some funds to private-sector investments. Discussions stalled on the details, mainly over the issue of individual versus government decision making in regard to investments.

The balance-of-payments deficit also remained a major concern and diplomatic issue as U.S. imports swelled, especially from economically depressed Asian nations, and exports remained static in the absence of economic strength in the same areas. Imports of $250 billion in the spring quarter, for example, exceeded by more than $20 billion the year-earlier figure and resulted in a net deficit for the quarter alone of nearly $85 billion. The deficit narrowed later but still remained on a course to exceed 1998's $247 billion total.

The most troubling trade relationships were with Japan and increasingly with China. The latter's deficit with the United States reached an astonishing $6.87 billion in August alone. The imbalance added friction to trade negotiations and delayed until November an agreement calling for China's entry into the World Trade Organization (WTO). Negotiations among trading nations deteriorated into a fiasco in Seattle as the year neared its end. Nations failed to agree on major issues, and demonstrators for human rights and for environmental and other causes claimed most of the headlines. Economists speculated that, unless corrected, the American imbalance of trade eventually might erode the trading power of the dollar. The dollar, however, held its own against major currencies. On December 20, for example, it traded at 103.07 yen and 1.9391 German marks, and was at par with the euro. Meanwhile, the price of gold remained without its old-time luster. After briefly spurting to $339 an ounce in October, it settled back to between $280 and $290.

For most people, however, such issues and problems were distant abstractions that hardly concerned them immediately. Their minds instead were on more personal things, such as the high cost of medical care, the future of Medicare and Social Security, and rising college tuitions.

JOHN CUNNIFF, *The Associated Press*

Foreign Affairs

In 1999, U.S. foreign-policy makers grappled with dilemmas that were likely to persist well into the new millennium. These included "world-order" issues such as intervention in sovereign states for humanitarian or self-interested reasons, the future of the North Atlantic Treaty Organization (NATO) and the United Nations (UN) as security organizations, the viability of arms control, the tenor of relations with major states such as China and Russia, and the benefits and curses of the "global economy." Secretary of State Madeleine Albright was highly visible in the developing world in 1999, visiting Southeast Asia and six African states, and seeing national leaders as well as rural villagers. She was concerned particularly about the future of democracy and the place of women in those regions, as she pledged stepped-up foreign assistance. Still, in the year in which the West celebrated the tenth anniversary of the Berlin Wall's fall, it

© Georges Merillon/Liaison Agency

President Bill Clinton was in Europe for nine days in November 1999. During a stopover in Italy, he joined other Western leaders in Florence for the Conference on Progressive Governance for the 21st Century, above.

appeared that the U.S. role in the post–Cold War world had yet to be defined clearly.

Europe. Early in the year, the long-simmering Kosovo dispute in Yugoslavia boiled over into violence, with the ultimate displacement of thousands of ethnic Albanians by Serb police, militia, and military forces. Washington and NATO threats did not deter Yugoslav (Serb) President Slobodan Milosevic's offensive. After prolonged interallied debate, and in the face of strong Russian objections, NATO, in its first organized European military combat, dispatched bombers over Serbia. At first hastening the pace of Serb ethnic cleansing, the bombardment, which resulted in numerous civilian casualties, ultimately paved the way for the entry of NATO ground forces as occupying peacekeepers. Despite Clinton's own record of support for the strategic bombing, he later joined European states in criticizing Russia for its attacks on the breakaway republic of Chechnya.

Russian forces also raced into Kosovo, and a complicated joint occupation was worked out painstakingly with NATO. Albanians returned, and later turned to vendettas against their Serbian neighbors, facing the peacekeepers with the challenge of assuring security, disarming the Kosovo Liberation Army (KLA), and convincing Serbs to remain in the province. As cold weather approached, the administration reversed itself and backed European Union (EU) plans to ship heating oil to opposition-held cities in economically depressed Serbia. (*See also* THE KOSOVO CRISIS, page 78.)

In March, Poland, the Czech Republic, and Hungary officially joined NATO, while in June the EU's decision to establish its own common-defense arm met with U.S. concern.

Meanwhile, U.S., West European, and Russian forces continued to patrol nearby Bosnia, where the Dayton Accords of 1995 remained only partly fulfilled. The president attended a summer summit in Sarajevo on stabilizing the Balkans, offering a plan to promote economic development, trade, and regional investment. During a European summit in November, the president visited earthquake-torn Turkey as well as Italy and Bulgaria, and encountered vigorous anti-American protest in Greece over his Balkan policies. Clinton frankly addressed conflicting perspectives, promised disaster relief, celebrated a long-sought agreement for a Central Asian oil pipeline, and joined in a new accord on reducing conventional forces in the region.

In November, after weeks of mediation and some blunt words from Clinton, special

While in Europe in November, President Clinton attended the Organization for Security and Cooperation in Europe (OSCE) summit and met with Russia's President Boris Yeltsin (left) *in Turkey. Developments in the Russian separatist republic of Chechnya dominated discussions at the two-day OSCE meeting.*

© David Scull/The White House/AP/Wide World Photos

envoy George Mitchell announced a tentative agreement to implement the Northern Ireland power-sharing accords of 1998. A new presidential envoy, Al Moses, was dispatched to the stalled Cyprus negotiations.

Money-laundering and currency-transfer corruption scandals in the former USSR and Africa led to proposed new banking and regulatory legislation in November. In February former Ukraine Prime Minister Pavlo Lazarenko was detained for financial offenses and requested asylum in the United States. After a Russian delegation agreed to a program of economic reform, the International Monetary Fund (IMF) approved a $4.5 billion aid package for Russia to tide the economy over through pending elections. Given the IMF's pivotal world economic role, Washington sought to influence the choice of the next IMF director as the new year approached, and some Republicans began to press for slowing Russian loans if attacks on Chechnya continued. In symbolic efforts to improve security at U.S. installations abroad, the State Department decided to authorize the "voluntary departure" of U.S. government workers in Russia, Ukraine, Moldova, and Belarus for fear of "Y2K" computer breakdowns in those countries.

Asia. The situation in the Indonesian province of East Timor erupted into a bloodbath after Jakarta allowed free UN-supervised elections in August. When the province voted for independence, pro-Indonesian militia rampaged, again posing difficult choices for Washington. As in Turkey's wars against Kurdish rebels, the United States traditionally had refrained from interfering with big, regionally strategic states confronting domestic unrest. However, the humanitarian tragedy in Timor, oil and economic interests, and the affront to UN election monitors meant that the Security Council had to act. President Clinton applied considerable pressure on the politically shaky Indonesian government, and determined to assist the dispatch of regional forces from Australia and a few other Asian states to occupy the province with Indonesian permission. The question remained whether this constituted a new U.S. doctrine regarding "ethnic cleansing," or just ad-hoc policy responses to specific events.

The Clinton administration sparred all year both with Beijing and with Congress over China policy. Sensitive to charges that advanced missile technology had been leaked to the Chinese, the administration rejected in February a commercial-satellite sale to a business group with Chinese ties, though in July the president loosened computer-sales restrictions.

When Secretary Albright visited Beijing in March, she carried assurances that China's ultimate admission to the World Trade Organization (WTO) still could happen. Tensions worsened in the spring, as a NATO plane mistakenly bombed the Chinese embassy in Belgrade during the Kosovo crisis. Chinese protests against the United States persisted. So did a spate of disagreements over Beijing's human-rights policies, U.S. aid and security (potential missile-defense) commitments to Taiwan that had moved toward a " two China" policy in July, missile proliferation through North Korea, Chinese nuclear developments, China's permanent favored trade status, and U.S. trade deficits. It was not until November that intensive talks paved the way for resumption of U.S.-Chinese military consultations and for a sweeping trade agreement, which was subject to congressional approval.

Washington quietly backed efforts to set up a war-crimes tribunal for former top Cambodian Khmer Rouge leaders. U.S.-Vietnamese trade and technological-cooperation deals also were readied for ratification.

The United States kept up contacts with and pressure on Afghanistan to capture suspected terrorist leader Osama bin Laden. In November, Afghan Taliban party leaders warned that U.S.-backed, UN-imposed sanctions would bring the wrath of "God Almighty," and there was speculation that rocket attacks near U.S. and UN facilities in nearby Islamabad, Pakistan, might have been the first shots.

Middle East and Africa. In terms of the Middle East, the Clinton administration's main effort was devoted to hastening Palestinian-Israeli agreements to move toward "final status" talks after the Israeli turnover of additional territory. In Oslo in November, President Clinton met with new Israeli Prime Minister Ehud Barak and Palestinian leader Yasir Arafat, aiming for a February 2000 "framework" agreement on the way to a planned September 2000 conclusion. During the year, Secretary of State Albright visited the Middle East and met with Jordan's new King Abdullah, who later toured Washington, reportedly bringing communications from Iraq's Saddam Hussein. President Clinton joined former President George Bush and former Secretaries of State Warren Christopher and James Baker in paying respects at the funeral of Morocco's King Hassan II in July. In November, Egyptian and U.S. officials became embroiled in controversy surrounding the cause of a crash of an Egyptian airliner off the coast of Nantucket. In December the president announced that Syria and Israel would resume peace talks. The first such negotiations in four years occurred in Washington at midmonth.

American and British warplanes continued to undertake bombing runs against Iraqi positions throughout the year. More information came to light that American intelligence operatives had served with UN monitors in Iraq. The administration, meanwhile, was staging a campaign to urge Iraq to accept a new arms-control regime in return for the easing of UN sanctions. U.S. government funds continued to be channeled to the Iraqi National Congress, a shaky and diverse coalition of opposition groups. Touring the region in March to promote security and support for Washington's Iraqi hard line, Defense Secretary William Cohen proposed massive arms sales to Egypt, Saudi Arabia, Israel, and several Persian Gulf states.

Secretary Albright took a definitive stand in supporting a regional peace initiative for the Horn of Africa, a region affecting the Middle East as well. In addition, the president's national security adviser for Africa held talks trying to strengthen the shaky agreement to defuse fighting in and around the Congo. (*See also* AFRICA.)

Arms Control. Severe difficulties surfaced on the arms-control front. In October the Senate surprised the administration with a quick vote to defeat the long-stalled Comprehensive Test Ban Treaty. This shook global, and particularly NATO, confidence in U.S. treaty commitments. The vote happened as the Clinton administration was pressing India and Pakistan to restrain their nuclear-arms race and amid concerns about the fall of Pakistan's civilian government in a military coup. Russia also rejected American inducements to authorize changes in the Antiballistic Missile (ABM) Treaty of 1972 to allow the development of missile defenses.

On the positive side, in May the administration reported that inspection of suspected North Korean nuclear sites proved negative. Former Defense Secretary William Perry became the first American diplomatic envoy to visit that country. After North Korea pledged to end its long-range-missile program, the United States agreed to lift some economic sanctions.

In the fall the trade in small and conventional arms was debated at international forums. At the UN Security Council, Secretary Albright somewhat vaguely promised that the United States, despite its global lead in arms sales, would refrain from selling such arms to "regions of conflict." The State Department was given the power to restrict sales of communication satellites, and Congress moved to require better reporting of incentives in arms-sales contracts.

Latin America. Antidrug and security policy continued to predominate in Latin America, making Colombia—caught in a persistent domestic rebellion—the third-largest global recipient of U.S. aid, and raising Latin concerns about possible future U.S. military intervention. In September, U.S. and Colombian customs services signed a protocol to stem drug smuggling and money laundering. Washington opened the year pressing Brazil not to prop up its currency, and later watched governmental developments in Venezuela.

In the winter, Clinton traveled to Mexico and Central America, promoting trade and drug interdiction, and also apologizing for prior U.S. aid to right-wing repression in Guatemala. Amid well-publicized baseball games between the Baltimore Orioles and the Cuban national team, and the opening of additional limited direct airline routes and eased financial restrictions, U.S.-Cuban dialogue progressed. A custody case regarding a young boy who escaped Cuba and was living with relatives in Florida, while his father wanted him returned to Cuba, seemed to dampen any improvement in relations late in the year. In August, Cuba President Fidel Castro strongly criticized Washington's immigration-policy enforcement. The last of the regular U.S. forces in Haiti prepared for a January 2000 departure, raising fears for that country's stability and economic viability. In December the Panama Canal was turned over to Panamanian control.

United Nations, Budget Issues, and Diplomatic Appointments. Despite persistent concern over payment of more than $1 billion in past dues, the possible loss of American voting rights, and friction over NATO's handling of the Kosovo crisis, President Clinton addressed the UN General Assembly in September. The previous month the Senate had confirmed the long-delayed nomination of Richard Holbrooke as U.S. ambassador to the world body. In September the United States was restored to its seat on the important UN budget committee, clearing the way for positive congressional action on UN payments.

Foreign-policy-budgetary issues remained a focus of congressional tension. The administration sought $3 billion to upgrade security at U.S. embassies abroad. A panel recommended shifting the maintenance budget to a multiagency board. An additional $2.8 billion was requested to prevent chemical, biological, and "cyber" terrorism.

Talks on the foreign-aid and -operations budget came down to the 11th hour prior to congressional adjournment. As part of IMF global strategy, the president had hoped to include debt forgiveness for the poorest of the developing states. After Clinton vetoed a reduced $12.6 billion aid budget, agreement was reached at the $15.3 billion level. Funds were included for the Mideast peace process, aid to former Soviet republics, and payment of UN dues and assessments in return for restrictions on aid to global-population-planning groups dealing with abortions.

Congress considered several other diplomatic appointments, including that of former Sen. Carol Moseley-Braun, an African-American, as ambassador to New Zealand. Amid charges of racial prejudice, Sen. Jesse Helms (R-NC) objected to her past financial dealings, meetings with discredited African leaders, and attacks on flying the confederate flag. Her nomination was confirmed in November.

Trade. The late-1999 meeting of the World Trade Organization (WTO) in Seattle, WA, saw both massive "antiglobalization" protests from American labor and interest groups and continuing disagreement among the major trading states over the trade-liberalization agenda. Negotiations on a global treaty for biotechnology-trade safeguards stalled in February, as the United States and five other major agricultural exporters objected to restrictions on genetically altered crops. In June agreement was reached with Canada on allocation of Pacific salmon fishing quotas.

FREDERIC S. PEARSON
Wayne State University

© Georges De Keerle/Liaison Agency

During a White House conference on May 10, 1999, President Clinton congratulated Brazil's President Fernando Henrique Cardoso (left) *on the recovery his Latin American nation had made from an early-in-the-year financial crisis.*

Uruguay

In the presidential election held in October 1999, no clear winner emerged, leading to a runoff a month later. Meanwhile, the economy continued to struggle.

Elections. Uruguay's major political parties chose their presidential candidates in April primaries. The centrist Colorado Party and the rightist National (Blanco) Party, the members of the governing coalition, selected Sen. Jorge Batlle and former President Luis Alberto Lacalle, respectively. The leftist Broad Front backed Tabaré Vásquez, a former mayor of Montevideo. For most of the campaign, it looked as though one of the coalition-party candidates would come out ahead, but Vásquez made a late surge, and he earned the most votes (38.5%) in the October 31 balloting. However, because he failed to get the 50% majority required to win the presidency outright, he faced the second-place finisher, Batlle, in a runoff on November 26. Batlle obtained almost 52% of the vote to only 44% for Vásquez in that contest.

At the same time as the first presidential vote in October, elections were held for 99 deputies and 30 senators. The Broad Front made a good showing, winning 12 Senate seats and 40 in the House of Deputies. The Colorado Party came in second, electing ten senators and 32 deputies.

Economy. During the first five months of 1999, imports exceeded exports by $1.3 billion to $840 million. Exports to Brazil fell by nearly 44% and to Argentina by 29%. Manufacturing activity, which had accounted for more than 80% of all exports in 1998, declined by 6.5% in the second trimester. The gross domestic product (GDP) was expected to fall by 2% for 1999, and unemployment in August stood at 10.5%. A controversial project to build a $1 billion, 26-mi (42-km) pontoon-type bridge linking Colonia, Uruguay, to Buenos Aires, Argentina, across the Río de la Plata estuary was approved by the House of Deputies in August 1999; it already had been approved by the Senate at the end of 1998. The construction was expected to take five years.

Foreign Relations. The foreign ministry rejected a request made in August by Paraguay for the extradition of José Segovia Boltes, defense minister in the Raúl Cubas administration. Accused by Asunción of misusing $450,000 in public funds, he was granted asylum in Uruguay in March after Cubas had been forced to step down. Paraguayan authorities sharply criticized Uruguay for allowing its foreign ministry to decide on the request, while it was a criminal matter.

President Sanguinetti traveled to Brazil in February to meet with his counterpart, Fernando Henrique Cardoso, to address the crisis that emerged in the Mercosur trade pact after Brazil, its principal member, devalued its currency, the real, by 40% in January. Sanguinetti pleaded with his host to honor all trade deals on the terms negotiated prior to the devaluation. A few days later, President Sanguinetti returned to Brazil with heads of Southern Cone governments and agreed to intensify regional integration. The Uruguayan chief executive hosted a meeting on August 6 in Montevideo, but the foreign and economy ministers from Mercosur partner states were unable to make any progress in resolving the crisis.

On January 29, Uruguay arrested an Egyptian Islamic militant, Said Hazan al-Mohammad, as he entered the country from Brazil using a false Malaysian passport. Wanted in several countries, Mohammad apparently was headed to London on a terrorist mission aimed at Israeli and U.S. diplomatic targets in Europe. Egypt requested his extradition, as it attributed a 1997 massacre of 70 tourists in Luxor to him, but it has no extradition treaty with Uruguay. Mohammad was jailed in Montevideo while his case was under study.

LARRY L. PIPPIN, *University of the Pacific*

URUGUAY • Information Highlights

Official Name: Oriental Republic of Uruguay.
Location: Southeastern coast of South America.
Area: 68,039 sq mi (176 220 km²).
Population (July 1999 est.): 3,308,523.
Chief City (May 1996 est.): Montevideo, the capital, 1,240,503.
Government: *Head of state and government,* Julio Maria Sanguinetti, president (took office March 1995). *Legislature*—General Assembly: Chamber of Senators and Chamber of Representatives.
Monetary Unit: Peso (11.6460 pesos equal U.S.$1, Dec. 29, 1999).
Gross Domestic Product (1998 est. U.S.$): $28,400,-000,000 (purchasing power parity).
Economic Index (Montevideo, 1998; 1990 = 100): *Consumer Prices,* all items, 1,839.4; food, 1,444.4.
Foreign Trade (1998 U.S.$): *Imports,* $3,808,000,000; *exports,* $2,769,000,000.

Venezuela

Newly elected President Hugo Chávez Frias immediately spearheaded the election of a new assembly and the complete rewriting of the constitution. Oil prices collapsed early in 1999, contributing to a severe economic recession, before rising again under a new Organization of Petroleum Exporting Countries (OPEC) strategy.

Politics. The December 1998 election of Chávez, a former lieutenant colonel and the leader of two failed coup attempts in 1992, ended the 40-year domination of Venezuelan politics by two major parties—Democratic Action (AD) and the Social Christian Party (COPEI). Chávez' alliance, the Patriotic Pole, won only 35% of the Congress, and the president moved quickly to fulfill his campaign promise to elect a new Constituent Assembly that not only would draft a new constitution, but also would have the power to dissolve Congress and the courts. A referendum on April 25 overwhelmingly approved the Constituent Assembly, and on July 25, voters elected 131 members (90% of whom were the president's candidates) for a six-month mandate. The assembly immediately moved to intervene in the other branches of government, restricting (and ultimately stripping) the powers of Congress and investigating and dismissing judges.

The assembly worked to produce a final draft of a new constitution in a little more than three months. On December 15, 45% of eligible voters turned out to approve the constitution in a referendum, with 71% in favor and 29% against. The new constitution extends the presidential term from five to six years and allows for reelection, giving President Chávez the potential of being in office for 13 years. It reduces civilian control over the military; moves to a unicameral legislature; creates the post of an appointed vice-president; and establishes two new branches of government—electoral and citizens' powers. The latter is to focus on corruption.

The day of the referendum, an unusual period of heavy rains culminated in severe flooding and mud slides in Caracas and the surrounding northern states. The tragedy was the worst natural disaster for Venezuela in at least three decades.

Economy. Chávez inherited a difficult economic situation, with oil prices at a two-decade low of about $8.00 per barrel and a fiscal deficit of 9% of gross domestic product (GDP). But he also had $14 billion in international reserves and an agreement with OPEC, Mexico, and Norway to cut oil production and raise prices. As a result, the price of oil doubled by midyear. Chávez reversed Venezuela's petroleum-exporting strategy, from one of cheating on OPEC quotas to expand global market share to one that defended production cuts to raise prices. Observers became concerned when Roberto Mandini, head of the state-owned oil company PDVSA, resigned, and Chávez named Hector Ciavaldini, a loyal but inexperienced confidant, to the top post. Worries that the well-run independent company would be politicized emerged with indications that the government wanted to place it under the control of the Ministry of Energy and Mines.

Although many feared that the new president would be a radical populist, he spent his first months in office trying to control the fiscal deficit, while still increasing social spending. He introduced a financial-transactions tax and took advantage of higher oil prices to cut the fiscal deficit to about 5%, but he failed to define a long-term economic strategy. The economy was expected to contract as much as 7% in 1999.

Under pressure to address the high unemployment and inflation rates, Chávez created Plan Bolívar 2000, giving 45,000 soldiers a visible role repairing schools and roads and participating in other public-works projects. He further demonstrated his reliance on the military when he named more than 100 retired and active-duty officers to mid- and upper-level government jobs.

Foreign Policy. Several actions by the Chávez administration during 1999 raised the ire of some of Venezuela's neighbors. For instance, in spite of protests from Bogotá, Chávez expressed vigorous interest in meeting with guerrilla leaders in Colombia to end the three-decade-old uprising there, and the Constituent Assembly discussed proposals to include a disputed portion of Guyana in Venezuela's territory.

JENNIFER L. MCCOY
Georgia State University

VENEZUELA • Information Highlights

Official Name: Republic of Venezuela.
Location: Northern coast of South America.
Area: 352,143 sq mi (912 050 km²).
Population (July 1999 est.): 23,203,466.
Chief Cities (1992 est.): Caracas, the capital, 1,964,846; Valencia, 1,034,033; Barquisimeto, 692,599.
Government: *Head of state and government,* Hugo Chávez Frias, president (inaugurated Feb. 2, 1999). *Legislature*—Congress of the Republic: Senate and Chamber of Deputies.
Monetary Unit: Bolívar (648.150 bolívares equal U.S.$1, Dec. 29, 1999).
Gross Domestic Product (1998 est. U.S.$): $194,500,-000,000 (purchasing power parity).
Economic Index (1997, 1990 = 100): *Consumer Prices,* all items, 1,818.8; food, 1,559.7.
Foreign Trade (1997 U.S.$): *Imports,* $14,573,000,000; *exports,* $21,067,000,000.

Vietnam

Foreign investment slowed greatly in 1999, reducing Vietnam's economic growth. Hanoi and Washington reached agreement on a major trade accord.

Politics. Communist Party leadership factions continued to haggle over whether or not to move ahead with reforms to create a market economy and encourage foreign investment. Early in the year, anonymous party veterans addressed a seven-page letter to leaders of the party's conservative faction, blaming all of Vietnam's troubles on the reform faction, led by former Prime Minister Vo Van Kiet. The letter, addressed to party chief Le Kha Phieu and senior advisers Do Muoi and Le Duc Anh, accused Vo Van Kiet and his allies of being capitalists at heart. Kiet was denounced for choosing officials on the basis of merit rather than party loyalty. The letter also decried the widespread corruption infecting the party and government, and revived the Cold War theory that Vietnam was being undermined by the U.S. Central Intelligence Agency (CIA).

In January the Central Committee of the Communist Party debated the problem of corruption and placed new limits on public dissent within the party. Retired Gen. Tran Do was expelled from the party for advocating political reform.

In February, Gen. Pham Hong Song criticized the party for corruption and lack of democracy. The following month a prominent scientist, Nguyen Thanh Giang, was arrested for criticizing the regime. However, he was released in May, after the United States appealed on his behalf.

In its August plenum session, the Central Committee discussed restructuring the party and government, but no major personnel changes were announced.

VIETNAM • Information Highlights

Official Name: Socialist Republic of Vietnam.
Location: Southeast Asia.
Area: 127,243 sq mi (329 560 km^2).
Population (July 1999 est.): 77,311,210.
Chief Cities (mid-1993, provisional): Hanoi, the capital, 2,154,900; Ho Chi Minh City, 4,322,300; Haiphong, 1,583,900.
Government: *Head of state,* Tran Duc Luong, president (took office September 1997). *Head of government,* Phan Van Khai, prime minister (appointed June 1997). *Legislature*—National Assembly.
Monetary Unit: Dong (14,026.5 dongs equal U.S.$1, Dec. 29, 1999).
Gross Domestic Product (1998 est. U.S.$): $134,800,-000,000 (purchasing power parity).
Foreign Trade (1998 est. U.S.$): *Imports,* $11,400,000,-000; *exports,* $9,400,000,000.

© Apichart Weerawong/AP/Wide World Photos

Vietnam's Prime Minister Phan Van Khai welcomed U.S. Secretary of State Madeleine Albright to Hanoi in September. A new U.S. consulate in Ho Chi Minh City was dedicated during the secretary's visit.

Economy. Foreign investment was expected barely to reach the level of $1 billion in 1999, a sharp drop from $9.2 billion in 1996, the last year before the economic-reform program stagnated. Many foreign firms—including Raytheon, Chrysler, and Sheraton Hotels—had pulled out, and others had reduced their operations in Vietnam. Because of falling foreign investment and the economic weakness of some of Vietnam's Asian trading partners, gross domestic product (GDP) was expected to grow at a rate of 4% to 4.5% in 1999, down from 9.3% in 1996. Unemployment was close to 20%. Devastating floods, particularly in the central provinces, further reduced productivity.

The political stalemate between the conservative and reform factions prevented Vietnam from meeting the International Monetary Fund's (IMF's) criteria for receiving loans. The IMF wanted Vietnam to fix its state-dominated banking system, which often has loaned money to state firms for political rather than financial reasons. In August, 77 people were convicted of obtaining bank loans falsely; six were condemned to death. The World Bank also urged Vietnam to make its state enterprises more competitive, but even though Hanoi largely failed to comply, the bank continued to provide development aid.

In July, after three years of negotiations, the United States and Vietnam reached agreement in principle on a trade accord. The lengthy document specified certain economic reforms that Vietnam must enact over the next few years to improve the climate for foreign investors. U.S. Ambassador Douglas "Pete" Peterson lobbied hard for the agreement in Washington and Hanoi.

One week after the agreement was reached, the U.S. Congress voted to allow U.S. firms trading with Vietnam to receive loans and guarantees from the U.S. Export-Import Bank and the Overseas Private Investment Corporation. However, a number of issues still had to be resolved before the trade agreement could be signed and ratified by the two governments. Only then would the United States reduce its tariffs on Vietnamese imports. In recent years, the United States had imported about $600 million worth of goods a year from Vietnam and exported $350 million a year. Vietnamese exports of shoes, clothing, and other light manufactured goods to the United States were expected to double after the agreement was ratified.

The Vietnamese government began an on-line lottery, and it even set up a number of public terminals in Hanoi to compensate for the small number of computers in the country. A few cyber cafes were allowed to exist in Ho Chi Minh City (formerly Saigon), but customers were warned that they would be fined if they attempted to download information.

Foreign Relations. In August the United States opened a new consulate in Ho Chi Minh City. Secretary of State Madeleine Albright visited the country in September, and Hanoi continued to assist the United States in resolving the status of American soldiers missing in action (MIAs). Some Vietnamese criticized their government for doing nothing to resolve the status of 300,000 Vietnamese MIAs, but a national census was established in 1999 to assess the health of Vietnamese who had been exposed to Agent Orange.

Le Kha Phieu, secretary-general of the Vietnamese Communist Party, visited Cambodia in June, and the two governments agreed to resolve all territorial disputes over the next few years. In late December, Vietnam and China signed a border treaty. The agreement settled all disputes along their common 740-mi (1 190-km) border.

PETER A. POOLE
Author, "Eight Presidents and Indochina"

Washington, DC

During 1999, his first year as mayor of Washington, DC, Anthony Williams worked toward returning the District to self-government. The National Capital Planning Commission approved a 4-acre (1.6-ha) site for a Washington memorial in honor of the late civil-rights leader Martin Luther King, Jr. Ground was broken near the Capitol for the National Museum of the American Indian.

The Mayor's First Year. In January, Mayor Williams signed a Memorandum of Understanding (MOU) with the DC Control Board that returned responsibility for much of the day-to-day management of government to the mayor's office. The MOU outlined the mayor's authority to oversee "all executive branch departments, agencies, boards, commissions, offices, and other entities of the District government and their personnel." The District's drive toward home rule was advanced further during the year, as the U.S. Congress passed several bills intended to shift even more of Washington's operational authority from the Control Board to the city's elected officials.

The mayor planned several measures for reforming the DC government, including the reclassification of 900 mid-level managers so that they could be fired without explanation if they were performing poorly. Some of these managers questioned the fairness of the plan, noting that hundreds of the people who might lose their jobs were black women. The managers also argued that they were being scapegoated for the government's past excesses and inefficiencies.

Williams faced a campaign-finance inquiry in June that resulted in his being fined $1,000 for not promptly disclosing two consulting jobs he had held in the summer of 1998 (as his electoral campaign was going on), for which he was paid $40,000. The mayor contended that there was no conflict of interest involved, and that his eight-month delay in revealing the income was due to an oversight.

DC Budget. In late November, President Bill Clinton signed a DC budget that included $435.8 million of federal funding and approved the spending of another $6.8 billion in local funds. Clinton and Congress had disagreed over social-policy provisions in the budget, with the result that Clinton vetoed two previous versions. The president rejected the first bill in September because of riders attached to it that would have barred the District from implementing social programs such as a needle-exchange program to fight the spread of disease; he vetoed the second a few weeks later, because congressional Republicans had added a 0.97% cut in discretionary spending. The final version of the bill still prohibited the use of federal or local money for needle

© Dennis Cook/AP/Wide World Photos

During 1999 government and police reform, the child-welfare system, and a curfew for children concerned Anthony Williams (above), *the new mayor of Washington, DC.*

exchanges, but it allowed groups that ran such programs to receive public funding for other uses.

Child-Welfare System. Beleaguered by a shortage of social workers, disorganization, and inconsistent payments to foster parents and day-care providers, the DC child-welfare system was under extreme duress. As of September, 3,334 DC children were in the foster-care system, and that figure was likely to rise. A city audit completed in 1999 reported that, partly due to shoddy accounting and lack of financial expertise, DC Child and Family Services had spent its $107 million annual budget by August, two months before the end of the fiscal year. Mayor Williams was considering a number of modifications, including a program in which DC would reduce its number of foster children by aggressively encouraging adoption.

Police Reform. A taxpayer-funded investigation of the 3,500-member police force by the DC Council committee, which began in December 1997, uncovered 65 instances of misconduct and mismanagement. In late 1999 the committee complained that its report's 46 recommendations to remedy the situation were not being implemented quickly enough. DC Police Chief Charles Ramsey refuted the charge, saying that he already had started a new performance-evaluation system; launched a 40-hour-per-year mandatory in-service training for all sworn personnel; and ordered all officers to requalify twice a year to use their weapons.

Curfew. After four years of court challenges, a City Council–approved curfew for the District began in September. The curfew prohibited children under 17 years old from being in a public place unaccompanied by a parent, guardian, or other person 21 or older between 11 P.M. and 6 A.M. Monday through Thursday, and between midnight and 6 A.M. Friday through Sunday. The mayor supported the new curfew in spite of concerns by DC police and the American Civil Liberties Union (ACLU) that the logistics of enforcing the law were untenable.

LYNDI SCHRECENGOST, *Freelance Writer*

Yugoslavia

The Federal Republic of Yugoslavia experienced severe turmoil during 1999. The regime of President Slobodan Milosevic maintained tight controls over the country's political and economic systems and stifled any organized opposition. Yugoslavia also lost the war with the North Atlantic Treaty Organization (NATO) over the Serbian province of Kosovo (*see* THE KOSOVO CRISIS, page 78), and disputes accelerated between the federal government in Belgrade and the reformist administration in the republic of Montenegro.

Political Repression. The Milosevic government was able to survive in office through a mixture of political repression, police intimidation, the fanning of Serbian nationalism, and the manipulation of the opposition. Milosevic's Socialist Party maintained a government with the neo-communist United Yugoslav Left—led by the president's wife, Mirjana Markovic—and the ultranationalist Serbian Radical Party, led by Serbian Deputy Prime Minister Vojislav Seselj.

Milosevic had at his disposal a network of agents and informers, and a special police force that harassed the independent media, political opponents, student leaders, civic groups, and the country's ethnic minorities. A number of outspoken journalists and human-rights campaigners were either

YUGOSLAVIA • Information Highlights

Official Name: Federal Republic of Yugoslavia.
Location: Southeastern Europe.
Area: 39,518 sq mi (102 350 km^2).
Population (July 1999 est.): 11,206,847.
Chief Cities (1991 census): Belgrade, the capital, 1,168,454; Novi Sad, 179,626; Nis, 175,391.
Government: *Head of state,* Slobodan Milosevic, federal president (sworn in July 23, 1997). *Head of government,* Momir Bulatovic, federal prime minister (took office May 1998). *Legislature*—Federal Assembly: Chamber of Republics and Chamber of Citizens.
Monetary Unit: Dinar (10.06 dinars equal U.S.$1, noncommercial rate, July 1999).
Gross Domestic Product (1998 est. U.S.$): $25,400,000,000.
Foreign Trade (1998 U.S.$): *Imports,* $4,622,000,000; *exports,* $2,604,000,000.

assassinated or physically attacked by perpetrators who never were apprehended by the police. Through a system of patronage and corruption, the regime's loyal supporters were given ownership over the most-lucrative sectors of the economy.

In the aftermath of the failed war with NATO over the province of Kosovo, the opposition parties became more active in seeking to dislodge Milosevic from power. A number of protest rallies and marches were organized during the summer by the Alliance for Change, the broadest opposition movement in Serbia. However, Milosevic refused to resign and launched a major propaganda campaign against his opponents through the state-controlled mass media. The protests largely fizzled out.

The opposition remained split between the Democratic Party, led by Zoran Djindjic, and the Serbian Renewal Movement, led by Vuk Draskovic. They failed to agree on a common platform or a joint strategy for unseating Milosevic. Moreover, Draskovic was believed to be corrupt and maintained clandestine contacts with Milosevic, having served in the Yugoslav federal government until the onset of the war with NATO. While much of the opposition demanded early general elections, the ruling party said that it would allow only for the holding of local elections in 2000.

Conflict with Montenegro. The reformist Montenegrin government of Prime Minister Milo Djukanovic grew increasingly impatient with Belgrade's policies. It refused to recognize the legitimacy of the federal government and took steps to assert its economic and political sovereignty while appealing for international assistance and protection.

Montenegro did not support the Serbian crackdown in Kosovo. Montenegrin recruits were not required to serve in the Yugoslav army during its actions in Kosovo, and the Montenegrin government allowed in tens of thousands of Albanian refugees. After the Kosovo conflict ended in June, large numbers of paramilitaries, many of them heavily armed, crossed the border into Montenegro, allying themselves with the Serbian government. Some observers feared this military buildup might lead to full-fledged armed combat. Meanwhile, a group of prominent intellectuals formed the Montenegrin Independence Movement and called for a referendum on statehood.

In July the Montenegrin government proposed a platform for an equal relationship with Serbia in a looser confederal arrangement, a move that largely was ignored by Belgrade. In a measure designed to further the republic's economic independence, in September, Montenegro introduced the German mark as legal tender in the republic. This step was condemned as separatist by the Serbian authorities.

Economy. The Yugoslav economy continued to decline because of a combination of factors, including international sanctions, damage inflicted during the war over Kosovo, corruption, mismanagement, and lack of foreign investment. Little statistical information was available from Yugoslavia, although economists believed that Serbia-Montenegro soon would be the poorest country in Europe in terms of industrial output and per-capita income. According to United Nations (UN) estimates, 63% of the population subsisted below the poverty line. Observers also feared a new wave of hyperinflation and a precipitous drop in the value of the Yugoslav currency, the dinar.

JANUSZ BUGAJSKI
Center for Strategic and International Studies

Zaire. *See* CONGO, DEMOCRATIC REPUBLIC OF THE.

Zimbabwe

Zimbabwe slipped deeper into political and economic crisis during 1999, in part as a result of President Robert Mugabe's unpopular and costly military intervention 600 mi (965 km) away in the Democratic Republic of the Congo (DRC). While the opposition press frequently criticized the government, there was only limited organized political opposition to Mugabe's ruling Zimbabwe African National Union–Patriotic Front

(ZANU-PF). Morgan Tsvangirai, secretary-general of the Zimbabwe Congress of Trade Unions, helped to found the Movement for Democratic Change (MDC) to challenge Robert Mugabe and ZANU-PF.

Tsvangirai publicly charged the government with widespread corruption and with squandering millions of dollars to maintain more than 10,000 Zimbabwean troops—one third of the army—in an "unwanted military adventure in the Congo," and he personally charged President Mugabe with betraying the ideals of the liberation war that brought Zimbabwe to independence after 100 years of colonial rule.

Economy. Tsvangirai maintained that the country's economy was in a state of crisis, with 75% of Zimbabwe's population living below the poverty line. He urged international donors to get tougher with the government. Indeed, international lenders such as the International Monetary Fund, the World Bank, and the European Union (EU) announced that loans and aid programs to Zimbabwe worth more than $340 million were "under review." The depreciation of the Zimbabwe dollar by more than 200% since 1997, inflation estimated at as high as 70%, and unemployment now said to be above 50% had led to civil and labor unrest. At a time when funds were needed desperately at home, Zimbabwe's support for Congolese President Laurent Kabila intensified internal and international criticism.

Mugabe remained unmoved by the criticism, and, in fact, the 2000 budget, released by Finance Minister Herbert Murerwa in October, proposed a significant increase in defense spending, a move that analysts believed could compromise the country's ability to service its foreign debts. In addition, concessions were made to tobacco growers, whose crops are Zimbabwe's single largest currency earner. An additional 3% tax was levied on personal and corporate earnings to combat the AIDS epidemic in Zimbabwe, which is among the countries with the highest rates of infection in the world.

The government also exacerbated Zimbabwe's economic troubles with its attempts to keep certain food prices artificially low. This resulted in farmers switching to more-lucrative crops, which in turn necessitated the use of foreign-exchange earnings for increased importation of grain from South Africa and the United States.

Doctors' Strike. In September, 50% of the country's 800 doctors went on strike, bringing much of the health system to a stop. Their drastic action was precipitated by shortages of drugs and medical equipment and low wages. Salaries for doctors averaged about $160 per month. The doctors' anger was shared by many Zimbabweans, who believed that the health budget was totally inadequate to combat the severity of endemic and epidemic diseases—including, in particular, HIV-AIDS cases, which had increased dramatically in recent years.

In November doctors in government hospitals ended their strike when they received assurances that their demands for salary increases and improved conditions would be met. After the doctors ended their strike, nearly 6,000 nurses at the same hospitals went on strike over the same grievances.

The Constitution. The Zimbabwe constitution, which was agreed to at Lancaster House in London in 1979, led to an end to white-minority rule in 1980. It had been amended 15 times over the years, and many of its protective clauses had been diluted. During 1999, President Mugabe appointed a commission of inquiry to rewrite the present constitution. However, the National Constitutional Assembly (NCA)—a broad-based civil-society organization that includes opposition parties, women's organizations, and trade unions—was left out. A majority of those Mugabe appointed to the commission, the NCA claimed, had strong ties to ZANU-PF and could be counted on to uphold the extensive powers of the presidency. At a number of public hearings held throughout the country, people demanded curbs on the president's powers and a limit of two terms in office.

Joshua Nkomo. On July 1, Joshua Nkomo, considered by many the founding father of Zimbabwe, died of prostate cancer at the age of 82.

PATRICK O'MEARA and N. BRIAN WINCHESTER
Indiana University

ZIMBABWE • Information Highlights

Official Name: Republic of Zimbabwe.
Location: Southern Africa.
Area: 150,803 sq mi (390 580 km²).
Population (July 1999 est.): 11,163,160.
Chief Cities (August 1992 census): Harare, the capital, 1,189,103; Bulawayo, 621,742; Chitungwiza, 274,912.
Government: *Head of state and government,* Robert Mugabe, executive president (sworn in Dec. 31, 1987). *Legislature* (unicameral)—House of Assembly.
Monetary Unit: Zimbabwe dollar (38.30 Z dollars equal U.S.$1, Dec. 29, 1999).
Gross Domestic Product (1998 est. U.S.$): $26,200,-000,000.
Economic Indexes (1998, 1990 = 100): *Consumer Prices,* all items, 636.9; food, 893.2. *Industrial Production,* 88.1.
Foreign Trade (1998 est. U.S.$): *Imports,* $2,000,000,000; *exports,* $1,700,000,000.

Zoos and Zoology

Several brand-new aquariums and a number of major zoo exhibits opened to the public during 1999. In June, Moody Gardens in Galveston, TX, unveiled the Aquarium Pyramid, a companion to its ten-story Rainforest Pyramid and the Discovery Pyramid. The 130,000-sq-ft (12 077-m^2) blue-glass aquarium displays more than 10,000 aquatic animals in 1.5 million gallons (5.7 million l) of water. Guests begin in the North Pacific exhibit, featuring fur seals and a spectacular kelp forest, then move on to the Great Barrier Reef and Coral Sea exhibit, which displays 200 species of colorful fish and stingrays. King penguins rule in the Antarctic realm, and the Caribbean Sea exhibit includes a glass tunnel in which visitors are surrounded by views of the ocean floor.

The new aquatic facility in Denver, CO, aptly is called Ocean Journey. The high-tech $93 million aquarium transports visitors along replicas of two major river systems—the Colorado and the Kampar of Sumatra, Indonesia—as they flow from their mountain origins to the sea. The trip on the Colorado begins with fossilized ancient sea creatures embedded in canyon walls, plummets down a waterfall in the Rocky Mountains, and ends in the crystal-clear Sea of Cortez. The Kampar River is followed from the Asian monsoon season high in the Indonesian volcanoes and through a tropical rain forest; it ends in a mangrove-bordered coral lagoon, home to two impressive-looking Sumatran tigers.

There are five special underwater tunnels at Oceanic Adventures Newport Aquarium (KY), which take visitors diving with sharks and into the colorful world of the coral reef. In addition, this new aquarium features king penguins in icy Antarctica, a humid and swampy 'gator bayou, a jellyfish gallery, and an overview of the Ohio River.

The aquatic ecosystem of southern Florida is the focus of Manatee Springs, which opened in May at the Cincinnati Zoo and Botanical Garden (OH). This new exhibit has a twofold purpose: highlighting the man-made threats to the endangered West Indian manatee, American crocodile, sea grasses, and other animal and plant species native to this highly developed region; and providing a home for rescued and rehabilitated manatees that are unable to survive in the wild.

Two exhibits re-creating the tropical rain forest of central Africa made their debuts during the year. The first was the Ituri Forest, which opened in May at San Diego Zoo (CA). This 2-acre (0.8-ha) jungle habitat features okapis (a distant cousin of the giraffe that lives only in this forest), river hippopotamuses, forest buffalos, guenons (monkeys), and six species of birds. Also featuring okapis, but much more elaborate, is Congo Gorilla Forest, which opened in June at the Bronx Zoo in New York to celebrate the 100th anniversary of the zoo. The hallmark species of this exhibit is the western lowland gorilla. The zoo's 19 gorillas roam spacious outdoor displays in two breeding groups, each headed by a mature silverback male. Among other Congo species are colobus

© Pat Sullivan/AP/Wide World Photos

The new Aquarium Pyramid at Moody Gardens in Galveston, TX, is home to more than 10,000 aquatic animals, whose native habitats range from the Northern Pacific to the tropics. Visitors can view many of them close up through clear walls, right.

© Brent Stirton/Liaison Agency

In the Bronx Zoo's newly opened Congo Gorilla Forest exhibit, 19 western lowland gorillas can roam their outdoor habitat or, if they choose, can interact with human visitors, left.

monkeys, mandrills, guenons, red river hogs, and a host of reptiles, fish, and invertebrates.

July 1 marked two milestones for the Philadelphia (PA) Zoo: It was the zoo's 125th anniversary and the opening of PECO Primate Reserve. A tragic fire on Christmas Eve 1995 had destroyed the old World of Primates, killing 23 animals. The new facility houses 11 primate species, including western lowland gorillas, Sumatran orangutans, white-handed gibbons, golden lion tamarins, and blue-eyed lemurs.

As the start of its Zoo 2002 project, Riverbanks Zoo in Columbia, SC, opened two new exhibits. The Bird Conservation Center and ten aviaries already had produced toucan chicks and provided homes for rare Bali mynahs, king vultures, and various parrots and macaws. The Riverbanks Farm was renovated to include black rat snakes, barn owls, and box turtles, in order to help visitors better understand the connections between farms and humans and between farms and the natural world.

Zoology. Ever since the cloning of the sheep named Dolly, scientists have been dreaming of other uses for this reproductive technique. In June researchers at the Chinese Academy of Sciences made news by boasting that cloning possibly could save China's national treasure—the giant panda. About 1,000 giant pandas remain in the wild in 32 separate areas; their forests are threatened by logging and human development. There is little opportunity for exchange of genes among the wild populations, and the giant panda is under serious threat of extinction. Chinese researchers took cells from a giant panda and multiplied them under laboratory conditions. A successful embryo was created and nurtured. Plans were under way to implant the embryo into the uterus of a host—probably a female of a closely related species, because of the ethical implications of experimenting with an endangered animal. According to experts, successful cloning could help maintain the diminishing genetic diversity of the giant panda and slow its decline. But conservationists are afraid that such a quick-fix solution will take the pressure off the issue of halting habitat destruction in China. This pressing problem threatens a host of other native species.

In November two giant pandas—on a ten-year loan from China—arrived at Zoo Atlanta, bringing the U.S. panda population to six. The 2-year-old pair would be on display at a new $7 million habitat. Their U.S. stay is part of a project to ascertain why pandas often will not mate in captivity. Late in November the National Zoo's giant panda Hsing-Hsing, 28, died.

Biologists from the Wildlife Conservation Society in New York discovered a new species of rabbit hopping around the forests of Laos, in the remote Annamite Mountains. This area is where the saola (a distant relative of wild cattle) and several new species of small deer were discovered in the mid-1990s. According to the researchers, the new rabbit's closest relative is a critically endangered species in Sumatra, about 1,000 mi (1 600 km) away.

The number of California condors in the wild was soaring, relatively speaking, with the release of eight young birds in northern Arizona. This brought to 28 the number of captive-bred birds released in the region. Another 28 were gliding in the California skies, and nearly 100 birds were in captivity.

DEBORAH A. BEHLER, *Executive Editor*
"Wildlife Conservation" magazine

STATISTICAL AND TABULAR DATA

Nations of the World[1]
A Profile and Synopsis of Major 1999 Developments

Andorra, S.W. Europe

Population: 65,939 **Capital:** Andorra la Vella
Area: 174 sq mi (450 km²)
Government: Marc Forne Molne, head of government

Angola, W. Africa

Population: 11,177,537 **Capital:** Luanda
Area: 481,351 sq mi (1 246 700 km²)
Government: José Eduardo dos Santos, president. (See also AFRICA.)

Antigua and Barbuda, Caribbean

Population: 64,246 **Capital:** St. John's
Area: 170 sq mi (440 km²)
Government: James B. Carlisle, governor-general; Lester Bird, prime minister

In March elections, Prime Minister Lester Bird's ruling Antigua Labour Party won 12 of the 17 seats in Parliament, a one-seat increase over the previous Parliament. (See also CARIBBEAN.)

Bahamas, Caribbean

Population: 283,705 **Capital:** Nassau
Area: 5,382 sq mi (13 940 km²)
Government: Sir Orville Turnquest, governor-general; Hubert A. Ingraham, prime minister. (See also CARIBBEAN.)

Bahrain, W. Asia

Population: 629,090 **Capital:** Manama
Area: 239 sq mi (620 km²)
Government: Hamad bin Isa Al Khalifa, emir; Khalifa bin Salman Al Khalifa, prime minister

Emir Isa bin Salman Al Khalifa, ruler of Bahrain since 1961, died on March 6. He was succeeded by his son, Crown Prince Hamad bin Isa Al Khalifa, who had been serving as commander of the nation's defense forces. In December, Bahrain and Qatar agreed to exchange ambassadors and improve relations. Bahrain's term as a member of the United Nations Security Council ended on December 31.

Barbados, Caribbean

Population: 259,191 **Capital:** Bridgetown
Area: 166 sq mi (430 km²)
Government: Sir Clifford Husbands, governor-general; Owen Arthur, prime minister. (See also CARIBBEAN.)

Benin, W. Africa

Population: 6,305,567 **Capital:** Porto Novo
Area: 43,483 sq mi (112 620 km²)
Government: Mathieu Kerekou, president

In March elections, a coalition of opposition parties, including former President Nicephore Soglo's Renaissance of Benin Party, won a majority of seats in the 83-seat National Assembly. In August, Benin, along with Ghana and Togo, signed an agreement with the Chevron Corp. and Royal Dutch/Shell Group to finance a West African gas pipeline, which would bring Nigerian gas to the three nations. Also during the summer, the government asked the public to help in an awareness campaign about an increasing national problem, the sexual abuse of children.

Bhutan, S. Asia

Population: 1,951,965 **Capital:** Thimphu
Area: 18,147 sq mi (47 000 km²)
Government: Jigme Singye Wangchuck, king

In December, in an effort to improve its human-rights standing in the international community, Bhutan released 200 political prisoners from jail. The nation had been condemned for forcing thousands of people, most of them ethnic Nepalis, out of the country.

Botswana, S. Africa

Population: 1,464,167 **Capital:** Gaborone
Area: 231,803 sq mi (600 370 km²)
Government: Festus Mogae, president

President Festus Mogae was reelected in October, and his ruling Botswana Democratic Party won 33 of the 40 seats in the National Assembly. The World Court ruled in December that Kasikili (Sedudu), a tiny uninhabited island in the Chobe River, belongs to Botswana, not Namibia, thus ending a dispute between the two countries.

Brunei Darussalam, S.E. Asia

Population: 322,982 **Capital:** Bandar Seri Begawan
Area: 2,288 sq mi (5 770 km²)
Government: Hassanal Bolkiah, sultan and prime minister

Burkina Faso, W. Africa

Population: 11,575,898 **Capital:** Ouagadougou
Area: 105,869 sq mi (274 200 km²)
Government: Blaise Compaoré, president; Kadre Desire Ouedraogo, prime minister

Burundi, E. Africa

Population: 5,735,937 **Capital:** Bujumbura
Area: 10,745 sq mi (27 830 km²)
Government: Pierre Buyoya, president. (See also AFRICA.)

Cameroon, Cen. Africa

Population: 15,456,092 **Capital:** Yaoundé
Area: 183,568 sq mi (475 440 km²)
Government: Paul Biya, president; Peter Mafany Musonge, prime minister

Cape Verde, W. Africa

Population: 405,748 **Capital:** Praia
Area: 1,556 sq mi (4 030 km²)
Government: Antonio Mascarenhas Monteiro, president; Carlos Wahnon Veiga, prime minister

Central African Republic, Cen. Africa

Population: 3,444,951 **Capital:** Bangui
Area: 240,533 sq mi (622 980 km²)
Government: Ange-Félix Patasse, president; Anicet-Georges Dologuele, prime minister

In September, President Ange-Félix Patasse was reelected to a six-year term; his victory was disputed by the opposition.

Chad, Cen. Africa

Population: 7,557,436 **Capital:** Ndjamena
Area: 495,753 sq mi (1 284 000 km²)
Government: Idriss Déby, president; Nagoum Yamassoum, prime minister

Comoros, E. Africa

Population: 562,723 **Capital:** Moroni
Area: 838 sq mi (2 170 km²)
Government: Azaly Assoumani, president and prime minister

On April 30 the Comoran army ousted the government of President Tadjidine Ben Said Massoundi. Col. Azaly Assoumani, who was installed as president on May 6, promised to put into effect an agreement to give greater autonomy to the separatist-minded islands of Anjouan and Moheli and thus keep the three-island nation from falling apart. The two islands had declared their independence in 1997, a move that was contested bitterly by the people of Grande Comore, the largest island in the Indian Ocean nation.

[1]Independent nations not covered in pages 110–581.

Congo, Republic of, Cen. Africa

Population: 2,716,814 **Capital:** Brazzaville
Area: 132,046 sq mi (342 000 km^2)
Government: Denis Sassou-Nguesso, president

Congo's civil war continued in 1999 despite a split in the rebel movement. At midyear, United Nations (UN) Secretary-General Kofi Annan called for the sending of an international peacekeeping force to Congo. In late December the rebels agreed to a new peace accord.

Djibouti, E. Africa

Population: 447,439 **Capital:** Djibouti
Area: 8,494 sq mi (22 000 km^2)
Government: Ismail Omar Guelleh, president; Barkat Gourad Hamadou, prime minister

In April elections, Ismail Omar Guelleh was elected president. He succeeded Hassan Gouled Aptidon, who had been president since Djibouti became independent of France in 1977.

Dominica, Caribbean

Population: 64,881 **Capital:** Roseau
Area: 290 sq mi (750 km^2)
Government: Crispin Anselm Sorhaindo, president; Edison James, prime minister. (See also CARIBBEAN.)

Dominican Republic, Caribbean

Population: 8,129,734 **Capital:** Santo Domingo
Area: 18,815 sq mi (48 730 km^2)
Government: Leonel Fernandez Reyna, president. (See also CARIBBEAN.)

Equatorial Guinea, Cen. Africa

Population: 465,746 **Capital:** Malabo
Area: 10,830 sq mi (28 050 km^2)
Government: Teodoro Obiang Nguema Mbasogo, president; Angel Serafin Seriche Dougan, prime minister

Eritrea, E. Africa

Population: 3,984,723 **Capital:** Asmara
Area: 46,841 sq mi (121 320 km^2)
Government: Isaias Afeworki, president

Eritrea's border war with Ethiopia, which erupted in May 1998, began anew in February 1999. Each side claimed to have killed thousands of enemy troops. (See also ETHIOPIA.)

Fiji, Oceania

Population: 812,918 **Capital:** Suva
Area: 7,054 sq mi (18 270 km^2)
Government: Kamisese Mara, president; Mahendra Chaudhry, prime minister

In May elections, the Fiji Labour Party and its opposition-coalition allies won a majority of Fiji's 71 legislative seats. The election was the nation's first since political rights were restored to the nation's ethnic Indians in 1998. Mahendra Chaudhry was named premier; he was the first ethnic Indian to hold that post.

Gabon, Cen. Africa

Population: 1,225,853 **Capital:** Libreville
Area: 103,348 sq mi (267 670 km^2)
Government: El Hadj Omar Bongo, president; Jean-François Ntoutoume-Emane, prime minister

Gambia, W. Africa

Population: 1,336,320 **Capital:** Banjul
Area: 4,363 sq mi (11 300 km^2)
Government: Yahya Jammeh, head of state

Ghana, W. Africa

Population: 18,887,626 **Capital:** Accra
Area: 4,363 sq mi (238 540 km^2)
Government: Jerry Rawlings, president

King Otumfuo Opoku Ware II, leader of Ghana's Ashanti people since 1970, died on February 25 at 79. He was succeeded by Nana Kwaku Dua, a 49-year-old businessman who took the title King Osei Tutu II. In August, Ghana—along with Togo and Benin—signed an agreement with the Chevron Corp. and Royal Dutch/Shell Group to finance a West African gas pipeline, which would bring Nigerian gas to the three nations.

Grenada, Caribbean

Population: 97,008 **Capital:** St. George's
Area: 131 sq mi (340 km^2)
Government: Daniel Williams, governor-general; Keith Mitchell, prime minister

Following the collapse of his government in 1998, Prime Minister Keith Mitchell led his New National Party to victory in January elections, winning all 15 seats in Parliament. Mitchell was sworn in the following day. (See also CARIBBEAN.)

Guinea, W. Africa

Population: 7,538,953 **Capital:** Conakry
Area: 94,927 sq mi (245 860 km^2)
Government: Lansana Conté, president; Lamine Sidime, prime minister. (See also AFRICA.)

Guinea-Bissau, W. Africa

Population: 1,234,555 **Capital:** Bissau
Area: 13,946 sq mi (36 120 km^2)
Government: Malam Bacai Sanha, interim president; Francisco Fadul, interim prime minister. (See also AFRICA.)

Guyana, N.E. South America

Population: 705,156 **Capital:** Georgetown
Area: 83,000 sq mi (214 970 km^2)
Government: Bharrat Jagdeo, president; Samuel Hinds, prime minister. (See also CARIBBEAN.)

Haiti, Caribbean

Population: 6,884,264 **Capital:** Port-au-Prince
Area: 10,714 sq mi (27 750 km^2)
Government: René Préval, president; Jacques-Edouard Alexis, prime minister. (See also CARIBBEAN.)

Ivory Coast (Côte d'Ivoire), W. Africa

Population: 15,818,068 **Capital:** Yamoussoukro
Area: 124,502 sq mi (322 460 km^2)
Government: Gen. Robert Gueï, president

On December 24, President Henri Konan Bédié was ousted in a military coup. Gen. Robert Gueï, former chief of the armed forces, proclaimed himself president and promised an "orderly return" to democracy.

Jamaica, Caribbean

Population: 2,652,443 **Capital:** Kingston
Area: 4,243 sq mi (10 990 km^2)
Government: Sir Howard Cooke, governor-general; P.J. Patterson, prime minister

A tax that increased fuel prices by 30%, as well as increases in some other taxes, led to three days of protests and rioting in mid-April. Nine people were killed before order was restored. Prime Minister P.J. Patterson appointed a committee to find alternative revenues, and within days he announced that the fuel taxes would be rolled back by 50%. (See also CARIBBEAN.)

Kazakhstan, Cen. Asia

Population: 16,824,825 **Capital:** Astana (Akmola)
Area: 1,049,155 sq mi (2 717 300 km^2)
Government: Nursultan A. Nazarbayev, president; Kasymzhomart Tokayev, prime minister

In January, President Nursultan A. Nazarbayev was reelected. Western observers said that harassment of opposition candidates had marred the election seriously. At an August meeting in Bishkek, the capital of Kyrgyzstan, the leaders of Kazakhstan, Kyrgyzstan, and Tajikistan—along with China and Russia—pledged to increase economic cooperation and security along their borders. In September, Nazarbayev apologized to the United States for selling MiG jet fighters to North Korea.

Kiribati, Oceania

Population: 85,501 **Capital:** Tarawa
Area: 277 sq mi (717 km²)
Government: Teburoro Tito, president

Kiribati became a member of the United Nations on September 14.

Kuwait, W. Asia

Population: 1,991,115 **Capital:** Kuwait
Area: 6,800 sq mi (17 820 km²)
Government: Jabir al-Ahmad al-Sabah, emir; Saad al-Abdallah al-Sabah, prime minister

In July elections, 34 of the 50 contested seats in the nation's parliament were won by candidates from the Shiite and Sunni branches of Islam. In November the parliament rejected giving women the rights to vote and to run for political office.

Kyrgyzstan, Cen. Asia

Population: 4,546,055 **Capital:** Bishkek (Frunze)
Area: 76,641 sq mi (198 500 km²)
Government: Askar Akayev, president; Amangeldy Muraliyev, prime minister

At a meeting in Bishkek, the leaders of Kyrgyzstan, Kazakhstan, and Tajikistan—along with China and Russia—pledged in August to increase economic cooperation and security along their borders. On October 24, Islamic militants released four Japanese geologists and an interpreter who had been held captive for two months. Other hostages had been released earlier, and it was believed that one had been killed.

Lesotho, S. Africa

Population: 2,128,950 **Capital:** Maseru
Area: 11,718 sq mi (30 350 km²)
Government: Letsie III, king; Bethuel Pakalitha Mosisili, prime minister

Ntsu Mokhehle, Lesotho's prime minister (1993–98), died at age 80 on January 6.

Liberia, W. Africa

Population: 2,923,725 **Capital:** Monrovia
Area: 43,000 sq mi (111 370 km²)
Government: Charles Taylor, president

In August, Liberian Defense Minister Daniel Chea accused forces from neighboring Guinea of using artillery to support rebel attacks against Liberia's northern Lofa county.

Liechtenstein, Cen. Europe

Population: 32,057 **Capital:** Vaduz
Area: 62 sq mi (160 km²)
Government: Hans Adam II, prince; Mario Frick, prime minister

In a power struggle with Liechtenstein's parliament in September, Prince Hans Adam II threatened to move to Austria if the parliament attempted to curtail his powers.

Luxembourg, W. Europe

Population: 429,080 **Capital:** Luxembourg
Area: 998 sq mi (2 586 km²)
Government: Jean, grand duke; Jean-Claude Juncker, premier

In June elections, Premier Jean-Claude Juncker's Social Christian Party won 19 of 60 parliament seats. The composition of Luxembourg's representation in the European Parliament remained about the same following separate elections. U.S. President Bill Clinton appointed James Hormel ambassador to Luxembourg. He was the first openly homosexual U.S. ambassador, and his appointment stirred controversy. In December it was announced that 78-year-old Grand Duke Jean would abdicate in 2000, relinquishing his position to Prince Henri, his oldest son.

Madagascar, E. Africa

Population: 14,873,387 **Capital:** Antananarivo
Area: 226,656 sq mi (587 040 km²)
Government: Didier Ratsiraka, president; Tantely Andrianarivo, premier

Malawi, E. Africa

Population: 10,000,416 **Capital:** Lilongwe
Area: 45,745 sq mi (118 480 km²)
Government: Bakili Muluzi, president

In June, Bakili Muluzi, leader of the ruling United Democratic Front and president of Malawi since 1994, was reelected.

Maldives, S. Asia

Population: 300,220 **Capital:** Malé
Area: 116 sq mi (300 km²)
Government: Maumoon Abdul Gayoom, president

Mali, W. Africa

Population: 10,429,124 **Capital:** Bamako
Area: 478,764 sq mi (1 240 000 km²)
Government: Alpha Oumar Konare, president; Ibrahim Boubacar Keita, prime minister. (See also AFRICA.)

Malta, S. Europe

Population: 381,603 **Capital:** Valletta
Area: 124 sq mi (320 km²)
Government: Guido De Marco, president; Edward Fenech Adami, prime minister

Marshall Islands, Pacific Ocean

Population: 65,507 **Capital:** Majuro
Area: 70 sq mi (181 km²)
Government: Kessai Note, president

Mauritania, W. Africa

Population: 2,581,738 **Capital:** Nouakchott
Area: 397,954 sq mi (1 030 700 km²)
Government: Maaouya Ould Sid Ahmed Taya, president; Cheikh El Avia Ould Mohamed, prime minister

Mauritius, E. Africa

Population: 1,182,212 **Capital:** Port Louis
Area: 718 sq mi (1 860 km²)
Government: Casseem Uteem, president; Navin Ramgoolam, prime minister

Micronesia, Federated States of, Pacific Ocean

Population: 131,500 **Capital:** Kolonia
Area: 271 sq mi (702 km²)
Government: Leo A. Falcam, president

Moldova, Europe

Population: 4,460,838 **Capital:** Chisinau (Kishinev)
Area: 13,067 sq mi (33 843 km²)
Government: Petru Lucinschi, president; Dumitru Braghis, prime minister

Six weeks after the resignation of Ion Ciubuc, prime minister since 1997, Parliament approved Ion Sturza as prime minister on March 12. Sturza, a reform-oriented former economic minister, was ousted by the legislature in a November no-confidence vote. He was replaced by Dumitru Braghis, the deputy economic minister.

Monaco, S. Europe

Population: 32,149 **Capital:** Monaco-Ville
Area: 0.7 sq mi (1.9 km²)
Government: Rainier III, prince; Michel Lévêque, minister of state

In May, Prince Rainier III marked the 50th anniversary of his reign.

Mongolia, N. Asia

Population: 2,617,379 **Capital:** Ulan Bator
Area: 604,247 sq mi (1 565 000 km²)
Government: Natsagiin Bagabandi, president; Rinchinnyamiin Amarjargal, prime minister

On July 22, following a no-confidence vote by the Mongolian parliament, Prime Minister Janlaviin Narantsatsralt and his government resigned. He had been in office only seven months, and his government was the third to collapse in 15 months. On July 30, Foreign Minister Rinchinnyamiin Amarjargal took over.

Mozambique, E. Africa

Population: 19,124,335 **Capital:** Maputo
Area: 309,496 sq mi (801 590 km^2)
Government: Joaquim Chissano, president; Pascoal Mocumbi, prime minister. (See also AFRICA.)

Namibia, W. Africa

Population: 1,648,270 **Capital:** Windhoek
Area: 318,696 sq mi (825 418 km^2)
Government: Sam Nujoma, president; Hage Geingob, prime minister. (See also AFRICA.)

Nauru, Oceania

Population: 10,605 **Capital:** Nauru
Area: 8 sq mi (21 km^2)
Government: Rene Harris, president

Nauru became a member of the United Nations on September 14.

Nepal, S. Asia

Population: 24,302,653 **Capital:** Katmandu
Area: 54,363 sq mi (140 800 km^2)
Government: Birendra Bir Bikram Shah Deva, king; Krishna Prasad Bhattarai, prime minister

Following Prime Minister Girija Prasad Koirala's resignation in December 1998, King Birendra dissolved Parliament on January 15 and ordered new elections, held in May. The Nepali Congress Party (NCP) won a majority in the House of Representatives, the lower house of Nepal's Parliament. Krishna Prasad Bhattarai of the NCP was sworn in as prime minister on May 31; due to intraparty dissent, Bhattarai announced late in the year that he would step down early in 2000.

Niger, W. Africa

Population: 9,962,242 **Capital:** Niamey
Area: 489,189 sq mi (1 267 000 km^2)
Government: Mamadou Tandja, president; Hama Amadou, prime minister. (See also AFRICA.)

Oman, W. Asia

Population: 2,446,645 **Capital:** Muscat
Area: 82,031 sq mi (212 460 km^2)
Government: Qaboos bin Said Al Said, sultan and prime minister

Palau, N. Pacific Ocean

Population: 18,467 **Capital:** Koror
Area: 177 sq mi (458 km^2)
Government: Kuniwo Nakamura, president

Papua New Guinea, Oceania

Population: 4,705,126 **Capital:** Port Moresby
Area: 178,259 sq mi (462 840 km^2)
Government: Sir Silas Atopare, governor-general; Mekere Morauta, prime minister

Facing a certain vote of no-confidence in parliament, Prime Minister Bill Skate, leader of the ruling First Party, resigned on July 7. Skate's problems were the result of his government's collapse ten days earlier, economic decline, and his decision to establish diplomatic relations with Taiwan. Sir Mekere Morauta, leader of the opposition People's Democratic Movement, was elected prime minister by the parliament on July 14. He reversed the decision to establish diplomatic ties with Taiwan.

Qatar, W. Asia

Population: 723,542 **Capital:** Doha
Area: 4,416 sq mi (11 437 km^2)
Government: Hamad bin Khalifa Al Thani, emir and prime minister

In March, Qatar held its first-ever elections—for a 29-seat Central Municipal Council. It was notable for the fact that women both voted and ran for office. During a March visit to Qatar by U.S. Secretary of Defense William Cohen, Foreign Minister Sheik Hamad bin Jasim al-Thani called on the United States to halt its air strikes against Iraq. In December, Qatar and Bahrain agreed to exchange ambassadors and improve relations.

Rwanda, E. Africa

Population: 8,154,933 **Capital:** Kigali
Area: 10,170 sq mi (26 340 km^2)
Government: Pasteur Bizimungu, president; Pierre Celestin Rwigema, prime minister

In May, to help end the civil war in neighboring Congo (Kinshasa), Rwanda declared a unilateral cease-fire for its troops there. They had been supporting Congo rebels in their effort to oust President Laurent Kabila. In December, Hutu rebels killed some 30 villagers in northwest Rwanda. Earlier, the government had announced that it would replace its flag, coat of arms, and national anthem, because they were symbols of the Hutu-dominated regime that had ruled the country until 1994.

Saint Kitts and Nevis, Caribbean

Population: 42,838 **Capital:** Basseterre
Area: 104 sq mi (269 km^2)
Government: Cuthbert M. Sebastian, governor-general; Denzil Douglas, prime minister

Saint Lucia, Caribbean

Population: 154,020 **Capital:** Castries
Area: 239 sq mi (620 km^2)
Government: Perlette Louisy, governor-general; Kenny Anthony, prime minister. (See also CARIBBEAN.)

Saint Vincent and the Grenadines, Caribbean

Population: 120,519 **Capital:** Kingstown
Area: 131 sq mi (340 km^2)
Government: David Jack, governor-general; James F. Mitchell, prime minister. (See also CARIBBEAN.)

Samoa, Oceania

Population: 229,979 **Capital:** Apia
Area: 1,104 sq mi (2 860 km^2)
Government: Malietoa Tanumafili II, head of state; Tuilaopa Sailele Malielegaoi, prime minister

Tofilau Eti Alesana, prime minister of Samoa (1982–85; 1988–98) and leader of Samoa's ruling Human Rights Protection Party, died on March 19.

San Marino, S. Europe

Population: 25,061 **Capital:** San Marino
Area: 23 sq mi (60 km^2)
Government: Loris Francini and Alberto Cecchetti, captains-regent

São Tomé and Príncipe, W. Africa

Population: 154,878 **Capital:** São Tomé
Area: 386 sq mi (1 000 km^2)
Government: Miguel Trovoada, president; Guilherme Posser da Costa, prime minister

Guilherme Posser da Costa was chosen to head a new government in January. The cabinet subsequently was reshuffled in July, with the ministers of foreign affairs and justice switching positions.

Senegal, W. Africa

Population: 10,051,930 **Capital:** Dakar
Area: 75,749 sq mi (196 190 km^2)
Government: Abdou Diouf, president; Mamadou Lamine Loum, prime minister

On January 24, Senegal established a bicameral legislature by creating a 60-member Senate. Members of the lower house of the legislature, the National Assembly, elected 45 members of the Senate, all of whom belonged to the ruling Socialist Party. President Abdou Diouf appointed 12 members, and Senegalese living in other countries elected three. Also in January, Senegal banned female circumcision.

Seychelles, E. Africa

Population: 79,164 **Capital:** Victoria
Area: 176 sq mi (455 km^2)
Government: France Albert René, president

Sierra Leone, W. Africa

Population: 5,296,651 **Capital:** Freetown
Area: 27,699 sq mi (71 740 km^2)
Government: Ahmad Tejan Kabbah, president. (See also AFRICA.)

Solomon Islands, Oceania

Population: 455,429 **Capital:** Honiara
Area: 10,985 sq mi (28 450 km^2)
Government: John Lapli, governor-general; Bartholomew Ulufa'alu, prime minister

On June 12 increasing tensions on Guadalcanal between Guadalcanalese and settlers from the nearby island of Malaita erupted into violence. Guadalcanalese militants attacked a plantation, killing three people. Two weeks later, the Solomon Islands government and the governments of the two islands signed an agreement to work toward a peaceful resolution.

Somalia, E. Africa

Population: 7,140,643 **Capital:** Mogadishu
Area: 471,776 sq mi (637 660 km^2)
Government: No functioning government as of December 1999

In June it was reported that Ethiopian armed forces had entered Somalia and occupied the city of Garba Harre, effectively placing southern Somalia under Ethiopian control.

Suriname, S. America

Population: 431,156 **Capital:** Paramaribo
Area: 63,039 sq mi (163 270 km^2)
Government: Jules Wijdenbosch, president

In June, to forestall his removal from office, President Jules Wijdenbosch called for elections to be held no later than May 25, 2000. Earlier, he had come under fire and lost a vote of no confidence in the National Assembly due to his failure to improve the sagging economy. On July 16 a Dutch court convicted Desi Bouterse, Suriname's former military leader, of cocaine trafficking. Bouterse, who had been Wijdenbosch's chief adviser until his dismissal in April, was convicted in absentia and was the subject of an international police hunt.

Swaziland, S. Africa

Population: 985,335 **Capital:** Mbabane
Area: 6,703 sq mi (17 360 km^2)
Government: Mswati III, king; Sibusiso Barnabas Dlamini, prime minister

Togo, W. Africa

Population: 5,081,413 **Capital:** Lomé
Area: 21,927 sq mi (56 790 km^2)
Government: Gnassingbé Eyadéma, president; Eugene Koffi Adoboli, prime minister

In August, Togo—along with Ghana and Benin—signed an agreement with the Chevron Corp. and Royal Dutch/Shell Group to finance a West African gas pipeline, which would bring Nigerian gas to the three nations.

Tonga, Oceania

Population: 109,082 **Capital:** Nuku'alofa
Area: 289 sq mi (748 km^2)
Government: Taufa'ahau Tupou IV, king; Baron Vaea, prime minister

Tonga became a member of the United Nations on September 14. In early January 2000, Baron Vaea was replaced as prime minister by King Taufa'ahau Tupou's youngest son, Prince Ulukalala Lavaka Ata. Vaea had applied for retirement almost five years earlier.

Trinidad and Tobago, Caribbean

Population: 1,102,096 **Capital:** Port-of-Spain
Area: 1,981 sq mi (5 130 km^2)
Government: Arthur Robinson, president; Basdeo Panday, prime minister

In June nine members of a drug gang were hanged for the 1994 murder of four people. There had been few executions in the former British colonies in the Caribbean; it was thought that these executions would open the door for others. *(See also CARIBBEAN.)*

Turkmenistan, Cen. Asia

Population: 4,366,383 **Capital:** Ashkhabad
Area: 188,457 sq mi (488 100 km^2)
Government: Saparmurad Niyazov

In December, Turkmenistan's parliament voted to make President Saparmurad Niyazov president for life. Also in December, the nation ended the practice of capital punishment.

Tuvalu, Oceania

Population: 10,588 **Capital:** Funafuti
Area: 10 sq mi (26 km^2)
Government: Sir Tomasi Puapua, governor-general; Ionatana Ionatana, prime minister

United Arab Emirates, W. Asia

Population: 2,344,402 **Capital:** Abu Dhabi
Area: 32,000 sq mi (82 880 km^2)
Government: Zayid bin Sultan Al Nuhayyan, president; Maktum bin Rashid Al Maktum, prime minister

In July the government of the United Arab Emirates stated that it would "take steps to clean up" the Dubai Islamic Bank, after the U.S. State Department charged the bank with channeling funds for accused terrorist Osama bin Laden.

Uzbekistan, Cen. Asia

Population: 24,102,473 **Capital:** Tashkent
Area: 172,742 sq mi (447 400 km^2)
Government: Islam Karimov, president

As the government's fight against Islamic militants continued, several car bombs exploded in Tashkent in February. Sixteen people were killed, and 120 were wounded. Six of those responsible for the bombings were sentenced to death in June; 16 others were sentenced to prison terms. In May the United States pledged more than $32 million in economic aid to Uzebekistan.

Vanuatu, Oceania

Population: 189,036 **Capital:** Port-Vila
Area: 5,699 sq mi (14 760 km^2)
Government: John Bani, president; Barak Sope, prime minister

Walter Lini, Vanuatu's first prime minister (1980–91), died February 21 at age 57.

Vatican City, S. Europe

Population: 870 **Capital:** Vatican City
Area: 0.17 sq mi (0.438 km^2)
Government: John Paul II, pope

Yemen, W. Asia

Population: 16,942,230 **Capital:** Sanaa
Area: 203,850 sq mi (527 970 km^2)
Government: Ali Abdullah Saleh, president; Abdul Ali al-Karim al-Iryani, prime minister

In May three Islamic militants were sentenced to death for the 1998 abduction of 16 Western tourists and the murder of four of them, who died in a failed rescue attempt. The leader of the militants was executed in October. In August a car bomb exploded in Sanaa, killing several people. And in October members of the Bani Jabr tribe kidnapped but quickly released three Americans. In September, in Yemen's first direct presidential election, President Ali Abdullah Saleh was reelected overwhelmingly. Opposition groups boycotted the voting.

Zambia, E. Africa

Population: 9,663,535 **Capital:** Lusaka
Area: 290,583 sq mi (752 610 km^2)
Government: Frederick Chiluba, president

Lusaka was the scene of 14 bomb attacks on February 28. Authorities speculated that the bombings were the result of Zambian support of rebels in neighboring Angola. On March 31 the High Court ruled that former president Kenneth Kaunda was not a Zambian citizen. Kaunda's son, Wezi Kaunda, was assassinated in November. In March the International Monetary Fund approved a $349 million loan to Zambia.

THE UNITED STATES GOVERNMENT

Executive Branch

(selected listing as of Jan. 1, 2000)

President: William J. (Bill) Clinton

Vice-President: Albert Gore, Jr.

Executive Office of the President

The White House

Chief of Staff to the President: John Podesta
Assistant to the President: Sidney Blumenthal
Assistant to the President and Cabinet Secretary: Thurgood Marshall, Jr.
Assistant to the President and Chief of Staff to the First Lady: Melanne Verveer
Assistant to the President and Deputy Chief of Staff: Maria Echaveste
Assistant to the President and Deputy Chief of Staff: Steve Ricchetti
Assistant to the President and Director of Communications: Loretta Ucelli
Assistant to the President and Director for Intergovernmental Affairs: Mickey Ibarra
Assistant to the President and Director of Legislative Affairs: Lawrence J. Stein
Assistant to the President and Director of Management and Administration: Mark Lewis
Assistant to the President and Deputy Counsel: Bruce Lindsey
Assistant to the President for Domestic Policy: Bruce Reed
Assistant to the President for Economic Policy: Gene Sperling
Assistant to the President for National Security Affairs: Samuel Berger
Counselor to the President: Ann F. Lewis
Assistant to the President and Press Secretary: Joseph Lockhart
Senior Adviser to the President for Policy and Strategy: Douglas B. Sosnik
Senior Adviser to the President for Policy and Communications: Joel Johnson
Office of Management and Budget, Director: Jacob J. Lew
Council of Economic Advisers, Chairman: Martin N. Baily
Office of the United States Trade Representative, United States Trade Representative: Charlene Barshefsky
Office of Science and Technology Policy, Assistant to the President for Science and Technology and Director: Neal Lane
Office of National Drug Control Policy, Director: Barry R. McCaffrey

The Cabinet

Secretary of Agriculture: Dan Glickman
Secretary of Commerce: William M. Daley
Secretary of Defense: William S. Cohen
  Deputy Secretary: John J. Hamre
  Joint Chiefs of Staff, Chairman: Henry H. Shelton
Secretary of Education: Richard W. Riley
Secretary of Energy: Bill Richardson
Secretary of Health and Human Services: Donna E. Shalala
  Surgeon General: David Satcher
  Commissioner of Food and Drugs: Jane E. Henney
Secretary of Housing and Urban Development: Andrew M. Cuomo
Secretary of Interior: Bruce Babbitt
  National Park Service, Director: Robert Stanton
Department of Justice, Attorney General: Janet Reno
  Federal Bureau of Investigation, Director: Louis Freeh
  Immigration and Naturalization Service, Commissioner: Doris Meissner
Secretary of Labor: Alexis M. Herman
Secretary of State: Madeleine K. Albright
  Chief of Protocol: Mary Mel French
  Deputy Secretary: Strobe Talbott
  United Nations Representative: Richard Holbrooke
Secretary of Transportation: Rodney E. Slater
Secretary of the Treasury: Lawrence H. Summers
  Internal Revenue Service, Commissioner: Charles O. Rossotti
Secretary of Veterans Affairs: Togo D. West, Jr.

Independent Agencies (selected listing)

Central Intelligence Agency, Director: George J. Tenet
Consumer Product Safety Commission, Chairman: Ann Brown
Environmental Protection Agency, Administrator: Carol M. Browner
Equal Employment Opportunity Commission, Chairman: Ida Castro
Export-Import Bank of the United States, President and Chairman: James A. Harmon
Farm Credit Administration, Chairman: Marsha P. Martin
Federal Communications Commission, Chairman: William E. Kennard
Federal Deposit Insurance Corporation, Chairman: Donna Tanoue
Federal Election Commission, Chairman: Darryl R. Wold
Federal Emergency Management Agency, Director: James Lee Witt
Federal Labor Relations Authority, Chairman: Phyllis N. Segal
Federal Maritime Commission, Chairman: H. J. Creel, Jr.
Federal Mediation and Conciliation Service, Director: C. Richard Barnes (acting)
Federal Reserve System, Chairman: Alan Greenspan
Federal Trade Commission, Chairman: Robert Pitofsky
General Services Administration, Administrator: D. J. Barram
National Aeronautics and Space Administration, Administrator: Daniel S. Goldin
National Foundation on the Arts and Humanities
  National Endowment for the Arts, Chairman: Bill Ivey
  National Endowment for the Humanities, Chairman: William Ferris
National Labor Relations Board, Chairman: John C. Truesdale
National Science Foundation, Director: Rita R. Colwell
National Transportation Safety Board, Chairman: James E. Hall
Nuclear Regulatory Commission, Chairman: Richard A. Meserve
Occupational Safety and Health Review Commission, Chairman: Thomasina V. Rogers
Office of Government Ethics, Director: Stephen D. Potts
Office of Personnel Management, Director: Janice Lachance
Peace Corps, Director: Mark L. Schneider
Postal Rate Commission, Chairman: Edward J. Gleiman
Securities and Exchange Commission, Chairman: Arthur Levitt
Selective Service System, Director: Gil Coronado
Small Business Administration, Administrator: Aida Alvarez
Social Security Administration, Commissioner: Kenneth S. Apfel
Tennessee Valley Authority, Chairman: Craven Crowell
U.S. Commission on Civil Rights, Chairman: Mary Frances Berry
U.S. Information Agency, Director: Penn Kemble (acting)
U.S. Agency for International Development, Administrator: J. Brady Anderson
U.S. International Trade Commission, Chairman: Lynn M. Bragg
U.S. Postal Service, Postmaster General and Chief Executive Officer: William J. Henderson

The Supreme Court

William H. Rehnquist, chief justice
John Paul Stevens
Sandra Day O'Connor
Antonin Scalia
Anthony M. Kennedy
David H. Souter
Clarence Thomas
Ruth Bader Ginsburg
Stephen G. Breyer

The 106th CONGRESS
Second Session

SENATE MEMBERSHIP

(As of January 2000: 55 Republicans, 45 Democrats.) Letters after names refer to party affiliation—D for Democrat, R for Republican, I for Independent. Single asterisk (*) denotes term expiring in January 2001; double asterisk (**), term expiring in January 2003; triple asterisk (***), term expiring in January 2005; quadruple asterisk (****), appointed in 1999 to fill vacancy, term expiring in January 2001.

Alabama
R. C. Shelby, R***
J.B. Sessions III, R**

Alaska
T. Stevens, R**
F. H. Murkowski, R***

Arizona
J. McCain, R***
J. Kyl, R*

Arkansas
T. Hutchinson, R**
B. L. Lincoln, D***

California
D. Feinstein, D*
B. Boxer, D***

Colorado
B. N. Campbell, R***
W. Allard, R**

Connecticut
C. J. Dodd, D***
J. I. Lieberman, D*

Delaware
W. V. Roth, Jr., R*
J. R. Biden, Jr., D**

Florida
B. Graham, D***
C. Mack, R*

Georgia
P. D. Coverdell, R***
J. M. Cleland, D**

Hawaii
D. K. Inouye, D***
D. K. Akaka, D*

Idaho
L. E. Craig, R**
M. Crapo, R***

Illinois
R. J. Durbin, D**
P. Fitzgerald, R***

Indiana
R. G. Lugar, R*
E. Bayh, D***

Iowa
C. E. Grassley, R***
T. Harkin, D**

Kansas
P. Roberts, R**
S. Brownback, R***

Kentucky
M. McConnell, R**
J. Bunning, R***

Louisiana
J. Breaux, D***
M. L. Landrieu, D**

Maine
O. J. Snowe, R*
S. Collins, R**

Maryland
P. S. Sarbanes, D*
B. A. Mikulski, D***

Massachusetts
E. M. Kennedy, D*
J. F. Kerry, D**

Michigan
C. M. Levin, D**
S. Abraham, R*

Minnesota
P. D. Wellstone, D**
R. Grams, R*

Mississippi
T. Cochran, R**
T. Lott, R*

Missouri
C. S. Bond, R***
J. D. Ashcroft, R*

Montana
M. Baucus, D**
C. Burns, R*

Nebraska
J. R. Kerrey, D*
C. Hagel, R**

Nevada
H. Reid, D***
R. H. Bryan, D*

New Hampshire
B. Smith, R**
J. Gregg, R***

New Jersey
F. R. Lautenberg, D*
R. G. Torricelli, D**

New Mexico
P. V. Domenici, R**
J. Bingaman, D*

New York
D. P. Moynihan, D*
C. E. Schumer, D***

North Carolina
J. Helms, R**
J. Edwards, D***

North Dakota
K. Conrad, D*
B. L. Dorgan, D***

Ohio
M. DeWine, R*
G. Voinovich, R***

Oklahoma
D. Nickles, R***
J. M. Inhofe, R**

Oregon
R. Wyden, D***
G. H. Smith, R**

Pennsylvania
A. Specter, R***
R. J. Santorum, R*

Rhode Island
L. Chafee, R****
J. Reed, D**

South Carolina
S. Thurmond, R**
E. F. Hollings, D***

South Dakota
T. A. Daschle, D***
T. Johnson, D**

Tennessee
W. H. Frist, R*
F. Thompson, R**

Texas
P. Gramm, R**
K. B. Hutchison, R*

Utah
O. G. Hatch, R*
R. F. Bennett, R***

Vermont
P. J. Leahy, D***
J. M. Jeffords, R*

Virginia
J. W. Warner, R**
C. S. Robb, D*

Washington
S. Gorton, R*
P. Murray, D***

West Virginia
R. C. Byrd, D*
J. D. Rockefeller IV, D**

Wisconsin
H. Kohl, D*
R. Feingold, D***

Wyoming
C. Thomas, R*
M. B. Enzi, R**

HOUSE MEMBERSHIP

*(As of January 2000: 222 Republicans, 212 Democrats, 1 Independent.) "At-L" in place of congressional district number means "representative at large." *Indicates elected in special election in 1999. **Switched to Democratic Party in 1999.*

Alabama
1. S. Callahan, R
2. T. Everett, R
3. R. Riley, R
4. R. Aderholt, R
5. B. Cramer, D
6. S. Bachus, R
7. E. F. Hilliard, D

Alaska
At-L. D. E. Young, R

Arizona
1. M. Salmon, R
2. E. Pastor, D
3. B. Stump, R
4. J. B. Shadegg, R
5. J. Kolbe, R
6. J. D. Hayworth, Jr., R

Arkansas
1. M. Berry, D
2. V. Snyder, D
3. A. Hutchinson, R
4. J. Dickey, R

California
1. M. Thompson, D
2. W. Herger, R
3. D. Ose, R
4. J. T. Doolittle, R
5. R. T. Matsui, D
6. L. Woolsey, D
7. G. Miller, D
8. N. Pelosi, D
9. B. Lee, D
10. E. Tauscher, D
11. R. W. Pombo, R
12. T. Lantos, D
13. F. P. Stark, D
14. A. G. Eshoo, D
15. T. Campbell, R
16. Z. Lofgren, D
17. S. Farr, D
18. G. A. Condit, D
19. G. Radanovich, R
20. C. M. Dooley, D
21. B. Thomas, R
22. L. Capps, D
23. E. Gallegly, R
24. B. J. Sherman, D
25. H. P. McKeon, R
26. H. L. Berman, D
27. J. E. Rogan, R
28. D. Dreier, R
29. H. A. Waxman, D
30. X. Becerra, D
31. M. G. Martinez, Jr., D
32. J. C. Dixon, D
33. L. Roybal-Allard, D
34. G. Napolitano, D
35. M. Waters, D
36. S. Kuykendall, R
37. J. Millender-McDonald, D
38. S. Horn, R
39. E. Royce, R
40. J. Lewis, R
41. G. Miller, R
42. J. Baca, D*
43. K. Calvert, R
44. M. Bono, R
45. D. Rohrabacher, R
46. L. Sanchez, D
47. C. Cox, R
48. R. Packard, R
49. B. Bilbray, R
50. B. Filner, D
51. R. Cunningham, R
52. D. Hunter, R

Colorado
1. D. L. DeGette, D
2. M. Udall, D
3. S. McInnis, R
4. B. Schaffer, R
5. J. Hefley, R
6. T. Tancredo, R

Connecticut
1. J. Larson, D
2. S. Gejdenson, D
3. R. L. DeLauro, D
4. C. Shays, R
5. J. H. Maloney, D
6. N. L. Johnson, R

Delaware
At-L. M. N. Castle, R

Florida
1. J. Scarborough, R
2. A. Boyd, Jr., D
3. C. Brown, D
4. T. Fowler, R
5. K. L. Thurman, D
6. C. B. Stearns, R
7. J. L. Mica, R
8. B. McCollum, R
9. M. Bilirakis, R
10. C. W. B. Young, R
11. J. Davis, D
12. C. T. Canady, R
13. D. Miller, R
14. P. J. Goss, R
15. D. Weldon, R
16. M. A. Foley, R
17. C. P. Meek, D
18. I. Ros-Lehtinen, R
19. R. Wexler, D
20. P. Deutsch, D
21. L. Diaz-Balart, R
22. E. C. Shaw, Jr., R
23. A. L. Hastings, D

Georgia
1. J. Kingston, R
2. S. Bishop, Jr., D
3. M. Collins, R
4. C. McKinney, D
5. J. Lewis, D
6. J. Isakson, R*
7. B. Barr, R
8. S. Chambliss, R
9. N. Deal, R
10. C. W. Norwood, Jr., R
11. J. Linder, R

Hawaii
1. N. Abercrombie, D
2. P. Mink, D

Idaho
1. H. P. Chenoweth, R
2. M. Simpson, R

Illinois
1. B. Rush, D
2. J. L. Jackson, Jr., D
3. W. O. Lipinski, D
4. L. V. Gutierrez, D
5. R. R. Blagojevich, D
6. H. J. Hyde, R
7. D. K. Davis, D
8. P. M. Crane, R
9. J. Schakowsky, D
10. J. E. Porter, R
11. J. Weller, R
12. J. F. Costello, D
13. J. Biggert, R
14. J. D. Hastert, R
15. T.W. Ewing, R
16. D. Manzullo, R
17. L. Evans, D
18. R. LaHood, R
19. D. Phelps, D
20. J. M. Shimkus, R

Indiana
1. P. J. Visclosky, D
2. D. M. McIntosh, R
3. T. Roemer, D
4. M. E. Souder, R
5. S. Buyer, R
6. D. Burton, R
7. E. A. Pease, R
8. J. N. Hostettler, R
9. B. Hill, D
10. J. Carson, D

Iowa
1. J. A. Leach, R
2. J. Nussle, R
3. L. L. Boswell, D
4. G. Ganske, R
5. T. Latham, R

Kansas
1. J. Moran, R
2. J. Ryun, R
3. D. Moore, D
4. T. Tiahrt, R

Kentucky
1. E. Whitfield, R
2. R. Lewis, R
3. A. M. Northup, R
4. K. Lucas, D
5. H. Rogers, R
6. E. Fletcher, R

Louisiana
1. D. Vitter, R*
2. W. J. Jefferson, D
3. W. J. Tauzin, R
4. J. McCrery, R
5. J. Cooksey, R
6. R. H. Baker, R
7. C. John, D

Maine
1. T. H. Allen, D
2. J. E. Baldacci, D

Maryland
1. W. T. Gilchrest, R
2. R. L. Ehrlich, Jr., R
3. B. L. Cardin, D
4. A. R. Wynn, D
5. S. H. Hoyer, D
6. R. G. Bartlett, R
7. E. E. Cummings, D
8. C. A. Morella, R

Massachusetts
1. J. W. Olver, D
2. R. E. Neal, D
3. J. McGovern, D
4. B. Frank, D
5. M. T. Meehan, D
6. J. F. Tierney, D
7. E. J. Markey, D
8. M. Capuano, D
9. J. J. Moakley, D
10. W. D. Delahunt, D

Michigan
1. B. T. Stupak, D
2. P. Hoekstra, R
3. V. J. Ehlers, R
4. D. Camp, R
5. J. A. Barcia, D
6. F. Upton, R
7. N. Smith, R
8. D. Stabenow, D
9. D. E. Kildee, D
10. D. E. Bonior, D
11. J. Knollenberg, R
12. S. M. Levin, D
13. L. N. Rivers, D
14. J. Conyers, Jr., D
15. C. C. Kilpatrick, D
16. J. D. Dingell, D

Minnesota
1. G. W. Gutknecht, R
2. D. Minge, D
3. J. Ramstad, R
4. B. F. Vento, D
5. M. O. Sabo, D
6. W. P. Luther, D
7. C. C. Peterson, D
8. J. L. Oberstar, D

Mississippi
1. R. F. Wicker, R
2. B. Thompson, D
3. C. W. Pickering, Jr., R
4. R. Shows, D
5. G. Taylor, D

Missouri
1. W. Clay, D
2. J. M. Talent, R
3. R. A. Gephardt, D
4. I. Skelton, D
5. K. McCarthy, D
6. P. Danner, D
7. R. D. Blunt, R
8. J. Emerson, R
9. K. Hulshof, R

Montana
At-L. R. Hill, R

Nebraska
1. D. Bereuter, R
2. L. Terry, R
3. W. E. Barrett, R

Nevada
1. S. Berkley, D
2. J. A. Gibbons, R

New Hampshire
1. J. E. Sununu, R
2. C. F. Bass, R

New Jersey
1. R. E. Andrews, D
2. F. A. LoBiondo, R
3. J. Saxton, R
4. C. H. Smith, R
5. M. Roukema, R
6. F. Pallone, Jr., D
7. B. Franks, R
8. W. J. Pascrell, Jr., D
9. S. Rothman, D
10. D. M. Payne, D
11. R. P. Frelinghuysen, R
12. R. Holt, D
13. R. Menendez, D

New Mexico
1. H. Wilson, R
2. J. R. Skeen, R
3. T. Udall, D

New York
1. M. P. Forbes, D**
2. R. A. Lazio, R
3. P. T. King, R
4. C. McCarthy, D
5. G. L. Ackerman, D
6. G. Meeks, D
7. J. Crowley, D
8. J. L. Nadler, D
9. A. Weiner, D
10. E. Towns, D
11. M. R. Owens, D
12. N. M. Velázquez, D
13. V. J. Fossella, R
14. C. B. Maloney, D
15. C. B. Rangel, D
16. J. E. Serrano, D
17. E. L. Engel, D
18. N. M. Lowey, D
19. S. W. Kelly, R
20. B. A. Gilman, R
21. M. R. McNulty, D
22. J. Sweeney, R
23. S. L. Boehlert, R
24. J. M. McHugh, R
25. J. T. Walsh, R
26. M. D. Hinchey, D
27. T. Reynolds, R
28. L. M. Slaughter, D
29. J. J. LaFalce, D
30. J. Quinn, R
31. A. Houghton, R

North Carolina
1. E. Clayton, D
2. B. Etheridge, D
3. W. B. Jones, R
4. D. Price, D
5. R. Burr, R
6. H. Coble, R
7. M. McIntyre, D
8. R. Hayes, R
9. S. Myrick, R
10. C. Ballenger, R
11. C. H. Taylor, R
12. M. Watt, D

North Dakota
At-L. E. R. Pomeroy, D

Ohio
1. S. Chabot, R
2. R. Portman, R
3. T. P. Hall, D
4. M. G. Oxley, R
5. P. E. Gillmor, R
6. T. Strickland, D
7. D. L. Hobson, R
8. J. A. Boehner, R
9. M. Kaptur, D
10. D. Kucinich, D
11. S. T. Jones, D
12. J. R. Kasich, R
13. S. Brown, D
14. T. C. Sawyer, D
15. D. Pryce, R
16. R. Regula, R
17. J. A. Traficant, Jr., D
18. R. W. Ney, R
19. S. C. LaTourette, R

Oklahoma
1. S. Largent, R
2. T. A. Coburn, R
3. W. Watkins, R
4. J. C. Watts, Jr., R
5. E. J. Istook, Jr., R
6. F. D. Lucas, R

Oregon
1. D. Wu, D
2. G. Walden, R
3. E. Blumenauer, D
4. P. A. DeFazio, D
5. D. Hooley, D

Pennsylvania
1. R. Brady, D
2. C. Fattah, D
3. R. A. Borski, D
4. R. Klink, D
5. J. Peterson, R
6. T. Holden, D
7. C. Weldon, R
8. J. C. Greenwood, R
9. B. Shuster, R
10. D. Sherwood, R
11. P. E. Kanjorski, D
12. J. P. Murtha, D
13. J. Hoeffel, D
14. W. J. Coyne, D
15. P. Toomey, R
16. J. R. Pitts, R
17. G. Gekas, R
18. M. F. Doyle, D
19. W. F. Goodling, R
20. F. R. Mascara, D
21. P. S. English, R

Rhode Island
1. P. J. Kennedy, D
2. R. A. Weygand, D

South Carolina
1. M. C. Sanford, Jr., R
2. F. Spence, R
3. L. Graham, R
4. J. DeMint, R
5. J. M. Spratt, Jr., D
6. J. E. Clyburn, D

South Dakota
At-L. J. R. Thune, R

Tennessee
1. W. L. Jenkins, R
2. J. J. Duncan, Jr., R
3. Z. P. Wamp, R
4. V. Hilleary, R
5. B. Clement, D
6. B. Gordon, D
7. E. Bryant, R
8. J. S. Tanner, D
9. H. E. Ford, Jr., D

Texas
1. M. Sandlin, D
2. J. Turner, D
3. S. Johnson, R
4. R. M. Hall, D
5. P. Sessions, R
6. J. Barton, R
7. B. Archer, R
8. K. Brady, R
9. N. V. Lampson, D
10. L. Doggett, D
11. C. Edwards, D
12. K. Granger, R
13. W. Thornberry, R
14. R. E. Paul, R
15. R. Hinojosa, D
16. S. Reyes, D
17. C. W. Stenholm, D
18. S. J. Lee, D
19. L. Combest, R
20. C. Gonzalez, D
21. L. Smith, R
22. T. DeLay, R
23. H. Bonilla, R
24. M. Frost, D
25. K. Bentsen, D
26. D. Armey, R
27. S. P. Ortiz, D
28. C. Rodriguez, D
29. G. Green, D
30. E. B. Johnson, D

Utah
1. J. V. Hansen, R
2. M. Cook, R
3. C. B. Cannon, R

Vermont
At-L. B. Sanders, I

Virginia
1. H. H. Bateman, R
2. O. B. Pickett, D
3. R. C. Scott, D
4. N. Sisisky, D
5. V. H. Goode, Jr., D
6. R. W. Goodlatte, R
7. T. J. Bliley, Jr., R
8. J. P. Moran, D
9. R. Boucher, D
10. F. R. Wolf, R
11. T. M. Davis, R

Washington
1. J. Inslee, D
2. J. Metcalf, R
3. B. Baird, D
4. D. Hastings, R
5. G. R. Nethercutt, Jr., R
6. N. D. Dicks, D
7. J. McDermott, D
8. J. Dunn, R
9. A. Smith, D

West Virginia
1. A. B. Mollohan, D
2. R. E. Wise, Jr., D
3. N. Rahall II, D

Wisconsin
1. P. Ryan, R
2. T. Baldwin, D
3. R. Kind, D
4. G. D. Kleczka, D
5. T. M. Barrett, D
6. T. E. Petri, R
7. D. R. Obey, D
8. M. Green, R
9. F. J. Sensenbrenner, Jr., R

Wyoming
At-L. B. Cubin, R

AMERICAN SAMOA
Delegate, E. F. H. Faleomavaega, D

DISTRICT OF COLUMBIA
Delegate, Eleanor Holmes Norton, D

GUAM
Delegate, R. A. Underwood, D

PUERTO RICO
Resident Commissioner, Carlos Romero-Barceló, D

VIRGIN ISLANDS
Delegate, Donna MC Christensen, D

Mining

Coal[a]
(thousand metric tons per month average)

	1997	1998
China[b]	113,523[c]	94,806
United States[d]	82,398	83,897
India	24,688	24,805
Australia	20,200[c]	20,677
Russia	13,317	12,779
Poland	11,496	9,735[c]
Ukraine	6,412	6,431
Kazakhstan	6,268	5,672
Indonesia	4,352	5,027
Germany[f]	4,267	3,776

Lignite and Brown Coal[a]
(thousand metric tons per month average)

	1997	1998
Germany	14,758	13,833
Turkey	4,885	5,148
Greece	4,861	5,127
Russia[c]	7,400	5,050
Poland	5,264	5,036[c]
Czech Rep.	4,787	4,285
Yugoslavia	3,522	3,627
Bulgaria	2,467	2,570
India	1,914	1,973
Romania	2,361[c]	1,886

Natural Gas[a]
(terajoules per month average)

	1997	1998
United States	1,711,216	1,713,389
Russia	1,608,012	1,665,726
Canada	521,791	538,236
Indonesia[c]	288,839	273,739
United Kingdom	270,136	N/A
Netherlands	201,193	198,554
Mexico[c]	169,405	184,022
Uzbekistan	145,183	151,078[c]
Saudi Arabia	138,000[c]	N/A
Argentina	123,456	134,483

Crude Oil[g]
(thousand barrels per day average)

	1997	1998
Saudi Arabia	8,562	8,389
United States	6,452	6,252
Russia	5,920	5,938
Iran	3,664	3,634
China	3,200	3,198
Venezuela	3,315	3,167
Mexico	3,023	3,070
Norway	3,143	3,017
United Kingdom	2,518	2,616
Nigeria	2,332	2,153
World total	66,420	66,874

Aluminum (primary smelter)
(thousand metric tons)

	1997	1998[e]
United States	3,600	3,700
Russia	2,910	2,960
Canada	2,330	2,340
China	2,000	2,200
Australia	1,500	1,580
Brazil	1,200	1,200
Norway	919	950
South Africa	660	660
Venezuela	640	600
France	390	420
Other Countries	5,290	5,550
World total[r]	21,400	22,200

Bauxite
(thousand metric tons)

	1997	1998[e]
Australia	44,100	45,000
Guinea	16,500	16,500
Jamaica	11,900	12,600
Brazil	12,300	12,500
China	8,000	8,500
India	5,800	6,000
Venezuela	5,080	4,500
Suriname	4,000	4,000
Russia	3,350	3,400
Guyana	2,500	2,600
Other countries	9,290	9,370
World total[r]	123,000	125,000

Cement
(thousand metric tons)

	1997	1998[e]
China	492,600	495,000
Japan	91,938	91,000
United States[h]	84,255	87,200
India	80,000[e]	85,000
Korea, South	59,796	59,000
Brazil	38,096	39,000
Germany	37,000[e]	37,000
Turkey	36,035	37,000
Thailand	36,000[e]	34,000
Italy	33,721	33,500
Other countries	379,000[e]	357,000
World total[r]	1,515,000[e]	1,500,000

Copper (mine)
(thousand metric tons)

	1997	1998[e]
Chile	3,390	3,660
United States	1,940	1,850
Indonesia	529	750
Canada	657	710
Australia	545	600
Russia	505	450
Peru	491	450
China	414	440
Poland	414	420
Mexico	391	400
Other countries	1,450	1,550
World total[r]	11,400	11,900

Iron Ore
(thousand metric tons)

	1997	1998[e]
China	243,000	240,000
Brazil	183,000	180,000
Australia	158,000	155,000
Russia	71,000	70,000
India	67,000	65,000
United States	63,000	62,000
Ukraine	53,000	50,000
Canada	37,000	37,000
South Africa	33,000	33,000
Sweden	22,000	22,000
Other countries	81,000	75,000
World total[r]	1,040,000	1,020,000

Iron (raw steel)
(thousand metric tons)

	1997	1998[e]
European Union	165,000	170,000
China	108,000	111,000
United States	98,500	102,000
Japan	105,000	95,100
Russia	48,400	42,800
Korea, South	42,600	41,100
Brazil	25,100	25,800
Ukraine	25,600	24,800
Other countries	177,000	170,000
World total[r]	795,000	783,000

Lead (mine)
(thousand metric tons)

	1997	1998[e]
China	650	600
Australia	531	590
United States	459	460
Peru	258	250
Canada	186	190
Mexico	175	170
Sweden	100	100
South Africa	84	90
Morocco	77	70
Kazakhstan	35	40
Other countries	455	520
World total	3,010	3,080

Phosphate rock
(thousand metric tons)

	1997	1998[e]
United States	45,900	44,600
Morocco	23,400	24,000
China	20,000	22,000
Russia	7,500	9,500
Tunisia	7,070	7,100
Jordan	5,900	6,000
Israel	4,050	4,000
Brazil	3,850	3,900
South Africa	3,000	3,000
Togo	2,630	2,600
Other countries	11,500	11,500
World total[r]	138,000	141,000

Salt
(thousand metric tons)

	1997	1998[e]
United States[i]	41,400	42,100
China	29,300	30,000
Germany	15,700	15,000
Canada	13,264	13,000
India	9,500	9,400
Australia	8,722	8,800
Mexico	7,933	7,900
France	7,160	7,200
United Kingdom	6,600	6,600
Brazil	5,520	5,700
Other countries	40,433	38,900
World total[r]	201,000	200,000

Sulfur (all forms)
(thousand metric tons)

	1997	1998[e]
United States	12,000	11,300
Canada	10,200	10,200
China	6,750	6,500
Russia	3,750	3,750
Japan	2,800	2,800
Saudi Arabia	2,000	2,000
Poland	1,820	1,800
Germany	1,130	1,110
France	1,110	1,100
Kazakhstan	945	1,000
Other countries	7,500	8,800
World total[r]	53,600	54,000

Zinc (mine)
(thousand metric tons)

	1997	1998[e]
China	1,200	1,250
Canada	1,060	1,100
Australia	1,040	1,100
Peru	865	870
United States	632	730
Mexico	379	380
Other countries	2,290	2,370
World total[r]	7,460	7,800

Note: Numerals are annual production unless otherwise indicated.

[a]Source: Monthly Bulletin of Statistics, UN Dept. of Economics and Social Affairs. [b]Includes lignite and waste. [c]Average of available monthly information. [d]Includes lignite. [e]Estimated. [f]Low-grade coal at its hard-coal equivalent. [g]Source: International Petroleum Monthly, U.S. Dept. of Energy. [h]Includes Puerto Rico. [i]Excludes Puerto Rico. [r]Totals rounded.

Source: U.S. Geological Survey, U.S. Department of the Interior, unless otherwise indicated.

CONTRIBUTORS

ADRIAN, CHARLES R., Professor Emeritus of Political Science, University of California, Riverside; Author, *A History of City Government: The Emergence of the Metropolis 1920–1945*; Coauthor, *State and Local Politics, A History of American City Government: The Formation of Traditions, 1775–1870, Governing Urban America*: ***Los Angeles***

AMICK, GEORGE, Author, *Linn's U.S. Stamp Yearbook*: ***Stamps and Stamp Collecting***

ANDERSON, JIM, Freelance writer and editor: ***20th Century Chronology****—Sports;* ***Biography****—Andre Agassi, Lance Armstrong;* ***Sports****—Overview;* ***States, U.S.****—(in part)*

ARNOLD, ANTHONY, Author, *Afghanistan: The Soviet Invasion in Perspective, Afghanistan's Two-Party Communism: Parcham and Khalq, The Fateful Pebble: Afghanistan's Role in the Fall of the Soviet Empire*: ***Afghanistan***

ATKIN, MURIEL, Professor, Department of History, George Washington University: ***Tajikistan***

ATTNER, PAUL, Senior Writer, *The Sporting News*: ***Obituaries****—Wilt Chamberlain;* ***Sports****—Basketball, Football*

BALDWIN, LOU, Staff Writer, *The Catholic Standard & Times*: ***Religion****—Roman Catholicism*

BATRA, PREM P., Professor of Biochemistry, Wright State University: ***Biochemistry***

BEHLER, DEBORAH A., Executive Editor, *Wildlife Conservation* magazine: ***Zoos and Zoology***

BEST, JOHN, Chief, *Canada World News*, Ottawa: ***Canada****—Provinces and Territories, Nunavut*

BETTELHEIM, ADRIEL, Medical and Science Writer, *CQ Researcher*: ***Environment***

BOWER, BRUCE, Behavioral Sciences Editor, *Science News*: ***Anthropology; Archaeology; Medicine and Health****—Mental Health*

BRAASCH, BARBARA, Freelance Travel Writer, Palo Alto, CA: ***Travel; Travel****—Adventure Travel*

BROWNE, MALCOLM W., Senior Science Writer, *The New York Times*: ***Breitling Orbiter 3—A Dream Is Realized***

BRUSSO, CHARLENE, Member, New England Science Writers: ***Physics***

BUGAJSKI, JANUSZ, Director of East European Studies, Center for Strategic and International Studies, Washington, DC; Author, *Ethnic Politics in Eastern Europe: A Guide to Nationality Policies, Organizations and Parties*: ***The Kosovo Crisis; Albania; Bosnia and Herzegovina; Bulgaria; Croatia; Hungary; Macedonia; Romania; Slovenia; Yugoslavia***

BURKS, ARDATH W., Professor Emeritus, Asian Studies, Rutgers University; Author, *Third Order of the Rising Sun*: ***Japan***

BUSH, GRAHAM W. A., Associate Professor of Political Studies, University of Auckland; Author, *Advance in Order: The Auckland City Council 1971–89*: ***New Zealand***

CHAMETZKY, PETER, School of Art and Design, Southern Illinois University: ***Art***

CLARK, CATHY L., American Numismatic Association: ***Coins and Coin Collecting***

COLLINS, BUD, Sports Columnist, *The Boston Globe*; Author, *My Life with the Pros*: ***Sports****—Tennis*

CONRADT, DAVID P., Professor of Political Science, East Carolina University; Author, *The German Polity, West European Politics*: ***Germany***

COOPER, ILENE, Children's Book Editor, *Booklist Magazine*: ***Literature****—Children's, Harry Potter*

COOPER, MARY H., Staff Writer, *CQ Researcher*; Author, *The Business of Drugs*: ***Energy; Taxation***

CUE, EDUARDO, Freelance Writer, Paris, France; Correspondent in France for *U.S. News & World Report*: ***France***

CUNNIFF, JOHN, Business News Analyst, The Associated Press; Author, *How to Stretch Your Dollar*: ***Business and Corporate Affairs; Industrial Production; United States****—The Economy*

CURRIER, CHET, Financial Writer, *Bloomberg News*; Author, *The Investor's Encyclopedia, The 15-Minute Investor*; Coauthor, *No-Cost/Low-Cost Investing*: ***Stocks and Bonds***

CURTIS, L. PERRY, Professor of History, Brown University: ***Ireland***

DALTON, MARGARET A., Project Director, Information Clearinghouse on Children, and Adjunct Professor, Child Advocacy Clinic, University of San Diego, School of Law; Editor in Chief, *Children's Regulatory Law Reporter*: ***Family****—Today's Teenager*

DAVID, LEONARD, Director, Space Data Resources and Information: ***Space Exploration***

DECKER, ANDREW, Freelance Art Journalist: ***Art****—The Art Market*

DENNIS, LARRY, Freelance Golf Writer: ***Sports****—Golf*

Di SCALA, SPENCER M., Research Professor, University of Massachusetts—Boston; Author, *Italy: From Revolution to Republic, 1700 to the Present*: ***Italy***

DUFF, ERNEST A., Professor of Politics, Randolph-Macon Woman's College; Author, *Agrarian Reform in Colombia, Violence and Repression in Latin America, Leader and Party in Latin America*: ***Colombia***

DYER, RICHARD, Chief Classical Music Critic, *The Boston Globe*: ***Music—****Classical*

EBERHART, GEORGE, *American Libraries* magazine, American Library Association: ***Libraries***

ENSTAD, ROBERT, Writer, Formerly, *Chicago Tribune*: ***Chicago***

FALLESEN, LEIF BECK, Editor in Chief, *Boersen*, Copenhagen: ***Denmark; Finland; Norway; Sweden***

FISCHER, MARTIN, Assistant Professor, Terman Engineering Center, Stanford, CA: ***Engineering, Civil***

FRANCIS, DAVID R., Senior Economics Correspondent, *The Christian Science Monitor*: ***Biography****—Robert Mundell, Lawrence Summers;* ***International Trade and Finance***

FRATTAROLI, SHANNON, Johns Hopkins Center for Gun Policy and Research: ***Crime****—Gun Control*

GAILEY, HARRY A., Professor of History, San Jose State University; Author, *History of the Gambia, History of Africa, Road to Aba*: ***Congo, Democratic Republic of the; Nigeria***

GILL, BATES, Director, Center for Northeast Asian Policy Studies, The Brookings Institution; Author, *China's Arms Acquisitions from Abroad: A Quest for "Superb and Secret Weapons"*: ***China****—The Espionage Case*

GOODMAN, DONALD, Associate Professor of Sociology, John Jay College of Criminal Justice, City University of New York: ***Prisons***

GORDON, MAYNARD M., Senior Editor, *Ward's Dealer Business* magazine; Author, *The Iacocca Management Technique*: ***Automobiles***

GRAYSON, GEORGE W., Class of 1938 Professor of Government, College of William and Mary; Author, *The Politics of Mexican Oil, The United States and Mexico: Patterns of Influence, Oil and Mexican Foreign Policy*: ***Brazil; Mexico; Portugal; Spain***

GROSSMAN, LAWRENCE, Associate Director of Research, The American Jewish Committee; Editor, *American Jewish Year Book*: ***Religion****—Judaism*

GROTH, ALEXANDER J., Professor Emeritus of Political Science, University of California, Davis; Author, *People's Poland, Contemporary Politics: Europe, Comparative Resource Allocation, Public Policy across Nations*: ***Poland***

HELMREICH, JONATHAN E., Professor Emeritus of History, Allegheny College; Author, *Belgium and Europe: A Study in Small Power Diplomacy, United States Relations with Belgium and the Congo 1940–1960*; Coauthor, *Rebirth: A History of Europe Since World War II*: ***Belgium; Netherlands***

HELMREICH, PAUL C., Professor Emeritus of History, Wheaton College; Author, *From Paris to Sèvres: The Partition of the Ottoman Empire at the Peace Conference of 1919–1920*; Coauthor, *Rebirth: A History of Europe Since World War II*: ***Switzerland***

HOLLOBAUGH, JEFF, Track Columnist, ESPN.com; Author, *100 Stars of American Track & Field*: ***Sports****—Track and Field*

HOPKO, THE REV. THOMAS, Dean, St. Vladimir's Orthodox Theological Seminary, Crestwood, NY: ***Religion****—Orthodox Eastern*

HOWARD, DAVE, Freelance Writer and Photographer: ***Photography***

HOYT, CHARLES K., Fellow, *American Institute of Architects*; Author, *More Places for People, Building for Commerce and Industry*: ***Architecture***

HUFFMAN, GEORGE J., NASA/Science Systems and Applications: ***Meteorology; Meteorology****—Avalanches*

HULBERT, DAN, *Atlanta Journal & Constitution*: ***Television and Radio; Theater***

ISIDORE, CHRIS, Freelance Transportation Writer: ***Transportation***

JENNERMANN, DONALD L., Director, University Honors Program, Indiana State University; Author, *Born of a Cretan Spring, Literature for Living*: ***Literature****—English*

JOHNSON, LONNIE, Author, *Central Europe: Enemies, Neighbors, Friends*: ***Austria***

JONES, GRAHAME L., Soccer Columnist, *Los Angeles Times* and ESPN's *SportsZone*: ***Sports****—Soccer, The 1999 Women's World Cup—A Milestone for Women's Sports*

JONES, STEPHEN F., Associate Professor of Russian and Eurasian Studies, Mount Holyoke College: ***Armenia; Azerbaijan; Georgia***

KARNES, THOMAS L., Professor of History Emeritus, Southwestern University; Author, *Latin American Policy of the United States, Failure of Union: Central America 1824–1960*: ***Central America; Central America****—The Panama Canal*

KELLER, EDMOND J., Professor/Director, James S. Coleman African Studies Center, University of California at Los Angeles; Author, *Revolutionary Ethiopia: From Empire to People's Republic*: ***Africa***

KERMOND, JOHN, Office of Global Programs, National Oceanic and Atmospheric Administration: ***Oceanography***

KESSLER, ANN, American Bankers Association: ***Banking and Finance***

KIM, HAN-KYO, Professor Emeritus, Political Science, University of Cincinnati; Author, *Korea and the Politics of Imperialism 1876–1910, Studies on Korea: A Scholar's Guide*: ***Korea***

KISSELGOFF, ANNA, Chief Dance Critic, *The New York Times*: ***Dance***

KUSHIDA, CLETE A., Director, Stanford Center for Human Sleep Research; Staff Physician and Clinical Instructor, Stanford Sleep Disorders Clinic: ***Sleep and Its Disorders***

LAWRENCE, ROBERT M., Professor of Political Science, Colorado State University; Author, *The Strategic Defense Initiative*: ***Military Affairs***

LEEPSON, MARC, Freelance Writer: ***Drugs and Alcohol; Social Welfare; Social Welfare****—Defining the Disabled*

LEVINE, LOUIS, Professor, Department of Biology, City College of New York; Author, *Biology of the Gene, Biology for a Modern Society*: ***Biotechnology; Genetics; Microbiology***

LEWIS, ANNE C., Education Policy Writer: ***Education; Education****—The Homework Issue*

LOESCHER, GIL, Professor of International Relations, University of Notre Dame; Author, *Refugees and International Relations, The Global Refugee Crisis: A Reference Handbook, Beyond Charity: International Cooperation and the Global Refugee Crisis*: ***The Kosovo Crisis****—The Spotlight Turns to the Refugees;* ***Refugees and Immigration***

MacLEOD, ALEXANDER, British Isles Correspondent, *The Christian Science Monitor*, London: ***Great Britain***

MAMMANA, DENNIS L., Reuben H. Fleet Space Center and Science Theater: ***Astronomy***

MARCOPOULOS, GEORGE J., Professor of History, Tufts University: ***Cyprus; Greece***

MATHESON, JIM, Sportswriter, *Edmonton Journal*: ***Sports****—Ice Hockey*

MAXON, ROBERT M., Professor of History, West Virginia University; Author, *Conflict and Accommodation in Western Kenya; East Africa: An Introductory History; Struggle of Kenya: the Loss and Reassertion of Imperial Initiative, 1912–23*: ***Kenya; Tanzania; Uganda***

MAYERCHAK, PATRICK M., Professor of Political Science, Virginia Military Institute; Author, *Scholar's Guide to Southeast Asia*; Coauthor, *Linkage or*

Bondage: US-ASEAN Economic Relations: ***Malaysia; Singapore***

McCLINTOCK, CYNTHIA, Professor of Political Science and International Affairs, George Washington University; Author, *Revolutionary Movements in Latin America: El Salvador's FMLN and Peru's Shining Path*; *Peasant Cooperatives and Political Change in Peru*: ***Peru***

McCONNELL, SHELLEY A., Associate Director, Latin American and Caribbean Program, The Carter Center: ***Ecuador***

McCOY, JENNIFER L., Associate Professor of Political Science and Senior Associate at the Policy Research Center, Georgia State University; Senior Associate, The Carter Center; Author, *Venezuelan Democracy under Stress*: ***Venezuela***

McGEE, GLENN, Center for Bioethics, University of Pennsylvania School of Medicine; Author, *The Perfect Baby*: ***Medicine and Health***—*Bioethics*

MICHIE, ARUNA NAYYAR, Department of Political Science, Kansas State University: ***India; Sri Lanka***

MIDDLETON, RICHARD, Freelance Writer, *Iceland Review* magazine: ***Iceland***

MILLER, RANDALL M., Department of History, St. Joseph's University; Author, *Shades of the Sunbelt: Essays on Ethnicity, Race and the Urban South*: ***Ethnic Groups, U.S.; Ethnic Groups, U.S.***—*Racial Profiling*

MILWARD, JOHN, Freelance Writer and Critic: ***Pop Music's New Diversity: Latin, Jazz, Swing...; Biography***—*Lauryn Hill, Ricky Martin;* ***Music***—*Popular and Jazz*

MORRIS, BERNADINE, Fashion Journalist; Author, *The Fashion Makers, American Fashion*: ***Fashion***

MORTIMER, ROBERT A., Professor, Department of Political Science, Haverford College; Author, *The Third World Coalition in International Politics;* Coauthor, *Politics and Society in Contemporary Africa*: ***Algeria***

MORTON, DESMOND, Director, McGill Institute for the Study of Canada; Author, *Working People: An Illustrated History of the Canadian Labour Movement, A Military History of Canada, Bloody Victory: Canadians and the D-Day Campaign, 1944:* ***Canada***

NASATIR, JUDITH, Freelance design journalist and editor; Former senior editor, *Interior Design* magazine: ***Interior Design***

OCHSENWALD, WILLIAM, Professor of History, Virginia Polytechnic Institute and State University; Author, *The Middle East: A History, The Hijaz Railroad, Religion, Society and the State in Arabia*: ***Saudi Arabia; Turkey***

O'MEARA, PATRICK, Dean of International Programs, Indiana University; Coeditor, *Africa, International Politics in Southern Africa, Southern Africa, The Continuing Crisis*: ***Biography***—*Thabo Mbeki;* ***South Africa; Zimbabwe***

PAUL, BIMAL KANTI, Kansas State University: ***Bangladesh***

PEARSON, FREDERIC S., Director, Center for Peace and Conflict Studies, Wayne State University, Detroit; Coauthor, *International Relations: The Global Condition, Fuel on the Fire? Effects of Armament During Warfare*: ***United States***—*Foreign Affairs*

PEARSON, RUTH, Freelance United Nations Correspondent: ***United Nations***

PERETZ, DON, Professor Emeritus of Political Science, State University of New York at Binghamton; Author, *The West Bank—History, Politics, Society and Economy, Government and Politics of Israel, The Middle East Today*: ***Biography***—*Ehud Barak;* ***Egypt; Israel***

PERKINS, KENNETH J., Professor of History, University of South Carolina: ***Libya; Religion***—*Islam*

PERRY, DAVID K., Associate Professor, Department of Journalism, The University of Alabama: ***Publishing***

PIPPIN, LARRY L., Professor of Political Science, University of the Pacific; Author, *The Remón Era*: ***Argentina; Argentina***—*Fernando de la Rúa;* ***Paraguay; Uruguay***

POOLE, PETER A., Author, *The Vietnamese in Thailand, Eight Presidents and Indochina*; Coauthor, *American Diplomacy*: ***Vietnam***

QUIÑONES, ERIC, Freelance Writer; Formerly, The Associated Press: ***20th Century Chronology***—*Business and Industry;* ***Biography***—*C. Michael Armstrong*

RICHTER, LINDA K., Professor of Political Science, Kansas State University; Author, *Land Reform and Tourism Development, Policy-Making in the Philippines, The Politics of Tourism in Asia*: ***Myanmar; Philippines***

RICHTER, WILLIAM L., Associate Provost for International Programs, Kansas State University: ***India***—*India-Pakistan Relations;* ***Pakistan***

RIGGAN, WILLIAM, Associate Editor, *World Literature Today*, University of Oklahoma; Author, *Pícaros, Madmen, Naïfs, and Clowns, Comparative Literature and Literary Theory*: ***Literature***—*World*

ROVNER, JULIE, Health-Policy Writer: ***Medicine and Health***—*Health Care*

RUBIN, JIM, Editor, *Bloomberg News*: ***Crime; Law***

RYAN, ROSE, Executive Editor, *The North Africa Journal*: ***Morocco; Tunisia***

SCHLOSSBERG, DAN, Baseball Writer; Author, *The Baseball IQ Challenge, The Baseball Catalog, The Baseball Book of Why, Cooperstown: Baseball's Hall of Fame Players*: ***Biography***—*Pedro Martinez;* ***Obituaries***—*Joe DiMaggio;* ***Sports***—*Baseball*

SCHRECENGOST, LYNDI, Freelance Writer based in Washington, DC: ***States, U.S.***—*(in part);* ***Washington, DC***

SCHROEDER, RICHARD, Freelance Writer, Specialist on the Caribbean and Latin America: ***Bolivia; Caribbean; Chile; Latin America***

SCHUYLER, ED, JR., Freelance Boxing Writer: ***Sports***—*Boxing*

SCHWAB, PETER, Professor of Political Science, Purchase College, State University of New York; Author, *Ethiopia: Politics, Economics, and Society, Human Rights: Cultural and Ideological Perspectives*: ***Ethiopia***

SEIDERS, DAVID F., Chief Economist and Senior Staff Vice-President, National Association of Home Builders, Washington, DC: ***Housing***

SENSER, ROBERT A., Editor, *Human Rights for Workers*: ***Human Rights***

SEYBOLD, PAUL G., Professor, Department of Chemistry, Wright State University: ***Chemistry***

SHAPIRO, WILLIAM E., Freelance Writer and Editor, New York City: ***20th Century Chronology***—*International Affairs, U.S. Affairs;* ***United States***—*The Kennedy Family: Another Tragedy;* ***Nations of the World***

SHARLET, ROBERT, Chauncey Winters Professor of Political Science, Union College; Author, *Soviet Constitutional Crisis*: ***Baltic Republics; Belarus; Russia; Ukraine***

SHOGAN, ROBERT, National Political Correspondent, Washington Bureau, *The Los Angeles Times*; Author, *A Question of Judgment, Promises to Keep*: ***Biography***—*Dennis Hastert;* ***United States***—*Domestic Affairs, The Bill Clinton Impeachment Trial*

SIMON, JEFFREY D., Freelance Writer; Author, *The Terrorist Trap*: ***Terrorism***

SIMON, SHELDON W., Professor of Political Science, Arizona State University–Tempe; Author, *The Future of Asian-Pacific Security Collaboration*: ***Asia***

SNODSMITH, RALPH L., Ornamental Horticulturist; Author, *Ralph Snodsmith's Tips from the Garden Hotline*: ***Gardening and Horticulture***

SPENCE, MIKE, Sportswriter, *Colorado Springs Gazette*: ***Sports****—The 2002 Salt Lake City Olympics Come under Fire*

STAEDTER, TRACY, Managing Editor, *Scientific American Explorations*: ***Geology***

STARR, JOHN BRYAN, Managing Director, Annenberg Institute for School Reform, Brown University; Author, *Continuing the Revolution: The Political Thought of Mao*; Editor, *The Future of U.S.-China Relations*: ***China; China****—Macao;* ***Taiwan***

STEIN, LANA, Associate Professor of Political Science, University of Missouri–St. Louis; Author, *Holding Bureaucrats Accountable: Politicians and Professionals in St. Louis*: ***Cities and Urban Affairs***

STIEBER, JACK, Professor Emeritus, School of Labor and Industrial Relations, Michigan State University; Author, *U.S. Industrial Relations: The Next Twenty Years, Governing the UAW, Public Employee Unionism*: ***Labor; Obituaries****—Lane Kirkland*

STUART, ELAINE, Managing Editor, *State Government News*: ***States, U.S.****—(in part)*

SUTTON, STAN, Freelance Sportswriter based in Bloomington, IN: ***Sports****—Auto Racing, Horse Racing*

TERET, STEPHEN, Director and Professor of Health Policy and Management, Johns Hopkins Center for Gun Policy Research: ***Crime****—Gun Control*

TESAR, JENNY, Freelance Science Writer; Author, *The New Webster's Computer Handbook, Introduction to Animals, Parents as Teachers*: ***20th Century Chronology****—Medicine and Health, Science and Technology;* ***Computers and Communications; Medicine and Health****—Overview, The West Nile Virus—A Deadly Visitor*

TURNER, ARTHUR CAMPBELL, Professor Emeritus of Political Science, University of California, Riverside; Coauthor, *Ideology and Power in the Middle East*: ***Biography****—King Abdullah;* ***Iran; Iraq; Jordan; Lebanon; Middle East; Obituaries****—King Hussein;* ***Syria***

TURNER, DARRELL J., Former Religion Writer, *The Journal Gazette*, Fort Wayne, IN; Former Associate Editor, Religious News Service, New York, NY: ***Religion****—Far Eastern, Protestantism*

VAN ZANDT, CHRISTINE, U.S. Government Analyst on East Asian Affairs, Washington, DC: ***Cambodia; Laos***

VAUGHAN, KRISTI, Freelance Writer: ***Biography****—Eileen Collins, Judi Dench, David E. Kelley;* ***Family; States, U.S.****—(in part)*

VEALE, SCOTT, *The New York Times*: ***New York City***

VOLL, JOHN O., Professor of History, Georgetown University; Author, *Islam: Continuity and Change in the Modern World*; Coauthor, *Sudan: Unity and Diversity in a Multicultural Society*; Editor, *Sudan: State and Society in Crisis*: ***Sudan***

VOLSKY, GEORGE, North-South Center, University of Miami: ***Cuba***

WALTON, DAVID, British Antarctic Survey; Author, *Antarctic Science*: ***Polar Research***

WEATHERBEE, DONALD E., Department of Government, University of South Carolina: ***Indonesia; Indonesia****—East Timor;* ***Thailand***

WHITTEN, PHILLIP, Editor in Chief, *Swimming World*: ***Sports****—Swimming*

WILLIAMS, PAUL, Assistant Professor of Law, Washington College of Law, American University: ***Law****—International*

WILLIS, F. ROY, Professor Emeritus of History, University of California, Davis; Author, *France, Germany and the New Europe, 1945–1968, Italy Chooses Europe*: ***The Kosovo Crisis****—NATO at 50* ***Europe***

WINCHESTER, N. BRIAN, Center for the Study of Global Change and Former Director, African Studies Program, Indiana University: ***Biography****—Thabo Mbeki;* ***South Africa; Zimbabwe***

WISNER, ROBERT N., Professor, Iowa State University; Coeditor, *Marketing for Farmers;* Author, *World Food Trade and U.S. Agriculture*: ***Agriculture; Food***

WOLCHIK, SHARON LEE, Director of the Russian and East European Studies Program and Professor of Political Science, George Washington University; Author, *The Social Legacy of Communism, Czechoslovakia in Transition: Politics, Economics and Society*: ***Czech Republic; Slovakia***

WOLF, WILLIAM, New York University; Author, *The Marx Brothers, Landmark Films, The Cinema and Our Century*: ***Motion Pictures; Motion Pictures****—Shakespeare—From Stage to Screen;* ***Obituaries****—George C. Scott*

WOLFE, JOHN, Senior Vice-President, American Association of Advertising Agencies: ***Advertising***

YARBROUGH, SCOTT, Assistant Professor of English, Charleston Southern University: ***Literature****—American*

YOUNGER, R. M., Journalist and Author; Author, *Australia and the Australians, Australia! Australia! A Bicentennial Record*: ***Australia***

ZELENAK, MEL J., Department of Family/Consumer Economics, University of Missouri–Columbia: ***Consumer Affairs; Retailing***

Acknowledgements

Illustration credits, page 4: Adolf Hitler—© H. Roger Viollet; Ed Sullivan and the Beatles—© CBS Photo-Warnecke & Lautenberger; Joe Namath and Super Bowl III—Walter Iooss, Jr./*Sports Illustrated*/© Time Inc.; New York Stock Exchange—© Jeff Christensen/Liaison Agency; Kosovar refugee—© Yannis Behrakis/Reuters/Archive Photos; Nigel Kennedy—© NTB/Corbis; *Breitling Orbiter 3*—© AP/Wide World Photos. Page 6: Computer—© Jacques Chenet/Liaison Agency; World War II leaders—Signal Corps, Photo, courtesy, Franklin D. Roosevelt Library; Babe Ruth—UPI/Corbis-Bettmann; Mother Teresa—© Jean-Pierre Laffont/Corbis-Sygma; atomic bomb—Hulton Getty/Liaison Agency. Page 7: 1963 March on Washington—Archive Photos; Martin Luther King, Jr.—AP/Wide World Photos; Edwin E. Aldrin, Jr., on the Moon—NASA; Elvis Presley—UPI/Corbis-Bettmann; *The Honeymooners*—Viacom; Mohandas Gandhi—Margaret Bourke-White/*Life* Magazine/© Time Inc.; Michael Jordan—UPI/Corbis-Bettmann.

We also wish to thank the following for their services: color separations and electronic file output, Quebecor World Digital Services; text stock printed on 60# Somerset Matte; dust jacket and covers printed by The Leigh Press; cover materials provided by Ecological Fibers, Inc.; and printing and binding by Quebecor World Book Services, KY.

INDEX

Main article headings appear in this index as bold-faced capitals; subjects within articles appear as lower-case entries. Bold-faced page numbers indicate the location of the article about the subject. Both the general references and the subentries should be consulted for maximum usefulness of this index. Illustrations are indexed herein. Cross references are to the entries in this index.